TURTLES

the United States and Canada

H. Ernst, Roger W. Barbour, and Jeffrey E. Lovich

D0002016

ISONIAN INSTITUTION PRESS, WASHINGTON AND LONDON

This book was edited by Nancy P. Dutro and designed by
Linda McKnight.

Library of Congress Cataloging-in-Publication Data
Ernst, Carl H.
    Turtles of the United States and Canada / Carl H.
    Ernst, Jeffrey E. Lovich, Roger W. Barbour.
      p.   cm.
    Includes bibliographical references (p.   ) and index.
    ISBN 1–56098–346–9
    1. Turtles—United States. 2. Turtles—
    Canada. I. Lovich, Jeffrey E. II. Barbour, Roger
    William, 1919-1993. III. Ernst, Carl H. Turtles of
    the United States. IV. Title.
    QL666.C5E76   1994
    597.92′0973—dc20   93–34939
                             CIP

British Library Cataloguing-in-Publication Data is
available.

   The paper in this publication meets the minimum
requirements of the American National Standard for
Permanence of Paper for Printed Library Materials
Z39.48–1984.

Manufactured in the United States of America.

Front cover: Barbour's map turtle, *Graptemys barbouri*;
photo by Roger W. Barbour.

Color illustrations printed in Hong Kong.

10 9 8 7 6 5 4 3 2 1
01 00 99 98 97 96 95 94

*Dedicated to the memory of
Roger W. Barbour,
nature photographer,
distinguished scientist,
and friend*

Contents

Illustrations

All photographs not otherwise credited are by Roger W. Barbour.

TEXT FIGURES

COLOR PLATES

The following species are illustrated in the color section. The page number is that of the text discussion of the species.

Preface

It has been more than twenty years since Ernst and Barbour (1972) published *Turtles of the United States,* which was, in turn, an attempt to summarize the knowledge of the life histories of North American turtles gained since the 1952 publication of the *Handbook of Turtles* by Archie F. Carr. The present volume continues this trend in twenty-year updating.

Although much was known about the turtles of the United States and Canada in 1952 and even more in 1972, almost twice as much information has been published since 1972. Several new and exotic taxa have been described or discovered, including *Graptemys caglei, G. ernsti, G. gibbonsi, Kinosternon sonoriense longifemorale, Pseudemys concinna metteri, P. gorzugi,* and *Trionyx steindachneri*. Several systematic rearrangements of established taxa have occurred; startling new discoveries have been made about the biology of our turtles, such as temperature-dependent sex determination; and new techniques, such as those used in karyology and the study of mitochondrial DNA relationships, have been developed.

The conservation movement to protect our turtles, beginning in the 1960s, has come to the forefront with the enactment of the United States Endangered Species Act in 1973 and the Canadian Government Organization Act, which includes fisheries and wildlife regulations, in 1979. A number of species are now protected by state or federal legislation (see species accounts). However, despite our efforts, turtle populations continue to decline. The major causes are habitat degradation, or outright destruction, and collection for commercial trade. There is much to be done if we are to save the North American turtle fauna. A current knowledge of the life histories of all threatened species is needed before adequate recovery plans can be formulated. The primary purpose of this book is to present the known data regarding each species, and to point out where critical knowledge is lacking. To do this, all pertinent literature through September 1992 has been reviewed for all freshwater and terrestrial species. New literature on marine turtles has been particularly voluminous, so that for these species only a selection could be included here. We refer the reader to Bjorndal (1982a) for a summary of marine turtle biology and the conservation movements regarding them.

A number of persons have contributed in various ways to the publication of this book. Richard D. Bartlett, Stephen D. Busack, Justin D. Congdon, Roger Conant, Ronald J. Crombie, Llewelyn M. Ehrhart, J. Whitfield Gibbons, Steve W. Gotte, James H. Harding, W. Ronald Heyer, John B. Iverson, Trip Lamb, C. J. McCoy, Roy W. McDiarmid, Joseph C. Mitchell, Robert P. Reynolds, Michael E. Seidel, Richard A. Seigel and, especially, George R. Zug gave advice and encouragement. Bruce J. Brecke, Vincent J. Burke, David M. Carroll, Joseph T.

Collins, Charles R. Crumly, Michael A. Ewert, Wayne Frair, Steve W. Gotte, John B. Iverson, Trip Lamb, Paul Licht, David A. Ross, Anton D. Tucker, Thomas G. Vermersch, Paul J. Weldon, and Robert T. Zappalorti supplied data or copies of submitted manuscripts. Harold W. Avery, Timothy P. Boucher, Ronald J. Brooks, Justin D. Congdon, C. Kenneth Dodd, Jr., Nat B. Frazer, J. Whitfield Gibbons, James H. Harding, J. Alan Holman, John B. Iverson, Trip Lamb, Joseph C. Mitchell, Richard A. Seigel, and George R. Zug reviewed accounts and the bibliography, and offered valuable suggestions for their improvement. Christopher W. Brown, Dale E. Fuller, Steve W. Gotte, Arndt F. Laemmerzahl, John F. McBreen, Anthony M. Mills, Gregg W. North, Joshua Schachter, and Steven W. Sekscienski helped with field collections and studies. The following persons provided specimens or photographs: Richard D. Bartlett, James F. Berry, Charles M. Bogert, J. Kevin Bowler, Christopher W. Brown, James R. Butler, Charles C. Carpenter, Roger Conant, William A. Cox, Bill Davis, James R. Dixon, James L. Dobie, Sean Doody, Llewelyn M. Ehrhart, George W. Folkerts, Wayne Frair, Frederick R. Gehlbach, J. Whitfield Gibbons, Steve W. Gotte, Frank Groves, John D. Groves, James H. Harding, Brian D. Horne, John B. Iverson, Donald P. Kelso, John R. MacGregor, Ken R. Marion, Ralph G. Martell, Ardell Mitchell, Joseph C. Mitchell, Paul E. Moler, Kenneth T. Nemuras, Charles W. Painter, William H. Randel, Al Redmond, Charles E. Shaw, Ramon A. Velez, Harold Wahlquist, Robert G. Webb, Peter R. Wilson, William H. Woodin, and George R. Zug. Bernice L. Barbour, Jay C. Shaffer, Addison H. Wynn and George R. Zug helped with photography, and Evelyn M. Ernst prepared the line drawings and maps. Evelyn M. Ernst and Sharon C. Lovich patiently typed parts of the manuscript.

Research, travel, and manuscript preparation for this project were subsidized in part by the American Philosophical Society; Department of Biology, George Mason University; George Mason University Foundation; Kentucky Research Foundation; Division of Amphibians and Reptiles, United States National Museum of Natural History, Smithsonian Institution; and contract number DE-AC9-76SROO-819 between the United States Department of Energy and the University of Georgia, Savannah River Ecology Laboratory.

During the final preparations of this book, the biological community suffered a great loss in the passing of Roger W. Barbour. Dr. Barbour was one of the nation's top nature photographers, and a distinguished scientist. During his career he authored or coauthored more than 100 scientific papers and twelve books. His illustrations enhanced all of the latter. He is greatly missed by his coauthors, and we dedicate this book to his memory.

Introduction

Everyone recognizes a turtle, of whatever size, shape, color, or origin. Would that the names applied to them were so straightforward—"turtle," "tortoise," "terrapin"—they mean one thing to one person, something else to another. Biologically all members of the order Testudines are correctly called turtles. Terrapins and tortoises are certainly turtles; **tortoise** is usually applied to terrestrial turtles, particularly the larger ones; **terrapin** is usually applied to edible, more or less aquatic hardshelled turtles. Of the 12 living families of turtles (Ernst and Barbour, 1989), only one, the Testudinidae, is considered to be composed of true tortoises. Of the remaining 11 families, two are sea turtles, and nine are aquatic or semiaquatic terrapins.

From the human viewpoint turtles are slow, harmless creatures, and in this characterization they have an important role in mythology and folklore. Everyone has heard, for example, the story of the race between the hare and the tortoise. But although turtles have always been the object of much interest and speculation, surprisingly little is known of their biology; indeed, some species are known only as to their appearance.

REPTILE EVOLUTION

Together with lizards, amphisbaenians, snakes, crocodilians, and the tuatara, turtles constitute the living members of the vertebrate class Reptilia. Reptiles are ectotherms that evolved walking limbs and a dry, scaly skin (snakes evolved from four-legged lizards). They evolved from the amphibians during the Pennsylvanian Period about 320 million years ago, toward the close of the Paleozoic Era (Carroll, 1969). During the following Mesozoic Era the reptiles underwent rapid adaptive radiation and became the dominant animals on earth. Along with the amphibians, reptiles represent a transitional stage in vertebrate evolution that diverged from the aquatic fishes and eventually gave rise to two separate terrestrial groups, the birds and the mammals. Reptiles were the first vertebrates completely adapted to life in dry places. Though many amphibians spend much time on land, their eggs must be laid in water or damp places. Reptiles were able to lay a specialized egg, which has a calcareous or parchmentlike shell that retards moisture loss. Hence, reptiles could take advantage of the great expanses of dry land not previously available to their ancestors. Their eggs also have embryonic membranes (amnion, chorion, and allantois) that are not found in amphibian eggs, as well as a yolk sac that contains nutrients. The amnion forms a fluid-filled compartment surrounding the embryo, thus bringing the aquatic environment within the egg.

Other characteristics also evolved that contributed to the reptiles' freedom from the water requirements of their amphibian predecessors. The scaly skin had few surface glands, and relatively little moisture is lost cutaneously. The well-developed lungs provided ample oxygen for the heart, now a three-chambered organ in most reptiles, but four-chambered in the crocodilians. The partitioning of the ventricle into two chambers was more efficient, produced higher blood pressure, and led indirectly to the development of more efficient kidneys. Other major developments include the appearance of claws on the toes, a palate separating the oral and nasal passages, and the evolution of a male copulatory organ (absent in the tuatara) which facilitates internal fertilization.

TURTLE EVOLUTION AND SYSTEMATICS

Turtles are ancient animals that evolved a shelled form more than 200 million years ago, long before mammals appeared on earth. Turtles are the only living members of the reptilian subclass Anapsida, and constitute the order Testudines, which is considered the oldest and most primitive of living reptiles (Romer, 1956; Carroll, 1969; Reisz, 1992). It is apparently close to the ancestral reptilian lineage (as indicated by its unspecialized skull). Living turtles are found on all continents except Antarctica. The marine species occur predominantly in tropical waters of the Atlantic, Pacific, and Indian oceans, but several also range far poleward in these waters. In maximum size, adult North American turtles range from 11.5 cm (*Clemmys muhlenbergii*) to 189 cm and 916 kg (*Dermochelys coriacea*).

The order Testudines is subdivided into the suborders Pleurodira and Cryptodira. The Pleurodira are the side-necked turtles: they withdraw their heads by bending their necks laterally. Pleurodirans are aquatic turtles now restricted primarily to the Southern Hemisphere in Australia, Africa, Madagascar, and South America; however, fossils indicate that they lived in North America until Cretaceous times. The Cryptodira are the hidden-necked turtles which withdraw their heads by bending the neck vertically into a sigmoidal curve. Cryptodirans inhabit the land, fresh water, and the seas, and occur on all continents except Antarctica (although only as marine turtles in Australia). All modern turtles living in North America are cryptodirans.

Members of seven cryptodiran families live in North America and its adjacent marine waters (Table 1). The Chelydridae, snapping turtles, are a New World family with two species in the United States and Canada. The Kinosternidae, mud and musk turtles, are a tropical American family, nine species of which range northward into the United States and Canada. The Emydidae, semiaquatic freshwater and marsh turtles, are found on all continents except Australia and Antarctica. This is the most populous family in North America, with 31 species. The Testudinidae, terrestrial tortoises, also are found on all continents except Australia and Antarctica; three species occur in the southern United States. The Cheloniidae, hard-shelled sea turtles, occur in the marine waters off the coasts of North America and the Hawaiian Islands; this family is represented by five species. The family Dermochelyidae has only one living species, the leatherback (*Dermochelys coriacea*), which is widely distributed in tropical and subtropical seas; it,

TABLE I
Turtle diversity in the United States and Canada

Family	Genus	Species	Subspecies
Chelydridae	2	2	2
Cheloniidae	4	5	4 (?)
Dermochelyidae	1	1	2 (?)
Trionychidae	1	5*	8
Kinosternidae	2	9	9
Emydidae	9	31	37
Testudinidae	1	3	0

*Two species introduced into Hawaii.

too, occurs off the Hawaiian Islands and continental United States and Canada. The Trionychidae, the softshells, are found in Asia, Africa, and North America; three species live in North America, two others have been introduced from Asia into Hawaii.

We follow, with some modification, the higher classification of turtles proposed by Gaffney and Meylan (1988). In their taxonomic scheme, living North American turtles belong to the gigaorder Casichelydia and the megaorder Cryptodira (hidden-necked turtles). See Dundee (1989) for a discussion of the proper ordinal name for turtles.

Common names for turtles are not subject to rigorous nomenclatural rules, as are their scientific names, and may vary from place to place. We use, with minor changes, the standard common names as listed by J. T. Collins (1990).

The oldest fossil turtles have been found in the Triassic deposits of Germany and Thailand. These fossils have been assigned to the genus *Proganochelys* (=*Triassochelys*), which, along with the fossil genera *Proterocheris, Saurischiocomes,* and *Chelytherium,* belongs to the gigaorder Proganochelydia (Romer, 1956; Gaffney, 1975a). Only some skeletal features of these are known completely. The skull is solidly roofed, with the external parts sculptured. The postfrontal, lacrimal, and supratemporal are (or may be) present, and the external nares are divided by a bony bar. The quadrate lacks the strong curvature around the stapes that is characteristic of most turtles. There are small teeth on bones of the palate and rudimentary teeth on the jaw margins. Proganochelydians have seven cervicals—the eighth vertebra is a dorsal rather than a cervical, its arch fused to the nuchal—and the cervicals are amphicoelous, with two-headed ribs. The bones of the pectoral girdle, although partially fused with the plastron, can still be identified individually as clavicle, interclavicle, and cleithrum. The pelvis probably was more or less firmly attached, some even fused, to the plastron. The peripherals of the carapace apparently were very numerous, the neurals are long and narrow, and there are nine costals. The plastron contains several extra bones, in the form of two pairs of mesoplastra, which are absent in most modern turtles. The buttress elements of the plastron do not reach the carapacial costals. There are dermal tubercles on the neck and tail, and presumably the head and limbs could not be pulled into the shell. Likely these primitive turtles were amphibious (Romer, 1956).

All other turtles are assigned to the gigaorder Casichelydia. Gaffney (1975a, 1984) compared the skulls of proganochelydians and casichelydians, and found the floor of the middle ear (acoustic-jugular cavity) and the interpterygoid vacuity to be open in proganochelydians but closed in casichelydians. The quadrate does not form the lateral wall of the middle ear in proganochelydians, but does so in casichelydians, and the following features are present in Proganochelydia but not in Casichelydia: a bladelike process on the parasphenoid, palatal teeth, a well-developed median tubercle on the basioccipital, and a dorsal premaxillary process dividing the external opening of the nostrils. In contrast, casichelydians have both an expanded supraoccipital crista and an antrum postoticum which are absent in proganochelydians. The Casichelydia became dominant during the Jurassic and have remained so ever since. They were mainly amphibious, but some species have become marine (Cheloniidae, Dermochelyidae) or terrestrial (Emydidae, Testudinidae). Two modern megaorders of turtles have arisen from early casichelydians: the Cryptodira, during the Jurassic, and Pleurodira (side-necked turtles) during the Cretaceous. The Cryptodira continued as the main evolutionary line of turtles, with the Pleurodira appearing as an aberrant but structurally conservative side branch living today in South America, Africa, Madagascar, Australia, and New Guinea.

The oldest known cryptodirans are from the Early Jurassic. By the Early Cretaceous they had become the dominant turtles of northern regions, and some species had invaded the oceans. Their heads can be withdrawn in a vertical flexure, because the cervical vertebrae can be bent into a sigmoid curve. The Cryptodira is considered to be the more advanced group of turtles. According to Gaffney and Meylan (1988) the cryptodiran line is composed of two subdivisions called capaxorders. The extinct capaxorder Kayentachelydia contains only one family, Kayentachelyidae, and the single genus, *Kayentachelys,* the oldest cryptodiran from the Early Jurassic of Arizona. The second capaxorder, Selmacryptodira, contains both living and extinct families and is further subdivided into two hyperorders. The extinct hyperorder Pleurosternoidea is composed of the family Pleurosternidae (=Glyptopsidae, Jurassic). The second hyperorder, Daiocryptodira, includes the parvorder Baenoidea (family Baenidae, Cretaceous-Eocene), and the parvorder Eucryptodira, which includes living cryptodirans.

Pleurosternids and baenoids retain several primitive characters. They retain nasal bones and thus have the prefrontals separated and not in contact at the midline of the skull. The foramen for the internal posterior cortical canal lies midway along the length of the basisphenoid-pterygoid suture. They also have a well-developed stapedial artery and reduced orbital and palatine arteries. The neck vertebrae lacked mechanisms to retract the head, and no formed central articulations were present in the early species. Mesoplastral bones and paired intergular scutes were also present.

We recognize the parvorder Eucryptodira as composed of two suborders (living species belong to the Polycryptodira) and several superfamilies: the Trionychoidea (Cretaceous-Recent), including the living families Kinosternidae, Dermatemydidae, Carettochelyidae, and Trionychidae; the marine Chelonioidea (Jurassic-Recent), including the extinct family Toxochelyidae (Cretaceous-Eocene) and the living family Cheloniidae; the marine Dermochelyoidea (Eocene-Recent), including the extinct family Protostegidae and the living family Dermochelyidae; the Testudinoidea (Paleocene-Recent), including the living families Bataguridae (considered by some authorities as either a subfamily of Emydidae or Testudinidae), Emydidae, and Testudinidae; and the Chelydroidea which includes the living families Chelydridae and Platysternidae.

If known, the fossil history of each North American turtle is given in its account. We have adopted the method of Holman (1981a) in presenting the subdivisions of geological time units as North American mammal ages. These are as follows: Miocene—Arikareean (early), Hemingfordian (medial), and Barstovian (late); Pliocene—Clarendonian (early), Hemphillian (medial), and Blancan (late); Pleistocene—Blancan (early), Irvingtonian (medial), and Rancholabrean (late). Following Roth and Laerm (1980), Pleistocene mammal ages are further subdivided into glacial stages thus (older to younger): Blancan—Nebraskan, Aftonian, and Kansan; Irvingtonian—Yarmouthian and Illinioan; Rancholabrean—Sangamonian and Wisconsinian.

TURTLE MORPHOLOGY

The exceptional feature of the turtle is its shell. This conservative character has remained little changed for many millions of years. It is divided into two parts: an upper part, the carapace, and a lower part, the plastron. The two parts may be joined on each side by a bony bridge or a ligamentous connection.

The carapace commonly consists of about 50 bones. The nuchal is the most anterior bone along the midline; behind it are eight neurals, two suprapygals, and a pygal, in that order.

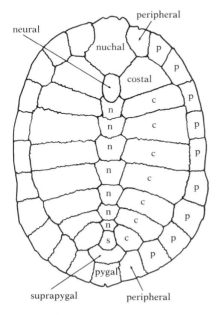

Carapacial bones of turtles

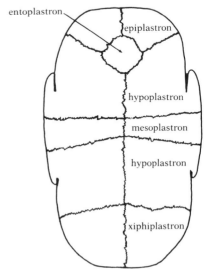

Plastral bones of turtles

Occasionally a preneural may be found, between the nuchal and the first neural. The neurals are attached to the neural arches of the dorsal vertebrae, but the other bones of the series are free from the vertebrae. On each side of the neurals are eight costal bones; in some species a precostal is also present. Outside the costals and extending along each side from the nuchal to the pygal is a series of about 11 peripherals. Each carapacial bone articulates with the adjacent bones along a suture.

The forepart of the plastron is composed of a median bone: the entoplastron, which is surrounded anteriorly by two epiplastra and posteriorly by two hyoplastra. Behind these are a pair each of hypoplastra and xiphiplastra. In some primitive species a pair of mesoplastra occur between the hyoplastra and hypoplastra. Between the forelimbs and the hind limbs the hyoplastra and hypoplastra articulate with the third to seventh peripherals. The forelimb emerges from the axillary notch, the hind limb from the inguinal notch. In many species just behind the axillary notches the axillary buttresses solidly attach the hyoplastra to the first costals, and in front of the inguinal notches the inguinal buttresses solidly attach the hypoplastra to the fifth costals.

The bones of the shell are covered with horny scutes. The division between adjacent scutes is called the seam. A seam often leaves an impression, termed a sulcus, on the underlying bones.

We follow the terminology for the various scutes proposed by Zangerl (1969), but other systems of scute nomenclature have been proposed (see Ernst and Barbour, 1989). Along the anterior midline of the carapace is a single cervical scute. This is followed posteriorly by a series of five vertebral scutes. Along each side and touching the vertebrals is a series of four pleurals. Outside the pleurals and extending along each side from the cervical are 11–12 marginal scutes. In the alligator snapping turtle (*Macroclemys*) a series of small scutes, called supramarginals, appears between the posterior pleurals and the marginals.

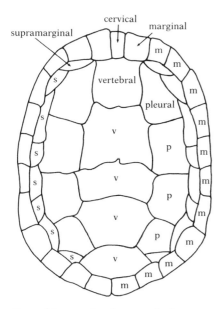

Carapacial scutes of turtles, generalized

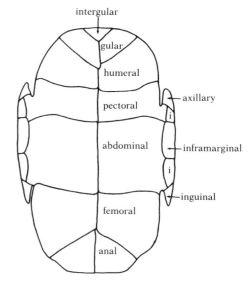

Plastral scutes of turtles

The scutes of the plastron are divided into pairs by a median longitudinal seam. Anteriorly lie a pair of gular scutes (except in the family Kinosternidae where a single gular is normal); in some species an intergular is also present. Paired humerals, pectorals, abdominals, femorals, and anals follow, respectively, and in some Cheloniidae an interanal is present. At the posterior edge of each axillary notch there may be an axillary scute, and at the front edge of each inguinal notch there may be an inguinal scute. Inframarginals, a series of small scutes lying between the carapacial marginals and the sides of the adjacent plastral scutes, are present in the families Cheloniidae and Chelydridae.

Hutchison and Bramble (1981) analyzed the scutes of fossil and living species of the Kinosternidae and the related family Dermatemydidae, and compared these scutes to those of testudinoid turtles. They found that the gular scute of kinosternids is really a new scale of different origin, which they term an intergular. They also found that the humeral scute of extant kinosternids is divided into two scutes by the development of the anterior plastral hinge between the epiplastron and hyoplastron; thus, kinosternids are unique in not having true pectoral or abdominal scutes. Consequently, Hutchison and Bramble prepared an alternate plastral scute terminology for the Kinosternidae, Dermatemydidae, and the chelid genus *Chelodina*. In it the gular scute, humerals, pectorals, and abdominals become the intergular, gulars, anterior humerals, and posterior humerals, respectively, in the Kinosternidae. The femoral and anal scutes retain their names. Although we feel their conclusions are accurate, we have not incorporated them in this book to avoid confusion, and instead call the attention of the reader to their paper. The more conservative approach is also used in the latest edition of the popular field guide by Conant and Collins (1991).

Growth of the epidermal scutes in those turtles that do not periodically shed is stimulated presumably by growth of the bony shell. The scutes adjust to the growth of the bones beneath them by eccentric growth around the granular infantile scute. A layer of germinal epithelium lies beneath the scute, and, as the bones of the shell grow, this layer increases correspondingly. The scute is enlarged by new material applied over the entire undersurface. When growth ceases, at the beginning of hibernation or estivation, the thin edges of the scutes are sightly depressed where they meet the seams. When growth is resumed, the germinal layer of the epidermis, rather than continuing to add to the edge of the existing scute, forms an entirely new layer. It is thin and indistinct under the central part of the scute but becomes more distinct toward its periphery. Near the edge of the scute the new layer becomes greatly thickened, and it bulges upward where it passes under the edge; this recurves the free edge of the scute above, forming a major growth-ring, or annulus, that may or may not represent one year of growth. The newly formed epidermis, projecting from under the edges of the scute, is paler and softer than the older parts; from this one is able to determine readily whether a turtle is growing. The epidermal scutes arc like low pyramids only in appearance; their apparent thickness is enhanced by the contours of the bony shell, which correspond to the contours of the scutes.

In *Chrysemys, Deirochelys, Graptemys, Pseudemys, Trachemys,* and some *Malaclemys,* a fracture zone develops between the old and new layers of the scute as the new layer of epidermis is formed, and the older layer is shed, annually and in one piece.

North American turtles of the genera *Sternotherus, Emydoidea,* and *Terrapene* have a transverse hinge located on the anterior edge of the abdominal scutes, and in *Kinosternon* a pair of hinges borders the abdominals. These hinges allow the plastron to be folded up to partially or completely enclose the head and limbs.

Turtles of the families Dermochelyidae, and Trionychidae have lost the horny covering of scutes, and the bony material in their shells is much reduced. Instead, they have a tough, leathery skin. These turtles are often referred to as leatherbacks or softshells.

Another exceptional characteristic of turtles is the migration of the limb girdles to positions inside the rib cage (which, along with the vertebral column, helps form the shell). The limbs of turtles are adapted to the medium through or on which they travel. For instance, the terrestrial tortoises of North America have evolved elephantine hind limbs, which help to support them, and shovellike forelimbs, which aid in digging. The limbs of the marine species are modified as flippers with which they quite literally fly through the seas. The semiaquatic turtles have developed various degrees of webbing between the toes: the more webbing, the more aquatic the turtle.

Although the turtle skull is highly modified it is basically primitive, evidenced by the solid cranium with no temporal openings, the ancestral anapsid form. Posteriorly the cranium has a large otic notch on either side of an elongated supraoccipital bone. The pterygoids are solidly fused to the braincase, and the quadrate is closely attached to a lateral expansion of the otic capsule. The jaws are toothless and are modified as sharp shearing beaks. The upper jaw is composed of two pairs of bones: the small premaxillae, in front (fused in soft-shelled turtles), and the maxillae along the sides; the lower border of the maxilla may be either a sharp cutting surface or a flat crushing surface. The maxilla forms the lateral border of the nasal cavity and the lower border of the orbit. Posteriorly it articulates with the jugal. The posterior rim of the orbit is formed by the jugal ventrally and the postorbital dorsally.

The paired bones along the dorsal midline of the skull are the prefrontals, frontals, and parietals. The parietals form the roof and much of the lateral walls of the braincase. Laterally the parietal has a strong process projecting downward and joining the pterygoid. The lower border of the parietal also articulates with the prootic and supraoccipital bones. The elongated supraoccipital extends backward and forms the upper border of the foramen magnum. Paired exoccipitals form the lateral borders, and a basioccipital forms the lower border; these three bones constitute the occipital condyle. The cheek bones are the large posterior squamosal and the smaller anterior quadratojugal (a small bone lying between the quadrate and jugal bones). The squamosals are connected to the supraoccipital by the exoccipitals.

The palatal complex is composed, from front to rear, of the single vomer and palatine bones and the paired pterygoids. These are often covered with a secondary palate. Anteriorly the vomer meets the premaxillae. The palatines form part of the roof of the nasal passage. Between each palatine and the adjacent maxilla is an opening, the posterior palatine foramen. The pterygoids are separated posteriorly by the basisphenoid. The free lateral projections of the pterygoids are the ectopterygoid processes. A pair of quadrate bones, which lie posterior to the pterygoids, forms the lower-jaw articulation.

Lateral view of turtle skull:

bo, basioccipital; *bs,* basisphenoid; *ex,* exoccipital; *fr,* frontal; *ju,* jugal; *mx,* maxilla; *op,* opisthotic; *pa,* parietal; *pal,* palatine; *pf,* prefrontal; *pm,* premaxillae; *po,* postorbital; *pt,* pterygoid; *qj,* quadratojugal; *qu,* quadrate; *so,* supraoccipital; *sq,* squamosal; *vo,* vomer

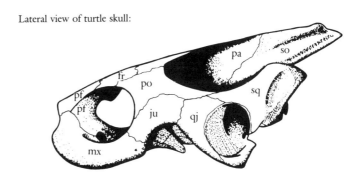

Ventral view of turtle skull

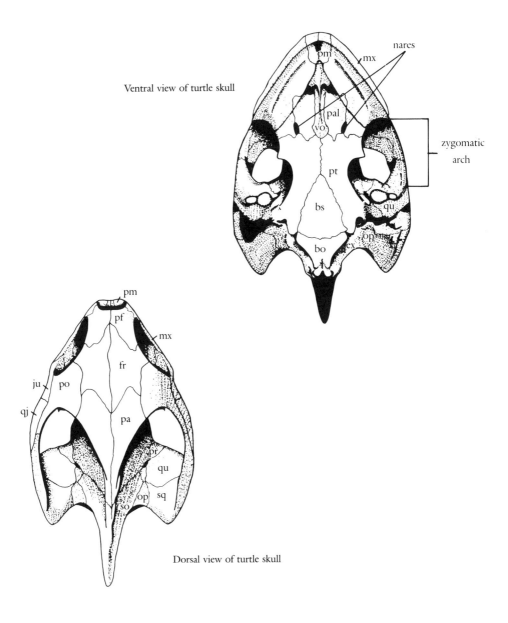

Dorsal view of turtle skull

Each half of the lower jaw is composed of six bones. The most anterior is the dentary, which forms the crushing or cutting surface; the two dentaries are firmly united at the symphysis. On the ventral border of the jaw the dentary extends backward nearly to the articulation with the quadrate. On the dorsal side behind the crushing surface are the coronoid and supraangular bones. At the inner posterior end of the lower jaw are, ventrally, the angular bone and, dorsally, the prearticular. The articular bone forms the articulation with the quadrate. We refer the reader to the works of Gaffney (1972, 1979) for detailed discussions and illustrations of the anatomical variations in turtle skulls.

Head scalation illustrated in the figure is typical. Members of the families Chelydridae and Kinosternidae have barbels—small fleshy protuberances, commonly conical—on the skin of the chin, throat, or neck.

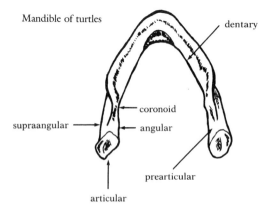

Mandible of turtles

Head scalation of turtles

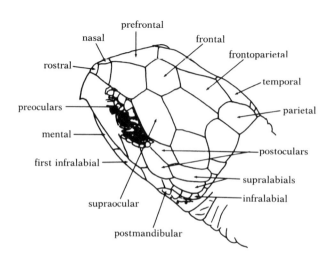

KARYOTYPE

The karyotype, or number and physical appearance of the diploid chromosome pairs, varies between families, genera, and some species of turtles. Each chromosome has a small, unstaining, constricted region called the centromere which may be located at different positions in different pairs of chromosomes. Its position is used to designate the chromosome as either metacentric, having the centromere located near the center so that the two arms are of equal or near equal length, acrocentric, having the centromere nearer one end of the chromosome so that the two arms are of unequal length (one long, one short), or telocentric, where the centromere is very near one end of the chromosome.

Karyotypes can be used as evidence of phylogenetic relationships. The more similar the karyotypes of two species, the more closely they are related. If known, the karyotype of each turtle is presented in its account.

TURTLE DISTRIBUTION IN NORTH AMERICA

Turtles are common in North America. They occur on land or in the fresh waters of all of the United States except Alaska and in all of the lower provinces of Canada, and marine turtles reach the coasts of both Alaska and Canada. The greatest number of species is found east of the Mississippi River in Florida and the Gulf coastal states (35), but many species are found in the Mississippi valley (16), the Atlantic coastal states (27), and Texas (29). The least number of species occur in the states west of the Rocky Mountains (12) and in Canada (13).

Only one turtle, *Chrysemys picta*, ranges from the Atlantic Coast to the Pacific Coast. It also ranges from Canada to Mexico, as do *Chelydra serpentina* and *Sternotherus odoratus*. Other species with extensive ranges in North America are *Kinosternon subrubrum*, *Graptemys geographica*, *Trachemys scripta*, and *Terrapene carolina*; *Malaclemys terrapin* occurs along the coast of the United States from Cape Cod to Texas. In contrast to these are *Pseudemys nelsoni*, which is restricted to Florida, *Pseudemys alabamensis*, which occurs only in the vicinity of Mobile Bay, Alabama, *Pseudemys gorzugi* and *Trachemys gaigeae*, which are restricted to the Rio Grande watershed, and many species of map turtles, *Graptemys*, which live in single river systems. *Clemmys muhlenbergii* has an interesting disjunct distribution: it occurs only in relict populations over a once rather large range. Several populations of *Trachemys scripta* apparently originated from released or escaped captives, and the only freshwater turtles on Hawaii, *Trionyx sinensis* and *T. steindachneri*, were introduced.

TURTLE HABITATS

Although a turtle species may be widespread it shows a preference for a particular habitat. Many North American species are aquatic to a considerable extent; these are found in lakes, ponds, cypress swamps, marshes, bogs, rivers, streams, and other freshwater habitats. Some prefer deep water, but most occur only in relatively shallow water, and nearly all avoid swift currents. Other aquatic species live in the brackish water of estuaries and coastal salt marshes, particularly *Malaclemys terrapin*. The sea turtles inhabit the warmer oceans and seas but occasionally enter bays and river mouths.

Several North American turtles have evolved a terrestrial way of life. The box turtles (*Terrapene*) vary in habitat preferences from deciduous hardwood forests in the eastern United States to the semiarid grasslands of the southwest. The tortoises (*Gopherus*) are found in the sandy pine woods of Florida, in the open dry woodlands of Texas, and in the deserts of the southwest. They somewhat overcome the rigors of their environment by burrowing.

ACTIVITY PERIODS

In the United States most turtles are active from April through October, but in Canada the annual activity period may be shorter. Feeding and other activities begin when the water or air temperature warms to 15–20°C. Typically, mating occurs in the spring, the eggs are laid in June and July, and hatching begins in late August and lasts through September. Many turtles are forced to estivate during dry, hot periods. In winter they hibernate in the soft bottom of some waterway or under the soil and vegetable debris of the woodland or prairie. In some southern states, notably Florida, turtles may remain active all year.

The daily cycle normally includes sleeping, basking in the sun, and foraging for food. Most turtles are diurnal, but mud turtles, musk turtles, and snappers are decidedly nocturnal.

TURTLE REPRODUCTIVE BIOLOGY

In North America spermatogenesis begins in the testes of the mature male in the spring and is completed in the early fall. The sperm pass from the testes and are stored over the winter in the epididymides. Ovulation in the female typically occurs in May and June, and new ova start to mature soon after.

A courtship precedes the actual mating. Courtship varies with the species: it may include a stroking (titillating) of the female's head region with the forefoot claws, as in *Chrysemys, Graptemys, Pseudemys,* and *Trachemys*; chasing, ramming, or biting, as in *Gopherus*; or some combination of these. Sperm may be stored by the female and may remain viable for a long time; for example females of the diamondback terrapin, *Malaclemys terrapin,* and eastern box turtle, *Terrapene carolina,* have laid fertile eggs after four years in isolation (Hildebrand, 1929; Ewing, 1943).

The digging of the nest, the arranging of the eggs in the nest, and the covering of the nest are completed with the hind feet only. All of this is done instinctively; the female never turns to look into the nest. After filling the nest she walks away, never to return: the eggs are left to hatch or not, as environmental conditions dictate. After hatching, the young receive no parental care and are strictly on their own. Several clutches of eggs may be laid each season.

With the exception of a few genera, turtles lack heteromorphic sex chromosomes (either XY male heterogamety, or ZW female heterogamety); their mechanism for sex determination is different than in humans. No turtle species living in either the United States or Canada has heteromorphic sex chromosomes, but the spiny softshell, *Trionyx spiniferus,* and the wood turtle, *Clemmys insculpta,* have homomorphic sex chromosomes and genetic sex determination (Janzen and Paukstis, 1991). All other North American turtles that have been studied have temperature-(environmental-) dependent sex determination (Bull, 1980; Bull and Vogt, 1979; Bull et al. 1982a,b; Paukstis and Janzen, 1990; Ewert and Nelson, 1991; Janzen and Paukstis, 1991). The incubation temperature of the eggs at a sensitive period of development in the middle trimester triggers the gonadal development leading to the sex of the hatchling (Bull and Vogt, 1981). Two patterns of temperature-dependent sex determination have been discovered in turtles (Bull, 1980; Ewert and Nelson, 1991; Janzen and Paukstis, 1991). Pattern I, common among emydine turtles, has a single transition zone of temperature below which incubation yields nearly or totally 100% males and above which only females are produced. Pattern II, known only from *Kinosternon* and *Sternotherus* in North America, has two transition zones, with males predominating at intermediate temperatures and females predominating at both extremes; in most species no constant incubation temperatures within the transition zone yield 100% males (however, exceptionally, constant temperatures do yield 100% males in *Sternotherus carinatus* and *Chelydra serpentina*). Pattern I occurs chiefly in turtles in which the adult females are larger than adult males; Pattern II is found mainly in turtles with females smaller than males or in which body size is not dimorphic (Ewert and Nelson, 1991). The smaller sex is typically produced at the coolest incubation temperatures. Ewert and Nelson (1991) proposed four possible explanations for the various patterns of sex determination in turtles: phylogenetic inertia, temperature-dependent differential fitness, sib-avoidance, and group-structured adaptation in sex ratios, and we refer the reader to their paper for details.

GROWTH AND LONGEVITY

Growth is rapid in young turtles but slows considerably after maturity is reached. As long as environmental conditions are favorable some growth occurs; the ability to grow is probably never lost.

The relative lengths of the abdominal scutes and the plastron remain approximately the same throughout the turtle's life. The original abdominal scutes of hatchlings do not increase in size; rather, they remain constant as new growth is initiated around them. Thus, an approximation of the growth rate can be obtained by measuring the plastron length, the abdominal-scute length, and the lengths of the various annuli of the abdominal scutes and then applying the equation $L_1/L_2 = C_1/C_2$, where C_1 represents the length of the annulus, C_2 the length of the abdominal scute, L_2 the plastron length, and L_1 the unknown length of the plastron at the time the annulus was formed. More sophisticated mathematical methods to predict growth rates have also been developed, particularly for known-age turtles.

Some turtles grow to very large size. The leatherback may become more than 180 cm long and weigh over 500 kg. Green turtles and loggerheads occasionally weigh over 400 kg. The giant tortoises of the Galapagos Islands may weigh more than 200 kg. The alligator snapping turtle can grow to more than 90 kg: it is the largest freshwater turtle in the United States.

Turtles may live longer than any other living vertebrate; the great longevity of some species is well documented. Box turtles (*Terrapene carolina*) have lived for more than a century, and several giant tortoises (*Geochelone*) are thought to have lived for 120–150 years.

FEEDING HABITS

Although some species have rather exclusive diets, most of our turtles are omnivorous opportunists. Animal food taken includes many kinds of invertebrates and vertebrates. Various algae and the fruits, stems, and leaves of terrestrial and aquatic plants are eaten. The green turtle (*Chelonia mydas*) and the tortoises (*Gopherus*) are strict herbivores. Some map turtles (*Graptemys*) feed almost exclusively on mollusks. Many species are carnivorous when young but become herbivorous with advancing age.

Turtles usually stalk their prey or actively seek it out, but some may lie in ambush. After the food is seized it is torn apart by the sharp, horny beak and the forefoot claws; then it is swallowed in portions. If the morsel is small it may be ingested whole.

IMPORTANCE OF TURTLES

Turtles may be of considerable importance to humans in several aspects. They serve as a ready source of meat and are eaten locally; the diamondback terrapin, various cooters, and the snapping turtle are still marketed commercially for their flesh. The hawksbill turtle, *Eretmochelys imbricata,* is the source of the tortoiseshell long used in jewelry and toilet articles. Importation of tortoiseshell into this country has been illegal since 1970, when *Eretmochelys* was placed on the U.S. Endangered Species List. Some species of turtles with specific environmental requirements serve as excellent indicators as to the health of their particular habitats. This is especially true of the bog turtle, *Clemmys muhlenbergii,* that lives only in extremely shallow wetlands, and the map turtles of the genus *Graptemys* that need relatively unpolluted waterways to support their primary molluscan prey. Probably more than a million dollars is spent on turtles annually in the pet trade. On the negative side, several common species are known to transmit the *Salmonella* bacteria to humans.

STATUS AND CONSERVATION

Turtle populations have been decreasing at an alarming rate in North America. If this trend continues all turtle species in the United States and Canada will be threatened with extinction in the twenty-first century. The major causes of decline are now quite clear, but each species is affected by a different suite of problems and must be examined individually. The life history traits of late maturity and high juvenile mortality make most species particularly vulnerable to human consumptive uses for these ancient animals. For many species we do not have an adequate knowledge of their life histories to understand where they are most vulnerable and how we can best help them. Good life history data are critical to the survival of all species, and important gaps in our knowledge are evident in the species accounts presented in this book. These knowledge gaps *must* be filled if we are to formulate a conservation and management plan for each species.

Two factors seem dominant in the decline of our turtles: habitat destruction (in its many forms) and overcollection for the pet trade and foreign food market. We are all aware that environmental quality in North America has been compromised in this century and that this has resulted in important conservation legislation directed toward improving the habitat of humans. The National Environmental Protection Act and the various clean air and water acts are good examples, and although these certainly also improve turtle habitats when implemented properly, turtles face a number of more specific problems. Loss of habitat is the worst of these. A turtle cannot live if its habitat is eliminated! If bogs and seepage areas are drained, bog turtles, *Clemmys muhlenbergii*, disappear. If woodlands are clear-cut, box turtles, *Terrapene carolina*, are eliminated. As a coastal tidal marsh becomes degraded, its population of diamondback terrapins, *Malaclemys terrapin*, declines. Swamps and marshes have been drained for additional farmland or for the construction of highways, housing developments, shopping centers, office complexes, and the like. Many rivers have been impounded and low-lying woodlands and marshy ground flooded, thus eliminating shallow-water and terrestrial habitats. And humans have polluted many bodies of water so badly that turtles can no longer live in them. One of the authors is well aware of how habitat degradation can affect local turtle populations. From 1965 to 1975, Ernst studied a community of six aquatic species, totalling approximately 4,000 individuals, in a wetland complex in Lancaster County, Pennsylvania. By 1985 the total number of turtles had decreased 90% to about 400, as farmers drained a large pond and channelized the adjacent marsh and boggy pastures. By 1985 the area which held the pond had become a dry cattle pasture, forcing the remaining turtles into feeder streams and artificial ponds.

Our freshwater and terrestrial species are not the only ones affected by habitat degradation. Suitable nesting beaches are critical to the survival of marine turtles (National Research Council, 1990), yet these are disappearing to waterfront development, floodlighting, and an increase in human disturbance. Nest and hatchling predators associated with humans, such as domestic dogs (*Canis familiaris*) and cats (*Felis cati*), and scavenging raccoons (*Procyon lotor*) which flourish in the company of humans, have also increased (see the accounts of individual marine turtle species for further discussion).

Residues of chemical pollutants in turtles (Hall, 1980; Stone et al., 1980; Hall et al., 1983; Olafsson et al., 1983; Ryan et al., 1986; Bryan et al., 1987; Bishop et al., 1991) are serious indicators of habitat breakdown. Pesticides can poison turtles as well as other wildlife (Herald, 1949; Ferguson, 1963; Hall, 1980). Formerly many of these contained large quantities of long-lasting chlorinated hydrocarbons which are stored in body fat. When these are later released as the fat is metabolized during hibernation, estivation, or migration, they may slowly poison the turtle. Pesticides and other pollutants may also adversely affect populations of prey species. Snail and clam feeders, such as the map turtles (*Graptemys*), diamondback terrapin (*Malaclemys terrapin*), and musk turtles (*Sternotherus*), are especially vulnerable in this regard.

The modern increase in mechanized vehicular traffic has also caused declines in many turtle populations. Although major studies on the effects of vehicles on reptilian populations are generally lacking, it is common knowledge that thousands of turtles lose their lives crossing highways each year. The carnage is particularly severe in May and June when females wander overland searching for nesting sites. When new multilane highways are constructed through forests or along waterways, adjacent turtle populations may be extirpated in only a few years.

The other major cause of decline in our turtle populations has been overcollecting for the pet trade or foreign food trade (particularly Japanese; see *Trachemys scripta*). The volume in commercial collection has resulted in the removal of many adults from populations. If a turtle displayed in a pet store is an adult, it was almost certainly taken from a wild population and not raised in captivity. The gathering of eggs and juveniles reduces the rate of replacement of those adults left to die of natural causes. With their slow rates of maturation and reproduction our turtles cannot withstand heavy cropping and still maintain their numbers. Such behavior is irreparable since few turtles that enter the pet trade survive as long as a year in captivity. Most states now regulate the commercial capture of turtles. However, some unscrupulous persons illegally harvest our turtles. Hardest hit are the rare species, such as *Clemmys muhlenbergii* and *Sternotherus depressus,* the "personality" species *Clemmys insculpta, C. guttata, Terrapene carolina* and *T. ornata,* and the pretty species *Graptemys flavimaculata* and *G. oculifera.* For example, the type population of the bog turtle (*Clemmys muhlenbergii*) in Lancaster County, Pennsylvania, has been extirpated by a pet dealer (Ernst, pers. obs.). If a turtle is illegally collected in a state where it is protected and then transported to another state for sale, provisions of the federal law, the Lacey Act, have been violated and the law enforcement division of the U.S. Fish & Wildlife Service can prosecute both the collector and the seller. Several pet trade dealers have been shut down (including the one mentioned above) or have been heavily fined for violating the Lacey Act.

As a result of population decline, 13 turtles are now federally protected in the United States under the Endangered Species Act (Table 2), and several other species, such as the bog turtle (*Clemmys muhlenbergii*), wood turtle (*Clemmys insculpta*), and Blanding's turtle (*Emydoidea blandingii*), are protected by some states (see individual species accounts).

If turtles are to remain a conspicuous part of our fauna we must initiate additional conservation measures. Although we do not yet know enough about turtle biology to formulate an adequate conservation plan for many species, certain needs are obvious. The waterways and lands harboring important populations must be protected from undue human disturbance and pollution. The trend away from the use of the dangerous residual pesticides and other chemical pollutants must be continued. States must pass and enforce legislation controlling the capture of these creatures in the wild, and the pet trade must be strictly monitored.

Equally important, more people must become acquainted with the many fascinating aspects of turtle biology. Such awareness should make people more interested in the protection of these shy creatures. The creation of such an attitude—not only toward turtles but also toward our dwindling wildlife resources generally—is a major purpose of this book.

TABLE 2

North American turtles protected under the Endangered Species Act as of 29 August 1992
(E=endangered, T=threatened)

Species (Common Name)	Date		Status
Caretta caretta (Loggerhead)	1978	T	Entire population
Chelonia mydas (Green turtle)	1978	E	Breeding populations in Florida and on Mexican Pacific coast
		T	All other populations
Eretmochelys imbricata (Hawksbill)	1970	E	Entire population
Lepidochelys kempii (Kemp's ridley)	1970	E	Entire population
Lepidochelys olivacea (Pacific ridley)	1978	E	Breeding population on Mexican Pacific coast
		T	All other populatons
Dermochelys coriacea (Leatherback)	1970	E	Entire population
Sternotherus depressus (Flattened musk turtle)	1987	T	Black Warrior River upstream from Bankhead Dam
Graptemys flavimaculata (Yellow-blotched map turtle)	1991	T	Entire population
Graptemys oculifera (Ringed map turtle)	1986	T	Entire population
Pseudemys alabamensis (Alabama red-bellied turtle)	1987	E	Entire population
Pseudemys rubriventris (Red-bellied turtle)	1980	E	Massachusetts populations
Gopherus agassizii (Desert tortoise)	1980	T	Entire, except Arizona south and east of Colorado River
Gopherus polyphemus (Gopher tortoise)	1987	T	West of Mobile and Tombigbee rivers

Identification of turtles

The accompanying key to the turtles of the United States and Canada is designed to enable one to identify the animal in hand. The characters most often used are those of the shell, limbs, and head—usually the least variable characters within a species. Occasionally it is necessary to refer to some character of the skull for positive identification.

Within a population of turtles any character will show individual variation; the larger the sample the greater the extremes. In most cases, however, a specimen will have the character as described in the key or at least can be placed within the middle range of measurements. Still, one may encounter a turtle in which the character is quite different or in which the measurements fall outside the given range. For this and other reasons no key is infallible, so after one has arrived at a name by use of the key, the animal should be compared with the photographs and the description in the species account.

Difficulties in keying are most frequent when the turtle is immature (or, sometimes, a preserved specimen). Then one should follow each alternative down to species and in each case examine that possibility by reference to the photographs and text.

If the reader still cannot identify the turtle, it is likely foreign—someone's pet, escaped or released. In this case we suggest the reader consult the work of Ernst and Barbour (1989).

KEY TO THE TURTLES OF THE UNITED STATES AND CANADA

Identification characters apply to living *adults*. Before attempting to key immature or preserved specimens see the introductory remarks.

1a. Shell covered with horny plates 2
 b. Shell covered with leathery skin 52
2a. Limbs paddlelike; strictly marine (Family Cheloniidae) 3
 b. Limbs not paddlelike; not strictly marine ... 7
3a. Four pairs of pleurals; cervical not in contact with the first pleurals 4
 b. Five or more pairs of pleurals; cervical touches the first pleurals 5
4a. One pair of prefrontal scales; lower jaw strongly serrated .... *Chelonia mydas*
 b. Two pairs of prefrontal scales; lower jaw only

weakly serrated .... *Eretmochelys imbricata*
5a. Bridge with three inframarginal scales
 .... *Caretta caretta*
 b. Bridge with four inframarginal scales 6
6a. Commonly only five pairs of pleurals; color gray .... *Lepidochelys kempii*
 b. Commonly more than five pairs of pleurals; color olive .... *Lepidochelys olivacea*
7a. Hind feet elephantine and not webbed; forefeet shovellike and modified for digging; strictly terrestrial (Family Testudinidae) 8
 b. Hind feet not elephantine and more or less

webbed; forefeet not shovellike; aquatic or semiaquatic 10

8a. Distance from base of first claw to base of fourth claw on forefoot approximately equal to the same measurement on hind foot; restricted to southern Texas or the southwestern United States 9

b. Distance from base of first claw to base of third claw on forefoot approximately equal to the distance from the base of first claw to base of fourth claw on hind foot; restricted to southeastern United States .... *Gopherus polyphemus*

9a. Paired axillary scutes; restricted to southern Texas .... *Gopherus berlandieri*

b. Single axillary scute; restricted to southwestern United States .... *Gopherus agassizii*

10a. Plastron small and cross-shaped; tail more than half the carapace length (Family Chelydridae) 11

b. Plastron not cross-shaped; tail length less than half the carapace length 12

11a. A row of supramarginal scutes above the marginals on each side; upper jaw strongly hooked; carapace with three prominent keels extending the entire length ...... *Macroclemys temminckii*

b. No supramarginals; upper jaw not strongly hooked; carapacial keels not extending the entire length .... *Chelydra serpentina*

12a. Plastron covered with 10 or 11 horny scutes; pectoral scute not in contact with marginals (Family Kinosternidae) 13

b. Plastron covered with 12 horny scutes; pectoral scute touches marginals (Family Emydidae) 21

13a. Pectoral scutes rectangular; some skin showing between plastral scutes; a single, indistinct transverse hinge between pectoral and abdominal scutes 14

b. Pectoral scutes triangular; no skin showing between plastral scutes; two prominent transverse hinges bordering abdominal scutes 17

14a. Two light stripes on side of head; barbels on chin and throat; nonoverlapping carapacial scutes .... *Sternotherus odoratus*

b. Light stripes absent from side of head; barbels on chin only; overlapping carapacial scutes 15

15a. Gular scute absent; very prominent vertebral keel .... *Sternotherus carinatus*

b. Gular scute present; vertebral keel not strongly developed (two dorsolateral keels may also be present on young individuals) 16

16a. Carapace wide and flattened, its sides slope at an

angle greater than 100°; mean angle/height ratio is 8:1 or greater .... *Sternotherus depressus*

b. Carapace not greatly flattened, its sides slope at an angle less than 100°; mean angle/height ratio is about 5:1 in those with a vertebral keel .... *Sternotherus minor*

17a. Ninth marginal much higher than eighth .... *Kinosternon flavescens*

b. Ninth marginal as high as or only slightly higher than eighth 18

18a. Carapace with three longitudinal light stripes; abdominal scute long ..... *Kinosternon baurii*

b. Carapace plain, not striped; abdominal scute not particularly long 19

19a. First vertebral widely separated from second marginals .... *Kinosternon subrubrum*

b. First vertebral touches second marginals .. 20

20a. Carapace medially keeled (keel well-developed at least posteriorly), arched as viewed directly from front; shell less than twice as broad as deep .... *Kinosternon hirtipes*

b. Carapace depressed, flattened when viewed directly from front, but some individuals may have a single low medial keel and others a low medial keel and two low dorsolateral keels; shell twice as broad as deep .. *Kinosternon sonoriense*

21a. Plastron with well-developed hinge between pectoral and abdominal scutes 22

b. Plastron without well-developed hinge 24

22a. Upper jaw notched; chin and throat bright yellow .... *Emydoidea blandingii*

b. Upper jaw without a notch; chin and throat not yellow 23

23a. Carapace keeled; pattern variable .... *Terrapene carolina*

b. Carapace not keeled; pattern of radiating lines on pleurals and plastron constant .... *Terrapene ornata*

24a. Neck extremely long (distance from snout to shoulder approximately equal to plastron length); forelimb stripe very broad .... *Deirochelys reticularia*

b. Neck not long (distance from snout to shoulder approximately equal to half plastron length); forelimb stripes narrow 25

25a. Upper jaw with a prominent notch which may or may not be bordered on each side by toothlike cusps 26

b. Upper jaw without a prominent notch 35

26a. Carapace keelless, not serrated posteriorly .... *Chrysemys picta*

b. Carapace with or without a keel but serrated posteriorly 27

27a. Crushing surface of upper jaw without a tuberculate ridge extending parallel to its margin 28

b. Crushing surface of the upper jaw with a row of tubercles on ridge extending parallel to its margin 29

28a. Red, orange, or yellow postorbital stripe touches orbit; pleural scutes patterned with parallel-sided stripes, not reticulations; plastron patterned with black blotches or ocelli .... *Trachemys scripta*

b. Large, black-bordered orange postorbital stripe separated from orbit; pleural scutes patterned with light reticulating lines; plastron patterned with a large, dark central figure .... *Trachemys gaigeae*

29a. Prefrontal arrow present on dorsal surface of snout, formed by a sagittal stripe passing anteriorly between the eyes to meet right and left supratemporal stripes *above* nostrils 30

b. Prefrontal arrow absent 32

30a. Paramedial stripes end in back of eyes .... *Pseudemys nelsoni*

b. Paramedial stripes continue forward between eyes and onto snout 31

31a. Carapace elevated medially; restricted to area around Mobile Bay, Alabama .... *Pseudemys alabamensis*

b. Carapace flattened medially; restricted to Atlantic Coastal Plain .... *Pseudemys rubriventris*

32a. A light C-shaped mark or a series of light whorls present on second pleural scute; plastron with dark markings 33

b. No light C-shaped mark on second pleural scute; plastron immaculate yellow .... *Pseudemys floridana*

33a. Second pleural patterned with a light C-shaped mark or vertical light bar; ranges no farther west than east-central Texas and eastern Oklahoma and Kansas .... *Pseudemys concinna*

b. A series of distinct light whorls on second pleural 34

34a. Second pleural patterned with 4–5 light-centered whorls of concentric black and yellow or orange enclosed in a wide, yellow or orange branching stripe; restricted to Rio Grande drainage .... *Pseudemys gorzugi*

b. Second pleural patterned with 5–6 dark-centered whorls; restricted to central Texas .... *Pseudemys texana*

35a. Crushing surface of upper jaw narrow 36

b. Crushing surface of upper jaw broad 39

36a. Carapace with some indication of a keel ... 37

b. Carapace smooth, without a keel 38

37a. Temporal region of head with a conspicuous orange blotch; carapace weakly keeled .... *Clemmys muhlenbergii*

b. Temporal region of head without an orange blotch; carapace strongly keeled .... *Clemmys insculpta*

38a. Carapace blue-black and marked with rounded yellow spots; found east of Mississippi River .... *Clemmys guttata*

b. Carapace mottled but without rounded yellow spots; found west of Rocky Mountains .... *Clemmys marmorata*

39a. Scutes of carapace rough, with concentric ridges or striations; head and neck without longitudinal stripes .... *Malaclemys terrapin*

b. Scutes of carapace smooth, without concentric ridges or striations; head and neck striped 40

40a. Vertebral keel low, without prominent spines or knobs 41

b. Vertebral keel well-developed, with prominent spines or knobs 42

41a. Horizontal or J-shaped reddish to orange mark behind eye; scutes of carapace distinctly convex; small size .... *Graptemys versa*

b. Yellowish spot behind eye; scutes of carapace not convex; medium to large size .... *Graptemys geographica*

42a. Vertebral keel with blunt, rounded black knobs .... *Graptemys nigrinoda*

b. Vertebral keel with sharp, narrow spines .. 43

43a. A large solid orange or yellow spot on each pleural scute .... *Graptemys flavimaculata*

b. Solid orange or yellow spot absent from pleural scutes 44

44a. A light ring or oval mark on each pleural scute .... *Graptemys oculifera*

b. No ring or oval mark on pleural scutes ... 45

45a. Large, solid light mark behind the eye 46

b. Narrow light lines behind eye 49

46a. A curved or transverse bar under chin; narrow light bars on marginals ... *Graptemys barbouri*

b. A longitudinal light bar under chin: broad light bars on marginals 47

47a. Interorbital blotch not connected or, rarely, narrowly connected to postorbital blotches; well-developed trident-shaped light mark present on dorsal surface of snout; a pair of supraoccipital spots or bulbous anterior projections of first pair of paramedial neck stripes present .... *Graptemys ernsti*

b. Interorbital blotch well connected to postorbital blotches; trident-shaped light mark present or absent on dorsal surface of snout; pair of supraoccipital spots or bulbous anterior projections of first pair of paramedial neck stripes rarely present 48

48a. Nasal trident commonly present, and a single, wide, yellow bar (16–21% as wide as scute) present on dorsal surface of each marginal scute .... *Graptemys gibbonsi*

b. Nasal trident absent, and a series of narrow, concentric, yellow ocelli (broadest only 10% as wide as scute) present on dorsal surface of each marginal scute .... *Graptemys pulchra*

49a. Light postorbital stripe originates beneath orbit and continues onto dorsal surface of head, commonly preventing neck stripes from reaching orbit 50

b. Light postorbital stripe originates behind orbit, does not prevent neck stripes from reaching orbit 51

50a. Chin with transverse cream-colored bar; no longitudinal yellow mark at symphysis of lower jaw; carapacial scutes lumpy
.... *Graptemys caglei*

b. Chin lacking a transverse cream-colored bar; a longitudinal yellow mark at symphysis of lower jaw; carapacial scutes smooth, not lumpy
.... *Graptemys pseudogeographica kohnii*

51a. Postorbital mark narrow; spots on lower jaw, if present, small
. *Graptemys pseudogeographica pseudogeographica*

b. Postorbital mark square, rectangularly elongate, or oval; large light spot just beneath orbit, and another on lower jaw
.... *Graptemys ouachitensis*

52a. Limbs paddlelike; snout blunt, not tubular; entirely marine (Family Dermochelyidae) .... *Dermochelys coriacea*

b. Limbs not paddlelike; snout an elongate tube; entirely freshwater (Family Trionychidae) 53

53a. Nostril round with no ridge projecting from septum; anterior rim of carapace without tubercles .... *Trionyx muticus*

b. Nostril crescentic with ridge projecting inward from septum; anterior rim of carapace with knobs or tubercles 54

54a. Marginal ridge present 55

b. Marginal ridge absent ...... *Trionyx spiniferus*

55a. Large cluster of coarse tubercles (wattles) at base of neck; restricted to Hawaiian Islands .... *Trionyx steindachneri*

b. No coarse tubercles (wattles) at base of neck 56

56a. Head plain or with a yellow band from posterior corner of eye to base of lower jaw; restricted to extreme southeastern United States .... *Trionyx ferox*

b. Head plain or with fine black lines radiating from eyes; no yellow band on side of head; restricted to Hawaiian Islands
.... *Trionyx sinensis*

Chelydridae
Snapping turtles

This New World family contains two monotypic genera, *Chelydra* and *Macroclemys,* that range from Canada to Ecuador. The fossil record of the family dates from the Paleocene of North America (*Hoplochelys*).

The temporal region of the skull is only slightly emarginate, and the frontals do not enter the orbit. No contact occurs between the parietal and squamosal bones. The maxilla is not connected to the quadratojugal, and only rarely is its crushing surface ridged. The quadrate encloses the stapes. No secondary palate is present, and the tip of the upper jaw is hooked. The tenth dorsal vertebra lacks ribs, and the neck has only one biconvex vertebra. The well-developed, rough carapace is keeled, strongly serrated posteriorly, and does not become fully ossified until late in life. The nuchal bone has rib-shaped lateral processes, which extend below the marginals. The costals are reduced laterally, and 11 peripherals lie on each side. Neural bones total seven or eight and one or two suprapygals are present. Only 11 marginal scutes occur on each side of the carapace. *Macroclemys* has inframarginal scutes and a series of supramarginals. The carapace is connected to the reduced, cross-shaped, hingeless plastron by a narrow bridge. Plastral features include a T-shaped entoplastron and a median plastral fontanelle. The abdominal scutes are reduced to the bridge and commonly do not touch medially. Limbs are well developed, webbed and heavily clawed. The saw-toothed tail is as long or longer than the carapace.

Both living species have a diploid chromosome total of 52, but they differ in the morphology of certain chromosomes (Bickham and Carr, 1983). Haiduk and Bickham (1982) concluded that *Chelydra* and *Macroclemys* do not share any derived chromosomal characteristics with each other or with any other families of cryptodiran turtles. However, the karyotype of *Macroclemys* could be derived from that of *Chelydra* (which is considered to be the primitive karyotype of the family). In a study of the penial morphology of cryptodiran turtles Zug (1966) found that the glans penis is nearly identical in *Chelydra* and *Macroclemys,* except for an additional fold in the latter, further suggesting close relationship between the two genera, and possible evolution of the latter from the former.

Chelydra serpentina (Linnaeus, 1758)
Snapping turtle

PLATE I

RECOGNITION: The snapping turtle is a large freshwater turtle with a posteriorly very serrated carapace (to 49.4 cm; Gerholdt and Oldfield, 1987) that has three low keels composed of knobs placed near to or well behind the centers of the scutes. The keels become less conspicuous with age, and old turtles may be smooth shelled. The carapace varies from tan, brown, or olive to black, and each scute may have a pattern of radiating lines. The bridge is short (10% or less of plastron length) and the yellowish to tan plastron is reduced, giving a cross-shaped appearance. The head is large with dorsolateral orbits and a somewhat hooked upper jaw. The yellow to cream-colored jaws are large and powerful, and many are patterned with dark streaks; two barbels lie on the chin. The neck is relatively long, its dorsal surface adorned with tubercles, and the tail is as long or longer than the carapace and bears three longitudinal rows of tubercles. The legs are large and powerful with webbed toes and heavy claws. Skin color is gray to black or yellow to tan, commonly patternless, but with whitish flecks on some individuals.

Males have the anal opening posterior to the carapacial rim. Their preanal tail length is commonly more than 120% of the length of the posterior plastral lobe, but that of females is generally less than 110% (R. J. Brooks, pers. comm.). Males generally grow larger than females (Gibbons and Lovich, 1990).

KARYOTYPE: Diploid chromosomes number 52: 24 macrochromosomes and 28 microchromosomes (Stock, 1972; Bickham and Baker, 1976; Killebrew, 1977b; Haiduk and Bickham, 1982).

FOSSIL RECORD: The oldest fossils of *Chelydra serpentina* are from the Pliocene Hemphillian and Blancan of Kansas (Galbreath, 1948; Hibbard, 1963; Schultz, 1965), and Blancan of Nebraska (Holman and Schloeder, 1991). Pleistocene remains have been found in Irvingtonian deposits from Kansas (Hibbard and Taylor, 1960; Holman, 1972, 1986a,b) and Maryland (Hay, 1923), and at Rancholabrean sites in Florida (Hay, 1916; Weigel, 1962; Holman, 1978), Illinois (Holman, 1966), Michigan (Wilson, 1967; Holman, 1988), Nevada (Van Devender and Tessman, 1975), Ohio (Holman, 1986b), Pennsylvania (Hay, 1923), Tennessee (Corgan, 1976) and Texas (Holman, 1964).

DISTRIBUTION: *Chelydra serpentina* ranges from Nova Scotia, New Brunswick, and southern Quebec west to southeastern Alberta, and southward east of the Rocky Mountains to southern Florida and the Texas coast in the United States. Populations also occur in Veracruz, Mexico, and thence southward, with some breaks, through Central America to western Ecuador. In North America it has been found from sea level to altitudes over 2,000 m.

GEOGRAPHIC VARIATION: Four subspecies are known, but only two reside in the United States or Canada (Ernst and Barbour, 1989). *Chelydra serpentina serpentina* (Linnaeus, 1758), the common snapping turtle, ranges from southern Canada to the Texas coast and at least as far as southern Georgia. The temporal region and back of the head are covered with flat juxtaposed plates, the dorsal surface of the neck with rounded, wartlike tubercles; the width of the third vertebral scute is much less than the height of the second pleural scute and less than 33% of the combined length of the five vertebral scutes, and the length of the plastral forelobe (from the level of the hyo-hypoplastral suture to the anterior tip) is less than 40% of the carapace length. *Chelydra s. osceola* Stejneger, 1918, the Florida snapping turtle, seems restricted to peninsular Florida. The temporal region and back of the head are covered with granular scales and a scattering of low tubercles, the dorsal surface of

Chelydra serpentina serpentina

Chelydra serpentina osceola

the neck with long pointed tubercles; the width of the third vertebral is about as long as or more than the height of the second pleural and about 33% of the combined length of the five vertebrals, and the length of the plastral forelobe is less than 40% of the carapace length. The forelobe of the two tropical subspecies is commonly longer than 40% of carapace length.

Some researchers consider *Chelydra s. osceola* to be a separate species rather than conspecific with *C. serpentina* (Richmond, 1958). Recent treatment of this form has relegated it to subspecific rank (Medem,

1977; Gibbons et al., 1988), on the basis of a report of supposed intergradation between *serpentina* and *osceola* by Feuer (1971b). However, Feuer examined relatively few turtles and found only seven he thought intergrade. A more thorough study is needed of the relationships between these two snapping turtles in northern Florida and southern Georgia.

CONFUSING SPECIES: *Macroclemys temminckii* has a row of supramarginals between the lateral marginal scutes and the pleurals, a strongly

Plastron of *Chelydra serpentina*

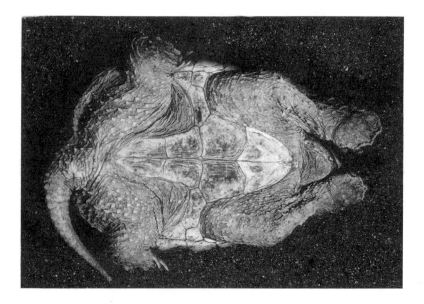

Tail of *Chelydra serpentina*

hooked beak, lateral orbits, and three high carapacial keels at all ages. *Kinosternon* and *Sternotherus* have short tails and better developed plastrons with one or two hinges.

HABITAT: *Chelydra serpentina* has been found in almost every kind of freshwater habitat within its range. It prefers slow-moving water with a soft mud or sand bottom and abundant aquatic vegetation or an abundance of submerged brush and tree trunks. Most of the water bodies in which it lives are shallow, but it may occur along the edges of deep lakes and rivers. Laboratory studies of habitat preferences of juvenile snapping turtles have confirmed field observations (Froese, 1978).

The Florida snapping turtle is often found in

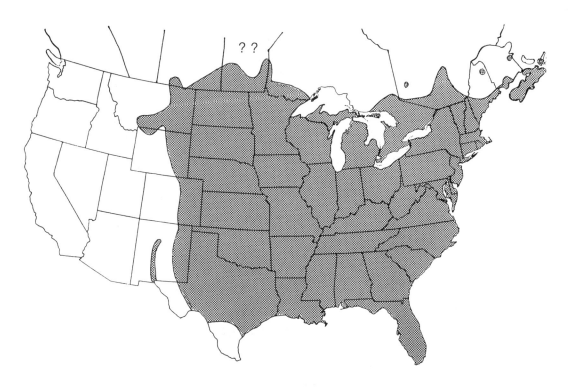

canals, sloughs, and pools and is one of the few tetrapods regularly found in acidic, muck-bottomed hammock streams. Large adults may even share holes with bull alligators. Juveniles often take refuge in clumps of water hyacinth.

The snapping turtle also enters brackish coastal waterways (Kiviat, 1980; Dunson, 1986). Salt marsh populations of *Chelydra serpentina* may represent a very early stage in evolution toward an estuarine life style; however, osmoregulatory adaptation is incomplete (Dunson, 1986). Subadults and adults immersed in sea water for extended periods by Dunson (1986) showed a continual, gradual loss of body water and an increase in plasma osmotic pressure. No evidence of extracloacal excretion by salt glands was found. Hatchlings derived from eggs of *C. serpentina* living in a saline creek grew much faster in 35% sea water, but slower in fresh water, than those from a freshwater marsh, but the saline-adapted hatchlings could not grow in salinities greater than 41% sea water. Behavioral osmoregulation seemed important, inasmuch as adults moved between the more and less saline portions of the tidal creek, thus avoiding long exposures to harmful salinities. Adult skin was quite permeable to water, but essentially impermeable to

sodium, and net water loss in sea water was inversely proportional to body mass. Large individuals had a considerable advantage over smaller turtles in attempting to osmoregulate in saline water.

BEHAVIOR: The snapping turtle is one of the more aquatic species of turtles. It spends most of its time lying on the bottom of some deep pool or buried in the mud in shallow water with only its eyes and nostrils exposed. The depth of the water above the mud is usually comparable to the length of the neck, for the nostrils must be periodically raised to the surface. The turtle also hides beneath stumps, roots, brush, and other objects in the water and in muskrat burrows and lodges.

Although thought to be most active at night over much of the southern range, studies at Algonquin Park, Ontario, indicate only rare nocturnal activity at northern sites (Obbard and Brooks, 1981b). Most summer activity in Ontario is in the morning or early evening. In laboratory studies, juvenile *Chelydra serpentina* were most active between 0500–0600 and 0800–0900, and least active at 1200–1300 and 2300–2400, but some activity occurred at all hours (Graham, 1978).

Chelydra serpentina serpentina

Chelydra serpentina osceola;
note long tubercles on neck

Chelydra usually moves about by creeping slowly over the bottom; however, when disturbed it can swim rapidly. By day it often floats lazily just beneath the surface with only its eyes and nostrils protruding. A social relationship in which *Chrysemys picta* basked on the back of floating snapping turtles has been described by Legler (1956). In contrast, other species of aquatic turtles usually avoid basking sites occupied by *Chelydra*.

In the deep South, particularly peninsular Florida, *Chelydra serpentina* may be active year round, but even there cold winter temperatures will drive it to dormancy. Activity increases during March in southern populations, but most northern snapping turtles do not emerge from hibernation before April, or even May in Canada. In summer, if their waterway dries, some snappers estivate in the mud, but others migrate to wetter nearby areas. Captives kept under natural conditions in Germany had annual activity cycles corresponding to those of wild North American turtles (Haas, 1985).

Most enter hibernation by late October: they burrow into the mud bottom, settle beneath logs or plant debris, crawl up under overhanging banks, or retreat into muskrat burrows or lodges. Overwintering snappers may even bury themselves in the soil of boggy pastures. Large congregations sometimes hibernate together (Meeks and Ultsch, 1990), and other species of turtles may join them. Not all become totally dormant in winter, even in the North; individuals have been seen crawling along under the ice in midwinter. In a study of winter movements using radiotelemetry, snappers collected from the Connecticut River were released into a small pond in Rhode Island during October by Ultsch and Lee (1983). Movements of up to 450 m occurred until 4 December, with the frequency of burial in mud increasing as winter approached. By that date all the turtles had moved into the inlet stream of the pond and had buried themselves in mud near the shore, where they remained dormant until 24 March. The flowing water of the stream may have provided needed oxygen, but two turtles froze. Submerged hibernating snapping turtles studied by Penn (in Brattstrom, 1965) had body temperatures of 5°C which matched the surrounding mud and water, and were similar to the above turtles, but captives kept outdoors in Germany had a lowest thermoactivity limit of 9°C (Haas, 1985).

Additional studies of hibernating *Chelydra serpentina* by Meeks and Ultsch (1990) in Ohio have confirmed a decrease in activity in early autumn. Snapping turtles spend a great deal of time buried in mud during the fall once water temperatures fall below 15°C, probably because they do not feed below this temperature and therefore do not forage (Obbard and Brooks, 1981b). All autumn movements cease at water temperatures of 5°C. Preferred hibernacula seem to have some combination of: (1) water shallow enough to let the turtle reach the surface to breathe without having to swim upward, but deep enough to prevent its freezing to the bottom; (2) a location that is likely to be the last to freeze over and/or the first to thaw; (3) mud deep enough for the turtle to bury itself; and (4) some additional cover, such as vegetation, brush, muskrat dwelling, or overhanging bank (Meeks and Ultsch, 1990). During the study by Meeks and Ultsch, a few of the Ohio snappers moved slightly during a brief thaw. *C. serpentina* survives better in normoxic waters during the winter because of its ability to use extrapulmonary gas exchange, and it can derive more than 11% of its aerobic oxygen demand at 4°C from the water (Gatten, 1980). Mud, however, is anoxic, so if the turtle buries too deep and

becomes torpid, it could die, probably from severe metabolic acidosis; however, Canadian *Chelydra* have spent the entire winter buried in anoxic mud with no apparent ill effects (R. J. Brooks, pers. comm.). Snapping turtles studied by Ultsch and Lee (1983) had cardiac blood lactate of 44.8 mM (Ultsch and Jackson, unpubl.) after about 3.5 months of hibernation (normal values for air-breathing turtles are <2 mM; Ultsch et al., 1984).

In Pennsylvania, *Chelydra serpentina* usually becomes active in the spring when water temperatures rise above 5°C (Ernst, pers. obs.), but in Canada, water temperatures of about 7.5°C may be necessary to bring it out of hibernation (Obbard and Brooks, 1981b). Turtles at both localities apparently do not feed until water temperatures have risen to 15°C. The mean critical maximum of eight *C. s. serpentina* studied by Hutchison et al. (1966) was 39.5°C (37.4–40.6); this was one of the lowest maxima among several species examined. The thermoactivity range of several *C. s. osceola* observed by Punzo (1975) was 18.7–32.6°C; he also found that a direct linear correlation exists between cloacal temperature and that of the environment.

Snapping turtles subjected to an aquatic thermal gradient of 21–23°C to 35–36°C by Schuett and Gatten (1980) showed a mean preferred body temperature of 28.1°C and mean hourly temperature preferences of 22.3–32.8°C. Sixty-six percent of the records fell between 25.5 and 30.5°C. No diurnal cycle in preferred temperature was evident. Williamson et al. (1989) acclimated juveniles at either 25°C or 15°C. When placed in a terrestrial temperature gradient, turtles from both 15°C and 25°C regimes selected similar body temperatures in fall/winter and spring (mean 24.6). In spring, turtles from both regimes selected a mean temperature of 28°C in an aquatic gradient. The critical thermal maximum of 25°C turtles was significantly higher (mean 41.1) than that of 15°C turtles (mean 39.1). The 15°C turtles were transferred to 25°C and the 25°C turtles to 15°C. After a week the critical thermal maxima of the two groups were the same, but after three weeks the 15°C to 25°C snappers had significantly higher averages (41.4°C) than the 25°C to 15°C turtles (39.6°C). The critical thermal maximum seems to be directly related to the acclimation temperature, but selected temperature is independent of acclimation temperature.

In Ontario, Canada, the body temperature of hibernating *Chelydra* may drop to 1–2°C for most of the winter, but if the turtle freezes it will probably die, as individuals cooled to 0°C, or slightly below, in the laboratory die immediately (R. J. Brooks, pers. comm.).

Brown et al. (1990) radio-monitored the body temperatures of eight adults at Algonquin Provincial Park, Ontario, to determine if they would use a combination of aquatic and atmospheric basking to maintain their temperatures within the range of 28–30°C selected by *Chelydra* in experiments within a controlled aquatic thermal gradient. The mean body temperature of all eight turtles over the study period was 22.7°C even though they had ample opportunity to select temperatures near 28°C. The mean temperature of each turtle was well below the mean selected range in the thermal gradient. However, the mean body temperatures differed significantly among the turtles despite no significant difference between air temperature or operative environmental temperature recorded at the same time. Brown et al. thought different foraging tactics, metabolic rates and home range structure may have contributed to these differences. Snapping turtles from northern populations may be adapted to lower temperatures than those from more southern parts of the range.

The effect of nutritional state on the selection of environmental temperature was studied in seven-month-old *Chelydra serpentina* by Knight et al. (1990). Satiated juveniles occupied a cooler mean selected position on a temperature gradient than did any other turtles, and the authors concluded that hatchling snappers do not exhibit a thermophilic response associated with feeding. Nutritional status affects the mean selected temperature only because recently fed turtles tend to be more sedentary. In similar studies on the thermal responses of fed wild adults in Canada, the turtles did not bask or seek a warmer habitat, nor did they experience significantly warmer temperatures than did unfed controls. Instead the fed turtles buried in the substrate and were less active and remained in shallower water than unfed controls (Brown and Brooks, 1991).

Gatten (1978) measured the oxygen consumption of resting and active snapping turtles at 10, 20, and 30°C after acclimation to either 10 or 25°C. Cold acclimation resulted in depressed resting and active rates of oxygen consumption and also in a decreased aerobic metabolic scope for activity (changes which facilitated hibernation). Warm acclimation resulted in high aerobic ability which supported aquatic and terrestrial activity.

Chelydra serpentina had a water-loss gradient of 0.64 g/h, which was the greatest among five species of turtles from Pennsylvania examined by Ernst (1968b). Water and electrolyte compositions of various-sized snapping turtles were studied by Dunson and Heatwole (1986). Differences in water, sodium, and potassium concentrations of entire turtles were related to the relative size of their shell: those with smaller shells had higher water and potassium concentrations, but lower sodium levels. These effects are associated with variation in the amount of shell bone, which is lower in both water and potassium than other tissues.

Aerial basking in *Chelydra serpentina* probably is restricted by intolerance of high temperatures and by rapid loss of moisture. Nevertheless, snapping turtles do occasionally bask out of water, but at a lesser frequency than do sympatric emydid turtles (Boyer, 1965; Feuer, 1979; Ernst, pers. obs.). Usually, basking occurs either while floating at the surface with just the head and top of the carapace exposed, or on some low perch close to the water. Normally only one snapper occupies a basking site at a time. Obbard and Brooks (1979) reported aerial basking to be common in Ontario; perhaps cooler environmental temperatures at that latitude require more frequent basking to maintain proper physiological activities (this point is supported by Brown et al., 1990, who found much less basking in *Chelydra* in the same population in a warmer summer than that reported by Obbard and Brooks). The number of aerial baskers in Ontario is positively correlated with total daily solar radiation and maximum air temperature, but negatively correlated with the total daily amount of precipitation. Maximum water temperature has little influence. The mean (27.6°C) and maximum (34.0°C) cloacal temperatures of Ontario baskers are significantly above ambient air temperatures.

Snapping turtles, at least nesting females, sometimes travel considerable distances, both overland and in water (Obbard and Brooks, 1980). In Canada, Brooks (pers. comm.) has recorded adult males making extensive (>1 km) overland trips over steep terrain and through dry maple woods. Trips by two males seemed to be annual movements between water bodies. Barbour (1950) found a juvenile on top of Big Black Mountain, Kentucky, more than 2 km from the nearest stream large enough to support fish and more than 8 km from the nearest pond. A pair of *Chelydra serpentina* observed by Klimstra (1951) moved overland 558 m from a drying pond to a stream, at an overland speed of 0.2 km/h, but they made two brief stops. In Pennsylvania nine adults, recaptured a total of 16 times, moved an average of 74.5 m between recaptures and had estimated home ranges averaging 1.8 ha (Ernst, 1968c). This is less than the overall average 3.4-ha home range of the 10 turtles carrying radio transmitters in Ontario studied by Obbard and Brooks (1981b); six males had an average home range of 3.21 ha (0.95–8.38) and three females, 3.79 ha (2.50–5.19). No significant difference was detectable in home range area for either sex, or for the correlation of area to carapace length. An additional five marked, but not radio-equipped, animals had home ranges averaging 1.54 ha (0.79–2.75). This area was also not significantly different from that of the radio-equipped turtles. Considerable overlap of home ranges between and within the sexes occurred with no apparent territoriality. Some individuals shifted their home ranges during Obbard and Brooks's two-year study.

Home ranges of four males fitted with radio transmitters at a lake near the study site of Obbard and Brooks (1981b) overlapped. Average size and location of the home ranges were relatively stable during the two summers of study. Though spacing may be maintained by aggressive interactions, male *Chelydra* do not seem truly territorial (Galbraith et al., 1987). Combat between large male snapping turtles does at times occur (Kiviat, 1980; Janzen and O'Steen, 1990), but is this territorial or merely social dominance? Do the winners of these bouts gain a reproductive advantage by influencing female mate choice? These are pertinent questions to be answered through further research.

The average distance traveled by 107 snapping turtles studied by Hammer (1969) was 1.1 km (0–6.05). The mean distance moved in one year was 0.92 km. One female moved 3.4 km in 10 days, but most traveled considerably less and many were recaptured in the same location 4–6 days later. Most of the movements occurred within the same marsh. Fifty-three percent of the recaptures were on a dike where nesting females were originally marked, and 74% had not left the pool where they had been marked; that is, there was little movement between pools.

Hatchlings are attracted to large areas of intense illumination and thus find their way from nests to the water. Escape from the nest is aided by a marked negative geotropism in the dark. Hatchlings are also attracted toward areas of high humidity; but the presence of a light source in a drier area will counteract any tendency to move into a wet area (Noble and Breslau, 1938). Adult *Chelydra* may use the sun as a directional guide while traveling overland (Gibbons and Smith, 1968). Two individuals chose blue 69% of the time and red 25% in trials with a choice of red-, yellow-, green- or blue-lighted compartments; the significance of this is not known (Ernst and Hamilton, 1969).

Although it prefers shallow waters, *Chelydra serpentina* is capable of diving to depths of at least 2–3 m (Ernst, pers. obs.), where it may remain for some time. A male in Ontario regularly stayed on the bottom of a lake in 5–10 m of water (R. J. Brooks, pers. comm.).

Deep diving may present an oxygen uptake strain. Gatten (1980) made simultaneous determinations of aerial and aquatic oxygen uptake by voluntary diving snapping turtles at 4°C and 20°C. The standard rates of aerial oxygen consumption were equivalent in cold- and warm-acclimated turtles in water and in cold-acclimated animals in air, but these rates were all lower than those of warm-acclimated turtles in air. Either cold acclimation or voluntary submergence reduces the standard metabolic rate but the effects are not additive. Aquatic oxygen uptake during voluntary submergence is more important at low than at moderate temperatures and probably contributes greatly to gas exchange in these animals as they overwinter beneath the ice of ponds and streams.

Chelydra totally submerged at 10°C in anoxic waters can survive as long as 8.5 days (Ultsch et al., 1984). Snappers submerged under identical conditions in normoxic waters can survive over 14 days; however, the differences in survival times in the two waters are not significant. Apparently snapping turtles lack efficient aquatic respiratory mechanisms as they exhibit a continual decrease in both blood pH and buffering compounds during such tests (buffering capacity of the blood is −8.81). Hematocrit is increased. Death occurs when the blood pH falls by about 1.0 unit. Additional studies on the changes in plasma ion balance of submerged *C. serpentina* show that lactate, potassium, calcium, and magnesium increase, but bicarbonate and chloride decrease (Jackson et al., 1984). Plasma ion adjustments only compensate about 47% of the added lactate. The rate of lactate accumulation, the initial plasma weak ion buffering, and the magnitude of the respiratory acidosis all influence the development of anoxic acidosis, and eventually death. The most important stimulus triggering the resumption of breathing in a submerged snapping turtle is the rise in blood CO_2 concentration to a critical value during the preceding nonventilatory period (West et al., 1989). Breathing episodes following submergence usually contain multiple breaths.

REPRODUCTION: In Iowa, males of *Chelydra serpentina* mature at four or five years of age and plastron lengths of 149–155 mm (Christiansen and Burken, 1979). Male snapping turtles from Tennessee have mature sperm in their testes and epididymides when about 145 mm in plastron length; some may undergo spermatogenesis at plastron lengths as short as 123–135 mm, but their epididymides are not fully developed and contain few sperm (White and Murphy, 1973). This probably represents the first season of sperm production and these males would be capable of reproducing the next year. In Quebec, the smallest snapping turtle with sperm had a carapace length of 210 mm, corresponding to a plastron length of approximately 140–150 mm (Mosimann and Bider, 1960).

The spermatic cycle of snapping turtles from Tennessee and Wisconsin was studied by White and Murphy (1973) and Mahmoud and Cyrus (1992), respectively. The respective cycles at these two latitudes have similar phases, but differ in their timing: males from Tennessee have longer cycles. The cycle can be divided into an active phase (late June to mid-November in Tennessee and mid-May to September in Wisconsin) and a non-active phase (late November to mid-June in Tennessee and November to April in Wisconsin). The cycle of cell division begins in mid- to late May, with the early stages of spermatogonia (primary and secondary spermatocytes) present, and Sertoli cells located near the basement membrane. Spermatogenesis is in full progress by mid-July, with about six times as many spermatogonia as Sertoli cells. From July to mid-October groups of spermatozoa attach to the Sertoli cells. Testes are at their greatest mass in July and August. Spermiogenesis occurs rapidly in mid-July to August with spermatogonial divisions greatly reduced. By late September few primary or secondary spermatocytes remain. Spermatozoa occupy the epididymides in October, but small numbers still remain scattered in the lumina of the seminiferous tubules in Tennessee. Sertoli cells are prominent. No spermatogenic activity occurs during the winter. April males have Sertoli cells throughout the seminiferous tubules, outnumbering spermatogonia about 10 to 1. Tubule lumina contain some scattered spermatozoa and much detritus. Interstitial cell proliferation and regression are negatively correlated with fluctuations in seminiferous tubule diameter; interstitial cells are most abundant from November to May when tubules are smallest in diameter, and are least abundant in July and August. Epididymides contain sperm throughout the year, but are usually largest from November to May. The testosterone level is highest in May and October, but relatively low during the rest of the year (Mahmoud et al., 1985).

The presence of either oviducal eggs or of ovarian follicles at least 44 mm in diameter suggests that female *Chelydra serpentina* in Tennessee mature at about 145-mm plastron length (White and Murphy, 1973). However, females from Iowa enter a period of ovarian follicle development without ovulations between four and seven years of age at plastron lengths of 123–175 mm, and ovulations first occur during the sixth or, more often, later years of growth (Christiansen and Burken, 1979). The youngest known age of maturity for females from Michigan is 12 years (Congdon et al., 1987). Females from Quebec become mature at about 200-mm carapace length (approximately 150-mm plastron length, Mosimann and Bider, 1960). At Algonquin Provincial Park, Ontario, females mature at a larger size and greater age; mean age at first enlargement of ovarian follicles in immature females is about 11–13 years, and the mean age at first nesting is 17–19 years at carapace lengths of 24.9–25.8 cm (Galbraith et al., 1989). This suggests that age at first reproduction is less important to reproductive success than is female body size. Larger body size may increase fecundity and also improve ability to survive during hibernation.

The ovarian cycle of Tennessee females may be divided into three phases: a prereproductive phase from August to mid-May, a reproductive or egg laying season from mid-May to mid-June, and a postreproductive phase from mid-June through late July (White and Murphy, 1973). During the reproductive phase (mid-May to mid-June) ovarian follicles 4.4–25.0 mm in diameter are ovulated, fertilized, shelled, and laid, while follicles with diameters of 2.0–4.4 mm grow to a size comparable to the former group. Little further enlargement of follicles occurs during the postreproductive period (mid-June to late July). From August to mid-May (the prereproductive phase), a rapid enlargement of the follicles (vitellogenesis) occurs, as well as an increase in size of the ovaries and oviducts. The largest follicles average 6.8 mm in diameter in late July, 10.8 mm in August, and 23.3 mm in November. Little additional yolk is added over winter. Corpora lutea are detectable in females containing oviducal eggs, or in those that have recently nested, but these disappear by July, 3–6 weeks after the nesting season (Cyrus et al., 1978). Most clutches are deposited in May and June, and only one clutch is laid a year. The plasma albumin level remains unchanged throughout most of the ovarian cycle except during vitellogenesis, the plasma cholesterol level rises slowly throughout vitellogenesis and reaches a peak in late vitellogenesis (it remains at a low level throughout the rest of the ovarian cycle), and plasma phosphate levels remain relatively low throughout the cycle (Mahmoud et al., 1985). Estrogen levels coincide with follicular growth, rising during vitellogenesis and reaching a peak during the preovulatory period. Blood calcium levels follow this same pattern.

Mating occurs from April to November. Each encounter may be preceded by courtship, but pre-coital behavior varies (Legler, 1955). A male may directly approach a submerged female and mount her at once, or he may crawl or swim after her for several minutes and then mount her near the surface, with the pair slowly sinking to the bottom. The male and female may face each other on the bottom with necks extended and snouts almost touching. The hind quarters of each are usually elevated, the anterior edges of their plastrons touching the bottom. The heads and necks may be swung sideways in opposite directions and then brought slowly back to the original position. This sequence is usually repeated about 10 times at intervals of approximately 10 seconds (Legler, 1955). Courting snappers have also been seen with their heads close together in shallow water gulping water and violently expelling it out of their nostrils, causing upheaval of the water surface above their heads (Taylor, 1933).

In coital position the male is astride the carapace of the female, gripping its rim firmly with all four feet. When in place he curls his tail under her body and at the same time extends his chin over her snout so that she cannot extend her neck forward. He then begins a series of violent, coordinated muscular contractions of the legs, neck and tail. The neck is thrust forward and downward. He may bite the female about the head and neck or grasp a fold of loose skin. Flexure of the tail elevates her tail and improves cloacal contact. Muscular spasms occur before, during, and after intromission. The female is passive, except that at times she may struggle violently and attempt to retaliate as the male bites her.

Sperm may possibly remain viable in the female for several years. Gist and Jones (1989) found sperm stored in tubules in the posterior albumin-producing region of the oviduct, but no free sperm in the oviductal lumen after 15 days isolation. Ducts, restricted to this region, connect these tubules to the oviductal lumen, allowing motile sperm entrance to the tubules.

Over most of its North American range, *Chelydra serpentina* has an approximately three-week nesting period between 15 May and 15 June, but oviposition might occur prior to this in the south, or afterward in the north. In southern Florida, *C. s. osceola* has oviposited as early as late February or March (Ewert, 1976), and other nests have been found from early May to the first week of June in that state (Punzo,

1975; Ewert, 1976; Iverson, 1977a). In Canada, nesting may not begin until mid-June, with the season extending into July (Robinson and Bider, 1988).

In southeastern Pennsylvania, most nesting takes place in the evening, but in northern Virginia most females nest in the morning. Females from New York nest both in the morning (44%) and evening (56%; Petokas and Alexander, 1980). A similar bimodal nesting cycle occurs in Michigan, but there most females excavate in the morning (60%; Congdon et al., 1987).

Warming ambient temperatures seem to trigger the nesting response in female *Chelydra serpentina*. An accumulation of heat units (degree days) in an Ontario lake were used to predict the onset of the annual nesting season by Obbard and Brooks (1987). The technique assumed a minimum threshold of body temperature in *C. serpentina* that has physiological importance. By measuring minimum and maximum daily temperatures of the air, water, and soil, the daily heat accumulation was quantified. The minimum number of heat units necessary for females to nest was 344. The lake temperature in early June was about 20–25°C, and about 15–20 heat units accumulated each day. The date of the first nesting attempt varied by only 15 days over six years, but the number of heat units accumulated prior to nesting varied by only 7.5%. In South Dakota, nesting activity is influenced by air temperature and by precipitation (Hammer, 1969). Rising air temperatures above a minimum of 10–16°C result in greater nesting activity. Light rain coincident with or slightly preceding rising night temperatures also increases the activity. Most nesting takes place between 0500 and 0900 and between 1700 and 2100. Large females in a population may oviposit before smaller ones (Hammer, 1969; Petokas and Alexander, 1980), and possibly a synchronization of nesting by several females may decrease the overall rate of nest predation (Robinson and Bider, 1988).

An open site is usually selected and the nest is dug with the hind feet in relatively loose sand, loam, vegetable debris, or sawdust piles left at old sawmills. Muskrat and beaver lodges are sometimes used as nesting sites. Where nest sites are hard to find females rely extensively on manmade sites, such as roadsides, railways, and dams. In areas lacking artificial sites in Ontario, Brooks and his co-workers found nests in beaver lodges, small clearings where trees had been uprooted near shorelines, and even in the soil accumulated in cracks in granitic rocks on shorelines.

The nest normally is bowl shaped: a slightly narrower opening descends at an angle to a large egg chamber below. The depth of the nest generally ranges from 7 to 18 cm, but may be even deeper in nests dug by large females, and other nest dimensions vary accordingly.

Females may make considerable migrations from their home ranges to a suitable nesting area. In Ontario, the maximum round-trip distance traveled between home range and nest site was 16 km (mean 10.6 km; Obbard and Brooks, 1980); in Michigan, females moved as far as 1.6 km (straight-line distance) in preparation for nesting (Congdon et al., 1987). After reaching the nesting area, females may make an additional relatively long overland journey before choosing a site to excavate. *Chelydra* in Ontario moved as far as 0.5 km overland to nest (Obbard and Brooks, 1980), and a gravid female from Pennsylvania taken in early June was approximately 1.0 km from the nearest water (Ernst, pers. obs.). Nests dug by Michigan females averaged 37 m (1–183) straight-line distance from the nearest relatively permanent water (Congdon et al., 1987); the distance in Florida averaged 94 m (38–141; Punzo, 1975). Some Michigan females that were observed nesting in more than one year dug nests within 5 m of a previous year's nest, but others changed sites to areas up to 1 km away (Congdon et al., 1987). In Ontario, 74% of the females tagged the previous year returned to a nesting site on a sand-gravel dam (Loncke and Obbard, 1977), and a particular female nested in the same 5-m² area for 17 consecutive years (R. J. Brooks, pers. comm.). Most females return to the same site year after year, but some switch sites with differing regularity.

The effects of varying levels of progesterone and estrogen on the contractility of the uterine wall during the different phases of the ovarian cycle was studied by Mahmoud et al. (1987). Treatment of the uterine tissue segments with arginine vasotocin increased contractility while decreasing the latent period between contractions, except during the early postovulatory phase when the corpora lutea are actively producing steroids. Pretreatment of female *Chelydra* with progesterone decreased contractility during the early postovulatory phase but had no effect during the rest of the cycle. Pretreatment with estrogen increased contractility in all phases of the ovarian cycle except early postovulation when no effect on contractile amplitude was noticeable. Total time of rhythmic contractions increased greatly during all phases, but was lowest during the early postovulatory period. Females will occasionally retain the shelled eggs in the uterus beyond the nesting period (Galbraith et al., 1988b). The reason for this is unclear, and under such conditions the eggs would probably be resorbed.

The eggs are laid at intervals of approximately one to three minutes and are put in place by alternate movements of the hind feet. When the clutch is complete the nest is filled and concealed by alternate scraping with the hind feet. The area about the nest is considerably disturbed during the digging and filling processes. If the female is visited by an intruder while she is nesting, she may go steadily on with the job or else wait quietly until the disturbance ends.

The total number of eggs in a clutch may be as low as 6 or as high as 104, but a typical clutch contains 20–40. Clutch size seems to increase with latitude. Female *C. s. osceola* lay between 6 and 21 eggs in Florida (Punzo, 1975; Iverson, 1977a), but farther north most clutches average about 35 eggs. The record clutch of 104 eggs is from Nebraska (Miller et al., 1989a). The larger females lay the most eggs. Whether all mature females lay each year is not known. The white, tough, spherical eggs are 23–33 mm in diameter and weigh 5–15 g. In a fresh egg one pole is white and the other pinkish, and an air chamber occupies nearly half the space within the shell. The shell is moderately pliable with a rather thick calcareous layer and visible pores. Its inner membrane is about 67% as thick as the outer crystalline aragonitic layer (Hirsch, 1983). Within the crystalline layer, the basic units are as high as wide, arranged in groups, and not interlocking with adjacent units. Water composes an average of 68–73% of the wet weight of the egg (Congdon and Gibbons, 1985; Wilhoft, 1986). Both the outer mineral layer of the shell and the inner membrane offer strong resistance to diffusion of water vapor and oxygen (Feder et al., 1982), but still the eggshell conducts water vapor at a rate 55 times higher than predicted for birds' eggs of similar size (Packard et al., 1979b). The membrane accounts for 24–76% of the total resistance to the passage of water vapor. The shell constitutes about 23.5–30.0% of the dry weight of the egg, and the dry lipid and protein contents, about 55% (Congdon and Gibbons, 1985; Wilhoft, 1986). Each egg has an average dry lipid mass of 0.5 g, with the yolk containing about 23.5% lipids (Congdon and Gibbons, 1985); whole eggs contain about 12.4 kcal of energy (Wilhoft, 1986). The ash content of the eggshell is approximately 40% (Lamb and Congdon, 1985). During development approximately 40% of the lipid content, 53% of the protein, and 40% of the energy of the egg are utilized by the embryo (Wilhoft, 1986).

Natural incubation may take 55–125 days, but 75–95 days are more common; clutches from northern populations seem to have longer incubation periods

(Obbard and Brooks, 1981a; Congdon et al., 1987). The incubation period is inversely related to incubation temperature. During a study by Yntema (1978), snapping turtle eggs were incubated at constant temperatures of 20–35°C, with successful development occurring at 22–30°C. Mean incubation times for various temperatures were 93 days at 22°C, 73 days at 24°C, 70 days at 26°C, 63 days at 28°C, and 62 days at 30°C. The rate of development during the final weeks appeared to be independent of temperature.

Eggs from Canadian *Chelydra serpentina* incubated at 28.6°C produced smaller hatchlings which grew more slowly than those from eggs incubated at 22.0°C or 25.6°C, but eggs incubated at 25.6°C produced larger turtles at seven months posthatching than did eggs incubated at either the lower or higher temperatures (Brooks et al., 1991a). These results indicate that egg size and size at hatching may not be useful indicators of intraspecific variation in egg quality or posthatching success in turtles.

The incubation temperature affects the blood pH of developing snapping turtles. Birchard et al. (1990) incubated eggs on moistened vermiculite, and on the 59th day placed them in individual containers in incubators set at 18.5 and 30°C. Embryonic blood samples on day 60 showed the pH varied in a manner similar to that of adults, declining with increasing temperature. This decrease may be accomplished passively, with blood CO_2 partial pressure increasing as a result of greater metabolic production of the gas while the diffusive excretion of the gas remains constant. No effect of substrate water potential on blood pH was noted, but low water potential does inhibit embryonic growth (Morris et al., 1983; Packard et al., 1987). Accumulation of nitrogenous waste products (NH_3, soluble urea) seems to be unaffected by hydration of the eggs, but more urea may accumulate late in incubation in eggs on wet substrates than in those on dry materials. Thus embryos are ureotelic throughout development, and the pattern of the primary nitrogenous waste is influenced by hydration of the environment (G. C. Packard et al., 1984a). Embryos of *Chelydra serpentina* incubated under wet conditions attain larger size and consume more oxygen than embryos from drier conditions (Gettinger et al., 1984). Packard and Packard (1989) incubated snapper eggs in wet and dry environments to see if metabolism and growth of the embryos are correlated inversely with the concentration of waste urea in the eggs. Turtles hatching from eggs that were in positive water balance had larger bodies, smaller residual yolks, and lower concentrations of urea in their blood than turtles emerging from eggs in negative water balance. Further studies by them showed that the reduction in metabolism and growth of the embryos developing in dry environments does not result from an inhibition of intermediary metabolism caused by urea.

Embryos developing in a wetter environment utilize both lipid and protein faster (Janzen et al., 1990). Canadian eggs incubated in wet substrates by Brooks et al. (1991a) produced larger hatchlings than those incubated in dry substrates, but posthatching growth is independent of these effects of moisture. Hydric conditions during incubation also influence the walking and swimming abilities of hatchling *Chelydra serpentina*. Those from eggs incubated on wet surfaces are faster in both distance and body lengths moved per unit time (Miller, 1987). This may stem from a greater aerobic capacity, because these animals accumulate lactate more slowly during locomotion. Effects of the hydric environment on metabolism of the embryos do not seem the result of altered patterns of sexual differentiation (G. C. Packard et al., 1984b). Eggs may be totally submerged in water for a short period after laying and still develop and hatch (Lardie and Lardie, 1980); just before hatching, however, oxygen consumption peaks (Ewert, 1991), so duration of submergence is probably critical.

Eggs laid near the periphery of a nest produce hatchlings with a living mass greater than those from eggs laid near the center of the clutch (Packard et al., 1980, 1981b). The difference can be attributed to the absorption of water across the shell membrane during the first half of incubation, with those on the outside of the clutch in contact with more soil water than those nearer the center. However, tests by Hotaling et al. (1985) seem to indicate that environmental factors which vary throughout the incubation period (rather than remain constant, as in the experiments by Packard et al., 1980, 1981b) actually decrease the variation among nests in hatchling weights rather than increase it.

Studies of physical disturbance on snapper eggs seem to indicate that egg rotation during the first week of development possibly reduces hatching success in some clutches (Feldman, 1983).

Chelydra has temperature-dependent sex determination. Snapping turtle eggs incubated at 20°C produce only females, eggs incubated at 21–22°C produce both male and female hatchlings, those incubated at 23–24°C produce only males, eggs incubated at 25–28°C produce hatchlings of both sexes but predominantly males at the lower end of this range, and eggs incubated at 29–31°C produce only females (Yntema, 1976; Dimond, 1983; Crews et al., 1989). Exposure to at least four hours a day at 30°C ensures female development, but shorter exposures produce males if a male-determining temperature is used over the remaining interval (Wilhoft et al., 1983). In natural nests, eggs on top of the clutch are much warmer (>30°C) than those at the bottom (<30°C), resulting in all females from top eggs, and commonly all males from the bottom eggs (Wilhoft et al., 1983).

The temperature-sensitive embryological stages (Yntema, 1968) for sex determination are 14–16 in eggs shifted from 20 to 26°C, and stages 14–19 for eggs shifted from 30 to 26°C during incubation (Yntema, 1979). Injection of estradiol benzoate into snapping turtle eggs causes all embryos to become females; a similar but less consistent female-determining effect is associated with the injection of testosterone propionate (Gutzke and Bull, 1986). Hormonally induced gonadal differentiation of embryos injected with estradiol benzoate occurs only between embryonic stages 10 and 19, inclusive (Gutzke and Chymiy, 1988).

At hatching, oviducts are absent or incomplete in males, but the testes are differentiated; in females the oviduct is intact at hatching, but the gonad is bisexual (Yntema, 1976).

Emergence from the nest normally occurs from mid-August to early October, but may be earlier in the south or delayed until the following spring (southeastern Pennsylvania; Ernst, 1966). More northern populations in the United States and Canada have very low frequencies of successful overwintering in the nest by hatchlings (Obbard and Brooks, 1981a), as lower soil temperatures, at many localities below freezing, kill hatchling *Chelydra serpentina* (Packard and Packard, 1990b). After emerging from the nest cavity, hatchlings often bury themselves in soil near the nest or crawl under leaf litter or debris. When they first reach water they almost immediately drink, and then when full crawl under some object to hide.

Hatchlings have nearly round, dark-gray to brown, wrinkled carapaces with three distinct keels. A common pattern on the underside of each marginal consists of a light spot, and the plastron is black with some light mottling. The skin is dark gray, and the head and jaws may be somewhat mottled. A buttonlike yolk sac 7–10 mm in diameter is attached to the center of the plastron; it usually is absorbed within the first three days. The mean weight of this yolk sac on the day of hatching is about 0.16 g and it averages 60% water, 36% lipid, 58% protein, and 0.53 kcal of energy (Wilhoft, 1986). The caruncle, or egg-tooth, usually is shed within the first three weeks. Hatchlings are about 24–31 mm in carapace length and 22–29 mm in carapace width. They have a total weight of about 5–9 g. Wet weight of hatchlings, minus yolk sac, is about 7.6 g; hatchlings average 82% water, 19.7% lipid, 32% protein, and 6.7 kcal of energy (Wilhoft, 1986). Hatchling mass is highly correlated with egg mass, but neither egg nor hatchling mass is related significantly to posthatching survival or rate of growth (Brooks et al., 1991a).

Juvenile *Chelydra* have some prehensile ability in their tails. Brode (1958) reported they would grasp a stick with their tails and could hang for several minutes. R. J. Brooks (pers. comm.) suggested that the long tail of hatchlings can hold them in place and may provide buoyancy in open water so as to counterbalance the head and allow the small turtle to keep its head out of the water.

GROWTH AND LONGEVITY: The age/size classes of six *Chelydra serpentina* taken from the polluted Kalamazoo River near Otsego, Michigan, were: one year, 54–66 mm; two years, 83–108 mm; three years, 124–145 mm; four years, 146–184 mm; five years, 177–211 mm; and six years, 204–238 mm (Gibbons, 1968e). The mean carapace length of five snappers increased 32 mm/year from the first through sixth year, but the rate of growth declined each year; for example, the average increase in length in a 15-year-old, 257-mm turtle was about 18.5 mm/year through the 14th year but less than 10 mm/year for the last two years. However, Gibbons (1968e) found no indication that the growth rate slows more rapidly once maturity is attained. In Iowa, shell growth begins in the last two weeks of May, but is most rapid in June through August, and all annual growth is accomplished in an activity period of 204 days and a 145-day feeding period (Christiansen and Burken, 1979). At a polluted marsh in Massachusetts which received directly effluent containing high phosphorus levels from a sewage treatment plant, the carapace length of snapping turtles increased a mean 26.5 mm/year through the sixth year. Two turtles grew an average of 48.2 mm between their fifth and sixth years, possibly due to a dietary shift (Graham and Perkins, 1976). Length/weight relationships of Michigan *Chelydra* were calculated as 197 mm/1.87 kg, 248 mm/3.36 kg, 298 mm/6.03 kg, 349 mm/9.98 kg, and 375 mm/13.61 kg by Lagler and Applegate (1943). A 470-mm adult taken in 1968 from a pond on a horse farm in Woodford County, Kentucky by Ernst and Bobby Gene Jett weighed 34 kg!

The annual growth increments of *Chelydra serpentina* from South Dakota are large in young turtles but small in older ones (Hammer, 1969). However, growth annuli may not be formed each year, at least on the fourth vertebral scute, in some adults from Canadian populations, and this could complicate calculations of the annual growth rate. Juveniles in Algonquin Park, Ontario, formed one growth annulus each winter, whereas approximately 50% of the adults did not add a growth annulus between captures a year apart (Galbraith and Brooks, 1987a, 1989). At this site recaptured hatchlings did not grow between the time of hatching and the first posthatching spring, but grew an average of 10 mm/year during the next three years (Galbraith and Brooks, 1989).

Shell growth is strongly influenced by environmental temperature. In laboratory studies hatchlings ate little and did not grow when kept at 15°C, but those kept at 25°C ate freely and increased from 7.4 to 50.7 g in one year (Williamson et al., 1989).

As *Chelydra* grows the carapacial keels become less conspicuous, the carapace becomes smoother, the length increases faster than the width, and the tail becomes relatively shorter.

The longevity record for this species is 38 years, 8 months and 27 days for an unsexed adult at the Philadelphia Zoo (Snider and Bowler, 1992). In an Ontario population, adult females have an average life span of 40 years (Galbraith and Brooks, 1989). In southeastern Pennsylvania, adults of both sexes have survived to be recaptured 20–25 years later (Ernst, pers. obs.), and Congdon and Gibbons (1989) estimated the mean longevity to be 28 years at a pond in South Carolina.

FOOD HABITS: *Chelydra serpentina* is omnivorous, essentially consuming anything it can fit into its jaws. It eats insects, spiders, isopods, amphipods, crayfish, fiddler crabs, shrimp, water mites, clams, snails, earthworms, leeches, tubificid worms, planarians, freshwater sponges, fish (adults, fry and eggs: *Cyprinus, Notropis, Lepomis, Ictalurus*), frogs and toads (adults, tadpoles and eggs: *Scaphiopus, Bufo, Acris, Hyla, Pseudacris, Eleutherodactylus, Rana*), salamanders (*Necturus, Eurycea, Pseudotriton*), small turtles (*Chelydra, Kinosternon, Sternotherus, Chrysemys, Pseudemys, Trachemys, Trionyx*), snakes (*Elaphe, Nerodia, Regina, Thamnophis, Agkistrodon*), birds (particularly aquatic or semiaquatic species: *Anas, Aix, Aythya, Branta, Cygnus, Larus, Tringa, Fulica, Agelaius*), and small mammals (*Ondatra, Oryzomys, Rattus*). Among the plants it eats are various algae, *Brasenia, Elodea, Potamogeton, Polygonum, Nymphaea, Lemna, Typha, Vallisneria, Nuphar, Sagittaria, Wolffia, Najas, Carex.* Budhabhatti and Moll (1990) observed a large Illinois snapper feed predominantly on *Lemna* (92% of fecal

matter) which it ingested using neustophagia (surface feeding), and water shield (*Brasenia odorata*) may be the main food of snappers in Ontario in late summer and early fall (R. J. Brooks, pers. comm.).

Fish, invertebrates, and plant material occurred most frequently in *Chelydra* from Michigan examined by Lagler (1943). Alexander (1943) found that plants composed 36.5% by volume (60% frequency) and animals 54.1% by volume (64.7% frequency) of the contents of 470 stomachs of *C. s. serpentina,* and crayfish occurred in 31% of 569 stomachs examined by Penn (1950). Fifty-nine *C. s. osceola* examined by Punzo (1975) contained worms, arthropods, insects (nine orders), snails, anurans, turtles, snakes, and plant material (seven genera); 100% had eaten triclad flatworms, oligochaetes, water boatmen, dragonflies, vertebrates, and plants.

Carrion is often consumed; when baits in turtle traps begin to decay, *Chelydra* is more likely to be attracted (Ernst, 1965). The snapping turtle sometimes comes into disrepute because it takes game fish and ducklings; Coulter (1957) reported that predation by snappers resulted in losses of 10–13% of the estimated duckling crop in two study areas in Maine, and Abel (1992) reported the loss of swan cygnets in Wisconsin. Its pugnacious nature may cause it to attack even larger animals. The large snapper mentioned above (see growth and longevity section) was notorious for biting the snouts of horses as they attempted to drink.

Young snappers actively forage for food, but older individuals often lie in ambush to seize their prey. Small prey is seized and swallowed intact; larger prey is held in the mouth and torn to pieces with the aid of the strong foreclaws. Larger animals are sometimes dragged beneath the surface and held until they drown. Feeding usually takes place underwater, but can occur on land. Ernst has seen two large adults graze on young *Carex* shoots while on land in a Pennsylvania pasture.

Prey capture is usually accomplished through a high-speed inertial pharyngeal mechanism during a head strike that allows the buccopharyngeal cavity to expand rapidly creating a low-pressure area into which the food item is drawn (Bramble, 1973; Lauder and Prendergast, 1992).

Burghardt and Hess (1966) fed three groups of hatchlings either meat, fish, or worms. When tested after a period of 12 daily feedings, each group preferred the diet to which it had become accustomed. Thereafter, for 12 days, each group was given an uncustomary food, and at the end of this period each still preferred its initial diet. Burghardt and Hess concluded that food-imprinting may influence the feeding behavior of this turtle. Competition and dominance behavior may occur during feeding in captivity (Froese and Burghardt, 1974). Digestive turnover, from initial ingestion to elimination, occurs within 31 hours at 25°C (Parmenter, 1981).

PREDATORS AND DEFENSE: *Chelydra serpentina* is most vulnerable to predation in the nest stage, and many species of animals excavate nests: hognose snakes (*Heterodon*), crows (*Corvus*), bears (*Ursus americanus*), mink (*Mustela*), skunks (*Mephitis*), foxes (*Urocyon*, *Vulpes*), wolves (*Canis lupus*), and raccoons (*Procyon*). Some predators may even visit a nest more than once. In a study by Hammer (1969), mammals destroyed 48% of 102 nests at the first predatory visit; 11% were visited more than once before all eggs were destroyed. Nests in which some of the eggs remained intact comprised 12% of the total. Twenty-five percent of the nests escaped destruction by predators or by the actions of men repairing dikes. Considerably more nests were destroyed by predators in 1966 (63%) than in 1967 (46%): abnormally high rainfall in 1967 apparently helped conceal the nests. Skunks destroyed 25% of the nests, raccoons 22%, and minks 9%. A high correlation existed between nest concentration and predation levels: dikes having the highest number of nests per km also had the highest percentage of nests destroyed. At some sites, 100% of the nests may be destroyed, or at least raided, during some years (Ernst, pers. obs.), and predation may occur anytime during the incubation period. In Michigan, nest predation rates averaged 70% during a seven-year study, ranging from 100% in two years to 30% in one year; most nests were plundered within 24 hours of oviposition. Foxes preyed on nests that were older and farther from water than nests preyed on by raccoons (Congdon et al., 1987).

Predation may take place either without the predator having seen the female nesting, or in the absence of egg scent, so the specific method of detection has not been discovered (Wilhoft et al., 1979). Nests dug in the open or near ecotonal areas suffer the highest predation (Temple, 1987; Robinson and Bider, 1988). Most female *Chelydra* in a population nest within a very short period of time, and this nesting synchrony may be a strategy to decrease total predation of the nests in a given area (Robinson and Bider, 1988).

Hatchlings and juveniles are the prey of herons (*Ardea*), egrets (*Casmerodius*), bitterns (*Botaurus*), shrikes (*Lanius*), crows (*Corvus*), large hawks (*Buteo*,

Circus), bald eagles (*Haliaeetus*), bullfrogs (*Rana*), various large fish, water snakes (*Nerodia, Agkistrodon*), alligators (*Alligator*), and larger snapping turtles. Humans are the chief predators of adults, but alligators, otters (*Lutra*), coyotes (*Canis*), and bears (*Ursus*) also eat them.

Almost all snapping turtles have leeches (*Placobdella*) attached to their skin, particularly at the limb sockets (Brooks et al., 1990). Some turtles may harbor hundreds of these blood suckers, which may result in considerable blood loss, particularly among smaller turtles.

When first disturbed, *Chelydra* will try to escape; if it cannot, it will tilt its body so that the broadest surface of the carapace faces the danger (Dodd and Brodie, 1975). This turtle has a short temper and should be handled carefully. It strikes with amazing speed and its jaws are capable of tearing flesh severely. The strike often carries the forepart of the body off the ground, and when the jaws make contact they sometimes lock and the turtle holds on for some time. The safest way to carry a snapping turtle is to grasp it by the hind limbs while keeping its head down and the plastron toward you and well away from your legs. Do not carry large individuals by the tail: they can be severely injured by having their caudal vertebrae separated or the sacral region stretched. When handled, snappers emit a musk as potent as that of musk turtles. Snapping turtles normally are docile when submerged, but even then they can and sometimes do bite viciously.

POPULATIONS: *Chelydra serpentina* composed 1–11% of five southern Illinois turtle populations (Cagle, 1942), and from 2.4 to 17.2% of six Louisiana populations (Cagle and Chaney, 1950). At White Oak, Pennsylvania, snapping turtles composed about 17% of more than 6,000 individual turtles collected in 25 years, and at Lake Reba, Madison County, Kentucky, 32.6% of 43 turtles collected were snapping turtles. Because *Chelydra* is secretive and may not be attracted to baits in traps as readily as are other species, these figures probably do not accurately reflect the relative abundance of snapping turtles. We feel they are among the more abundant aquatic turtles and are common throughout most of their North American range. However, overcollecting has seriously reduced many populations. About 860 mature females were estimated to be in the snapper population at the Lacreek Refuge, South Dakota, in the areas sampled by Hammer (1969). An estimate of the mature population was obtained by doubling that number, for the sex ratio was approximately 1:1; thus

1,720 mature turtles were believed to exist in the portions of the refuge Hammer sampled. Extrapolation to include areas not adequately sampled gave an estimate of 2,415 sexually mature snappers on Lacreek Refuge: approximately one turtle for every 0.8 ha, or 1.2 turtles per ha, of marsh (a biomass of 9.1 kg/ha; Iverson, 1982a).

In the fall of the year when the young hatch and enter the population, the hatchling and juvenile size and age classes may predominate (at least for a short period, as juvenile mortality is high due to predation).

In two 0.4-ha ponds in western West Virginia, the density of snapping turtles was estimated at 60.5 turtles/ha with a 1:1.3 male to female ratio (Major, 1975). At an 0.8-ha pond in Tennessee, Froese and Burghardt (1975) found a density of 59 adults/ha (sex ratio, 1:1; biomass, 181.3 kg/ha; Iverson, 1982a). At the 10-ha Ellenton Bay, South Carolina, Congdon and Gibbons (1989) calculated a density of 8/ha, a biomass of 21.6 kg/ha, and an annual egg biomass production of 0.4 kg/ha. Eleven snappers (total biomass 61.2 kg; sex ratio 1.75:1) were trapped in one small pond in North Carolina (Brown, 1992). Lagler (1943) found a density of five turtles/ha in Michigan. Petokas (1981a) corrected Pearse's (1923) estimate of *Chelydra* density in a Wisconsin lake to 1.9 individuals/ha. In a nutrient-enriched pond in Ontario the density was 66 turtles/ha (biomass, 340 kg/ha) with a male-biased 1.96:1 sex ratio (Galbraith et al., 1988a); but at a more northern oligotrophic pond in Ontario the density was only 2.4 turtles/ha (biomass, 16 kg/ha) with an approximately equal sex ratio (Galbraith et al., 1988a). Apparently, warmer, more productive water bodies can support larger populations of *C. serpentina*.

The sex ratio of hatchlings is about 1:1, and this seems to be the ratio maintained into adulthood (Mosimann and Bider, 1960). Deviation from this ratio in a series of large individuals is often due to the fact that males may attain a larger size, but it may also be caused by sex-biased collecting methods.

Survivorship of the lower age classes is low. Nest survivorship in New York and Quebec were only 56% and 15.7%/year, respectively (Petokas and Alexander, 1980; Robinson and Bider, 1988). Mean egg to hatchling survivorship varies from 12 to 22%/year (Hammer, 1969; Congdon et al., 1987).

The 13-year average of survivorship of adult female *Chelydra* in a marked population in Algonquin Provincial Park, Ontario, was 96.6% per year with an annual mortality of 1%; only six dead turtles were discovered (Galbraith and Brooks, 1987b; Brooks et al., 1991b). However, from 1987 to 1989 a great

decline occurred in the population, and 34 dead snappers were found at the site, almost all of which had been killed by otters (*Lutra canadensis*) during winter hibernation. Consequently, the population estimate of adults in the study area dropped from 38 and 47 in 1978–1979 and 1984–1985, respectively, to 31 in 1988–1989, and only 16 adults were definitely known to be alive in 1989. In 1986 and 1987 annual female survivorship was estimated to be 80% and 55%, respectively, and the estimated numbers of nesting females declined from 82 in 1986 to 71 in 1987 and 55 in 1988. The actual number of nests found declined by 38% and 20% over the same periods, but no significant differences occurred in mean egg mass or mean clutch size between 1987 and 1989 and earlier years, as the mean clutch mass in 1988 was larger than in 1977 or 1978. Brooks et al. (1991b) thought this difference due to a gradual increase in the mean age and body size of breeding females rather than to density-dependent changes. Recruitment into this population was inversely low (<2%), and between 1987 and 1989 less than two individuals entered the population per year (Brooks et al., 1991b). Hatchling survival and the number of juveniles were low throughout the study. These observations support the view that turtle populations with high juvenile mortality and long adult life spans may be decimated quickly by increased adult mortality, particularly if the numbers of juveniles and immigrants are low. Recovery of turtle populations will be very slow because of a lack of effective density-dependent response in reproduction and recruitment.

Brooks et al. (1988), while developing management guidelines for snapping turtles, have constructed a life table for females in Algonquin Park, Ontario, and we refer the reader to their paper for additional information.

REMARKS: The flesh of the snapping turtle is tasty and eaten throughout the range; an excellent soup can be made from it. The fresh eggs are edible if fried (they will not hard-boil). A detailed account of the economic value of this species was given by Clark and Southall (1920). Human taste for this species has recently severely decimated some populations (Harding and Holman, 1990).

The snapping turtle, like other aquatic animals, has shown a recent uptake and storage of chemical toxicants within its body. High levels of organochlorines, especially PCBs, were found in the fat of adults and in eggs from the Hudson River, New York (Stone et al., 1980; Olafsson et al., 1983; Bryan et al., 1987), and Ryan et al. (1986) found tetrachlorodibenzo-p-dioxin and other related dioxins and furans in the fat and liver of *Chelydra* from the upper St. Lawrence River. Such stored poisons may cause a hazard to persons who eat snapping turtles, and eventually also reduce the turtle population (Bishop et al., 1991). More importantly, they indicate the poor quality (due to chemical pollution) of our waterways. Cleanup of our rivers and lakes will benefit both humans and wildlife.

The most recent summaries of the literature of this species are in Ernst et al. (1988a) and Gibbons et al. (1988).

Macroclemys temminckii (Harlan, 1835)
Alligator snapping turtle
PLATE 2

RECOGNITION: The alligator snapping turtle is the largest freshwater turtle in North America, some attaining a carapace length of 80 cm (Pritchard, 1980b) and a weight of 113 kg (Pawley, 1987). It has a hooked jaw, lateral eyes, three keels on the carapace, and a row of supramarginal scutes along the upper carapacial rim. The large, rough, dark carapace is strongly serrated posteriorly and has three prominent keels: a central keel on the vertebrals and two lateral keels on the pleurals; knobs on the keels are elevated and somewhat curved posteriorly. A row of three to eight supramarginal scutes lies between the marginals and the first three pleurals on each side. The bridge is small and the hingeless plastron is reduced, giving a cross-shaped appearance. The plastron is grayish brown; in juveniles it may be somewhat mottled with small whitish blotches. The skin is dark brown to gray above and lighter below; darker blotches may be present on the head. The tail is about as long as the carapace and has three rows of low tubercles above and many small scales below. The eyes are placed to the side of the huge, pointed head so that the orbits cannot be seen from above. The eye is surrounded by a ring of small, fleshy, broad-based, flattened, pointed projections (Winokur, 1982). Numerous branching dermal projections are present on the side of the head, chin, and neck. The jaws are large and powerful, and the upper jaw is strongly hooked. A wormlike process on the tongue is used to lure prey within biting range.

Sexual dimorphism is pronounced. Precloacal tail length increases rapidly with body size in males but not in females: mature males have an average precloacal length of about 169 mm, whereas the average for females is about 84 mm. The largest male examined by Dobie (1971) weighed 44.4 kg, almost double that of the heaviest female (23.5 kg).

KARYOTYPE: The diploid chromosome number is 52: 24 macrochromosomes (14 metacentric or submetacentric and 10 telocentric or subtelocentric; the third pair lacks the conspicuous short arm, secondary constriction and telocentric condition found in *Chelydra*), 26 microchromosomes, and a large metacentric chromosome pair unique to *Macroclemys* (Killebrew, 1977b; Haiduk and Bickham, 1982). Bickham and Carr (1983) concluded that the karyotype of *Macroclemys* may be derived from that of *Chelydra*.

FOSSIL RECORD: The genus *Macroclemys* once had a much wider geographic distribution; remains of *M. schmidti* are known from Miocene, Hemphillian, Hemmingfordian, and Marsland deposits in Nebraska (Zangerl, 1945; Whetstone, 1978; Parmley, 1992), and *M. auffenbergi* is known from the Pliocene (Hemphillian) of Alachua County, Florida (Dobie, 1968a), a location south of the present distributional limit of the genus. Fossils referable to *M. temminckii* have been found in Pliocene (Clarendonian) deposits in South Dakota (Zangerl, 1945), Pliocene (Blancan) remains from Kansas (Hibbard, 1963), presumed Pleistocene (Rancholabrean) deposits in Hillsborough County, Florida (Auffenberg, 1957), and late Pleistocene (Rancholabrean) to Recent deposits from the Brazos River, Texas (Hay, 1911).

DISTRIBUTION: The alligator snapping turtle is confined to river systems that drain into the Gulf of Mexico. It is widely distributed in the Mississippi Valley from as far north as Kansas (Clarke 1981), Illinois (Galbreath, 1961), and Indiana to the Gulf, and has been found in almost all river systems from the Suwannee River, Florida (Iverson and Etchberger, 1989), to eastern Texas (Conant and Collins, 1991). *Macroclemys* had been considered extirpated in Indiana until one was caught in the White River, Morgan County, in March 1991 (Grannan and Anderson, 1992).

Macroclemys temminckii

Plastron of *Macroclemys temminckii*

GEOGRAPHIC VARIATION: No subspecies have been described, but according to Pritchard (1989) individuals from the Mississippi drainage of Louisiana have three or four supramarginal scutes on each side, whereas those from the Flint/Apalachicola River system in Georgia and Florida have only two or three.

CONFUSING SPECIES: *Chelydra serpentina* lacks supramarginal scutes, has low keels on the carapace, or none at all, and its eyes are situated high enough so that the orbits can be seen when viewed from above.

HABITAT: Adult alligator snapping turtles are typically found in the deeper water of large rivers and their major tributaries, but have also been found in canals, lakes, oxbows, swamps, ponds, and bayous. Juveniles are occasionally found in small streams (Allen and Neill, 1950); Ernst has taken them in

Distribution of *Macroclemys temminckii*

northern Arkansas and Missouri from shallow mud and gravel-bottomed streams 20–46 cm deep.

The presence of barnacles (*Balanus improvisus*) on some *Macroclemys* suggests the species is capable of spending prolonged periods in brackish water (Jackson and Ross, 1971a), and Dundee and Rossman (1989) reported that alligator snappers are common in the brackish, tidally influenced areas between Lake Pontchartrain and Lake Maurepas in southern Louisiana.

BEHAVIOR: Little is known of the behavior of this species under natural conditions. Adults are highly aquatic; typically only nesting females venture onto land. A single observation of aerial basking was reported by Ewert (1976) who saw an approximately 20-cm juvenile on the Texas side of the Sabine River at about 1700 on 13 July under slightly overcast skies, on a truncated branch lodged in the center of the 1.5–2.0-m-deep main channel. The turtle appeared to be dry, and was completely out of the water with the anterior portion of the body facing upward at 45°. Its basking position required negotiating a slight current in relatively deep water.

Movements of a 23-kg *Macroclemys* were reported by Wickham (1922). It was collected in the Washita River, Oklahoma, held in captivity for three years, then tagged and released in another Oklahoma river in late July 1918. In September 1918 the turtle was recaptured only 274 m from the release point, but by the last time it was seen, in July 1921, it had moved 27–30 km upstream from the release point.

Radiotelemetry was used to study the daily movements, home range, and habitat use of 11 adult *Macroclemys* in Louisiana from 8 August 1984 to 6 November 1985, at Black Bayou Lake, a shallow 610-ha lake, and an adjacent impounded bayou (Bayou Desiard) that was seasonally connected to the lake (Sloan and Taylor, 1987). Six turtles were residents and five were introduced. Three introduced turtles used culverts to travel between the two study sites; two of these made the trip only once, remaining in Bayou Desiard for the rest of the study period. One resident and one introduced turtle stayed within Bayou Desiard, and one introduced and four resident turtles spent the entire time within Black Bayou Lake, the original release site. A resident of Black Bayou Lake was intentionally released in Bayou Desiard to test homing ability, and was located 1 km from its original capture site three days later, and 400 m from the capture site three months later. An introduced turtle from the Ouachita River moved 6.8 km (one way) in six days. Mean daily distance traveled ranged from 27.8–115.5 m/day for all turtles, but mean daily distances moved by introduced and resident turtles were not statistically different. The minimum home range varied from 18 to 247 ha, but was not statistically different between resident and introduced turtles. All the *Macroclemys* had core activity areas, and journeys from these areas were usually short in both distance and duration. The two turtles that stayed in Bayou Desiard spent an average of 74.6% of the monitoring period in cypress-bordered channels. Habitat use was in close proportion to habitat availability; three turtles that occupied both the lake and the bayou spent 56.4% of the monitoring period in cypress-bordered channels. Specific habitat use for lake and bayou combined was three times its availability. The six turtles in Black Bayou Lake spent 76.8% of the study period in areas with densely vegetated floating mats of detritus, cypress, and buttonbush. Habitat use was more than three times greater than its availability in Black Bayou Lake.

A 24.7-kg radio-tagged female in Kansas moved upstream 7 km in a river between 11 April 1986 and 31 May 1991. During the first two weeks she moved upstream 0.46 km. Her fastest rate of travel was 8.4 m/minute for 12 minutes. Activity began between 0200 and 0700 and lasted for one to three hours. Up to eight days of inactivity were recorded between movements (Shipman et al., 1991).

The two upstream movements of *Macroclemys* observed by Wickham (1922) and Shipman et al. (1991) hardly give credence to Pritchard's (1989) hypothesis that certain individuals may continually migrate upstream in the Mississippi drainage until they are very old, large, and few in numbers. Not only is his theory unsubstantiated, but Pritchard does not explain the presence of small juveniles in small upstream tributaries.

The tails of small *Macroclemys* are reportedly prehensile. Brode (1958) observed that 1.8- and 3.6-kg juveniles could grasp a stick or broom handle with their tails when tapped on the posterior part of the plastron with a pencil. Their grip was sufficient to allow them to be raised off the ground for intervals of a few seconds to several minutes.

Compared to other aquatic turtles, alligator snappers cannot remain submerged for long periods of time: submergence times range from 40 to 50 minutes at water temperatures between 21 and 24°C. After 15 to 20 minutes of involuntary submergence, medium-sized turtles will extend the neck upward in an attempt to breathe. While submerged, *Macroclemys* slowly opens and closes its mouth while pulsating the throat slightly (addition of dye to the water confirms the presence of swirling currents near the mouth). The rate of these pumping actions increase as involuntary submergence time increases, and eventually the turtle begins gulping water. From these observations, Allen and Neill (1950) speculated that *Macroclemys* is perhaps capable of pharyngeal respiration; detailed physiological tests will be necessary to confirm this hypothesis, however.

Captives maintained in an outdoor enclosure in Tulsa, Oklahoma, crawled about and surfaced for air at water temperatures as low as 8°C, but remained buried in detritus on the bottom of the pool when the surface froze (Grimpe, 1987). Captives refuse to eat when the air temperature falls below 18°C (Allen and Neill, 1950), but according to Pritchard (1989) professional turtle trappers collect these turtles on baited hooks from mid-March to mid-October. Hutchison et al. (1966) recorded mean critical thermal maximum temperatures of 38.5 and 40.7°C for two *Macroclemys*.

Adults maintained in small enclosures may exhibit aggressive behavior toward one another. Allen and Neill (1950) introduced a 29-kg individual into the tank that a 42-kg *Macroclemys* had occupied for several years (judging from the reported sizes, both turtles were probably males). The larger resident repeatedly attacked the smaller turtle, biting it on the shell and front leg. The smaller turtle made no effort to bite back and tried to escape. The larger turtle eventually clamped its jaws onto the shell of the intruder, lifted it off the tank bottom, and turned it over. At this point the smaller turtle was removed from the enclosure; surprisingly, it had suffered no visible injuries. Aggressive behavior was observed frequently between a captive 34-kg male and 17-kg female by Grimpe (1987). The male was dominant and aggressive, especially during and after feeding, biting the female on the shell, head, neck, and limbs, but never inflicting noticeable damage. When both turtles approached a food item simultaneously, the female always retreated.

The biting ability of alligator snappers is legendary but often overstated. Cahn (1937) and others have reported that large individuals are capable of snapping a broom handle in two as if it were cut by a sharp axe. In contrast Allen and Neill (1950) observed that 16–18-kg *Macroclemys* are "scarcely capable of biting an ordinary pencil in two, although they can deeply score the wood," and those weighing 41–45 kg only dented a broom handle. However, Allen and Neill noted that a large recently captured *Macroclemys* once bit a chunk of spruce wood out of a canoe gunwale. In an effort to put the controversy of alligator snapper bite strength to rest, Pritchard (1989) taunted a 75-kg specimen with a brand new household broom. It scored the wood deeply on the first bite, but did not sever it. When he attempted to get the broom away from the turtle, it bit down harder and cut completely through the handle. The ability of large specimens to inflict damage to human flesh is far less controversial.

REPRODUCTION: Mating behavior and copulation have been observed in captive specimens in Florida during February, March, and April (Allen and Neill, 1950), and in Oklahoma during October (Grimpe, 1987). Mounting may be preceded by vigorous pursuit in which the male attempts to crawl onto the female carapace. The male mounts the female and grasps the front and rear edges of the carapace with all four feet (Allen and Neill, 1950; Grimpe 1987). He then extends his neck so that his chin touches the back of her head; she may in return attempt to bite his head and neck at this time (Grimpe, 1987). The male moves his body slightly to the side and pushes his tail downward beneath the female's tail as she pulls her tail upward and to one side. Contact time lasts from 5 to 25 minutes (Allen and Neill, 1950).

Dobie (1971) described the gonadal anatomy of male *Macroclemys* from Louisiana. The smallest mature male, as determined by coiling of the vas deferens and the presence of sperm in the testes, had a carapace length of 39 cm and a combined testicular length of 58 mm. The largest male examined (59 cm) had a combined testicular length of 160 mm. Testes of adult males collected in every month from March to July, inclusive, and in December contained viable sperm, leading Dobie to conclude that Louisiana populations produce sperm year round.

In adult females, mature ovarian follicles are bright yellow, atretic follicles are normally brown or orange, and corpora lutea are creamy white (Dobie, 1971). Ovaries of adult females collected from mid-April to late July vary in length from 85 to 165 mm. Ovulated eggs have diameters of approximately 20–28 mm. The relative proportion of follicles in the 20–31-mm-size class decreases in April whereas the number of follicles in the 8–19-mm-size class increases dramatically. Follicles reach an ovulation diameter (20–31 mm) in December, and are present in postovulated females in May. No evidence exists that *Macroclemys* lays more than one clutch per season, and it is unlikely that 20–31-mm ovarian eggs are retained until the next year, as no eggs of that size are found in July (Dobie, 1971). Mean diameter of corpora lutea decreases from about 13 mm at ovulation in April to about 6 mm in July. The mean number of luteal scars in 35 specimens was 13.6 on the left ovary and 10.7 on the right (Dobie, 1971).

The reproductive tract of a female that laid nine eggs on 3 June contained one oviducal egg with a diameter of 35.3 mm and weight of 21.3 g, 10 corpora lutea, and 23 ovarian follicles greater than 8 mm in diameter, including three that were larger than 20 mm, when examined two days later (Powders, 1978).

Eggs may pass down either oviduct; Dobie (1971) reported that seven of nine females examined had exchanged eggs between ovaries and their opposite oviducts. A single shelled egg was observed in the body cavity of one female, and two shelled eggs were observed in the urinary bladder of another female with a deformed carapace (Dobie, 1968b). These eggs may have eroded through the oviductal wall.

The spherical eggs are chalky white (nearly opaque), turgid, and have a rough granular appearance (Dobie, 1971). The mean maximum and minimum diameter of clutches of shelled eggs in 13 females collected between 16 April and 28 May varied from 36.2 to 40.0 mm and 36.0 to 39.2 mm, respectively. Others have reported egg dimensions as follows: mean length 34.8 mm (34.0–36.0), with one egg weighing 24.5 g, for a female from southwestern Georgia (Powders, 1978); and mean length 33.9 mm (32.6–37.0), mean width 33.0 mm (31.4–34.0), and mean weight 20.3 g (18.5–22.8) for a captive female (Grimpe 1987). Allen and Neill (1950) reported that the eight bottom eggs in the nest of a captive female ranged from 38.4 to 40.9 mm, but they were measured seven days after oviposition.

Reported clutch sizes range from 9 (Powders, 1978) to 44 (Allen and Neill, 1950), although counts of corpora lutea led Dobie (1971) to suggest that up to 52 eggs may be produced in a season. He also reported that larger females (as measured by skull length) had more corpora lutea than smaller females.

The eggshell is composed of 58.9% fibrous material and 41.1% mineral material, and ranges in thickness from 0.21 to 0.24 mm. Major components of fresh eggs account for the following percentages by weight: shell, 9.4%; albumin, 52.7%; and yolk, 37.9% (Ewert, 1979a).

The nesting season in western Florida extends from 1 to 11 May (Ewert, 1976), but in western Georgia a female was observed completing a nest on 3 June (Powders, 1978). Females in Louisiana contain shelled eggs from 19 to 28 April (Dobie, 1971). Captive specimens have oviposited from 26 June to 11 July (Allen and Neill, 1950; Drummond and Gordon, 1979; Grimpe, 1987).

Nesting is diurnal (Allen and Neill, 1950). Of 16 nests along the Apalachicola River in Florida examined by Ewert (1976), seven were located on sandy mounds that appeared to be dredging heaps, five were on the upstream, overgrown ends of a sandbar, three were placed on the elevated, upstream end of an island, and the last was on top of a 1.5-m-high bank. Another nest, at Lake Iamonia, Florida, was located 1.7 m into a field of low corn, 72 m from the nearest water and about 5 m above water level. Three others were placed in more mesic locations varying from partly to deeply shaded. All nests were dug in sand or sand mixed with silt and organic alluvium. The list of nest site conditions would perhaps indicate that alligator snappers are not particularly selective regarding placement; however, Ewert (1976) noted a conspicuous absence of nests on open sandbars and in low forested areas with leaf litter and matted roots. Twelve nests along the Apalachicola River had a mean distance from nearest water of 12.2 m (2.5–22.0) and a mean approximate altitude of nest surface above water of 1.6 m (0.5–2.5). Powders (1978) observed a single alligator snapper nest in western Georgia that was 30 m from the normal water line, 18 m from the maximum high waterline, and 75 cm above the normal high-water mark of Muckalee Creek.

Nesting is accomplished by lifting soil out of the nest cavity with alternating hind limbs (Allen and Neill, 1950). The Lake Iamonia female observed by Ewert (1976) did not construct a large body pit. She was discovered at 0900 on a cloudless day over a completed egg chamber. The first egg was dropped at 0915 and the last (36th) at 0956. Intervals between the dropping of eggs 1–12 were 45–50 seconds; at least one drop involved two eggs. The interval between the laying of eggs 35 and 36 was two minutes. Eggs were wet when deposited, but not slimy. Extensive rearrangement was never attempted by the female and she did not usually touch the eggs with her hind feet between drops. When oviposition was complete the female filled the nest with her hind limbs.

Interestingly, the tail may be used to pack dirt (Powders, 1978) or to support the female while moving both hind limbs (Ewert, 1976). Allen and Neill (1950) reported that the nest cavity was packed down and smoothed over when the female crawled over it, but this was not observed by Ewert (1976). In the latter case the female simply walked forward

leaving a disturbed, vaguely oval area with a superficially churned appearance. The surface area disturbed at three nests had mean dimensions of 90 × 130 cm (70 × 98–110 × 180).

The mean and range of the nest chamber variables for six nests measured by Ewert (1976) were as follows: soil depth to top egg 19.5 cm (15.0–22.5), depth of egg chamber 32.5 cm (28.0–39.0), and horizontal diameter of egg chamber 20.0 cm (15.0–25.5). Ewert estimated that the nesting process observed at Lake Iamonia required at least four hours. A Georgia female discovered in the last phases of nest construction took 3.5 hours from the time she began to lay nine eggs until the nest was covered (Powders, 1978).

Incubation time for eggs maintained under artificial conditions ranges from 79 to 107 days (Allen and Neill, 1950; Grimpe 1987). Most of this variation is undoubtably due to differences in incubation temperature. Ewert (1979a) reported the following mean incubation periods for various temperatures: 25–25.5°C, 113.3 days; 26–30°C, 90 days; and 29.5–30°C, 81.4 days. Hatching takes place over several days (Drummond and Gordon, 1979).

Possible hatchling overwintering behavior was observed in an Oklahoma zoo (Grimpe, 1987). Three eggs were removed from a clutch of 28 eggs laid 8 July. Of these, two hatched 79 days later and the third was stillborn. The remaining 25 eggs were left in the nest and their temperature was monitored with a probe in the top layer of eggs. Nest temperatures ranged from 24.5 to 26°C in July and August, dropped to 15.5°C in September, 5°C in December and remained at 0°C for several days in February. On 18 February the nest was opened and two healthy hatchlings were removed. Nest temperatures never exceeded 16°C through May and on the 15th the nest was reopened. Seven living, but emaciated, hatchlings were found at various depths, some still in cracked eggs. All other hatchlings were dead, and one of the seven alive eventually died. Grimpe believed that the hatchlings probably would not have survived if the nest had not been opened.

The only observation of incubation under natural conditions was reported by Powders (1978), who periodically visited a Georgia nest containing eight eggs, deposited on 3 June, until 25 September. Up to this time no evidence of hatching was observed. He returned on 22 October and discovered what he considered to be a hatchling escape tunnel with opening dimensions of 2.5 × 3.5 cm, and the shell fragments of three eggs. The remaining five eggs contained two well-developed but dead embryos (34 and 38 mm); the other three eggs were infertile. Assuming that hatchlings emerged from this nest the minimum estimated incubation period would have been 114–142 days.

Clutch success is variable. Grimpe (1987) reported that a clutch of 29 eggs had 10 infertile eggs, 14 live hatchlings, and 5 dead embryos in various stages. Another clutch of 25 eggs had 13 infertile eggs, 6 live hatchlings, and 6 dead embryos. However, Redmond (in Pritchard, 1989) reported 80% hatching success in oviducal eggs incubated in shallow pans of sand in a greenhouse.

As in many species of turtles, the sex of *Macroclemys* is determined by the incubation temperature. Eggs incubated under controlled conditions produce 11% males at 22.5°C, 69% at 25°C, 71% at 27°C, and no males at 30°C (Ewert and Nelson, 1991).

Hatchling *Macroclemys* look much like adults. They are brown, with a roughened carapace and a long, slender tail. The head is covered with elaborate papillae, and the eye is ringed with conical tubercles. The dark skin may show some lighter mottling. The jaws are long, relatively narrow, and pointed at the tip, and the inside of the mouth is light gray-brown with black mottling. A yolk sac may be present at hatching and an egg tooth measuring 1.0 x 0.75 mm is present for about eight days. Hatchlings exhibit the following mean measurements: carapace length, 35.5–42.0 mm; total tail length, 62.0 mm; weight, 14.2–20.1 g (Dobie, 1971; Drummond and Gordon, 1979; Grimpe, 1987). Mean hatchling weight is 69.3% of freshly laid egg weight (Ewert, 1979a).

GROWTH AND LONGEVITY: The only published information on growth in juvenile *Macroclemys* is for captives. Hatchlings fed on a diet of live mosquitofish (*Gambusia*) starting 11–14 days after hatching, increased in mean carapace length and mean weight from 42 mm and 15.1 g at hatching to 43 mm and 17.7 g after 47–50 days (Drummond and Gordon, 1979). *Macroclemys* hatched in captivity attained carapace lengths of 84 and 90 mm after five years (Allen and Neill, 1950).

As with most temperate species of hardshelled turtles, *Macroclemys* scutes develop rings that are generally assumed to represent annual growth intervals; but examination of one turtle led Powders (1978) to conclude that some annuli do not represent a full year of growth. In addition, a 49.5-cm alligator snapper collected in Illinois had 17 annuli on the right second pleural and 28 on the left second pleural, but this discrepancy may have been caused by uneven wear between the two pleurals (Morris and Sweet,

1985). Scute annuli are poorly correlated with internal bone annuli in the vertebrae and lower jaw (Dobie, 1971). Louisiana turtles collected from mid-March until mid-July showed scute growth intervals of 1–5 mm suggesting that growth starts in March and continues at least through July. Growth is rapid until attainment of maturity at about 11–13 years of age, but slows appreciably after 15 years of age. The smallest mature female and male specimens examined by Dobie had carapace lengths of 34 and 38 cm, and skull lengths of 114 mm and 115 mm, respectively.

Alligator snappers are capable of living for many years in captivity. Snider and Bowler (1992) reported that a male lived for 70 years, 4 months, and 26 days at the Philadelphia Zoo.

FOOD HABITS: The diet of the alligator snapper is incredibly variable. Redmond (1979) listed the contents from several thousand stomachs as including fish, crayfish, freshwater mussels, snakes, and small alligators. Fifty percent of alligator snapping turtles collected in small creeks contained briar roots and, in the fall, wild grapes, small animals, and water birds. Redmond further stated that they feed year round by taking advantage of warm winter days. The list was expanded by George (1987), Spindel et al. (1987), and Shipman et al. (1991) to include large salamanders (*Amphiuma, Siren*), fish (*Amia, Micropterus, Cyprinus, Lepisosteus,* and various catfish, Ictaluridae), crabs, clams, snails, mammals (*Procyon, Ondatra, Castor*) as evidenced by bones, acorns, tupelo fruit, palmetto fruits, and turtles (*Graptemys, Trachemys, Pseudemys, Sternotherus, Macroclemys, Trionyx*). Captives ate many of the above-mentioned food items but also worms, beef, pork, frogs, various aquatic grasses, and the turtle genera *Kinosternon* and *Deirochelys* (Allen and Neill, 1950).

The propensity of *Macroclemys* to eat turtles appears to have been an important selective agent on the predator-specific defense behavior of *Sternotherus carinatus* and *S. minor peltifer.* Jackson (1990) tested the response of both *Sternotherus* to water from tanks containing *Pseudemys concinna* and *Trachemys scripta,* and to water from a tank containing a single large male *Macroclemys.* Because *Pseudemys* and *Trachemys* do not normally eat live turtles, the *Sternotherus* were not expected to avoid water bearing their chemical cues. Individual *Sternotherus* were placed in divided tanks and allowed to chose between the side to which water from a tank containing the other turtle species was added or to a control side receiving only dechlorinated water. Both *Sternotherus* spent statistically equal amounts of time in "*Pseudemys/Trachemys* water" and plain water. In contrast, mean time spent in the *Macroclemys* side was only 19% for *S. carinatus* and 29% for *S. minor*. Additional responses by both *Sternotherus* included moving less in *Macroclemys*-treated water relative to *Pseudemys/Trachemys* water, and increased gular pumping in *Macroclemys*-treated water. These results suggest that both species of *Sternotherus* can detect the unseen presence of *Macroclemys* using chemical cues, and avoid proximity to such a formidable turtle predator.

The alligator snapping turtle is the only reptile in the world with a predatory lure inside its mouth (Drummond and Gordon, 1979). The lure, or "worm" as it is sometimes called, is a small, movable appendage on the tongue used to attract fish into biting range. The attractive power of the lure is presumably due to its resemblance to a worm or insect larva. The unique lingual appendage is a branching tissue mass that is attached to the anterior third of the oral cavity in front of the glottis (Spindel et al., 1987). The structure is functionally subdivided into a main body, an anterior horn, and a posterior horn. Its color varies ontogenetically, being white or pale pink in juveniles and mottled or smoky gray in subadults and adults. These colors contrast with the gray-black coloration of the oral cavity. The hyoid skeleton appears to be the primary supportive structure of the lingual appendage. Ten pairs of muscles were identified that may be responsible for hyoid movement, and thus lure manipulation. These may be divided into three groups on the basis of their sites of insertion. Muscles of the first group, including Musculus intermandibularis and M. constrictor colli, have no direct connection to the hyoid skeleton or lingual appendage. When contracted, M. constrictor colli would tend to pull M. intermandibularis caudally, thus indirectly influencing the appendage. The second group, including M. geniohyoideus, M. hypoglossohyoideus, M. branchiohyoideus, M. branchiomandibularis visceralis, and M. coracohyoideus, have an insertion on at least one element of the hyoid skeleton but no attachment to the submucosa. These muscles protract, elevate, and otherwise shift the position of the hyoid skeleton. The third group of muscles, including M. genioglossus, M. hypoglossoglossus, and M. hyoglossus all have insertions in the submucosa. Contraction of these muscle pairs presumably results in lateral deviations in the position of the hyoid skeleton and insertion of the lingual process into the body of the lingual appendage. The blood supply of the lingual appendage is supplied by terminal branches of the common carotid arteries. The branch of a nerve trunk that gives rise to

numerous other branches that innervate various hyoid muscles enters the lingual appendage. The main nerve trunk has a complex origin on the middle and caudal regions of the medulla and may be composed of the glossopharyngeal, vagus, spinal accessory, and hypoglossal cranial nerves. The lingual nerve has three branches: one enters the posterior horn and two enter the anterior horn; virtual absence of muscle fibers in the horns of the lingual appendage suggests a sensory function for the lingual nerve. Histologically, the lingual appendage is composed of two main layers including the tunica mucosa and the tunica submucosa. The tunica mucosa is composed of the lamina epithelialis, basement membrane, and lamina propria. Melanocytes are present in the lamina epithelialis, lamina propria, and the tunica submucosa. The lamina propria contains the greatest density of melanin, which is partly responsible for the pigmented appearance of the lingual appendage in subadults and adults. Structures resembling taste buds, but lacking the direct innervation expected of taste buds, are scattered over the distal three-fourths of both anterior and posterior horns.

When the turtle is luring, the hyoid skeleton is protracted, elevating and extending the lingual appendage. Engorgement with blood and the buoyancy of water allow the lingual appendage to achieve a partially erect stature. The flexibility of the appendage appears to allow it to wriggle as the base is shifted by the hyoid skeleton. Flexibility may also make it less susceptible to injury when grasped by prey that are lured to it.

Luring has rarely been observed under natural conditions, but Allen and Neill (1950) reported an example in which a small *Macroclemys* (18 cm) was observed, at night near Biloxi, Mississippi, moving its appendage while fish were swimming nearby. Detailed observations of luring behavior in captive hatchlings were made by Drummond and Gordon (1979). Experiments conducted in the presence of mosquitofish (*Gambusia*) indicated that the hunting sequence had four phases. The first phase (waiting) is characterized by the turtle remaining motionless in a shallow pit dug in the gravel substrate. Turtles assume a posture with legs spread outward and head held horizontal or tilted upward. Sometimes only the head of the turtle protrudes above the substrate. During the second phase (luring) the jaws are opened at an angle of about 70°; opening sometimes takes one or two minutes. The red, wriggling lure is seen as soon as the dorsal surface of the lower jaw is visible. Most episodes of luring are initiated after vigorous movements by the nearest fish; mean distance between the fish and a turtle head at the onset of luring is about 6.2 cm. Turtles make frequent eye movements and occasionally orient their jaws toward fish. The mean duration of luring episodes that did not end in an attack was 336 seconds. The third phase (attack) only occurs when turtles are luring. In most cases an attack consists of rapidly closing the jaws without moving the head toward a fish. Most attacks occur when fish dart into the jaws, apparently at the same moment that the lure is seized. All fish passing through the turtle's jaws and 75% of those biting the lure are captured. The fourth (last) phase of the hunting sequence is prey handling. After a fish is captured it is held in the jaws 1–83 seconds (mean, 16.2) before being swallowed whole. Swallowing is facilitated with several snaps of the jaws (mean, 6.2). Large fish are swallowed by extending the head forward with the mouth open as the hyoid apparatus expands the buccopharyngeal cavity creating low pressure that draws in the fish (Bramble, 1973). Occasionally a turtle will mutilate the posterior portion of the prey with its claws, while holding the anterior end in its jaws. Prey handling time decreases with experience.

One of the littermates demonstrated feeding behavior in sharp contrast to the preceding description, even though it was raised under identical conditions. It moved about frequently and oriented toward fish. This behavior was unsuccessful and after the third feeding session it adopted a more typical luring pattern.

Subjects from a second litter were tested to determine if (1) visual and mechanical cues or (2) chemical cues elicit first luring, and then attack. A third experiment tested the importance of tactile stimuli to attack. To eliminate any effects due to learning, Drummond and Gordon (1979) used hatchlings that had never been presented with food. In the first experiment, visual cues were tested by presenting turtles with fish sealed in a clear plexiglass container. Mechanical stimuli were generated by squirting water near the turtles' head through a small plastic tube. Mechanical and visual stimuli were not applied in the same trial. Turtles lured in all but one of 37 trials when visual stimuli were applied. The number of turtles luring in the presence of mechanical stimuli was not significantly different from the control condition when no fish or stimuli were present. In the second experiment, water from tanks containing mosquitofish (*Gambusia*) and minnows (Cyprinidae) was added to experimental tanks with turtles. The number of trials in which luring was observed when fishy water was added did not differ from the number when control water was added. These results suggest that chemical stimuli alone do not elicit luring behavior. In the third experiment, various parts of a luring turtle's mouth and head were tapped gently with a piece of wire. Touching the lure and tongue produced attacks in 7 of 11 turtles. Taps to the upper jaw and head produced two attacks and three turtles attacked after the lower jaw was tapped. Drummond and Gordon concluded that in ingestively naive hatchling alligator snappers, luring occurs in response to visual signals and attack occurs in response to tactile stimuli.

PREDATORS AND DEFENSE: Eggs and hatchlings of alligator snapping turtles are probably susceptible to the same predators as other aquatic turtles. Redmond (1979) reported that raccoons (*Procyon*) destroy many nests and that large fish, wading birds, and otters (*Lutra*) take their toll of hatchlings and juveniles. From a defensive standpoint, Allen and Neill (1950) noted that the alligator snapper is less aggressive than the common snapping turtle and lunges with less agility. Disturbed individuals usually sit passively, mouth agape, striking out only when a threatening object approaches the head. If it makes contact with its mouth, severe damage may result. When lifted from the ground, it may evert the glottal opening for a few seconds exposing the bright white lining of the respiratory tract against the dark lining of the mouth. Other responses to molestation include malodorous excretions and discharge of copious streams of clear liquid from the cloaca. Defensive stances may be maintained for as long as 10 seconds (Hayes, 1989).

The human is the only enemy of an adult alligator snapping turtle. The species has been heavily exploited for its meat; the impact of concentrated harvesting is controversial, however, because there are no rigorous studies of past or present population trends.

POPULATIONS: The relative abundance of various turtle species was assessed by Cagle and Chaney (1950) at 14 sites in Louisiana during summer 1947. *Macroclemys* composed 4.2% of the sample at Caddo Lake, 12.5% at Lake Iatt, 12.1% at Tensas Bayou, and 4% at Lake Arthur, but alligator snappers may have been more abundant than indicated, as trap design made it difficult for large *Macroclemys* to enter.

George (1987) and Pritchard (1989) reviewed anecdotal information provided by turtle trappers and state wildlife biologists suggesting that *Macroclemys* populations have declined drastically throughout the range. Although protected to varying extents by several states (George, 1987), Pritchard (1989) concluded that the species should receive Federal protection as a threatened species. We concur.

REMARKS: The relationships of chelydrid turtles were examined by Gaffney (1975b) using shell and skull characters; he concluded that the group was strictly monophyletic, and that *Macroclemys* was derived from *Chelydra*.

Bour (1987) discussed the controversy surrounding the holotype of *Macroclemys temminckii*, and we refer the reader to that reference.

Cheloniidae
Marine turtles

Five living genera and six species of hard-shelled sea turtles belong to this family. Most of their feeding and nesting range is in the warmer marine waters, and they occur in all tropical oceans with several species ranging well into the temperate zones. Five species inhabit the coastal waters of the United States and Canada. Cheloniids have a long history in North America, dating from the late Cretaceous (Nicholls et al., 1990). Morphologically and serologically they are most closely related to *Dermochelys coriacea* (Dermochelyidae) and the extinct sea turtle families Plesiochelyidae, Protostegidae, and Toxochelyidae, but they also show some affinities to the terrapin family Emydidae.

These large turtles have a carapace that is covered with horny scutes. The carapace retains the embryonic spaces (peripheral fenestrae) between the ribs; thus the neurals and pleurals are greatly reduced in size. Neurals are hexagonal, shortest anteriorly, and variable in number. The nuchal lacks riblike processes, but is attached ventrally to the neural arch of the eighth vertebra. The carapace and plastron are connected by ligaments; the hingeless plastron is somewhat reduced and has a small entoplastron. A small intergular scute and small postanal scutes may be present. Inframarginal scutes are common. The forelimbs are paddlelike, with elongated digits. The deltopectoral crest of the humerus is positioned far down the shaft, the trochanteric fossa of the femur is greatly restricted, and the trochanters are united. The neck is short, and the ability to retract the head has been lost. The fourth vertebra is biconvex. The temporal region of the skull is completely roofed; parietal-squamosal contact occurs. The premaxillae are not fused, meet the vomer, and separate the internal nares and palatines. A secondary palate is present, but the palatine fenestrae are missing. Bony trabeculae of the basisphenoidal rostrum lie close together or are fused. The pterygoids separate the basisphenoid from the palatines, but do not meet the maxillae. The maxilla does not contact the quadratojugal, and the quadrate encloses the stapes. The dentary is confined to the anterior half of the lower jaw.

Chelonia mydas (Linnaeus, 1758)
Green turtle

PLATE 3

RECOGNITION: *Chelonia mydas* is a medium to large sea turtle that has paddlelike forelimbs with only one claw on each, two prefrontal and four postocular scales on the head, and a serrated cutting edge on the lower jaw. Its broad, low, heart-shaped carapace is commonly less than 105 cm long, but may possibly reach 153 cm. In adults the large carapacial scutes are not (or only slightly) juxtaposed. No vertebral keel is present and the carapace is only slightly serrated posteriorly. Four pairs of pleurals are present; the first pair does not touch the cervical. Carapacial scutes are olive to brown, or even black, and may contain a mottled radiating or wavy pattern. The bridge has four poreless inframarginal scutes, and the hingeless plastron is immaculate white or yellowish. Epidermis of the shell is heavily keratinized and commonly two to four cells thick (six cells thick at growing points); during development the pigment bodies migrate toward the surface layers (Solomon et al., 1986). The skin is brown or, in some, gray to black, and many of the head scales have yellow borders. The horny inner surface of the upper jaw has well-developed vertical ridges, and the cutting edge of the lower jaw is strongly serrated.

In males the carapace is more tapering posteriorly and the hind lobe of the plastron is narrower than in females. In some populations the males are much flatter than the females (Hirth, 1980c). The male tail is strongly prehensile in a vertical plane, is tipped with a heavy, flattened nail, and extends far beyond the posterior carapacial rim; the female tail barely reaches the rim. The male forelimb has a large, curved claw.

The common name of this turtle is derived from the greenish color of its fat.

KARYOTYPE: The chromosomes total 56 in both sexes (Makino, 1952, mistakenly reported that females have only 55): 14 metacentric and submetacentric macrochromosomes, 10 telocentric and subtelocentric macrochromosomes, and 32 microchromosomes (Bickham et al., 1980; Bachère, 1981).

FOSSIL RECORD: The genus *Chelonia* is known from late Cretaceous deposits in Europe, the Miocene of Japan, and the Eocene to Recent of Australia and North America (Tachibana, 1979; Limpus, 1987; Ernst and Barbour, 1989). Probable North American fossils of *C. mydas* are from the Miocene of California (Gilmore, 1937) and possibly New Jersey (Zug, in press), Pliocene of Florida and North Carolina (Dodd and Morgan, 1992; Zug, in press), and Pleistocene (Rancholabrean) of Florida (Weigel, 1962).

DISTRIBUTION: The green turtle ranges through the Atlantic, Pacific, and Indian oceans, chiefly in the tropics. In the eastern Atlantic it has been recorded from the Shetland Islands, England, Ireland (Eire) and the Netherlands southward to Portugal (Brongersma, 1972), and in the western North Atlantic from Massachusetts (Lazell, 1980) southward to Bermuda, the Florida Keys, and the Bahamas. Those in the North Atlantic, particularly off the United States, are usually juveniles or subadults. *Chelonia mydas* also ranges throughout the Gulf of Mexico and Caribbean Sea, and southward in the western South Atlantic to Uruguay and Argentina. North Pacific records are from Eliza Harbor, Admiralty Island (57°16′ N) and Point Macartney, Kuprenoff Island (57°03′ N), Alaska (Hodge, 1981; Stinson, 1984) south to Baja California and the Gulf of California (Stinson, 1984). Its range continues south along the Pacific coast of Central and South America to Chile. A population is resident in San Diego Bay, California; the turtles are usually there from November to April when water and sediment temperatures and salinity are annually lowest, but only in areas where the temperature and salinity are

Female *Chelonia mydas mydas*

Male *Chelonia mydas mydas;*
note elongated tail

highest and the species diversity and biomass of benthic invertebrates are greatest (Stinson, 1984). More *Chelonia* are seen off the northern Pacific Coast in years of hot water temperatures, especially during the influence of El Nino (Stinson, 1984).

GEOGRAPHIC VARIATION: Two sub-species are recognized. *Chelonia mydas mydas* (Linnaeus, 1758), the Atlantic green turtle, ranges in the Atlantic Ocean from New England and the British Isles to Argentina and extreme South Africa. It is often abundant about Ascension Island, in the Cape Verde Islands and the Cayman Islands, and off Bermuda. This subspecies is predominantly brown and has an elongated, shallow carapace that is not markedly indented above the hind limbs. It attains a greater carapace length than its Pacific counterpart (see Growth and longevity section below). *Chelonia mydas agassizii* Bocourt, 1868, the Pacific green turtle, ranges from Ethiopia and Yemen around the Cape of Good Hope to western Africa, and east through the Indian and Pacific oceans to the western coast of the

Plastron of *Chelonia mydas*

Chelonia mydas; note single pair of prefrontal scales

New World, from Alaska to Chile. This turtle is greenish or olive brown and has a broad, deep shell that is commonly markedly indented above the hind limbs. Some individuals are melanistic, becoming slate gray to black in overall color. Caldwell (1962c) described *C. m. carrinegra* from the Gulf of California on the basis of this dark pigment; however, inasmuch as black turtles also occur along the coast of Central America and in the Galapagos Islands and paler individuals can be found in the Gulf of California, there seems to be no geographic distinction between the two color morphs and all eastern Pacific green turtles should be considered *C. m. agassizii.* Western Pacific green turtles may yet prove to be a third subspecies, *C. m. japonica* (Thunberg, 1787).

Hirth (1980c) suggested that *C. mydas* not be split into subspecies until more precise definitions and demarcation of their ranges are available. Others studying marine turtles would elevate *C. m. agassizii* to specific status. Atlantic and Pacific green turtles differ in size, carapace shape, and coloration, but these differences are no more striking than those between subspecies of some emydid turtles, such as *Trachemys scripta* and *Terrapene carolina*. Examination of karyotype morphology reveals little difference (Bachère, 1981), although myoglobin and protein electrophoretic studies indicate that some genetic differentiation exists between breeding aggregations of *Chelonia* in both the Atlantic and Pacific oceans (Williams and Brown, 1976; Bickham et al., 1980; Bowen, 1988; Meylan et al., 1990a; Bowen et al., 1992). This is to be expected because the green turtle has great nest site tenacity which acts as a reproductive barrier between nesting populations.

Overall similarity of mitochondrial DNA genotypes within Atlantic nesting populations indicates either recent divergence or that gene exchange only occurs at very low levels (Bowen, 1988; Bowen et al., 1992). Hawaiian *C. m. agassizii* are also very similar to some Atlantic populations, but differ by having five restriction enzymes (Bowen et al., 1989; Avise et al., 1992). The Atlantic and Pacific green turtles have presumably been separated for at least three million years, over which time a nucleotide sequence divergence of only 0.2% per million years has occurred, or about 10% the conventional pace. Even at this decreased rate, many restriction site changes should have taken place if these two populations have speciated. This is supported by an electrophoretic survey of 23 gene loci in populations of *C. mydas* from the Atlantic, Pacific, and Indian oceans by Bonhomme et al. (1987) which revealed virtually no genetic heterozygosity or geographical differentiation.

The above studies of nesting females show only contemporary restriction of gene flow between the Atlantic and Pacific populations (such as in Atlantic and Pacific populations of *Caretta* and *Lepidochelys*; Bowen et al., 1991). In addition, study of male DNA from several breeding populations in the Atlantic, Pacific, and Indian oceans by Karl et al. (1992) revealed moderate rates of male-mediated gene flow. Positive relationships between genetic similarity and geographic proximity suggest the existence of historical connections and/or contemporary gene flow between particular rookery populations, likely via matings on overlapping feeding grounds, migration corridors, or nonnatal rookeries.

These studies support our continuing to regard *C. m. mydas* and *C. m. agassizii* as subspecies of one species rather than separate species.

CONFUSING SPECIES: *Eretmochelys imbricata* has four prefrontal and three postocular scales, juxtaposition of the large scutes of the carapace, and a strongly serrated posterior carapacial rim. *Caretta* *caretta* and the two species of *Lepidochelys* have five or more pairs of pleurals, with the first pair touching the cervical scute.

HABITAT: The green turtle migrates across the open seas but feeds in shallow water supporting an abundance of submerged vegetation. It has been seen in the ocean more than 160 km from land (Fritts et al., 1983), and some migrate across 2,000 km of the Atlantic Ocean from Brazil to Ascension Island (Carr and Coleman, 1974), but most individuals travel much closer to shore. Water depths in which Hoffman and Fritts (1982) and Fritts et al. (1983) observed swimming *Chelonia mydas* were 11–461 m; all but one were in water less than 50 m deep. Sea surface temperatures at the sighting locations were 24–27°C (mean 25.6), and seven of eight turtles seen off the Atlantic coast of Florida were inshore (west) of the Gulf Stream Current (Hoffman and Fritts, 1982).

Juvenile development and adult foraging areas are typically quiet, shallow (3–5 m), well-lighted places, ideal for algal and sea-grass production and enhancement of invertebrate diversity and biomass. Nearby reefs or rocky areas may provide resting or sleeping shelters. Once hatchlings enter the open sea they apparently associate with floating mats of sargassum (Frick, 1976; Carr and Meylan, 1980a; Carr, 1987), and they may spend a year or more there slowly drifting around the Gulf of Mexico or Caribbean Sea.

BEHAVIOR: The annual cycle of *Chelonia* is poorly known, and may vary between populations. Some populations are apparently resident in the breeding area and do not migrate to and from the nesting beach, but others have nesting and foraging areas that are widely separated (sometimes by over 1,000 km). During reproductive years individuals from these populations must first travel to the reproductive area, then mate and oviposit, and then migrate back to the foraging locality. Even immature green turtles must have some pattern of annual movements as they are more numerous in some months than in others (Mendonça, 1983; Henwood, 1987b). A fourth annual subdivision occurs in some more northern populations where green turtles hibernate during the colder months (see below).

Daily activity is usually diurnal, with foraging in the shallows in midmorning and midafternoon, and resting in deeper waters over midday in summer, but no definite diel activity cycle occurs in the winter (Mendonça, 1983). At night *Chelonia* sleeps on the bottom or on a ledge above the water level.

Subadult *Chelonia mydas* at Cape Canaveral, Florida, are active until water temperatures reach 34°C (adults become inactive at water temperatures of 26–28°C; Heath and McGinnis, 1980). When water temperatures climb above 25°C they adopt a defined home range (Mendonça, 1983). Feeding does not begin, however, until the water temperature reaches 18°C, thus cold waters retard growth.

Chelonia mydas has some localized endothermic capabilities. Standora et al. (1982) and Spotila and Standora (1985) reported that a green turtle swimming vigorously had a pectoral body temperature of 37°C in water of 29°C, but that inactive turtles were only 1–2°C above the water temperature (Heath and McGinnis, 1980, found that juveniles in thermal equilibrium with the environment had deep body temperatures 1.0–2.5°C above ambient temperature). Apparently only active tissues are involved in elevated regional endothermy, not the entire body. Heat is retained in active tissues due to the turtle's large body size and the insulating properties of its shell and fat. Standora et al. (1982) thought elevated pectoral muscle temperature increases the turtle's swimming ability, particularly during long-distance migrations.

Heat production seems solely from muscular activity (Heath and McGinnis, 1980). The green turtle heats faster than it cools when placed in different temperature regimes, and smaller turtles heat and cool faster than large ones (Smith et al., 1986). Heart rate increases with increasing body temperature (Davenport et al., 1982; Smith et al., 1986), as does the breathing rate and oxygen uptake (Jackson et al., 1979; Kraus and Jackson, 1980; Davenport et al., 1982), but blood pH decreases (Kraus and Jackson, 1980; Lutz and Lapennas, 1982). *Chelonia* hyperventilates during exercise (Prange and Jackson, 1976); the breathing rate may increase to seven times the resting rate (West et al., 1992). Pulmonary blood flow increases in proportion to oxygen uptake with rises in temperature, so that constant oxygen content differences are maintained between pulmonary arterial and venous blood (Gatz et al., 1987). Most increases in pulmonary and aortic blood flow can be attributed to an increase in cardiac output; however, pulmonary flow increases more than aortic flow, suggesting that pulmonary resistance is reduced during exercise (West et al., 1992). Mean lung volume is 56 ml/kg body weight and physiological dead space volume is about 3.6 ml/kg (Gatz et al., 1987). The large tidal volume relative to functional residual capacity promotes fast exchange of alveolar gas when the turtle breathes. Resting green turtles breath in bursts (West et al., 1992).

Above 30°C arterial carbon dioxide increases (Kraus and Jackson, 1980). Fixed acid and carbon dioxide Bohr effects are strongly saturation dependent (low at low saturation, highest at higher saturation; Lapennas and Lutz, 1982). *Chelonia mydas* may have a small (net) intracardiac shunt which allows the high arterial oxygen saturation (90%) of arterial blood (Wood et al., 1984).

Cold water temperatures not only retard feeding and growth, but if low enough can stun green turtles. Cold-stunned *Chelonia* have been found in Long Island Sound, New York (Meylan and Sadove, 1986; Morreale et al., 1992); Indian River Lagoon, Florida (Witherington and Ehrhart, 1989); and at several sites in Texas (Shaver, 1990). Cold-stunning usually happens when water temperatures drop to 10°C or below, and can result in death if the cold period is extended and the temperature drops to 5.0–6.5°C. At these temperatures *Chelonia* will die in 9–12 hours (Schwartz, 1978). Green turtles lose the ability to dive at 9°C and remain floating horizontally with neck extended until they either warm up or die.

Body temperatures of nesting females may rise. Cloacal temperatures of seven females were recorded just after they had crawled out of the 27.5–28.5°C ocean to nest. The average cloacal temperature taken 3–20 minutes after they had left the water, but before laying, was 29.9°C; that taken 1–2 hours after emerging, by which time laying had been completed, was 30.0°C (Hirth, 1962). Body water may be lost by evaporation from the skin surface at this time, and is usually correlated with the turtle's mass (Smith et al., 1986), but the loss causes no major problem if the female returns promptly to the sea.

Chelonia mydas is the only marine turtle that habitually leaves the water to bask, and it can raise its body temperature as much as 5°C above the ocean temperature (Spotila and Standora, 1985). Emergent basking seems restricted to *C. m. agassizii*, and is common in the Hawaiian Islands (Balazs and Ross, 1974a; Balazs, 1979a, 1980; Sheekey, 1982; Whittow and Balazs, 1982; Kam, 1984). There *Chelonia* crawls out onto coral and sand beaches, lava rock ledges, and even old exposed shipwrecks. Although usually spatially separated from other basking *Chelonia* and other animals, Balazs (1979a) has published a photograph of a monk seal (*Monachus*) and a green turtle basking together with the seal partially lying on the turtle. The highest cloacal temperature recorded from a basking *Chelonia* was 31.3°C, but the surface temperature of the carapace may reach 42.8°C (Whittow and Balazs, 1982). Basking turtles often flip sand onto their carapaces, but do not seem to orientate their position toward the sun. Duration of basking is inversely related to the mean temperature of a black globe placed on the beach even though the beach is relatively cool (Whittow and Balazs, 1982). Basking may last 450–600 minutes. Ventilation while basking consists of periods of breath-holding (50–635 seconds) alternating with single inhalations. Warming in the sun may aid digestion and egg maturation, or avoidance of marine predators (Whittow and Balazs, 1982; Snell and Fritts, 1983).

Basking may also occur while the turtle is floating at the surface, at which time seabirds may perch on the turtle's back (Booth, 1975). Apparently some solar heat is absorbed through the dark carapace: hatchlings in an aquarium set below a radiant heat source had cloacal temperatures 1.1–2.3°C above an ambient temperature of 22°C, but when their dark carapaces were painted white their cloacal temperatures were maintained only 0–0.6°C above the ambient temperature (Bustard, 1970).

One population of *C. m. agassizii* overwintering at approximately 29° N latitude is known to hibernate for extended periods underwater in the Infiernillo Channel in the Gulf of California (Felger et al., 1976), and Ogren and McVea (1982) also reported the possibility of hibernation in the Gulf of Mexico at about the same latitude. Hibernating turtles partially bury themselves along muddy or sandy edges of undersea troughs, often beside patches of eelgrass (*Zostera*), at depths of 4–8 m.

As in other sea turtles, the kidneys of the green turtle cannot alone rid the body of the excess salts ingested while drinking seawater or swallowing marine prey (Prange, 1985). To aid osmoregulation, *Chelonia* has large secretory orbital glands consisting of closely packed, branched secondary tubules radiating from larger ducts and a saclike main duct (Schmidt-Nielsen and Fange, 1958; Marshall and Saddlier, 1989). Distally the large ducts consist of large columnar cells, more proximally these canals and the main duct are lined with stratified or pseudostratified epithelia. At the luminal borders of the epithelia in the secondary and main ducts is a layer of monocytes. A green turtle in seawater has the following concentrations of sodium and potassium (expressed as millimoles/liter) in its salt gland secretions, plasma, and urine, respectively: 388 and 26 (osmolality 768 milliosmoles/kg), 157.8 and 1.48 (osmolality 390), and 22 and 34 (osmolality 320) (Prange, 1985). Obviously, most sodium is removed by the orbital glands, whereas most potassium passes out in the urine (although the amount passed by the orbital glands is relatively high). The orbital glands also secrete high amounts of chloride, 401 milliosmols/liter (Prange, 1985). The two eye glands do not always

secrete at the same rate or concentration (Nicolson and Lutz, 1989). If the green turtle is dehydrated, urine osmolarity may rise (Prange and Greenwald, 1980) and the secretion of ammonia and urea by the kidney increases (Bjorndal, 1979b).

Swimming is accomplished by oaring through the water with the elongated foreflippers. The downstroke is the power movement, and the positive propulsive force peaks as the flipper reaches its most posterior position close to the body (Davenport et al., 1984). During the turning and twisting of the flipper at this position propulsive force declines rapidly, almost to zero, but forward motion is again developed during the flipper upswing, although the propulsive force then is only 20–40% of the force during the downstroke. At the top of the forelimb cycle, another twisting motion and momentary cessation of forward movement are followed by a small amount of backward thrust which is quickly reversed (Davenport et al., 1984). The mean flipper cycle takes about 0.37–1.13 seconds, depending on the size of the turtle. *Chelonia* can generate twice the propulsive force and swim six times as fast as some freshwater turtles. Juveniles tested by Davenport et al. (1984) achieved swimming speeds of 5.9–143.0 cm/second, and Prange (1976) reported that young *Chelonia* swimming in a water channel were able to sustain speeds of 0.14–0.35 m/second (their oxygen consumption when at rest was 0.07 l/kg/hour, but at the above swimming speeds increased 3–4 times). Hatchlings can be stimulated to speed up their swimming rate with chemical stimuli, such as food odors (Bennett and Kleerekoper, 1978).

In the ocean adult green turtles are powerful swimmers that may migrate long distances. Some breeding populations regularly travel more than 1,000 km between their nesting beaches and principal foraging areas. Those nesting on Ascension Island in the middle of the Atlantic Ocean forage off the coast of Brazil, 2,200–2,300 km west (Carr and Coleman, 1974; Mortimer and Carr, 1987); a round trip to and from this island would require the equivalent of about 21% of body mass in fat stores to cover the energetic cost of swimming (Prange, 1976). The maximum possible recorded direct trip by a *Chelonia* was 3,085 km, 4,439 if the turtle moved along the coast between captures (Carr, 1975). Several female *C. m. mydas* tagged at nesting beaches have been recaptured more than 2,000 km away (Carr, 1975; Schulz, 1975; Carr et al., 1978; Green, 1984; Mortimer and Carr, 1987). Balazs (1976) reported that a Hawaiian *C. m. agassizii* swam at least 1,075 km between captures, and Márquez (1990) reported a female tagged in Michoacán, Mexico, was next captured 3,500 km away in Colombia. The maximum speed recorded for a long migration was 93 km/day (Carr et al., 1978), but a review of all long distance records indicates that swimming speeds near 25 km/day are normal.

Carr and Coleman (1974) proposed a theory to explain why the Ascension Island breeding population makes the long trip from Brazil when other suitable beaches to the north are much closer. According to them the Ascension Islands may once have been much nearer the Brazilian coast, but as the sea floor spread because of plate tectonics involved in continental drift since the Cretaceous, the islands slowly shifted position to the middle of the Atlantic Ocean, approximately midway between the western bulge of Africa and the eastern one of Brazil. This forced the green turtles using Ascension for nesting to slowly migrate farther and farther from their foraging area. Although intriguing, this hypothesis is unproven, but the turtles breeding there do constitute a distinct genetic stock (Meylan et al., 1990a).

The factors leading to long-range remigrations of green turtles are probably not the same for all breeding populations. Hirth (1978) proposed that some of the better known remigrations had their origins in short-distance movements between feeding pastures and nearby nesting beaches. The foraging site was the center of activity, and movements to the nesting beach were based upon familiarity with the local environment. Changing conditions on either the feeding pasture or the nesting beach (or both) influenced selection for the semipermanent residents. Passive drift in dominant surface currents probably gave rise to some of the first distant remigrations. A refinement of passive drift includes an adult's identification of a previous nesting site, and this short-range discriminatory ability may have been a precursor to long-range, unidirectional homing, and this in turn to true navigation. Some of the long-distance remigrations seen today, although highly developed, may be only remnants of more widespread patterns that have evolved.

Short-range homing behavior in feeding waters has been shown for Pacific green turtles in Hawaii (Balazs et al., 1987). Turtles captured on Palaau and released at either Kaunakakai, 8 km away, or Kawela, 17 km distant, were recaptured at Palaau in 0.3–31.7 months. Immature Atlantic green turtles in Mosquito Lagoon, Florida, make random long-distance movements of 5–10 km/day (mean 8.2) when water temperatures are 11–18°C (Mendonça, 1983), so possibly the distances between the Hawaiian release points used by Balazs et al. (1987) were still within an area familiar to the turtles. Mendonça (1983) has reported that when water temperatures in Mosquito Lagoon are above 25°C the immature turtles adopt a defined home range and move only an average of 2.6 km/day (1.2–4.1).

Several studies have been made to discover how green turtles find their way. Some have concerned vision inasmuch as optokinetic behavior is present at the time of emergence from the nest (Ireland, 1979). However sea-finding orientation in *Chelonia* cannot be explained solely in terms of some photic mechanism permitting progress in the brightest direction (Rhijn, 1979). Probably the turtle also orients visually with the help of a multiple input system of some type (Rhijn, 1979). Experiments by Verheijen and Wildschut (1973) indicate that *C. mydas* moves in the brightest direction of the angular light distribution and not in the direction opposite to the darkest direction, and that it obtains data about the brightest direction by processing of photic stimuli coming through an input cone with a very large horizontal angle of acceptance. Also, studies by Ehrenfeld and Koch (1967) on the visual accommodation of *C. mydas* indicate that the species is extremely myopic in air but approximately enmetropic in seawater. Nevertheless, hatchlings orient toward the most intensely illuminated direction, but move away from dark silhouettes (Salmon et al., 1992).

Hatchlings prefer the shorter wavelengths near ultraviolet to green over the longer wavelengths yellow and red (Mrosovsky and Carr, 1967; Witherington and Bjorndal, 1991b). Mrosovsky and Shettleworth (1968) found that in blue-red and yellow-red preference tests the attractiveness of red could be boosted by increasing its intensity relative to the blue or yellow alternative. Although there was a preference for blue over red of equal intensity, this preference could be reversed if the intensity of the red was made sufficiently high, an indication that brightness was an important factor. Mrosovsky and Shettleworth (1968) also reported that if there is a blue preference, the part it plays in sea-finding can only be secondary compared with brightness. Simultaneous comparison of differential brightness from a wide field of view enables the turtle to head for the center of an open horizon. The underlying mechanism involves a balancing of brightness inputs in both eyes, and the hatchling orients itself to maintain such a balance. For *Chelonia* on the nesting beach the most open horizon is nearly always seaward and is nearly always brighter than the landward direction. Because it has a brightness preference and a tropotatic reaction to light, the bright illumination from the open horizon may be the turtle's principal cue in sea-finding. The preference of blue over red light of equal intensity was also observed by Dickerson and Nelson (1988), who thought that the shorter wavelengths are the primary disorientation stimuli for hatchlings. Witherington and Bjorndal (1991b) reported that in two-choice tests hatchlings oriented toward near-ultraviolet (360 nm), violet (400 nm), and blue-green (500 nm) light, but preferred standard white light over yellow-orange (600 nm) and red (700 nm) light (there was a positive correlation between intensity and preference with 360, 400, and 500 nm light). When given a choice of either a darkened window or one lighted by one of eight monochromatic colors at each of two intensities, the green turtles responded poorly to 600 and 700 nm light at either intensity, indicating the ability of spectral quality assessment (Witherington and Bjorndal, 1991b).

Experiments by Ehrenfeld (1968) in which spectacles holding a variety of color filters were placed over the eyes of green turtles confirmed that light-intensity discrimination rather than color discrimination is the basis for sea-finding. In preference tests between flashing and continuous light, hatchlings were not influenced much by the flashing light unless it considerably reduced illumination averaged over time, suggesting that the turtles integrate brightness data over time in their sea-finding behavior (Mrosovsky, 1978).

Turtles have two fields of visual orientation: a temporal field in which light enters from the side of the head and a nasal field located in front of the head. To test the effect of each on green turtles, Mrosovsky and Shettleworth (1974) designed experiments using opaque goggles. These tests showed that the nasal field inputs are associated with contralateral turning and those of the temporal field with ipsilateral turning, demonstrating that inputs from different directions contribute differently to sea-finding orientation.

Hatchling *Chelonia mydas* orient down slopes when exposed to infrared light, but this response is weakened in the presence of nocturnal levels of visible light (Salmon et al., 1992).

No evidence exists of an innate compass-direction preference based on celestial information, or that a direct view of the sea or surf is not necessary for seaward orientation, or that light polarized by reflection from the surface of the sea is not used as a primary cue when the water is out of sight (Ehrenfeld and Carr, 1967).

The sound of the waves breaking onto the beach may also guide hatchlings and postnesting females to the water. *Chelonia* has a maximum cochlear sensitivity in the region of 300–400 Hz and an upper limit of about 2,000 Hz (Ridgeway et al., 1969).

Nonrandom departure courses are maintained by hatchlings even after they have swum over the horizon from all fixed objects on the shore (Frick, 1976). The cues guiding *Chelonia* in the open ocean are unknown, but several possibilities have been proposed. Once in the water, hatchlings consistently swim toward approaching waves and oceanic swells for 24 hours in what has been termed a "frenzy" period (Wyneken and Salmon, 1992). Wave tank experiments have confirmed this orientation (Lohmann et al., 1990). Most swimming is diurnal, and after 24 hours swimming duration drops continually for several days (Wyneken and Salmon, 1992). This behavior exists whether or not the hatchling has first made a beach crawl. Such orientation would take the small turtle to the open sea and away from the beach and its many predators.

Visual accommodation has effectively eliminated open-sea navigation by the stars: the turtles cannot see them (Ehrenfeld and Koch, 1967). The location of nesting grounds on mainland beaches and feeding areas near the mainland makes it difficult to prove that at least some turtles do not locate these places by following shorelines. However, many major nesting beaches are located on isolated islands, and apparently *Chelonia* has no difficulty in finding them. The Brazil-to-Ascension migration has been discussed at length by Carr (1967b), Carr and Coleman (1974), and Mortimer and Carr (1987). Ascension Island is only about eight kilometers across and lies in the westward flow of the Equatorial Current, directly upstream from the bulge of Brazil. Before the current strikes the mainland, it splits—some of its waters flowing to the West Indies and the Caribbean Sea and becoming the Gulf Stream, the rest turning southward along the coast as the Brazilian Current. The Ascension nesting colony consists of turtles that come from both north and south of the point on the bulge opposite which the current splits. Two advantages are at once apparent in the Brazil—Ascension migration. One is the current that comes directly from the island toward the feeding area. The other is the position of Ascension: it is on the same parallel of latitude as the nearest point on the mainland. These special features may have favored development of the Ascension-seeking pattern, but they increase our difficulty in defining the mechanics of the guidance process as they favor no one navigation process over another. Celestial, inertial, magnetic field, and Coriolis-force guidance would all be simplified to some extent by the geography of the situation. In addition, the relationship between the direction of the current and the direction of the shortest course between the island

and the mainland makes it impossible to rule out a fifth possibility, namely landmark-piloting by an odor emanating from the island, possibly detectable from far out at sea. Koch et al. (1969) evaluated the possibility of orientation based in part on the detection of some chemical substance originating at the island. Calculations based on the turbulences and structure of the oceanic currents in the South Atlantic showed that the concentration of any substance emanating from the island would be only 100–1,000-fold lower in the Brazilian coastal waters than in the upstream waters in the immediate vicinity of Ascension. To follow this chemical trail to the island the turtle would have to be able to follow the gradient of increasing concentration to the center of the stream and then travel against the current in an easterly direction. In doing so *Chelonia* would have to solve four problems: (1) It must be able to selectively detect an odor from the target islands. (2) It must be able to detect the direction of the current or else must be provided with a time-compensated sun compass sense and a knowledge of the approximate direction of the goal (doubtful, considering its myopic vision). (3) It must be able to detect a difference in concentration at one time compared with another time—hours apart. (4) It must be capable of going far enough in a fixed direction with a crosscurrent component to sense a meaningful change in concentration and alter course accordingly.

If chemical orientation occurs, then obviously the imprinting of hatchlings with the taste or odor of the waters near their nesting beach would be a tremendous advantage. Despite having a regressed olfactive epithelium compared to that of the Emydidae (Saint-Girons, 1991), *Chelonia* can detect very low concentrations of chemicals dissolved in water (Manton et al., 1972a,b), supporting the theory of an odor memory in the species. Tests by Manton et al. (1972a,b) showed that the green turtle uses olfactory chemical reception, not taste, for discriminatory behavior, and that the odor memory may last at least a year after the initial training to a particular chemical. Further experiments by Owens et al. (1985) and Grassman and Owens (1987, 1989) have supplemented these results by showing that sea turtles can identify specific chemical cues learned earlier in their lives without initial formal conditioning, and that they can orientate to and distinguish between low concentrations of solutions prepared from natural beaches. If no other stimuli are present, subadults seem to imprint to chemicals to which they have had an early exposure. Tests further indicate that exposure both in the nest and in the early waters is necessary for any consistent

subsequent response, and that this exposure should be fairly long, at least several weeks. Although these experiments do not prove the existence of natal beach olfactory imprinting, they do suggest its possibility.

One other sense may be involved in open sea orientation and navigation by *Chelonia mydas*: the detection of magnetism. Green turtles examined by Perry et al. (1986) had magnetic remanence in their head regions with the greatest concentration in the anterior portion of the dura mater (although it was also diffuse throughout the facial muscle). This magnetic material was later identified as small particles of magnetite, with adult *Chelonia* containing more than juveniles or hatchlings. How this may aid in detecting the earth's magnetic lines is not clear, but should be a fruitful field for research.

We still do not know how turtles find their way in the open sea. Many explanations have been proposed and many have been rejected; the research continues. The use of radio transmitters attached to free-swimming oceanic turtles, with signals reflected from a satellite to a receiving station, is providing valuable clues.

Chelonia mydas may spend considerable time underwater, particularly at night. A captive female observed by Schwartz and Jenzen (1991) was more active (75.8% of the time) than female loggerheads, but not as active as male loggerheads kept with it. It had a greater breathing rate during the day than at night (14–33 breaths/hour versus 3–9 breaths/hour); its longest period of total submergence was 13 hours. Lutz and Bentley (1985) calculated an average dive duration of about 4.5 minutes with a maximum duration of 26.9 minutes at 21–25°C. When *Chelonia* is resting on the bottom it closes its nostrils (Walker, 1959). Closure occurs within each nostril, not at the tip, and is effected by the meeting of three bulges from the wall of each nasal passage. When the turtle is prowling underwater it keeps its nostrils open and slowly moves the floor of the mouth up and down, apparently for olfaction.

Berkson (1966, 1967) studied the physiologic adjustments to prolonged and deep diving in *Chelonia mydas*. He found that in prolonged dives the green turtle can survive up to five hours with no measurable oxygen in the trachea or in the blood of the carotid artery and that as long as nine minutes may elapse between heartbeats; intervals of four to five minutes are common. The green turtle's lungs are complexly subdivided and multicameral with small terminal air spaces through which a high flux of oxygen (at up to 10 times the resting state) can occur (D. C. Jackson, 1985); the respiratory epithelium consists largely of ciliated pseudostratified columnar cells (Solomon and Purton, 1984). Gas exchange areas occur at all levels from the bronchi down to the capillary-rich alveoli (Solomon and Purton, 1984). Support of the airways prevents physical collapse during expiration (Tenney et al., 1974), allows rapid emptying of the lungs during normal breathing, and prevents gas entrapment during deep dives. Chemical control of breathing is through sensitivity to both decreased and increased inspired oxygen (Jackson, 1985). Blood pH is regulated at the normal body temperature range of 25–35°C by controlling blood carbon dioxide levels through the relationship of ventilation and metabolic rate (D. C. Jackson, 1985). *Chelonia* has a high anaerobic capacity (Lutz and Bentley, 1985), and during prolonged dives (to 13 hours, see above) all tissues may become anaerobic as large changes in blood pH and carbon dioxide content are tolerated. The brain can function in the absence of oxygen for many hours. Also, the hemoglobin can become saturated at rather low oxygen levels (Lapennas and Lutz, 1982). When oxygen availability is limited by vasoconstriction, working muscles in diving *Chelonia* simultaneously ferment carbohydrates and amino acids, resulting in an increase of succinate and minor amounts of alanine from amino acid catabolism and pyruvate and lactate from glycolysis (Hochachka et al., 1975).

Balazs (1980) and Balazs et al. (1987) reported an interesting relationship between *C. m. agassizii* and wrasses (Labridae) and surgeonfish (*Acanthurus,* and possibly *Ctenochaetus*). The fish were seen grazing on algae and other detritus attached to the turtle's shell; in fact, discrete cleaning stations were established for the turtles. Cleaning mutualism of this type may play an important role in reducing the amount of algal and, possibly, invertebrate fouling of the shell.

REPRODUCTION: Sexual maturity in both sexes of *Chelonia* is reached sometimes between 6 and 13 years in captivity (Wood and Wood, 1980), but most probably mature at an older age in the wild. Ehrhardt and Witham (1992) estimated the age of maturity in free living Atlantic green turtles to be between 19 and 24 years. Males begin to show the lengthened mature tail at 64–65 cm and those with 75-cm carapaces have fully developed tails (Caldwell, 1962c; Balazs, 1980); but the female carapace length at maturity varies between populations. Of 1,146 nesting female *C. m. mydas* at Tortuguero, Costa Rica, the smallest had a 69.2-cm carapace (Carr and Ogren, 1960). Elsewhere the shortest ovipositing female Atlantic green turtles are longer than 83 cm, and the

average mature size for the Atlantic subspecies is over 100 cm (Hirth, 1980a). The shortest known mature Hawaiian female *C. m. agassizii* is 65 cm (Balazs, 1980), but most nesting Pacific females average over 81 cm (Hirth, 1980a). (See Growth and longevity section for additional data on maturity.)

The annual physical changes occurring in the male testes have not been adequately documented, although mature sperm is present at the time of spring mating and testis mass and spermatogenic behavior are greater in January than in September (Licht et al., 1985c). Two mature males examined by Owens (1980) three to four months prior to the nesting season had loose packed sperm in the epididymides and testicular spermiogenesis.

Male hormonal cycles are better known. Testosterone levels closely follow testicular enlargement and spermatogenesis instead of showing a separate peak during the spring mating period (Licht, 1982); in fact, gonadotropins remain low and androgen levels are lower during copulation than in the prebreeding season (Licht et al., 1979, 1985c). Plasma testosterone is lowest in male *C. m. mydas* in September–November and then increases progressively to a peak in April; levels begin to decline immediately thereafter, coincident with the beginning of the mating season (Licht et al., 1985c). Testosterone levels are relatively constant over a 24-hour period at any time of the year, and plasma thyroxine levels remain constant throughout the year (Licht et al., 1985c). Follicle-stimulating hormone promotes spermatogenesis and androgenesis, and brings on mating behavior, but luteinizing hormone and progesterone seem to have no effects (Owens and Hendrickson, 1978; Owens and Morris, 1985). Follicle-stimulating hormone is orders of magnitude more potent than luteinizing hormone in controlling both testis growth and androgen production (Licht and Papkoff, 1985), but from March to late May, amounts of either hormone in the plasma are not measurable (Licht et al., 1979).

During a nonreproductive year adult females have ovarian weights of 43–100 g and follicles of several size classes (1, 2, 6, and 13 mm; Owens, 1980). Ovarian weight in a reproductive year is high prior to the first copulation, rises until ovulation of the first clutch, drops below the precopulatory weight, and then rises again until the first clutch is laid and the second clutch is ovulated. This cycle is repeated after each successive nesting with ovarian weight decreasing after each ovulation until all mature eggs have been deposited and ovarian weight reaches its lowest level for the cycle (Owens and Morris, 1985).

The oviduct has two glandular subdivisions, each of which appears to be homogenous (Aitkin and Solomon, 1976). The more anterior functions only in albumen secretion, whereas the more posterior has the dual functions of adding both shell membrane materials and calcareous shell.

A clear relationship occurs between luteinizing hormone, ovulation, and a pronounced progesterone peak, which takes place as albumen is secreted in the oviduct. Ovulation coincides with a luteinizing hormone and progesterone surge a day following oviposition (Licht, 1980; Owens, 1980; Owens and Morris, 1985; Wibbels et al., 1992). Follicle-stimulating hormone surges during the periovulatory stage (Wibbels et al., 1992), but shows only a transient peak during oviposition (Licht, 1980); its exact role has not been determined, but it may regulate estrogen production (Owens and Morris, 1985). Plasma estrogens are at low concentrations with peaks in the spring, which may correlate with migration and ovarian maturation, as well as during the internesting interval when vitellogenesis occurs and subsequent follicle classes mature (Owens and Morris, 1985). Plasma progesterone rises progressively during the prebreeding and mating seasons and up to oviposition, and testosterone peaks in the plasma during the mating period and then drops in concentration during the remainder of the nesting season (Licht et al., 1979; Wibbels et al., 1992).

Mating occurs during the laying season in the water off the nesting beaches. Although mated pairs have been seen more than a kilometer from shore, the greatest activity is in relatively shallow water close to shore. Copulation takes place at any hour, and usually occurs before the nesting emergence. A female may mate sequentially with several males, but once she begins to oviposit is no longer interested in copulation (Simon et al., 1975; Ulrich and Parkes, 1978). Whether the males accompany the females from the foraging waters or whether they make a separate synchronized migration that brings them to the nesting area at the same time as the females is unknown. The sex ratio off the nesting beaches often is skewed toward females, but at some beaches approaches unity. All females are not receptive at a given time, so several males may court or attempt to copulate with a single female at the same time, and the sight of copulation seems to stimulate previously uninterested males to join the action (Simon et al., 1975). Perhaps secretions from the Rathke glands situated on the bridge (Ehrenfeld and Ehrenfeld, 1973) act as sex attractants (Parkes, 1981).

Courtship involves several behaviors (Hirth, 1971;

Booth and Peters, 1972; Bustard, 1973; Crowell Comuzzie and Owens, 1990; Márquez, 1990; Alvarado and Figueroa, 1991). The male may nuzzle the female about the head and neck, or he may rub his gular scutes along her head or carapace. Biting may occur at any place on the female's body, but especially in the soft skin of the shoulders, neck, and mouth. After this the male shifts to the rear and checks the female's cloaca by placing his nostrils against her inguinal region between the Rathke glands and cloacal vent. He may also bite her hind flippers. Females attempt to avoid male attention by either pulling in the limbs or splaying them widely while lying on the bottom, resting in female sanctuary areas, circling to always face the male, biting him, or breaking out and swimming away. Circling behavior usually brings on more biting by the male, and if she flees he chases her. When the female shows receptivity, or is caught after a chase, the male attempts to mount her carapace from the rear, holding on by hooking his foreclaws over the anterior rim and placing his rear flippers at the posterior rim of her shell. This may result in deep, bleeding wounds on the female's carapace. He then pushes his elongated tail around and under hers to bring their vents together and intromission soon follows.

The mating act takes some time, usually several hours; Ulrich and Parkes (1978) reported copulations lasting as long as 52 hours. Mating may occur at the surface or underwater; while it is taking place, other males commonly attempt to dislodge or bite the mating male.

Females may be able to store sperm from a mating to fertilize later clutches, possibly up to several years, although this has not been proven (Parkes, 1981; Ehrhart, 1982). Ulrich and Parkes (1978) reported that four captive females nested without having been seen mating and that three of them laid fertile eggs with two of the clutches producing the average hatch rate. It is possible that these females had in fact mated unobserved that year. Indirect evidence, however, suggests that a female *Chelonia mydas* may store enough sperm from a single mating to fertilize all of her clutches that season (Ulrich and Parkes, 1978): once oviposition begins, she no longer shows interest in mating (Simon et al., 1975; Ulrich and Parkes, 1978). Also, sperm has been found in glands at the junction of the shell-forming zone and vagina, and at the junction of the oviductal magnum with the aglandular zone (Solomon and Baird, 1979). If several males copulate with a female before oviposition, the resulting fertile eggs in each clutch possibly may have different male parents.

The principal nesting season in the western Atlantic extends from March to October, but the prime period is May to September, depending on latitude. Oviposition occurs 21–95 days after mating (but most frequently within 30–34 days) which also results in clutches producing the most viable hatchlings (Ulrich and Parkes, 1978).

Extralimital nesting beaches that possibly serve the green turtles found along the Atlantic Coast of the United States occur in northern Brazil, French Guiana, Surinam, Guyana, Venezuela, Trinidad and Tobago, Aves Island, Colombia, Costa Rica, Guatemala, Belize, Mexico (Quintana Roo, Yucatán, Veracruz, Tamaulipas), Lesser and Greater Antilles, U.S. Virgin Islands, Mona Island, Puerto Rico, Cuba, Cayman Islands, Bahamas and Bermuda (Carr, 1952; Hirth 1980c; Hildebrand, 1982; Márquez et al., 1982a; Pritchard and Trebbau, 1984; Moll, 1985; Ernst and Barbour, 1989; Higginson, 1989; Márquez, 1990; Durán Nájera, 1991). On the continental United States, *Chelonia* nesting has been recorded in Texas (Kenedy County; Shaver and Amos, 1988; Shaver, 1989), Florida (Loggerhead Key; Dade, Broward, Palm Beach, Martin, St. Lucie, Indian River, Brevard, and Volusia counties; Stoneburner et al., 1979; Dodd, 1981; Conley and Hoffman, 1987); Georgia (Jekyll Island, Glynn County; Litwin, 1981), and North Carolina (Camp Lejeune, Onslow County; Schwartz et al., 1981; Peterson et al., 1985).

Nesting in the eastern Pacific occurs any time between February—March and January, with the peak periods varying with latitude and population. On French Frigate Shoal, Hawaii, the nesting season is from mid-April through June (Balazs, 1980). Southern nesting beaches which may provide the *Chelonia* seen along the Pacific Coast of North America include those in Panama, Costa Rica, Nicaragua, Guatemala, El Salvador, and Mexico (Chiapas, Baja California, Michoacán, and the Revillagigedo and Tres Marías islands) (Carr, 1952; Hirth, 1980c; Hildebrand, 1982; Márquez et al., 1982a; Awbrey et al., 1984; Márquez, 1990).

Most female *C. m. mydas* nest every third year and others commonly either the second or fourth year (Wood and Wood, 1980), although renestings have been recorded at intervals of one to five years, and one female nesting on Ascension Island had a nine-year interval (Carr, 1975; Carr et al., 1978; Ehrhart, 1982). *Chelonia m. agassizii* nesting in Michoacán, Mexico, seem to oviposit annually (Cliffton, in Pritchard and Trebbau, 1984). In Hawaii, Balazs (1980) documented the reproductive intervals of 21 nesting females: 14 (66.7%) laid their eggs every two years, six (28.6%) every three years, and one (4.7%) returned to lay its eggs after six years.

Up to seven clutches have been laid in a season by wild females (Carr et al., 1978), and some captive females have laid eight clutches in one season (Ulrich and Parkes, 1978). Usually clutches are deposited at 12–14 day intervals (Carr et al., 1978; Balazs, 1980), but this may vary between populations, and intervals of 10 to more than 30 days may occur.

Females show a high degree of nest site fidelity, renesting on the same beach at least 70% of the time (Mortimer and Portier, 1989). Between nesting emergences females usually travel parallel to the shore in waters shallower than 24 m (Meylan, 1982a), and most longshore movements are less than 10 km (Carr and Carr, 1972; Meylan, 1982a; Mortimer and Portier, 1989). If a female is prevented from nesting and returns to the water, she remains in shallow water traveling back and forth near the nesting beach until daylight, and then moves into deeper water (Mortimer and Portier, 1989).

Beaches used most frequently for nesting by *Chelonia* are flat, rising only about 2–3 m above the water, with low wave energy. Hendrickson (1958) found that the nesting beaches on islands commonly were on the leeward side, and in Sarawak (Borneo) the principal ones had fringing coral reefs below mean low tide. Hirth and Carr (1970) compared the characteristics of the nesting beaches at South Yemen, Aldabra Island, Ascension Island, Aves Island, and Tortuguero, Costa Rica. They found that the sand varied from fine to coarse in texture and from olive-gray to white in color. The pH ranged from 6.9 to 8.0, and the carbonate content was high in all beaches except at Tortuguero. Organic content was 0.30–1.18%. Stancyk and Ross (1978) found that the sand color, grain size, and water content of the nesting beaches on Ascension Island varied so much as to encompass the ranges of these parameters for *Chelonia* nesting beaches throughout the world. The nest beaches on Hawaii and in Indonesia consist of broken coral and mollusk fragments, and contain a high calcium content (Balazs, 1980; Nuitja and Uchida, 1983).

Clutch mortality is strongly tied to the nest site. In Surinam only 12% of green turtle nests are occasionally washed over by seawater; most nests are situated in the beach sand or along the beach-vegetation border, with only about 13% of the nests dug among fringing vegetation (Whitmore and Dutton, 1985). Too dry sand is a major factor in egg mortality (Mortimer, 1990). Mortality is also positively correlated with mean particle diameter, suggesting physiological distress (possibly due to desiccation) in coarser sands (Mortimer and Carr, 1984; Mortimer, 1990). On Ascension Island, clutch survival is positively correlated with nest depth and negatively correlated with both the electrical conductivity and volume of air-filled pore space in the substrate (Mortimer, 1990).

At Tortuguero, the nesting beach can be divided into three zones from the surf line to the forest behind it depending on the extent of vegetative cover: the open full-sun zone, the border zone between the open and vegetative zone, where vegetation provides some shade, and the vegetative zone, where shade is complete (Spotila et al., 1987; Bjorndal and Bolten, 1992a). All three zones are used by nesting females. The amount of shading affects the nest temperature and, ultimately, the sex of the hatchlings in that nest (see below). Distribution of nests among the three zones varies among years, and females that lay several clutches a season nest in more than one zone more often than in a single zone. These females are more likely to conform to the population's pattern of nest distribution each year than to develop their own nesting pattern between years. Annual factors apparently have a greater effect on the nest placement than do individual nesting preferences. This lack of a consistent pattern may lead to varying hatchling sex ratios from year to year, and between subsequent nestings in one season.

Several detailed accounts of the nesting behavior of *Chelonia* have been published (Carr and Giovannoli, 1957; Carr and Ogren, 1960; Hendrickson, 1958; Hirth and Carr, 1970; Hirth, 1971; Ernst and Barbour, 1972; Pritchard and Trebbau, 1984; Hirth and Samson, 1987), and the description presented below is a composite of these.

Most nesting occurs at night, although diurnal nesting has been reported (Fritts and Hoffman, 1982). The female leaves the water and crawls up the beach, using a simultaneous pushing or pulling of the pairs of limbs at a speed of about 1.8 m/min (Cribb, 1972). She stops this laborious crawling periodically to place her nostrils to the sand, presumably to test the coarseness or moisture of the sand and to gain olfactory information. When a suitable area is reached on the upper beach, she makes a few tentative swipes at the sand with the forelimbs. Soon she starts to dig purposefully with her front flippers and scoops out a body pit by throwing the sand backward and toward the side while rotating the body. The body pit of *Chelonia mydas* is generally the deepest of the cheloniids. As the pit is deepened, the posterior 75% of the turtle's body is lowered into it. The hind

flippers may aid in digging at this point, working in an alternate sequence. This phase of the nesting process may take 20–35 minutes.

When the female is satisfied that the body pit is deep enough, digging of the actual egg chamber begins. She pushes the distal edge of her hind flipper against the bottom of the pit, curls it, and scoops out the sand. The hind limbs are used alternately during excavation of the nest cavity, and about a cupful of sand is removed in each scraping sequence. As the working flipper is thrust into the hole for its load of sand, the other flipper is spread firmly on the beach beside the mouth of the hole (particularly in *C. m. agassizii*). The excavating limb raises its burden of sand out of the hole, slowly moves it to the side, and drops it. Immediately the off flipper shoots out laterally and upward and strikes the under margin of the carapace a hard backhand blow producing a loud thudding sound. This behavior is continuously executed throughout this stage of digging. As the flippers alternate in digging, the process is repeated in reverse, and the whole operation of excavating the flask-shaped egg chamber is a series of such bilateral reciprocal actions. Excavation of the egg chamber usually takes 20–35 minutes.

After the nest cavity is completed, the turtle stops digging, places her tail into the hole, and begins to lay her eggs. During oviposition the rear flippers may be either spread together over the nest or else one or both flippers are projected posteriorly into and pressed against the rear of the egg chamber. One to four eggs are dropped at a time, but usually one to three, the intervals between extrusions of eggs vary between one and 10 seconds except for a few periods of rest of as long as 30–60 seconds toward the end of the operation. Oviposition lasts about 10–20 minutes.

When laying is completed, the filling of the egg chamber begins. The female reaches laterally with alternately working hind flippers, rakes in sand, and kneads it into the hole. When the cavity is full the raking and packing continue, so that a mound grows beneath the rear edge of the shell. From time to time she bunches and squeezes this mound between the flippers, and as it continues to grow the back end of her body is pushed upward until it is nearly horizontal, instead of being inclined on the slope of the nest pit as it had been throughout the nesting process. Filling of the nest chamber takes approximately 10–18 minutes.

Next the body pit is obliterated and the nest site camouflaged. This takes about 40–50 minutes. The hind flippers stop and the forelimbs begin to thrash and sling sand. After a few strokes, the hind flippers join in this work. As the turtle throws sand, she shifts the orientation of her body, and the indiscriminately flung sand gradually fills the body pit and sprinkles the surroundings through a radius of 2–3 m. As the pit fills, the shifting stops, but the scooping and throwing of sand with the forelimbs continues, and eventually produces two good-sized basins (one for each flipper) at some distance from the former rim of the now disguised nest excavation. Gradually the scattering of sand is stopped, and the female begins shuffling and scuffing about, over and near the site. When filling is completed the two depressions scooped out during the process by the front flippers remain as the most conspicuous features of the local topography. After this she orientates herself and crawls back to the sea at a speed of 1.9–3.9 m/min (Cribb, 1972). The entire nesting sequence may consume as much as two hours.

Carr and Hirth (1962) reported that the high threshold of alarm of the emerging Ascension Island green turtle is the most striking behavioral difference between it and a female of the Tortuguero population. When the latter lands and starts up the beach she can be turned back into the surf by the slightest show of artificial light or by movement of something silhouetted against the starlit sky. In the Ascension population the pattern of behavior, which in most turtles begins with the digging process and thereafter keeps the female oblivious to outside interference, appears to take over at the time of emergence onto the beach. The turtles could thus be watched at close quarters, permitting the observation of sand-smelling.

Data on nest dimensions are generally lacking, but the body pit may be 30–50 cm deep and the bottom of the egg chamber 76 cm deeper than the beach surface (Solomon and Baird, 1979; Pritchard and Trebbau, 1984).

Clutches have contained 3–238 eggs, but 100–120 eggs are more common, and clutch size varies between populations (Hirth, 1980a). Usually eastern Pacific *C. m. agassizii* lay fewer eggs per clutch than the larger Atlantic *C. m. mydas* (Cliffton et al., 1982). Female body size is significantly correlated with both clutch size and individual egg diameter (Simon et al., 1975; Balazs, 1980; Bjorndal and Carr, 1989), but it accounts for only a small proportion of the variation in clutch size at any particular beach. Clutch size also increases significantly with the age of the female (Bjorndal and Carr, 1989), and may either increase or decrease with successive ovipositions during a season, depending on the particular female. Hirth (1988) found that among first-time nesters at Tortuguero, a significantly positive relationship exists between carapace length and clutch size, but that a negative relationship occurs between female size and hatchling size. The relative clutch weight of first-time nesters is 3.42–5.54% of female body weight.

The nearly spherical, pliable, white eggs are 35–58 mm (usually 40–45) in diameter and weigh 28–65 g (usually 35–45). Under normal conditions dehydration sets in after deposition, and within 48 hours the shell is somewhat shriveled and brittle.

Simon et al. (1975) reported that captive females laid an average of 593 eggs per season. Hirth (1971) calculated that the average green turtle female weighs 125 kg (wet weight), that she lays 550 eggs per season, and that each egg weighs 38 g. From these figures he concluded that the average adult female *C. mydas* produces 21 kg of eggs per season, or an amount equivalent to about 17% of her body weight.

The outer calcified surface of the eggshell is primarily composed of crystalline aggregates of calcium carbonate in its aragonite form (Solomon and Baird, 1976); in captivity these are arranged in distinct regions of blocks of calcite and spherulites of aragonite, but shells from eggs laid in the wild have only aragonite spherulites (Baird and Solomon, 1979). Perhaps dietary differences cause this discrepancy. The soft membrane protein-carbohydrate fibers of the eggshell consist of a dense core surrounded by a less dense mantle. In oviposited eggs the core material is homogeneously dense, but in oviducal eggs it is pitted (Solomon and Baird, 1977). Analyses of eggs by Bustard et al. (1969) revealed the following mean values of calcium, magnesium, and phosphorus (expressed as mg/specimen) in the shell, yolk and albumen, respectively: calcium—412, 46.2, 1.06; magnesium—1.27, 12.1, 0.25; and phosphorus—2.09, 88.3, 0.71. Total egg content (in mg/specimen) was 459.3 for calcium, 13.5 for magnesium, and 91.1 for phosphorus.

Hatchling success may vary from zero to over 90% in natural, undisturbed nests, but may average lower in clutches removed and reburied elsewhere or artificially incubated.

The incubation period is normally 50–55 days, but may range from 30 to 90 days depending on the incubating temperature. For some unknown reason clutches laid on mainland beaches hatch sooner (mean 52.7 days) than those laid on island beaches (mean 60.8 days; Hirth, 1980a). The lower temperature limit for successful incubation is 23–24°C and the upper temperature limit is 35–38°C (Bustard, 1971).

Tests conducted at Ascension Island by Carr and Hirth (1962) indicated that metabolic heating raises the temperature in nests of developing eggs and

suggested that this may constitute thermal cooperation affecting the fitness of the sets of eggs and young
as evolutionary units. Hendrickson (1958) recorded
nest temperature gains of 5.9°C over the outside
average at the same depths during a two week period.
At Ascension Island the average gain was 2.3°C in
nests. Metabolic heating begins after about 50–62%
of the incubation period has passed (Mrosovsky and
Yntema, 1982) and may affect the hatchling sex ratio
(see below).

Gas exchange is related to both the incubation and
metabolic temperatures of a clutch. The rate of
embryonic growth and the hatching success may be
related to gas exchange; the best developmental rates
(incubation period about 60 days) and hatching
success occur in a respiratory environment quite
similar to that found in a natural nest (Ackerman,
1977, 1980, 1981b). Any limitation of gas exchange
between clutch and environment retards embryonic
development and reduces hatching success, and a
drop below naturally occurring levels causes death.
Oxygen consumption by the embryo is sufficiently
low and the gas conductance of the shell sufficiently
high that only small gas partial pressure gradients
occur across the individual eggshells, but the metabolic demand of an entire clutch is very large, and,
inasmuch as gas movement through beach sand is
restricted (only 30–50% that occurring in the nest;
Ackerman, 1977), increasing gas partial pressure
gradients are established between the center and
periphery of a clutch and between the clutch and
surrounding beach (Ackerman, 1980).

Water exchange also occurs during incubation.
Exchange of water vapor rather than liquid water
seems to account for observed changes in egg mass,
and water exchange is related to nest temperature
(Ackerman et al., 1985). Eggs incubated in natural
nests usually gain mass during incubation after an
initial loss.

Hatchlings in a nest are not independent individuals but a group that meets the shared predicament of
its interment with group action (Carr and Hirth,
1961). The first young that hatch do not start digging
at once but lie still until some nestmates are free of the
egg. Each new hatching adds to the working space,
because the spherical eggs and the spaces between
them make a volume greater than that of the young
and the crumpled shells. The vertical displacement
that will carry the turtles to the surface is the upward
migration of this chamber, brought about by a
collaboratory action that is really a loose sort of
division of labor. Noise can induce hatchling activity
(Balazs and Ross, 1974b), and possibly the sounds of

scrapping by some hatchlings activate others to thrash
about. Although the movements involved are only a
generalized thrashing, similar to those that free the
turtle from the egg, they accomplish four different
and perhaps indispensable things, depending on the
position of the turtle in the mass (Carr and Hirth,
1961). Hatchlings on the top layer scratch down the
ceiling. Those around the sides undercut the walls.
Turtles on the bottom have two roles, one mechanical
and the other psychological. They either trample and
compact the sand that drops down from above, or
they serve as a receptor motor device for the hatchling
group, stirring it out of recurrent periods of inactivity.
Lying passively for a time under the weight of the
turtles above, one will suddenly burst into a spasm of
squirming that triggers a new concerted group work
action. Thus by fits and starts, the ceiling falls, the
floor rises, and the group of collaborating turtles is
carried upward to the surface.

Hatchlings emerge from the nest after dark. Nocturnal emergence has marked survival value, because a
high temperature of the surface sand would kill them,
and because the danger of predation is greater by day.
Bustard (1967) found nests in which a few hatchlings
were visible at the sand surface during the heat of day;
in most cases only the head protruded, but occasionally part of the anterior region of the carapace also was
exposed. They gave no sign of life, remaining
completely immobile for many hours; detailed observation, however, showed that in this position they
were able to remain alive under conditions in which
total exposure would have been fatal. After dark they
became active, emerged from the nest with the rest of
the brood, and made for the water. Bustard (1967)
never saw diurnal-emergent hatchlings bury themselves, but this has been described by Moorhouse
(1933). Any account of the mechanism preventing
daytime emergence must include an explanation of
how inactivity, caused by bright light or high temperature, is transmitted to the hatchlings deeper down
which are unable to experience these conditions
directly. Bustard (1967) suggested that the comatose
condition of a few turtles that reach the surface has a
damping effect on the activity of those below.
Furthermore, those at the surface act like corks in a
bottle, occupying the opening of the nest shaft and
making exit difficult if not impossible for those below.
Experimental removal of individuals whose heads are
protruding from the sand, together with the removal
of others then immediately visible, has led to activity
within the nest and emergence of the brood within
minutes, during the day. Mrosovsky (1968) found
that diurnal activity is inhibited at temperatures above

28.5°C, and that the heat of the sand on the nesting beaches usually is high enough to confine the hatchlings to the nest until after dark. Once the temperature falls to 28.5°C at night, they become active. He pointed out that in the morning the temperature just beneath the surface frequently is below 28.5°C. This is most often the case on rainy days, and in fact hatchlings often emerge after a rain, sometimes by day.

The hatchling carapace is keeled and dark green to brown; it may have a mottled pattern and a light border. The plastron is white or yellowish with two longitudinal ridges. In *C. m. agassizii* the plastron is at first dark but lightens in the first four months (Balazs, 1986), which may give added protection in the open sea. The skin is blackish, and the flippers have white borders. The upper jaw is light in color, and the caruncle is merely its sharply pointed but smoothly continuous upper-anterior projection. Hatchlings are 35–59 mm (normally 49–53) in carapace length, and weigh about 22–30 g (17.7–35.0).

The color pattern of the hatchling is an example of countershading. Bustard (1970) thought that the black dorsal coloration is disadvantageous: the hatchlings are conspicuous to predators when crossing pale-colored beaches to the sea. He suggested that the dark carapace plays an important role in elevating the body temperature when the little turtle is floating at the surface (see above). The increased body temperature would result in faster growth, due to heightened digestion and metabolism. A more rapid growth rate during this extremely vulnerable life history stage would have a decided survival value.

Sex of *Chelonia mydas* is determined by its incubation temperature. An incubation temperature of 26°C produces almost all males (84%), 27–28°C produces 61–68% males, incubation at 29–30°C results in 0–43% males, and an incubation temperature of 33°C hatches only 14% males (Paukstis and Janzen, 1990). The pivotal temperature is about 29°C. Although *C. mydas* does not have sex chromosomes, it does have sex-specific DNA (Demas et al., 1990), but how this functions is not understood.

In a study of the sex ratio of hatchlings from a Surinam beach, Mrosovsky et al. (1984a) found that more males were produced from clutches laid in the wetter, cooler months of the nesting season, whereas more females hatched from eggs laid in the drier, warmer months. These almost balanced to produce an overall 53.9% females. Nest location also plays a role in sex determination. The beach at Tortuguero, Costa Rica, is divided into three distinct thermal zones: (1) low beach, above the high water mark to sparse vegetation, (2) midbeach, areas of sparsely vegetated sand up to dense jungle vegetation, and (3) high beach, areas of dense vegetation (Spotila et al., 1987; Bjorndal and Bolten, 1992a). At depths of 30 and 50 cm, sand temperatures in the high beach are significantly lower than those in the other two zones. Nest temperatures below 28.5°C produce males and those above 30.3°C produce primarily females. Nests in the low and midbeach zones produce 72 and 87% females, respectively, whereas nests from the high beach produce only 7.4% females. The overall seasonal sex ratio is about 67% females.

The above has implications for some modern conservation practices. The removal of eggs for incubation in styrofoam boxes, which are 1.0–1.5°C cooler than sand on a beach, not only causes embryonic mortality from mechanical disturbance, but has also resulted in an estimated 23% decrease in female hatchlings (Mrosovsky, 1982). Cool incubation at less than 28°C produces almost no females (0–10%) whereas warm incubation at temperatures above 29.5°C produce 95–100% females (Morreale et al., 1982). Because the natural sex ratio needed to maintain *Chelonia* populations is unknown, these artificial practices may be doing severe damage to the survival of the species (Mrosovsky and Yntema, 1980, 1982; Morreale et al., 1982). The best policy may be simply to protect the nesting beaches allowing the clutches to remain intact and incubate naturally. The well-intentioned "head start programs" for hatchling sea turtles which treat eggs in this manner and then raise the hatchlings to a size large enough to avoid most predation before they are released seem reasonable in theory, but in practice may be contributing to the decline of sea turtles (Woody, 1990, 1991). It is interesting that sea turtle populations as a whole seem to be declining at an even faster rate since these programs have been initiated. Perhaps we should not interfere with nature!

GROWTH AND LONGEVITY: *Chelonia mydas* grows more slowly than either *Eretmochelys* or *Caretta* of similar size (Bjorndal and Bolten, 1988a,b), but growth rates vary between populations (possibly due to differences in nutrition and water temperature, as well as genetics).

In the U.S. Virgin Islands, juvenile *C. m. mydas* with 20–30-cm carapaces grow an average of 6.9 cm per year. Growth slows after this and 30–40-cm turtles increase about 5.0 cm annually; those 40–50 cm, 3.0 cm; 50–60-cm turtles, 3.5 cm; and 60–70-cm individuals grow only 1.9 cm a year (Boulon and Frazer, 1990). Atlantic green turtles from Mosquito

Lagoon, Florida, have the following average annual growth rates: 30–40 cm long, 5.3 cm; 50–60 cm, 3.1 cm; 60–70 cm, 2.8 cm; and 70–80 cm, 2.2 cm (Mendonça, 1981). In the Bahamas the early growth rate is faster, turtles 30–40 cm long average 8.8 cm per year and those with 40–50-cm carapaces increase about 4.9 cm annually; however, in the larger size classes the growth rate slows considerably to 1.8 cm a year for those 60–70 cm long and only 1.2 cm for turtles of 70–80 cm (Bjorndal and Bolten, 1988b). Puerto Rican *C. m. mydas* take about 10 years to grow from 25 to 75 cm at an annual rate of about 5 cm, with the fastest carapacial growth occurring between 40 and 50 cm (Collazo et al., 1992). Carr (1952) reported that yearlings of *C. m. mydas* are commonly 20–25 cm in carapace length, mature females about 89 cm, and 10-year-olds as much as 111 cm. Body weight has the following average annual increases in the Bahamas (Bjorndal and Bolten, 1988b): carapace length 30–35 cm, 3.7 kg; 40–45 cm, 3.5 kg; 45–50 cm, 3.8 kg; 60–65 cm, 2.7 kg; 65–70 cm, 3.0 kg; 70–75 cm, 1.7 kg; and 75–80 cm, 2.2 kg. Frazer and Erhart (1985) have prepared a preliminary von Bertalanffy growth model for increases in length in *C. m. mydas,* and Bjorndal and Bolten (1989) have calculated equations for converting over-the-curve carapace measurements to straight-line carapace measurements. Ehrhardt and Witham (1992) published a preliminary equation, based on a generalized von Bertalanffy growth model, for calculating increases in weight in *C. m. mydas.* We refer the reader to these papers for details.

Captive *C. m. mydas* may grow faster than wild individuals; the average carapace length and weight of pen-reared turtles at age one was 21.4 cm and 1.3 kg (Witham and Futch, 1977). Caldwell (1962b) recorded the growth rates of four captive hatchlings as 10 cm the first year and 11.5 cm in each of the following two years. The mean weight gain was about 1.35 kg the first year, 2.7 kg the second, and 5.0 kg the third.

Carr and Caldwell (1956) found that the relationship between carapace length and body weight in 208 *C. m. mydas* (mostly young turtles) from Florida could best be expressed by the following equation: log weight = −2.195 + 2.87 log carapace length.

Caldwell (1962d) reported that male *C. m. agassizii* from the Gulf of California are smaller (maximum 90 cm) than the females (maximum 98 cm). A tendency for males to weigh less than females begins at a carapace length of about 75 cm, when sexual dimorphism first becomes evident. The female becomes somewhat deeper bodied, the posterior portion of the male's carapace becomes proportionally more pointed and the length of his tail increases greatly by comparison with the female's. Caldwell found the relationship between length and weight in these turtles could best be expressed by the equation log weight = −2.14 + 2.60 log carapace length. In Hawaiian *C. m. agassizii* the average growth rate per month for immature turtles varies from island to island: Hawaii, 0.44 cm (0.38–0.52); Oahu, 0.20 cm (0.19–0.21); Necker Island, 0.14 cm; French Frigate Shoal, 0.08 cm (0.01–0.13); and Lisianski Island, 0.13 cm (Balazs, 1982a). At these growth rates it would take 8.7–47.9 years to reach maturity if the turtles mature at 81 cm carapace length, or 10.8–59.4 years if maturity is gained at 92 cm.

Two male Pacific green turtles lived 33 years, 6 months in the Sea Life Park, Hawaii (Snider and Bowler, 1992), and 11 Atlantic green turtles were kept for more than 20 years at Marineland, Florida (Ernst and Barbour, 1972). Maximum longevity in the wild is unknown but, on the basis of skeletal data, Zug and Balazs (1985) estimated that a 93-cm Hawaiian female had possibly lived 66 years. The longest survival for released Florida head-started *Chelonia* has been 10–13 years (Witham, 1991).

FOOD HABITS: The most important adult feeding areas are pastures of sea grasses or algae in relatively shallow, protected waters; juveniles, however, may forage among coral reefs, rocky outcroppings, sargassum mats, and in lagoons and bays.

Chelonia mydas is omnivorous; adults prefer plant food but the juveniles are more carnivorous. Principal plants consumed include green (Chlorophyceae, including *Sargassum*), brown (Phaeophyceae), and red (Rhodophyceae) macroalgae (particularly red), blue-green algae (Cyanophyta), red mangrove (*Rhizophora*) roots and leaves, and the sea grasses *Cymodocea, Diplanthera, Halodule, Halophila, Posidonia, Syringodium, Thalassia,* and *Zostera.* Young leaves and roots seem to be the preferred parts of sea grasses, which may make up to 88% of the turtle's diet in Florida (Mendonça, 1983). Animals eaten (particularly by immatures) include sponges (*Chondrilla, Chondrosia, Craniella, Geodia, Haliclona, Spongia*), jellyfish (*Physalia, Velella; Cassiopea* in captivity; Witham and Futch, 1977), bryozoans (*Hippoporina, Schizoporella*), annelid worms, snails (*Cerithium, Nassarius, Neritina*), tuskshells (*Dentalium*), bivalves (*Brachiodontes, Mytilus*), squid (*Janthina*), crabs (*Planes*), amphipods, echinoderms, tunicates (*Botryllus, Pyrosoma, Styella*), and fish (*Pervagor*; and eggs of either a needlefish, Belonidae, or halfbeak, Exocoetidae) (sources: Chace, 1951;

Carr, 1952, Hirth, 1971; Brongersma, 1972; Ernst and Barbour, 1972; Carr and Stancyk, 1975; Balazs, 1980; Fritts, 1981a; Mortimer, 1981, 1982; Garnett et al., 1985; Balazs et al., 1987; Márquez, 1990).

Most feeding is diurnal, especially in midmorning and mid- to late afternoon, and up to nine hours a day may be devoted to foraging (Mendonça, 1983; Ogden et al., 1983; Williams, 1988). When eating *Thalassia testudinum* in the Bahamas, green turtles do not forage randomly, but instead maintain grazing plots of young leaves by constant recropping (Bjorndal, 1980a). Thus they consume a more digestible forage, which is higher in protein and lower in lignin, than the ungrazed, older leaves. This is not the case in the U.S. Virgin Islands where *Chelonia* grazes on all available *Thalassia* and may be contributing to a decline in the sea grass there (Williams, 1988). However, *Thalassia* in grazed areas may grow faster as a consequence of increased light penetration into the beds, but leaf width is reduced, and the leaf bases contain higher proportions of nitrogen and lower amounts of lignin than the leaf tips (Zieman et al., 1984). Sea grass beds may be abandoned by the green turtle if the sediment ammonium content is reduced and the plant's growth retarded. Beds of *Thalassia testudinum* may have a biomass of 5.66 kg/m², of which 80–90% is underground; the leaves contain 13% protein, 25% ash, 36% carbohydrates, and 16% crude fiber, but only 0.5% fat (Burkholder et al., 1959). In Nicaragua *Thalassia* composes 80% of the food of *Chelonia* (Mortimer, 1981).

Individual *Chelonia* consume about 280 g dry weight of *Thalassia* leaves per day (Thayer et al., 1982). Symbiotic cellulose breakdown by postgastric bacterial and protozoan fermentation occurs (Bjorndal, 1979a, 1985; Fenchel et al., 1979; Bjorndal et al., 1991), and 71.5–93.7% of the cellulose may be digested (Bjorndal, 1980a). Bacterial and protozoan numbers are comparable to those in the rumen of a domestic cow (Fenchel et al., 1979; Fenchel, 1980), and these microbes may be obtained as a juvenile by ingesting the fecal pellets of adult *Chelonia* (scatophagy; Witham, 1991). Other digestive values are 32.6–73.9% for organic matter, 21.5–70.7% for energy, 40.3–90.8% for hemicellulose, and 14.4–56.6% for protein (Bjorndal, 1980a). Digestive efficiency increases with increases in water temperature and body size (Bjorndal, 1980a), as does also consumption (Davenport et al., 1989). By one year of age juveniles can absorb 68% of the energy available in *Zostera* (Davenport et al., 1989). The major end products of symbiotic fermentation are volatile fatty acids which are very important energy sources (Bjorndal, 1979a;

Joseph et al., 1985). The energy required for an adult female is approximately 805,800 kJ/year; if she feeds on *Thalassia* the turtle may only be able to allocate 10% of her annual energy budget for reproduction, but if she eats more easily digested algae rich in volatile fats, 24% of the budget can go to reproduction (Bjorndal, 1982b).

Total clearance time for food passing through the hatchling digestive tract is about 394 hours, with most time spent in the large intestine (Davenport and Oxford, 1984; Davenport et al., 1989). The hatchling's requirement for the amino acids lysine (4.8% of crude protein intake), tryptophan (0.63%), and methionine (1.5%) was determined by Wood and Wood (1977).

Digestive tracts of Nicaraguan adults contained only 1.4% animal prey, 67% of which was sponge (Mortimer, 1981). Sponges may be more nutritious, but are more difficult to digest owing to their high collagen content and the irritation of their spicules, and probably provide the green turtle little supplemental dietary material (Bjorndal, 1990).

The serrated jaw of *Chelonia* probably is an adaptation to grazing. Green turtles are the only marine turtles subsisting mainly on plants, a diet poor in vitamin D. They are also the only marine turtles that habitually come ashore to bask, perhaps as a means of producing the needed vitamin D through the action of sunlight on skin sterols.

Hobart Smith (1961) proposed that the papillalike rakers in the choanae (the internal openings of the nasal passage in the roof of the mouth) of *Chelonia* are correlated with a distinctive behavior whereby the choanae are used specifically as strainers. Because the green turtle is more herbivorous than other sea turtles, he believed that a reasonable possibility exists that the so-called choanal rakers and a unique (among sea turtles) compressive role of the tongue evolved as adaptations to a primarily vegetarian diet. Development of the rakers seems closely correlated with the shift from a carnivorous to a herbivorous diet.

PREDATORS AND DEFENSE: *Chelonia* is most vulnerable when on the nesting beach; humans, feral dogs (*Canis familiaris*), and jaguars (*Panthera onca*) are known to kill or molest adult females in the Americas. American nests are robbed by ghost crabs (*Ocypode*), scarab beetles (*Trox*), fly maggots, ants, vultures (*Carthartes, Coragyps*), ruddy turnstones (*Arenaria*), golden plovers (*Pluvialis*), white-tailed shearwaters (*Puffinus*), opossums (*Didelphis*), peccaries (*Tayassu*), feral pigs (*Sus*), coatis (*Nasua*), raccoons (*Procyon*), mongooses (*Herpestes*), skunks (*Meph-*

itis), dogs (*Canis*), jaguars (*Panthera*), and humans. Fungus may also attack the eggs (Solomon and Baird, 1980). Hatchlings in the nest or crossing the beach are eaten by ghost crabs (*Ocypode*), ants, fleshflies (*Megaselia*), snakes (*Masticophis*), vultures (*Cathartes, Coragyps*), ravens (*Corvus corax*), gulls (*Larus*), frigate birds (*Fregata*), ruddy turnstones (*Arenaria*), night herons (*Nycticorax*), opossums (*Didelphis*), rats (*Rattus*), mongooses (*Herpestes*), feral cats (*Felis catus*), feral dogs (*Canis*), and peccaries (*Tayassu*). Hatchlings and juveniles are not safe in the water either, as a host of predators await them: dolphin fish (*Coryphaena*), needlefish (*Tylosurus*), groupers (*Epinephelus, Promicrops*), jackfish and ulua (*Caranx*), kingfish (*Menticirrhus*), snook (*Centropomus*), sharks (*Galeocerdo*), and bottlenosed dolphins (*Tursiops truncatus*). Besides humans, adult green turtles have few marine enemies, but groupers (*Epinephelus*), and tiger sharks (*Galeocerdo*) take a few. (Sources for predation data on American populations: Hirth, 1971; Brongersma, 1972; Ernst and Barbour, 1972; Witham, 1974; Fowler, 1979; Balazs, 1980; Allgower, 1980; Witzell, 1981; Small, 1982; Awbrey et al, 1984; Pritchard and Trebbau, 1984; Seabrook, 1989; Márquez, 1990.)

The green turtle is a rather inoffensive creature. If disturbed at sea it will dive and attempt to swim away. When picked up *Chelonia mydas* may flail its forelimbs and beat its handler; only an occasional individual will bite. The volatile secretion from the Rathke's glands situated at the bridge may ward off predators (Ehrenfeld and Ehrenfeld, 1973).

POPULATIONS: Since serious study of *Chelonia mydas* began in the 1950s it has become apparent that populations around the world have declined (Cliffton et al., 1982; King, 1982; National Research Council, 1990). Assuming a 1:1 sex ratio, Carr et al. (1978) calculated the total number of sexually mature green turtles in the western Caribbean as 62,532, or just over 31,000 reproductive females. No comparable figures are available for the eastern Caribbean, but some beaches may serve as many as 5,000 females (Schulz, 1982). Relatively few females nest in the southeastern United States, and most nesting is in Florida (Dodd, 1981; Conley and Hoffman, 1987).

Adult *Chelonia* frequent the waters off southwestern Florida in most months, except those of winter, and increase their numbers off the Atlantic coast of Florida during and immediately after the nesting season, but still the species does not occur in great numbers (Hoffman and Fritts, 1982; Fritts et al., 1983). Carr and Caldwell (1956) estimated approximately 5,600 turtles in the feeding population of immature *C. mydas* along the western coast of Florida. However, the estimate was based on recaptures of tagged turtles by commercial fishermen, who were selective and took only turtles weighing more than 9 kg, and many smaller turtles probably were not accounted for. Also, the tagged turtles were not released on the fishing grounds; that is, not all of them were likely to have entered waters where recapture was possible. Unfortunately, the Florida population is probably much smaller today. From 1976 to 1981 only 199 green turtles were captured in the Florida's Indian River lagoon system, most of them immature (Ehrhart, 1983), and at Mosquito Lagoon, Florida, from July 1976 to March 1979 108 were captured (40% weighed less than 70 kg, only 6% were over 80 kg; Mendonça and Ehrhart, 1982).

Only 10 immature green turtles were stranded along the southern coast of Texas from 1976 to 1979, indicating that the population there is small (Rabalais and Rabalais, 1980). From 1979 to 1986 only five *Chelonia* were recorded in Virginia waters (Keinath et al., 1987).

A juvenile population of *C. m. mydas* inhabits the waters of the Culebra Archipelago, Puerto Rico, where carapace lengths are about 25–75 cm, with most in the 40–50-cm range, and the ages are 2–14 years (Collazo et al., 1992).

At French Frigate Shoal, Hawaii, only 94–248 female *C. m. agassizii* nest annually (Balazs, 1982b), and basking counts also confirm a rather small resident population. The size composition of the Hawaiian population is approximately 71% juvenile, 22% subadult, and 6.5% adult (Balazs, 1980).

The sex ratio of a population of green turtles may be skewed toward females (Hirth, 1971), but in any given season it can approach equality (Pritchard and Trebbau, 1984). Male to female ratios of two groups of the Atlantic subspecies caught on Miskito Bank by commercial fishermen were, respectively, 0.41:1.00 and 0.39:1.00 (Carr and Giovannoli, 1957). Hirth and Carr (1970) reported a sex ratio of 0.78:1.00 among 4,376 *C. m. agassizii* caught on the feeding grounds between Aden and Ras al Ara, but at Masirah Island, Oman, females make up only about 47% of the foraging population (Ross, 1984). Adult females are almost twice as abundant during basking turtle surveys in Hawaii (Balazs, 1980). In the future, new radioimmunoassay techniques (Owens et al., 1978) and tests for the presence of cytotoxicity to H-Y antiserum and amounts of H-Y antigen (males have higher amounts; Standora and Spotila, 1985; Wellins, 1987) may allow a better estimation of sex ratios in juvenile populations.

Survivorship may be low in some populations, but higher in others, and varies with the age class sampled. The mortality rate in hatchlings and nesting females is high; that of adult males is unknown, but they seem to be declining due to commercial harvesting. In some cases none of the hatchlings from a given nest survive the trip to the sea. Hendrickson (1958) estimated the rates of loss to various factors during the early stages of the life cycle of *C. m. agassizii* in Malaysia (presented as percentage of loss per survival stage): nondeveloping eggs, 40%; nest destruction by later excavating females, 50%; nest predation, 25%; beach predation on hatchlings, 40%; shallow-water predation on hatchlings during the first hour or so in the sea, 50%; and deep-water predation on hatchlings during the first week at sea, 75%(?). He calculated that, as a result of these losses, only 1.7% of the eggs laid per clutch survive. A summary of papers calculating annual survivorship from egg to hatchling by Iverson (1991a) lists survival rates of 39.6–86.0%. Bustard and Tognetti (1969) found that nest destruction is dependent on population density and is a means of regulating population size. Adult females nesting at Tortuguero, Costa Rica, survive at an annual rate of only 60.7% (Bjorndal, 1980b). Márquez and Doi (1973) thought the average overall annual survival rate in the Gulf of California is 80%. Hirth and Schaffer (1974) calculated that even in constant environments no fewer than 2.2, and perhaps as many as 10, hatchlings per 1,000 must survive to maturity to maintain stability in a population of *Chelonia*.

Smith et al. (1977) found that the level of genetic heterozygosity in green turtle populations from Florida and Grand Cayman Island is 11.9% with a range in percentage of polymorphic loci of 46.2–69.2%. The similarity coefficient for these populations is 0.904. The high level of genetic variability shown by these populations is encouraging from a survival standpoint.

The major cause of the decline of *Chelonia mydas* has been the exploitation of it on both the nesting and feeding grounds. Populations have been severely depleted and not allowed to recuperate, and because of the high demand for its eggs and flesh for food, the turtle has already disappeared from many nesting beaches where it formerly was plentiful. Collection of eggs on the nesting beaches is particularly injurious to the species, as it retards juvenile recruitment for replacement of lost adults. If *Chelonia mydas* is to survive, conservation methods must be applied wherever the turtle breeds or feeds. A worldwide moratorium on the taking of adults may be needed, and

nesting beaches must be rigorously protected by governmental regulation and adequately patrolled during the breeding season.

Economically *Chelonia mydas* is the most important reptile in the world. Its flesh and its eggs serve as an important source of protein in many third-world nations where protein is scarce. More affluent societies have long relished delicious turtle soup, the demand for which has supported commercial fisheries since the 17th century. Green turtles formerly provided fresh meat to the crews of naval, whaling, and pirate ships. Also, a thin oil is obtained from the turtle and its eggs. Parsons (1962) gave a detailed historical account of the commercial exploitation of this animal.

Degradation of the nesting and feeding habitats is a serious problem to be corrected. Even the type of artificial lighting used near nesting beaches can be a problem; far fewer females emerge to nest on beaches illuminated by mercury vapor lights (Witherington, 1992). Other causes of decline are entanglement in nets and trawls, dredging, ingestion of plastic refuse, and slow pesticide poisoning (Clark and Krynitsky, 1980; McKim et al., 1983; Balazs, 1985; Thompson, 1989; Caillouet et al., 1991). Another question to be answered by the marine turtle researcher is whether or not current practice of handling females and collecting data on the nesting beaches is not, in fact, stressing populations and lowering survivorship. Human interference during research has been shown to stress other animals, particularly bats, possibly contributing largely to their disappearance.

Under the Endangered Species Act, the U.S. Fish and Wildlife Service considers endangered the breeding populations in Florida and on the Pacific coast of Mexico; all other breeding populations are considered threatened.

REMARKS: Various serological tests show that *Chelonia mydas* is more closely related to the other genera of hard-shelled sea turtles than to the leatherback, *Dermochelys coriacea;* however, *Caretta, Eretmochelys,* and *Lepidochelys* are more closely related to each other than to *Chelonia* (Frair, 1979). Proteins in *Chelonia* are more similar to those of *Caretta* and *Lepidochelys* than those of *Eretmochelys* (Frair, 1982), and amino acid analysis of shell scutes shows significant differences between *Chelonia* and *Eretmochelys* (Hendrickson et al., 1977).

Bowen et al. (1989) and Meylan et al. (1990a) have found fixed or nearly fixed mitochondrial DNA restriction site differences between some Atlantic rookeries, suggesting a severe restriction on contemporary gene flow. The extremely close similarity in overall mitochondrial DNA sequences in Atlantic nesting populations is incompatible with the Carr and Coleman (1974) vicariant biogeographic hypothesis that plate tectonics and sea-floor spreading resulted in natal homing to the Ascension Island beaches, colonization of Ascension Island, or that any gene flow into the Ascension population has been evolutionarily recent.

According to Wallin (1985) the Linnaean type series of *C. mydas* also included specimens of *Caretta caretta*.

Hirth (1971, 1980b,c) and Márquez (1990) summarized the life history and literature of the green turtle.

Eretmochelys imbricata (Linnaeus, 1766)
Hawksbill

PLATE 4

RECOGNITION: *Eretmochelys* is a small to medium-sized sea turtle with four pairs of pleurals (the first does not touch the cervical), two pairs of prefrontal scales, and commonly three postoculars. Its carapace (to 114 cm) is shield shaped (heart shaped in the young, but more elongated and straight sided in the adult), has a keel on the last four vertebrals, and is serrated posteriorly. In the young the carapacial scutes strongly overlap the next posterior ones, but as the turtle grows the overlapping becomes progressively less, until finally the scutes lie side by side. The carapace is dark greenish brown; in the young it shows a tortoiseshell pattern. Four poreless inframarginal scutes reside on the yellow bridge. The plastron is hingeless and yellow; in juveniles it may have two longitudinal ridges and a few dark blotches, especially on the anterior scutes. Head scales are black to chestnut brown at the center and lighter at their margins; the jaws are yellow with some brown streaks or bars. The chin and throat are yellow, and the neck is dark above. The cutting edge of the lower jaw is without strongly elevated vertical ridges on the inner surface. The snout is elongated and narrow—rather like a hawk's beak—and lacks a notch at the tip. The floor of the mouth is deeply excavated at the mandibular symphysis. The forelimbs have two claws.

Males have somewhat soft, concave plastra, long, thick tails, which extend beyond the posterior carapacial rim, and long, heavy claws. Males may also be more brightly pigmented. Females have hard, less concave or flat plastra, shorter tails hardly extending beyond the posterior carapacial rim, and shorter, thinner claws.

KARYOTYPE: The karyotype is 2n = 56, with 10 metacentric, 2 submetacentric, 2 subtelocentric, and 8 acrocentric macrochromosomes, and 34 microchromosomes (Bickham, 1981; Kamezaki, 1990).

FOSSIL RECORD: Five specimens have been identified from the Bone Valley Formation, Pliocene (early Hemphillian), of Polk County, Florida (Dodd and Morgan, 1992).

DISTRIBUTION: The hawksbill is predominantly tropical, but is known in the Atlantic, Pacific, and Indian oceans from California, Japan, the Red Sea, the British Isles, France and Massachusetts south to Peru, New Zealand, Australia, Madagascar, northwestern Africa, southern Brazil, and St. Helena. *Eretmochelys* infrequently occurs in Hawaiian waters, and occasionally enters the Mediterranean Sea.

GEOGRAPHIC VARIATION: Two subspecies have been described. *Eretmochelys imbricata imbricata* (Linnaeus, 1766), the Atlantic hawksbill, ranges through the warmer parts of the western Atlantic Ocean, from Massachusetts through the Gulf of Mexico to southern Brazil. It also has been recorded from Ireland, Scotland, Morocco, and St. Helena. This subspecies has a nearly straight-sided carapace that tapers posteriorly; a keel that is continuous on only the last four vertebrals; ridges that converge posteriorly on only the last two vertebrals; and the upper surfaces of the head and flippers with less black, and little black plastral blotching in juveniles. *Eretmochelys imbricata bissa* (Ruppell, 1835), the Pacific hawksbill, ranges through the tropical portions of the Indian and Pacific oceans, from Madagascar to the Red Sea on the east coast of Africa and east to Australia and Japan in the western Pacific, to the Hawaiian Islands in the central Pacific, and from Peru to Baja California in the eastern Pacific. Stragglers occasionally reach California. It has a more heart-shaped carapace, a fully continuous vertebral keel, all vertebrals with ridges that converge posteriorly, the head and flippers almost solid black, and, in the young, black plastral pigmentation.

Eretmochelys imbricata imbricata

Plastron of *Eretmochelys imbricata*

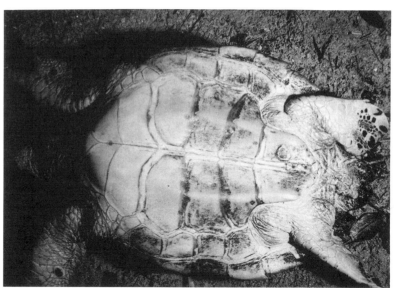

The characters used to separate these supposed races may be of little value. Carapace shape changes with age and growth, as probably also does the extent of carapacial keeling, and the degree of melanism is quite variable in every population (see discussions in Witzell, 1983; and Pritchard and Trebbau, 1984). A quantitative study is needed to determine the true relationship between the Atlantic and Pacific populations.

CONFUSING SPECIES: *Chelonia mydas* has two prefrontals, four postoculars, and a strongly serrated lower jaw. *Caretta caretta, Lepidochelys kempii,* and *L. olivacea* have five or more pairs of pleurals with the first touching the cervical. *Dermochelys coriacea* lacks horny shell scutes.

HABITAT: *Eretmochelys* is characteristically a tropical inhabitant of shallow (<20 m) rocky places and coral reefs. It also occurs in shallow coastal waters, such as mangrove-bordered bays, estuaries, and lagoons with mud bottoms and little or no vegetation, and in small, narrow creeks and passes. It

Eretmochelys imbricata; note two pairs of prefrontal scales

is occasionally found in deep waters, and juveniles associate with floating patches of *Sargassum* weed.

BEHAVIOR: Relatively little data regarding this species have been added since 1970. The hawksbill's more or less solitary life style has hampered study. It nests individually instead of in groups, thus further hindering the gathering of both reproductive and population data.

As in other marine turtles, its annual cycle during nesting years is probably divided into four phases: prereproductive migration to a nesting beach, nesting, postreproductive migration to feeding habitats, and foraging.

Apparently it is diurnal except during the nesting season. Night is spent on the bottom sleeping, the turtles surfacing every 30–45 minutes for air (Parrish, 1958). Diurnally resting hawksbills surface for air every 10–56 minutes, whereas active turtles come up to breathe every 30 seconds to 10 minutes. Active individuals submerged for short periods usually take only one breath when surfacing, but those that have stayed down longer than 10 minutes take 5–11 breaths at intervals of five seconds to three minutes.

Salt and water balance is a problem faced by *Eretmochelys* in its marine environment. Apparently, most osmoregulation is accomplished through large orbital salt-secreting glands (Dantzler and Holmes, 1974). These work intermittently in tandem with the kidneys, most often following a meal during which seawater has been swallowed. Dantzler and Holmes

(1974) thought that the hawksbill may drink seawater to gain sodium, which in turn increases salt-gland activity so that both excess sodium and potassium ions from foods are excreted.

Overheating on the nesting beach is another environmental problem faced by ovipositing females. However, *Eretmochelys* can nest during the day, if exposed to wind, because it is less affected by solar radiation than the larger species of marine turtles as it loses more heat by convection (Spotila and Standora, 1985). Hirth (1962) took the cloacal temperatures of two hawksbills just after they had finished nesting; one had a temperature of 28.5°C, the other 29.0°C. Shallow water offshore varied only 1.0°C during the period of the study, averaging 27.9°C (27.5–28.5). Basking has been reported, principally on uninhabited or sparsely inhabited beaches (Márquez, 1990).

A relatively limited number of hawksbills have been tagged, as females emerge singly onto nesting beaches. Evidence available, however, seems to indicate that this species is the least migratory of marine turtles. Extensive migrations are not the regular mode of behavior, but some tagged individuals have made long journeys between captures. Females tagged at Tortuguero, Costa Rica, have dispersed over 400 km northward to the Miskito Cays, Nicaragua, and Honduras, and south to Panama (Carr and Stancyk, 1975; Bjorndal et al., 1985). A female moved 496 km from Big Miskito Cay to Pedro Keys near Jamaica in less than five months (Carr and Stancyk, 1975), and another swam 625 km after nesting (Nietschmann; in

Pritchard and Trebbau, 1984). Of course, those *Eretmochelys* that strayed to Massachusetts and the British Isles traveled much farther from their probable Caribbean nesting beaches, and may have traveled across the Atlantic on the Gulf Stream. The record trip by a tagged hawksbill is 1,400 km straight-line distance from the Solomon Islands to Papua New Guinea in less than three years (Vaughan and Spring, 1980).

A Nicaraguan record from the Miskito Coast gives a little evidence on the speed of travel; that turtle had traveled about 460 km in not more than 60 days (Carr et al., 1966). Malaysian *Eretmochelys* traveled 713 km in 40 days, 17.8 km/day (de Silva, 1982). Oliver (1955) reported the cruising speed of a medium-sized hawksbill as around 1.6 km/hour.

Carr et al. (1966) studied the sea-finding orientation in hatchling *Eretmochelys* at Tortuguero. The hatchlings were able to find the sea from a wide range of release situations, including all conditions of topography and seaward outlook that occur at Tortuguero between the surf and the coconut-grove or shore-forest vegetation. The most immediate orientation and most active locomotion occurred when the nest was in sight of ocean surf and separated from it by beach that sloped toward the water. Orientation was successful, however, in rolling or cluttered ground, where the traveling turtle had to go over or around obstacles and climb long, blind, seaward slopes before the ocean came into view. Although most of the natural emergences are at night or at dawn, orientation in the trials was equally successful by day and by night. The greatest single natural hazard, other than exceptional concentrations of predators, appeared to be the heat of the midday sun, which immobilized or slowed the hatchlings within a few minutes—either killing them in the open or causing them to take refuge under debris, whence they rarely emerged. The sea-finding feat was clearly shown to be, in most cases at least, not a single-stimulus event but a composite behavior in which environmental information of diverse kinds is used. The dominant cue is some aspect of the sky over the ocean. What aspect of exposure or illumination is involved has not been shown.

The sea-finding ability and drive are retained by hatchlings long after they have been placed in tanks of water. Tank-held turtles seem less strongly motivated, however, and are easily confused by situations in which they had no direct visual contact with the sea. Pope (1939) reported that hatchlings are noticeably influenced by light when on the shore, but once placed in water they no longer are attracted by light.

Philibosian (1976) also reported that bright lights disorient hatchling *Eretmochelys,* causing them to move inland instead of toward the sea.

When hatchlings were released by Carr et al. (1966) on a spit between a river and the sea, the seaward tendency dominated across much of the width of the land. However, where the ocean was hidden and the river was visible from a few yards away, the turtles quickly entered the river.

During their first day in the water the hatchlings use their forelimbs chiefly as balancers while swimming largely by means of alternate strokes of the hind limbs. The presence of internal yolk material makes diving efforts ineffectual for several days. This inability affects the hatchlings' feeding habits, exposes them to predators, and allows them to be dispersed by wind and current.

The orientation processes that guide the nesting female inland are not understood, nor are those by which she returns to the sea. Clearly, however, more than sand-smelling and direct appraisal of the landscape is involved. The orientation of the mature female in going from a nest back to the sea seems identical with that of the sea-finding feat in hatchlings; that is, it probably is a composite process dominated by a response to illumination, not a compass sense. Like hatchlings, the female has no trouble turning directly toward the ocean from any nest site, even when her view of the water is blocked. Whatever the nature of the process, the back-azimuth orientation that takes the turtle from the water to the upper beach must be the opposite of it (Carr and Ogren, 1960).

Captives may be aggressive while feeding, biting at each other, and some limited territoriality over nesting spots has been seen in captivity (Witzell, 1983).

An interesting behavioral association between *Eretmochelys* and angelfishes (*Pomacanthus paru*) has been observed in waters off Grand Cayman Island (Smith, 1988). Two *Pomacanthus* actively swam over the hawksbill and bit at it, apparently performing a cleaning service, while the turtle remained perfectly still with forelimbs extended downward and to the side. The fish moved up and down over the front flippers, under the plastron and around the turtle's mouth.

REPRODUCTION: Mature females nesting on Atlantic Ocean beaches have straight-line carapace lengths of 62.5–94.0 cm (Witzell, 1983; Bjorndal et al., 1985) and minimum weights of 35.7–46.0 kg (Carr et al., 1966; Bjorndal et al., 1985). Carr (1952) thought Costa Rican *Eretmochelys* mature sexually at three years of age and 13.4 kg; Harrison (1963) believed that Sarawak hawksbills are fully grown at a mean carapace length and weight of 49.5 cm and 12.8 kg, and Witzell (1980) thought Samoan *Eretmochelys* mature at 50 cm and 3.5 years of age (based on captive growth). The gonadal cycles are unknown.

Mating has been observed in the shallow waters off nesting beaches (Carr, 1954; Caldwell and Rathjen, 1969; Carr and Stancyk, 1975; Carr et al., 1978); amorous males may even follow females onto the beach. Whether it also occurs elsewhere in open water or at feeding sites is unknown. Copulation usually takes place at the surface and may last several hours. The male hooks his heavy foreclaws onto the anterior rim of the female's carapace and presses his soft, concave plastron against the posterior dorsal surface of her carapace to hold fast. His tail is then wrapped beneath hers, and his penis is inserted into her cloacal vent. When copulating, *Eretmochelys* shows little response to outside disturbance. Several males may pursue a female until one catches her; perhaps females mate with more than one male per nesting season.

The Atlantic hawksbill nests, at least rarely, on beaches in Brazil (Bahia), French Guiana, Surinam, Guyana, Trinidad, Tobago, Venezuela (mainland and offshore islands), Colombia (offshore islands), Panama (mainland and San Blas Islands), Costa Rica, Nicaragua, Guatemala, Belize, Mexico (Yucatán, Quintana Roo, Veracruz, Campeche), the Lesser Antilles (Anguilla, St. Martin, St. Barthélemy, St. Eustatius, St. Kitts, Barbuda, Antigua, Montserrat, Guadeloupe), Barbados, the Grenadines, Dominican Republic, Puerto Rico (Isla Mona), Cuba (Isle of Pines), Aves Island, Jamaica (Pedro and Morant cays), Cayman Islands, Virgin Islands, Grenada, the Bahamas, and Florida (Elliot and Soldier's keys, Dade County; Port Everglades, Broward County; Juno Beach, Palm Beach County; Jupiter Island, Martin County; Canaveral National Seashore, Volusia County) (Meylan, 1983; Pritchard and Trebbau, 1984; Dalrymple et al., 1985; Lund, 1985; McMurtray and Richardson, 1985; Wyneken and Hicklin, 1988; Meylan, 1989; Horrocks and Scott, 1991). *Eretmochelys* rarely oviposits in the Hawaiian Islands, its nests having only been found on Hawaii and Molokai (Ernst and Barbour, 1972; Balazs, 1982b). In the eastern Pacific, hawksbill nesting has been reported from Ecuador, Panama, Costa Rica, Nicaragua, Guatemala, El Salvador, Mexico (Chiapas, Revillagigedo Islands) (Cornelius, 1982; Pritchard and Trebbau, 1984).

Although usually a dispersed, solitary nester, the hawksbill does nest in small concentrations on Antigua (National Research Council, 1990). Its habit of coming ashore singly has made the gathering of reproductive data more difficult than with other marine turtles. Most nesting in the western Atlantic and Caribbean takes place during April to October with the usual peak from May through July, but southern sites may experience nesting earlier or later and nesting occurs year round in the Bahamas (Hirth, 1980a; Witzell, 1983; Márquez, 1990). Nesting in Florida has been recorded from April to August (Witzell, 1983). The nesting season in the eastern Pacific is generally from June through December (Witzell, 1983).

Emergence may be either at night or occasionally during the day, often on a rising tide (Witzell, 1983). On Barbados, most nests were dug on west coast beaches rather than those on the south or east coast, suggesting *Eretmochelys* prefers beaches with low wave energy and steeper beach slopes (Horrocks and Scott, 1991). Sheltered beaches may be chosen because of the mechanical difficulties and energetic costs of moving onto and off high-energy beaches. Also, such beaches usually have less debris, and *Eretmochelys* is known to clean its nest site before excavating. Most nesting occurs within 100 m of the sea, and such short, steep beaches may reduce the energy needed to travel on land by both the gravid female and the hatchling. Nests are often dug among vegetation, and hatchling success is often greater in these nests, possibly owing to less compaction of the soil (Horrocks and Scott, 1991) or more concealment for the nest. The sand is of medium diameter (1.76–2.77 mm) and often composed of ground coral mixed with shells or roots (Nuitja and Uchida, 1983), but varies from beach to beach.

The hawksbill does not crawl up the beach by laboriously dragging itself along with its forelimbs as do most other marine turtles. Instead it uses an alternating sequence of both front and hind limbs with the diagonal flippers working simultaneously together. This allows it to rapidly "walk" over the sand. When the female first comes ashore, she appraises the beach by pushing her snout against the sand and holding it there for several seconds, apparently receiving olfactory and tactile information. She also cranes her neck and peers about. If all is well, she moves up the beach until a suitable site is chosen, sand-smelling and peering may occur as she frequently stops to assess the situation. The final site seems to be chosen visually.

Before digging the nest cavity, a shallow body pit cleared of debris is scraped out, first by the forelimbs then by both front and back limbs. Once this has been completed, the egg cavity is scooped out by the hind feet working alternately. The foot is brought in beneath the hind rim of the shell, and its edge is pressed against the sand and curled to lift a small amount of sand. The cupped foot is then lifted and swung laterally, and the sand is dropped several centimeters out from the rear rim of the carapace. As the sand falls, the other hind foot, which until then has rested on the sand beside the egg cavity, is brought forward, throwing sand from beside the hole to the front and side. This entire process is then reversed and repeated over and over until the flask-shaped cavity is completed. Both hind limbs are then withdrawn from the nest and spread on either side of the hole. The tail is then placed into the hole and oviposition begins. Two or three eggs are usually extruded at a time. Once the entire clutch is laid, the hind feet ladle sand, picking it up and dropping it into the cavity, and occasionally knead it. When the cavity is filled, the forelimbs begin throwing sand backward, first working alternately, then together, as the pressing action of the hind flippers is gradually converted into kicking strokes. This action obliterates the body pit, conceals the nest, and moves the turtle forward across the beach, but leaves a trail of upthrusted sand to 2–3 m beyond the nest cavity. The female then quickly returns to the sea in a straight path using the alternate limb gait. She may sand-smell and peer about on the return trip. The total nesting sequence from stranding to the return to the sea may take one or two hours. For a more detailed description of the nesting process, we refer the reader to Carr et al. (1966).

Nests may be placed more than 25 m from the waterline, sometimes in the vegetation bordering the beach. Body pits average about 25 cm (22.8–30.5) in depth, and the depth from the beach surface to the bottom of the nest cavity is about 43 cm (43–44) (Carr et al., 1966). Egg chambers average 23 × 28 cm.

Nesting usually occurs at intervals of two to three (1–6) years (Carr et al., 1966; Pritchard and Trebbau, 1984; Márquez, 1990), and hawksbills may nest four or five times a season (Corliss et al., 1989) at intervals of 18–19 days (13–28 days; Hirth, 1980a). Nest fidelity is not standardized within a season, as some females seek other beaches for subsequent oviposition, but a greater degree of site-fixity is exhibited between nesting seasons (Bjorndal et al., 1985).

The white, calcareous eggs usually are spherical, averaging about 38–40 mm (31–45) in diameter and about 25 g (20.0–32.5) in weight (Hirth, 1980a; Witzell, 1983; Márquez, 1990), but a few in each clutch may be slightly elongated. The eggshell is composed of two layers, a calcareous outer layer formed by groups of needlelike aragonite crystals and an inner fibrous layer (Acuña-Mesén, 1989a). Eggs contain 22% protein, 16% lipid, 3% ash, 59% water, but no fiber (Suwelo, 1971). Eggs examined by Deraniyagala (1939) were thinly covered with a mucilaginous secretion, which appeared to absorb water and was found to remain moist for 48 hours. Clutches of 32–250 eggs have been reported (Hirth, 1980a; Witzell, 1983), but most clutches average about 160 eggs (Ehrhart, 1982). Hatch success of unplundered nests is about 80%, and each female produces about 560 hatchlings a season in Antigua, West Indies (Corliss et al., 1989).

Incubation period varies with beach temperature, 43–91 days, but probably averages from 60 to 70 days; hatching success may be 0–100% for an individual nest and 47–97% for an entire season at a particular beach (Witzell, 1983). Nest success is strongly correlated with nest site location, and is greatest from nests close to mean beach elevation and less at higher or lower elevations (Horrocks and Scott, 1991). Emergence from the nest cavity takes place in either the morning or evening (Fernando, 1983) and is accomplished by sporadic movements and thrashing. This action, usually begun by one turtle, quickly spreads throughout the clutch; it dislodges sand from the walls and ceiling and packs it up on the floor of the chamber, slowly pushing the hatchling group upward. Once just under the surface, the little turtles settle down until the proper surface temperature is reached (<28°C), usually near dawn, and then emerge onto the beach. The young disappear from view when they enter the sea after hatching and are rarely seen again until they reach a carapace length of 125–150 mm. Once in the ocean, hatchlings may either associate with patches of drifting sargassum (Redfoot et al., 1985), or remain on the coastal reef habitats of adults.

The hatchling carapace is heart shaped and has a vertebral keel; the plastron has two longitudinal ridges. Hatchlings are black or very dark brown except for the keels, the shell edge, and areas on the neck and flippers, which are light brown. Sizes and weights are as follows: carapace length, 39–46 mm, carapace width, 27–35 mm, plastron length, 30–37 mm, and weight, 12–15 g (Fernando, 1983; Witzell, 1983).

Eretmochelys has its sex determined by the incubation temperature of its eggs, as in other cheloniids. The pivotal temperature at which 50% of each sex is produced is 29.2°C (Mrosovsky et al., 1992). Embryonic phases are described by Witzell (1983).

Natural hybridization has occurred between *Eretmochelys* and *Chelonia mydas* in Surinam (Wood et al., 1983), and Conceição et al. (1990) reported a hybrid *Eretmochelys* × *Caretta* from Brazil that was both morphologically and electrophoretically intermediate, but with proteins more similar to *Eretmochelys*.

GROWTH AND LONGEVITY: *Eretmochelys* grows fast. Wild individuals are estimated to have straight-line carapace lengths of about 20–23 cm at the end of one year, 33–40 cm at two years of age, and 60–65 cm in three years (Schmidt, 1916; Kajihara and Uchida, 1974; Uchida, 1979). Well-fed captives grow even faster. Jamaican hatchlings grew to 19 cm in six months and 26 cm in one year (Brown et al., 1982). One maintained by Caldwell (1962b) for nearly three years increased in length approximately 10 cm the first year, 6 cm the second, and 10 cm the third; respective increases in weight were approximately 160, 900, and 2,330 g. Deraniyagala (1939) reported that in 16 months two captive juveniles grew 33 cm and put on 45 kg. Lewis (1940) reported a 127-kg hawksbill from the Cayman Islands—apparently the record weight for this species, but most adults weigh about 50–60 kg (Márquez, 1990). Kaufmann (1975) reported a nine-fold increase in carapace length over two years for captives.

Carapace length is approximately 1.3 times carapace width in both juveniles and adults (Kaufmann, 1975). Witzell (1980) calculated regression relationships of four morphological parameters to carapace length: carapace width, $y = 1.47 + 0.72x$; plastron length, $y = 1.45 + 0.69x$; head width, $y = 0.78 + 0.14x$; and eye width $y = 0.40 + 0.04x$.

The horny scutes of the hawksbill's shell change in character as the length increases. In juveniles the scutes lie side by side until the turtles reach a length of more than 10 cm. Then the scutes develop the shinglelike form of the adult. The scutes remain this way until the turtle reaches a length of 36–40 cm, when they return to a juxtaposed condition. This change usually begins first in the plastral scutes (Deraniyagala, 1939).

A captive in the Berlin Zoological Garden lived at least 16 years, and four females and a male were kept for more than 20 years at Marineland, in Florida. Longevity in the wild is unknown.

FOOD HABITS: *Eretmochelys* is an omnivorous opportunist that seems to prefer invertebrates, particularly sponges. In fact, it feeds almost exclusively on sponges in the Caribbean (Meylan, 1988). Its diet is taxonomically narrow and highly uniform geographically. It includes sponges that are toxic to other vertebrates and contains more silica than that of other vertebrates (Meylan, 1988). By affecting space competition, spongivory by *Eretmochelys* may influence succession and diversity of reef communities. However, such a specific diet of filter-feeders in hard-bottomed communities makes this turtle particularly vulnerable to deteriorating reef conditions, adding to it problems for survival.

In addition to sponges, it is known to eat coelenterates (Portuguese man-of-war, anemones, hydroids, coral), bryozoans, platyhelminthes, polychaetes, sea urchins, mollusks (gastropods, bivalves, cephalopods, scaphopods), barnacles, crustaceans (crabs, rock lobsters), tunicates (*Salpa*), and fish; plants consumed are algae (green, brown, red), sea grasses (*Thalassia, Syringodium, Cymodocea*), and mangrove (*Rhizophora*; wood, bark, leaves, fruits) (Carr, 1952; Carr and Stancyk, 1975; Den Hartog, 1980; Witzell, 1983; Pritchard and Trebbau, 1984; Bjorndal et al., 1985; Meylan, 1988). Odd items such as stones and plastic have also been found in hawksbill stomachs. Captives eat fish, meat, bread, octopi, squid, crabs, mussels, and oysters. Hatchlings seem to be herbivorous, doing particularly well on *Sargassum,* but become more omnivorous as they age.

When seizing a crab, a hawksbill kept by Deraniyagala (1939) would swim up to it and examine it for a couple of seconds. If the prey was small it would be seized without further ado, but if it was large the turtle would maneuver for position and then wait until the crab moved, whereupon the turtle would seize the crab by one side and break its carapace by a sharp bite, preventing the use of the pincers. When eating a Portuguese man-of-war a hawksbill closes its eyes, presumably to avoid being stung (Carr, 1952).

Hawksbill flesh and eggs are eaten in many parts of its range. This requires caution, for *Eretmochelys* tends to store in its tissues the toxins of several poisonous organisms that it eats. Deraniyagala (1939) cites an instance in which 24 persons were poisoned by eating hawksbills that had fed on poisonous weeds. Seven died after two days; the others recovered. More recently 18 people became sick and two died from eating hawksbill flesh in Tonga (Balazs, 1984).

PREDATORS AND DEFENSE: Hawksbill nests are robbed by humans, dogs (*Canis*), raccoons (*Procyon*), coatimundis (*Nasua*), mongooses (*Herpestes*), and rats (*Rattus*); and thrashers (*Margarops*), gulls (*Larus*), and ghost crabs (*Ocypode*) eat hatchlings crossing the beach. Humans, sharks (*Carcharhinus, Galeocerdo*), red snappers (*Lutjanus*), groupers (*Epi-*

nephelus), saltwater crocodiles (*Crocodylus porosus*), and octopi (*Octopus vulgaris*) attack adults and juveniles in the water (Gilbert and Kelso, 1971; Brongersma, 1972; Ernst and Barbour, 1972; Witzell and Banner, 1980; Buxton and Branch, 1983; Nellis and Small, 1983; Witzell, 1983; Young, 1992). Captives may be cannibalistic (Witzell, 1983).

In addition to predation, some *Eretmochelys* lose their lives through accidents, usually related to human activity or pollution, such as becoming fouled with tar or oil (Critchley, 1987) or entangled in fishing nets or lines (Balazs, 1985).

The hawksbill's chief claim to fame is the translucent scutes of the carapace—the tortoiseshell of commerce. The scutes are a clear amber, streaked with red, white, green, brown, and black. Usually the turtle is killed before the scutes are removed by the application of heat. There is evidence that if the scutes are removed carefully and the turtle is returned to the sea it can regenerate the lost scutes. This may be possible if the mitotic Malpighian cells of the epidermis are not damaged. However, most turtles so treated probably die (Carr and Meylan, 1980b). A single turtle can yield 4.5–5.5 kg of tortoiseshell (called "carey" by the Caribbeans).

Eretmochelys is not defenseless. Newly caught individuals may be aggressive, biting and snapping at anything within their reach. When it seizes an object the turtle does not release it readily, and the strong, sharp jaws inflict a painful bite. Furthermore, the sharp edges of the overlapping scutes can cause deep wounds if a struggling specimen is carelessly handled.

POPULATIONS: The hawksbill's reproductive strategy of using scattered nesting beaches has made accurate population estimates difficult. However, most authorities agree that the numbers of *Eretmochelys* in the Caribbean and off the Pacific Coast of the Americas have declined until most populations are depleted or endangered (King, 1982; National Research Council, 1990). Meylan (1989) reported that in the Greater Caribbean only nesting beaches in Brazil, the Dominican Republic, Grenada, Jamaica, and Turks and Caicos Islands are visited by 100–500 females per year, and only Mexico has over 500 nestings per season.

Undisturbed nests may have survivorship rates of 80–97%, but this rate drops drastically if the clutch is transported to another site or disturbed in any other way (Limpus, 1980; Small, 1982; Brooke and Garnett, 1983; Witzell, 1983; Pritchard and Trebbau, 1984; Iverson, 1991a). Survivorship of females during the internesting years may be low; Brooke and Garnett (1983) reported that in the Seychelles only 25–30% of the females tagged were recaptured in a later season.

Mrosovsky et al. (1992) found that although the sand temperatures at the depth of hawksbill nests on Antigua were sometimes higher than the pivotal sex-determining temperature of 29.2°C, more often they were lower, and thought it unlikely that hatchling hawksbills produced there have highly female-biased sex ratios.

REMARKS: Immunoprecipitation and electrophoretic tests of cheloniid serum indicate that *Eretmochelys*, *Caretta*, and *Lepidochelys* share many proteins and are closer to each other than to *Chelonia* (Frair, 1979, 1982). However, *Caretta* and *Lepidochelys* are more closely related to each other than to *Eretmochelys*. Comparison of the amino acids in the shell scutes of *Eretmochelys* and *Chelonia* show considerable distinction between the two genera (Hendrickson et al., 1977), and an analysis of the body fat composition of *Eretmochelys* also indicates a significant difference from the other members of the Cheloniidae (Pathak and Dey, 1956).

The hawksbill was one of the first endangered turtles protected under Endangered Species Act, but its survival is still problematic. Throughout its range it is hunted for the plates of its shells and for food. Existing conservation laws are ineffectively enforced and as long as there is a ready market for tortoiseshell the numbers of this turtle will continue to dwindle (Carr and Meylan, 1980b). The key to saving this turtle is to restrict the market in tortoiseshell. Fortunately, Japan, the leading importer of hawksbill shell products, has banned import of hawksbill shell effective December 1992 (Donnelly, 1991). Nesting preserves will not work well to save this species because of its scattered nesting behavior.

A review of the pertinent literature regarding the life history of *Eretmochelys* is provided by Witzell (1983).

Caretta caretta (Linnaeus, 1758)
Loggerhead
PLATE 5

RECOGNITION: *Caretta caretta* is the largest hard-shelled turtle living; its maximum length and weight are exceeded only by the leatherback (*Dermochelys coriacea*). The typical adult carapace length is 85–100 cm, and most mature individuals weigh about 135 kg, but some attain truly massive size. The maximum known carapace length is 213 cm, and weights of up to 453.6 kg have been reported (Brongersma, 1972). Pritchard and Trebbau (1984) reported a skull 27.6 cm wide from a turtle that probably would have weighed over 500 kg, and Smith and Smith (1979) reported a Pacific loggerhead weighing 545 kg.

The elongated carapace has five or more pairs of pleurals (the first touch the cervical scute), commonly 12–13 (11–15) marginals on each side, a vertebral keel that becomes progressively smoother with age, and a serrated posterior rim. It is reddish brown but may be tinged with olive, and many scutes have yellow borders. Three poreless inframarginals lie on the bridge. The bridge and plastron are cream to yellow. The plastron is hingeless and has two longitudinal ridges, which disappear with age. The large head is broad posteriorly and rounded in front; the snout is short and broad, and two pairs of prefrontals are present. Head pigmentation varies from reddish or yellowish chestnut to olive brown, with many scales yellow bordered. The jaws are yellowish brown, and the bony surface of the lower jaw is smooth at the symphysis. Limbs and tail are dark above, and yellowish toward the borders and below.

The carapace is heavily pigmented; during development the pigment granules migrate toward the surface layers. The epidermis is commonly two to four cells thick, but at growing points there may be six cell layers. The keratinized scales are hard with microfolds on the carapacial scutes which may lower frictional drag while swimming (Solomon et al., 1986).

Compared to females, mature males have wider shells, which gradually taper posteriorly; long, thick tails, which extend beyond the rear carapacial rim; a large, recurved claw on each forelimb; and more yellow pigment on the head.

KARYOTYPE: As in other species of Cheloniidae, the loggerhead has 56 diploid chromosomes: 32 macrochromosomes (12 metacentric, 2 submetacentric, 6 subtelocentric, 12 acrocentric) and 24 microchromosomes (Kamezaki, 1989).

FOSSIL RECORD: Few fossils of the living species *Caretta caretta* have been found. Pliocene remains are known from Florida and North Carolina (Dodd and Morgan, 1992; Zug, in press), and Pleistocene (Rancholabrean) fossils have been found in Florida (Hay, 1917) and in caves in Puebla, Mexico (Alvarez, 1976). An archeological specimen was uncovered from an Indian mound in Palm Beach County, Florida (Johnson, 1952). Other fossil sea turtles possibly referable to the genus *Caretta* have been discovered in European late Cretaceous to Pliocene deposits, from the Eocene of northern Africa, and from the late Cretaceous to Pleistocene of North America (Romer, 1956).

DISTRIBUTION: *Caretta* occurs in the Pacific, Indian, and Atlantic oceans from Alaska and eastern Russia, India, Kenya, the British Isles, Norway, northern Russia, and Newfoundland south to Chile, Australia, South Africa, tropical western Africa, and Argentina (Brongersma, 1972; Hodge, 1982, 1992; Stinson, 1984; Dodd, 1988c, 1990b,c; Bane, 1992). The loggerhead also occurs in the Caribbean and Mediterranean seas. It has been rarely observed in the Hawaiian Islands, where it is considered only a visitor (Balazs, 1982b). In southern California *Caretta* occurs in low numbers from July to September in any year, but there are more in warm years and the

Caretta caretta

Plastron of *Caretta caretta*

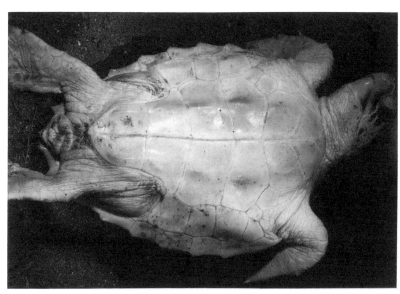

activity period is extended to include October to June (Stinson, 1984).

GEOGRAPHIC VARIATION: Two poorly marked subspecies have been described. *Caretta caretta caretta* (Linnaeus, 1758), the Atlantic loggerhead, ranges from Newfoundland and the British Isles south to Argentina, the Canary Islands, and the western coast of tropical Africa; occasionally it enters the Mediterranean Sea. This turtle commonly has seven or eight

neural bones in the carapace and averages 12 marginal scutes on each side. *Caretta c. gigas* Deraniyagala, 1933, the Pacific loggerhead, occurs from Alaska, Russia, India, and Kenya south through the Pacific and Indian oceans to Chile, Australia, and South Africa; it has also been recorded from the eastern Atlantic. This form has 7–12 neural bones in the carapace, the last 1–5 commonly interrupted by costal bones, and 13 marginal scutes on each side.

The validity of these subspecies has been ques-

Head of *Caretta caretta*

tioned (Dodd, 1990c; Márquez, 1990). Pritchard (1979) noted much overlap in number of both neural bones and marginal scutes between several populations around the world, and suggested abandoning the trinomial distinction, and Stoneburner (1980) found little variation in body depth between nesting populations of Atlantic loggerheads. Also, recent comparison of mitochondrial DNA restriction sites by Bowen et al. (1991) has revealed low divergence (0.007–0.008) between the Atlantic and Pacific populations of *Caretta*, indicating only recent separation of the two. It is probably best to consider the two named races as invalid.

CONFUSING SPECIES: The ridleys (*Lepidochelys*) have pores and four inframarginals at the bridge; *L. kempii* is gray, and *L. olivacea* is olive colored and commonly has more than five pairs of pleurals on the carapace. *Chelonia mydas* and *Eretmochelys imbricata* have only four pairs of pleurals, with the first pair not touching the cervical scute. Also, *Chelonia* has but one pair of prefrontal scales. None of the other marine turtles is reddish.

HABITAT: The loggerhead wanders widely throughout the marine waters of its range; it has been found as far as 240 km out in the open sea, but rarely is it seen east of the western boundary of the Gulf Stream, where it occupies cooler waters than those of the Gulf Stream (Hoffman and Fritts, 1982). It enters bays, lagoons, salt marshes, creeks, and the mouths of large rivers. Subadults and adults are free swimming, but hatchlings and juveniles are most often found along current fronts, downswells, or eddies associated with drifting mats of *Sargassum* (Caldwell, 1969; Fletemeyer, 1978; Pritchard and Trebbau, 1984; Carr, 1987). One posthatchling was found, however, inshore on an artificial reef (Collard and Hansknecht, 1990).

BEHAVIOR: The reproductive year of female *Caretta* has the same four phases found in other marine turtles: (1) migration to the reproductive area, (2) the nesting period, (3) remigration from the nesting beach to the feeding range, and (4) a period of active foraging which includes much of the year and may involve, for individuals near the northern limits of the winter range, some weeks spent in hibernation (see below).

The daily activities of three captives, each about 38 cm long, appeared to Layne (1952) to be about equally divided between swimming and resting on the bottom of the tank. When resting, they always selected a corner and would lie completely motionless with the head thrust into the corner, eyes open or half-shut, and flippers extended to about the normal midstroke swimming position. They were alert, and the slightest movement above the water brought them to the surface. Possibly the turtles slept in this same position; on one occasion, when the loggerheads were observed at night by dim light, they were found in their corners with eyes tightly closed and were slower to rouse than during the daylight hours. Nocturnal activity in wild loggerheads has not been documented (Mendonça and Ehrhart, 1982). Parrish (1958) reported that captives at Marineland, Florida, did most of their sleeping before 0100, but showed little activity in the predawn hours.

In the open sea loggerheads spend a great deal of time floating on the surface, presumably sleeping; but Carr (1952) never saw them do this in the sounds or estuaries, where they stay in the deeper parts of the channels and come up only to breathe.

Low water temperatures affect loggerhead activity patterns. Loggerheads become lethargic at about 13–15°C and adopt a stunned floating posture in water of about 10°C (Mrosovsky, 1980). Off northeastern North America loggerheads seem generally restricted to a maximum latitude of about 38° N in waters with mean surface temperatures of 22.2°C (Shoop and Kenney, 1992). Incidents of natural cold stunning after sudden drops in the environmental temperature have been reported from Long Island Sound, New York (Meylan and Sadove, 1986; Morreale et al., 1992), Florida (Witherington and Ehrhart, 1989), and Texas (Shaver, 1990). Water temperatures below 6.5°C may be lethal (Schwartz, 1978), but some *Caretta* have the ability to hibernate on the bottom during periods of adverse water temperature. This is apparently not an uncommon event in the Port Canaveral Ship Channel in eastern Florida (Carr et al., 1981). An age difference exists in cold tolerance by *Caretta*. Younger turtles seem more resistant, and are not affected until the water temperature falls below 9°C, and hatchlings do not react to cold until the water temperature drops below 4.5°C (Schwartz, 1978). Loggerheads lack a well-developed counter-current heat exchange system, such as that of the leatherback, *Dermochelys coriacea* (Mrosovsky, 1980).

High temperatures also affect *Caretta,* but its critical thermal maximum is unknown. Probably it seeks out cooler water when becoming overheated. The loggerhead docs bask while floating at the surface, possibly to raise its body temperature. Sapsford and Van der Riet (1979) reported that a loggerhead raised its body temperature 3.75°C above the water temperature by surface basking on a sunny day, but that on overcast days its body temperature equaled that of the water.

During nesting the loggerhead's body temperature may also rise if she has come from colder water, but not very much: only 1.1–2.5°C when loggerheads came from 23.0–24.5°C water, and 1.75–4.50 when they emerged from 25.00–25.25°C water (Sapsford and Hughes, 1978).

During physiological tests over a temperature range of 15–30°C, Lutz et al. (1989) discovered that moderate activity by *Caretta* caused a threefold increase in oxygen consumption, accommodated by a twofold increase in ventilation (due to a faster breathing rate), and a 60% increase in oxygen uptake by the lungs. Oxygen consumption also increased ($Q_{10} = 24$), primarily because of an increase in oxygen uptake, inasmuch as neither the tidal volume nor the breathing frequency changed. Venous blood pH decreased but P_{CO_2} and P_{O_2} increased with temperature, suggesting that ventilatory adjustments alone are insufficient for regulating thermally dependent shifts in blood pH. Plasma potassium levels increased with temperature, possibly related to cellular-mediated adjustments in blood pH.

Living in the ocean may cause dehydration problems for the loggerhead. Bennett et al. (1986) reported that hatchlings may lose as much as 12% of their initial hatched weight from water loss during emergence from the nest. After additional water loss when entering the sea, hatchlings will drink seawater and return to their initial weight within 10–15 days, without feeding. No significant changes in plasma osmolarity or sodium levels occur during this period. *Caretta* can regulate levels of the majority of the solutes (the monovalent ions) in its body fluids through secretions (mMol/liter) of the postorbital salt glands: sodium, 732–878; potassium, 18–31; and chloride, 810–992 (Prange, 1985). Normal plasma concentrations (mMol/liter) of these and other important ions are: sodium, 140; potassium, 3.5; chloride, 111; calcium, 1.2; and magnesium, 2.2. Normal urine concentrations are: sodium, 4.9; potassium, 69.4; chloride, 10.0; and magnesium, 8.8 (Prange, 1985).

An adult loggerhead may travel a long distance from its nesting beach to its feeding range, and some may even wander great distances beyond their reproductive and feeding ranges. Australian *Caretta* tagged on the nesting beach have made journeys of 2,177 km and 1,774 km between captures (Bustard and Limpus, 1970, 1971), and other females tagged in Tongaland, Africa, have been recaptured between 2,400 and 2,655 km away (Hughes, 1974; Hughes et al., 1967). A female loggerhead equipped with a radio transmitter and released near Biloxi, Mississippi, swam to near Brownsville, Texas, and then retraced its path to near Port Arthur in eastern Texas before the transmitter was lost (Timko and Kolz, 1982).

Juveniles may also journey far from their nesting beach or release site. A large juvenile tagged in the Canary Islands was caught 154 days later in Cuban waters after having traveled at least 6,900 km at a minimum rate of 45 km/day (Bolten et al., 1992). One released offshore from Padre Island, Texas, was later captured in the Adriatic Sea off southeastern Italy (Manzella and Fontaine, 1988), another released in Brazil traveled to the Azores (Bolten et al., 1990), and a juvenile released at Okinawa crossed the Pacific Ocean to be recaptured two years later off San Diego, California (Uchida and Teruya, in Márquez, 1990). Another long migration by a juvenile covered a minimum distance of 5,140 km from Cape Canaveral, Florida, to São Jorge Island, Azores (Eckert and Martins, 1989), and a juvenile tagged at Newport, Rhode Island, swam 1,571 km south to Cumberland Island, Georgia (Shoop and Ruckdeschel, 1989).

Nesting females are only short-term residents in the vicinity of nesting beaches, migrating into these areas every two or three years and residing elsewhere during nonreproductive years (Richardson et al., 1978; Henwood, 1987a).

During migration adults are capable of maintaining minimum average swimming speeds of 28–70 km/day (Meylan, 1982b; Meylan et al., 1983), and Stoneburner (1982) reported swimming speeds in excess of 20 km/hour. Swimming speeds may be influenced by water temperature. In tests using heated water in laboratory tanks, hatchling loggerheads maintained a swimming speed of approximately 20 cm/sec at 25.6–28.9°C, but when the water temperature was increased to 30 and 33°C the turtles slowed considerably until one was only moving 15.5 cm/sec (O'Hara, 1980). Cold water temperatures probably also slow swimming speed.

Numerous records confirm that female *Caretta* returns to the same beach to nest several times during its lifetime (Dodd, 1988c). How can these turtles find their way to such a small area when their feeding waters may be a thousand kilometers away? Several possible orientation and navigational systems are available to them. Light cues may aid in offshore orientation. Witherington (1991) reported that hatchlings swimming from a lighted beach swim more slowly than those from a dark beach and have a larger angle of dispersion, but Salmon and Wyneken (1990) found that once in the water hatchlings respond more to natural horizons than brighter horizons and thought it unlikely that such photic stimuli are of primary importance in guiding movements offshore. However, during the trip across the beach, brightness cues seem very important in directing hatchlings from nest to water; the young turtles even orient away from dark silhouettes (Hooker, 1908, 1911; Daniel and Smith, 1947; McFarlane, 1963; Fehring, 1972; Kingsmill and Mrosovsky, 1982; Salmon and Wy-

neken, 1990; Witherington and Bjorndal, 1991a,b; Salmon et al., 1992). Some hatchlings even perform orientation circles to choose the brightest horizon (Kingsmill and Mrosovsky, 1982). Hooker (1908, 1911) demonstrated that hatchling *Caretta* prefer blue over red, orange, or green. Witherington and Bjorndal (1991a,b) also observed that shorter wavelengths are preferred over longer ones; the turtles orient toward near-ultraviolet (360 nm), violet (400 nm), and blue-green (500 nm), but choose standard white light over yellow-orange (600 nm) and red (700 nm) light. Their responses are positively correlated with intensity and color preference with near-ultraviolet, violet, and blue-green light. When given a choice between a dark window or one lighted with monochromatic colors at each of two intensities, they also orient toward the lower wavelength colors, and away from green-yellow to yellow-orange. Loggerheads orient toward red light only at high intensity. The aversion to yellow light suggests a spectral quality assessment in sea-finding.

Under infrared light, hatchling *Caretta caretta* orient down slopes, but in the presence of nocturnal levels of visible light they ignore slope cues (Salmon et al., 1992).

Once in the water, hatchlings seem to respond to wave activity, swimming away from shore and into oceanic swells and wind-generated surface waves (Salmon and Lohmann, 1989; Wyneken et al., 1990; Witham, 1991). Hatchlings swim almost continuously during the first 24 hours, but eventually become inactive at night (Wyneken and Salmon, 1992). Such behavior quickly moves them away from the dangerous near-shore predators.

Loggerheads avoid sources of low-frequency sound in the 25–1,000-Hz range (O'Hara and Wilcox, 1990), but how this relates to sea- or beach-finding orientation is unknown. O'Hara and Wilcox (1990) suggested this be explored as a possible deterrent resource to keep turtles from entering nets where they may become entangled and drown.

Caretta caretta possibly has an odor-memory capacity which may guide them home to their original nest beach (Grassman and Owens, 1981; Owens et al., 1982, 1985). Such a sense would require the turtle to be imprinted with the odor characteristics of the beach, or possibly ground or offshore water, while either still in the egg, digging out of the nest, crossing the beach, or swimming away after entering the ocean. Later, when mature, the loggerhead would then retrace its original migration route by following the odor cues emitted by the nesting area. This requires a very sensitive olfactory system, but *Caretta* does possess the ability to imprint on very small concentrations of chemicals (Grassman and Owens, 1981; Owens et al., 1982). Possibly, a loggerhead can follow odor trails from the secretions of the Rathke's glands of other individuals (Radhakrisna et al., 1989; Weldon et al., 1990; Weldon and Tanner, 1990; Rostal et al., 1991). Such an ability would allow them to congregate off nesting beaches or in feeding waters; unfortunately this has not been adequately demonstrated.

Magnetic material has been discovered in the head of hatchling loggerheads that is comparable in amount to that in a honey bee (Kirschvink, 1980), and Lohmann (1991) has demonstrated that hatchling *Caretta* can detect the magnetic field of the earth and possibly use it as an orientation cue. Apparently, *Caretta* has several means of orientation and navigation at its disposal, and the turtle probably uses a combination of these during its migrations to and from the nesting beach.

Young *Caretta* swim differently than adults: 95% of their swimming is accomplished by a simultaneous double hind-limb kick, with the forelimbs folded against the carapace (Davenport and Clough, 1986; Witham, 1991). This behavior is progressively replaced by alternate-limb swimming as the juvenile grows beyond 400 g, and entirely disappears by age one.

Hatchling loggerheads possess positive buoyancy and cannot sink (Milsom, 1975); adults use changes in lung volume to regulate buoyancy (Milsom and Johansen, 1975). The ability to dive develops gradually, and improves by the time they weigh 300–400 g when they can dive to about two meters (Davenport and Clough, 1986). The ability to dive is positively related to lung volume which increases relatively with age (Milsom, 1975). The gross anatomical and histological structure of the hatchling lung, like that of adults, is very similar to that of marine mammals, the main points of convergence being the broad major intrapulmonary airways, the abundance of smooth muscle and connective tissue, and the double capillary network on the gas exchange surfaces (Perry et al., 1989). Vascularization of the breathing surface is essentially complete by one day before hatching (Perry et al., 1989). Aquatic respiration is negligible in *Caretta,* accounting for less than 2% of the resting oxygen consumption (Lutz and Bentley, 1985). There are no special adaptations for increased oxygen capacity in blood or tissue (but the hemoglobin readily releases oxygen to the tissues; Friedman et al., 1985); the lung acts as the major oxygen reservoir and it can supply sufficient oxygen for most aerobic dives

up to 20 minutes (Lutz and Bentley, 1985). *Caretta* can endure substantial changes in its blood gas and pH levels (detailed discussion of the physiology and biochemistry of diving are beyond the goals of this book; we refer the reader to the following papers which cover these in depth: Lapennas and Lutz, 1982; Lutz and Lapennas, 1982; Baldwin and Gyuris, 1983; Lutz and Bentley, 1985; Friedman et al., 1985; Lutz and Dunbar-Cooper, 1987; Lutcavage et al., 1987, 1989; Lutcavage and Lutz, 1991; and Nilsson et al., 1991).

By the end of the first year, diving ability has developed, and adults have no trouble swimming to the bottom to feed or sleep. While offshore, *Caretta* may demonstrate a circadian diving rhythm that is obscured when the turtle is near the beach where tides affect it (Sakamoto et al., 1990a). The circadian rhythm is closely related to sunrise and sunset; mean diving depth of the female monitored by Sakamoto et al. (1990a) was shallower than 10 m during the day, but deeper than 15 m at night. This turtle was capable of maintaining a stomach temperature several degrees warmer than its environment (Sakamoto et al., 1990a,b). This was largely due to the thermodynamic transfer of heat from the skin, but the turtle also drank cold seawater during deep dives, thereby cooling its body from within. Coming out of the cooler deep water again, she would make continuous and repeated dives in the shallower, warmer water layer to raise her body temperature.

Males are more active swimmers and divers than females, usually frequenting midwater to surface depths; females tend to remain on the bottom except when breathing (Schwartz and Jensen, 1991). Breath intervals vary by sex and size of turtle from hourly breathing up to 20 hours for one female (Schwartz and Jensen, 1991), and loggerheads may spend as much as 85% of the day submerged (Lutcavage and Lutz, 1991). Walker (1959) noted that when moving underwater *Caretta* keeps its nostrils open and moves the floor of its mouth slowly up and down. The turtle also moves the lower jaw slightly. Presumably it passes water through the nostrils for olfaction. When asleep or resting on the bottom, there is no such movement and the nostrils are closed. Closure occurs partway within each nostril and is effected by the meeting of bulges from the laterodorsal and medioventral walls of the nasal passages. It takes 23–45 seconds for the nostrils to open completely.

Schooling aggregations of wild loggerheads, both juveniles and adults, have been reported (see Dodd, 1988c). In captivity, however, some individuals may be very aggressive toward other *Caretta* and other species of sea turtles. Pope (1939) reported that Atlantic loggerheads kept at Beaufort, North Carolina, were gentle during the first two years of life, but later became decidedly aggressive and frequently fought each other and bit at any hand within reach. Caldwell (1963) found a Pacific loggerhead extremely pugnacious: it killed two *Chelonia mydas* kept in a dry pen with it. After a stay out of water of some 10 days—in the pen and during airplane and automobile rides—the turtle still bit at a stick placed near its mouth. Layne (1952) found evidence of possible territoriality in captive loggerheads. Usually each turtle occupied a particular corner of the tank while at rest, and once the regular occupant of a corner delivered a vicious snap at the head of another that attempted to occupy the same place.

Some captives do not seem overly aggressive; for example, one large individual freely allowed its head to be scratched. However, such action is not recommended with wild loggerheads, if you value your fingers. Perhaps captive aggression is fostered by restricted movement.

REPRODUCTION: Mature females from several nesting beaches have straight-line carapace lengths of at least 65.1–87.0 cm and average 79.2–96.4 cm; their body masses are 70.3–180.7 kg (average 100.7–118.2) (Dodd, 1988c). Females composing the Atlantic nesting population in the United States are morphologically uniform in carapace length, width, and depth (Stoneburner, 1980). Straight-line carapace lengths of mature males throughout the world are 75.2–104.1 cm (Dodd, 1988c). Inasmuch as these measurements were taken from obviously mature turtles, maturity is probably attained at a shorter carapace length, perhaps 60–70 cm (Hughes, 1974).

The age of maturity may also vary between populations, possibly owing to genetics, but more probably because of differential feeding and growth rates. Captives have been predicted to mature in 16–17 years (Frazer and Schwartz, 1984), and wild North American *Caretta* seem to reach mature size in 10–30 years (Mendonça, 1981; Frazer, 1983a; Zug et al., 1983, 1986; Frazer and Ehrhart, 1985) and may have a maximum reproductive life span of 32 years (Frazer, 1983a).

Limpus et al. (1982) reported that an Australian loggerhead with a male-like tail contained not only functional testes, but also oviductal-like tissues.

The physical changes occurring during the gonadal cycles of North American *Caretta* have not been adequately described for either sex, but some endocrine data are available. Data on the spermatogenic

cycle of males from Australia indicate that during January–March, the seminiferous tubules are involuted with only spermatogonia, or some primary spermatocytes and abundant secondary spermatocytes and early spermatids, and tubules have some spermatozoa in the lumen (Wibbels et al., 1990). Transforming spermatids and some spermatozoa are present in July, and from late July to October spermatids and spermatozoa are abundant, with maximal spermiogenesis from September to November. By the end of November spermatozoa are abundant, but spermatids and spermatocytes have become reduced in numbers. The spermatogenic cycle is coincident with increased concentrations of serum testosterone (Wibbels et al., 1987a, 1990), and serum testosterone is high during the months when migration and mating occur. This suggests an annual breeding cycle for males, but Wibbels et al. (1987a) reported that during certain months adult male loggerheads along the Atlantic Coast of the United States exhibit a wide range in titers of serum testosterone, suggesting that some are not sexually active all year. Reproductive North American males have high serum testosterone levels in February–April followed by a drop in titer during May.

Female *Caretta* may reproduce over a multiple of years (see below); however, according to Nat B. Frazer (pers. comm.), the phenomenon may not be cyclic, but possibly related to nutrition, as individuals "switch" from nesting in the second year to the third year or vice versa (such nutritional-driven female reproduction is well known in rattlesnakes of the genus *Crotalus*, where the females feed sparingly during the reproductive year and need the next year to replenish their fat and energy reserves before again bearing young; Ernst, 1992b). During a nesting year, females have hundreds of vitellogenic follicles about 1.5 cm in diameter four months prior to the nesting season (Wibbels et al., 1990). About four to six weeks before migrating to the nesting area, serum estradiol concentrations increase significantly and remain high for approximately four weeks, suggesting a period of increased vitellogenesis. During a one-to-two-week period prior to migration, serum estradiol levels decrease significantly, whereas serum testosterone increases at least until the time of migration; immature females have low serum testosterone levels throughout the year, and adult females sampled on the nesting beach have higher titers than those captured in the water the same months (Wibbels et al., 1987a). At ovulation the ovarian follicles are approximately 3.0 cm in diameter.

Serum testosterone, estradiol, and progesterone are elevated during nesting if the female will oviposit again during that season; surges of follicle-stimulating hormone, luteinizing hormone, and progesterone occur within 26–50 hours after oviposition (Wibbels et al., 1992). Emerging females have no detectable prostaglandins, but these become greatly elevated during nest excavation, and are further elevated during egg laying. Serum prostaglandins decline during the covering of the nest. This prostaglandin cycle may indicate an active role during oviposition consistent with the hypothesis that these stimulate uterine contractions and cervical relaxation (Guilette et al., 1991). Arginine vasotocin is low in females which are not reproductively active and at the time of emergence onto the nesting beach by reproductive females, but greatly increases during oviposition and then declines as the turtles return to the water (Figler et al., 1989). Neurophysin increases in concert with arginine vasotocin, also reaching the highest levels during oviposition, but does not decline as the turtle crawls back to the sea. Arginine vasotocin is a physiological regulator of oviducal contractions.

The prenuptial pattern of gonadal recrudescence and gonadal steroid production in both sexes of *Caretta* contrasts with those of many temperate freshwater turtles, and this type of reproductive pattern may have been facilitated by adaptation to a tropical marine environment (Wibbels et al., 1990).

Although Pritchard and Trebbau (1984) stated that "copulation takes place at the beginning of the nesting season," it may in fact occur several months before the turtles arrive at the nesting beach. Matings have been observed as early as 19 March off Sanibel Island, Florida (LeBuff, 1990), and have been recorded from late March to June elsewhere in North American waters (Caldwell, 1959; Fritts et al., 1983; Bearse, 1985; Henwood, 1987a). Mating only rarely takes place off the nesting beach (Dodd, 1988c), but most often in open water (Bearse, 1985), as females migrate through territories of resident males on their way to the nesting area (Limpus, 1985).

Courtship involves circling, a final approach from the rear, and neck or shoulder biting by the male (Limpus, 1985). Perhaps odors from Rathke's gland secretions bring the sexes together (Radhakrisna et al., 1989; Weldon et al., 1990; Weldon and Tanner, 1990; Rostal et al., 1991). Mating has been observed at every hour from dawn to dark but doubtless also occurs at night. Paired loggerheads may copulate for extended periods—for more than three hours according to Wood (1953)—and females may remate after each nesting (Harry and Briscoe, 1988). Mating usually occurs at the surface of the water. Although the female is completely or partially submerged, the highest part of the male's carapace usually is out of the water. He grasps the anterolateral rim of her carapace with the claw of each foreflipper and the posterolateral rim with the claw of each hind flipper. He sometimes bites the nape of her neck. His head surfaces every few minutes for breathing; she struggles to the surface about every five minutes. His tail is bent beneath hers, so that the cloacal openings touch. Behavior of the female during mating ranges from passive acceptance to violent resistance. Several males may contribute sperm to a single clutch of eggs; 33% of the clutches from the Mon Repos rookery, Australia, contained genotypic ratios indicating multiple parentage (Harry and Briscoe, 1988).

Caretta is the only species of marine turtle with a nesting range that lies mostly beyond the tropics. Nestings have been recorded from New Jersey (Brandner, 1983) south to Florida and west to Texas (Dodd, 1988c), but most of the North American breeding range lies in South Carolina, Georgia, and Florida. Other breeding beaches which possibly contribute loggerheads to Atlantic waters off the United States and Canada are located in Brazil, French Guiana, Surinam, Guyana, Venezuela, Colombia, Costa Rica, Nicaragua, Honduras, Guatemala, Belize, Mexico (Quintano Roo, Yucatán, Campeche, Tabasco, Veracruz, Tamaulipas), Trinidad, Tobago, Grenada, St. Lucia, Dominica, Antigua, Hispaniola, Cuba, Cayman Islands, Dry Tortugas, and the Bahamas (Dodd, 1988c; Pritchard, 1988). Depending on latitude, the Atlantic nesting season lasts from January to September, but the peak months are May through July. No nests have been recorded from the Pacific Coast of the United States, but loggerheads seen there may be from nesting beaches on Panama (and possibly adjacent Costa Rica) and Nicaragua (Cornelius, 1982). The nesting season in the eastern Pacific extends from May to December.

Nests are primarily excavated on continental beaches seaward from the dune front or, secondarily, island beaches. Nests are usually located above the high-tide line on open beaches, but sometimes even among the shrubs and grasses behind the beach. In Mississippi loggerheads have adopted man-made beaches as nest sites (Hoggard, 1991). Most females return to the same beach during successive seasons, but some do not possess such strong site fidelity and nest elsewhere (Bjorndal and Meylan, 1983; LeBuff, 1974, 1990).

In the United States, nesting has occurred at one-to-seven-year intervals (Richardson et al., 1978). The mean interval at Cumberland, Georgia, is 2.5 years, with 55.8% returning to nest after two years, 31.0%

after three years, 7% after four years, 2.9% in one year, and 1.7% in five years (Richardson et al., 1978). At Melbourne, Florida females returning in two to three years lay 81.4% of the clutches (Bjorndal and Meylan, 1983). Possibly, those recorded after four years were missed in the intervening seasons, nested elsewhere those seasons, or may have shifted intervals (Dix and Richardson, 1972). Hughes (1982) found so much irregularity (1–9 years) in Natal, Africa, that he thought no regular female reproductive cycle exists there. However, irregular cycles may be due to periods of female infertility (possibly due to a lack of mating); Seyle (1987) reported that a female that laid several fertile clutches in 1981 and 1986 produced four infertile clutches of 118–143 eggs each in 1984.

Most nests are dug at night, usually within four or five hours of sunset, but diurnal emergences do occur and may be of higher frequency than previously thought (Fritts and Hoffman, 1982). Female loggerheads come ashore more often at high tides on gently sloping beaches, but emergences are not related to tidal action on steep sloping beaches (Frazer, 1983b; Brooks and Webster, 1988). Beaches artificially illuminated by mercury vapor lights are used less than either unlighted beaches or those lighted by low-pressure sodium vapor lights (Witherington, 1992).

Several good descriptions of loggerhead nesting behavior have been published (Caldwell et al., 1959; Bustard, et al., 1975; Pritchard and Trebbau, 1984; Dodd, 1988c), and a ten-phase nesting ethogram has been proposed by Hailman and Elowson (1992). The following is a compilation of these.

When approaching the beach in shallow water, the female rests on the bottom and extends her head, possibly to view it. She is most sensitive to disturbance at this time, and if disturbed will quickly swim seaward. If not disturbed she swims directly to the beach and begins to ascend it, first pausing in the surf for 10–30 seconds then hauling herself up the beach with a synchronous movement of forelimb with the opposite hind limb. She frequently pauses, lies prostrate, and places her snout to the sand, sometimes plowing a furrow in it. This has thought to be for olfactory cues, but possibly she is measuring the temperature of the sand, as the beach temperature may be important in final nest site selection, sand temperatures of 19.4–22.7°C usually being selected (Stoneburner and Richardson, 1981). The female then elevates her head to a horizontal position, and she may move the head from side to side and raise and lower the throat. Ascent of the beach usually takes about seven minutes (2.0–13.5). Much wandering on the beach may occur before the proper site is located.

Next a body pit is constructed. The female uses all four flippers in this process until she has lowered herself several centimeters below the surface of the sand. Usually the head and foreflippers are still above the front of the pit and the carapace is well above the sides. This usually takes only 5–10 minutes, and digging of the actual nest follows almost immediately by the hind flippers working alternately. With its outer edge downward, one flipper is inserted into the sand or into the growing hole. It is then cupped, and the outer edge is rotated inwardly. A small amount of sand is now scooped up, lifted to the top of the hole, and deftly laid to one side. Meanwhile the opposing flipper remains flat, palm down on the sand near the edge of the hole. The turtle now shifts her body so this other flipper comes into position over the hole. Just before she inserts it into the hole to dig, she flicks it out laterally and upward to brush the loose sand, deposited when this flipper last excavated, away from the edge of the hole. The digging process is then repeated as the turtle shifts to bring the first flipper into play again. About 10–15 (3–29) minutes are needed to complete excavation of the egg chamber.

Almost as soon as the nest is finished (in about 15–20 seconds) the flippers are laid straight back or pointed slightly outward, palms down, and the everted cloaca is inserted. During the digging process the head is held flat on the sand and the eyes kept open, although blinking occasionally. The eyes secrete copiously during both digging and laying. Just before each group of eggs falls (in groups of 1–4 at 5–10-second intervals) the neck is arched with the head still down, and the hind flippers are curled upward. As each group of eggs falls, the neck is lowered to the position held during digging and the flippers come down and lie flat again between extrusions. During this interval, the head may be raised slightly, and the turtle may snort or sigh by expelling air from the nostrils or mouth. The female does not urinate into the cavity, but quite a bit of mucous accompanies the eggs as they are laid. Egg laying may take 6–25 minutes.

When the nest is filled with eggs the female rests for one to three minutes before covering it. Sand is drawn in by the hind flippers, usually working alternately, sometimes together. The outer edge of the flipper is used, the limb reaching well forward and out from the body to drag sand back to the hole. As filling proceeds, the front flippers join in sweeping sand backward to replenish that pushed into the nest cavity by the hind legs and, like the hind flippers, the front ones are used either alternately or together. When the hole is full of loose sand, the hind flippers press it down firmly. During the filling and packing process the head and front part of the body are sometimes raised as if to shift weight to the hind flippers and help them exert more force. Perhaps this shifting and raising of the body to increase pressure at the hind flippers accounts for the impression that the site is pounded, but females do not seem to pack or pound the nest with their plastra. Packing may take 10–15 minutes. As the filling reaches completion, the front flippers aided somewhat by the hind ones begin to fling sand backward. This increased exertion pivots the turtle on the pedestal of sand her digging leaves under her plastron. Twenty-five to 45 minutes may be spent filling the nest and body cavity.

As the turtle moves away from the site she raises her head high with the eyes still open, as they have been throughout the nesting process, and the hyoid apparatus becomes quite prominent as it moves in and out. When she leaves the nest, the actual nest is so camouflaged that the eggs are hard to find without the aid of a probing rod, but a disturbed path leading from the nest area is quite evident.

The return trip to the surf is usually made quickly (2–12 minutes) at a rate of a meter per 3.0–4.5 seconds. Although the head is slightly raised while the turtle drags herself along, on reaching the water she drops her head into it, and after a moment she raises it again before moving rapidly out of sight into the sea directly perpendicular to the beach.

The egg chamber is 15–25 cm deep, 20–25 cm wide, and somewhat flask shaped, being slightly wider at the bottom than at the top. The depth of the uppermost eggs in 317 nests was 13–56 cm with 67% of them between 28 and 41 cm (Caldwell, 1959).

A female may lay several clutches a season (see below) at intervals of 9–28 days (Dodd, 1988c), but more frequently at 11–15 days on North American beaches (Caldwell, 1962a; Ehrhart, 1982; Dodd, 1988c). As the water temperature increases over the nesting season, the internesting period may decrease; conversely subsequent internesting intervals may increase if a cold front decreases the water temperature (Nelson, 1988). Both mean annual clutch size and frequency vary yearly (Frazer and Richardson, 1985b), and some females tend to lay fewer eggs in later clutches each season (Frazer and Richardson, 1985a).

Between nestings females often migrate to natural or artificial reefs or estuaries where food is more abundant (Stoneburner, 1982). Internesting movements may be extensive, often over 100 km (Stoneburner, 1982), with a record of 725 km (Stoneburner and Ehrhart, 1981).

The spherical, white eggs have soft, leathery shells. Clutch size ranges from 23 to 198, 43 to 198 in North America (Dodd, 1988c), but most clutches laid in the United States probably contain 110–130 eggs (Ehrhart, 1982; LeBuff, 1990; Márquez, 1990). Two nest cavities found near Charleston, South Carolina, that contained 219 and 341 eggs, respectively (Caldwell, 1959), may have resulted from several females laying at the same place. Correlation between clutch size and female body size is positive (Frazer and Richardson, 1986).

One to seven clutches may be laid in a nesting season (Lenarz et al., 1981; Lund, 1986; Dodd, 1988c), but one to three clutches per season is more normal for North America females (Dodd, 1988c). Clutch frequency is not correlated with female body size (Frazer and Richardson, 1986).

The greatest diameter of normal fertile eggs is 34.7–55.2 mm, 35–55 mm in the United States (Caldwell, 1959; Dodd, 1988c; LeBuff, 1990; Márquez, 1990). Eggs weigh 26–47 g (Dodd, 1988c). A weak positive correlation exists between egg size and female size in Florida loggerheads (Ehrhart, 1982), but only a very weak positive relationship between egg size and oviposition date (Ehrhart, 1980). Total egg volume has a higher positive correlation with female size than with either clutch or egg size (Pinckney, 1990). Hays and Speakman (1991) found a positive correlation between the number of clutches into which eggs could be divided and the total time spend by a nesting female on the beach, therefore a negative correlation between time invested on the beach per egg and clutch size (Frazer, 1984, developed a rigorous model for predicting age-specific fecundity in sea turtle populations, particularly those of *Caretta,* to which we refer the reader).

The ideal soil moisture level for development of loggerhead eggs is 25%; far fewer eggs hatch at higher or lower levels of moisture. However, hatchling carapace length decreases significantly with increasing soil moisture (McGehee, 1990). Hatchling plastron lengths are greatest at 25% moisture, but much less at other levels. The average moisture content in natural nests of *Caretta* is about 18% (McGehee, 1990). This explains the high egg mortality witnessed after excessive rainfall by Kraemer and Bell (1980).

Most naturally incubated clutches have rather high hatching success, 60–85% (Dodd, 1988c), but those from which the eggs have been moved between the twelfth and fourteenth day and artificially incubated elsewhere can have hatching success reduced by 30–67% (Limpus et al., 1979). Inversion of the egg between the twelfth hour and fourteenth day after oviposition can cause high egg mortality (Limpus et al., 1979). If the eggs are relocated before the twelfth hour, mortality is greatly reduced, and, in such cases, artificially incubated clutches may actually have higher hatching success than undisturbed naturally incubated nests (Wyneken et al., 1988).

Caldwell (1959) discovered that 5.3% of the eggs laid among stands of the spike grass *Uniola paniculata* were destroyed by its roots. The root hairs formed thick mats around the individual eggs, eroded the shells, and desiccated them; often the sharp-pointed stolons pierced the eggs. A small number of the turtles that pipped their eggs were prevented from leaving the egg. Others escaped from the shell but were trapped in the nest, either because of their inability to climb through the tightly packed deposit of fractured eggshells and matted roots or because of their tendency to burrow horizontally into hard sand instead of perpendicularly to the surface. Other reasons for egg failure, other than predation, are infertility, bacterial or fungal invasion, erosion, desiccation, and flooding (Stancyk et al., 1980; Andre and West, 1981; Wyneken et al., 1988).

The incubation period for loggerhead eggs ranges from 46 to 80 days, depending on the incubating temperature, and from 49 to 76 days in the United States (Dodd, 1988c); most naturally incubated clutches probably hatch in about 60–65 days. Seven clutches collected and reburied within six hours on Little Cumberland Island, Georgia, had incubation periods of 59–78 days, with four producing hatchlings in 59–63 days; hatch success was 64–94%, the percentage of emergence, 74–100 (Christens, 1990). The increase in mass of embryonic *Caretta* with incubation period is sigmoidal, and depends on the incubating temperature (Ackerman, 1981b).

A volumetric reduction of nest contents occurs prior to hatching owing to loss of egg turgor (Kraemer and Richardson, 1979). The maximum depth of the air space thus created above the eggs is about 4 cm, and the amount of egg-mass reduction is significantly correlated to the number of hatchlings and full-term embryos in the nest but is not correlated with the number of eggs in the clutch. The rate of volumetric change varies seasonally, and is apparently related to temperature.

Hatchlings usually emerge at night, and their emergence seems cued to lower surface temperatures. A surface temperature greater than 28.5°C does not inhibit young *Caretta*, as it does *Chelonia* or *Eretmochelys* which remain underground (Neville et al., 1988). Once they leave the nest the hatchlings crawl immediately across the beach, with few interruptions, to the sea, often in a "frenzy"-like charge (Dial, 1987). This frenzy may last about four minutes and results in speeds averaging 6.5 m/minute, but results in a 22-fold increase in lactate concentration over resting level (Dial, 1987); obviously some anaerobic metabolism is occurring during the event. After hatching the relative amount of yolk is decreased considerably, but the hatching mass does not change appreciably as this yolk is absorbed; the yolk seems to function as an energy source to the hatchling as it digs out of the sand and crosses the beach (Kraemer and Bennett, 1981). The remaining yolk can probably support swimming activity for a few days after the *Caretta* enters the water.

Hatchling loggerheads have heart-shaped carapaces with three dorsal keels. Carapace color varies from yellowish brown or grayish black in Pacific populations to brown or reddish brown in hatchlings on Atlantic beaches. The plastron has two longitudinal ridges, and may be cream colored or gray with black and white mottling. In the United States, hatchlings have carapace lengths of 33.5–52.0 mm, carapace widths of 26.8–40.0 mm, and weights of 12.2–27.6 g (Dodd, 1988c). Carapace length may greatly decrease with increasing moisture above 25% in the nest, but carapace width and turtle mass are not affected (McGehee, 1990).

Caretta caretta has temperature-dependent sex determination (Yntema and Mrosovsky, 1979, 1980, 1982; Mrosovsky, 1980, 1988; Mrosovsky and Yntema, 1980; Limpus et al., 1983; Mrosovsky et al., 1984b; Standora and Spotila, 1985; Gouveia and Webster, 1988; Provancha and Mrosovsky, 1988; Paukstis and Janzen, 1990). The pivotal temperature is 29–30°C (Yntema and Mrosovsky, 1982; Mrosovsky, 1988); above this clutches produce a preponderance of females, and at incubation temperatures of 32–34°C clutches commonly contain only females. Incubation temperatures of 24–27°C produce mostly males with those at 24–26°C generally 100% males (Paukstis and Janzen, 1990). The critical embryonic period for sex determination is between stages 12 and 22 (Yntema and Mrosovsky, 1982). Developing 32°C females possess heterogeneous nuclear ribonucleic proteins in their urinogenital tissue until stage 25 that are not expressed in the developing 26°C male urinogenital tissue after stage 24 (Harry et al., 1990). Once sex has been determined, growth patterns differ for the male and female urinogenital tracts during embryonic stages 22–27 (Harry and Williams, 1991). Seasonal changes in the sex ratios of hatchlings from naturally incubated nests are consistent with the role of temperature-directed sexual differentiation. The sex ratio of nests from South Carolina and Georgia changes from no females in those laid in late May to 80% females in those laid in early July, and then decreases to about 10% females from clutches oviposited in early August (Mrosovsky et al., 1984b).

Hybridization is rare, but may occur; hybrid offsprings from *Eretmochelys* × *Caretta* crosses have been found in Japan and Brazil (Kamezaki, 1983; Conceição et al., 1990).

GROWTH AND LONGEVITY: Most growth data are based on captive juveniles. At one year of age laboratory raised captives averaged 18.4 cm in carapace length and 1.3 kg in weight (Witham and Futch, 1977). Parker (1929) kept a 4.8-cm, 20-g hatchling *C. c. caretta* for 4.5 years, during which it grew to 63 cm and 37 kg. Hildebrand and Hatsel (1927) reported that an Atlantic loggerhead, obtained as a yearling, grew in carapace length from 13.6 cm to 53.8 cm in 3.5 years. At age 4.5 years it weighed 20 kg; at 6 years, 27 kg. Smith (1968) reported that a young individual 6.4 cm in carapace length grew 4.2 cm in three months. Two captive hatchlings each grew 4.5 mm in 13 days. In a group of mixed juveniles one was 4.8 cm long about two weeks after hatching; others, 5.3–7.1 cm long, were approximately 11 weeks old; and one, 8.1 cm long, was about 13 weeks old (Caldwell et al., 1955b). Five Atlantic loggerheads 4.7–5.2 cm in length when hatched had a mean length increase of 2.2 cm in two months (Caldwell, 1962b). Hughes et al. (1967) reported that 2.5-year-old Pacific loggerheads were 20–25 cm in length.

Three *Caretta* confined in a fenced-off section of tidal creek in the Bahamas increased from 23.8 to 24.8 cm (2.2 kg) in carapace length to 67.0–75.0 cm (35.5–49.5 kg) in 35 months at growth rates of 14.8–17.2 cm/year and weight increases of 11.4–16.2 kg/year (Bjorndal and Bolten, 1988a). One of these turtles then grew from 68.5 cm (39.0 kg) to 81.0 cm (68.0 kg) in another 26 months (5.8 cm and 13.4 kg/year), and another, 75 cm (49.5 kg) long, increased to 78.8 cm (62.5 kg) in 10 more months (4.6 cm and 15.6 kg/year).

Wild *Caretta* from Florida studied by Mendonça (1981) had the following annual average growth rates: 50–60 cm, 7.4 cm; 60–70 cm, 6.0 cm; and 70–80 cm, 5.0 cm. A 29.0-cm juvenile grew 17 cm in about 39.5 months in the sea between captures (Bolten et al., 1990). Two tagged *Caretta* grew 1.9 cm and 3.0 cm and increased in weight 1.5 kg and 2.7 kg after 1.0 and 1.5 months foraging in the Delaware Bay, respectively, equating to an average growth rate

of approximately 2.0 cm and 1.5 kg/month during the summer (Eggers et al., 1992).

Several growth models for size or weight change in *Caretta* based either on logistic or von Bertalanffy equations have been proposed (Uchida, 1967; Hirth, 1982; Frazer, 1983a; Zug et al., 1983; Frazer and Ehrhart, 1983, 1985; Frazer and Schwartz, 1984); the reader is referred to these for details.

Caretta caretta has lived for 33 years (from 1898 to 1931) in the Vasco da Gama Aquarium, Lisbon, Portugal, and one lived at least 23 years and possibly 25 years at the Berlin Zoological Gardens (Flower, 1925). Nine Atlantic loggerheads were kept in captivity for more than 20 years at Marineland, in Florida (Ernst and Barbour, 1972). Dodd (1988c) estimated that the maximum life span of a wild female *Caretta* is 47–62 years.

FOOD HABITS: *Caretta* is omnivorous. It commonly noses about coral reefs, rocky places, and old boat wrecks for food. Invertebrates seem the most important food groups, and the loggerhead's large head and massive jaws seem well adapted for crushing hard-shelled prey. Prey consumed include: sponges, hydroids, jellyfish (including *Physalia*), polychaete worms, cephalopods (squid, cuttlefish), snails, whelks, conchs, pennshells, bivalves (clams, mussels, oysters, scallops), barnacles, amphipods, shrimp, crabs, brachiurans, isopods, insects, horseshoe crabs, bryozoans, sea urchins, basket stars, tunicates, fish (eggs, juveniles and adults—*Brevoortia, Ceratoscopelus, Diodon, Entelurus, Hippocampus, Macrorhamphosus, Sardinops, Scomber*), young turtles (*Caretta*), algae (*Ascophyllum, Sargassum, Ulothrix, Urospora*), and vascular plants (*Cymodocea, Thalassia, Zostera*); Van Nierop and Den Hartog (1984), Dodd (1988c), and Márquez (1990) give detailed lists of the invertebrate genera known to have been eaten by *Caretta*. Many of its prey species are bottom dwellers, but others (jellyfish) are probably taken in the water column. Juveniles feed on insects and marine invertebrates while residing in sargassum mats (Richardson and McGillivary, 1991).

Captive loggerheads grew slowly on a diet of 100% dry, prepared chow pellets, but the more herbivorous *Chelonia mydas* grew rapidly on this diet (Stickney et al., 1973).

Prey may be located either visually or by odor. Fehring (1972) successfully trained hatchling *Caretta* to discriminate between broadband hues to obtain food when spatial, intensity and other confounding cues were randomized with respect to the correct choice, so possibly colors play a role in prey recognition. Juveniles may also be imprinted to food odors (Steele et al., 1989).

Juvenile *Caretta* may use the enlarged, projecting scale points on the anterior margin of the forelimb to manipulate food (Davenport and Clough, 1985). These "pseudoclaws" have two feeding functions: (1) they may be used as a saw to tear food held in the mouth but too large to swallow whole; (2) small pieces of food material may adhere to the pseudoclaws after they have been used to tear apart large pieces; hatchlings eat such small pieces by turning the head sideways and cleaning off the pseudoclaw row of that forelimb.

The rate of digestion is temperature dependent in *Caretta* (Birse and Davenport, 1987). Total time for a food bolus to pass through a loggerhead's digestive tract decreases with increasing temperature (Q_{10} = 1.6). Digestive clearance is 33 hours less in juvenile turtles kept at 25°C than in those kept under 20°C; but a further reduction of only six hours occurs in turtles maintained at 30°C. At 25 and 30°C the satiation ratio is about 3.7% of body weight, but at 20°C it is only 0.9%. The ratio of intestine length to carapace length increases with age: hatchling *Caretta* have a ratio of 3.32, whereas that of subadults and adults is 8.55 (Bjorndal, 1985).

PREDATORS AND DEFENSE: Many animals feast on loggerhead eggs: ants (*Solenopsis*), sand crabs (*Ocypode*), crows (*Corvus*), hogs (*Sus*), armadillos (*Dasypus*), raccoons (*Procyon*), dogs (*Canis*), foxes (*Urocyon*) and humans are known nest robbers (Caldwell, 1959; Ernst and Barbour, 1972; Richardson, 1978; Dodd, 1988c; Nelson, 1988; Drennen et al., 1989; LeBuff, 1990), and snakes (*Coluber*), opossums (*Didelphis*), bears (*Ursus*), skunks (*Mephitis*), cats (*Felis, Lynx*) and rats (*Rattus*) are potential predators in the southeastern United States (LeBuff, 1990). Nest predation rates vary per beach and season, but may be very high where the raccoon, the major egg predator, is common. Hatchlings crossing the beach are eaten by ghost crabs, snakes (*Masticophis*), crows (*Corvus*), gulls (*Larus*), frigate birds (*Fregata*), kites (*Milvus*), vultures (*Coragyps*), rats (*Rattus*), raccoons, mongooses (*Atilax*), dogs, and possibly herons (*Ardea, Nyctanassa, Nycticorax*) (Caldwell, 1959; Ernst and Barbour, 1972; Pritchard and Trebbau, 1984; Dodd, 1988c; Nelson, 1988; LeBuff, 1990). Once in the water hatchlings find sharks (*Carcharhinus, Galeocerdo*), other large fish (*Caranx, Coryphaena, Centropomus, Centropristes, Lutjanus, Sphyraena*), and gulls (*Larus*) ready to devour them (Caldwell, 1959; Brongersma, 1972; Witham, 1974; Rudloe, 1980; Stancyk, 1982; Dodd, 1988c;

Nelson, 1988; Collard and Hansknecht, 1990; LeBuff, 1990). On the beach adult females are killed by dogs (*Canis*) and humans, and pestered by salt marsh mosquitoes (*Aedes*) (Day and Curtis, 1983). In the water juveniles, subadults, and adult *Caretta* may be attacked by sharks (*Carcharhinus, Carcharodon, Galeocerdo*), killer whales (*Orcinus*), and humans (Caldwell, 1959; Brongersma, 1972; Ernst and Barbour, 1972; Balasz, 1979b; Dodd, 1988c; Nelson, 1988; LeBuff, 1990; Márquez, 1990; Small and Ragan, 1991). As many as 40% of nesting females exhibit wounds presumably from shark attacks (LeBuff, 1990).

Unmolested *Caretta* are shy, and if encountered in the ocean either dive or try to swim away. However, if they are trapped while crossing the beach, or if an attempt is made to haul them into a boat, some adults may be quite aggressive, flailing their forelimbs and biting. A bite from their massive jaws can cause severe damage.

POPULATIONS: *Caretta caretta* remains the most populous sea turtle in North American waters, but an accurate estimate of the total population is difficult as most numerical data concern only nesting females. Ross (1982) reported that the approximate number of nesting females in the southeastern United States, where over 90% of nesting in North America occurs (Murphy and Hopkins-Murphy, 1984), varies annually from 6,000 to 25,000. Estimated nesting densities on Atlantic Florida beaches range from 35.7 to more than 300 nests/km; probably 20,000 clutches are laid each year (Dodd, 1988c).

The adult sex ratio of *Caretta* is unknown as males seldom come onto the beaches, but a 1:1 ratio would indicate that 12,000–50,000 adults are involved in the nesting populations from Cumberland Island and Cape Romain south to the Atlantic beaches of central Florida. If the adult sex ratio is one male for every two females, as has been used in some models of population dynamics (Hughes, 1974), the adult population would be 9,000–37,500. This estimate does not include those turtles involved in sporadic nesting northward along the Atlantic Coast or along the Gulf Coast, or the number of females that nest on the islands off Florida's Gulf Coast. Fritts et al. (1983) reported that 1,715 (96%) of the 1,791 turtles observed in aerial surveys of coastal waters in the Gulf of Mexico and nearby Atlantic Ocean were loggerheads, and Rabalais and Rabalais (1980) reported that 202 (78%) of the 259 sea turtles stranded along 208 km of the south Texas coast were *Caretta*. From 1979 to 1986, 1,024 (91%) of the 1,124 identifiable sea turtles in the Chesapeake Bay were *Caretta*

(Keinath et al., 1987) and from 1976 to 1981, 205 (50.2%) of 408 marine turtles observed in the Indian River Lagoon system, Florida, were loggerheads (Ehrhart, 1983). Mendonça and Ehrhart (1982) estimated that 253 (65.7%) of 388 sea turtles using Mosquito Lagoon, Brevard and Volusia counties, Florida, were *Caretta* (mostly juveniles); the population density was 4.2/km².

For the most part, the above population figures do not include juveniles, so *Caretta caretta* may be our least threatened species of cheloniid. This is deceiving, however, because in the western Atlantic the United States is the major nesting area, and other beaches that could supply individuals to our waters probably have fewer than a maximum of 500 ovipositing females visit them each year (Ross, 1982). Further, there has been a slow but steady decline in the numbers of females returning to nest on some of the more important beaches, such as Cumberland and Little Cumberland islands, Georgia, over the last quarter of a century (Talbert et al., 1980; Richardson and Richardson, 1982; Dodd, 1988c; National Research Council, 1990). The causes of the decline are discussed below.

The size and age classes of loggerhead populations are difficult to calculate, as they may vary seasonally (Henwood, 1987a). Those about the nesting beaches are mostly large adults, whereas at some feeding areas juveniles predominate (Mendonça and Ehrhart, 1982). The largest groups of loggerheads caught in trawls off Cape Canaveral, Florida, have 60–80-cm carapaces, with those 90–105 cm long second most numerous, and turtles less than 45 cm are absent (Henwood, 1987a). Most turtles stranded in the Chesapeake Bay are 60–90 cm curved length (Lutcavage and Musick, 1985), and along the south Texas coast those 50–93 cm predominate, with most smaller than 76 cm (Rabalais and Rabalais, 1980). In New England waters, 2,200–11,000 *Caretta* may be present each summer at a density of about 21.6 turtles/1,000 km of shoreline (Shoop and Kenney, 1992).

Sparse data are available on sex ratios. Henwood (1987a) recorded a 1.16:1.00 male to female ratio for 586 adult loggerheads caught in trawls off the Atlantic coast of Florida, and Limpus (1985) reported adult sex ratios in Australia favoring males by as much as 2.4–7.0:1.0; but Wibbels et al. (1987b) calculated an adult ratio of 1.94 females per male at Cape Canaveral, Florida.

The sex ratio of hatchling *Caretta* is determined by the incubation temperature (see above), and may vary seasonally. Sex ratios of hatchlings taken from beaches in South Carolina and Georgia ranged from 100%

males in nests laid in late May to 80% females in those laid in early July, and back to 90% males for early August nests (Mrosovsky et al., 1984b). At Cape Canaveral, over 93% of the hatchlings produced in 1986 were females (Mrosovsky and Provancha, 1989). The ratios are consistent with sand temperature and depth of nests; in 1986 most sand temperatures were in the female range for sex determination. Mrosovsky and Provancha (1989) point out that turtles in which high incubation temperatures produce females will have difficulty overcoming the feminizing effect of global warming. A sample of 256 immature *Caretta* captured at four locations along the Atlantic Coast had a pooled sex ratio of 1.94 females per male, significantly skewed toward females (Wibbels et al., 1987b).

Inasmuch as the overall population of *Caretta* in North American waters is decreasing, mortality must be outpacing survivorship. Estimates of an egg surviving on a North American beach range from 3 to 90%; annual juvenile survivorship is 43–94%, and that of adult females, 81% (Iverson, 1991a). Frazer (1986) estimated the survivorship rate for a loggerhead from egg through adulthood is only 0.09–0.18% at Little Cumberland Island, Georgia, and that a value of 0.25% is needed to maintain the population at a stationary level. He later estimated the annual survivorship of wild juveniles 8–16 years old to be 69.5% (Frazer, 1987). From 1974 to 1979, loggerhead stranding mortality on the beach at Cumberland Island increased annually from approximately 20 turtles to 187, with most mortality in subadults and juveniles (Ruckdeschel and Zug, 1982). At these survivorship rates, adult females have a reproductive life of only four years, and within two three-year reproductive cycles most nesting populations will turn over completely. Any age class of loggerheads contributes to its species' success as a result not only of its reproductive value (for instance, adults higher than immatures), but also of its differential rate of survival and growth rate, both of which are greater in the larger juvenile classes (Crouse, 1989); therefore this group should probably be given the most protection (Crouse et al., 1987).

Several mortality factors have contributed to the steady loss of loggerheads (Dodd, 1988c). Anything that interrupts the nesting act ultimately reduces recruitment into the population, and along the Atlantic coast of the southeastern United States increased development for home sites and recreational areas has brought about additional stress on nesting females. Some beaches have been physically altered, human beach activity has increased (although actual egg poaching has probably decreased), and many nesting areas are now subject to additional lighting pressures; all of these may cause females to return to the water without ovipositing. Eggs now contain insecticide residues and breakdown products and increased heavy metal concentrations (Clark and Krynitsky, 1980, 1985; Stoneburner et al., 1980; McKim and Johnson, 1983). With increased human development has come an increase in some nest predators, particularly the raccoon whose coastal populations have grown tremendously in the last 30 years. Increased rainfall on some beaches has raised the egg mortality rate, and recent severe hurricanes in the Carolina-Georgia region may have damaged some good nesting areas, and, if true, the current trend in global warming could skew sex ratios toward all females. Besides natural predation, some adults are still taken for food. Others may be killed by collisions with the increased boat traffic. Many are drowned in shrimp trawls and other nets (Ogren et al., 1977; Lipske, 1979; Talbert et al., 1980; Shoop and Ruckdeschel, 1982; Thompson, 1989; Caillouet et al., 1991), and channel dredging (particularly using a vacuum) also results in some mortality. Offshore blasting at oil rigs may be a mortality or disturbance factor, and pollution certainly is, particularly that resulting from oil spills or the dumping of clear plastic refuge, which may be mistaken for jellyfish and swallowed. Natural mortality may also increase with the incidence of poisonous red tides. Loggerhead populations from South Carolina, Georgia, and Florida have relatively low genetic variability which may further reduce their chances of survivorship (Smith et al., 1977).

Caretta caretta was listed as threatened under the Endangered Species Act in 1978.

REMARKS: Morphological and blood protein studies by Zangerl (1958) and Frair (1979, 1982) indicate that *Caretta* is more closely related to *Lepidochelys* and *Eretmochelys* than to *Chelonia*.

Summaries of the biology and literature of *Caretta caretta* are found in Dodd (1987, 1988c, 1990b,c), Nelson (1988), and LeBuff (1990).

Lepidochelys kempii (Garman, 1880)
Kemp's ridley or Atlantic ridley
PLATE 6

RECOGNITION: Kemp's ridley has a maximum carapace length of 74.9 cm, two pairs of prefrontals, four pairs of pore-bearing inframarginals on the bridge, and five pleurals (rarely more or less) on each side of the carapace. The heart-shaped, grayish-green carapace commonly is wider than long in adults, is highest anterior to the bridge and serrated behind, and has a series of three to five raised middorsal knobs, which become proportionally lower with age until totally absent in some old adults. The first pair of pleurals touch the cervical, and 12–14 marginals are present on each side. The bridge and the hingeless plastron are immaculate white, and the head and the paddlelike limbs are gray. The head is wide and somewhat pointed anteriorly, with a short, broad snout and a distinctly hooked upper jaw. The bony alveolar surface of the upper jaw has a conspicuous ridge running parallel to the cutting edge.

Males have long prehensile tails which extend beyond the posterior carapacial rim, a thick curved claw on each forelimb, and soft, slightly concave plastra. The female tail, which is less developed, barely extends beyond the carapacial rim; she lacks recurved claws on the forelimbs, and her plastron is flat and ridged.

KARYOTYPE: The karyotype has not been described, but presumably involves 56 chromosomes as in other members of the Cheloniidae (Bickham, 1981).

FOSSIL RECORD: The only possible fossils of *Lepidochelys kempii* are from the Pliocene (early Hemphillian) Bone Valley Formation of Polk County, Florida (Dodd and Morgan, 1992). An archeological record from an Indian Mound in Palm Beach County, Florida, was reported by Johnson (1952).

DISTRIBUTION: Adult *Lepidochelys kempii* are rarely found beyond the limits of the Gulf of Mexico, and are most frequently sighted off southwestern Florida but only occasionally observed in the western Gulf. Juveniles have been reported from Bermuda, Nova Scotia, Newfoundland, Ireland, the Scilly Isles, Great Britain, France, Netherlands, Morocco, Malta, the Azores, Cameroon, and Venezuela (Brongersma, 1972; Ernst and Barbour, 1972; Pritchard and Márquez, 1973; Chavez and Kaufmann, 1974; Wibbels, 1983; Fontaine et al., 1988; Wilson and Zug, 1991), and regularly occur in Long Island Sound, New York (Morreale et al., 1992). An adult has nested on a beach in Colombia, but Pritchard and Trebbau (1984) consider this a misidentified *L. olivacea,* and some of the other extralimital records may really be *L. olivacea.* Some adults and juveniles visit the east coast of Florida (Ehrhart, 1983) and juveniles regularly migrate to the Chesapeake Bay, Long Island Sound, and New England coast (Lazell, 1980; Keinath et al., 1987; Burke et al., 1991).

GEOGRAPHIC VARIATION: No subspecies have been described.

CONFUSING SPECIES: *Lepidochelys olivacea* is olive colored and commonly has more than five pairs of pleurals on each side of the carapace. *Chelonia mydas* and *Eretmochelys imbricata* have only four pleurals on each side of the carapace, with the first not touching the cervical. *Caretta caretta* has only three inframarginals in the bridge and is reddish brown.

HABITAT: Kemp's ridley prefers shallow water, 11–409 m deep, usually less than 50 m deep (Fritts et al., 1983). In the Florida Keys it is closely associated with the subtropical shoreline of red mangrove. Young *Lepidochelys kempii* may use sargassum mats or sea-grass mats for refugia and foraging (Manzella and Williams, 1991).

Lepidochelys kempii

Plastron of *Lepidochelys kempii*

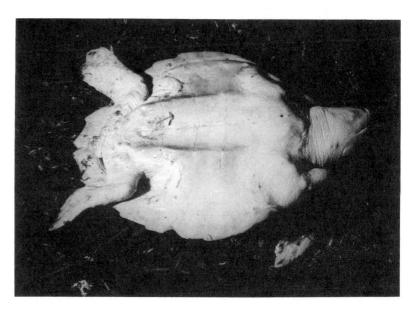

BEHAVIOR: Although *Lepidochelys kempii* has been extensively studied the last 20 years, we still know very little of its behavioral characteristics and ecology.

Oviposition occurs from April to July and mating probably occurs off the nesting beach at this time. After the nesting season adults of both sexes migrate to the principle feeding areas in the Gulf of Mexico off Louisiana and Campeche, Mexico, and remain there until the next reproductive season. Some Kemp's ridleys possibly hibernate on the bottom during the winter.

The daily cycle is largely unknown, but must include foraging and sleeping periods. Nights are presumably spent sleeping on the bottom, such as occurs in captives (Wood and Wood, 1988). Captives at the Cayman Turtle Farm, Cayman Islands, occasionally come onto the beach, cover themselves with sand and seemingly sleep for up to eight hours, both during the night and day (Wood and Wood, 1988).

Lepidochelys kempii

Parrish (1958) reported that captives sleep with their eyes open and are never seen with their eyes more than half-closed.

Kemp's ridleys are vulnerable to cold water temperatures (Ross et al., 1989). Schwartz (1978) kept *Lepidochelys kempii* in a large outdoor tank from November to March during the winters of 1968–1976. The turtles responded to the cold water by bobbing to the surface tail first, then horizontally when water temperatures dropped below 10°C, but some individuals could still swim and dive in water above 10°C. Individuals larger than 300-cm carapace length died at 6.5°C within 20–24 hours; smaller ridleys tolerated 5.0°C before expiring. *L. kempii* in waters generally north of 29° latitude must migrate south before the critical water temperature of 10°C is reached. If not, they become cold-stunned and either sink to the bottom to die or float onto the beach and are stranded. Such events have been recorded in Florida (Ehrhart, 1983; Witherington and Ehrhart, 1989), Long Island Sound (Meylan and Sadove, 1986; Burke et al., 1991; Morreale et al., 1992), and Cape Cod Bay (Danton and Prescott, 1988). Most turtles involved were immatures. As long as bottom water temperatures do not drop below 7°C, *L. kempii*, although dormant (hibernating?), may possibly survive until the next spring. *L. kempii* is capable of closing its nostrils underwater. Closure occurs part way within each nostril, and is effected by the meeting of bulges from the laterodorsal and medioventral walls of the nasal passages (Walker, 1959). It takes *L. kempii* approximately two years to acquire the blood

oxygen system needed to allow it to remain on the bottom for extended periods (Davis, 1991).

Adult female *Lepidochelys kempii* after ovipositing at their major nesting beach at Rancho Nuevo, Tamaulipas, Mexico, seldom leave the Gulf of Mexico, but do migrate close to shore either northeastward to the Gulf Coast of the United States from Louisiana east to the Florida Keys or south along the Mexican coast as far as Campeche (Chavez, 1969; Pritchard and Márquez, 1973; Zwinenberg, 1977). These trips may involve swimming great distances. The longest recorded migration by a tagged female was 5,400 km from Rancho Nuevo to the coast of Colombia, a rare event because the turtle left the Gulf of Mexico and crossed the western Caribbean (Zwinenberg, 1977). Zwinenberg (1977) reported seven additional long migrations (>1,000 km); one of 1,060 km to Campeche took only 33 days, and another of 1,311 km to Louisiana took 64 days. Atlantic ridleys are capable of migratory rates of 20–32 km per day.

Hatchling *Lepidochelys kempii* also make long journeys, and are essentially pelagic for about two years. Once across the narrow continental shelf off Rancho Nuevo they are caught up in the western boundary current of the Gulf of Mexico formed by anticyclonic eddies derived from the main Loop Current and transported eastward to the Loop Current (Collard, 1990; Collard and Ogren, 1990). Eventually those caught in this current are swept out of the Gulf of Mexico through the Florida Straits and carried northward by the Florida Current and Gulf Stream (Ogren, 1989). If, however, they are caught in a Loop

Current eddy, the hatchlings may remain in the northeastern Gulf, or be carried back to the central-southwestern Gulf. The size distribution of post-pelagic juveniles suggests the smallest individuals found in coastal waters off western Louisiana and the Florida Panhandle have spent two years in the Gulf of Mexico. Intermediate-size postpelagic ridleys are found in Long Island Sound and off New England, and the largest juveniles occur along the Atlantic coast of Florida (Henwood, 1987b; Ogren, 1989). Once swept by the northward Atlantic currents to the Northeast, these turtles must actively migrate southward before winter.

When the immature *Lepidochelys kempii* enter the Gulf of Mexico, they move randomly relative to geographical and wind direction, but nonrandomly to current directions (Wibbels, 1984). Although displaced by a current, the turtles tend to swim against it, canceling the effects of the current. Three- to seven-month-old Kemp's ridleys in a lagoon orientation arena swam randomly relative to shore position and the brightest direction, but they too swam against the current (Wibbels, 1984).

Studies of sea-finding behavior by hatchlings indicates that they have a phototropic orientation mechanism toward brightness, but they also seem to use an unidentified orientation mechanism that does not rely on light intensity as a cue (Wibbels, 1984). Preliminary studies in a planetarium by Fontaine et al. (1985) using hatchlings that had never seen the stars showed that they had a particular preference for the western half of the test sky as compared with the eastern half, but whether or not this represents celestial orientation could not be determined.

How females find their way back to the narrow nesting beach in Tamaulipas, Mexico, is uncertain, but hatchlings may detect differences in natural water samples and remember olfactory cues to which they were exposed neonatally (Grassman et al., 1984: Owens et al., 1985; Grassman and Owens, 1989). Such imprinting may affect their orientation behavior, and, as adults, they may possibly use chemoreception to navigate to the beach on which they were hatched.

REPRODUCTION: Mature females ovipositing at Rancho Nuevo, Tamaulipas, Mexico, are at least 60 cm in carapace length (Chavez, 1967; Pritchard and Márquez, 1973), but Márquez (1990) thought the minimum carapace length for female maturity could be 52.5 cm. The size at which male *Lepidochelys kempii* mature is unknown, as are also the gametic cycles of both sexes. Captives of both sexes have gained maturity in five to seven years (Wood and Wood, 1988), but wild individuals may need 10–12 years to mature (Márquez, 1990; Zug, 1991a).

Courtship and mating occur shortly before nesting, at the surface of the water just off the beaches, and the males are quite active at this time. Carr (1967a) reported that one even followed a nesting female onto the beach and attempted to mount her all the way. Chavez et al. (1968b) observed a copulating pair at 1100 hours off Rancho Nuevo where copulation begins in early April (Pritchard and Márquez, 1973), and Shaver (1992) reported a noon mating off Texas that occurred in early June. At the Cayman Turtle Farm, Cayman Islands, captive April matings were observed by Wood and Wood (1984, 1988) that lasted 129–139 minutes. Typically, a male pursued a female, circled to approach her head, and then bit her neck and shoulders. Next he swung his body to bring his tail near that of the female while continuing to bite her. Using the claws in his front flippers, the male secured a hold on the anterior rim of the female's carapace, while his rear flippers were placed over her posterior carapacial rim. Insertion soon followed. Shaver's (1992) description of the wild mating, although brief, is similar.

Both sexes have Rathke's glands which open at the pores on the bridge and produce a secretion containing various glycoproteins and lipids, but not glycogen (Radhakrisna et al., 1989; Weldon et al., 1990; Rostal et al., 1991; Weldon and Cannon, 1992). These glands are particularly active in young turtles, but also function in mature adults of both sexes (Rostal et al., 1991), and, although the prime function of the secretion may be antipredator, the chemical produced may also serve to bring the mature sexes together.

Almost 100% of the nests are dug on or near the beach at Rancho Nuevo, but scattered nesting has also been reported from beaches in Veracruz, Tabasco, and Campeche, Mexico (Pritchard and Márquez, 1973; Zwinenberg, 1977; Ross et al., 1989), Colombia (Zwinenberg, 1977; Ross et al., 1989), Padre Island, Texas (Anon., 1991), Pinellas County, Florida (Meylan et al., 1990b,c), and Georgetown County, South Carolina (Anon., 1992b). Kemp's ridley has also attempted to nest in Palm Beach County, Florida (Fletemeyer, 1990).

Before Hurricane Gilbert scoured the beach at Rancho Nuevo, most nesting occurred on approximately 18 km of the beach, but particularly on one 1–2-km stretch; however, after the storm the beach was much more gravelly and rocky, forcing the turtles to extend the primary nesting area more than 15 km northward.

The nesting season at Rancho Nuevo usually lasts from mid-April to mid-July, with the peak period in May and June (Hirth, 1980a). Nesting is usually diurnal; Chavez et al.(1968b) reported that it takes place between 0825 and 1825, but a few females may lay their eggs at night.

Females return to the nesting beaches every one to three years, with most ovipositing annually or every two years. One to four (mean 1.4; Márquez, 1990) clutches are laid each season at intervals of 10–49 days, but usually 20–28 days (Ernst and Barbour, 1972; Pritchard and Márquez, 1973; Hirth, 1980a; Wood and Wood, 1988; National Research Council, 1990). Upon returning to the sea between nestings females make random movements for one or two days, after which they make rapid, directed longshore movements for at least 10 km north or south of the nesting site, but possibly up to 100 km (Mendonça and Pritchard, 1986).

Some females come up to nest individually, but most do so in large groups, formerly involving thousands of individuals, but now only a few hundred. The turtle traffic was once so dense at the place of maximum emergence that the eggs laid by one female were often dug up by a later-nesting female. At the time of nesting the ridleys gather offshore from the nesting beaches in groups that Carr (1967a) has termed arribadas (Spanish, "arrivals"). These gatherings usually take place during a time of strong wind from the northeast and heavy surf, but they may also occur at full moon, and ambient temperatures may play a role in their formation (Casas-Andreu, 1978). Group nesting is inherent, and arribadas are also formed by *Lepidochelys olivacea*. Arribadas also occur in captivity (Wood and Wood, 1988).

The ideal nesting beach for this species is broad, with relatively low-amplitude tides, white sand, and a well-defined or elevated vegetated dune area behind it (Pritchard and Márquez, 1973).

The nests are dug in fine sand, either on the beach or on the dunes, at distances of 5–60 m from the water (Pritchard and Márquez, 1973). On the nesting beach at Tamaulipas the sea is to the east, so females leaving the water travel in a westerly direction, and even while they deposit their eggs they keep their heads pointed toward the west. When they have finished nesting they generally turn counterclockwise—that is, they start toward the left, or south—until they face the water; then they return to the sea (Chavez et al., 1968b).

Chavez et al. (1968b) observed a female leave the water at 1234 hours. She crawled, using an alternate sequence of limbs, in a more or less diagonal direction toward the dunes. On the way she stopped 11 times,

apparently to rest. Sometimes while crawling she slightly buried the front of her jaw, apparently to test the texture of the sand. She reached the base of a dune at 1242; there she stopped, buried her jaw in the sand, and, while moving her head from side to side, began digging with her front flippers until a shallow body pit was excavated. She then began to dig the nest, alternately using the posterior flippers, the outer edges of which were curled so as to lift out the sand; the front flippers were at this time buried firmly in the ground for balance. When the nest was deep enough she lifted the forepart of her body, burying the flippers even deeper. At 1257, she finished the 41-cm excavation and, keeping her hind flippers on the sand, started to lay a clutch of 106 eggs. Most of the time two or three eggs fell together, but sometimes only one, and at intervals a clear, viscous liquid was secreted over the eggs. While she was depositing the eggs the turtle lifted her head and expanded the hyoid apparatus; her mouth remained slightly open and at times a sound was produced by the exhaled air. From the beginning of nesting she kept her eyes almost completely closed; a lachrymal fluid was secreted from them. She finished laying at 1309 and immediately began to cover the nest. When it was almost filled she began to press down by dipping (pounding) the sides of her body, alternately producing a sound, and at intervals she threw more sand with her hind limbs. The nest was completely covered at 1315. Then she turned to the left (south), made a complete turn to face the sea, and departed. On the way she stopped five times, finally arriving at the water at 1322. Her stay on the beach lasted exactly 48 minutes.

Body pits are normally only 10–15 cm deep. The nest is flask shaped; its surface diameter is 26–33 cm, but the cavity widens a few centimeters toward the bottom. The maximum depth is 37–49 cm, and the depth from the surface to the level of the eggs is 11–38 cm. The temperatures of eight nests, recorded after nesting, were 23–30°C (Chavez et al., 1968b).

The spherical eggs have soft white shells containing a thin calcareous layer in which the basic units are about twice as wide as tall and spherulitic (Hirsch, 1983). These units are loosely arranged and commonly do not touch each other, and the shell membrane is 1.5–2.0 times thicker than the heights of these basic units. The eggshell structure suggests it will expand considerably with water absorption or collapse during dehydration. Chavez et al. (1968b) reported that after being buried in the sand for two days the shell becomes even softer and dark spots appear on the embryonic side.

Clutch size varies from 51 to 185 eggs, with most

nests containing 100–110 eggs (Chavez et al., 1968b; Pritchard and Márquez, 1973). The first clutch laid per season usually contains the most eggs; succeeding clutches normally are composed of fewer and fewer eggs. Possibly older females may lay larger clutches. A 61.8-cm female laid 118 eggs and when dissected was found to contain 258 large oviducal eggs (diameters 26.0–31.2 mm) and 11 smaller eggs (12.9–16.6 mm) (Chavez et al., 1968b). Newly matured females (5–7 years old; curved carapace length, 48–57 cm) at the Cayman Turtle Farm laid only 11–103 egg clutches with a hatching rate of only 5–45% per clutch (Wood and Wood, 1988).

Egg diameter is 34.6–45.5 mm (mean, 39) and weight 24.1–41.0 g (mean, 30). The incubation period is usually 45–60 days, but some transported clutches have taken as long as 70 days to hatch. Hatching success of clutches in beach nests is 43.0–95.5% (usually 65–75%). If the eggs are removed to hatching corrals or various types of boxes, the hatching success may be as low as 5–25% or as high as 95%, but usually averages 50–60% (Chavez et al., 1968b; Pritchard and Márquez, 1973; Zwinenberg, 1977; Weedy, 1981; Márquez, 1983; Márquez et al., 1987).

Chavez et al. (1968b) removed almost 30,000 eggs from 271 nests within 48 hours of their being laid and reburied them in a protected part of the beach. After an incubation period of 50–70 days 1,664 hatched. Most hatching occurred after 53–56 days, and all took place between 0517 and 0850; 87% occurred before 0700. Hatchings took place in any kind of weather—even when it was raining or a strong wind was blowing. Two or three days before hatching the upper and central parts of the nests sank, producing a circular depression about 5 cm deep. From 27 to 31 hatchlings were seen emerging from a nest at intervals of 30–40 minutes, and some left the same nest on different days.

Lepidochelys kempii has temperature-dependent sex determination like other species of the Cheloniidae (Shaver et al., 1988). All clutches incubated in styrofoam chests at mean temperatures exceeding 30.8°C during the midtrimester of the incubation period produce only females, and those at 30°C produce 83.0–99.6% females. Clutches with an average incubation temperature of 28°C result in only about 28% females. Using estimates based on these figures, Shaver et al. (1988) predicted that clutches undergoing their middle third of incubation early in the nesting season at Rancho Nuevo would produce primarily males, later parts of the season primarily females, and the middle of the nesting season a mixture of sexes. Standora and Spotila (1985) had previously proposed this pattern for *L. kempii*. This species also contains sex-specific DNA with replicates of the male Bkm satellite of DNA in male chromatin (Demas et al., 1990).

Hatchlings have relatively elongated, oval carapaces with three tuberculate keels and a plastron with four longitudinal ridges. The inframarginal pores are already developed. The little turtles are dark gray to black, with a white border on both the flippers and the carapace. The measurements and weights of 124 examined by Chavez et al. (1968a) were as follows: carapace length, 38–46 mm (Zwinenberg, 1977, reported a 50-mm hatchling, and Carr, 1987, a 20.9-mm individual); carapace width, 30–40 mm; plastron width, 27–41 mm; head length, 17–22 mm; and weight, 13.5–21.0 g. In the hatchlings they examined, the carapace always was longer than wide—the opposite of the usual condition in adults. The mean length of the foreflippers was 38.9 mm (33–44) and that of the hind flippers was 26.0 mm (20–31). The front flippers are proportionately longer than those of adults.

The first two years of life are apparently spent drifting about the Gulf of Mexico in floating patches of sargassum weed (Fontaine et al., 1988; Manzella et al., 1991).

GROWTH AND LONGEVITY: *Lepidochelys kempii* has one of the fastest growth rates of all sea turtles. In captivity, some juveniles fed high-protein foods can grow as much as 20 cm in 10 months (Klima and McVey, 1982), but total growth is usually less. Captives kept by Márquez (1972) grew 87 mm their first year, 117 mm the second, and 111 mm the third. In 23 days hatchlings measured and weighed by Casas-Andreu (1971) grew approximately 6 mm and increased more than 4 g in weight. At capture a Kemp's ridley was 260 mm long and weighed 3,178 g, but after 316 days on a cut-fish diet it had increased 45 mm in length and 1,589 g in weight, and had changed from wider than long to longer than wide. Another measured 279 mm and weighed 2,838 g at capture. After 330 days on a cut-fish diet it had increased only 15 mm and 1,362 g. Almost exactly a year later this turtle had increased an additional 46 mm in length and 1,816 g in weight (Caldwell, 1962b). Four captive hatchlings averaging 44.5 mm in carapace length and 16.2 g in weight increased an average of 46.7 mm and 252.8 g in 188 days.

Growth in the wild is also rapid. Standora et al. (1989) reported that three juveniles tracked and recaptured in Long Island Sound gained about 548 g/

month during the summer. Eighteen captive-raised *Lepidochelys kempii* released into the Gulf of Mexico and later recaptured showed an average weight gain of 5.1 g/day and an average increase in carapace length of 0.024 cm/day (McVey and Wibbels, 1984). Another head-started Atlantic ridley captured 289 days after its release in the Gulf of Mexico had grown from 17.7 cm to 25.5 cm in carapace length and had increased its weight from 1,037 g to 2,746 g. Three adult females, tagged while nesting, grew 50–100 mm in carapace length in 349–373 days (Chavez, 1969), and Márquez (1972) calculated a growth rate of 32.6–37.3 mm/year for adult females he measured on the beach at Rancho Nuevo.

Carr and Caldwell (1956) found that the length-weight relationship in *Lepidochelys kempii* is best expressed by the following equation: log weight = −1.69 + 2.49 log carapace length. They reported that at a carapace length of 42.5 cm an Atlantic ridley had a mean empirical weight of about 9 kg and a calculated weight of 10.4 kg; turtles 50.8 cm long had a mean empirical weight of 16.1 kg (14.1–17.3) and a calculated weight of 16.1 kg; and those 64.8 cm long had a mean empirical weight of 26.5 kg (26–27) and a calculated weight of 26.6 kg. They calculated that the carapace length of a 42.3-kg turtle would be 74.9 cm. The great variation in the length-width proportion of the carapace makes for correspondingly wide ranges in the length-weight ratios, because Kemp's ridleys that have shells as wide as, or even wider than, long are heavier than those of more usual widths for the length class. Hirth (1982) calculated the same regression equation on another set of weight-length data for adult *L. kempii* to be log weight = −1.28 + 1.61 log carapace length. Increase in weight of 10 ridleys held in captivity for five years followed a sigmoid pattern described by a fitted Gompertz growth function; the upper asymptotic weight was 29.2 kg, much smaller than that recorded (39–49 kg) for nesting adults (Caillouet et al., 1986). Other morphometric comparisons are presented by Landry (1989).

Emerging hatchlings at Rancho Nuevo average about 3.8 cm; the posthatchling stage, which lasts from months to several years, encompasses the approximate carapace lengths of 3.8–19.0 cm; juveniles to subadults are 5–15 years old and 19–56 cm long; and adulthood is achieved at 56–72 cm in length (Ross et al., 1989).

Female *Lepidochelys kempii* have been kept in captivity for more than 20 years at Marineland, in Florida (Ernst and Barbour, 1972), and a wild-caught adult male survived over 18 years in captivity at the New England Aquarium, Boston (Snider and Bowler, 1992).

FOOD HABITS: *Lepidochelys kempii* is predominantly carnivorous, feeding in the wild on crabs (particularly *Callinectes* and *Ovalipes,* but at least nine other genera), shrimp (*Penaeus, Sicyonia*), barnacles, insects, sea urchins, snails (mostly *Nassarius,* but other genera as well), bivalves (*Corbula, Mulinia, Nuculana, Polinices,* and other genera), cephalopods (including egg cases of squid), jellyfish (*Physalia*), fish (*Leiostomus, Lutjanus, Stellifer*), and marine plants and algae (*Cymodocea, Gracilaria, Halodule, Sargassum, Thalassia, Ulva,* and several other genera) (Carr, 1952; Liner, 1954; Dobie et al., 1961; Pritchard and Márquez, 1973; Zwinenberg, 1977; Lutcavage and Musick, 1985; Shaver, 1991).

The most complete study on the prey of *L. kempii* (Texas) was that of Shaver (1991) who lists about 50 genera of animals and plants as food of wild or captive Atlantic ridleys. The most frequently eaten prey in that study were the crabs *Callinectes rapidus* (44%) and *Persephona mediterranea* (40%), and *Sargassum* weed (44%).

Captives do well on fresh fish, crabs, and shrimp, but best on specially prepared, high-nutrient (protein, vitamin) pellets (Fontaine et al., 1985; Caillouet et al., 1986). Juvenile ridleys prefer red foods over those colored yellow, blue, or green in controlled diets (Fontaine et al., 1985). The mean amount of food consumed per month by captives increases proportionately with an increase in body mass (Wood, 1982).

Hatchlings and small juveniles probably feed at the surface, possibly among floating mats of vegetation, but adult stomachs and intestines often contain mud and other debris indicating they are feeding on the bottom at least some of the time.

PREDATORS AND DEFENSE: The nests are robbed and the eggs eaten by ghost crabs (*Ocypode*), boat-tailed grackles (*Quiscalus major*), black vultures (*Coragyps atratus*), coyotes (*Canis latrans*), coatis (*Nasua narica*), skunks, and humans (Chavez et al., 1968b; Pritchard and Márquez, 1973; Márquez et al., 1989; Márquez, 1990); the hatchlings are attacked on the beach by ghost crabs and black vultures, and in the water by fish (*Caranx, Sciaenops*) (Chavez et al., 1968b; Pritchard and Márquez, 1973) and the leatherback turtle (*Dermochelys coriacea*); and adults are preyed on by coyotes, probably sharks, and, most often, humans. A cluster of mites (*Macrocheles*) were found on the neck of a hatchling at Rancho Nuevo (Mast and Carr, 1985), but the significance of this is not certain. Remora fish sometimes attach to the shell of adult *L. kempii,* but apparently do no harm.

Lepidochelys kempii is generally bad tempered, and freshly caught individuals exhibit hysterical violence and obstinacy. If kept out of water and placed on their backs they thrash about frantically with their flippers and often bite at nearby objects. Although captives become somewhat tame, they often remain nervous. Secretions from the Rathke's glands located on the bridge are similar in chemical composition to several snake neurotoxins, and may possibly act as predator repellants (Radhakrisna et al., 1989; Weldon et al., 1990; Rostal et al., 1991).

POPULATIONS: When the principal nesting beach at Rancho Nuevo was first discovered thousands of females emerged in a single arribada to oviposit; in 1947, an estimated 42,000 females nested on a single day (Hildebrand, 1982). Since then the number of females nesting there has steadily declined until during the 1988 nesting season less than 200 females crawled onto the beach in the largest arribada (Byles, in Ross et al., 1989). This was less than 0.05% of a typical arribada of the 1940s; the estimated number of females nesting at Rancho Nuevo throughout the 1988 season was only 648 (Byles, in Ross et al., 1989). In 1989, the number of nesting females dropped further to 362–545 (Ross et al., 1989; Pritchard, 1990), and these estimates of the numbers of nesting females may be exaggerated. In 1990, only two arribadas occurred with more than 150 nests each, and about 530 females were tagged the entire season (Márquez et al., 1992). If the adult sex ratio is 1:1, possibly fewer than 3,000 mature *Lepidochelys kempii* exist today, making it the most endangered species of marine turtle, and it has been so listed under the federal Endangered Species Act since 1970.

The numbers of juveniles and subadults also declined between the 1940s and 1960s, but seem to have increased in recent years; most Kemp's ridleys observed in the sea today are between 30 and 40 cm long (Ross et al., 1989). In the Chesapeake Bay during 1979–1981, juvenile *Lepidochelys kempii* amounted to only 43 (3.1%) of 1,382 marine turtles observed (Lutcavage and Musick, 1985); and during 1979–1986 juvenile *L. kempii* constituted only 80 (7.1%) of 1,124 live or dead identifiable marine turtles stranded on the beaches of the Chesapeake Bay and adjacent waters (Keinath et al., 1987). Along the Florida Gulf Coast from June 1981 to September 1989 most Kemp's ridleys stranded on the beach were juveniles or subadults (Meylan et al., 1990c). Only juveniles (19–49 cm) are present in New England waters and Long Island Sound (22.5–37.6 cm), but in the Atlantic Ocean 81–87% of the individuals are juveniles, 11–15% are subadults (49.5–59.0 cm), and 2–4% are adults (>59.5 cm), and in the Gulf of Mexico (based on strandings) 70% of the *L. kempii* are juveniles, 11% are subadults, and 17% are adults (Ross et al., 1989; Morreale et al., 1992).

The increase in the lower size classes may be due to the so-called head-start programs now functioning in which eggs are removed from the nests and incubated elsewhere, with the resulting hatchlings raised to a sufficient size to avoid most predation and then released either at Rancho Nuevo or at other historic nesting beaches, particularly Padre Island, Texas. However, the total value of head-start programs for *Lepidochelys kempii* has been questioned by Woody (1991), who recommends they be stopped. He points out that the population of nesting females continues to decline despite the head-start program, and believes the 25 clutches used each year in this "experiment" (about 3% of the annual production of hatchlings) are probably unnecessarily sacrificed. Woody may be right; so little evidence of success is available for the head-start program that it might be best just to protect these clutches on the beach at Rancho Nuevo (see also the article on the head-start program by Taubes, 1992a, and the resulting letters published in Science 257:465–467, 1992).

Frazer (1992) objects to the head-start program, which he terms "halfway technology," for several other reasons. The program only acts as a bandaid, and does not address the real reasons for the decline of *Lepidochelys kempii* and the other sea turtle species. Also, recent demographic models of sea turtle populations indicate that increasing the survival rate of adults and larger juveniles would result in a greater recovery response (Crouse et al., 1987; Frazer, 1989). Further, restricting the influx of hatchling turtles from the nesting beaches and the later release of larger turtles into the sea may disrupt food webs, creating adverse ecological implications for the entire marine community. Frazer believes more emphasis should be placed on controlling disruptive lighting on nesting beaches and on requiring turtle exclusion devices on various fishing nets. We add that control of development of beachfront property and of predators, such as the raccoon (*Procyon lotor*), on nesting beaches is necessary if breeding populations of sea turtles are to survive in the United States.

A variety of factors have contributed to the decline of *Lepidochelys kempii* (Ross et al., 1989). Egg poaching (now apparently under control) caused the initial decline, and since then drowning in shrimp trawls, entanglement in other fishing gear (particularly gill and pound nets), vacuum dredging, explosions at offshore oil rigs, and oil pollution (Delikat, 1981; Hall et al., 1983; Lutz and Lutcavage, 1989; Ross et al., 1989; Thompson, 1989; National Research Council, 1990; Caillouet et al., 1991) have all taken their toll.

Although the sex ratio of wild adults is unknown, that of head-start turtles examined from 1978 to 1984 indicates that a preponderance of males are being released from this program. Wibbels et al. (1989) reported the following male to female ratios: 1978, n = 32, 1.9:1; 1979, n = 22, 1.4:1; 1981, n = 4, 0:1; 1982, n = 92, 2.9:1; 1983, n = 12, 1:1; and 1984, n = 159, 2.5:1.

Using data from Márquez et al. (1982a), Iverson (1991a) calculated the annual survivorship rate of *Lepidochelys kempii* at Rancho Nuevo from egg to one year to be only 59%.

REMARKS: Immunoprecipitation, electrophoretic, and immunoelectrophoretic tests of blood proteins run by Frair (1979, 1982) indicate that *Lepidochelys kempii* is most closely related to *L. olivacea*, *Caretta*, and *Eretmochelys*, but less so to *Chelonia*, and the chemical composition of the fatty acids in depot fats and the glycoproteins in Rathke's gland secretions further support a close relationship with *Caretta* (Ackman et al., 1971; Radhakrisna et al., 1989). The ridleys (*Lepidochelys*) long were confused with the loggerhead (*Caretta*), and even today *L. kempii* is sometimes referred to as "Kemp's loggerhead," but obvious differences exist between the loggerhead and the ridleys; see the account of *Caretta caretta*.

Hendrickson (1980) viewed *Lepidochelys kempii* as recently separated from *L. olivacea* following the final emergence of the Panamanian land bridge and its isolation from the major eastern Pacific populations of *L. olivacea*. Using mitochondrial DNA studies, Bowen et al. (1991) have dated this divergence at about 3–6 million years ago (dating consistent with Hendrickson's theory). The studies by Bowen et al. have also shown *L. kempii* and *L. olivacea* are more closely related to each other than either is to *Caretta*, but that *L. kempii* is phylogenetically distinct from *L. olivacea*.

Summaries of the life history and status of Kemp's ridley are presented in Pritchard and Márquez (1973), Caillouet and Landrey (1989), and Ross et al. (1989); a review of the literature on the species is in Wilson and Zug (1991) and Zug and Ernst (in press).

Lepidochelys olivacea (Eschscholtz, 1829)
Pacific ridley or olive ridley

PLATE 7

RECOGNITION: This small sea turtle has two pairs of prefrontals, four pairs of pore-bearing inframarginals on the bridge, and commonly six to eight (some have five to nine) pleurals on each side. The heart-shaped, olive carapace (to 73.5 cm) is flattened dorsally, highest anterior to the bridge, and serrated posteriorly in young individuals but smooth in old turtles. The first pair of pleurals touches the cervical, and one side of the carapace may have more pleurals than the other; in individuals from the eastern Pacific the higher number usually is found on the left side. On each side of the carapace lie 12–14 marginals. The bridge and the hingeless plastron are greenish white or greenish yellow. Four inframarginal scutes reside at the bridge and two longitudinal ridges extend along the plastron. The skin is olive above and lighter below. The wide triangular-shaped head has concave sides, especially on the upper part of the short, broad snout. The bony alveolar surface of the upper jaw may have a gentle elevation extending parallel to the cutting edge, but it lacks a conspicuous ridge. Each paddlelike forelimb has two anterior claws.

Males have longer shells (Frazier, 1983) and long thick tails, which extend well beyond the rear carapacial rim; the heavier female shell is broader, and the tail commonly does not reach the carapacial rim. Males have concave plastrons, a more gently sloping lateral profile, and a strongly developed, curved claw on each front flipper. Males may also have softer plastra than females (Wibbels et al., 1991b).

The pleural scutes of *Lepidochelys olivacea* are clearly divisible into whole and half scutes—the whole scutes being homologous with the five pleurals of *L. kempii*. Displacement of the homologues of the seams of *L. kempii* generally is slight, although in cases of extreme splitting (to 8–9 pleurals) the seams become displaced to lessen the size of the small first pleural and the large last vertebral. In almost every case division takes place in the posterior pleurals; for example, a six-

six count is produced by division of the fifth pleurals on each side or an eight-eight count by division of the third, fourth, and fifth pleurals. The number of pleural scutes does not adequately distinguish the two species of *Lepidochelys* (Frazier, 1983).

KARYOTYPE: The diploid chromosome number is 56: 24 pairs of macrochromosomes (12 metacentric, 2 submetacentric, 2 subtelocentric, and 8 telocentric) and 32 acrocentric microchromosomes (Bhunya and Mohanty-Hejmadi, 1986). Nakamura (1937) had previously reported the karyotype consisted of only 52 chromosomes, but this is questionable as all other cheloniid sea turtles have 56 chromosomes (Ernst and Barbour, 1989).

FOSSIL RECORD: Unknown.

DISTRIBUTION: *Lepidochelys olivacea* lives in the tropical waters of the Indian and Pacific oceans from Arabia, India, Japan, and Micronesia south to southern Africa, Australia, and New Zealand; in the Atlantic Ocean off the western coast of Africa and the coasts of northern Brazil, French Guiana, Surinam, Guyana, and Venezuela in South America; and occasionally, in the Caribbean Sea as far north as Puerto Rico. In the eastern Pacific it is found from Chile and the Galapagos Islands northward to the Gulf of California, and along the Pacific Coast at least, in Oregon, as far north as Seaside, Clatsop County (46° N) and just north of Yachats, Lincoln County (42°20′45″ N) (Stinson, 1984). Márquez (1990) stated that *L. olivacea* may even reach the Gulf of Alaska during El Nino years.

GEOGRAPHIC VARIATION: No subspecies are recognized, but the possibility exists that the eastern Pacific and southern Atlantic populations are distinct. Variations in carapace width and numbers of

Lepidochelys olivacea

pleural scutes occur between populations (Pritchard and Trebbau, 1984).

Breeding populations of *Lepidochelys olivacea* from Surinam in the Caribbean Sea and from the Pacific coast of Costa Rica, 25,000 km apart, were indistinguishable in assays of their mitochondrial DNA (Bowen et al., 1991; Avise et al., 1992).

CONFUSING SPECIES: *Lepidochelys kempii* is gray and commonly has only five pleurals on each side (but so occasionally may *L. olivacea*; see Frazier, 1983). *Chelonia mydas* and *Eretmochelys imbricata* have only four pleurals on each side, with the first not touching the cervical. *Caretta* is reddish and has three inframarginals on the bridge.

HABITAT: Most records are from protected, relatively shallow marine waters (24–55 m; Pritchard, 1976) typically within 15 km of mainland shores, but the Pacific ridley occasionally occurs in the open sea. Deraniyagala (1939) reported the habitat in Sri Lanka to be the shallow water between reefs and shore, and larger bays, and lagoons.

BEHAVIOR: In 1972 Ernst and Barbour commented on the paucity of behavioral data concerning this species. Since then little has changed, and most knowledge of *Lepidochelys olivacea* is concerned either with reproduction or long-distance movements.

The annual cycle consists of trips to and from the nesting beach depending on what months constitute the nesting season of the particular population. The

daily cycle is generally unknown, but foraging probably occurs in the morning followed by surface basking in the afternoon. *L. olivacea* may also sleep at the surface (Pritchard and Trebbau, 1984).

Body temperatures of three *Lepidochelys olivacea* taken by Pritchard (1969) were 28.0–29.5°C when sea temperature was approximately 28°C. Temperature may vary at different parts of the turtle. Mrosovsky and Pritchard (1971) recorded cloacal temperatures of 27.3–28.0°C and body temperatures below the carapace or plastron of 29.0–29.25°C from three nesting females while the sea temperatures were 27.25–28.0°C. Temperatures of freshly laid clutches from two of the females were 28.0–28.75°C, fairly close to the female's body temperatures. Large species of sea turtles (*Caretta*, *Chelonia*, *Dermochelys*) may become heat stressed if they nest during the day, but the smaller *L. olivacea* practices diurnal nesting. It can do so, if exposed to wind, because it is less affected by solar radiation and loses more body heat through convection (Spotila and Standora, 1985).

In the eastern Pacific, large numbers of *Lepidochelys olivacea* may be seen sleeping or basking at the surface. Floating is most developed where coastal waters are deep and cold, and this behavior may allow the turtle to raise its internal temperature by direct insolation of the upper carapace (Pritchard and Trebbau, 1984). In Surinam floating does not occur, but the waters there are shallow and warm.

Lepidochelys olivacea must rid its body of the excess ions ingested from the ocean when it feeds and drinks. To do this, it excretes urine containing sodium and potassium concentrations of 20.5 and 8.6 mMol/L, respectively, and, although the potassium concentration is rather high, that of sodium is low. Most sodium (713 mMol/L), chlorine (782 mMol/L), and potassium (28.8 mMol/L) are secreted by extrarenal salt-secreting glands in the orbital regions (Prange, 1985).

Although *Lepidochelys olivacea* is not as strong or as fast a swimmer as either *Chelonia* or *Eretmochelys* (its shorter scapula results in a less extensive forearm), it may migrate long distances from its nesting beach. Those tagged on nesting beaches in Surinam spread out along almost 4,000 km of the coast of northern South America from Isla de Margarita to Amapá, Brazil, and as far north as Trinidad and Barbados (Pritchard, 1973, 1976). Most females, however, have been recaptured within 200 km of their nesting beach. Individuals occasionally caught off the coast of Puerto Rico probably also come from northern South America. Pacific ridleys from nesting beaches in western Mexico have been recaptured almost 200–400 km from the point of tagging (Vargas Molinar, 1973); and those tagged on Pacific beaches of Costa Rica have dispersed to Ecuador and Mexico (Cornelius and Robinson, 1982). The minimum average swimming speed for long-distance migrations is about 28 km/day (Meylan, 1982b); one turtle covered 1,900 km in 23 days, a speed of 82 km/day against a major current (Schulz, 1975). When returning to the nesting beaches from distant feeding areas, *L. olivacea* may use olfactory behavior (chemoreception) to identify the proper beach (Mora and Robinson, 1982; Owens et al., 1982, 1985).

Hatchlings studied by Acuña-Mesén (1988) took 13–24 minutes to cover 20 m of beach (length of track on sand, 23–33 m). The sea-finding efficiency, as measured by speed, was 2.08 and 1.32 m/min for groups of hatchlings with 49–60 and 37–48 hours of captivity, respectively.

REPRODUCTION: The complete sexual cycle, size, and age at which males mature are unknown. Owens (1980) examined three males collected by fishermen in late April on the Nicaragua feeding grounds, as well as three others collected on 29 October by fishermen off the nesting beach in Oaxaca, Mexico. Two April adults (101–107 cm curved carapace length) had testes weights of 237–369.6 g, epididymides with loosely packed sperm weighing 48.7–74.5 g, and appeared to be in early to peak spermiogenesis. The third 72.3-cm male was immature. The three males examined in October had curved carapace lengths of 62.3–69.0 cm, testes

weights of 27.5–100 g, epididymides with tightly packed sperm weighing 23.5–36.5 g, and were in the spermiation stage of their cycle. Their testes were rather small with folded (regressing) seminiferous tubule walls and depleted sperm, and the epididymides had much more active tubular epithelium.

Most nesting females are over 60 cm in carapace length, but Cornelius (1983) reported that females mature at 55 cm in seven to nine years in Costa Rica, Hughes and Richard (1974) observed a 54-cm female nest, and Pritchard (1969) found some matured at 58 cm in Surinam.

The ovary of reproductive females demonstrates a distinct hierarchy of follicles. October reproductive females from Oaxaca, Mexico, with curved carapace lengths greater than 62 cm had ovaries that weighed 200–845 g, with four to many large follicles that averaged 27 mm in diameter and a second set of smaller follicles about 11 mm in diameter (Owens, 1980). Also present were 0–55 corpora hemorrhagia, 17–52 large corpora lutea, up to 69 small corpora lutea, and 0–51 oviducal eggs.

Licht (1982) and Licht et al. (1982) studied changes in luteinizing hormone and progesterone associated with the nesting cycle and ovulation in *Lepidochelys olivacea* on the Pacific coast of Mexico. Ovulation is completed by most females within a few days after nesting in this multiclutched turtle. By three days post oviposition, eggs in the oviduct contain thin partially calcified shells, even though these may not be laid for up to a month. Some females off the nesting beaches hold mature eggs in their oviducts, apparently delaying oviposition until the number of females is adequate for an arribada. Ovulation coincides with a surge of more than one order of magnitude in luteinizing hormone and progesterone within a day after oviposition. Hormonal levels return to near base level within two or three days, by the time the eggshell membrane appears. Testosterone and estrogen levels show little concentration change in the periovulatory period; in fact, estrogen levels in nesting *L. olivacea* are quite low (Owens and Morris, 1985). Estrogen levels peak in the spring and may correlate with migration and ovarian maturation as well as during the interesting interval when subsequent follicle size classes are maturing (Owens and Morris, 1985). Gonadotropin-releasing hormone and a potent agonistic analog are inactive in both sexes of adult breeding *L. olivacea*.

Arginine vasotocin is in low concentration in females which are not reproductively active (Figler et al., 1989). It is also low at the time the turtles emerge from the surf to nest, but greatly increases during oviposition, and then drops as the females return to the sea (Figler et al., 1989). Apparently arginine vasotocin is a physiological regulator of reproductive tract contractions. Neurophysin increases in concert with arginine vasotocin, reaching its highest levels during oviposition, but neurophysin levels remain elevated over prenesting levels during the return trip to the water (Figler et al., 1989).

Environmental temperature may directly affect the endocrine cycles. The pineal complex produces the hormone melatonin which is reduced in the circulation and cerebrospinal fluid by the exposure to light (Owens and Morris, 1985).

Mating is thought to occur off the nesting beaches before the first ovulation. After a single mating, sperm is stored for the season in tubules in the oviductal wall (Owens, 1980; Gist and Jones, 1989). However, some mating probably occurs in the open ocean at other times of the year; Hubbs (1977) reported a copulation by *Lepidochelys olivacea* at about 300 m offshore from La Jolla, California, at 1130 on 21 August 1973. The pair was floating at the surface with the male riding on the female's carapace with a claw from each forelimb attached at times to the forward rim of the female's shell, but sometimes one claw was attached to the corresponding flipper of the female (Márquez et al., 1976, reported the tail may also help hold the male in place). There was much flapping of the turtles' flippers as they slowly drifted southward, but the female did the swimming for the pair. The turtles submerged when swimmers approached, but rose to the surface again 15 minutes later when the humans had departed, but soon disappeared again. At 1400 the pair, still embraced, resurfaced. The female escaped at 1410 when the male was dislodged and captured. Márquez et al. (1976) observed mating pairs of *L. olivacea* near nesting beaches in both morning and early afternoon. Unusual development occurs in the series of Rathke's glands on the bridge (Ehrenfeld and Ehrenfeld, 1973). Secretions from these glands may include pheromones which attract the opposite sex, enabling the turtles to congregate off the nesting beaches for mating.

The Pacific ridley nests in almost every month of the year in various parts of the range. In those populations producing individuals that may reach the coast of North America the eggs are laid from May through January in the eastern Pacific from Costa Rica to Jalisco and Baja, Mexico, and from March through August along the northern coast of South America from French Guiana to Colombia, and Trinidad and Tobago. Females start to emerge from the sea with a rising tide and are finished nesting by the advent of a low tide. Most nesting is done from twilight into the night, but many diurnal ovipositions occur. During the peaks of activity the nesting arribada may consist of several thousand females. Prior to emergence some females swim back and forth parallel to the shoreline just beyond the breaking waves, diving for brief periods of less than five minutes. These turtles disappear after nesting, lying immobile on the bottom (Plotkin et al., 1991). Emerging females crawl up the beach using an alternate gait of all four limbs. Once a site is selected, seldom more than 50 m from the water, the turtle scoops out a shallow body pit with all four flippers, the front ones usually working together. When this has been completed, excavation of the actual nest cavity is begun in the rear of the body pit with the hind flippers. The final nest cavity is flask shaped and 30–55 cm deep (commonly 38–43; Zwinenberg, 1976); the egg chamber may be 17–30 cm wide (Carr, 1952). Prior to oviposition the hind limbs are withdrawn from the cavity and extended outward, and the forelimbs are braced in the sand. One to four eggs are deposited at one time until the entire clutch has been laid. Sand is then scraped into the cavity by the hind flippers, and the shell is used to pound the sand compact. After the nest cavity has been filled, the body pit is obscured with sand by alternate sweeps of the forelimbs. When this is completed, the female returns to the sea. The complete nesting, from emergence to reentering the water usually takes less than an hour. Successful oviposition may be dependent upon beach configuration and recent rainfall patterns that affect the friability of the sand, and many abandoned nest holes occur where sand is too loose to maintain the shape of the egg cavity (Fritts et al., 1982).

Females may oviposit three times a season, but most usually do so only once or twice. In Surinam, the usual intervals between successive nestings are about 17 days, 30 days, and possibly 44 days, but one female oviposited after a 60-day interval (Pritchard, 1969). On the Pacific coast of Central America, the internesting period may be 4–75 days, but most lay again in 15–17 days (Minarik, 1985). Nesting often occurs during periods of strong winds, and the interval between nestings may be controlled more by environmental factors, such as the tide and water, than by physiological factors. However, the mechanism that brings so many females on to the nesting beach at one time is still unclear.

Lepidochelys olivacea, like its relative *L. kempii*, shows a high incidence of nesting in successive seasons, but some females may nest at two- to three-year intervals.

Clutch size of Surinam nests was 30–168 eggs (mean 116); only four nests contained fewer than 70 eggs and only four had more than 155 (Pritchard, 1969). Females from the eastern Pacific laid 74–126 eggs, mean 105 (Cornelius, 1976). The second or third clutches of the season contained fewer eggs than were laid in the first.

The oval-to-spherical, white eggs have soft, leathery shells, and are 32.1–45.4 mm in diameter. Most weigh 30–38 g. When newly laid they adhere to one another, owing to the strongly mucilaginous mucus that covers them; these agglutinated eggs have a morulalike appearance. Under natural conditions eggs laid on beaches hatch in 45–51 days, but if weather conditions are unfavorable the period may extend to 70 days. The embryological stages of *Lepidochelys olivacea* have been described by Crastz (1982), and we refer the reader to that publication for details.

Eggs incubated at temperatures of 28°C or less produce only males, those incubated at 31–32°C produce only females, and incubation temperatures of 29–30°C result in mixed sex clutches (McCoy et al., 1983; Standora and Spotila, 1985; Mohanty-Hejmadi et al., 1985; Mohanty-Hejmadi and Dimond, 1986). Gonadal development at 28°C and 32°C has been described by Merchant-Larios et al. (1989) and Merchant-Larios and Vallalpando (1990).

Hatching success varies according to environmental conditions and the rate of nest predation, which both vary yearly and between nesting beaches. Pritchard (1969) found strikingly high hatching percentages for *Lepidochelys olivacea* nests in Surinam. All the eggs in a clutch of 88 hatched producing normal offspring. In another clutch, of 126 eggs, three that he opened before hatching contained living embryos; of the remainder 118 hatched, two were infertile, and three were slow developers. In contrast, Cornelius et al. (1991) reported that only about 27–35% of more than 268,000 nests produced hatchlings at two Pacific beaches in Costa Rica during August and September 1984; predation, beach erosion, and exposure by later nesting females were the leading causes of clutch loss. Also, only 8–31% of the eggs hatched in successful nests.

The relatively elongated, oval carapace of the hatchling commonly has three well-developed pale keels. The plastron has four longitudinal ridges. Hatchlings are gray black to olive black, with a small white mark at each side at the supralabial scale, another on the hind part of the umbilical protuberance, and several where the ridges of the plastron cross the abdominal and femoral scutes. The skin and plastron may be dark grayish brown. A fine white line borders the carapace and the trailing edge of both the fore and hind flippers. Hatchlings are 37–50 mm in carapace length, 31–45 mm in carapace width, and weigh 16–19 g. Acuña-Mesén (1990) pointed out that the neonatal skin is characterized by multiple, ornamented coriaceous plates resulting from the presence of conical pores, which he thought may function as physicochemical receptors for water, thus producing a specific imprinting that allows reproductive females to eventually return to the beaches which produced them. This needs confirmation.

GROWTH AND LONGEVITY: Growth data on wild *Lepidochelys olivacea* are scarce, but juveniles may increase their carapace lengths by about 50 mm/year (Carr and Caldwell, 1958). Deraniyagala (1939) recorded the following growth data for individuals from the Indian Ocean: at age 30 days, carapace length, 85 mm; 210 days, 170 mm; and 307 days, 185 mm. One grew from 43 mm to 74 mm from 1 February to 3 August 1929, and another grew from 45 mm to 490 mm from 18 January 1934 to 30 May 1936.

Captive growth data are more plentiful. Hatchlings in Thailand grew from a mean carapace length of 43 mm to 100 mm in six months, 188 mm in one year, and 320 mm in 18 months (Phasuk and Rongmuangsart, 1973). Captives kept in seminatural conditions in Mexico were 117–200 mm (0.26–1.3 kg) at eight months, and 182–237 mm (1.0–2.3 kg) when one year old (Márquez et al., 1976). Mexican hatchlings fed a daily ration of chopped fish and pellets containing 36% protein grew from an average of 41.9 mm to 225 mm curved carapace length (175–235) and increased in weight from an average of 13 g to 1.25 kg (0.78–1.3) in 15 months (Silva-Batiz et al., 1992).

Body weight is positively correlated with carapace length (Hirth, 1982).

The natural life span of *Lepidochelys olivacea* is unknown.

FOOD HABITS: The Pacific ridley is predominantly carnivorous, particularly in the immature stages. Most animal prey are invertebrates or protochordates that can be caught in shallow marine waters or estuarine habitats: jellyfish, sea urchins, bryozoans, sipunculid worms, bivalves, snails, small shrimp, crabs, rock lobsters, and tunicates. However, pelagic feeding may be indicated by its consumption of jellyfish and both adult fish (*Sphoeroides*) and fish eggs (Fritts, 1981a). Some filamentous algae may also be eaten, and occasional captives have been cannibalistic.

PREDATORS AND DEFENSE: Nests are robbed by pigs (*Sus*), opossums (*Didelphis marsupialis*), raccoons (*Procyon lotor*), coatimundi (*Nasua narica*), coyotes (*Canis latrans*), caimans (*Caiman, Paleosuchus*), the sunbeam snake (*Loxocemus bicolor*), and ghost crabs (*Ocypode*) (Schulz, 1975; Hughes and Richard, 1974; Mora and Robinson, 1984; Márquez, 1990; Cornelius et al., 1991). Hatchlings are preyed upon as they crawl across the beach to the water by crabs (*Gecarcinus, Ocypode*), vultures (*Cathartes, Coragyps*), and frigate birds (*Fregata*) (Cornelius, 1983), and once in the water probably by crocodiles (*Crocodylus acutus*), sharks, and other oceanic fishes. Hatchlings have even been found in the stomach of the leatherback turtle (Pritchard, 1971). Adults have few enemies other than humans, but, evidenced by the wounded shells and amputated limbs of some, sharks must occasionally attack them. Mosquitoes plague females while they nest.

The leading predators on *Lepidochelys olivacea* are humans who not only collect the eggs from the nests, but also slaughter some females on the beach, and take other adults at sea for commercial sale of the meat and hides or for use as fish bait.

Defensive behavior has not been studied in this species, but if handled on the beaches they will flail their forelimbs. In the water, *L. olivacea* will dive or swim away if disturbed.

POPULATIONS: *Lepidochelys olivacea* is seasonally abundant off its nesting beaches, and it may have the highest populations of hard-shelled marine turtles. Its habit of synchronized mass nesting (arribadas) gives some clue to its numbers, and along the Pacific coast of Mexico and Costa Rica 20,000 to 200,000 females may visit a nesting beach in one season (Ross, 1982). Cliffton et al. (1982) estimated the lower limits of the adult female population of western Mexico to be almost 600,000 prior to 1969. If the adult sex ratio is approximately equal, some eastern Pacific nesting areas may serve populations of at least 400,000 adults, and records from three populous Mexican nesting beaches indicate a population of almost 1,200,000 adults in 1969 (Cliffton et al., 1982). Márquez (1990) reported that still as many as 200,000 nests may be dug annually in both western Mexico and Nicaragua. Unfortunately, for many reasons, Pacific ridley populations have declined and today probably only a few hundred thousand adult females survive. Arribadas no longer appear on some formerly heavily used beaches. Fewer females nest on northern South American beaches, only about 1,000 at Eilanti, Surinam (Ross, 1982).

Iverson (1991a) summarized the available survivorship data concerning *Lepidochelys olivacea:* from egg to hatchling, 0.2–59%; from egg to one year, 58%.

REMARKS: Serological tests show a close affinity among the five North American genera of marine turtles (Frair, 1979). *Lepidochelys, Caretta,* and *Eretmochelys* are more closely related to each other than to *Chelonia,* and these hard-shelled genera are distinct from *Dermochelys. Lepidochelys* seems closest to ancestral sea turtles.

Although *Lepidochelys olivacea* is still numerous at some reproductive sites, its overall decline in the last 30 years, apparently due to exploitation of nesting females for commercial leather and meat, has earned it an endangered species listing. Governmental protection of the nesting beaches and control of commerce in meat and hides should help the recovery of this species. However, owing to its relatively long maturation period, this may take decades.

Dermochelyidae
Leatherback sea turtles

This family is represented by a single extant species, *Dermochelys coriacea,* the leatherback or luth, the largest species of living turtle, reaching 219 cm (Holland et al., 1990) and weighing over 900 kg (Eckert and Luginbuhl, 1988; Holland et al., 1990), which ranges widely in tropical and subtropical seas. Other extinct leatherbacks are known from the Eocene to Miocene of Africa, Europe, and North America (*Cosmochelys, Eosphargis, Psephophorus*), and from the Oligocene of Germany (*Pseudosphargis*) (Pritchard and Trebbau, 1984).

The carapace lacks horny scutes but is covered with a ridged, leathery skin. Shell bones, except the nuchal and those at the rim of the plastron, are lost; their place is taken by a mosaic of small bony plates embedded in the skin. The largest of these polygonal bones form seven prominent longitudinal keels, which divide the carapacial surface into eight sections. The nuchal is attached to the neural arch of the eighth cervical vertebra. A series of 10 dorsal vertebrae runs medially along the carapace; free dorsal ribs, except the last, articulate with the neural arch and two adjacent centra and are embedded in a layer of cartilage. Ribs 1–10 are short. The hingeless plastron has five longitudinal ridges underlined with polygonal bones. No entoplastron is present, but the bones at the rim are apparently homologous to the epiplastra, hyoplastra, hypoplastra, and xiphiplastra of other turtles. The skull roof is complete. The vomer touches the premaxillae, separating both the nares and palatine bones, and the choanae lie posterior to the alveolar surfaces of the vomer. No basisphenoid-palatine contact occurs, and the maxilla is separated from both the pterygoid and the quadratojugal. Neither a secondary palate nor a palatine fenestra is present. The quadrate is open posteriorly and so does not enclose the stapes. The supraoccipital process is short. Both jaws are very short behind the coronoid process, and the anterior maxillary ridge is cusped. The neck is short and incompletely retractile; its fourth cervical vertebra is biconvex. Limbs are paddlelike and clawless.

Dermochelys coriacea (Linnaeus, 1766)
Leatherback or luth
PLATE 8

RECOGNITION: This huge marine turtle has a brown to black, smooth, elongated, lyre-shaped carapace that tapers to a supracaudal point above the tail. Some small, white to yellowish, scattered blotches are present on the carapace, and the head and neck are black or dark brown with a few scattered white, yellowish, or pink blotches. Limbs are also black with some white spotting. The snout is blunt and nonprojecting, and a toothlike cusp lies on each side of the gray upper jaw.

Males have concave plastra and are rather depressed in profile. They also have a narrower carapace that is more tapered posteriorly, little or no pink pigment on the dorsal surface of the head, and tails longer than their hind limbs. Most females have extensive pink pigment on the top of the head and a tail that is barely half as long as that of the male.

KARYOTYPE: A full chromosomal complement consists of 56 chromosomes: 24 macrochromosomes (14 metacentric and submetacentric, 10 telocentric and subtelocentric) and 32 microchromosomes; chromosomal numbers and morphology are similar to those of cheloniid turtles (Medrano et al., 1987).

FOSSIL RECORD: No fossil *Dermochelys coriacea* has been discovered.

DISTRIBUTION: *Dermochelys* may be the most widely distributed reptile, owing in part to its habit of following drifting flotillas of jellyfish, its primary food. It ranges throughout the tropical waters of the Atlantic, Pacific, and Indian oceans, where its primary nesting beaches are located, but also has been recorded from Norway, the British Isles, and Iceland (Brongersma, 1972; Petersen, 1984), Labrador (Threlfall, 1978), Newfoundland (Goff and Lien, 1988), Nova Scotia (Bleakney, 1965) and possibly also

Baffin Island (Shoop, 1980) in the North Atlantic; the Bering and Barents seas (Bannikov et al., 1971), Alaska (Hodge, 1979; Stinson, 1984), and British Columbia (MacAskie and Forrester, 1962) in the North Pacific; the Cape of Good Hope and Argentina in the South Atlantic; and Chile, New Zealand, Tasmania, Australia and Tongoland, South Africa in the South Pacific and Indian Ocean. It also enters the Mediterranean Sea.

GEOGRAPHIC VARIATION: Two subspecies have been described. *Dermochelys coriacea coriacea* (Linnaeus, 1766), the Atlantic leatherback, ranges through the Atlantic Ocean, the Gulf of Mexico, and the Caribbean Sea, from Labrador to Norway southward to Argentina and the Cape of Good Hope. It supposedly has longer forelimbs in comparison to total body length, a shorter head, and is darker with less light mottling on the back, lower jaw and throat. *Dermochelys c. schlegelii* (Garman, 1884), the Pacific leatherback, occurs in the Pacific and Indian oceans from Alaska to Chile and west to Japan and eastern Africa. It has shorter forelimbs, a longer head, and is paler, with more light mottling on the back, lower jaw, and throat.

These supposed races are poorly differentiated, and a detailed study will be necessary to determine their validity. Also an additional small third subspecies may occur in the eastern Pacific Ocean off the western Americas; if it proves valid, the name *angusta* (Philippi, 1899) is available.

CONFUSING SPECIES: All other marine turtles in American waters have claws and a bony carapace covered with horny scutes.

HABITAT: The leatherback is pelagic, but occasionally enters the shallow waters of bays and estuaries. Even the juveniles appear to be pelagic, as they are seldom observed along the coast.

Dermochelys coriacea coriacea

Plastron of *Dermochelys coriacea*

BEHAVIOR: Almost nothing is known of the behavior of free-living leatherbacks other than that of nesting females. The annual cycle is divided into three phases during reproductive years. Nesting (and probably also mating) occurs from March to July in Atlantic *Dermochelys*, but along the Pacific coast of Mexico and Central America, nesting takes place later, usually from September through March, and is most frequent in November and December. The second phase starts after the nesting season ends when the leatherbacks follow the drifting schools of jellyfish from tropical to temperate waters. Cooling water temperatures or decreasing day length probably cue the third phase of the yearly cycle, the remigration to the tropics. This is timed to bring gravid females to nesting beaches from temperate latitudes just prior to oviposition (Eckert and Eckert, 1988).

The daily cycle must include foraging periods, but the hours of feeding are generally unknown. While free swimming, mean time spent at or near the surface is correlated with the time of day, and peaks between 0900 and 1200 EDT (Standora et al., 1984). Sleeping is accomplished while floating at the surface (Pope, 1939).

Dermochelys is subject to a wide range of temperatures during its annual migrations. It is remarkable for occurring in waters too cold for normal activity by most turtles, even near the Arctic Circle in Alaska during years of high water temperatures (Stinson, 1984). Active leatherbacks have been taken off Labrador from waters that could not have exceeded 6°C (Threlfall, 1978), and occur in 9–15°C waters off British Columbia, Labrador, and Newfoundland (MacAskie and Forrester, 1962; Goff and Lien, 1988). These turtles often have stomachs full of jellyfish, so have been feeding despite these relatively low water temperatures (Bleakney, 1965). Deep body temperatures recorded from *Dermochelys* experimentally exposed to water temperatures as low as 7.5°C were 18°C above the water temperatures (Frair et al., 1972; Spotila and Standora, 1985). As the water temperature was slowly lowered from about 27°C to 1°C, the turtle's body temperature fell only about 9°C from 31°C to 22°C.

Cloacal temperatures of four females on a nesting beach were 30.00–31.25°C, the temperatures of the egg clutches they had laid were 30–31°C, and the water offshore was 28.25°C (Pritchard, 1969; Mrosovsky and Pritchard, 1971). Body temperatures of nesting females recorded by Sapsford and Hughes (1978) were 5.3–6.25°C above the temperatures of adjacent water, and Standora et al. (1984) reported a leatherback heated internally from 29.6°C to 30.1°C while active on land for 2.5 hours although the air temperature dropped from 26.4°C to 25.3°C. While in air, another *Dermochelys* had pectoral temperatures as much as 4.8°C warmer than the surface temperature of the carapace, and 8.3°C above the air temperature of 21.8°C (Standora et al., 1984).

How can *Dermochelys* function properly at such low water temperatures, and how can it maintain a deep body temperature so far above that of the ambient temperature? Multichannel telemetry demonstrates that its internal temperature when resting is higher than either carapace surface or surrounding air temperatures, indicating that heat can be generated to some extent metabolically and not from either locomotor muscle activity or absorbed from the environment (Spotila and Standora, 1985). Is the leatherback homeothermic? It certainly seems as if it must have some adaptations for preventing heat loss, but what are these? Cardiovascular adaptations may be involved. Apparently *Dermochelys* has a countercurrent heat exchanger consisting of a single well-formed, deeper than broad, bundle of closely packed arteries and veins near the junction of each of the front and rear flippers with the body (Greer et al., 1973), and

recordings of exhaled air temperatures suggest that the leatherback may also use another countercurrent exchanger system in its nares (Sapsford and Hughes, 1978). Also, the lipid of flipper adipose tissue freezes at a lower temperature than lipids from within the shell (Davenport et al., 1990).

Body heat generated metabolically or through muscle action while swimming may also be trapped by a thick insulating layer of oil-saturated, subepidermal fat (Frair et al., 1972). These fats are unique in containing nearly 10% lauric acid (possibly replacing palmitic acid) in contrast to 0.2–2.0% in the fat of other turtles, and trans-6-hexadecenoic acid not found in any other turtle (Ackman et al., 1971); however, the fatty layer compares chemically to that of the green fat of *Chelonia mydas,* and Ackman and Burgher (1965) thought it may be primarily intended for bouyancy. Total lipid forms about 87–95% of the dry weight of the subepidermal fat, 43% of the liver, and 5% of the pectoral muscle (Holland et al., 1990). The high levels of neutral lipid in the liver (79% of total lipid) and subepidermal fat (87–99% of total lipid) indicate an important energy storage function for these tissues. Neutral lipid composes about 1–11% and phospholipids 0.6–15.5% of the total fatty acids. The fatty acid composition of *Dermochelys* lipids is very similar to that of its jellyfish prey (Holland et al., 1990).

There are in fact two distinct subdermal adipose tissues beneath the shell of *Dermochelys,* a depot layer and a second layer of shell fats, composed of almost pure triglycerides (Ackman et al., 1972; Goff and Stenson, 1988). Apparently these layers have different functions. The most superficial layer is over 30% thicker (with nearly crisscrossing connective tissue fibers), white in color, and solid in consistency; the deeper, less thick, more vascularized layer is of softer, brown tissue (Goff and Stenson, 1988). The outer, thicker layer probably helps support the shell, in lieu of bone, as well as insulates. The brown, inner layer is more likely thermogenic (heat-generating), as in mammals.

The large body mass of *Dermochelys* may also aid in heat retention (Neill and Stevens, 1974; but also see Mrosovsky and Frair, 1974). Mathematical modeling indicates that this turtle can use its large body size, peripheral insulating fat layers, and countercurrent circulatory adjustments to maintain warm temperatures in the northern oceans, and also to avoid overheating on tropical beaches (Paladino et al., 1990).

Osmoregulation is another problem for vertebrates living in desiccating marine waters: water must be conserved while excess salts, particularly NaCl, must be excreted. The kidney of marine turtles does not seem to be the major organ for salt removal; instead ionic and osmotic balance is accomplished primarily by specialized cephalic salt-secreting glands. As the leatherback's primary food is jellyfish, which are isotonic to sea water, it experiences great osmotic strain. *Dermochelys* has a very large pair of postorbital lachrymal glands presumed to be for salt removal. After fasting 22 hours under experimental conditions, *Dermochelys* secreted lachrymal gland fluids of considerably higher osmotic pressure that those from either *Caretta, Chelonia,* or *Eretmochelys* (Hudson and Lutz, 1986). The total osmotic pressure of the fluids from *Dermochelys* was almost twice those from the three cheloniids: a mean of 1,163 mOz/kg versus means of 492–685 mOz/kg. Blood plasma osmotic pressure in *Dermochelys* was close to that of the other marine turtles, but the ratio of lachrymal fluid osmotic pressure to that of the plasma was 3.3 versus 1.5–2.3. Apparently the orbital lachrymal glands in the leatherback are extremely active salt-secreting tissues, possibly responding to its high-salt jellyfish diet. However, Den Hartog and Van Nierop (1984) thought that most excess sea water, including that from jellyfish, is orally expelled and that excess salts are not primarily excreted by either the kidneys or lachrymal glands.

Dermochelys is a powerful swimmer. Swimming is accomplished by synchronized beating of the forelimbs whether moving slowly or quickly. Tests on hatchlings have shown that they can only swim forward (Davenport, 1987). Hatchlings have two swimming speeds, subsurface and fast (30 cm/sec) or surfaced and slow (8 cm/sec). Intermediate speeds are transitory. They seldom seem to rest without movement, nor do these turtles exhibit any gliding between strokes. During the night, hatchlings typically swim between 15% and 45% of the time (Wyneken and Salmon, 1992). Power during fast swimming is developed on both the up and down strokes of the limb cycle, but during slow swimming power is generated only by the upstroke. This is owing to an orientation of the limb axis opposite that of other sea turtles. The maximum speed developed by a subadult during an 18-hour experiment was 5 km/h; mean speed was 3.1 km/h (Standora et al., 1984). Maximum swimming speed recorded by Duron-Dufrenne (1978) was 9.3 km/h.

Leatherbacks travel great distances; some of these trips are either regular migrations outward from nesting beaches or following jellyfish schools, but others may be random wanderings. Although some movement may be far from shore, most migration is probably fairly close to the coastline, particularly along the east coast of North America (Ernst and Gilroy, 1979), where leatherbacks can be found west of the Gulf Stream in water less than 70 m deep (Hoffman and Fritts, 1982). *Dermochelys* usually reaches New England in late spring at about the same time as the jellyfish flotilla.

Some evidence of the migrational ability of *Dermochelys* has come from subsequent recaptures of females tagged on nesting beaches. Six females tagged in Surinam were later recaptured more than 5,000 km away in Ghana, Campeche, Mexico, Texas, South Carolina, and New Jersey (Pritchard, 1973, 1976, 1985). Another female tagged in Trinidad was later found dead on Rockaway Beach, New York (Lambie, 1983). Other females tagged in Costa Rica and the Virgin Islands have been recovered 1,000–3,100 km away (Carr and Meylan, 1984; Hirth and Ogren, 1987; Boulon et al., 1988), and a radio-equipped, satellite-tracked female swam 840 km in a preferential direction in 23 days, averaging over 30 km/day, from its nesting beach in French Guyana (Duron-Dufrenne, 1987).

These animals show movements away from nesting areas, but only one tagging record indicates a return trip from temperate to tropical waters. A leatherback caught in a pound net in the Chesapeake Bay, tagged, and released was caught over a year later off southern Cuba, a minimum distance of 2,168 km (Keinath and Musick, 1990).

Dermochelys sometimes travel in groups. Leary (1957) observed a concentration of about 100 leatherbacks along a 50-km line off the Texas coast on 17 December 1956. The turtles seemed to be most numerous in a dense school of the jellyfish *Stomolophus meleagris*.

Not all swimming is at the surface, and *Dermochelys* spends much time each day underwater for various reasons. Surface swimming is correlated with time of day and peaks between 0900 and 1200 (Standora et al., 1984). Standora et al. (1984) found that during the day time spent at the surface by a leatherback off Rhode Island was similar to duration of submergence, but at night submergence time was twice that of surface activity. However, Eckert et al. (1986, 1989b) noted that mean surface time is greater during the day in leatherbacks from the Virgin Islands. They also found that mean diving depth is greater in daylight and less variable at night (but there was no significant difference in mean diving time between day and night for either of their two turtles). Submergence intervals are greater at dawn, then decline through the day to become shortest at dusk (Eckert et al., 1989b). The leatherback is an active diver during internesting periods (maximum diving duration, 27.8 and 37.4 minutes for two turtles studied by Eckert et al., 1986). Lutcavage et al. (1992) estimated, based on maximum and minimum rates of oxygen uptake, that dives of 5–70 minutes can be supported aerobically.

How deep does *Dermochelys* dive? This probably depends on the reason for the dive and proximity to the shore. Those closest to shore probably dive more shallowly than those diving in open water (Hughes, 1978; Limpus, 1984). Maximum diving depths recorded by Eckert et al. (1986) were 475 m for their smallest turtle and 314 m for the largest, and another gravid female from the Virgin Islands dove to a depth greater than 1,000 m (Eckert et al., 1989b). Davenport (1988) and Davenport and Balazs (1991) suggested that leatherbacks diving to great depths are possibly seeking bioluminescent abyssal jellyfish and glowing tunicates.

Some physiological and anatomical adaptations may aid *Dermochelys* during deep dives. Tidal volume of the lungs is considerably less than in other sea turtles, suggesting that the leatherback has relatively small lungs; however, its blood has an extremely high hemoglobin concentration and hematocrit, and a higher oxygen-carrying capacity than other marine turtles (Lutcavage et al., 1990, 1992). Potential oxygen stores seem almost equally divided between the small lungs and the blood and tissues; however, pectoral muscle myoglobin, indicative of oxygen store, is twice that of other sea turtles, suggesting that leatherbacks rely more on enhanced blood and tissue oxygen stores than on oxygen held in the lungs during deep dives.

The leatherback also has an intracardiac blood shunt controlled by a sphincter muscle in the pulmonary artery which directs blood away from the lungs and back to the body during dives (Sapsford, 1978). Skeletal features similar to those of deep-diving marine mammals are also present which may aid in achieving the great depths recorded (Rhodin et al., 1980, 1981).

Carr and Ogren (1959) studied the sea-finding orientation of hatchling leatherbacks at Tortuguero, Costa Rica, and found that they have a positive reaction to open areas and to large areas of illumination (such as the horizon over the sea). Carr and Ogren also discovered that this basic attraction to open areas of illumination is supplemented by the capacity to use information of various sorts to repeatedly reorient in the complex beach landscape: on their way across the beach the hatchlings regularly execute circles, presumably for orientation by visual cues. Orientation circles are performed more frequently in overcast weather or rain than when it is sunny (Mrosovsky and Shettleworth, 1975; Mrosovsky, 1977). Circling tends to be more in the direction of the sun (Mrosovsky and Kingsmill, 1985), and more circles are completed on the upper beach than on sand below the high-tide lines. Hatchlings emerging at night may also circle. Not all circle; some hatchlings crawl directly to the sea at a rapid pace.

Once in the water a hatchling swims almost continuously during the first 24 hours, in what Wyneken and Salmon (1992) term the "frenzy" period. It does not swim as often after the first day; swimming duration decreases through the fifth day, but increases slightly on the sixth day (Wyneken and Salmon, 1992). Swimming is not limited to the light hours. Such activity quickly moves the small turtle away from the waters off the nesting beach which abounds with predators.

REPRODUCTION: The size and age of maturity in males is unknown, but nesting females average about 150 cm in carapace length (Pritchard, 1969; Bacon, 1970). The annual gametic cycles of both sexes are unknown.

Mating was thought to occur in tropical waters at the time of nesting, but may actually take place prior to or during the migration from temperate to tropical waters (Eckert and Eckert, 1988). The only recorded observation of copulating *Dermochelys* took place at 1630 in water 44 m deep on 5 April off Culebra Island, Puerto Rico (Carr and Carr, 1986). The two turtles surfaced about five meters apart, and the female remained stationary while the male swam quickly to her with head held high above the water. When about a meter behind her, he lunged forward, lodging the center of his plastron on the posterior dorsal surface of her carapace. She immediately dove, but he took a breath and followed. The two turtles emerged a second time about two meters apart, and the male lunged onto her back again. She again dove, only more slowly. When the leatherbacks surfaced for the third time, they were very close together and she did not resist his subsequent lunge. He positioned the center of his plastron just posterior to the center of her carapace, his weight forcing her beneath the waves. Both turtles began to list, and then roll laterally back and forth. At this time the male's tail and semierect penis were visible. The turtles then separated, submerged, and surfaced a fourth time. The male repeated his behavior, curving his tail beneath the base of her tail. Her forelimbs became rigid and slightly elevated above the water, while his forelimbs and neck became rigid. At this point the turtles quivered slightly and slowly sank beneath the surface until lost from view. *Dermochelys* nests on this island, so this may have been a mating involving a female about to oviposit.

Western Atlantic nesting beaches, possibly producing individuals that eventually reach the shores of North America, include: northern South America—Brazil, French Guiana, Surinam, Guyana, Venezuela, Trinidad, Tobago, and Colombia; Central America—Panama, Costa Rica, Nicaragua, Belize, and Mexico (Yucatán, Veracruz, and possibly Tamaulipas); Caribbean Islands—Antigua, Barbados, Culebra, Dominica, Dominican Republic, Grenada, Guadalupe, Jamaica, Martinique, Nevis, St. Lucia, St. Kitts, St. Maarten, St. Vincent, and St. Thomas. Of these, only the beaches of French Guiana, Surinam, and Costa Rica can be considered major nesting areas; all other beaches produce few nests annually.

In the United States, rare leatherback nesting has been reported on Padre Island, Texas (but not recently), and along the Atlantic Coast less than 50 *Dermochelys* nest annually on beaches ranging from Dade to St. Johns counties, Florida (Caldwell, 1958; Nichols and DuToit, 1983; Anon., 1992a), and on Cumberland Island, Camden County, Georgia, and Blackbeard Island, McIntosh County, Georgia (Ruckdeschel et al., 1982). Nesting by western Atlantic *Dermochelys* may occur from February to August, but mostly from April into July.

Eastern Pacific nesting areas from which leatherbacks may migrate northward include: Ecuador, Panama, Costa Rica, Guatemala, and Mexico (Oaxaca, Guerrero, Michoacán, Jalisco, and Baja California). Nesting populations in Oaxaca, Guerrero, and Michoacán are apparently large (Pritchard, 1982). Nesting on eastern Pacific beaches occurs from September to March, and possibly to May, but is most concentrated from November into January.

Based on a von Bertalanffy growth model estimating the age of barnacles colonizing female leatherbacks, Eckert and Eckert (1988) extrapolated the dates on which individual turtles arrived at their nesting beaches and suggested that gravid females do not arrive from the temperate zone until just before nesting. They also thought that the females travel directly to a preferred nesting beach rather than oviposit opportunistically at some beach along the route. Nesters at the Virgin Island site they studied apparently arrive asynchronously over a four-month period, and, irrespective of date, begin to oviposit within relatively few days of arrival.

Typical nesting beaches have a slope of 8–12° and are free of much abrasive material (coral, rocks), as the female's plastron is soft and easily scuffed. The sand varies in particle size, but usually is course with a high silica content, and broken mollusk shells may be common. If driftwood or other obstructions are present on the beach, the emerging female manipulates around them until reaching a chosen spot to excavate her nest. If she becomes lodged in these, mortality from overheating or predation may follow (Fretey, 1977). Normally a deep-water approach is necessary so the female can ride the waves high onto the beach. Possibly, the sound of the breakers may be a supporting navigational cue (Mrosovsky, 1972).

Nesting leatherbacks usually land singly or in small groups at night. Bacon (1970) found that on Trinidad all observed females emerged from the sea between 2100 and midnight, and spent about 1.5 hours on the beach.

Leatherback females are much less disturbed by lights or movements once they have beached than are cheloniid sea turtles. Once ashore the female begins a labored dragging forward of the body by simultaneous movements of all four limbs, and slowly progresses up the beach (Renous and Bels, 1991). Visual obstructions may cause her to perform a circling motion to get her bearings, and orientation circles seem phototactic (Bacon, 1973). Circling behavior is most frequent on cloudy, moonlit nights, and it is possible that the changing illumination during the crawl may disorient her and lead to the circling behavior. On steep unobstructed beaches with a dark background and constant light conditions, the tract is usually short (>10 m) and direct. On flat beaches the direct tract may be relatively long (<10 m).

After crawling a distance over dry sand, the female stops and begins scraping away sand with bulldozerlike sweeps of the forelimbs working mostly together, while the hind limbs scrape and push sand independently of the forelimbs and of each other, to construct a concealing pit in which she lies while excavating the actual nest cavity. This body pit is at first deeper anteriorly, but eventually is leveled. When the sand under the posterior portion of the plastron has been brought to the same level as the anterior floor of the pit, the hind feet continue to dig at this point, and the cavity that grows there becomes the nest. Once the actual nest cavity is begun, the female becomes essentially oblivious to disturbance. The hind feet work alternately in digging the nest, the body pivoting on its forward end to swing the working flipper directly over the hole. Digging stops when the cavity is as deep as the hind foot can easily

Nesting *Dermochelys coriacea*

reach. The hind flippers are then spread out flat behind the body, over and partly within the opening of the nest, into which the tail and cloaca are lowered. Almost immediately oviposition begins. Throughout the egg-laying process part of one of the hind flippers remains in the nest, its distal sections pressed against the back edge of the nest.

Shortly after the last egg has been dropped, and while the forelimbs are still anchored motionless, the hind flippers begin to fill the cavity. Again they work alternately, each pulling and pushing in sand from the accumulation on its side of the opening. When the fill, rising in the nest, is high enough to be felt by the working flippers, the edges of these tilt downward anteriorly in such a way as to press the forerim into the sand over the nest. This is the beginning of a packing operation which increases as filling nears completion. For several minutes the flippers keep up the packing work, sometimes pressing downward so hard that the plastron is raised from the sand. After a while the forelegs join in the filling. Working together they sweep with lateral strokes that begin far forward and throw sand back over the sides of the body and into the pit. At the same time, the hind legs slowly drag sand into the cavity, resulting in the building of a growing mound under the back end of the body. The forelimb strokes drag the turtle slowly forward away from the original body pit, leaving behind a character-istic trail marked by an irregular ridge (the mounding work of the hind limbs) and two deep crescent-shaped cavities where the front flippers made their last scrape.

Nesting *Dermochelys coriacea*

Dermochelys coriacea returns to the sea

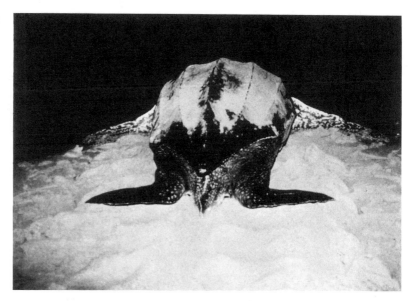

After the female has thus moved several meters, she stops concealment behavior and begins the return trip to the sea. Once again an orientation circle may be performed to determine the correct direction.

More complete descriptions of the nesting behavior are presented in Carr and Ogren (1959), from which the above notes were modified, and Pritchard and Trebbau (1984). Nesting *Dermochelys* emit a variety of sounds (Mrosovsky, 1972). Some are sighs accompanying breathing, but others are sharper and resemble a human belch. The sounds are relatively intense, in the 300–500-Hz range, and although they may simply be related to labored breathing, their role may possibly be communicative to offshore males waiting to mate (Mrosovsky, 1972) or to other emerging females to prevent being crawled upon.

The nest may be flask shaped or not, depending on whether the turtle digs down to damp sand. Data regarding nest dimensions are scanty, but Deraniyagala (1939) found a nest in Sri Lanka 100 cm deep, including the body pit. In Australia, Limpus and McLachlan (1979) found an egg mass 61–103 cm below the beach surface in a chamber measuring 47 × 30 cm, and McAlpine (1980) reported that Panamanian nests had the first egg laid at depths of 95–110 cm and the last at depths of 30–61 cm below the surface. Most nests are dug within 15 m of the high-tide mark.

Poor nest selection may result in high egg mortality. Females often nest in places where their eggs are destroyed by high tides, and such behavior seems related to beach topography (Mrosovsky, 1983b). In the Virgin Islands, short-term erosion and accretion

cycles result in an annual loss of 45–60% of the nests (Eckert, 1987; Eckert and Eckert, 1990). Also, some nest sites may be more prone to predation that others.

Leatherbacks usually nest at 8–12-day intervals, but the internesting period may be much longer. Dutton et al. (1992) reported that a female may lay as many as 11 clutches a year in the Virgin Islands, but probably about 6 clutches a season are normal. Clutch frequency is positively correlated with female carapace length (Tucker and Frazer, 1991).

During the internesting period many females remain close to the nesting beach, frequently diving for as long as 37 minutes (Eckert et al., 1986), but others may stray away and lay their next clutch on another beach. A three-year study in the Virgin Islands showed that 0–27% of the females strayed each year (Eckert et al., 1989a). A few may even migrate away without laying their last clutch. Such seems the case of a stranded, gravid female found in New Jersey 1,500 km north of the nearest nesting beach on 24 August 1979 who contained 23 shelled eggs; three, 51–52 mm in diameter, contained yolk, the others, 15–41 mm, were yolkless (Rhodin and Schoelkopf, 1982).

Female leatherbacks have a multiyear nesting interval, usually returning to the beaches to oviposit every two or three years (Pritchard, 1971), but whether or not these represent cycles is questionable (see comments under *Caretta caretta*).

The usual clutch contains 50–166 eggs; females laying on Atlantic beaches normally oviposit more eggs per clutch than those nesting on eastern Pacific beaches. Midseason clutches are often larger that those laid before or after. A rather large proportion of the eggs is yolkless; nests from Atlantic beaches average 80–90 yolked eggs but those from the eastern Pacific average only 60–66 yolked eggs. The smaller, yolkless eggs usually do not appear until after 30–40 yolked eggs have been laid (Pritchard, 1971). Normal yolked eggs are spherical, have soft, white shells, are 49–65 mm in diameter, and weigh 70–90 g. The shell contains several crystalline forms consistent with the presence of both aragonite and calcite, but not phosphorus, within their organic matrix (Solomon and Watt, 1985). Eggs in whose shells the normal aragonite configuration is partially replaced by large calcite crystals are more prone to attack by fungi, resulting in the death of the embryo (Solomon and Tippett, 1987). After four or five days of incubation, fertile eggs develop a white spot on the shell which enlarges to make the entire shell opaque and white. Infertile eggs fail to develop white spots and remain creamy beige throughout incubation (Chan, 1989). Yolkless eggs may be ellipsoidal, small and spherical, or somewhat dumbbell shaped, and are 13–45 mm in greatest diameter.

Tucker and Frazer (1991) found no correlation between clutch size and female carapace length at Isla Culebra, Puerto Rico, but Hall (1988) had previously found a positive correlation at the same area and Hirth and Ogren (1987) reported a strong correlation in Costa Rica. Hirth and Ogren also found positive correlations between both egg diameter and mass and female size, and Hall (1988) reported a positive correlation between egg size and female length.

Incubation periods of leatherback eggs are 50–78 days (Márquez, 1990), but most undisturbed clutches probably hatch in 60–65 days. Transplanted clutches are somewhat delayed, and often take over 70 days to hatch. Miller (1985) and Renous et al. (1989) have described the embryonic development of *Dermochelys*. Ossification of the embryo skeleton occurs mainly in the last half of incubation and is well advanced at the time of hatching; 75% of the calcium is obtained from outside the egg, so the eggshell is not structurally altered by the developing embryo (Simkiss, 1962).

Hatchlings are dark brown or black, with white or yellow carapacial keels and flipper rims. The skin is covered with small scales and the tail is dorsally keeled; the scales and keel soon disappear. Neonate carapace length is 51–68 mm; hatchlings weigh 35–50 g. Carr and Ogren (1959) gave the following mean measurements for 30 hatchlings from Caribbean Costa Rica: carapace length, 62.8 mm; carapace width, 41.8 mm; plastron length, 53.6 mm; depth, 26.3 mm; and head width, 18.04 mm.

Hatchlings remain in the nest cavity for a time after breaking out of the egg, apparently waiting for proper surface thermal conditions. Emergence from the nest usually is nocturnal. The rise to the surface from the nest cavity is achieved by sporadic thrashing activity, usually begun by one turtle and quickly spreading throughout the rest of the hatchlings. Such activity scrapes sand from the ceiling and walls of the nest chamber and deposits it on the floor below the bottommost hatchlings. This buildup of the floor beneath the turtles slowly pushes them upward until they are only a few centimeters below the surface. There they remain until the surface reaches the proper temperature, often near dawn, and then they scrape away the remaining sand, emerge, and make their way to the surf (see section on behavior for a description of their orientation behavior).

Hatchling sex is determined by incubation temperature. Incubating temperatures at or below 28.75°C produce only males, incubating temperatures at or above 29.75°C produce only females (Mrosovsky et al., 1984a; Rimblot et al., 1985; Rimblot-Baly et al., 1987). An incubation temperature of 29.5°C produces some individuals of each sex, and is considered the pivotal temperature for sexual differentiation of the gonads (Rimblot-Baly et al., 1987).

In Surinam more males are produced from eggs naturally incubated in the wetter, cooler months of the nesting season, but more females are produced in the warmer, drier months; the overall sex ratio favors males 51% to 49% (Mrosovsky et al., 1984a).

That low incubating temperatures produce only males becomes a problem if the eggs of *Dermochelys*, and also those of other marine turtles, are taken from the natural nest and artificially incubated in styrofoam boxes, as has been the practice in the past. As these boxes are well insulated, incubation temperatures are normally below 29.5°C and produce only males (Dutton et al., 1985). Head-start juveniles released from cool incubated clutches may tremendously bias the sex ratio.

GROWTH AND LONGEVITY: Few data are available on the growth rate of *Dermochelys*, and those are predominantly from captives or semi-captives (this in itself is interesting, as leatherbacks generally do poorly in captivity). Hatchlings kept at the Hassanal Bolkiah Aquarium, Malaysia, and fed Spanish mackerel, prawns, and pieces of water-buffalo heart grew about 10 mm/week to carapace lengths of 93–112 mm in five weeks, 120–151 mm in 10 weeks, 190 mm in 15 weeks (the lone survivor), 247 mm at 20 weeks, 315 mm at 25 weeks, 375 mm at 30 weeks, and 400 mm in 33 weeks (Birkenmeier, 1971). The largest survivor of this group weighed 45 g on arrival and 4.54 kg at the age of 29 weeks when 370 mm long. Deraniyagala (1939) kept a leatherback until it died after 169 days; at that time it was 160 mm in carapace length, 133 mm in plastron length, and 40 mm in head length, and the extended forelimbs, tip to tip, were 280 mm. Another individual kept by him reached the following carapace lengths (mm) at the ages specified: 195 days, 225; 218 days, 302 (3 kg); 308 days, 350 (4.53 kg); 624 days, 433 (6.8 kg); and 662 days, 545 mm. From 25 September 1975 to 26 May 1976 a captive juvenile grew in carapace length from 60 to 216 mm, and it increased its weight from 255 g on 3 December 1975 to 1,035 g on 26 May 1976 (Phillips, 1977). A hatchling survived nine months at the Miami Seaquarium at which time it weighed 5.9 kg (Edwards, 1976), and Pritchard and Trebbau (1984) reported that two leatherbacks kept at that institution weighed 16 kg after eight months, and that one of these increased its weight from 3 kg to 7 kg in less than a month.

Skeletal growth is different in *Dermochelys* from that in other species of marine turtles. Primary vascular irruption occurs into the noncalcified hypertrophied cartilage of the metaphysis with rapid extension of vascularity also into the nonhypertrophied epiphyseal cartilage of long bones. Endochondral ossification of the metaphysis advances continuously from the diaphysis, no calcified subphyseal cartilage plate is formed, nor is there isolation of a cartilaginous metaphyseal cone. The noncalcified epiphyseal cartilage remains thick with transphyseal, as well as perichondral, blood vessels running through cartilage canals (Rhodin, 1985). This ossification pattern may be due to very rapid skeletal growth leading to a huge body size, and resembles skeletal growth in marine mammals (Rhodin, 1985; Rhodin et al., 1980, 1981).

Maximum natural longevity is unknown, but Pritchard (1985) reported that a nesting female tagged in French Guiana on 14 June 1970 was found dead in New Jersey on 5 June 1984.

FOOD HABITS: *Dermochelys* is highly carnivorous on invertebrates, but it may at times ingest, possibly secondarily, some algae and vertebrates. Preferred prey are the numerous oceanic jellyfish (particularly Scyphomedusae). This is a relatively open marine food niche, as the only other large predator on this group is the ocean sunfish, *Mola mola*. Prey reported for wild leatherbacks include: jellyfish (*Aequorea, Apolemia, Aurelia, Chrysaora,*

Cyanea, Pelagia, Physalia, Rhizostoma, Stomolophus), hydrozoans (*Obelia*), sea urchins, octopi, squid, snails (*Buccinum, Conus, Crepidula, Hipponyx, Lunatia, Murex, Natica, Strombus*), bivalves (*Pecten, Pinna*), amphipods (*Hyperia,* possibly symbiotic with jellyfish), crabs (*Carcinus, Libinia*), tunicates (*Pyrosoma, Salpa*), small fish (*Trachurus, Urophycis;* possibly symbiotic with jellyfish), a hatchling ridley turtle (*Lepidochelys*), small bird feathers, blue-green algae, green algae (*Enteromorpha*), and floating kelps (*Fucus, Ulva*) (Glusing, 1973; Den Hartog, 1980; Eisenberg and Frazier, 1983; Den Hartog and Van Nierop, 1984; Limpus, 1984; Pritchard and Trebbau, 1984; Márquez, 1990; Davenport and Balazs, 1991).

Captives have eaten jellyfish (*Cassiopea*), octopi, prawns, fish (*Scomberomorus*), raw meat, chicken liver, cattle heart, green algae, and bread (Deraniyagala, 1939; Birkenmeier, 1971; Pritchard and Trebbau, 1984). Chan (1988) was successful in feeding captive hatchlings blended squid mantle incorporated into agar discs.

The jaw apparatus of *Dermochelys* lacks the massive construction, crushing plates, and musculature for taking hard-shelled prey found in some cheloniid sea turtles, but the jaw rims are sharp and well adapted for a jellyfish diet. In the relatively long esophagus are numerous keratinized, posteriorly pointing spines which probably prevent soft prey, such as jellyfish, from being regurgitated and escaping from the mouth; these are illustrated in Den Hartog and Van Nierop (1984).

Duron-Dufrenne (1978) calculated that an adult leatherback would ingest about 8–10 kg of organic matter/day, but, based on dietary studies, Den Hartog and Van Nierop (1984) thought total ingestion more on the order of 2.5 kg/day, representing an energy intake of 11,000–16,000 kcal/day. Using volumetric oxygen consumption data, Lutcavage and Lutz (1986) calculated that an average-weight hatchling (53 g) consumes 0.36 liter of oxygen/day, or the equivalent of 1.76 kcal/day energy consumption. Complete combustion of a 100-g jellyfish (*Cassiopea*) yields 1.62 g ash-free dry weight. Assuming an overall assimilation rate of 76% (Bjorndal, 1980a), this results in 3.2 kcal assimilable energy or 0.03 kcal energy/jellyfish gram. Therefore, the typical hatchling may need 55.3 g of jellyfish each day for maintenance and growth.

Many jellyfish are consumed from schools floating at or near the surface (Duron-Dufrenne, 1978; Eisenberg and Frazier, 1983; Collard, 1990). When feeding at the surface, the slow-swimming turtle swallows jellyfish rapidly, possibly drawing them into its mouth by pharyngeal inflation, and raises its head periodically out of the water, presumably to assist in swallowing this slippery prey. Not all feeding is done at the surface, however, and much of the prey is benthic. Limpus (1984) reported that a *Dermochelys* was hooked on a handline baited with octopus suspended just off the bottom at about 50 m depth, and Eckert et al. (1989b) thought the dive pattern in the Virgin Islands suggests nocturnal foraging within the deep scattering layer. Davenport (1988) has gone so far as to suggest that deep-diving leatherbacks are pursuing bioluminous jellyfish. Obviously, leatherbacks swim to the habitat of their prey. If near enough to the shore for ample food species to be supported, *Dermochelys* probably dives to feed, but when in a pelagic situation, more likely feeds on floating jellyfish.

Predilection for clear jellyfish has created a serious problem for *Dermochelys*. As increasing volumes of human trash have been dumped into the oceans, the numbers of floating clear plastic bags has increased tremendously. Apparently, leatherbacks cannot tell these strips of plastic from jellyfish and swallow them, resulting in blockage of the gastrointestinal tract. Such accidents are more and more frequently implicated in the deaths of stranded leatherbacks (Mrosovsky, 1981; Fritts, 1982; Den Hartog and Van Nierop, 1984).

After feeding on jellyfish, the flesh of *Dermochelys* may store nematocyst toxins and become poisonous if eaten. Taylor (in Halstead, 1970) reported that in the Philippines 14 deaths occurred among 33 persons who became ill from eating leatherback meat in 1917.

PREDATORS AND DEFENSE: Traditionally, humans have been the worst nest predators, gathering the eggs for both commerce and personal consumption, but other animals also raid nests and eat the eggs, including: ghosts crabs (*Ocypode*), monitor lizards (*Varanus*), gulls (*Larus*), turnstones (*Arenaria*), knots (*Calidris*), plovers (*Pluvialis*), vultures (*Cathartes, Coragyps*), opossums (*Didelphis*), raccoons (*Procyon*), coatis (*Nasua*), feral dogs (*Canis*), genets (*Genetta*), mongooses (*Herpestes, Ictonyx*), and pigs (*Sus*). On the perilous trip across the beach, hatchlings are eaten by ghost crabs, gulls, crows (*Corvus*), vultures, frigate birds (*Fregata*), various hawks and possibly owls, and coatis. Once in the water hatchlings are still not safe as cuttlefish, octopi, sharks (*Carcharhinus*) and other large fish prey on them. Adults seem relatively free of predators other than humans, but jaguars (*Felis onca*) may occasionally injure nesting females, and large sharks (*Carcharhinus*) and killer whales (*Orcinus orca*) may attack them at sea (Gilbert

and Kelso, 1971; Mrosovsky, 1971; Pritchard, 1971; Ernst and Barbour, 1972; Zwinenberg, 1974; Fretey and Lescure, 1981; Pritchard and Trebbau, 1984; Hirth and Ogren, 1987; Horrocks, 1989; Godley et al., 1991).

Several species of barnacles and remora fish often attach to the skin, and although their presence probably causes little local damage, they may cause drag as the turtle swims, making it more vulnerable to predation (Ernst and Barbour, 1972; Fretey, 1978).

Accidents also cost many leatherbacks their lives. Females perish on beaches when they become trapped or disoriented by downed trees and other large debris, which eventually causes them to heat beyond their lethal point (Fretey, 1977). Besides perishing from the ingestion of plastic refuse (see above), leatherbacks often drown after entangling in fishing nets and lines (Balazs, 1982b; Caillouet et al., 1991).

Dermochelys has great strength and is a formidable adversary when captured: it flails its flippers violently and may bite viciously. It may even vocalize when in distress. If disturbed in open water, the leatherback normally dives and swims quickly away beneath the surface, but individuals may behave differently. An approximately 1.5-m adult was seen chasing a shark (*Carcharhinus*) that had apparently attacked it, and, after driving off the shark, the *Dermochelys* attacked the boat of the observers (Engbring et al., 1992).

POPULATIONS: Unfortunately, few data are available concerning population size of *Dermochelys coriacea*. Most estimates are based on the numbers of females that emerge to nest on a particular beach during a three-year period. Adding these together may not be the best way to calculate the total world population of leatherbacks, especially as the adult sex ratio has not been confirmed; nevertheless, Pritchard (1982) estimated the world population of mature females to be 115,000. If this number of females is accurate and is further divided among the numerous American, African, and Asian beaches where *Dermochelys* is known to regularly nest, it presents a rather bleak survival picture for the species.

Although some major nesting beaches are visited by relatively large numbers of females each year, most nesting areas service only 25–100 females annually. Of 19 known nesting beaches listed by Ross (1982), only 4 are used by more than 1,000 females a year. Of nesting populations which may provide the turtles that reach North American coasts, only those at French Guiana (6,000 females/year) in the Caribbean and Chacahua (2,000) and Tierra Colorada (5,000), Mexico, in the eastern Pacific (Ross, 1982; Márquez et al., 1981) can be considered large. As many as 80,000 nests may be dug each year on the beaches of western Mexico (Márquez, 1990). Ross (1982) estimated that only 14,325 females nest each year worldwide. If the females at Tierra Colorada nest on a two-year cycle, the total population of females there would be about 10,000 (Márquez et al., 1981). Aerial surveys show *Dermochelys* to be uncommon throughout the entire Gulf of Mexico, averaging about 50 turtles/10,000 km^2 (Lohoefener et al., 1988); only 36 leatherbacks were stranded on beaches in Texas during the period 1981–1989 (Judd et al., 1991).

Two areas of relatively high summer abundance occur in the northeastern United States, south of Long Island and in the central and eastern Gulf of Maine, with a mean density of 6.9 and a range of 1.7–60 leatherbacks per 1,000 km (Shoop and Kenney, 1992). Maximum density is higher than in the Gulf of Mexico, and 100–900 *Dermochelys* may be present during the summer months.

Egg poaching by humans has caused population declines at most leatherback nesting beaches, but on protected beaches in Surinam, Florida, and South Africa, nesting by *Dermochelys* has increased in recent years (Ross, 1982). The overall trend in decline could mean extinction of this species from all but a few protected beaches. The leatherback is listed as endangered under the Endangered Species Act.

No estimates of adult survivorship have been published, but Iverson (1991a) estimated the annual natural survivorship from egg to hatchling to be only 63%, and the National Research Council (1990) listed the mean emergence success as varying from 25 to 71% at different beaches. On some beaches subject to erosion 40–60% of the nests may be lost each year (Whitmore and Dutton, 1985; Eckert, 1987). To further complicate survivorship, several papers have noted that moving clutches for artificial incubation may induce higher egg mortality (Wyneken et al., 1988; Eckert and Eckert, 1990).

A leatherback stranded in Wales had relatively high concentrations of some heavy metals and PCB in its flesh, indicating that chemical pollution of the oceans may also pose a problem for survival.

The only reports on the sex ratio of *Dermochelys* are those of Mrosovsky et al. (1984a), who calculated that during an entire nesting season in Surinam 51% of the hatchlings were males (a 1:1 ratio at hatching), and Márquez et al. (1981), who estimated a 1:1.5 adult male to adult female ratio at Tierra Colorada, Guerrero, Mexico.

REMARKS: Both immunoprecipitation and electrophoretic tests of serum have shown *Dermochelys* to be the most distinct species of living sea turtle (Frair, 1979, 1982). However, these tests also indicate a closeness that caused Frair (1982) to suggest that the family Dermochelyidae be either placed in a superfamily containing all living sea turtles or relegated to subfamily rank within the family Cheloniidae. Zangerl (1980) also proposed that *Dermochelys* be placed in the same family as the cheloniids, and chromosome morphology supports this view (Bickham, 1979; Medrano et al., 1987). The minimum chronologic separation of modern hard-shelled sea-turtle lines is probably no less than 30 million years, and that leading to leatherbacks is probably at least 50 million years old (Carr, 1982). Studies on the comparative histology of the nasal epithelium of *Dermochelys* and species of the Cheloniidae by Saint-Girons (1991) supports the conclusion that the leatherback was adapted to an aquatic existence long before the cheloniids.

There has been some controversy regarding the authorship of the specific name *coriacea* (Fretey and Bour, 1980; Rhodin and Smith, 1982; Bour and Dubois, 1983a), but Linnaeus (1766) is usually judged the original describer of the species as his designation was in the acceptable binomial style.

Additional references on *Dermochelys* are listed in Pritchard (1971, 1980a).

Trionychidae
Soft-shelled turtles

Living species of softshells are found today in North America, Africa, Asia, and the Indo-Australian archipelago. Fossils, possibly dating back to the late Jurassic, indicate a greater geographic range in the past which included South America and Europe. Five species live in the United States and Canada; two of these are of Asian origin and have been introduced and established in Hawaii.

Softshells are a highly derived group, certainly not primitive, with rounded, flattened carapaces that lack horny scutes, but are covered with a leathery skin. The neck is long and retractile, and the limbs are paddlelike with three claws on each. The snout is commonly a long proboscis.

The bony elements of the shell are secondarily reduced; peripherals and pygals are absent, and the distal ends of the ribs project freely in the American species. Neurals bones total 7–8 and 7–10 costals are present, with the last pairs meeting centrally in some species. The plastron is reduced and has central lacunae and lateral fontanelles, but no entoplastron. Several callosities (superficial ossifications closely connected to the underlying bones) are present on the adult plastron. The neck vertebrae are slender, and none is biconvex. The fourth digit has four to six phalanges; the fifth has two to four. The temporal region of the skull is widely open. Neither the parietal nor the postorbital touches the squamosal, and the premaxillae are fused. The reduced vomer does not separate the palatines, is separated from the premaxillae, touches the maxillae, and separates the internal nares. The nasopalatine foramen is large; the palatine fenestra is small. The jugal touches the parietal. The maxilla contacts the pterygoid, but not the quadratojugal. The basisphenoid is separate from the pterygoid but touches the palatines. The quadrate encloses the stapes, and an epipterygoid is present. The jaw is very deep at the level of the coronoid process, and the dentary reaches laterally nearly to the posterior end of the jaw. The family is divided into two subfamilies, but all American species belong to the subfamily Trionychinae (typical softshells).

In a cladistic study of 113 skeletal characters, Meylan (1987) subdivided the genus *Trionyx* into nine genera (six monotypic). Webb (1990) thought this premature, but an important first step toward our understanding of the relationships within the genus *Trionyx* (*sensu lato*). As there seems to be doubt regarding the wisdom of Meylan's systematic arrangement, we agree with Webb, but believe some of Meylan's genera will prove valid, and others will probably be relegated to subgeneric rank. Until further study is completed by Webb and others, we follow Webb (1990)

103

Carapacial bones of *Trionyx*

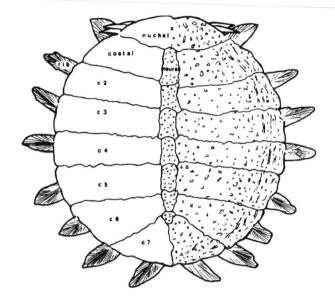

Plastral bones of *Trionyx*

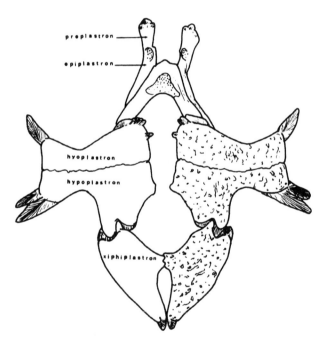

in retaining the five American softshells in the genus *Trionyx*. The relationships of North American softshell turtles have been reviewed by Stejneger (1944), Neill (1951a), Schwartz (1956b), Webb (1962, 1990), Frair (1983), and Meylan (1984, 1987).

Trionyx muticus Le Sueur, 1827
Smooth softshell

PLATE 9

RECOGNITION: *Trionyx muticus* is medium-sized to large turtle (carapace length to 17.8 cm in males, 35.6 cm in females) with a round, flat, leathery shell lacking spines or raised knobs. The carapace is olive to orangish brown, with a pattern of darker dots, dashes, or blotches; many have a lighter marginal band bordered on the inside by a darker area. The hingeless plastron is immaculate white or gray, and the underlying bones are commonly visible through the skin as callosities on the preplastra, epiplastra, hypoplastra, and xiphiplastra. The head, neck, and limbs are olive to orange above and gray to white below. A black-bordered, light line extends through the eye and onto the neck. The tubular snout commonly terminates somewhat obliquely, and the round nostrils are usually inferior. The nostrils lack the septal ridge that is present in other North American softshell turtles. The mandibles are very sharp. The limbs are usually patternless, but may have a few scattered dark dots, and the anterior surface of each forelimb has four cornified antebrachial scales. The feet are webbed, and the webbing extends up the shank of the hind limbs.

Adult males have long thick tails, with the anal vent near the tip, and lose the juvenile carapacial pattern of dark dashes with age until it is entirely absent or, more frequently, present only posteriorly. Adult females have short tails with the vent beneath the carapace, and a mottled or blotched carapacial pattern. Females have longer hind claws and males have longer foreclaws. Sexual size dimorphism is pronounced; adult females are, on average, about 1.5 times larger than adult males (Gibbons and Lovich, 1990).

KARYOTYPE: Diploid chromosomes total 66, including 16 metacentric and submetacentric, 12 subtelocentric, and 38 acrocentric and telocentric chromosomes, with a total of 94 arms (Stock, 1972). The diploid chromosome total of only 56 reported by

Forbes (1966) was questioned by Bickham et al. (1983).

FOSSIL RECORD: Although the genus *Trionyx* has existed in North America from at least the Miocene Barstovian (Holman, 1973, 1982; Holman and Sullivan, 1981; Holman and Corner, 1985; Voorhies et al., 1987; Joeckel, 1988), and possibly as long ago as the Cretaceous (Quammen, 1992), no fossil of *T. muticus* has been found. An archeological record exists from Havana, Mason County, Illinois (Adler, 1968).

DISTRIBUTION: The smooth softshell turtle ranges from the Ohio River drainage of Ohio, Indiana, and Illinois, the upper Mississippi watershed from Minnesota and Wisconsin, and the Missouri River of the Dakotas south to the western Florida Panhandle west to central Texas. An isolated population occurs in eastern New Mexico. Although formerly present in the Allegheny River in Pennsylvania, the species is now considered extirpated in that state (Ernst, 1985d).

GEOGRAPHIC VARIATION: Two subspecies are recognized. *Trionyx muticus muticus* Le Sueur, 1827, the midland smooth softshell turtle. ranges in the central United States from Ohio to southern Minnesota and the Dakotas, south to Tennessee, Louisiana, and Oklahoma and west to Texas and New Mexico. It is distinguished by a juvenile pattern of dusky dots and short lines, ill-defined pale stripes on the snout, and pale postocular stripes with thin black borders less than half their width, except in some individuals in the Colorado River drainage of Texas. *Trionyx m. calvatus* Webb, 1959, the Gulf Coast smooth softshell turtle, lives along the Gulf Coast from the Escambia River system of Alabama and the Florida Panhandle west to southeastern Louisiana and

Plastron of *Trionyx muticus*

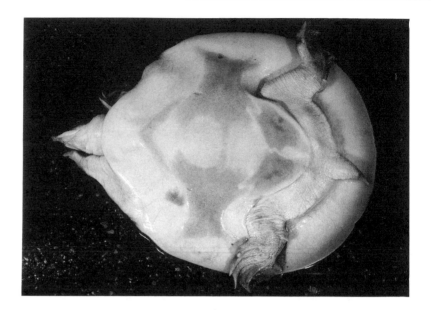

Trionyx muticus muticus

eastern Mississippi, including the Pearl River drainage. It has a juvenile carapacial pattern of large round (some are ocellate) spots, no stripes on the dorsal surface of the snout, a pattern of fine markings on the dorsal surface of the limbs, and pale postocular stripes having thick black borders approximately half their width on adult males.

CONFUSING SPECIES: All other North American softshells have ridges on the internasal septum, spines or knobs on the anterior border of the carapace, and heavily patterned forelimbs.

HABITAT: The smooth softshell occurs in large rivers and streams with moderate to fast currents. *Trionyx m. calvatus* has been taken only from the habitats described above, but *T. m. muticus* is also known from lakes, impoundments, and shallow bogs. Waterways with sandy bottoms and a few rocks or aquatic plants are preferred.

Distribution of *Trionyx muticus*

Smooth softshells from Iowa are limited to the large, downstream portions of rivers (Williams and Christiansen, 1981). Ponds are occasionally occupied there, but they are always connected to large rivers at least during floods.

Studies by Plummer (1977b) in the Kansas River, Kansas, show that, although males live in every habitat of the river, they are most abundant in shallow water near sandbars. Subadult females are more inclined to sandbars than adult females, but less than males. Adult females are not often captured on sandbars except during the nesting season. Basking adult females are not often seen, and most of these emerge on steep mud banks near deep water. Hatchlings prefer small, shallow, warm puddles created by the highly dissected shoreline of sandbars. In Indiana, adult females frequent seasonally flushed oxbow ponds and main river channels; males are rare in oxbows but common in the main channels (Ewert, 1979c).

BEHAVIOR: *Trionyx muticus* emerges from hibernation in late March or early April in Kansas, but most annual activity takes place from May through September (Plummer, 1977b). The winter is spent underwater buried in the bottom (Plummer and Shirer, 1975). Daily activity seems almost entirely diurnal (Plummer and Shirer, 1975). When not browsing or basking it spends long periods underwater, buried in the bottom at a depth that just allows the snout to reach the surface. Smooth softshells bury themselves by thrusting the head into the substrate and then pulling with the forelimbs while pushing with the hind limbs as the body is tilted downward toward the front. This is followed by a shuffling motion that stirs up the bottom, causing the loose materials to settle over the turtle. When finished, the carapace is concealed and only the head is visible. While in water, *T. muticus* may lose about 64% of its respiratory carbon dioxide by nonpulmonary means, primarily through the skin (D. C. Jackson et al., 1976), allowing it to remain submerged for extended periods.

Smooth softshells bask aerially on sandy or muddy beaches within a few meters of the water (Fitch and Plummer, 1975), or on logs or rocks, with head fully extended and the limbs usually tucked under the shell. Aquatic basking also occurs in the shallow water around beaches (Williams and Christiansen, 1981).

A single smooth softshell in Iowa outfitted with a

Trionyx muticus muticus

Trionyx muticus calvatus

radiotransmitter and followed for four days appeared to select environments that were roughly the same temperature as the surface water, implying surface activity (Williams and Christiansen, 1981).

Because *Trionyx muticus* has a shell covered with skin, it has a high rate of water exchange, and consequently does not spend long periods on land. In fresh water, the rate is 6.3 ml/100 g wet mass/h. Median skin influx permeability to water and sodium is 1154 μmol/cm^2·h and efflux permeability is 1049 μmol/cm^2·h. Values of influx and efflux for plastral skin and cartilage combined are 608 and 420 μmol/cm^2·h, respectively (Dunson, 1986). Generally, smaller smooth softshells have a relatively larger overall water concentration, a lower overall sodium concentration, and a larger relative wet mass of shell (Dunson and Heatwole, 1986). A striking inverse size-related difference exists in the proportion of overall exchangeable sodium.

The smooth softshell is a powerful swimmer. Cahn (1937) saw one capture a small brook trout, one of the fastest of our freshwater fish. The turtle rapidly overtook the darting fish and when within reach shot out its head capturing the prey.

Most movements are aquatic, but females wander on sandbars during the nesting season (Fitch and Plummer, 1975). Radio-equipped *Trionyx muticus* in Kansas were often recaptured in areas extending 2–3 km along their river (Plummer and Shirer, 1975). Mean linear home-range length (and 95% confidence limits) of males was 474 m (346–623); of subadult females, 750 m (512–1,033); and of adult females, 1,228 m (814–1,726). All three home-range lengths are significantly different from each other. Utilization of the home range differed between the sexes in several aspects. Mean movement per day within the home range was significantly greater in females: adult females, 165 m (131–204); subadult females, 116 m (80–158); and males 61 m (46–78). Males were inactive a greater amount of time (38%) than either subadult females (26%) or adult females (25%). Females tended to occupy both sides of the river, whereas males tended to live on one side. Female movements were very extensive. One moved a total of 21.8 km in 20 days, although she did not move at all on 5. She ranged 4 km downstream from the release point and 6.8 km upstream, passing the release point twice. Another subadult female moved 10.5 km in 16 days (2 days spent with no movement) to a distance 6.8 km upstream from the release point, averaging 658 m/day. Males moved as much as 1.9–3.5 km upstream in one to four days, and 2.9 km downstream in one day. Females swam 2.1–2.3 km upstream in one day, 7.8 km in two days, and 3.3–4.1 km downstream in a day. Studies of homing ability by Plummer and Shirer (1975) seemed to indicate that the softshells could return from long distances (2.4–4.0 km) if displaced, but the results are not conclusive as some individuals wander farther than this and may have knowledge of extensive stretches of the river.

Anderson (1958) studied the photic response and water approach behavior of hatchlings along the Pearl River in Mississippi. Hatchlings move toward water even when it is not visible from their perspective. If artificial light is introduced along their path to the water they may orient toward the source. Hatchlings kept in cans filled with sand were active on the surface at night but buried into the substrate during the daytime. In maze experiments, hatchlings orient more often toward artificial light (both moonlight and flashlight) than toward darkness. Hatchlings also orient away from dark masses erected between them and water.

REPRODUCTION: Males mature in their fourth year at plastron lengths of 80–85 mm; the largest immature male found by Plummer (1977c) was 90 mm, and the smallest mature male was 79 mm. Females mature in their ninth year at 140–150 mm plastron length; the largest immature female found by Plummer (1977c) was 151 mm, and the smallest mature female was 131 mm.

In Kansas, the volume of the male testes varies seasonally, reaching maximum diameter before hibernation, decreasing in the spring, and increasing again in midsummer (Plummer, 1977c). In April–May the vas deferens are about 2 mm in diameter, highly convoluted, and turgid with sperm, but by June they are flaccid and translucent with some empty. In September–October they once again fill with sperm.

Vitellogenesis begins in July in Kansas females, and by September some ova are of ovulatory diameter (16–20 mm; Plummer, 1977c). By May females contain only enlarged ova, but smaller follicles 1–5 mm in diameter are present throughout the year. Females collected in June have both enlarged ova and corpora lutea, indicating that ovulation occurs in mid-May. By late June two sets of corpora lutea are present, indicating two clutches are produced each year.

Mating occurs after emergence from hibernation (Plummer and Shirer, 1975). Courtship behavior was observed in Kansas by Plummer (1977a) in April–June and August. Males actively search for females in the water and at basking sites. Searching males often pass from one basking turtle to another, presumably investigating their sex by probing with their snouts under the edge of the carapace of the basking individual. If the basking turtle is a male the response is usually passive, but occasionally a basking male will respond aggressively with an open mouth causing the investigator to retreat. Basking females often turn and bite at the searching male in an effort to prevent mounting, and semicircular bleeding wounds, presumably from bites, are common on the posterior margins of male carapaces during the spring. Receptive females remain passive while the male investigates and then mounts. Some females move back into the water while the male attempts to mount, and several males may attempt to mount one female. Successful mounting seems to take place only in deeper water. Since males do not grasp females with their forelimbs, they are forced to continually swim in place to maintain their position. One pair, presumably copulating, was observed swimming about for 20 minutes. Plummer also observed captives courting in September.

Legler (1955) observed a captive male *T. spiniferus hartwegi* actively courting a female *T. muticus*. The male generally followed the female, but at times, she suddenly turned and followed him. Occasionally, the male bit the anterior part of her carapace. The rear rim of the female's carapace was upturned while that of the male was downturned. The female sank to the bottom of the tank several times and remained motionless. The male then approached from the rear, crawled onto her back and positioned his tail beneath her carapace bringing their vents together. The turtles remained in this position for about 15 seconds, possibly in intromission. This behavioral sequence was repeated five times in 30 minutes.

The nesting season encompasses late May through July, and nests are usually excavated on the high ridges of exposed sand bars (Muller, 1921; Goldsmith, 1945; Anderson, 1958; Webb, 1962; Fitch and Plummer, 1975; Plummer, 1976). Most are fully exposed to the sun and located within 30 m (4–90) of the water and about 1.34 m (0.5–6.1) above it (Fitch and Plummer, 1975). A few nests may, however, be dug in small patches of sand among dense, permanent vegetation. Often nests are in close proximity, with two or more in a space of a meter, so close, in fact, as to have connected chambers (Fitch and Plummer, 1975). The cavity is dug entirely by the hind feet and is 15–30 cm deep (Goldsmith, 1945; Ernst, pers. obs.); depth from the sand surface to the tops of the eggs in Kansas averages 16.2 cm (7.6–25.4; Fitch and Plummer, 1975). As the eggs are laid they are arranged into two layers within the nest chamber by the hind feet; the sand is often slightly damp but not saturated (Fitch and Plummer, 1975). After laying, the female uses her hind feet to fill the cavity and rake soil over the nest. In sandy soil the completed nests appear as small craters, and in pebbly places they are marked by circular patches of clear sand. Immediately after nesting, females often burrow, forming a shallow trough, usually about 1 m long but occasionally up to 4 m in length, with the nest in one end and the female at the other (Plummer, 1976).

Periodic flooding of sandbars is a major problem. Eggs submerged for over 24 hours have decreasing survivorship, and those submerged over four days have little chance of hatching (Plummer, 1976).

Clutches consist of 1–33 eggs; in Kansas most contain 11–14 (Fitch and Plummer, 1975; Plummer, 1976, 1977c), but farther north 18–22 eggs is usual (Muller, 1921; Cahn, 1937; Goldsmith, 1945; Webb, 1962; Vogt. 1981a). Second clutches of the season may contain slightly fewer eggs than the first (Fitch and Plummer, 1975). The number laid is proportional to the size of the female. The eggs are ovid to spherical and have thick brittle, white shells. They are 20–24 mm in diameter and weigh 3.4–9.0 g. Ewert

(1979a) reported that 9.2% of the weight is shell, 43.8% is albumen, and 47% is yolk.

The incubation period is 65–77 days. In the laboratory the average incubation time for eggs from Minnesota incubated at 25–25.5°C is 101.7 days (Ewert, 1979a). Eggs from Minnesota incubated at 29.5–30°C hatch in an average 59.0 days, but eggs from Texas require an average of 62.7 days (Ewert, 1979a).

Emergence from the nest takes place in August or September. Hatchlings leave the nest within the first three hours after sunset and all emerge within two hours (Anderson, 1958). Instead of using the caruncle, the hatchling escapes from the egg by means of its forelimbs.

The nearly circular, dull-olive carapace of the hatchling is marked with many short, black dashes and bordered with a pale margin, which broadens posteriorly. Hatchlings are 30–45 mm in carapace length, 21–32 mm in plastron length, and weigh about 3–7 g. Mean weight of hatchlings from Minnesota is 5.5 g, or about 74.3% of freshly laid egg weight; Texas hatchlings weigh 6.2 g, or about 76.3% of freshly laid egg weight (Ewert, 1979a). The umbilical scar is approximately 2 mm in diameter. The caruncle drops off in about a week.

Trionyx muticus appears to have genetic sex determination. Roughly equal numbers of males and females are produced at incubation temperatures ranging from 27–33°C (Ewert and Nelson, 1991).

GROWTH AND LONGEVITY: All we know about increase in size of *Trionyx muticus* comes from studies by Fitch and Plummer (1975) and Plummer (1977c) in Kansas.

Through allometric growth the carapace changes from an almost round shape in hatchlings to an ovoid shape in adults, but there is no corresponding change in plastral shape, so that the carapace/plastron ratio changes little with increasing size. In a sample of 164 individuals, the mean carapace/plastron ratio was 1.38; for those near hatchling size (80) the mean was 1.39, adults and large juveniles (33) had a mean of 1.40, but for medium-sized young 40–50 mm (51), the ratio was 1.34 (Fitch and Plummer, 1975).

Unfortunately, softshell turtles do not form growth annuli on their shells, as do many hard-shelled species, and this has made correlation of growth with age impossible except in those marked as hatchlings. Except in some rapidly growing small *Trionyx muticus* in midseason, a minimum of two months between captures is required for sufficient growth to occur to overcome random errors in measurement (Plummer,

1977c). Growth decreases with size in *T. muticus,* and the annual growth period in Kansas covers May through September. Plastron lengths of hatchlings in that population average 24.5 mm (19.5–28.8). Those that hatch in August and early September may feed and grow several weeks before hibernating, but hatchlings that emerge in late September have little time to grow before their first hibernation. By late May the young turtles have plastra averaging 30.1 mm in length, by mid-June they are 35.1 mm, in mid-July, 38.5 mm, in late August, 45.4 mm, and by mid-September of their first full year, 47.1 mm. Fourteen 48–60 mm juveniles showed a mean monthly growth rate of 2.9 mm (1.0–5.4). *T. muticus* can be sexed after it has grown to 60-mm plastron length. Males 61–65 mm long grow an average of 1.95 mm/month; at 66–75 mm they grow 2.1–2.5 mm/month; and at 76–80 mm males grow 1.9 mm/month. After this the monthly growth rate decreases rapidly: at 81–85 mm, 1.03 mm; 91–95 mm, 0.7 mm; 101–105 mm, 0.2 mm; and by 111–115 mm the monthly rate is only 0.09 mm. Females grow faster than males, but the mean rate per month declines as maturity is approached at 135–140-mm plastron length: 61–70 mm, 2.8 mm; 71–80 mm, 3.2 mm; 81–90 mm, 2.2 mm; 91–100 mm, 2.8 mm; 101–110 mm, 2.1 mm; 111–120 mm, 2.5 mm; 121–130 mm, 3.9 mm; 131–140 mm, 1.4 mm; and at 151–160 mm, 0.7 mm. Growth in all age classes and sexes is most rapid in midseason, 16 June–31 August (Plummer, 1977c).

Natural longevity is unrecorded, but surely some smooth softshells survive over 20 years in the wild. Captives have lived over 11 years in Ernst's laboratory.

FOOD HABITS: *Trionyx muticus* is decidedly insectivorous, but other animals are sometimes consumed, as is also some plant material. Prey is taken both in the water and on land. It (and the other North American softshells) obtains food prowling about on the bottom, on submerged debris, or over exposed sandbars, by actively pursuing and capturing prey or ambushing it. Often a method of pharyngeal gulping is used to suck in small aquatic animals. Prey taken includes worms, snails, clams, isopods, crayfish, spiders, insects (mostly aquatic and more often larvae—Coleoptera, Diptera, Ephemeroptera, Hemiptera, Homoptera, Hymenoptera, Isoptera, Lepidoptera, Neuroptera, Odonata, Orthoptera, Plecoptera, Trichoptera), fish (*Catostomus, Hypentelium, Cyprinella, Notropis, Lepomis, Morone, Perca*), adult frogs and tadpoles, mudpuppies (*Necturus maculosus*), young birds, small mammals, algae, elm (*Ulmus*) seeds, cottonwood (*Populus*) seeds, mulberries (*Morus*), and

"hard nuts" (Cahn, 1937; Carr, 1952; Webb, 1962; Anderson, 1965; Plummer and Farrar, 1981; Williams and Christiansen, 1981). Captives feed readily on canned or fresh fish and various meats.

The diet of smooth softshells in Iowa is about 75% insects. Pieces of large fish were found in the stomachs of 8% of individuals examined, but 20% contained small fish, presumably eaten alive. Crayfish were present in 4% and plant material occurred in 12% of the turtles. The percent volume occupied by various food items in 25 smooth softshells was as follows: crayfish, 1.0%; large fish, 4.4%; small fish, 12.0%; plant material, 1.2%; insects—Ephemeroptera (26.5%), Hemiptera (2.4%), Diptera (15.6%), Coleoptera (6.0%), Odonata (0.6%), Trichoptera (6.3%); unidentified and miscellaneous animal material, 4.2%; unidentified and miscellaneous insect material, 18.4%; sand and gravel, 1.0% (Williams and Christiansen, 1981).

In Kansas, smooth softshells eat mostly insects, fruits, and fish carrion. Males have a more diverse diet that is significantly different from females. Females consumed 71% by volume aquatic prey (especially *Hydropsyche* larvae), but males ate 67% by volume terrestrial items including mulberries and cottonwood seeds. Food size was unrelated to turtle size or sex. Dietary differences between male and female turtles are related to microhabitat preferences. Females foraged in deep water and males foraged along the shallow interface between water and land (Plummer and Farrar, 1981).

PREDATORS AND DEFENSE: Nests are destroyed by a variety of predators: fly larvae (Diptera), crows (*Corvus*), moles (*Scalopus aquaticus*), raccoons (*Procyon lotor*), skunks (*Mephitis mephitis*), and dogs (*Canis familiaris*) (Muller, 1921; Goldsmith, 1945; Webb, 1962; Fitch and Plummer, 1975). Juveniles are eaten by large fish, turtles, snakes, wading birds, and various mammals. Adults have few enemies other than humans and alligators.

Trionyx muticus is very wary while basking or nesting, and will quickly flee to the water if disturbed. When caught many simply pull into their shells, and in this respect the species is generally milder tempered than other North American softshells, but some, especially large females, may deliver a nasty bite.

POPULATIONS: Plummer (1977b), using Jolly's method, derived an average of weekly estimates of the size of his population in the Kansas River of 1,801 adults (à8 males, 463 females). Using the Hayne method, the estimate was 2,251 adults (1,610 males, 641 females) if the entire 1973 season was used in the calculations and 1,762 (1,180 males, 582 females) if only the period 1 May to 15 June was used. Similarity in the results indicated that probably about 1,400 males and 550 females were in the main study area. The sex ratio was approximately 2.5:1.0. Density at some parts of the study area was sometimes great. Plummer once counted 88 smooth softshells basking within 100 m length of a sandbar, and, at the same time, a large, but undetermined, number of heads were visible in the adjacent water. At one 4 × 12 m area he captured 73 burrowed turtles by hand in about 30 minutes. On another occasion at another sandbar approximately 1.5 × 10 m, 48 *T. muticus* were captured in one day and 64 more the succeeding day. Only two of those captured the second day had been captured the day before. Most *T. muticus* recorded during Plummer's study were 80–110 mm in plastron length, and he estimated that possibly 37% of the population was composed of immature individuals.

Annualized survivorship in this population was about 43% (Fitch and Plummer, 1975; Iverson, 1991a). Survivorship of eggs, owing to submergence, predation, and other hazards, varies from year to year and at times may be very low. In 1973 only 2% of the eggs in nests that were located at the time of oviposition eventually hatched, whereas 49% of such eggs hatched the next year (Plummer, 1976).

REMARKS: Other references on *T. muticus* are summarized by Webb (1973b, 1990).

Trionyx spiniferus (Le Sueur, 1827)
Spiny softshell
PLATE 10

RECOGNITION: *Trionyx spiniferus* is a medium-sized to large (males to 21.6 cm, females to 54.0 cm carapace length and 11.7 kg; Halk, 1986) turtle with a flat, round, keelless, leathery carapace. Conical, spiny projections are present along the anterior edge of the carapace, and its surface is roughened like sandpaper. The carapace is olive to tan, with a pattern of black ocelli or dark blotches and a marginal dark line. The hingeless plastron is immaculate white or yellow, and the underlying bones can often be seen through the leathery covering. Well-developed callosities are present on the hyoplastra, hypoplastra and xiphiplastra; poorly developed callosities occur on the preplastra and epiplastra less frequently. The head and limbs are olive to gray, with a pattern of dark spots and streaks. Two separate, dark-bordered, light stripes are found on each side of the head: one extending backward from the eye, the other backward from the angle of the jaw. The tubular snout is truncated, with large nostrils, each of which contains a septal ridge; the lips are yellowish with dark spotting, and the jaws are sharp. The anterior surface of each forelimb has four cornified antebrachial scales. All four feet are webbed, and the webbing extends up the shank of the hind limbs.

Adult males have long thick tails with the anal opening near the tip. They retain the juvenile pattern of ocelli, spots, and lines. Adult females have short tails situated beneath the carapace. They develop a mottled or blotched pattern when about 52 mm in carapace length that is not correlated with the attainment of sexual maturity (Webb, 1956; Graham, 1991a). Adult females are more than 1.6 times larger, on average, than adult males.

KARYOTYPE: Diploid chromosomes total 66, including 16 metacentric and submetacentric, 12 subtelocentric, and 38 acrocentric and telocentric chromosomes, with a total of 94 arms (Stock, 1972).

The diploid chromosome number of 58 reported by Forbes (1966) was questioned by Bickham et al. (1983).

FOSSIL RECORD: *Trionyx spiniferus* is included in the Pleistocene Blancan fauna of Oklahoma (Hay and Cook, 1930) and Texas (Holman, 1969b), the Irvingtonian of Kansas (Holman, 1972) and Texas (Hay, 1924; Parmley, 1988), and the Rancholabrean of Alabama (Holman et al., 1990) and Illinois (Holman, 1966). Other 5,840-year-old bones of this turtle have been found in Michigan (Wilson, 1967; Holman, 1988), and archeological records exist from Illinois and Michigan (Adler, 1968).

DISTRIBUTION: The spiny softshell turtle ranges from western New York, western Pennsylvania and southern Ontario west to southern South Dakota, Nebraska, and Wyoming, and south to the Gulf coastal states and New Mexico. Disjunct populations occur in Lake Champlain and the lower reaches of the Ottawa River in Vermont, Quebec, and Ontario, and in Montana and Wyoming, and it has also been introduced into Salem County, New Jersey, and the Gila–Lower Colorado river system in Arizona, California, Nevada, Utah, and New Mexico. In California, populations have spread westward from the Colorado River in the irrigation canals of Riverside and Imperial counties. Other populations also occur in the northern parts of Tamaulipas, Nuevo León, Coahuila, and eastern Chihuahua, Mexico.

GEOGRAPHIC VARIATION: Seven subspecies are recognized, but only six live north of Mexico. *Trionyx spiniferus spiniferus* (Le Sueur, 1827), the eastern spiny softshell turtle, ranges east of the Mississippi River, from Vermont and extreme southeastern Canada west to Wisconsin and south to North Carolina, western Virginia, and Tennessee. It can be

Enlarged spines on anterior carapacial rim of *Trionyx spiniferus*

Plastron of male *Trionyx spiniferus*

distinguished from the other subspecies by the presence of large black ocelli in combination with only one dark marginal line. *Trionyx s. hartwegi* (Conant and Goin, 1948), the western spiny softshell turtle, ranges west of the Mississippi River, from Minnesota, southern South Dakota, and Montana south to northern Louisiana, Oklahoma, and north-eastern New Mexico. It has uniform small dots and ocelli on the carapace and only one dark marginal line.

Trionyx s. asper (Agassiz, 1857), the Gulf Coast spiny softshell turtle, occurs from south-central North Carolina to Mississippi and southeastern Louisiana; its range includes the Florida Panhandle, but not peninsular Florida. This race has more than one black line following the contour of the rear margin of the carapace, and on many specimens the postlabial and postocular stripes on each side of the head are fused. *Trionyx s. pallidus* Webb, 1962, the pallid spiny

Nostril of *Trionyx spiniferus;* note septal ridge

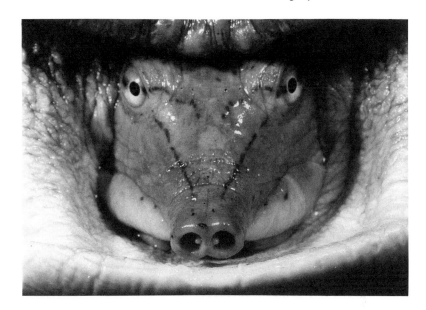

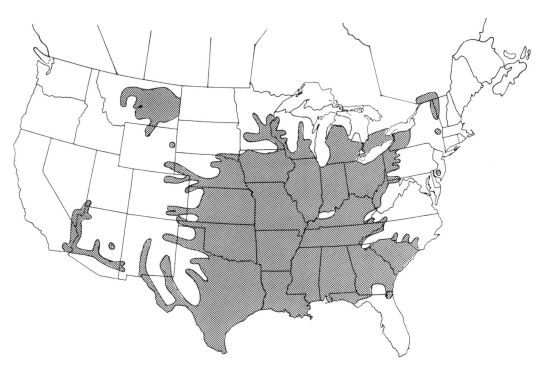

Distribution of *Trionyx spiniferus*

Male *Trionyx spiniferus spiniferus*

Female *Trionyx spiniferus spiniferus*

softshell turtle, is found east of the Brazos River in eastern Texas and in the upper Red River drainage of northwestern Louisiana and Oklahoma. It is pale and has white tubercles on the posterior half of the carapace; the tubercles gradually decrease in size anteriorly and are indistinct or absent on the anterior third of the carapace, and they are not surrounded by black ocelli. *Trionyx s. guadalupensis* Webb, 1962, the Guadalupe spiny softshell turtle, lives only in the Nueces and Guadalupe–San Antonio watersheds in south-central Texas. It is dark and has white tubercles and narrow black ocelli scattered over the entire surface of the carapace; some tubercles are as large as 3 mm in diameter. Some have small black dots interspersed among the white tubercles. *Trionyx s. emoryi* (Agassiz, 1857), the Texas spiny softshell turtle, resides in the Rio Grande and Pecos drainages of Texas and New Mexico and the Colorado River drainages in California, Utah, Nevada, Arizona, New Mexico. It has a pale rim on the carapace that is four

Trionyx spiniferus hartwegi

Trionyx spiniferus asper

or five times wider posteriorly than laterally. There is a dark, slightly curved line connecting the anterior margins of the orbits, and most postocular stripes are interrupted, leaving a pale blotch behind each eye.

Four of the subspecies—*T. s. spiniferus, T. s. hartwegi, T. s. pallidus,* and *T. s. asper*—intergrade in the Mississippi River drainage of Louisiana; *T. s. asper* is the subspecies least represented there (Webb, 1962).

CONFUSING SPECIES: *Trionyx muticus* lacks ridges on the internasal septum and spines or knobs on the anterior border of the carapace. *Trionyx ferox* has a marginal ridge on its carapace.

HABITAT: *Trionyx spiniferus* is primarily a riverine species, but it also inhabits marshy creeks, bayous, oxbows, lakes, and impoundments. A soft bottom with some aquatic vegetation seems essential,

Trionyx spiniferus pallidus

Trionyx spiniferus emoryi

and sandbars and mud flats are usually present. Fallen trees with spreading underwater limbs are frequented.

In Iowa, spiny softshells are found throughout the length of most rivers and in permanent and temporary ponds adjacent to them. The preferred microhabitat appears to be dominated by areas with much submerged brush, fallen trees, and other debris. Females seem to prefer open water more than do males (Williams and Christiansen, 1981).

BEHAVIOR: The annual activity cycle in Kentucky lasts from April through October, but in the south it may be active in all months, or become active as early as March. Farther north, emergence from hibernation may not take place until May, and *Trionyx spiniferus* often becomes inactive in September. Adults appear earlier in the spring and remain active longer in the fall than do juveniles.

Daily activity takes place almost entirely during the daylight hours. At night this turtle sleeps buried in the

bottom substrate or among the branches of submerged trees.

Trionyx spiniferus is highly aquatic, spending most
of its time in well-oxygenated water, either foraging,
floating at the surface, or buried in the soft bottom
with only the head and neck protruding. It buries
itself by first thrusting its head into the substrate and
then retracting it as powerful thrusts are made with
both the fore and hind limbs, allowing the turtle to
virtually crawl beneath the soft bottom (Graham and
Graham, 1991). The anterior end of the body is
drawn down into the substrate as the forelimbs are
first extended and then swept to the side to pull the
animal forward. While the forelegs are pulling, the
hind legs are pushing forward and upward as the
posterior portion of the body is raised. After moving
forward several centimeters, the animal rapidly wig-
gles the rear of its carapace causing the bottom
material to settle smoothly over the carapace. Often it
lies buried under water shallow enough to allow the
nostrils to reach the surface when the neck is
extended, but it also burrows in deep water, where it
remains submerged for relatively long periods.

Gage and Gage (1886) demonstrated that when
submerged both it and *T. muticus* pump water in and
out of the mouth and pharynx at an average rate of 16
times/minute by alternately raising and lowering the
hyoid apparatus. Such behavior is probably olfactory.

Dunson (1960) reported that either dermal or
cloacal respiration is sufficient to sustain life during
forced submersion up to five hours in a closed system
at room temperature. However, prolonged diving
requires certain physiological adjustments. Acid-base
adjustments of submerged *T. spiniferus* are apparently
the result of efficient use of extrapulmonary gas
exchange. Prolonged submersion at 10°C under
anoxic conditions increases plasma lactate and decreases plasma bicarbonate (Jackson et al., 1984).
Potassium, calcium and magnesium also increase in
the plasma, but chloride content is lowered. These
changes are probably compensatory, serving to balance the increase in lactate and resulting lowering of
the blood pH, and are associated with exchanges of
weak ions that buffer the buildup of hydrogen ions.
About 34% of the added lactate is neutralized in this
way. *Trionyx spiniferus* will die if the blood pH falls by
about one unit (Ultsch et al., 1984). Spiny softshells
survive less than three days under such conditions,
but can live more than 14 days when submerged in
normoxic water (Ultsch et al., 1984; Ultsch, 1985,
1989). The hematocrit of the blood is also increased
during prolonged diving. After 100 days of normoxic

submergence the increase is about 10%, from 26% to
35% (Ultsch et al., 1984). Since *T. spiniferus* has
effective aquatic extrapulmonary respiration and can
remain submerged for a relatively long time in
normoxic water, plasma ion concentrations tend to
fall (except potassium and lactate) due to dilution by
water uptake (Ultsch and Wasser, 1990). Limitation
of prolonged submergence is largely osmoregulatory
rather than by acidosis.

The spiny softshell has a large cutaneous surface
area and is capable of exchanging gas through its skin
while in both air and water (Stone et al., 1992a).
When in water, 38% of the oxygen and 85% of the
carbon dioxide are exchanged via the skin. An inverse
pattern occurs in air.

In studies by Stone et al. (1992b) the duration of
voluntary immersion by *T. spiniferus* exceeded 50
minutes only under conditions of hyperoxia: the vast
majority of the turtles remained underwater less than
20 minutes/dive, and the duration decreased linearly
with decreasing aquatic oxygen. When surfacing,
water is typically ejected from the nostrils, and breath
durations are 1.7–5.0 seconds (mean 3.0). Ventilation
begins within two seconds or less in 67% of surfacing
events, and precedes submergence by less than two
seconds in 43% of dives. Ninety-nine percent of all
breathing bouts involve only a single breath. Since
hibernation takes place beneath the surface of the
water, usually under 5–10 cm of bottom substrate, the
above physiological adjustments are critical during the
winter. In addition, plasma protein levels are lowered
during the winter (Seidel, 1974), perhaps as a safe-
guard against clotting.

Because of its soft, leathery shell, this species has
different osmoregulatory problems than hard-shelled
turtles. The skin is three or four times more permeable
to water than that of the hard-shelled *Trachemys
scripta,* whether in air or in hypotonic or hypertonic
solutions (Bentley and Schmidt-Nielsen, 1970). Water efflux rates of 6.3–10.3 ml/100 g wet mass/hour
have been reported for *T. spiniferus* and *T. muticus* kept
in fresh water (Dunson, 1986). In air *T. spiniferus*
loses water relatively fast through its skin, and, if kept
out of water for two or three days, may die of
dehydration (Ernst, pers. obs.). Apparently, neither
total evaporative water loss nor cutaneous water loss
are size dependent (Robertson and Smith, 1982).

Osmoregulation of two populations of *T. s. emoryi*
was examined by Seidel (1975). One population
occurred in fresh water (total ions = 26.9 meq/l) and
the other lived in brackish water (total ions = 238.0
meq/l) that was hypoosmotic to turtle blood. The

turtles were maintained in water similar to their respective natural environments and then acclimated to tap water or brackish water. Brackish water turtles acclimated to tap water demonstrated the lowest plasma osmotic concentration of all groups. Both populations elevated plasma urea levels in response to high solute concentrations; however, turtles from the brackish water habitat possessed greater concentrating ability than those living in fresh water.

Spiny softshells spend much time basking on rocks, logs, mud or sandbanks, or floating debris. When basking on the shore they usually turn to face the water, ready to make a rapid escape. Normally they bask alone, but occasionally several will use the same site simultaneously. Basking seldom begins before 1000 hours.

Thermal relationships of an active adult male in Iowa were reported by Williams and Christiansen (1981). Midday temperatures of the radiotransmitter were well below those of surface water, suggesting that the turtle spent most of the time near the bottom. During a period of falling water levels the individual crossed 250 m of hot sand (57°C) in bright sunlight to get to another pond.

When in either air or water, *Trionyx spiniferus* heats faster than it cools (Smith et al., 1981). Heart rates during warming exceed those during cooling at the same body temperature in either air or water. The species, despite its extensive surface-to-volume geometry (flat, disk-shaped), has a high degree of physiological thermoregulation, with small (0.5 kg) individuals heating twice as fast as they cool. *T. spiniferus* is capable of altering heat-exchange rates to a greater extent than any previously reported ectotherm of similar size (Smith et al., 1981).

Trionyx spiniferus has a mean critical thermal maximum of 41.05°C (39.9–42.3; Hutchison et al., 1966), but it cannot withstand freezing temperatures for long. It dies if its underwater hibernaculum is exposed to freezing air temperatures as water levels drop during the winter (Christiansen and Bickham, 1989).

The spiny softshell seems to move less often than its congener *T. muticus* (Williams and Christiansen, 1981); however, it has orientation mechanisms for long migrations (DeRosa and Taylor, 1980, 1982). When tested in a large circular terrestrial arena, *T. spiniferus* displayed a significant degree of orientation in the homeward direction on clear days, but this ability was lost on overcast days. The orienting behavior was contingent upon time-dependent solar cues synchronized with an internal biological clock (a sun compass mechanism), and the turtle did not appear to use the plane of polarized light to orientate.

It also showed a positive geotaxis at a 2.5° incline. The spiny softshell possibly also uses colors in some way to orient itself. Ernst and Hamilton (1969) reported that in a four-choice situation of red, yellow, green, and blue compartments, a *T. spiniferus* entered the yellow compartment in 10 of 12 trials.

Spiny softshells are aggressive toward members of their own species. Larger individuals tend to dominate in interactions with smaller ones in captivity. Such interactions invariably involve a considerable amount of biting. However, when kept with hard-shelled species such as *Kinosternon, Sternotherus, Graptemys, Chrysemys, Pseudemys,* or *Trachemys,* spiny softshells usually are not pugnacious (Lardie, 1965; Ernst, pers. obs.).

REPRODUCTION: Male *T. s. emoryi* in Oklahoma mature at plastron lengths between 8 and 9 cm, and males of the other subspecies at 9–10 cm (Webb, 1956, 1962). Females mature at plastron lengths between 18 and 20 cm (Webb, 1956, 1962). In Tennessee, males of *T. s. spiniferus* mature at a body weight of approximately 130 g, but females do not mature until they weigh about 15 kg (Robinson and Murphy, 1978).

During April in Tennessee, spermatogonia and Sertoli cells are abundant in the walls of the male seminiferous tubules, and mature sperm reside in the lumen (Robinson and Murphy, 1978). By May a weblike network of fibers, possibly Sertoli cell extensions, fills most of the lumen, and the spermatocytes in the wall have increased in number and moved closer to the lumen. Spermatocyte production peaks in June or July, spermatids are present but not abundant, and the fibrous network has receded to the periphery of the lumen. In August spermatids attached to Sertoli cells are plentiful, but both spermatogonia and spermatocytes are fewer in numbers. Mature sperm are present in some tubules and testes weight is greatest in July and August. By September few spermatocytes or spermatogonia are present, and several rows of mature sperm line the lumen. These pass into the epididymides during September and October, and are apparently stored there over the winter.

Ovarian follicles enlarge throughout the year, with the possible exception of winter, in Tennessee *T. spiniferus* (Robinson and Murphy, 1978). Ovaries weigh the least in August and early September after the nesting season has concluded. Yolking (vitellogenesis) starts thereafter and by mid-September to mid-October enlarged follicles, 12–22 mm in diameter, are abundant. Follicles of these same diameters are present in the spring, and ovulation occurs in May and June, with nesting in June and July.

Mating occurs in April or May (see the account of *T. muticus* for a description). Viable sperm may be stored in small tubules in the walls of the oviduct for later use (Gist and Jones, 1989).

The nesting season may begin in late May and last to August, but June and July are the primary months for oviposition. Two clutches of eggs are produced each year (Robinson and Murphy, 1978). Most nests are dug in full sunlight close to the water, often in adjacent sand or gravel bars, but females may wander up to 100 m inland to nest (Vogt, 1981a). If nesting habitat is limited, several females may lay their eggs in a small area (Minton, 1972). Nests are dug entirely with the hind feet, and bladder water may be voided into the cavity to facilitate digging. Nests are flask shaped, 10–25 cm deep, with a 2.5–7.5-cm neck, and an egg chamber 7.5–12.5 cm wide. Female *T. spiniferus* usually cease digging and retreat into the water if disturbed before egg deposition begins. Breckenridge (1960) reported that a female spiny softshell from Minnesota dug a cavity in 15 minutes, laid a clutch of 17 eggs in six minutes, and filled and covered the nest in another five minutes.

The white, brittle eggs are spherical or nearly so, average about 28 mm (24–32) in diameter, and usually weigh 10–11 g. Clutch size is 4–39 eggs, with 12–18 being most common (Webb, 1962; Ernst and Barbour, 1972; Minton, 1972; Vogt, 1981a; Miller et al., 1989b). Large females contain more oviducal eggs than do small ones, but the difference may not be statistically significant (Robinson and Murphy, 1978). The shell of the egg is 0.15–0.19 mm thick, or almost two times thicker than in eggs of *Chrysemys picta;* it is brittle, smooth, and composed of 27.3% fibrous layers and 72.7% mineral layers (Ewert, 1979a). The eggshell is morphologically very similar to that of birds (Packard and Packard, 1979). The outer crystalline layer is composed of roughly columnar aragonite aggregates of calcium carbonate. Interior to this are two tertiary, multilayered membranes: the outer shell membrane and the inner shell membrane. The outer shell membrane is firmly attached to the inner surface of the shell, and the two membranes are in contact except at the air cell, where the inner membrane separates from the outer one. The inner shell membrane is the more fibrous of the two. Numerous pores occur in the eggshell.

The brittle eggshell of *T. spiniferus* allows for little exchange of water with the nest environment. It exchanges water at a rate less than five times higher than that of a bird's egg (Packard et al., 1979b). Developing embryos convert most of the ammonia released during catabolism of proteins into soluble urea rather than insoluble urate. In the process they commit a portion of their limited water reserve as a solvent for metabolic wastes (Packard and Packard, 1983). The effect of different levels of urea concentration on developing embryos was tested by Packard and Packard (1990a), who injected a physiologically realistic range of urea concentrations into eggs at the midpoint of development. Under their experimental conditions, high levels of uremia did not inhibit the growth rate of developing embryos, suggesting that uremias normally generated during natural incubation are insufficient to inhibit intermediary metabolism.

Spiny softshell eggs incubated on wet substrates contain more water at the end of incubation than do eggs incubated on dry substrates, in spite of the heavily calcified and rigid eggshells (Packard et al., 1979a, 1981c; Gettinger et al., 1984). Differences in the amount of water contained in eggs has no detectable effect on patterns of metabolism, growth of embryos, or hatching success (Packard et al., 1979a, 1981b). Mass specific oxygen consumption is unaffected by the hydric condition of the incubating substrate (Gettinger et al., 1984). Developing embryos obtain about 75% of their calcium from the eggshell and all of their magnesium and phosphorus from the yolk. All three elements are virtually depleted from the yolk by the end of development (Packard and Packard, 1991).

The incubation period varies as a function of temperature as follows: 25–25.5°C, 95.4 days; 25–30°C, 69.0 days, 29.5–30°C, 57.9 days, mostly above 30°C, 52.2 days. Under natural conditions, eggs hatch in 82–84 days in Wisconsin (Ewert, 1979a). Hatching normally occurs from late August to October, but some hatchlings may overwinter in the nest (Minton, 1972).

Unlike most other turtles, *T. spiniferus* is not temperature-dependent sex determinate (Bull and Vogt, 1979; Janzen and Paukstis, 1991). Sex ratios are essentially 1:1 under a wide range of incubation temperatures. Although this suggests the existence of heteromorphic sex chromosomes, none have been reported in this species.

Hatchlings resemble adult males in shape, color, and pattern. The pale, olive to tan, rounded carapace has a well-marked pattern of small, dark ocelli, spots or dashes, and a yellowish border set off by a black line. The granulation of its surface is pronounced, but the spines along the anterior edge are small and poorly developed. Hatchlings are 30–40 mm in carapace length. They weigh about 8.2 g in Florida and 9.6 g in Wisconsin, or approximately 75.6% and 74.1% of freshly laid egg weight, respectively (Ewert, 1979a).

GROWTH AND LONGEVITY: The smallest Minnesota *T. spiniferus* from which Breckenridge (1955) obtained growth-rate data was 5.7 cm long and about one year old. He estimated that the growth rate for a hatchling 3.8 cm long is 4.8 cm/year, but when it has grown to 5 cm its rate of growth decreases to about 4.2 cm/year. Breckenridge estimated that a 10-year-old female is about 25 cm in carapace length; a 15 year old, 29.7 cm; a 20 year old, 33.3 cm; and one 30 years old, 38.1 cm. By his estimation a 43-cm female would be approximately 53 years old. He calculated that a 10-year-old male is approximately 16 cm in carapace length and a 15-year-old male is only 17 cm long. Long (1984) reported the allometric equation for the length-volume for 30 *T. spiniferus* to be carapace length = 19.63 volume$^{0.355}$.

A female spiny softshell lived 25 years, 2 months, and 17 days at the Racine Wisconsin Zoo (Snider and Bowler, 1992).

FOOD HABITS: The spiny softshell is predominantly carnivorous. The stomach contents of individuals collected in the upper Mississippi River in Minnesota contained numerous insects including ephemeropteran nymphs (*Hexagenia*); trichopteran larvae (Hydropsychidae, Limnephilidae); Odonata (Anisoptera and Zygoptera nymphs and adults); dipteran larvae (Stratiomyidae and Chironomidae); Coleoptera (*Donacia* adults); Lepidoptera (terrestrial adults and larvae); Hemiptera (Corixidae); and other invertebrates (decapods, isopods, oligochaetes, gastropods, crayfish, and pelecypods). Pieces of fish including fingerlings of the white crappie (*Pomoxis annularis*) were also found in some stomachs (Cochran and McConville, 1983). Fish remains were found more often in female stomachs and dragonfly naiads (Odonata) were found more often in male stomachs. Relatively equal numbers of males and females ate crayfish and *Hexagenia* naiads. Cochran and McConville (1983) concluded that spiny softshells in Minnesota were habitat generalists capable of utilizing a variety of prey bases.

The diet of spiny softshells in Iowa is about 25% insects, 36.5% fish (probably eaten as carrion), 5.8% small fish (probably eaten alive), and 55% crayfish (Williams and Christiansen, 1981). Plant material, including acorns, leaves, and other items, was observed in the stomachs of 61% of the sample of turtles. The percent volume occupied by various food items in 52 spiny softshells was as follows: crayfish, 24.2%; large fish, 17.2%; small fish, 2.2%; plant material, 12.8%; Ephemeroptera, 6.7%; Hemiptera, 1.9%; Diptera, 0.6%; Coleoptera, 3.0%; Odonata,

2.4%; Trichoptera, 0.5%; unidentifiable animal material, 19.5%; unidentifiable insect material, 6.5%; sand and/or gravel, 2.0%.

Lagler (1943) examined the stomachs of 11 *T. spiniferus* from Michigan and found crayfish in 47% and insects in 52%. Breckenridge (1944) reported that 18 spiny softshells in Minnesota contained 44% crayfish, 29% aquatic insects, and 8% fish. In Missouri, stomachs of 11 held remains of crayfish (61.2%), insects (34.8%) and fish (2%) (Anderson, 1965). Penn (1950) found crayfish constituted 46% (58% frequency) of the food. Lagler (1943) reported cryptograms in *T. spiniferus,* and Surface (1908) found one stomach full of corn. Captives readily consume fresh and canned fish, chicken, beef, pork, and newborn and full grown mice. Juveniles will also eat commercial dry trout chow.

While feeding, spiny softshells crawl or swim along the bottom in a somewhat random fashion, thrusting their snouts under stones and into masses of aquatic vegetation. They sometimes actively pursue and capture small animals, but they also take prey from ambush on the bottom with a gape and suck behavior. Large prey may be held by the forefeet while torn into smaller pieces by the sharp jaws, but sometimes the turtles swallow it whole, using the forefeet to assist in forcing it down.

PREDATORS AND DEFENSE: Skunks (*Mephitis*) and raccoons (*Procyon lotor*) destroy many nests, and the young are eaten by fishes, other turtles, snakes, wading birds, and mammals (Webb, 1962). Parmalee (1989) reported that a muskrat (*Ondatra*) ate a *T. spiniferus* in Tennessee. Alligators and humans eat the adults, and many are decapitated by fishermen after being hooked on their lines.

The disposition of spiny softshells is generally bad. They bite and scratch savagely when handled, and Platt and Brantley (1991) reported that a female even squirted blood from both eyes in response to handling. Large females withdrew their head and forelimbs and completely extended the hind limbs when tapped on the front of the carapace (Stuart and Clark, 1990). Another behavior involves extension of the hind limb opposite the stimulus, but not the corresponding forelimb, resulting in an oblique carapace orientation. Some bend the rear portion of the carapace downward when disturbed. Frontal approach generally elicits either biting or head withdrawal, and bites of large *T. spiniferus* can be serious.

Trionyx spiniferus is capable of changing the amount of melanism of its carapace over time, possibly to match the bottom shading of its waterway. An adult female *T. s. asper* from Alabama taken from a stream with many dark, algae-covered rocks had numerous large, well-developed, olive carapacial blotches which made it appear dark when caught. When brought to Ernst's laboratory and placed in a large, white plastic bin, she lightened over the next few months until the blotches were barely visible. Bartley (1971) found that such blotches in spiny softshells are due to increased cell populations and/or differences in the degree of pigment dispersion within melanin-containing cells. Analysis of the epidermis demonstrated the existence of functional units of melanism production and distribution-epidermal melanin units. Changes in coloration seem physiological in nature, which, with time, may be enforced by secondary morphological changes. Bartley's (1971) studies strongly suggest that regulation of color change is endocrine rather than neural.

POPULATIONS: Spiny softshells composed less than 1% of more than 1,000 turtles collected from a drainage ditch near Jacob, Illinois; however, they made up 16% of 214 turtles at Elkville, Illinois (Cagle, 1942). Cagle and Chaney (1950) found that Louisiana *T. spiniferus* were most abundant in streams with some current (Caddo Dam Spillway, 52.9% of the turtles caught; Lacassine Refuge, 25.3%; Sabine River, 66.6%), but that they also occurred in quiet waters (Caddo Lake, 31.2%; False River, 8.6%; Lake Providence, 12.8%).

The adult sex ratio of three populations of *T. spiniferus* in Mississippi and Alabama was not significantly different from 1:1 (Vogt and Bull, 1982a). Statistically unbiased sex ratios have also been reported for Illinois and Minnesota populations by Cagle (1942) and Breckenridge (1955), respectively.

REMARKS: Frair (1983) examined the relationship of trionychid turtles to other turtle families using antigens reacting with antiserums against *T. spiniferus*. Other literature on *T. spiniferus* is summarized by Webb (1973c, 1990).

Trionyx ferox (Schneider, 1783)
Florida softshell

PLATE II

RECOGNITION: This medium to large, flat softshell turtle has a marginal ridge on its leathery carapace (<60 cm; Allen, 1982). The oval, keelless carapace has blunt, knobby tubercles clustered along its anterior edge and in the marginal ridge. Many have longitudinal rows of indentations and raised areas on the dorsal surface. The carapace is gray, brown, or olive and may have darker blotches. The hingeless adult plastron is gray to white; that of juveniles is two-toned, lighter anteriorly, darker posteriorly. Underlying bones can be seen through the leathery covering of many plastra. Hyo-hypoplastral and xiphiplastral callosities are present, but callosities are usually lacking or poorly developed on the preplastra and epiplastra. The head and limbs are gray to brown, some with light mottlings or reticulating lines. On many specimens, a red or yellow stripe extends from the posterior corner of the eye to the base of the lower jaw. The lips are fleshy and the jaws are sharp. Older individuals may develop an expanded crushing surface on the upper jaw. The tubular snout is terminally truncated, and each nostril has a lateral ridge that projects from the nasal septum. The anterior surface of each forelimb has four cornified antebrachial scales. All four feet are webbed and the webbing extends up the shank of the hind legs.

Adult females may grow larger than 60 cm in carapace length, but males only to about 33 cm. Males have long thick tails with the anal vent near the tip; the female tail is short and barely extends beyond the carapacial rim.

KARYOTYPE: The normal chromosomal complement is 66 (Becak et al., 1964; Bickham et al., 1983) consisting of 16 macrochromosomes (8 metacentric, 2 submetacentric, 4 acrocentric, 2 telocentric) and 50 microchromosomes. The karyotype is identical to those of *T. sinensis* and *T. spiniferus* (Bickham et al., 1983).

FOSSIL RECORD: Florida Pleistocene records are from the Irvingtonian of Levy County (Holman, 1959) and Rancholabrean of Hillsborough and St. Lucie counties (Hay, 1908, 1917).

DISTRIBUTION: *Trionyx ferox* ranges from southern South Carolina and southern Georgia through peninsular Florida and west through the Florida Panhandle and extreme southern Alabama to Baldwin County, Alabama. It does not naturally occur on the Florida Keys, but has recently been introduced into Blue Hole Pond on Big Pine Key (Iverson and Etchberger, 1989).

GEOGRAPHIC VARIATION: No subspecies have been described.

CONFUSING SPECIES: All other softshells within the range of *T. ferox* lack a marginal ridge on the carapace, and *T. muticus* does not have a septal ridge in its nostrils.

HABITAT: This softshell occurs in all freshwater habitats. We have taken them from waterbodies varying from shallow drainage canals (juveniles) and streams to marshes, swamps, lakes, and deep rivers. It seems to be more at home in still waters in the northern parts of the range than in southern Florida. It prefers water with sand or mud bottoms, or bubbling mud-sand springs where there is foliage overhead. *Trionyx ferox* sometimes occurs in brackish water near the mouths of streams; there the tides occasionally carry it out to sea.

BEHAVIOR: Although a common species, surprisingly little has been published on its life history.

During years with warm winters the Florida softshell is active in all months on the peninsula, but if Florida experiences an extended cold spell it remains

Trionyx ferox

Plastron of *Trionyx ferox*

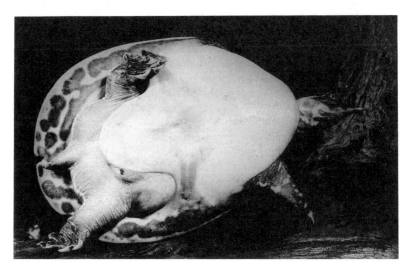

relatively inactive until water temperatures again rise. In the northern and western parts of the range, *T. ferox* may hibernate during cold winters.

The daily cycle of *T. ferox* has not been studied. *Trionyx ferox* spends much time buried in the soft bottom in either shallow or deep water, with only its head protruding. Marchand (1942) stated that when buried in mud it appears to consider itself perfectly concealed and protected; at such times the carapace may be handled or even pulled about, and the snout may be rubbed without the turtle's showing any concern. It can burrow into and tunnel through mud and sand with amazing speed. According to Mar-

chand (1942) some areas on the bottom of Crystal Springs, Florida, have been so thoroughly disturbed by the burrowing of softshells that these places are bare and soft. An area treated thus by *T. ferox* assumes a characteristic appearance and can be easily recognized. Rainbow Run, Marion County, Florida, has bottom areas of bare white sand, and softshells are fond of burrowing there. Whenever they do so a school of fish invariably is attracted to the spot—a clue to the location of the turtles (Marchand, 1942).

While submerged, *T. ferox* may practice pharyngeal or cloacal breathing. Marchand (1942) dropped a small amount of silt directly in front of the nostrils of

Anterior view of *Trionyx ferox*. Spines on leading edge of carapace gradually transform into a marginal ridge

a submerged *T. ferox* and easily detected the water currents set up by the intake and expulsion of water. He presumed this for pharyngeal respiration, but probably it was for olfaction, not breathing. Other softshells derive much of their oxygen through their skin when underwater, and *T. ferox* should be no different.

Trionyx ferox can withstand rather high water temperatures and may be exposed to them in shallow waters during much of the Florida summer. Hutchison et al. (1966) reported that two Florida softshells lost the righting response at 36.9°C and 37.4°C and had critical thermal maxima of 38.9°C and 39.1°C; but Brattstrom (1965) reported that the critical maximum temperature appears to be about 42.3°C.

Trionyx ferox spends much time floating on the surface or lying on sandbars or banks, and seems quite fond of basking.

This softshell occasionally migrates overland, and can be commonly seen on the highways of Florida.

REPRODUCTION: Some males mature at a plastron length of 12 cm (Webb, 1962). The smallest recorded mature female had a carapace length of approximately 22 cm (Hamilton, 1947); but Iverson (1985c) thought females reach maturity between 28 and 30 cm, because those shorter than 28 cm lacked ovarian follicles larger than 3 mm in diameter, while females over 30 cm long were clearly mature.

The annual gonadal cycles of both sexes are largely unknown. A female collected on 27 April contained oviducal eggs, 18 ovarian follicles 19–25 mm in diameter, 12 follicles 13–18 mm in diameter, and two different size classes of corpora lutea; two others collected in June contained 12 and 24 oviducal eggs, respectively, and two series of enlarged follicles 17–24 mm and 10–17 mm in diameter (Iverson, 1985c).

The courtship and mating behaviors of *T. ferox* have not been described.

Nesting occurs from mid-March to July in southern Florida (Lardie, 1983a; Iverson, 1977a, 1985c), and from June through July in the northern and western portions of the range. Sandy soil in full sunlight usually is chosen as the nest site, and the nest is normally dug in the morning. A typical nest has an entrance about 5 cm in diameter and an enlarged egg chamber 10 cm in diameter; the total depth is about 8–13 cm. The nest is dug by alternate scraping of the hind feet, and the bladder contents may be used to soften the earth and moisten the cavity (Hamilton, 1947). The eggs are covered by scraping soil into the hole with the hind feet. *Trionyx ferox* occasionally lays its eggs in the vegetative nest mounds of alligators (Deitz and Jackson, 1979).

After the female has completed nesting she may move a few meters away and then vigorously scratch up the ground, scattering the earth about and leaving a conspicuous trace of her presence. Harper (in Hamilton, 1947) suggested that this may serve to draw the attention of predators away from the actual nest.

The spherical, white eggs have thin, brittle shells; they are 24–33 mm in diameter and weigh 10–12 g (Goff and Goff, 1935; Goode, 1983; Iverson,

Distribution of *Trionyx ferox*

1985c). Oviducal eggs are slightly smaller: about 25–27 mm in diameter. Clutches consist of 4–24 eggs, most commonly 17–22 (Ernst and Barbour, 1972; Goode, 1983; Iverson, 1985c). Two to possibly as many as six clutches may be laid a year, and there is a tendency for large females to lay more eggs per clutch (Iverson, 1985c). A 35-cm female contained five sets of corpora lutea and one set of 30 preovulatory follicles (17–19 mm). Her luteal scars totalled 115, and with the 30 follicles, this turtle had an annual reproductive potential of 145 eggs, far more than the maximum confirmed for any other North American *Trionyx* (Jackson, 1991b).

Eggs are composed of about 71% water; the total dry mass of egg components is 3 g (Congdon and Gibbons, 1985). The shell has a dry weight of about 0.95 g, and the dry lipid content weighs approximately 0.58 g; about 28% of the yolk is lipid (Congdon and Gibbons, 1985).

Development takes 56–83 days (most clutches hatch in 60–70 days), depending on the incubation temperature (Goff and Goff, 1935; Goode, 1983; Lardie, 1973a; Iverson, 1985c). Hatchlings are less round than those of *T. muticus* or *T. spiniferus*. The carapace is yellowish olive with dusky spots and a narrow yellow or orange border. The spots are large, and the narrow light lines separating them present a reticulated appearance. The posterior portion of the plastron is dark gray. The olive skin is mottled with lighter color. A Y-shaped light figure extends from the anterior edge of each orbit to the middle of the snout. Neonates are usually 38–39 mm (28.8–40.2) in carapace length, and they weigh 8.5–9.3 g (Goff and Goff, 1935; Ernst, pers. obs.).

GROWTH AND LONGEVITY: A captive hatchling grew from 39 to 49 mm in carapace length in 45 days, another grew from 41 to 61 mm in 166 days, and a third increased in carapace length from 41 to 70 mm in 422 days (Lardie, 1973a).

Snider and Bowler (1992) reported a longevity record of 19 years, 2 months, and 22 days for a *T. ferox* at the Cincinnati Zoo; but Goode (1983) noted that a male captured as an adult had lived at least as long in the Columbus Zoo, and so was probably over 20 years old; and Pope (1939) reported that a captive lived 25 years at the Frankfurt Zoo, Germany.

FOOD HABITS: *Trionyx ferox* is thought to be omnivorous but not fond of plant materials. The bulk of the diet apparently consists of invertebrates, and the turtle is known to do some scavenging. Natural foods include plants, snails (*Pomacea, Viviparus*), bivalves (*Anodonta*), crayfish, insects, fish (*Lepisosteus, Cyprinidae*), frogs (*Rana*), turtles (*Pseudemys, Sternotherus*), snakes (*Nerodia, Regina*), and birds (passerines, waterfowl) (Pope, 1939; Carr, 1952; Dalrymple, 1977; Ashton and Ashton, 1985; Ernst, pers. obs.). Captives readily feed on canned and fresh fish, shrimp, canned dog food, raw beef, chicken, earthworms, and commercial trout chow.

In the wild, small *T. ferox* feed mostly on insects (54.4% of total number of prey items) and snails (40.4%); medium-sized turtles eat more snails (54.1%), but also consume many insects (32%) and fish (9%); and large individuals feed predominantly on snails (45%), some insects (25%), and fish (17.5%) (Dalrymple, 1977). There is an obvious reduction in insect consumption, but an increase in fish eating, with growth.

Females grow larger than males and show more variation in diet. The age variation in jaw morphology seen in large adults is part of the physiological adaptation of the feeding mechanism to a changing diet of larger, harder prey (Dalrymple, 1977).

Small foods are readily seized and swallowed whole; usually a form of inertial feeding, or "gape and suck," is used. Large prey are seized and then chewed or torn with the foreclaws into smaller pieces before swallowing (Ernst, pers. obs.). Mollusks or crayfish are repeatedly crushed in the posterior expanded portions of the jaws (Dalrymple, 1977).

PREDATORS AND DEFENSE: Crows (*Corvus*), spotted skunks (*Spilogale*), bears (*Ursus*), raccoons (*Procyon*) and foxes (*Urocyon*) rob the nests; and large fish, turtles (*Chelydra, Macroclemys*), snakes (*Agkistrodon, Nerodia*), everglades kites (*Rostrhamus*),

wading birds, and various predatory mammals eat the young (Pope, 1939; Hamilton, 1947; Woodin and Woodin, 1981; Beissinger, 1990; Ernst, pers. obs.). Other potential predators on eggs and juveniles are armadillos (*Dasypus*), striped skunks (*Mephitis*), and otters (*Lutra*). Alligators probably feed on all size classes of Florida softshells (Pope, 1939; Ernst, pers. obs.).

However, humans are still the greatest destroyer of *T. ferox,* with their habitat destruction, pollution, and automobiles. Meehean (in Carr, 1952) used large amounts of derris (a toxic plant) in Florida lakes to collect fish for population analyses. He found that in nearly all lakes numbers of *T. ferox* were incapacitated although no other turtles were affected. Rotenone, the active ingredient of derris, works through the respiratory system to kill fish and possibly also in *T. ferox* through its cutaneous respiration. Herald (1949) reported that a field observer found a *T. ferox* eating a DDT-killed bluegill on the morning after spraying. An attempt was made to capture the turtle but it escaped. Ten days later a softshell of approximately the same size was found dead, and it was suspected that this was the same turtle. It is likely that turtles that feed often on carrion, including the bodies of animals killed by pesticides, ingest enough poison to harm them.

Large *T. ferox* can be quite pugnacious when first caught, snapping at any thing within reach.

POPULATIONS: No data are available.

REMARKS: *Trionyx ferox* shares the marginal ridge and the longitudinal ridges of small knobs on the carapace with the Asiatic species of *Trionyx*. These characters are lacking in other native North American softshells.

Webb (1973a) summarizes the literature regarding the Florida softshell up to that date.

Trionyx sinensis Wiegmann, 1835
Chinese softshell
PLATE 12

RECOGNITION: This small to medium-sized soft-shelled turtle has a flattened, keelless carapace (to 25 cm) which is slightly longer than wide and contains a marginal ridge. It is grayish green, and in juveniles is patterned with round, light-bordered, black spots. The hingeless, white to yellow plastron is immaculate in adults but has large black blotches in juveniles. Callosities, totaling seven, occur on the hyo- and hypoplastra, the xiphiplastra and, in some specimens, the epiplastra. The head and limbs are olive to yellowish white, and the head and neck may have fine black lines. The throat is either light with vermiculations or dark with yellow spots, and many have fine black lines radiating from the eyes. The tubular snout has a lateral ridge projecting from each side of the nasal septum; the lips are fleshy and the jaws are sharp. Each forelimb bears cornified antebrachial scales on its anterior surface. All four feet are webbed, and the webbing extends up the shank of the hind limbs.

Males differ from females in being smaller, shallower, and in having long thick tails, with the anal vent near the tip. Females are more domed, and their tails barely extend past the carapacial rim.

KARYOTYPE: The 66 chromosomes of the karyotype are as follows: 16 macrochromosomes (8 metacentric, 2 submetacentric, 4 acrocentric, 2 subtelocentric) and 50 microchromosomes (Bickham et al., 1983). Oguma (1937) reported 64 diploid chromosomes in males (12 macrochromosomes and 52 microchromosomes) and 63 in females; however, several chromosomes were probably lost during preparation.

FOSSIL RECORD: Fossil remains of *T. sinensis* have been reported from Pliocene deposits in China (Yeh, 1963).

DISTRIBUTION: *Trionyx sinensis* inhabits central and southern China, Vietnam, and the islands of Hainan and Taiwan. It has been introduced into the Hawaiian Islands, one of the Bonin Islands, Timor, and Japan. This species is apparently the rarer of the two softshells introduced into the Hawaiian Islands, where it seems to be restricted to Kauai (McKeown and Webb, 1982).

GEOGRAPHIC VARIATION: No subspecies are currently considered valid; however, variation in patterns exists. The population on Chusan Island has been named *tuberculatus* (Cantor, 1842), and the Japanese softshells, *japonicus* (Temminck and Schlegel, in Siebold, 1835), but these are usually placed in the synonymy of *T. sinensis*. A thorough study of variation in *T. sinensis* is needed.

CONFUSING SPECIES: *Trionyx sinensis* can be distinguished from all other American softshells by the presence of a juvenile plastral pattern, the dark lines radiating from the eye, and the absence of a dark-bordered, pale stripe passing through the eye.

HABITAT: In China *T. sinensis* is found in rivers, lakes, ponds, canals, and creeks with slow current (Pope, 1935). On Kauai, Hawaii, it occurs in the marshlands and the drainage canals and many small streams feeding the Kapaa Canal.

BEHAVIOR: Almost nothing is known of this turtle's natural behavior. The basking habit is not well developed, but *T. sinensis* occasionally suns itself on the bank. Captives in Japan hibernate in the mud bottom of ponds from October to April or May (Mitsukuri, 1905), and captives in China hibernate when the water temperature drops below 15°C, often losing 10–15% of their body weight in the

Juvenile *Trionyx sinensis*

Plastron of juvenile *Trionyx sinensis*

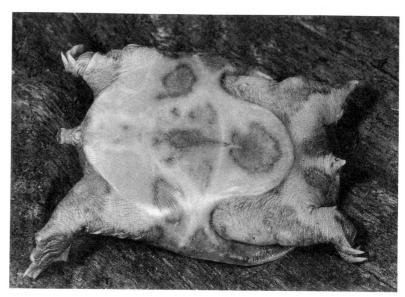

process (Chu, 1989). Outdoor winter survivorship in China may be only 20–30% (Chu, 1989). To lower this mortality, Chinese culturists construct special overwintering rooms that utilize ground heating to keep the water temperature at 23–30°C and eliminate the need for hibernation. In such a setting 95% of the turtles survive and they gain an average 11% in weight during the winter months (Chu, 1989).

In the laboratory the preferred ambient temperature range of *T. sinensis* is 20–25°C (Khosatzky,

1981). In 20–23°C water, the Chinese softshell is normally calm, and after remaining for a long period of time at these conditions, the temperatures of the various parts of the body equalize. Frequently, some increase of 0.1–0.7°C above the water temperature is observed in the cloaca and also at parts of the body surface. Sometimes this increase reaches 1°C in the cloaca and in the axillary and inguinal cavities. When the turtle is removed from the water, surface temperatures often are lowered by evaporative cooling to below that of the original water temperature, but the

Adult *Trionyx sinensis*

Distribution of *Trionyx sinensis* in Hawaii

cloacal temperature remains high, sometimes exceeding that of the water by 0.5–1.0°C. Once stabilized in air, the surface temperatures again rise to above that of the ambient temperature, indicating a high metabolic rate in this turtle. Active wild *T. sinensis* were netted at 0800 and 2000 on 7 October when the water temperatures were 5.5 and 8.5°C, respectively (Khosatzky, 1981).

Like other soft-shelled turtles, *T. sinensis* spends much time totally submerged, resting buried in the substrate with only its nostrils showing. During total submergence, its heartbeat slows to 4–33% of the rate before diving (Wang and Liu, 1986). While diving, much of its oxygen demand is satisfied through either buccopharyngeal or cutaneous respiration. Wang et al. (1989) totally submerged three groups of *T. sinensis* in water at 16–18, 21–22, and 28–30°C, respectively, and found the mean aquatic oxygen uptake of the three groups was 7.5, 11.1, and 12.3 ml/kg/h. The rhythmic pharyngeal movements of these three groups corresponded to the temperature of the water, slower (10–25/min) at 16–18°C and faster (24–40/min) at 28–30°C. Buccopharyngeal respiration accounted for an estimated 67% of the oxygen uptake, cutaneous uptake for only 33%. During forced submersion experiments the heart rate dropped to 4–33% of that before diving (Wang and Liu, 1986). The heart rate slowed gradually in all turtles tested, but the rate of decline varied from individual to individual.

REPRODUCTION: Sexual maturity is reached in four years in China (Yun et al., 1984), but not until five or six years in Japan (Mitsukuri, 1905; Fukada, 1965).

Lofts and Tsui (1977) studied the male sexual cycle of *T. sinensis* from southern China and found well-marked seasonal differentiation between the functional activity of the seminiferous tubules and the interstitial tissue. In the March–April breeding period, the interstitial cells are large and lipid free with rounded turgid nuclei, and a significant reduction of about 48% in epididymal weight occurs as spermatozoa are evacuated from the epididymal canals. Testicular weights are low and do not vary much during this phase. The seminiferous tubules remain regressed and sperm are not matured; the germinal epithelium is composed only of Sertoli cells and spermatogonia. Spermatogenesis begins in May, and by the middle of the month the germinal epithelium shows several stages of developing sperm. At the onset of spermatogenesis, there is a rapid clearance of intratubule lipids. Sperm production continues through June and July, accompanied by an increase in diameter of the seminiferous tubules, but slows toward the end of August. Spermiogenesis becomes more prevalent in September, and by October the germinal epithelium is mainly composed of spermatids and spermatozoa. During this period, numerous free spermatozoa crowd the lumina of the tubules, and the testes achieve their maximum size as the epididymal canals decrease in diameter. Lofts and Tsui thought there is an inverse relationship between sperm production by the tubules and hormone production by the interstitial tissue. A rapid reduction in testis weight and seminiferous tubule diameter occurs as sperm production ceases and the spermatozoa pass into the epididymides from November to February. Only inactive spermatogonia and Sertoli cells are found in the germinal epithelium. The epididymides gradually increase in weight during November and December.

Licht (1982) reported a similar cycle in epididymal and testicular weight, with the testes reaching maximum weight in October–November and rapidly decreasing in mass in December as sperm is released to the epididymides. However, on the basis of direct measurement of plasma testosterone levels, Licht believes the concept of the separation of steroid secretion and spermatogenesis, as reported by Lofts and Tsui (1977), is not supported. Plasma testosterone is virtually undetectable through most of the year, especially in the spring when Leydig cells appear active in the interstitial tissue and breeding occurs, increases only after testes are fully recrudesced, and reaches peak levels in November.

Sperm may remain viable in the female's oviduct for almost a year after copulation (Yun et al., 1984).

In female *T. sinensis*, fully mature ova are 17–20 mm in diameter versus oogonia which are only 8–10 mm (Yun et al., 1984). The entire female sexual cycle is divided into four stages: oogonia, primary follicles, growing follicles, and mature follicles. Females may ovulate two to five times per year, laying 8–12 to 20–30 eggs each time (Fukada, 1965; Yun et al., 1984). The whitish, spherical eggs average about 20 mm in diameter but may be as large as 24 mm.

Mating takes place from May to July in Japan (Mitsukuri, 1905; Fukada, 1965). The copulatory act occurs at the surface or underwater and may last 5–30 minutes (Thieme, 1979) with the male holding the female's carapace with his forelimbs and sometimes biting at her neck, head, and limbs. Fukada (1965) reported that nesting starts about two weeks after mating.

In Japan, nesting begins in late May and continues to mid-August (Mitsukuri, 1905). Licent (in Pope, 1935) discovered quantities of eggs on 14 June in southeastern Kansu, China.

The digging of the nest is done entirely by alternating actions of the hind legs. Each leg, with claws extended, is moved firmly from side to side while the body also sways, in rhythm with the motion of legs. The force put into the lateral sweeps of the feet is so great that soil is sometimes thrown three meters or more, although most of it is piled up around the hole.

The rounded nest generally is about 7–10 cm across at the entrance and 10 cm or more in depth and width. When the cavity is finished the eggs are deposited in a disordered pile; the entire clutch may be deposited in 20 minutes. The hind feet then scrape in soil and fill the nest.

Incubation lasts about 60 days (23–83), depending on soil temperatures. By the time the last clutches are laid, in August, those deposited in May or June are ready to hatch. Mitsukuri (in Fukada, 1965) reported a mean hatching success for seven clutches of 74.3%

(26.3–100). Choo and Chou (1987) found that the temperature tolerance range of Chinese softshell eggs is between 23 and 34°C. The optimum temperatures for minimum incubation and hatchability are 34°C and 28°C. The incubation period can be reduced by as much as 10 days without adversely affecting hatching success when the eggs are incubated at a constant 28°C.

Hatchlings average 27 mm in carapace length and are about 25 mm wide. The carapace is olive, and it may have a pattern of small, dark-bordered ocelli. The marginal fold is prominent, as are also the longitudinal rows of spiny tubercles. The plastron is white to yellow, with large dark blotches. The limbs and head are olive above and lighter below. The head has dark flecks, and dark lines radiate from the eyes. The throat is mottled, and the lips may have small, dark bars. A pair of dark blotches lie in front of the tail, and a black band is present on the posterior side of each thigh.

Sex determination in *Trionyx sinensis* is independent of incubation temperature. Eggs incubated at constant temperatures of 23, 25, 28, 31, and 34°C yielded 73 males and 93 females, and, although slightly more females were produced at each temperature, no significant difference in the sex ratio occurred at any individual temperature (Choo and Chou, 1992).

GROWTH AND LONGEVITY: Captive juveniles averaged 45 mm in carapace length and 23 g in weight at the end of their first year, 105 mm and 169 g after the second year, 125 mm and 300 g after the third year, 160 mm and 563 g after the fourth year, and 175 mm and 750 g after the fifth year (Mitsukuri, 1905). Chu (1989) reported that it takes four or five years for a captive turtle to reach a weight of 100–800 g in China.

A *Trionyx sinensis* sent to Ernst as a hatchling from Hawaii in 1968 died in March 1992 at almost 24 years of age.

FOOD HABITS: *T. sinensis* is predominantly carnivorous. Heude (in Pope, 1935) found the remains of fish, crustaceans, mollusks, insects, and seeds of marsh plants in the stomachs he examined. Mitsukuri (1905) reported that juveniles feed on fish and that adults eat fish and bivalves. Captives eat canned and fresh fish, canned dog food, raw beef, newborn mice and rats, and chicken.

Captives kept in water of 20–28°C consumed seven times as much food as did turtles in water only 13–22°C. The former also grew by a factor of 5–10, but the latter individuals increased only by a factor of 1.6–6.0 (Kanamoto and Teruya, 1978).

PREDATORS AND DEFENSE: The young are sometimes eaten by the adults, but little else is known of predation. Surely many other vertebrates prey on the eggs and young.

Individuals we have kept have been ill tempered, biting hard and scratching when handled.

POPULATIONS: The population inhabiting Kauai is quite limited, as only two individuals have been recorded (McKeown and Webb, 1982).

REMARKS: The Chinese and the Japanese make wide use of *T. sinensis* as food and have propagated it in turtle ponds. The turtles were exported to the Hawaiian Islands for food, and it is believed that the Kauai turtles arrived in this way before World War II, when importation was interrupted (Brock, 1947). Mitsukuri (1905) reported that the *T. sinensis* sold in Osaka, Tokyo, Nagoya, and a few other Japanese cities in a single year weighed over 7000 kg and were worth about $3.25 to $3.75 each. Brock (1947) reported that the price in Hawaii during World War II reached $2.72/kg, and in 1947 they were selling for about $0.54/kg. Paul Kawamoto told us that during the 1950s Hawaiian *T. sinensis* averaging 0.5–1.4 kg sold for $15 to $20 each (this probably refers more to *T. steindachneri*). Meats of *T. sinensis* analyzed by Suyama et al. (1979) contained extractive nitrogen ranging from 253 to 289 mg/100g.

Trionyx sinensis is most closely related to the Asiatic softshells *T. steindachneri* and *T. subplanus* (Meylan, 1987).

Trionyx steindachneri Siebenrock, 1906a
Wattle-necked softshell
PLATE 13

RECOGNITION: The oval carapace has several longitudinal rows of small raised tubercles in younger individuals, but the surface becomes smoother with age. The carapace is longer (to 42.6 cm) than broad and has a well-defined marginal ridge with enlarged blunt tubercles along the anterior rim. The adult carapace is brown to gray-brown or olive and patternless. Most of the yellow to cream or gray plastra lack dark markings. Callosities occur on the hyo- and hypoplastra, xiphiplastra, and epiplastra. The head and limbs are olive to brown. Black preorbital, suborbital, and postorbital streaks, and shorter black streaks and dots are present on top of the head, and a pale yellow stripe begins behind the eye and extends backward onto the side of the neck, becoming narrower toward the body. A yellowish spot is present at the corner of the jaws. These head and neck markings are lost with age. The most diagnostic character in large adults is a large clump of coarse tubercles (wattles) at the base of the neck. A lateral ridge projects from each side of the nasal septum. The anterior surface of each forelimb bears cornified antebrachial scales. All four feet are webbed, and the webbing extends up the shank of the hind limbs.

Males are smaller than females and have longer, thicker tails with the vent closer to the tip. The female tail barely extends past the carapacial rim at best and its vent is beneath the carapace.

KARYOTYPE: Lin et al. (1988) reported that the karyotype of *T. steindachneri* is composed of 66 chromosomes, including 44 macrochromosomes (8 metacentric, 8 submetacentric, 4 subtelocentric, 24 telocentric) and 22 microchromosomes.

FOSSIL RECORD: None.

DISTRIBUTION: *Trionyx steindachneri* ranges in China from Guangdong, Guangxi, and Hainan Island southwestward into northern Vietnam. It has been introduced and established on Mauritius, and in the Hawaiian Islands on Kauai and Oahu (Webb, 1980; McKeown and Webb, 1982).

GEOGRAPHIC VARIATION: Unknown.

CONFUSING SPECIES: *Trionyx sinensis* is the only other soft-shelled turtle in Hawaii. It lacks neck wattles and a yellowish stripe behind the orbit, but has seven plastral callosities (*T. steindachneri* has only four) and a juvenile plastral pattern of large dark blotches.

HABITAT: In Hawaii, it lives in marshes, drainage canals, and streams.

BEHAVIOR: As in *T. sinensis,* the basking habit is not well developed, but captives occasionally emerge to lie in the sun. Apparently, hibernation is not necessary in Hawaii, so *T. steindachneri* is active in every month.

REPRODUCTION: Nesting in Hawaii probably occurs in June, with hatching in late August or September (McKeown and Webb, 1982). Clutches vary from 3 to 28 eggs. The eggs are spherical, averaging 22 mm in diameter, with brittle shells. Hatchlings have rounded carapaces (54–58 mm) which are orangish brown with scattered black spots. The longitudinal rows of tubercles on the carapace are prominent, as are also the dark head streaks and the yellow neck stripe.

FOOD HABITS: Both juveniles and adults are primarily carnivorous. Captives at the Honolulu Zoo consume fish, raw beef, horse meat, chicken parts, mice, crickets, crawfish, mollusks, amphibians, and some plant materials (McKeown and Webb, 1982).

134

Trionyx steindachneri

Distribution of *Trionyx steindachneri* in Hawaii

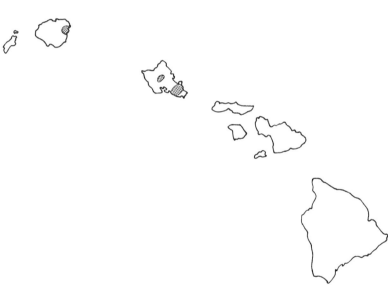

REMARKS: The life history of *Trionyx steindachneri* is poorly known; no information is available on its growth rate, longevity, predators, defensive behavior, or population dynamics. It is most closely related to the Asiatic species *T. subplanus* and *T. sinensis* (Meylan, 1987). Meylan (1987) created the monotypic genus *Palea* for this species.

The specific name, *Aspidonectes californiana* Rivers, 1889, attributed to a softshell from the Sacramento River, California, is a senior synonym of *Trionyx steindachneri* (Webb, 1975). Since the seldom-used name *californiana* has priority over the better known *steindachneri*, Webb (1978) petitioned the International Commission of Zoological Nomenclature (ICZN) to use its plenary powers to suppress *californiana* and place it on the Official Index of Rejected and Involved Specific Names in Zoology. This the ICZN did in 1982.

The flesh is palatable and it is eaten in Asia. This was probably the reason the turtle was introduced into Hawaii.

Kinosternidae
Musk and mud turtles

The family Kinosternidae is composed of the small to medium-sized, freshwater, mud or musk turtles that range from Canada to South America. The four genera—*Sternotherus, Kinosternon, Staurotypus,* and *Claudius*—contain 23 species; most of them are Central American, but the four species of *Sternotherus* and five of the 16 species of *Kinosternon* occur in the United States or Canada. The genera *Kinosternon* and *Sternotherus* compose the subfamily Kinosterninae. Kinosternid turtles apparently evolved in Mexico or Central America, and later migrated northward. Their center of diversification is Mexico, but the oldest known fossil kinosternid, *Xenochelys formosa* (Oligocene, Chadronian), is from South Dakota.

There are only 10 or 11 scutes on the single- or double-hinged plastron. Musk glands, associated with the bridge, exude malodorous secretions when the turtle is disturbed. The carapace has a nuchal bone with riblike lateral processes extending below the marginals, 10 peripheral bones, and 23 marginal scutes. The 10th dorsal vertebra lacks ribs and there is only one biconvex vertebra in the neck. The temporal region of the skull is moderately emarginated. The frontal bones are reduced and do not enter the orbit. The maxilla contacts the quadratojugal, and its crushing surface lacks a ridge. The quadrate does not enclose the stapes. A secondary palate is present. The entoplastron is absent in *Kinosternon* and *Sternotherus.*

In a study of kinosternid shell kinesis, Bramble et al. (1984) concluded that the anterior plastral kinesis of *Kinosternon* and *Sternotherus* evolved independently of the other genera in the family. A movable plastron originated to open the front of the shell. This function seems correlated with relatively large head size, the consumption of hard-shelled prey (durophagy), and a defensive behavior in which the jaws are opened wide while the head is pulled back into the shell. *Sternotherus* has retained this primitive form of shell kinesis, but in *Kinosternon* the ancestral opening mechanism has been converted to one which closes the shell. This reversal of function is associated with a secondary reduction in head size, a shift away from durophagous feeding, and a change in defensive behavior. *Kinosternon* has converged with the emydid box turtles *Terrapene* in using the neck retractor musculature to elevate the anterior plastral lobe. Kinesis of the posterior plastral lobe in *Kinosternon* may also have begun as an opening mechanism. The method of closing the posterior lobe is mechanically similar to that of *Terrapene,* except that the M. attrahens pelvium (rather than M. testoliacus) is the chief adductor muscle. A special form of midline kinesis permits an exceptionally tight seal between the posterior lobe and the carapace in some of the more terrestrial species, and relative plastral development and kinesis within *Kinosternon* seems strongly influenced by local environmental conditions, especially whether or not the aquatic habitat periodically dries completely.

Seidel et al. (1986) placed *Sternotherus* in the synonymy of *Kinosternon* based on electrophoretic studies which showed little protein variation among most species of *Kinosternon*, but that the North American *K. baurii* and *K. subrubrum* were more closely related to the four species of *Sternotherus*. Other biochemical data supported this arrangement, indicating the genus *Kinosternon* may be a paraphyletic taxon. After analyzing 27 morphological characters, Iverson (1991b) relegated *Sternotherus* to subgeneric status under *Kinosternon*, but did little else to solve the question of the status of *Sternotherus*. Previous studies on plastron morphology by Bramble et al. (1984), neural bone patterns by Iverson (1988b), karyotypes by Sites et al. (1979), and by Frair (1972) on biochemistry also indicated that *K. baurii* and *K. subrubrum* are less divergent from the sympatric species of *Sternotherus* (sensu Zug, 1986) than from the Mexican and tropical species of *Kinosternon*. *K. baurii* and *K. subrubrum* seem to share a more immediate ancestor with the species of *Sternotherus*.

Several questions arise from the lumping of *Sternotherus* with *Kinosternon*. If the genus *Kinosternon* evolved in Mexico and *K. baurii* and *K. subrubrum* occupy the most distant ranges from the center of diversity, would these two turtles not be genetically more diversified than other *Kinosternon* sympatric in the tropics? If the genus *Sternotherus* evolved from *Kinosternon* in what is now the United States, which is probable, would its species not be more closely related to the two members of the parent genus with which they share mutual geographical ranges? Also, why not relegate *K. baurii* and *K. subrubrum* to the genus *Sternotherus* rather than the four *Sternotherus* species to *Kinosternon*? Obviously, the answers to these questions are not readily available; therefore, we have adopted a conservative view and continue to recognize *Kinosternon* and *Sternotherus* as separate genera.

Iverson and Iverson (1980) published a bibliography on the turtles of the genera *Kinosternon* and *Sternotherus*.

Sternotherus odoratus (Latreille, in Sonnini and Latreille, 1802)
Stinkpot or common musk turtle
PLATE 14

RECOGNITION: The stinkpot is a small turtle with two prominent light stripes on the side of the head (see below), a small plastron with 11 scutes, and an inconspicuous single hinge. Its carapace (to 13.7 cm) is highly arched, deep and narrow, with the scutes not overlapping, and the posterior marginals not serrate. In younger individuals a prominent vertebral keel is present, but this is lost in adults. The carapace is gray brown to black; in adults it is unmarked, but many juveniles have a pattern of scattered spots or radiating dark streaks. The plastron ranges in color from yellowish to brown. A single, well-developed gular scute is present. The skin is gray to black, and the sides of the head and neck commonly have a pair of conspicuous yellow or white stripes beginning on the snout and extending backward, passing above and below the eye; these stripes may be faded or broken, and in some Florida individuals they may be lacking. Barbels are present on both the chin and the throat.

Males have longer, thicker tails, which end in a blunt terminal nail, and more exposed skin around the median plastral seams than females; they also have two small patches of tilted scales on the inner surface of each hind leg. Mount (1975) reported that the plastron length of 32 males more than 75 mm in carapace length averaged 69.1% (63.0–77.3) of the carapace length, but plastron length averaged 73.3% (68.0–78.1) for 24 females larger than 75 mm in carapace length.

KARYOTYPE: The diploid chromosome number is 56: 26 macrochromosomes (14 metacentric, 8 submetacentric, 4 telocentric) and 30 microchromosomes (Stock, 1972; Killebrew, 1975).

FOSSIL RECORD: Fossil remains of *Sternotherus odoratus* are known from the Pliocene (Clarendonian) and Pleistocene (Blancan) of Kansas (Holman, 1972; 1981b). Pleistocene (Rancholabrean) fossils are also known from Florida (Weigel, 1962), Kansas (Holman, 1987) and Texas (Holman, 1969b), and 5800-year-old Holocene bones have been found in Michigan (Holman, 1990).

DISTRIBUTION: *Sternotherus odoratus* ranges from New England, Quebec and southern Ontario south to Florida and west to Wisconsin and central Texas. An old record from Chihuahua, Mexico, is doubtful (Conant and Berry, 1978; Smith and Smith, 1979).

GEOGRAPHIC VARIATION: No subspecies are recognized, but differences exist between populations in maximum carapace length and the degree of carapacial melanism. Florida *S. odoratus* are shorter and much darker than those from more northern localities. Seidel et al. (1981) reported high overall heterozygosity in *S. odoratus,* but found little difference between populations. Similarly, Reynolds and Seidel (1983) found much intrapopulational variation in 19 morphological characters, but relatively little divergence among populations.

CONFUSING SPECIES: All other species of *Sternotherus* lack the two light stripes on the side of the head, have barbels only on the chin, and have each large carapacial scute slightly overlapping the one behind it. The mud turtles (*Kinosternon*) have large plastra with two prominent hinges.

HABITAT: The stinkpot occurs in almost any waterway with a slow current and soft bottom: rivers, streams, lakes, ponds, sloughs, canals, swamps, bayous, and oxbows. It may, however, occasionally occur in almost any sort of stream. We have taken a specimen on a gravel-bottomed stream in northwestern Arkansas. The fall line may limit the distribution of *Sternotherus odoratus*, which is found only above it

Sternotherus odoratus

Sternotherus odoratus; note
striped face and neck

in rivers draining into the Gulf of Mexico (Tinkle,
1959a).

Although this species usually prefers the shallow
water of littoral zones, McCauley (1945) and Carr
(1940, 1952) found it in water 3–9 m deep. *S.
odoratus* apparently is not tolerant of brackish water.
Conant and Bailey (1936) reported that it disappeared when a habitat in New Jersey became brackish

owing to the opening of a canal, and Dunson (1986)
found that it has essentially zero tolerance to seawater.

BEHAVIOR: In Florida and south-central Texas,
Sternotherus odoratus may be active all year long
(Bancroft et al., 1983; Vermersch, 1992), but farther
north stinkpots are usually forced to hibernate in
winter. In southeastern Pennsylvania they are active

Plastron of *Sternotherus odoratus*

Juvenile *Sternotherus odoratus*

for about 200 days from April to October (Ernst, 1986b). This annual cycle is similar to that reported from Michigan (Risley, 1933) and Ohio (Conant, 1951a), but not as long as that of populations in Oklahoma. Mahmoud (1969) found them active in Oklahoma most of the year, with a decline in activity from December to February. He estimated their annual activity period to be about 330 days.

Sternotherus odoratus is chiefly nocturnal (Bancroft et al., 1983; Ernst, 1986b). During the daylight hours it is generally inactive, remaining buried in the mud or resting on the bottom. However, an occasional individual may be found crawling along the bottom at any time. The 24-hour cycle in Oklahoma and Pennsylvania shows morning and evening activity from April to September (Mahmoud, 1969; Ernst, 1986b). Most activity is from 0400 to 1100 and from 1700 to 2100. From September to April most of the activity occurs between 1000 and 1600.

Daily activity may be controlled by the ambient

Distribution of *Sternotherus odoratus*

temperature cycle. Under cyclic thermal acclimation (15–25°C), *S. odoratus*'s activity is bimodal with major peaks at hours 10 and 16 (Graham and Hutchison, 1979a). Its activity minimum is not synchronized with the high of the ambient temperature cycle, but instead takes place at the 12th hour.

Most bottom activity is at depths of less than 60 cm, but Minton (1972) observed stinkpots at a depth of 9 m. Prolonged diving results in several physiological adjustments. Submerged *S. odoratus* is a bimodal breather, exchanging gases with both air and water. While underwater it requires only one-eighth the oxygen normally used in air and so can remain submerged for long periods (Root, 1949); however, most dives are less than 20 minutes duration (Stone et al., 1992b). Submerged stinkpots have average blood volumes of 26% saturation for oxygen and 56% for carbon dioxide; when in air these are reversed (Stone et al., 1992a). Buccopharyngeal respiration contributes little to the ability of the turtle to remain submerged; throat movements that are prominent while the turtle is underwater are primarily concerned with olfaction. Stinkpots submerged in anoxic water die in about five days (Ultsch et al. 1984; Jackson et al., 1984), indicating that some oxygen is absorbed

from the water. Acid-base responses in *S. odoratus* blood in normoxic water indicate efficient use of extrapulmonary gas exchange while diving (Ultsch et al., 1984). Stinkpots can balance about 60% of the added lactate when submerged in anoxic waters, but will die if their blood pH drops a full unit, thus oxygen uptake from the water is essential.

Because it spends extended periods underwater, the stinkpot often supports a rich growth of algae and many leeches on its shell (Ernst and Barbour, 1972; Reilly, 1983; Ernst, 1986b).

The basking habit is poorly developed: *S. odoratus* is seldom found out of the water. Most basking occurs while the turtle rests in shallow water with just the top of the carapace exposed to the sunlight or when floating at the surface among aquatic vegetation. The stinkpot occasionally climbs onto the bank or onto fallen trees to bask. It sometimes climbs almost 2 m or more above the surface of the water on small tree trunks. Older individuals drop into the water when disturbed, but the younger ones hold on with such a grip that it is sometimes difficult to remove them. In Pennsylvania most basking takes place from April to July (Ernst, 1986b).

Temperature relationships of Oklahoma and Pennsylvania *S. odoratus* have been studied by Mahmoud (1969) and Ernst (1986b). Mahmoud found a mean difference between the cloacal and environmental temperature, throughout the year, of +0.58 to −0.05°C. The thermal activity range was 10–34°C and the field-preferred body temperature was 24.14°C. The minimum and maximum body temperatures at which *S. odoratus* would accept food in the laboratory were 13 and 35°C. In captivity the stinkpot showed greater activity at water temperatures of 21–26°C. Mahmoud's turtles had a mean critical thermal maximum of 40.25°C (39.5–41.9) and lost their righting ability at an average temperature of 38.7°C (38.4–39.0). Ernst (1986b) recorded the cloacal and environmental temperatures during 547 captures. Active turtles (536) had cloacal temperatures ranging from 14 to 30°C (mean 21.7); 67% of these temperatures fell between 16 and 24°C. The highest cloacal temperature, 30°C, was much lower than the critical thermal maximum of 40.1–41.7°C reported by Hutchison et al. (1966). Basking turtles had cloacal temperatures of 14–27°C; those feeding, 18–30°C; stinkpots moving in water, 17–26°C; moving on land, 22–27°C; courting or mating 16–22°C; nesting, 20–25°C; dormant in warm water, 24–28°C; and dormant in cold water, 6–12°C. Edgren and Edgren (1955) found that temperatures of stinkpots are higher than the water temperatures when the water temperatures are low (17–19°C) and lower when the water temperatures are high (28–30°C); but in the laboratory the turtles' cloacal temperatures and the water temperatures are about the same, which suggests that thermoregulation resulting from behavioral mechanisms was precluded by laboratory conditions. Graham and Hutchison (1979b) found that stinkpots acclimated at 15°C to longer photoperiods in laboratory studies have higher mean preferred temperatures.

When fully grown stinkpots are kept out of water for a period of time with like-sized turtles of other species, such as *Chrysemys picta*, *Clemmys guttata*, and *Kinosternon subrubrum*, they usually are the first to show signs of distress. Ernst (1968b) compared evaporative loss of water in *S. odoratus*, *Chelydra serpentina*, *Clemmys guttata*, *C. insculpta*, and *Terrapene carolina*, and found that *S. odoratus* suffered the greatest total weight (water) loss (20%) and had a weight-loss gradient of 0.24 g/h. Two juveniles died during the study after losing 33.4% and 33.1% of their weight, respectively.

Stinkpots hibernate buried 30 cm or so in the mud bottom underwater, beneath rocks, logs, or detritus in or near the water, in recesses beneath banks, or in muskrat dens or lodges. They begin to burrow when

the water temperature falls below 10°C. Stinkpots sometimes congregate in numbers at suitable hibernacula. Thomas and Trautman (1937) found an estimated 450 stinkpots in an area approximately 14 m by 1.8 m in the mud bed of a drained canal at Buckeye Lake, Ohio. In studies by Ultsch (1985, 1988) on *S. odoratus* submerged at 3 and 10°C in normoxic and anoxic water, those subjected to anoxic conditions died quickly as their acid-base status deteriorated rapidly, plasma lactate rose, and plasma bicarbonate fell, resulting in a lowering of blood pH.

Maximum and minimum distances between successive points of capture of Oklahoma *S. odoratus* were 525 and 1.8 m. The average first-last capture distances for periods of more than 100 days were 50 m for females and 69 m for males; for less than 100 days, 38 m for females and 66 m for males. The average distance traveled by 39 males was 68 m, by females 46 m. Average home range of Oklahoma stinkpots was 0.2 ha for males and 0.05 ha for females (Mahmoud, 1969).

Ernst (1986b) calculated the mean home range of Pennsylvania males to be 1.75 ha, and that of females, 0.94 ha. Among 109 *S. odoratus* recaptured, the average distance between recaptures was 93.6 m for males, 89.5 m for females, and 117.3 m for juveniles.

Williams (1952) studied homing ability of stinkpots in a Michigan lake, and 15 of 50 animals showed site fidelity by returning to close proximity of original capture. One returned to within 15 m eight times, which involved straight-line movements of at least 213 m from the release point. This turtle traveled a minimum distance of at least 1,707 m during the 34 days of trials. The 15 turtles that homed averaged over 122 m/day during the return trips.

Stinkpots occasionally move overland, but the home range is probably confined to one body of water. Overland movements are likely seasonal or forced. Both Bancroft et al. (1983) and Ernst (1986b) have reported habitat shifts over periods of time. Three Pennsylvania males moved 0.59, 0.64 and 0.70 km, respectively (Ernst, 1986b). If their aquatic habitat dries up during the summer, stinkpots may or may not move out to seek water. Gibbons et al. (1983) reported that the number of *S. odoratus* emigrating from a South Carolina pond during a drought year exceeded the mean number of emigrants during the previous five years; and Ernst (1986b) observed the same behavior when a pond in Pennsylvania was drained.

Newly hatched stinkpots find their way from the nest to the water primarily through the attraction of large areas of intense illumination. Escape from the nest is facilitated by their marked negative geotropism in the dark. They are attracted toward areas of high humidity, but the presence of a light source in a drier area will counteract any tendency to move toward a wet area (Noble and Breslau, 1938).

The retina of *S. odoratus* contains both rods and cones; that is, the stinkpot can see color (Ernst et al., 1970). Ernst and Hamilton (1969) reported that *S. odoratus* chose red or yellow compartments over green or blue in 64% of trials; this color selection, they thought, may aid orientation.

REPRODUCTION: Although it has been reported that males mature in three or four years at carapace lengths of 60–70 mm (Risley, 1933; Tinkle, 1961), Mitchell (1988) found male stinkpots from Virginia with typical secondary sex characteristics (enlarged tail base, scale patches on the hind legs) at carapace lengths as short as 51 mm. Histological examination revealed Virginia males first produced sperm at the end of their second year. Oklahoma males mature in four to seven years at carapace lengths of 65 mm (Mahmoud, 1967).

Risley (1933) thought that females from Michigan matured in 9–11 years, but Tinkle (1961) reported females mature in 2–7 years at lengths above 80 mm. The youngest Virginia female with at least one shelled egg was four years old and 65.7 mm long (Mitchell, 1988). However, Mitchell found no mature three-year females. In Florida, the smallest mature female was 57 mm and the largest immature female 64 mm (Bancroft et al., 1983). Oklahoma females mature in five to eight years at carapace lengths of 65–85 mm (Mahmoud, 1967).

Southern stinkpots mature faster than those in the north. Tinkle (1961) found that the minimum size at maturity of southern males was 54 mm (mean 65 mm), and of southern females 61 mm (mean 82 mm). Comparable figures for northern males and females were 63 mm (mean 73 mm) and 80 mm (mean 96 mm). No mature northern female had fewer than three growth annuli, and most had four or more; the oldest immature female examined had seven. The youngest mature northern male had three annuli, but several with this number were immature. Northern males four years old or older were mature. The youngest mature southern female had three annuli; no specimens were available with more than three annuli, but all of the southern females with three were mature. The youngest mature southern male had three annuli, and none with more than three was immature. A southern male with a single annulus was mature, but all others with one or two annuli were immature.

The male sexual cycle has been studied in various parts of the United States: Alabama (McPherson and Marion, 1981a); Michigan (Risley, 1934, 1938), Oklahoma (Mahmoud and Klicka, 1972), and Virginia (Mitchell, 1985b, 1988). The timing of histological changes varies with locality, but generally conforms with the following description. Spermatogenesis begins with multiplication of spermatogonia in May or June. Primary spermatocytes and maturation divisions appear from mid-June into July with the peak in sperm production occurring from mid-July to mid-August. Spermiogenesis begins as early as late July, is in full progress by late August or early September, and is completed in late September or October. Testes are of maximum size and weight, and seminiferous tubules of greatest diameter, in late August and early September, followed by an increase in the diameter of the epididymides. Restoration of germinal epithelium occurs primarily from March to early May, with some recovery in the winter.

Plasma testosterone is undetectable through most of the year (especially from February to July). It then increases to its highest levels from August to October after the testes are fully recrudesced (McPherson et al., 1982; Licht, 1982). However, males show little seasonal change in total plasma lipid levels (McPherson and Marion, 1982); the testosterone peak might be important for the onset of fall mating behavior (McPherson et al., 1982). Mendonça and Licht (1986) reported that monthly mean follicle-stimulating hormone levels are correlated significantly with the level of plasma testosterone. Both are at minimal levels in the spring when the testes are small and at high levels in the fall when spermiation has begun and the testes are regressing. Plasma luteinizing hormone remains undetectable throughout the year in males.

Decreasing day length is the key environmental stimulus for male sexual activity, but rising temperatures may help to correlate mating behavior (Mendonça and Licht, 1986; Mendonça, 1987). Testosterone is effective in bringing on male mating behavior only under certain environmental conditions (Mendonça, 1987). Increased testosterone helps initiate and maintain sexual behavior, but its action may vary seasonally according to photoperiod (and, to a lesser extent, temperature).

The female cycle begins in mid- to late July after the last eggs of the year have been ovulated (Edgren, 1960; Mahmoud and Klicka, 1972; Iverson, 1977a; McPherson and Marion, 1981b; McPherson et al., 1982; Mitchell, 1985d, 1988). At this time the ovarian follicles are of minimal size. Vitellogenesis begins in late July causing follicular enlargement and continues until December, after which further increase is slowed or stopped during winter hibernation. Some additional yolk material may be added to the ova in the spring until they reach maximum size just prior to ovulation. Ovulation may begin in February in Florida or as late as April or May farther north, and females usually produce more than one clutch each year. The eggs may be retained for 20–35 days while the albumen and shell are formed; Edgren (1960) calculated that the life of the egg in the oviduct is five to eight weeks.

Testosterone levels increase during the periovulatory period of the first clutch, but during vitellogenesis, ovulation, and oviposition of the second and third clutches, plasma levels remain low (McPherson et al., 1982). A small increase in testosterone level is associated with vitellogenesis. High estrogen levels are associated with the vitellogenic periods during the fall and spring into early summer. Progesterone concentrations increase markedly during the periovulatory period but decline as the eggshells are formed in the oviducts, and increase slightly again in the fall. Ho et al. (1982) reported a similar estrogen cycle, and also that the plasma levels of egg-yolk proteins (vitellogenins) synthesized in the liver show a positive correlation with plasma estrogen levels and ovarian growth.

Vitellogenesis appears to be an estrogen-specific dose-dependent response that can be inhibited by progesterone and testosterone. Females have seasonal peaks in plasma lipids associated with ovarian development and body-fat storage (McPherson and Marion, 1982). Ovarian concentrations of lipids are lowest after nesting and increase during the fall. Females have nondetectable levels of plasma luteinizing hormone and follicle-stimulating hormone throughout the year (Mendonça and Licht, 1986).

Generally, prolonged exposure to high temperature (28°C) inhibits follicular growth but lower temperature (18°C) promotes it (Mendonça, 1987). Photoperiod has no apparent effect in any season. High temperature in the fall initially stimulates vitellogenesis when the follicles are partially enlarged.

Courtship and mating occur sporadically throughout the year, with peaks in the spring and fall. Most mating occurs in April and May (Ernst, 1986b) before the nesting period. A second period of mating occurs in September and October but may extend into December. All 12 matings observed in Pennsylvania by Ernst (1986b) took place in the morning (0915–1027) in water shallower than 30 cm. In all cases the male was slightly larger than the female (average

difference, 2.04 mm). One 85.8-mm female was found copulating with two different males in 1973 (29 April, 20 May). Cloacal temperatures of mating turtles averaged 18.4°C (16.0–22.2) and water temperatures 18.5°C (16.0–23.1).

There is evidence that sperm from fall matings may be retained through the winter in viable condition in the oviducts. Gist and Jones (1989) using an electron microscope identified sperm-containing tubules in the oviduct of female *Sternotherus odoratus*. These sperm-storage tubules are located in the posterior portion of the albumen-secreting section of the oviduct between the infundibulum and uterus.

Mahmoud (1967) studied the sexual activities of *S. odoratus*, *S. carinatus*, *Kinosternon subrubrun*, and *K. flavescens*, and has given a most detailed composite account of their courtship and mating. There are three phases: tactile, mounting and intromission, and biting and rubbing. During the tactile phase a male with head extended approaches another turtle from behind and touches or smells its tail, apparently to determine sex. Courtship usually proceeds no further if the approached turtle is a male; if a female, the male, with head still extending forward, moves to her side and nudges the region of her bridge with his nose. This movement apparently is directed at the musk glands there. If the female is not receptive she moves away. The male responds either by giving chase or by going elsewhere. If chasing occurs, the male, with head fully extended, persistently attempts to nudge or bite the female about the head as he follows. If initially receptive, the female remains immobile while the male, with head fully extended, gently nudges her just behind the eye and a few seconds later assumes the mounting position. This tactile phase may vary in length from a few seconds to three minutes.

The mounting phase usually follows the tactile phase. Males approach females either from behind or from the side. The male positions himself with his plastron directly over the female's carapace by grasping the rims of her carapace with the toes and claws of all four feet. By flexing one knee the male holds the female's tail between the two scaly patches on the opposing posterior surfaces of the upper and lower leg throughout coitus. The male's tail is looped so that the terminal nail touches the skin at one side of the female's cloaca; this brings the vents together, and insertion of the penis follows. The male's head extends forward to gently touch the top of the female's head and neck. These actions occur simultaneously. When the coital position is attained the rubbing and biting phase begins. The time between mounting and penial insertion is about 5–10 seconds.

Finneran (1948) discovered a pair of Connecticut *S. odoratus* copulating plastron-to-plastron with the male holding the female with all four feet. This is the only record of mating in this position, and it must be considered exceptional.

The nesting season varies with latitude: in the south, egg-laying lasts from February through July, in south-central Texas, from April through July, and in the north, from May through July. Nesting takes place from early morning into the night, although in Ernst's (1986b) experience most in the north occur in the evening (1910–2048). Nests have been dug as far as 45 m from the water, but excavations are usually nearer the water.

Some females lay their eggs on the open ground; others dig well-formed nests as deep as 10 cm. Most nests, however, are shallow and are formed by scraping away debris such as decaying vegetable matter, leaf mold, or rotting wood. Many eggs are laid under stumps and fallen logs and in the walls of muskrat lodges. When a nest is excavated it usually is dug with the hind feet only; however, Newman (1906) saw a female dig with all four feet and her snout.

Female stinkpots are noted for sharing nesting sites; often several lay their eggs at the same place. Cagle (1937) found 16 nests under one log about a meter long; these nests were so close together that many of them were intermingled. Edgren (1942) found 130 eggs buried in the debris of an abandoned duck blind. Of 32 nests found by Ernst (1986b), 17 were in full sunlight and 10 in shade.

The eggs are elliptical, with a thick, white, brittle shell that appears slightly glazed when dry. Length varies from 22 to 31 mm, and width from 13 to 17 mm. The eggs weigh 3–5 g. Clutches contain one to nine eggs (although the latter number may represent that of more than one female). Usually, however, two to five eggs are laid. In Pennsylvania, 32 clutches contained 104 eggs, an average of 3.25 (Ernst, 1986b), but females from more southern populations may lay smaller clutches (mean 2.5, Tinkle, 1961; 2.4, Gibbons, 1970b; 2.6 for riverine and 2.75 for pond dwellers, McPherson and Marion 1981b, 1983), although Iverson (1977a) reported a mean clutch size of 3.2 eggs for Florida females. This may be correlated with the shorter carapace lengths of southern stinkpots. Clutch size seems to increase with a decrease in the isotherm zone: at an isotherm zone of 21–23°C the mean clutch size is 1.8, at 10–13°C it is 3.5, and at 7–10°C it is 5.5 (Tinkle, 1961).

A correlation exists between clutch size and the body size of the female; the largest females lay the most eggs

per clutch (Mitchell, 1985d; Ernst, 1986b), and two to four clutches may be laid each year (Gibbons, 1970b; Iverson, 1977a; Mitchell, 1988).

Total hatching success of 104 Pennsylvania eggs laid was only 15.4% (Ernst, 1986b). Predators destroyed 25 (78%) of the 32 nests containing 79 (76%) eggs; 2 (6%) other nests containing 5 (5%) eggs were lost to dehydration. Of the remaining 20 eggs, only 16 hatched; 4 were either infertile or suffered prenatal mortality. Assuming Pennsylvania *S. odoratus* lay 3.25 eggs per clutch and that natural prenatal mortality eliminates 20%, the reproductive potential is 2.6 young per clutch, the number of young is further reduced 80% by predators and climatic factors until the realized potential is about 0.5 young per clutch. If multiple clutches are laid by each female, the reproductive potential will be enhanced accordingly. Dissections of females by McPherson and Marion (1981b, 1983) revealed potentials of three to four clutches per season, and they estimated the reproductive potential to be 8.25 eggs per nesting season in those laying three clutches and 11.0 in those laying four clutches. If *S. odoratus* in Pennsylvania lay multiple clutches, the potential would be 6.5 eggs for two clutches, 9.25 eggs for three, and 13 eggs for four clutches. The number of eggs laid and females ovipositing may vary from year to year depending on weather conditions (Gibbons, 1982).

The natural incubation period ranges from 65 to 86 days, and the hatchlings emerge from August to November depending on latitude. Carr (1952) gave the following account of the hatching of a stinkpot egg. At 1800 hours he noticed a small crescentic piece of shell, about 2.5 mm long and 1 mm wide, that was loose but remained in place. By 2300 this hole was enlarged to 3.5 mm in diameter and another hole, on the opposite side of the same end, appeared, giving the egg two separate openings. From the larger (the first) of these the toenails of the hatchling protruded. The next day at 1100 no change was evident except the holes were slightly larger, now irregularly so, and with jagged outlines; the inner membrane was not broken under the new hole. At 2100 the two holes were now continuous, the band of shell separating them having been fractured. On the third day at 0900 several cracks radiated from the single large hole in the end. At noon, the hatchling was out of the shell; it had not emerged by forcing its way through the initial hole but by breaking the entire end of the egg in one large or two small pieces. Ewert (1985) has given a detailed discussion of the embryonic development of *S. odoratus*.

Hatchling *Sternotherus odoratus*

Gibbons (1970b) believed hatchlings overwinter in the nest in South Carolina, but Ernst has not observed this phenonema in Pennsylvania nor has Mitchell (1988) in Virginia.

The hatchling carapace is rough and has a prominent vertebral keel and two smaller lateral keels. It is black, with a light spot on each marginal. The plastron lacks a hinge and is rough in texture; it is dark with lighter mottlings. The skin is black and the two light stripes on the head are prominent; with head and limbs retracted hatchlings look like blackened nuts or bits of driftwood (Minton, 1972). Newly hatched young have carapaces 18.5–22.8 mm long, 15.5–16.6 mm wide, and 11.5–12.8 mm high.

Incubation temperature determines the sex of the hatchling (Vogt et al., 1982; Clark et al., 1986). Incubation at 28°C or higher produces nearly all females, but cooler temperatures produce both sexes. An incubation temperature of 25°C produces as much as 80% males.

GROWTH AND LONGEVITY: As *Sternotherus odoratus* grows it becomes more elongated and flattened. Risley (1933) reported that stinkpots with carapaces over 80 mm in length are at least 10 years old. He showed that stinkpots averaged approximately 32.5 mm, 52 mm, 61 mm, 67 mm, 71 mm, 74.5 mm, 77.6 mm, and 80 mm in length, respectively, for each of their first nine years. Mahmoud (1969) found that Oklahoma males having a carapace

length of 41–60 mm increased an average of 12.1 mm (21%) per growing season; those 61–80 mm increased 1.6 mm (2.3%); and those over 81 mm increased only 0.78 mm (0.96%). Females having a carapace length of 41–60 mm increased 26.6 mm (52%); those 61–80 mm increased 0.88 mm (1.3%); and those over 81 mm increased only 0.23 mm (0.25%). Three *S. odoratus* over 10 years old did not grow during the two years they were kept in captivity.

Ernst (1986b) found growth in Pennsylvania stinkpots fell between those reported by Risley (1933) and Mahmoud (1969), but his animals had only a 150-day annual feeding period compared to 190 days in Oklahoma.

In one month, the hatchlings of a clutch increased in length from 18.3 mm to 19.9 mm and in width from 14 mm to 18.2 mm, and those of another clutch increased from 22 mm to 23.7 mm in length and from 16.3 mm to 20.9 mm in width (Adler, 1960).

A stinkpot lived for more than 54 years, 9 months in the Philadelphia Zoo (Snider and Bowler, 1992). Ernst (1986b) estimated that a wild female in his Pennsylvania population was at least 28 years of age and a male was at least 27 years old at the time they were last captured.

FOOD HABITS: *Sternotherus odoratus* is omnivorous. Stinkpots under 5 cm in carapace length feed predominantly on small aquatic insects, algae, and carrion, whereas those above 5 cm feed on any kind of food. They are bottom feeders, often walking about with head extended in search of prey. They probe soft mud, sand, and decaying vegetation with their heads, apparently looking for prey. A piece of food too large to be swallowed whole is held between the jaws while the claws tear the main mass away from the part in the mouth.

The stinkpot is known to eat earthworms, leeches, clams, snails, crabs, crayfish, aquatic insects, fish eggs, minnows, tadpoles, algae, and parts of higher plants. These usually are eaten underwater, but Newman (1906) observed stinkpots, at dusk, crawling about on land and seizing and eating slugs. He also reported that they scavenge, feeding on all sorts of material, from dead mollusks to kitchen refuse. Lagler (1943) reported that insects and snails were the foods most often found in the stomachs (34.2% and 28.3% of occurrence, respectively). Mahmoud (1968b) found the following percentages of frequency and volume, respectively, of food items in Oklahoma *S. odoratus:* Insecta 98.3, 46.4; Crustacea 61.1, 5.0; Mollusca 96.1, 23.7; Amphibia 5.2, 1.1; carrion 37.4, 3.4; and aquatic vegetation 97.4, 20.4. In Florida, Bancroft et al. (1983) found that 99% of the plant biomass in stinkpot stomachs was accounted for by *Nuphar* (56%), *Vallisneria* (26%), filamentous algae (9%), and *Eichhornia* (8%). Dominant animal prey items by biomass were mollusks (94.%) and aquatic insects (38%). Ernst (1986b) observed those in Pennsylvania eating algae (*Cladophora, Spirogyra*), leeches, snails, crayfish, larval and adult aquatic insects, tadpoles and adult frogs (*Rana*), and dead fish (*Catostomus, Lepomis*). Berry (1975) observed that *S. odoratus* in Florida fed primarily on crayfish in areas where *S. minor* was absent. The diet of *S. odoratus* was more generalized in areas where both species occupied the same body of water.

Diet may vary seasonally according to what is most available, and sexual differences in preferred prey may exist. Bancroft et al. (1983) found that, in general, males are more dependent than females on aquatic insects and less so upon snails.

Parmenter (1981) reported that the digestive turnover rate for one stinkpot (plastron length, 58 mm, body weight, 76 g) was 49 hours at 23–27°C.

PREDATORS AND DEFENSE: Stinkpot eggs are eaten by snakes (*Cemophora, Lampropeltis*), skunks (*Mephitis*), raccoons (*Procyon*), various herons, and crows (*Corvus*) and, probably, by other animals on occasion. Forks (1979) and Knight and Loraine (1986) reported instances of stinkpot eggs passing through kingsnakes (*Lampropeltis getula*) and later

hatching. Red-shouldered hawks (*Buteo*) are predators of juveniles and adults, and the remains of juveniles have been found in largemouth bass (*Micropterus*), bullfrogs (*Rana catesbeiana*), and cottonmouths (*Agkistrodon piscivorus*). Adults are eaten by alligators (Delany and Abercrombie, 1986). Clark (1982) listed several observations of bald eagle (*Haliaeetus leucocephalus*) predation on *S. odoratus,* and Bancroft et al. (1983) reported the apparent killing of four adults by mammals and birds (probably boat-tailed grackles, *Quiscalus major*). Some evidence exists that muskrats (*Ondatra, Neofiber*) sometimes feed on adults.

Humans occasionally take them on hook and line and usually destroy the turtle for its efforts. Another major human problem is the wounding of turtles by boats; Bancroft et al. (1983) thought boat propellers a major source of mortality, as they found three dead from propeller strikes and 77 others showing boat damage. The worst human effects, however, come from habitat destruction (wetland drainage, pollution).

The temperament of individuals varies. Some are shy, pulling into their shells when handled, but many bite and scratch viciously. In addition to biting and scratching they may void the contents of their musk glands, and the resulting odor is vile enough to have earned them the common name, stinkpot. The odor arises from a yellowish volatile fluid secreted by two glands located on each side beneath the border of the carapace: one gland is located at the posterior end of the bridge, the other about midway between the bridge and anterior edge of the carapace (Ehrenfeld and Ehrenfeld, 1973). Similar glands are found in all kinosternids. The secretion contains four ω-phenylalkanoic acids: phenylacetic, 3-phenylpropionic, 5-phenylpentanoic, and 7-phenylalkanoic acids (Eisner et al., 1977). The last two are quite malodorous and responsible for the stench from which the common name is derived. Several aliphatic acids are also present. Only a few milligrams of fluid are secreted at one time. Eisner et al. (1977) tested its deterring effects on potential fish predators, but thought the turtle did not ordinarily discharge enough fluid to prevent an attack. They thought the smelly liquid was used only as an aposematic signal to warn predators of the turtle's more generalized undesirability. However, the secretion is quite volatile and perhaps is more directed toward attacks in air than in water.

POPULATIONS: Mahmoud (1969) estimated there were 150/ha in his Oklahoma study area, and Mitchell (1988) reported an estimated density in a

Virginia lake of 194/ha. In contrast to these high estimates, Ernst (1986b) found the density of a small population from Pennsylvania to be only 24/ha. The biomass estimation for Mahmoud's Oklahoma stinkpots was 10.2 kg/ha (Iverson, 1982a) and in Mitchell's (1988) Virginia population, 13.6 kg/ha, but Congdon et al. (1986) reported that in small ponds in South Carolina, where the density varied from only 7.5 to 21.8/ha, the biomass was less than 1.5 kg/ha. At a northern Alabama lake, Dodd (1989a) estimated the density to be 148.5/ha (a biomass of 10.6 kg/ha). Obviously, the number of *Sternotherus odoratus* that can be supported varies with the carrying capacity of the aquatic habitat.

Most populations are composed predominantly of adults. Ernst (1986b) reported that adults made up over 70% of his Pennsylvania population. Juvenile mortality seemed high since 51 of his 68 juveniles were never recaptured; however, Mitchell (1988) calculated an 84–86% survivorship rate in all age and sex groups in Virginia. At Dodd's (1989a) Alabama lake, juveniles made up 16.3% of the captured turtles.

Some populations of *S. odoratus* have sex ratios favoring one sex over the other. Risley (1933) reported that of 255 adults taken in the field, 77 were males and 178 were females—a sex ratio of 1.0:2.3. Cagle (1942) found that males composed 41% of his samples. The sex ratio of all *S. odoratus* examined by Tinkle (1961) in which sex could be determined was slightly skewed in favor of females; among 51 hatchlings there were 36 females and 15 males, and of 647 stinkpots over 50 mm in carapace length 339 (52%) were females and 308 (48%) were males. Dodd (1989a) reported a 1.0:2.8 male to female ratio, but this was not significantly different from equality, and Ernst (1986b) reported a sex ratio of 1.34:1, but, although favoring males, it also was not significantly different. Mitchell (1988) reported a 1:1 sex ratio for his population, and Bancroft et al. (1983) recorded a ratio not significantly different from 1:1 for almost 3,000 adults in a Florida lake.

REMARKS: Zug (1966) found that in *Sternotherus* the structure of the glans penis is of two general types: a *minor-odoratus* type and a *carinatus* type. He gave a thorough description of each. Electrophoretic studies by Seidel et al. (1981) have showed *S. odoratus* to be closest phylogenetically to *S. carinatus*.

Zug (1971) and Smith and Smith (1980) have discussed the past use of the name *Sternothaerus* for the American musk turtles and have presented evidence that *Sternotherus* is the valid spelling. Lists of the literature pertaining to *S. odoratus* are in Reynolds and Seidel (1982) and Zug (1986).

Sternotherus depressus Tinkle and Webb, 1955
Flattened musk turtle

PLATE 15

RECOGNITION: This small musk turtle has an oval carapace (to 12.5 cm) which is broad and very flat. Its sides always slope at an angle greater than 100°, and in juveniles the mean angle/height ratio is 9.5:1. A blunt middorsal keel is present, the vertebral scutes are juxtaposed, and the posterior marginals are serrate. The carapace is yellowish brown to dark brown with small, dark-brown or black spots or streaks and dark seams. The immaculate pink to yellowish-brown plastron contains a single gular scute, and has an indistinct hinge between the pectoral and abdominal scutes. The head is moderately wide with a projecting tubular snout and a slightly hooked (some are notched) upper jaw. Two pairs of barbels are present on the chin. Fine black mottling is present on the olive head, and dark bars on the jaws. Some individuals have a yellow stripe from the nostril to the orbit, and others may have alternating light and dark longitudinal stripes on the upper neck, reminiscent of *Sternotherus minor peltifer,* but the stripes are commonly narrower. Other skin is olive with fine black mottling. All four feet are webbed.

Males have long, thick tails, with the vent posterior to the carapacial rim, and roughened patches of scales on their thighs and crura.

KARYOTYPE AND FOSSIL RECORD: Unknown.

DISTRIBUTION: *Sternotherus depressus* is restricted to the Black Warrior River system in west-central Alabama (see Ernst et al., 1989).

GEOGRAPHIC VARIATION: No subspecies have been described. *Sternotherus depressus* was originally described as a full species (Tinkle and Webb, 1955), but Wermuth and Mertens (1961, 1977) relegated it to a subspecies of *S. minor* (which

was followed by Ernst and Barbour, 1972). This was because specimens from drainages in extreme west-central Alabama north of Tuscaloosa were thought to be intermediate between it and *S. m. peltifer* (Estridge, 1970; Mount, 1975). More recent morphological studies and studies of the electrophoretic properties of proteins from these two turtles have shown them to be related but distinct species (Iverson, 1977c; Seidel and Lucchino, 1981; Seidel et al. 1981; Ernst et al. 1988b). Ernst et al. (1988b) showed these "intermediate" populations to be *S. depressus*. Although some individuals from western Alabama have head and neck patterns (characters quite variable in kinosternid turtles) similar to those in *S. m. peltifer,* carapacial configuration clearly indicates they are *S. depressus*.

CONFUSING SPECIES: *Kinosternon subrubrum* has a double-hinged plastron. *Sternotherus carinatus* lacks a gular scute and has a high peaked shell with sides always sloping at an angle less than 100°. Both *S. m. minor* and *S. m. peltifer* have shells with sides that always slope at an angle less than 100°, and their mean angle/height ratio is about 5:1. *Sternotherus odoratus* does not have overlapping vertebral scutes, always has the sides of its carapace sloping at an angle less than 100°, and bears two distinct yellow stripes on each side of its face.

HABITAT: Clear, shallow (to 150 cm), rock-bottomed to sandy, permanent streams above the fall line seem preferred. In such places it hides during the day in rock crevices, under sunken logs, or buried in the sand. Since it is mostly a bottom dweller, heavy infestations of leeches and algae may occur on the carapace (Dodd, 1988a).

BEHAVIOR: The flattened musk turtle is inactive during the winter months, but where it spends this period has not been determined. Mount (1981)

Sternotherus depressus

Sternotherus depressus

reported earliest and latest capture dates of 18 April and 20 October. Juveniles are more active during the day than adults. Most adult activity is nocturnal. During a summer study of this turtle in central Alabama, Ernst et al. (1989) found fewer active adults than juveniles during the daylight hours, and those juveniles collected are usually of the smaller size classes. Juveniles become more active at twilight, and as darkness increases, so does musk turtle activity. There seems to be a correlation between the amount of darkness (time?) and the size of the active musk turtles. In early evening more juveniles are observed foraging, but as it gets darker, more young adults emerge, and still later the very large (old) adults become active. Trapping revealed that most large adults become active after 2200. Early in the year when water temperatures are rather cool, *Sternotherus depressus* normally is diurnal, but some are active either crepuscularly or nocturnally (Dodd et al., 1988). As the season progresses and the water warms, diurnal activity becomes less obvious but nocturnal activity increases. The critical thermal minimum and maximum are unknown, but Mount (1981) trapped turtles at water temperatures of 17–27°C.

Plastron of *Sternotherus depressus*

The basking habitat is not well developed, but Dodd et al. (1988) recorded 67 instances from 16 May to 14 September, with the majority of observations occurring between 14 August and 4 September. Basking most frequently occurred in the morning, and the cloacal temperatures of eight basking *S. depressus* were 22.2–33.1°C. Mount (1981), Dodd (1988b), and Dodd et al. (1988) thought most basking occurred in sick turtles (60%), but healthy individuals also bask.

Dodd et al. (1988) followed 13 radio-equipped *S. depressus* from 4 to 40 days. Males moved during 69% of the days, females only 50%. Males traveled greater distances (mean 31.2, 0.5–460 m) than females (mean 19.2, 0.5–160 m). The turtles tended to stay in the same area and returned continuously to the same cover sites, which were often simultaneously occupied by several individuals. The longest distances moved were upstream and for durations of only one or two days. Dodd et al. (1988) applied several methods to determine the home range of an adult male located 39 times, and found it to vary between 77 m^2 and 123 m^2.

REPRODUCTION: There is a paucity of information on the reproductive biology of this species. Tinkle (1958a) thought *Sternotherus depressus* matured in four years: females at a carapace length of 90–100 mm, males at about 75 mm. However, Close (in Mount, 1981) examined a large series of flattened musk turtles, and thought that males require four to six years to mature (60–65-mm carapace lengths) but

females take six to eight years (70–75-mm carapace lengths). Tinkle (1958a) dissected females and found the mean number of potentially ovulatory follicles to be 5.5.

Females apparently come out of the water individually at separate sites and deposit their eggs in shallow nests dug in the fringing woodlands along their waterways. Dodd et al. (1988) reported that a shallow nest found on 31 July had been dug in a high, sandy bank under slight vegetative cover 6.5 m from water in such a position as to receive the afternoon sun. The two freshly laid eggs were 31.1–33.1 mm long, 15.7–16.1 mm wide, and weighed 5.5–6.0 g. Estridge (1970) reported that an oblong, brittle shell egg laid by a captive on 16 June was 32 × 16.4 mm.

Dodd et al. (1988) incubated the two eggs at 25°C and hatching began on 14–16 September (45–47 days). The egg incubated by Estridge (1970, temperature unknown) hatched on 16 October (122 days). Carapace length of Estridge's hatchling was 25 mm (27.1 mm fully expanded). The smallest juvenile caught by Ernst et al. (1983) had a 26-mm carapace. Complete emergence from the egg takes from 12 hours to two days. The yolk scar disappears within a few days. The carapacial pattern is faintly developed, but small individuals have typical head and neck patterns.

GROWTH AND LONGEVITY: Dodd et al. (1988) collected 50 *Sternotherus depressus* previously measured and marked by Ernst et al. (1983). Growth and weight change analysis showed that these turtles

Distribution of *Sternotherus depressus*

increased less than 1.15 mm/year in carapace length during the two-year interval, and that weight changes were minor. Growth did not slow uniformly with sexual maturity, and individual variation in growth rate was not correlated with shell length. Some large adults grew at the same rate as shorter, newly matured, adults. The smallest turtle grew the fastest, and small *S. depressus* probably grow much faster than 1–2 mm/year. The maximum growth recorded for any individual was 6.7 mm (3.35 mm/year).

Natural longevity is unknown, but some wild individuals probably live more than 20 years.

FOOD HABITS: Marion et al. (1991) analyzed the diet of *Sternotherus depressus* by examining fecal contents. The percent volumetric displacement and percent dry weight were calculated for each prey. Snails composed 69.5% by volumetric displacement and 71.7% by percent dry weight of the fecal contents; bivalve shells made up 16% and 20.7%, respectively. Mollusks were found in fecal samples from all collecting sites. Where *S. depressus* populations were dense, the amount of snails consumed was greater than at sites with low turtle density. Most of the bivalve shell fragments were those of the introduced Asiatic clam, *Corbicula maniliensis*. Remains of

crayfish (2.0 and 1.2%) and three orders of insects (Trichoptera, 1.8 and 0.6%; Coleoptera, 1.9 and 0.7%; and Orthoptera, 0.3 and 0.1%; respectively) were also identified, as also were the seeds of several plants (6.0 and 4.0%, respectively) including *Sambucus, Prunus* and *Ulmus*. Fish bones made up only 0.1% by both volumetric displacement and dry weight. Tinkle (1958a) found a prevalence of haliplid beetles in stomachs (mostly juveniles) he examined, but remains of arachnids, isopods, crayfish, and clams were also present.

As in *S. minor,* larger adults develop expanded crushing surfaces on both jaws and heavy lower-jaw musculature, probably in response to an increased diet of snails and clams.

PREDATORS AND DEFENSE: Ernst et al. (1983) found only two adult *Sternotherus depressus* victims (apparently killed by raccoons, *Procyon lotor*), but several other individuals were missing legs or tails. Juveniles are probably more heavily preyed upon by raccoons and large wading birds, and possibly by bass (*Micropterus*) and hellbenders (*Cryptobranchus*) which occur in the same habitats. Nests may be destroyed by raccoons, skunks (*Mephitis*) and foxes (*Urocyon, Vulpes*).

Overexploitation for the pet trade is still a major cause of declining populations (Muir, 1984; Dodd, 1988b; Dodd et al., 1988). *Sternotherus depressus* has been federally listed as a threatened species.

When handled, *S. depressus* expels musk and attempts to bite. If disturbed in the water, it will attempt to swim away or hide under objects.

POPULATIONS: Dodd et al. (1988) estimated the population size, using the Schumacher-Eschmeyer test, of what is considered the largest population in north-central Alabama as 600 individuals (498–762), and at another nearby site as only 88. At many sites, populations appear to be composed of predominantly or all adults, especially those near surface mines. Prior to 1970, 55% of all of *Sternotherus depressus* collected were juveniles, but Mount (1981) found juveniles represented only 14% of the turtles he collected, and in 1983 Ernst and his colleagues found juveniles were only 15% of their overall sample. Although these data seem to indicate a decline in the number of juvenile *S. depressus,* we caution the reader to consider that the first figure is for several collections combined, and therefore cannot accurately be compared to either Mount's or Ernst's results. Also, population studies on turtles often show low numbers of juveniles owing to their secretive habits, and 14–15% is not unusually low.

Dodd et al. (1988) reported that *S. depressus* made up 87% of all turtle species collected at the populous site in north-central Alabama, or 28.8/ha (a biomass of 24 kg/ha), so this turtle can occur in high densities at suitable localities.

The sample of *S. depressus* collected by Tinkle (1958a) included 10 (24%) males to 32 (76%)

females. In studies by Dodd (1989b), the overall male to female ratio was 2:1, but each collecting site and sample period yielded a different ratio. At sites not near surface mines this ratio was 1.6:1, but at those affected by mines it was 1.4:1 (Dodd et al., 1988).

According to Dodd (1990a), *S. depressus* has disappeared from more than 50% of its former range because of habitat modifications to stream and river channels in the Black Warrior River watershed, and that only 6.9% of its probable historic range contains relatively healthy populations, which are further fragmented by extensive areas of unsuitable habitat. These statements are misleading and based on the assumption that *S. depressus* was evenly dispersed throughout the Black Warrior basin. No aquatic turtle occupies 100% of a river system. Its distribution is determined by the patches of suitable habitat available, which are of variable length along the river channel and separated by stretches generally unsuitable to the ecology of the species. There are no adequate data regarding the distribution of *S. depressus* prior to the 1980s, so Dodd's statements are unsubstantiated. We have no doubt that the flattened musk turtle has declined in numbers in this century, as have most turtle species in North America, but to what extent is still open to conjecture, especially since Ernst et al. (1988b) showed that turtles in west-central Alabama, believed to be hybrids with *S. minor peltifer,* are *S. depressus,* increasing both the overall population size and range. Nevertheless, the flattened musk turtle is listed as threatened under the Endangered Species Act.

REMARKS: Reviews of the literature concerning *S. depressus* are in Iverson (1977c) and Zug (1986).

Sternotherus minor (Agassiz, 1857)
Loggerhead musk turtle
PLATE 16

RECOGNITION: *Sternotherus minor* is a small turtle with overlapping vertebral scutes, a small plastron with a single indistinct hinge and 11 scutes, and no prominent facial stripes. The deep carapace (to 14.5 cm) is slightly serrated behind and has a vertebral keel and two lateral keels; the latter often disappear with age. The sides of the carapace form an angle of less than 100°, and mean angle/height ratio is about 5:1 in those with a vertebral keel. The carapace is dark brown to orange with dark-bordered seams; many juveniles have a pattern of scattered spots or radiating dark streaks. The plastron is pink to yellowish and commonly immaculate; it has a single gular scute, and the hinge is located between the pectorals and the abdominals. The skin is gray-brown to pinkish, with dark dots on the head, neck, and limbs; some have orange skin with dark stripes on the neck. The jaws are tan with dark streaks. The snout is somewhat tubular, and there are two barbels on the chin. All four feet are webbed.

Males have thick, long, spine-tipped tails, and the anal opening is posterior to the carapacial margin.

KARYOTYPE: Chromosomes number 56: 12 macrochromosomes with median or submedian centromeres, 12 macrochromosomes with terminal or subterminal centromeres, and 16 additional pairs of chromosomes, including microchromosomes (Sites et al., 1979).

FOSSIL RECORD: No fossils have been discovered.

DISTRIBUTION: *Sternotherus minor* ranges from southwestern Virginia and eastern Tennessee and eastern Georgia south to central Florida and west to the Pearl River system, in south-central Mississippi, and Washington Parish, Louisiana (Dundee and Rossman, 1989). It is replaced in the Black Warrior drainage of central Alabama by *S. depressus*.

GEOGRAPHIC VARIATION: Two subspecies have been described. *Sternotherus minor minor* (Agassiz, 1857), the loggerhead musk turtle, ranges from eastern Georgia and southeastern Alabama to central Florida. This subspecies commonly lacks stripes on the head and neck, has three carapacial keels in the juvenile (these may disappear with age). *S. m. peltifer* Smith and Glass, 1947, the stripeneck musk turtle, ranges from southwestern Virginia, eastern Tennessee, and Alabama to the Pearl River in south-central Mississippi. It has distinct wide stripes on the neck and a vertebral keel (which disappears with age).

The subspecies *peltifer* was thought to hybridize with *S. depressus* in west-central Alabama (Mount, 1975); however, Ernst et al. (1988b) proved that these populations exhibit variation within the range of *S. depressus* and should be included in that species. They also reported that *S. m. peltifer* has a different slope to its growth curve than either *S. m. minor* or *S. depressus* and may represent a separate species; however, this needs additional verification.

CONFUSING SPECIES: *Sternotherus depressus* has a wider, flatter carapace with a slope greater than 100° and a mean angle:height ratio of 8:1 versus an angle less than 100° and a mean angle:height ratio of about 5:1 in *S. minor*. *Sternotherus carinatus* has a very prominent vertebral keel and lacks a gular scute, and *S. odoratus* has two light stripes on each side of its face and nonoverlapping carapacial scutes. North American mud turtles of the genus *Kinosternon* have two prominent plastral hinges and triangular pectoral scutes.

HABITAT: This species inhabits rivers, creeks, spring runs, oxbows, ponds, lake margins, and swamps. It occurs most commonly around snags and fallen trees, and it prefers a soft bottom. Although most occupy relatively shallow waters (0.5–1.5 m), we have seen them walking on the bottom of clear

Plastron of *Sternotherus minor*

Anterior view of *Sternotherus minor*

Florida springs at depths of 3–5 m. The subspecies *peltifer* seems to be more of a river and stream dweller, but *minor* occurs most often in waters with less current.

BEHAVIOR: In Florida springs, *S. minor* may be active in every month, but farther north it is forced to hibernate, usually from December through February. Hibernation most often takes place in the soft bottom of some waterway or in submerged rock crevices. Muskrat bank burrows may also be used.

Sternotherus minor is active both day and night, but is most often seen in the morning. At this time it can be found prowling along the bottom, probing for food, or else resting on submerged objects. Although it is an adept climber that can reach high and difficult perches for basking, the basking habit is poorly developed and it seldom leaves the water. Apparently it cannot long withstand the direct rays of the sun. Its mean critical thermal maximum is 40.4°C (39.7–41.4) and the loss of righting response occurs at a mean temperature of 38.3°C (37.8–38.7; Hutchison et al., 1966).

Distribution of *Sternotherus minor*

Three juvenile *S. minor* (two *S. m. minor,* one *S. m. peltifer*) chose a red-lighted compartment in 46% of the trials over yellow (25%), blue (25%), and green (4%), but the significance of this to orientation is unknown (Ernst and Hamilton, 1969).

Sternotherus minor often remains submerged for long periods of time, and can obtain oxygen from the water via the buccopharyngeal lining (Belkin, 1968b). Gatten (1984) studied aerobic and anaerobic metabolism in *S. minor.* The turtles generate lactate rapidly during vigorous swimming but not during long periods of voluntary diving and surfacing. The greatest use of anaerobiosis occurs during pursuit of prey, emergencies, and possibly during aquatic hibernation. Under minimal resting conditions, oxygen uptake from the water amounts to only about 12% of that consumed. Involuntary immersion brings about a threefold increase in extraction of oxygen from the water. While breathing in air, nonpulmonary surfaces may account for almost 31% of total carbon dioxide loss (D. C. Jackson et al., 1976).

REPRODUCTION: Males mature at a carapace length of 55–60 mm (50–70) in four years (3–9; Etchberger and Stovall, 1990; Cox et al., 1991); females mature at an average age of eight (5–9 years) at about 80 mm (70–85) carapace length (Tinkle, 1958a; Etchberger and Ehrhart, 1987; Etchberger, 1988; Cox et al., 1991). The testes begin to enlarge from March or April to June when spermatogonia proliferate and become abundant, and continue to enlarge into July when there is a great increase in testicular mass (Etchberger, 1988; Etchberger and Stovall, 1990). Testes are largest in August and September when spermatozoa are abundant. The period September–October marks the peak in spermatogenesis; regression begins in late September and October. Testicular size declines rapidly through October and November but then stabilizes after December. The lowest spermatogenic activity occurs in February and March, and by March the testes have shrunk to the size of those found in immature males. Shrinkage presumably results from the passage of sperm into the epididymides. The testicular cycle peaks about five months before that of the ovarian cycle.

Female follicular enlargement begins in late August or September, and continues through the following June (Iverson, 1978a; Etchberger and Ehrhart, 1987). Ovulation and oviposition occur from October through June or July; follicular regression then begins, followed by a brief period of quiescence in

Female *Sternotherus minor minor*

Sternotherus minor peltifer

August. Tinkle (1958a) found the mean number of potentially ovulatory follicles in *S. m. minor* to be 2.7, and in *S. m. peltifer,* 7.0.

Courtship and mating have been described only recently (Cox et al., 1980; Bels and LiBois, 1983). Mating activities have been observed in nature by Cox et al. (1980) on 15 March, 25 April, 8 September, and 26 November, and in the laboratory on 12 April. Several similarities in behavior were noted. All mating pairs were: (1) completely submerged and situated upon some substrate, (2) at least partially concealed,

(3) found in shaded areas (and in one instance, appeared to actively avoid exposure to direct sunlight), and (4) observed in the early to midmorning. Furthermore, all uncoupled quickly if sufficiently disturbed, and exhibited similar copulatory postures (in all observations, both sexes were of approximately equal size). The complete behavioral sequence for coitus observed in the laboratory was as follows: At 0605 CST on 12 April 1976, the male began closely following the female about the sink. He made several approaches from the female's left side, with his head

Copulating *Sternotherus minor minor*

and neck fully extended, and appeared to make contact with his nostrils at the posterior edge of her bridge. At no time was any other precopulatory behavior evident, such as biting, caressing, or titillating. The male made several futile attempts to mount the female (0610–0615), but in each instance he was unable to retain his balance atop her carapace and slipped off. His lack of success in attaining the "riding" position was attributed to the shallow water and the relatively large size of the animals (carapace lengths: male = 102 mm, female = 110 mm). Following these unsuccessful attempts, mounting and intromission were effected at 0615. The male attained a position with his plastron superimposed over the left half of the female's carapace, with the claws of his left forefoot grasping the left margin of her carapace anterior to the bridge and his right forefoot holding to the top of her carapace (this position was not observed in the field). The claws of his hind feet were grasping the edge of her posterior marginals. The tail of the female was curved laterally toward her right side away from the male, with his tail curled under hers. On four occasions during copulation, the female began moving rapidly about the tank for intervals of 15–30 seconds. At these times the grip of the male's forelimbs was broken, and he was dragged along upside down behind the female for 10–20 seconds. At the conclusion of each of these bursts of activity, the male righted himself and regained his original position relative to the female. His continued grip on

the posterior margin of her carapace with the claws of his hind feet, as well as the mutual grasping of the tails, maintained uninterrupted sexual contact. The male dismounted at 0722, and subsequently returned for several unsuccessful attempts (0821–0825, 0832–0834, and 0840–0845). During these approaches, the female would snap repeatedly at him until he discontinued his efforts. The total time elapsed from initiation to completion of mating behavior was two hours and 40 minutes.

As many as six smaller males may attempt to mate with one female, pushing and shoving each other off her back as she is mounted (Ashton and Ashton, 1985). C. G. Jackson, Jr. (1969) reported agonistic behavior between males, and possibly this was related to reproduction.

Iverson (1978a) reported the clutch size in *S. m. minor* from Florida as one to five; Etchberger and Ehrhart (1987) found a similar range and a mean clutch size of 3.0 for Florida females. Eight clutches laid by captive *S. m. minor* contained an average of 3.6 eggs (2–5) (Sachsse, 1977b). Two to five clutches of one to five eggs may be deposited each year, and the number of eggs laid is positively correlated to female size (Iverson, 1977a, 1978a). The annual reproductive potential may range from 6 to 12 eggs (Etchberger and Ehrhart, 1987). Lehmann (1984) reported a case of two young *S. m. minor* produced from a single egg.

The eggs are 21.2–32.8 mm in length, 12.7–20.0

mm in width, and weigh 1.97–6.70 g; the shells are about 0.32 mm thick (M. J. Packard et al., 1984a). Eggs are laid singly or in groups in shallow holes in the soil, often at the bases of trees or beside logs (Carr, 1952; Mount, 1975).

Chilling may delay embryonic development; unchilled eggs incubated at constant 25°C reached developmental stage in 11–12 days, but eggs chilled to 18–22°C took about 48 days to reach this stage (Ewert, 1991). Hatching may also be delayed by the embryo reducing its oxygen consumption toward the end of development (Ewert, 1991).

The young hatch after an incubation period of 61–119 days. Hatchlings of both races have a medial keel and two lateral keels. The carapace is only slightly longer than wide and bears a pattern of streaks, blotches, or spots. The plastron of *S. m. minor* is pinkish white; that of *S. m. peltifer* is yellow-orange. Hatchlings of *S. m. peltifer* have strongly striped necks. Most hatchlings have carapace lengths of 22–27 mm, and plastra 16–21 mm long.

Hybridization between a captive male *S. odoratus* and a captive female *S. m. minor* was reported, with a description of the progeny, by Folkerts (1967).

GROWTH AND LONGEVITY: The rate of growth declines after *S. minor* reaches 10 years and a carapace length of 80–100 mm (Cox et al., 1991). The carapace in both subspecies becomes progressively flatter with increasing size (Tinkle, 1958a). Detailed analysis via multiple comparisons among shapes of the growth curve log carapace height versus log carapace length indicates that the growth curve slope of *S. m. peltifer* is significantly greater than that for *S. m. minor* (Ernst et al., 1988b).

The longevity record for this species is 23 years, 11 months for a male caught wild as a juvenile and subsequently kept at the Philadelphia Zoo (Snider and Bowler, 1992).

FOOD HABITS: Tinkle (1958a) found insects, millipedes, snails, clams, fish, and aquatic plants in *S. m. minor,* and Ashton and Ashton (1985) reported this race eats aquatic invertebrates, carrion, small vertebrates, algae, and other aquatic plants. Folkerts (1968) found snails and insects to be the leading food of *S. m. peltifer* in Alabama; he also found that they had consumed filamentous algae, vascular plants, clams, crayfish, spiders, fish, bits of rock, and detritus. A captive juvenile *S. m. minor* kept by Barbour killed and partially ate two juvenile *Trachemys scripta,* a hatchling *S. m. minor,* and a juvenile *S. m. peltifer* over a two-year period. It is

likely that older individuals are somewhat cannibalistic and that they prey on small turtles of other species as well.

In *S. m. minor* increasing size brings a shift from an insectivorous to a molluscivorous diet. This subspecies develops heavy lower-jaw musculature and an expanded crushing surface on both jaws, apparently adaptations to eating mollusks. This parallels the crushing-apparatus development in *Graptemys barbouri* and *G. pulchra,* but Sachsse (1977b) proposed that development of large jaws in *S. minor* is not dependent on the hardness of the prey, but rather on its dietary contents.

Folkerts (1968) watched *S. m. peltifer* feeding on algal mats or mats of riverweed (*Podostemum*). On several occasions individuals bit down on clumps of algae, drew the head back, and pulled the algae between the jaws. These clumps were covered with tiny snails, and many were scraped off by this action.

Trapping evidence indicates that *S. m. minor* feeds at twilight and in the forepart of the night but not during the morning; *S. m. peltifer* feeds mostly during the morning but not at night. Prey may be eaten both in the water or on land (Ashton and Ashton, 1985). Digestive turnover (ingestion to defecation) takes about 57 hours (Parmenter, 1981).

Where *S. minor* and *S. odoratus* are sympatric in northern Florida, they compete for food resources, as they overlap considerably in food selection and hunt in the same microhabitats at the same time (Berry, 1975). At such sites, or where the snail *Goniobasis* is absent, *S. minor* loses its specialized molluscivorous adaptations. Berry (1975) interpreted this as a case of character convergence with *S. odoratus* resulting from competition of generalized resources.

Feeding on the snail *Goniobasis* may bring about some health problems. Cox et al. (1988) found that *S. minor* that eat these snails are often heavily parasitized by the lung fluke *Heronimus mollis;* these snails are intermediate hosts of the worm.

PREDATORS AND DEFENSE: Nests are destroyed by a variety of small mammals, crows (*Corvus*), and reptiles, and the juveniles fall prey to larger vertebrates of all classes. Adults, however, are relatively immune to predation except by alligators and humans.

Habitat destruction is probably the most serious threat to the continued existence of *S. minor.* Pollution often affects its mollusk and insect foods, and eliminates the turtle from formerly suitable waterbodies.

This turtle is pugnacious, often biting viciously and expelling a strong musk when handled. The young are capable of emitting musk even before hatching (Neill, 1948b).

POPULATIONS: Marchand (1942) reported that 500 or more *S. minor* could be seen during a day of water-goggling in Rainbow Springs River, Marion County, Florida. Based on data in Cox and Marion (1979), Iverson (1982a) estimated the population density in one Florida spring to be 2,857/ha, or a biomass of 45.7 kg/ha.

Samples collected by Tinkle (1958a) had sex ratios of 169 (49%) males to 178 (51%) females in *S. m. minor*, and 32 (52%) males to 30 (48%) females in *S. m. peltifer*, and Cox et al. (1988) collected 47 (47%) males and 52 (53%) females at a site in Jackson County, Florida; these sex ratios are not significantly different from equality. Sachsse (1977b) reported the sex ratio in a clutch of young hatched in the laboratory was three males to nine females (0.33:1); however, this is still not significantly different from 1:1.

REMARKS: Seidel and Lucchino (1981) electrophoretically examined 11 protein systems (17 loci) and used discriminent analysis to examine 15 morphological characters in a study of speciation among *S. m. minor*, *S. m. peltifer*, *S. depressus*, and *S. carinatus*. They found *S. carinatus* to be strongly divergent from the others, which formed a close group. Seidel (1980) compared the concentrations of blood proteins and urea in *S. carinatus*, *S. depressus*, *S. minor*, and *S. odoratus*. Interspecific variation in total plasma protein was not observed, but different levels of plasma urea were present. *Sternotherus minor* and *S. depressus* had much higher urea concentrations than the other two species.

Additional references are listed in Iverson (1977d) and Zug (1986).

Sternotherus carinatus (Gray, 1856)
Razorback musk turtle
PLATE 17

RECOGNITION: This is a small turtle with a prominent vertebral keel and a small plastron with 10 scutes and an indistinct hinge. The deep, steeply sloping carapace (to 17.6 cm) is slightly serrated posteriorly, and each vertebral scute commonly overlaps the one behind it; the marginals are slightly flared. The carapacial scutes are light brown to orange, with dark spots or radiating streaks and dark posterior borders on each; this pattern may be lost with age. The immaculate yellow plastron lacks a gular scute, possessing only 10 of the 11 scutes commmonly found in other kinosternids. The pectoral scute is rhomboid in shape. An indistinct hinge is located between the pectoral and the abdominal scutes. The skin is gray to brown or pinkish, with small dark spots, and the jaws are tan with dark streaks. The snout is somewhat tubular, and the chin has two barbels. All four feet are webbed.

Males have thick, long tails, with the anal opening located posterior to the carapacial rim. Males also have a patch of rough tilted scales on the posterior surface of the thigh and crus of each hind limb.

KARYOTYPE: The karyotype consists of 56 chromosomes (26 macrochromosomes, 30 microchromosomes): 16 metacentric and submetacentric, 8 subtelocentric, and 32 acrocentric and telocentric (Stock, 1972; Killebrew, 1975).

FOSSIL RECORD: No fossils have been found.

DISTRIBUTION: *Sternotherus carinatus* ranges from southeastern Oklahoma and central Arkansas south to east-central Texas, and from south-central Mississippi south to the Gulf of Mexico.

GEOGRAPHIC VARIATION: No subspecies are recognized, but variation within this species has been inadequately studied.

CONFUSING SPECIES: Other *Sternotherus* lack a pronounced vertebral keel and have a gular scute. Mud turtles (*Kinosternon*) have two well-developed plastral hinges, two gular scutes, and triangular pectoral scutes.

HABITAT: This species lives in rivers, slow streams, and swamps. Little current, soft bottoms, abundant aquatic vegetation, and some basking sites are the preferred conditions.

BEHAVIOR: In Oklahoma, *Sternotherus carinatus* has an annual active period of about 310 days, from March through November. It hibernates in cavities beneath overhanging banks as well as beneath rocks on river bottoms. In summer it apparently does not estivate, but instead retires to deep water. From June to September these turtles are most active from 1500 to 2200 in the afternoon and evening and from 0440 to 1100 in the morning (Mahmoud, 1969).

This musk turtle basks more often than other *Sternotherus*. Boyer (1965) conducted heat gain experiments with three turtle models. The flattened *Trionyx*-like model heated the fastest, but his "high-roofed" model patterned after *S. carinatus* was the slowest to heat. Perhaps the peaked carapace of this species receives less direct radiation.

Sternotherus carinatus shows differences between the cloacal and the environmental temperature, throughout the year, of +1.0°C to -0.11°C. The temperature range for active individuals is 14–34°C, and the field-preferred body temperature is 33.29°C. Captives accept food at body temperatures of 16–34°C. The mean critical thermal maximum is 40.25°C

Sternotherus carinatus

Plastron of *Sternotherus carinatus;* note absence of gular scute

(39.5–41.9), and the righting ability is lost at a mean of 38.7°C (38.4–39.0) (Mahmoud, 1969). Boyer (1965) reported a lethal temperature of 42.1°C.

The maximum and minimum distances between successive captures of Oklahoma *S. carinatus* were 94 and 4.5 m. The average distance between first and last captures during more than 100 days of activity was 17 m for females and 39 m for males (Mahmoud, 1969).

REPRODUCTION: Females mature at a carapace length of about 10 cm, which is reached in four or five years; males, at 100–120 mm, in five or six years.

Spermatogenesis begins in June and reaches a peak by mid-August when the testes attain maximum size (Mahmoud and Klicka, 1972). During May, there is a decrease in the diameter of the seminiferous tubules caused by sperm release, but by the end of June the

Distribution of *Sternotherus carinatus*

testes gradually increase in size as new sperm mature. During the last half of August through the middle of September the testes shrink in size, possibly owing to a decrease in spermatogenic activity and release of mature sperm to the epididymides. Testes diameter continues to decline from mid-September through December as almost all mature sperm descend into the epididymides, and testes weigh least at the end of this period. No spermatogenesis occurs from January to April, but mature sperm pack the epididymides in January and February and then descend into the vas deferens in March and April.

The female reproductive cycle is similar to that of *S. odoratus* (Mahmoud and Klicka, 1972). Follicular growth proceeds slowly from September to November, and possibly also from December through February. In March and April follicles enlarge at a faster rate (presumably by adding yolk material), and during May and June grow at their fastest rate. Ovulation, mating, and oviposition also occur then (Tinkle, 1958a, reported that females from the Pearl River Mississippi had oviducal eggs in early April and early June). The largest corpora lutea are present when eggs are still in the oviducts, but begin to degenerate to corpora albicantia shortly after oviposition. There is no significant follicular growth during July and August.

The courtship of this turtle is divisible into three phases: tactile, mounting and intromission, and biting and rubbing. These phases are identical with those of *S. odoratus* (see that account for details). A captive male mated several times with a female between 17 and 31 March, resulting in two clutches of two and four eggs, respectively, laid on 10 May and 7 June (Becker, 1992).

The only data on a natural nest are those of Tinkle (1958a), who found a clutch of two eggs laid halfway up a steep bank on the Pearl River. By dissection Tinkle estimated that a female lays an average of 7.3 eggs a season, in two clutches. Ewert and Legler (1978) induced female *S. carinatus* to lay more than one clutch a season by injecting them with the hormone oxytocin. However, Mahmoud and Klicka (1972) reported the mean clutch size is five eggs (4–5), and thought that only one clutch is laid each year. The eggs are elliptical (24–31 × 14.4–18.0 mm) with hard, white shells. Incubation periods of two clutches kept at 28–30°C and 95% humidity were 120–139 days (first clutch) and 109–120 days (second clutch) (Becker, 1992).

Hatchling *Sternotherus carinatus*

The hatchling carapace is 23–31 mm long and nearly as wide as long. Hatchlings are similar to adults, differing only in their greater tendency toward overlapping of the vertebral scutes, more accentuated markings of the head and upper shell, and paler coloration. Many have three carapacial keels, and they weigh 3.4–4.2 g (Becker, 1992).

GROWTH AND LONGEVITY: The growth period in Oklahoma is 180 days during the warm months. The growth rates of two groups of Oklahoma *Sternotherus carinatus* were determined by Mahmoud (1969). In the first group, females having an initial carapace length of 21–40 mm increased an average of 12.7 mm (42.3%) per growing season; those 41–60 mm increased 26.6 mm (52%); those 61–80 mm increased 0.88 mm (1.3%); and those over 81 mm increased only 0.23 mm (0.25%). Males having an initial carapacial length of 21–40 mm had the same growth rates as those of the first group; those 41–60 mm grew 13 mm (37.3%); and those 61–80 mm increased 15.3 mm (21%) per growing season. Males of the second group were 61–80 mm in carapace length initially and grew only 0.2 mm (0.18%). Mahmoud also found that the growth rate continued at approximately the same rate beyond the first six years. Three *S. carinatus* ranging from 11.3 to 14.2 cm in carapace length showed no apparent growth for one to three years, and two individuals more than 10 years old showed no growth during the two years they were captive.

A captive *S. carinatus* lived 21 years, 10 months, and 10 days (Snider and Bowler, 1992).

FOOD HABITS: *Sternotherus carinatus* is omnivorous. Mahmoud (1968b) recorded the following percentages of frequency and volume of food items, respectively, in this turtle: Insecta 91.6, 42.9; Crustacea 38.7, 2.8; Mollusca 96.7, 24.3; Amphibia 3.1, 2.5; carrion 61.2, 10.6; and aquatic vegetation 88.9, 16.6. Individuals under 50 mm in carapace length fed predominantly on small aquatic insects, algae, and carrion, whereas larger *S. carinatus* fed on any kind of food, regardless of its size, but preferred mollusks. Tinkle (1958a) reported that *S. carinatus* fed predominantly on insects, snails, and clams, and that some took decapods and plants. Captives feed readily on any kind of earthworm, meat, or fish offered them, but seem to particularly relish small mollusks.

Razorback musk turtles are bottom feeders. They frequently walk along the bottom, with neck fully extended, searching for food. They also probe with their heads in soft mud, sand, and decaying vegetation, apparently for food. Occasionally they feed at the surface.

PREDATORS AND DEFENSE: Nests of this turtle are robbed by many species of mammals. Fish, water snakes, and other turtles prey on the hatchlings. Humans destroy the adults; for example, Mahmoud (1969) reported that two fishermen caught and killed 51 adults in two hours on the Blue River near Milburn, Oklahoma.

Razorback musk turtles are more shy than other *Sternotherus*. When handled they seldom bite or expel musk.

POPULATIONS: Mahmoud (1969) estimated 229 *Sternotherus carinatus* per hectare of suitable habitat in Oklahoma, an estimated biomass of 14.35 kg/ha (Iverson, 1982a). He found an adult sex ratio of 36 females to 22 males. Tinkle (1958a) reported a ratio of 73 females to 50 males.

REMARKS: Formerly, *Sternotherus carinatus* was thought to be most closely related morphologically to *S. depressus* and *S. minor* (Tinkle, 1958a; Ernst and Barbour, 1972); however, more recent electrophoretic studies have shown it to be strongly divergent from these two species, and closer to *S. odoratus* (Seidel and Lucchino, 1981; Seidel et al., 1981). As can be seen from the above discussions on the life history of *S. carinatus*, very little has been added to our knowledge of its behavior and ecology since 1972 (see Iverson, 1979a, and Zug, 1986, for literature reviews). A thorough study of its ecological parameters would be rewarding.

Kinosternon subrubrum (Lacépède, 1788)
Eastern mud turtle
PLATE 18

RECOGNITION: This small mud turtle grows to a maximum carapace length of 12.5 cm. It has 11 scutes on the double-hinged plastron, a keelless carapace lacking stripes, and the ninth marginal not enlarged. Its carapace is oval and smooth, and many are depressed; the sides are straight, and the carapace drops abruptly behind. The first vertebral scute is widely separated from the second marginal. Color of the patternless carapace varies from yellowish to olive or black. The immaculate yellow to brown plastron has a single gular scute and two well-developed transverse hinges bordering the abdominal scute (which tend to ossify in old individuals); structure and kinesis of these hinges are described by Bramble et al. (1984). The plastral forelobe is longer than the hind lobe, and the abdominal scute is also shorter than the forelobe. The skin is brown to olive and may exhibit some markings. The head is medium sized and commonly dark brown with yellow mottling; on some, two light stripes lie on each side of the face and neck. The rostral scute may or may not be posteriorly forked. All four feet are webbed.

Males have larger heads; longer, thicker, nail-tipped tails; deeper posterior plastral notches; longer and more curved foreclaws; and two tilted patches of scales on the inner side of each hind leg. Although the male carapace may be longer than that of the female (Ernst et al., 1973), the male has a much shorter plastron (Mahmoud, 1967; Iverson, 1979d).

KARYOTYPE: The full diploid set of chromosomes is 56. Killebrew (1975), using a squash technique, reported 26 macrochromosomes and 30 microchromosomes, but Sites et al. (1979), using a banding technique, found 24 macrochromosomes (6 pairs of metacentric or submetacentric chromosomes and 6 pairs of telocentric or subtelocentric chromosomes) and 32 microchromosomes.

FOSSIL RECORD: Pliocene (Hemphillian) remains of *Kinosternon subrubrum* have been found in Seward County, Kansas (Fichter, 1969), and fossils dating from the Pleistocene (Rancholabrean) have been unearthed in Levy County, Florida (Weigel, 1962; Holman, 1978).

DISTRIBUTION: *Kinosternon subrubrum* ranges from Long Island, New York, south through peninsular Florida and to the Gulf Coast, west to east-central Texas, and north in the Mississippi Valley to Missouri, southern Illinois, and southern Indiana. Isolated colonies exist in northwestern Indiana.

On the basis of specimens in the Peabody Museum, Yale University, the eastern mud turtle was previously thought to occur in Connecticut. These have proved to be *Sternotherus odoratus* rather than *K. subrubrum,* and, as apparently no populations of *K. subrubrum* exist in Connecticut, the northern limit of the range in the Northeast is Long Island (Craig et al., 1980). Similarly, the southeastern range of the species supposedly extended onto the Florida Keys, but the Stock Island, Monroe County, specimen upon which this record was based (Carnegie Museum of Natural History 26725) is in reality *K. baurii* (John B. Iverson, pers. comm.).

GEOGRAPHIC VARIATION: Three subspecies are recognized. Characters listed are from Ernst et al. (1974a) and Iverson (1977b). *Kinosternon subrubrum subrubrum* (Lacépède, 1788), the eastern mud turtle, ranges from Long Island, New York, to northern peninsular Florida and the Gulf Coast northwest through Kentucky to Indiana and Illinois. It has a long plastron (75–101% of the carapace length), a wide bridge (13–22% of the carapace length), the anterior lobe of the plastron shorter than the posterior lobe, the posterior plastral lobe width 45–53% of the carapace length, and a spotted or

Kinosternon subrubrum
subrubrum

Kinosternon subrubrum
hippocrepis

mottled head. *K. s. hippocrepis* Gray, 1855, the Mississippi mud turtle, ranges in the Mississippi Valley from Louisiana and eastern Texas northward to Missouri, western Kentucky and southern Illinois. It has a long plastron (84–98% of the carapace length), a wide bridge (15–24% of the carapace length), the anterior lobe of the plastron shorter than the posterior lobe, the posterior plastral lobe width 45–52% of the carapace length, and a pair of distinct light stripes on each side of the face. *K. s. steindachneri* (Siebenrock,

1906b), the Florida mud turtle, is restricted to peninsular Florida. The plastron is shorter (73–90% of the carapace length), the bridge is narrow (6–14% of the carapace length), many anterior plastral lobes are longer than the posterior lobe, the posterior lobe is only 38–42% as wide as the carapace, and the head is plain or mottled.

Where the geographic ranges of the three subspecies meet, interbreeding results in narrow zones of intergradation (Ernst et al., 1974a; Iverson, 1977b).

*Kinosternon subrubrum
steindachneri*

Distribution of *Kinosternon subrubrum*

Plastron of *Kinosternon subrubrum subrubrum*

Plastron of *Kinosternon subrubrum hippocrepis*

CONFUSING SPECIES: *Kinosternon flavescens* has an enlarged ninth marginal scute, most *K. baurii* have a striped carapace (Lamb and Lovich, 1990), and the musk turtles, *Sternotherus,* have small plastra with a single hinge.

HABITAT: The eastern mud turtle prefers slow-moving bodies of shallow water with soft bottoms and abundant aquatic vegetation. Frequently it inhabits the lodges of muskrats (*Ondatra, Neofiber*), and has been taken from ditches, sloughs, streams, rivers, wet meadows, ponds, Carolina Bays, marshes, bayous, lagoons, and cypress swamps. Waterbodies occupied by this turtle in Florida often experience wide daily variations in pH, especially after rainfall (Ernst et al., 1972). Coastal and barrier island populations show a

Plastron of *Kinosternon subrubrum steindachneri;* note narrow hindlobe

marked tolerance for brackish water, and *K. subrubrum* may be abundant in tidal marshes.

BEHAVIOR: The annual activity period of *Kinosternon subrubrum hippocrepis* in Oklahoma is about 265 days. Most of the turtles disappear in late October and remain secluded until early April, but a few are active during the winter (Mahmoud, 1969). The earliest and latest dates on which Nichols (1947) found active *K. s. subrubrum* on Long Island were 11 April and 11 November. In Virginia, we have found them emerging as early as 4 April, but others were still digging out of hibernation sites on 27 April, and in the fall active individuals have been observed as late as 18 October. *Kinosternon s. steindachneri* may be active in all months in Florida, providing winter temperatures do not drop too low.

The diel cycle of Oklahoma *K. s. hippocrepis* shows two activity periods during June through August: between 0400 and 0900 with a peak between 0520 and 0800, and between 1640 and 2200 with a peak between 1900 and 2000 (Mahmoud, 1969). In Florida, *K. s. steindachneri* has a similar summer cycle. Most northern Virginia captures have been between 0700 and 0830.

Most aquatic activity takes place in relatively shallow waters where *K. subrubrum* can reach the surface with ease, but it can dive to depths of up to 3 m or more (Ernst, pers. obs.). Usually only about 20 minutes is spent underwater between breaths, and dive duration is independent of the oxygen content of the water (Stone et al., 1992b). It is a bimodal breather,

however, capable of utilizing oxygen from both air and water. When submerged its blood saturation levels for oxygen and carbon dioxide average 14% and 46%, respectively (Stone et al., 1992a). When in air an inverse gas exchange pattern is evident.

The eastern mud turtle can be seen basking at times on submerged brush or on the shore, but it does not bask often. Mahmoud (1969) found a mean difference between cloacal and environmental temperatures throughout the seasons of +0.46 to—0.8°C; The thermoactivity range in Oklahoma is 16–36°C, the field preferred temperature was 23.65°C. In the laboratory, *K. subrubrum* takes food at body temperatures of 13–38°C. Its mean critical thermal maximum is 40.95°C (39.0–42.5) and it loses righting ability at 38.8°C (38.1–39.4) (Mahmoud, 1969).

Kinosternon subrubrum is quite terrestrial and prowls about on land from late spring to fall. Most terrestrial surface activity is in the morning or evening. Some individuals leave the water in late spring or early summer and remain on land until the next spring, both estivating and hibernating underground (Bennett et al., 1970). Carr (1952) found Florida *K. s. steindachneri* in holes in clay canal banks, and watched a large male dig such a hole just below the waterline, using all four feet to remove the soil. When finished the turtle emerged, turned around, and backed into the burrow. Several mud turtles in northern Virginia have been found in summer occupying shallow burrows (or "forms") under leaf litter, and others have been seen digging out of deeper hibernacula in April.

When kept in fresh water, 64.1% of the body, 77.5% of the soft parts, and 41.1% of the bony shell are water (Dunson and Heatwole, 1986). Under terrestrial conditions, evaporative loss of body water can be a major problem for *K. subrubrum*. Two *K. s. steindachneri* lost moisture at hourly rates of 0.46% and 0.61% of their initial weights. The larger lost 23.6% of its initial body weight in 51 hours in a drying-chamber at 38°C and 37% relative humidity (Bogert and Cowles, 1947). To avoid drying, the turtle spends much of its terrestrial stay in humid sites, such as the burrows mentioned above, under leaf litter, or within pulpwood of rotting logs. Most surface activity follows rains.

When the aquatic habitat dries, mud turtles may burrow into the mud and estivate, or they may leave the area. They are often plowed up at the edges of ponds and swamps. A large population of mud turtles inhabited a pin oak flatwoods in southern Illinois that was covered with water during the early spring; the woods dried by late April, and the turtles dug burrows and estivated. The 1963 population was estimated to be active only about six weeks (Skorepa and Ozment, 1968).

During a drought in South Carolina, 76 *K. subrubrum* emigrated from a waterbody, compared to an average 61 during the predrought period, almost a 25% increase (Gibbons et al., 1983), but the drought did not seem to significantly affect the reproductive rate, as 23 females oviposited as compared to a predrought range of 19–54 per year.

Strecker (1926) observed a migration of *K. s. hippocrepis* near Waco, Texas. A marsh was rapidly drying, and as he walked along the levee 45 mud turtles were seen traveling overland in the same direction. At first he thought they were moving to a ditch along a railroad track less than 200 m away, but he found that there was very little water there and that the mud turtles were scattered over a damp meadow on the other side. Strecker followed the line of march and discovered that the turtles were headed for a large tank more than 0.8 km away.

With the onset of cold weather in the north (usually in late October) the eastern mud turtle enters hibernation. It may dig into the soft bottom of a waterway, dig a burrow some distance from the water, or retreat into rotting logs or piles of vegetable debris. In the south, however, mud turtles may remain active all year, but less so from December to March (Ernst et al., 1972).

Two *K. subrubrum* that had moved 100 and 300 m from a waterbody in South Carolina were located by Bennett (1972). They spent the winter on land in burrows 2–11 cm below the surface. Most excavation occurred in December after surface movement had ceased in November. One turtle dug from 2 cm to 9.5 cm and then back to 2 cm while the other burrowed from 2 cm to 11 cm and then maintained a depth of 8 cm. Minimum soil temperatures of the burrows were below freezing 64% and 18% of the time in January and February, respectively. Maximum temperatures increased slightly after mid-February and were higher than 21°C when turtles left their burrows in early March. Initial moves from the hibernacula were 1.6 and 7.8 m before the two turtles burrowed again.

Mahmoud (1969) reported that the maximum and minimum distances between successive points of capture for Oklahoma *K. subrubrum* were 408 m and 0.6 m. The average first-last capture distances for periods of more than 100 days were 81 m for females and 57 m for males; for less than 100 days, 42.7 m for females and 46.9 m for males. Eleven were recaptured at their original capture point. During July 1957 he released 15 *K. subrubrum* into Lake Texoma at one place and during August 1959 recovered seven within an estimated radius of 45.7 m from the release point. This restricted movement suggests a limited aquatic home range, which Mahmoud estimated to average 0.05 ha for both sexes.

In South Carolina, radioactively tagged *K. subrubrum* spent 3–142 days on land and traveled 1–600 m from capture sites. They generally moved short distances (>2 m/day), burrowed beneath litter or sand to depths of 2–11 cm for up to two weeks in one location, and then moved longer distances (10 m/day). The time spent in the first burrow was seven days (2–16). The cycle—short movements, burrowing, then longer moves—was repeated until December, when the turtles ceased to move. The mean rate of travel was 3.6 m/day (Bennett et al., 1970).

Kinosternon subrubrum may swim at speeds of 5.0–12.8 cm/sec with a mean limb cycle period of 0.72 sec (Davenport et al., 1984).

The orientation and navigation mechanisms used by *K. subrubrum* have been scarcely studied. Gibbons (1970a) found only random directional movements in individuals leaving or entering a South Carolina pond. Ernst and Hamilton (1969) reported that *K. subrubrum* selected a blue-lighted compartment in 60% of the trials and a red-lighted compartment in 22%; it entered yellow and green compartments in only 9%, each, of the trials. They thought that color selection may have some significance to orientation.

Eastern mud turtles occasionally fight among themselves. An agonistic encounter between two individuals was observed by Rigley (1974). The two turtles pushed each other back and forth up to 50 cm in a head-to-head confrontation. When one turtle began to crawl away after about 10 minutes, the other turtle chased it and bit its left hind leg. After a struggle the first turtle finally broke free. When the turtles were captured, that which had been bitten had its left hind leg amputated at the knee joint, and its aggressor still had the severed limb in its mouth. Unfortunately, the sex of the two turtles was not reported. The purpose of such aggressive encounters is unknown.

REPRODUCTION: Attainment of sexual maturity may vary in its onset from population to population. Oklahoma *K. subrubrum* usually mature at a carapace length of 8–12 cm: males when four to seven years of age, females when five to eight years of age; however, two females 6.8 and 7.1 cm examined by Mahmoud (1967) were mature. The largest immature females from Arkansas were 7.1 and 8.2 cm, and the smallest mature females had carapaces 8.0–8.6 cm long (Iverson, 1979d). These females were five to seven years old. Florida *K. subrubrum* of both sexes also mature at carapace lengths of about 8 cm in their third or fourth year (Ernst et al., 1973). Iverson (1979d) doubted that females normally mature at carapace lengths less than 8 cm. However, in South Carolina, females are mature at 7–8 cm; Gibbons (1983) found none shorter than 7 cm was mature, 5% of those 7.0–7.9 cm contained eggs, whereas 28–43% of those larger than 8 cm had eggs. Almost all South Carolina males are mature at 8 cm, and the critical size for transition seems to be 7–8 cm (Gibbons, 1983; Frazer et al., 1991a). Both males and females reach maturity during their fourth year in South Carolina.

The male sexual cycle for *K. subrubrum* collected in Arkansas, Oklahoma, and Texas was studied by Mahmoud and Klicka (1972). In January and February the testes are small in diameter with no evidence of spermatogenesis, but the epididymides contain viable sperm. From March to April, the testes are still small with no spermatogenetic activity, but the sperm has now descended from the epididymides to the vas deferens. During the period May to July the sperm ducts decrease in diameter (probably due to sperm release during copulation), but the testes gradually increase in diameter and weight as the sperm-producing cycle begins. Presumably, if mating does not occur, involuntary sperm release from the vas deferens is possible (captive males sacrificed by Mahmoud and Klicka in late April had much sperm in their vas deferens, but other captives sacrificed in early

June had small vas deferens with few sperm). The testes begin to enlarge during the last half of June and continue to grow until reaching maximum size in mid-August when spermatogenesis peaks, and then shrink as spermatogenesis declines. Mature sperm may remain temporarily in the seminiferous tubules before descending into the epididymides. In June and July, sperm passes into the epididymides, which increase in diameter. Sperm production ceases during the period September–December, and testes diameter decreases to its lowest point of the year, but the epididymides are swollen with sperm at this time. Licht (1972) introduced the mammalian gonadotropins follicle-stimulating hormone and luteinizing hormone into male *K. subrubrum* in mid-July; follicle-stimulating hormone stimulated testes development but luteinizing hormone tended to inhibit endogenous gonadotropin activity.

Mahmoud and Klicka (1972), Iverson (1979d), and Houseal and Carr (1983) described the reproductive cycle for females collected in Arkansas, Oklahoma, and Texas. From September to November, little follicular growth takes place, and that at a rather slow rate (follicles probably begin to enlarge in late August). No females were examined during December through February. The rate of growth increases in March and April, and during May and June there is a rapid rate of vitellogenesis with follicles reaching their peak diameter. Ovulation and nesting occur during May and June. By the end of May shelled eggs occupy the oviduct and corpora lutea are present; shelled eggs may be found in the oviducts as late as July. Corpora lutea degenerate to corpora albicantia shortly after oviposition. Several sets of corpora lutea may be present, indicating more than one set of eggs is be laid each season. In the last phase, July–August, the remaining ovarian follicles experience no significant growth. Any follicles larger than 10 mm present at this time either are held until the next season or become atretic.

Mating occurs from mid-March through May; copulations are earliest in the south. Courtship and mating behaviors are as in *Sternotherus odoratus* (see for details). Mating usually takes place underwater but sometimes occurs on land. The oviducts contain sperm-storage tubules in the posterior portion of the albumen-secreting section between the infundibulum and uterus (Gist and Jones, 1989), so presumably sperm from a single mating may be stored to fertilize several clutches of eggs.

Most nesting is during May and June, but oviposition has been observed from February through September in various parts of the range. Eastern mud turtles from Florida may nest continuously throughout the year (Iverson, 1977a). The nest site is usually open ground not far from water. Sandy, loamy soils are preferred, but piles of vegetable debris also are used, and eggs are sometimes laid in the walls of American alligator nests (Deitz and Jackson, 1979). In northern Virginia, Ernst's former graduate student Steve W. Gotte found that female *K. subrubrum* most frequently nested in the rotting pulpwood of downed logs. In some localities mud turtles nest in muskrat tunnels, and eggs have also been found on the surface of the ground and under piles of boards.

A female may try several places before finding a site that suits her. When satisfied she starts digging with her forefeet, thrusting the dirt out laterally until she is almost concealed; then she turns around and completes the nest with her hind feet. At this time, and while she is laying, only the head of the turtle is visible. After the eggs are deposited she crawls out and may proceed directly to the water, or she may make a slight effort to conceal the nest cavity by leveling the site and scratching around it. Of the 14 completed nests examined by Richmond (1945) only three showed indications that the turtles had tried successfully to conceal them.

The completed nest usually is a semicircular cavity 7.5–13 cm deep and entering the ground at about a 30° angle. The cavity is dug slightly higher and wider than the space to be occupied by the clutch and, after the eggs are laid, soil is packed firmly around and above them. In loose sandy soil the nest cavity may be soon obliterated by rains.

One to eight eggs may be ovulated at a time (Gibbons, 1983; based on oviducal eggs), but probably clutches with two to four eggs are most common. Tinkle (1959b) found six eggs beneath a pile of boards, and McCauley (1945) found one clutch of eight eggs and another of nine eggs, but these latter clutches may represent the contributions of more than one female. Clutches laid by northern females may contain more eggs than those from southern populations (Gibbons, 1983). The average clutch size of a population remains relatively stable over time (Gibbons et al., 1979b, 1982; Gibbons, 1983), but decreases each season with successive clutches.

Most females lay a single clutch each year, but a few may lay as many as three clutches a season at intervals of about 30 days (9–66). Only about 75% of the females in a population reproduce each year (Gibbons, 1983; Frazer et al., 1991a).

The eggs are elliptical, pinkish white or bluish white, and brittle shelled. The shell surface is covered with a fine, irregular network of impressed lines, which cause the surface to appear finely granular or pebbled, although not evenly so. The eggs are 22.0–32.3 mm long, 12.8–18.0 mm wide, and weigh 3.0–4.9 g. They do not take up water as fast during incubation as do parchment-shelled eggs; only about 61.2% of the egg mass can be attributed to water (Congdon and Gibbons, 1985). Mean shell dry mass is 0.67 g, which is approximately 23% of the total egg dry mass; the average ash content of the shell is 52.8% (Lamb and Congdon, 1985). A typical egg has a lipid dry mass of 0.27 g (17.7% of the egg dry mass), and the yolk is 31.6% lipid (Congdon and Gibbons, 1985).

Most hatching probably occurs in late August and September, but cool temperatures may retard development (Ewert, 1991). Hatchlings may overwinter in the nest after hatching and emerge the following spring (Lardie, 1975c). The nesting season in Florida may be extended; Iverson (1977a) found recently hatched young from 10 December to 21 February, and Lardie (1975c) discovered one on 15 April. Natural incubation probably takes about 90–100 days; laboratory incubated eggs have hatched in 76–158 days (Iverson, 1979d; Houseal and Carr, 1983; Gibbons, 1983).

The hatchling carapace is shaped like that of the adult but has a vertebral keel and two low lateral keels, is rough, and not depressed anteriorly or sharply turned down posteriorly. It is dark brown or black, with light spots along the marginals. The plastron is irregularly mottled with orange or red, and the hinges are poorly developed. The skin is brown or black. Hatchling *K. s. hippocrepis* have two faint light stripes on each side of the head and neck, and those of *K. s. steindachneri* may have a broad light postorbital stripe. Carapace length is 16.7–27.0 mm, width 13.1–20.0 mm, and depth 9.4–12.2 mm; most hatchlings weigh 3.5–4.0 g.

A clutch of six eggs incubated at 22.5°C by Ewert and Nelson (1991) produced one (17%) male and five (83%) females; however, until more data are available, it cannot be definitely established that the sex of *K. subrubrum* is determined by its incubation temperature.

Hybrid crosses between a captive female *K. subrubrum* and male *K. flavescens* produced young (Schipperijn, 1987).

GROWTH AND LONGEVITY: Studies have been conducted on the growth rate of both the carapace and plastron of *Kinosternon subrubrum*. Mahmoud (1969) found the growth period of *K. s. hippocrepis* in Oklahoma to be 170 days, limited to the warm months. Females having an initial carapace

Plastron of hatchling
*Kinosternon subrubrum
subrubrum*

length of 21–40 mm increased an average of 16.6 mm (44%) per growing season; females 41–60 mm increased 13.7 mm (27.5%); those 61–80 mm increased 2.6 mm (3.5%); and females longer than 80 mm increased only 0.38 mm (0.39%). Males 61–80 mm initially increased 3.0 mm (1.24%) and those longer than 81 mm increased only 0.83 mm (0.98%) per growing season. There was an increase in length in both sexes during the first six years, after which growth steadily slowed. Sixteen were kept two years in captivity without any apparent growth; annual rings indicated that these individuals were more than 10 years of age.

In South Carolina, *K. s. subrubrum* grow to 70–80 mm in carapace length in four to six years, when sexual maturity is attained by both sexes (Gibbons, 1983). After this the growth rate decreases, that of mature turtles being less than 1.0 mm/year, support-ing the concept of indeterminate growth in this species. Gibbons (1983) found no adult turtles that had not grown during a five-year or more period, and could not attribute the variability of growth among adults to either sex or body size of the individual.

Plastral growth was determined in a mixed sample of *K. s. subrubrum* and *K. s. steindachneri* from Florida by Ernst et al. (1973). Females were slightly longer at hatching (mean, 18.2 mm) than males (mean, 17.6 mm) and maintained a slight size advantage thereafter in samples up to 15 years of age. Plastral growth was more rapid in juveniles and slowed once maturity was reached in both sexes. Hatchlings with 9–19-mm

plastra increased an average of 63–108% during their first year. Individuals 20–29 mm long grew an average of 33.8% in plastron length; those 30–39 mm, 22.4%; 40–49 mm, 16.9%; 50–59 mm, 12.5%; 60–69 mm, 8.1%; 70–79 mm, 6.8%; 80–89 mm, 5.8%; and those with plastron lengths of 90 mm or more increased only 4.2% per growing season. The longer growing season in Florida allows a greater annual growth rate than is found in more northern populations and in the Oklahoma population studied by Mahmoud (1969). The growth rate of *K. s. hippocrepis* from Arkansas reported by Iverson (1979d), surprisingly, falls be-tween those of the Florida mud turtles reported by Ernst et al. (1973) and the Oklahoma population studied by Mahmoud (1969), indicating possible differential growth rates in geographically separated populations.

Kinosternon subrubrum has a potentially long life-span. A female, which was an adult when received, lived 38 years in captivity (Pope, 1939), and Snider and Bowler (1992) reported that another unsexed *K. s. hippocrepis*, also collected as an adult, lived over 18 years at the St. Louis Zoo.

FOOD HABITS: *Kinosternon subrubrum* is an omnivorous feeder. Mahmoud (1968b) reported the following percentages of frequency and volume, re-spectively, of food items: Insecta 98.3, 30.4; Crustacea 15.0, 1.4; Mollusca 93.1, 31.8; Amphibia 30.0, 2.2: carrion 68.6, 11.9; and aquatic vegetation 89.6, 22.3. Individuals under 50 mm in carapace length feed predominantly on small aquatic insects, algae, and carrion; those longer than 50 mm eat any kind of food.

Sixty fecal samples of *K. subrubrum* from North Carolina, examined from March to August, included 26 with crayfish remains, 18 with mollusks (aquatic snails, sphaeriid bivalves), 22 with beetles, 11 with other insects (dragonfly nymphs, caddisfly cases, etc.), 14 with plant remains (*Carex* seeds, *Sambucus, Rubus,* unidentified cereal grains), four with spiders, two with amphibian vertebrae, and one each with an amphibian egg mass, earthworm egg capsule, planarian egg case, clusters of a small colonial ciliate, and cycloid scales from a small fish (Brown, 1992). Crustacean prey besides crayfish included amphipods, isopods, and ostracods.

Captives feed readily on canned and fresh fish, canned beef, dog food, earthworms, snails, insects, newborn mice, commercial trout chow, tomatoes, and watermelon.

This species occasionally feeds at the surface, but when in water is predominantly a bottom feeder, probing into soft mud, sand, and decaying vegetation with its head. We have observed terrestrial feeding on two occasions in northern Virginia: a female was seen eating a caterpillar and a male, an earthworm. That this turtle may feed while on land is not surprising since it spends so much of the year out of water.

PREDATORS AND DEFENSE: Kingsnakes (*Lampropeltis getula*) eat the eggs (Wright and Bishop, 1915), and we have seen opossums (*Didelphis*), weasels (*Mustela*), skunks (*Mephitis*), raccoons (*Procyon*), gray foxes (*Urocyon*), and fish crows (*Corvus*) raid nests. Juveniles are attacked by blue crabs (*Callinectes*) (Nichols, 1914), gars (*Lepisosteus*), water snakes (*Nerodia*), hognose snakes (*Heterodon*), cottonmouths (*Agkistrodon*), and crows (*Corvus*). The shells of adults are sometimes gnawed by rodents, and bald eagles (*Haliaeetus*) take some (Clark, 1982). Humans have eliminated many through road kills and, more importantly, habitat destruction.

The disposition of *K. subrubrum* is variable. Some are very timid and retreat completely into their shells, but others bite fiercely. Individual *K. s. steindachneri* that we have handled have been particularly bad tempered. The musk secreted by this species is weak compared to that of either *Sternotherus* or *Chelydra*.

POPULATIONS: *Kinosternon subrubrum* may occur in high numbers in suitable habitats. Mahmoud (1969) estimated 159.3/ha of suitable habitat in Oklahoma during 1956 and 258.5 in 1957. Skorepa and Ozment (1968) reported that it was often possible to find 10 adults within an estimate 7 m² area in the southern Illinois population they studied. Gibbons (1983) estimated a density of 22–56/ha and a mean population size of 371 (224–556) individuals for a 10-year span in the approximately 10-ha basin of Ellenton Bay, South Carolina. Norman (1989) found *K. subrubrum* to be the second most numerous turtle to *Sternotherus odoratus* during a survey of the freshwater turtles in the Blackwater River in southeastern Virginia; 73 individuals (20%) were collected at 19 of 33 stations.

The biomass of *K. subrubrum* at particular localities may also be high; that of the Oklahoma creek studied by Mahmoud (1969) was approximately 25.9 kg/ha (Iverson, 1982a). However, at other sites it may be contrastingly low; Congdon et al. (1986) and Congdon and Gibbons (1989) estimated biomasses of only 3.7 kg/ha for the 10-ha Ellenton Bay and 0.7 kg/ha for the 1.1-ha Risher Pond in South Carolina. Ellenton Bay had an average annual egg biomass production of only 0.1 kg/ha. Apparently, permanently running streams may support greater numbers of eastern mud turtles than waterbodies subject to periodic drying.

Male to female ratios of mature Oklahoma *K. subrubrum* were 1.0:1.5 in both Cowan Creek and the Tishomingo Fish Hatchery, but 1.0:1.75 at Lake Texoma (Mahmoud, 1969); however, the sample sizes of all three collections were small and they probably do not differ significantly from equality. A 1:1 sex ratio is the rule in South Carolina (Gibbons, 1983). At Mahmoud's study area, adults greatly outnumbered juveniles, and we have observed the same apparent phenomenon in Kentucky and northern Virginia, but is this really due to fewer juveniles than adults, or to the more secretive nature of small *K. subrubrum* making them much harder to capture?

At the Savannah River Site in South Carolina the annual survival rate is 87.6% for adult females and 89.0% for adult males. Survival from oviposition until the hatchling enters the water is 26.1%. Survivorship of mud turtles at this locality may be high, as almost 90% of adults live until the next year. Eight individuals recaptured after 12–13 years by Gibbons (1983) were of adult size and presumably a minimum of four to six years of age when first captured. Thus, their ages at last capture were at least 16–17 years. Since this is a late-maturing, relatively long-lived species, Gibbons thought the maximum survivorship in nature is probably over 30 years. Frazer et al. (1991a) prepared a life table for this population.

REMARKS: Additional literature references are included in Iverson (1977b), and Iverson and Iverson (1980).

Kinosternon baurii (Garman, 1891)
Striped mud turtle
PLATE 19

RECOGNITION: This small mud turtle has 11 plastral scutes; some have three variable light stripes on the tan-to-black carapace. The broad, smooth carapace (to 12.7 cm) lacks a keel, is unserrated, and may have the vertebrals depressed, forming a broad, shallow, middorsal groove. The broad plastron has two well-developed transverse hinges bordering the abdominal scutes; it is olive to yellow and either plain or with dark seam borders. The skin is tan to black, and the neck and head may bear dark mottling. The small, conical head has two light, continuous or broken stripes extending posteriorly from the orbit—one above and one below the tympanum. A canthal stripe typically extends anterior of the eye to the tip of the snout. All feet are webbed.

Females are about 1.1 times larger than males and have short, stubby tails. Males have long, thick, spine-tipped tails and two patches of tilted scales on the inner surface of each hind leg.

KARYOTYPE: The diploid chromosome number is 56 (Killebrew, 1975; Sites et al., 1979; Bickham and Carr, 1983). According to Killebrew (1975) *Kinosternon baurii* has 26 macrochromosomes and 30 microchromosomes, but Sites et al. (1979) reported 24 macrochromosomes (12 metacentric or submetacentric, 12 telocentric or subtelocentric) and 32 microchromosomes.

FOSSIL RECORD: Pleistocene (Rancholabrean) remains have been found at Vero Beach, St. Lucie County, Florida (Weigel, 1962).

DISTRIBUTION: The striped mud turtle is found from the Florida Keys northward throughout peninsular Florida, and along the Atlantic Coastal Plain as far north as King and Queen County, Virginia (Lamb and Lovich, 1990).

GEOGRAPHIC VARIATION: No subspecies are currently recognized (Iverson, 1978c). At one time mainland populations were considered to be distinct from populations in the Florida Keys. Most specimens in peninsular Florida have head and carapace stripes characteristic of the species. In many specimens from some parts of Florida (including the Lower Keys) as well as those north of Florida, carapace and, to a lesser extent, head stripes are greatly obscured and may be absent altogether (Lamb and Lovich, 1990).

CONFUSING SPECIES: The striped mud turtle is often confused with *Kinosternon subrubrum*, particularly in the northern portion of the range. In *K. subrubrum*, a canthal stripe, if present, does not extend anterior of the eye. In *K. subrubrum*, the ratio of the abdominal scute length to plastron length ranges from 0.25 to 0.28 in males and 0.24 to 0.28 in females. In contrast, the same ratio in *K. baurii* ranges from 0.29 to 0.33 in males and 0.28 to 0.35 in females. Turtles of the genus *Sternotherus* have a single plastral hinge, not two as in *Kinosternon*.

HABITAT: The striped mud turtle is most often found in quiet fresh waters at least 60 cm deep with a soft bottom, such as swamps, sloughs, canals, ponds, and Carolina bays. Individuals have been found in the lodges of the round-tailed muskrat (*Neofiber alleni*). Although *Kinosternon baurii* sometimes inhabits brackish water, it requires water with less than 15 ppt salinity, and prefers water where the salinity is 8.5 ppt (25% sea water) or less (Dunson, 1981).

BEHAVIOR: *Kinosternon baurii* is active all year in Florida, both on land and in water; however, seasonal activity seems bimodal as two growth annuli are often produced during any one year (Iverson, 1979e). Winter annuli are apparently always pro-

Kinosternon baurii

Plastron of *Kinosternon baurii*

duced and are usually distinct from those produced in the summer. Annual terrestrial activity is also bimodal, with northern Florida striped mud turtles most often encountered on land during March when spring rains are filling the ponds and marshes and again in October as water levels are dropping.

Wygoda (1979) studied the behavior of a population in west-central Florida centered on a riverine forest pond and adjacent seasonal swamps. From February to July, turtles disperse to estivation sites in the surrounding forest as the pond habitat dries. With the arrival of summer rains they migrate back to the pond, but then disperse to newly formed shallow swamps. As these swamps dry from September to December turtles return to the ponds. Terrestrial activity is correlated with water depth, and mass migrations appear to be initiated by heavy rainfall.

Seasonal activity of *K. baurii* was studied using a drift fence and buckets in a sandhill adjacent to a hardwood swamp forest in central Florida by Mu-

Distribution of *Kinosternon baurii*

shinsky and Wilson (1992). Only gravid females and hatchlings were collected, suggesting the sandhill was a nesting site. Females were captured during most months, with a peak capture rate in June. Most hatchlings were captured from February through April. The smallest female collected had an 83-mm carapace, and the mean female carapace length was 98 mm. The hatchlings had a mean carapace length of 23 mm. Peak abundance of females followed that of the hatchlings by eight months. The data suggest that hatchlings delay emergence from the nest, but empirical verification is required. Hatchling emergence was uncorrelated with monthly temperature or rainfall data.

During phases of terrestrial activity striped mud turtles construct shallow burrows or forms. Most forms are constructed in soil beneath leaf litter, and soil depth above the carapace is 0–25 mm. Some forms are located in natural debris-filled depressions or beneath logs. Striped mud turtles travel from 1.1 to 48.8 m (mean, 12) when moving from the aquatic habitat to the first form of the season, and from 0.8 to 33.5 m (mean, 7.3) between subsequent forms. Time spent in forms ranged from 1 to 50 days (mean, 17). Wygoda (1979) observed no relationship between size or sex and distance traveled to forms, time spent in forms, number of forms occupied, or type of form constructed. Up to four forms may be used by a single turtle each season, and single retreats may be used repeatedly. Evaporative water loss is quite low (0.5%/ mass/day in the laboratory, and presumably also in the field; Dunson, 1981).

Hutchison et al. (1966) found the mean critical thermal maximum to be 40.6°C (39.9–41.2). The mean loss of righting response occurs at 39.1°C (38.2–40.4).

REPRODUCTION: Wild female *Kinosternon baurii* mature at 70–75 mm carapace length in five or six years (Iverson, 1979e); wild males contain mature sperm when 75 mm long (Einem, 1956). Captive males have matured at 23 months of age, and captive females at 29 months (Praschag, 1983).

The male gametic cycle has not been described, but the female ovarian cycle is nearly continuous with only a short summer quiescent period (Iverson, 1979e). Ovulation occurs from late August or early September to early June, and follicles are yolked to replace those ovulated during all but the last of this period. Einem (1956) found eggs in the oviducts from late February through mid-April and ovarian follicles with diameters greater than 15 mm present from late February to early May. Follicular growth stops from late May through June. During the remainder of the year enlarged follicles greater than 7 mm are present, along with oviducal eggs and/or corpora lutea. Females examined by Einem (1956) had follicles less than 10.8 mm in diameter, with most 4–5 mm, during August and September. Females may retain their eggs until suitable nesting sites and conditions are found without possibility of subsequent ovulation, as oviducal eggs can be found when corpora lutea are regressed (Iverson, 1977a, 1979e).

Lardie (1975a) observed a captive mating on 16 March and reported that the courtship and mating behaviors are divisible into three phases: tactile, initial mounting, and copulation. During the tactile phase, the male approaches the female, stretches out his neck, nudges about her tail, and sometimes bites her head. In the mounting phase, he grasps the rim of her carapace with the claws of all four feet, usually in the vicinity of marginals 1–2 and 9–10. He also uses his tail to hold on by placing it under the posterior rim of her carapace with the terminal spine touching either the top or sides of her tail and the area about her anal vent. At this time he may continue to bite at the female's head. To achieve coitus, the male slides to a more posterior position on the female's carapace, still grasping it with his toe claws, and brings the vents together. Insertion soon follows.

Carr (1940) observed aggressive behavior, which may have been related to courtship, between two males in the presence of a female on 2 May along the banks of a small stream. After a brief struggle lasting about five minutes, one of the males fell into the stream. The victor immediately turned to the female, thrust his snout beneath her plastron, and crawled under her. She remained balanced on the male's carapace for 30 minutes.

Like many other turtles, female *Kinosternon baurii* appear to be capable of storing sperm. A captive female, isolated from males of the same species for at least 397 days, produced a fertile egg that subsequently hatched (Nijs and Navez, 1990).

Females typically possess oviducal eggs in the fall (Iverson, 1979e; Lamb and Lovich, 1990). Florida females produce at least three clutches per year (Lardie, 1975c; Iverson, 1979e). Nests are constructed in sand or in piles of decaying vegetation. Clutch size varies from one to seven eggs (Sachsse, 1977a), and is positively correlated to female size (Iverson, 1979e). Each clutch constitutes about 8% of female body weight (Iverson, 1979e). The eggs are

elliptical, whitish to pinkish white, and have brittle shells with a dull finish. Eggs range in length from 22.8 to 32.8 mm, in width from 13.6 to 19.3 mm, and weigh 3.3–5.3 g (Iverson, 1979e; Praschag, 1983). Measurements apparently remain constant throughout the incubation period. Resistance to desiccation is indicated by the fact that eggs left completely dry will develop normally (Einem, 1956). Thickness of the eggshell averages 0.31 mm (M. J. Packard et al., 1984a).

If chilled, eggs of *K. baurii* enter a period of diapause (arrested development) until warmed (Ewert, 1985, 1991). The embryos respond to 30°C and, almost always, to 28°C with active development, but cool temperatures (22.5–24.0°C) will hold some embryos in diapause. Embryos at 22.5–24.0°C will assume active development within five to nine days of transfer to 30°C, even though they have been in diapause for several weeks. Once development proceeds, it continues to completion even if the egg is returned to its former cooler temperature. Diapause may persist for as long as 95 days in advance of heating, but once it is broken, viability through hatching is high.

Eggs incubated at room temperature under artificial conditions hatch in 80–145 days (Einem, 1956; Nicol, 1970; Iverson, 1979e; Praschag, 1983). After two to three months of incubation and at least one month before hatching, eggs develop a single longitudinal crack around the eggshell. Small amounts of albumen leak from the crack as it expands. As hatching nears, the egg is ruptured again near the end of the egg next to the hatchling's eyes. Using its forefeet, the hatchling makes two jagged holes about 3 mm in diameter, first in the eggshell and then in the shell membrane. Hatchlings typically emerge from this end of the egg without halving the egg longitudinally. The process of emergence takes from 2 to 65 hours (Einem, 1956).

The ground color of the 16.5–27.0-mm hatchling carapace is mahogany or reddish brown to black with light-yellow to orange-yellow stripes and marginal spots. Three distinct keels are present. The yellow plastron has a dark central blotch that extends outward along the seams. Plastral hinges are not functional until about three months after hatching. Hatchlings have yolk sacs that are 5–7 mm long, and egg teeth are lost 27–31 days after hatching (Einem, 1956).

GROWTH AND LONGEVITY: Einem (1956) reported that hatchling *Kinosternon baurii* increased their dimensions in three months as follows: carapace length, 1.0–5.2 mm; plastron length, 0.8–

3.7 mm; carapace width, 3.9–8.8 mm; and carapace height, 0.4–1.4 mm. During this time, the carapace height of two turtles decreased 1.2 and 1.5 mm (possibly due to measurement error). Praschag (1983) reported that a captive male grew from 80 mm to 89 mm carapace length in about 16 months, at the same time its body weight increased from 89 g to 104 g, and two captive females grew from 90 mm to 94 mm (128 g to 155 g) and from 87 mm to 95 mm (126 g to 160 g), respectively, in about 18 months. Another captive female 96 mm long did not grow in length, but increased its weight 12 g in 70 months.

A female captured in Florida when she was about 10 years old lived in captivity for 49 years, 7 months, and 13 days before having her life cut short in a fire (Johnson, 1984).

FOOD HABITS: *Kinosternon baurii* is omnivorous. In Florida natural foods include large numbers of the seeds of cabbage palmetto (*Sabal palmetto*), juniper leaves, and other vegetable debris (including algae), small snails, insects and their larvae, and unidentified bone fragments. This turtle may forage in cow dung when on land, perhaps seeking insects. Captives do well on fresh, frozen or canned fish, newborn mice, earthworms, commercial trout chow, and romaine lettuce; interestingly, captive hatchlings snap indiscriminately when blood is added to their water (Einem, 1956). Our captives have accepted food out of water.

PREDATORS AND DEFENSE: Eggs are undoubtedly eaten by a variety of mammalian predators and king snakes (*Lampropeltis getula brooksi*). *Kinosternon baurii* were found in the stomach contents of 5.7% of 350 alligators (*Alligator mississippiensis*) collected in Orange, Lochloosa, and New-

nans lakes, Florida, by Delany and Abercrombie (1986). On Lake Okeechobee, Florida, 69.8–89.8-mm *K. baurii* compose 31.3% of the turtles eaten as alternative prey by the snail kite, *Rostrhamus sociabilis* (Beissinger, 1990).

Unlike its close relative *K. subrubrum*, *K. baurii* rarely bites if disturbed, but withdraws into its shell, relying on it for total protection.

POPULATIONS: The male to female sex ratio observed by Wygoda (1979) in Florida varied according to habitat as follows: pond, 1:2; swamps, 1:1; road captures, 1:7. Iverson (1982a) used Wygoda's data to estimate a biomass of 5.2 kg/ha.

REMARKS: The taxonomic status and exact distribution of *Kinosternon baurii* have been clouded by pattern variation and similarity to *K. subrubrum*. Verification of populations of *K. baurii* north of Florida was provided by Lamb (1983a,b), and later the species was confirmed as far north as Virginia (Lamb and Lovich, 1990).

Seidel et al. (1986) analyzed biochemical variation in kinosternid turtles and concluded that *K. baurii* and *K. subrubrum* are more closely allied to *Sternotherus* than to congeners. The close relationship of *K. baurii* to *K. subrubrum* has also been identified by Iverson (1988b, 1991b).

An apparent case of DDT poisoning in *K. baurii* was reported by Herald (1949). A female was discovered a day after an application of DDT had killed many fish. She was unable to retract her head or legs when captured. On the fourth day she laid two eggs (which failed to hatch following incubation), and on the twelfth day she died.

Other references on this species are summarized in Ernst (1974c).

Kinosternon flavescens (Agassiz, 1857)
Yellow mud turtle
PLATE 20

RECOGNITION: This small desert/grassland species has 11 scutes on the plastron, and both the ninth and tenth marginals elevated. Its broad smooth carapace (to 18.2 cm) is not serrated, lacks a vertebral keel and may be depressed medially. The first vertebral touches the second marginal. The carapace is olive to brown and the scutes are dark bordered. The bridge and venters of the marginals are yellow with dark pigment along the seams. The plastron has two well-developed transverse hinges bordering the abdominal scutes; it is yellowish to brown, with dark pigment along the seams. The skin is immaculate yellow to gray. The head is flattened. The jaws are hooked and commonly whitish to yellow; some bear dark spots. All four feet are webbed.

Males have short, concave plastra, long, thick, spine-tipped tails, and two patches of rough scales on the inner surface of each hind leg. Most adult females are shorter than males.

KARYOTYPE: The diploid chromosome number is 56: 26 macrochromosomes, 30 microchromosomes (Killebrew, 1975). Stock (1972) reported 16 metacentric and submetacentric chromosomes, 8 subtelocentric, and 32 acrocentric and telocentric.

FOSSIL RECORD: Pliocene (Hemphillian) fossils have been found in northeastern Nebraska (Parmley, 1992), and Pliocene (Blancan) fossils exist from Meade County, Kansas (Fichter, 1969), Garden County, Nebraska (Holman and Schloeder, 1991), and Scurry County, Texas (Rogers, 1976). Pleistocene records are from the Blancan of Cochise County, Arizona (location of the type specimens of *K. f. arizonense* Gilmore, 1922), and Brown County, Nebraska (Fichter, 1969), Irvingtonian of Meade County, Kansas (Holman, 1986a), and Travis County, Texas (Holman and Winkler, 1987), and the Rancholabrean of Sonora, Mexico (Van Devender et al., 1985).

Parmley (1990) described late Holocene (150 B.P.) material from Montague County, Texas.

DISTRIBUTION: The yellow mud turtle occurs in northwestern Illinois and adjacent Iowa and Missouri, northern Nebraska, southwestern Missouri, and from southern Nebraska south through Texas, New Mexico, and southern Arizona to Sonora, Durango, Tamaulipas, and Veracruz, Mexico. It has been found at elevations to 1,500 m.

GEOGRAPHIC VARIATION: Three subspecies are recognized, but only two occur north of Mexico (Iverson, 1992b). *Kinosternon flavescens flavescens* (Agassiz, 1857), the yellow mud turtle, ranges from northwestern Illinois, eastern Iowa, northeastern Missouri, and Nebraska south to Texas, New Mexico, and southeastern Arizona in the United States, and to the Rio Panuco Basin of Veracruz, Mexico. Its short gular scute is approximately 41% as long as the anterior lobe of the plastron. *Kinosternon f. arizonense* Gilmore, 1922, the Arizona mud turtle, occurs mainly in Sonora, Mexico, and southern Arizona. Its extensive gular scute is approximately 63% as long as the anterior lobe of the plastron. Collins (1991) suggested that *K. f. arizonense* be elevated to specific rank, as there is no demonstrable gene flow between it and *K. f. flavescens*.

The populations in Illinois and adjacent Iowa and Missouri were formerly designated a separate race (*K. f. spooneri*, Smith, 1951), but studies by Houseal et al. (1982) and Berry and Berry (1984) synonymized it with *K. f. flavescens* (although quite a controversy raged over its status; Dodd 1982, 1983; Bickham et al., 1984; Gallaway et al., 1985).

CONFUSING SPECIES: No other *Kinosternon* in the United States typically has an elevated ninth marginal. Musk turtles (*Sternotherus*) have

182

Kinosternon flavescens flavescens

*Kinosternon flavescens
arizonense*

rectangular pectoral scutes and a single, indistinct plastral hinge, and *S. carinatus* lacks a gular scute.

HABITAT: *Kinosternon flavescens* inhabits almost any quiet water within its range: swamps, sloughs, sinkholes, rivers, creeks, ponds (particularly temporary ones), lakes, reservoirs, cisterns, and cattle tanks in semiarid grasslands, open woodlands, or deserts. A mud or sand bottom is preferred, and aquatic vegetation is often present within the waterbody; in the north, *K. flavescens* seems tied to sandhill habitats that allow it to dig below the frost line in winter. Ninety percent of the variation in the abundance of *K. flavescens* in three Missouri populations could be

accounted for by the amount of very course sand in their habitats (Kangas, 1986a). Of nine other variables tested in a stepwise multiple regression, three, area in marsh (0.95), area under human influence (0.18), and area in pasture (0.08), were also significant predictors of yellow mud turtle abundance (Kangas, 1986a).

Webster (1986) tested substrate preference and found that *K. flavescens* from Kansas prefer tan-colored loess "mud" to a dark-brown sandy-loam bottom. Addition of aquatic plants to the sandy loam causes a shift to the vegetated area. The turtles can also discriminate between a substrate of dark or light contact paper, but prefer dark loess to a light-colored loess. Webster's experiments tested turtles from mud-

Plastron of *Kinosternon flavescens*

bottomed farm ponds, and their preference was similar to that in their home pond, but whether this was learned or innate is not known.

Kinosternon f. arizonense is confined to lowlands (200–800 m) in the Sonoran Desert where it resides in temporary created presas, ponds, tanks, and road-side ditches as well as in some permanent lentic waters. Arizona mud turtles seem to avoid permanent streams and rivers (Iverson, 1989).

BEHAVIOR: In New Mexico, *Kinosternon flavescens flavescens* is active for approximately 183 days each year from approximately 15 April to 15 October (Christiansen and Dunham, 1972). In Oklahoma, the annual activity period lasts 140 days (Mahmoud, 1969), and in Missouri and Iowa the species is aquatically active for 100–128 days, from late April to mid-July and then again from mid- to late August to September or October (Christiansen et al., 1985; Johnson, 1987). A period of terrestrial estivation usually occurs in midsummer, when the turtles bury to depths of 25 cm in the sandy soil. The yellow mud turtle maintains the highest carcass lipid index of all reported turtles (Long, 1985), which may provide needed energy and insulation during periods of estivation and hibernation. Most activity is diurnal, but some limited nocturnal activity occurs; in Nebraska nocturnal activity occurs mostly from 0800 to 1000 and 1700 to 2000 (Iverson, pers. comm.).

Iverson (1989) trapped few *K. f. arizonense* at night, suggesting that it is primarily a diurnal feeder. In the Sonora Desert it is most active from 1 July to 15 August, and is brought forth from its terrestrial estivation-hibernation sites by summer rains.

Kinosternon f. flavescens spends much time basking or moving on land, and it occasionally migrates overland between bodies of water, so at times it may be greatly influenced by air temperatures. *Kinosternon f. arizonense* sometimes basks when air temperatures are near 45°C (Iverson, 1989).

Mahmoud (1969) found a mean difference between cloacal and environmental temperatures of Oklahoma *K. f. flavescens* throughout the year of +0.3°C to −20°C. The thermoactivity range was 18–32°C; the field preferred body temperature was 25.06°C. His captives accepted food at body temperatures of 16–38°C. Their mean critical thermal maximum was 43.25°C (39.2–43.7), and they lost the ability to right themselves at a mean temperature of 39.7°C (38.1–40.1). With the onset of cold weather *K. flavescens* burrows into natural depressions, such as old stumpholes, and beneath shrubs, brushpiles, logs, or litter. Some dig burrows in loose sandy soil (particularly in the north); others hibernate in muskrat dens or in the mud at the bottom of pools. Carpenter (1957) found them terrestrially overwintering in close association with *Terrapene ornata* and *T. carolina*. Some *K. flavescens* can remain terrestrially dormant for up to two years (Rose, 1980). They accumulate a great store of lipids, which probably provides the energy needed during such long durations. The total lipid index of this species is 0.45, among the highest reported for any North American ectotherm (Rose, 1980).

Distribution of *Kinosternon flavescens*

Seidel (1978a) experimentally induced terrestrial dormancy in yellow mud turtles which resulted in physiological adjustments that reduced oxygen consumption and carbon dioxide release. Reduced peripheral circulation, decreased integumental permeability, and breath holding brought about retention of carbon dioxide. Sharply elevated oxygen consumption upon emergence from dormancy indicated presence of an oxygen debt and supported the hypothesis of increased anaerobic metabolism. While buried beneath soil during dry conditions *K. flavescens* avoids dehydration by reducing respiration. During dehydration, *K. flavescens* increases the thickness of the horny epidermal layer of its skin (Seidel and Reynolds, 1980); this layer is shed after the turtle returns to the water (Iverson, pers. comm.). A devastating winterkill of *K. flavescens* occurred in Iowa in 1977 resulting from unusually cold weather combined with low water levels (Murphy and Corn, 1977; Christiansen and Bickham, 1989).

Yellow mud turtles often move overland from one waterbody to another (Mahmoud, 1969). This has allowed them to occupy ponds scattered throughout their range. One such site in eastern New Mexico grasslands harboring a large population was an isolated stock pond at least 8 km from the nearest

natural depression periodically holding water and 48 km from the nearest permanently flowing stream (Degenhardt and Christiansen, 1974). During a severe drought in 1988, some *K. f. flavescens* in Spring Lake, a Mississippi River oxbow in Iowa, sought out the only water available when the oxbow dried, a small artificial pool 2 m deep, instead of estivating on land (Watts and Christiansen, 1989). During rainy periods *K. f. arizonense* wanders considerable distances over the desert floor.

The maximum and minimum distances between successive points of capture of Oklahoma *K. f. flavescens* were 435 m and 3.3 m. The average distance between first and last capture during more than 100 days of activity was 258 m for females and 135 m for males; for periods of less than 100 days, 170 m for females and 244 m for males. The areas traversed averaged 0.11 ha for males and 0.13 ha for females (Mahmoud, 1969).

In Iowa, all terrestrial habitats utilized by radio-equipped *K. f. flavescens* are 100–450 m from water in areas of sparse herbaceous cover in elevated sandy dunes (Christiansen et al., 1985). Burrowing is usually to a depth of 5–15 cm, and the turtles often change locations. Rainfall stimulates movement, and most journeys occur at night. In contrast, most overland migrations in the Nebraska sandhills take place in the morning (0800–1000) or late afternoon (1700–2000) (Iverson, 1990).

Male yellow mud turtles sometimes engage in combat behavior. Lardie (1983a) has observed aggressive male-to-male interactions in both field (Oklahoma) and laboratory. Aggressive interactions occurred regardless of the presence of a female. A definite sequence was followed in these bouts: touching, initial mounting, genital biting, and chasing and biting. These are all intimidating and threatening, and are usually performed by the stronger or more dominant male. Lardie thought this an example of territoriality, with the dominant male defending a small aquatic area with its available food supply and any females within it.

REPRODUCTION: Males become sexually mature at carapace lengths of 8–9 cm in their fifth or sixth year; females mature at about 8–12.5 cm at age 4–16 (Mahmoud, 1967; Christiansen and Dunham, 1972; Long, 1986a; Iverson, 1989, 1991c). Age of maturity is positively related to latitude. At the northern limit of the range in Nebraska female *Kinosternon flavescens flavescens* mature at about 9-cm carapace length (the smallest gravid female was 8.8 cm) after an average of 11 years (11–16; Iverson, 1991c).

The annual male and female sexual cycles are essentially like those reported under *Sternotherus odoratus* (Mahmoud and Klicka, 1972; Christiansen and Dunham, 1972; Christiansen et al., 1984; Long, 1986a). Incorporation of lipids in ovarian follicles occurs at a constant rate and at direct expense of the female's lipid reserve (Long, 1985).

Courtship and mating behavior of *K. flavescens* resembles that of *Sternotherus odoratus*, but varies in several actions (Mahmoud, 1967; Lardie, 1975a, 1978). Lardie (1978) divided it into three general phases: tactile, initial mounting, and copulating. The tactile phase is essentially the same as described by Mahmoud (1967). The male approaches the female with neck outstretched, nudging her about the tail and sometimes biting her about the head. Although this phase may last up to five minutes, it usually takes one or two. The tactile phase is sometimes omitted and the male tries directly to mount. The entire procedure seems to depend on cooperation of the female and on male eagerness. It is not unusual to find the female uncooperative, whereupon prolonged chasing usually ensues, including both swimming and crawling along the bottom until the male catches and mounts the female.

The initial mounting phase comprises several more or less simultaneous procedures as the male mounts the female with his plastron directly over her carapace. He grasps the edges of the female's carapace with the claws of all four feet; the large second and third digits of his forefeet seem to be used most effectively in holding onto her carapace, generally in the areas of the first and second marginals. The large claws of the first three digits of the hind feet are used in grasping at about the ninth and tenth marginals, depending somewhat on the relative size of the pair. The male also uses his tail for grasping by inserting it under the posterior margin of the female's carapace; at this time the terminal nail on his tail may touch the area on either side or above the female's tail and vent. A female may attempt to close her plastron, furthering the male's attachment by holding his tail tightly. The male then extends his neck and head, expanding his yellow throat while biting or rubbing at the top of the female's head. At this point the turtles may proceed without struggle or the female may attempt to free herself; the male may be dislodged several times before gaining a secure hold. (Captive males occasionally perform this phase with other males and in a reversed position from that with females. When this occurs, the tactile phase is omitted.) During this mounting phase the male attempts to maintain his hold and bring his cloacal area into contact with that of the female. This phase may last from about 30 seconds to 45 minutes. Biting and rubbing begin when mounting is initiated and do not stop until coitus is finished.

In Mahmoud's (1967) courtship description the male flexes either the left or right hind leg at the knee during the mounting phase and grasps the female's tail between the scaly patches on the inner surfaces of the upper and lower leg; the male's tail is looped under the female's so the cloacal areas meet and the penis inserted. Furthermore, the biting and rubbing phase does not begin until the coital position is reached. Lardie's (1978) observations of *K. flavescens* differ in that the very short female tail is not long enough to be held by the scaly patches of the male's hind legs as it is in such species as *Sternotherus odoratus* or *S. carinatus*. Also, in *K. flavescens,* the male and female cloacal areas are farther from the tail tip than in *Sternotherus.*

The copulatory phase is initiated as the male reaches a more posterior position on the female's carapace to bring the vents together. The male flexes either the left or right rear leg at the knee, holding the female's carapace edge at about the tenth and eleventh marginals between the scaly patches on the inner surfaces of the upper and lower leg throughout the coital period. His tail is looped under that of the female, guided and held into place by the foot of this same leg; the penis is inserted at this point. The toes and claws of the other rear foot continue to hold the female's carapace at the edge of the ninth and tenth marginals, the exact location again depending upon the relative size of the two turtles. The foot used to hold the carapace edge also may be used to counter the female's foot when she attempts to push his tail away. The terminal nail of the male's tail is usually placed into the plastral notch between the anal scutes, although it is sometimes positioned elsewhere along the plastron to facilitate balance. In order for the vents to touch, the male must move his forefeet backward from the anterior margins of the female's carapace and place them in the general vicinity of the second and third pleurals. Occasionally, he may momentarily grasp the female's carapace rim at the sixth and seventh marginals to regain balance. He will continue to stretch his head forward, making biting motions while expanding his throat. The procedure creates a considerable angle between the male's plastron and the female's carapace, exaggerated more when the two are floating, as they may be touching only at their extreme posteriors. During this phase, a cooperative female rests quietly, her head and all four legs jerking rhythmically (each 4–8 seconds). The copulatory phase lasts from about 5.5 minutes to 2.5 hours. Mahmoud (1967) reported that coitus lasts from 10 minutes to three hours.

Courtship usually takes place in water varying in depth from 2.5 cm to almost a meter, but Mahmoud (1967) saw a pair mating on the bank of a pond.

Oviposition by *K. f. flavescens* begins in May and peaks in the first half of June. In Nebraska, females move nonstop in an essentially straight path 21–191 m from water to sparsely vegetated, generally south-facing slopes, and bury in the sandy soil to depths of 5–10 cm (Iverson, 1990). A female may relocate on the slope as many as three times before she finds a suitable nest site. When the proper place is found she digs to a depth of about 13 cm by pushing the sand laterally with her forelimbs and posteriorly with the hind limbs. When buried horizontally at this depth, she excavates a nest with her hind feet, deposits her eggs, and releases bladder water into the cavity. Nest depths are 17–23 cm beneath the soil surface. She then remains with the eggs for one to more than 38 days, and possibly some females may not return to the water until the next spring. The annual incidence of nest attendance seems inversely related to the amount of rainfall between May and mid-June. Egg mortality

may be reduced by the effects of the female's presence on both predation on the eggs and soil moisture at the nest.

The activity and reproductive cycles of *K. f. arizonense* are asynchronous with those of *K. f. flavescens*. In Arizona and Sonora the subspecies is most active from July to the middle of October, copulates in July, and nests in July and August (Iverson, 1989).

Females have proportionally larger pelvic canals than do males, and Long and Rose (1989) thought this difference in pelvic girdle size exists to favor the development and passage of larger eggs. Iverson (1991c) did not find this true in Nebraska; pelvis size did not constrain egg size, and increases in female reproductive output with body size are accomplished both by increases in egg size (mainly width) and egg number.

One to nine elliptical, hard, white eggs are laid in each clutch; females in most northern populations lay only one clutch per year, *K. f. flavescens* from the southern populations may occasionally oviposit twice, and *K. f. arizonense* typically lays two to three clutches per year. In Nebraska only 75% of the mature females oviposit in any given year (Iverson, 1991c). Annual frequency in nesting is not related to female body size but is positively correlated with late spring temperature of the current and past year. Eggs of *K. f. flavescens* are 22.7–31.4 mm long, 14.1–18.3 mm wide, and weigh 3.0–5.8 g (Iverson, 1991c). Those of *K. f. arizonense* are larger, 29.9–35.2 mm long, 16.2–19.5 mm wide, and 5.8–6.8 g in mass (Iverson, 1989). In *K. f. flavescens* the width, dry mass, clutch dry mass, and clutch size increased with female size, and egg width is positively correlated with egg mass (Long, 1986a; Iverson, 1991c), but these seem not correlated with female size in *K. f. arizonense* (Iverson, 1989). When the effect of body size is removed, egg size is inversely correlated with clutch size in *K. f. flavescens* (Iverson, 1991c). Clutch mass in Nebraska averages 10.9% of female mass and is correlated with both female size and clutch size, but energy expenditure per hatchling (clutch mass/clutch size) is inversely correlated with female size and only weakly correlated to egg size (Iverson, 1991c).

Structure and formation of the eggshells has been described by M. J. Packard and co-workers (1984a,b). The shells are thinner (0.18 mm) than those of *S. minor, K. baurii,* and *K. hirtipes,* and have a rigid calcareous layer composed of calcium carbonate (aragonite). This layer is organized into individual units with needlelike crystallites radiating from a common center. This layer constitutes most of the shell's thickness, but a fibrous membrane is also present. The outer surface of the shell is sculptured and may have thick, scattered organic layers. Calcium may be withdrawn from the shell during embryonic development.

Hatching occurs from August to October in most populations, but probably in July and August in southern Arizona. Lardie (1975c, 1979) recorded incubation periods of 94–118 days for eggs of *K. f. flavescens* incubated in the laboratory at 22–33°C, and Iverson (1989) reported an incubation period of 320 days for an egg of *K. f. arizonense* kept at 25°C. This last figure probably is typical of the natural pattern, with eggs of *K. f. arizonense* laid in July and August of one year hatching at the beginning of the next summer rainy period. Natural incubation periods have not been reported.

Ewert (1985, 1991) studied embryonic development in *K. f. arizonense*. When the eggs are incubated at 25°C, development occurs between days 22 and 134, with a period of delayed hatching or estivation within the eggshell for up to 232 additional days (a total period of 366 days from oviposition to hatching). The young are stimulated to hatch by a substantial wetting of the incubation medium. Some eggs hatched in 0.4–3.0 hours after submersion in water, but others endured four to eight hours submersion without hatching and had to be assisted because of the weak condition of the hatchling, presumably due to hypoxia. Experiencing cool or warm temperatures (16.5/32.0°C) did not initially bring on hatching of eggs incubated at 27°C. Eventually, two months after initial testing, hatching accompanied the cooling phase. Increased moisture seems the stronger natural stimulus, but the most natural form of application is unclear.

In Iowa the young hatch in mid-September but remain underground until the following spring (Christiansen and Gallaway, 1984). In western Texas, hatchling also seem to overwinter underground and emerge in early summer (Long, 1986b); those in Nebraska hatch and then dig down to avoid frost (Iverson, pers. comm.). Sufficient rainfall, coupled with warming soil temperature, apparently cues emergence. Eggs of *K. flavescens* contain large lipid stores, which may facilitate hatchling survival over the winter.

Hatchling *K. f. flavescens* have 17.7–23.9-mm carapaces, 15.8–21.7-mm plastra, and weigh 2.0–3.7 g (Iverson, 1991c); those of *K. f. arizonse* have 24.8–28.4-mm carapaces, 20.0–24.3-mm plastra, and weights to 5.1 g (Iverson, 1989). The shell is slightly

keeled and the ninth and tenth marginals are the same height as or slightly lower than the eighth. Cahn (1937) reported that elevation of the marginals first appears at a shell length of about 67 mm. Hatchling coloration of both *K. f. flavescens* and *K. f. arizonense* is similar to that of adults.

Incubation temperature influences the sex of hatchlings. Eggs incubated at 25°C yielded 79% males, but those incubated at 31°C yielded 100% females (Vogt et al., 1982). Schipperijn (1987) reported captive hybridization between *K. flavescens* and *K. subrubrum*.

GROWTH AND LONGEVITY: At hatching, females are larger than males, but males are larger than females in all age classes older than three years (Iverson, 1991c). Juvenile growth rates are faster in the south and seem inversely correlated with latitude. The growth period in Oklahoma is only 90 days (Mahmoud, 1969). Turtles having an initial carapace length of 21–40 mm increased 7.7 mm (22%) per growing season; those 41–60 mm increased 7.9 mm (16.5%); those 61–80 mm increased 3.1 mm (4.5%); and those more than 81 mm increased only 2.7 mm (0.3%).

Multivariate comparisons of continuous shell characters indicate that shell shape in *Kinosternon flavescens flavescens* is highly correlated to shell length and strongly allometric (McCord et al., 1990). Long (1984) reported the following allometric equations for growth of *K. f. flavescens:* carapace length = 15.65 (mass$^{0.354}$), r = 0.99; carapace length = 13.16 (volume $^{0.379}$), r = 0.98. Growth rates of captive juvenile *K. f. flavescens* indicate a greater potential for carapace lengthening than is achieved in the wild. A 23-mm hatchling grew to 39.5 mm in 5.5 months (Lardie, 1975c), a 39-mm juvenile grew 18.5 mm (47.4%) in one year, and another 58.3-mm turtle increased in size 13.7 mm (23.5%) in less than four months (Lardie, 1979). A captive hatchling grew from 23 mm to 49.5 mm (115.2%) in one year, and three others grew 9.5% in 36 days, and 22.9% and 24.1% in 93 days (Lardie, 1979).

Mean plastron lengths (mm) of *K. f. arizonense* reported by Iverson (1989) are as follows: age 2, males 41.2, females 46.4; age 4, males 71.2, females 73.5; age 6, males 86.9, females 88.0; age 8, males 107.3, females 102.4; and at age 10 a male and a female were 121.6 and 112.1, respectively. During a three-year span, recaptured adults longer than 124-mm plastron length grew 0.53–1.25 mm/year, and a 104-mm female grew to 117 mm at a rate of 4.4 mm/year.

The longevity record for a captive *K. flavescens* is 10 years, 4 months, and 25 days (Snider and Bowler, 1992), but wild individuals in northern Nebraska have a typical generation time of 28.2 years (Iverson, 1991c).

FOOD HABITS: *Kinosternon flavescens* seems omnivorous, but plants may be only secondarily ingested. Mahmoud (1968b) found the following percentages of frequency and volume, respectively, of food items in *K. flavescens* from Oklahoma: Insecta 94.7, 27.8; Crustacea 99.2, 27.7; Mollusca 93.7, 23.5; Amphibia 91.2, 9.2; carrion 13.2, 3.2; and aquatic vegetation 37.2, 8.5. Turtles shorter than 5 cm in carapace length fed predominantly on small aquatic insects, algae, and carrion, whereas those more than 5 cm ate a greater variety of items.

In Iowa, Christiansen et al. (1985) found that fish, crustaceans, insects (particularly beetles) and plant material occurred in the highest percentage of stomachs from May through July in 1973–74, but in 1979, a year following a drought, snails were the dominant food item. Duckweed was found in 61% of the stomachs on 6–7 June 1979. Nebraska yellow mud turtles feed mainly on snails, tadpoles, earthworms, and carrion (Iverson, 1975); and in northeastern Missouri, snails, crayfish, fish, and plant material are the most prevalent foods (Kofron and Schreiber, 1985). In Texas, planarians, nematodes, oligochaetes, isopods, crayfish, insects, and amphibians were heavily preyed upon, but snails were the most common animals eaten (Punzo, 1974).

Yellow mud turtles collected in July usually show little or no new growth (Christiansen et al., 1985). This corresponds to the period of terrestrial estivation when feeding is usually curtailed. Feeding on land may occur, and *K. flavescens* may eat earthworms when beneath the soil surface (Moll, 1979).

PREDATORS AND DEFENSE: The black hawk (*Buteogallus*), fish, water snakes (*Nerodia*), and other turtles prey on hatchlings and juveniles. The nests are plundered by hognose snakes (*Heterodon*) and several species of mammals, particularly rodents, raccoons (*Procyon*) and skunks (*Mephitis*), and predator control greatly enhances nesting success (Christiansen and Gallaway, 1984). Humans seem to be the only important enemy of the adults, killing them on the roads and through habitat drainage and pesticide contamination (Flickinger and Mulhern, 1980).

In disposition these turtles are shy and retiring and seldom bite, but do expel their pungent musk.

POPULATIONS: Population sizes for *Kinosternon flavescens flavescens* vary with the suitability of the habitat and extent of the waterbody. Mahmoud (1969) estimated 27.9/ha of suitable habitat in an Oklahoma stream, and Iverson (1982a) calculated that this density would be equivalent to a biomass of 1.83 kg/ha. The male/female ratios of mature individuals at three Oklahoma localities were 0.7:1, 0.7:1, and 1.5:1; probably the sex ratio does not differ significantly from unity.

The numbers of turtles at four Missouri sites were 206 (pond), 34 (pond), 32 (slough), and 2 (canal) (Kofron and Schreiber, 1985). At the pond site where 34 turtles were caught, 20 were males, 12 females, and 2 of undetermined sex. Three other sites in Missouri had populations (Schnabel estimates) of 932 (655–1,610), 61 (43–101), and three turtles (Kangas, 1986a).

At a 1,050-ha Iowa site (Christiansen et al., 1985), Gazey and Staley (1986), using a sequential Bayes algorithm, estimated the population size to be 1,574 (410–3,470) turtles, but later estimates show this large population to consist of 2,925–3,207, or possibly more, *K. f. flavescens* (Christiansen et al., 1990). Population density of the entire tract was 2.79–3.05 turtles/ha, but as only about 33% of the total area was sampled (Christiansen et al., 1990), the density of the tract could have been as high as 8.37–9.15 turtles/ha. The increase in numbers apparently resulted from strict predator control, particularly of raccoons.

Density of *K. f. arizonense* in very small ponds may be extremely high. One 0.15-ha pond yielded 25 adults (estimated biomass, 58.3 kg/ha) in 45 minutes of trapping, and additional trapping would probably have caught more turtles (Iverson, 1989).

Most populations in Illinois were apparently always small, and the yellow mud turtle has disappeared from several localities in that state since the 1950s (Brown and Moll, 1979; Moll and Brown, 1976).

Despite temperature-dependent sex determination, cohort sex ratios in Nebraska are not significantly different from 1:1, nor do they seem to be correlated with annual midsummer air or soil temperatures (Iverson, 1991c).

Survivorship from egg to hatchling emergence the following spring in Nebraska is only 19% (Iverson, 1991a,c). This is due primarily to egg predation, but egg infertility, overwintering mortality, and death during migration from nest to water also account for small losses. The annual survivorship of Nebraska juveniles is 30–70%, and the survival rate increases to 90% by six years of age and 95% by the eighth year of life. Overall survivorship in two Missouri populations, estimated using age-frequency distributions, was 50–55% for *K. flavescens* five years or older, corresponding to a range of mortalities of 60–69%; age group estimates ranged from 17% for hatchlings to 100% for several age groups in several years (Kangas, 1986b).

REMARKS: *Kinosternon flavescens* is most closely related to *K. baurii* and *K. subrubrum* (Iverson, 1991b).

Additional references are listed in Seidel (1978b).

Kinosternon sonoriense Le Conte, 1854
Sonoran mud turtle

PLATE 21

RECOGNITION: *Kinosternon sonoriense* is a dark, medium-sized turtle with 11 scutes on the plastron, an elongated carapace, and a mottled pattern on the head, neck, and limbs. The carapace (to 17.5 cm) is smooth and many are depressed, but one or three low keels may be present (the two lateral keels usually disappear with age). The first vertebral touches four marginals. The posterior marginals are flared, and the tenth on each side is higher than either the ninth or eleventh. The carapace is olive-brown to dark brown with dark seams; venters of the marginals and the bridge are yellowish to brown with a dark mottled pattern. The plastron has two well-marked transverse hinges bordering the abdominal scutes; it is yellow to brown with dark-bordered seams. The skin is gray, and the head, neck, and limbs have mottled dark markings. Light-colored mottlings tend to form at least one pair of stripes on each side of the head (one extending above the tympanum and another below it to the corner of the mouth). The head is flattened with hooked, cream-colored jaws, which may bear dark flecks, and rather long chin barbels. All four feet are webbed.

The shorter males (to 15.5 cm) have concave plastra, long, thick, spine-tipped tails, and two patches of tilted scales on the inner surface of each hind leg. The larger females (to 17.5 cm) have short tails and flat plastra. Many males develop ventral melanism (Hulse, 1976b).

KARYOTYPE: Unknown.

FOSSIL HISTORY: Pleistocene (Rancholabrean) remains are known from Arizona and Sonora, Mexico (Moodie and Van Devender, 1974; Van Devender et al., 1985).

DISTRIBUTION: The Sonoran mud turtle ranges from the Lower Colorado and Bill Williams rivers in Arizona and California and eastward in the Gila River watershed to New Mexico, southward in Mexico to the Rio Yaqui basin of the continental divide, and eastward through the Rio Casas Grandes basin of northwestern Chihuahua (Iverson, 1981; Stebbins, 1985). A mud turtle observed at Pyramid Canyon, Clark County, Nevada, may have been this species (Stebbins, 1985).

GEOGRAPHIC VARIATION: Two subspecies have been described. *Kinosternon sonoriense sonoriense* Le Conte, 1854, the Sonoran mud turtle, lives in New Mexico, Arizona, California, Sonora, and western Chihuahua. It has a long interanal seam (19.5% of carapace length in males, 23.0% in females), a short interfemoral seam (10.1% of carapace length in both sexes), a first vertebral scute of medium width (24.4% of carapace length in males, 25.5% in females), and a relatively wide gular scute (20.0% of carapace length in males, 19.4% in females). *Kinosternon s. longifemorale* Iverson, 1981, the Sonoyta mud turtle, occurs only in the Sonoyta River basin in Arizona and adjacent Sonora, Mexico. It has a short interanal seam (14.4% of carapace length in males, 18.5% in females), a long interfemoral seam (12.8% of carapace length in males, 13.5 in females), a wide first vertebral scute (28.9% of carapace length in males, 28.8% in females), and a narrow gular scute (17.7% of carapace length in males, 17.8% in females).

CONFUSING SPECIES: *Kinosternon flavescens* has the ninth marginal higher than the eighth, and *K. hirtipes* has a strongly keeled carapace, which is arched as viewed from the front; neither has a posterior plastral notch. Species of *Sternotherus* have rectangular pectoral scutes and a single, poorly developed hinge.

Kinosternon sonoriense sonoriense

Anterior view of *Kinosternon sonoriense sonoriense*

HABITAT: This mud turtle occurs at elevations to 2,042 m in permanent streams, creeks, ditches, ponds, springs, and waterholes, usually in woodlands; only rarely does it enter temporary bodies of water. Degenhardt and Christiansen (1974) reported that New Mexican *K. sonoriense* may occasionally migrate considerable distances from one waterbody to another, as indicated by their presence in farm ponds as far as 8 km from permanent water.

BEHAVIOR: *Kinosternon sonoriense* may be active in all months (Iverson, 1981). In Tule Stream, Yavapai County, Arizona, Hulse (1976a) found individuals moving about on warm days in December and January, and estimated the annual activity cycle there to be about 340 days; however, populations at higher altitudes in Arizona may be forced to hibernate. *K. sonoriense* is diurnally active during the fall, winter, and spring, but becomes more nocturnal with the

Distribution of *Kinosternon sonoriense*

approach of hot summer weather (Hulse, 1974; 1976a).

It sometimes leaves the water to bask, particularly in cold-water habitats, but, judging from the amount of algal and epizoic attachment to its carapace (Hulse, 1976a), basking must be a rather rare event. Instead, most activity takes place on the bottom of the waterbody as it creeps along searching for food. Occasional rains stimulate sporadic movements overland, but it does not normally migrate very far, and probably has only a small home range. *K. sonoriense* congregates in waterholes during dry periods. Apparently it is harshly affected by dehydration, but closure of its plastron greatly inhibits water loss in air (Wygoda and Chmura, 1990).

REPRODUCTION: On the basis of sperm in the vas deferens, Hulse (1982) found that males at the Tule Stream site attained sexual maturity at five or six years of age at carapace lengths of 76–82 mm. Maturity was delayed at two other higher, cooler streams, however, where the smallest mature males were 91 mm (eight years old) and 97 and 98 mm (no age given), respectively.

The testes of this turtle undergo an annual cyclic change in weight reaching maximum size in June and then maintaining this size through August (Hulse, 1982). Testicular regression begins in September and the testes probably reach minimum size in January and early February. Rapid testicular growth then occurs and continues to June.

Hulse (1982) also studied the attainment of maturity and sexual cycles in female *Kinosternon sonoriense*. He considered females mature if follicles greater than 5 mm, enlarged oviducts, or corpora lutea were present. The largest immature female in the Tule Stream population had a 93-mm carapace and was eight years old. All females shorter than 93 mm were immature. The smallest mature female was also 93 mm long, but her age could not be determined owing to shell erosion. Several mature females were eight or nine years old and 96–99 mm long. As with males, females at a higher, cooler site mature later at a greater carapace length. The largest immature female collected there was 116 mm and probably 10–11 years of age. The smallest mature female was 130 mm and more than 12 years old. Elsewhere in Arizona, females may mature in six years with carapace lengths of at least 112 mm (Rosen, 1987).

Females from Tule Stream contain, to some degree,

Plastron of *Kinosternon sonoriense sonoriense*

Plastron of *Kinosternon sonoriense longifemorale*

follicles 5.0–9.9 mm in diameter throughout the year (Hulse, 1982). The female sexual cycle begins in March when follicles start enlarging to 10.0–12.9 mm in diameter as yolk is added. Rapid follicular growth continues until May when ovulatory size reaches 13–15 mm in diameter. By August these large follicles disappear. Follicles 10.0–12.9 mm in diameter are present until December when they begin to decrease in size and number, and by February, only follicles less than 10 mm in diameter are present.

Hulse thought this reduction in size was due to atresia. Turtles at Tule Stream contain oviducal eggs from June to September, but those at higher altitude have none after early July. No unshelled oviducal eggs were found, so shell deposition must occur almost immediately.

Hulse (1982) observed March courtship in captivity and copulation in nature in April at a water temperature of 21°C, and Iverson (1981) reported a May copulation at another Arizona site. The late July mating reported by Wiewandt et al. (1972) was not of *K. sonoriense,* but of *K. alamosae* instead (Iverson, pers. comm.).

Courtship varies little from that described by Mahmoud (1969) for other kinosternids (Hulse, 1982). A swimming male, with neck fully extended, approaches the female from the rear and forces his neck under her anal scutes, presumably to test her sexual odor. This procedure lifts the female off the bottom of the pond. If she moves away the male chases her, but if she remains motionless he approaches and gently nudges the posterior portion of her plastron with his head. When a chase occurs, the necks of both animals are fully extended, and whenever she stops the male nudges her. Finally, when the female is receptive and remains stationary, the male mounts from the rear with his forelegs clutching the female's carapace near the bridge.

In Arizona, nesting begins in late May and continues through September at lower elevations, but ceases in July at higher sites (Hulse, 1982). Females at Tule Stream are capable of laying two clutches of two to four eggs each year; clutch size for non-Tule females is two to nine eggs (Hulse, 1982). Elsewhere, however, up to four clutches of 1–11 eggs may be laid a year (Iverson, pers. comm.). The white eggs are elliptical (28–35 × 13.8–19.0 mm) with calcareous, brittle shells. Typically, they weigh 4.2–5.6 g (Iverson, 1992c). The shell surface is granular in texture and pitted with small irregular pores. The correlation between female shell length and size of individual eggs is positive (Hulse, 1982). The eggs undergo embryonic diapause and require chilling before development begins. This lengthens the developmental period to almost a year, possibly as an adaptation to synchronize hatching during the next summer's rainy season (Iverson, pers. comm.). Eggs incubated by Ewert (1991) did not begin to develop until 265 days after oviposition and hatched after 345 days.

Hatchlings are only a little longer than wide. One figured by Agassiz (1857) was 28.5 mm in carapace length, 24.0 mm in carapace width, 14.0 mm in depth, 23.5 mm in plastron length, and 14.5 mm in plastron width. The smallest Sonoran mud turtles measured by Iverson (1981) were 22.3–25.7 mm in carapace length (plastra, 18.3–20.0 mm). The carapace of most hatchlings has a low, broad central keel and two elongated lateral ridges, the upper posterior edge of each marginal has a black smudge, and the tenth marginal is not noticeably elevated. The plastral seams are dark bordered. Head stripes are distinctly yellow in hatchlings and juveniles.

Hatchling sex is temperature dependent, with a higher proportion of females produced at higher temperatures (Iverson, pers. comm.).

GROWTH AND LONGEVITY: Populations differ in growth rate (depending on the size and age of attainment of sexual maturity), as do sexes in a given population (Hulse, 1976b). Males grow at a slower rate and reach a shorter maximum size than females. In both sexes growth rates slow abruptly at the onset of sexual maturity. At Tule Stream the annual increase in linear carapace length is 1.57 mm for mature males and 1.50 mm for mature females; growth rates of both sexes are similar through the first four years (Hulse, 1976b). Multivariate comparison of continuous shell characters indicates that the shell shape of *K. sonoriense* is highly correlated with its length and strongly allometric (McCord et al., 1990).

A *K. sonoriense* of unknown sex lived 36 years, 6 months and a day at the Baltimore Zoo (Snider and Bowler, 1992); however, Iverson has told us that some wild individuals probably live more than 40 years.

FOOD HABITS: Sonoran mud turtles in central Arizona are basically carnivorous, opportunistic feeders, with a shift to omnivorous feeding in streams with poor benthic faunas (Hulse, 1974). While foraging, *Kinosternon sonoriense* creeps slowly and methodically over the bottom in shallow water with its neck fully extended. As it moves along the head is swung back and forth to search the substrate for prey. In soft substrates, such as mud, the head will often be partly covered. Vision and odor seem to be the main cues in prey detection. When potential prey is discovered, the turtle partially retracts its head and then makes a rapid lunge, often moving its entire body forward. If the prey is small it is swallowed whole, but if large, it must be torn apart or chewed before swallowing. Foraging turtles surface to breathe every 5–10 minutes.

Kinosternon sonoriense is predominantly a diurnal feeder in the spring and fall, but shifts to nocturnal foraging during the hot summer weather. Little feeding occurs in the colder months of December and January, and perhaps resorption of ovarian follicles helps supply necessary energy to females (Hulse, 1982).

Plant material consisting of aquatic angiosperms, green algae, and *Chara* constitutes about 18% of the total food volume (Hulse, 1974); however the amount of plant material consumed varies between populations. Animals make up about 82% of the total food volume. Most prey are benthic dwellers or attached to submerged vegetation: water bugs (Naucoridae) constitute about 4% of the total volume. Insects are found in about one third of the stomachs. Other animals eaten are snails (*Physa*), crayfish, fish, and frogs (*Rana*). Ostracods are also heavily consumed when seasonally available.

Captives readily eat earthworms, fresh and canned fish, and various kinds of meat.

PREDATORS AND DEFENSE: Introduced bullfrogs (*Rana catesbeiana*) prey on young *Kinosternon sonoriense,* and the eggs and juveniles are probably also eaten by a host of mammals and birds. Archeological evidence from southern Arizona indicates that Indians ate *K. sonoriense* (Schneider and Everson, 1989), and the modern practices of irrigation and water diversion are damaging its habitat.

This species is shy, and those we have kept have seldom attempted to bite, but instead pull into the shell if disturbed. The expulsion of musk also ceases after a short time in captivity.

POPULATIONS: At Tule Stream, Arizona, Hulse (1982) estimated the population size to be between 315 and 328 individuals using two different methods. The study site encompassed about 0.4 ha of suitable habitat, so the population density was 750–825/ha. Iverson (1982a) estimated the biomass of this population to be approximately 100.3 kg/ha. Of the 190 *Kinosternon sonoriense* marked, 79 (41.5%) were mature males, 40 (21.0%) were mature females, and 71 (37.5%) were juveniles. The estimated numbers of mature males, females, and juveniles based on recapture data were 136, 69, and 123, respectively.

REMARKS: *Kinosternon sonoriense* is closely related to the Mexican species *K. leucostomum, K. scorpioides,* and, especially, *K. hirtipes* (Frair, 1972; Seidel et al., 1986; Iverson, 1991b).

Additional references on *K. sonoriense* may be found in Iverson (1976) and Iverson and Iverson (1980).

Kinosternon hirtipes (Wagler, 1830)
Mexican mud turtle
PLATE 22

RECOGNITION: This chiefly Mexican species has 11 scutes on the plastron, an elevated tricarinate carapace (to 18.5 cm), and commonly a finely reticulated head pattern. The oval carapace is smooth and is less than twice as broad as deep. The well-developed medial keel appears somewhat arched when viewed from the front, and it slopes gently anteriorly but rather abruptly posteriorly, forming a hump over the sacral region. The first vertebral touches the second marginals. The marginals are narrow except for the tenth, which is elevated, and those posterior to the bridge are somewhat flared. The carapace is olive to brown with distinctly black-bordered seams. The plastron is short and narrow, with the hind lobe narrower or the same width as the front lobe. Two well-developed hinges border the abdominal scutes. The plastron ranges from brown to tan, and the seams are bordered with darker brown. The gular scute is twice as long as the interhumeral seam and more than half as long as the anterior lobe of the plastron. The bridge is rather short. The limbs are gray to tan. The head and neck are tan to black, with light reticulations if black or with dark reticulations or spotting if tan. The large adult nasal scale is commonly forked posteriorly. The jaws are tan to gray and may be finely streaked with dark brown or black. The chin bears three pairs of barbels. All four feet are webbed.

Males have long, thick tails, rough scale patches on the back of the thigh and crus, dark chins, shorter concave plastra, and the posterior marginals more flared than those of females. Females have lighter chins. Iverson (1985b) discussed geographic variation in sexual size dimorphism in this species.

KARYOTYPE: The diploid chromosome number is 56: 26 macrochromosomes and 30 microchromosomes (Killebrew, 1975).

FOSSIL RECORD: Alvarez (1975) reported fossil remains of *K. hirtipes* from a cave at Tepeyolo, Puebla, Mexico, but, as *K. hirtipes* is not present in the region, these are probably either *K. herrerai* or *K. integrum,* which do live there (Iverson, pers. comm.).

DISTRIBUTION: *Kinosternon hirtipes* ranges from the Big Bend Presidio County, Texas, and Chihuahua, Mexico, south and east on the Mexican Plateau to the Chapala, Zapotlán, San Juanico, Pátzcuaro, and Valle de México basins of southern Mexico at elevations of 800–2,600 m (Iverson, 1985a).

GEOGRAPHIC VARIATION: Six subspecies are recognized (Iverson, 1981), all but one limited to Mexico. *Kinosternon hirtipes murrayi* Glass and Hartweg, 1951, the Big Bend mud turtle, barely reaches the United States in Presidio County, Texas. Its description is presented above.

CONFUSING SPECIES: In *Kinosternon flavescens,* the ninth marginal is elevated above the eighth; the shell of *K. sonoriense* is more than twice as broad as deep, and its nasal scale is not posteriorly forked. Musk turtles of the genus *Sternotherus* have a small plastron with a single, poorly developed hinge and rectangular pectoral scutes. See Conant and Berry (1978) and Ernst and Barbour (1989) for additional characters separating these species.

HABITAT: This mud turtle usually inhabits permanent bodies of water in mesquite grasslands, such as marshes, lakes, ponds, streams or rivers. In Texas, it seems only to live in spring-fed cattle tanks.

BEHAVIOR: Little is known of the life history of this turtle. It is highly aquatic and thought to be

197

Kinosternon hirtipes murrayi

Anterior view of *Kinosternon hirtipes murrayi*

chiefly nocturnal. Frederick R. Gehlbach (pers. comm.) found Mexican mud turtles in Texas to be most active between 2100 and 2400, but J. B. Iverson has told us that those from Chihuahua are predominantly diurnal with some nocturnal foraging.

Beltz (1954b) reported that a captive adult female kept in southern California escaped and overwintered under a pile of leaves and debris without ill effect. He thought this same individual, when placed out of water in the sun, became uneasy and seemed to search for water. Seidel and Reynolds (1980) found that *K. hirtipes* consistently demonstrated a greater rate of evaporative water loss than the more terrestrial *K. flavescens,* and thought the greater degree of keratinization of the horny epidermal layer of the skin may account for the superior ability of *K. flavescens* to withstand cutaneous water loss.

REPRODUCTION: Females mature in six to eight years at 95–100-mm carapace length (Iverson et

Posterior view of *Kinosternon hirtipes murrayi;* note medial keel

Plastron of *Kinosternon hirtipes murrayi*

al., 1991). Ovulation occurs from early May to late September. Nothing has been reported on the attainment of maturity by males, their sex cycle, or courtship patterns.

In Mexico the nesting season varies by locality from May until September (Iverson, 1981; Iverson et al., 1991), with two to four clutches of one to seven (usually three) elliptical, white, brittle-shelled eggs laid each year (Ernst and Barbour, 1972; Iverson, 1981; Iverson et al., 1991). Most females lay two clutches by July. Clutch size is positively correlated with female shell length and mass. Ewert (1979a) reported that an average egg measured 28 × 17 mm, but Iverson (1981) and Iverson et al. (1991) found average egg dimensions at several Mexican localities to be 24.2–33.2 × 14.6–18.6 mm. Egg mass averages 4.8 g (3.8–6.6). Egg length is not correlated with female size, but egg width and mass are positively correlated with female shell length and mass. Egg width and mass are negatively correlated with clutch size (Iverson et al., 1991). M. J. Packard et al. (1984a) noted that the mean thickness of the eggshell was 0.28 mm.

Distribution of *Kinosternon hirtipes*

Hatchlings are 20–27 mm in carapace length and 17–19 mm in plastron length. The hatchling carapace is brown, and the plastron bears red or orange marks. Incubation period at 29°C is 196–201 days (Rudloff, 1986); the eggs undergo embryonic diapause until they are chilled (Ewert, 1985, 1991).

GROWTH AND LONGEVITY: Males grow faster and larger than females by age five (Iverson et al., 1991). Iverson (1981) reported that Mexican *K. hirtipes* less than one year of age had carapace lengths of 22.8–26.5 mm and plastra 16.8–18.9 mm long. Frederick R. Gehlbach (pers. comm.) found the following plastron lengths for Texas *K. hirtipes* with countable growth annuli: two- to three-year juveniles, 51–70 mm; five- to six-year males, 116–121 mm; a six-year female, 109 mm; and a nine-year male, 125 mm. Ernst and Barbour (1972) showed that the plastral growth rate of a 13-year-old, 128-mm male, wild caught in Texas, began to slow at about seven years of age, and almost stopped between 10 and 13 years. In a Chihuahuan population adult turtles larger than 90-mm carapace length grew an average of only 0.78 mm/year (Iverson et al., 1991). Mean plastron lengths of males two to eight years old from this population were, respectively, 55.2, 67.6, 78.7, 83.7,

83.0, 86.7, and 91.7 mm; of females two to seven years of age, 51.1, 63.5, 74.7, 79.0, 85.0, and 89.2 mm.

Multivariate comparisons of continuous shell characters indicate that shell shape in *K. hirtipes* is highly correlated with shell length and therefore allometric (McCord et al., 1990).

The longevity of *K. hirtipes* is unknown.

FOOD HABITS: In Mexico this turtle is almost completely carnivorous, feeding primarily on snails, aquatic insects, and crustaceans, but also taking worms, fish, and amphibians (Iverson, pers. comm.). Captives readily eat canned and fresh fish. Legler (1960b) reported that *K. hirtipes* are attracted to nets baited with canned sardines in soybean oil.

PREDATORS AND DEFENSE: Unknown.

POPULATIONS: Frederick R. Gehlbach (pers. comm.) collected six adults (two females 109–122 mm in plastron length, four males 116–125 mm) and two juveniles (51–70 mm), and observed three other individuals in a 580-m², 4-m-deep, *Chara*-choked stock pond in Texas. This is a density of 189.5/ha, and a biomass of about 47.2 kg/ha (Iverson, 1982a).

Kinosternon hirtipes is very common in the streams

and arroyos in the vicinity of Yepómera, Chihuahua, and probably throughout most of the high Sierra Madre in Chihuahua (Van Devender and Lowe, 1977). It inhabits the Rio Papigochic watershed west of the continental divide, but is apparently replaced by *K. integrum* to the west in Sonora where the river becomes the Rio Yaqui.

In the Rio Grande at Lajitas, Brewster County, Texas, *Trionyx spinifera emoryi* was the most abundant turtle, *Trachemys gaigeae* was uncommon, and *K. hirtipes* was rare, and about the same situation prevailed in the Rio Conchos, about 1.5 km northwest of Ojinaga, Chihuahua. However, at the junction of the Rio San Pedro and the Rio Conchos in Chihuahua, *K. hirtipes* was the dominant turtle (Legler, 1960b).

Williams et al. (1960) found a similar situation in the Rio Florida, 1.3 km east of La Cruz, Chihuahua, where they collected 17 *K. hirtipes* and only two each of *Trionyx s. emoryi* and *Trachemys gaigeae*.

REMARKS: Seidel et al. (1986) have shown by electrophoretic allele studies and subsequent phenetic and cladistic analyses that *Kinosternon hirtipes* is most closely related to *K. flavescens, K. herrerai,* and the *K. scorpoides* group, but additional research by Iverson (1991b) indicates that *K. hirtipes* and *K. sonoriense* are parapatric.

Iverson (1985a) reviewed the literature on this species. Studies are needed on the ecology and behavior of this turtle.

Emydidae:
Semiaquatic pond and marsh turtles

The Emydidae is the largest family of living turtles, with 33 genera and almost 100 species (the exact number is debatable). Today it is represented in the Americas, Europe, and Africa, and the fossil record indicates that it was formerly more widespread in Europe than at present. The oldest fossil emydids are *Gyremys sectabilis* from the Upper Cretaceous Judith River Formation of Montana and *Clemmys backmani* from the Paleocene Ravenscrag Formation of Big Muddy Valley, Saskatchewan. Another genus, *Echmatemys,* is known from Eocene deposits in North America. Thirty-one species in nine genera live today in the United States and Canada.

The carapace forms a low arch in most members of the Emydidae but it may be considerably domed in some species. A vertebral keel may be present or absent, and some species also have a pair of lateral keels. Dorsal rib heads are well developed. Carapace and plastron are commonly united by a broad bridge. The plastron is large, and in several genera may bear a moveable hinge between or near the seam separating the pectoral and abdominal scutes. Mesoplastral bones are absent, as are intergular and inframarginal scutes. Skulls are relatively small and similar to those of the batagurines (Bataguridae) and tortoises (Testudinidae). The temporal region of the skull is widely emarginated posteriorly preventing squamosal-parietal contact. The frontal bone enters the orbit, and the postorbital is wider than that found in Testudinidae. The maxilla and quadratojugal are separated, and the quadrate is exposed posteriorly. The premaxillae commonly do not meet to form a hooklike process. The triturating surface of the upper jaw varies from broad to narrow, and may be ridged. There is a tendency toward the development of a secondary palate. A vestigial splenial bone may be present. Limbs are developed for swimming, and have at least remnants of toe webbing. The second and third digits commonly bear more than two phalanges, and the femoral trochanteric fossa is reduced. In the pelvic girdle, the pubis normally touches the ischium of the same side; however, cartilage along the ventral midline of the girdle prevents the pubis and ischium from touching those from the other side.

Formerly the family was divided into two subfamilies, but the subfamily Batagurinae was elevated to full family rank by Gaffney and Meylan (1988). The remaining species (the former subfamily Emydinae), except those of the European genus *Emys,* are entirely New World ranging from southern Canada to South America with representatives on some of the West Indies.

Two complexes seem to exist in the former Emydinae (McDowell, 1964; Bramble, 1974b; Gaffney and Meylan 1988; Seidel and Adkins, 1989). The *Clemmys* complex includes the genera *Clemmys, Emydoidea, Terrapene,* and the Old World *Emys.* The plastron of *Clemmys* is rigid, but that of the other three genera is hinged and movable. *Clemmys* is thought to be ancestral to the hinged forms of which *Emys* is most primitive, *Emydoidea* intermediate, and *Terrapene* most derived (Bramble, 1974b). These turtles have the triturating surfaces of the jaws narrow and ridgeless with the upper triturating surface lacking parts of the palatine or pterygoid bones. The orbitonasal foramen is small. The interorbital region is coarsely sculptured, and the postorbital bar is relatively wide. The jugal bone does not touch the palatine. On the plastron, the humero-pectoral seam crosses the entoplastron. The cervical vertebrae are not elongated in *Clemmys, Emys,* or *Terrapene,* but are in *Emydoidea,* in which also the cervical extensor muscles are hypertrophied. Musk glands are present in all four genera, and they share an electrophoretic myoglobin band not found in the second complex (Seidel and Adkins, 1989). Formerly, *Emydoidea* was included in a separate complex with the genus *Deirochelys* (Loveridge and Williams, 1957; McDowell, 1964). The two genera share similar neck, jaw, and rib structure, but these are probably convergent features related to similar feeding mechanisms (Bramble, 1974b). Also, D. R. Jackson's (1978b) studies on fossil *Deirochelys* and the electrophoretic studies of Seidel and Adkins (1989) indicate that it is more closely related to the genera of the *Chrysemys* complex.

The *Chrysemys* complex includes the freshwater genera *Chrysemys, Trachemys, Pseudemys, Deirochelys, Graptemys,* and the brackish-water genus *Malaclemys*. All have a rigid plastron with the humero-pectoral seam crossing posterior to the entoplastron. The triturating surface is commonly broad (narrow in *Deirochelys*), with or without ridges, and with the upper surface containing parts of the palatine or pterygoid bones (except in *Deirochelys*). The orbitonasal foramen is commonly much larger than the posterior palatine foramen (but not as large in *Deirochelys*). The interorbital region is not coarsely sculptured, and the postorbital bar is not wide. Jugals and palatines touch. With the exception of *Deirochelys,* the cervical vertebrae are not elongated, nor the cervical extensor muscles hypertrophied. Musk glands are present. Members of this complex share an electrophoretic myoglobin band not found in the *Clemmys* complex (Seidel and Adkins, 1989).

Seidel and Adkins (1989) believe that the distinct patterns of myoglobin polymorphism suggest dividing the family Emydidae into two subfamilies, representing the two generic complexes; the Emydinae (*Clemmys, Terrapene, Emydoidea, Emys*) and the Deirochelyinae (*Deirochelys, Chrysemys, Trachemys, Pseudemys, Graptemys, Malaclemys*) as originally proposed on morphological grounds by Gaffney and Meylan (1988).

Clemmys guttata (Schneider, 1792)
Spotted turtle
PLATE 23

RECOGNITION: This small black turtle has a pattern of small, round yellow spots on its broad, smooth, keelless, unserrated, to 12.5-cm carapace. The spots are transparent "windows" in the scutes overlying deposits of yellow pigment (Yerkes, 1905), which may fade with age so that some older turtles are spotless (a few hatchlings and small juveniles may also be spotless or nearly so). The ventral surface of the marginals is yellow, and young individuals have a pattern of black blotches at its outer edge. The bridge is marked with an elongated black mark. The yellow or yellow-orange plastron has a large black blotch on each scute. With age, melanism increases until the entire plastron may be black in older turtles. The black head is moderate in size, has a notched upper jaw, and many are spotted. A broken yellow band is near the tympanum and another may extend posteriorly from the orbit. Skin on the upper surfaces of the neck, limbs, and tail is gray to black with scattered yellow spots on the neck and limbs. Skin on the lower surface of the limbs can be orange, pink, or salmon-red.

Males have tan chins, brown eyes, slightly concave plastra, and long, thick tails with the vent beyond the carapacial rim. Females have yellow chins, orange eyes, a flat or convex plastron, and shorter tails with the vent beneath the posterior marginals (Blake, 1922; Grant, 1935). The sexual dichromatism can already be seen in hatchlings. Unlike other members of the genus, female *C. guttata* are, on average, larger than males (Gibbons and Lovich, 1990).

KARYOTYPE: Diploid chromosomes total 50: 8 pairs of macrochromosomes with median to submedian centromeres, 5 pairs of macrochromosomes with terminal to subterminal centromeres, and 12 pairs of microchromosomes (Bickham, 1975, 1976).

FOSSIL RECORD: The only reported fossil *C. guttata* is an approximately 5,800-year-old, mid-Holocene epiplastron from Shiawassee County, Michigan (Holman, 1990), but there are Pleistocene (Rancholabrean) carapacial elements from South Carolina in the South Carolina State Museum, Columbia (James L. Knight, pers. comm.). Archeological records exist for Louisiana (Kozuch, 1989), Illinois , Michigan, and Wisconsin (Adler, 1968).

DISTRIBUTION: *Clemmys guttata* ranges from southern Ontario, Quebec (Cook et al., 1980) and Maine southward along the Atlantic Coastal Plain and Piedmont to northern Florida (Berry and Gidden, 1973; Banicki, 1981), and westward through Ontario, New York, Pennsylvania, central Ohio, northern Indiana, and Michigan to northeastern Illinois. The Illinois population has declined until relatively few spotted turtles now exist in that state (Johnson, 1983), and the numbers of *C. guttata* are also dropping in other Midwestern states (J. Harding, pers. comm.).

GEOGRAPHIC VARIATION: No subspecies have been described. Morphological variation between spotted turtle populations is not significant (Laemmerzahl, 1990), but differences exist in the light pigmentation (cream, yellow, orange, or pinkish) of the skin (Ernst, pers. obs.).

CONFUSING SPECIES: *Emydoidea blandingii* has a hinged plastron and bright yellow chin and throat. Older unspotted spotted turtles may be confused with *C. muhlenbergii*, but the latter has a slightly keeled carapace and a large orange blotch on each side of the head.

HABITAT: Spotted turtles occupy a wide variety of shallow wetland habitats including swamps, bogs, fens, wet pastures, marshes, the edges of Carolina bays and ponds, tidally influenced brackish streams, and small woodland streams (Finneran,

Plastron of *Clemmys guttata*

Male *Clemmys guttata*

1948; Nemuras, 1966). Habitat requirements include soft substrate and some aquatic vegetation. In some parts of the range and during certain times of the year, *C. guttata* spends considerable time on land (Ward et al., 1976).

BEHAVIOR: Spotted turtles are active during daylight hours (only nesting females are active after dark). As darkness approaches they burrow into the mud bottom of the wetland or crawl into mammal burrows or under vegetation and become inactive until dawn. Activity begins at sunrise, with turtles basking until warm or foraging for food. During periods of cool weather they spend more time basking and less time foraging, and few are active during rainy weather. Daily activity peaks vary from around noon in March to early morning later in the summer (Ernst, 1976).

Clemmys guttata has one of the shorter annual activity cycles of North American turtles. The seasonal cycles of spotted turtles in Maryland, Pennsylvania,

Female *Clemmys guttata*

Ohio, and South Carolina were contrasted and compared by Lovich (1988a). Levels of activity, as measured by frequency of capture, were highest in the spring for all populations. Activity levels peak in May for all states except South Carolina, which peaks in March, and decline in June for all states except South Carolina, which begins to decline in April. Percentages of spotted turtles captured between March and May in Maryland, Pennsylvania, and Ohio were 74%, 68%, and 93%, respectively. In South Carolina 50% of yearly captures were in February and March. Statistically significant differences in seasonal activity were detected between all possible pairs of states except for Pennsylvania vs. Maryland. Differences between South Carolina and other states are due largely to low levels of activity from April to July in South Carolina.

Clemmys guttata is most active in the cooler parts of the year. Activity levels reach a peak when mean monthly air temperature is between 13.1 and 18.0°C (mean 15.5), at least two months before the month with the highest mean air temperature. Activity then declines when mean monthly air temperature is between 17.8 and 22.3°C (mean 20.3), and then approaches or reaches a minimum level during the month with the highest mean air temperature. Activity peaks seem to be associated with temperatures at which feeding occurs. In spite of favorable temperatures in the fall, spotted turtles do not become active in large numbers until the following spring, possibly owing to decreased food supplies (see also Ward et al.,

1976). Spotted turtles become dormant when the water temperature reaches 32°C. At this time they enter estivation in muskrat burrows or the bottom of pools of running water (Ernst, 1976; Kiviat, 1978b).

Cloacal temperature of active spotted turtles from Lancaster County, Pennsylvania, range from 3 to 32°C (mean 20.16; Ernst, 1982b). The 3°C cloacal temperature of a male crawling slowly beneath the ice in shallow water is apparently the lowest known for an active turtle. As expected for an ectotherm, cloacal temperatures are closely correlated with environmental temperatures. Spotted turtles initiate activity at water temperatures as low as 3°C in the early spring. They become dormant at water temperatures of about 30°C, and shift their diel activity cycle from afternoon to morning as summer approaches. Some individuals begin to feed when water temperatures reach 14°C, and mating occurs at cloacal temperatures as low as 8°C in water of 8.5°C. Males feed and are generally more active than females in waters of cooler temperatures: a probable result of females remaining active longer into the warmer part of the annual cycle. Mean cloacal temperatures (°C) associated with other activities are as follows: basking, 21.50; moving in water, 19.29; moving on land, 21.00; dormant in water (high temperature), 21.93; dormant in water (low temperature), 9.75; and nesting females, 23.50 (Ernst, 1982b). The highest cloacal temperature recorded by Ernst (1982b), 32°C, is much lower than the mean critical thermal maximum of 41.98°C recorded for the species by Hutchison et al. (1966).

Distribution of *Clemmys guttata*

Spotted turtles express a unimodal rhythm of locomotor activity when acclimated and tested at 15°C, and a bimodal rhythm at 25°C (Graham and Hutchison, 1979a). Under cyclic thermal acclimation between 15 and 25°C, activity is unimodal with a peak before noon and an afternoon minimum coinciding with an ambient temperature peak. *Clemmys guttata* are most active under long photoperiods of 16 hours light and 8 hours dark, and least active under photoperiods of 8 hours light and 16 hours dark (Graham and Hutchison, 1979a).

At temperatures between 10 and 29°C and relative humidities between 45 and 95%, spotted turtles lose about 0.11% of their weight per hour when deprived of food and water. After five days, individuals under these conditions lose about 8.9% of their original weight. This water-loss gradient is intermediate between *Terrapene carolina* and *Clemmys insculpta* (Ernst, 1968b).

Seasonal microhabitat selection of a population of spotted turtles in Maryland was studied by Ward et al. (1976). They tagged 105 turtles with small radioactive markers that allowed location with a radiation detection device from up to 10 m away. In early May *C. guttata* occupies puddles and flooded areas in fields and ecotones between forest and marsh. Water depth

at these sites is 8–10 cm and they contain grasses, algae, and leaves. Starting in mid-May the turtles leave the pools (in response to drying and increasing water temperatures) and burrow into mats of decaying vegetation at the edges of fields. From May through July turtles crawl into their "forms" for several days of estivation and then emerge to reoccupy flooded areas.

Most sites occupied by estivating turtles are located in early successional paludal woods. The form microhabitat is characterized by heavy organic soils, shallow water, and an overstory of dense leaves, grasses, and ferns. The forms used by *C. guttata* are usually filled with water so that only the top of the carapace is above the surface. Spotted turtles in Pennsylvania use muskrat burrows in the banks of shallow streams, muskrat lodges, or the soft substrate of streams deeper than 20 cm to both estivate and hibernate (Ernst, 1982b). In a Maryland study, Ward et al. (1976) found most spotted turtles hibernating in puddles that were irregularly shaped, usually about 4.6 m in longest dimension, and from 0.6 to 0.9 m deep near the center. They selected positions under 10–15 cm of water near the edge of the pools. Sporadic activity continued until March when the turtles became active in large numbers.

Clemmys guttata in South Carolina behave similarly

to those from Maryland (Ward et al., 1976). David Scott (pers. comm.) of the Savannah River Ecology Laboratory has noted migrations of spotted turtles into Carolina bays in the month of March. These turtles may have been emerging from hibernation sites in adjacent woodlands. Spotted turtles in Pennsylvania have been reported to migrate to and from hibernation sites (Netting, 1936; Ernst, 1976).

Spotted turtles may hibernate in congregations of up to 12 conspecifics (Bloomer, 1978). Bloomer (1978) also found 5 *C. guttata* and 12 *C. insculpta* hibernating within the burrow complex of a muskrat (*Ondatra zibethica*) at a site in New Jersey, and seven *C. guttata* hibernating in November under about a meter of water in a dilapidated spring house. Hibernacula in Pennsylvania are located in the soft bottoms of streams 10–25 cm deep. These sites never freeze completely, but are shallow enough to thaw quickly in the spring Ernst (1982b). Warm days during the winter may bring spotted turtles temporarily out of hibernation (Belmore, 1980; Legere, 1989).

Clemmys guttata has some homing ability. Ernst (1968a) collected 25 adults of each sex during the spring at a site in Pennsylvania. Each individual was transported in a lightproof container 0.31 km upstream from the point of capture and released. The study area was searched, and turtles recaptured within 27 m of the original point of capture were considered to have homed. Eight females and six males homed, and four males and three females were observed within 27–73 m of their original points of capture. Three turtles returned to within 1.5 m of the point of first capture. There was no significant difference between the number of returns for each sex.

The home ranges of male and female spotted turtles in Pennsylvania are not significantly different (Ernst, 1970a). Both males and females have mean home ranges of 0.50–0.53 ha. Normal daily movements of spotted turtles in Pennsylvania are usually less than 20 m. Foraging turtles may move up to 50 m, and males may move up to 250 m away from water. Nesting females may travel up to 50 m from water in search of a suitable nesting site (Ernst, 1976).

Spring movement patterns of two radio-tagged male spotted turtles in an extensive South Carolina aquatic system in 24-hour periods ranged from 0 to 423 m (Lovich, 1990a). Of all daily changes in location, 22% were greater than 100 m. Rates of movement reached 20.7 m/h (mean 2.7). Total distance moved by each turtle from 6 March to 23 April was 2.75 and 1.84 km, respectively. Straight-line distances from the original points of capture were more than a kilometer for both turtles. During the study each animal occupied three separate aquatic habitats, staying in each pond or marsh 4–20 days before moving to another. Overland movements lasted up to two days. Return to a previously occupied aquatic habitat was observed only once during the study. In view of these extensive movements, the short movements reported for Pennsylvania males by Ernst (1970a) are unusual, inasmuch as males of many turtle species move greater distances and more often than females, perhaps to increase reproductive success (Morreale et al., 1984), but Ernst's total study area contained only about 3.2 ha of habitat suitable for *C. guttata*, and further movement was restricted by cultivated fields. The local habitat must be considered when interpreting movement data.

REPRODUCTION: Both sexes mature by the time they grow to a carapace length of 8.0 cm, probably in about 7–10 years (Ernst, 1970b; Ernst and Zug, in press).

The sexual cycle of males from southeastern Pennsylvania was described by Ernst and Zug (in press). In March, at the time of spring emergence, the spermatogenic cycle is at a low ebb. The seminiferous tubules are thin-walled with a single layer of spermatogonia and Sertoli cells locally along the basement membrane; the tubule lumen may be empty or contain small, diffuse clusters of cell debris. The spermatogenic cycle remains in regression during April. Spermatogenic activity begins in May. The tubule lumens remain large and open; the spermatogonia are actively dividing and the primary spermatocytes lie in two to four layers with the exception of the single basal layer of spermatogonia. In June, the lumens remain open although compressed by the many layers of germ cells. By July some lumen are packed with secondary spermatocytes and small clusters of transforming spermatids, suggesting that some spermiogenesis occurs as the germ cells move downward through the tubules. Aggregations of spermatozoa occur in Sertoli plumes embedded in the germ cell layers, not in the lumens. Spermatogenesis and spermiogenesis conclude in August. The tubule walls consist mainly of spermatozoa plumes arising from a one- or two-cell-thick layer of secondary spermatocytes above the basal spermatogonia; the lumens are large and broadly open with many small clusters of spermatozoa. Tubules begin to regress in September. The lumens contain loose and diffuse aggregations of cell debris and spermatozoa; tubules have thin ragged walls, sparsely populated with spermatogonia and secondary spermatocytes. Seminiferous tubule enlargement matches the spermatogenic cycle, reaching a maximum in July and rapidly declining thereafter.

The ovarian cycle of female *C. guttata* is similar to that of other North American emydid turtles (Ernst and Zug, in press). Commonly four size classes of follicles occur in mature females with or without oviducal eggs: class I, <2 mm diameter, previtellogenic; class II, 2.0–5.9 mm, early vitellogenic; class III, 6.0–9.9 mm, midvitellogenic; and class IV, 10.0+ mm, late vitellogenic phase. Shelled oviducal eggs are found only in May. Class IV follicles occur in April–June and August, and class III follicles in April–May and September females. All females have class I and II follicles. More than 10 class I follicles are found on each ovary; in contrast, seldom more than three class II follicles are found on each ovary. Of three females with oviducal eggs examined by Ernst and Zug (in press), one had both class III and IV follicles, another only class III follicles, and the third only class IV follicles. Clutch size varied from three to four oviducal eggs, but examination showed three to five class IV follicles.

The timing of the mating season varies geographically. In Ontario, mating has been reported on 30 May and 17 June (Chippindale, 1989), but courtship behavior in Pennsylvania begins in March and lasts into June (Ernst, 1970b, 1982b; Ernst and Zug, in press). Mating may occur in either the morning or the afternoon. Water and air temperatures during courtship range from 8.8 to 18.9°C, and 10.0 to 22.3°C, respectively. Courtship involves frantic chases of a female by one or more males, covering 30–50 m, and lasting from 15 to 30 minutes. Courtship activity takes place in shallow water and adjacent land. Males sometimes bite the female's legs and tail, and may even bite each other while pursuing a female.

When the pursuit is over the male mounts the female from the rear, grasping her carapace and placing his tail under hers. Occasionally the male slides off the female giving the copulating pair an L-shaped appearance (Ernst, 1967c). Copulation usually takes place in the water (Ernst, 1967c, 1970b) and may take as long as an hour to complete (Ernst, pers. obs.), although Chippindale (1989) reported it lasting only two or three minutes. Mating aggregations of up to 16 turtles (including four copulating pairs, one clasping pair, and three pairs of unpaired males and females) have been reported (Ernst, 1967c).

Ernst (1983) reported a hybrid mating between a female *C. muhlenbergii* and a male *C. guttata* under free-living conditions that resulted in a female offspring with traits of both parents.

The egg-laying season lasts from May to July,

varying geographically (Adler, 1961; Ernst, 1970b; Chippindale, 1989; Ernst and Zug, in press). Nests are dug in well-drained areas exposed to full sunlight. Nest sites include grass tussocks, hummocks of moist sphagnum moss, and the loamy soil of marshy pastures (Ernst, 1970b; Belmore, 1980; Chippindale, 1989).

Nesting takes place either in the late afternoon or evening, or in the morning (Adler, 1961; Ernst, 1970b; Chippindale, 1989; Ernst and Zug, in press). In southeastern Pennsylvania, 50% of the females nested in the morning (most before 0900) and 50% in the later afternoon after 1700 (most after 1800) (Ernst and Zug, in press). Female spotted turtles may repeatedly smell the ground when searching for a nest site. The flask-shaped nests are usually 45.0–65.0 mm deep, have a chamber 45.2–53.8 mm wide, and a neck diameter of 29.3–32.5 mm (Ernst, 1970b; Chippindale 1989). The deepest nests are dug by the largest females (Ernst, 1970b).

Ernst (1970b) described the nesting process in Pennsylvania. Several test holes may be dug before the final site is selected. Once a suitable site is found the female faces the water, braces her front legs, and excavates the nest cavity with alternating movements of the hind feet. Digging lasts from 29 to 75 minutes, and oviposition begins about five minutes after the cavity is completed. The female extends her neck before each egg is laid and contracts it as each egg is expelled. The eggs are arranged in the nest with alternating movements of the hind feet. The duration of egg laying ranges from 12.5 to 22.4 minutes, and the mean interval between the laying of individual eggs is 1.0–2.5 minutes. The female begins to cover the nest about five minutes after oviposition is completed. After using her feet to fill the nest with soil and grass, she rubs her plastron from side to side over it before returning to the water. The entire process takes from 45 to 120 minutes. Females may return to the same nesting area year after year, and some may nest near other females (Belmore, 1980).

One or two clutches of one to eight eggs are deposited in a year (Wilson, 1989; Ernst and Zug, in press). Blake (1922) reported females from Massachusetts with 9–11 oviducal eggs. Larger females appear to lay more and larger eggs than smaller females (Ernst, 1970b). Egg dimensions are as follows: length, 25–33.7 mm; width, 15.9–18.5 mm; and weight, about 6 g (Adler, 1961; Ernst, 1970b; Chippindale, 1989). Eggs are elliptical, white, and have a flexible membranous shell. Indentations, sometimes present after laying, disappear as the eggs develop. The shell is about 0.21 mm thick, and is

Hatchling *Clemmys guttata*

composed of 64.9% fibrous layers and 35.1% mineral layers (Ewert, 1979a).

The reproductive parameters of a population of spotted turtles in Pennsylvania were described by Ernst (1970b). Of 43 eggs observed during the study, 18 did not survive. Six were destroyed by predators or drought, and 12 were either infertile or underwent prehatching mortality. Twenty-five of the 37 eggs not destroyed by predators hatched. Assuming that 3.6 eggs are laid per clutch and that prehatching mortality is about 32%, then the realized reproductive potential per clutch is 2.4 young.

The natural incubation period to hatching may last 70–83 days, although in captivity the period may be as short as 44 days (Ernst, 1970b; Belmore, 1973; Ewert, 1979a).

The earliest emergence of hatchlings in Pennsylvania is 18 August (Ernst, 1970b), and some hatchlings may overwinter in the nest (Ernst, 1975). Belmore (1973) reported that hatchling emergence occurs at night. Hatchling *C. guttata* will usually bury themselves in nearby soil or hide under debris shortly after emerging from the nest.

Clemmys guttata has temperature-dependent sex determination. Eggs incubated at temperatures from 22.5 to 27.0°C produce a predominance of males, but those incubated at 30°C produce 100% females (Ewert and Nelson, 1991).

Hatchlings are blue-black and most bear a single yellow spot on each carapace scute, except the cervical which has none; some hatchlings have no spots on the shell. The head is always spotted and the neck may be. Hatchlings weigh about 4.7 g, or 75.2% of the freshly laid egg weight (Ewert, 1979a). Other hatchling dimensions are as follows: carapace length, 28.0–31.2 mm (mean 29.8), carapace width, 28.5–33.1 mm (mean 31.3), and plastron length, 25.2–26.9 mm (mean 26.4). The tail of the hatchling is proportionally longer than that of the adult. The egg tooth (caruncle) drops off by the end of the first week, and the yolk sac averages 16.5 mm in diameter (Ernst, 1970b).

GROWTH AND LONGEVITY: The growth rate of 11 Rhode Island spotted turtles was estimated by Graham (1970) using the relationship between scute annuli and plastron length. Mean plastron length increased 7.5 mm/year from ages one to five. Annual growth rates decreased from 10.6 to 4.9 mm/year from ages two to six, and then increased to 7.7 mm/year in the seventh year. Annual percent increase in plastron length ranged from 42.98% in the first year to 8.08% in the seventh year. The mean and estimated plastron lengths (mm) for each age class studied were as follows: hatchlings, 24.73 (22.9–26.7); one year, 35.36 (30.5–46.2; two years, 42.57 (35.6–52.8); three years, 48.80 (39.6–58.9; four years, 54.89 (44.6–64.8); five years, 59.82 (4.5–70.1); six years, 67.47 (53.1–78.2); seven years, 72.92 (57.0–83.8). The estimated growth rate of

Pennsylvania spotted turtles is slightly greater than the rate reported for those from Rhode Island (Ernst, 1975). Growth in the first year ranges from 4.2 to 17.5 mm, an annual increase of 66.93%; however, it is important to note that Ernst's calculated figures for plastron length slightly underestimate actual plastron length. Overwintering hatchlings grow more in their first year owing to a longer first growing season. Adults grow at a rate of about 2–3% annually, but some turtles larger than 90 mm fail to show measurable annual growth. Males and females seem to grow at the same rate, but as mean female size is greater than males, Gibbons and Lovich (1990) hypothesized that females continue growing after the size at which males attain sexual maturity. Annual increases in plastron length range from 26.88% at age one to 2.25% at age 18. The mean weight of mature males (155.5 g) is not significantly different than the weight of mature females of the same size.

Wild spotted turtles of both sexes have lived over 30 years in Pennsylvania (Ernst, pers. obs.).

FOOD HABITS: In Pennsylvania, foraging does not seriously begin until water temperature exceeds 15°C. Spotted turtles have been observed feeding at temperatures as low as 14.2°C on 5 April, and as early in the year as 9 March at a water temperature of 16.8°C. Feeding continues as long as turtles are active (March–September).

Spotted turtles are omnivorous scavengers and feed in the water. Usual plant foods include aquatic grasses and filamentous green algae (Chlorophyta), and Lazell (1976) observed New England *C. guttata* eating cranberries. Animal foods, eaten live or as carrion, include aquatic insect larvae, small crustaceans (including amphipods and isopods), snails, tadpoles (*Bufo, Rana*), salamanders (*Ambystoma*), fish (*Catastomus, Cyprinus, Ictalurus, Lepomis, Notropis*), and a mallard duck (*Anas platyrhynchos*) (Manns, 1969; Ernst, 1976; Lovich, pers. obs.).

In a study of the food color preferences of *C. guttata* from Ontario, Humphreys and Mallory (1977) discovered that a captive specimen showed a definite preference for lighter colors of dyed fish (white, yellow) compared with darker colors (red, green, blue). The significance of this observation is not clear.

PREDATORS AND DEFENSE: Spotted turtles and their eggs are preyed upon by bald eagles (*Haliaeetus;* Clark, 1982), skunks (*Mephitis*), and especially raccoons (*Procyon*). The rate of predation may be high, and it differs between populations. In Pennsylvania 13.5% of the spotted turtles collected showed signs of predator attacks or injuries caused by farm grass mowers, and 17.9% of all adults showed signs of predation or injuries. Injuries included amputated limbs and tails, and damaged shells (Ernst, 1976). Iverson (1991a) estimated that the annual rate of survivorship of eggs and hatchlings in this population was only 58%. Of the spotted turtles from Cedar Bog, Ohio, 31% showed signs of predator-related injuries (Lovich, 1989a). The proportion of injuries there was not significantly different between sexes, but did vary over time in response to suspected increases in raccoon population density. Grant (1936a) found spotted turtles in northern Indiana whose shells had been gnawed by rodents and others that had been mutilated or killed by unknown predators.

In the water this turtle is shy and attempts to burrow into the bottom when disturbed. If basking, it dives into the water at the first sign of disturbance. Spotted turtles will rarely bite, but some will void their bladders when held. The spotted carapacial pattern of *C. guttata* may imitate floating duckweed (*Lemna, Spirodela*), which may be seasonally common in the turtle's habitat, providing a selective advantage in reducing vulnerability to predation (Ross and Lovich, 1992).

POPULATIONS: The yearly estimated population size at a 3.2-ha marsh in Pennsylvania ranged from 127 to 258 individuals between 1967 and 1974 (Ernst, 1976). Density ranged from 39.5 to 79.1 turtles per hectare and biomass ranged from 4.3 to 8.7 kg/ha (Iverson, 1982a). The population was composed of 40.6% males and 59.4% females; 32.3% of these were juveniles. The largest proportion of turtles had a plastron longer than 60 mm and were older than six years. Between 1965 and 1967 *C. guttata* constituted 10.2% of all turtles captured at the study site. Frequencies for other species are as follows: *Chrysemys picta,* 76.3%; *Sternotherus odoratus,* 4.5%; *Chelydra serpentina,* 3.5%; *Terrapene carolina,* 2.3%; *Clemmys insculpta,* 2.3%; and *Clemmys muhlenbergii,* 0.8% (Ernst, 1976).

REMARKS: Spotted turtle populations are declining in many areas owing to habitat destruction and collection for the pet trade (Lovich and Jaworski, 1988; Lovich, 1989a; J. Harding, pers. comm.). Additional information on the species is summarized by Ernst (1972a), Bury and Ernst (1977), and Carroll (1991).

Clemmys muhlenbergii (Schoepff, 1801)
Bog turtle
PLATE 24

RECOGNITION: The bog turtle is a small species with a large, bright blotch on each side of the head. The elongated carapace (to 11.4 cm) is moderately domed and has a low keel. Growth annuli on the carapace produce a rough appearance in young individuals, but older turtles may be almost completely smooth. The sides of the carapace are nearly parallel or slightly divergent behind, and the posterior rim is smooth or only slightly serrated. Carapace color varies from light brown to rich mahogany or black; each scute may have a light center or a pattern of radiating lines. The lower marginals and bridge are the same color as the rest of the carapace. The hingeless plastron is dark brown to black, with a few light marks. The small head is brown with a marbled appearance and has a large yellowish-orange or red blotch, broken or unbroken, above and behind the tympanum. The blotch is commonly posteriorly forked or lobed (variation in the shape of the blotch is illustrated in Wright, 1918). The snout is not prominent and the upper jaw is medially notched. The skin is brown and may be mottled with red dorsally and orange or red ventrally.

Males have long, thick tails, with the vent posterior to the rim of the carapace, concave plastra, and thick foreclaws. Females have high, wide carapaces and flat plastra. Males are larger, on average, than females.

KARYOTYPE: The diploid chromosome number is 50 including 8 pairs of macrochomosomes with median or submedian centromeres, 5 pairs of macrochromosomes with terminal or subterminal centromeres, and 12 pairs of microchromosomes (Bickham, 1975).

FOSSIL RECORD: Early Pleistocene (Blancan) plastral elements have been found in Cumberland Cave, Allegany County, Maryland (Holman, 1977b).

DISTRIBUTION: The range of Clemmys muhlenbergii is discontinuous and confined to the eastern United States. The main range is from western Massachusetts, Connecticut, and eastern New York southward through eastern Pennsylvania and New Jersey to northern Delaware and northern Maryland. Isolated populations exist, or previously existed, in northwestern New York, northwestern Pennsylvania, southern Virginia, western North Carolina, northwestern South Carolina, northern Georgia, and eastern Tennessee. A record from Rhode Island is questionable, and an earlier record from northern Virginia has been discounted (Mitchell, 1989). Additional details on the distribution of bog turtles in the southern part of the range are summarized in Herman (1981) and Tryon (1988, 1990).

GEOGRAPHIC VARIATION: No subspecies are recognized. Dunn (1917) described a single variant of C. muhlenbergii from North Carolina as C. nuchalis, largely on the basis of differences in the shape of the head blotch (see above). The taxon has since been synonymized with C. muhlenbergii (Ernst and Bury, 1977). Our research has shown that blotch pattern may vary geographically, but the extent of variation is insufficient to warrant recognition of separate taxa.

CONFUSING SPECIES: Clemmys guttata has a black, unkeeled carapace with yellow spots, and a light plastron patterned with large dark blotches. Terrapene carolina and Kinosternon subrubrum have hinged plastra, and the much larger Clemmys insculpta has a sculptured shell, a strongly serrated posterior carapace rim, and a light plastron with large dark blotches.

HABITAT: The bog turtle lives in spring-fed sphagnum bogs, tamarack and black spruce swamps,

Clemmys muhlenbergii

Plastron of *Clemmys muhlenbergii*

and marshy meadows from sea level to over 1300 m in the southern portion of the range (Herman and Pharr, 1986). Clear, slow-moving rivulets or brooks with soft, highly organic substrates are required habitat features (Pitts, 1978). In Maryland, high population densities are usually associated with circular drainage basins containing spring-fed pools of shallow water, substrates of soft mud and rock, vegetation dominated by low grasses and sedges, and a heterogeneous habitat with wet and dry areas

(Chase et al., 1989). The most frequently associated plants in Pennsylvania are sedge (*Carex* sp.), sphagnum moss (*Sphagnum* sp.), poison sumac (*Rhus vernix*), swamp magnolia (*Magnolia virginiana*), alder (*Alnus* sp.), Juneberry (*Amelanchier spicata*), swamp honeysuckle (*Rhododendron viscosum*), swamp blueberry (*Vaccinium corymbosum*), sundew (*Drosera rotundifolia*), swamp orchids (*Arethusa bulbosa, Nymphaea tuberosa, Pogonia ophioglossoides*), various *Lycopodium* sp., and ferns. Dominant plants in southern

A bright orange blotch behind the eye is characteristic
of *Clemmys muhlenbergii*

Juvenile *Clemmys
muhlenbergii*

habitats include alders (*Alnus serrulata*), willows (*Salix* sp.), sphagnum moss, jewelweed (*Impatiens capensis*), arrow arum (*Peltandra virginica*), red maple (*Acer rubrum*), skunk cabbage (*Symplocarpus foetidus*), bulrushes (*Scirpus* and *Juncus* sp.), and a variety of ferns (*Onoclea sensibilis, Osmunda cinnamomea, O. regalis, Dryopteris cristata, Thelypteris novaboracensis,* and *T. palustris*) (Herman and George, 1986). Plant

diversity can be very rich in southern bog turtle habitat: over 150 species have been recorded in a Tennessee bog smaller than 0.13 ha (Tryon, 1990).

In an extensive survey of bog turtles south of Maryland, Tryon and Herman (1991) located 96 populations, of which 52 have the potential for sustained viability. North Carolina and Virginia contain the most populations with 37 and 13,

Distribution of *Clemmys muhlenbergii*

respectively. Southern habitats range in size from about 0.4 to 30 ha.

Three bog turtle habitats in Delaware have the following physicochemical ranges: pH, 5.5–7.4; air temperature in the shade at ground level, 0–29.5°C; water temperature, 2.0–28.0°C; water color, clear-turbid; current, slow-fast; flow, low-high; salinity always zero (Arndt, 1977).

From an ecological perspective bog turtle habitat is largely ephemeral because plant succession causes a relatively rapid transition toward dryer habitats, and the transition period is often accelerated by human activity such as draining wetlands and fire control.

BEHAVIOR: *Clemmys muhlenbergii* is primarily diurnal, although Holub and Bloomer (1977) report nocturnal feeding, breeding, and nesting in New Jersey. Ernst (1977) reported that most captures of a Pennsylvania population occurred during late morning. In Delaware hourly rates of capture based on 44 turtles were 0800, 2.28%; 0900, 0; 1000, 2.28%; 1100, 0; 1200, 18.18%; 1300, 34.09%; 1400, 11.36%; 1500, 9.09%; 1600, 13.63%; 1700, 6.81%, and 1800–1900, 2.28% (Arndt, 1977). Bog turtles emerge from cover early in the morning and bask until they move off in search of food or mates. During

the hottest part of the day they seek shelter until the evening when activity is resumed. In New Jersey, activity has been observed until 2300 (Holub and Bloomer, 1977).

Clemmys muhlenbergii has traditionally been thought to be active primarily in the spring of the year. The annual cycle of surface activity begins as early as March or April (Nemuras, 1967; Ernst, 1977; Holub and Bloomer, 1977; Lovich et al., 1992). In Delaware, 82% of all captures occur before July (Arndt, 1977), and in Pennsylvania 87% of all captures occur in the same period (Ernst, 1977). A bimodal activity pattern was reported by Ernst and Barbour (1989) with turtles coming out of estivation to become active again in September. Although some geographic variation in activity cycles might be expected, Lovich et al. (1992) found no statistically significant difference between the seasonal activity cycles in North Carolina and those reported for Delaware by Arndt (1977).

In North Carolina both the number of turtles captured per month and the number of turtles captured per man-hour were highest in the spring; 64% of all adult captures were made prior to June (Lovich et al., 1992). There is no statistically significant difference in the monthly frequency of captures between males and females during the period from April to June. However, data based on radiotelemetry indicate that *C. muhlenbergii* is active from August to December in North Carolina when hand captures are minimal or absent. The discordance between techniques used to judge activity is probably due to collecting bias: hand collecting efforts are usually concentrated in the spring before vegetation effectively conceals turtles from researchers. Ernst has found *C. muhlenbergii* active in Pennsylvania from March to November.

Bog turtles are active at air temperatures between 16 and 31°C (Ernst, 1977; Arndt, 1977; Herman, 1981). Activity generally begins when air temperatures remain above 21.3°C (Zappalorti, 1976), but in Pennsylvania, 65% of activity occurs at temperatures below 23°C (Ernst, 1977). The cloacal temperatures of Pennsylvania turtles during various activities are as follows: basking, 22.0–31.0 (mean 25.3); feeding, 17.0–25.3 (mean 21.0); moving in water, 16.2–23.1 (mean 18.2); moving on land, 19.5–22.4 (mean 20.8).

The basking habit is well developed. In New Jersey, the predominant activity of bog turtles captured by Arndt (1986) was basking (58.3% on land, 12.3% in shallow water). Basking Pennsylvania *C. muhlenbergii* had cloacal temperatures 3.2°C higher than that of the air (Ernst, 1977).

As temperatures increase during the summer, bog turtles may estivate. Ernst and Barbour (1972) found a Pennsylvania *C. muhlenbergii* embedded in hard clay under a board on 8 August. In contrast, many become subterranean, congregating in wet areas and inhabiting networks of tunnels partly or completely filled with water (Holub and Bloomer, 1977), or entering muskrat (*Ondatra zibethica*) bank burrows or lodges (Arndt, 1977; Kiviat, 1978b; Ernst, pers. obs.).

Hibernation begins from late September to November and ends in March or April. During winter warm spells, bog turtles may become aroused and move in and out of their hibernacula (Chase et al., 1989). Hibernacula in New Jersey and Pennsylvania include the soft bottoms on waterways, tussocks of the sedge *Carex,* the base of tree stumps, and meadow vole (*Microtus pennsylvanicus*), white-footed mouse (*Peromyscus leucopus*), meadow jumping mouse (*Zapus hudsonius*), and muskrat burrows. Turtles in muskrat burrows are usually 1.0–1.8 m from the entrance in 3.0–7.5 cm of water and mud. Those in the bottoms of waterways hibernate under 20–25 cm of water and mud, and those using other rodent burrows spend the winter under 5–55 cm of water and mud. Turtles may return to the same hibernation site two or more years

in a row, and may hibernate singly or in association with others (Ernst et al., 1989). Congregations of up to 141 individuals have been overwintering in the same general vicinity (Bloomer, 1978).

Hatchlings usually hibernate in the immediate vicinity of the nest site, and some overwinter in the nest. Turtles younger than two or three years hibernate in shallow habitats, but as they become older and reach a carapace length size of about 45–50 mm they hibernate in deeper areas (Holub and Bloomer, 1977).

Cloacal temperatures of hibernating bog turtles are highly correlated with environmental temperatures. Turtles are capable of varying their depth in soft-bottomed hibernation sites in response to substrate temperature. An individual female turtle was captured 14 times over four successive winters in New Jersey and her hibernation depth increased with decreasing substrate temperature (Ernst et al., 1989).

Movement activity, as determined with thread-trailers, indicates a six-month activity period in Maryland. Point-to-point movements between recaptures during July and August ranged from 1 to 2 m. However, the thread trail showed that movements of up to 30 m were made in an area of about 4 m² in less than 24 hours. Home ranges of males (mean 0.176 ha) were significantly larger than those of females (mean 0.066 ha), with males showing greater variance. Home ranges overlapped considerably among turtles of both sexes (Chase et al., 1989).

Data from other studies confirm the tendency of males to move greater distances and more frequently than females. Ernst (1977) reported that male Pennsylvania bog turtles also have larger home ranges (mean 1.33 ha) than females (mean 1.26 ha). The longest movement observed by Ernst was 225 m in eight days by a male, but overland movements of up to 750 m have been recorded for bog turtles wearing radio transmitters in New York (Eckler et al., 1990).

The movements of three males and two females fitted with radio transmitters were monitored in North Carolina by Lovich et al. (1992). Males and females had significantly different rates of movement of 2.1 m/day and 1.1 m/day, respectively. Small movements were observed during December and January. Distances between relocations ranged from 0 to 87 m (mean 24.3 m) for males and 0 to 67 m (mean 15.8 m) for females. Arndt (1977) reported distances between recaptures of 5.1–59.4 m (mean 29.4 m) for males and 0–41.7 m (mean 16.3 m) for females in Delaware.

Bog turtles are capable of homing. In New Jersey, both males and females returned to the general area of capture when released within a 0.32–0.80-km radius (Holub and Bloomer, 1977). Some of these turtles made the return trip in 30 hours, but others released beyond these limits or outside of the bog habitat did not return. Ernst had a Pennsylvania male displaced 0.80 km return in four days, and another male released 0.40 km away return in one day.

Bog turtles in some populations are aggressive toward members of their own kind (Zappalorti, 1976; Holub and Bloomer, 1977; Ernst, pers. obs.). Adult males almost always threaten or attack smaller males. The defensive posture consists of extending the neck with the mouth open or closed while advancing toward the intruder. Just before contact, the aggressor will partially withdraw the head and tilt the carapace forward by raising the hind legs and lowering the front legs. If the threatened turtle responds with similar behavior, both turtles push against each other and occasionally bite at each other's head and legs. The duration of aggressive interactions rarely exceeds a few minutes before the vanquished turtle either withdraws into its shell or flees, sometimes with the winning male in pursuit. The attacking male is almost always the winner. Females defend the vicinity of their burrow from other adult females, but will retreat from approaching males, except during the mating season. Territories rarely exceed a radius of 1.2 m. Juveniles are ignored by defending females. Males defend an area within about 15 cm of wherever they happen to be.

Adult male bog turtles in the wild, as well as those in captivity, will move away from approaching *Chelydra serpentina* or *Clemmys insculpta*, but not *C. guttata* or *Chrysemys picta* (Holub and Bloomer, 1977).

REPRODUCTION: Reproductive cycles have not been described for either sex. The timing of sexual maturity may vary geographically. Bog turtles in Pennsylvania mature at a plastron length of about 7.0 cm, a size attained by some individuals of both sexes during the sixth year of growth (Ernst, 1977). In New Jersey, males may mature in the fourth year at a minimum size of 6.5 cm, and most females mature in the fourth or fifth year at a minimum size of 7.0 cm (Holub and Bloomer, 1977).

Mating usually occurs in the afternoon from March to June with most activity in the first two months (Zappalorti, 1976; Arndt, 1977, 1986; Holub and Bloomer, 1977; Ernst, pers. obs.). Courtship may take place in or out of water. Zappalorti (1976) recognized three phases of courtship and breeding: sexual recognition, aggressive biting, and mounting

and intromission. During the first phase the male approaches the female and uses visual and olfactory cues to determine her sex. He then circles her, probing her tail and cloacal region with his nose, and may bite at her head and neck during this phase. If she crawls away, the male may or may not follow her but, if the female moves away during the second phase, he will bite her legs and head and attempt to get in front of her. A chase may last a few seconds to more than half an hour, but usually only about 10 minutes. If the female is receptive the male gently bites her head and neck before mating, and she may withdraw her front limbs and head during this time. During the third phase the male approaches the female from behind, climbs onto her carapace, bites her head and neck, and hooks all four of his feet onto the edges of her marginals. Occasionally he bites and holds onto her neck while positioning himself on her carapace. The weight of the male may force the female completely beneath the water and into the bottom substrate, creating an anoxic condition for her (Sachsse, 1974). If mounting is achieved underwater the male may blow bubbles through his nostrils as he attempts to bite the female. Copulation lasts from 5 to 20 minutes, and the entire courtship and mating ritual normally takes about 35 minutes (Zappalorti, 1976; Holub and Bloomer, 1977). Additional details of courtship and mating behavior are summarized by Arndt (1977) and Holub and Bloomer (1977).

Males and females will mate with more than one partner during the mating season, although females may become nonreceptive after one or two matings. In contrast, males will attempt to mate with as many females as possible. Not all adult bog turtles mate every year (Holub and Bloomer, 1977).

The bog turtle occasionally hybridizes with *C. guttata* under natural conditions (Ernst, 1983). Arndt (1977) observed a male bog turtle mounted on a female *C. guttata* at a Delaware study site, but it is important to note that the *C. guttata* lacked the conspicuous yellow carapace spots characteristic of that species. Holub and Bloomer (1977) concluded from experiments with captives that color pattern, particularly of the head, was important to the bog turtle for interspecific discrimination.

The nesting season lasts from May to July (Zappalorti, 1976; Holub and Bloomer, 1977; Ernst and Barbour, 1989). Most nesting activity occurs in the late afternoon or early evening hours, 21–31 days after copulation. Females move away from wetter areas of the habitat toward higher ground to find nest sites. Most lay their eggs in elevated sedge tussocks or sphagnum moss above the water line. Other sites

Hatchling *Clemmys*
muhlenbergii with yolk sac

include the soft soil above springs, adjacent pastures, or even the sides of railroad embankments. Nest sites are exposed to sunlight for most of the day.

Nesting behavior in New Jersey was described by Holub and Bloomer (1977). At 2100 a female was observed crawling upstream within a small rivulet. At 2115 she arrived at a site above the source of the rivulet, an area of open, dry ground covered with short pasture grasses grazed by cattle. She occasionally nosed the ground until 2144 and then began excavation of a nest cavity with alternating motions of her hind feet. At 2210, excavation was completed. The cavity was flask shaped with a circular bottom. At 2216 the female laid the first egg and moved it slightly with her foot. The next egg was expelled 40 seconds later, and after another 50 seconds a third and fourth egg were laid. The female began to cover the nest nine minutes after the first egg appeared. Covering was completed at 2315, and she rested five times, for an average of three minutes each, during the process. The female then circled the nest pressing her plastron to the ground, smoothing the surface. The entire process lasted 165 minutes. Arndt (1972) provides an additional description of nesting by a captive.

Females ovipositing in sedge tussocks climb into the center and separate the moss or blades of grass with alternate movements of the hind feet. In Pennsylvania, some merely tunnel through the tussock, depositing their eggs behind them as they crawl (Ernst, pers. obs.). Elsewhere a nest may actually be dug in soil or sphagnum moss. The depth of such

nests are 3.8–5.1 cm and their diameter is about 5 cm (Zappalorti, 1976; Herman, 1981).

Bog turtles lay from one to six eggs (Ryan, 1981; Herman, 1983); older females lay more eggs than younger ones. Typical clutch size is three eggs (Zappalorti, 1976; Holub and Bloomer, 1977). Probably only one clutch is laid per year, but Herman (1986b) reported a captive female living under seminatural conditions laying two clutches: one on 30 May containing two eggs and another on 30 June containing five eggs that were considerably smaller than those in the first set.

Bog turtle eggs are elliptical and white. Ranges for various egg dimensions are as follows: length, 21.8–36.0 mm; width, 13.0–16.2 mm; weight, 2.5–5.4 g (Zovickian, 1971a; Arndt, 1977, 1986; Holub and Bloomer, 1977; Ewert, 1979a; Ryan, 1981; Herman, 1986b). Eggs increase significantly in weight and width prior to hatching (Arndt, 1972, 1977). The shell consists of a tough fibrous membrane packed with appositions of calcium carbonate (Sachsse, 1974).

Of 27 eggs deposited by six females in captivity, one was partially eaten by the female that laid it, seven were infertile, one young was dead upon hatching, and another hatchling was deformed (Arndt, 1977).

Incubation time varies as a function of temperature taking from 42 to 80 days under natural or artificial conditions (Zovickian, 1971a; Zappalorti, 1976; Arndt, 1972, 1977; Holub and Bloomer, 1977; Tryon and Hulsey, 1977). Hatchlings usually emerge from the nest in late August and September, but Ernst collected a single hatchling in Pennsylvania in May that had overwintered in the nest. Overwintering behavior has also been reported in New Jersey (Bloomer and Bloomer, 1973). Usually the hatchlings spend some time hiding in the tussock under the nest before venturing out into the world.

While hatching the young turtle makes small slits in the eggshell, through which it soon shoves its head (Zappalorti, 1976). Complete emergence takes from 28.0 to 104.5 hours (mean 51.2; Arndt, 1977).

Hatchlings have carapaces that are 21.1–28.5 mm long, 19.5–23.4 mm wide, and 11.5–12.9 mm high; they weigh 3.7–4.2 g (Arndt, 1972, 1977; Ernst, 1977). Hatchling weight is approximately 83.7% of freshly laid egg weight (Ewert, 1979a). No correlation exists between weight of eggs at laying and hatchling weight. The caruncle disappears in several days and the yolk sac is absorbed in 48 hours (Zappalorti, 1976).

Twinning has been reported in captive bog turtles. A nest destroyed by ants contained an egg with two full-term embryos in one egg. The egg containing the dead twins was 33.5 mm long, 16.1 mm wide, and 5.4 g at laying. Sixty days after oviposition the twins were 14.0 and 16.0 mm long, and 12.5 and 13.0 mm wide, respectively (Herman, 1987).

The method of sex determination in *C. muhlenbergii* is unknown.

Details of captive propagation are summarized by Zovickian (1971a), Sachsse (1974), Tryon and Hulsey (1977), Herman and George (1986), and Herman (1991).

GROWTH AND LONGEVITY: Ernst (1977) calculated the growth rate of Pennsylvania bog turtles using the relationship between scute length and plastron length. His calculations predict that female hatchlings are slightly smaller and have slower growth rates than male hatchlings; however, this relationship requires confirmation using animals of known age. The mean percentage calculated growth per year for various ages is as follows: hatchling, 34.6; age 1, 22.9; age 2, 15.6; age 3, 13.1; age 4, 10.8; age 5, 8.6; age 6, 8.4; age 7, 7.4; age 8, 6.4; age 9, 4.0; age 10, 3.6; age 11, 4.9; age 12, 5.2. The total annual growing period in Lancaster County, Pennsylvania, is about 140 days. A New Jersey hatchling had a carapace length of 32 mm when captured in August and a 40-mm carapace length when recaptured in April of the following year (Holub and Bloomer, 1977).

An increase in temperature and humidity seems to stimulate growth in young bog turtles. Three hatchlings, ranging in carapace length from 24 to 26 mm

and kept at 23°C, grew only 3.5–6 mm in five months. After this period they were maintained at 25°C and a higher humidity. By the end of the next five months they had grown to between 51 and 58 mm. Zovickian (1971b) attributed most of this dramatic increase in the growth rate to higher humidity.

A bog turtle has lived for 23 years, 1 month in captivity (Snider and Bowler, 1992), and Ernst has recaptured some wild adults after 20 years in Pennsylvania.

FOOD HABITS: The bog turtle is omnivorous and will feed on land or in water. Surface (1908) reported that the stomach of one specimen contained 80% insects and 20% berries. Barton and Price (1955) observed that stomachs of two specimens contained mostly insects, with one species of lepidopterous larva constituting nearly half the total amount in each stomach. Other items, in order of importance, were beetles, seeds of pondweed (*Potamogeton*), and large numbers of *Carex* seeds. Other items found in a larger sample of turtles included caddisfly larvae and other insects, snails (*Succinea*), a millipede, and a cranefly wing. The most abundant food item in the stomachs of specimens captured in August was the Japanese beetle (*Popillia japonica*).

Other food items in the catholic diet include wood frogs (*Rana sylvatica*), bullfrogs (*R. catesbiana*), pickerel frogs (*R. palustris*), crickets, slugs, nestling birds, crayfish, dead water snakes, butterflies (*Euphydryas phaeton*), salamanders, earthworms, mice, skunk cabbage (*Symplocarpus foetidus*), cattails (*Typha*), duckweed (*Lemna*), and berries (Nemuras, 1967; Zappalorti, 1976; Holub and Bloomer, 1977).

PREDATORS AND DEFENSE: Bog turtles are preyed upon by a wide variety of animals including raccoons (*Procyon*), snapping turtles (*Chelydra serpentina*), foxes (*Vulpes, Urocyon*), skunks (*Mephitis*), and possibly opossums (*Didelphis*) (Holub and Bloomer, 1977; Herman, 1986a). Herman (1987) reported ant predation on unhatched eggs.

Three of 17 turtles collected at three sites in Delaware were found dead on a highway (Arndt, 1977).

The hard shell of *C. muhlenbergii* offers limited protection from large predators owing to the small size of the turtle. Most individuals are inoffensive and will not bite when handled.

POPULATIONS: Under undisturbed conditions, bog turtle habitat in New Jersey will support about 49–62 turtles per hectare, with a sex ratio of about 2.5 adult females per adult male (Holub and Bloomer, 1977). At one New Jersey site only one juvenile was found in a sample of 37 turtles, and 58% of the adults were males (Arndt, 1986). In Maryland, the sex ratio of 174 adults was 1:1 and population densities varied from 7 to 213 turtles per hectare of wetland habitat. Of all captures in Maryland, 24% were juveniles. Previously published estimates of population density in Pennsylvania range from 125 to 140 turtles per hectare (Chase et al., 1989). The biomass of bog turtles at Pennsylvania and North Carolina sites was estimated to be 10.9 and 12.3 kg/ha, respectively (Iverson, 1982a).

REMARKS: Humans pose the chief threat to the continued survival of *C. muhlenbergii*. Destruction of wetland habitat required by the bog turtle and collection for the pet trade have caused the extinction of some populations (D. E. Collins, 1990) and severely reduced others. As a result, in the Conven-tion of International Trade in Endangered Species (CITES), Appendix I, the species is classified in Category 2 of the list of animals considered for protection of the Federal Endangered Species Act, and, as of 1989, listed as "in need of special management," threatened, or endangered in the states of Massachusetts, New Jersey, New York, North Carolina, Pennsylvania, Tennessee, and Virginia (Tryon, 1990). The need for effective conservation measures is discussed by Herman (1981), Holub and Bloomer (1977), Tryon (1990), and Tryon and Herman (1991).

Clemmys muhlenbergii seems to be closely related to *C. guttata*. However, analysis of plastron morphology suggests that *C. muhlenbergii* is in a separate group from the other three members of the genus, including *C. guttata* (Lovich et al., 1991a).

Additional information on *C. muhlenbergii* is sum-marized by Anderson and Curcione (1973), Ernst and Bury (1977), Bury and Ernst (1977), Kiviat (1978a), Bury (1979b), and Landry (1979).

Clemmys insculpta (Le Conte, 1830)
Wood turtle

PLATE 25

RECOGNITION: The wood turtle is medium sized with a keeled, heavily sculptured carapace (to 23.4 cm). Growth annuli are conspicuous and give the scutes a raised, irregular pyramidal appearance in some individuals. The posterior marginals are strongly flared in juveniles and females, and serrated in all individuals. The carapace is tan, grayish brown, or brown, and a pattern of black or yellow lines radiating from the upper posterior corners may be present on the vertebrals and pleurals. The undersides of the marginals and bridge commonly have dark blotches along the posterior, outer corner of each scute. The hingeless plastron is yellow with an oblong dark blotch on each scute. The head is black, and locally speckled with faint yellow dots. It has a nonprojecting snout and a notched upper jaw. The skin is dark brown except on the throat, neck, tail, and especially the underside of the forelegs, where it is yellow, orange, or red. The intensity of color has been reported to vary seasonally in New Jersey populations (Harding and Bloomer, 1979).

Adult males are, on average, 1.07–1.10 times larger than adult females (Lovich et al., 1990a) and have long, thick tails, with the vent posterior to the carapacial rim, a concave plastron, and prominent scales on the anterior surface of the forelimbs. On some older males, the carapace is slightly indented at the bridge.

KARYOTYPE: The diploid chromosome number is 50: 8 pairs of macrochromosomes with median or submedian centromeres, 5 pairs of macrochromosomes with terminal or subterminal centromeres, and 12 pairs of microchromosomes (Bickham, 1975).

FOSSIL RECORD: Pleistocene remains of *Clemmys insculpta* have been found in Irvingtonian deposits in Pennsylvania (Hay, 1923) and Rancholabrean deposits in northwestern Georgia (Holman, 1967), Pennsylvania (Richmond, 1964), and Tennessee (Parmalee and Klippel, 1981). The latter two records indicate that *C. insculpta* had a much more southerly range during the late Pleistocene.

DISTRIBUTION: The wood turtle is found from Nova Scotia and New Brunswick south to at least Rockingham County, Virginia (Buhlmann and Mitchell, 1989), and west through southern Quebec, southern Ontario, and New York to northern Michigan, Wisconsin, eastern Minnesota, and northeastern Iowa.

GEOGRAPHIC VARIATION: No subspecies are recognized, but wood turtles in the Great Lakes region and Midwest have light-yellow or yellow-orange lower soft parts, while individuals from east of the Appalachians in Pennsylvania and New York tend to be brighter with orange or reddish pigment.

CONFUSING SPECIES: *Clemmys insculpta* is found in association with several other turtles. *Terrapene carolina* and *Emydoidea blandingii* have hinged plastra. *C. muhlenbergii* is small and has an orange blotch on each side of the head, and *C. guttata* has a keelless, unserrated, black, yellow-spotted carapace. None of these other species has a deeply sculptured carapace.

HABITAT: *Clemmys insculpta* is always found in close association with water, but the degree of association varies geographically. In Michigan and Wisconsin, wood turtles may be quite aquatic occupying habitats in or near moving water including rivers, streams, and associated shoreline habitats (Vogt, 1981a; Harding, 1991). Drainages with hard sand or gravel bottoms are preferred over those with soft clay or muck bottoms. Moderate current and clear streams are also preferred. As the name implies, wood turtles

Female *Clemmys insculpta*

Plastron of *Clemmys insculpta*

are found in forests, but areas with openings in the stream-side canopy form the best habitat. Streams are utilized almost daily in Michigan (Harding, 1991).

Wood turtles in the eastern portion of the range are decidedly terrestrial in the summer, but even there they are never found far from water and may enter streams every few days (Strang, 1983; Ernst, pers. obs.). In Virginia, *C. insculpta* is found near clear brooks and streams in deciduous woodlands (Ernst and McBreen, 1991c). Other habitats include swamps, bogs, wet meadows, upland fields and pastures and the matrix of habitats in between (Harding and Bloomer, 1979; Ross et al., 1991).

Habitat use in central Pennsylvania is not in proportion to its availability. During the active season, turtles spend more time in water than in any one terrestrial habitat. In May, turtles spend more time in alder (*Alnus*) thickets than in other habitats. Hemlock (*Tsuga*) forests are used very little, except in July and August when mushrooms (a favorite food) are sprouting. Deciduous forests are hardly used at all in central Pennsylvania (Kaufmann, 1992a), but

Head of *Clemmys insculpta*

Distribution of *Clemmys insculpta*

Basking *Clemmys insculpta*

elsewhere in the range where conifer stands or alder thickets are absent, such as in southeastern Pennsylvania and northern Virginia, deciduous woods are heavily used.

Males spend more time in the creek than do females, possibly because they are searching for mates. Females spend more time than males in habitats dominated by grasses, sedges, and forbs (Kaufmann, 1992a).

BEHAVIOR: The wood turtle is primarily diurnal, but mating and nesting behavior may continue until 2300. During the night, turtles rest in sheltered areas of creeks or shallow forms on land (Kaufmann, 1992a). In New Jersey, wood turtles become active at 0700 and retire at about 1900; 85% of all sightings occur between 1000 and 1500. *Clemmys insculpta* is active at air and water temperatures as low as 3°C and 6°C, respectively, but it does not start to feed until water temperatures climb to about 15°C (Ernst, 1986a), and may become inactive on very hot summer days. Wood turtle activity is stimulated by rain in New Jersey, but not in northern Michigan, possibly because of the frequent temperature drops there during rain storms (J. Harding, pers. comm.). In contrast, those from Pennsylvania move about the same distance during rainy and nonrainy days (Strang, 1983). Preferred periods for feeding and moving are during early morning and late afternoon. At night, wood turtles either enter the water or shelter in shallow forms in the soil under grass, leaves, and brush

(Harding and Bloomer, 1979; Ernst, 1986a; Farrell and Graham, 1991).

Michigan wood turtles spend a considerable part of their daily cycle basking. Most basking activity occurs in late morning and late afternoon on sunny days. Basking sites include emergent logs over deep stream channels, stream banks, and woodland openings with low ground cover. Emergent logs are used by both sexes in the spring and fall, but females seem to prefer terrestrial sites from late June through August (Harding and Bloomer, 1979). In Pennsylvania, the basking habit is not as well developed as in either *C. guttata* or *C. muhlenbergii*. Basking occurs before noon, at air temperatures of at least 14°C, primarily on stream banks; the mean time spent basking is 140 min (Ernst, 1986a). Farrell and Graham (1991) observed basking behavior in New Jersey as late as 1625. They described preferred basking sites as "depressions on the stream bank oriented at an angle of 25--80° from horizontal."

In Pennsylvania, the annual activity cycle lasts from March until late November. Males are more active than females in the early spring. In April, when air temperatures are consistently below 10°C at night, 84% of the turtles monitored by Kaufmann (1992a) stayed in a creek, compared to 54% on warmer nights. On April days when maximum air temperatures did not exceed 20°C, 90% of the turtles stayed in the creek, compared to 39% on warmer days. From April to May, wood turtles are generally aquatic owing to their underwater mating preference, but from mid-June until autumn, they are more terrestrial (Ernst, 1986a), but return to creeks during cool periods (Kaufmann, 1992a). In Michigan, wood turtles are active from April or May until early October (Harding, 1991). Farrell and Graham (1991) reported that the mean time of capture in each month of the activity cycle in New Jersey changed very little. In contrast, wood turtles in Virginia shift daily activity from afternoon in the spring to morning in the summer, and then back to afternoon in the fall (Ernst and McBreen, 1991c). Of yearly captures in New Jersey, 49% occurred from March to May and 42% occurred in October and November. No captures were made in January or February. The bimodal activity pattern may be a result of spring and fall mating tendencies (Farrell and Graham, 1991).

As temperatures increase in the summer, wood turtles may estivate. One Pennsylvania male sheltered in a shallow puddle in a pasture for several days, and other dormant terrestrial *C. insculpta* occupied shaded forms under vegetation, fallen logs, or flood debris near creeks (Ernst, 1986a). Turtles kept in outdoor pens estivated for 7–28 days during July and August in New Jersey (Farrell and Graham, 1991). A female in Wisconsin spent all her time in a river when air temperature ranged from 26 to 35°C (Ross et al., 1991).

Wood turtles enter hibernation sometime between October and November, depending on geographic location and yearly variations in weather, and resume activity between early March and mid-May. Most hibernate underwater. Hibernation sites include deep pools (exposed on top of the substrate or under 18–30 cm of mud or sand), under overhanging roots or logs along the stream, in beaver (*Castor canadensis*) lodges, and in muskrat (*Ondatra zibethica*) burrows (Bishop and Schoonmacher, 1921; Ernst, 1986a; Ernst and McBreen, 1991c; Farrell and Graham, 1991). In Pennsylvania, waterways selected for hibernation were flowing streams, 1.0–2.3 m deep, that never froze completely (Ernst, 1986a). In Massachusetts, wood turtles have been observed hibernating on the bottom of flowing streams in 0.3–0.6 m of water. Resting sites were often adjacent to submerged logs or rocks. Turtles made small movements within an area of about 6–8 m² (Graham and Forsberg, 1991). Hibernating groups of up to 70 turtles, some resting shell-to-shell, have been reported in New Jersey (Bloomer, 1978). This particular aggregation was found on the bottom of an 18 x 6 m pond under about 1.8 m of water. Individuals may show perennial hibernacula fidelity (Garber, 1989). Although little movement is observed during hibernation, one indi-

vidual in Pennsylvania moved about 10 m upstream in two days (Ernst, 1986a).

Brewster (1985) reported on wood turtles hibernating under artificial conditions. A female was maintained in a plastic container in a refrigerator from 28 September until 22 April, and misted with water and weighed weekly (no temperature given). During the experimental period she lost 3.4 g, but her weight fluctuated from a maximum gain of 7.2 g to a maximum loss of 5.8 g. A male, hibernated at 2°C in a bucket of water from 5 March until 22 April, lost a total of only 0.3 g while fluctuating from +0.2 g to −3.7 g.

Subadult wood turtles have higher weight-specific rates of metabolism while hibernating than adults. The ability to hibernate in streams with high oxygen tension that do not freeze over seems to be an adaptation that has allowed the species to avoid a wintertime exclusive dependence on anaerobiosis (Graham and Forsberg, 1991).

Hutchison et al. (1966) reported that the mean critical thermal maximum for four *Clemmys insculpta* was 41.3°C (39.6–42.5), and that the mean loss of the righting response occurred at 39.8°C (39.0–40.5).

Active Pennsylvania wood turtles have cloacal temperatures of 7.5–30.0°C (mean 21.0); the lowest air and water temperatures at which wood turtles have been observed to feed are 23 and 17.2°C, respectively (Ernst, 1986a). Cloacal temperatures of active wood turtles in New Jersey range from 3.4 to 31.0°C (mean 16.2), and for dormant wood turtles from 0 to 28.1°C (mean 9.5; Farrell and Graham, 1991).

Graham and Dadah-Tosti (1981) tested the locomotor patterns of three female wood turtles under a 14:10 hour light:dark cycle and three thermal treatments as follows: treatment 1—constant 25°C for five days; treatment 2—a transition to 15°C at 2°C per day over five days; and treatment 3—constant 15°C for three days. At a constant 25°C the "typical" *C. insculpta* had multiple activity peaks during a 24-hour cycle. During the transition period to 15°C the number of peaks was reduced until, at a constant 15°C, activity was unimodal, with well-defined daily peaks between 1100 and 1200. Activity time per day and mean number of movements per hour in each treatment were as follows: 18.4 hours/day and 108.8 movements/hour at 25°C; 11.6 hours/day and 153.4 movements/hour at 25–15°C; and 6.7 hours/day and 84.7 movements/hour at 15°C. Activity was 96–97% diurnal at 25°C, but all activity occurred during daylight hours at 15°C.

Brenner (1970) examined the influence of different

light and temperature regimes on fat utilization in a laboratory population of female wood turtles. Both light and temperature influenced the rate of fat utilization in skeletal muscle, but not in liver tissue. The fat content of cardiac tissues in turtles exposed to dark conditions at room temperature (21°C) was significantly higher than that of turtles exposed to dark conditions at 5°C. The rate of evaporative water loss in *C. insculpta* is intermediate between aquatic *Chelydra serpentina* and *Sternotherus odoratus* and terrestrial *Terrapene carolina* under experimental conditions (Ernst, 1968a).

Clemmys insculpta can travel at a relatively rapid pace compared to other turtles. An 18.6-cm adult moved 137 m in 25 min at a rate of 0.32 km/h (Woods, 1945). Wood turtles may move considerable distances during the active season. The movements of wood turtles in Pennsylvania were studied with thread trailers by Strang (1983) during several summers. The mean 24-hour path length of nine turtles was 108 m, although the straight-line displacement was only about 60 m. The home ranges, measured as the greatest distance between a pair of mapped location points, were elongated due to the propensity to follow stream courses. Mean home range size was 447 m.

The movements and microhabitat use of captive-raised juvenile (5.25–6.0 cm carapace length) wood turtles were studied by Brewster and Brewster (1991) in Wisconsin using radiotelemetry. The turtles were raised in captivity and then released into a wood turtle population different from that of their parents. Turtles released in May moved longer distances per day than those released in later months. Movements between relocations reached a peak between five and eight days following release, and declined thereafter. Some were relocated while they were being carried downstream short distances in the current of a small river. When daytime temperatures fell below 17°C and during periods of rain, turtles became sedentary for two to eight days. All turtles remained within 40 m of the Wisconsin River channel during the period of study.

In Michigan, wood turtles seem to have small home ranges. Harding and Bloomer (1979) observed that of 47 turtles captured at least twice, 64% were located within 150 m of the original point of capture, and 32% were captured less than 305 m from the starting point. Two individuals traveled more than 800 m from the original point of capture. Most movement occurred along waterways: observed overland movement never exceeded 150 m. The mean minimum daily movement of males (41.9 m) in Wisconsin was significantly longer than that of gravid females (27.4

m) from June to August. Home ranges of males (0.08––0.41 ha) and females (0.27–0.91 ha) were not significantly different (Ross et al., 1991). A male and a female in Pennsylvania had mean distances moved between captures of 90 m and 15 m, and home ranges of 2.5 ha and 0.07 ha, respectively (Ernst, 1968b). Kaufmann (1992b) noted that although the home ranges of wood turtles in Pennsylvania overlapped considerably, they were not defended.

Learning ability of *C. insculpta* is great compared to that of other reptiles. Tinklepaugh (1932) concluded from food-finding experiments using mazes that its learning ability was comparable to that of rats under similar conditions. This may play a role in homing when displaced to an unfamiliar place. A New Jersey male returned to its original point of capture within five weeks of being displaced a distance of 2.4 km: a journey across three roads, a small stream, woodlands, hills, and fields, and wood turtles in Michigan homed a distance of up to 8 km in less than two months (Harding and Bloomer, 1979).

Of New York *C. insculpta* displaced less than 2 km, 83% returned, but of those released at distances greater than 2 km, only 17% returned (Carroll and Ehrenfeld, 1978). Homing ability was independent of displacement direction, sex, or age, and the turtles showed no evidence of having learned the route home when displaced and recaptured several times. Carroll and Ehrenfeld (1978) considered the orientation used to be "intermediate-range homing"; the wood turtles were displaced far enough, in most cases, to be in unfamiliar terrain, but too close to enable them to use celestial navigation methods. They hypothesized that orientation was probably via either olfactory cues or magnetic inputs.

Aggressive interactions between males have been observed under both natural and artificial conditions (Harding, 1979; Barzilay, 1980; Brewster and Brewster, 1988; Kaufmann, 1992b). Dinkins (1954), Harding and Bloomer (1979), and Harless (1970) reported dominance hierarchies based on size, sex, and maturity among captive wood turtles. In these aggressive encounters the larger individual is not always the victor (Barzilay, 1980). Barzilay thought aggression to be related to territorial defense. In captivity, males may be very aggressive toward other species of turtles kept with them, particularly *Terrapene carolina* (Harding, 1979; Ernst, pers. obs.).

The most thorough investigation of social behavior in wood turtles is based on the studies in central Pennsylvania by Kaufmann (1992b). He listed 27 types of nonreproductive behaviors observed during social interactions of wood turtles including 15 aggressive acts, 8 defensive acts, and 4 neutral acts. Neutral acts included feeding or resting within a meter of another turtle. Spring and fall peaks in social activity were from mid-April until mid-May and late August through October, respectively. Social interactions were uncommon between late May and early August.

Observed interactions between females were rarely neutral, and only two aggressive interactions were observed. Interactions between males and females included 22 neutral encounters and 24 aggressive encounters (including three staged encounters). Males were judged the winners in all but three of the aggressive interactions, and males outweighed females in all but four of the aggressive interactions. In cases where the winning males were lighter, the losing females were older and 70–300 g heavier than the males. Of the cases where the male did not win, one involved a large female feeding near a similar-sized male, one involved a female that ignored attacks by the male, and the third involved a female that was about twice the weight of the male.

Most interactions observed during the study were between males. During the study 494 out of 560 encounters were aggressive. Of these, 66% included physical contact, and of the encounters without physical contact 76% resulted in active displacement and the rest ended in passive displacement of the loser. Aggressive and nonaggressive encounters were more common in the fall (17.2 per week) than in the spring (5.8 per week) (aggressive behavior between males in New Jersey occurred only during the spring and fall mating seasons; Farrell and Graham, 1991). Of all fall encounters, 98% were aggressive, compared to 81% in the spring. The increase in aggressive behavior in the fall coincides with an increase in mating behavior at that time. Encounters between males were most frequent from 1000 to 1200 and 1800 to 2000. Males interacted more often in the creek than on land, and more aggressive interactions occurred in the creek than on land. Kaufmann thought that the difference in behavior between turtles on land relative to the creek was due to competition for females.

Aggressive encounters had several possible scenarios. Sometimes the subordinate individual would flee from an approaching dominant turtle without any outward display of aggression from either. At other times turtles would bite, shove, ram, and otherwise attempt to subdue or intimidate each other. Encounters lasted as long as 3.5 hours, but most were over very quickly. Most fights involved only two males, but groups of up to five occasionally engaged in combat. Fights rarely resulted in injury, although bites some-times produced minor bleeding. Homosexual mounting occurred in 33% of the physical encounters observed. This behavior was more frequent in the fall. Mounting was usually attempted by the winner or turtles known to be dominant.

Kaufmann's (1992b) work shows that male wood turtles have a linear rank hierarchy of dominance: dominant males almost always won encounters with subordinate males. This was confirmed, with few exceptions, by both field observations and staged encounters. Strong positive correlations existed between rank and age rank and weight: older and larger males tended to be dominant. Using DNA fingerprinting of 11 clutches, he determined that the number of fertilized eggs is positively correlated with male rank.

A possible cleaning symbiosis may exist between *Clemmys insculpta* and the blacknose dace, *Rhinichthys atratulus* (Kaufmann, 1991). Several times in May and June schools of the fish were seen cleaning wood turtles who sat very still in water 18–30 cm deep with head and legs extended while the dace nipped at the skin. The turtles actually appeared to solicit cleaning.

REPRODUCTION: Elements of the female reproductive cycle of *Clemmys insculpta* in Nova Scotia were described by Powell (1967). A single female collected in September contained 10 follicles ranging in size from 11 to 17 mm, representing one clutch. Others collected on June 5 contained oviducal eggs, and nesting activity was observed in the same area on June 21. Only one clutch is laid per season as virtually all large follicles are ovulated at one time. Of 12 gravid females, 8 lacked large follicles and 4 had only one each. The amount of ovarian fat is correlated with maturation of ova and increases as ova dry weight increases. The increase in ovarian fat is accompanied by a corresponding decrease in the fat content of other body tissues (Brenner, 1970). The male reproductive cycle has not been described.

The timing of sexual maturity varies within and among populations (Lovich et al., 1990a). Maturity in males, as determined by courtship activity, occurs at plastron lengths of 14.1–17.9 cm and carapace lengths of 19.2–20.0 cm. Maturity in females, as determined by courtship and nesting activity, occurs at plastron lengths of 13.4–16.0 cm and carapace lengths of 15.8–18.5 cm. Both sexes mature between the ages of 14 and 18 years (Garber, 1989; Farrell and Graham, 1991; Ross et al., 1991; Brooks et al., 1992).

Mating can occur at any time during the active season but peaks are evident in the spring and the fall. In Virginia the greatest numbers of copulating pairs are found in the fall (Ernst and McBreen, 1991c), but McBreen (pers. comm.) has also seen mating *C. insculpta* in December. Most courtship occurs in late afternoon (Harding and Bloomer, 1979; Ernst and McBreen, 1991c). Mating usually takes place in water at depths of 0.1–1.2 m, although copulation has been observed on land (Ernst, 1986a). In Pennsylvania, courtship and mating take place at water temperatures of 10.0–20.0°C (Ernst, 1986a). In the Appalachians of Pennsylvania and New York the only aquatic breeding habitats may be swift, cold trout streams (Swanson, 1952), and males may patrol shorelines of nesting beaches and attempt to copulate with any female that approaches or leaves (Ratner, in Vogt, 1981a; Harding, pers. comm.).

Courtship is usually started by the male, but cases of female-initiated courtship have been reported. Although accounts vary, the following composite description of courtship behavior summarizes the mating ritual (Evans, 1961, 1967; Harding and Bloomer, 1979; Brewster and Brewster, 1988; Kaufmann, 1992b). The male approaches the female and begins nosing her shell, head, tail, and legs. She may move away from the male or direct nosing behavior toward him; if she flees, he pursues her. The pair may face each other and bob or sway their heads simultaneously for an hour or more. Mounting occurs suddenly, with the male locking his claws under the female's marginal scutes. Once mounted he shakes her from side to side for up to several hours. Typical bouts consist of 1–14 shakes at rates of 0–5 bouts/minute. Bouts may be separated by periods of inactivity or other behaviors. The male then rubs his plastron on her shell, and bites at her head and shell. This phase alternates with thumping behavior in which he audibly pounds his plastron against her carapace. Thumping lasts for about 30 minutes before the male dismounts; typical thumping behavior has up to five thumps/bout with up to six bouts/minute. Thumping periods last from 5 to 117 minutes.

Copulation occurs after the male curls his tail to bring the vents into alignment. Female movement at this time may cause him to bite her. Mounting time varies from 1 to 12 hours, but a male may clasp a female for as long as two days in the water or up to five days on land! Actual coitus lasts one or two hours. While mounted underwater the male breathes periodically, but the female often has to struggle toward shallow water to gain a breath of air. Copulatory ties, or clasping locks, may be formed that last 22–33 minutes. In Pennsylvania, copulatory ties have been observed only in pairings that were not preceded by thumping, and sperm transfer is usually accomplished only in pairings that culminate in a copulatory tie (Kaufmann, 1992b). Up to 84.5% of the mountings observed by Kaufmann (1992b) in Pennsylvania probably did not result in sperm transfer. More pairings result in sperm transfer in the fall than in the spring. Kaufmann's observations are detailed and interesting, but it is not known if they represent standard behavior throughout the range.

Meritt (1980) noted that copulation was accompanied by vocalization, a behavior that was questioned by both Harding and Bloomer (1979) and Kaufmann (1992b), and we have never observed this.

Kaufmann (1992b) reported that individual females may be mounted by males up to eight times in one fall season and up to five times in one spring season. Females have also been observed to mate in five out of six years. Individual females have been observed to mate with four different males in the fall and three in the spring. Kaufmann (1992b) observed one female known to be inseminated by at least two different males: one in the fall and another the following spring. DNA fingerprinting of 11 clutches demonstrated that several clutches had two or more fathers.

Mature Pennsylvania males that notice mating pairs attempt to dislodge the mounted male, usually causing him to dismount and fight, regardless of the rank of the challenging male. After the fight, the winning male mounts the female if she is still in the area. Dominant males force subordinate males to dismount 93% of the time, whereas subordinate males displace dominants only 67% of the time. Subordinate males rarely win or retain their mounts. The number of mounts and inseminations by a male per week are positively correlated with his social rank (Kaufmann, 1992b).

The nesting season lasts from May to early July depending on geographic location (Ernst and McBreen, 1991c). In Nova Scotia, nesting occurs in July and may last only one week (Powell, 1967). Nesting usually takes place in the afternoon and may continue until 2315. Nest site requirements in Michigan include ample exposure to direct sunlight, well-drained but moist sand or soil substrate not subject to flooding, and a substrate free of rocks and thick vegetation (Harding and Bloomer, 1979)

An account by Pallas (1960) of the nesting act of a captive is the most complete on record. On 12 June a female was discovered digging at 0850, during a fine drizzle (nesting does not occur in the rain in Michigan, perhaps because of accompanying drops in air temperature; Harding, pers. comm.). At that time she had already dug a hole perhaps half the depth her hind legs could reach. Digging continued until 1024; it was done entirely with the hind feet, which alternated without once missing a turn. After digging the hole she formed an egg chamber at the bottom by scraping the right side with her left foot, and vice versa. Her head was stretched far out during the digging, and the front feet were stationary. She dug slowly and did not pause to rest.

At 1025 the first egg was laid. Seven more followed, the last at 1034. During oviposition, her head was partly withdrawn, and one hind leg rested on the ground, the other at the edge of the hole or just inside it. As each egg appeared she raised her posterior high and lifted her tail. After each egg was dropped she inserted one foot inside the cavity—the feet alternated in this—but pulled it out as the next egg appeared.

She rested for two minutes, and then began to fill the nest with earth. Filling and tamping continued until about 1120; during this period the turtle retained her original position while pivoting farther and farther to the sides. Then, for another 20 minutes, filling and tamping continued, but she moved her front feet from their stations and swung in an irregular circle that finally brought her some centimeters from the nesting site.

The filling behavior consisted of scratching with her claws at the sides of the cavity, scraping with her toes and the sides of her feet to bring dirt from the surface into the hole, packing with the soles of her feet held flat and the feet rapidly alternating, and tamping with the sides of the feet, the back of the feet, and occasionally with the whole side of the lower leg. She also pounded the dirt with the rear of her plastron, until the nesting site was indistinguishable from the surrounding ground. Her head was extended during this stage, and she rested several times, for as long as two to four minutes. At 1148 she left the site.

Harding and Bloomer (1979) reported that after leaving the water, females in Michigan flip sand over their carapaces, perhaps to camouflage themselves. They also stop periodically to sniff the substrate, and occasionally dig test pits. Although the nest cavity is usually dug entirely with the hind feet, females in New Jersey sometimes use their forelimbs to excavate a body pit prior to excavating the actual nest chamber (Farrell and Graham, 1991). The nest cavity may be 5–10 cm deep (Swanson, 1952; Combs, 1971). Some females may void bladder water into the cavity during the filling process. The entire nesting process, from leaving the water to returning to it, may take three to four hours.

Only one clutch of 4–18 eggs is laid per year (Ernst and Barbour, 1972; Harding, 1977), but individual females may not nest every year (Ross et al., 1991). Mean clutch size is 10.4 eggs in Michigan, 8.5 eggs in New Jersey (Harding and Bloomer, 1979; Farrell and Graham, 1991), 8.8 eggs in Ontario (Brooks et al., 1992) and 11 eggs in Wisconsin (Ross et al., 1991).

The oval, white, thin-shelled eggs have the following dimensions: length, 27.0–49.0 mm; width, 19.5–26.3 mm; weight, 6.3–14.9 g (Combs, 1971; Harding and Bloomer, 1979; Ernst and McBreen, 1991c; Farrell and Graham, 1991). The mean wet mass of clutches from Ontario is 96 g (Brooks et al., 1992). The eggshell constitutes 6.1% of the total egg weight (Ewert, 1979a).

Egg width and mass, but not length, are positively correlated with female size and clutch size in Ontario (even after removing the effect of body size in the latter). Smaller females produce relatively longer eggs than larger females; those of large Ontario females are smaller than the eggs laid by small New Jersey females (Brooks et al., 1992).

The incubation period varies as a function of temperature. In the laboratory, hatching time ranges from 67 days at 25–25.5°C to about 40 days at temperatures above 30°C (Ewert, 1979a). Of 161 eggs incubated under artificial conditions by Farrell and Graham (1991), 12% were infertile, 14% died during incubation, and 74% hatched. *Clemmys insculpta* does not have temperature-dependent sex determination (Bull et al., 1985; Ewert and Nelson, 1991).

Hatchlings leave the nest as early as mid-August and as late as early October. Apparently none overwinter in the nest (Harding, 1991; Ernst, pers. obs.). The young turtles may wander a considerable distance on land before entering water, but once in the water they immediately drink and then hide under nearby objects. The gray-brown hatchlings lack the bright pigment on the head and legs characteristic of adults and are 78.5% of the weight of freshly laid eggs (Ewert, 1979a). Their low, keelless carapaces are 28.0–37.9 mm long, 27.4–35.9 mm wide, and 13.0–17.4 mm high and they weigh 4.6–10 g (Farrell and Graham, 1991). The ratio of hatchling size to maximum size is about 1:7.4 (Bury, 1979a). Yolk sacs and caruncles are lost prior to emergence or shortly thereafter.

Captive propagation is discussed by Herman (1991).

GROWTH AND LONGEVITY: Growth rings are highly reliable indicators of age in wild

Hatchling *Clemmys insculpta;* note egg tooth (caruncle) on upper jaw

Juvenile *Clemmys insculpta*

specimens as old as 15–20 years (Harding and Bloomer, 1979; Ernst, pers. obs.). A hatchling kept in an outdoor enclosure in New Jersey grew from 34 mm to 56 mm in its first year and 71 mm by the end of the second growing period, and a second 35-mm hatchling grew to 126 mm by the end of the seventh growing season (Harding and Bloomer, 1979). The annual increment of growth in New Jersey wood turtles ranges from 84.0% during the first growing season to about 2.0% from age 14–20 or more (Farrell and Graham, 1991).

Growth in males and females from Pennsylvania is rapid and similar until reaching a plastron length of about 16.0 cm, after which males grow at a slightly faster rate. Straight-line carapace length increases faster than plastron length in males owing to the development of plastron concavity as they mature. Wood turtles continue to grow after reaching sexual maturity. The mean individual growth rate of *Clemmys insculpta* exceeding 16.0 cm at first capture was 0.8 mm per year (Lovich et al., 1990a).

The mean age of adult male and female wood

turtles in Michigan was reported as 21.5 and 20.2 years, respectively (Harding and Bloomer, 1979), but possibly these were underestimated (Harding, pers. comm.). Wild *C. insculpta* have survived for more than 33 years (Ross et al., 1991), and captives to 58 years of age (Oliver, 1955).

FOOD HABITS: The wood turtle is omnivorous. Farrell and Graham (1991) observed wood turtles in New Jersey feeding on the green leaves of strawberries (*Fragaria*) in April and May, and strawberries and blackberries (*Rubus*) in June and August. A large male ate a dead fish in May and a juvenile consumed a slug in September. The diet of wood turtles in Pennsylvania consists of fungi, invertebrates, and flowers and fruits, in descending order of importance (Strang, 1983). Of 51 food items consumed, 31.4% are leaves including cinquefoil (*Potentilla canadensis*) and various violets (*Viola*). Fungi figure prominently in the diet after the first heavy rains of July. Surface (1908) found plant remains in 76% and animal remains in 80% of the Pennsylvania *C. insculpta* he examined.

Other food items consumed under natural and seminatural conditions include algae, moss, blueberries (*Vaccinium*), leaves of willows (*Salix*) and alders (*Alnus*), grasses, mollusks, insects (including the nymphs of the 17-year cicada), earthworms, tadpoles, newborn mice, possibly the eggs and young of ground-nesting birds, other turtle eggs, and whatever else they can find (Reid and Nichols, 1970; Czarnowsky, 1976; Harding and Bloomer, 1979; Ernst and McBreen, 1991c).

One of the most unusual feeding habits of any turtle has been observed in some wood turtle populations in central Pennsylvania and Michigan. Wood turtles sometimes cause earthworms to come to the surface by stomping their front feet. This behavior, or "worm stomping," was described by Harding and Bloomer (1979), Kaufmann (1986, 1989), and Kaufmann et al. (1989). A stomping turtle typically takes a few steps forward and then stomps several times with one front foot and then the other at a rate of about one stomp per second. Any worm brought to the surface is eaten. The whole sequence usually lasts 15 minutes or more and may include 2–19 stomps (mean 8.1) from the time stomping begins until a worm is eaten. Sequences start with light stomping with the force of each successive stomp increasing, and some stomps are audible for several meters. The plastron may also be banged against the ground in the process. All worm stomping observed in Pennsylvania by Kaufmann and co-workers oc-

curred in damp areas within 30 m of a creek, at any time of the day, but not on days following rain. Wood turtles captured about 2.4 worms/hour.

As fantastic as this seems, the behavior may have a relatively simple explanation. It is a well-known fact that worms come to the surface when it rains. Surface activity in worms may be stimulated by the vibrations produced when raindrops hit the soil. People in some areas mimic these vibrations by rubbing a stick against another notched stick driven into the ground. When worms come to the surface they are collected and used for fish bait. It is likely that wood turtles are exploiting the tendency of earthworms to respond to vibrations by coming to the surface. Kaufmann tested the theory by drumming his fingers against the ground with rhythm and force comparable to that generated by wood turtles. On average, he observed one worm on the surface every 9–10 minutes. Some were noticed when they responded to vibrations by contracting toward their hole. Another explanation may be that the earthworms mistake the vibrations for those made by a tunneling mole, a natural predator, and surface to escape (Harding, pers. comm.). Whatever the mechanism behind this unusual behavior, some *C. insculpta* seem to have mastered the ability to collect worms. However, worm stomping may be a learned trait of only some populations, as wood turtles elsewhere do not seem to practice this behavior.

PREDATORS AND DEFENSE: Farrell and Graham (1991) observed 53 living wood turtles (18 males, 19 females, and 16 juveniles) in New Jersey with injuries that were probably caused by predators. Of these, 27 had missing limbs, 11 had mutilated carapaces, and one had a mutilated plastron. Three turtles were found dead with their heads chewed.

During a fifteen-year study in northern Michigan, 12.5% of marked wood turtles had mutilated or amputated limbs, most a result of injuries sustained as adults. Two percent were missing two limbs. Raccoons (*Procyon lotor*) were suspected to be the predator. The recapture rate of injured turtles was significantly lower than that for noninjured turtles, suggesting that limb loss compromises long-term survival. Some females with mutilated limbs were recaptured several years in a row, indicating that wood turtles can live with major injuries. Other *Clemmys insculpta* had shells that had been gnawed by large rodents, perhaps porcupines (*Erithizon dorsatum*) or beavers (*Castor canadensis*) (Harding, 1985; Harding and Bloomer, 1979).

Raccoons and striped skunks (*Mephitis mephitis*) are accomplished egg predators and may destroy 100% of the clutches in some years. Less damaging nest predators include ravens (*Corvus corax*) and coyotes (*Canis latrans*). Hatchlings and juveniles are preyed upon by raccoons, skunks, feral cats (*Felis catus*) and dogs (*Canis familiaris*), opossums (*Didelphis marsupialis*), various birds, snapping turtles (*Chelydra serpentina*) and large fish (Harding and Bloomer, 1979).

Wood turtles are often infested with the leech, *Placobdella parasitica* (Koffler et al., 1978; Hulse and Routman, 1982; Brewster and Brewster, 1986; Farrell and Graham, 1991).

Habitat destruction, human exploitation, and highway mortality are probably the greatest causes of adult mortality in wood turtles (Harding, 1991; Ernst and McBreen, 1991c). Of these, the most serious recent threat to wood turtles is commercial collecting for the pet trade. Most states have laws to protect the wood turtle (Harding, 1991).

Most wood turtles are inoffensive when captured, but some large males may bite hard and scratch, and others may void bladder water. *Clemmys insculpta* has good hearing which helps it escape from predators. It responds quickly to sounds up to about 500 cycles/second (cps), but its response declines rapidly above 1,000 cps, and no measurable response occurs to sounds above 3,000–4,000 cps (Wever and Vernon, 1956a,b; Peterson (1966).

POPULATIONS: Wood turtle density estimates (as calculated yearly) in New Jersey are 9.9–11.4 turtles per hectare (Farrell and Graham, 1991). In another study of New Jersey turtles, Harding and Bloomer (1979) estimated a density of about 12.5 adults per hectare in habitats ranging in size from 40 to 120 ha, and thought that population densities in Michigan were much lower than those in New Jersey.

Sex ratios of adults range from male-biased to female-biased. Lovich et al. (1990a) noted that females tend to predominate numerically in large samples, perhaps because males mature at a later age than females in some populations. Partial confirmation of this hypothesis was subsequently provided by Brooks et al. (1992), who reported a sex ratio of 0.38:1 males to females in Ontario, Harding (1991),

who reported a sex ratio of 0.82:1 in Michigan, and Ross et al. (1991), who reported a predominance of males in a small sample of turtles from Wisconsin. In contrast, Farrell and Graham (1991) recorded a male:female ratio of 1.6:1 in New Jersey, and Kaufmann (1992b) found no significant difference in the number of males and females in his Pennsylvania population.

Details of population structure were provided by Farrell and Graham (1991) for a New Jersey population. The hatchling and juvenile to subadult and adult ratio was 1.0:1.2; over 45% of the turtles were adults with plastron lengths greater than 14.0 cm. Other age groups were represented in the following percentages: hatchlings (age 1), 3%; juveniles (age 1–8), 42%; subadult females (age 9–13), 11%; subadult males (age 9–13), 10%; adult females (age $\geq$14), 13%; and adult males (age $\geq$14), 21%. Garber (1989) reported that turtles under 14 years of age composed 37% and 44% of two populations in Connecticut. In contrast, Ross et al. (1991) noted an abundance of older adults in Wisconsin, and Harding (1991) found that 82% of his study population in Michigan were adults.

REMARKS: The wood turtle is declining in many parts of its range because of overcollecting and habitat destruction. Like most turtles, it is especially vulnerable to increased mortality because of the traits of slow growth, late maturity, and the high natural mortality of eggs and juveniles. As a result of the increasing threats to the continued survival of this species it is listed in Appendix II of the Convention of International Trade in Endangered Species (CITES). Conservation problems and efforts are discussed by Harding and Bloomer (1979) and Harding (1991).

Merkle (1975), using starch electrophoresis to study relationships among members of the genus *Clemmys*, showed *C. insculpta* to be the most primitive, sharing the fewest protein bands with other species of the genus. However, plastron scute relationships examined by Lovich et al. (1990a) indicate *C. insculpta* is most similar to *C. marmorata*.

Additional information on this species is summarized by Ernst (1972b).

Clemmys marmorata (Baird and Girard, 1852)
Western pond turtle
PLATE 26

RECOGNITION: This is a small to medium-sized turtle with a low carapace and, commonly, a pattern of spots or lines that radiate from the centers of the scutes (a pattern which closely resembles that of some European *Emys orbicularis*). The short (to 20 cm; Buskirk, 1991), broad carapace is smooth, widest behind the bridge, and keelless. It is olive, dark brown, gray, or black, and may be patternless in some individuals. The first vertebral touches four marginals and the cervical. The ventral side of the marginals and the bridge are marked with irregular dark blotches or lines along the seams. The hingeless, pale-yellow plastron in places bears a pattern of dark blotches along the posterior margins of the scutes. The skin is gray, with some pale yellow on the neck, chin, forelimbs, and tail. The head is plain or reticulated.

In males the plastron is concave; in females it is flat. The male's anal vent is posterior to the carapacial rim; the female's is ventral to the rim. Males have lighter throats; females have more heavily patterned carapaces.

KARYOTYPE: The karyotype is 2n = 50: 16 macrochromosomes with median or submedian centromeres, 10 macrochromosomes with terminal or subterminal centromeres, and 24 microchromosomes (Bickham, 1975).

FOSSIL RECORD: Remains of *Clemmys marmorata* have been identified from Pliocene (Blancan) deposits in California and Oregon and Pleistocene (Irvingtonian, Rancholabrean) deposits from California and Washington (Brattstrom, 1953, 1955; Brattstrom and Sturn, 1959; Miller, 1971; Gustafason, 1978). Archeological sites in California have yielded remains of *C. marmorata* that indicate Indians had apparently eaten them (Schneider and Everson, 1989).

DISTRIBUTION: *Clemmys marmorata* ranges chiefly west of the Cascade-Sierra crest from western Washington to northern Baja California. Isolated colonies existed in the Truckee and Carson rivers in Nevada, but these are apparently extinct (Buskirk, 1991). Another isolated, but extant, population is found in the interior-draining Mojave River of California as far into the Mojave Desert as Afton Canyon. There is a questionable record from Jerome County, Idaho, and an individual has been seen in Grant County, Oregon (Nussbaum et al., 1983). *C. marmorata* collected on Vancouver Island, British Columbia, may have been escaped or released captives originally from the United States (Cook, 1984); however, western pond turtles have also been reported in the adjacent lower Fraser River watershed on the mainland of British Columbia (Nussbaum et al., 1983), but Buskirk (1991) questions these records.

GEOGRAPHIC VARIATION: Two poorly defined subspecies are recognized. *Clemmys marmorata marmorata* (Baird and Girard, 1852), the northwestern pond turtle, ranges from western Washington south to San Francisco Bay, and also occurs in western Nevada. It has a pair of well-developed triangular inguinal scutes on the bridge, and its brown or grayish neck and head are well marked with dark dashes. The throat is pale in contrast with the sides of the head. *C. m. pallida* Seeliger, 1945, the southwestern pond turtle, is found from San Francisco Bay south into northern Baja California. It can be distinguished by its poorly developed inguinal scutes (absent in 60% of individuals), and by the uniform light color of the throat and neck. A large area of intergradation occurs in central California (Bury, 1970; Stebbins, 1985).

Buskirk (1991) reviewed the characters used by Seeliger (1945) to separate the two subspecies, and

Clemmys marmorata

Plastron of *Clemmys marmorata*

questioned their validity because of the ambiguity of several.

CONFUSING SPECIES: The only other freshwater turtle within its range in the United States or Canada is *Chrysemys picta bellii,* which has a large, dark blotch spreading along the seams of the plastron, a notched upper jaw, a reticulate pattern of light lines on the carapace, red pigment on the marginals, and yellow stripes on the neck and limbs.

HABITAT: The western pond turtle is primarily riparian, most often living in sloughs, streams (both permanent and intermittent), and large rivers, although some may inhabit impoundments and irrigation ditches and other artificial waterbodies. In streams, pools are preferred over shallow reaches (Bury, 1972). Habitats may be either rocky or mud bottomed, but usually contain some aquatic vegetation and basking sites. *Clemmys marmorata* has been collected from brackish estuarine waters at sea level to

Head of *Clemmys marmorata*

over 1,800 m elevation in mountain streams (Stebbins, 1954; Bury, 1963).

BEHAVIOR: Evenden (1948) reported that the earliest occurrence of *Clemmys marmorata* in the central Willamette Valley, Oregon, was 28 February, the latest was 19 November, but in northern California, Bury (1972) found active turtles from late May to October. In California, at least north to Shasta County, it may be active every month (Stebbins, 1985; Buskirk, 1991). Hibernation is spent underwater, often in the mud bottom of a stream pool. *Clemmys marmorata* may also estivate during summer droughts by burying itself in the soft bottoms of its stream.

The daily activity cycle consists of a period of foraging at sunrise (0530–0800) followed by a period of basking (0800–dusk), with most basking occurring from 0900 to 1000 (Bury, 1972). At other times the turtles either remain inactive in the water or forage. In summer, turtles may forage in the late afternoon or early evening (to 1930), but most forage earlier in the day (Bury, 1972). In the early morning or evening these turtles move up or downstream from pool to pool (Pope, 1939).

Clemmys marmorata apparently avoids body temperatures over 34°C, usually terminating aerial basking at about 32–34°C, well below its critical thermal maximum of 40°C (Bury, 1972). Mean time of basking by undisturbed turtles steadily decreases from about 68 minutes at 0800–0859 and 40 minutes at 0900–0959 to only 11–15 minutes at 1200–1359

(Bury, 1972). When too hot, the western pond turtle either dunks itself in the water or seeks shade. Some turtles reemerging to bask remain partially submerged for some time before climbing entirely out of the water. Basking is usually on a rock or log or on the bank, but some may even climb a short way onto tree branches that dip into the water from bank vegetation (Nussbaum et al., 1983). Very seldom does *C. marmorata* bask by floating at the surface, possibly so it will not be swept downstream.

Brattstrom (1965) found afternoon body temperatures of three *C. marmorata* to be 21.8°C, 25.5°C, and 27.0°C. One collected at 0930 in water of 8.3°C had a body temperature of 9.0°C. The preferred range of body temperatures for normal activity is 24–32°C (Bury, 1972).

Home range sizes and lengths in a population congregated in pools in a northern California stream were, respectively: adult males 0.98 ha (0.22–2.42), 976 m (275–2,425); adult females 0.25 ha (0–0.75), 248 m (0–750); and juveniles 0.36 ha (0–1.15), 363 m (0–1,150) (Bury, 1972). During the summer these turtles moved from pool to pool within the stream system; 53.5% of males, 27.5% of females, and 32.6% of juveniles moved upstream, while 34.0% of males, 38.9% of females, and 27.1% of juveniles traveled downstream. The average male moved 354 m during Bury's (1972) study, while the average female and juvenile moved only 169 m and 142 m, respectively. More than 81% of the males moved over 200 m, but only 36.6% of females and 22.5% of juveniles traveled a distance greater than 200 m; 26.6% of the

Distribution of *Clemmys marmorata*

males, 6.1% of females, and 6.2% of juveniles migrated over 500 m. In three years, the average male moved approximately 817 m. These turtles were capable of moving distances of at least 1.6 km overland to adjacent waterbodies and later returning. The orientation or navigational cues used during these journeys are unknown.

At another site in southern California, four radio-equipped females averaged daily movements of 28.0, 54.6, 60.5, and 87.1 m during the period 20 May to 21 June 1989 (Rathbun et al., 1992).

Aggressive behavior may be initiated by a basking *C. marmorata* toward an approaching turtle (Bury and Wolfheim, 1973). Most common is an open-mouth gesture, during which the yellow jaws and pinkish-red mouth lining are displayed. Other turtles usually pull in their heads or slide into the water when an open-mouth gesture is directed at them. Adults emerging to bask sometimes direct the open-mouth gesture at juveniles already occupying good sites. If this gesture does not work, some turtles bite or ram to push the other turtle off its perch. Most basking aggression takes place before noon (0900–1159).

REPRODUCTION: The reproductive biology of *Clemmys marmorata* is poorly known. Ovipositing females are at least 135–140 mm in carapace length (although Nussbaum et al., 1983, reported the size of maturity in females to be 120 mm), and are probably 8–10 years old, but detailed information on the size and age of maturity and annual gametic cycles of both sexes is unavailable.

Copulation has been observed in the field in May, June, and late August, and in captivity in late August and early September (Holland, 1988; Buskirk, 1991). The only description of courtship is that provided by Holland (1988) from an observation on 30 August at 1242–1247 in San Luis Obispo County, California. The incident occurred on the bottom at a depth of two meters (surface temperature 19°C, bottom temperature 16°C). At first both turtles moved slowly along the bottom. The female had pulled in her head but partially extended her legs. The male swam to one side 4–5 cm behind and slightly above (2–3 cm) her with his head and limbs fully extended. He made several scratching motions to the anterior left rim of her carapace with his right front foot, which caused her to stop, retract her front legs, and elevate the posterior portion of her shell 2–3 cm off the bottom by extending her hind legs. The male then swam in front of the female, turned to face her, and scratched the anterior rim of her carapace 17 times with his foreclaws. His extended head touched her carapace four times, but Holland saw no biting. The male proceeded 15–20 cm to the front and slightly to the left of the female, fully extended his head, partially extended his left front and hind legs, and made several short (<2 cm) horizontal, coordinated sweeping/fanning movements which lasted about 25 seconds. He then repeated the scratching and limb-sweeping sequences, while elevating his entire body at a 45° angle directly in front of the female while extending his head and all four limbs. The male at this point surfaced for air, discovered Holland and eventually attempted to swim away.

The nesting season extends from late April through August, depending on the latitude; the peak period is late May to early July. Some females may travel along a waterway as far as 2 km to distant nesting areas if suitable excavating habitat is not available locally (Rathbun et al., 1992). Nests may be dug in either the morning or evening. Usually they are located along stream or pond margins; however, nests have been found in fields over 100 m above and distant from the water. Full sunlight seems to be a requirement; all six terrestrial locations where Rathbun et al. (1992) found a radio-equipped female during the nesting season were in open, grassy areas with a southern exposure. On two of these occasions she was observed digging nests. Both times she first moistened the soil with bladder water, but deposited no eggs and left the cavities open. All of her trips onto land began between 1700 and 2000, and she spent the night ashore, returning to the water the next morning between 0815 and 0900. A second female also made overnight trips to a similar habitat, presumably to nest.

Three flask- or pear-shaped nest cavities examined by Rathbun et al. (1992) were surrounded by a "turtle-shaped" bare area that was trampled and scraped clean of vegetation. The nests were 6.5–8.0 cm deep with a 6.5–7.0-cm-wide egg chamber and a 3.5–4.0-cm mouth.

Clutch size ranges from 2 to 11 eggs (mean 6.3 for 15 clutches). Evidence presented in tabular form by Storer (1930) seems to indicate that two clutches may be laid a season. The hard, white eggs are elliptical-oval, 30.0–42.6 mm long × 18.5–22.6 mm wide, and weigh 8.3–11.1 g. The eggs are approximately 71% water, 16% lipid, and 40% shell; the yolk is about 27% lipid (Congdon and Gibbons, 1985).

The natural incubation period is unknown, and may vary with altitude and latitude. Eggs incubated at 25–33°C by Lardie (1975b) and Feldman (1982) hatched in 73–81 days. Eggs incubated on saturated vermiculite failed to hatch, while 13 of 18 eggs incubated on a screen over a waterbath developed normally (Feldman, 1982). Feldman noted that hatchlings did not leave the egg if the temperature exceeded 27°C, but, once moved to a cooler environment, emerged within two or three hours. The embryology of *Clemmys marmorata* is discussed and illustrated by Noble and Noble (1940). Hatchling sex is determined by incubation temperature (M. A. Ewert, pers. comm.).

Hatchling emergence may occur in late summer or fall, but Feldman (1982) and Buskirk (1991) presented data indicating some little turtles overwinter in the nest and emerge the next spring.

Hatchlings are usually 25–29 mm in carapace length. The rounded and keeled carapace is brown or olive, with yellow marks at the edge of the marginals. Carapacial scutes have many small tubercles, giving them a grainy appearance. The plastron is yellow and has a large, irregular, dark central blotch. The head, limbs, and tail are marked with pale yellow. The tail is nearly as long as the carapace.

GROWTH AND LONGEVITY: Storer (1930) found that at the beginning of their second season, *Clemmys marmorata* were 27.8–33.9 mm in carapace length. A 48.7-mm juvenile was in its second season of growth; one 58.0 mm long was in its third season; two, 58.5 and 64.0 mm long, were commencing their third growing season; and one 66.0 mm long was well into its third growth period. Those in their fourth growing season were 71.5–79.5 mm long, and one in its fifth year was 95.0 mm long. These rates indicate that *C. marmorata* may be expected to reach a carapace length of about 135–140 mm in 8–10 years.

The granular condition of the hatchling carapace disappears with age. Seeliger (1945) gave the following average carapace lengths in relation to the progressive changes: granular condition at 30.1 mm; partly granular with radiating and concentric ridges on each scute at 67.9 mm; concentric ridges only at 125.7 mm; and smooth shell at 145.9 mm.

Lardie (1975b) noted that the plastron is a uniform light yellow in the embryo, and that a hatchling he had contained black coloration only along the edges of the scutes at the center of the plastron, but that this pigmentation gradually spread from the center, in an irregular oval pattern, until it covered 50% of the plastron in just over three months. This supports

Slater's (1962) conclusion that there is an increase of dark plastral pigment with age.

Clemmys marmorata has lived over 12 years in captivity (Snider and Bowler, 1992), but wild individuals probably survive over 20 years.

FOOD HABITS: *Clemmys marmorata* is a generalist feeder. Most food is obtained by opportunistic foraging or scavenging, but neustophagia (modified filter feeding) may also be used for capturing small, plentiful foods at the surface (Holland, 1985; Bury, 1986). Although Bury (1986) reported it does not select prey based on its general availability, the observation of filter feeding on *Daphnia,* a temporary abundant resource, by Holland (1985) indicates at least occasional predation on the most plentiful food item at a given time. Bogert (in Carr, 1952) saw a captive pick up a large sowbug on land and carry it to the water before attempting to swallow it, and Ernst has also observed this behavior in captives.

Known foods are: algae, various plants (including the pods of the yellow water lily, *Nuphar polysepalum*), snails, crustaceans (crayfish, *Daphnia*), isopods, insects (Coleoptera adults and larvae, Diptera adults and larvae, Ephemeroptera nymphs, Hemiptera adults and larvae, Neuroptera larvae, Odonata nymphs, Orthoptera adults, Trichoptera larvae), spiders, fish (*Catostomus, Lampetra*), frogs (tadpoles and adult *Rana*), mallard duck (*Anas platyrhynchos,* carrion), and a mouse fragment (cricetid?) (Pope, 1939; Evenden, 1948: Carr, 1952; Holland, 1985; Bury, 1986). Captives feed well on canned and fresh fish, liver, raw beef, canned dog food, trout chow, earthworms, and romaine lettuce.

Diets of adult males and females and of juveniles differ in prey size and proportions of prey items, which may reduce intraspecific competition between the age and sex classes (Bury, 1986). Males consume more insects and vertebrates than do females, who eat more algae, and males seem to prefer larger food items. Juveniles eat smaller foods and take higher numbers of prey than do adults (Bury, 1986).

PREDATORS AND DEFENSE: Reports on natural predation are unavailable, but eggs and juveniles most likely fall victim to a variety of larger vertebrates. The pet trade has seriously reduced some populations, and this along with habitat alteration and pollution may be the greatest threat to the survival of *Clemmys marmorata*. Bury (1989) reported that one pet wholesaler obtained about 500 western pond turtles from a southern California lake and shipped them to Europe.

Clemmys marmorata is shy and tries to escape as soon as an intruder is detected. If picked up, some will try to bite, scratch, or release bladder water on the handler, but most remain rather passive.

POPULATIONS: Bury (1972, 1989) captured, marked, and released 578 *Clemmys marmorata* in a 3.5-km stretch of a stream in northern California, and estimated the density to be 214 turtles/hectare. This density is somewhat deceiving as the turtles were usually congregated in separated pools in the stream. One such 0.9 × 3 m pool yielded 12 adults, and another deeper pool contained about 50 turtles. Each meter of stream deeper than 0.5 m had an estimated 0.6 turtles. During the four summers of Bury's study, 70% of the marked turtles were recaptured for a total catch of 1,500 turtles. The estimated biomass for this population was 137 kg/ha. The adult sex ratio was 1.7 males for every female. Thirty-five percent of the population was juvenile.

Populations are declining in southern California and over most of the northern range; habitat destruction seems the major cause (Brattstrom, 1988; Brattstrom and Messer, 1988). Today only northern California and southern Oregon support extensive populations. The U.S. Fish and Wildlife Service was petitioned to list *Clemmys marmorta* as an endangered species (Federal Register, 1992).

REMARKS: Aspects of the shell morphology of *Clemmys marmorata* are more similar to *C. guttata* and *C. insculpta* than to *C. muhlenburgii* (Lovich et al., 1991a), but, from a biochemical standpoint, *C. marmorata* is closest to *C. muhlenbergii* (Merkle, 1975).

The common name "western pond turtle" is a misnomer, as this species seldom lives in ponds. A more accurate common name would be "western stream turtle."

The comparative anatomy of *C. marmorata* is presented in Noble and Noble (1940), Bury (1970) has reviewed the literature concerning this turtle up to that time, and Buskirk (1991) gives the most recent update on the status of the species.

Emydoidea blandingii (Holbrook, 1838)
Blanding's turtle
PLATE 27

RECOGNITION: This northern turtle has an elongated, smooth carapace (to 27.4 cm) that is neither keeled nor serrated. The broad first vertebral touches four marginals. The carapace is black, and each scute commonly has tan to yellow irregular spots or slightly radiating lines, but some individuals are patternless or their spots are faded to the point of being almost invisible. A movable hinge lies between the pectoral and abdominal scutes on the plastron. The plastron is connected to the carapace by ligaments; it has no plastral buttresses. It varies from yellow with a large, dark blotch at the outer, posterior corner of each major scute to almost totally black. The flattened head is moderate in size with a nonprotruding snout, a notched upper jaw, and protruding eyes. The top and sides of the head are blue-gray with tan reticulations, and the chin, throat, and neck are bright yellow. The upper jaw may be marked with dark bars. The triturating surfaces of the jaws are narrow and ridgeless. Other skin is blue-gray; some yellow scales occur on the tail and legs. The neck is very long, and the feet are webbed.

Males have dark pigmentation in their upper jaws, the cloacal vent behind the posterior rim of the carapace, and a slightly concave plastron. Females have yellow upper jaws, the cloacal vent under the posterior marginals, and flat plastra. Females also have longer plastra and higher carapaces than males (Rowe, 1992).

KARYOTYPE: The diploid chromosome number is 50: 20 metacentric or submetacentric, 10 subtelocentric, and 20 acrocentric or telocentric chromosomes (Stock, 1972).

FOSSIL RECORD: A late Pliocene (Blancan) fossil of a Blanding's turtle has been found in Kansas (Preston and McCoy, 1971; McCoy, 1973); Pleistocene remains are known from the Irvingtonian of Kansas and Oklahoma (Taylor, 1943; Preston and McCoy, 1971; Holman, 1986a), and the Rancholabrean of Kansas, Mississippi, Missouri, and Ontario (Preston and McCoy, 1971; Jackson and Kaye, 1974a, 1975; Churcher et al., 1990). A 5,000-year-old postglacial fossil was discovered in Michigan (Holman, 1990), and archeological records exist for Illinois, Maine, New York, and Ontario (Bleakney, 1958a; Adler, 1968; Preston and McCoy, 1971; French, 1986). The Rancholabrean fossils from Jones Spring, Hickory County, Missouri, reported to be Emydoidea blandingii by Van Devender and King (1975) have been reidentified as Terrapene carolina putnami by Moodie and Van Devender (1977), and fossils of Emys twentei Taylor, 1943, from Kansas are now considered E. blandingii (Preston and McCoy, 1971; McCoy, 1973).

A Miocene (Barstovian) hypoplastron from an Emydoidea seems ancestral to E. blandingii (Hutchison, 1981).

DISTRIBUTION: The main range of Emydoidea is from southwestern Quebec and southern Ontario south through the Great Lakes region, and west to Iowa, northeastern Missouri, southeastern South Dakota, and west-central Nebraska. It also occurs in scattered localities in southeastern New York, eastern Massachusetts, southern New Hampshire and adjacent Maine, and on Nova Scotia (Graham et al., 1987). Blanding's turtles occasionally cross Lake Erie to northwestern Pennsylvania (Ernst, 1985c).

GEOGRAPHIC VARIATION: No subspecies are recognized.

CONFUSING SPECIES: Box turtles of the genus Terrapene have a well-developed plastral hinge, but none have a yellow throat and chin, or, com-

Emydoidea blandingii

Plastron of *Emydoidea blandingii*

monly, a notched upper jaw; *T. carolina* has a keeled carapace. Turtles of the genus *Clemmys* lack a plastral hinge, and *C. insculpta* has a sculptured, keeled carapace with a strongly serrated posterior rim.

HABITAT: In general, *Emydoidea blandingii* lives in productive, eutrophic habitats, with clean shallow water, a soft but firm, organic bottom, and abundant aquatic vegetation. It is found in lakes, ponds, marshes, creeks, wet prairies, and sloughs.

Ross and Anderson (1990) noted that *Emydoidea* in Wisconsin seem to spend most of the time in marshes, rather than ponds; but marshes are used less than expected based on habitat availability, as are also terrestrial habitats, and ponds with sand bottoms and no aquatic vegetation are rarely used. Wetlands covered by cattail (*Typha*) mats are not used either, but areas cleared of cattails by muskrats (*Ondatra zibethica*) are entered by the turtle, possibly for foraging. Habitat preferences may vary seasonally; in

Distribution of *Emydoidea blandingii*

early summer, marsh habitat is used in proportion to availability, but terrestrial and stream/ditch habitat use exceeds availability (Ross and Anderson, 1990; Rowe and Moll, 1991). Habitat in Wisconsin is characterized by high dissolved oxygen and high nitrogen and phosphorus concentrations, but not correlated with either water color or biochemical oxygen demand (Ross and Anderson, 1990).

In Minnesota, small juveniles primarily use emergent sedge (*Carex comosa*) habitats and alder (*Alnus rugosa*) hummocks (Pappas and Brecke, 1992). Other larger juvenile *Emydoidea* use sedge/water interfaces, and the largest juveniles are found in open water. As with adults, significant seasonal differences occur in the use of these various habitats.

BEHAVIOR: *Emydoidea* is primarily active during daylight. Under experimental conditions, at a 14:10-hour light:dark cycle and 25°C, its daily activity patterns are bimodal with peaks at about 0700 and 1600. At 15°C, activity tends to be unimodal with a peak at about noon (Graham, 1979b).

From May to August in northeastern Illinois, most activity begins between 0600 and 0800 and ends between 1900 and 2200. The turtles are more active in the morning than at any other time. At night, they sleep suspended in aquatic vegetation or on pond bottoms beneath aquatic vegetation (Rowe and Moll, 1991).

Activity begins as early as April in Michigan and Missouri and lasts until September (Gibbons, 1968d; Kofron and Schreiber, 1985). In northeastern Illinois, Blanding's turtles are first seen in late March when water temperatures climb to 19°C, but data based on radiotelemetry indicate that some may be active at temperatures as low as 10°C (Rowe and Moll, 1991). They respond to baited traps from May through August. Rowe and Moll (1991) captured none in March, April, September, or October; the numbers captured per trap day in various months were: May, 0.095; June, 0.216; July, 0.055; August, 0.140. Most *Emydoidea* were trapped either in the morning or in the evening.

Hutchison et al. (1966) found the mean critical thermal maximum of 12 *Emydoidea* to be 39.5°C (38.2–40.6). This is one of the lowest maxima among the 25 species they examined, and probably is a reason for the species restriction to northern latitudes.

Several studies have shown that Blanding's turtles

may travel considerable distances. Movements in a Wisconsin wetland complex ranged from 212 to 652 m (mean 396; Ross, 1989a). Minimum daily movements of females (mean 95 m) were significantly greater than those of males (mean 48 m), perhaps because of postnesting movements of females. Of female movements, 43% were over 100 m. In contrast, only 14% of male and 19% of juvenile female movements were greater than 100 m (Ross, 1989a).

Wisconsin *Emydoidea* have well-defined, widely separated, activity centers (areas in which individuals spend at least five days) (Ross and Anderson, 1990). The location of these centers changes over time, and the size of the centers of two males (0.57 and 0.94 ha) studied by Ross and Anderson did not differ significantly from those of adult females (mean 0.64 ha). Activity centers of juvenile females averaged 0.40 ha. Centers of females overlapped both those of males (mean overlap 12%) and other females (mean overlap 26%); activity centers of the two males were not shared. Distances between activity centers for two males (260 and 635 m) did not differ significantly from those of six females (mean 489 m), nor did the range lengths within activity centers between males (15 and 635 m) and females (mean 159 m). Center shape was largely determined by that of the wetland occupied.

Activity centers in an Illinois population were identified as clusters of relocations within an area of overall activity. Individuals occupied two to four activity centers ranging in size from 0.1 to 1.2 ha (mean 0.6 ha), and totaling 0.4–2.3 ha (mean 1.3 ha) in the summer (Rowe and Moll, 1991). During the summer, 84.5% of all activity was confined to these areas; all other activity was transient movement between or away from the centers. As in Wisconsin, both range length and total center area did not differ significantly between the sexes. Daily movements in activity centers were 1–230 m and peaked in July, but individuals occasionally made trips of up to one kilometer. Males moved significantly greater distances per day than females, except in May (Rowe and Moll, 1991).

Several studies have reported terrestrial tendencies in Blanding's turtles. Gibbons (1968d) found nesting females on land in Michigan in June, but both sexes were seen on land in April and September. Most terrestrial movement in an Illinois population occurs in May and June when both sexes periodically move between aquatic habitats. Long-distance displacements of up to 1.4 km at a rate of up to 550 m/day take place as males move between aquatic habitats.

Female trips are shorter and associated with nesting. From 18 to 29 May some Illinois *Emydoidea* moved inland 2–21 m under a variety of weather conditions and rested in leaf litter or vegetation for up to six hours (Rowe and Moll, 1991).

Some Wisconsin Blanding's turtles estivated for 0.5–5 days between late July and late August when air temperatures were 18–33°C. One turtle estivated repeatedly beneath herbaceous growth on land, and two others rested, partly buried, in the silt at the bottom of a creek under 30 cm of matted cattails. Aquatic estivation occurred in July and August at maximum air temperatures of 27–37.5°C (Ross and Anderson, 1990).

Blanding's turtle is fond of basking and has been seen sunning itself on muskrat lodges, steep banks of dikes and ditches, stumps, logs, piles of driftwood, sedge clumps, and cattail debris, both singly and with several other *Emydoidea* or with *Chrysemys picta*. The earliest spring sighting of this species in Nova Scotia was of one basking on 30 April (Dobson, 1971). Atmospheric basking occurs infrequently from late March to late August in Illinois. The turtles bask from 0758 to 1729, at air temperatures of 15–27°C, under sunny to partly cloudy conditions (Rowe and Moll, 1991). Juveniles in Minnesota bask on sedge (*Carex comosa*) tussocks and the roots of alder (*Alnus rugosa*), or perch on the branches of alders 20–90 cm above the water. When disturbed, these juveniles often crawl into holes or burrows at the base of the sedge tussocks (Pappas and Brecke, 1992).

Most Blanding's turtles enter overwintering sites between September and late November, depending on location, when water temperatures are 6–13°C (Kofron and Schreiber, 1985; Ross and Anderson, 1990; Rowe and Moll, 1991). In Wisconsin, hibernacula include the deepest parts of ponds and creeks with organic substrates. Dormant turtles lie partially buried in the substrate at mean water depths of 0.9 m, and several may hibernate within 10 m of each other. Hibernacula are not far from summer habitats, and five of six individuals found by Ross and Anderson (1990) hibernated within a summer activity center. At the Toledo Zoo, two spent the winter under wet leaves on land, but most hibernated successfully beneath masses of soggy leaves in their pool (Conant, 1951a).

Blanding's turtles do not immediately become dormant in winter. Evermann and Clark (1916) saw them swimming slowly beneath the ice in November in northern Indiana. Two Missouri *Emydoidea* overwintered in the mud among roots of grasses and shrubs in the shallow part of a marsh where water depth was 9.5–21 cm and maximum mud depth, 15 cm. Both made frequent movements of up to 13 m, but when the water temperature dropped to 2–3°C, they moved only 1–2 m (Kofron and Schreiber, 1985).

REPRODUCTION: The sexual cycles of *Emydoidea* are poorly known. That of the male has not been studied. Michigan females ovulate in May; a female collected in April contained numerous follicles 7 mm in diameter, but no eggs or enlarged follicles (Gibbons, 1968d). The urogenital morphology of both sexes is described in detail by Nicholson and Risley (1942).

Size and age at attainment of sexual maturity varies among populations and individuals of *Emydoidea*. Data collected during a 24-year study of Blanding's turtles in Michigan (Congdon and van Loben Sels, in press) provide the only information on maturation of the species. The youngest female found in its first mature season (primiparous) was 14 years old, 18.3 cm in plastron length, and 19.2 cm in carapace length, but 59% of all reproductive females in the population were smaller. The smallest sexually mature female (15.7-cm plastron, 16.3-cm carapace) was also one of the oldest at 20 years. The largest primiparous female (21.0-cm plastron, 22.5-cm carapace) was 18 years old. Primiparous females were 14–20 years of age, with 15.7–21.0 cm plastra and 16.3–21.5 cm carapaces. No relationship was detected between body size and age at first oviposition.

Other studies have determined the timing and size at maturation based on the age and size of reproducing females or the appearance of secondary sexual characteristics. Females in Wisconsin appear to mature at a plastron length of about 17 cm and at a minimum age of 18 years (Ross, 1989a). Graham and Doyle (1977) suspected that male Blanding's turtles in Massachusetts matured at plastron lengths of 18–19 cm in the 12th year of growth, based on the appearance of secondary sexual characteristics. Secondary sexual characters become evident in Missouri at plastron lengths of between 17 and 18 cm (Kofron and Schreiber, 1985).

Courtship and mating have been observed in every month from March to November, but are most common from March to July (Conant, 1951a; Graham and Doyle, 1979; Vogt, 1981a). The mating in Illinois on 17 November reported by P. W. Smith (1961) was surely a belated one, because these turtles are less active at that time of the year.

Courtship behavior, under seminatural conditions, was documented by Baker and Gillingham (1983),

and involves eight different male behaviors: (1) chase—pursuit of the female, often in contact with her posterior carapace; (2) mount—climbing onto the females carapace; (3) gulping—drawing water into the mouth and expelling it from mouth or nostrils over the females snout; (4) chinning—placement of the chin on the female's snout and exerting a downward or inward pressure; (5) chin-rubbing—lateral movement of the head while the chin or gular region is in contact with the female's snout; (6) swaying—horizontal movement of the head and neck without contacting the female's snout, and with neck extended and head bent downward at a sharp angle; (7) violent swaying—rapid horizontal swinging of the head and neck, arched in such a way as to allow the head to pass under the female's plastron, sometimes producing audible sounds when the male's plastron rubbed on the female's carapace; and (8) snorkel—at termination of a behavior, the male remained motionless, and then slowly raised his neck to the surface to breathe.

The courtships observed by Baker and Gillingham (1983) took place in water and from 20 April to 28 May at water temperatures of 7–21°C. A typical courtship sequence begins when a male approaches a female, climbs onto her carapace, and clasps her marginal scutes with his claws. If she moves away, he chases her. Once mounted, the male begins chinning for up to 70 minutes (mean 4), but stops if either turtle surfaces to breathe. Breathing periods last 7–22 seconds (mean 12) and males breathe significantly more often than females. Chin-rubbing usually follows a male snorkel behavior or female breathing attempt. If the female moves forward while mounted, the male ceases chinning and begins to gulp. Gulping bouts include 16–37 pulsations (mean 22) and individual gulps last about one or two seconds (mean 1.3). Gulping may be associated with the behavior observed by Graham and Doyle (1979) in which Massachusetts males expelled bubbles while mounted. Swaying usually follows gulping. A complete swaying sequence lasts one to three seconds (mean 1.2). If the female retracts her head at this stage the male resumes chinning her, but if she remains motionless, swaying changes to violent swaying, especially when the female retracts her head, limbs, and tail. Copulation occurs only when the female extends her tail. Each cycle of violent swaying lasts 0.27–0.66 sec (mean 0.33), and often causes the male to lose his grip on the female and fall off.

Intromission occurs only after swaying behavior. The male slides his tail beneath hers and inserts his penis as their tails touch. The male then releases his grip on the female and tilts backward. Mating may last 16.5–29.3 min (mean 23.0). If a male accidentally mounts another male the duration is short (<60 sec).

The order of the various male courtship behaviors is not random. The mount-chase interaction is important early in the sequence, snorkeling is frequently followed by the chin-rub and eventually chinning, and there appears to be a linear sequence from chinning to gulping to swaying and then violent swaying. Finally, dismounting is also associated with violent swaying (Baker and Gillingham, 1983).

The nesting season lasts from late May to early July, depending on geographic location and weather conditions (Bleakney, 1963; Congdon et al., 1983b; Rowe and Moll, 1991; Rowe, 1992). During six years in Michigan, nesting activity began between 23 May and 9 June, and lasted from 16 to 30 days (mean 23) (Congdon et al., 1983b). The onset of nesting was significantly correlated with April, but not May, temperatures. Females from northeastern Illinois nest between 26 May and 22 June (Rowe and Moll, 1991). Seventeen females from Nebraska collected by Rowe (1992) were gravid between 11 June and 10 July; of these, nine were collected on land from 19 June to 3 July between 1700 and 1900, when they were presumably searching for a nest site. In Massachusetts, the nesting season covers the first 24 days in June (Linck et al., 1989).

Nesting is usually completed at night, although it is initiated in the early evening. Most nests are completed by 2300, but some females finish later. A complete Massachusetts nesting sequence was reported by Linck et al. (1989). At 1920 the female entered a cornfield. She lowered her head until it almost touched the ground and made several alternating sweeps with her front legs. At 1933 she turned 180° and began digging the nest with alternating hind feet. She rested for intervals of up to a minute. The first egg was laid at 2049 and 10 more followed at intervals of about one minute each. She paused for about two minutes between deposition of eggs 10 and 11 to move the eggs in the chamber with her hind feet. The final egg was deposited at 2102 followed by 10 minutes of egg manipulation with the hind feet. At 2115 she began to fill the nest cavity, a process that was completed in five minutes. She then smoothed the nest site by rocking her plastron over the cavity and "kneading" the soil with her knuckles. The process of rocking and kneading lasted for about 90 minutes, and was interrupted by occasional sweeping of soil from the area around the cavity. Most Massachusetts females observed by Linck et al. (1989) faced the water while digging the nest.

The nest is flask shaped and about 18 cm deep; the opening is 7.5–10.0 cm in diameter, and the egg chamber is about 18 cm wide.

In Michigan the nesting process lasts about 2.5 hours once the site is selected (however, Snyder, 1921, observed a nesting sequence that took only 45 minutes to complete), and some females may remain on land for two to seven days (mean 4.5) to complete nesting (Congdon et al., 1983b). Females in Illinois may move overland for 5–17 days before nesting 650–900 m (mean 815) from their home ponds (Rowe and Moll, 1991). In Wisconsin, mean distance of the nest from the nearest water is 168 m (Ross and Anderson, 1990). During periods of prolonged terrestrial activity, females seek cover in dense vegetation or under leaf litter when not searching for a nest site or excavating.

Eight of 11 Michigan females observed nesting in more than one year showed nest site fidelity, but other females nested up to 1.3 km from previous nest sites (Congdon et al., 1983b). Nests were dug from 2 m to over 1 km from the nearest water (mean 135 m). Most females nest in areas adjacent to marshes where they are not considered to be residents. There is no relationship between the size of nesting females and the day of the nesting season they oviposit (Congdon et al., 1983b).

Most nests in Wisconsin are located in grasslands larger than six hectares and characterized by well-drained, sandy loam soil or sand (Ross and Anderson, 1990). Cover in this microhabitat is composed of 50.6% grasses and sedges, 25.5% other herbaceous plants, 23.9% bare soil, and very few woody species. Nests are located, on average, 18.4 m from shrubs, 36.3 m from trees, and 246 m from nonnesting activity centers.

Only a single clutch is deposited each year, but not all sexually mature females nest in a given year. On average, only 48% of the sexually mature Michigan females lay eggs in one year (Congdon et al., 1983b). Clutch size ranges from 3 to 22 eggs, but averages between 10 and 15 eggs (Rowe, 1992; Congdon and van Loben Sels, in press). The ellipsoidal, dull-white, hard-shelled eggs have a nodular surface and are 28.0–40.7 mm long, 17.7–26.0 mm wide, and weigh 8.9–15.8 g. The eggshell is 9.6% of egg weight and is composed of 45.2% fibrous layers and 54.8% mineral layers (Bleakney, 1963; Ewert, 1979a; Graham and Doyle, 1979; Brewster, 1982; Graham and Forsberg, 1986; DePari et al., 1987; MacCulloch and Weller, 1988; Congdon et al., 1983b; Congdon and van Loben Sels, 1991, in press; Rowe, 1992). Some of the data on egg dimensions are based on measurements of x-radiographs and may result in 6.4–15.4% overestimations of actual size (Graham and Petokas, 1989; Congdon and van Loben Sels, 1991).

Clutch size in Michigan varies significantly among individuals and among years, although body size (carapace and plastron length) of reproductive females does not (Congdon et al., 1983b; Congdon and van Loben Sels, 1991, in press). Clutch size is positively correlated with female carapace length, but body size does not account for much of the variation in egg dimensions. Clutch size is not correlated with female age. It does not differ significantly between females with a mean age of 21 years and those with a mean minimum age of 47 years, nor between first-year breeders and veteran nesters. Females at least 55 years old reproduce more often (mean 0.57 clutches/year) than those 20–30 years old (mean 0.35 clutches/year). Clutch wet mass is 60.4–183.4 g (mean 111.7) and is also positively correlated with female length. The mean ratio of clutch wet mass to female wet mass is only 0.12. Mean clutch egg width, measured from x-radiographs, is positively correlated with clutch size. DePari et al. (1987) found no significant relationship between clutch size and female length in Massachusetts females ranging from 20.0 to 22.0 cm, but MacCulloch and Weller (1988) showed that both clutch mass and relative clutch mass are related significantly to both female mass and length in Ontario, and that clutch size is also related to female shell length, but that mean egg mass is not related to either clutch size or female length. However, in Nebraska, no measure of reproductive output is significantly related to female carapace length (Rowe, 1992).

The eggs of *Emydoidea blandingii* have a relatively small lipid fraction, perhaps because the species does not usually overwinter in the nest (Gibbons and Nelson, 1978; Congdon et al., 1983b). Eggs contain 12.5–18.6% (mean 15.56) lipid by total weight; egg lipid weight is 0.45–0.63 g (mean 0.55), and the lean component dry weight ranges from 2.64 to 3.50 g (mean 3.0). Approximately 38% of the egg lipid stores are utilized by the embryo during development (Congdon et al., 1983b).

Incubation time varies as a function of temperature. Incubation time in the laboratory at various temperatures is as follows: 24°C, 81.6 days; 25–25.5°C, 71.3 days; 25–30°C, 52.4 days; 29.5–30°C, 49.3 days; and above 30°C, 47.4 days (Ewert, 1979a). In Michigan, hatchlings emerge from the middle of August to early October; the time between laying and emergence is 73–104 days (mean 84). Emergence usually occurs between 1000 and 1500 and may take

one to eight days. An average of 2.2 eggs per nest fail to develop, and in some years, all nests have some inviable eggs (Congdon et al., 1983b). Hatchlings hide almost immediately after emergence from the nest (David M. Carroll, pers. comm.).

Eggs were incubated under hydric conditions eliciting different patterns of net water exchange between eggs and air and substrate by G. C. Packard et al. (1982). Those incubated on wet and intermediate substrates increased in weight during the first half of incubation, but became lighter during the second half until their mass just before hatching was slightly lower than at oviposition. Eggs incubated on dry substrates and on platforms above substrates lost weight throughout incubation, with a rate of decline greater in the second half of incubation. Hatchling size was related to the amount of moisture in the environment in which its egg was incubated, and, possibly, to the net flux of water across the eggshell. Variation in hatchling size was not as great as has been reported for other turtles with flexible-shelled eggs, possibly owing to the constraints on water exchange imposed by the more complex shells of *Emydoidea* eggs.

In the laboratory, the proportion of Blanding's turtle eggs that hatch is affected by the incubation temperature (Gutzke and Packard, 1987). Hatching success is greatest (95.2%) when eggs are incubated at 26.5°C, and slightly, but significantly, decreased (77.3%) when they are incubated at 31.0°C. No embryos develop in eggs incubated at 22°C.

The rounded, keeled carapace of the hatchling is dark brown to black, sometimes with spots, and is 29.0–38.8 mm long. The plastron has a large, black, central blotch on each scute, and the future hinge is suggested by a crease. The plastron is 25–35 mm long. The tail is proportionately much longer than that of adults. Hatchlings weigh 6–13 g (Graham and Doyle, 1979; Congdon and van Loben Sels, 1991). They constitute 66.2% of egg weight (Ewert, 1979a), and their body dry mass averages 14.7% lipid (Congdon et al., 1983b). Mean dry weight of hatchling lean and lipid components is 1.78 g and 0.31 g, respectively (Congdon et al., 1983b). The initial mass of the egg significantly affects the hatching mass of the young (Gutzke and Packard, 1987).

Sex determination in *Emydoidea* is temperature dependent. Eggs incubated at 22.5–26.5°C produce 97–100% males, and eggs incubated at 30–31°C produce only females (Gutzke and Packard, 1987; Ewert and Nelson, 1991).

Gutzke and Packard (1987) have pointed out that

Juvenile *Emydoidea blandingii*

Plastron of juvenile
Emydoidea blandingii

the effect of temperature on the development of *Emydoidea* poses two questions regarding the distribution of the species. First, how does it maintain a limited northern range when its embryos cannot complete development at low temperatures? Second, why, inasmuch as it is omnivorous, semiaquatic, capable of long overland migrations, and has eggs that are tolerant of dry conditions (G. C. Packard et al., 1982) and relatively high temperatures, has it not extended its range southward? Gutzke and Packard believe the answer to the first question is that,

apparently, females simply avoid nesting in cool woodland or shaded sites. They believe the answer to the second, more interesting, question is related to influences other than those of the environment on eggs and hatchlings. One possibility is that *Emydoidea* is excluded from the South through competition with other established emydids.

GROWTH AND LONGEVITY: Growth in Michigan Blanding's turtles is essentially linear until age 13, and averages about 10.4 mm and 75.3 g (between age 4 and 13) per year. Growth rates decline sharply between the ages of 16 and 18 at about 20.0 cm carapace length and a weight of 1.2 kg. Some, but not all, females grow indeterminately after age 20. Those that do grow have yearly increases ranging from 0.1 to 1.9 mm (mean 0.66) (Congdon and van Loben Sels, 1991). In Wisconsin, growth is 85.9% in the first year of life and declines until year eight when scute annuli are indiscernible (Ross, 1989a). Similar, but somewhat slower, growth rates occur in Massachusetts (Graham and Doyle, 1977). Blanding's turtles from Nebraska show an approximately 70% lengthing of the abdominal scute during their first year, but growth declines rapidly after this and becomes more constant at 4–9% about the fourth year (Rowe, 1992).

Congdon and van Loben Sels (in press) concluded that differences in juvenile growth rate and age of maturity, but not indeterminate growth, are responsible for most of the variation observed in the size of adult females. Individual growth rates of juveniles are significantly and negatively related to the age at which females mature; individuals that grow rapidly as juveniles mature at younger ages than individuals that grow slowly. Body size differences between fast- and slow-growing females are not related to age at sexual maturity inasmuch as both groups mature at similar sizes.

Blanding's turtles are capable of living well beyond 25 years (Gibbons, 1987; Congdon and van Loben Sels, in press). An individual was collected in Minnesota in 1988 inscribed with initials dated 1926. The condition of the initials was such that they were likely carved when the specimen was mature (older than 15 years). Thus, the turtle probably had a minimum reproductive period of 56 years and a minimum age of 77 years (Brecke and Moriarty, 1989), the oldest individual ever reported from a natural population.

FOOD HABITS: Feeding in Missouri begins in early April approximately two weeks after water temperatures reach and remain at 18°C. Feeding continues through June, ceases by mid-July, and resumes again when water temperatures fall to 21°C. The feeding period lasts only about 4.5 months. Crayfish are the dominant prey, but insects (Odonata, Trichoptera, Coleoptera, Diptera, Orthoptera), fish (*Lepomis cyanellus*) and their eggs, frogs (*Rana catesbeiana*), and plant material (filamentous algae and duckweed) are also ingested (Kofron and Schreiber, 1985). Lagler (1943) observed that crustaceans make up more than 50% of the food volume of Michigan *Emydoidea*, with insects providing another 25% of the

volume, and fish, other vertebrates, snails, leeches, and plants the remainder. Crayfish constituted 78% prey frequency and 58% volume in 92 Blanding's turtles examined by Penn (1950). Blanding's turtles in Massachusetts eat pondweed (*Potamogeton*), seeds, golden shiners (*Notemigonus crysoleucas*), and brown bullheads (*Ictalurus nebulosus*) (Graham and Doyle, 1977).

Cahn (1937) noted that this species eats leaves, grasses, berries, and other succulent vegetation, slugs, grubs, insect larvae, and earthworms on land, and insect larvae, crayfish, minnows, tadpoles, and frogs in water. Harding (1989) reported that Blanding's turtle will occasionally grab prey on land and then drag it into the water, and that no swallowing is done on land; however, Ernst and Barbour (1972) had captives eat dog food from a dry dish. Juveniles are very aggressive aquatic feeders (Harding, 1989).

Although prey may be captured by rapid thrusts of the long neck, and *Emydoidea* sometimes waits in small pools to ambush prey such as tadpoles (Ross, 1987), the main feeding strategy probably involves an entirely different behavior (Bramble, 1973). Blanding's turtle uses a pharyngeal mechanism that exploits the relatively high density and viscosity of water. Function of this mechanism relies chiefly on the generation of large negative pressures within the buccopharyngeal cavity through the rapid expansion of the chamber by the hyoid apparatus; coupled with fast inertial feeding thrusts of the head, such negative pressures quickly draw water and prey into the mouth. Lingual movements play little or no role in feeding. Morphological adaptations of this mechanism include a massive hyoid apparatus, small tongue, broad, flat palate, nonserrated or ridged jaws, and no appreciable cranial flexure.

PREDATORS AND DEFENSE: Of the turtles collected in Missouri by Kofron and Schreiber (1985), 31% had injuries or were missing body parts. Thirteen had injuries to the feet, eleven had damaged shells (cracks or chips), and five had lost part of their tails. Injuries were distributed evenly among adult males, adult females, and subadults. Like many turtles, *Emydoidea* are frequently killed on roads by cars (Kofron and Schreiber, 1985; Harding, 1990).

Blanding's turtle nests are frequently destroyed by predators. Nests located near the edges of habitats (ecotones) are more often plundered than are those dug more than 60 m from such edges (Temple, 1987). Nest predation in Michigan ranged from 42 to 93%. The most common predators were raccoons (*Procyon lotor*) and foxes (*Urocyon, Vulpes*); one nest was destroyed by ants. Following oviposition, 47% of nests were destroyed in the first 24 hours, 84% within five days, and 12% between days 6 and 30, but after the 30th day no nests observed were attacked. Some nests were preyed upon as hatchlings emerged. Observed nests that survived predation were not significantly farther from water than those attacked. Nests in open areas such as fields were preyed upon more frequently than nests in areas where a predator's search pattern was linear (Congdon et al., 1983b).

All 16 nests found by Ross and Anderson (1990) in Wisconsin were destroyed by predators. Ten of these were located within 50 m of a habitat edge (see Temple, 1987). Nine of the nests were destroyed by skunks (*Mephitis mephitis*), but raccoons and opossums (*Didelphis marsupialis*) also are egg predators in Wisconsin (Temple, 1987).

The color pattern of *Emydoidea* seems to imitate the floating leaves of duckweed (*Lemna*), which is abundant in many wetland habitats throughout the range of the turtle. This cryptic pattern may confer an advantage to the turtle by reducing vulnerability to predation (Ross and Lovich, 1992).

When handled, these turtles withdraw into their shells and close the movable lobes of the plastron as tightly as possible. They are timid and usually make no attempt to bite. Those touched on the ground may pull into their shells or tilt the shell in the direction of the disturbance. Defensive postures are discussed by Hayes (1989).

POPULATIONS: Blanding's turtle density estimates for Michigan range from 8.8 to 10.0 individuals per hectare, with a biomass of 7.9–8.8 kg/ha. Biomass and energy equivalents for eggs produced in the same hectare are 1.11 kg and 7,908 kilojoules (Congdon et al., 1986; Congdon and Gibbons,

1989). Density and biomass in Wisconsin are greater, 27.5 individuals per hectare and 45 kg/ha (Ross and Anderson, 1990). Blanding's turtle densities from various other localities are as follows: Missouri, 55/ha (Kofron and Schreiber, 1985); Massachusetts, 6.3/ha (Graham and Doyle, 1977); and Michigan, 15.8/ha (Gibbons, 1968d).

Sex ratios of Blanding's turtle populations range from essentially 1:1 to strongly female biased (Ross, 1989a; Gibbons, 1990b; Congdon and van Loben Sels, 1991). In Wisconsin, immatures represent 35% of one population, where the immature to adult ratio is 1.8:1 (Ross, 1989). Most studies have noted the rarity or absence of small Blanding's turtles in samples (Gibbons, 1968d; Kofron and Schreiber, 1985; Ross, 1989a; Congdon and van Loben Sels, 1991), but some researchers have managed to find large numbers (Pappas and Brecke, 1992). The size distributions of all Michigan males and females greater than 15.5-cm plastron length are not significantly different (Congdon and van Loben Sels, 1991).

The annualized survivorship of eggs and hatchlings in a Michigan population is only 18% (Congdon et al., 1983b; Iverson, 1991a).

REMARKS: Bramble (1974b) concluded that *Emydoidea* is most closely related to *Emys* and *Terrapene*, not *Deirochelys* as was previously believed. He based his conclusion on a shared plastron closing mechanism, other morphological similarities, and convergent feeding systems between *Deirochelys* and *Emydoidea*. This conclusion is strengthened by similar findings in an electrophoretic study of turtle myoglobins by Seidel and Adkins (1989).

Additional information on *Emydoidea* is summarized by McCoy (1973).

Terrapene carolina (Linnaeus, 1758)
Eastern box turtle

PLATE 28

RECOGNITION: This is a small terrestrial turtle with a hinged plastron and a keeled, high-domed, elongated carapace highest posterior to the plastral hinge. The carapace (to 21.6 cm) is rounded dorsally and not serrated posteriorly; a dorsal keel is commonly present on vertebral scutes 2–4. The first vertebral is elevated at a steep angle (50° or more), and the first marginal is usually rectangular in shape. The carapace is brownish, commonly with an extremely variable yellow or orange pattern of radiating lines, spots, bars, or irregular blotches on each pleural and vertebral scute. The plastron lacks a bridge and has a strong hinge between the pectoral and abdominal scutes forming two movable lobes. The hinge usually arises at the fifth marginal. The plastron is commonly as long or longer than the carapace, and its lateral rim may not be indented at the femoroanal seam. Frequently an axillary scute is present, at the fourth marginal. The plastron is tan to dark brown; it may be patternless, show dark blotches or smudges, have radiating light lines, or have a dark central area with branches along the seams. The skin is black to reddish brown, with yellow, red, or orange spots and streaks; on the head the markings are variable. The upper jaw is hooked terminally and is commonly without a notch.

In most adult males the iris is red (although in some populations this may not be true); in females it is usually yellowish brown. The carapace of the female is more domed than that of the male; the posterior lobe of the plastron is concave in males, flat or slightly convex in females (Wilbern and Ingold, 1983). The claws of the hind foot are, in males, fairly long, stocky, and considerably curved; those of females are shorter, more slender, and straighter. Males have longer, thicker tails than females.

KARYOTYPE: The diploid chromosome number is 50 (26 macrochromosomes and 24 mi-crochromosomes): 20 metacentric or submetacentric, 10 subtelocentric, and 20 acrocentric or telocentric (Stock, 1972; Killebrew, 1977a).

FOSSIL RECORD: In addition to the extant subspecies, several fossil forms of *Terrapene carolina* have been described (Auffenberg, 1958; and see Milstead, 1967, 1969, for a summary). Based on this broader concept of the species, fossils are known from the Miocene Clarendonian of Kansas and Nebraska (Holman, 1975, 1981b), Pliocene Hemphillian and Blancan of Florida and Maryland (Milstead, 1969; Holman, 1977b), Pleistocene Irvingtonian of Florida, Kansas, Maryland, Nebraska, Texas, and West Virginia (Milstead, 1969; Holman, 1987; Holman and Winkler, 1987; Holman and Grady, 1989), and Pleistocene Rancholabrean of Florida, Georgia, Mississippi, Missouri, Tennessee, Texas, and Virginia (Milstead, 1969; Holman 1967, 1969a,b, 1978; Corgan, 1976; Holman and Clausen, 1984; Holman and Winkler, 1987; Gillette, 1974; Jackson and Kaye, 1974b; Moodie and Van Devender, 1977; and Fay, 1984). Remains of *T. carolina* are also frequently found during archeological digs; summaries of such records in Canada, the United States, and Mexico are presented by Bleakney (1958a), Adler (1970), and Alvarez (1976).

DISTRIBUTION: In the United States, *Terrapene carolina* ranges from southern Maine south to the Florida Keys and west to Michigan, Illinois, eastern Kansas, Oklahoma, and Texas. It also has been reported from isolated localities in New York and western Kansas. In Mexico, it occurs in the states of Campeche, Quintana Roo, San Luis Potosí, Tamaulipas, Veracruz, and Yucatán.

The peripheral boundaries of the range have been somewhat clouded as this is a popular pet trade species and individuals are often released in places

Terrapene carolina carolina

Variation in carapacial pattern of *Terrapene carolina carolina*

near as well as far from the normal distributional range. The species has even been found on the island of Hawaii (Mull, 1987), and Bleakney (1958a) and Adler (1968, 1970) have presented evidence that prehistoric humans may have transported *T. carolina* north of its present range.

GEOGRAPHIC VARIATION: Of the six recognized extant subspecies, four reside in the United States (Ernst and McBreen, 1991b). *Terrapene carolina carolina* (Linnaeus, 1758), the eastern box turtle, ranges from New England south to Georgia and west to Michigan, Illinois, Tennessee, and northern Alabama. The carapace is short, broad, and brightly patterned with the marginals nearly vertical or slightly flared, and each hind foot has four toes. *T. c. major* (Agassiz, 1857), the Gulf Coast box turtle, ranges along the Gulf Coastal Plain from northwestern Florida to eastern Texas. This is the largest of the box turtles: some slightly exceed 20 cm in carapace length. The carapace has few to no markings, or marks obscured by black or tan pigment in males, but

Plastron of *Terrapene carolina*

Distribution of *Terrapene carolina*

The four North American subspecies of *Terrapene carolina*, from left: *T. c. bauri*, *T. c. carolina*, *T. c. triunguis*, and *T. c. major*

Terrapene carolina major

radiating yellow spots or dashes in females; the posterior marginals are strongly flared, and four toes occur on each hind foot. *T. c. triunguis* (Agassiz, 1857), the three-toed box turtle, ranges from Missouri (and possibly southwestern Illinois; Paukstis and Janzen, 1988; Gilbert and Gilbert, 1992) south to Alabama and Texas. The highest point on the carapace is more posteriorly positioned than in the other subspecies, in cross-section it appears peaked, and is typically tan or olive with an obscure pattern of radiating dashes and, commonly, dark seam borders.

Orange, red, or yellow spots usually are conspicuous on both head and forelimbs, and some have alternating white and black pigment on the upper jaws; males may have totally red heads. Each hind foot has three toes. *T. c. bauri* Taylor, 1895, the Florida box turtle, is restricted to peninsular Florida and the Keys. The dark brown carapace has a bright pattern of yellow radiating lines, is highest posterior to the center, and has little or no posterior flaring. The plastron also bears a pattern of radiating light lines on each scute, and two light, longitudinal stripes are present on each

The head of male *Terrapene carolina triunguis* is sometimes brick red

Terrapene carolina bauri

side of the head. Each hind foot usually has only three toes.

Studies of the phalangeal formulae of the subspecies of *T. carolina* by Minx (1992) showed that *bauri* and *major* share a common forefoot pattern, that of *carolina* is slightly different and intermediate between the pattern of the former two subspecies and that of *triunguis*, which is the most divergent of the four. Similarly, the hind-foot formulae of *bauri, carolina* and *major* are similar, while that of *triunguis* is divergent. Both the forefoot and hind-foot formulae of *triunguis* are most similar to that of the Mexican subspecies, *T. c. mexicana*.

Much confusing intergradation occurs between the subspecies where the ranges of several meet; this is particularly true in southern Alabama and western peninsular Florida.

CONFUSING SPECIES: *Terrapene ornata* lacks a vertebral keel and has an irregularly oval or

Variation in carapacial pattern in *Terrapene carolina bauri*

triangular first marginal, the plastral hinge commonly arising at the seam between the fifth and sixth marginals or at the sixth marginal, commonly a plastron pattern of radiating yellow lines, and normally four toes on each hind foot. *Emydoidea blandingii* has a notched upper jaw, a bright yellow neck and chin, and no carapacial keel. Tortoises of the genus *Gopherus* and turtles of the genus *Clemmys* lack plastral hinges. Mud turtles (*Kinosternon*) have two plastral hinges.

HABITAT: The eastern box turtle is predominantly a species of open woodlands, although it also occurs in pastures and marshy meadows, and in Florida may be found in palmetto thickets.

Reagan (1974) conducted a quantitative study of habitat selection by *T. c. triunguis* in Arkansas. He measured 33 microenvironmental variables in the vicinity of 201 resting forms. Principal component analysis indicated that temperature, cover, and moisture were the basic microhabitat factors. Canonical correlation of the microhabitat and microclimatic variables indicated that the microclimate at the forms was influenced most by the ground cover present. Moisture variables immediately surrounding the turtle were not correlated with the microhabitat features, suggesting that the turtles select humidity levels independent of prevailing conditions at the surface. Measurements of 55 active turtles revealed temperatures and humidity levels similar to those taken at forms, indicating that the box turtles live within a relatively limited microclimatic range at all times during the annual activity period.

Form locations and trailing data revealed that Reagan's turtles experienced a seasonal shift in habitat from grasslands in late spring and early fall to forested areas in summer, early spring, and late fall. Activity in the grasslands coincided with moderate temperature and peak moisture conditions. At other seasons the turtles buried under leaf litter in the woodlands to avoid temperature extremes and maintain high humidity.

In Maryland, resting forms are almost always quite shallow and frequently involve burial in little more than the superficial layer of leaf litter and top 1–3 cm of soil on the forest floor (Strass et al., 1982). Such forms probably contribute little to thermoregulation as compared to deeper hibernacula, but may be important for preventing desiccation, particularly during hot, dry periods. Since daily forms are shallow, *T. carolina* does not experience the buildup of carbon dioxide that occurs in the burrows of the gopher tortoise, *Gopherus polyphemus,* and does not seem as physiologically adapted to high carbon dioxide stress levels as the tortoise (Ultsch and Anderson, 1986).

BEHAVIOR: The annual cycle in most of the United States begins in early April and ends in October, but in the South, box turtles may emerge from hibernacula in March and in Florida may be active in every month during warm years. In the northernmost parts of the range, *Terrapene carolina* may be forced into hibernation as early as late September, and emergence may be delayed until late April or early May during cold springs. A warm autumn may allow individuals to remain active into December, and warm spells in November and December may arouse some from hibernation. Final entrance into hibernation usually is brought about by the first severe autumn frost, and the last killing frost of spring usually marks the beginning of annual activity. In Virginia and Pennsylvania, juveniles emerge later in the spring than adults and become inactive in the fall before adults; however, Brisbin (1972) reported that there is no significant difference in the times of spring emergence between juveniles and adults in Georgia. There is no adult sexual difference in the timing of either spring emergence or the beginning of hibernation. Extended hot, dry periods in summer cause many individuals to estivate, but rains and the return of cooler air temperatures bring about increased activity and the resumption of foraging. In Virginia and Pennsylvania, May and June are the most active months.

In spring, much basking occurs in the morning with the turtle returning to a form at night (Carr and Houseal, 1981). Basking may occur in the form, and foraging is restricted to the afternoon. A second period of basking may follow foraging. In summer, activity is largely restricted to mornings and after rain; box turtles may be active as early as 0550. Evening activity is largely restricted to nesting females (although some may also excavate nests in the morning), and apparently little or no nocturnal activity occurs. The fall diel cycle parallels that of spring, except that fewer individuals move then than in the spring.

Often these turtles avoid the heat of day by sheltering under rotting logs or masses of decaying leaves, in mammal burrows, or in mud; in the hottest weather they frequently enter shaded shallow pools and puddles and remain there for periods varying from a few hours to days. In other words, thermoregulation is accomplished by changing the microenvironment; by this means the body temperature is kept within a range of 29–38°C. Hutchison et al. (1966) reported that loss of the righting response by *T. carolina* occurs at 39.0–42.2°C, and that its critical thermal maximum is 41.5–43.9°C; they found no significant variation in the critical thermal maximum in *T. carolina* from five widely separated states.

Heat stress affects several blood components; the white and red cell counts and the hematocrit are reduced (Sturbaum, 1981; Sturbaum and Bergman, 1981). Ten *T. c. triunguis* exposed to 40, 45, and 50°C established and maintained air to core temperature

gradients of 0.56 and 3.88°C with efficiencies of evaporation of 3.7 and 8.7% in the 40 and 45°C environments, respectively (Sturbaum, 1981). In the 50°C environment core temperatures climbed steadily to the lethal temperature of 43°C. The effects of thermal acclimation at 25 and 5°C on electrical activity in the heart were investigated by Risher and Claussen (1987); the durations of the electrocardiogram QRS wave complex and the intervals between several of the wave types (P-R, R-T, R-R) increased with decreasing body temperature.

The pineal hormone melatonin may play a role in thermoregulation. Intraperitoneal injections of melatonin (4 and 8 mmg/kg body weight) will significantly decrease the mean selected temperatures of *T. c. triunguis* when compared with control animals over 24 hours. Chlorpromazine (25 mg/kg), which may block the breakdown of endogenous melatonin, also causes a significant decline in mean selected temperature. Both exogenous and endogenous melatonin appear to play a role in behavioral and physiological thermoregulation (Erskine and Hutchison, 1981).

Metabolic heat may be produced by *T. carolina*. After a fast of three days, each of 10 *T. c. carolina* resting in the dark at about 24°C studied hourly by thermometer readings for a 12-hour period showed a steady mean heat production of 0.12 cal/h/g (Elghammer and Johnson, 1976). Three *T. carolina*, after fasting for 14 days and resting quietly in the dark for 24 hours at 25°C, had mean heat production of 0.74 J/h on day 8, 0.95 on day 10, and 0.89 on day 12 (Swan and Johnson, 1977). The consistency of the heat production possibly involves regulatory systems.

Terrapene carolina apparently can establish a fever in response to a bacterial infection. Monagas and Gatten (1983) injected live bacteria (*Aeromones hydrophila*) into 10 turtles, resulting in the mean body temperature being behaviorally increased 4–5°C.

Under natural conditions of temperature (10–29°C) and humidity (45–95%), unfed, catheterized *T. c. carolina* studied by Ernst (1968b) lost 3.6% of their total weight; this was a weight-loss gradient of 0.14 g/h for five days. During the same period, the semiaquatic *Clemmys guttata* and *C. insculpta* lost 10.0%, and the aquatic *Chelydra serpentina* and *Stenotherus odoratus* lost 17.8%. Obviously, there is a significant difference in the water-holding ability of turtles from different habitats: greatest in terrestrial species, least in aquatic species. *Terrapene c. carolina* studied by Olson (1989) lost an average of 2.3 g/day during activity in both 180–280-g and 300–450-g weight groups, with 0.93 and 0.76% body weight lost, respectively, for the two weight groups. During dormancy at 5°C, the averages for the 180-g turtles were 0.39 g/day and 0.2% body weight loss; for the larger turtles, 0.47 g/day and 0.16% body weight loss. Similar data collected by Olson for *T. c. triunguis* was comparable to that of *T. c. carolina*. Bogert and Cowles (1947) found *T. c. bauri* lost 17.3% of its weight (gradient of 0.38 g/h) in 45 hours at 39°C and 37% relative humidity in a drying chamber. *T. c. bauri* apparently requires a more humid habitat than *T. c. carolina* and *T. c. triunguis,* and those we keep in the laboratory spend significantly more time soaking in water pans than do the other subspecies.

The major function of a high rate of evaporative water loss in turtles is probably to protect the brain from overheating during thermal stress, as determined by Morgareidge and Hammel (1975) during experiments on *T. c. major.*

Nitrogen wastes of *T. carolina* are eliminated in the urine as ammonia (8.4%), urea (75%), and uric acid (7.5%) (Baze and Horne, 1970).

When entering hibernation eastern box turtles burrow into the loose soil, sand, vegetable debris, the mud of ponds or stream bottoms, or old stump holes, or they may enter mammal burrows. The same hibernaculum may be used in successive winters. They dig deeper as the soil temperature drops: as much as 60 cm deep before winter is over, although hibernation depths are usually much shallower (Dolbeer, 1971). Turtles monitored in an Ohio woodland hibernated at variable depths but never deeper than 14 cm; the average depth was 4–5 cm and the amount of leaf litter varied but averaged 8 cm (Claussen et al., 1991). The depth to which the soil freezes seems to be a factor limiting the northern distribution. We have observed that the hibernacula often are shared by as many as four turtles, and Carpenter (1957) found Oklahoma *T. carolina* hibernating in close association with *T. ornata* and/or *Kinosternon flavescens* and *Chelydra serpentina.*

Box turtles usually emerge from hibernation in April. In Ohio, hibernation lasts about 142 days (Claussen et al., 1991). Carpenter (1957) reported that the longest period an Oklahoma individual remained in the same hibernaculum in one season was 154 days, from 11 November to 8 April, and found that many *T. carolina* changed hibernacula during the winter. The average length of time that 73 turtles remained in one place was 63.4 days. Some Ohio *T. carolina* also shift hibernation sites early or late in the winter (Claussen et al., 1991). Dolbeer (1971) recorded movements of 0.6–122.3 m by Tennessee box turtles from late October to late January; these movements were clearly related to rainfall.

During warm spells in winter or early spring many emerge and soon thereafter are killed by rapid declines in temperature. Neill (1948a) thought that more box turtles are killed by cold than by all other natural factors together, and suggested that the wholesale destruction may actually be of advantage to the species by eliminating weaker individuals. Many of the turtles caught in early spring after warm, wet winters suffer from eye and respiratory diseases (Evans, 1983; Ernst, pers. obs.). Oliver (in Brattstrom, 1965) thought that box turtles (mostly *T. carolina*) that do not hibernate or otherwise lower their body temperature during the winter usually die the following summer. However, we have kept both *T. carolina* and *T. ornata* in captivity at room temperature for several years with no mortality.

Cahn (1937) compared the hibernation of several individuals of *T. carolina* and *T. ornata* under the same environmental conditions in Illinois. *Terrapene ornata* burrowed into the ground in October two weeks before *T. carolina,* and continued to burrow to a maximum of 12 cm. Some individuals of *T. carolina* spent the entire winter in the mud bottom of a puddle and became active on warm winter days; others burrowed nearly as deep as *T. ornata. Terrapene ornata* emerged from hibernation one or two weeks later in the spring than did *T. carolina.*

Overwintering activity of *T. carolina* was studied in South Carolina by Congdon et al. (1989). The turtles were equipped with temperature-sensitive transmitters and released into a fenced wooded old-field habitat with well-drained sandy soil. Air and soil temperatures were also monitored, and were found to play important roles influencing winter behavior. The proportion (32%) of turtles walking about during November and December was more than twice that of those that moved in January and February (12%). Mean transmitter temperature of turtles on the surface (20.5°C) was significantly higher than those buried both deeper (12.3°C) and shallower (11.9°C) than 2 cm. Mean transmitter temperature of partially buried turtles was 14.7°C. At the end of November the hibernaculum of completely buried turtles had a vertical extension to the surface, and during that month the *T. carolina* in these burrows faced these openings. However, after the coldest days in January and February the turtles turned 180° and faced away from the opening to the surface. All burrows were less than 4 cm deep. In the spring, just prior to emergence, the turtles once again faced the opening. By burrowing only to shallow depths the box turtles probably avoided problems in gas exchange (Gatten, 1987); perhaps farther north, where *T. carolina* hibernates deeper in the soil, this may be a problem.

To investigate freeze tolerance in *T. carolina*, Costanzo and Claussen (1990) froze 19 adults to body temperatures as low as −3.6°C under controlled laboratory conditions. The turtles withstood the freezing of at least 58% of their body water and remained frozen without injury for at least 73 hours. Supercooling occurred in 63% of the turtles, but only lasted from 0.1 to 2.0 hours, and the high supercooling points (mean −1.1°C) show this is not an effective strategy to avoid freezing. Body ice contents (7–58% of total body water) of turtles frozen 0.7–50 hours were inversely related to core body temperature. Freeze tolerance is an important adaptation to a shallowly buried terrestrial hibernator such as *T. carolina*.

During a study of hibernation in Ohio, Claussen et al. (1991) discovered that body temperatures of *T. carolina* were sometimes lower than adjacent soil temperatures. In spite of the insulation provided by a cover of leaf litter, some turtles experienced body temperatures of −0.3 to −1.4°C during the winter but survived. Although freezing can be a significant cause of winter mortality (especially in exposed individuals), the data presented by Claussen et al. (1991), and the research of Costanzo and Claussen (1990) discussed above, suggest that body freezing is neither rare nor necessarily lethal to *T. carolina*. Lesser amounts of body freezing may occur routinely in the northern parts of the range.

Grobman (1990) studied the effect of soil temperature on emergence from hibernation in *T. carolina* near St. Louis, Missouri. The turtles moved upward in the soil toward a minimum ambient temperature of about 7°C and emerged after five consecutive days of subsurface temperatures of 7°C or higher. The occasional individual that emerged prematurely was not likely to survive. If the subsurface temperature dropped substantially below 7°C, the turtles remained underground. After emerging they remained near their hibernacula, and reentered them if surface temperatures dropped. Movement away from the hibernacula occurred during and after the first warm spring rains.

The rate of movement by *T. carolina* increases with increasing ambient temperature. Adams et al. (1989) examined voluntary locomotion in a laboratory racetrack at six temperature regimes from 9.7 to 31.9°C. The mean number of strides and the mean total time stopped in the first meter decreased as temperature increased. Both the mean velocity and the mean fastest nonstop velocity increased with increasing temperature. Voluntary locomotion seemed to be maximal at body temperatures of 24–32°C.

Several investigators have reported data concerning home range dimensions in *T. carolina*. Unfortunately, several methods were used to calculate home range size, making them generally incomparable.

The home ranges of Long Island, New York, *T. c. carolina* had a diameter of 228 m or less, and shifted somewhat with the passage of years. One exceptional turtle wandered more than 0.3 km (Nichols, 1939b). Dolbeer (1969) estimated the home range of Tennessee *T. c. carolina* to be only 74.4 m; only 2.8% of the turtles exhibited major displacements of home range, and 8.4% minor changes in location. Stickel (1950) reported that in Maryland the average diameter of the ranges of adult males was 100.6 m, that of females 112.8 m. Thirty-nine years later, Stickel (1989) calculated that the average elliptical home range of males occupied an area of 1.2 ha (146 m long × 105 m wide) and that of females 1.13 ha (144 × 100 m). Strang (1983) reported the home ranges of *T. c. carolina* in Pennsylvania were 167 m long, and Williams and Parker (1987) found home range diameters of 171 m for males and 176.4 m for females during a 27-year study in Indiana.

Home range data are also available for *T. c. triunguis* in Missouri. Schwartz and Schwartz (1974) and Schwartz et al. (1984) studied three-toed box turtles for 19 years and reported overall home range areas of 5.1 ha (0.6–10.6): males 5.2 (0.6–10.2), females 5.1 (1.8–10.6). Home range size in their population increased with age and shell length of the turtles, and open woods had the highest density of home ranges.

Ranges of box turtles of all ages and both sexes overlap; the turtles frequently occur together and seldom show antagonism. Movements within the home range vary from random meanderings to fairly direct traverses. In many cases certain routes are used repeatedly. Some box turtles use only one part of the home range at a time and may take several days or weeks to use the entire range. Some have a divided home range and travel between the divisions at infrequent intervals. Occasional trips outside the range are made by some individuals; these trips include searches for nesting sites. Hibernacula are usually located within the home range.

A substantial proportion of a box turtle population at any time and place consists of transients (Schwartz and Schwartz, 1974; Schwartz et al., 1984; Williams and Parker, 1987; Ernst, pers. obs.). This makes estimation of population size and density difficult, but promotes gene flow between adjacent populations (Kiester et al., 1982).

Nichols (1939b) found most adults (89.5%) showed some homing tendency. All adults displaced 0.8–1.2 km moved in a homeward direction 0.91–1.28 km. Only three of seven young showed any tendency to home; the greatest distance they returned was 640 m. Two adults displaced 6.45 and 32.25 km remained near the places they were liberated. Posey (1979) displaced 10 *T. c. carolina* 500–900 m and three others 1.6 km, 4 km and 8 km from their home ranges. Of the 10 displaced less than 900 m, nine returned to their home ranges; none of the three turtles released more than 1.6 km away attempted to travel home. Schwartz and Schwartz (1974) reported a similar experience with seven *T. c. triunguis* displaced 1.6–3.2 km from their capture points.

Gould (1957) reported that 22 of 43 *T. carolina* moved in a homeward direction when released in open fields up to 3 km from their original points of capture. They oriented themselves by the sun: homeward headings were inaccurate or lacking on overcast days, and light reflected from a mirror caused them to alter course. Later studies by Gould (1959) revealed that box turtles released in unfamiliar localities sometimes headed in a direction other than that of home. Lemkau (1970) released 14 eastern box turtles in unfamiliar territory and found that each individual tended to move in a single direction; however, for the group as a whole no particular direction was discernible. These data suggest that *T. carolina* is able to move in a predetermined direction over periods of several days and for considerable distances; this would facilitate the maintenance of a direct course when orientation cues are temporarily obscured. DeRosa and Taylor (1982) tested *T. carolina* in a terrestrial arena and found the turtles to be dependent on an internal clock and time-dependent celestial cues for orientation. Ernst and Hamilton (1969) found that this species has no significant color choice, so individual colors may not be important in orientation.

Geomagnetism may play a role in orientation. In tests conducted by Mathis and Moore (1988) using a circular arena, control *T. carolina* oriented significantly more toward a training direction, while experimental box turtles with magnets attached to their carapaces seemed disoriented and chose directions randomly. In additional field tests, in which the turtles were displaced from their home ranges to four sites located symmetrically about the home site, more control turtles moved in a homeward direction. Experimental turtles bearing magnets, which increased the magnetic field 15% over normal background, again showed more random directional choice. However, both control and experimental

animals clustered in an eastward orientation regardless of the home direction. This eastward orientation masked, to some degree, the homeward orientation of the *T. carolina*.

Terrapene carolina may enter water during its wanderings. We have seen them swim across small waterbodies several times, and McCauley (1945) and Tyler (1979) have observed swimming behavior.

Some climbing ability is present, but perhaps not as well developed as in *T. ornata* (Wilbern, 1982); however, *T. carolina* will climb high embankments, and they sometimes bask on top of logs or off the ground in very low branches of shrubs.

A social hierarchy may be established when several captives are kept together, particularly with regard to feeding order (Boice, 1970; Shalet, 1977; Ernst, pers. obs.). Dominance of one turtle over another may take the form of biting or pushing with shell or feet, with the dominant animal feeding first and usually consuming the most food.

Aggressive behavior between wild male *T. carolina* is known (Stickel, 1989; Ernst, pers. obs.). Males may crawl on top of other males or even bite them. Whether or not this behavior is a mistaken courtship or true aggression against another male is not clear, for many times two wild males can be found literally side by side without any aggression.

REPRODUCTION: Although sexual maturity has been reported in both sexes at 5–10 years of age by Minton (1972), a captive male received by Mertens (1973) when about 2.5 years old did not mate until it was about 18 years of age.

Increases in male hormone levels bring on maturity. Endocrine studies by Evans (1952) showed that 18 months after injection with testosterone propionate the first to third hind claws of juvenile *Terrapene carolina* became hypertrophied, as compared to untreated juveniles. The claws became thicker and more abruptly curved, as in adult males. The penis of treated males also enlarged to some degree, but still could be withdrawn into its cloacal sheath. Intensity of red pigment in the iris increased in some treated turtles, and their plastra began to develop a concavity.

The sexual cycles of both sexes are fairly well known, thanks to the research of Altland (1951) on *T. carolina* from Maryland and Pennsylvania. Spermatogonia divide from May to July. Primary spermatocytes appear in June, peak in July, and decrease in numbers until autumn. Maturation divisions and spermiogenesis occur in July, and both increase greatly in early August. Spermatogenesis is past its peak by mid-September, after which the seminal epithelium is greatly reduced in size. Following hibernation the testis is composed chiefly of Sertoli cells, lipid debris, and spermatogonia; the epididymis is filled with spermatozoa throughout the year. Interstitial cells are large and heavily laden with lipids during May, but are small in July and August. In the fall they increase in size, but there is little increase in lipid material.

The oogenetic cycle begins in July and August, when the oogonia divide and grow in the germinal ridges located at sites scattered about the periphery of the ovary. New follicles are formed at this time, and usually two to eight accumulate yolk during the fall. Ovarian weight is greatest in May. In June, after ovulation in late May, the collapsed follicles are transformed into corpora lutea, which atrophy by mid-August (Altland, 1951). Egg-bearing *T. c. carolina* can be found in North Carolina from May to July (Stuart and Miller, 1987).

Courtship and mating activity usually begins in May, although Dundee and Rossman (1989) and Jackson (1991a) reported March and April copulations in Louisiana and Florida, and extends through the summer to October (Schwartz and Schwartz, 1974; Williams and Parker, 1987; Jackson, 1991a; Ernst, pers. obs.). In Missouri most pairing takes place in October (Schwartz and Schwartz, 1974). Mating partners usually occupy broadly overlapping or contiguous home ranges (Stickel, 1989), but transients may mate with resident turtles (Ernst, pers. obs.). Males may copulate with more than one female, or the same female several times during a several-year period (Williams and Parker, 1987). Copulation takes place on land or in shallow water (particularly in *T. c. major*; Ernst, 1981).

Courtship is divided into three phases: a circling, biting, and shoving phase; a preliminary mounting phase; and a coital phase (Evans, 1953; Ernst, 1981; Levell, 1985). In phase 1 the male approaches the female but stops when about 10 cm away if she remains still, with his legs straightened, his head held high, and often with one leg raised above the ground. The female retracts her head but watches him. He then walks around the female, nipping her shell as he goes, or pushes her shell a few degrees upon its axis, bites it, and then pushes it farther around and bites it again. He may actually tip her over or roll her continuously during this behavior. If the female crawls away, the male moves after her, with head and neck extended, and places his nose close to her vent, apparently smelling it. He will also smell her bridge area if she remains still. Up to one hour may elapse during this phase, depending on the readiness of the female to open her plastron. He eventually mounts

and almost instantly hooks his toes into the posterior plastral opening, where she holds them tightly. Titillation of the claws upon the posterolateral edges of the female's carapace may be the final stimulus inducing her to open the rear of her plastron.

In phase 2 the male's hind feet follow the edge of the plastron forward and, when near the hinge, the claws hook on and the rear plastron closes upon them.

The stimuli that bring about phase 3 are the contact of plastron and carapace, the downward projection of the male's head in front of the female's face as he bites the forward rim of her shell, the touch of his forefeet upon her shell, and the slight motion of his pinioned claws on the plastral rim. For copulation, the male slips backward until his carapace rests on the ground, while the rear ankles of the female press downward and medially upon his feet, which have shifted farther beneath her carapace. After several seconds he leans still farther back and then returns to the vertical position, in which intromission occurs.

The courtship pattern of *T. c. carolina* is perhaps the ancestral type (Evans, 1968). The *T. c. triunguis* male stops a few centimeters from the female and, with head held high, pulsates his bright throat. She comes alongside; he mounts, scratches her scutes with all four feet, is pinioned, and then for several minutes exposes his pulsating throat to her. The *T. c. bauri* male climbs upon the female's carapace with all four feet. After a moment of rubbing and scratching her he pulsates his yellow throat above her head. When pinioned in the usual manner he nibbles gently at her neck. The mating of *T. c. major* sometimes takes place in shallow water, but, except for having the olfactory behavior described above, in other respects resembles that of *T. c. carolina*.

Males sometimes die as a result of falling on their backs after copulation in a place where they cannot gain sufficient leverage to right themselves (Allard, 1939).

A female may lay fertile eggs for up to four years from one successful mating (Ewing, 1943). Tubular albumen-secreting ducts in the oviducts of *T. carolina* can serve as seminal receptacles. The glands containing the stored sperm are restricted to the caudal portion of the albumen region of the oviduct, and open into the oviductal lumen either by breaks in the mucosal epithelial lining or through ducts formed by invaginations in this lining (Hattan and Gist, 1975).

Natural nesting occurs from May through July, but oviposition has been recorded as late as 17 August in captivity (Jackson, 1991a). Most nests are started in the evening and finished after dark; but some females have been found excavating nests in the morning.

Suitable nest sites may not be found within a female's home range, and she may have to make a foray outside of the range to lay her eggs, usually on damp, overcast days (Stickel, 1950). The nest site usually is in an open elevated patch of sandy or loamy soil, although some females will nest in the woods (Ernst, pers. obs.). The 7.5–10.0-cm flask-shaped cavity is dug entirely with the hind feet and its size is correlated with the length of the hind leg. Most nests are dug on stormy evenings (Congello, 1978), perhaps either to facilitate digging or to hide their odor from predators. At the beginning of excavation the forefeet are braced and subsequently not moved; the hind feet dig alternately. The eggs are deposited at intervals of one to six minutes and are arranged in the nest by the hind feet; the entire nesting process may take as long as five hours to complete. Bladder contents may be voided into the cavity during excavation. When the clutch is complete, the nest cavity is filled by broad lateral sweeps of one hind foot or by scooping soil and grass forward with both hind feet in unison. Filling also involves much tamping and treading with the toes, feet, knees, and plastron. Trial nests may be dug before the true nest is constructed. Females may soak in water for several days immediately before and 12–30 hours after nesting (Jackson, 1991a). Congello (1978) has given an excellent description of nesting behavior and oviposition to which we refer the reader.

The eggs are elliptical and have thin, white, flexible shells with nodular surfaces. They are 24.5–40.2 mm in length, 17.0–25.1 mm in width, and 6–13 g in weight. Clutch size is 1–11 (Congello, 1978; Warner, 1982; Jackson, 1991a); 4–5 is the usual number. Most of the thickness (63.5%) of the eggshell consists of fibrous layers; mineral layers constitute only 36.5% (Ewert, 1979a). The shell, albumen contents, and yolk, respectively, compose 8.1, 44.2, and 47.7% of the fresh egg weight (Ewert, 1979a). The eggs are approximately 68% water, 25.8% lipid by weight, and the shell is about 20.7% of the dry mass (Congdon and Gibbons, 1985).

The maximum number of clutches laid in one season was five by a *T. c. major* (Tucker et al., 1978), but two clutches are more normal for the other subspecies (Finneran, 1948; Minton, 1972; Riemer, 1981). *Terrapene c. major* lays clutches at intervals of 23–30 days (Jackson, 1991a). Not all eggs laid are fertile; Ewing (1933) recorded a fertility rate of 78%, but Dodge et al. (1978) and Congello (1978) reported rates as low as 54 and 24%, respectively, and Stuart and Miller (1987) found some clutches totally infertile.

The incubation period depends on soil temperature, which in turn depends on such factors as mean air temperature, shading, soil characteristics, rainfall, and exposure. The lowest and highest lethal temperatures for incubation are 22 and 34°C (Dodge et al., 1978; Dimond, 1985). About 70–80 days normally are required before hatching, which usually takes place from early September into October, but Schwartz (1968) reported a December emergence in Philadelphia. Sometimes hatchlings overwinter in the nest (Gibbons and Nelson, 1978; Ernst, pers. obs.). The shortest incubation period recorded was 57 days (Iverson, 1977a), the longest, 136 days (Allard, 1948).

Terrapene carolina has temperature-dependent sex determination. Clutches incubated at temperatures of 22.5–27.0°C produce a preponderance of males, while those incubated at 28.5°C or above produce almost all females (Dimond, 1983; Ewert and Nelson, 1991).

Hatchlings have a flat, brownish-gray carapace with a vertebral keel and a yellow spot on each large scute. The plastron is yellow to cream, with a brown central blotch; the hinge is nonfunctional. The tail is long compared to that of the adult. Newly hatched young have the following dimensions: carapace length, 28–35 mm; carapace width, 24–33 mm; carapace height, 15–18 mm; plastron length, 26–33 mm; and weight, 5.7–10.0 g. Hatchling *T. c. major* measured 10–20 days after pipping, but before feeding, by Jackson (1991a) had 31.8–39.7-mm carapaces, 28.5–38.8-mm plastra, and weighed 8.3–11.3 g. At hatching a caruncle is present between the nostrils; it is lost and the yolk sac is retracted within a week. The plastral hinge does not become functional until the turtle grows to about 50 mm. Neill (1948c) commented that during the early months young *T. carolina* emit a strong odor when molested which is lost upon further development; we have never noticed this.

GROWTH AND LONGEVITY: Several studies have been published on the growth rate of the eastern box turtle.

Allard (1948) followed for several years the growth of 22 turtles hatched in 1934. Their average weight on 11 July 1935 was 11.5 g; on 15 September 1935, 20.6 g; and on 17 October 1936, 39.6 g. They were weighed again on 14 May 1937 and found to have an average weight of 38.6 g, which meant an average loss of 1 g after almost seven months; during this period they had hibernated and subsequently had probably been without food (on 14 May they had barely begun

Hatchling *Terrapene carolina carolina*

Plastron of hatchling *Terrapene carolina carolina*

to feed). On 28 October 1937, at the end of their third year after hatching, their average weight was 53.9 g. Yahner (1974) found that weight is a poor indicator of age in *Terrapene carolina;* some turtles recaptured after four years weighed more but others weighed less. There seems to be no significant effect of season on either total body water or total body fat reserves in *T. carolina* (Brisbin, 1972).

Ditmars (in Pope, 1939) reported that a Connecti-

cut *T. c. carolina* attained a carapace length of 12.7 cm in slightly more than five years. Rosenberger (in Pope, 1939) reported that a male grew to 12.1 cm in plastron length and a female to 10.1 cm in four years. Carr (1952) stated that during the first four or five years box turtles may grow at a rate of 12.7–19.1 mm/yr, and Nichols (1939a) found the maximum growth rate to be 9.5 mm/yr. These latter growth rates are closer to those found in the wild.

Stickel and Bunck (1989) studied the growth of *T. c. carolina* in a Maryland woods from 1944 to 1981. A bivariate analysis of age-related growth showed that between 8 and 13 years males grow an average of 6.7%/yr in carapace length, while females only grow at a rate of 5.3%/yr. Both sexes grow slower between 14 and 19 years of age (males, 2.3%/yr; females, 3.4%/yr), and growth slows even more once the turtles pass 20 years of age. Allometric analysis of different carapace and plastron dimensions showed that among males length increased proportionally more than either width or height, and that width increased more than height. Among females, only the greater increase of length over width was statistically significant. Fully grown males were larger in all dimensions except height. Leuck and Carpenter (1981) found a reduction in the dorsal keel, a lightening in color of the carapace and plastron scute rims, and pronounced carapace flaring with age in *T. c. triunguis.*

Incubation temperature may affect the post-hatching growth rate of juvenile *T. carolina* (Dodge et al., 1978). Hatchling growth from eggs incubated constantly at 24 and 30°C was nearly equivalent, but the growth rates of both these groups were four times those of hatchlings reared under field conditions.

The eastern box turtle's shell has great regenerative powers: Smith (1958) and Rose (1986) reported cases of total regeneration of the carapace of badly burned *T. carolina.*

Oliver (1955) reported that a *T. carolina* lived 138 years in the wild, and Graham and Hutchison (1969) gave evidence for centenarian box turtles in New England. Stickel (1978) and Dundee and Rossman (1989) thought some certainly live 80 years in Maryland and Louisiana. However, from our observations and the studies of Stickel (1978), only a few wild individuals live more than 30–40 years.

FOOD HABITS: Feeding may take place on land or in shallow water, and *Terrapene carolina* is omnivorous. When young it is chiefly carnivorous, but it becomes more herbivorous with age; however, apparent differences in the diets of juveniles and adults may be influenced by seasonality or availability of certain food items (Stuart and Miller, 1987). Babcock (1939) kept a young box turtle for six years after hatching before it took any plant material. Stomachs of 40 individuals of various sizes examined by Surface (1908) had animal material in 80% and plant material in 62% of those containing food. Stickel (1950) reported that the principal food is fungi (71.6% frequency by volume). Klimstra and

Newsome (1960) found plant remains in 89% and animal remains in 98% of stomachs containing food. Barbour (1950) noted snails 60%, crayfish 15%, and plant material 12.5%, by volume. Bush (1959) found snails and slugs 52.5%, mushrooms 10%, caterpillars 10%, carabid beetles 4%, and centipedes 3.5%, by volume. Strang (1983) found that *T. carolina* did not eat green leaves in nature, but instead took flowers and fruits 11% of the time, fungi 55%, invertebrates 28%, and vertebrates 6%.

Roots, stems, fruits, and some seeds are eaten. *Terrapene carolina* may even be a potential seed disperser for some wild plants (Braun and Brooks, 1987). Among the plants consumed are mushrooms, blackberries, blueberries, elderberries, mulberries, wild grapes, plums, strawberries, sweet cicely, tomatoes, mayapple, wintergreen, ground cherry, mosses, *Rubus, Polygonum, Ambrosia, Galium, Vitis,* and the grasses *Bromus, Paspalum,* and *Hordeum.* Invertebrates eaten include snails, slugs, earthworms, spiders, crayfish, isopods, millipedes, centipedes, wood roaches, grasshoppers, crickets, flies, beetles, ants, termites, cicadas, moths, caterpillars, insect grubs, and maggots. Vertebrate food includes fish, frogs (*Acris, Pseudacris, Hyla, Rana*), toads (*Bufo*), salamanders (*Ambystoma*), lizards (*Phrynosoma*), and small snakes (*Carphophis, Coluber, Storeria, Thamnophis*), and birds (*Passer, Catharus;* Alsop and Wallace, 1978; Anton, 1990). *Terrapene carolina* also consume carrion: they have been seen feeding on dead ducks (*Anas*), green herons (*Butorides*), amphibians, mice (*Microtus*), shrews (*Sorex*), cottontails (*Sylvilagus*), and even a dead cow (*Bos*). Conant (1951a) saw captives feeding on a broken duck egg, and Ernst has seen wild *T. carolina* feeding on snapping turtle (*Chelydra*) eggs and a captive female eat several of her own eggs.

Myers (1956) reported an unusual feeding habit. When confronted with several mealworms a captive subadult picked up each in turn and with a few bites killed or disabled it. Only when all were incapable of escape did the turtle start to feed. This behavior was observed several times when more that one mealworm was offered.

A strange social facilitation may exist between *T. carolina* and the American toad, *Bufo americanus,* in which intraspecific pairings of both female turtles and female toads produce significantly faster eating of a fixed amount of food per animal in both species than in individual animals (Overmann and Boice, 1970). No satisfactory explanation has been presented for this behavior.

Our captives feed well on earthworms, canned dog food, newborn mice (*Mus*), tomatoes, romaine lettuce, bananas, apples, watermelon, cantaloupe, strawberries, shaved carrots, hard-boiled eggs, and bread. Cahn (1937) reported that if his young captives were not permitted to hibernate during the winter they ceased to eat, no matter what food was offered, and starved to death. We have found this not to be the case as long as the turtles are kept at 24–27°C and well hydrated.

PREDATORS AND DEFENSE: Large numbers of nests are destroyed by badgers (*Taxidea*), skunks (*Mephitis*), foxes (*Urocyon, Vulpes*), raccoons (*Procyon*), crows (*Corvus*), and snakes (*Cemophora, Heterodon, Lampropeltis*). Crows, vultures (*Cathartes, Coragyps*), Mississippi kites (*Ictinia*), barn owls (*Tyto*), and snakes (*Agkistrodon contortrix, A. piscivorus, Coluber constrictor*) are known predators of juveniles, but surely many other species take the young. The numerous limb mutilations seen on adults are probably caused by such carnivores as raccoons, skunks, coyotes and dogs (*Canis*), and foxes. Few species are able to prey effectively on adults; however, Culbertson (1907) observed hogs (*Sus*) crushing and eating them, and Clark (1982) found adult shells in bald eagle nests (*Haliaeetus*), but these were probably taken as carrion.

Box turtles are sometimes infested by fleshfly larvae (*Sarcophaga, Phaenicia*); if severe, such parasitism may be fatal (Ewing, 1926; Peters, 1948; King and Griffo, 1958; Jackson et al., 1969; McAllister, 1987).

Humans are the leading killers of box turtles: thousands die annually on our highways, and thousands more are now being shipped overseas for the foreign pet trade. Adler (1970) has suggested that the Indians (primarily the Iroquois) were responsible for the elimination of *Terrapene carolina* in western New York and possibly in southern Ontario by using them for food, medical, ceremonial, burial, and hunting purposes.

The box turtle's best defense is to withdraw completely within its shell and close its plastral hinge. Often individuals will release bladder water on their handler, kick or scratch, but seldom do they bite.

POPULATIONS: Dolbeer (1969) collected 270 *Terrapene carolina carolina* in a 8.9-ha woodland near Knoxville, Tennessee, and by recapture estimated the population to be 17–22/ha with a male to female ratio of 1.61:1.00. By 1972 males were favored 3:1 over females at this site (Yahner, 1974).

Stickel (1950) collected 245 adult *T. c. carolina* on 11.7 ha at Laurel, Maryland, and estimated the population to be 9.9–12.4/ha (a biomass of 3.1–3.9

kg/ha; Iverson, 1982a). Her recapture records showed that some of these adults had home ranges entirely within the study plot and that others ranged beyond it. Still others were transients, so the number of box turtles collected was somewhat greater than the permanent population. Transients were estimated to compose about 6.7% of the total at any one time. Juveniles constituted less than 10% of the total population, or about 0.25–1.23/ha. The adult male to adult female ratio was 1.00:1.09.

Continued studies of this same Maryland population for over 30 years (Stickel, 1978) showed a pronounced decline in population size from 1945 to 1975, when the numbers were reduced by half. Proportions of females and of young also declined. The number of older males in 1975 was 57% of those in 1945, older females 29%, and juveniles 38%. Changes typical of declining populations were apparent: the proportion of females to males declined, as did the proportion of younger turtles. Females made up 53.3% of the population more than 20 years old in 1945, but only 36.4% in 1975. Turtles under 20 years old composed 19.4% of the population in 1945, but only 17.9% in 1975.

Williams (1961) marked 255 *T. c. carolina* in Allee Woods, Indiana, from 1958 to 1960, and estimated the density to be 8.9/ha. This population was subsequently sampled in 1964, 1965, 1967, 1970, and 1983 (Williams and Parker, 1987). The population density in the 1960s was 4.4–5.7/ha, but both population size and density declined substantially to a density of only 2.7/ha in 1983. Sex ratios favored males in most years, but not significantly. In a North Carolina population of *T. c. carolina*, adult males made up 35.6% of the population, adult females 41.3%, and juveniles 23.1% (Stuart and Miller, 1987). In Illinois, Elghammer et al. (1979) recorded a 1.00:3.40 male:female ratio in *T. c. carolina*.

Population dynamics of *T. c. triunguis* have also been extensively studied. Schwartz and Schwartz (1974) and Schwartz et al. (1984) marked 1,568 different turtles at a 22.2-ha site near Jefferson City, Missouri, from 1965 to 1983. The density to 1973 was 17.3–34.6/ha (a biomass of 5.4–10.8 kg/ha; Iverson, 1982a). The juvenile to adult ratio from 1965 to 1970 varied from 1.00:7.69 to 1.00:3.03; the adult sex ratio was 1.22:1.00 in favor of males. Population density in 1979 was estimated as 21.4/ha. Schwartz et al. (1984) believed the population had remained fairly stable with only 27–134 new turtles entering the population each year, and a nearly comparable number leaving annually. The adult sex ratio was approximately equal. Juveniles composed about 46% of the population, adults 54%. The sex ratio of a population of *T. c. triunguis* in Cleveland County, Oklahoma, was also equal (Leuck and Carpenter, 1981).

Survival rates for *T. carolina* are rather high. Yahner (1974) recorded an average 25.9% survival rate from 1968 to 1972 in Tennessee *T. c. carolina* weighing up to 250 g, and an average survival rate of 42.5% for turtles heavier than that. At Allee Woods, Indiana, among original cohorts, only 44–71% of the individuals were recaptured in subsequent years, but in those captured a second year, 88–100% were recaptured later (Williams and Parker, 1987). Survival to 20 years or more after first marking as adults averaged 18.1% in older males, 36% in growing males, 15.6% in older females, and 13.8% in growing females. Among 136 turtles marked in 1958, 11.4% of the males and 10.5% of the females survived at least 25 more years. In the population of *T. c. triunguis* studied by Schwartz and Schwartz (1974) and Schwartz et al. (1984), once a turtle was present, its average probability of survival to the next year was 81.9% (74–92). Juveniles averaged a 66.3% (43–91) survival rate, and adults varied from 68 to 100% survival per year. However, by 1989 only 22 individuals (6%), 10 males, 12 females, of the original population remained alive in the study area (Schwartz and Schwartz, 1991). All of these spent their known lives in permanent home ranges of 2.2–10.6 ha. Most turtles left the population (found dead or no longer collected) in two to eight years after initial capture.

In spite of the abundance of *T. carolina* in some regions, hatchlings and juveniles are rarely found. The young, apparently, immediately seek shelter and hide in vegetation or beneath debris. So younger age classes may be underrepresented in most population studies.

A large population of *T. c. bauri* lives on the offshore Egmont Key, Hillsborough County, Florida, where Franz et al. (1992) marked 215 individuals in January, March, and April 1991.

REMARKS: Hybridization between *Terrapene carolina* and *T. ornata* occasionally occurs where their ranges overlap (see summary in Ernst and McBreen, 1991b).

Carpenter (1956) reported carapace-pitting in Oklahoma *T. c. triunguis*. This involved both the scute and underlying bone of the anterior borders of the third pleural scutes. The condition was more common in females, and it was positively correlated, in both sexes, with increasing carapace length. Neither the cause nor the significance of the pitting is known.

Stickel (1951) found no significant difference in either population size or growth rate of *T. carolina* in an area treated with DDT annually for five years, but subsequent long-term studies of this population showed considerable reduction in population size over 30 years (Stickel, 1978). Could this have been, in part, due to accumulative pesticide poisoning? Ferguson (1963) reported a *T. carolina* death possibly from heptochlor poisoning. Perhaps the mortality from pesticides and herbicides is higher than we know.

Terrapene carolina is sometimes eaten by humans, but this is risky: Babcock (1919) reported that Pennsylvania miners ate box turtles (during a strike) and became ill. It is likely that the turtles had fed on a poisonous fungus, which did not affect them but made their flesh temporarily poisonous. Carr (1952) retold an anecdote of his father's: box turtles accidentally roasted in burning brushpiles in Mississippi were eaten by several boys, all of whom later became ill.

The latest literature reviews of *T. carolina* are by Ernst and McBreen (1991a,b).

Terrapene ornata (Agassiz, 1857)
Ornate box turtle

PLATE 29

RECOGNITION: This is a small terrestrial turtle with a hinged plastron, a keelless carapace (most individuals), and a conspicuous pattern of radiating light lines. The carapace (to 15.4 cm) is round to oval and high domed; its highest point is directly above or anterior to the plastral hinge. No posterior serrations are present, and the carapace is flattened dorsally; rarely a weakly developed middorsal keel occurs on the posterior half of the third and anterior half of the fourth vertebral scutes. The first vertebral is elevated at a low angle (45° or less), and the first marginal commonly is irregularly oval or triangular. The carapace is dark brown to reddish brown, commonly with a yellow middorsal stripe; each scute shows radiating yellowish lines. The plastron has a strong hinge between the pectoral and abdominal scutes; this divides the plastron into two movable lobes. The hinge normally arises at the seam between the fifth and sixth marginals or at the sixth marginal. The plastron is commonly as long or longer than the carapace, and its lateral rim is commonly entire (not indented). No bridge is present; normally axillary scutes are absent, but, if present, are at the fifth marginal. The plastron has a pattern of radiating lines on each scute. The skin is dark brown with yellow spotting, especially on the dorsal surface of the head and limbs; the chin and the unnotched upper jaw are yellow. In some individuals, head coloration is greenish. The tail may have a yellow dorsal stripe. Each hind foot has four toes (rarely only three).

Adult males have a red iris; in females it is yellowish brown. In males but not females the first toe on the hind foot is thickened, widened, and turned in. The hind lobe of the plastron is slightly concave in males, flat or convex in females.

KARYOTYPE: The karyotype is 2n = 50: 26 macrochromosomes (16 metacentric, 6 submetacentric, and 4 telocentric) and 24 microchromosomes

(Stock, 1972; Bickham and Baker, 1976; Killebrew, 1977a; Bickham, 1981).

FOSSIL RECORD: Middle Pliocene (Hemphillian) *Terrapene ornata* have been identified from deposits in Kansas and Oklahoma, late Pliocene—early Pleistocene (Blancan) fossils are known from Kansas, Texas, and possibly Arizona. Remains of Pleistocene (Irvingtonian) age have been found in Kansas (Holman, 1986a), and Pleistocene (Rancholabrean) bones and shells and Recent archeological remains have been found in Arizona, Kansas, New Mexico, and Texas (Milstead, 1969; Rogers, 1976; Ward, 1978; Moodie and Van Devender, 1978; Parmley, 1986; Schneider and Everson, 1989).

DISTRIBUTION: *Terrapene ornata* ranges from northwestern Indiana, Illinois, southcentral Wisconsin, eastern and western Iowa, southern South Dakota, and eastern Wyoming (Goshen County) south to southwestern Louisiana, Texas, eastern and southern New Mexico, southeastern Arizona, and Sonora, Chihuahua, and southwestern Coahuila, Mexico. Its range extends from near sea level to over 2,000 m elevation.

GEOGRAPHIC VARIATION: Two subspecies are recognized. *Terrapene ornata ornata* (Agassiz, 1857), the ornate box turtle, ranges from Indiana, Illinois, Wisconsin, and eastern Wyoming south to Louisiana and New Mexico. It is distinguished by five to nine radiating lines on the second pleural and by its generally dark appearance. *T. o. luteola* Smith and Ramsey, 1952, the desert box turtle, ranges from the Trans-Pecos region of Texas and southeastern Arizona south into northern Mexico. This turtle has 10–16 radiating lines on the second pleural and is generally yellowish. The shells of old individuals often lose their pattern and become uniformly pale greenish or

Terrapene ornata ornata

Plastra of *Terrapene ornata,* from left: *T. o. ornata* and *T. o. luteola*

straw colored; this pigment loss does not usually occur in *T. o. ornata.*

CONFUSING SPECIES: *Terrapene carolina* normally has a middorsal keel on the second to fourth vertebral scutes, has the first marginal nearly rectangular, has the plastral hinge usually at the fifth marginal, commonly has only three toes on the hind foot, and, except in the Florida subspecies, lacks a plastral pattern of radiating yellow lines on each scute. *Emydoidea blandingii* has a notched upper jaw and a bright yellow neck and chin. The tortoises,

genus *Gopherus,* do not have a hinged plastron. Aquatic mud turtles, *Kinosternon,* in the United States have two plastral hinges and heavily webbed toes.

HABITAT: This is generally a prairie turtle, inhabiting treeless, sandy plains and gently rolling country with grass and scattered low brush as the dominant vegetation. However, it may enter woodlands, particularly along streams, and in Arizona and New Mexico may also be found on the fringes of deserts.

Distribution of *Terrapene ornata*

BEHAVIOR: Over most of its range, *Terrapene ornata* is active from March to November, but Blair (1976) found one active in December in Texas. In the north, turtles emerge from hibernation around the middle of April, and most are usually underground again by mid-October. Most activity occurs from late April through June, the primary reproductive season, but a second peak of movement may take place in September, probably as the turtles migrate back toward hibernating areas.

The daily cycle of activity consists of periods of basking, foraging, and rest that vary in length depending on environmental conditions. These turtles emerge from their nightly retreats, or forms, and other places of concealment soon after dawn and ordinarily bask for at least a few minutes before setting off to forage. Although foraging sometimes continues in shady spots throughout the day, it usually ceases between midmorning and noon, when the turtles seek shelter. They remain under cover until mid-or late afternoon, when they again forage. Activity of all except nesting females ceases at dusk.

As temperatures rise in summer the period of midday quiescence is lengthened and the turtles sometimes spend the warmest hours in pools of water. At least in the southwestern portion of its range, *T. ornata* activity seems to be largely controlled by rainfall: it becomes specially active during and after thunderstorms. In the north it is less active during rains or on cool, overcast days.

Legler (1960a) took about 500 body temperatures under natural conditions and found 30°C to be the optimum temperature for activity. Turtles usually emerge when the body temperature is 24°C or higher and almost never when it is below 15°C. Body temperature is raised to optimum by basking; if this is impossible, activity begins at suboptimal body temperatures. Shelter in dens, burrows, or forms is sought when the body temperature rises above 30°C. A temperature of 40°C for a prolonged period is lethal; prolonged exposure at 0°C or below is also fatal. Brattstrom (1965) found the mean body temperature of 57 active ornate box turtles to be 28°C (13.0—35.9).

Twenty-two adult *T. ornata* kept with 12 adult *Gopherus berlandieri* in an outdoor enclosure in Texas consistently maintained lower body temperatures than the tortoises. Rose et al. (1988) thought this possibly a result of differences in the foraging strategies of the two species. The *Gopherus* is a cropper that spends little time at one place while feeding; it swallows much hard-to-digest plant material and its feces contain a high amount of roughage. *Terrapene*, however, is an opportunistic feeder that eats a variety

Terrapene ornata luteola

of more easily digested animal foods as well as vegetable matter.

Several studies have been conducted on the physiological effects of environmental temperature on *T. ornata*. Bethea (1972) found that the heart rate is directly proportional to body temperature, and that at low body temperatures (5–11°C) mean heart rates during warming are significantly lower than during cooling; the rate of cooling is greater than the rate of warming (Spray and May, 1972, reported that cooling occurs twice as fast as heating in *T. ornata*; however, Costanzo, 1982, found that *T. ornata* in 40°C water heat faster than they cool). Heart rate is inversely proportional to body weight, especially at 10°C or higher, but the cooling rate of individuals less than 300 g is directly proportional to body weight. The percentage contribution of increased heart rate to increased oxygen transport during activity may be 14–42% (Gatten, 1974b). Adams and deCarvalho (1984) heated and cooled *T. ornata* in water at 35 and 15°C, and found no significant differences between warming and cooling rates when thermal time constants were calculated. Heart rate is only slightly higher during warming. However, Legler (1971) recorded an increase in heart rate from approximately 28 beats/minute to almost 50 beats/minute after 60 minutes of basking.

A pronounced diurnal rhythm of breathing frequency is present at all temperatures (Glass et al., 1979). At 5°C the mean breathing rate is 3.7 breaths/h, at 15°C it is 16 times higher with a 17-fold increase of ventilation. Oxygen uptake changes from 3.4 to 12.7 ml/kg/h; however, a decrease occurs at 25°C. The following ranges of standard/active metabolic rates (cm³ O_2/g × h at STPD) were recorded by Gatten (1974a): 10°C, 0.0008/0.0167; 20°C, 0.0093/0.2055; 30°C, 0.0149/0.3625; and 40°C, 0.0912/0.7316. Total body lactate (mg/g) when at rest and during two minutes of maximal activity were: 30°C, 0.39/0.98; and 40°C, 0.55/1.00. Arterial blood percentage saturation with oxygen, lactate concentration, and pH in *T. ornata* at rest and during two minutes of maximal activity were, respectively, at 40°C, 56.4, 55.1, and 7.18 versus 59.6, 115.3, and 7.12; and at 30°C, 92.8, 31.6, and 7.56 versus 53.0, 97.0, and 7.20 (Gatten, 1975).

In studies on preferred temperatures by fasted and recently fed *T. ornata* by Gatten (1974c), fed turtles were less variable in body temperature than starved ones, but had a thermal preference of 29.8°C, only 1.5°C above that for animals deprived of food for 7–14 days. Sturbaum and Riedesel (1974, 1977) studied the responses of *T. ornata* acclimated to 30°C core temperature when exposed to air temperatures of 38–55°C. Exposure to 38–41°C was not a heat stress. At 51°C, frothing occurred in approximately 68 minutes, but at 55°C copious saliva (extreme frothing) was produced and spread over the head and forelimbs. Urine may also be rubbed onto the hind legs, and urination ordinarily occurs before salivation (Riedesel et al., 1971). Ambient temperatures of 65–75°C bring on acute stress, but are probably never experienced in the wild.

Ornate box turtles begin to enter hibernation in September in the north (Doroff and Keith, 1990) and October in the south; by the end of November most or all are underground. In Kansas autumn activity is characterized by movement into ravines and other low places and into wooded strips along fields or small streams (Legler, 1960a)—locations well suited for basking and burrowing as well as protected from the wind. The turtles often use animal burrows along the banks of a ravine for temporary shelter, and the overhanging sod at the edge of the ravine provides cover beneath which the turtles can easily dig.

Low air temperature is probably the primary stimulus for hibernation. A decrease in general activity usually follows the autumn rains. Rain probably facilitates burrowing by softening the soil; more often than not, ornate box turtles excavate their own hibernacula. These are deepened gradually during the winter; depth seems to be governed by the temperature of the soil (and the depth of soil frost may be the limiting dispersal factor at the northern extremes of the range). Hibernacula in woods and other sheltered places ordinarily are shallower than those in open grassland.

Terrapene ornata hibernates alone. In the rare instances in which more that one are found in a hibernaculum, the association has no social significance; it is simply a reflection of the availability and suitability of the hibernaculum.

Legler (1960a) reported that body temperatures of hibernating *T. ornata* approximated that of the surrounding soil. In November and December body temperatures tended to be slightly higher than soil temperatures; in February and March slightly lower. The lowest body temperature of any turtle that survived the winter was 2.7°C; body temperatures 1–3°C higher than this were common in the coldest part of the winter.

In Wisconsin, burrow temperatures declined from late November to late February from an average of 5°C (3.6–7.5) to 1.2°C (−0.3–2.7), with deeper burrows tending to have the warmest temperatures (Doroff and Keith, 1990). From late February to early April, mean burrow temperatures rose to 3.9°C (2.2–5.0). Shade played no role during the winter, but shaded hibernacula warmed more slowly in the spring. Burrow depths ranged from 0.5 to 1.8 m, with no difference between the sexes. The next year eight of fourteen turtles hibernated within a meter of their previous year's hibernaculum; five of the turtles were within 0.5 m of each other.

Emergence from hibernation usually takes place in April, but in some years a few emerge as early as the first week of March (particularly in the south). Emergence is delayed until the ground has been sufficiently moistened and air temperatures have reached 26°C (Fitch, 1956). In early March, turtles face upward in their hibernacula, and as the soil temperature rises they move slowly toward the surface, usually following the route by which they entered. They remain just below the surface of the ground for a week or two before actually emerging; emergence is probably hastened by the ground-softening spring rains. Some fat is built up for energy and, possibly, insulation over the winter; the total lipid index is about 0.1 (Rose, 1980).

Studies of *T. ornata* near St. Louis, Missouri, showed that in the spring the turtles move from their hibernacula toward the soil surface as they follow a minimum ambient temperature of about 7°C (Grobman, 1990). They emerge after five consecutive days of subsurface (10–20 cm) temperatures of 7°C or higher. If the subsurface temperature dips below this about the time of emergence, the *T. ornata* remain underground until conditions improve. After emergence they remain near their hibernacula and, if the surface temperature drops, reenter. During and after the first warm spring rains they move away from the vicinity of the hibernacula.

Cahn (1937) compared the hibernation of *T. ornata* and *T. carolina* in an outdoor pen. The ornate box turtles entered hibernation before the eastern box turtles; every individual disappeared fully two weeks before the first *T. carolina* made any effort to burrow. Once *T. ornata* had dug into the ground, it did not emerge until spring. Like *T. carolina,* they were only a few centimeters under the surface of the ground in October but dug deeper as the temperature dropped. Eastern box turtles ceased their descent at 48 cm, but the ornate box turtles dug to a depth of 57 cm. *Terrapene ornata* did not emerge until a week or two after the *T. carolina* had become active. Altogether, *T. ornata* spent nearly a month longer in hibernation than did *T. carolina.* The greater depth of the hibernaculum may explain the longer period of inactivity. Peters (1959) noted the existence of an air dome above hibernating *T. ornata.* This space was about half the size of the turtle and was filled with loose dirt, which provided a little air space.

In a study of the effects of hibernation on the physiology of this species, Peters (1959) found an increase of 19% in the number of red blood cells, an increase of 30% in the number of white blood cells, an increase of 57% in the amount of blood sugar, no significant change in the amount of serum protein, a 50% decrease in liver fat, and a total weight loss of 1.2–10.4 g.

Hibernation mortality may be high during severe winters, particularly among shallowly buried turtles, and may result in lower population densities the next summer (Metcalf and Metcalf, 1979).

Living in relatively dry habitats, water retention is a problem for *T. ornata*. Olson (1989) reported that 200–400-g turtles at an activity temperature of 33°C showed an average body weight loss (due to evaporative water loss) of 1.1 g/day, equal to 0.30–0.47% body weight loss. Riedesel et al. (1971) recorded body weight losses due to salivary evaporative water loss of 6.6–8.1% at 45°C, 4.3–9.8% at 55°C, 1.4–8.9% at 65°C, and 2.9–10.8% at 75°C as turtles tried to cool themselves. When the rostral brainstem is heated the rate of evaporative water loss increases (Morgareidge and Hammel, 1975); the magnitude of the response is proportional both to the change in hypothalamic temperature and to the ambient temperature with which the turtle is in equilibrium. The major function of this response is probably to protect the brain from overheating during heat stress.

To alleviate the problem of water loss, *T. ornata* adjusts its daily activity period, seeking shade when environmental conditions produce thermal stress. Lost water may be replaced through drinking or from food. Blair (1976) reported the frequent use of prickly-pear cacti (*Opuntia*) as food, and suggested this provides at least part of the water needs of this species in the dry southwestern part of its range.

Fitch (1958), who recovered 14 marked *T. ornata* a total of 30 times in seven years, found the average radius of the home range to be 83.5 m, indicating an area of approximately 2.2 ha; a female, possibly gravid, moved 558 m in 53 days. Legler (1960a) found that the ranges of males and females did not differ significantly. The radius of the home range of 44 adults (146 captures) averaged 85 m (21.6–278.0); the average area of the home range was 2.3 ha. Blair (1976) reported that five females had a range of 67–119 m (mean, 94) for the longest axis of their home range, but six males had long axes of 76–137 m (mean, 111).

In Wisconsin, Doroff and Keith (1990) found that home range varied greatly among adults (0.2–58.1 ha). Male home ranges averaged 8.2 ha in 1986 (13) and 3.4 ha in 1987 (5); whereas, females averaged 12.0 ha in 1986 (17) but only 6.9 ha in 1987 (12). Means between years or sexes were not significantly different. The mean home range of five juveniles (3–7 years) in 1987 was only 1.5 ha, significantly less than that of either adult sex. Three hatchlings from a single nest were each located at least 40 times during the summer of 1987 within a 16-m^2 area that included the

nest cavity. These hatchlings were often near or under rocks in dense vegetation. Home ranges of *T. ornata* of all ages and sexes overlap broadly with no indication of territoriality or social hierarchy.

Blair (1976) recorded the rates of normal movements for two turtles in Texas. A female moved 76 m in an hour, and a male crawled 100 m in 3.75 hours. Of two *T. ornata* removed more than 400 m from their home range by Legler (1960a), one homed but the other did not. A female studied by Metcalf and Metcalf (1970) homed from 1.7 km to the approximate site of original capture, between 23 August 1965 and 21 July 1966. Another displaced female (studied with a trailing device) traveled 442 m in 9.67 hours. Metcalf and Metcalf (1978) repeated their homing experiments by displacing 100 *T. ornata* distances of 1.6–2.8 km east, west, and south of their original points of capture (no roads ran north). All were larger than 80-mm plastron length, and adults of both sexes and juveniles were involved. Eighteen were retaken near the point of original capture: a female and four males homed 1.6 km, four females and five males homed 2 km, two females 2.4 km, and a female and a male returned from 2.8 km. The least time recorded between release and recapture was 31 days. Of the 18 that successfully homed, 2 returned from the south, 13 from the west, and 3 from the east. In addition, three turtles were displaced 3.2 km, and one of these (a male that had previously homed 2 km) was retaken in its home range the following year.

Terrapene ornata is a relatively good swimmer, and often enters puddles or cattle ponds to cool itself. It also has fair climbing ability, and some individuals may be quite good at this; Wilbern (1982) reported it capable of scaling a 77-cm vertical wire fence, and that it seemed to have better climbing ability than *T. carolina* kept with it.

REPRODUCTION: Sexual maturity seems more closely correlated with size than with age. There is evidence that males mature when smaller and younger than females: 76% of the males studied in Kansas by Legler (1960a) were mature at 100–109 mm in plastron length and at age 8–9 years, and 66% of the females were mature at 110—129 mm in plastron length and at age 10–11 years. Blair (1976) reported that males from Texas matured at seven years, but that females first reached maturity at eight years of age.

The spermatogenic cycle begins in May in all parts of the range and reaches its peak in September, when large numbers of sperm and spermatids are present in the testes. The cycle is completed in October, when sperm pass into the epididymides, where they are stored over the winter; thus females are inseminated with sperm produced the previous year.

The ovarian cycle begins in July, soon after ovulation, and continues until the next spring. Follicular growth is rapid during the period from spring emergence to ovulation. Large follicles remaining after ovulation represent, in many instances, eggs that will be laid later the same season.

Courtship and mating are most common in spring, soon after emergence from hibernation, but sometimes occur in the summer and fall. The earliest and latest dates of matings observed by Blair (1976) in Texas were 5 April and 13 October. Both males and females may copulate several times a season, particularly during the spring, with more than one partner.

The best description of mating in *Terrapene ornata* has been presented by Brumwell (1940). A male pursued a female for nearly 30 minutes, first nudging the margins of her shell and later approaching rapidly from the rear and hurling himself on her back while emitting a stream of liquid from each nostril. Presumably the liquid was water: both turtles had imbibed in a pond just before courtship began (Brumwell suggested that pressure on the plastron of the male had forced the water out his nostrils). After the male had achieved intromission the pair remained in coitus for 30 minutes; however, the act may last as long as two hours. At another time Brumwell saw four males pursuing a single female; they exhibited the same nudging and lunging behavior. Males that attempted to mount other males were repelled by defensive snapping. The female, too, snapped at some of the males that tried to mount her (female biting was also reported by Harless and Lambiotte, 1971). One male was finally successful and thereafter was unmolested by the other males. In the several matings observed by Legler (1960a), the male, after mounting the female, gripped her just beneath her legs or on the skin of the gluteal region with the first claws of his hind feet and used the remaining three claws to grip the posterior edges of her plastron. In most instances she secured his legs by hooking her own around them. This coital position differs from that of *T. carolina*, at least in the position of the male's legs.

Nesting extends from early May to mid-July and is most frequent in June. However, Ernst's captive *T. ornata*, which remain active all year, have laid as early as mid-March and as late as August. About 33% of females lay a second clutch in late June or early July (Legler, 1960a). In a two-year period in Wisconsin, only 57% of the females oviposited (Doroff and Keith, 1990).

Nesting sites that are open, well-drained, and have a soft substrate are preferred. The site is selected after a period of wandering during which the female tests the substrate at a number of places; the search may continue for more than a week. Nest excavation begins in the evening and is usually completed after dark. The female uses her hind feet only. She prepares a preliminary cavity, in which she lies while digging the main cavity. Often the bladder is voided on the surface and inside the cavity, softening the soil. The typical nest is flask shaped: roughly 55 mm deep, 80 mm wide at the bottom, and 60 mm wide at the opening. Females have a much larger pelvic aperture than males, presumably to aid in egg passage (Long and Rose, 1989).

Clutches include two to eight eggs; four to six are usual. The ellipsoidal eggs have a finely granulated but somewhat brittle white shell. Data from 42 eggs in nine clutches from Kansas were as follows: length 36.06 mm (31.3–40.9), width 21.71 mm (20.0–26.3), and weight 10.09 g (8.0–14.3). The smaller clutches tended to have the largest eggs: the largest and heaviest were in a clutch of two eggs, the smallest in a clutch of eight (Legler, 1960a). Elgar and Heaphy (1989) gave the mean weight of the eggs as 10.8 g. Mean clutch size in Wisconsin was 3.5 eggs (Doroff and Keith, 1990) versus 4.7 eggs in Kansas (Legler, 1960a). No evidence of double clutching was observed in Wisconsin.

Incubation periods for 49 eggs kept in a laboratory were 56–127 days, depending on the air temperature. Eggs kept at a daily average temperature of 33°C had a mean incubation period of 59 days (56–64); at 28°C, 70 days (67–73); and at 24°C, 125 days (124–127) (Legler, 1960a). The incubation periods averaging 59 and 70 days more nearly reflect natural conditions than does the excessively long period of 125 days. Naturally incubated clutches in Wisconsin hatched in an average of 80 days (79–84) (Doroff and Keith, 1990). Embryos close to hatching can survive two days' exposure to approximately 4.5°C, which may be necessary in late-season nests (Legler, 1960a). Minton (1972) reported an apparent case of a hatchling overwintering in the nest in Indiana.

During incubation the eggs expand by absorption of water. A temporary lack of moisture usually will not kill embryos, but prolonged dryness may be lethal. Packard et al. (1985) incubated eggs of *T. ornata* at 29°C on wet and dry substrates. Those on wet substrates absorbed water and increased in mass by 6% over the course of incubation, while eggs on dry medium lost water throughout development and weighed 17% less late in incubation than when first laid. However, only one of the dry-incubated, fertile eggs failed to hatch. Eggs developing on the wet medium incubated three days longer, mobilized more nutrient reserve in their yolk, and grew larger before hatching (possibly affecting later survivability). All 28 hatchlings that emerged from eggs incubated at 29°C were females. The young usually hatch and emerge from the nest in August and September.

The almost round hatchlings are approximately 30 mm in carapace length and weigh about 7 g. The carapace is dark brown to black, with yellow spots on the scutes and a yellow dorsal stripe along the vertebral ridge. The plastron is yellow to cream colored, with a large, dark central blotch; the hinge is not yet developed. The caruncle remains on the beak for a variable period of time.

Hybridization with *T. carolina* may occur naturally (see references listed in Ernst and McBreen, 1991b), and in captivity interspecific matings are common. A female *T. o. luteola* kept by Ernst often mated with a large male *T. c. major* and produced several clutches of fertile eggs, although none hatched.

GROWTH AND LONGEVITY: Scute growth in *Terrapene ornata* begins with the spring formation of a new layer of epidermis beneath the existing scute (Legler, 1960a). The peripheral projection of the new layer is distinct in texture and color and is separated from the older part of the scute by a major growth ring or annulus. Minor growth rings form when growth slows or temporarily stops during periods of quiescence and no new layer of epidermis is formed. The scutes are not shed.

Early hatching and early emergence from the nest are factors contributing to maximum growth of the shell in the first season. Hatchlings that overwinter in the nest do not grow there, but they emerge early the following year. Growth is rapid at first but slows gradually until maturity is reached, and it all but stops two or three years later; the total growing period is probably not more than 15–20 years of an ornate box turtle's lifespan. Legler (1960a) recorded mean increments in plastral length of 68%, 29%, and 18% for the first three years of life.

The average number of growing days for *T. ornata* in Kansas is approximately 160 per year; the amount of growth depends on climatic influences on food supply and foraging conditions. Growth rate is directly correlated with precipitation, and is highest when large populations of grasshoppers and long periods of favorable weather occur in the same year (Legler, 1960a).

Several carapace growth increments for wild ornate

box turtles from Texas were reported by Blair (1976): a 40-mm juvenile grew to 57.2 mm in 25 months; an 80-mm female five years old grew to 100 mm by age eight; another female continued to grow until she was 110 mm at 15 years and then ceased to grow (she was still 110 mm long when 23 years old); a three-year-old female with a 62.1-mm carapace reached 97.2 mm at age eight, and by age 10 she was 111 mm; and a male first captured at a length of 76.1 mm and estimated to be five years old grew rapidly to 85 mm by age six and 102 mm at age seven.

Long (1984) measured the carapace lengths and body masses of nine *T. ornata*: the averages were 132.0 mm and 429.9 g, respectively. The allometric equation for the length-mass relationship was length $= 18.96$ mass$^{0.318}$ $+ 0.045$ (r $= 0.98$). Shell volume was also calculated for 26 *T. ornata*, and the allometric equation for length-volume was length $= 14.33$ volume$^{0.356}$ $+ 0.029$.

A number of changes in structure and appearance occur in the period from hatching to maturity. Fontanelles of the bony shell close at or before maturity, and the hinge of the plastron becomes functional the fourth year. The markings on the carapace and plastron change with age to distinct, straight-sided radiating lines, and this results in some older *T. o. luteola* becoming much lighter in hue.

Field studies over 23 years by Blair (1976) indicate a relatively long life span, but do not suggest that wild *T. ornata* survive to 100 years. Individuals living 50 years are also probably rare (although expected by Legler, 1960a); in fact, Blair's oldest turtles were two males estimated to be 31 years old, and a female with an estimated age of 32 years.

Metcalf and Metcalf (1985) studied *T. o. ornata* over 26 years in Kansas, and for individuals observed for 10 or more years gave the following average ages: 59 females, 22.5 years; 56 males, 21.8 years. They estimated the oldest of their turtles was about 28 years old, and that almost a complete turnover of the population occurred within 25 years.

A captive adult female *T. o. luteola* received by Ernst in May 1968 at an estimated age of 20 years (based on growth annuli) lived until July 1990, and was probably 42 years old at death. A female *T. o. ornata* survived seven years, six months and 27 days at the Milwaukee County Zoo (Snider and Bowler, 1992).

FOOD HABITS: Under natural conditions *Terrapene ornata* is chiefly carnivorous; captives, however, eat a variety of vegetable matter as well as meat. Insects (chiefly beetles, caterpillars, and grasshoppers) compose approximately 90% of the food (Legler,

1960a). Dung beetles constitute the most important staple element of the diet: the disturbance of piles of dung by turtles in the course of their foraging is a characteristic sign of *T. ornata*. In the past when bison and cattle roamed the plains there must have been a constant supply of dung beetles during the warmer months. Insects form the bulk of the diet most of the year, but certain other foods (for example mulberries) are eaten in quantity when especially abundant—sometimes to the exclusion of other foods. The ornate box turtle also eats carrion (Legler, 1960a; Metcalf and Metcalf, 1970; Blair, 1976; Lardie, in Black, 1987), and even cacti (*Opuntia, Coryphantha:* Legler, 1960a; Metcalf and Metcalf, 1970; Blair, 1976; Thomasson, 1980; Smith, in Black, 1987).

Metcalf and Metcalf (1970) observed *T. ornata* eating grasshoppers, caterpillars, scavenger beetles, fish, a dead woodrat (*Neotoma floridana*), mulberries, cantaloupes, tomatoes, strawberries, blackberries, a pod of a green bean, a ground-cherry (*Physalis*) fruit, and a dandelion during their study of these turtles in Kansas. They also found an individual stuck in a can that contained a small amount of honey. Another turtle, which had been confined in the trunk of an automobile in which honey had been transported, was found with some honey around its mouth. Whether these turtles were eating honey or were seeking bees attracted to it is not known.

Foods of a Texas population included a recently killed black rat (*Rattus rattus*), bird carrion, a land snail, June beetle, stick insect, mulberries, persimmons, prickly-pear cacti, and cow dung (Blair, 1976).

Legler (1960a) reported that ornate box turtles occasionally eat the eggs and young of ground-nesting birds, and several other observations indicate that individual *T. ornata* may feed on birds if the opportunity arises. Legler (1960a) and Blair (1976) both found turtles with feathers in their mouths, and Parker (1982) saw them foraging under the nests of a Mississippi kite (*Ictinia*), presumably on scraps dropped by the nestlings, but also possibly on the nestlings themselves if they fell to the ground. Captives have been seen chasing, catching, and biting domestic chicken peeps (Black, 1987).

Ornate box turtles displayed surprising agility in capturing and eating tadpoles of spadefoot toads (*Scaphiopus*) presented to them; this suggests that *T. ornata* may be an important predator upon the larvae of this anuran (Norris and Zweifel, 1950). We have observed captives rapidly pursue, catch, and devour hopping crickets.

Stones up to 7 mm in diameter have been found in the stomachs of ornate box turtles (Legler, 1960a). These stones were presumed to have been swallowed accidentally during the ingestion of food; however, Skorepa (1966) observed captives deliberately eating bits of stone 3–5 mm in diameter, and Kramer (1973) reported that a captive consumed two mouthfuls of sandy soil on one occasion and four more on another. This individual also voluntarily ate small pebbles and loamy soil lacking stones. The purpose of soil and pebble ingestion by *T. ornata* is unknown.

PREDATORS AND DEFENSE: Dogs and coyotes (*Canis*), badgers (*Taxidea*), skunks (*Mephitis, Spilogale*), raccoons (*Procyon*), cats (*Felis*), opossums (*Didelphis*), crows and ravens (*Corvus*), large hawks (*Buteo, Circus*), golden eagles (*Aquila*), copperheads (*Agkistrodon*), bullsnakes (*Pituophis*), hognose snakes (*Heterodon*), and bullfrogs (*Rana*) devour *Terrapene ornata* (particularly eggs and juveniles) if the opportunity arises. Adult *T. ornata* sometimes eat juveniles, and Rainey (1953) reported the apparent death of an ornate box turtle caused by an infestation of flesh flies (*Sarcophaga*) which are frequent parasites. A mole (*Scalopus aquaticus*) destroyed two nests in Wisconsin (Doroff and Keith, 1990).

Adult *T. ornata* have few enemies other than humans, but many shallowly buried, torpid individuals may be dug up and eaten in the winter by predatory mammals. More adults seem to be killed by automobiles than all predators combined. For 29 years Anderson (1965) kept road counts in Missouri on the number of live ornate box turtles encountered during late May and early June. He gave particular attention to one test stretch of 161 km in a region where they were common. One-way drives over the test road in 1940 yielded counts of 90–156 turtles. Counts made in 1959 when conditions of weather, time, and temperature were approximately the same showed counts of only 5–35 turtles. Anderson attributed this decline to the enormous highway-traffic toll, which seemed to have reduced the populations adjacent to the highway. If such a reduction occurred before 1960, think of the highway toll that must have taken place during the 1980s and will continue to occur in the 1990s!

In a study of *T. ornata* in Wisconsin, the only known causes of adult mortality were automobiles, farm machinery, and lawn mowers (Doroff and Keith, 1990), but habitat destruction and pesticides may be other causes of population decline.

Recently, a great number of adult *T. ornata* have appeared in the pet trade. Most of these are at least 20 years old, and it is extremely doubtful that they have been raised in captivity. Thus, some populations are probably being reduced by pet trade collectors.

When disturbed, this species, like its eastern cousin *T. carolina,* closes its shell for protection. The extent of timidness varies between individuals and some never close completely. Others may not withdraw into their shells at all, and instead may scratch or urinate on a handler, but seldom bite.

POPULATIONS: Density of *Terrapene ornata* in certain areas of favorable habitat in Kansas was 6.4–15.6/ha (Legler, 1960a); the biomass of these populations, as calculated by Iverson (1982a), was 1.8–4.3 kg/ha. The total number of individuals on Legler's study area was estimated to be 286. The marked population consisted of 53% adult or subadult females, 31% adult males, and 16% juveniles. Only six turtles had plastra shorter than 60 mm. Small box turtles are probably not as rare as these samples indicate; they are just more secretive and difficult to find. More females than males were found in all months of the activity season except April and August, when more males were found; the preponderance of females was greatest during the nesting season.

At another 0.5-ha Kansas locality, 15–44 active *T. ornata* were observed each year from 1957 to 1977 (Metcalf and Metcalf, 1979). Combined numbers for two mulberry groves inspected several times daily for turtles during the fruiting season in the years 1972–1977 ranged from 60 to 77 individuals in 1972–1974, but fell to only 12 in 1975. In 1976 and 1977, the number of turtles taken increased slightly, but was still only about 33% of the number of earlier years. The numbers of ornate box turtles taken annually by Metcalf and Metcalf (1979) in their central study area averaged 19.9/yr from 1957 to 1965. A marked increase after 1965 continued until 1974, followed by a noticeable decline between 1975 and 1977. They thought these figures suggested cyclicity in population density.

In Texas, Blair (1976) recorded densities of 0.53–0.89 adults/ha from 1952 to 1956. In a condensed 0.93-ha area, the number of adults ranged from 16 to 22/yr over 17 years, but only two or three juveniles were found each year.

At the northern limits of the range in Wisconsin, Doroff and Keith (1990) estimated a total of 54–56 adults on four occupied sites within their 8-km^2 study area. Adult densities at these sites ranged from 2.9 to 5.0/ha; the observed male:female ratio was 1.0:1.56.

Survivorship of adults is 81–96%/yr (Blair, 1976; Metcalf and Metcalf, 1985; Doroff and Keith, 1990).

REMARKS: The little life history data published on *Terrapene ornata luteola* is anecdotal, and most accounts of the behavior and ecology of the species are based on studies of *T. o. ornata. T. o. luteola* occupies a more arid range, so surely its behavior, ecology, and physiology must differ from those of *T. o. ornata.* Studies of *T. o. luteola* would increase our understanding of adaptation in this species.

The most recent literature summaries on *T. ornata* are those of Ward (1978) and Ernst and McBreen (1991a).

Chrysemys picta (Schneider, 1783)
Painted turtle

· PLATE 30

RECOGNITION: *Chrysemys picta* is a small, attractive turtle with red markings on the marginals and a notched upper jaw. Its carapace (to 25.1 cm) is smooth, oval, flattened, and keelless, and its posterior rim is not serrated. It is olive to black, with yellow or red borders along the seams and red bars or crescents on the marginals. Some individuals have a well-developed red or yellow middorsal stripe. The bridge is unmarked, and in some individuals, the yellow hingeless plastron has a black or reddish-brown blotch of varying size and shape (see Geographic variation below). The skin is black to olive; the neck, legs, and tail are striped with red and yellow. A yellow stripe extends rearward from below the eye and may meet a similar stripe from the lower jaw, and on each side of the head behind the eye are a large, yellow, dorsolateral spot and a yellow streak. The chin is marked with two wide yellow stripes, which meet at the tip of the jaw to enclose a narrower yellow stripe.

Compared to females, males have elongated fore-claws and long, thick tails, with the anal opening posterior to the carapacial margin. Females are larger in all shell dimensions (Ernst, 1971b; Gibbons and Lovich, 1990).

KARYOTYPE: The karyotype is 2n = 50: 26 macrochromosomes (16 metacentric, 6 submetacentric, 4 telocentric) and 24 microchromosomes (Stock, 1972; Killebrew, 1977a); however, DeSmet (1978) reported 24 macrochromosomes and 26 microchromosomes.

FOSSIL RECORD: Late Miocene (Barstovian) fossils of *Chrysemys picta* have been found in Nebraska (Holman, 1976; Holman and Sullivan, 1981), and Pliocene fossils which may represent *C. picta* have been reported from the Clarendonian of Kansas (Wilson, 1968) and from the Blancan of Texas (Rogers, 1976). Pleistocene remains are from the Blancan of Kansas (Rogers, 1982) and the Irvingtonian of Alabama (Holman et al., 1990), Indiana (Teller and Bardak, 1975; Graham et al., 1983), Kansas (Holman, 1986a, 1987), Maryland (Holman and Grady, 1989), Michigan (Wilson, 1967), Ohio (Holman, 1986b), and Virginia (Holman and McDonald, 1986). Bones of *C. picta* have been found at a Holocene site in Michigan (carbon-14 date, 5,840 B.P.; Holman, 1990) and at archeological sites in Illinois, Michigan, Ohio, Wisconsin, and eastern Canada (Bleakney, 1958a; Adler, 1968).

DISTRIBUTION: *Chrysemys picta* is the only North American turtle that ranges across the continent. They occur across southern Canada, from New Brunswick and Nova Scotia to British Columbia, and south to Georgia, Alabama, Mississippi, Louisiana, northeastern Texas, Oklahoma, eastern Colorado, Wyoming, Idaho, and Oregon. The species is also found in scattered localities in central and western Texas, New Mexico, southwestern Colorado, Arizona, Utah, and Chihuahua, Mexico.

GEOGRAPHIC VARIATION: Four subspecies are recognized. *Chrysemys picta picta* (Schneider, 1783), the eastern painted turtle, ranges from southeastern Canada through New England and the Atlantic coastal states to Georgia and thence west into eastern Alabama. This subspecies has the vertebral and pleural carapacial seams aligned, light borders along the carapacial seams, and an unmarked yellow plastron. The middorsal stripe is narrow; it may be poorly developed or absent. *Chrysemys picta marginata* Agassiz, 1857, the midland painted turtle, ranges from southern Quebec and Ontario south in the central United States to Tennessee and northern Alabama. Its range is east of the Mississippi River, and extends eastward into New England, Pennsylvania, West Virginia, Maryland, Virginia and the

Chrysemys picta picta

Chrysemys picta has an upper jaw notch bordered on each side by a toothlike cusp

Carolinas. It has alternating vertebral and pleural seams, dark-bordered carapacial seams, and a variable dark figure on the plastron. This figure commonly is no more than half the width of the plastron, and it does not extend outward along the seams. The middorsal stripe is normally absent or poorly developed. *Chrysemys picta dorsalis* Agassiz, 1857, the southern painted turtle, is found from southern Illinois and Missouri southward along both sides of the Mississippi River to the Gulf coast of Louisiana and eastward through northern Mississippi into Alabama. A relict population exists in southeastern

Oklahoma and adjacent Texas. It has a conspicuous red or yellow middorsal stripe, alternating vertebral and pleural seams, and an immaculate yellow plastron. *Chrysemys picta bellii* (Gray, 1831), the western painted turtle, ranges from western Ontario across southern Canada to British Columbia and south to Missouri, northern Oklahoma, eastern Colorado, Wyoming, Idaho, and northern Oregon. It is also found in many scattered localities in the southwestern United States, and in one locality in Chihuahua. This, the largest of the painted turtles, has alternating vertebral and pleural seams; a reticu-

Plastron of *Chrysemys picta picta*

Bright yellow spots behind the eye of *Chrysemys picta picta* enable it to be identified at a distance

late pattern of light lines on the carapace; and a large, dark plastral figure, which branches outward along the seams to occupy most of the plastral surface. The middorsal stripe is absent or poorly developed. Males in northern populations may develop reticulate melanism (Smith et al., 1969; Ernst and Ernst, 1973; MacCulloch, 1981a; Schueler, 1983).

Bleakney (1958b) offered an explanation for the present distribution of the subspecies of *C. picta*. He suggested that at the time of the latest retreat of the glaciers, painted turtles were divided into three separate populations, which may well have repre-

sented separate incipient species: *C. picta* in the southeastern Atlantic coastal region, *C. dorsalis* in the lower Mississippi River region, and *C. bellii* in the southwest. However, the populations did not develop complete reproductive isolation. The retreat of the glaciers was accompanied by northward extensions from the three localities. According to Bleakney, *C. dorsalis* spread up the Mississippi River and met *C. bellii* near the mouth of the Missouri River; hybridization of these two forms produced *C. marginata*, which spread up the Ohio River valley into the eastern Great Lakes Region. Meanwhile *C.*

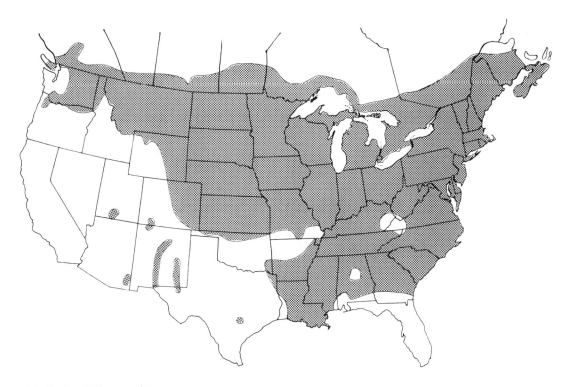

Distribution of *Chrysemys picta*

Chrysemys picta marginata

Plastron of *Chrysemys picta marginata*

Chrysemys picta dorsalis

picta spread northward along the Atlantic Coastal Plain and westward along the Gulf Coastal Plain, eventually meeting *C. marginata* in the north and *C. dorsalis* in the west. Wherever turtles from the three sites met, they eventually interbred, indicating that the whole complex consists of a single species with four subspecies. Intergradation between the subspecies has been well studied in several regions (Bishop and Schmidt, 1931; Johnson, 1954; Hartman, 1958; Waters, 1964, 1969; Ernst, 1967a, 1970d; Ernst and

Ernst, 1971; Ernst and Fowler, 1977; Pough and Pough, 1968; Groves, 1983; Muir, 1989; and Gordon, 1990).

CONFUSING SPECIES: North American turtles of the genera *Pseudemys* and *Trachemys* have the posterior rim of the carapace serrated, a medial carapacial keel, and are usually larger as adults. *Deirochelys reticularia* has a much longer neck, a wide foreleg stripe, and its rump vertically striped.

Plastron of *Chrysemys picta dorsalis*

Chrysemys picta bellii

HABITAT: *Chrysemys picta* prefers slow-moving shallow water, as in ponds, marshes, lakes, sloughs, oxbows, and creeks. A soft bottom, basking sites, and aquatic vegetation are preferred. Along the Atlantic Coast it sometimes enters brackish water.

BEHAVIOR: Painted turtles are most active from March through October, but Ernst has seen them bask in every month in northern Virginia and southeastern Pennsylvania. Even in some of the more northern populations, individuals may bask in February or early March during warm spells if the ice has melted enough to let them emerge (Vogt, 1981a; Ross, 1989a). March activity may be observed through the ice as the turtles swim beneath (Vogt, 1981a; Ernst, pers. obs.). In three years with very cold winters resulting in thicker ice cover than usual, western painted turtles did not become active at a lake in southwestern Minnesota until early May and were not trapped until the water temperature had risen above 18°C (Ernst and Ernst, 1973). Winter dormancy at that site began in mid-September as water temperatures fell below 20°C, and all turtles disappeared by October. Most *Chrysemys picta* do not feed until water temperatures rise above 15°C, but a few may feed lethargically at 14°C (Ernst, 1972c).

Sexton (1959a) divided the annual cycle of activity and movements of Michigan *C. picta* into the

Plastron of *Chrysemys picta bellii*

Reticulate melanism commonly occurs in some northern populations of *Chrysemys picta bellii*

following separate seasons: "prevernal," beginning with the final melting of the ice and lasting until 25 March, or when mass movements out of hibernation ponds first occur; "vernal," from 16 March to 31 May, or when submerged aquatic plants important to *C. picta* grow to the surface and most mating takes place; "aestival," from 1 June until 31 August, essentially beginning with the nesting season and ending when the turtles return to winter quarters; "autumnal," extending from 1 September until 1 December, or when the permanent cover of ice forms (some mating may occur at this time); and "hiemal," lasting while water is permanently covered with ice.

There is little activity during the prevernal season. During the vernal season the turtles emigrate from the hibernating ponds to outlying bodies of water. In the aestival season they gradually filter back into the hibernating ponds from these outlying water bodies, and congregate in the aquatic vegetation. Painted turtles tend to move into deeper water during the autumnal season, and dormancy occurs during the hiemal period.

Chrysemys picta is diurnal; it spends the night sleeping at the bottom or on a partially submerged object. It becomes active about sunrise and may bask for several hours before beginning to forage. Another period of basking follows, and foraging is resumed in the late afternoon, to continue into the early evening.

The basking habit is well developed in all age groups; as many as 50 painted turtles can be seen on a log at one time, and they also commonly share basking sites with other species of turtles. A period of basking usually lasts about two hours, and the periods are most common in the early morning, at midday, and in early afternoon. Summer basking activity peaks around 1100; however, some painted turtles can be found basking at any daylight hour. Basking is most frequent from April through September, and some individuals bask during warm spells in winter. Cloacal temperatures of eight basking painted turtles in Pennsylvania averaged 25.2°C (22.5–29.0) (Ernst, 1972c).

In northern populations basking peaks in the morning, probably to raise body temperatures to operational levels (21.4°C in Ontario, Canada; Schwartzkopf and Brooks, 1985b). Two patterns of hourly basking frequency occur in Ontario, bimodal and unimodal (Schwartzkopf and Brooks, 1985b). Bimodal basking involves a drop in basking activity at midday and a later rise in late afternoon. Unimodal basking is characterized by a rise in basking activity until noon and then a decrease in this activity in the afternoon. On days with bimodal basking patterns, fewer *C. picta* bask per hour, the first basking peak occurs earlier, and air and water temperatures are warmer than when unimodal basking patterns are observed. The turtles use available air and water temperature to maintain a high body temperature over the entire day.

Cloacal temperatures of active *C. picta* in southeastern Pennsylvania ranged from 8°C to 29°C, with a mean of 22°C; 50% fell between 17°C and 23°C, which may be the optimum temperature range (Ernst, 1972c). The most frequent records were for 23°C, 22°C, and 19°C, in that order. The critical thermal maximum of an adult female was 41.5°C. Brattstrom (1965) found the mean critical thermal maximum of *C. picta* to be 42.3°C; it was lower in smaller individuals. Hutchison et al. (1966) discovered a correlation between the critical thermal maximum and the habitat and geographic distribution of painted turtles. Differences in the critical thermal maxima were found in different parts of the range; the lowest (40.9°C) was recorded in *C. p. picta* from Rhode Island and *C. p. bellii* from Minnesota, the highest in *C. p. marginata* from Michigan (42.2°C) and *C. p. dorsalis* from Louisiana (41.6°C). *Chrysemys picta* exposed to longer photoperiods have higher critical thermal maxima than those exposed to shorter photoperiods at the same acclimation temperatures (Hutchison and Kosh, 1965). This probably results in seasonal variations in resistance to temperature extremes. Kosh and Hutchison (1968) found indications of a circadian rhythm in temperature tolerance.

The critical thermal minimum of *C. picta* is approximately −2°C. In laboratory studies conducted by Costanzo (1982), *C. picta* heated 12.3% and cooled 14.5% faster than *Terrapene ornata* tested at the same time.

Painted turtles acclimated at either 15°C or 25°C to longer photoperiods in the laboratory develop higher mean preferred temperatures (Graham and Hutchison, 1979b). When three *C. picta* were acclimated in the laboratory to a cycle of 8 hours of light and 16 hours of darkness and the ambient temperature shifted periodically from 15°C to 25°C for a one-hour exposure to either the high or low temperature allowing the turtle's body temperature to stabilize at that temperature, the turtle's locomotor activity showed a periodicity of 24 hours (Graham and Hutchison, 1978). When the light and temperature cycles were shifted two hours out of phase each day, the activity cycles of the turtles were not appreciably altered. Graham and Hutchison (1978) suggested that this close coupling of the locomotor activity to the biological clock is adaptive in that it probably serves as an effective synchronizer of the activity of this species in nature.

Renal function is also temperature dependent; however, it apparently does not undergo significant seasonal acclimation (Crawford, 1991a). Cold temperature has an antidiuretic effect, and the apparent lack of seasonal compensation may reflect an energetic constraint resulting from the need to conserve metabolic energy during hibernation when temperature and oxygen availability are low.

Painted turtles injected with the pathogen *Aeromonas hydrophila* raised their mean body temperature 4–5°C (Monagas and Gatten, 1983). Apparently this turtle is capable of behaviorally developing a fever as an immunological response to infection.

Chrysemys picta subjected to intense exercise in a dry metabolic chamber at 25°C raised their oxygen consumption rate and total body lactate content, while their lung oxygen concentration remained unchanged (Stockard and Gatten, 1983). In contrast a burst of swimming in 18 cm of water at 25°C brought on an insignificant change in oxygen uptake, a greater rise in lactate content, and decline in lung oxygen concentration. These results suggest that 56% of the ATP liberated during maximal activity in a terrestrial environment comes from anaerobic pathways, whereas 75% of the ATP used during a swimming burst comes from this source. Painted turtles that have sustained swimming speeds for as long as 30 minutes raise their oxygen consumption rate as much as nine times over the resting rate and three times that of the average rate (Lowell, 1990). However, Seidel (1977) found no difference in the oxygen consumption (metabolic) rate of *C. picta* tested at 12°C and 25°C terrestrially after acclimation at 25°C. Serum thyroxine levels also remain nearly identical when *C. picta* is exposed to 7°C and 28°C environments, suggesting a less active thyroid gland than that of mammals (Mason, 1977).

Painted turtles acclimated to temperatures between 5 and 30°C for at least 12 days showed an overproportional 6–7-fold increase in oxygen uptake as compared to a 4.4-fold increase in pulmonary ventilation when the temperature was raised from 10 to 30°C; at the same time the arterial carbon dioxide level rose from 13 mmHg at 5°C to 32 mmHg at 30°C as a result of a decrease in the ratio of pulmonary ventilation to oxygen uptake (Glass et al., 1985). An increase in arterial oxygen from 12 Torr at 5°C to about 60 Torr at 20 and 30°C resulted from intracardiac blood shunting combined with temperature-dependent shifts of the oxygen dissociation curve.

In the more northern populations *C. picta* may remain dormant for five or six months, but elsewhere hibernation is not prolonged, and they become active during warm periods. Winter dormancy may be spent in the soft bottom of some waterbody, within muskrat (*Ondatra*) lodges or bank burrows, underneath overhanging dirt banks, or on land in floodplain woods or pastures. The water of the hibernation site may be as much as two meters deep, but usually less, and the turtles bury themselves as deep as 95 cm in the soft bottom.

Cloacal temperatures of 22 hibernating Pennsylvania *C. picta* averaged 6.2°C; in 20 turtles the temperature was higher than that of the water, and in 15 it was higher than that of the soft bottom (Ernst, 1972c). In Ontario, temperatures of the sediment in which *C. picta* overwintered were 3–6°C, and, during the period of ice cover, the turtles maintained carapace surface temperatures of 4–6°C (Taylor and Nol, 1989). Movements continued after ice cover, but ended once the water became anoxic, and all turtles were buried in the soft bottom from January to March. In contrast to the findings of Ernst (1972c), Peterson (1987) reported that the deep core body temperature of hibernating *C. picta* he studied were never higher or lower than environmental temperatures; however, Peterson suggested the possibility of

behavioral temperature control by exploitation of a soft-bottom water thermal gradient.

At a site near Ann Arbor, Michigan, studied by Crawford (1991b) from 1981 to 1985, hibernating *C. p. marginata* experienced minimum water temperatures of 3.7–6.3°C, and ice covered the site for an average of 92 (56–117) days annually. Dissolved oxygen fell during the winter, and the water became severely hypoxic (<1 ppm oxygen) for an average of 43 (39–46) days each year. The turtles emerged from 1 March to 14 April, depending on the severity of the winter, so photoperiod or a circannual rhythm do not seem proximate cues for spring arousal. Turtles generally emerged after the ice cover had completely disappeared, when water and bottom temperatures were steadily rising, and spring overturn of vertical temperatures had taken place.

The stress of remaining underwater for very long periods is countered by several physiological adjustments, but the water temperature plays a major role in the length of survival. *Chrysemys picta* submerged at water temperatures of 1–3°C, regardless of the oxygen content of the water, survived longer (37–168 days) than those submerged in 5°C water (41–72 days) or 9–10°C water (10,8–48.3 days) (Ultsch, 1989). At 3°C, painted turtles submerged in normoxic waters had the following mean plasma parameters (ions in mMol/L): pH 7.75, osmium 105.6, potassium 3.57, chloride 57.4, bicarbonate 19.9, and hematocrit 38.7% (Ultsch and Jackson, 1982a,b; Jackson and Ultsch, 1982; Herbert and Jackson, 1985; Ultsch, 1985, 1989). The same plasma parameters in turtles submerged in anoxic waters were: pH 7.08, sodium 111.6, potassium 10.2, chloride 53.4, bicarbonate 3.8, and hematocrit 19%.

In the south, *C. p. dorsalis* may not hibernate at all, while at the extreme northern end of the range *C. p. bellii* may remain dormant for more than seven months (Ernst, pers. obs.). Ultsch et al. (1985) subjected *C. p. bellii* and *C. p. dorsalis* to simulated hibernation conditions by submerging them in anoxic water at 3°C without access to air to compare the physiological responses of the two subspecies. After acclimation at 3°C, initial acid-base and ionic conditions were the same for both turtles, but as anoxia continued both subspecies showed similar changes in all measured parameters, but the rates of change were greater in *C. p. dorsalis*. By day 46, plasma pH of *dorsalis* had dropped to 6.96; it took about 180 days for *bellii* to reach this level. By day 38 the acidosis was entirely due to lactate formation in both turtles, and it had induced compensatory changes in ionic concentrations, particularly large increases in total calcium and total magnesium in the blood. Apparently *C. p. bellii* is adapted to limiting lactate accumulation during its long hibernation, either by having a lower metabolic rate, or possibly by a greater ability to eliminate lactate.

Seasonal acclimation affects both the nonbicarbonate buffering capacity and lactate dehydrogenase activity in cardiac and skeletal muscles of *C. picta* (Olson and Crawford, 1989). Buffering capacity is highest in heart muscle in the autumn; it is lower in the other three seasons with no statistical difference among them. Buffering capacity is lowest during the winter in skeletal muscles (metabolic acidosis may be severe in winter; Maginniss et al., 1983), and that of spring, summer, and autumn acclimatized turtles shows no statistical difference. *Chrysemys picta* can maintain myocardial ATP reserves for at least four weeks through metabolic suppression at 3°C (Makris and Rotermund, 1989).

Blood samples taken from naturally hibernating *C. p. bellii* in British Columbia also indicated a progressive lactate acidosis through the winter, but not to the extent recorded in laboratory studies (St. Clair and Gregory, 1990). The turtles hibernated on top of the bottom substrate at one-meter depths in oxygen-rich areas, and remained essentially in place throughout the winter.

Blood viscosity is inversely related to the body temperature of *C. picta* (Langille and Crisp, 1980). During cold torpor, the blood of *C. picta* does not clot so easily as at warmer temperatures (Barone and Jacques, 1975), thus allowing flow at slower rates (heat rates are depressed at hibernation temperatures; Risher and Claussen, 1987).

During prolonged hypometabolism, such as occurs in aquatic hibernation, aerobic animals consume internal stores of fat, protein, and carbohydrate, while glycogen is the primary fuel supporting anaerobic hypometabolism. Since excretory processes are reduced, the accumulated chemical wastes must be dealt with internally. It was related above how some of this occurs, but what happens in the sensitive brain cells? Lutz (1989) discovered that the brain of *C. picta bellii* can lower its energy requirements by reducing activity through depression of synaptic transmission, membrane hyperpolarization through opening chloride channels, and slowing transmembrane ion flux by the selective closure of ion channels. Increased carbon dioxide and hydrogen ion and decreased bicarbonate reduce neural tissue activity.

Prolonged diving under warmer conditions during the annual activity period also requires physiological adaptation. A switch to anaerobic metabolism occurs during voluntary submergence and total body lactate content may increase fourfold (Gatten, 1981). Painted turtles forcibly submerged for two days at 25°C exhibit total body lactate levels up to 300 mg%, but it takes about two weeks to reach this level in winter turtles forcibly submerged at 5°C (Gatten, 1981). Summer turtles diving undisturbed outdoors have lactate levels of about 10 mg%. Submergence in anoxic waters at 10°C causes an increase in lactate and a corresponding decrease in bicarbonate; corresponding increases in potassium, calcium, and magnesium ions also occur, while the concentration of chloride ions decreases (Jackson et al., 1984). These are apparent changes to compensate for increases in plasma acidity, and *C. picta* can balance about 60% of the added lactate. Hematocrit also increases (Ultsch et al., 1984). *Chrysemys picta* will die if the blood pH falls by about one full unit (Ultsch et al., 1984). Nonpulmonary oxygen exchange decreases with increasing temperature from 21% at 3°C to only 5% at 20°C, but anoxic submergence at both temperatures causes a sharp drop in the metabolic rate (Herbert and Jackson, 1985). Turtles submerged in 3°C and 10°C aerated water experience less severe blood acid-base and ionic disturbances than those diving in anoxic waters, but aeration of the water has no beneficial effect at 15°C or 20°C (Herbert and Jackson, 1985). Blood pressure is directly affected by temperature under normal diving conditions, but normally unaffected by anoxic submergence. Heart rate is depressed under anoxic conditions at all water temperatures.

Since *C. picta* basks and also occasionally wanders about on land for days at a time, it also must adjust to evaporative body water loss to the air. Ernst (1972c) subjected six catheterized *C. picta* to dry terrestrial environments at normal summer temperatures (10–29°C) and humidities (45–95%). Percent weight loss per day varied from 11% in the lightest individuals to 8.2–8.5% in the heaviest. The weight loss gradient in gm/h ranged from 0.15 to 0.29, and was directly proportional to body mass.

Osmoregulation is also a problem faced by the painted turtle in its freshwater environment. The painted turtle loses sodium, calcium, and potassium ions to the water, but can also absorb sodium and calcium, but not potassium, from the water (Trobec and Stanley, 1971). Absorption of sodium and calcium contributes toward salt balance in this species. Influx of water is a greater osmoregulatory problem than is loss of ions. Uncompensated water inflow dilutes internal fluids by about 3% per day, whereas uncompensated sodium loss reduces sodium concentrations by only 0.2% per day (Trobec and Stanley,

1971). When placed in salt water, *C. picta* has a greater water influx, but lower sodium influx, than the estuarine turtle, *Malaclemys terrapin* (Robinson and Dunson, 1976).

Drought with its subsequent drying of the habitat may force the painted turtle to either seek a more permanent waterbody or estivate in the soft substrate. Mortality may be quite high at such times. Lindeman and Rabe (1990) reported an approximately 70% decrease in a Washington population of *C. p. bellii* following two years of drought, which they attributed to both mortality and emigration. Growth of individuals in this population was also markedly suppressed. Pond drying during the winter may also result in an increased rate of mortality due to extended exposure of hibernating turtles to freezing temperatures (Christiansen and Bickham, 1989).

Chrysemys picta often moves long distances, sometimes overland from one waterbody to an adjacent one or linearly along streams or rivers (MacCulloch and Secoy, 1983a). Consequently, the size of the home range has not been reported, and it probably depends on the specific locality. Zweifel (1989) found that on Long Island, painted turtles did not restrict their movements to any specific areas within the small ponds he studied, and Ernst (1969) found that turtles in Pennsylvania essentially traversed their entire 2.4-ha pond each day.

In Nebraska, *C. p. bellii* migrates several kilometers from shallow or dry marshes and basins to permanent bodies of water during the dry summer months (McAuliffe, 1978). These turtles also emigrate from semipermanent hibernacula to outlying areas in response to the filling of these areas by spring rains, and McAuliffe (1978) thought crowding effects and the generally greater productivity of aquatic plants in the shallower, less permanent areas were the reason for these movements. Male *C. p. bellii* of a riverine population in southern Saskatchewan traveled as far as 21.5–26.0 km between captures, while females moved up to 7–8 km and juveniles less than 2 km; 89–90% of the males moved at least 500 m during a two-year period, while 85–94% of the females moved, and 81–83% of the juveniles (MacCulloch and Secoy, 1983a).

Homing ability is well developed. Cagle (1944b) reported the return of many Illinois *C. p. marginata* that were released some distance from the collection point; a few of these returns required overland journeys, and one turtle returned four of five times it was removed. Williams (1952) released 98 *C. picta* at varying distances from their collection points; of 57 that were recovered 41 had returned. Ream (in Vogt,

1981a) found Wisconsin painted turtles could home in the water from 5.8 km away.

Ernst (1970e) found that *C. picta* returned from 1.6 km with the current and from 3.2 km against the current. Those returning upstream had to leave the water and climb a 20% grade beside a dam.

Forty-five turtles studied by Emlen (1969) displayed a marked tendency to orient homeward when displaced 100 m; however, none returned from 1.6 km. He thought that painted turtles do not orient by simple positive geotaxis, although downhill movements could partly explain his results. Homeward orientation did not correlate with wind direction at the time of release; therefore olfactory cues emanating from the home pond probably were not guiding stimuli. Turtles released under completely overcast skies displayed accurate homeward orientation. This argues against the use of celestial cues; however, Gould (1959) and DeRosa and Taylor (1978) reported painted turtles employ sun-compass orientation to get their directional bearings. Emlen found a deterioration in both homeward orientation and the straightness of the paths traversed by blindfolded *C. picta*. He thought that visual recognition of landmarks is important in enabling *C. picta* to home. The possession of such a simple, short-distance homing ability would seem well adapted to the needs of a relatively sedentary species like the painted turtle. In Ontario, female *C. picta* travel long distances to nesting areas, and Whillans and Crossman (1977) thought the turtles may locate the nest sites by some simple form of homing.

Ortleb and Sexton (1964) found positive responses to water temperatures and to light and negative responses to water current, aromatic water, and variously colored water. Heidt and Burbidge (1966) reported that painted turtles at hatching prefer red light over green or blue, and Ernst and Hamilton (1969) recorded similar results for adults. Noble and Breslau (1938) showed that hatchling *C. picta* were attracted toward the maximum area illuminated by the open sky.

It is not known whether or not *C. picta* has a social hierarchy in the wild, but captive animals establish one quickly when placed together in an aquarium, with the most dominant feeding first and the least aggressive last.

The only indications of agonistic behavior in nature have been observations by Bury et al. (1979) and Lovich (1988b) on aggressive basking behavior. Intraspecific interactions include pushing, open mouth gestures, biting, and lateral and vertical displacement. Turtles avoid potentially aggressive encounters by averting faces while basking and moving away from approaching turtles. Aggressive behavior is positively correlated with the number of turtles basking, the frequency of emergences, and water temperature. Aggression is rarely seen when interturtle spacing of about one carapace length is maintained. Smaller individuals are more likely to initiate lateral displacement toward a larger turtle than vice versa. Bury et al. (1979) suggested that the function of these acts during basking is to ensure individuals of positions on preferred basking sites and to maintain some distance between individuals at these sites.

Basking painted turtles occasionally gape, a behavior characterized by opening the mouth briefly and then reclosing it without directing the gesture toward another turtle in an aggressive manner. Gaping frequency does not increase as either environmental temperature or crowding at the basking site increase. The frequency appears to decrease with crowding, perhaps because of the similarity between gaping and aggressive open mouth gestures (Lovich, 1990b).

REPRODUCTION: Attainment of sexual maturity in male *C. picta* seems to be a correlate of size rather than age. Male painted turtles mature at plastron lengths of 70–95 mm, usually in their third or fourth year, but possibly as late as the fifth year in some northern populations (Cagle, 1954b; Ernst, 1971b; Ernst and Ernst, 1973; Callard et al., 1976; Tucker, 1978; Licht et al., 1985a; Mitchell, 1985a, 1988). If growth is enhanced, maturity is attained earlier. Cagle (1954b) reported that southern male *C. p. dorsalis* may mature during their first growing season, and Ernst and McDonald (1989) found that an enriched diet and longer annual feeding period in nutrient-rich Maryland sewage lagoons produced rapid growth with males reaching the normal size of maturity in two years instead of the usual four years in this region.

Females normally mature at plastron lengths of 97–128 mm in 6–10 years (Ernst, 1971b; Ernst and Ernst, 1973; Tucker, 1978; Mitchell, 1985c, 1988). Enhanced growth does not necessarily result in early maturity (Ernst and McDonald, 1989).

Spermatogenesis begins in March and reaches peaks in July and August. The cycle is completed in September, when the sperm pass into the epididymides (Ernst, 1971b; Mitchell, 1985a, 1988). Epididymal sperm have a cytoplasmic droplet of high lipid content attached at the midpiece (Gist et al., 1992). The lipid is closely associated with mitochondrial membranes and may function in either the formation or the destruction of mitochondria. The droplets detach from the sperm shortly before the beginning of the fall mating season, and are not found on sperm recovered from the oviduct of females.

Plasma levels of testosterone, thyroxine, and follicle-stimulating hormone have pronounced seasonality (Licht et al., 1985a), but plasma luteinizing hormone is not detectable (Callard et al., 1976). Plasma testosterone and follicle-stimulating hormone have both spring and fall peaks, whereas thyroxine peaks in summer coincident with the nadir in testosterone. Hormone levels are minimized when the turtles emerge from hibernation, testosterone and follicle-stimulating hormone then increase rapidly to peak in about a week and remain high for around two more weeks. Plasma testosterone and follicle-stimulating hormone rise again in September before hibernation and shortly after the late summer peak in spermatogenetic recrudescence. Plasma thyroxine increases slowly after spring emergence and does not peak for one or two months. High testosterone levels are coincident with large Leydig cells, but low levels occur during spermatogenesis (Callard et al., 1976; Dubois et al., 1988). Leydig cell atrophy is associated with a reduction in the volume of cytoplasm and smooth endoplasmic reticulum. Leydig cells again become active in the fall. In contrast, Sertoli cells show variations during the annual cycle, but no degeneration. Follicle-stimulating hormone alone is capable of stimulating testis growth, recrudescence of spermatogenesis, and hypertrophy of interstitial cells (Licht, 1972).

Temperature is a major cue for testis recrudescence (Ganzhorn and Licht, 1983; Licht and Porter, 1985b). Body temperatures above 17°C are required for the initiation of testis growth, spermatogenesis, and testosterone secretion, and Ganzhorn and Licht (1983) stimulated complete testicular recrudescence within seven weeks at 28°C in males with regressed testes starting in either fall or spring, while maintenance of males at 17°C or below completely suppressed the male sex cycle. Males exhibit spontaneous testicular regression even under constant warm temperatures.

The ovarian cycle begins with vitellogenesis in July or August. Yolking continues into the fall, but ceases when the female stops feeding and becomes dormant, and then begins again the next spring (Ernst, 1971b; Callard et al., 1978; Congdon and Tinkle, 1982; Mitchell, 1985c, 1988). Ovulation occurs in May after a further spring period of follicular growth. Photoperiod seems to be a major triggering cue of various events in the sexual cycle (Whillans and Crossman, 1977), although environmental temperatures probably also play an important role (Ganzhorn and Licht, 1983). Ovarian activity alternates: in any one season, one ovary produces more eggs than the other. Three major classes of ovarian follicles are present at all times of the year: those 12 mm or greater in diameter (although very few in July), those 8–11 mm in diameter, and small follicles usually smaller than 7 mm in diameter. Marked changes in the plasma steroid hormones progesterone, testosterone, and estrogen occur during the preovulatory period, increasing sharply prior to or around the time of ovulation, and declining rapidly thereafter. Smaller peaks of testosterone and estrogen, but not progesterone, occur during the autumn period of ovarian recrudescence. Progesterone completely inhibits ovulation and causes a reduction in the pituitary, oviduct, and follicle size (Klicka and Mahmoud, 1977). Embryonic nutrition is derived primarily from egg-yolk proteins (vitellogenins) synthesized in the liver and transported by the blood to the oocytes, and plasma vitellogenin levels are positively correlated with ovarian growth and with levels of plasma estrogen during the female sex cycle (Ho et al., 1980, 1982). Vitellogenesis seems to be an estrogen-specific, dose-dependent response that can be inhibited by progesterone and testosterone.

The walls of both the uterus and the glandular segments of the oviduct exhibit marked seasonal variations in the extent and content of their sub-mucosal and epithelial glands. Submucosal glands are most prominent during the preovulatory and post-ovulatory periods in May and June, regress in late summer after the female has oviposited, and recrudesce the next spring. These changes are correlated with variations in the muscle layer, number of uterine epithelial blebs, oviductal vascularity, and the presence of eosinophils in cross-sections of the cervix (Motz and Callard, 1991).

Like that of males, the female sex cycle may be influenced by environmental temperatures (Ganzhorn and Licht, 1983). Warm temperatures (28°C) inhibit follicular growth and cause regression of ovaries in females. Maximal ovarian growth and ovulation are observed only in spring in females kept at a constant 17°C or 17°C with several hours of daily basking. Follicles grow at lower temperatures (13°C), but ovulation does not occur. Injections of estrogen increase the amplitude of oviductal contractions; in contrast, progesterone injections significantly reduce the duration of contraction (Callard and Hirsch, 1976).

Injection of estradiol benzoate into eggs of the painted turtle will cause all embryos to develop as females; a similar but less consistent female-determining effect is associated with injection of testosterone propionate (Gutzke and Bull, 1986).

Courtship and mating normally occur from March to mid-June but Ernst (1971f) has observed courtship activity in August and September, and Gist et al. (1990) recovered large quantities of sperm from female oviducts in October (much more than from spring females). Electroejaculation of male *C. picta* yields sperm only in the autumn, coinciding with the time of sperm appearance in the female oviducts. Viable sperm may be stored (for up to 165 days) in tubules in a small region of the albumen-secreting section of the oviduct (Gist and Jones, 1989). Courtships observed by Ernst in Pennsylvania always took place in water less than 60 cm deep and at temperatures of 10.0–27.8°C. In the spring, males are possibly attracted by odors (pheromones?) released by females (Vogt, 1979a).

Courtship in this species begins with a slow pursuit of the female; when at last she is overtaken the male passes and turns to face her. He then strokes her head and neck with the backs of his elongated foreclaws. Receptive females respond by stroking his outstretched forelimbs with the bottoms of her foreclaws (Ernst, 1971b). Between the periods of stroking, the male swims away, seemingly trying to entice the female to follow. After this behavior has been repeated several times the female sinks to the bottom, the male swims behind and mounts her, and copulation begins.

Nesting occurs from late May until mid-July, with peak activity in June and early July. In Quebec, the beginning of the nesting season is consistently correlated with the mean temperature of the previous year rather than the mean April temperature of the current year (Christens and Bider, 1987). A female may lay at least two and possibly as many as three to five clutches during this period (Moll, 1973; Tucker, 1978; Snow, 1980); 30–50% of the females possibly do not reproduce every year, and in Michigan 15% to more than 30% lay two clutches a year (Tinkle et al., 1981; Congdon and Tinkle, 1982; Congdon, pers. comm.). Nussbaum et al. (1983) reported that apparently only one clutch is laid per year by *C. p. bellii* in the Pacific Northwest.

Most nests are dug in the late afternoon or early evening, but morning nestings are not uncommon. Congdon and Gatten (1989) reported that in Michigan 76% of the nests are started after noon and 24% before noon. Most (92%) nests there are completed between 1500 and 2200, the rest (8%) are completed between 0500 and 1200, and the body temperature of nesting females is usually 29–30°C.

The flask-shaped nests are dug with the hind feet in loamy or sandy soil, in the open. Nests are usually dug within 200 m of water, but may be as far away as 600 m, and ovipositing females may return to the same site for several seasons (Lindeman, 1992). The soil is often moistened with bladder water. Total nesting time may take over four hours, and if the day is warm, turtles may nest later in the evening (Christens and Bider, 1987). Average dimensions of 14 Pennsylvania nests were as follows: greatest diameter of cavity, 72 mm (65–72); diameter of the neck, 45 mm (41–51); and depth, 104 mm (99–111).

Whole-body lactate of females that have just completed nesting may be 3.7 times the resting level (Congdon and Gatten, 1989). Glycolysis provides only 1% of the ATP production during the nesting act, and the total energetic cost of nesting activity is less than 1% of the energy invested in eggs.

The number of eggs per clutch varies from 1 to 23 and differs with the subspecies. The largest race, *C. p. bellii*, lays the most eggs per clutch, up to 23 (MacCulloch and Secoy, 1983b), and MacCulloch and Secoy (1983b) recorded an average of 26 enlarged follicles per female in Saskatchewan. The medium-sized subspecies *C. p. picta* and *C. p. marginata* lay 2–10 and 3–14 eggs, respectively. Fifteen clutches of intergrade *C. p. picta* × *C. p. marginata* from Pennsylvania averaged 4.73 eggs (4–6). The smallest subspecies, *C. p. dorsalis,* lays only one to seven eggs per clutch. Michigan populations of *C. p. marginata* may produce an annual egg biomass of 1.2 kg/ha (Congdon and Gibbons, 1989).

Several aspects of painted turtle reproduction change with latitude (Moll, 1973). Age and minimum size at maturity are least in Louisiana (males two to three years, 60 mm plastron length; females four years, 100 mm plastral length) and greatest in Wisconsin (males four to five years, 96 mm; females eight years, 136 mm). Spermatogenesis begins earlier and ends later and seasonal changes in testicular size are more pronounced in southern populations. Female reproductive cycles are also prolonged in the south. The nesting season lasts 10 weeks in Louisiana, but only six weeks in Wisconsin. Mean clutch size and maximum number of clutches range from 4.1 eggs and four to possibly five clutches in Louisiana to 10.7 eggs in two clutches in Wisconsin and 6–20 eggs in one clutch in the Pacific Northwest. Within the subspecies *C. p. bellii* only moderate geographic variation occurs in the sexual cycles with increasing latitude (Christiansen and Moll, 1973). Mean clutch frequency also does not vary much, with about 14% of New Mexico females producing three clutches,

compared to only two in Wisconsin. In Quebec 40–80% of the 7–11-year-old female painted turtles reproduce each year; most females older than 11 years reproduce each year, and 5–32% of females lay two clutches per season (Christens and Bider, 1986). Females living in different microhabitats within a single waterbody may differ in reproductive capacity owing to variable nutritional levels (Tucker, 1978).

Painted turtle eggs normally are elliptical, white to cream in color, and have smooth, slightly pitted surfaces; they are flexible when first laid but become firmer as water is absorbed. Egg dimensions are 27.9–35.1 mm in length, 15.9–22.6 mm in width, and 4.5–9.1 g in weight. Clutch size, clutch mass, and egg width are positively correlated with female shell length (Congdon and Tinkle, 1982; Congdon and Gibbons, 1987) but individual egg length and mass may not be (Tucker et al., 1978; Schwarzkopf and Brooks, 1986). Egg width and egg mass are not correlated with clutch size, and mean clutch mass and mean egg size may vary from year to year (Schwarzkopf and Brooks, 1986). These facts do not support optimal egg size theory.

Congdon and Gibbons (1987) thought that pelvic girdle structure constrains egg size and therefore hatchling size. This is demonstrated by the correlation of the slopes of the increase of the pelvic aperture and egg width with increasing female shell length. Gutzke and Packard (1985) found that large painted turtle eggs have a significantly higher probability of hatching than do small eggs incubated under identical conditions. Surface area to volume considerations may account for differences in hatching rate between large and small eggs in dry nests. Natural selection for size in turtle eggs may therefore be more intense than has been suspected previously, because differential mortality is probably related to egg size in prenatal as well as early postnatal stages. Mahmoud et al. (1973) have described in detail the embryonic development of *C. picta.*

Energy allocation to the largest class of follicles begins at least ten months before nesting. The average female enters hibernation with half of the 222 kJ of an average clutch already in follicles that are approximately 14 mm in diameter (Congdon and Tinkle, 1982). Between spring emergence and nesting, stored body lipids probably supply the remaining 50% of the energy required to complete the clutch. The energy level of an entire clutch is high, about 29.2 kJ/g (Congdon and Tinkle, 1982). Egg lipids average 22.3% of the total dry mass and 28.2% of the dry mass of shell-less eggs. Hatchlings are 20.7% lipid by mass. Of the total egg lipids, 38% are used during embryonic development and 62% remain in the hatchling for maintenance and possible early growth. Levels of body lipids stored by females are more variable than reproductive output, indicating that *C. picta* may fit the "bet hedging" strategy for reproduction (Condgon and Tinkle, 1982).

Females may not oviposit if nesting conditions are not suitable (Lindeman, 1989). Hot weather and drought have delayed nesting for as long as three weeks during some years in Virginia (Ernst, pers. obs.). Rotation of eggs during the first seven weeks of incubation seems to have little effect on hatching success (Feldman, 1983).

Artificially incubated eggs in Pennsylvania took 65–80 days (mean 76) to hatch; those naturally incubated in the nest took 72–80 days (mean 76). The earliest natural hatching took place on 14 August, the latest on 29 August (Ernst, 1971g). The egg is able to develop normally following a month of near-freezing temperatures while the embryo remains in the late gastrula stage (Ewert, 1991).

The eggshell of *C. picta* is somewhat flexible with a well-defined calcareous layer and numerous pores (M. J. Packard et al., 1982). This allows the eggs to be relatively independent of the hydric environment so that hatching success is not unduly reduced by dry conditions; however, eggs in more favorable hydric environments nevertheless produce larger hatchlings than eggs exposed to less favorable conditions. Embryonic turtles developing in flexible-shelled eggs consume more yolk and grow larger before hatching when incubated in moist rather than dry environments (Packard et al., 1983; Packard and Packard, 1984, 1986). Embryos in relatively wet environments have different patterns of net water exchange which may cause different rates of metabolism. Water exchanges may exercise control over oxidative metabolism in embryos by altering the bulk water in cytoplasm, by affecting concentrations of urea in body fluids, by influencing growth of the allantois, and indirectly by affecting the incubation temperature (Packard et al., 1983; Packard and Packard, 1984). Water fluxes may influence duration of incubation by affecting the water potential in compartments such as the yolk. However, evidence supporting these hypotheses is fragmentary, and no single mechanism is applicable to all reptile species studied to date.

Apparently the influence of the hydric environment on hatching success, on duration of incubation, and on size of hatchlings is confined to the last two-thirds of incubation (Gutzke and Packard, 1986). The lack of effects during the first third of incubation is probably due to compensatory water exchanges during the middle trimester. During the middle third of incubation, water uptake is greater and more rapid in a moist environment if an egg previously was in dry conditions than if it was in wet conditions. Conversely, water loss is more pronounced on a dry substrate during the middle trimester if an egg was previously in wet conditions than if it had been dry. No compensatory water exchange occurs during the final trimester, but environmental hydric conditions during this period affect development.

Embryos rely on both yolk and eggshell to supply the calcium required for development, but those exposed to wet substrates use the eggshell for a greater proportion of their calcium (56%) than do embryos exposed to dry conditions (40%) (Packard and Packard, 1986). Residual yolk contains less than 1 mg calcium and cannot support growth of neonates at or near levels characteristic of late-term embryos. The larger energy reserve available to small hatchlings in the form of a large residual yolk probably can be used only to support maintenance metabolism, and newly hatched *C. picta* must begin to feed soon to promote further growth.

The magnitude and pattern of mass changes of painted turtle eggs in natural nests differ from those observed in the laboratory, and are probably due to the differences between the hydric and thermal environments of the natural nest and those used during laboratory tests (Ratterman and Ackerman, 1989). Exchange of water vapor rather than liquid water accounts for the changes in egg mass. Packard et al. (1981a) discovered that the conductance of painted turtle eggs to water vapor is 70 times higher than that of avian eggs of comparable mass, yet transpirational water loss from incubating turtle eggs nevertheless is small because of the small gradient in vapor pressure between eggs and air trapped inside the nest. Eggs exposed to wet substrates have longer incubation periods but higher success than eggs incubated on dry substrates. The thermal conductivity of the substrate also has an important effect on the exchange of heat and water through eggshells (Ackerman et al., 1985). Differences in the patterns of water exchange can be attributed to quantitative differences in the thermal regimes in which the eggs are incubated. The greater the thermal conductivity of the substrate in which eggs are incubated, the more water the eggs will absorb under wet conditions. Large eggs, owing to the relationships between mass, surface area, and water conductance, will exchange relatively little water compared to small eggs. The egg clutch may be viewed as a very large egg which will be much less sensitive to the hydric environment than a single, smaller egg. Temperature and water vapor pressure differences existing within a clutch will determine the exchange of heat and water within the clutch and influence the exchange between the clutch and the nest substrate.

In southeastern Pennsylvania, young turtles from clutches laid late in the season often are not ready to emerge from the nest before the onset of cold weather. They apparently hatch and then overwinter in the nest, as newly emerged hatchlings are found in late April and May. Overwintering in the nest seems a well-established mechanism in painted turtles, and it has been reported from many localities in the northern part of the range (Gibbons and Nelson, 1978). In Michigan, all hatchling *C. p. marginata* spend the winter in the nest (Breitenbach et al., 1984).

The nest cavity of *C. picta* is usually less than 12 cm beneath the surface of the soil, so overwintering hatchlings in northern populations may be exposed to subzero temperatures before emergence the next spring. Hatchlings of *C. picta* are unique in being the only reptile and highest vertebrate known to tolerate natural freezing of extracellular body fluids during winter hibernation (Storey et al., 1988). They have survived frequent exposure to temperatures from $-2°C$ to $-8°C$ in natural nests (Breitenbach et al., 1984; Storey et al., 1988), and laboratory cooling to $-8.6°C$ for at least 16 hours (Paukstis and Shuman, 1989; Packard and Packard, 1990b). Apparently, hatchlings have the ability to supercool to temperatures as low as $-8.9°C$ (Paukstis and Shuman, 1989), but freezing at $-10.9°C$, resulting in 67% ice, is lethal (Storey et al., 1988). Storey et al. (1988) found a two- to threefold increase in glucose content of liver and blood and a threefold increase in blood glycerol in response to freezing; these may act as the winter-active cryoprotectants.

Hatchling *C. p. marginata* from two Michigan nests excavated in February by Breitenbach et al. (1984) were responsive to touch and symmetrically arranged in the cavity with their heads directed upward. Data of hatchling survivorship in Michigan over five years suggest that winterkill may be an important source of hatchling mortality during winters with little insulating snow cover; no hatchlings died during the 1981–1982 winter characterized by deep snow cover (Breitenbach et al., 1984). In Idaho, overall survivorship for 193 overwintered eggs was only 21–33%, and the survivorship within seven successful nests was 38–60% (Lindeman, 1991). Overwinter mortality is also very high in British Columbia (St. Clair and Gregory, 1990).

Hatchling *C. picta* are often exposed to extended periods of freezing while overwintering in the nest (Storey et al., 1988). As related above, some survive, others do not. Glucose and lactate build up in the liver, muscle, brain, heart, kidneys, lung, and digestive tract for possible use as cryoprotectants (Churchill and Storey, 1991). The level of glucose in these organs declines over the course of the freezing exposure, suggesting that the main function of the sugar may be to serve as the substrate for lactate production. Glucose-6-phosphate also accumulates in the liver, an indication that liver glycogenolysis takes place during freezing.

The hatchling *C. picta* is essentially round and has a keeled carapace. The head, eyes, and tail are proportionally larger than in the adult. A deep crease crosses the abdominal plate. The pigmentation and patterns of the shell and skin are brighter and more pronounced than adults. The hatchling has an external yolk sac 10–25 mm in diameter, and a caruncle that usually drops off by the fifth day. Lindeman (1991) reported that in Idaho the average hatchling size is positively correlated with female size.

Chrysemys picta has temperature-dependent sex determination, with cooler incubation temperatures usually producing only male hatchlings (Ewert and Nelson, 1991). Only males are produced from clutches incubated at 22–27°C and 27°C, but incubation at 30–32°C produces 100% female hatchlings (Gutzke and Paukstis, 1984; Schwarzkopf and Brooks, 1985a; Ewert and Nelson, 1991). Both sexes are produced when eggs are incubated at 20°C and 28°C; threshold temperatures producing 50% males are 20°C and 27.5°C (Schwarzkopf and Brooks, 1985a). It is possible that females in some northern populations seldom, if ever, can find nest sites where the ground temperatures exceed 28°C, so pivotal temperatures such as 20°C and 27.5°C assure the production of females. To test if northern populations may experience lower threshold temperatures for sexual differentiation, Gutzke and Paukstis (1984) incubated 40 eggs from Nebraska females at 22°C and produced 18 hatchlings with six (33.3%) males, 11 (61.1%) females, and one (5.6%) of indeterminate sex, confirming that *C. picta* has two threshold temperatures for sex determination instead of the usual one.

Female *C. picta* do not pick particular nest sites to influence the sex ratio of their clutch. Schwarzkopf and Brooks (1987) found no evidence that individual females at Algonquin Park, Ontario, followed a simple pattern in choosing nest sites and no indication that they influenced the sex ratio by choosing sites with specific characteristics. Instead, females selected nest sites that maximized the probability that the eggs would complete development, rather than to influence offspring sex ratio.

Bull and Vogt (1981) discovered that sex determination is more readily influenced by an incubation temperature of 25°C than by one of 31°C, and that maleness is determined earlier in development than is femaleness. The primary sensitive period is in the middle trimester (embryonic stages 16–22; Yntema, 1968). If the incubation temperature is 25°C from laying to stage 16, maleness will develop, but incubation at 31°C is required from laying until stage 22 for femaleness (although some effect may arise as early as stage 19). The lower threshold for maleness possibly balances later higher male mortality in some northern female-biased populations (Gutzke and Paukstis, 1984).

Hatchling sex ratios are not correlated with any nest characteristic but temperature, and nest temperatures are more dependent on yearly variations in climate than on variations in site characteristics (Schwarzkopf and Brooks, 1987). Substrate moisture plays no significant role in sex determination in the painted turtle (Paukstis et al., 1984; Packard et al., 1991), but slightly more males emerge from eggs incubated on dry substrates (Paukstis et al., 1984).

GROWTH AND LONGEVITY: The growth period is limited by the temperatures of the air and water, amount of rainfall, and availability of food, and thus may vary between localities and years. Growth rates of painted turtles inhabiting a marsh in Kalamazoo County, Michigan, increased during the 1980s when compared to those from the 1960s, while the survival rates apparently declined (Frazer et al., 1991b). These enhanced growth rates were possibly the result of the warmer and drier weather during the 1980s.

In southeastern Pennsylvania the growth period, 92 days, is from 1 June until 31 August (Ernst, 1971c), and on Long Island, New York, it is about 100 days (Zwiefel, 1989). Cagle (1954b) thought the growing season of *Chrysemys picta* in Louisiana was from the end of February to the end of December, approximately 307 days, and in southern Illinois, from the end of May to the end of October, approximately 153 days; however, data from more northern populations indicate a growing season of only about 90 days (Ernst and Ernst, 1973; MacCulloch and Secoy, 1983b).

Growth during the first season depends on the date of hatching: hatchlings that overwinter and emerge the following spring grow more than those that hatch and emerge in late summer. Growth is initiated as soon as the shell unfolds, usually 7–10 days after hatching, and the youngsters start to feed. It is rapid the first season: some hatchlings double their size. After the first season, growth is variable, and smaller individuals usually grow faster than larger ones (Gibbons, 1967a; Ernst, 1971c; Ernst and Ernst, 1973; Tucker, 1978; Hart, 1982; Iverson, 1982b; MacCulloch and Secoy, 1983b; Balcombe and Licht, 1987; Ross, 1989a; Zweifel, 1989). Pennsylvania *C. picta* in their first year are as much as 45 mm in plastron length; in the second year, 60 mm; in the third year, 75 mm; and after the fourth year, 90 mm (Ernst, 1971c). Zweifel (1989) reported faster rates on Long Island: one year, 62 mm; two years, 84 mm; three years, 97 mm; four years, 107 mm. Growth in some of the larger subspecies, such as *C. p. bellii,* may be even more rapid (Ernst and Ernst, 1973; MacCulloch and Secoy, 1983b). Females grow larger than males and have faster growth rates (Ernst, 1971c; Iverson, 1982b; Rickard et al., 1989; Zweifel, 1989); male growth is sharply retracted once maturity is reached. Hart (1982) thought this a function of differences in size at maturity, and found that nongrowing adults consume increased amounts of plant foods. Once maturity is reached, growth slows or essentially ceases, and some adults show no growth whatever from one year to the next (Wilbur, 1975b, developed a growth model based on long-term studies of Michigan *C. p. marginata,* and Rickard et al., 1989, proposed a nonparametric method for comparing painted turtle growth curves; we refer the reader to these papers).

Growth rates may vary between separate populations in the same area (Gibbons, 1967a; Tucker, 1978), probably owing to differences in nutritional levels.

Quinn and Christiansen (1972) reported that *C. p. bellii* from southern Iowa lentic habitats with highly organic substrates grow faster than those from sand substrates with less apparent organic matter. Confirmation of this was published by Ernst and McDonald (1989) who reported that painted turtles living in nutrient-rich (organic) sewage lagoons in Maryland grow at enhanced rates and matured earlier than those from a nearby natural habitat.

Weight also increases with age and greater shell length. Zweifel (1989) reported the following mean weights by age for *C. picta* from Long Island, New York: first-year males, 32.4 g, females, 37.1 g; second-year males, 65.5 g, females, 85.0 g; third-year males, 104.2 g, females, 126.9 g; fourth-year males, 124.2 g, females, 171.4 g; fifth-year males, 138.3 g, females, 212.5 g; sixth-year males, 139.0 g, females, 262.4 g; seventh-year males, 149.9 g, females, 294.6 g; eighth-year males, 176.8 g, females, 320.4 g; ninth-year males, 193.8 g, females, 323.7 g; tenth-year males, 208.2 g, females, 335.7 g; and fifteenth-year males, 302.0 g, females, 380.0 g.

Carapace length is positively correlated with body mass, and females are significantly heavier than males at any given carapace length. Skeletal mass is also positively correlated with carapace length and body mass. Bone mass makes up less than 2% of body mass in hatchlings, and the ratio increases with body size up to about 100-mm carapace length, above which it nearly levels off at 20–27% (Iverson, 1982b).

Snider and Bowler (1992) reported a captive *C. p. dorsalis* of unknown sex collected as an adult lived 20 years, 6 months, and 24 days at the Columbus Zoo. Wild *C. picta* may live much longer than this. Some five- to eight-year-old turtles marked by Ernst at a Pennsylvania marsh in 1965 were still alive in 1988 at 28–31 years of age, Frazer et al. (1991a) reported 31–34-year-old painted turtles from Michigan, and Wilbur (1975a) estimated that some *C. picta* from Michigan survived 40 years.

FOOD HABITS: Spring feeding begins when water temperatures reach 15–18°C in April or May (Ernst, 1971c; Ernst and Ernst, 1973). Foraging ceases when the water temperature drops below this range in September. Water temperatures above 30°C may cause a temporary cessation of feeding in July or August. Feeding also stops if *Chrysemys picta* is forced to estivate in a dried-out waterbody.

Painted turtles obtain food by foraging along the bottom and among clumps of algae and aquatic plants. Most animal food is sought out and moving prey is detected and seized faster than that which is stationary (Feder, 1983). The turtle makes exploratory strikes with the head into vegetation to disturb potential prey sufficiently to make it move, then actively pursues it (Sexton, 1959a). Large prey is held in the jaws while the forefeet tear it apart. Occasionally *C. picta* will ambush its prey.

Belkin and Gans (1968) described surface-skimming feeding by *C. picta* which they termed "neustophagia." The head is projected out of the water at an angle of about 45°. The mandible is dropped so that its cutting edge is parallel to the surface; at the same time the hyoid is protracted, to increase the capacity of the pharynx. The head and neck are then slowly retracted until the surface film is broken and water flows into the throat. After several seconds, when the throat has been partially filled, the turtle closes its mouth, thus trapping the fine particulate matter (neuston) found on the water surface.

Painted turtles are omnivorous generalists in the broadest sense; most species of plants and animals, living or dead, found in their habitat may be eaten as opportunity arises. Fifty-six Pennsylvania adults examined by Ernst contained animal food in 65% of the stomachs (61.2% by volume) and plant remains in 100% (38.8% by volume). Known prey are algae—*Cladophora, Cosmarium, Lyngbya, Nitella, Oedogonium, Oöcystis, Oscillatoria, Pediastrum, Phacus, Pithophora, Rhizoclonium, Spirogyra, Ulothrix;* vascular plants—*Anacharis, Bidens, Ceratophyllum, Lemna, Myriophyllum, Najas, Nuphar, Nymphaea, Polygonum, Potamogeton, Sagittaria, Typha, Vallisneria* and *Zea;* invertebrates—bryozoans, planaria, earthworms, aquatic oligochaetes, leeches, rotifers, slugs, snails, small clams, crayfish, amphipods, cladocerans, water mites, spiders, various insects (some adults but mostly larval): water striders and true bugs, beetles, dragonflies, damselflies, mayflies, caddisflies, chironomids, springtails, mosquitoes, and sphingid moth caterpillars; vertebrates—fish, probably taken as carrion (*Catostomus, Culaea, Etheostoma, Lepomis, Micropterus, Notropis, Perca, Percina, Pimephales, Pomoxis*) and frogs (larval and adult *Rana*) (Surface, 1908; Raney and Lachner, 1942; Lagler, 1943; Ernst, 1969; Ernst and Barbour, 1972; MacCulloch and Secoy, 1983b; Brown, 1992). Brown (1992) observed young *C. picta* from North Carolina capturing cladocerans in early spring; a separate head lunge was required to secure each, and an adult from this same locality contained an estimated 1,200 of these small crustaceans in its digestive tract. Young painted turtles are at first carnivorous, but become more herbivorous as they mature.

Captive painted turtles have done well on romaine lettuce, cantaloupe, fresh and canned fish, frozen smelt, earthworms, frozen shrimp, newborn mice, commercial trout chow, and Reptomin.

The digestive turnover rate of *C. picta* kept at 25°C is 59 hours; digestive turnover times are inversely correlated with temperatures between 16 and 34°C (Parmeter, 1981). Kepenis and McManus (1974) reported that the lowest rate of food ingestion by juvenile painted turtles is 1.25 mg/g/day at 20°C and the highest is 5.01 mg/g/day at 35°C. Intake at 25°C and 30°C is similar, 3.67 and 3.68 mg/g/day, and assimilation efficiencies are 79.7%, 85.3%, 84.3%, and 88.8% at 20°C, 25°C, 30°C, and 35°C, respectively. Mean fecal and urine production in mg/g/day is directly correlated to temperature, ranging from 0.14 at 15°C to 0.78 at 35°C. The metabolic rate drops continually during fasting (Sievert et al., 1988).

The total annual energy budget for an adult female *Chrysemys* is approximately 1997 kJ, including 1718 kJ for maintenance, 6.2 kJ for growth, and 271 kJ for egg production (Congdon et al., 1982).

PREDATORS AND DEFENSE: Thirteen-lined ground squirrels (*Spermophilus*), chipmunks (*Tamias*), woodchucks (*Marmota*), gray squirrels (*Sciurus*), skunks (*Mephitis*), badgers (*Taxidea*), foxes (*Urocyon, Vulpes*), fish crows (*Corvus*), garter snakes (*Thamnophis radix*) and humans destroy some nests, but the raccoon (*Procyon*) is the major nest predator. Nest predation in some years may be as high as 95–100% (Ernst, pers. obs.); although Snow (1982) reported otherwise, new nests are usually preyed on more frequently than older ones. Rice rats (*Oryzomys*), muskrats (*Ondatra*), mink (*Mustela*), raccoons (*Procyon*), snapping turtles (*Chelydra*), snakes (*Agkistrodon, Coluber, Nerodia*), bullfrogs (*Rana*), large fish (*Micropterus, Ictalurus*), herons (*Ardea*), and water bugs (Hemiptera; Gotte, 1992) feed on young turtles, and alligators, raccoons, bald eagles (*Haliaeetus*), osprey (*Pandion*), and red-shouldered hawks (*Buteo*) may take adults. Raccoons are the worst natural enemy of all life stages (Ross, 1988). Leeches (*Placobdella*) are often found on *Chrysemys picta* (Ernst, 1971a; MacCulloch, 1981b). Nevertheless, humans with their automobiles, rifles, habitat destruction, pesticides, and pet trade are probably responsible for the death of most painted turtles each year.

When handled, a painted turtle may remain passive or, more often, it will attempt to escape by kicking and scratching, voiding bladder water, or sometimes biting. It is interesting that basking individuals from populations usually undisturbed by humans seem less wary (Moll, 1974).

POPULATIONS: *Chrysemys picta* is usually the most abundant turtle in suitable shallow waterbodies within its range. In a pond-marsh habitat at White Oak, Lancaster County, Pennsylvania, during a 23-year study, seven species were present, and *C. picta* made up 76% of the individuals caught. In all, 3,273 *C. picta* were marked, and the Petersen index estimate was over 2,100 individuals for most years—a mean density of 590/ha of water (Ernst, 1971e). According to Iverson (1982a) the biomass at this site was 106.4 kg/ha. Sexton (1959a) estimated the density of a Michigan population to be 410/ha during a dry period and 99/ha during high water. Gibbons (1968b) marked 1,001 turtles (biomass, 28.2 kg/ha; Iverson, 1982a) and estimated their density as 576/ha at Sheriff's Marsh, Michigan. By 1988 the estimation

of the population size had increased to 3,377 turtles, a density of 838/ha (Frazer et al., 1991b). McAuliffe (1978) recorded a density range of 160–333/ha in an oxbow lake off the Elkhorn River in Nebraska, and Mitchell (1988) reported a rather large population (approximately 517 turtles, biomass 28.3 kg/ha) living in a shallow impoundment and two small beaver ponds in central Virginia. In a marsh in Ontario, Balcombe and Licht (1987) caught 437 painted turtles in just over five years, and at another marsh in Missouri, Kofron and Schriber (1987) made 450 captures and recaptures of *C. picta* in two years. Density of a central Wisconsin wetland population was 104/ha (Ross, 1989a).

Density in smaller ponds may be greatly reduced or quite variable (Lindeman, 1990); Bayless (1975) recorded a painted turtle density of only about 25/ha in a three-hectare New York pond, and Zweifel (1989) calculated the average density for a total pond area on Long Island of just under 0.3 ha to be 137/ha (71–193) in spring, but, because the turtles congregated in one pond, mean spring density of that pond was 348 (150–525)/ha. Spring biomass estimates averaged 23.5 kg/ha (15.7–30.0). During the summer, densities of 210–560/ha occurred fairly often in one pond. At three individual sites at the E. S. George Reserve, Michigan, the densities and biomasses were 89.5/ha, 16.6 kg/ha; 39.9/ha, 7.2 kg/ha; and 41.6/ha, 7.2 kg/ha (Congdon et al., 1986).

Since painted turtles living in rivers can disperse longer distances, riverine populations usually are of low density. *Chrysemys picta* accounted for only 18.4% (67) of the turtles collected at 23 of 33 stations in Blackwater River, Virginia, by Norman (1989), and Harris (1983) saw only three in a pond associated with Morgan Creek, Saskatchewan. MacCulloch and Secoy (1983b) estimated the density of *C. picta* in the Qu'Appelle River, Saskatchewan, to be only 11.1/ha.

The ability to travel far may lower the density at any given area in an extensive lake system; at such a locality in Minnesota Ernst and Ernst (1973) recorded a painted turtle density of only 9.9/ha, and Pearse (1923), as corrected by Petokas (1981a), reported a density of about 32.8–33.3 painted turtles per hectare of lake-marsh habitat at Lake Mendota, Wisconsin. Of course, if most dispersing turtles immigrate into one area of the lake, population density at that site will increase accordingly.

The adult sex ratio found in most long-term population studies of this species has been 1:1 (Gibbons, 1968b; Ernst, 1971e; Mitchell, 1988; Ross, 1989a; Zweifel, 1989), but short-term fluctuations may occur yearly or monthly (Kofron and

Schreiber, 1987; Zweifel, 1989). Also, some populations may have skewed sex ratios, usually toward males (Ernst and Ernst, 1973; Bayless, 1975; Gibbons and Lovich, 1990). Even a few long-term studies have produced unequal adult sex ratios. Ream and Ream (1966) reported an adult male to female ratio of 1.36:1 at Lake Mendota, Wisconsin, and Balcombe and Licht (1987) found a 1:1.39 male to female ratio during a five-year study in Ontario. Sex bias may be introduced in population studies if only one collecting method is used and it is one that favors a particular sex (Ream and Ream, 1966).

Sex ratios of hatchling cohorts may also be skewed; Zweifel (1989) recorded an overall 1.3:1 ratio favoring males in cohorts from 1963 to 1977, yet the sex ratio of hatchlings produced by a single female from 1972 to 1976 was a perfect 1:1. One must be careful in interpreting hatchling sex ratios, as *C. picta* has temperature-dependent sex determination, and the availability of suitable nest sites with both male- and female-producing temperature regimes may be unequal at some localities (Vogt and Bull, 1984).

Age classes in most populations are skewed toward adults. In Pennsylvania, Ernst (1971e) found a 1:42 juvenile to adult ratio. Some other juvenile to adult ratios in the literature are: 1:0.92 (Michigan; Gibbons, 1968b), 1:3 (Quebec; Bider and Hoek, 1971), 1:4.6 (Saskatchewan; MacCulloch and Secoy, 1983b), 1:5 (New York; Bayless, 1975), 1:0.75–2.11 (Michigan; Wilbur, 1975a), 1:1.0–1.3 (Virginia; Mitchell, 1988), 1:0.45–6.3 (New York; Zweifel, 1989). Small turtles may not be as scarce as these ratios indicate; they are probably just more difficult to find and catch. In an investigation of the influence of sampling methods on the estimation of population structure in *C. picta*, Ream and Ream (1966) found that each method yielded a different size-class distribution.

Turnover rates have been calculated in several population studies of *C. picta*. During Ernst's (1971e) study in Pennsylvania, where no immigration or emigration occurred, the estimated annual turnover in population was 51%, with most of the mortality in the young. Bayless (1975) estimated that the losses by emigration and mortality at his New York site ranged from none to 0.09 turtles per year; gains from juvenile recruitment into his small population were 0.03–0.08/yr, and by immigration, 0–0.03/yr. Mitchell (1988) reported that the differences between recruitment (immigration and natality) and losses (emigration and mortality) indicated that his Virginia population was growing at a rate of 7.2%/yr. Zweifel (1989) calculated an annual mean actual recruitment of 10.3% of the estimated natality, or a mean of about

0.7 recruits per breeding female in his New York population.

Survivorship of individual painted turtles has also been given attention in several studies (Iverson, 1991a). From egg to hatchling the annual survivorship rate is 2–67% (Gibbons, 1968b; Tinkle et al., 1981); Wilbur (1975a) reported that mortality is about 92% between laying and the arrival of the hatchling at the water. Between the egg and one year of age, survivorship is 19% (Wilbur, 1975a). Mitchell (1988) calculated annual survivorship of juveniles in Virginia at only 46%. In southwestern Michigan, annual survivorship of juveniles under six years old is 21–51%, while that of adults at least six years old is 64–83% in males, but only 29–50% in females (Frazer et al., 1991b). In another southern Michigan population, the annual survival rate between the ages of 1 and 30+ is 76% (Wilbur, 1975a). Survivorship tables for individual populations are presented in Wilbur (1975a), Mitchell (1988) and Zweifel (1989).

Since males usually average younger in age than females, they probably experience a greater mortality rate. Once females reach age ten they have a high survival rate (Mitchell, 1988); prior to this more males probably enter the population than females. Juvenile females have about a 40% survival rate, while adult females have about a 95% annual survival rate (Mitchell, 1988).

Natural phenomena, such as severe flooding, may drastically alter size and age class characteristics of turtle populations. Severe flooding associated with Hurricane Agnes in June 1972 destroyed all nests of *C. picta* at White Oak, Pennsylvania, resulting in small juveniles not being recruited into the population that year. This caused shifts in size and age class distribution which favored adults. Habitat destruction also forced the turtles into more shallow areas resulting in increased predation on adults (Ernst, 1974a).

REMARKS: McDowell (1964) revised the New World emydine genus *Chrysemys* on the basis of skull and foot morphology, including in it *C. picta* and the cooter and slider turtles of the genera *Pseudemys* and *Trachemys*, and suggested that three subgenera were involved (*Chrysemys, Pseudemys,* and *Trachemys*). Similarities in the choanal structure of *Chrysemys picta* and various species of *Pseudemys* and *Trachemys* upheld both their placement within the genus *Chrysemys* and McDowell's subgeneric distinctions (Parsons, 1968). Zug (1966) found little variation in the penial structure of *Chrysemys picta* and *Trachemys scripta, Pseudemys nelsoni, P. floridana,* and *P. concinna,* strengthening the inclusion of these turtles within

Chrysemys. Weaver and Rose (1967) concurred with the inclusion of *Pseudemys* and *Trachemys* in *Chrysemys,* but showed the subgenera to be invalid, based on further examination of skull and shell characters. However, there remained much disagreement about the generic arrangement of these turtles, and many experts still maintained that *Pseudemys* (including *Trachemys scripta*) was a separate genus.

Holman (1977a) expressed doubts about the status of McDowell's (1964) genus *Chrysemys*. He pointed out that under McDowell's concept as many as four congeneric species may occur in the same waterbody in the southeastern United States and that, although they have similar courtship patterns, there are no records of hybridization between *Chrysemys picta* and other species of *Chrysemys*.

However, hybrids are known within the subgenus *Pseudemys: floridana* × *concinna* (P. W. Smith, 1961; Mount, 1975; Fahey, 1980), and *floridana* × *rubriventris* (Crenshaw, 1965). Holman (1977a) urged additional study of the relationships within the genus. Subsequently, the morphological, cytological, biochemical, and parasitological characteristics have been reevaluated (Ernst and Ernst, 1980; Vogt and McCoy, 1980; Seidel and Smith, 1986; McCoy and Jacobs, 1991). These new studies indicate that *Chrysemys, Pseudemys,* and *Trachemys* are best treated as separate genera.

Since *C. picta* is one of our more easily observable and popular experimental turtles, the literature concerning it is enormous, and has been reviewed by Ernst (1971d, 1988).

Trachemys scripta (Schoepff, 1792)
Slider

PLATE 31

RECOGNITION: *Trachemys scripta* is a medium to large freshwater turtle (males in the United States reach 20 cm, and females, 28 cm carapace length) with a prominent red, orange, or yellow postorbital stripe on each side of the head. Because there are three subspecies in the United States, the following description is highly generalized; see the section on Geographic variation for particulars on color and pattern.

The carapace is oval, weakly keeled, and has a slightly serrated posterior margin. It is olive to brown with yellow stripes or bars. Marks on the undersides of the marginal scutes commonly take the form of a dark blotch partly surrounded by a light band. The bridge pattern varies from dark blotches to bars. The hingeless plastron is yellow, and the pattern varies from a single dark blotch or ocellus on each scute to one dark blotch on each anteriormost scute (or, rarely, no pattern). The skin is green to olive brown, with yellow stripes. The yellow supratemporal and orbital headstripes are conspicuous; a postorbital stripe of red or yellow is present in most North American individuals, and a prefrontal arrow is formed as the supratemporal stripes pass forward from the eyes to meet a yellow sagittal stripe on top of the snout. The neck is marked with many yellow stripes, and a central yellow chin stripe runs backward and divides to form a Y-shaped mark. The limbs have many narrow yellow stripes.

Adult male *T. scripta* become darker, or melanistic, as they become larger and older. The bright-yellow pattern typical of females and juveniles becomes obliterated by dark-brown pigments. Melanistic males are so different in appearance from nonmelanistic ones that the two were once considered as separate species. The transformation occurs well past the age at which most males attain sexual maturity. The process is not strictly size- or age-dependent, but it is coincident with population-specific female body size

at maturity. For example, in populations where females usually mature at a plastron length of 16.0 cm, few if any melanistic males are smaller than 16.0 cm. Melanin proliferation is also coincident with maximal development of male foreclaw length. Melanistic individuals typically form a small part of the population but predominate within larger male size classes. The two color forms have physiological, hormonal, histological, and behavioral differences, and the reader is referred to Lovich et al. (1990c) and Garstka et al. (1991) for additional details and references.

Adult males have elongated, curved claws and long, thick tails, with the anal opening posterior to the carapacial rim. Mean adult male carapace and plastron lengths are greater than those of females in the same population. The degree of sexual size dimorphism varies due to sampling biases, growth pattern, predatory pressure, population sex ratio, and the size at which the sexes reach sexual maturity. Sexual dimorphism in slider turtle populations is reviewed by Gibbons and Lovich (1990), and methods of quantifying sexual size dimorphism are reviewed by Lovich and Gibbons (1992).

KARYOTYPE: The diploid chromosome number is 50: 26 macrochromosomes and 24 microchromosomes (Killebrew, 1977a). Of these, 20 are metacentric and submetacentric, 10 are subtelocentric, and 20 are acrocentric and telocentric, with a total of 80 arms (Stock, 1972). DeSmet (1978) reported *T. scripta* to have 52 chromosomes (32 macrochromosomes and 20 microchromosomes).

FOSSIL RECORD: Although the genus *Trachemys* is represented in Miocene and Pliocene deposits (Weaver and Robertson, 1967; Jackson, 1988b), the earliest fossil *T. scripta* dates from the Pliocene Blancan of Texas (Rogers, 1976). Pleistocene records

Trachemys scripta scripta

Trachemys scripta elegans

of *T. scripta* abound: Blancan—Texas (Hay, 1924; Holman, 1969b); Irvingtonian—Kansas (Schultz, 1965; Preston, 1971; Rogers, 1982), and Texas (Parmley, 1988); Rancholabrean—Florida (Weigel, 1962; Holman, 1978; according to Jackson, 1988b, all Pleistocene *Trachemys* from Florida are assignable to *T. scripta*), Illinois (Holman, 1966), Missouri (Moodie and Van Devender, 1977), and Texas (Holman, 1963). Mexican records are from Sonora

and Yucatán (Alvarez, 1976; Van Devender et al., 1985). Archeological records exist for Illinois, Michigan, and Wisconsin (Adler, 1968). Weaver and Robertson (1967), Weaver and Rose (1967), and Seidel and Jackson (1990) reviewed the evolution and fossil relationships of the genus *Trachemys*.

DISTRIBUTION: In the United States, *T. scripta* ranges naturally from southeastern Virginia

Trachemys scripta troostii

Distribution of *Trachemys scripta*

southwestward to northern Florida, north through Kentucky and Tennessee to southern Ohio, northern Indiana, Illinois, and southeastern Iowa, and west to Kansas, Oklahoma, and New Mexico. The natural range continues south, through Mexico and Central America to Colombia and Venezuela. The slider turtle has been introduced all over the world via the pet trade, including Japan, Germany (Ernst, pers. obs.), Israel (Bouskila, 1986), South Africa (Branch, 1988), the Mariana Islands (Rodda et al., 1991), and many other exotic localities. In the United States extralimital feral populations have been established in Arizona (Hulse, 1980), Florida (Hutchison, 1992), Hawaii (Lovich, pers. obs.), Michigan (Edgren, 1943, 1948), New Jersey (Stein et al., 1980), Pennsylvania (Manchester, 1982), and in Maryland and the vicinity of Washington, D.C. (Ernst, pers. obs.).

GEOGRAPHIC VARIATION: *Trachemys scripta* is the most variable of all turtles with from as few as 13 to as many as 19 subspecies, depending on whether one accepts the arrangement of Ernst (1990b) or that of Legler (1990). Much of the taxonomy of these races is confused, and more study is needed to clarify relationships. Most variation occurs in tropical America, and some populations now listed as subspecies may eventually prove to be species, such as the Rio Grande form *T. gaigeae* which has been elevated to specific status (Conant and Collins, 1991; Ernst, 1992a).

Three subspecies occur in the United States. *Trachemys scripta scripta* (Schoepff, 1792), the yellow-bellied slider, ranges from southeastern Virginia to northern Florida. It has a wide yellow stripe on each pleural scute, a conspicuous yellow postorbital blotch, which may join a neck stripe, and a yellow plastron, which commonly has a dark ocellus or blotch on each anteriormost scute. *Trachemys s. elegans* (Wied-Neuwied, 1839), the red-eared slider, occupies the Mississippi Valley from Illinois to the Gulf of Mexico. It has a wide red postorbital stripe, narrow chin stripes, a transverse yellow stripe on each pleural, and a plastral pattern of one large dark blotch or ocellus on every scute. *Trachemys s. troostii* (Holbrook, 1836), the Cumberland slider, is found in the upper portions of the Cumberland and Tennessee rivers, from southeastern Virginia and Kentucky to northeastern Alabama. It has a narrow yellow or orange postorbital stripe, broad chin stripes, a transverse yellow stripe on each pleural scute, and a dark ocellus on each plastral scute; see Burger (1952) and Ernst and Jett (1969) for more complete lists of characters.

Where the ranges of the three North American subspecies meet, interbreeding has established zones of intergradation, sometimes resulting in confusing individuals. This has been compounded by the release of so many pet trade *T. s. scripta* and *T. s. elegans* within the range of the other, and Ernst and Jett (1969) documented intergrade *T. s. elegans* × *T. s. troostii* in Madison County, Kentucky.

The slider turtle is one of the most genetically variable vertebrates known (Smith and Scribner, 1990). After study of mitochondrial DNA, Avise et al. (1992) noted a phylogenetic split by *T. scripta* into an eastern population and a western one, but found that the magnitude of change was less than that of five or six other turtle species with concordant phylogeography. Genetic similarities among populations in South Carolina and Georgia appear to be related to geographic proximity regardless of the structure of the intervening habitat and potential for dispersal and interpopulation gene flow (Scribner et al., 1984, 1986). The Savannah River seems to be a significant barrier to gene flow in *T. scripta* (Scribner et al., 1986), a species that prefers still water.

CONFUSING SPECIES: *Trachemys gaigeae* has a black-bordered, orange postorbital blotch that is separated from the orbit, a reticulate pattern of light lines on the carapace, and a large, central plastral figure. *Pseudemys rubriventris, P. nelsoni, P. alabamensis* and *P. texana* have deep shells and a prominently notched upper jaw bordered on each side by a cusp. *Pseudemys floridana, P. concinna,* and *P. gorzugi* have deep shells and lack a prefrontal arrow. *Chrysemys picta* has a notched upper jaw, with cusps, and an unserrated carapace. *Deirochelys reticularia* has an extremely long neck and a broad foreleg stripe.

HABITAT: *Trachemys scripta* occupies most freshwater habitats within its range, but prefers quiet waters with soft bottoms, an abundance of aquatic plants, and suitable basking sites (Ernst and Barbour, 1972). In Georgia and South Carolina this species is found in or near salt marshes (Gibbons and Coker, 1978; Gibbons et al., 1979b; Gibbons and Harrison, 1981; Lovich, pers. obs.). It is found above and below the fall line in the Alabama River, but is rare or absent above the fall line in the Tombigbee and Apalachicola rivers, respectively (Tinkle, 1959a).

BEHAVIOR: In the southern part of its range *T. scripta* may be active in every month, but farther north it must hibernate in winter. Even in the north,

Plastra of the three subspecies of *Trachemys scripta* occurring in the United States, from left: *T. s. scripta, T. s. troostii,* and *T. s. elegans*

Trachemys scripta elegans has a red bar behind the eye; in *T. s. troostii* this bar is yellow or orange

however, individuals may emerge on warm winter days (Anton, 1987). In Kentucky it is usually active from April to November (Ernst and Barbour, pers. obs.). Slider turtles in Illinois are not active until water temperatures reach 10°C or higher, but turtles can be observed basking in all months except January (Cagle, 1950). Similarly, in Louisiana, turtles are captured in baited traps in every month except January, but not at water temperatures below 20°C.

Active sliders were observed in a prairie stream in north-central Texas in the winter, swimming in water as cold as 2.4 C; some were even seen swimming under ice cover (Lardie, 1980). Most *T. scripta*

trapped in a Texas farm pond by Ingold and Patterson (1988) were collected between May and September. The summer-centered activity pattern was most conspicuous in turtles with plastron lengths less than 14.4 cm. Larger turtles were collected with relatively equal frequency throughout the year.

Slider turtles become inactive at water temperatures below 10°C and may hibernate in muskrat (*Ondatra zibethica*) burrows, hollow stumps, or other shelters. In Illinois, hibernating turtles sometimes freeze and large numbers of dead sliders may be found along the shores of larger ponds and lakes in March (Cagle, 1950). During hibernation, blood clotting time is increased dramatically (Barone and Jacques, 1975), thus assuring continuous, although slow, blood flow.

The slider is primarily diurnal. At night, slider turtles sleep by resting on the bottom or floating at the surface. Trap records compiled by Cagle (1950) suggest a concentration of feeding activity early in the morning, but turtles can be collected at baited traps at all hours of the day. Diurnal rhythms of activity in juveniles are not well developed under experimental conditions, either under normal room conditions or under a 12:12-hour light:dark cycle. Activity is suppressed at 30°C but increased at 20°C. Activity increases when turtles are exposed to 12 hours of ultraviolet light followed by 12 hours of darkness (Cloudsley-Thompson, 1982). Cloudsley-Thompson concluded that the activity of juvenile slider turtles is neither exogenous nor circadian. In contrast, Jarling et al. (1989) concluded that the temperature preference of adults exposed to different photoperiods is based on an endogenous circadian rhythm.

The most conspicuous part of the daily activity cycle is basking. The habit is well developed, even in hatchlings (Janzen et al., 1992).

The behavioral ecology of basking in a Florida population was studied in detail by Auth (1975). The number of times individual turtles basked atmospherically per day reached a peak at a daily mean water temperature of 28.5°C. Aquatic basking while floating at the surface reached a peak when water temperatures approached 31.5°C. Basking adults elevated their temperature as much as 10°C above near-surface water temperature. The duration of basking increased as sunshine and air and water temperatures decreased, but the number of turtles basking per day and number of times individual turtles bask on a given day decreased during overcast conditions. Basking duration was also related to body size; *T. scripta* with carapaces shorter than 10 cm basked more often per day than did larger turtles. Some basked up to five times a day but a substantial part of the population did not bask every day, even under optimum conditions. Basking began in earnest at about 0800 and peaked between 1000 and 1100 on clear days in August and September. Basking activity shifted later into the day during October and November. Cagle (1950) observed a peak in basking activity during midmorning and midafternoon.

The primary function of basking seems to be thermoregulatory, although many other advantages have been suggested (Boyer, 1965; Moll and Legler, 1971). The pineal gland is very sensitive to light (Meissl and Ueck, 1980) and may aid in determining how long *T. scripta* can safely bask without overheating.

Operative environmental temperatures, or T_e (an index of the thermal environment), were good predictors of basking behavior in a population of slider turtles in South Carolina. Turtles generally did not bask unless T_e was 28°C (the preferred body temperature) or higher, again suggesting that basking is thermoregulatory. T_e was positively correlated with short-wave and total solar radiation as well as air and substrate temperature, with the latter variable being the best single predictor of T_e. As the sun changes position throughout the day, so does the spatial variation in T_e's available to turtles, thus influencing their location and basking behavior (Crawford et al., 1983).

Sliders occupying the warm arm of a nuclear reactor cooling reservoir in South Carolina used aquatic basking even though atmospheric basking sites were available. Water temperature in the warm arm was as much as 9°C higher than areas with no thermal impact. Aquatic basking raised body temperature 1–3°C above water temperature. Turtles in normal-temperature parts of the reservoir used atmospheric basking on sunny days throughout the year (Spotila et al., 1984).

The effects of digestive state, acclimation temperature, sex, and season on basking behavior were studied in the laboratory by Hammond et al. (1988). During the spring and summer, there was a statistically significant difference between basking durations of fed and unfed turtles and between basking times of the sexes at all acclimation temperatures except 35°C, when basking was limited for fed and unfed turtles. Fed females basked longer than fed males and both basked longer than their unfed counterparts. Differences were greatest at 10 and 20°C but were also detected at 30°C. The basking times of fed and unfed turtles and males and females did not differ significantly during the fall and winter. However, the differences between basking times at all four acclimation temperatures were statistically significant.

Like other ectothermic animals the behavior of the slider turtle is controlled largely by environmental temperatures. *T. scripta* has a selected temperature of 28–29°C with its greatest capacity for activity between 25 and 30°C. Heat tolerance ranges from 41.0 to 41.7°C, although the critical thermal maximum is 40.2–42.3°C (Hutchison et al., 1966). The species can live in water temperatures from 1 to 40°C. Modeling indicates that in full sun the slider turtle can withstand 32°C in a wind of 400 cm/sec and 19°C in still air. Basically, a turtle basking in full sunlight can withstand higher temperatures only if air is moving over the shell to facilitate heat transfer by convection and evaporation. Under a clear night sky, *T. scripta* can withstand temperatures as low as 9°C in still air but, because convective heat transfer increases with wind speed, as low as 3°C at a wind speed of 400 cm/sec (Spotila et al., 1990). *Trachemys scripta* heats faster than it cools (Lucey, 1974), and larger individuals heat and cool slower than smaller individuals (Boyer, 1965; Glidewell et al., 1981).

Trachemys scripta has decided thermal preferences. Individuals acclimated to temperatures between 3 and 19°C usually select temperatures over 28°C within an hour when exposed to a thermal gradient, and eventually reach a final thermal preference between 31 and 33°C (Crawshaw et al., 1980). Turtles placed in the gradient for extended periods are more active during the day, but the temperature selected is not related to either activity or time of day. However, both the median and mean selected temperatures, calculated from the temperature of the plastral surface and that near the heart, are positively correlated with the time of day between 0700 and 1700 with slopes ranging from 0.42 to 0.60°C (Jarling et al., 1984). Nutritional state also plays a role in the thermoregulatory behavior of *T. scripta*. After feeding, sliders increased their thermal preference from 24.6 to 29.1°C (Gatten, 1974c).

In general, oxygen consumption increases with a rise in temperature, but breathing rate is independent of temperature (D. C. Jackson, 1971). Both arterial pH and plasma carbon dioxide concentration are correlated with the breathing rate (Jackson et al., 1974). Total plasma carbon dioxide does not appreciably change during heating or cooling, but while cooling the ventilatory rates of oxygen decrease (Jackson and Kagen, 1976). *Trachemys scripta* has a periodic breathing pattern in which ventilatory cycles occur in sequences separated by apneic periods of varying duration (Lucey and House, 1977). This pattern changes with body temperature. As the temperature increases, the frequency of the ventilatory cycles also increases, but the number of cycles per sequence decreases, as does also the duration of the cycle. Heart rate and blood pressure also increase with rising temperature, and heart rate is faster at the same temperature while heating than during cooling. Physical activity is also accompanied by an increase in heart rate.

During basking and terrestrial activity, water is lost through cutaneous evaporation. Boyer (1965) found that at normal summer temperatures and humidities his largest *T. s. elegans* lost 0.43 g/h and his smallest lost 0.23 g/h. He thought that heat loss from evaporation was negligible. Rates of water loss

increase as wind speed and air temperature increase, but are inversely proportional to body size (Foley and Spotila, 1978). Minimum rates of evaporative water loss occur in the largest *T. scripta* in wind or still air, regardless of air temperature. Small sliders, however, lose more water in moving air as the temperature increases. Urine may be retained in the bladder. While this occurs it is acidified by transporting carbon dioxide in the form of bicarbonate from the bladder lumen into the serosal layer of its wall (Schilb, 1978). The bicarbonate may enter the blood stream to be used elsewhere as a buffering agent. The urine is rich in ammonia, urea, and, to a lesser extent, uric acid (Baze and Horne, 1970).

Trachemys scripta may spend considerable time underwater, especially during winter hibernation, and such nonbreathing periods require physiological adjustments. Many physiological experiments have been conducted on diving *T. scripta*, but only the highlights are presented here. Lactate and carbon dioxide increase in body tissues and blood pH drops. At the end of a four-hour dive at 24°C, nonpulmonary carbon dioxide increases to a peak about twice the predive rate (D. C. Jackson, 1976). Carbon dioxide is eliminated from the body by shunting it to extracellular fluid (D. C. Jackson, 1976). Prolonged anoxic dives are associated with increased serum osmolality and decreased sodium chloride, suggesting that diuresis occurs. However, this may be secondary to the newly discovered diuresis-producing hormones long-acting sodium stimulator (proatrial natriuretic factors 1–30) and vessel dilator (proatrial natriuretic factors 31–67) which circulate as part of the atrial natriuretic factor prohormone. In the brain, anoxia causes increases in the levels of certain inhibitory amino acids in combination with concentration decreases of the excitatory amino acid glutamate, mediating or facilitating the lowering of brain activity and energy consumption (Nilsson et al., 1991). Also, a marked decrease in both heart and skeletal muscle cytochrome oxidase activity occurs, possibly owing to a need for oxygen in porphyrin biosynthesis, which may indicate either increased metabolic efficiency or possibly lowered (zero) mitochondrial oxygen consumption (Simon and Robin, 1970).

Submersion by a slider reduces heat production by as much as 80%. This reduction depends on the oxygen concentration available prior to the onset of diving. Uptake of oxygen from water is only about 6% of that from air. A profound reduction in the metabolic rate follows diving, but not until oxygen stores are depleted. Only a very low metabolism can be supported by oxygen extracted from water, and the metabolism of submerged *T. scripta* is primarily anaerobic (Jackson and Schmidt-Nielsen, 1966; Jackson, 1968).

The combined function of the cloacal bursae and urinary bladder on *T. scripta* is analogous to that of ballast tanks in a submarine. The cloacal bursae are used for water storage and for active, short-term adjustments of water volume. A larger volume of fluid usually occupies the urinary bladder, which acts as a relatively static depot involved in large or long-term buoyancy adjustments (D. C. Jackson, 1969).

Individual *T. scripta* may have extensive home ranges which may include several bodies of water between which they make frequent overland journeys (Cagle, 1944b). In a review of movement patterns in *T. scripta* and other turtles, Gibbons et al. (1990; also see Gibbons, 1986) identified four major purposes for movements within a population: feeding, reproduction (mate searching, courtship, and nesting), basking, and seeking favorable sites in which to hide or remain dormant for variable periods of time. Movements between populations occur seasonally or in response to changes in habitat (e.g. drought). Seasonal movements include migration of hatchlings from the nest to aquatic habitats, searching for resources that vary seasonally in their availability, departure or return from overwintering sites, searching for mates during the breeding season, and nesting movements.

Little is known of the movements of slider turtles within a population (Gibbons et al., 1990). The movements and home range of *T. s. scripta* in Par Pond, a thermally impacted 1,100-ha reservoir in South Carolina, were studied by Schubauer et al. (1990). Aquatic and total (aquatic + terrestrial) home range sizes of males (40 and 104 ha, respectively) were significantly greater than those of females (15 and 37 ha, respectively). The mean length of total home range, as determined by radiotelemetry, was 731 m for males and 401 m for females. Home range size was significantly positively correlated with body size for females, but not for males. The home range size of *T. scripta* in thermally altered portions of the reservoir did not differ significantly from those in normal temperature areas. Turtles did not occupy areas with lethal water temperatures, but no other major effects of thermal effluents on behavior were detected.

The homing ability of slider turtles was tested by Cagle (1944b). He marked and released 1,006 turtles in a drainage ditch in Illinois. Most remained within 0.8 km of the release point, but some moved greater distances. In 27 days one moved approximately 3.2 km up the ditch, then 0.4 km overland to a pond. Of 51 individuals released "at some point distant from the point of collection" and recaptured once, 16 were recovered in the original area, 4 remained in the area of release, 14 were found in another area, and 17 moved to an adjacent waterbody. He concluded from this and other data that individual turtles have home ranges.

A male recaptured by Webb (1961) had moved approximately 2.4 km between 23 July 1953 and 21 June 1954. Another male, which had moved about 1 km between 23 July 1953 and 18 June 1954, was recaptured on 20 June and found to have moved about the same distance in this two-day period. A female moved about 0.53 km between July 1953 and 22 June 1954.

Adult male slider turtles move greater distances than females at certain times of the year, probably in search of mating opportunities. This conclusion is based on the assumption that male reproductive success is based partly on the number of mating opportunities available. By increasing movements, males presumably encounter more females. Morreale et al. (1984) and Gibbons et al. (1990) showed that male slider turtles in South Carolina were more active than females in early spring and later autumn, and significantly more males made terrestrial and aquatic movements greater than one kilometer. The longest movements (>5 km) were made by males. Additional support for the theory of greater male movement was collected from a population inhabiting a radioactive habitat. Levels of female contamination were significantly higher than in males. The reason for this disparity is likely the more sedentary nature of females and its obvious effect on exposure to radionuclides in contaminated habitats. Adult males emigrated more often and farther than females in Mississippi (Parker, 1984).

Movement into and away from a Carolina bay in South Carolina was studied in detail by researchers at the Savannah River Ecology Laboratory. The direction of movement between the two parts of the bay defined by a causeway was nonrandom. The reason for the disparity is unknown. In contrast, movements into the bay were more or less random in terms of compass direction. Movements seemed to be correlated with rainfall (Gibbons, 1970a). When movements into and away from the bay were pooled, significant directional disparities were detected (Gibbons and Semlitsch, 1981). Movements between aquatic habitats were also evident. Of 4,768 individuals from Ellenton Bay, Par Pond, and the Lost Lake system, 244 *T. s. scripta* moved from other habitats ranging from 0.2 to 9.0 km distant (Gibbons et al., 1990).

During an eight-year study of immigration and dispersal of *T. s. elegans* living in a system of farm ponds in Mississippi, annual immigration increased from 18% to 61%, possibly as a result of algicide application in one of the ponds (Parker, 1984). The amount of time spent in a single pond is a function of turtle sex and age. Over 40% of older adult males spent only one year in the main study pond. Younger males and females were more sedentary. Immigrants of both sexes emigrated more often than resident turtles. Population size of a newly constructed farm pond in Mississippi peaked at 26 *T. s. elegans* after three years then declined slightly over the next two years. Most immigrants were immature turtles. Individual turnover rate between years was higher in adults than in immature turtles, and higher than in long-established ponds (Parker, 1990).

Slider turtle movements are occasionally motivated by droughts or seasonal fluctuations in water level. *Trachemys s. elegans* in Louisiana move out of deeper bayous and swamps to roadside pools and shallow swamps in the spring and remain there until receding water levels force them back into deeper areas in the late summer (Cagle, 1950). In South Carolina, most *T. s. scripta* departed from a drying Carolina bay and emigrated in the direction of the nearest body of water (Gibbons et al., 1983). According to Cagle (1950) sliders do not estivate. They may escape extreme temperatures by burrowing into the mud or finding shade, but under extreme conditions migrate overland in search of water.

Migrating adult *T. scripta* use the position of the sun to orient on a compass course that intersects their home shoreline at right angles (Murphy, 1970). This ability is used only when familiar landmarks are absent, and the adult slider does not seem to use celestial orientation at night.

Murphy (1970) studied the cues directing initial orientation of hatchlings upon emergence from the nest. In fall laboratory tests, hatchlings tested on a dry substrate showed a negative phototaxis at either high or low body temperatures. Conversely those tested in water had a positive phototaxis. In fall outdoor tests, hatchlings moved toward the highest horizon. Neither pretest treatment (exposure to desiccation, low temperatures, or light), test conditions (sand or grass substrate, sunlight, darkness, overcast skies, rain), nor lack of a distinct visual image altered the response toward the high horizon. Most hatchlings in groups retained overwinter under either a light:dark cycle at room temperature, darkness and alternating high and low temperatures, or a light:dark cycle at low temperature moved toward the lowest horizon when tested the next spring. Murphy (1970) thought this shift in behavior is probably related to maturation, and may reflect adaptations for overwintering in the nest followed by spring emergence.

Trachemys scripta are occasionally aggressive toward each other. Melanistic males in particular have a reputation for being more aggressive than nonmelanistic individuals (Lovich et al., 1990c). Observations in Oklahoma indicate that groups of turtles occupying pools in a stream habitat usually had one melanistic male that showed territorial behavior toward other males whenever they were present. Under laboratory conditions, melanistic males were observed to bite, shove, and ram conspecific and heterospecific turtles of about the same size and color. A possible dominance hierarchy existed with melanistic males dominating over other males during courtship behavior (Lardie, 1983b).

REPRODUCTION: The timing and size of sexual maturity varies dramatically among and within populations of *T. scripta*. In males, maturity is evidenced by elongation of the foreclaws, an increase in preanal tail length, and a significant reduction in rate of growth (Cagle, 1948a; Ernst and Barbour, 1972c, 1989; Gibbons and Greene, 1990; Gibbons and Lovich, 1990). Populations in warm, nutrient-rich areas grow faster and mature earlier than do populations in colder, nutrient-limited habitats. Reported minimum sizes or size ranges (CL = carapace length, PL = plastron length) and ages of sexual maturity for various populations are: Illinois *T. s. elegans*—males 9–10 cm PL and two to five years, females 15.0–19.5 cm PL (Cagle, 1944c, 1948a, 1950); Oklahoma *T. s. elegans*—males 9.0–10.0 cm PL, females 17.4–19.3 cm PL (Webb, 1961); Back Bay, Virginia, *T. s. scripta*—males 10.2 cm CL, females 23.2 cm CL (Mitchell and Pague, 1990); and Dismal Swamp, Virginia, *T. s. scripta*—females 22.6 cm CL (Mitchell and Pague, 1990).

Maturation of female *T. s. elegans* in a lake receiving thermal effluent in Illinois was compared to that of females in a nearby control lake by Thornhill (1982). Those in the thermally impacted lake matured at plastron lengths as small as 18.5 cm in three years, while those in the natural lake matured at 17.3 cm, or larger, in four years.

The most comprehensive studies of geographic variation in age and size of maturity of *T. scripta* turtle have been conducted at the University of Georgia's Savannah River Ecology Laboratory (Gibbons et al.,

1981). In all cases, maturity of the female *T. s. scripta* was verified through the use of dissections or the observation of oviducal eggs in x-ray photographs (Gibbons and Greene, 1979). Females living in Par Pond (a lake receiving thermal effluent from a nuclear reactor) matured at a larger size, but about the same age (8 years) as females in a nearby natural habitat (Ellenton Bay, nonthermally impacted). Par Pond females matured at plastron lengths between approximately 19.5 and 21.0 cm, while females in Ellenton Bay matured at between 16.0 and 17.5 cm. Male maturity was determined on the basis of foreclaw elongation. Par Pond and Ellenton Bay males matured at about the same plastron length, 9.0–12.0 cm, but at different ages: Par Pond, three to four years; Ellenton Bay, four to five years. The difference in maturity schedules for these two populations is remarkable given their proximity (about 20 km). However, the thermal conditions and food quality are more favorable for sliders in Par Pond (Christy et al., 1974). Males respond by growing faster and maturing earlier but at about the same size as turtles in more natural environments. In contrast, Par Pond females forego the opportunity to mature at an earlier age in favor of attaining a larger body size at maturity. The advantage of such a strategy, increased fecundity, is discussed below.

Populations of *T. s. scripta* on South Carolina's Atlantic barrier islands are also composed of large individuals in comparison to natural populations on the adjacent mainland (Gibbons et al., 1979b). Females in particular are exceptionally large, attaining sizes similar to those of sliders in Par Pond. The large size and rapid growth rate of the island sliders is attributed to a high protein diet (euryhaline fish) and optimal thermal conditions.

The foregoing discussion of timing and size of maturity in *T. scripta* suggests that size is a more important determinant of sexual maturity in males than age. In females, age may be more important than size (Gibbons and Greene, 1990); however, maturity in most organisms is not strictly size or age dependent but occurs at a point that minimizes a reduction in fitness caused by slower growth and smaller size (Stearns and Crandall, 1984). The size at which each sex matures is the underlying cause of sexual dimorphism in *T. scripta* (Gibbons and Lovich, 1990).

On the basis of male *T. s. elegans* from the Texas Panhandle, spermatogenesis begins in May in North America with proliferation of spermatogonia and the presence of Sertoli nuclei on or near the basement membranes of the seminiferous tubules (Brewer and Killebrew, 1986; Sprando and Russell, 1988). By mid-May the Sertoli cytoplasm extends midway into the tubule lumens which also contain some debris but no mature spermatozoa. Spermatogonia become more plentiful during the latter part of May and increasing numbers of spermatocytes appear in the latter part of June. At the same time, Sertoli cytoplasm is considerably reduced and the tubule lumens are relatively free of debris. Spermatocytogenesis begins in mid-June and continues through early September, peaking from mid-July into early August. Numerous spermatocytes and spermatids are present in the tubules by mid-July, and some males show differentiation of spermatids into mature spermatozoa. Spermiogenesis increases in early August and is well advanced by the end of the month. Spermatozoa clump in bunches at the distal ends of the Sertoli cells, but spermatocytes and spermatids are still abundant in most tubules. Spermiogenesis slows by late September and ends by mid-November. Spermiation begins in early to mid-September, peaks during October, and gradually declines until the end of November. The winter period of germinal quiescence is signified by a decline in spermatogenic activity in late November. Many spermatozoa are enmeshed in the Sertoli cytoplasm and some debris is present in the tubule lumens in early December. The testes appear to remain in a sexually quiescent state, following the completion of spermatogenic activity, pending the initiation of a new cycle the following spring.

The testes usually weigh the least at the time of emergence from hibernation, but gradually increase in weight as the next cycle of spermatogenic activity progresses. Initiation of a new spermatogenic cycle in *T. s. elegans* from the Texas Panhandle is followed by a gradual increase in testes weight. Mean testes weight is lowest in May as gonial proliferation progresses. The testes weigh the most in August, coinciding with the peak period of spermatogenic activity. Weight gradually regresses as spermatogenesis declines and spermatozoa pass into the epididymides. Seasonal changes in the diameter of the seminiferous tubules coincide with fluctuations in testes weight. Minimum and maximum mean seminiferous tubule diameters occur in May and August, respectively. About 45% of the observed variation in testes weight is associated with variation in total weight, plastron length, carapace length, and epididymal weight.

The epididymides are packed with mature sperm throughout the year. The epididymal tubules contain mature sperm in the spring through late June. Some of these tubules contain reduced numbers of sperm in mid-July. The epididymides weigh the least in July and the most in December. The mean diameter of the epididymal tubules is maximum in May and minimum in September. Almost 43% of the observed variation in epididymal weight is associated with variation in total weight, plastron length, carapace length, and testes weight. The adjusted monthly mean epididymal weights for December differ significantly from those for July–September. The cycle in Texas is similar to that described for male Panamanian *T. scripta* by Moll and Legler (1971) and Moll and Moll (1990), but varies in the timing of events.

Testes are smallest and lightest from early January to May and are largest and heaviest from early July to December in *T. scripta* populations in northern Alabama (Lovich et al., 1990c). These changes coincide with various stages of spermatogenesis, with maximum enlargement occurring during the time of greatest spermatogenic activity. Enlargement of the epididymides occurs after maximum testes enlargement, and they remain enlarged well after regression of the testes.

Leydig cells are most conspicuous from January to May (Bourne and Licht, 1985; Garstka et al., 1991). Lipid concentrations peak between March and April in the interim between spermatogenic cycles, and then decline to negligible levels between August and November. Lipid substances in the tubules are in or closely associated with Sertoli cells. Seasonal lipid concentrations generally follow those of interstitial cells.

The timing and extent of gametogenesis in melanistic and nonmelanistic males from northern Alabama was examined by Lovich et al. (1990c). Testis mass, relative to body size, is consistently greater in melanistic males throughout the year. Seminiferous tubule diameter is largest in September, but does not differ significantly between melanistic and nonmelanistic males. The timing of spermatogenesis is similar in the two color forms. Melanistic and nonmelanistic males differ dramatically in relative concentrations of sex steroid hormones, and the reader is referred to Lovich et al. (1990c) and Garstka et al. (1991) for details.

Photoperiodicity may play a controlling role in the male sexual cycles. An experimental group of male turtles kept at 10–24°C was artificially illuminated by Burger (1937). Artificial illumination began at 1900 and was gradually increased from three to seven hours per night. Two control groups were established. The first was kept in the same room as the experimental group, but was not provided with artificial illumination. The second control group was maintained in a barrel in a dimly illuminated basement at a temperature range of 5–20°C. The experiment began 18

November, and turtles were sacrificed for examination on 7 January to 5 February. Those sacrificed on 18 November had epididymides full of spermatozoa and testes with a large number of spermatids. Turtles in the artificially lighted group showed signs of starting a new spermatogenetic cycle with thickened walls in the seminiferous tubules and a slight proliferation of secondary spermatogonia when sacrificed on 7 January. By 23 January the cycle had advanced and mature sperm from the previous cycle had disappeared. Spermiogenesis was completed on 5 February as evidenced by the presence of free spermatozoa in the tubule lumens. Controls held in dark conditions showed no suppression of the original spermatogenetic cycle. The control group maintained in normal daylight did not exhibit uniform results. In two males the original cycle was arrested, and the testes of the other two were in the same condition as those of turtles kept in darkness. The results of Burger's experiment should be interpreted with caution since the turtles were maintained under rather unusual conditions, and groups were kept at different temperatures.

The sperm of *T. scripta* is representative of the flagellated type occurring in other vertebrates. Details of sperm morphology are summarized by Kaplan et al. (1966), and semen collection techniques are discussed by Platz et al. (1980).

The oogenetic cycle of Panamanian *T. scripta* was studied by Moll and Legler (1971), and although the events are probably similar, the timing of these events probably varies from that of the reproductive cycle in North American females. The ovarian cycle is divided into four phases (follicle diameter classes are as follows: Class I, ≤6 mm; Class II, 7–13 mm; Class III, 14–20 mm; Class IV, 21–27 mm): (1) follicular enlargement, (2) ovulation and intrauterine period, (3) oviposition, and (4) quiescence period. The first phase (vitellogenesis) begins in August or September with follicles reaching ovulatory size in late November or December. Follicle development is continuous until late May. When class IV follicles are ovulated, the next smaller class enlarges and becomes preovulatory. Ovarian weight is greatest from early January to March. During the end of the nesting season in April and May (May to July in the United States), the number and size of ovarian follicles and ovarian weight decrease. Class IV follicles are not present after oviposition but Class III follicles may be present for at least a month. It is not known if Class III follicles are retained until the next breeding season, or if they become atretic. Class I and II follicles are present throughout the year. Ovarian quiescence occurs from June to early August in Panama.

Following ovulation (in May in North America) the follicles become corpora lutea, the largest of which are 11–12 mm in diameter. Corpora lutea are obvious for up to 18 days following oviposition and are apparently glandular while intrauterine eggs are present. However, they may disappear within 30 days of ovulation, even if the eggs are retained in the oviducts. Webb (1961) thought that the corpora lutea of female *T. s. elegans* in Oklahoma decreased 3–4 mm in diameter between ovulation and oviposition, and possibly more between successive ovulations.

The mean ovary weight of females with oviducal eggs decreased during the egg-laying season in Louisiana and Illinois. Weight ranges for various months were as follows: May, 28.1–42.0 g (mean 35.05 g); June, 18.3–37.4 g (mean 22.72); July, 7.8–15.4 g (mean 11.6 g). Many females collected in September and October lacked follicles larger than 2 mm, but some contained follicles larger than 10 mm. Plastron length was not correlated with either follicle size or ovarian weight in females collected in the fall (Cagle, 1944c, 1950). Follicles of sexually mature females in Oklahoma ranged from 10 to 21 mm in diameter. Females collected 19 May to 21 July contained ovarian follicles larger than 15 mm. Oviducal eggs were found in some specimens until July (Webb, 1961). Cagle (1944c) reported that seven females, ranging in size from 21 to 22 cm, of a sample of 183 females had "senile ovaries." In spite of this statement reproductive senility has not been convincingly demonstrated in turtles (J. W. Gibbons, pers. comm.).

Courtship behavior in *T. scripta* is highly stereotyped and ritualized. A summary of courtship behaviors in subspecies found south of the Mexican border is provided by Lovich et al. (1990c). Courtship behavior is traditionally thought to occur in the spring and fall. Cagle (1950) observed that in Illinois *T. s. elegans* courtship activity peaks in May and September, but in Louisiana similar peaks occur in April and October, and in Kentucky, courtship lasts from March to early June (Ernst and Barbour, 1972). In northern Alabama, courtship may occur only in the spring (Lovich et al., 1990c). In South Carolina *T. s. scripta* courtship has been witnessed in October, December, and January, and copulation has been observed in December (Gibbons and Greene, 1990). Winter attempts at courtship by *T. s. elegans* have also been seen in north-central Texas (Lardie, 1980). Courtship is dissociated from male gametogenesis in the sense that gametogenesis occurs at a time other than the mating season (Brewer and Killebrew, 1986; Lovich et al., 1990b; Garstka et al., 1991).

Detailed descriptions of courtship behavior in *T. scripta* have been published by Cagle (1950), Carr (1952), Ernst and Barbour (1972), and Jackson and Davis (1972a). Courtship occurs in the water and begins with the male searching for a mate. When a female is found, the male begins trailing her and sniffing her cloaca. He then swims to the front of the female, turns to face her, and extends his forearms, soles outward. The female becomes stationary, and the male begins to vibrate (titillate) his elongated foreclaws along the side of her head near the eyes. She withdraws her head slightly and closes her eyes. After a variable length of time the male stops stroking her face and moves to her rear to mount. The female of *T. s. elegans* generally remains passive throughout the entire courtship sequence, slowly sinking to the bottom. A complete courtship bout is composed of the following actions: (1) extension and rotation of the male's forearms parallel to his neck, (2) movement of the male foreclaws over the female's eyes, (3) titillation of the foreclaws in proximity or contact with the female's head, (4) termination of step 3 with foreclaws maintained in position over the female's eyes, and (5) movement of the foreclaws away from the female's orbital region.

Similar courtship behavior and sequencing were reported by Lovich et al. (1990b) when male *T. s. scripta* (but not females) were implanted with various hormones in an attempt to stimulate courtship (Garstka et al., 1991). However, in sharp contrast to the behavior reported for *T. s. elegans*, female *T. s. scripta* were anything but passive. In fact, females courted males as often as males did the females. In several trials females titillated males while males remained passive. They were also observed nosing the cloacal region of males and actively trailing and orienting toward males. An unexpected observation was female blinking behavior involving closing the nictitating membrane, thus producing a white flash. As many as six blinks may occur per minute, but blinking was observed only when males were orienting near the female. Perhaps these female behaviors actively solicit male attention by communicating sexual readiness.

Three or four males may court the same female simultaneously. Males do not often fight while competing for the same mate, although larger males have an advantage over smaller ones (Cagle, 1950). In trials with hormonally implanted male slider turtles, Garstka et al. (1991) observed that melanistic males courted more frequently than did nonmelanistic males. Juvenile slider turtles may occasionally also court other small turtles (Cagle, 1955; Morris, 1976; Ernst, pers. obs.).

Copulation in *T. s. elegans* occurs after the male drops his tail and maneuvers the rear portion of his shell toward that of the female. The male then interlocks his tail with that of the female and intromission is effected when their cloacal vents are brought into close apposition. After attaining intromission the male withdraws his head and forelegs and drifts backwards until the pair essentially forms a right angle. During intromission the male makes occasional paddling motions, perhaps to maintain his posture. Separation occurs shortly after twitching of the tails, extension of the head and limbs by the male, and attempts by the male to swim to the surface (Davis and Jackson, 1970). While mating, male *T. s. scripta* form copulatory locks (Lovich, pers. obs.) that are strong enough to hold the pair together even when lifted out of the water with the female dangling from the male. Copulation may last as long as 15 minutes.

Sperm-storage tubules are present in a small region of the posterior portion of the egg albumen-secreting section of the oviduct between the infundibulum and the uterus. Sperm were identified in the oviducts of females isolated from males for an average of 79 days (Gist and Jones, 1987, 1989).

North of Mexico the nesting season generally occurs between April and July, with May and June the most important months (Cagle, 1950; Webb, 1961; Ernst and Barbour, 1972; Gibbons et al., 1982; Jackson, 1988a), but Ernst has observed a female *T. s. elegans* nest on 3 August in western Kentucky. At Ellenton Bay in South Carolina females nested in the following percentages during the nesting seasons between 1976 and 1987: April, 7%; May, 52%, June, 37%; and July, 4% (Gibbons and Greene, 1990). Not all adult females nest in a given year. The number of nesting females at Ellenton Bay was estimated to vary from a mean low of 27.2% to a mean high of 47.1% (Frazer et al., 1990b).

Most of what we know about nesting behavior of this species comes from Cagle (1950). The female selects an open, unshaded area where the soil is not muddy. Nests are often located on the nearest spot of land providing these conditions, but some females will move as far as 1.6 km from the water to find a suitable nest site. In Florida, females rarely move more than 180 m from water to nest (Carr, 1952). Barriers such as a highway or thick vegetation will cause a concentration of nesting activity on the water side. As in other species, female slider turtles often dig

several test holes. These holes usually contain rocks, roots, or other barriers. One female dug six different holes along a 15-m length of trail before completing a nest. In the vast swamps of Louisiana few suitable nest sites are available for slider turtles, and females may have to move several kilometers to find a nest site. Levees, drainage ditches, and railroad embankments are often the sites of concentrated nesting activity. Most nesting activity takes place in the early morning or late evening (Cagle, 1937).

The nest is excavated by the female with alternating scoops of her hind limbs. If the ground is hard the female releases fluid from the cloacal bladders to soften it. Once the initial entrance to the nest is excavated to a depth of 2.5–10.0 cm the female uses her hind feet to enlarge the cavity into a jug-shaped nest as much as 11.4 cm deep (Taylor, 1935). The actual shape of the nest varies as a function of soil type. In soft moist earth the nest is ovoid with an entrance about one quarter the diameter of the nest cavity. In hard soil the nest entrance is shallower and the nest cavity is spherical. The general overall appearance is flask shaped. The size of the nest varies with the size of the turtle (Carr, 1952). Nest excavation may last 26–187 minutes (Cagle, 1950).

The eggs are laid at intervals of about 40 seconds (Cahn, 1937). Following oviposition the female pushes loose soil into the nest, kneading it into place with the hind limbs and the rear portion of the plastron. Once again the female voids fluid from the cloacal bladders. This nest plug is usually not forced into the nest cavity and thus does not come in contact with the eggs. Eggs that are completely enclosed in the nest plug are often killed (Cagle, 1950). The mixture of wet soil and debris forming the nest plug has the appearance of a mud ball thrown against the ground.

Slider turtles in the United States lay 2–23 eggs per clutch (Cahn, 1937; Cagle, 1950; Carr, 1952; Webb, 1961; Iverson, 1977a; Gibbons and Greene, 1990), the actual number varying among populations (Gibbons, 1970c; Congdon and Gibbons, 1983) and as a function of body size. Gibbons (1982) and Gibbons et al. (1982) conducted long-term studies of slider turtle reproductive ecology in South Carolina. Mean clutch size (6.1 eggs) did not vary significantly among years once the effect of body size was removed. Monthly variation in clutch size was as follows: April, 8.9 eggs; May, 5.7 eggs; June, 6.0 eggs. Clutch size in individual slider turtles may vary as much as 86%, or remain the same from year to year. Variation in the year-to-year clutch size of individual turtles is significantly less than the within-population variation. Mean clutch sizes in a Florida population and two South Carolina populations were 10.6, 6.9, and 11.2 eggs, respectively (Jackson, 1988a).

Clutch size is positively correlated with both plastron length and weight, but not with age (Gibbons, 1982; Gibbons et al., 1982; Jackson, 1988a). Egg wet mass, the logarithm of clutch wet mass, and egg width are also positively correlated with plastron length, but egg length is not. Clutch size and egg wet mass are not significantly correlated. When the effect of body size is removed, mean clutch size, egg wet mass, and the logarithm of clutch mass are similar between populations of females experiencing rapid growth and large adult body size, and populations that experience slower growth and smaller adult body size. This suggests that the proportional investment per egg or clutch remains relatively constant under differing environmental conditions (Congdon and Gibbons, 1983; 1985). Clutch mass is about 5.1% of body mass (Congdon and Gibbons, 1985).

Egg width is not constrained by the width of the pelvic opening in *T. s. scripta* from South Carolina (Congdon and Gibbons, 1987). Instead, egg width remains relatively constant as pelvic opening width increases. This relationship supports the optimal egg size theory which predicts that egg size is optimized at the point where increased fitness associated with increased egg size is equal to a decrease in fitness caused by a reduction in egg number.

As many as five clutches may be deposited by an individual in a single year (Jackson, 1988a). Research in South Carolina indicates that the mean plastron length of females laying a single clutch per year does not differ significantly from the plastron length of those that lay more than one clutch per year. Individual clutch size varies within a year; some turtles lay the same number of eggs in the second clutch and others lay more or less. The timing between the first and second clutches ranges from 12 to 36 days. Since mean population-specific clutch size does not vary appreciably from year to year, clutch frequency has an important influence on variation in annual reproductive output (Gibbons, 1982; Gibbons et al., 1982; Congdon and Gibbons, 1990). Fewer females lay eggs in drought years than in normal years (Gibbons et al., 1983).

The ovoid eggs of sliders north of Mexico are 30.9–43.0 mm long, 19.4–25.6 mm wide (length:width ratio, 1.48–1.70), and weigh 6.1–15.4 g. The eggs are 72.2–74.4% water. Eggshell dry mass is 18.0–18.8% of the total egg mass, and yolk dry mass ranges from 2.35 to 2.78 g (Cagle, 1944c; Iverson, 1977a; Jackson, 1988a; Congdon and Gibbons, 1990). The eggshell is composed of 39.3% ash or inorganic components (Lamb and Congdon, 1985). Nonpolar lipid dry mass is composed of about 24.8% of total egg mass, and 30.4% of yolk mass. Figures for polar and nonpolar lipids are 33.4% and 40.7%, respectively. Egg lean dry mass for polar and nonpolar lipids is 1.64 g and 1.77 g, respectively. The underlying membrane fibers are physically modified to form saucer-shaped nucleation sites which dictate the orientation of crystal growth (Solomon and Reid, 1983). The mammillary layer projects above the surface of the membrane fibers and supports the layer of individual aragonite units which are covered with a cuticle. Pores are not present, but the arrangement of the aragonite units is such as to leave spaces through which gases can diffuse. The eggshell is relatively thin. Its outer layer is composed of multishaped structural units of aragonite crystals bordered by grooves that allow for expansion as the egg becomes turgid during development (Acuña-Mesén, 1989b).

Nests provide a stable thermal environment for egg development; the air in a nest cavity in Tennessee had a maximum temperature fluctuation of 8°C (Cagle, 1937). Late afternoon temperatures measured in Louisiana nests ranged from 22 to 25°C (Cagle, 1950). Average incubation time of eggs maintained under laboratory conditions varies according to temperature as follows: below 25°C, 112.5 days; 25–25.5°C, 93.0–100.9 days, 25–30°C, 68.9 days; 29.5–30°C, 58.7–69.0 days. Under field conditions the eggs hatch in 60–80 days (Ewert, 1979a). A single clutch of eggs in Florida hatched on 26 August after 88 days of incubation (Jackson, 1988a). Incubation in the laboratory may last 64–91 days (Cagle, 1950; Lardie, 1976; Iverson, 1977a).

Under laboratory conditions atmospheric gas concentration also affects incubation period. Total incubation time lengthens at low, but survivable, oxygen concentrations (Etchberger et al., 1991) and high carbon dioxide concentrations (Etchberger et al., 1992).

Eggs hatch in the late summer or early fall, although hatchlings in some populations overwinter in the nest, emerging the following spring (Cagle, 1944a; Gibbons and Nelson, 1978). In Louisiana, hatching has been observed from July to September. Prior to hatching some of the hardened calcareous layer of the egg falls away. While hatching, the eggs usually split along the end as the hatchling cuts through the shell and embryonic membranes with the egg tooth and the front legs. Twenty four to 106 hours may elapse before all the young in a clutch break the eggs. Hatchlings generally remain in the

Hatching *Trachemys scripta elegans*

broken eggshell for several days until the yolk sac is absorbed (Jackson, 1988a). The yolk mass is 1–3 cm in diameter and weighs 0.2–1.9 g (mean 0.8 g). Yolk absorption takes about five days under laboratory conditions. During this period the neonate turtle undergoes dramatic changes in shape. When first hatched the marginal scutes are bent downward and there is a deep fold across the plastron. As the yolk is absorbed the carapace lengthens and widens relative to carapace height (Cagle, 1950).

Hatchlings have carapaces 25.4–35.8 mm long, 25.4–34.2 mm wide, 13.5–18.4 mm deep. Their plastra are 15.3–35.5 mm long, and they weigh 4.4–10 g (Cagle, 1950).

The hatchling body is composed of about 24.5% lipids, and its weight is about 77% that of a freshly laid egg (Ewert, 1979a). Substrate moisture affects the size and weight of hatchlings with larger and heavier hatchlings produced under moist laboratory incubation conditions (Congdon and Gibbons, 1990). The yolk scar is visible on the hatchlings for the first few months of life and the egg tooth is present for a few days after the hatchlings enter the water.

Hatchling *T. s. elegans* from Louisiana can withstand freezing of extracellular body fluids for up to four hours at temperatures as low as −4°C (Churchill and Storey, 1992). At −2.5°C only 50% of an experimental group survived after six hours, but none survived after 24 hours of exposure when body ice content reached 54.7%. All recovered after four hours of exposure to −4°C after attaining a mean body ice content of 49.6%, and a few survived eight hours of

exposure and a mean body ice content of 64.5%. Overall, the ability to synthesize cryoprotectants, or natural antifreezes, seems poorly developed.

As in most emydid turtles, the sex of *T. scripta* is determined by incubation temperature (Paukstis and Janzen, 1990; Ewert and Nelson, 1991; Janzen and Paukstis, 1991). Eggs incubated at 22.5, 25, or 27°C produce 100% males but those incubated at 30°C produce only females (Ewert and Nelson, 1991). Sex determination is sensitive over a range of embryonic stages beginning prior to stage 16 and extending to stages 19–20. The effect of female-producing temperatures occurs at an earlier stage than the effect of male-producing temperatures. Embryos must experience a given temperature for the duration of several developmental stages before the effects become irreversible, but certain temperatures have a more potent effect on sex determination than others. Although temperature exerts an "all or none" effect on gonadal differentiation, the length of ovaries is affected in a graded fashion (Wibbels et al., 1991a). Injection of estrogen into eggs incubated at the male-producing temperature of 26°C causes dose-dependent feminization of hatchlings (Crews et al., 1991); however, other hormones are unable to induce male sex determination at a female-producing temperature (Wibbels and Crews, 1992). Sex determination is not influenced by oxygen concentrations (Etchberger et al., 1991), but is altered in favor of females by elevated carbon dioxide concentrations (Etchberger et al., 1992).

Genome size, a heritable genetic character that

varies within and among populations of *T. scripta* and is correlated with nuclear volume, cell volume, and the duration of mitotic and meiotic cycles, is not measurably affected by different incubation temperatures (Lockwood et al., 1991).

GROWTH AND LONGEVITY: Growth models for the slider turtle show that female asymptotic plastron length is greater than that of males. Both sexes grow at similar rates as juveniles until males attain sexual maturity. Females continue to grow at the juvenile rate until attaining maturity at some time later than males. Individuals in populations inhabiting areas of enhanced productivity have higher growth rates than those in populations in areas with lower productivity (Gibbons et al., 1981; Gibbons and Lovich, 1990; Dunham and Gibbons, 1990).

Laboratory growth studies, which began with unfed eight-week-old hatchlings subsequently kept under constant controlled conditions for over two years, were conducted by Sarnat et al. (1981). During the test, the increase in mean carapace length was from 32.5 mm to 75.2 mm, the mean increase in plastron length was from 30.8 mm to 68.3 mm, and mean weights increased from 6.9 g to 80.6 g. As the sliders aged the growth slowed, but no seasonal differences in growth rates were noted between the summer and winter periods as would normally occur in wild populations.

Cagle (1950) reported that, ordinarily, individuals 2.0–3.5 cm in length are hatchlings, those 3.5–5.5 cm are in their first season of growth, and those 5.5–6.5 cm are in their second season. Under excellent growing conditions an individual may attain a size greater than 5.5 cm in one growing season. Estimated growth in Illinois hatchling *T. s. elegans* ranged from 18 to 46 mm (mean, 30 mm) in their first season, an average of doubling their growth in this short interval of time (Cagle, 1948b). In Virginia *T. s. scripta,* average annual growth rate between ages one and six was 13.1 mm (Mitchell and Pague, 1990). Webb (1961) estimated the growth of Oklahoma *T. s. elegans* based on changes in scute annuli width. At the end of the first growing season seven males had plastron lengths of 4.1–6.3 cm (mean 5.4) and 18 females were 4.2–7.8 cm (mean 6.2) long. At the end of the second growing season six males were 6.0–8.3 cm (mean 7.1) and 12 females were 6.2–11.3 cm (mean 9.1). After the third season of growth four males were 7.4–10.9 cm (mean 8.9) and seven females were 8.0–14.0 cm (mean 11.4). Three females had grown to 12.9–17.6 cm (mean 14.5) in

their fourth growing season. For additional data on growth in this species examine the excellent papers by Cagle (1946, 1948b).

Growth curves based on animals of known age were compared to a growth model based on Faben's method of estimating increases in length when ages are not known. The utility of Faben's method has been confirmed by Frazer et al. (1990a), although accurate estimates of growth parameters may require data on large individuals.

Shape of the carapace outline becomes asymmetrical as juvenile *T. scripta* grow (Lestrel et al., 1989), but differences are not always visually obvious, underscoring the need for precise shape descriptors in the analysis of shell shape.

Due to differential growth rates, the weight of several brain regions varies between male and female *T. scripta* (Quay, 1972). Male cerebral weights, in particular, are greater than those of females of the same size and weight.

Body growth in *T. scripta* is dependent on thyroid activity (Denver and Licht, 1988, 1991; Stamper et al., 1990). Growth of thyroidectomized hatchlings is significantly reduced six to eight weeks after surgery. Growth hormone alone, however, may directly control growth, despite how much food is eaten by a juvenile (Brown et al., 1974).

Light intensity has little effect on hatchling growth rate, according to studies conducted by Chou and Venugopal (1982). Hatchlings subjected to 12-hour daily light-intensity treatments ranging from 1,000 to 5,000 lux grew at similar rates.

One of the most unusual experiments conducted on *T. scripta* examined the effect of high gravity on growth of juveniles. Turtles were placed in a centrifuge and spun to simulate 5–28 gravity forces (*g*'s) for five to nine weeks by Dodge and Wunder (1963). Continuous lighting and a temperature of 27°C were maintained throughout the experiment. Turtles were removed from the centrifuge for 20 minutes each day for feeding and cage cleaning. Experimental turtles grew approximately twice as fast as controls at 5 *g*'s during five weeks of exposure. At 6 *g*'s growth of control and experimental turtles was the same, and at higher simulated gravitational fields the experimental animals grew at a slower rate than controls. The relative shell mass of turtles exposed to 5 *g*'s was greater than that of controls suggesting that mechanical forces acting on a skeletal structure will enhance the growth of the stressed portion.

A captive *T. s. elegans* lived for 37 years, 9 months, and 10 days (Snider and Bowler, 1992).

FOOD HABITS: North American slider turtles are opportunistic omnivores subsisting on a catholic diet of various plant and animal foods. Recorded foods are: algae—*Cladophora, Oscillatoria, Spirogyra;* vascular plants—*Azolla, Bacopa, Brasenia, Cabomba, Caltha, Celtis, Ceratophyllum, Cornus, Egeria, Eichhornia, Lemna, Limnobium, Lippia, Myriophyllum, Najas, Nymphaea, Nyssa, Persicaria, Piaropus, Potamogeton, Sagittaria, Spirodela, Taxodium, Utricularia, Wolffia;* sponges; snails (Physidae); clams; bryozoans; cladocerans; ostracods; isopods; amphipods; crayfish; shrimp; spiders; insects (adults and larvae)—crickets, grasshoppers, beetles, flies, bumblebees, fire ants, diving hemipterans (true bugs), dragonflies, mayflies, homopterans, lepidopterans, trichopterans; fish—*Lepomis, Notropis, Perca, Umbra;* frogs (eggs, tadpoles, adults); turtle scutes; and snakes (*Nerodia*) (Cahn, 1937; Carr, 1952; Ferguson, 1962; Ernst and Barbour, 1972; Hart, 1983; Parmenter and Avery, 1990). Carrion is sometimes eaten (Ernst, pers. obs.). Captives readily consume commercial trout chow, fresh and canned fish, raw beef and chicken, canned dog food, earthworms, newborn mice, bananas, watermelon, cantaloupe, romaine lettuce, and various other green vegetables.

The food preferences of *Trachemys scripta* change with age (Clark and Gibbons, 1969; Ernst and Barbour, 1972; Hart, 1983). Juveniles are highly carnivorous, but as they become older they eat progressively larger quantities of vegetable matter. In South Carolina, carnivory by *T. s. scripta* continues into the second year, but decreases during the first year of growth (Clark and Gibbons, 1969). The percent animal material dry weight in the digestive tract declines to between 0 and 10% at a plastron length of about 4.0–6.0 cm. There is a positive relationship between shell calcium content and turtle plastron length, so juveniles have relatively less calcium in their shell than adults. The calcium-rich diet of juveniles seems to be a strategy for hardening the shell (Clark and Gibbons, 1969). Adults prefer animal food when it is available (Clark and Gibbons, 1969; Parmenter and Avery, 1990). Louisiana juvenile *T. s. elegans* prey predominantly on insects (mostly hemipterans and dragonfly nymphs), but shift gradually to plants (mostly waterweeds and duckweed) with increasing plastron length (Hart, 1983). This dietary shift parallels a habitat shift from foraging sites in shallow water (mean 81 cm) to others in deeper water (mean 95.5 cm). The shift in Louisiana is more gradual than that reported in sliders from South Carolina (Clark and Gibbons, 1969).

Mahmoud and Lavenda (1969) found that hatchling *T. s. elegans* established preferences for the initial diet fed them, but these preferences were not long lasting.

Webb (1961) thought its omnivorous habits allowed *T. scripta* to thrive in places subject to an alternating availability of different foods because of fluctuating water levels.

Thermal conditions and diet quality affect the behavior and bioenergetics of *T. scripta*, and ultimately its life history pattern (Spotila et al., 1989). Water temperature has a profound effect on the feeding behavior of the slider and other turtles. Enhanced growth rates and large body sizes of *T. s. scripta* in Par Pond, a thermally impacted reservoir in South Carolina, can be attributed to differences in diet quality and elevated water temperatures (Parmenter, 1980). Stomach flushing shows that sliders in Par Pond eat twice as much protein (mostly in the form of fish) as those in nearby natural bodies of water, but fish (except *Gambusia*) are absent in Ellenton Bay, the other major aquatic habitat studied. The elevated water temperature in Par Pond increases rates of ingestion, and extends the turtles' growing season. Ingestion is at a maximum at 29°C, decreasing at higher or lower temperatures.

A water temperature of about 18°C is required for feeding, and consequently growth, to begin in the spring. *Trachemys s. elegans* in north-central Texas feed from early March to early November, a maximum growth period of 248 days (Lardie, 1980), while in northeastern Missouri the feeding/growing period for this subspecies only lasts from May to early September (Kofron and Schreiber, 1987). In the thermally impacted reservoir in South Carolina mentioned above, *T. s. scripta* feed even in the winter. Out of 22 turtles captured in winter by Schubauer and Parmenter (1981), 17 had food in their stomachs; however, they concluded that the feeding behavior observed was not directly linked to the heated effluent coming into the reservoir. All turtles were collected in nonthermally impacted areas and as slider turtles in Par Pond were known to remain in resident areas there is little chance that they moved into thermally altered areas to feed.

Sliders forage during the day, preferring to patrol areas with shallow water (<3 m) and a profusion of aquatic vegetation, if available. Juveniles frequent shallower waters than do adults (Hart, 1983). Hatchlings begin foraging soon after emergence from the nest. The digestive systems of Illinois hatchlings contained food even though they still had yolk reserves (Cagle, 1946). While foraging, *T. scripta* swims slowly, periodically poking its head into clumps of vegetation, perhaps in an attempt to flush out hidden prey. It is attracted to prey movements and will pursue small fish, tadpoles, and frogs. Once captured, prey are swallowed whole if small, or ripped apart with the jaws and foreclaws. Prey detection is primarily visual, but olfactory cues are also important (Parmenter and Avery, 1990). Auth (1975) observed that *T. s. scripta* in Florida sometimes skim the surface of the water with their mouth open feeding on duckweed.

Avery et al. (1993) examined the effects of dietary protein level and ambient temperature on growth rates, food consumption rates, digestion rates, and digestive efficiencies of juvenile slider turtles. Growth of both the plastron and carapace and body mass are significantly greater in turtles eating 25% and 40% crude protein diets than those ingesting 10% crude protein (in this latter group plastron length and body mass actually decreased with time). Food ingestion rates increase with increasing ambient temperature, confirming the conclusions of Parmenter (1980). Increasing crude protein in the diet also causes an increase in ingestion rates. Digestive efficiency is highest at 15°C (99.5%) and decreases at higher temperatures (95.8% at 34°C). Protein concentration has no detectable effect on digestive efficiency.

The digestive turnover rate for *T. s. scripta* fed bologna in the laboratory at 25°C was 61 hours, and body size and digestive turnover rate were not correlated at this temperature (Parmenter, 1981). Bjorndal (1991) examined the potential for non-additive interactions among ingested food items. *Trachemys scripta* were fed one of three diets of duckweed, insect larvae, or duckweed and insect larvae mixed. Diet had a significant effect on digestibility and intake, but not on digestive turnover time. A significant nonadditive interaction was seen in the mixed diet. All food components, except lipids, experienced significantly greater digestive efficiencies in the mixed diet than those predicted from the digestive efficiencies for duckweed or larvae diets alone. The presence of larvae in the mixed diet probably improved digestive processing by providing greater numbers or diversity of cellulolytic microorganisms. Duckweed provided about 70% more energy and 20% more nitrogen to the turtle when ingested with the larvae than when ingested alone.

Slider turtles may prefer foods of certain colors over others. When offered a choice of white (uncolored), yellow, red, green, or blue fish chunks a captive showed a statistically significant preference for the lighter colors (white and yellow). Yellow was preferred over white. On some occasions the turtle would ignore all blue pieces offered and then immediately consume all white and yellow pieces placed in the tank (Humphreys and Mallory, 1977). When given a choice of several compartments lighted with different colors, *T. scripta* chose the yellow compartment in 57% and the blue compartment in only 14% of the trials (Ernst and Hamilton, 1969).

Young captive sliders often steal food from the mouth or claws of feeding conspecifics, with the frequency of kleptoparasitism being inversely related to the amount of food in the tank. Unlike other species of turtles, other aggressive behaviors rarely occur during feeding (Hayes, 1987).

PREDATORS AND DEFENSE: Alligators (*Alligator*), gars (*Lepisosteus*), crows (*Corvus*), mink (*Mustela vison*), raccoons (*Procyon lotor*), otters (*Lutra canadensis*), and coyotes (*Canis latrans*) (Minckley, 1966) are natural predators of North American adult sliders. Juveniles are eaten by fish (*Ictalurus;* Mather, 1982), frogs, snakes, carnivorous turtles, large wading birds, and various mammals (Cagle, 1950), including the rice rat (*Oryzomys palustris;* Goodpaster and Hoffmeister, 1952). Nests are frequently robbed by skunks (*Mephitis, Spilogale*) and raccoons (Cagle, 1949), and ants, fly maggots, and molds attack the eggs. Turkowski (1972) reported that a stem of grass (*Andropogon*) actually grew completely through a hatchling in a Virginia nest.

Under experimental conditions largemouth bass (*Micropterus salmoides*) did not eat live hatchling sliders. Turtles were ingested but then quickly spit out and ignored by the fish. In contrast, dead hatchlings with the margin of the carapace removed were usually eaten. These results suggest that either the behavior of live hatchlings or the architecture of their carapace rim inhibits predation by largemouth bass (Semlitsch and Gibbons, 1989).

Humans are the greatest enemy of *T. scripta*. Every year untold numbers of adults are shot while basking, beheaded after being hooked by uninformed fishermen, crushed as they wander across highways, or sacrificed for research and teaching, or lost to the pet and food industries.

Slider turtles can be aggressive and will often bite, scratch, or void bladder water when handled. Defensive postures are reviewed by Hayes (1989).

POPULATIONS: *Trachemys scripta* is an abundant turtle in most of its natural range in the United States. Cagle (1950) reported that in southern Illinois and Louisiana the slider turtle constituted 71–87% of the total turtle population. In Kentucky they constituted 75% of the turtles trapped by Ernst and Barbour (1972). Population density of *T. scripta* may sometimes be high. Brown and Haver (1952) found 81 *T. s. elegans* in a 3.6 × 0.6 m road culvert in Brazoria County, Texas, and Ingold et al. (1986) reported a density of approximately 28/ha in a small Texas pond. Ernst once trapped 61 *T. s. elegans* in an approximately one-hectare farm pond in central Kentucky, and did not capture all those present.

The size class distribution in a population of *T. scripta* varies according to environmental quality, predatory pressures, and many other variables. *Trachemys s. scripta* in thermally enhanced environments and Atlantic barrier islands are characterized by large body size (Gibbons et al., 1979b). Changes in the population structure of Mississippi *T. scripta* populations are reviewed by Parker (1984, 1990).

The biomass of slider turtle populations in the United States ranges from 40.6 kg/ha at a density of 88 turtles per hectare to 877.3 kg/ha at a density of 353/ha (Iverson, 1982a; Congdon et al., 1986). Total annual biomass production at Ellenton Bay, South Carolina, was estimated at 5.2 kg/ha/yr (4.4 kg/ha/yr for body mass and 0.8 kg/ha/yr for eggs). The energy equivalent for eggs produced at Ellenton Bay is estimated at 4862 kJ^{-1} (Congdon et al., 1986; Congdon and Gibbons, 1989).

The adult sex ratio of natural populations of the slider turtle is influenced by four demographic factors including hatchling sex ratios, differential mortality of the sexes, differential immigration and emigration of the sexes, and differences in age at maturity of the sexes (Gibbons, 1990b). Sampling biases can result from many causes and must be eliminated before a meaningful interpretation of sex ratio can be reached (Gibbons, 1970d, 1990b). In most well-studied populations, males outnumber females. Gibbons (1990b) attributed this to the fact that males mature at an earlier age than females in the same population. He concluded that in species in which males usually mature earlier then females, a male-biased sex ratio is expected, and could be considered a characteristic of the species. Other factors may also alter the sex ratio of a turtle population (see Lovich and Gibbons, 1990).

Frazer et al. (1990b) constructed a life table for the population of *T. s. scripta* in Ellenton Bay, South Carolina. They showed that the population was declining at an annual rate of 15% if both death and emigration are combined to calculate age-specific survivorship. The net reproductive rate was 0.137, with a realized intrinsic rate of increase of −0.1675.

The results of the exercise demonstrate that few if any sliders in the population live long enough to leave the nest, and of those that do, most die during their first or second year of life.

Data based on a 13-year mark recapture study in South Carolina indicate that approximately 10% of a population attains an age of 10 years and 1% can be expected to attain an age of 20 years (Gibbons, 1987). Maximum longevity in natural populations is about 30 years. Survivorship is approximated by a Type II survivorship curve with a constant rate of mortality at all ages (Gibbons and Semlitsch, 1982). Annual survivorship of turtles one to three years old ranges from 53.9 to 82.9% (Frazer et al., 1990b). Annual survivorship of males and females more than four years old is 84.4% and 81.4%, respectively (Frazer et al., 1990b).

REMARKS: Environmental contamination is a problem faced by all turtle populations. Some populations of *T. s. scripta* on the Savannah River Site in South Carolina are exposed to radioactive contaminants. The uptake of radionuclides by *T. scripta* is proportional to exposure time (Morreale et al., 1984; Brisbin et al., 1990; Gibbons et al., 1990). ^{137}Cesium retention by soft tissues (as a potassium analogue) is related to metabolic rate. ^{90}Strontium is deposited in calcareous skeletal tissue (as a calcium analogue). The absorption of these and other radionuclides by the turtles is higher than that previously reported for other organisms and differed significantly among isotopes (Hinton et al., 1992). High absorption rates were observed in juveniles and adults. Elimination rates were not affected by dietary differences, sex, or isotopic differences, but did vary among seasons. The greatest rate of elimination occurred in the summer and then declined to essentially zero during the winter (Scott et al., 1986; Hinton et al., 1992). Radiocesium elimination rates were positively exponentially related to turtle body mass (Peters and Brisbin, 1988). The biological half-lives of cesium and strontium in slider turtles are 64 and 365 days, respectively (Scott et al., 1986). Additional information on the radioecology of turtles is reviewed by Hinton and Scott (1990).

Slider turtles exposed to radioactive contaminants on the Savannah River Site have significantly greater variation in DNA content in blood cells than individuals from control populations. Variation increases as a function of plastron length and estimated age of turtles (Bickham et al., 1988; Lamb et al., 1991). The authors concluded that radiation or some unknown chemical contaminant in the habitat caused chromosomal rearrangements leading to deletions and duplications that increased DNA content variation in blood cells.

Pesticide poisoning is another environmental problem faced by *T. scripta* (Hall, 1980). Residues of the insecticides endrin, heptachlor, and mirex have been detected in the bodies and eggs of sliders (Rosene et al., 1961; Rosato and Ferguson, 1968; Holcomb and Parker, 1979).

Hatchlings of *T. scripta* were once the most popular turtle item in the pet trade, and an estimated 5–10 million turtles were exported annually around the world. Few survived the inadequate care to which they are so often subjected. Turtle farms were established in the southeastern United States (mostly in Louisiana) in response to declining wild stocks. By 1960 more than 150 farms were operating. Unfortunately these farms were not self sufficient and over 9,000 adults were taken from the wild each year to maintain breeding stocks, seriously depleting natural populations in some areas (Feehan, 1986; Warwick, 1986; Warwick et al., 1990). In 1975 the U.S. Food and Drug Administration banned the sale of turtles under "4 inches" (10 cm) carapace length in the United States and Canada because they transmitted the disease salmonellosis caused by the bacteria of the genera *Salmonella* and *Arizona* (Kennedy, 1969;

DuPonte et al., 1978; Shane et al., 1990). The turtle pet trade industry has continued to export large numbers of hatchlings and adults to other countries using various techniques to limit exposure to *Salmonella*. The use of the antibiotic gentamicin has led to the development of many antibiotic-resistant strains of *Salmonella* (D'Aoust et al., 1990). An estimated three to four million turtles continue to be exported to countries including Japan, France, Italy, Hong Kong, Spain, England, Belgium, Germany, Mexico, and the Netherlands, thus providing an important potential route for global dissemination of human salmonellosis (Gangarosa, 1985; Tauxe et al., 1985; D'Aoust et al., 1990).

Trachemys scripta has been the focus of several excellent life history studies and reviews (Cagle, 1950; Moll and Legler, 1971), the most recent being that of Gibbons (1990a) which contains 24 chapters on systematics, taxonomy, evolution, ecology, physiology, and parasitology. The reader is referred to these sources for information beyond that presented in this book. The complex taxonomic history and relationships of this species are discussed by McDowell (1964), Holman (1977a), Ernst and Ernst (1980), Vogt and McCoy (1980), Ward (1984), Obst (1985), Seidel and Smith (1986), Ernst and Barbour (1989), Ernst (1990b), and Legler (1990).

Trachemys gaigeae (Hartweg, 1939)
Big Bend slider
PLATE 32

RECOGNITION: This poorly studied aquatic turtle reaches a carapace length of 22.2 cm. Its oval, weakly keeled carapace has a slightly serrated posterior rim, and is light olive-brown with a reticulate pattern of curved orange lines, commonly surrounding small ocelli, on the pleurals and vertebrals. Each marginal has a single, curved, orange bar and a dark-bordered ocellus at its lower, posterior corner. Melanism may develop with age (Hartweg, 1939; Lovich et al., 1990c). The undersides of the marginals have large dark-bordered ocelli at the seams, and the bridge is patterned with narrow, transverse dark lines. The hingeless plastron is cream to orange or light olive, commonly with a large, dark, central figure formed by a series of elongated narrow lines that may spread laterally along the transverse seams. This central figure is commonly continuous from the gulars to the anals. The skin is light olive to orange-brown; the forelegs are striped with yellow, and the hind quarters are vertically striped. An oval, black-bordered, red to orange spot lies behind and well separated from the orbit. The chin is medially striped, with the lateral stripes shortened to ovals that are almost ocelli. The upper jaw is slightly notched, and the toes are webbed.

Males are usually smaller and less domed than females and have long, thick tails with the vent beyond the carapacial rim, and slightly concave plastra. Mature males do not have the elongated foreclaws found in male *T. scripta* from the United States.

KARYOTYPE: Unknown.

FOSSIL RECORD: Unknown.

DISTRIBUTION: *Trachemys gaigeae* is found in the Rio Grande River, from the Big Bend upstream at least to Bosque del Apache Refuge, New Mexico, and the Rio Conchos drainages of western Texas, New Mexico, Chihuahua, and Coahuila.

GEOGRAPHIC VARIATION: Unknown. This turtle was formerly considered a subspecies of *Trachemys scripta;* for an extensive taxonomic review, see Ernst (1992a).

CONFUSING SPECIES: In the United States, *Trachemys scripta* has an elongated yellow, orange, or red postorbital stripe that touches the orbit. *Pseudemys gorzugi* lacks the orange, black-bordered spot behind the eye, and has only a simple seam-following plastral pattern. *Pseudemys texana* has a red-tinged plastral rim.

HABITAT: In Texas, this species is found in scattered pools, often bordered by sand or gravel bars, and sloughs in the Rio Grande. Presumably *T. gaigeae* wanders from pool to pool as they dry in summer, but it seldom moves inland away from the river channel. Some also live in cattle ponds and tanks adjacent to the Rio Grande, and Axtel (1959) thought lack of permanent water has restricted eastward extension from the Rio Grande. The Big Bend slider has also been reported from the large, open Elephant Butte Reservoir, New Mexico (Degenhardt and Christiansen, 1974).

REMARKS: Only one publication discusses life history data of *T. gaigeae*. Legler (1960b) opened several stomachs and found only aquatic vegetation (but captives we have kept readily accepted fish). Few were observed basking, but there was a paucity of out-of-water objects at the site trapped by Legler; however, some were seen aquatic basking at the surface of the water, particularly in the morning and late afternoon. Sexually mature females were at least 16.9 cm, and four contained 6–11 oviducal eggs on

Male *Trachemys gaigeae*

Plastron of *Trachemys gaigeae*

Female *Trachemys gaigeae*

Head of *Trachemys gaigeae*

Distribution of *Trachemys gaigeae*

26 June. Eleven males thought to be mature were at least 11.5 cm long, and another 10.3-cm male showed development of some sexually dimorphic characters, so Legler concluded that most males attain sexual maturity at carapace lengths of 10.5–11.5 cm.

The male courtship of this species does not involve stroking the female's face with elongate foreclaws as in *T. scripta;* the male chases the female from the rear, possibly biting her tail and hind quarters (Ernst, pers. obs.).

Additional ecological and behavioral studies of *T. gaigeae* would be rewarding. A review of the literature regarding this species is in Ernst (1992a).

Pseudemys concinna (Le Conte, 1830)
River cooter

PLATE 33

RECOGNITION: This large (carapace to 43.7 cm, Pritchard, 1980b) freshwater turtle has a backward-facing C-shaped light mark on the second pleural and a patterned plastron. Its oval to elongated, narrow, flattened carapace (the low juvenile keel disappears with age) is highest at the middle, slightly serrated posteriorly, and brown with yellow to cream-colored markings; some carapaces are restricted in the region of the sixth marginals. Dorsally each marginal has a dark area, commonly in the form of two concentric circles, and some individuals have a light bar on each marginal. The ventral surface of each marginal has a dark light-centered spot bordering the seams. Many older turtles become melanistic, or their carapace may be covered with a dark stain which obliterates the light pattern. The bridge has one or two dark bars that extend onto the inguinal scute. The hingeless, yellow to orange plastron has a dark, seam-following pattern that may contain posteriorly facing swirls and may be present only on the anterior half. This pattern commonly resembles an X and fades with age. The skin is olive to brown, with yellow or cream stripes. On the head the narrow supratemporal and paramedial stripes lie parallel, and the sagittal stripe passes anteriorly between the eyes but does not meet the supratemporals. Head stripes may be indistinct in old turtles. Wide yellow stripes occur on the underside of the neck; the central chin stripe extends posteriorly and divides to form a Y-shaped mark. The outer rim of the lower jaw is adorned with many small denticulations, and the upper jaw has a shallow medial notch that is never flanked by toothlike cusps.

Adult males have elongated, straight foreclaws, and long thick tails with the anal vent positioned behind the carapacial rim. Females are larger and more domed than males (Buhlmann and Vaughan, 1991).

KARYOTYPE: Diploid chromosomes total 50: 26 macrochromosomes (16 metacentric, 6 submeta-centric, 4 telocentric) and 24 microchromosomes (Killebrew, 1977a).

FOSSIL RECORD: Pleistocene (Rancholabrean) remains of Pseudemys concinna have been found at Ladds Quarry, Bartow County, Georgia (Holman, 1967, 1985a,b) and Bell Cave, Colbert County, Alabama (Holman et al., 1990). Jackson (1976) thought the Florida Pliocene species, Chrysemys caelata, may be ancestral to P. concinna; the Pleistocene species Chrysemys (?Pseudemys) hibbardi resembles the river cooter (Holman, 1991).

DISTRIBUTION: Pseudemys concinna ranges along the Piedmont and the Atlantic and Gulf coastal plains from southern Virginia southward to those western Florida watersheds flowing into the Gulf of Mexico between Gulf and Hillsborough counties and westward to eastern Texas; inland in the Mississippi Valley to southern Indiana and Illinois (see Moll and Morris, 1991, for a report on the status of Illinois populations), southern Missouri, southeastern Kansas, and Oklahoma. The distribution of P. concinna in the Atlantic coastal states is almost entirely above the fall line (Seidel and Palmer, 1991). Isolated populations occur in the New (Bayless, 1972; Seidel, 1981; Buhlmann and Vaughan, 1991) and Ohio (Seidel and Green, 1982) rivers in West Virginia, and the Tennessee River watershed of eastern Kentucky and Tennessee.

GEOGRAPHIC VARIATION: We recognize five subspecies. Pseudemys concinna concinna (Le Conte, 1830), the eastern river cooter, ranges from Virginia to eastern Alabama in the streams of the Piedmont and the Atlantic Coastal Plain. Its markings are essentially as described above. Pseudemys c. suwanniensis Carr, 1937, the Suwannee River cooter, is found in western Florida rivers draining into the Gulf

A backward-facing C-shaped
mark on the second pleural
scute is characteristic of
Pseudemys concinna

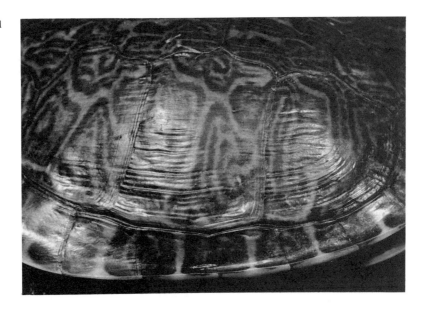

Pseudemys concinna concinna

of Mexico between Gulf and Hillsborough counties. Its range seems allopatric from other subspecies of *P. concinna*, and, because this apparently prevents inter-breeding with other populations of *P. concinna*, Collins (1991) has suggested that *P. c. suwanniensis* be elevated to full specific status. This turtle lacks stripes on the outer surface of its hind feet. The head stripes are yellow, and the plastron is yellow or orange, with a well-defined pattern. Older individuals may become almost totally black, and females may grow to over 40 cm in carapace length. *Pseudemys c. mobilensis* (Holbrook, 1838), the Mobile Bay cooter, occurs in the Gulf watersheds from the Florida Panhandle to extreme southeastern Texas. It is similar to the Suwannee River cooter but is paler, smaller, and has orange to red head stripes. Ward (1984) considered this race to be invalid and included these individuals, along with eastern examples of the taxon *P. floridana hoyi* (Agassiz, 1857), in *P. c. hieroglyphica*. We feel this combination wrong, and agree with Dundee and Rossman (1989) that *P. c. mobilensis* is a valid sub-species. *Pseudemys c. heiroglyphica* (Holbrook, 1836), the hieroglyphic river cooter, ranges from southern Indiana and Illinois southward in the Mississippi

Plastron of *Pseudemys concinna hieroglyphica*

Pseudemys concinna hieroglyphica

Valley to Mississippi and Louisiana and eastward through Alabama and the panhandle of Florida to western Georgia. The plastral pattern is usually not well developed, and the shell may be indented at the bridge. The light marks on the second pleural form a reticulate pattern with a well-developed C-shaped mark. We tentatively recognize *P. c. metteri* Ward, 1984, the Missouri River cooter. It ranges from southwestern Missouri, adjacent southwestern Kansas, and central and eastern Oklahoma through eastern Texas. The pattern on the second pleural is composed of curved vertical bars that do not form a reticulate pattern, and the C-shaped mark may not be present on all individuals. The dark plastral pattern is well developed. According to Ward (1984), this race includes those western populations once identified as *P. floridana hoyi*. Dundee and Rossman (1989) did not consider the erection of *P. c. metteri* justified, and we are also unsure about this arrangement. The pattern characters that supposedly set this form apart seem to us to fall within the variation of *P. c. hieroglyphica*. Additional study is needed to resolve this controversy.

Juvenile *Pseudemys concinna mobilensis*

Distribution of *Pseudemys concinna*

Four major problems seem apparent in Ward's (1984) analysis of variation within *P. concinna*. The first, and most minor, is the placement of *P. c. mobilensis* (Holbrook, 1838) in the synonymy of *P. c. hieroglyphica*. Ward stated that the type specimen of *mobilensis* appeared to be an intergrade between *hieroglyphica* and *P. c. concinna,* and that the population

it represents (Mobile Bay) is "unquestionably intermediate," thereby making Holbrook's description inappropriate. However, Ward gave no adequate data supporting the intergrade state of the Mobile Bay turtles, and neither does Mount (1975) from whom he apparently borrowed this interpretation. Ernst has examined the holotype of *mobilensis* and disagrees that

Pseudemys concinna
suwanniensis

Pseudemys concinna mobilensis

it is necessarily an intergrade. Also, some eastern Gulf Coast populations seem perfectly good *mobilensis*. Second, Ward presented a map depicting the distribution of the subspecies of *P. concinna* in which the zone of intergradation between *concinna, hieroglyphica,* and *metteri* is larger than the individual ranges of any one of the races. This is a major flaw. Zones of intergradation represent relatively narrow areas of gene exchange between adjacent subspecies, and never occupy a greater geographic area than those of the races involved. Third, the placement of *P. floridana hoyi* (Agassiz, 1857) in the synonymies of both *P. c. hieroglyphica* and the newly designated *P. c. metteri* is problematic. While *hoyi* and *hieroglyphica* certainly interbreed in the lower Mississippi Valley (Fahey, 1980; Dundee and Rossman, 1989), they are syntopic elsewhere without

evidence of interbreeding. Each is a fully recognizable entity in the Cumberland and Tennessee rivers of Kentucky. Eliminating *P. f. hoyi* is a convenient way of circumventing the overall question of the relationship between the species *concinna* and *floridana*. If this is ever to be adequately understood, a large sample of turtles must be examined and compared from each major drainage system throughout the ranges of each species, not just where they are thought to hybridize. Fourth, we question the statistical integrity of his analysis. The use of untransformed ratios and numerous univariate comparisons violates certain statistical assumptions and weakens the experimental design.

CONFUSING SPECIES: *Pseudemys gorzugi* has a pattern of four distinct whorllike blotches of

Male *Pseudemys concinna hiero-glyphica;* note the elongated foreclaws

Plastron of juvenile *Pseudemys concinna hieroglyphica*

concentric black and yellow rings on the second pleural, but no C-shaped light mark. *Pseudemys floridana* commonly lacks a plastral pattern, and has no notch at the tip of the upper jaw. *Chrysemys picta* lacks serrations on the carapace and has a notched upper jaw. *Pseudemys nelsoni, P. alabamensis, P. rubriventris,* and *P. texana* have a notched upper jaw and a prefrontal arrow formed by the junction of the sagittal and supratemporal head stripes. *Trachemys*

scripta has a prefrontal arrow, and vertical stripes on its thighs.

HABITAT: *Pseudemys concinna* is predominantly a turtle of rivers, preferring those with slow to moderate current, abundant aquatic vegetation, and rocky bottoms. Basking sites, such as partially submerged tree trunks or rocks, seem to be a necessary feature. It also inhabits lakes, ponds, deep springs, oxbows, floodplain pools, swamps, and large ditches, and has been taken in lagoons, brackish tidal marshes, and the Gulf of Mexico.

BEHAVIOR: Over most of its range the river cooter is active from April to October, but some may remain active all year in Florida and the lower Gulf Coastal Plain streams, and Buhlmann and Vaughan (1991) saw one basking on 4 March in southern West Virginia. It spends the colder winter months in the mud or on the bottom of some waterbody.

Most activity is diurnal, although some females may finish nesting after dark. River cooters forage during the early morning and late afternoon, and most of the time between is spent basking.

The river cooter is shy and leaves the water only to bask or nest. The basking habit is well developed, and many may share a log or other favored site. Carr (1940) once counted 47 on a single log. *Chrysemys picta, Trachemys scripta, Deirochelys reticularia,* and other species of *Pseudemys* may also occupy the same basking site. While basking it is very wary, and will dive into the water at the slightest alarm.

Pseudemys concinna seems less resistant to solar radiation than are some of the thicker-shelled *Pseudemys;* however, Hutchison et al. (1966) found the critical thermal maximum to be 41.8°C (40.4–42.8), and Pritchard and Greenhood (1968) thought the critical thermal maximum of *P. c. suwanniensis* may be even as high as 43–44°C. Smaller cooters heat and cool faster than larger individuals (Boyer, 1965). Hutton et al. (1960) reported that the heart beats faster when body temperature is increased, but at cloacal temperatures between 11 and 35°C, the heart rate is inversely related to body size.

Hennemann (1979) studied the frequency of basking by immature *P. c. suwanniensis* under both fasting and well-fed conditions. The turtles showed a slightly higher basking frequency after feeding, but the difference was not significant. Unfed turtles also frequently basked. Response of basking turtles to infrared radiation was greater than response to light alone and approximated the response to light and heat combined, so Hennemann concluded that juveniles bask for some benefit other than just the enhancement of digestion by elevated body temperatures.

Evaporative water loss may also be a problem during basking and terrestrial activity by this species. Jackson and Cantrell (1964) found total body water values ranging from 72.4 to 73.9% of gross body weight in newly hatched *P. c. suwanniensis,* which can desiccate rapidly in the journey between the nest and water.

The river cooter is highly aquatic, and is seen on land less often than other freshwater emydids. Much time is spent submerged in water 1.0–1.5 m deep, either resting on the bottom or walking slowly about in quest of food. When breathing, usually only the head is above the water surface, the body remaining at an angle of about 45° (Cahn, 1937). The turtle may remain in this position for a long time, slowly treading with its hind feet. Belkin (1964), however, reported that not even the tip of the snout protrudes above the surface when this species breathes. The lining of the nares is hydrophobic, so that once the turtle is at the surface the nares open at the bottom of a small depression in the surface film. The cooter is able to maintain this position with respect to the surface despite the bobbing of the body caused by breathing; thus, it can breathe without any part of its body projecting above the surface film.

Belkin (1964) studied the diving physiology and behavior of the subspecies *suwanniensis.* Each of his turtles spent most of the time lying quietly on the bottom of the aquarium with eyes closed; during this time a turtle stirred periodically to open its eyes, raise its head and the forepart of its body, breathe, and again submerge. Periods of submergence ranged from a few minutes to more than two hours; the average was about an hour. For some turtles the submerged periods were of equal length; for others they varied greatly. Breathing periods ranged from 30 seconds to about four minutes. On average, the duration of submergence was more than 50 times that of the breathing periods. Belkin discovered that, except in instances of unusually prolonged submergence, the time spent breathing after a dive was not influenced by the duration of the dive. Typically the turtle began to breathe as soon as its nares were emptied of water and continued to breathe for 5–20 cycles, each cycle consisting of an exhalation followed by an inhalation and lasting about three seconds. This was followed by a period of apnea and then another period of breathing; the last inhalation was followed almost immediately by submergence. Belkin also found that the oxygen-storage capacity was sufficient to allow a two- to three-hour dive at 22°C. In another study, Belkin (1968a) subjected *P. c. suwanniensis* to gas mixtures containing no free oxygen, during which the turtle's central nervous system continued to function. He attributed this ability to a comparatively high rate of anaerobic uptake or metabolism of glucose.

Ultsch (1985) also studied the ability of *P. concinna* to remain underwater for long periods. Adults totally submerged at 3°C in aerated water (normoxia) survived for almost 150 days, while those in N_2-

bubbled water (anoxia) survived only a little over 50 days. Those in the normoxic waters developed fungal infections, so occasional basking may be necessary to prevent infection.

River cooters usually venture away from water only to nest, but Minton (1972) reported they occasionally make short overland trips to ponds and swamps adjacent to rivers. When on land they are slow and awkward, and their orientation seems poor. Cahn (1937) remarked that fishermen at Reelfoot Lake, Tennessee, often throw them ashore into a maze of cypress knees and that many perish before they can find their way back to the water. When picked up these turtles withdraw into their shells and remain there for a considerable time.

Some *P. c. suwanniensis* marked by Marchand (1942) wandered 640 m or more between recaptures; one was recaptured 5 km downstream from the release site. He thought some of this movement could be attributed to abnormal population pressures created by releasing many individuals at one place.

Buhlmann and Vaughan (1991) reported home ranges varying between 1.2 and 1.6 ha for two radio-equipped adult *P. c. concinna* in West Virginia.

River cooters sometimes make strange sounds. Allen (1950) reported that he often heard *P. c. suwanniensis* utter a short, deep-throated grunt. The calling turtle always was afloat on the surface with head held high, and the call was given with the mouth closed; the neck pulsated with each grunt. He thought it likely that this utterance played a part in courtship. No other observations of this behavior have been reported, and it is more probable that the turtle had a respiratory problem.

REPRODUCTION: The smallest mature female *P. c. suwanniensis* recorded by Jackson (1970) was 14.0 cm in carapace length, the smallest male was 14.6 cm.

Mating usually occurs in the spring. The male pursues the female, sniffing at her tail, swims to a position dorsal to her, extends his neck and head outward and downward over hers, positions his elongated foreclaws just anterior and to the side of her snout, and vibrates them rapidly in front of her face. If properly stimulated, the female will sink to the bottom and allow the male to slide backward and mount her; if not interested she will try to outswim the male or duck under some submerged object to displace him.

A laboratory study of courtship by Suwannee River cooters was conducted by Jackson and Davis (1972b). Their observations were made from 10 to 20 April between 0900 and 1700, and vary somewhat from those reported by Marchand (1944) for the same race. Courtship begins with an aroused male swimming after a female, his snout in close proximity to her hindquarters, suggesting that he is following a pheromone released from her cloaca. This trailing behavior alternates with periods when the male swims around the female with his tail extended and hanging vertically. Occasionally the two turtles approach one another, necks extended, until they almost touch snouts, remaining in this snout-to-snout posture for as long as two minutes, while their snouts delicately bump together. The male then either resumes trailing the female, or positions himself above her, with his plastron resting on her carapace, his neck extended, and his head bent downward at nearly a right angle so that it becomes approximately vertical to her head. He then retracts his forelimbs so as to position his elongated foreclaws beside her face and then vibrates them. Prior to this foreclaw stroking phase, he may begin a series of very fine chewing movements with his jaws which increase in intensity until the titillations begin and then cease. Duration of the vibratory sequence is rather uniform, lasting an average of 506 milliseconds (Jackson and Davis detected no actual physical contact between the foreclaws and the female's face). She usually withdraws her head during the stroking phase, and occasionally displays some of the male courtship pattern to the male.

Petranka and Phillippi (1978) observed recently hatched *P. concinna* court. The turtles faced each other, extended their necks forward until their heads almost touched, and then rhythmically stroked each other with their foreclaws in a fashion like that of courting male *Trachemys scripta*. The hatchlings' claws were not elongated, as in adult males, so facial contact did not occur. The vibratory movements lasted for about 0.5 seconds and occurred at about three-second intervals. One turtle even displayed to the extended hind foot of the other. One-year-old *P. concinna* kept by Petranka and Phillippi performed normal male courtships.

Nesting normally takes place in late May or June, but some clutches may be laid as late as mid-July to late summer. Common nest sites are open areas within 30 m of the water with either sandy or friable loam soil. The flask-shaped nest cavity is dug entirely with the hind feet; Green and Pauley (1987) described a nest dug by a 30.5-cm female as 12.7 cm deep, with an opening 6.8 cm in diameter. The subspecies *suwanniensis* and *P. floridana* are unique in excavating a three-holed nest (Jackson, 1987), consisting of a central nest cavity and two adjacent false nests. The

Hatchling *Pseudemys concinna*

false nests are rarely covered, and up to two eggs may be deposited in them, possibly to lure predators away from the main nest cavity (Ashton and Ashton, 1985).

The pinkish-white, ellipsoidal (29.0–44.0 × 22.0–30.5 mm) eggs have parchmentlike shells bearing many fine nodules. They weigh 16.4–22.4 g (Jackson and Jackson, 1968). The total lipid content of a typical egg is 23.3%, with that of the yolk 27.7% (Congdon and Gibbons, 1985). Clutches range from 9 eggs (Cahn, 1937) to 29 eggs (Caldwell and Collins, 1981), although 19–20 eggs are probably more normal. Caldwell and Collins (1981) reported that in Kansas more than one clutch is laid per season, and that the later clutches contain fewer eggs. Most hatchlings emerge from the nest in August or September, after an incubation of 80–150 days (Caldwell and Collins, 1981), depending on soil temperatures. Three groups of eggs incubated in the laboratory by Jackson and Jackson (1968) hatched after 84–92 days; hatching percentages in these clutches varied from 47.0% to 91.3%. The eggs will develop continuously, but slowly, at 22.5°C, and closely approach term at 161–166 days, but many of the embryos are deformed (Ewert, 1991). In some of the more northern populations, hatchlings may over-winter in the nest cavity and emerge the next spring (Buhlmann and Vaughan, 1991); perhaps those that do so are from later clutches.

Hatchlings have green shells, and brighter light markings than do adults. The carapace is rounded and 27.0–36.5 mm long, 25.0–35.4 mm wide and 15–18 mm in depth; a medial keel is present. The plastron is yellow with a well-formed brownish-green seam-following pattern. Typical hatchlings weigh about 10–14 g.

Hatchling Suwannee River cooters examined by Jackson and Jackson (1968) retained yolk sacs that were 6.2–12.8 mm wide. Within a week the sacs were retracted through the umbilical opening of the plastron. The caruncle was lost in 8–17 days (average 11 days).

About two weeks after hatching, the typical juvenile pattern develops; the hatchling becomes brighter green, and the C-shaped mark on the second pleural becomes discernible.

GROWTH AND LONGEVITY: Shell proportions of 30 juveniles (of both sexes) from central South Carolina were compared by Carr (1952); as the turtles grew from the size group with carapaces 39–58 mm to that with 163–184 mm carapaces, carapace length increased over width by 17%, depth of the shell decreased 9.4%, and width of the head relative to carapace length decreased 7.7%.

Marchand (1942) calculated that in one year a young female *P. c. suwanniensis* increased 23% in shell length, and a young male, 17%. The average growth rate for all turtles he recaptured was 5–10% per year; smaller individuals grew faster. Jackson (1970) found the season of active growth in this race to be from March to November. He found a progressive decline in the growth rate with increasing size; the rate of increase of carapace length and five other morphological variables was greater in females than in males.

Snider and Bowler (1992) reported that a captive male *P. c. suwanniensis* lived 40 years, eight months and four days.

FOOD HABITS: As in other species of *Pseudemys*, adult river cooters are mostly plant eaters; however, the herbivorous tendencies appear to be less developed, and individuals of all ages may consume animal foods. Parker (1939) found that the stomach of a large *P. c. hieroglyphica* contained Phaeophyceae, *Oscillatoria,* and Lemnaceae, and he remarked that small captives will eat bits of meat and insects, as well as plants. Cahn (1937) thought *P. c. hieroglyphica* largely carnivorous, feeding upon almost any animal matter available. The stomachs he examined contained crayfish, tadpoles, small fish, snails, many kinds of insects, aquatic sedges, algae, and many shallow-water plant species. Cahn thought the scavenging habit well developed. However, Brimley (1943) found only filamentous algae in the intestine of a large individual.

Adult *Pseudemys c. concinna* from the New River, West Virginia, eat eelgrass (*Vallisneria*), elodea (*Elodea canadensis*) and crayfish, while juveniles consume vegetation, invertebrates (crayfish, trichopterans) and fish (*Percina caprodes*) (Buhlmann and Vaughan, 1991).

Apparently *P. c. suwanniensis* sometimes scavenges but does not seem to be predaceous; rather, it has a marked preference for both aquatic and terrestrial plants (Allen, 1938). Juveniles we have kept accepted fish, but adults ate only plants. Marchand (1942) examined the stomachs of 10 adults and found the following percentages, by volume, of plants present: *Najas* 82.3%, *Ceratophyllum* 5.5%, *Sagittaria* 2.5%, and filamentous algae 2.5%. In saltwater habitats this race feeds largely on turtle grass.

PREDATORS AND DEFENSE: Alligators take a few in the water, and nesting females may be harassed by raccoons (*Procyon*) or other carnivorous mammals. Skunks (*Mephitis*), raccoons, opossums (*Didelphis*) and hogs (*Sus*) prey on eggs. Juveniles fall prey to a multitude of mammalian, wading bird, reptile, and fish species. Rice rats (*Oryzomys*) account for a large percentage of juvenile mortality at Reelfoot Lake, Tennessee (Goodpaster and Hoffmeister, 1952). Humans are the greatest persecutor of this turtle: adults are eaten, are crushed on highways, and are driven from their habitats by pollution, drainage, or other forces of "progress," and the young formerly appeared in the pet trade.

If handled, most adults will pull into their shells, but some will kick, scratch, or void bladder water; only a few will bite.

POPULATIONS: Among the 1,022 turtles collected from Rainbow Springs Run, Marion County, Florida, Marchand (1942) found 37.3% *P. c. suwanniensis* and 33.3% *P. floridana peninsularis*. Carr (1940) reported that in the 1930s enormous aggregations of *P. c. suwanniensis* foraged on the flats off the mouth of the Suwannee River. Formerly, in relatively undisturbed waters, the numbers of basking individuals were the largest Carr (1952) had ever seen. Now, however, this turtle has been greatly reduced in numbers, and has been placed on the Florida threatened list (Auffenberg, in McDiarmid, 1978).

The adult population of *P. c. concinna* in an 11.2-km section of the New River, West Virginia, during the summer of 1985 was estimated by Buhlmann and Vaughan (1991) to be 67 individuals. At three study pools, juveniles composed 6%, 25%, and 35% of captures. The male:female ratios at these same pools were 1.1:1.0, 2.0:1.0, and 4.5:1.0, and the overall sex ratio was 1.9:1.0.

REMARKS: For an animal that is still extremely plentiful at some localities, we know practically nothing of its critical life history features. A thorough ecological study of this turtle is required.

Pseudemys gorzugi Ward, 1984
Rio Grande cooter
PLATE 34

RECOGNITION: The carapace (to 23.5 cm) is oval to elongated, flattened, slightly keeled, highest at the middle and widest behind the middle. The posterior marginals are serrated, and the surface of the pleurals is shallowly rugose. Ground color is olive to greenish brown with blotches of alternating black and yellow rings. The second pleural scute has a pattern of four distinct blotches (whorls) of concentric black and yellow rings. A similar mark of alternating yellow and black lies over the seam separating the ventral marginals. Two dark bars may be present on the bridge, particularly at the axillary scute. The hingeless plastron is yellow with dark borders along all seams in juveniles, but fading so that only those along the gular-humeral and humeral-pectoral seams remain in adults. The upper jaw lacks a medial notch and flanking toothlike cusps. The crushing surfaces of both jaws bear a series of well-developed cusps. Skin is green with yellow stripes on the head, neck, limbs, and tail. An oval postorbital blotch is present. The temporal stripe curves dorsally over the postorbital blotch, expands anteriorly, and ends at the level of the posterior corner of the mouth. A wide sagittal stripe runs from the tip of the snout backward to the neck, and a broad Y-shaped stripe is present on the chin.

Males have elongated straight foreclaws and thicker tails with the vent posterior to the carapacial rim. Females are larger, more domed, and have the anal vent beneath the carapacial marginals.

KARYOTYPE: Unknown.

FOSSIL RECORD: Unknown.

DISTRIBUTION: *Pseudemys gorzugi* is found in the Rio Grande watershed from Brownsville, Texas northwestward to the Big Bend, north of Del Rio, Terrell County, and in the Pecos River drainage of western Texas (Culberson, Reeves, and Loving coun-

ties) and southeastern New Mexico possibly as far north as the Bitter Lakes Wildlife Refuge, Chaves County (Degenhardt and Christiansen, 1974; Dixon, 1987). Ward (1984) thought that the apparent 161-km hiatus separating the populations in the Rio Grande and Pecos drainages was due to pollution of the intervening waterways by runoff from petroleum and natural-gas wells. Isolated populations occur in northeastern Coahuila, central Nuevo León, and northeastern Tamaulipas, Mexico (Smith and Smith, 1979; Powell et al., 1984), although the Coahuila colonies may possibly be in contact with the Rio Grande *P. gorzugi*. Degenhardt and Christiansen (1974) noted that this turtle has been taken at elevations as high as 1,082 m in New Mexico.

GEOGRAPHIC VARIATION: No subspecies are recognized. Ward (1984) discussed clinal variation in the characteristic head and shell markings in populations from New Mexico, Texas, and Mexico.

CONFUSING SPECIES: *Pseudemys texana* has a median notch often flanked by toothlike cusps on the upper jaw, and a plastron with a red-tinged rim. *P. concinna* has either a light backward-facing C-shaped mark or a vertical bar on the second pleural scute. *Trachemys gaigeae* has a large orange blotch behind the eye, an extensive medial plastral figure, and light reticulations on its carapace.

HABITAT: Degenhardt and Christiansen (1974) reported that the usual habitats of *P. gorzugi* in New Mexico are relatively clear pools with rocky or sandy bottoms, but that at the Bitter Lakes Wildlife Refuge, where they were first reported by Bundy (1951), the habitat consists of very turbid ponds with soft, muddy bottoms. Milstead et al. (1950) thought that this turtle was more limited to natural waters than to artificial cattle tanks.

Pseudemys gorzugi

Plastron of *Pseudemys gorzugi*

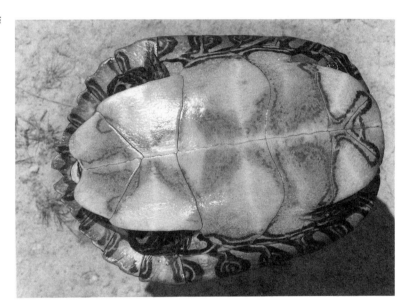

REMARKS: This recently described taxon has long been confused with both *Pseudemys concinna* and *P. texana*. The only published life history data is a comment by Legler (1958) that the stomach and intestines of a specimen from New Mexico were filled with finely chopped vegetable matter. A good behavioral and ecological study of this turtle is sorely needed.

Pseudemys gorzugi was originally designated a subspecies of *P. concinna* by Ward (1984). However,

Ward also pointed out that it is widely separated from the nearest *P. concinna* population, that of *P. c. metteri* in north-central Texas, and, in fact, that the range of *P. texana* lies between the two. Because of this allopatry and the apparent lack of gene exchange with *P. concinna*, we feel it best to consider *P. gorzugi* a separate species.

A summary of the literature on *P. gorzugi* is in Ernst (1990a).

Head pattern of *Pseudemys gorzugi*

Distribution of *Pseudemys gorzugi*

Pseudemys floridana (Le Conte, 1830)
Cooter

PLATE 35

RECOGNITION: This large freshwater turtle has a wide transverse stripe on the second pleural, and an immaculate, yellow, hingeless plastron. Its elongated and highly arched carapace (to 40.3 cm) is highest at the center, widest behind the center, and is posteriorly serrate. A low juvenile keel disappears with age. The carapace is brownish with yellow markings; the wide vertical stripe on the second pleural may be forked at the upper or lower end or at both. Each marginal has a central yellow bar on the dorsal surface and, on the ventral surface in some individuals, a dark, light-centered spot, which usually covers the posterior seam. The upper jaw bears no medial notch or cusps, and the lateral jaw ridge lacks denticulations. The skin is brown to black, with yellow stripes. The supratemporal and paramedial head stripes commonly join behind the eyes to form a hairpin-shaped mark. The underside of the neck is marked with wide yellow stripes, and a central chin stripe extends back and divides to form a Y-shaped mark.

Males have elongated foreclaws and long, thick tails, with the anal vent behind the carapacial rim. Males are slightly smaller and flatter than females.

KARYOTYPE: Each diploid cell has 50 chromosomes. Killebrew (1977a) found 26 macrochromosomes (16 metacentric, 6 submetacentric, and 4 telocentric) and 24 microchromosomes, but Stock (1972) reported 20 metacentric or submetacentric, 10 subtelocentric, and 20 acrocentric or telocentric chromosomes.

FOSSIL RECORD: Pleistocene (Rancholabrean) fossils have been found at Williston, Levy County, Florida (Holman, 1959), and Edisto Island, Colleton County, South Carolina (Roth and Laerm, 1980). Remains of *P. floridana* associated with 12,000-year-old Indian artifacts have also been found at Little Salt Spring, Sarasota County, Florida (Holman and Clausen, 1984).

Jackson (1976) thought the Pliocene species *Chrysemys caelata* possibly ancestral to both *P. floridana* and *P. concinna,* and the Pleistocene species *Chrysemys* (?*Pseudemys*) *hibbardi* also resembles these two species (Holman, 1991). Weaver and Rose (1967) assigned North American cooters and sliders to two evolutionary lines: an advanced branch including *P. floridana, P. concinna,* and several tropical forms of the *Trachemys scripta* complex, and a second more conservative branch including *P. alabamensis, P. nelsoni, P. rubriventris, Chrysemys picta,* and the rest of the *Trachemys scripta* complex.

DISTRIBUTION: *Pseudemys floridana* ranges along the Atlantic Coastal Plain from southeastern Virginia southward through peninsular Florida to about the Tamiami Trail, and westward across the Gulf Coastal Plain to Mobile Bay.

GEOGRAPHIC VARIATION: There are two subspecies. *Pseudemys floridana floridana* (Le Conte, 1830), the Florida cooter, occurs on the Atlantic Coastal Plain from Virginia to northern Florida and west on the Gulf Coastal Plain to Mobile Bay. This race has numerous head stripes which do not form hairpin markings and, in 74% of individuals, dark pigment on the inguinal scute (Seidel and Palmer, 1991). *Pseudemys f. peninsularis* (Carr, 1938a), the peninsula cooter, is restricted to peninsular Florida. It has a pair of light stripes which resemble hairpins on the top of its head, which may be broken or incomplete, and no dark pigment on the inguinal scute.

CONFUSING SPECIES: *Trachemys scripta, Pseudemys rubriventris, P. nelsoni,* and *P. alabamensis* have a prefrontal arrow, and in the latter three the upper jaw is notched. *Pseudemys concinna* has its upper

Pseudemys floridana floridana

Juvenile *Pseudemys floridana peninsularis*

jaw slightly notched, a C-shaped mark on the second pleural, and a patterned plastron. *Chrysemys picta* is much smaller and has a notched upper jaw and an unserrated carapace. *Deirochelys reticularia* has a net-like pattern of light lines on the carapace, an extremely long neck, and a wide foreleg stripe.

HABITAT: The cooter lives in almost any water-way having a slow current, soft bottom, basking sites, and abundant aquatic vegetation. It is particularly common in large slow-flowing rivers and their backwaters, lakes, and large ponds.

BEHAVIOR: Over most of its range, *P. floridana* hibernates in winter; however, the subspecies *P. f. peninsularis* may be active in all months. When forced to be inactive by a cold spell, it does not truly hibernate, but becomes less active, and sometimes burrows into the mud. The annual activity period in the north usually lasts from April to October.

Plastron of *Pseudemys flor-idana peninsularis*

Distribution of *Pseudemys floridana*

The cooter is predominantly diurnal, being most active early and late in the day. Carr (1952), however, observed on several nights that two or three were feeding when most were asleep or, at least, inactive. Marchand (1942) found that cooters spent midday in hiding along the edges of a stream, with concentrations in such places as caves, sunken trees, and patches of water lilies (*Nymphaea*). At night they slept on the bottom or among water lily stems.

Pseudemys floridana is quite fond of basking and spends many of the daylight hours so occupied. Cooters are gregarious, and often as many as 20–30 may bask on the same log. Such a group is difficult to approach, but individuals do not seem especially wary.

The paramedial stripes on *Pseudemys floridana peninsularis* form a pair of "hairpins" on the back of the head

The number of atmospherically basking *P. floridana* per day reaches a peak when the daily mean water temperature is 28.5°C (Auth, 1975). Aquatic basking increases in summer when the water temperature approaches 31.5°C, but basking decreases on overcast days, and ceases entirely when the water temperatures drops to 14°C. Thermoregulation is the primary function of basking (Auth, 1975).

In Florida, cooters often bask with *P. nelsoni, P. concinna suwanniensis,* and *Trachemys scripta;* however, they apparently cannot tolerate direct sun for as long as *P. nelsoni* (Pritchard and Greenhood, 1968). This is surprising, as Hutchison et al. (1966) found that *P. floridana* has a critical thermal maximum of 40.85°C (40.4–41.3), slightly above that of *P. nelsoni.* Bogert and Cowles (1947) kept a large cooter for 40 hours in a chamber in which the temperature was maintained at 38°C and the relative humidity at 37%. During this period the turtle maintained a body temperature of 35.0–36.9°C and lost 14.4% of its original weight. When replaced in water it regained its original weight plus 115 g.

Breathing and heartbeat increase with rising body temperatures until the energy costs can become considerable in a cooter. At a body temperature of 22°C, the oxidative cost attributable to ventilation in *P. floridana* is 0.0047 ml oxygen/ml gas ventilated, a value about 10 times that of a human (Kinney and White, 1977). The percentage of arterial hemoglobin saturation in cooters varies inversely with body temperature, but the arteriovenous oxygen difference remains constant; *P. floridana* consumes more oxygen per body mass than do lizards at the same body temperature (Kinney et al., 1977).

Pseudemys floridana is more often terrestrial than most other species of its genus. During unseasonably warm days in winter they often wander about on land; although sometimes this may be attributed to a migratory urge set up by low water levels in their home ponds, at other times no satisfactory explanation is evident (Carr, 1952). Both sexes wander; therefore a desire to nest cannot be the driving force in all cases. Many of the wandering cooters are killed by predators or automobiles, and others perish when they become overheated.

Gibbons et al. (1983) studied turtle movements in and out of a Carolina bay on the Savannah River Site, near Aiken, South Carolina. Unusually high numbers of *P. floridana* emigrated during drought conditions in 1981, and as of July 1982 most had not returned. Three to 19 cooters had been recorded emigrating in normal years, and only a total of 45 in the previous five years, compared to 40 in 1981. The increase was unquestionably due to the drought, and 70% of the 40 *P. floridana* that left the bay traveled toward the nearest body of water, a beaver pond 400 m away. Normally, *P. floridana* showed locationally random entry into the bay, but directional emigration (Gibbons and Coker, 1977). The most obvious habitat features with which the immigration of juveniles and emigration of adults corresponded were nearby aquatic areas (Gibbons and Coker, 1977). Emigration of adults in the general direction of the closest Carolina bays to that studied may indicate a tendency of individuals to associate with more than one body of water. *Pseudemys floridana* uses the sun to find a particular direction when moving overland, so long-distance directional movement between waterbodies is possible (Gibbons and Smith, 1968).

Marchand (1945) reported that of 33 marked peninsula cooters retaken once, 16 were at the release point; six of these were recaptured within a month, and the greatest elapsed time was seven months. Of the 17 cooters that had moved, eight wandered 91.5 m or less, and the greatest distance was 275 m (three cases; seven months, 1.5 months, and seven days, respectively). Of eight retaken twice, the greatest distance traveled was 243 m, in a month's time. Two showed no movement, and two had returned to the site of initial capture. Of three that were retaken three times, two showed site preferences, but the third wandered extensively, covering 366 m in 19 days, although the total distance from the initial capture point was only 206 m. One recaptured four times had not moved on one occasion, and the maximum distance covered in any of its travels was 160 m in 18 days. Marchand (1945) also studied the movements of *P. floridana* and *P. c. suwanniensis* at another Florida site where 20 returns, equally divided between the two species, were recorded, and 14 of the turtles wandered 640 m or more.

In studies of individual discrimination in a T-maze, *P. floridana peninsularis* did significantly better than chance (p <0.05), and performed better than *P. nelsoni* (Kramer, 1989).

REPRODUCTION: Males mature at plastron lengths of 12–14 cm and females at 24–25 cm; maturity may be reached in three to four years in males, but takes five to seven years in females (Jackson, 1988a). In Alabama, male testes are largest in spring, decline in size during the summer, and begin to enlarge again in the fall (Thomas and Mount, 1973). Females have enlarged follicles in late winter, which are probably ovulated in late April or May. Ovarian activity declines during summer and early fall. The ovaries of several large females collected on 30 July in Louisiana revealed that by then the breeding season is over for most, but two had enlarged follicles that presumably could have been deposited later that year (Dundee and Rossman, 1989).

In Alabama, courtship and mating take place in early April when water temperatures are 20–23°C (Thomas and Mount, 1973). Courtship behavior of *P. floridana* has not been described, but may be similar to that of its near relative, *P. concinna*.

Pseudemys f. peninsularis produces clutches throughout the year in Florida (Ernst and Barbour, 1972; Iverson, 1977a), but particularly in late fall, winter, or early spring (Jackson, 1988a); however, elsewhere the species' nesting season may be abbreviated. In southern Georgia and South Carolina, *P. f. floridana* nests in May and June (Carr, 1952; Gibbons and Coker, 1977), and early June through July is its nesting period in Alabama (Thomas and Mount, 1973). Farther north, it probably nests only in June and July.

The nest cavity is roughly flask shaped and is dug with the hind feet in friable soil in open places. Usually one or more additional cavities, ordinarily containing one or two eggs, are dug 5.0–7.5 cm from the principal nest. Depth of the central chamber averages 12.5 cm, that of the side cavities about 6 cm (Franz, 1986b). Carr (1952) observed that peninsula cooters kick out trenches on either side of the nest and rest their hind feet in these during oviposition.

Nesting usually begins in the afternoon and sometimes continues into the night. Cooters nest at least twice a year, and possibly as many as three to six times (Jackson, 1988a). Iverson (1977a) reported that a female collected on 4 May contained 15 oviducal eggs, and that her ovaries bore two distinct sets of corpora lutea. One set corresponded to the 15 oviducal eggs and the other to an earlier 10-egg clutch. Fifteen additional 18–22-mm follicles were also present on the ovary suggesting a possible third clutch. The number of eggs per clutch depends on the size of the female and on the number of times she has previously nested during the season. A clutch usually has about 20 eggs, but clutches ranging from 10 to 29 eggs are known. Goff and Goff (1932) found that an average of 46 seconds (25–105) elapsed between the laying of each of 13 eggs, but Allen (1938) reported an interval of 20–29 seconds for another ovipositing female.

The elliptical eggs have white, well-calcified, parchmentlike shells with a course granular surface; they are soft when laid but rapidly harden. Variable in size, they average 34 mm (29–40.5) in length, 25 mm (20–27) in width, and 11.5 g (8.7–16.3) in weight. Eggs are composed of 72% water and 24% lipids (29% of yolk) (Congdon and Gibbons, 1985). The total biomass and energy equivalents of eggs produced per hectare by females at a site in South Carolina were 0.28 kg and 1696 kJ (Congdon et al., 1986).

Natural incubation usually lasts 80–150 days, depending on soil temperature, but eggs we have incubated in the laboratory at a constant 25°C hatched in 66–69 days. Jackson (1988a) recorded incubation periods of 62–70 days for eggs incubated at 30°C, and temperatures of 22.5–25°C resulted in periods of 70–120 days. At 22.5°C, the eggs continuously develop at a slow rate and do enter diapause; at higher temperatures development is accelerated (Ewert, 1991).

In the north hatchlings may overwinter in the nest; Gibbons and Coker (1977) found that hatchling *P. floridana* in west-central South Carolina overwintered on land and initially entered the water in the spring. They observed five gravid or ovipositing females between mid-May and late June, so emerging hatchlings may have remained in the nests as long as 9–10 months.

Hatchlings are more brightly colored and more strongly patterned than adults. Their carapace is about as wide as long, has a well-developed keel, and is more highly arched and flared than that of adults. The immaculate yellow to orange plastron bears a yolk sac at hatching; this soon disappears, leaving a yolk scar. The caruncle persists for more than a week. Hatchlings are usually 27–24 mm in carapace length, 25–31 mm in width, 16–18 mm in depth, and have 26–34-mm plastra. They weigh 7–12 g. However, Ewert (1979a) reported that 21 hatchlings had mean carapace and plastron lengths of 36 and 32.4 mm, respectively.

Pseudemys floridana has temperature-dependent sex determination; 100% of hatchlings from eggs incubated at 25°C are males (Ewert and Nelson, 1991).

GROWTH AND LONGEVITY: The hatchling shell remains comparatively broad for some time; at maturity it has lost about 10% of its initial relative width. The depth of the shell relative to its length appears to remain fairly constant with growth. Carr (1952) measured a series of 30 *P. f. floridana* from North and South Carolina and found that in growing from a length of 46 mm to 24 cm the shell became 24% narrower and 9% lower and the head became 11.2% narrower, compared with the total shell length. The greatest growth shown by any *P. f. peninsularis* retaken by Marchand (1942) was that of a male, which increased its initial 16-cm carapace length about 12% per year; the next greatest was that of a 24-cm female, which gained 8%. The greater gains were made by the smaller adults; juveniles were not studied. In South Carolina, plastron length increases at approximately 2–4 cm per year in juveniles (Gibbons and Coker, 1977). The growth rate declines with increasing age.

The longevity record for a captive *P. floridana* is 12 years, six months and nine days at the Philadelphia Zoo (Snider and Bowler, 1992).

FOOD HABITS: Adult *Pseudemys floridana* are largely herbivorous; they consume a wide variety of aquatic plants, including *Sagittaria, Ceratophyllum, Myriophyllum, Najas,* and *Lemna,* and probably also eat algae. Hart (in Dundee and Rossman, 1989) reported that some insects, sponges, and bryozoans are eaten, but did not state by which age group. In captivity, cooters accept romaine lettuce, kale, spinach, cabbage, watermelon, cantaloupe, and bananas. The young take animal food (particularly fish and aquatic insects), but become less carnivorous as they grow older.

PREDATORS AND DEFENSE: Many eggs are destroyed by skunks (*Mephitis*), raccoons (*Procyon*), opossums (*Didelphis*), bears (*Ursus*), and hogs (*Sus*). The young are eaten by large wading birds, snail kites (*Rostrhamus*), large fish, snakes, carnivorous turtles, and various mammals. Adults are eaten by alligators (Delany and Abercrombie, 1986) and humans.

Carr (1952) thought the construction of shallow satellite pockets at the side of the central nest chamber was a strategy to reduce predation on the deeper main nest cavity in which most eggs are laid. Observations of the extent of raccoon (*Procyon lotor*) predation on cooter nests uphold Carr's theory; in 99 plundered nests, eggs were overlooked only in the main nest chamber (Franz, 1986b).

POPULATIONS: The total turtle population of Rainbow Springs Run, Marion County, Florida, included 33.3% *Pseudemys floridana* and 37.3% *P. concinna suwanniensis* (Marchand, 1942). At a South Carolina site, Gibbons and Coker (1977) captured 78 *P. floridana,* including 28 hatchlings, in an eight-year period. At this site, the maximum density was 7.0/ha; the biomass was 7.8 kg/ha, and the annual biomass production of eggs was 0.3 kg/ha (Congden et al., 1986; Congdon and Gibbons, 1989). Kramer (1986) marked 43 *P. floridana* (23 males, 20 females) along a 980-m section of Rock Springs Run near Orlando, Florida, and estimated a combined density at that site of 250 (±75) *P. floridana* and *P. nelsoni.*

REMARKS: Hybridization between *Pseudemys floridana* and the species *P. concinna* and *P. rubriventris* has been reported (Carr, 1952; Crenshaw, 1965; Mount, 1975; Pritchard, 1979; Fahey, 1980; Seidel and Palmer, 1991). However, Ward (1984), in his review of the relationships within the genus, thought no hybridization occurs, and that previous reports of it have been based on misidentified specimens or a poor understanding of the variation found in any given species. He conveniently eliminated hybridization in the Mississippi Valley between the resident subspecies of *P. concinna* and the taxon *P. f. hoyi* (Agassiz, 1857) by placing the latter in the synonymies of both *P. c. heiroglyphica* and a newly described *P. c. metteri*. For a discussion of the taxonomic confusion that has attended *P. floridana* and *P. concinna* in the Mississippi Valley, see the account of the latter species.

In the central Atlantic drainages, *P. floridana* inhabits the coastal plain and *P. concinna* lives on the piedmont (Seidel and Palmer, 1991). Populations in a relatively broad area overlapping the fall line of North Carolina are somewhat intermediate between the two species, and rare hybridization with *P. rubriventris* also occurs in North Carolina (Crenshaw, 1965; Martof et al., 1980; Seidel and Palmer, 1991). The relationship between *P. floridana* and *P. concinna* in the Atlantic drainages of North Carolina is more characteristic of subspecies than of species, which is similar to that observed elsewhere by Carr (1952) that brought about his proposal that the two taxa were merely subspecies of *P. floridana*. In spite of these observations, Seidel and Palmer (1991) believe it premature to propose a conspecific relationship for *P. floridana* and *P. concinna*.

As long ago as 1939, Pope reported a local decrease in *P. floridana* after pollution of waters by sewage and industrial wastes at Raleigh, North Carolina. It is depressing to think what further decreases in populations of this species and those of other aquatic turtles may have occurred between then and when our current clean water acts were implemented.

Pseudemys rubriventris (Le Conte, 1830)
Red-bellied turtle
PLATE 36

RECOGNITION: *Pseudemys rubriventris* is a large freshwater turtle that has a reddish plastron and a prominent notch at the tip of the upper jaw, with a toothlike cusp on each side. Its elongated carapace (to 40 cm) is commonly highest at the middle, widest behind the middle, flattened dorsally, and slightly serrated posteriorly. A low juvenile keel disappears with age. The carapace is brown to black, with red or yellow markings on the pleurals and marginals. The second pleural has a broad, light, vertical bar, which is forked at the upper or lower end or both. Each marginal has a red bar on the upper surface and a dark blotch with a light central spot on the lower surface. Melanism is common in old individuals. The plastron is reddish orange with a black pattern that spreads along the seams in juveniles but fades with age. A wide dark bar crosses the bridge. The head is moderate in size with a slightly protruding snout and a notched upper jaw (described above). Skin is dark olive to black with yellow stripes. A sagittal stripe passes anteriorly between the eyes and meets the joined supratemporal stripes on the snout, forming the prefrontal arrow that is characteristic of the red-bellied group. Five to eight stripes lie between the supratemporals behind the eyes. The paramedial stripes pass forward from the neck across the occipital region and terminate between the orbits. A supratemporal stripe bends upward from the neck on each side and enters the orbit.

Males have long, straight foreclaws; large, thick tails, with the vent behind the carapacial rim; and lower, slightly narrower shells than females. Females are slightly larger and more domed than males.

KARYOTYPE: Kiester and Childress (in Gorman, 1973) reported that the mitotic chromosomes total 50.

FOSSIL RECORD: Fossils of *Pseudemys rubriventris* are unknown, but archeological remains have been found in Massachusetts. Bullen (1949) and Waters (1962, 1966) reported red-bellied turtles from Indian middens on Martha's Vineyard, Dukes County, and Rhodin and Largy (1984) found bones of this turtle in the Concord Shell Heap, an Indian midden on the Sudbury River at Concord, Middlesex County. Many of the Concord bones were fire charred, so the turtles had probably been eaten.

DISTRIBUTION: The main range of *Pseudemys rubriventris* is along the Atlantic Coastal Plain from central New Jersey south to northeastern North Carolina and west up the Potomac River to eastern West Virginia. Relict populations also occur in Plymouth and Carver counties, and possibly Essex County, Massachusetts.

GEOGRAPHIC VARIATION: No subspecies are currently recognized. In the past, the small colonies in Massachusetts were considered a separate race, *Pseudemys rubriventris bangsi* Babcock, 1937, based on a supposedly more domed carapace (greatest carapace length in red-bellies from New England is 2.4 times its greatest height, that of turtles from more southern populations, 2.6). Conant (1951b) and Graham (1969) questioned this diagnostic character, and Ernst has observed that it is not valid in *P. rubriventris* from the Potomac River watershed. Recent statistical analyses of separate male and female data sets by Iverson and Graham (1990) revealed clinal variation in some male characters, but no obvious geographic variation in females. No geographic population showed enough morphological distinction to warrant subspecific status.

CONFUSING SPECIES: *Pseudemys floridana* and *P. concinna* lack a notch, or have only a weak one, at the tip of the upper jaw and have no prefrontal arrow, and *P. concinna* has a backward-facing C-shaped

Juvenile *Pseudemys rubriventris*

Plastron of adult *Pseudemys rubriventris*

figure on the second pleural (see Seidel and Palmer, 1991, for an extensive morphometric comparison of *P. rubriventris*, *P. c. concinna*, and *P. f. floridana*). *Chrysemys picta* lacks serrations on the carapace and has two large yellow marks on each side of the head. *Pseudemys nelsoni* has fewer head stripes, and less dark pigment on the juvenile plastron.

HABITAT: *Pseudemys rubriventris* is usually associated with relatively deep waterbodies: moderate gradient rivers and associated floodplain marshes, ponds, and oxbows. The colonies in Massachusetts are restricted to ponds. It often frequents brackish waters near the mouths of rivers, as evidenced by occasionally having barnacles attached to its shell (Arndt, 1975b). Habitat requirements include a soft bottom and many basking sites. Aquatic plants form the staple of its diet and must also be present.

Juveniles may utilize a different microhabitat than that of adults. McCauley (1945) reported that two

Plastron of juvenile *Pseudemys rubriventris*

small red-bellies he found had carapaces covered with a thick growth of algae, indicating that most of their time was spent in the water from which they seldom emerged to bask. However, Arndt (1975b) and Ernst and Norris (1978) have found colonies of the algal genus *Basicladia* on adult carapaces.

BEHAVIOR: Although nesting females may be active after dark, most activity by this turtle is diurnal. In the south, *Pseudemys rubriventris* is active from March to November, but in New England it first emerges from hibernation in mid-April and becomes inactive again in mid-October. The colder months are spent in hibernation, buried in or resting on some deep mud bottom.

Much of the day is occupied by lying in the sun on logs and rocks. It is shy and difficult to approach, and the basking sites usually are adjacent to deep water, into which it dives at the slightest alarm. Graham (1982a) reported that aerial basking may not be necessary, and that, when water temperatures are warm, the turtles may lie on or in supportive aquatic vegetation to achieve a preferred body temperature.

Interspecific basking aggression has been reported between this species and *Chrysemys picta* (Lovich, 1988b). Aggression was noted under crowded basking conditions when turtles frequently climbed on top of each other. Both species often tried to displace any turtle that attempted to climb onto them.

REPRODUCTION: Males first develop secondary sex characteristics at about 22-cm plastron length, and maturity is probably reached after nine years of age (Graham, 1971). Nothing is known about attainment of maturity by the female, or about the reproductive cycles of either sex.

Copulation probably occurs in the spring, but the courtship and mating acts have not been described. Nesting takes place from late May to July, but primarily in June. The nest is dug with the hind feet, most often in a sandy clay or loam soil. The site is usually in full sunlight, often in a cultivated tract adjacent to the water, and may be 10–250 m from the water's edge. Nests are flask shaped and average about 10 cm deep and 10 cm wide at the bottom, with a 7–8-cm opening. If disturbed before she has laid the first egg, the female will usually abandon the nest and crawl into the water, but once oviposition has begun, she will remain at the task. When laying is completed the female scrapes dirt into and over the hole, using only her hind feet. She packs the dirt firmly by rising as high as possible on all four legs and dropping heavily onto the nest site.

Nesting probably occurs more than once a season. Conant and Bailey (1936) reported that a New Jersey female, caught on 26 June, laid six eggs on 21 July and 12 more on 10 August. The eggs are elliptical, smooth surfaced, white shelled, 24–37 mm in length, about 19–24 mm in width, weigh 11–12 g, and vary in dimensions with size of the female. The usual

Distribution of *Pseudemys rubriventris*

complement totals 10–12, but Mitchell and Pague (1991) recorded a potential clutch of 29 oviducal eggs and Smith (1904) reported that the largest females lay as many as 35 eggs and possibly more.

Most young seem to hatch in late summer after an incubation period of 70–80 days, but some may overwinter in the nest and emerge the following spring. A recently emerged hatchling with caruncle and yolk sac was found in Fairfax County, Virginia, on 10 April 1980, and Mitchell (1974) found emerging hatchlings on 13 April 1974 in Middlesex County, Virginia. The light-green hatchlings are brightly colored, have rounded, keeled carapaces (29.0–37.5 mm), and weigh 7–11 g. The reddish plastron has a large dark figure that spreads somewhat along the seams. This pattern is similar to that of young *Pseudemys concinna,* but is larger and more pronounced.

GROWTH AND LONGEVITY: Graham (1969) reported that individuals 129.4 and 230.2 mm in carapace length were in their fourth and ninth growing seasons, respectively. In a later publication based on a more extensive sample size, Graham (1971) reported the following ranges in plastron lengths by age: hatchlings, 28.7–35.9 mm; 1 year,

45.9–72.9 mm (21.0% mean annual growth increment); 2 years, 61.3–96.0 mm (18.9% mean increase); 3 years 78.2–108.4 mm (17.4%); 4 years, 110.9–126.6 mm (27.6%); 5 years, 132.6–140.2 mm (18.7%); 6 years, 147.8–155.8 mm (15.9%); 7 years, 160.4–169.2 mm (13.4%); 8 years, 174.7–183.2 mm (13.5%); 9 years, 191.7–204.0 mm (19.3%); 10 years, 208.6–213.9 mm (12.4%); and 11 years, 220.3 mm (9.0%). The growth rate declines with size and age. Females longer than 300 mm in plastron length may weigh between 4 and 5 kg (Graham, 1971).

A wild-caught *Pseudemys rubriventris* survived 11 years, two months, and 26 days at the Brookfield Zoo (Snider and Bowler, 1992).

FOOD HABITS: Young red-bellied turtles are omnivorous, but older adults seem almost exclusively herbivorous. Known food items include snails, fish, tadpoles, crayfish, and aquatic vegetation (*Myriophyllum, Spirogyra, Utricularia, Sagittaria, Brasenia*). The fact that adults are not often lured into traps baited with fish seems to indicate that fish are not a normal part of their diet; however, captive juveniles and young adults readily eat fish. The median ridges on the crushing surfaces of the adult jaws are tuberculate, like those of other eastern species of *Pseudemys*. This probably is an adaptation to a herbivorous diet, so it is likely that adult *P. rubriventris* depend to a substantial degree on aquatic vegetation for nourishment.

Graham (1984b) reported that a large female from New Jersey defecated shell parts of an adult painted turtle, *Chrysemys picta,* and thought it had probably scavenged the remains of a dead turtle.

PREDATORS AND DEFENSE: Crows (*Corvus*), skunks (*Mephitis*), and especially raccoons (*Procyon*) rob nests and prey on hatchlings. Graham (1984a) found the remains of two hatchlings in a bullfrog (*Rana catesbeiana*). Humans are the chief destroyers of adults.

Adults may attempt to bite or void their bladder water when handled, but most retire shyly into their shells.

POPULATIONS: *Pseudemys rubriventris* is essentially a riverine species over much of its range, so population sizes are difficult to estimate, although they may contain many individuals. Only about 200 turtles constitute the entire population living in the several New England ponds, but Graham (1969) noted that these ponds contain a substantial number of juveniles, so further recruitment is possible.

REMARKS: *Pseudemys rubriventris, P. nelsoni, P. alabamensis,* and *P. texana* form the red-bellied, or *rubriventris,* group of the genus *Pseudemys*. They share external characters—notched upper jaw with cusps, prefrontal arrow, and reddish plastron—and have the skull with the vomer contributing to the triturating surface and with the middle ridge of the lower triturating surface set well to the side of the lingual margin of the surface.

In the northern part of its range the future of this species is bleak. It is endangered in Pennsylvania (Ernst, 1985a) where the continued existence of suitable habitat along the Delaware River is doubtful in view of industrial expansion, the demand for property, the drainage of wetlands, water pollution, and the application of pesticides to control mosquitoes. Fortunately, the Massachusetts colonies are now protected by the U.S. Fish and Wildlife Service.

Graham (1991b) has prepared a review of the literature concerning *P. rubriventris*.

Pseudemys nelsoni Carr, 1938b
Florida red-bellied turtle

PLATE 37

RECOGNITION: The carapace is high arched, elongated (to 37.5 cm), highest anterior to the middle, widest at the middle, posteriorly serrated, and bears a low vertebral keel, which may disappear completely in old individuals. It is commonly black, but may be olive or dark brown, with red or yellow marks on the pleurals and marginals. The light vertical stripe on the second pleural may be branched to form a Y-shaped figure. Each marginal has a red vertical bar on the dorsal surface and dark smudgelike blotches at its ventral seams. Melanism develops with age in both sexes. The bridge is deep; most are immaculate but some bear several dark blotches. The hingeless plastron is reddish orange and may be immaculate or have a medial pattern which fades with age. The upper jaw is medially notched with a toothlike cusp on either side. The skin is black with yellow stripes. A prefrontal arrow is formed by the junction of the sagittal and two supratemporal stripes on the snout, and one to three stripes lie between the supratemporals behind the eyes. The paramedial head stripes commonly are reduced and always end behind the eyes. *Pseudemys nelsoni* may have the sagittal and a paramedial stripe unite behind the eye to form the "hairpin" mark, as in *P. floridana*, but commonly on only one side of the head (Ward, 1984).

Males have elongated, slightly curved foreclaws, and long, thick tails with the vent posterior to the carapace. Females are slightly larger than males.

KARYOTYPE: The diploid chromosome number is 50: 26 macrochromosomes (16 metacentric, 6 submetacentric, 4 telocentric), and 24 microchromosomes (Killebrew, 1977a).

FOSSIL RECORD: D. R. Jackson (1978a) summarized the Pleistocene records of *P. nelsoni* from Florida: Blancan of Gilchrist County; Rancholabrean of Alachua, Citrus, Columbia, DeSoto, Gilchrist, Levy, Marion, Palm Beach, Polk, and Suwannee

counties. In addition to these records, fossil *P. nelsoni* have been found in late Pleistocene (Rancholabrean) deposits at Edisto Beach, Colleton County, South Carolina (Dobie and Jackson, 1979), and Ladds Quarry, Bartow County, Georgia (Holman, 1985a,b), which indicates that the ranges of this species and the more northern *P. rubriventris* may have overlapped at that time. Sub-Recent remains of *P. nelsoni* have been reported from Dade (Hirschfeld, 1968) and Sarasota (Holman and Clausen, 1984) counties, Florida. D. R. Jackson (1978a) also believes that Hay's (1908) Pleistocene *Trachemys? jarmani* and *Deirochelys floridana* from Hillsborough County, Florida, may be *P. nelsoni*.

Pseudemys caelata Hay, 1908, from Pliocene deposits in Levy County, Florida, is probably immediately ancestral to *P. nelsoni* (Jackson, 1976).

DISTRIBUTION: *Pseudemys nelsoni* ranges from Cumberland Island, Camden County (Shoop and Ruckdeschel, 1986), and Okefenokee Swamp, Ware County (Vitt and Dunham, 1980), Georgia, southwest to at least Taylor County, Florida, and south through peninsular Florida but not the Keys (Iverson and Etchberger, 1989). Reports of the Alabama red-bellied turtle, *P. alabamensis*, from Franklin and Wakulla counties, Florida, may be based on individuals of *P. nelsoni*.

GEOGRAPHIC VARIATION: No subspecies are recognized, and hybridization with *P. floridana* and *P. concinna* probably does not occur (Ward, 1984).

CONFUSING SPECIES: Most *Pseudemys floridana* and *P. concinna* individuals lack the notch and cusps on the upper jaw, and all lack the prefrontal arrow; also, *P. concinna* has a backward-facing C-shaped figure on the second pleural, and *P. floridana*

Juvenile *Pseudemys nelsoni;*
note "prefrontal arrow"

Female *Pseudemys nelsoni*

has hairpin head markings on both sides of the head behind both eyes. In *P. alabamensis* the prominent paramedial headstripes are rarely reduced, and they continue forward between the eyes. *Pseudemys rubriventris* has more head stripes and a greater amount of dark pigment on the juvenile plastron.

HABITAT: This turtle lives in ponds, lakes, alligator holes, ditches, sloughs, spring runs, marshes, mangrove-bordered creeks, and rivers. Most sites contain slow-moving water and abundant aquatic vegetation. It seems to prefer fresh to brackish water, but Dunson and Seidel (1986) found it to be intermediate in salinity tolerance between truly freshwater turtles and the salt-tolerant *Malaclemys. Pseudemys nelsoni* has low rates of mass loss, primarily net water loss, in 100% sea water (about 0.4%/day). Mean whole body water losses of adults larger than

Plastron of adult *Pseudemys nelsoni*

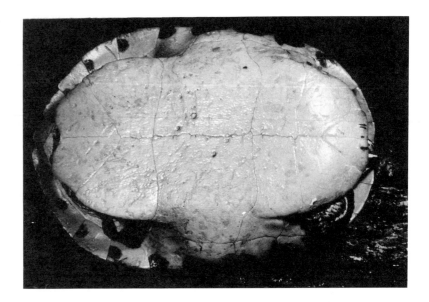

Distribution of *Pseudemys nelsoni*

60 g are only 0.24–0.47%/100g/hour, and sodium intake is also low.

BEHAVIOR: Florida red-bellied turtles are diurnal and active in all months, especially in southern Florida. This confirmed basker spends much of the day lying in the sun on logs or floating mats of vegetation. It often shares basking sites with *P. concinna* and *P. floridana*, but is capable of outcompeting them for access to preferred positions under crowded conditions (Pritchard and Greenhood, 1968). It also occasionally basks on alligator nest mounds (Goodwin and Marion, 1977; Ernst, pers. obs.). Pritchard and Greenhood (1968) studied the basking habits of *P. nelsoni* and stated that it seems to bask for longer periods than either *P. concinna* or *P. floridana*. Possibly *P. nelsoni* can tolerate longer basking periods because its thicker shell retards the conduction of heat to the viscera; however, it shows no marked tolerance for high body temperatures. Hutchison et al. (1966) reported a mean critical thermal maximum of 40.42°C (39.7–41.0), and Pritchard and Greenhood (1968) reported a lethal temperature range of 43–44°C. The critical thermal maximum is slightly lower than those of *P. concinna* and *P. floridana* and corresponds closely to that of *Trachemys scripta*.

The Florida red-bellied turtle has some limited learning ability. In tests using a T-maze conducted by Kramer (1989), *P. nelsoni* scored significantly better than chance (p = <0.05).

Kramer (1986) reported only weak attraction but high tolerance with other *P. nelsoni,* as agonistic interactions occur infrequently. Agonistic behavior is observed most frequently between males, typically involving gaping behavior but occasionally biting.

REPRODUCTION: Males mature at plastron lengths of 17–21 cm in three to four years; females mature at plastron lengths of 26–27 cm in five to seven years (Jackson, 1988a).

Courtship and mating have been observed from October to March, but possibly occur throughout the year. Courtship behavior is similar to that of *P. concinna,* rather lengthy, and consists of several distinct phases (the following description is adapted from Lardie, 1973b, and Kramer and Fritz, 1989). The first phase consists of several behaviors leading to the male positioning himself above the female once the two turtles are close together. The male trails the female, approaches her hindquarters and smells her thighs and cloacal area. If she swims away, he follows closely, neck extended, nuzzling her hindquarters. He may swim around to her side, stretching his neck fully then bending it to bring his head close to her face and touching her with his nose. This occurs in about 50% of the courtships and lasts about two minutes. Next, the male swims up to position himself above the female. At this point his neck is retracted and head pointed downward. He then rapidly strokes the sides of her face (10.8 vibrations/sec; 3–10 vibrations/sequence); titillation bouts average about 0.62 seconds. The male's tail is usually oriented vertically downward, but the penis is not protruded. The female withdraws her head, often turning it sideways and downward. She may also rub her face with her forefoot, as if brushing away an irritant. Titillation

never occurs when the female's head is above water while taking a breath. The male then bends his head downward even more and begins to bite the female's neck. He may protrude his penis at this time. The male may drop behind and then swim forward again, repeating this sequence several times. He finally slides backward and grasps her carapace in the inguinal region, as the female stops swimming and elevates her hindquarters. His tail is twisted around hers, and the penis is inserted into her cloaca. Copulation may last up to four minutes.

Juveniles sometimes stroke other juveniles, but always from a face-to-face position (Kramer, 1987), and Jackson (1987) has observed a female *P. nelsoni* initiate courtship by trailing a male, sniffing his vent, moving to a position in front of him, touching her nose to his, and then stroking his preorbital area with her foreclaws. Kramer (1987) thought face-to-face titillation primitive.

Most freshly excavated nests have been discovered in May and June, but Lardie (1973b) found a female ovipositing on 6 October. Iverson (1977a) thought *P. nelsoni* is a continuous breeder that may oviposit throughout the year, but Jackson (1988a) listed it as a spring and summer nester. Each female probably lays several clutches (possibly 3–6) in a reproductive year.

Nests are often dug in sandy soil at moderate distances from water, and nest sites may be shared with other turtles, particularly *P. floridana*. Lardie (1973b) reported that a nest along a sandy road was 14 cm deep. *Pseudemys nelsoni* frequently lays its eggs in holes dug in alligator nests (Goodwin and Marion, 1977; Deitz and Jackson, 1979; Kushlan and Kushlan, 1980; Ashton and Ashton, 1985; Jackson, 1988a; Hunt and Ogden, 1991; Ernst, pers. obs.). In northern Florida, 33–44% of alligator nests may contain eggs of *P. nelsoni* (Goodwin and Marion, 1977; Deitz and Jackson, 1979), but only 18–20% in the Everglades (Kushlan and Kushlan, 1980). However, of the turtle species identified in 22 of the 40 alligator nests with turtle eggs by Deitz and Jackson (1979), *P. nelsoni* eggs were present in 20 mounds (91%). Most clutches appeared to have been deposited before the alligator clutch was laid or after the mound was abandoned by the alligator because of hatching or egg loss (Kushlan and Kushlan, 1980).

An ecological trade-off occurs when female *P. nelsoni* lay their eggs in alligator nests. If laid before those of the alligator, the turtle's eggs receive the same protection given by the female alligator to her own eggs. Also, the rotting vegetation of the nest mound provides warm incubating temperatures; Goodwin and Marion (1977) reported the mean average

Plastron of juvenile *Pseudemys nelsoni*

incubating temperature was 30°C. The incubation period at this temperature may last only 50 days (Deitz and Jackson, 1979). On the negative side are the possibilities of turtle eggs being destroyed when the alligator tears open the mound to release her hatched young, and increased egg predation by mammals or humans attracted to the alligator nest. The nesting female may also be attacked by the alligator (Hunt and Ogden, 1991).

The total number of eggs per clutch is 6–31. Lardie (1973b) observed a female in the process of laying eggs. Six eggs had been placed in the flask-shaped nest; however, all other reported clutches total over 12 eggs, so this turtle may not have finished ovipositing. Goodwin and Marion (1977) and Jackson (1988a) reported mean clutch sizes of 24 (21–31) and 14 (7–26) eggs, respectively, in nests from northern Florida, but Iverson (1977a) found only 12 eggs in two females from the same area. Kushlin and Kushlin (1980) reported clutches averaging 12.6 eggs in the everglades of southern Florida, and Duellman and Schwartz (1958) removed 12 eggs from a southern Dade County female. Clutch size increases with female shell length (Jackson, 1988a).

The elliptical, white eggs average 36.5 mm (33–39) in length and 24.0 mm (19–26) in width. Hatchlings have been found from March and April to December (Lardie, 1973b); incubation lasts 45–80 days under artificial conditions (Jackson, 1988a) and probably takes about 60–75 days in nature. The eggs

cannot withstand exposure to 20°C for longer than 30 days (Ewert, 1991).

Hatchlings are brighter than adults with rounded, slightly keeled 28–32-mm carapaces. The plastron (27–33 mm) is orange or reddish, and the dark plastral markings are solid semicircles with the flat sides along the seams. A juvenile with a prominent umbilical scar found by Duellman and Schwartz (1958) had a carapace length of 32.4 mm; its plastron was 28.9 mm long.

GROWTH AND LONGEVITY: Two hatchlings raised by Lardie (1973b) grew from 35 to 72 mm in carapace length (35 to 67 mm in plastron length) from 4 April 1968 to 4 March 1979, and from 34 to 91 mm (plastron growth, 34 to 79 mm) from 16 October 1968 to 1 November 1970, respectively.

A female *P. nelsoni* lived 26 years, two months, and 15 days at the Columbus Zoo (Snider and Bowler, 1992).

FOOD HABITS: Adult *Pseudemys nelsoni* are highly herbivorous; the young, like those of other species of *Pseudemys*, probably are more carnivorous, feeding on aquatic insects and other small invertebrates. Adults prefer *Hydrilla*, *Eichhornia*, *Sagittaria*, *Lemna*, and *Najas*. Jim Butler, former naturalist at the Corkscrew Swamp Sanctuary, observed them eating lesser duckweed (*Lemna minor*), broad-leaved arrowhead (*Sagittaria latifolia*), climbing hempweed (*Mikania*), and water hemlock (*Cicuta*). Filamentous green algae may also be consumed; in fact, Meshaka (1988) saw *P. nelsoni* biting off algae from the carapaces of other individuals.

Pseudemys nelsoni feeding on *Hydrilla* has high digestive efficiencies for dry matter (80%), organic matter (81%), energy (75%), and cell walls (86%), and moderate digestive efficiency for nitrogen (58%) (Bjorndal and Bolten, 1990). Microbial fermentation occurs in the intestines and is responsible for the high cell wall digestibility.

The rate of digestion is a key factor in the amount of energy gained from foods, and, apparently, hatchlings can process foods faster than adult *P. nelsoni* (Bjorndal and Bolten, 1992b). Hatchling Florida red-bellied turtles have a significantly better digestive performance than adults. When fed duckweed (*Lemna*), hatchlings process nearly four times as much food on a mass-specific basis than do adults on the same diet while maintaining equivalent digestibilities as adults. Hatchlings gain more than four times the amount of energy and nitrogen daily on a mass-specific basis than do adults. On a diet of *Hydrilla* they feed selectively, ingesting parts significantly higher in energy and nitrogen and significantly lower in lignin than do adults. The small bite size of the hatchlings is a mechanism that enables them to meet higher mass-specific nutrient requirements by improving both the physical structure and, through selective feeding, the nutrient quality of their diet. The increased gains in energy and nitrogen help account for the more rapid growth rate of young *P. nelsoni*.

Bjorndahl (1986) noted a positive feeding interaction within groups of captive juvenile *P. nelsoni*. Solitary turtles ingested only a mean 2.8 mg dry weight per gram of live body weight per day, while those feeding in a group were stimulated, presumably by the sight of other turtles feeding, to consume 4.1 mg. Also, solitary turtles fed an average of only 1.95 minutes every 30 minutes but grouped animals fed an average of 2.59 minutes.

PREDATORS AND DEFENSE: Many nests of the Florida red-bellied turtle are destroyed by skunks (*Mephitis*), otters (*Lutra*), raccoons (*Procyon*), opossums (*Didelphis*), and hogs (*Sus*). Hatchlings and juveniles are eaten by various fish, alligators, snapping turtles (*Chelydra*), water snakes (*Agkistrodon, Nerodia*), mammals, ospreys (*Pandion*), bald eagles (*Haliaeetus*), snail kites (*Rostrhamus*), and wading birds, but adults are relatively free of predators. Besides humans, the only major predator on adults is the alligator (Delany and Abercrombie, 1986), and Pritchard and Greenhood (1968) suggested that the thick, heavily domed carapace of *P. nelsoni* evolved in response to alligator predation. Wiley and Lohrer (1973) found the remains of a 20 cm adult in an osprey (*Pandion*) nest.

This shy animal will flee if given a chance, but when handled often voids bladder water, and large individuals may deliver severe bites.

POPULATIONS: Marchand (in Carr, 1952) found *P. nelsoni* to compose 2.1% of a turtle population that included six other species, the most numerous of which were *P. concinna* and *P. floridana*. There is little difference in the habitat preference of *P. nelsoni* and *P. floridana*, but the latter seems more abundant nearly everywhere they are sympatric. Kramer (1986) marked 129 *P. nelsoni* (73 males, 56 females) and 43 *P. floridana* (23 males, 20 females) along a 980-m section of Rock Springs Run near Orlando, Florida. He estimated a total density of 250 (±75 individuals) of both species combined. The modal core home range size for *P. nelsoni* was between 75 and 100 m, as measured along the shoreline.

REMARKS: A review of the literature regarding *P. nelsoni* is presented by D. R. Jackson (1978a).

Pseudemys alabamensis Baur, 1893a
Alabama red-bellied turtle
PLATE 38

RECOGNITION: This large turtle has a reddish plastron and a prominent notch at the tip of the upper jaw, bordered on either side by a toothlike cusp. The oval, rugose carapace is elongated (to 33.5 cm), highly arched, and elevated along the vertebral scutes; in many, the highest point is anterior to the middle, and it is widest at the middle. With age, longitudinal ridges develop across the pleural scutes, and the low juvenile keel disappears. The posterior marginals are serrated. The carapace is olive to dark brown, with red to yellow bars on the pleurals and marginals. A wide, light, centrally placed vertical bar, which may be Y-shaped, is present on the second pleural. The broad, hingeless plastron is reddish yellow and, at least in younger individuals, may have a mottled pattern of dark vermiculations. Such dark markings may also occur on the bridge and carapace. The skin is olive to black with yellow to orange stripes. The supratemporal and paramedial head stripes are prominent and parallel, but do not join behind the orbits. A sagittal stripe passes anteriorly between the orbits and joins the supratemporal stripes at their junction to form the prefrontal arrow characteristic of the red-bellied turtle group.

Females (to 33.5 cm) grow larger than males (to 29.5 cm), and their carapaces are more domed (Mount, 1975). Males have long, straight foreclaws and long, thick tails with the vent behind the carapacial rim.

KARYOTYPE: Unknown.

FOSSIL RECORD: Unknown.

DISTRIBUTION: *Pseudemys alabamensis* is restricted to Mobile Bay and its tributary streams in Mobile and Baldwin counties, Alabama. Occasionally, individuals occur as waifs along the Gulf Coast as far west as Mississippi (a juvenile, #22218, from Biloxi,

resides in the Senckenberg Museum, Frankfurt, West Germany). It might also have once ranged as far east as Apalachee Bay, Florida (Carr and Crenshaw, 1957), but these records may have been based on specimens of the closely related Florida red-bellied turtle, *P. nelsoni*.

GEOGRAPHIC VARIATION: No subspecies are recognized.

CONFUSING SPECIES: Variants of *P. floridana* and *P. concinna* occasionally have the deep notch and toothlike cusps at the tip of the upper jaw, but neither has the prefrontal arrow. Also, *P. concinna* has a light, backward-facing C-shaped mark on the second pleural, and in *P. floridana* the supratemporal and paramedial head stripes are joined behind the eyes. In *P. nelsoni* the paramedial stripes are reduced or absent. *Trachemys scripta* has an orange or red postorbital stripe and vertical yellow stripes on its hindquarters.

HABITAT: This turtle is definitely *not* a salt marsh inhabitant, as we formerly reported (Ernst and Barbour, 1972). Instead it is found primarily in freshwater streams, rivers, and bays at shallow to moderate depths in areas with soft bottoms and extensive beds of submerged aquatic vegetation. The most important plants are *Myriophyllum*, *Potamogeton*, and *Vallisneria*. It also enters tidal brackish waters, as evidenced by the occasional fouling of its shell by bryozoans and encrusting barnacles (Jackson and Ross, 1974, 1975).

BEHAVIOR: During years with warm winters, *P. alabamensis* may be active in every month; however, it frequently is forced to hibernate in the soft bottoms for at least short periods in most winters.

Like other *Pseudemys*, it is diurnal. Most of the day

Pseudemys alabamensis

Plastron of adult *Pseudemys alabamensis*

is spent foraging in vegetated areas, or in basking. It is very wary while basking, and quickly submerges when disturbed.

REPRODUCTION: Nothing is known of the annual sexual cycles, or the size and age at maturity. Meany (1979) and Dobie and Bagley (1988) noted that several clutches of about six (3–9) eggs are laid between May and early July; however, commercial turtle collector Al Redmond (pers. comm.) believes

these clutch sizes to be too small and mistakenly based on eggs laid by *Graptemys nigrinoda* that also nests in the area. He has found the nests of *P. alabamensis* to contain 16–26 eggs (norm, 18–20).

The primary nesting area is Gravine Island, Baldwin County, although some females may oviposit at other scattered sites, including just north of the Highway 90 Causeway (Meany, 1979; Dobie and Bagley, 1988) and on the banks of nearby feeder streams (Al Redmond, pers. comm.). Nine presumed

Distribution of *Pseudemys alabamensis*

Alabama red-bellied turtle nests discovered on Gravine Island by Meany (1979) were in an open sparsely vegetated sand beach at varied distances from the water in fine moist sand at the base of vegetation. Nests were 8–16 cm deep. Eggs artificially incubated at 27.5°C by Meany hatched in an average of 63 days.

Hatchlings are nearly round and have a keeled carapace with a serrate posterior rim. The carapace is green with a pattern of dark-bordered yellow stripes on each scute, and each pleural scute may bear a dark-centered yellow ocellus. A dark-bordered ocellus covers both the dorsal and ventral marginal seams. The plastron and the bridge are orange-red to coral, usually with a variable, black, seam-following pattern (Mount, 1975, shows a juvenile with an immaculate plastron). The head, limbs, and tail are olive to black with many yellow stripes. The prefrontal arrow and maxillary cusps are well developed.

GROWTH AND LONGEVITY: No growth data have been published on this species. A *P. alabamensis* sent to Ernst as a hatchling in the fall of 1980 survived to 19 July 1991.

FOOD HABITS: This species seems to be chiefly herbivorous; Dobie (in Dobie and Bagley,

1988) reported finding only vegetation in digestive tracts. However, both juvenile and adults kept by Ernst readily ate fish and earthworms, as well as aquatic plants, lettuce, and commercial trout chow. In the wild, elodea (*Anacharis*) may be a primary food (Dobie and Bagley, 1988).

PREDATORS AND DEFENSE: Meany (1979) reported that fish crows destroyed 100% of the natural nests on Gravine Island. Domestic pigs were released on Gravine Island in the 1960s and took their share of eggs, as also did the human residents (Dobie and Bagley, 1988). Fire ants have been found in the nest chambers. Many adults bear tooth scars on their shells from alligator attacks. Probably many other large fish, snakes, wading birds, and mammals take their toll of juveniles.

POPULATIONS: Quantitative population data are scarce. The turtle is most abundant in beds of submergent aquatic plants. McCoy and Vogt (1979) trapped 20 animals in 1,008 hours (0.02 turtles/hour), but saw many more individuals than were collected. Dobie and Bagley (1988) presented some evidence that juveniles declined between 1970 and 1983, and related this to disturbance and nest predation. Adults were formerly collected for food.

Juvenile *Pseudemys alabamensis*

Plastron of juvenile *Pseudemys alabamensis*

REMARKS: Because of its limited range, and the dangers that development, pollution, pet trade collecting, and tropical storms pose to the nesting area on Gravine Island and to the population in general, *Pseudemys alabamensis* was officially desig-nated an endangered species by the U.S. Fish and Wildlife Service on 16 July 1987.

A literature survey of *P. alabamensis* is presented by McCoy and Vogt (1985).

Plate 1 (top). *Chelydra serpentina serpentina*, snapping turtle

Plate 2 (below). *Macroclemys temminckii*, alligator snapping turtle

Plate 3 (opposite top). *Chelonia mydas mydas*, green turtle

Plate 4 (opposite bottom). *Eretmochelys imbricata imbricata*, hawksbill

Plate 5 (below). *Caretta caretta caretta*, loggerhead

Plate 6 (opposite top). *Lepidochelys kempii*, Kemp's ridley, or Atlantic ridley

Plate 7 (opposite bottom). *Lepidochelys olivacea*, Pacific ridley

Plate 8 (directly below). *Dermochelys coriacea*, leatherback

Plate 9 (bottom of page). *Trionyx muticus muticus*, smooth softshell

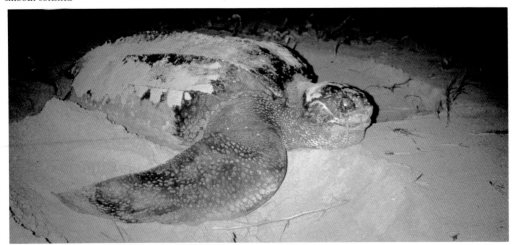

Plate 10 (below). *Trionyx spiniferus spiniferus*, spiny softshell

Plate 11 (opposite top). *Trionyx ferox*, Florida softshell

Plate 12 (opposite bottom). *Trionyx sinensis*, Chinese softshell

Plate 13 (left). *Trionyx steindachneri*, wattle-necked softshell

Plate 14 (below). *Sternotherus odoratus*, common musk turtle

Plate 15 (opposite top). *Sternotherus depressus*, flattened musk turtle

Plate 16 (opposite bottom). *Sternotherus minor minor*, loggerhead musk turtle

Plate 17 (opposite top). *Sternotherus carinatus*, razor-back musk turtle

Plate 18 (opposite bottom). *Kinosternon subrubrum subrubrum*, eastern mud turtle

Plate 19 (right). *Kinosternon baurii*, striped mud turtle

Plate 20 (below). *Kinosternon flavescens flavescens*, yellow mud turtle

Plate 21 (below). *Kinosternon sonoriense*, Sonoran mud turtle

Plate 22 (bottom of page). *Kinosternon hirtipes murrayi*,
Big Bend mud turtle

Plate 23 (opposite top). *Clemmys guttata*, spotted turtle

Plate 24 (opposite bottom). *Clemmys muhlenbergii*, bog turtle

Plate 25 (opposite top). *Clemmys insculpta*, wood turtle

Plate 26 (opposite bottom). *Clemmys marmorata marmorata*, western pond turtle

Plate 27 (top). *Emydoidea blandingii*, Blanding's turtle

Plate 28 (right). *Terrapene carolina carolina*, eastern box turtle

Plate 29 (left). *Terrapene ornata ornata*, ornate box turtle

Plate 30 (below). *Chrysemys picta picta*, painted turtle

Plate 31 (opposite top). *Trachemys scripta scripta*, slider

Plate 32 (opposite bottom). *Trachemys gaigeae*, Big Bend slider

Plate 33 (left). *Pseudemys concinna hieroglyphica*, hieroglyphic river cooter

Plate 34 (below). *Pseudemys gorzugi*, Rio Grande river cooter

Plate 35 (opposite top). *Pseudemys floridana peninsularis*, peninsular cooter

Plate 36 (opposite bottom). *Pseudemys rubriventris*, red-bellied turtle

Plate 37 (opposite top). *Pseudemys nelsoni*, Florida red-bellied turtle

Plate 38 (opposite bottom). *Pseudemys alabamensis*, Alabama red-bellied turtle

Plate 39 (right). *Pseudemys texana*, Texas river cooter

Plate 40 (below). *Deirochelys reticularia chrysea*, Florida chicken turtle

Plate 41 (below). *Graptemys geographica*, common map turtle

Plate 42 (opposite top). *Graptemys barbouri*, Barbour's map turtle

Plate 43 (opposite). *Graptemys pulchra*, Alabama map turtle

Plate 44 (opposite top). *Graptemys ernsti*, Escambia map turtle

Plate 45 (opposite bottom). *Graptemys gibbonsi*, Pascagoula map turtle

Plate 46 (below). *Graptemys caglei*, Cagle's map turtle

Plate 47 (below). *Graptemys pseudogeographica
pseudogeographica*, false map turtle

Plate 48 (opposite top). *Graptemys pseudogeographica
kohnii*, Mississippi map turtle

Plate 49 (opposite bottom). *Graptemys ouachitensis
ouachitensis*, Ouachita map turtle

Plate 50 (below). *Graptemys versa*, Texas map turtle

Plate 51 (opposite top). *Graptemys oculifera*, ringed map turtle

Plate 52 (opposite bottom). *Graptemys flavimaculata*, yellow-blotched map turtle

Plate 53 (opposite top). *Graptemys nigrinoda nigrinoda*, black-knobbed map turtle

Plate 54 (opposite bottom). *Malaclemys terrapin centrata*, Carolina diamondback terrapin,

Plate 55 (below). *Gopherus agassizii*, desert tortoise

Plate 56 (top). *Gopherus berlandieri*, Texas tortoise

Plate 57 (immediately above). *Gopherus polyphemus*,
gopher tortoise

Pseudemys texana Baur, 1893b
Texas river cooter
PLATE 39

RECOGNITION: The elliptical carapace (to 33 cm; Vermersch, 1992) is somewhat flattened (height only about 40% of length), highest just anterior to the middle, widest behind the middle, and posteriorly serrated. The juvenile carapace bears a vertebral keel which commonly disappears with age. Longitudinal rugose striations develop along the pleural scutes in adults. The carapace is olive-brown with a pattern of fine yellow reticulations, whorls, and ocelli; the second pleural has five or six concentric whorls with dark centers and each marginal has a narrow yellow vertical bar on its dorsal surface. The undersides of the marginals are patterned with ocelli. Adult males may become melanistic with age. The hingeless plastron is approximately the same width throughout. It is yellow with dark seams and a pattern of narrow black lines following the seams. This pattern tends to disappear with age. The rim may be tinged with red pigment. The bridge bears a pattern of wavy bars. The skin is black with white to yellow stripes. Head markings are variable, consisting of narrow and broad yellow stripes which may be broken into spots and dashes. A prominent postorbital stripe and a broad, vertical bar just behind the jaw articulation are commonly present. The upper jaw bears a medial notch flanked in some by toothlike cusps; the lower jaw is horizontally flattened.

Adult males are slightly shorter (to 25.3 cm) and more flattened than females, and have longer, thicker tails with the vent behind the carapacial rim. The foreclaws of adult males are long and very pronounced; those of adult females much shorter and thicker.

KARYOTYPE: Killebrew (1977a) reported 50 chromosomes: 26 macrochromosomes (16 metacentric, 6 submetacentric, 4 telocentric) and 24 microchromosomes.

FOSSIL RECORD: Unknown.

DISTRIBUTION: *Pseudemys texana* lives in central and south-central Texas in the Colorado (Concho, Llano, San Saba), Brazos, Guadalupe, and San Antonio watersheds.

GEOGRAPHIC VARIATION: Dixon (in Etchberger and Iverson, 1990) observed previously undocumented and significant geographic variation in color pattern, even within the Colorado River basin, which makes the relationship between *P. texana* and *P. concinna* uncertain. Further study of the closeness of these two species is needed.

CONFUSING SPECIES: *Pseudemys concinna* and *P. gorzugi* lack the medial notch and cusps on the upper jaw. Turtles of the genus *Trachemys* have rounded lower jaws, and adult *Graptemys* have a well-developed medial keel on the carapace.

HABITAT: *Pseudemys texana* is most often found in rivers, but may wander into impoundments, irrigation ditches, canals, and cattle tanks.

BEHAVIOR: The basking habit is well developed, and *Pseudemys texana* may bask for hours on logs on moderately hot days without periodically returning to the water to cool itself (Vermersch, 1992).

REPRODUCTION: Males may mature in three years, but it takes six or more years for females to be ready to breed (Vermersch, 1992). Courtship behavior in *Pseudemys texana* is similar to that of *P. nelsoni* (see that account) (Fritz, 1989).

Nesting probably takes place in May and June. Vermersch (1992) and his students observed three females digging shallow nests 10.2–12.7 cm deep in clay soil within 3.6 m of the water, but none

Plastron of *Pseudemys texana*

Distribution of *Pseudemys texana*

completed oviposition. The eggs are textured with fine granulations, dull white, and measure about 35 mm in length; 4–19 eggs are laid per clutch (Vermersch, 1992).

In south-central Texas, hatchlings emerge in August and September (Vermersch, 1992). Hatchlings and juveniles are more brightly marked than adults with a complex pattern of prominent yellow stripes, whorls, and ocelli on each pleural and vertebral scute (Smith and Sanders, 1952; Carr, 1952). The plastral pattern is also more intense. Pilch (1981) reported a two-headed, approximately two-month-old, 30.2-mm juvenile in which both heads were apparently fully functional.

GROWTH AND LONGEVITY: Unknown.

FOOD HABITS: Strecker (1927) found only mollusks (*Sphaerium, Planorbis, Lymnaea*) in digestive tracts of *Pseudemys texana*. Vermersch (1992) reported that young individuals actively pursue aquatic and terrestrial insects, crayfish, snails, and other invertebrates when offered.

PREDATORS AND DEFENSE: Opossoms, raccoons, and skunks are the normal nest predators in Texas (Vermersch, 1992). When disturbed, *Pseudemys texana* first tries to escape. If caught and handled, most will retreat within their shells, but some bite or void their bladder contents.

POPULATIONS: This turtle seems more common today in parts of the San Antonio River than it was 25 years ago; the river's polluted state does not seem to have adversely affected it (Vermersch, 1992).

REMARKS: Very little life history of *Pseudemys texana* has reached the literature under its name. Unfortunately most data have been published under *P. concinna* or *P. floridana,* and cannot be distinguished at this time. A thorough ecological and behavioral study is needed.

Etchberger and Iverson (1990) gave a literature review of *P. texana*.

Deirochelys reticularia (Latreille, in Sonnini and Latreille, 1802)
Chicken turtle

PLATE 40

RECOGNITION: *Deirochelys reticularia* is a small to medium-sized turtle with an extremely long neck and a reticulate pattern of yellow lines on its tan to olive, pear-shaped carapace. The long narrow carapace (to 25.4 cm) is not keeled or posteriorly serrated, and the surface is rough with small longitudinal ridges. Vertebral scutes are very broad and the first touches four marginal scutes instead of the usual two. The undersides of the marginals are yellow and may have a dark blotch at the seam. One or two dark blotches may also occur on the well-developed bridge. The hingeless plastron is yellow, and in the western subspecies may have a dark pattern bordering the seams. The head is long and narrow with a pointed snout, and the upper jaw is neither hooked nor notched. The skin is olive to brown, with yellow or white stripes. A characteristic pattern of vertical light stripes occurs on the rump, and the foreleg stripe is very wide. The length of the head and neck combined is approximately equal to the length of the plastron, or about 75–80% of the carapace length. The toes are webbed.

Adult males have long, thick tails, with the vent posterior to the rim of the carapace. Adult females are more than 1.5 times larger than adult males (Gibbons and Lovich, 1990).

KARYOTYPE: The diploid chromosome number is 50: 26 macrochromosomes and 24 microchromosomes with a total of 80 arms. Chromosome types, according to centromere placement, include 20 metacentric or submetacentric, 10 subtelocentric, and 20 acrocentric or telocentric configurations (Stock, 1972; Killebrew, 1977a).

FOSSIL RECORD: Fossil *Deirochelys reticularia* are known from Pliocene (Blancan), Pleistocene (Irvingtonian, Rancholabrean) and sub-Recent sites in Florida (C. G. Jackson, Jr, 1964, 1974b; D. R.

Jackson, 1978b; Holman, 1978). *Deirochelys carri* D. R. Jackson, 1978b, from the Pliocene (Hemphillian) of Florida is the presumed ancestor of *D. reticularia*, and even older, more primitive fossil *Deirochelys* from the Miocene (Hemingfordian) of Florida may represent an important link in the gradual evolutionary sequence from a generalized emydine ancestor, like *Trachemys*, to the more specialized *D. carri* and *D. reticularia* (Jackson, 1978b).

DISTRIBUTION: *Deirochelys reticularia* ranges from southeastern Virginia (Mitchell and Buhlmann, 1991) and eastern North Carolina south along the Atlantic Coastal Plain to southern Florida, west along the Gulf Coastal Plain to Texas, and northward, west of the Mississippi River, to southeastern Oklahoma and southeastern Missouri. Although present in some Atlantic coastal localities, the species is found on few barrier islands (Gibbons and Coker, 1978).

GEOGRAPHIC VARIATION: Three subspecies are recognized. *Deirochelys reticularia reticularia* (Latreille, in Sonnini and Latreille, 1802), the eastern chicken turtle, occurs along the Atlantic and Gulf coastal plains from southeastern Virginia to the Mississippi River. This subspecies has narrow netlike lines on the olive to brown carapace, a narrow yellow carapacial rim, and in most cases a spot at the juncture of the femoral and anal scutes. Black spots are present on the ventral surface of the marginals at the level of the bridge in about 72% of individuals (Schwartz, 1956a). *Deirochelys r. chrysea* Schwartz, 1956a, the Florida chicken turtle, is restricted to peninsular Florida. This subspecies has a network of broad, bright, orange or yellow lines on the carapace and a wide, orange carapacial rim. Black spots are present on the ventral surface of the marginals in about 43% of individuals (Schwartz, 1956a). *Deirochelys r. miaria*

Male *Deirochelys reticularia reticularia*

Plastron of *Deirochelys reticularia reticularia*

Schwartz, 1956a, the western chicken turtle, occurs in western Mississippi and west of the Mississippi River from southeastern Missouri and southeastern Oklahoma south to the Gulf of Mexico. It is flattened, has a network of broad, faint lines on the carapace, and has a plastral pattern of dark markings along the seams. Adults have unstreaked chins and throats.

CONFUSING SPECIES: The neck of *Deirochelys* is much longer than those of *Trachemys, Chrysemys, Pseudemys, Graptemys* or *Malaclemys,* and none of these turtles has its first vertebral scute in contact with four marginal scutes. *Trachemys scripta* has narrow yellow stripes on the front legs, and, along with *Pseudemys* and *Graptemys,* has a posteriorly serrated carapace.

HABITAT: The chicken turtle inhabits still waters including ponds, lakes, ditches, marshes, cypress swamps, and Carolina bays. Normally ample amounts of aquatic vegetation and a soft bottom are present.

Deirochelys reticularia has "striped-pants"

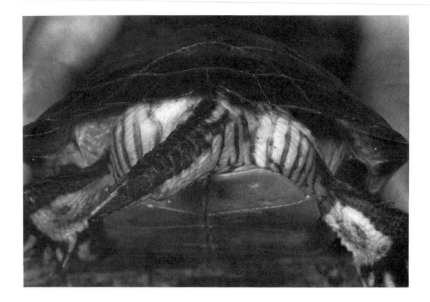

Note wide foreleg stripe on female *Deirochelys reticularia*

BEHAVIOR: Most of what is known of the behavior of this species is based on long-term studies using terrestrial drift fences by researchers at the Savannah River Ecology Laboratory in South Carolina (Gibbons, 1969b; Gibbons and Semlitsch, 1981). Terrestrial activity there is evident from March through April, and some individuals were captured entering a Carolina bay in August when other habitats dried up (Gibbons, 1969b; Gibbons and Greene, 1978). Both sexes periodically migrate between aquatic habitats, although males move greater distances than females (Gibbons, 1986). Gibbons (1970a) reported a direc-

tional trend in emigrating turtles but a random movement by immigrants into the same Carolina bay.

Some movement is prompted by drought. Gibbons and Green (1978) noted that fewer chicken turtles left the Carolina bay in high-water years than during a drought year; however, response by *Deirochelys* to drought varies within and among populations. During a severe drought in 1967–1968, only a few individuals left the natural Carolina bay (Gibbons, 1969b), but the number was not significantly greater than that in non-drought years. In contrast, chicken turtles emigrated in large numbers when a man-made pond was drained

Distribution of *Deirochelys reticularia*

Male *Deirochelys reticularia chrysea*

(Gibbons et al., 1983; Gibbons, 1986). The species is well adapted to living in ephemeral habitats and coping with varying water levels (Gibbons et al., 1990), and individuals burrow during protracted periods of terrestrial activity, presumably to escape drought conditions (Bennett et al., 1970; Gibbons et al., 1983).

Data concerning long-distance movements by *Dei-rochelys* are sparse, but a marked chicken turtle in Florida moved 612 m in slightly more than eight months (Marchand, 1945).

Deirochelys spends much time basking, but little has been reported on the thermal ecology of this species. Active animals have been found with cloacal temperatures of 25.5–25.6°C (Brattstrom, 1965), and Hutchi-

Plastron of *Deirochelys
reticularia chrysea*

Plastron of *Deirochelys
reticularia miaria*

son et al. (1966) found that three *D. reticularia* lost the righting ability at 39.1°C (38.5–39.5) and that their mean critical thermal maximum was 41.3°C (40.8–42.2).

At least in the northern part of the range, the chicken turtle hibernates in mud and aquatic vegetation. In Florida it does not hibernate, but remains active except on cold days.

REPRODUCTION: Male *Deirochelys* in South Carolina attain sexual maturity at plastron lengths of between 7.5 and 8.5 cm during their second or third growing season. Males in northern Florida probably mature at about the same size (Jackson, 1988a). Testes volume increases with body size and is greatest from May through July (Gibbons, 1969b).

Females in South Carolina mature at a plastron length of about 16.0 cm (Gibbons, 1969b), although a few may come into breeding condition as small as 14.1 cm (Gibbons and Greene, 1978).

The largest ovarian follicles are present in the largest females, but some 16.1–18.8-cm females had follicles of 6 mm or less in diameter. Ovarian activity is asymmetrical with one oviduct producing more eggs than the other, and ovarian dominance appears to alternate between clutches (Jackson, 1988a). Gibbons (1969b) noted an absence of enlarged follicles in several females larger than 18.0 cm, prompting him to suggest that they may have been reproductively senile. However, there is no convincing evidence of reproductive senility in turtles. Gibbons (pers. comm.) told us that the females in question were sampled outside the period of the sexual cycle when larger follicles would be expected (his 1969b reference was published before *Deirochelys* in South Carolina was known to have both spring and fall nesting seasons). Jackson (1988a) detected what he called "signs of potential senescence" (reduced number and size of clutches, and high percentage of atretic follicles during the reproductive season) in only one Florida female.

During courtship the male vibrates his foreclaws against the female's face (Krefft, 1951; Fritz, 1991).

Deirochelys is one of the few North American turtle species with a "winter"-nesting pattern (Jackson, 1988a). No evidence is available to document that chicken turtles nest throughout the year as suggested by Iverson (1977a). The egg-laying season in South Carolina is divided into two periods: a late winter and spring period from mid-February to May, and a fall and early winter period from August to November (Gibbons, 1969b; Gibbons and Greene, 1978, 1979, 1990). The percentage of nesting females (based on x-ray data) from a single area in South Carolina in various months from 1976 to 1987 was as follows: January, 1%; February, 14%; March, 37%; April, 5%; August, 13%; September, 24%; October, 1%; November, 2% (Gibbons and Greene, 1990). Farther south in Florida, the nesting season is continuous from mid-September until early March, but may be delayed temporarily by cold weather (Jackson, 1988a). Fewer females nest in drought years than in non-drought years (Gibbons et al., 1983).

Egg retention is another interesting variant in the biology of chicken turtles. Free-living females in Florida retain shelled eggs in the oviducts less than two weeks according to Jackson (1988a). However, Gibbons informed us that a free-living female in South Carolina x-rayed on 23 September 1977 and 2 April 1978 was found to be carrying the same clutch of eggs both times (as demonstrated by the size of the eggs and their position in the oviducts). She was recaptured on 17 November 1978, after laying the clutch of five eggs, and on this date contained 11 eggs. When recaptured a third time on 16 March 1979, she had not yet oviposited the latter clutch. A captive female was reported to retain shelled eggs for over eight months (Cagle and Tihen, 1948).

The abbreviated nesting season of *Deirochelys* populations in the northern part of the range may be derived from the more continuous nesting season seen in Florida (Iverson, 1977a; Jackson, 1988a). The genus has existed in the subtropical climate of Florida for at least 10 million years. As the species moved northward, the nesting season was interrupted in response to colder winters. Potential advantages of protracted winter nesting include more favorable timing of hatchling emergence relative to food availability, reduction of interspecific competition among hatchlings, and the ability to reproduce when predators are not accustomed to finding turtle eggs.

Relatively little has been published on the nesting habits of *Deirochelys*. On 11 May, a 20.9-cm Texas *D. r. miaria* dug a "goblet"-shaped nest 16.5 cm deep 30 m from the water (David, 1975). The nest was excavated in sandy soil on an approximately 15° slope in low weeds and grass. No trees or brush were within 50 m of the nest site, which was noticeably moister than the surrounding soil. The female deposited eight eggs in 20 minutes, laying them at approximately two-minute intervals. After the last egg was laid, about five minutes passed before she filled in the nest with dirt and debris using semicircular sweeping movements of the hind legs. Filling required just over 15 minutes. Ernst and Barbour (1972) reported nests to be cylindrical, 7.6 cm wide at the mouth and 10 cm deep, and a captive female observed by Nicol and Nicol (1985) dug a flask-shaped nest 5 cm across and 8 cm deep. In Florida, nests are often dug in the heavy soil of plowed lakeside fields (Carr, 1952).

The flexible, oblong, white eggs are 28.0–40.0 mm long, 17.0–23.6 mm wide, and weigh 8.7–13.3 g. Eggs laid in the fall in South Carolina are larger, have a higher percentage of shell and lipids, have a heavier dry and wet mass, and have less water relative to spring eggs. The wet mass of eggs is positively correlated with female body size, and the proportion of lipid content in the yolk increases with egg size. Egg wet mass is not significantly correlated with clutch size (Congdon et al., 1983a; Congdon and Gibbons, 1985; Jackson, 1988a; Gibbons and Greene, 1990). Nicol and Nicol (1985) reported a clutch of infertile eggs laid by a captive that were between 40 and 45 mm in length.

Egg width is constrained by the width of the pelvic opening in *Deirochelys* from South Carolina (Congdon et al., 1983a; Congdon and Gibbons, 1987); in other words, egg width increases at the same rate as body size. This relationship challenges the ecological concept of optimal egg size theory. Achievement of an optimal egg size may be constrained by structural requirements of the pelvic girdle related to locomotion. The pelvic constraint appears to be relaxed in large Florida females since clutch size, not egg size, is responsible for the relationship between clutch mass and body size (Jackson, 1988a).

Clutches usually contain about eight eggs (5–12) in South Carolina (Gibbons et al., 1982) and nine eggs (2–19) in Florida (Jackson, 1988a). Females from South Carolina may lay two clutches a year; some lay both clutches in the spring (Gibbons, 1969b), others lay one clutch in the spring and one the following fall (Gibbons and Greene, 1978). Females may lay more or fewer eggs in the second clutch than the first clutch in the same year. Of 25 individual females, captured while gravid more than once over several years, 2 laid the same number of eggs in the second clutch, 15 laid more eggs, and 8 laid fewer eggs. The clutch size of fall (mean 7.4) and spring (mean 7.2) nesters does not differ significantly. Mean clutch size by month is as follows: February, 7.1; March, 7.2; April, 8.6; August, 8.2; September, 6.8 (Gibbons et al., 1982). Variation in the clutch size within individuals and among individuals in a Carolina bay was similar (Gibbons, 1982). Florida females may deposit two to four clutches per season for a mean annual reproductive potential of 28.5 eggs (Jackson, 1988a).

Clutch size appears to increase with plastron length in the fall, but not in the spring; but the difference may be an artifact of sample size (Gibbons et al., 1979a). Weak but significant positive relationships were detected between plastron length and clutch size in South Carolina (Gibbons et al., 1982; Congdon et al., 1983a), but in Florida, where female *Deirochelys* attain larger sizes relative to those from South Carolina, the relationship is stronger (Jackson, 1988a). In Florida, the increase in clutch mass relative to body size is due to an increase in clutch size rather than egg size. In South Carolina, the increase in clutch mass relative to body size is due to an increase in egg size.

Mean clutch wet mass (72.5 g) in South Carolina is about 9% female body mass (Congdon and Gibbons, 1985), and relative clutch mass (clutch mass divided by body mass including clutch mass) of Florida females is 10.3% (Jackson, 1988a). No significant difference exists between the wet mass of spring and fall clutches in South Carolina when adjusted for female body size (Congdon et al., 1983a).

Eggs of *Deirochelys* have a high proportion of lipids, possibly as a provision for a long incubation period. The mean weight of various egg components varies between fall and spring (in parentheses) clutches as follows: lean dry mass, 1.759 g (1.345 g); lipid dry mass, 0.896 g (0.617 g); shell dry mass, 0.569 g (0.494 g). The dry mass of spring and fall eggs is 26.2% lipids and the dry mass of the yolk is 32.42% lipids. The eggshell is 6.87% of total egg dry weight (Congdon et al., 1983a; Congdon and Gibbons, 1985). The mean weight of the eggshell is about 0.5 g, including about 36% inorganic ash (Lamb and Congdon, 1985).

Embryos of chicken turtles undergo a period of diapause with development arrested in the late gastrula stage. A period of chilling is required before development continues (Ewert, 1985, 1991).

Eggs of South Carolina *Deirochelys* hatch in 152 days at 29°C (Congdon et al., 1983a); those laid in Florida hatch in 78–89 days at temperatures from 25 to 29°C (Iverson, 1977a; Jackson, 1988a). Some hatchlings in South Carolina remain in the nest over winter (Gibbons, 1969b; Gibbons and Nelson, 1978; Gibbons et al., 1990).

The nearly round 28.0–31.6-mm hatchling carapace is keeled and rugose, the plastron is 28–32 mm long, and the little turtles weigh 8.1–9.0 g (Ewert, 1979a; Jackson, 1988a). Congdon et al. (1983a) reported that mean South Carolina hatchling wet mass is 6.7 g of which mean lipid content is 27.4% and mean water content is 78.7%. Mean dry mass lean and lipid components are 1.03 g and 0.39 g, respectively. Hatchling mass is correlated with egg mass (Jackson, 1988a). Hatchling *D. r. miaria* have dark pigment along the plastral seams.

Sex determination is influenced by incubation temperature; 100% of eggs incubated at 25°C produce males, but at 30°C, only 11% are males (Ewert and Nelson, 1991).

GROWTH AND LONGEVITY: During periods of drought, *Deirochelys* in South Carolina grow 25–30 mm/yr up to a size of 9.0–10.0 cm for males and 13.0–15.0 cm, or more, in females (Gibbons, 1969b). During non-drought years, individuals captured in their first year grow 32–44 mm/yr. Some adults may not grow every year, while others grow at a modest rate (Gibbons and Greene, 1978).

Individual chicken turtles in South Carolina have been recaptured at intervals of up to 15 years after the first capture, and some have attained maximum known, or estimated, ages of at least 20–24 years (Gibbons, 1987).

FOOD HABITS: During the first year of life chicken turtles are at least partially carnivorous (D. R.

Juvenile *Deirochelys reticularia reticularia*

Juvenile *Deirochelys reticularia chrysea*

Jackson, 1978b), but adults probably are more omnivorous. Competition with other emydid turtles is assumed to be negligible owing to the specialized feeding behavior of the chicken turtle. *Deirochelys* probably uses a "pharangeal" feeding method similar to that described by Bramble (1973) for other species. For capturing rapid prey, such as aquatic arthropods, the chicken turtle's well-developed hyoid apparatus allows it to literally suck in food items. In southern Florida, *D. r. chrysea* forages mostly in the morning, crawling or swimming slowly along with neck out-stretched, occasionally probing into clumps of aquatic vegetation (Ernst, pers. obs.).

Carr (1952) observed wild chicken turtles eating tadpoles, crayfish, and what appeared to be a bud of the water plant *Nuphar*. Cagle (1950) reported that chicken turtles respond best to decayed bait, whereas other turtles may not enter a trap containing rotten bait.

Captive adults readily ingest romaine lettuce, newborn mice, fish, and commercial trout chow. Juveniles refuse plant materials, feeding instead on fish, newborn mice, earthworms, and trout chow.

PREDATORS AND DEFENSE: Little has been published regarding predation on *Deirochelys*. Predators such as raccoons (*Procyon lotor*), skunks (*Mephitis mephitis*), and others undoubtedly prey on eggs, juveniles, and adults, and alligators (*Alligator mississippiensis*) occasionally eat them. Chicken turtles are also eaten by some people—their palatable flesh is the source of their common name. Many are traffic fatalities each year (Ernst, pers. obs.).

Wild *Deirochelys* are wary, and often difficult to approach. Their disposition varies: some bite and scratch viciously, others are shy and retiring. Chicken turtles are especially wary while basking.

POPULATIONS: The size structure of adult and subadult females in a South Carolina population did not differ appreciably between 1967–1970 and 1975–1976 (Gibbons and Greene, 1978); a scarcity of females with 8.1–11.2-cm plastra was noted in this same population by Gibbons (1969b).

The density and biomass of *Deirochelys* in a 10-ha Carolina bay in South Carolina were 40.1 turtles/ha and 8.18 kg/ha (Iverson, 1982a). Later estimates for the same site and a man-made pond in the region were 17.7 turtles/ha and 5.1 kg/ha, and 7.2 turtles/ha and 3.1 kg/ha, respectively (Congdon et al., 1986). Minimum total biomass and energy equivalents of eggs produced per hectare of aquatic habitat each year at the Carolina bay were 0.22 kg and 1391 kJ (Congdon et al., 1986).

Sex ratios for South Carolina populations range from 1.12 to 2.79 adult males for every adult female (Gibbons, 1990b).

Cagle and Chaney (1950) reported that *Deirochelys* composed only 4.4% of the turtles trapped in southwestern Louisiana during 456 trap hours.

Survivorship curves indicate that fewer than 10 individuals out of 1,000 live past the age of 15 years (Gibbons, 1987).

REMARKS: Baur (1889) first proposed a close relationship between *Deirochelys* and *Emydoidea* on the basis of similar rib and skull specializations, and this was accepted by Loveridge and Williams (1957), McDowell (1964), and Ernst and Barbour (1972), among others. Most authors also noted that *Deirochelys* closely resembles *Chrysemys*, *Trachemys*, and *Pseudemys* in shell features. Bramble (1974b) in his study of shell kinesis and other skeletal and muscle morphology indicated that *Emydoidea* is more closely related to *Emys* and *Terrapene* than to *Deirochelys*, and that *Deirochelys* is more closely related to *Chrysemys*, *Trachemys* and *Pseudemys*. The findings of D. R. Jackson (1978b, 1988a) support the presumed relationship with the three latter genera, and electrophoretic studies of skeletal muscle myoglobin also show *Deirochelys* to be closely related to *Chrysemys*, *Trachemys*, *Pseudemys*, *Graptemys*, and *Malaclemys* (Seidel and Adkins, 1989).

Additional information on *Deirochelys* is summarized by Zug and Schwartz (1971).

Graptemys geographica (Le Sueur, 1817)
Common map turtle

PLATE 41

RECOGNITION: This widely distributed species is large (female carapace to 27.3 cm) and broad headed (females). Its oval carapace is posteriorly serrated and bears a distinct but low vertebral keel. Vertebral spines are present on juveniles and low in adult males, but are essentially absent on adult females. Carapace color is olive-green with a reticulate pattern of fine yellow lines. The hingeless plastron is cream to yellow in adults, but juveniles have a dark seam-following pattern. The lower marginal scutes are yellow with circular dark markings, and the bridge bears longitudinal dark lines. The skin is olive to brown-black with yellow to greenish-yellow stripes. The postorbital mark is roughly triangular and is not connected to the head stripes, but the anterior end of one neck stripe may turn upward across the tympanum, and a few neck stripes always reach the orbit. The lower jaw is patterned with longitudinal yellow stripes, of which the medial is widest.

Adult males are smaller (to 16 cm) than females (see above), have an oval carapace, and long, thick tails, with the anal vent posterior to the rim of the carapace. Females have a broader head and a more rounded carapace.

KARYOTYPE: The diploid chromosome number is 50: 26 macrochromosomes and 24 microchromosomes (Killebrew, 1977a).

FOSSIL RECORD: Pleistocene remains of *Graptemys geographica* are known from Irvingtonian deposits in Kansas and Rancholabrean deposits in Tennessee, Texas, Virginia, and various midwestern sites (Fay, 1988; Guilday et al., 1978; Holman, 1969b, 1972; Jenkins and Semken, 1972; Preston, 1979; Slaughter et al., 1962). Archeological specimens have been reported from several digs about the Great Lakes (Adler, 1968).

DISTRIBUTION: The common map turtle ranges from southern Quebec and northwestern Vermont in the St. Lawrence drainage west through the Great Lakes into southern Wisconsin and eastern Minnesota, and, west of the Appalachians, south to Kansas, northeastern Oklahoma, Arkansas, Tennessee, Alabama (above the fall line) and northwestern Georgia. It also occurs in the Susquehanna River system of Pennsylvania and Maryland and in the Delaware River (Arndt and Potter, 1973) of Pennsylvania and New Jersey. An isolated population apparently exists in the Hudson River. This is the only species of map turtle that inhabits watersheds emptying into the Atlantic Ocean.

GEOGRAPHIC VARIATION: No subspecies are recognized. The lack of mitochondrial DNA variation within or among populations is unusual given the wide range of this species (Avise et al., 1992).

CONFUSING SPECIES: All other *Graptemys* have well-developed vertebral keels with prominent spines. In addition, *G. pseudogeographica kohnii* has a crescent-shaped postorbital mark that separates the neck stripes from the orbit, *G. p. pseudogeographica* has a narrow postorbital mark, and *G. ouachitensis* has large postorbital marks and prominent large white spots on each side of the face, one just below the orbit and another on the lower jaw.

HABITAT: The common map turtle is typically an inhabitant of large bodies of water such as rivers and lakes. Areas with abundant basking sites are preferred. Habitat preferences in a Pennsylvania river, as measured by frequency of capture, were as follows: deep, slow-moving areas, 52.9%, shallow areas, 2.3%, and riffles and other areas, 27.0%. Large turtles

Graptemys geographica

Plastron of *Graptemys geographica*

were captured in deep, slow areas more often than expected and small turtles were collected in shallow, slow areas more often than expected. Large adults avoided areas with emergent vegetation, but congregated in areas with fallen limbs (Pluto and Bellis, 1986).

BEHAVIOR: *Graptemys geographica* is primarily diurnal, foraging in the morning and late afternoon and basking at midday (Ernst and Barbour, pers. obs.). In Kentucky, Pennsylvania, and Wisconsin it is active from April to late October or early November during warm years, but may become inactive in late September if the weather turns cold (Ernst, pers. obs.; Vogt, 1980). In Pennsylvania, deep riverine pools are used as hibernacula (Pluto and Bellis, 1988), and in Kentucky impoundments are often used as overwintering sites (Ernst, pers. obs.).

Females begin to bask in April soon after emerging from winter dormancy; perhaps warming of their bodies during the spring raises metabolism and speeds up eggshelling (Vogt, 1980). Generally, a basking site is selected that is offshore, near deep water, and exposed to the sun. Sites include fallen trees and rocks (Gordon and MacCulloch, 1980; Pluto and Bellis, 1986). At far northern localities in the spring, they

Head pattern of *Graptemys geographica*

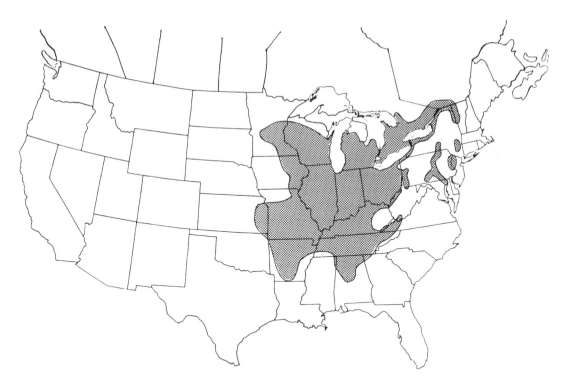

Distribution of *Graptemys geographica*

may even bask on ice floes (Gordon and MacCulloch, 1980).

Mean characteristics of basking sites in a Quebec lake are: site length, 185 cm; width, 40 cm; distance from land, 486 cm; distance from emergent aquatic vegetation larger than 1 m, 139 cm; height above water, 20 cm; and water depth below site, 54 cm. The site is usually composed of roots or stumps with an easterly exposure, separated from shore, stationary, and not obviously protected from prevailing west winds. Sites used for basking are significantly longer than unused places, farther from land and both aquatic and terrestrial vegetation, and lie in deeper water (Flaherty and Bider, 1984).

Meteorological factors affecting fall basking behavior of *G. geographica* in Michigan were examined by Ecksdine (1985). Step-wise multiple regression analysis revealed that the average difference between basking-site temperature and water temperature explained 26.5% of the variability in the number of turtles observed basking in one day. Site type explained an additional 16% of the variance. Another step-wise model using size estimates of each basking turtle as the dependent variable revealed that 8.3% of variance was attributable to wind speed. The negative correlation observed suggests that as wind speed increases it has less effect on the basking behavior of larger turtles than it does on smaller ones. Site temperature minus water temperature explained another 6% of the variance, and water temperature explained an additional 4% given that the other two variables were already present in the model.

Basking activity in Quebec is bimodal with peaks occurring in May–June and August (Gordon and MacCulloch, 1980). Large numbers of turtles may bask at the same site. Medium-sized turtles are pushed off the basking log by large-sized turtles more often than the opposite occurs. Most physical interactions take place when an emerging individual makes contact with another that is already basking. Smaller individuals generally emerge away from large basking turtles (Pluto and Bellis, 1986).

Map turtles are extremely wary while basking, and they dive into the water at the slightest disturbance. Their gregariousness makes them difficult to approach, for when one becomes alarmed and slides into the water all promptly follow.

Graptemys geographica does not always remain in the same place throughout its annual activity period. Gordon and MacCulloch (1980) observed that 27% of marked males and 60% of marked females in a lake population in Quebec moved from previous points of capture during the prenesting period in late June.

During the postnesting period 56% of the marked males changed locations. These differences in behavior may be due to females moving greater distances than males (but see below), or basking less than males.

In a central Pennsylvania river, *G. geographica* has three annual movement patterns (Pluto and Bellis, 1988): (1) late spring and summer movement, primarily by males, upstream from a deep slow-current area and return downstream to it in late summer, (2) late spring downstream migration, mainly by males, from the deep pool and upstream return to it in late summer, and (3) confinement to small areas along the river. High water in spring aids downstream movement while it retards upstream travel. Although the overall movement pattern of females was not determined, gravid females swim mostly upstream. Juveniles move mainly downstream, possibly aided by the current. Four hatchlings moved 1.2 km, 4.4 km, and 5.3 km downstream, and 2.3 km upstream, respectively, from their original capture site. A juvenile male migrated in late summer from a shallow area 4.7 km upstream to the deep pool. Five gravid females moved 0.63–5.35 km (mean, 3.2) upstream during June and July. One adult male traveled upstream 5.8 km in four days (1.46 km/day). Overall, males had mean linear home ranges along the river of 2.1 km (0.17–6.07), and females, 1.2 km (0–5.3); these differences are significant (Mann-Whitney test).

Maximum swimming speed, as determined by maintaining position in current, shows a significant positive association with body size. Mean swimming speeds for various sizes (carapace length) is as follows: >12.5 cm, 56.8 cm/sec; 6.65–12.5 cm, 46.9 cm/sec; and <66.5 cm, 37.0 cm/sec (Pluto and Bellis, 1986).

REPRODUCTION: Little is known regarding the attainment of sexual maturity by this turtle. Newman (1906) reported that none of the females he found nesting was smaller than 19 cm or less than 14 years old. Females in Wisconsin are still immature at 10–12 years (Vogt, 1980).

Courtship and mating apparently occur both in spring and autumn. Evermann and Clark (1916) reported that on 4 October and later, pairs of *G. geographica,* a small one trailing a larger one, frequently were seen walking about on the bottom of Lake Maxinkuckee, Indiana, and that on 27 April smaller ones were again seen following larger ones about, as if to mate. Ernst and Barbour have also observed such spring behavior in Kentucky streams. No vibration of the forelimbs occurs during court-

Hatching *Graptemys geographica*

ship; instead the male may swim to the front of the female, make snout-to-snout contact, and then bob his head rapidly up and down (Vogt, 1980). The male may attempt to mount after cloacal contact. He hooks his tail around that of the female to maintain his balance and bring the vents together for intromission.

The nesting period lasts from late May to mid-July, depending on location, with a peak during the second and third weeks of June. Preferred nest sites are characterized by soft soil or sand and full sunshine. Three nests located along the margin of a lake in Quebec were within 3 m of the water's edge and less than a meter above the water level (Gordon and McCulloch, 1980). Several trial cavities may be dug before oviposition, and soft, plowed soil or clean, dry sand away from beaches seem to be preferred, although clay is sometimes used. Most nesting is early in the day, usually before 0800.

The nest is flask shaped, and the dull white, ellipsoidal eggs are soft and easily dented when fresh but become firmer as water is absorbed. The eggs are 32–35 mm long and 21–22 mm wide. The mean lipid content of eggs of *G. geographica* from Michigan was 0.399 g, or about 15.9% of egg mass. The mean dry mass of the lean, or nonlipid, part of these eggs was 2.11 g (Congdon et al., 1983c). Clutch size usually is 9–17 (Gordon and McCulloch, 1980), but Thompson (in Babcock, 1919) reported nests containing as many as 20 eggs. A female dissected by Thompson contained 14 eggs in the oviducts and about the same number of well-developed eggs in the ovaries.

Female *Graptemys geographica* from the Niangua River, Missouri, lay an average of 10.1 eggs per clutch (6–15), and contain 1–24 (mean, 10.9) enlarged follicles, and 5–15 (mean, 9.4) corpora lutea (White and Moll, 1991). These data indicate that at least two clutches of eggs are deposited each year, and the existence of two sets of corpora lutea of different sizes and a set of enlarged follicles by May suggests that as many as three clutches may be produced per year. A female captured there on 28 April had 13 enlarged follicles and nine oviducal eggs, and two sets of corpora lutea (one set of nine and a set of five small corpora lutea). Eight (67%) of 12 females had one set of corpora lutea and one set of enlarged follicles; four (33%) females had two sets of corpora lutea and one set of enlarged follicles by 1 May. Assuming 10 eggs per clutch, White and Moll (1991) estimated that the annual reproductive potential of 100 typical, fertile females to be 23.3 eggs per female. In Wisconsin, females lay two clutches of 8–19 eggs (mean 13.6) a year (Vogt, 1980). The average length, width, and weight of the eggs are 32.4–37.4 mm, 17.9–24.7 mm, and 5.9–11.2 g, respectively.

Hatchlings may emerge from the nest in August–September or overwinter, depending on locality (Gibbons and Nelson, 1978). Overwintering behavior was not observed at Stoddard, Wisconsin, perhaps in response to maggot infestation of turtle nests (Vogt, 1981c).

Graptemys geographica has environmental sex determination. Under experimental conditions a predominance of males is produced at an incubation

Plastron of juvenile
Graptemys geographica

temperature of 25°C but an incubation temperature of 30°C or higher produces predominantly females (Bull and Vogt, 1979; Ewert and Nelson, 1991). Experimentally manipulated eggs incubated under natural conditions produce predominantly males when placed in the shade and mostly females when placed in sites exposed to the sun (Bull and Vogt, 1979). The observed hatchling sex ratio in seven natural nests in Wisconsin was 21% male (Vogt and Bull, 1984).

Hatchlings are nearly round and possess a prominent dorsal keel. The reticulate pattern of the carapace and the plastral markings are well developed.

GROWTH AND LONGEVITY: The estimated size of two juveniles from Vermont at hatching and one year using the size of growth annuli relative to carapace length were 29.9–31.3 mm and 55.0–55.9 mm, respectively (Graham, 1989). Growth rates of *Graptemys geographica* in Quebec ranging from 2 to 18 cm were estimated by Gordon and McCulloch (1980) using growth annuli on the pectoral scutes. The slope of the growth curve for females is significantly greater than that for males, which is not surprising given the degree of sexual size dimorphism in this species.

In Indiana, female *G. geographica* studied by Iverson (1988c) grew significantly larger than males after their second year and reached significantly larger body sizes, but, overall, both sexes averaged smaller than the Canadian map turtles examined by Gordon and MacCulloch (1980). Yearling males averaged 42.3-mm plastron length; two-year-olds averaged 59.4 mm; three-year males, 69.6 mm; four-year-olds, 75.9 mm; five-year-olds, 81.3 mm; and seven-year males, 84.7 mm. In contrast, females averaged 44.1 mm at one year of age, 61.8 mm at two years, 80.5 mm at three years, 96.2 mm at four years, 114.4 mm at five years, 143.2 mm at seven years, and 180 mm when 10 years old. Between ages two and four the male growth rate dropped from 40.4% to 9.1%, while that of females declined only from 40.1% to 19.5%. The female growth rate declined only to 8.7% by age nine; males older than five years showed negligible plastron growth.

The common map turtle does not usually do well in captivity, but an adult lived for 18 years, 21 days at the Brookfield Zoo (Snider and Bowler, 1992). However, wild individuals may live at least 20 years (Ernst, pers. obs.).

FOOD HABITS: According to unpublished field notes of the late Fred Cagle, males from the White River, Arkansas, eat small snails and some insects including trichopterans. All snails were crushed, but appeared to be of a size that could easily have been swallowed whole. Females contained large crushed snails and some earthworms. No other prey items were detected in spite of an abundance of other invertebrates in the habitat. Ernst and Barbour (1972) listed freshwater snails, clams, insects (especially the immature stages), crayfish, water mites, fish, and aquatic vegetation as natural foods. Penn (1950) reported that crayfish made up 24% of the diet in the eastern United States.

Adults of both sexes rely heavily on gastropods for food. The small snail, *Elimia potosiensis,* made up 94.1% by volume and had a 98.9% frequency in the digestive tracts of adult *Graptemys geographica* from the Niangua River, Missouri (White and Moll, 1992). Crayfish were found in 19.8% (2.9% by volume) of the adult stomachs, and insects and plant material collectively composed 3.0% by volume and were each found in 2.8% of the turtles. *Elimia potosiensis* made up 100% of the food in four juvenile digestive tracts.

In Wisconsin, *G. geographica* consumes mostly mollusks (81% of stomachs examined), fish, caddisflies, mayflies, damselflies, and some plant material; it avoids competition with sympatric, predominantly insect- and plant-eating *G. p. pseudogeographica* and *G. ouachitensis* by specializing on mollusks (Vogt, 1981b).

Newman (1906) noted that *G. geographica* uses two feeding methods. The first is to bite off the extended parts of mollusks and leave the rest behind. The other method was to swallow the shell, crush it, and pick out the broken pieces with the foreclaws.

Cahn (1937) reported that basking *G. geographica* catch passing insects; however, Moll (1976b) noted that the jerky head motions of basking map turtles are more likely a response to annoying flies and other insects, especially as the movements occur with the mouth closed.

PREDATORS AND DEFENSE: As with other species of turtles, the eggs and hatchlings of *Graptemys geographica* are preyed upon by a wide variety of vertebrates. Goodpaster and Hoffmeister (1952) reported that juveniles are eaten by rice rats (*Oryzomys palustris*) at Reelfoot Lake, Tennessee.

Females may be attacked by vertebrate predators when they leave the water to oviposit. At a nesting site in eastern Minnesota, in a five-day period, Cochran (1987) found remains of 13 adult females and the bones of other turtles which he thought were most likely also map turtles. Potential predators in the area included opossums (*Didelphis*), raccoons (*Procyon*), skunks (*Mephitis*), and coyotes (*Canis*).

Human activities, such as water pollution that eliminates its molluscan prey, waterfront development that destroys nesting habitat, and automobile traffic that kills females traveling overland to nest, have reduced populations in some parts of the range.

The shyness of this species protects it from much predation when in the water or basking. It is most vulnerable when on shore. A few large individuals will bite or void bladder water if handled, but most retire into their shells to await developments.

POPULATIONS: Populations may be substantial in waterways with abundant mollusks (Ernst and Barbour, pers. obs.). The relative abundance of *Graptemys geographica* in the Tombigbee River of Alabama varies little in relation to the fall line (Tinkle, 1959a).

Mature males outnumber mature females. Pluto and Bellis (1986) captured 92 males (51%), 76 females (42%), and 11 juveniles (6%) along a 6.6-km section of a Pennsylvania river, an adult male to female ratio of 1.2:1, a juvenile to adult ratio of 0.06:1, and a total population density of 27 turtles/km of shoreline. Gordon and McCulloch (1980) captured 132 males (61%), 79 females (36%), and 5 juveniles (2%) in a Quebec lake where the density of turtles two years of age and older was approximately 15/km of shoreline. The adult male to female ratio was 1.67:1, but the juvenile to adult ratio was only 0.024/1.

REMARKS: Additional literature on this species is summarized in McCoy and Vogt (1990).

Graptemys barbouri Carr and Marchand, 1942
Barbour's map turtle

PLATE 42

RECOGNITION: *Graptemys barbouri* is a large (females to 33-cm, males to 13-cm carapace length) broad-headed map turtle with an oval, posteriorly serrated, high-domed carapace that is highest anterior to the middle. A strong vertebral keel is present with laterally compressed dark spines on the anterior of each vertebral; the second and third are most prominent. The spines become lower and less conspicuous with age, especially in females. A low longitudinal keel is present on the pleural scutes of smaller individuals. Carapace color is olive to olive-brown with yellow, C-shaped markings on the pleural scutes and a relatively wide yellow bar on the upper surface of each marginal scute. The yellow-white plastron is hingeless and some have a pattern of dark pigment along the transverse seams; nearly concentric dark marks are present on the ventral surface of the marginals. Juveniles have prominent ridges and spines on the pectoral and abdominal scutes. Skin color is dark brown or black with light-yellow or yellowish-green markings. The dorsal head pattern consists of a large interorbital blotch connected to the postorbital blotches. A heart-shaped or Y-shaped dark pattern, containing a light concentric pattern within, is present behind the orbits. The chin has a transverse or curved light bar that generally follows the curve of the jaw. Dorsal neck stripes are relatively wide and are roughly equal in size. Toes are webbed and the tail and limbs are striped.

Adult females are more than twice the size of males and have grotesquely widened heads with broad alveolar surfaces. The anal vent of males is posterior to the carapacial rim.

KARYOTYPE: McKown (1972) reported the diploid chromosome number as 52, including 48 macrochromosomes and 26 microchromosomes, but Killebrew (1977a) reported a diploid number of 50 (26 macrochromosomes—16 metacentric, 6 submeta-centric, and 4 telocentric—and 24 microchromosomes), suggesting the need for further study on the karyology of the genus *Graptemys*.

FOSSIL RECORD: Pleistocene (Rancholabrean) remains tentatively referred to *Graptemys barbouri* have been found along the Santa Fe River, Columbia and Gilchrist counties, Florida (Jackson, 1975).

DISTRIBUTION: Barbour's map turtle is restricted to the Apalachicola River and larger tributaries including the Chipola, Chattahoochee, and Flint rivers in eastern Alabama, western Georgia, and western Florida. An old record (Cagle, 1952b), perpetuated by McDowell (1964) and Newman (1970), extending the range west to the Escambia River, is erroneous (Dobie, 1972).

GEOGRAPHIC VARIATION: No subspecies have been described.

CONFUSING SPECIES: *Graptemys ernsti, G. gibbonsi,* and *G. pulchra* lack the curved or transverse bar on the underside of the chin, and also the heart- or Y-shaped pattern on the dorsal aspect of the head. In addition, the interorbital and postorbital blotches on the head of *G. ernsti* are not connected. *Graptemys barbouri* is not found with any other species of *Graptemys*.

HABITAT: Barbour's map turtle is found in clear, limestone-bottomed streams and large rivers with abundant basking sites in the form of snags and fallen trees.

BEHAVIOR: Much of what is known of the behavior of this species was reported by Sanderson (1974). *Graptemys barbouri* basks year-round on the

Male *Graptemys barbouri*

Female *Graptemys barbouri*

Chipola River in Florida. Basking sites are usually in full sun and consist of living or dead trees that extend over the river and contact the water, cypress knees (*Taxodium*), vines, and exposed limestone ledges. Turtles move from the west to the east side of the river during the day to take full advantage of the sun. Turtles bask during all parts of the day but most frequently at about 1400. Basking takes place at temperatures as low as 10°C and is most intense after periods of inclement weather. Cloacal temperatures of basking turtles range from 12.0 to 35.4°C (Sanderson, 1974).

The average home range of *G. barbouri* with three or more captures ranged from 0 to 1750 m (mean 365) for males, and 0 to 638 m (mean 273) for females (Sanderson, 1974). Three males traveled more than 1000 m during Sanderson's study and one immature turtle moved over 1300 m downstream in six months. Flooding associated with Hurricane Agnes had little effect on movement, in contrast to data reported for *Chrysemys picta* by Ernst (1974a). During periods of high water, turtles moved into the flooded margins of the river where the current was weakest.

Plastron of *Graptemys bar-bouri*

REPRODUCTION: Males are sexually mature at a plastron length of about 6.9 cm and an age of four years (Cagle, 1952b). The smallest sexually mature female examined by Cagle (1952b) had a plastron length of 17.6 cm. Females may require from 15 to more than 20 years to reach sexual maturity (Sanderson, 1974).

Chin pattern of *Graptemys barbouri*; note transverse bar

Courtship behavior was observed in captivity by Wahlquist (1970). Males that were two years old attempted to mate with other species of *Graptemys* that shared their enclosure. They approached other turtles with neck extended and attempted to orient themselves face-to-face. Nose contact was observed and the males titillated the sides of the head of the other turtles with the inner sides of their forelegs for several seconds. Captives have been observed courting in the winter (Stuart, 1974).

The nesting season on the Chipola River, Florida, lasts from June through early August (Sanderson, 1974). A 24.0-cm female examined by Cagle (1952b) had three oviducal eggs and eight corpora lutea, and a 24.2-cm female had nine oviducal eggs and 18 corpora lutea, suggesting the potential for multiple clutches in a single year. Other females containing oviducal eggs had 4–33 follicles more than 1 cm in diameter. The total number of eggs that seven females could have laid in a season ranged from 11 to 51, and the number of oviducal eggs in the same females ranged from 4 to 11. Shelled oviducal eggs ranged from 31.0 to 40.4 mm (mean 37.1) in length and from 22.2 to 29.3 mm (mean 25.9) in width. The largest eggs were removed from the female containing the most oviducal eggs (11) and the smallest oviducal eggs were found in a female containing six (Cagle, 1952b). Two clutches of eight and nine eggs found on the Flint River in Georgía on 27 August by Wahlquist and Folkerts (1973) were 38.3–41.6 mm (mean 39.4) long, 27.6–30.8 mm (mean 29.5) wide, and weighed 17.7–21.7 g

Note extreme size differences between female (above) and male (below) *Graptemys barbouri*

Distribution of *Graptemys barbouri*

(mean 18.9). A clutch of nine eggs deposited by a captive hatched after 58 days (Stuart, 1974).

Eight hatchlings found in their nest along the Flint River, Georgia, on 27 August had carapaces 35.2–38.0 mm (mean 37.0) long and 36.7–38.5 mm (mean 37.5) wide, and weighed 10.0–12.9 g (mean 10.7) (Wahlquist and Folkerts, 1973). All had egg teeth, but their yolk sacs had been absorbed. They were patterned much the same as adults, but appeared somewhat faded.

Barbour's map turtle has environmental sex determination. Eggs incubated at 25°C produce 100% males, but those incubated at 30°C produce only females (Ewert and Nelson, 1991).

GROWTH AND LONGEVITY: Males increase in plastron length at a rate of about 45% per year shortly after hatching, but the growth rate declines to almost zero at a plastron length of approximately 10 cm. The growth rate of females is similar to that of males until they reach a plastron length of about 6 cm. Between plastron lengths of 9 and 13 cm, female growth rate stabilizes at about 4.2% per year. The growth rate of females slows after attainment of sexual maturity and is essentially zero in large individuals (Sanderson, 1974).

Cagle (1952b) calculated the estimated plastron sizes of *Graptemys barbouri* at various ages as follows: first year, 3.09–5.10 cm (mean 4.36); second year, 4.94–6.50 cm (mean 5.89); third year, 6.78–9.09 cm (mean 7.86); and fourth year, 9.63–10.22 cm (mean 9.93). The smallest male that showed no evidence of recent growth was 8.8 cm in plastron length. One female with a plastron length of 18.2 cm showed traces of recent growth: females larger than this size showed no signs of growth.

A *G. barbouri* survived 31 years, eight months, and nine days at the National Zoo (Snider and Bowler, 1992).

FOOD HABITS: Large *Graptemys barbouri*, particularly females, feed primarily on mollusks including snails and some clams (Cagle, 1952b). Two adult males collected on the Chipola River (11.8 and 13.5 cm) contained mostly small insect larvae including trichopterans (Limnephilidae; Hydropsychidae, *Cheumatopsyche;* Helicopsychidae, *Helicopsyche*) and lepidopterans (Pyralidae). Other prey found in the stomachs included wings of adult trichopterans, shell fragments of aquatic snails (*Lioplax pilsbryi, Goniobasis athearni*), and some plant material. The digestive tract of the larger male contained well over 1,000 insects. The various prey of males normally live on limestone ledges and in riffle areas. In contrast, females feed mostly on bivalves (*Corbicula* and others), snails and crayfish (Lee et al., 1975). The stomach contents of one unsexed and two female Barbour's map turtles contained the following additional food items: insects—Ephemeroptera (Baetidae), Odonata (Coenagrionidae, adult *Argia*), Trichoptera (Hydropsychidae, *Hydropsyche, Cheumatopsyche;* Leptoceridae, *Leptocella;* Hydroptilidae, *Stactobiella, Neotrichia;* Glossosomatidae, *Glossosoma;* Helicopsychidae, *Helicopsyche*), Lepidoptera (Pyralidae), Diptera (Chironomidae, Ceratopogonidae), Coleoptera (Elmidae, *Gonielmis dietrichi*), and algae (Chlorophyta) (Sanderson, 1974).

The following categories of prey items, by percent occurrence and percent volume (in parentheses) were found in the stomachs of 20 *G. barbouri* of various carapace lengths from the Chipola River (Sanderson, 1974): gastropods—immatures, 20 (0.9), males, 37.5 (6.0), females less than 10.0 cm, 66.6 (1.7), females greater than 10.0 cm, 100 (96.7); bivalves—immatures, 20 (0.7), males, 0 (0), females less than 10.0 cm, 33.3 (trace), females greater than 10.0 cm, 20 (3.3); insects—immatures, 100 (97.9), males, 100 (93.8), females less than 10.0 cm, 100 (88.3), females greater than 10.0 cm, 20 (trace); plants (algae)—immatures, 20 (0.5), males, 12.5 (0.2), females less than 10.0 cm, 0 (0), females greater than 10.0 cm, 0 (0).

Females over 20.0 cm in plastron length excreted large quantities of *Corbicula* and *Goniobasis* when captured and held overnight (Sanderson, 1974). Females in the same size range of males eat more mollusks by volume than males. In captivity, females over 20.0 cm readily feed on *Corbicula* up to 2.4 cm long. The shells are crushed in the mouth and swallowed with the soft parts. Smaller turtles eat large numbers of small prey items, whereas large females eat relatively small numbers of larger prey. The jaws of adult females have broad crushing surfaces: an adaptation for feeding on hard-shelled prey.

In addition to mollusks, captives will eat fish, raw beef, chicken, commercial trout chow, and romaine lettuce.

PREDATORS AND DEFENSE: Eggs and hatchlings of *Graptemys barbouri* are preyed upon by a variety of vertebrate predators. Neill (1951c) reported that a scarlet snake (*Cemophora coccinea*) was observed raiding a turtle nest on the banks of the Chipola River. The snake would puncture an egg and thrust its head into the shell to consume the liquid contents. Although the turtle species responsible for depositing the clutch was not identified, Neill noted that *G. barbouri* was present in the river, so the scarlet snake may be an important predator of its eggs.

Humans occasionally eat this turtle, and Newman (1970) reported that three people collected 50 *G. barbouri* from a one-mile section of the Chipola River in a single afternoon.

Large numbers of dead adult females have been found along the Flint River in Georgia in recent years, possibly victims of pollution (Al Redmond, pers. comm.).

If disturbed, *G. barbouri* will immediately try to flee, but, if captured, large females will bite.

POPULATIONS: Sanderson (1974) reported densities ranging from one turtle per 33.3 m to one turtle per 9.1 m of shoreline on the Chipola River.

Assuming that marked turtles composed 65% of the actual population, the adjusted density is one turtle per 9 m of shore. The sex ratio reported by Sanderson was 57.7% males and 42.3% females. Males over 7.0 cm in plastron length constituted over 90% of all males captured. Only 20% of all females captured were mature (plastron length > 16.5 cm).

From 12 to 24 July 1950 Cagle (1952b) collected 393 *Graptemys barbouri*, two *Trachemys scripta scripta*, one *Pseudemys concinna mobilensis*, two *Sternotherus minor*, and a *Macroclemys temminckii* in the Chipola River. The sex ratio of adult male Barbour's map turtles to adult females was 1.64:1.

REMARKS: Barbour's map turtle is closely related to *Graptemys pulchra*, *G. ernsti*, and *G. gibbonsi*. Collectively, these species form the *G. pulchra* group: an association defined by the combination of large female size with extreme sexual size dimorphism, head pattern with large interorbital and postorbital blotches, enlarged heads and hypertrophied jaws in females, presence of prominent vertebral spines, and a diploid chromosome number of 52 (Lovich and McCoy, 1992).

Variation in plastron scute morphology was examined by Lovich et al. (1991a). Additional references on this species are summarized in Sanderson and Lovich (1988).

Graptemys barbouri is losing its battle for survival against the ravages of pollution and overcollecting for the pet trade. It should be federally listed at least as threatened.

Graptemys pulchra Baur, 1893b
Alabama map turtle

PLATE 43

RECOGNITION: The Alabama map turtle is a moderate-sized (carapace length to 27.3 cm), relatively low-domed, medially keeled map turtle with a series of concentric yellow markings on the dorsal surface of each marginal scute. The keel is composed of laterally compressed knobs that are most prominent on the posterior portions of the second and third vertebrals. A black, often interrupted, medial stripe divides the dark-olive carapace, and narrow yellow vermiculations are present on each pleural scute. The hingeless, pale-yellow plastron is characterized by seam-following, and occasionally isolated, areas of dark pigment. Each marginal has a wide concentric set of dark rings on its ventral surface. The skin is brown to olive with light-yellow or yellowish-green stripes and blotches. The head pattern resembles a mask, with a large interorbital blotch broadly fused to a pair of relatively narrow postorbital blotches. Neck stripes are relatively wide and vary little in width.

Adult females are over twice the size of mature males, and have conspicuously enlarged heads with broad crushing jaw surfaces. Males have longer tails with the vent posterior to the rim of the carapace. Both sexes have relatively flat plastra.

KARYOTYPE: McKown (1972) reported that *Graptemys pulchra* (sensu lato) has 52 diploid chromosomes: 26 macrochromosomes with 48 arms and 26 microchromosomes with 26 arms. All other members of the genus *Graptemys*, except *G. barbouri*, have a total of 50 diploid chromosomes (McKown, 1972).

FOSSIL RECORD: None.

DISTRIBUTION: The Alabama map turtle is restricted to the Mobile Bay drainage system in Alabama, Georgia (Harris et al., 1982; Santhuff and Wilson, 1990), and possibly Mississippi. Individuals have been collected in the Alabama, Cahaba, Tombig-

bee, Coosa, and Black Warrior Rivers, but it is apparently absent from the Tallapoosa River above the fall line in Alabama (Mount, 1975). *Graptemys pulchra* is expected in the Tombigbee River system of Mississippi as the sympatric *G. nigrinoda* has been collected there (Shoop, 1967).

GEOGRAPHIC VARIATION: No subspecies are recognized.

CONFUSING SPECIES: The Alabama map turtle is sympatric with two other species of *Graptemys*. *Graptemys nigrinoda* has a narrow head and round, knoblike projections on the vertebrals, and *G. geographica* lacks the distinctive mask. Allopatric, but similar, species differ as follows: *G. ernsti* has an interorbital blotch that is not connected to the pair of postorbital blotches, *G. gibbonsi* has a single wide bar of yellow pigment on each marginal, and *G. barbouri* has a narrow interorbital blotch that ends anteriorly in a narrow point, a curved or transverse bar under the chin, and, in small specimens, a conspicuous bump on each of the anterior pleural scutes.

HABITAT: The Alabama map turtle is an inhabitant of relatively large, swift creeks and rivers. Stream sections with abundant basking sites in the form of logs and brush are preferred. In rocky piedmont habitats males are usually found in shallow stretches (often in association with *Sternotherus depressus* and *Trionyx spiniferus*), but females seem to be restricted to deep pools or impoundments (Ernst, pers. obs.).

BEHAVIOR: *Graptemys pulchra* is primarily diurnal, and it is active from late March to November (although warm winters may bring on activity in all months). It is extremely wary when basking, dropping into the water at the first sign of danger.

Male *Graptemys pulchra*

Plastra of male *Graptemys pulchra*

Hatchlings and juveniles bask close to shore in thick brush. Adults typically bask on larger structures near deep water. Little else is known of the behavior of this species.

REPRODUCTION: Males sometimes rapidly bob their heads at both sexes of *Graptemys pulchra*, and at other species of *Graptemys*. Perhaps this is courtship behavior.

Nesting activity in *G. pulchra* (sensu lato) begins in late April or early May, reaches a peak in June, and continues through July and August (Mount, 1975). Six to seven clutches of four to six eggs are laid each year. Many nests are destroyed by predators. Hatchlings have been collected along the Cahaba River of Alabama in October (Lovich, pers. obs.).

GROWTH AND LONGEVITY: Ernst has kept males from the Black Warrior drainage of Alabama for over ten years, and Snider and Bowler (1992) reported that *G. pulchra* (sensu lato) has lived in captivity for over 15 years.

Distribution of *Graptemys pulchra*

FOOD HABITS: The introduced Asian mussel *Corbicula* may be an important source of food for this species, particularly of the females (Marion, 1986; Ernst, pers. obs.). In captivity, males eat fresh fish, newborn mice, snails, shrimp, trout chow, and occasionally romaine lettuce.

PREDATORS AND DEFENSE: The eggs and hatchlings of *G. pulchra* are undoubtedly preyed upon by a wide variety of vertebrate predators. The wary behavior of this species while basking is its greatest defense. Unfortunately, this behavior is not effective when unethical shooters use basking turtles as targets.

Water pollution, which adversely affects its molluscan prey, and other degradation of its waterways may be reducing *G. pulchra* populations.

POPULATIONS: In the Cahaba River of Alabama *G. pulchra* is often seen basking with *G.*
nigrinoda, Trionyx spiniferus asper and *Pseudemys concinna*. Populations of *G. pulchra* occur in almost equal abundance above and below the fall line (Tinkle, 1959a).

REMARKS: Map turtles tend to have small ranges restricted to a single drainage system. As originally described, *G. pulchra* had the most extensive range of any of these turtles. Lovich and McCoy (1992) demonstrated that *G. pulchra* (sensu lato) is composed of three distinct species, most confined to a single drainage system: *G. pulchra*—the Mobile Bay watershed, *G. ernsti*—the Escambia River drainage system, and *G. gibbonsi*—the Pearl and Pascagoula rivers.

Additional references on *G. pulchra* (sensu lato) are given in Lovich (1985). Lovich and McCoy (in press) provide a summary of information on *G. pulchra*.

Graptemys ernsti Lovich and McCoy, 1992
Escambia map turtle
PLATE 44

RECOGNITION: *Graptemys ernsti* is a moderate-sized (carapace length to 28.5 cm in females), high-domed, medially keeled map turtle with a single yellow bar on the dorsal surface of each marginal scute. Dark smudges lie between the marginals at the rim of the carapace. The vertebral keel is composed of laterally compressed knobs that are most prominent on the posterior parts of the second and third vertebrals. A pronounced, broken, black stripe runs down the center of the olive carapace. Relatively wide yellow rings and vermiculations are present on the distal parts of the pleural scutes. The hingeless, pale-yellow plastron has a dark seam-following pattern, especially along seams running perpendicular to the long axis of the body. The ventral surface of each marginal scute has a dark, wide, diffuse border, which forms one or two semicircles on some scutes. The brown to olive skin is broken with light-yellow or yellowish-green stripes and blotches. The head has a large interorbital blotch that is not connected to the large postorbital blotches on each side of the head. A distinct three-pronged mark is present on the anterior part of the interorbital blotch. A pair of supraoccipital spots commonly lie between the posterior extensions of the postorbital blotches, and may fuse to the first paramedial neck stripes. Dorsal neck stripes are relatively thick and, commonly, roughly equal in size, but some stripes may be thin. Some individuals have a light blotch beneath each eye.

Adult females are more than twice the size of adult males, and have conspicuously enlarged heads with broad crushing jaw surfaces. Large females appear hump-backed owing to a dramatic incline of the first vertebral scute. Males have longer tails with the vent posterior to the rim of the carapace. Both sexes have relatively flat plastra.

KARYOTYPE: McKown (1972) reported that *Graptemys pulchra* (sensu lato) has a diploid chromosome number of 52 including 26 macrochromosomes with 48 arms and 26 microchromosomes with 26 arms.

FOSSIL RECORD: None

DISTRIBUTION: *Graptemys ernsti* is restricted to rivers flowing into Pensacola Bay, including the following in Alabama and Florida: Yellow River, Escambia River, Conecuh River, and Shoal River.

GEOGRAPHIC VARIATION: No subspecies are recognized.

CONFUSING SPECIES: *Graptemys ernsti* is not sympatric with any other species of map turtle. *Graptemys pulchra* and *G. gibbonsi* have an interorbital blotch that is connected to the lateral postorbital blotches. *Graptemys barbouri* has a narrow interorbital blotch that ends anteriorly in a narrow point, a curved or transverse bar under the chin, and, in small individuals, a conspicuous bump on each of the anterior pleural scutes.

HABITAT: The Escambia map turtle is found in relatively large, swift creeks and rivers, with sandy or gravelly bottoms. Stream sections with an abundace of basking sites in the form of snags, logs, and brush are preferred.

BEHAVIOR: Basking occurs during all months, even when the water temperature is as low as 11°C, but peaks in March and April in association with high water levels, warmer temperatures, and bright skies. Individuals do not bask on cloudy days when water temperature exceeds air temperature. Basking behavior is frequent from May through July but declines from July to October. Basking occurs at any time of day and may last for several hours. Partially shaded

Female *Graptemys ernsti*

Plastron of *Graptemys ernsti*

basking sites are preferred by females and hatchlings, especially in late summer and during periods of high water. Preferred basking sites are separated from the shore, located near deep water, and are well established. Recently created sites, such as freshly fallen trees, are shunned in preference for older sites. Basking individuals invariably move to the highest prominence offered by a particular site, perhaps for the purpose of securing a clearer view of possible danger. *Graptemys ernsti* is extremely wary while basking and will plunge into the water at the first sign of danger. The stimulus of other species of turtles falling into the water evokes a similar response in basking *G. ernsti* (Shealy, 1976).

From November to February *G. ernsti* is generally inactive, resting on the bottom of deep, silted pools, wedged among limestone boulders or sunken trees. While inactive, individuals have their head and limbs partially withdrawn. Feeding and activity are strongly curtailed at water temperatures below 19°C.

Shealy (1976) studied homing behavior in *G. ernsti* by releasing six males and 15 females 24

Head of *Graptemys ernsti*

Distribution of *Graptemys ernsti*

channel km upstream of the point of capture, and seven males and 19 females downstream of the point of capture. Half of the recovered females returned to the point of capture but none of the males returned. However, 42% of nondisplaced males were captured near the point of previous release during Shealy's study.

REPRODUCTION: Shealy (1976) provided detailed information on the reproductive ecology of *G. ernsti* in the Conecuh River of Alabama.

Males mature three or four years after hatching at a minimum carapace length of 80 mm. Females are judged to be sexually mature if corpora lutea or ovarian follicles larger than 15 mm in diameter are present. Based on this criteria, females mature in about 14 years at a carapace length of 22 cm. The largest immature female in the population studied by Shealy (1976) was 22 cm, and the smallest mature female was 21.2 cm.

Active sperm are present in the epididymides of mature males throughout the year. Shealy (1976) thought this indicated that mating could occur at any time of the year, but mating activity has only been observed from September to November. Testis diameter is greatest in September, a time when follicular development is most rapid in females.

The percentage of follicles larger than 10 mm in diameter, relative to the maximum number of eggs produced in a season, decreases from May to September. Ovulation begins in late April and continues through July. Shealy (1976) suggested that some follicles are not ovulated during the normal nesting season. Atretic follicles account for no more than 5% of the reproductive potential, leading Shealy to suggest that some follicles are ovulated after the normal nesting season or held over to the following year. The number of follicles larger than 10 mm in diameter and the number of eggs produced are positively correlated with female carapace length. The number of large ovarian follicles produced in a season ranges from 7 to 71 (mean = 29). Almost all follicles larger than 10 mm are ovulated. As the mean number of ovulatory follicles in a given season is 29 and the mean clutch size is 7.2 eggs, then the mean estimated number of clutches per season is four. The number of clutches laid per season is also correlated with female size. Data based on autopsies and nesting signs suggest that large females ovulate earlier and later in the nesting season than smaller females. In addition, one or two clutches per season is typical of small females in their first reproductive season, but the largest females may produce six or seven clutches per season.

Courtship starts with the male approaching the cloacal region of the female with his neck outstretched. He then swims in front of the female assuming one of three positions face-to-face: slightly to either side, slightly above, or slightly below her head. Next he begins to rapidly vibrate his head vertically against the side of the female's snout, alternating sides at intervals of approximately 15 seconds. During this action the female withdraws her head somewhat and partially closes her eyes. Following head bobbing, the male swims to the rear of the female and attempts to copulate by looping his tail beneath hers in an effort to appose the cloacae. This sequence is often repeated several times before successful copulation. Oviducal scrapings in March and May contain active sperm, demonstrating the potential for sperm storage.

The nesting season lasts from late April to late July. Most nests are dug in large sandbars located at sharp bends in rivers. Most are excavated in very fine sand at elevations 2–3 m above the existing water level, and 3–15 m from the water's edge. Nesting may occur at any time of day. Females intent on oviposition appear to move onto shore very cautiously, pausing occasionally to press their noses to the substrate as if searching for olfactory cues. Possible additional substrate-testing behavior includes sweeping the sand with the front legs to form furrows 1–5 cm deep, and digging test holes with the hind legs. Such holes often have stones, leaf litter, roots, or other potential obstacles at the bottom. The actual nest cavity is constructed with alternating sweeps and scrapes of the hind legs. It is flask shaped, about 15 cm deep, with a lower spherical chamber diameter of about 10 cm, and a neck diameter of about 4 cm. After depositing the eggs the female packs the nest with sand and smooths the area over the nest entrance with lateral movements of her body before crawling directly back to water.

Oviducal eggs have mean dimensions of 38 × 26 mm, and eggs from nests have mean dimensions of 38 × 27 mm; the slight difference is due to rapid water absorption. During incubation the eggs assume an almost spherical shape.

Eggs incubated under artificial conditions closely approximating those of natural nests hatch in 74–79 days (mean = 76) (Shealy, 1976). Nest temperatures of natural nests range from 23 to 31°C (mean 29). Nests may be submerged by high water for up to a week or more and still produce hatchlings. Nine of 64 eggs collected in the field and incubated under artificial conditions by Shealy were infertile. Eggs from one fertile clutch had mean dimensions of 29.5 × 43 mm just prior to hatching.

Hatchlings pierce the apex of the eggshell and then remain in the shell for about four days while the yolk is absorbed. The yolk sac is 12–15 mm at hatching, but disappears after three days. Hatchlings apparently do not overwinter in the nest, and move directly to water after leaving the nest. In the Conecuh and Yellow rivers, free-living, recently hatched juveniles have carapace lengths ranging from 34 to 44 mm (mean 40.8) when collected in late September (Lovich, pers. obs.).

GROWTH AND LONGEVITY: Growth is rapid in both sexes of *Graptemys ernsti* until the attainment of sexual maturity. In females, growth is steady from 45- to 160-mm carapace length, then peaks just prior to maturation at 160–220 mm. Males show much less variation in size after maturity than do females. The earliest seasonal growth is observed in May and is then roughly linear until August when it averages 67% of that of the previous year. Growth declines dramatically after August. Maximum size in females is attained after an estimated 23 years, but males reach maximum carapace length after an estimated 8.4 years. Signs of advanced age include wandering plastral seams, a decrease in pectoral scute length and an increase in humeral scute length, loss of contrast in head pigmentation, and areas of erosion on the shell and jaws; however, no evidence of reproductive senility accompanies these changes (Shealy, 1976).

Snider and Bowler (1992) reported that *G. pulchra* (sensu lato) has been kept in captivity for more than 15 years.

FOOD HABITS: Hatchling *Graptemys ernsti* begin feeding shortly after entering the water. Individuals less than 100 mm in carapace length are essentially insectivorous. The fecal samples of turtles collected by Shealy (1976), including adult males, contained Trichoptera, Coleoptera, Odonata, Hymenoptera, and millipedes. Females shift to mollusks, including gastropods and the imported mussel *Corbicula maniliensis,* at a carapace length of 90–100 mm, and *Corbicula* composes at least 95% of all food consumed by adult females. Females under 150 mm prey mostly on mussels from 2 to 12 mm in length, and females over 150 mm utilize all sizes of mussels, especially those 5–20 mm long. Females over 220 mm feed primarily on mussels 15–25 mm in length.

The remainder of the female diet is composed of native mussels (usually smaller than 50 mm), aquatic snails, and occasionally crayfish. Adult males are primarily insectivorous, but 15% of the fecal volume of a sample of 11 turtles was composed of small aquatic snails, and some small *Corbicula* shells were also observed (Shealy, 1976).

PREDATORS AND DEFENSE: Nest predation can exceed 90% in a given year. Fish crows (*Corvus ossifragus*) prey on nests by day and raccoons (*Procyon lotor*) by night. Nesting females may also be killed by raccoons (Shealy, 1976), but humans are the most serious predators of this species. Basking individuals are sometimes shot for target practice (Shealy, 1976).

POPULATIONS: Shealy (1976) estimated the density of *Graptemys ernsti* to be one turtle per 3–4 m of channel length in the Conecuh River. During the period of Shealy's study, juvenile and female size class distributions had pronounced peaks between 50 and 75 mm and 225 and 250 mm, respectively. The size frequency distribution of males was "normally distributed" centering around the size class 90–95 mm; 58% of mature males were 85–100 mm long.

REMARKS: This species was formerly considered only a variant of *Graptemys pulchra*. Lovich and McCoy (1992) demonstrated that *G. pulchra* (sensu lato) is actually composed of three distinct species. Additional references on *G. pulchra* (sensu lato) are given in Lovich (1985). McCoy and Lovich (in press a) summarize information on *G. ernsti*.

Graptemys gibbonsi Lovich and McCoy, 1992
Pascagoula map turtle

PLATE 45

RECOGNITION: This moderate-sized (carapace length to 29.5 cm), high-domed, medially keeled map turtle has a single vertical yellow bar on the dorsal surface of each marginal scute. The medial keel is composed of a laterally compressed knob on the posterior part of each vertebral scute; those on the second and third vertebrals are most prominent. The olive-brown carapace is divided by a black medial stripe (interrupted in some individuals), and relatively wide yellow rings and vermiculations lie on each pleural scute. Each marginal has a single relatively narrow band of dark pigment on its ventral surface. The hingeless, pale-yellow plastron is characterized by seam-following dark pigment. The skin is brown to olive with light-yellow or yellowish-green stripes and blotches. Head pattern consists of a large interorbital blotch connected by thin stripes to a pair of broad postorbital blotches. The anterior part of the interorbital blotch forms a three-pronged trident between the eyes and nose on most individuals.

Adult females are about twice the size of mature males and have conspicuously enlarged heads with broad crushing jaw surfaces. Males have longer tails with the vent posterior to the rim of the carapace. Both sexes have relatively flat plastra.

KARYOTYPE: McKown (1972) reported that *Graptemys pulchra* (sensu lato) has a diploid chromosome number of 52: 26 macrochromosomes, with 48 arms, and 26 microchromosomes, with 26 arms.

FOSSIL RECORD: None.

DISTRIBUTION: *Graptemys gibbonsi* is restricted to the Pascagoula and Pearl rivers and their major tributaries (including the Chickasawhay, Leaf, and Bogue Chitto) in Mississippi and Louisiana.

GEOGRAPHIC VARIATION: No subspecies have been described. Individuals from the Pearl River have slightly narrower yellow bands on the dorsal surface of the marginals, but slightly wider dark bands on the ventral surface of the marginals (Lovich and McCoy, 1992).

CONFUSING SPECIES: *Graptemys gibbonsi* is sympatric with three other species of *Graptemys*. *Graptemys flavimaculata* and *G. oculifera* both have narrow heads and more extensive yellow pigmentation, and *G. pseudogeographica kohnii* has a crescent-shaped yellow mark behind each eye. A similar broad-headed species, *G. barbouri*, has a curved or transverse bar under the chin and a narrow bar between the eyes instead of a broad interorbital blotch.

HABITAT: The Pascagoula map turtle lives in the main channel of rivers, often in swift currents. Sand or gravel bottoms and an abundance of basking sites in the form of logs and brush contribute to ideal habitat.

BEHAVIOR: The water approach behavior of hatchlings was studied along the Pearl River by Anderson (1958). Hatchlings leave their nests within the first three hours after sunset. In daylight tests, hatchlings showed negative reactions to bright sunlight by moving to the nearest shade, even when placed within 60 cm of the water. During nocturnal tests in a "Y" maze, most hatchlings moved toward an artificial light source and away from darkness. Without discriminating between the response of *Graptemys gibbonsi* and *G. oculifera*, Anderson demonstrated a transition between diurnal and nocturnal behavior by running Y-maze tests at sunset. Collectively, both species avoided the sun under bright conditions, but oriented toward the sun as it set. When mazes were set up so that a line of trees separated the hatchlings from the water, most oriented away from the trees,

Male *Graptemys gibbonsi*

Plastron of *Graptemys gibbonsi*

and thus away from the water. Anderson concluded that orientation of hatchling *G. gibbonsi* is mainly driven by a negative response to dark masses such as the forest edge.

This species rests at night by clinging to the branches of submerged trees a few centimeters below the surface (Chaney and Smith, 1950; Cagle, 1952b).

REPRODUCTION: Cagle (1952b) listed the sizes and sexual conditions of four male *Graptemys pulchra* (sensu lato), including two *G. gibbonsi*

(Tulane University specimens 13447 and 13798). Without discriminating between species he indicated that the plastron length of the smallest mature male in the series was 89 mm. Males may mature in their fourth year. Of three female *G. gibbonsi* from the Pearl River with plastron lengths of 13.3, 17.0, and 19.5 cm, only the two largest specimens were sexually mature. The 17.0-cm female collected on 8 June contained two eggs in the left oviduct and one in the right oviduct; egg lengths and widths were 42.7–47.3 mm and 25.0–27.0 mm, respectively.

Head of *Graptemys gibbonsi*

Distribution of *Graptemys gibbonsi*

The right ovary had three ovulation scars (corpus luteum and corpus albicans), but the left had none. Three enlarged oocytes, 8, 9, and 20.5 mm in diameter, were present on the left ovary, and the right ovary contained oocytes 14, 21, and 22 mm in diameter. Cagle thought the oviducal eggs represented the first clutch of the season; the enlarged oocytes probably would have matured and been laid later the same season.

GROWTH AND LONGEVITY: Cagle (1952b) calculated the plastron lengths of hatchling *Graptemys gibbonsi* and *G. ernsti* from growth rings on 29 specimens whose lengths ranged from 21.5 to

35.3 mm (mean, 30.2 mm). Calculated plastron lengths for subsequent years and various subsamples were as follows: age one, 35.3–51.4 mm, mean 43.7 mm; age two, 45.6–59.3 mm, mean 51.1 mm; age three, 56.0–65.7 mm, mean 60.9 mm; and age four, 63.2–69.0 mm, mean 67 4 mm. A juvenile female *G. gibbonsi* from the Pearl River was 22.7 mm at hatching, 42.4 mm at the end of the first growing season, and 59.3 mm at the end of the second season of growth.

FOOD HABITS: Unpublished field notes of the late Fred Cagle indicate that *Graptemys gibbonsi* eats insects (including trichopterans), snails, and clams.

PREDATORS AND DEFENSE: Raccoons and other predators undoubtably eat the eggs and hatchlings, but habitat destruction is the greatest threat to this species. The Pearl River and parts of the Pascagoula River are degraded by industrial pollution.

In 1986, a lengthy section of the Leaf River (a Mississippi tributary of the Pascagoula) below the outflow of a pulp processing plant was conspicuously devoid of *Graptemys,* while upstream they were plentiful.

Large females may bite if handled.

POPULATIONS: In 26 hours of collecting along 9 km of the Pearl River in the summer of 1950, Chaney and Smith (1950) caught 64 *Graptemys gibbonsi* and *G. oculifera* (combined), nine *Trachemys scripta,* four *Pseudemys floridana,* and four *Sternotherus carinatus.* Of 98 *G. gibbonsi* collected by Cagle (1952b) in the Pearl River, 75 were juveniles, 12 were adult males, and 11 were females (including five adults).

REMARKS: This species was formerly considered a variant of *Graptemys pulchra,* but Lovich and McCoy (1992) demonstrated that *G. pulchra* (sensu lato) is composed of three distinct species. Additional information on this species is summarized by McCoy and Lovich (in press b).

Graptemys caglei Haynes and McKown, 1974
Cagle's map turtle

PLATE 46

RECOGNITION: This Texas resident has a narrow head, a cream-colored transverse bar on the chin, and a yellow V -shaped mark on the dorsal surface of the head. Its somewhat flattened carapace (to 21.3 cm) is elliptical, serrated posteriorly, and bears a vertebral keel of sharp spinelike projections. Medially raised vertebral scutes give the carapace a lumpy appearance. The carapace is greenish to brown; each scute has yellowish, contourlike markings, and the posterior midline of each vertebral is brown or black. The hingeless plastron is cream colored with a dark seam-following pattern, and black flecking may occur on each scute. The cream-colored bridge is crossed by four black longitudinal bars, as are the undersides of the fifth to eighth marginals. The head of both sexes is narrow, and the snout is somewhat pointed. The black head has several cream-colored stripes on its dorsal surface, with the medial stripe widest. Another broad stripe begins below and in front of the orbit, runs backward and upward on the side of the face to form a complete crescent-shaped mark around the orbit and meet the stripe from the opposite side at the midline just behind the orbits to produce a V -shaped mark when viewed from above. Several other narrower stripes also follow this path, but do not meet. A cream-colored bar extends transversely across the lower jaw. The black neck, limbs, and tail bear many cream to yellow stripes.

Adult males are 7.0–12.6 cm in carapace length, adult females, to 21.3 cm. Adult females have more rounded shells and lower vertebral spines, but the male tail is longer with the vent beyond the carapacial rim.

KARYOTYPE: The diploid number of mitotic chromosomes is 50: 11 pairs of metacentric or submetacentric and two pairs of acrocentric macrochromosomes, and 12 pairs of microchromosomes (McKown, 1972; Killebrew, 1977a).

FOSSIL RECORD: None.

DISTRIBUTION: This species was restricted to the Guadalupe and San Antonio river watersheds of south-central Texas (Dixon, 1987; Conant and Collins, 1991) but may now be extirpated in the San Antonio drainage (Vermersch, 1992).

GEOGRAPHIC VARIATION: Intraspecific variation has not been studied.

CONFUSING SPECIES: *Graptemys versa*, *G. pseudogeographica kohnii*, *G. ouachitensis* have a longitudinal yellow mark at the symphysis of the lower jaw instead of a transverse cream-colored bar, and lack the characteristic V -shaped dorsal head pattern. *Trachemys scripta elegans* lacks a pronounced vertebral keel and has black smudges on the plastron. *Pseudemys texana* also lacks a vertebral keel and has broad stripes, spots, or vertical bars on the head.

HABITAT: Habitat in the Guadalupe River system consists of limestone- or mud-bottomed streams with moderate current, and numerous pools of varying depth. *Graptemys caglei* may also live in the slow-moving waters 1–3 m deep behind impoundments (Vermersch, 1992).

BEHAVIOR: Cagle's map turtle is diurnal and spends much time basking on logs, cypress knees, and rocks. According to Haynes and McKown (1974) it avoids emerging onto logs connected to the bank. Like other map turtles, it is wary and difficult to approach, and seldom comes onto land except to nest (Vermersch, 1992).

REPRODUCTION: Clutches contain one to six oval eggs (Wibbels et al., 1991a), which are

392

Head pattern of *Graptemys caglei*

Plastron and chin patterns of *Graptemys caglei*

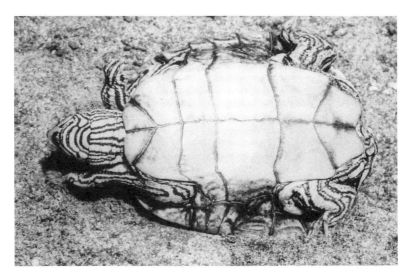

deposited near the water in a cavity approximately 15 cm deep (Vermersch, 1992). Possibly two or three clutches may be laid by a single female each year (Vermersch, 1992).

Haynes and McKown (1974) observed and collected hatchlings from September through November, indicating a late spring to early summer nesting season.

Graptemys caglei has temperature-dependent sex determination (Wibbels et al., 1991a). Eggs incubated at 28°C or lower produce 100% males, those incubated at 30.5°C, 100% females, and incubation temperatures of 29.0–29.5°C hatch 80–82% males.

The estimated pivotal temperature producing more females than males is approximately 30°C, higher than those reported for other species of *Graptemys*.

Incubation temperature also influences the length of ovaries in hatchlings. Ovaries of hatchlings from eggs incubated at 29 and 29.5°C were statistically significantly shorter than those of hatchlings incubated at 30.5°C (means of 3.05 and 3.42 mm, respectively) (Wibbels et al., 1991a). Temperature did not have a significant effect on the size of testes. Oviducts developed normally in females but not in males from low incubation temperatures, but males from clutches incubated at intermediate temperatures

Distribution of *Graptemys caglei*

sometimes developed regressed or nonregressed oviducts (Wibbels et al., 1991a).

GROWTH AND LONGEVITY: No growth data have been published. A male, adult when caught, survived 14 years, six days in captivity (Snider and Bowler, 1992).

FOOD HABITS: The stomach contents of several juveniles and adult males and two subadult females collected in July were examined by Haynes and McKown (1974). Large amounts of plant and animal material were found in each specimen. Plant matter consisted mostly of bark and algae that may have been ingested incidentally while feeding on insects and snails, but included fragments of grass like those found on the larval cases of caddisflies (Trichoptera). Juveniles contained large amounts of bark and pieces of grasses embedded in larval caddisfly cases as well as many small gnatlike insects. The stomachs of adult males contained caddisfly larvae and larval cases.

The contents of female stomachs were essentially the same as in males, but females also contained fragments of snail shells.

PREDATORS AND DEFENSE: Nothing has been published on predators or defense mechanisms of this species.

POPULATIONS: Cagle's map turtle may be the dominant turtle in certain parts of the Guadulupe watershed (Vermersch, 1992).

REMARKS: *Graptemys caglei* is morphologically intermediate between *G. versa* and *G. pseudogeographica kohnii* (Haynes and McKown, 1974), and belongs to the narrow-headed group of map turtles (Dobie, 1981). Bertl and Killebrew (1983) concluded that *G. ouachitensis, G. p. pseudogeographica,* and *G. p. kohnii* are its closest biogeographical relatives. Additional information on this species is found in Haynes (1976).

Graptemys pseudogeographica (Gray, 1831)
False map turtle
PLATES 47, 48

RECOGNITION: The false map turtle is a fairly large freshwater species (male carapace length to 15 cm, females to 27 cm) with a concave anterior profile, a distinct medial keel bearing conspicuous low spines, and a strongly serrated posterior rim. Its carapace is olive to brown with yellow oval markings and dark blotches on each pleural. Both the upper and lower marginal surfaces have a yellow ocellus at each seam. The bridge is marked with light bars, and the plastron is immaculate cream to yellow in adults, but small individuals have a pattern of dark lines bordering the seams. The head is narrow to moderately broad with a nonprotruding snout and no medial notch or hook on the upper jaw. Skin is olive to brown, with many narrow yellow stripes on the legs, tail, chin, and neck. The small postorbital mark is variable but commonly consists of a narrow downward extension of a neck stripe behind the orbit which allows four to seven neck stripes to contact the orbit (or prevents any from reaching the orbit; see section on Geographic variation).

Adult males have long, thick tails, with the vent posterior to the carapacial rim, and elongated foreclaws (especially the third). Adult females are, on average, 1.50–1.74 times larger than adult males and have wider heads (Gibbons and Lovich, 1990).

KARYOTYPE: The diploid chromosome number is 50: 20 metacentric and submetacentric, 10 subtelocentric, and 20 acrocentric and telocentric chromosomes with a total of 80 arms (Stock, 1972; Killebrew, 1977a).

FOSSIL RECORD: The fossil record of *G. pseudogeographica* is neither extensive nor old. A 4,000–6,000-year-old Holocene hypoplastra from Bay County, Michigan, has been assigned to this species by Wilson and Zug (1966) and Wilson (1967), but Holman (1988) questioned the identification, believing the bone more likely to have been from a *G. geographica*. An archeological record of *G. pseudogeographica* exists for Rock Island County, Illinois (Adler, 1968).

DISTRIBUTION: *Graptemys pseudogeographica* occurs primarily in large streams of the Missouri and Mississippi river systems from Ohio, Indiana, Illinois, Wisconsin, Minnesota, and the Dakotas southward possibly to extreme southwestern Alabama, southern and western Mississippi, Louisiana, and eastern Texas.

GEOGRAPHIC VARIATION: Two subspecies are currently recognized (Vogt, 1993). *Graptemys pseudogeographica pseudogeographica* (Gray, 1831), the false map turtle, is described above. It occurs from Ohio, Indiana, Illinois, Wisconsin, Minnesota, and the Dakotas southward to western Kentucky, Tennessee, and Missouri. *Graptemys p. kohnii* (Baur, 1890), the Mississippi map turtle, differs from the nominate race in having the curved stripe behind the eye so long that it usually prevents any neck stripe from reaching the orbit, a white iris, and a more extensive plastron pattern. It is found in the Mississippi River watershed from western Tennessee, central Missouri, and possibly southeastern Nebraska south to eastern Texas, Louisiana, and southern and western Mississippi. There is also a questionable record from the vicinity of Mobile, Alabama (Mount, 1975). Most of its range lies west of the Mississippi River. Jones et al. (1991) thought the *G. p. kohnii* recently found in the Pearl River, Mississippi, came from the pet trade, but McCoy and Vogt (1992) suggested these turtles may have been introduced into the Pearl watershed during the April 1979 flood of the Mississippi River.

Cagle (1953b) originally described *G. ouachitensis ouachitensis* and *G. o. sabinensis* as subspecies of *G. pseudogeographica*. Studies by Vogt (1993) have

Head pattern of *Graptemys*
pseudogeographica
pseudogeographica

Plastron of *Graptemys*
pseudogeographica
pseudogeographica

shown that *G. ouachitensis* and *G. pseudogeographica* are separate species. Separation of *G. ouachitensis, G. p. kohnii,* and *G. p. pseudogeographica* is mostly on the basis of head pattern, but Ewert (1979a) and Vogt (1980, 1993) noted that various head patterns may be produced by different incubation temperatures, and that a single clutch may produce several head patterns.

CONFUSING SPECIES: *Graptemys ouachitensis* may have a pair of light spots on each side of the face, one just under the eye and another on the lower jaw; *G. geographica* has a low, spineless vertebral keel and a relatively broad head; and *G. gibbonsi* has a wide, light interorbital mark.

HABITAT: This species lives primarily in large rivers and their backwaters, but also occupies lakes, ponds, sloughs, bayous, oxbows, and occasionally marshes. It prefers water with abundant aquatic vegetation, places to bask, and slow currents, but can

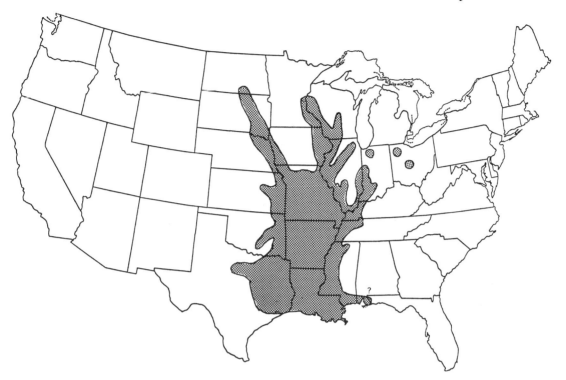

Distribution of *Graptemys pseudogeographica*

be found in swiftly flowing main channels of large rivers.

BEHAVIOR: The life history of the false map turtle has been obscured because data on both it and *G. ouachitensis* have been reported under the name *pseudogeographica*.

The behavior of *Graptemys p. pseudogeographica* was studied by Vogt (1980) in the Mississippi River of western Wisconsin. Emergence from overwintering sites occurs in April when water temperatures are 4–7°C. In May, females move out of river channels and concentrate around islands with nesting sites. During the summer, most males move into quiet backwaters to forage. Females apparently move into backwaters to feed after depositing their first clutch of eggs for the year.

In October, Wisconsin *G. p. pseudogeographica* move into wing dams along sloughs and channels and lodge themselves into rock piles to hibernate for the winter, and Vogt (1981a) found over 100 individuals of *G. geographica, G. p. pseudogeographica,* and *G. ouachitensis* hibernating in the same area. In the northern part of the range *G. p. pseudogeographica* may remain inactive until after the ice has melted, but in western Kentucky

and Tennessee it sometimes can be seen basking on warm winter days. When it gets cold again the turtles return to the water and burrow 10–30 cm into the soft bottom. The underground entrance of a muskrat lodge or bank burrow is often used as an overwintering site (Ernst, pers. obs.). A drop in the water level during winter may cause some individuals to freeze, and winterkill may be an important mortality factor during dry winters (Christiansen and Bickham, 1989). *Graptemys p. kohnii* from Missouri are active from late March to mid-October (Johnson, 1987).

Graptemys pseudogeographica spends most of the day basking (from 0900 to 1800) on muskrat (*Ondatra zibetheca*) lodges, logs, rock piles, sand bars, or stumps. Basking sites are rarely located on or near the shore, and some may be 2 m above the water. Emerging turtles usually orient themselves anterior to posterior or posterior to posterior with respect to other basking turtles, possibly to minimize aggressive interactions by avoiding face-to-face contact. They often bask with the anterior end of the plastron resting on the posterior end of another turtle's carapace. Basking aggression does not seem to occur, and individuals may sun themselves as long as 100 minutes (Vogt, 1980).

Head pattern of *Graptemys pseudogeographica kohnii*

Plastron of *Graptemys pseudogeographica kohnii*

Basking turtles are extremely wary and difficult to approach. They are more likely to slide into the water within the first five minutes of emergence if disturbed by a passing boat. Submergence by one basking turtle often triggers others to do the same, but they warily return to the basking site within 5–10 minutes of the disturbance.

Basking turtles stretch their hind limbs, spread the webbing between the toes, and extend the head and forelimbs, and this has led to an interesting feeding and cleaning symbiosis with common grackles (*Quiscalus quiscula*) in Wisconsin. The birds remove leeches (*Placobdella*) from the leg and neck cavities of basking turtles as they move along a basking site carefully inspecting the leg cavities of each turtle. The map turtles appear to be oblivious of the grackles, even when rocked back and forth while the leech is pulled free (Vogt, 1979b).

Movement data are sparse. Three days after a female *G. p. pseudogeographica* nested, Vogt (1980) recaptured her 1.6 km away from the nesting site. Another female moved 8 km in less than five months. Some false map turtles are repeatedly recaptured in the same area, suggesting an established home range.

REPRODUCTION: The reproductive cycles of both sexes have been barely studied. That of female *G. p. pseudogeographica* begins between late June and mid-July after she has laid her last eggs for the year. Females enter hibernation with their coelomic cavity encroached upon by enlarged ovarian follicles (Vogt, 1980). Male testis size in *G. p. pseudogeographica* is largest in the fall and smallest in the summer (Vogt, 1980).

In the upper Missouri River, male *G. p. pseudogeographica* as small as 10.3 cm in plastron length contain live sperm, but their testes are small and they have poorly developed secondary sexual characteristics. Females in the same population mature between 18 and 19 cm and have ovarian follicles 8 mm or larger (Timken, 1968). In Wisconsin, males of this subspecies mature as small as 7.5 cm at four to six years of age, but females take eight years to mature (Vogt, 1980).

Mating in Wisconsin *G. p. pseudogeographica* probably occurs in April and again in October and November (Vogt, 1980), but Ernst (1974b) observed a captive male *G. p. pseudogeographica* courting a female *G. flavimaculata* in July. Courtship has not been observed in either subspecies in nature, although Cagle (1955), Ernst (1974b) and Vogt (1980) observed courtship in captives. A male seems to identify a conspecific female by visual and olfactory cues. Courtship often begins after a male places his nostrils near a female's anal vent. He approaches the female with his forelimbs raised above his head and arched laterally. When his nose is within 3 mm of that of the female, he positions his forelimbs near her head with palms facing outward. The foreclaws are vibrated against the female's ocular region for 344–834 milliseconds (mean, 470); the mean number of contacts per vibration bout is about ten, and he may bob his head up and down in accompaniment. Mounting is attempted if the female remains motionless, and mounting seems independent of the number of courtship bouts. Copulation is facilitated by the male hooking the tip of his tail around that of the female. Copulation lasts from 15 seconds to over four hours, with male *G. p. pseudogeographica* passively floating at a 45° angle to the female with his forelimbs arched over his head (Vogt, 1980). Copulation in *G. p. kohnii* usually takes place at the bottom of the water (Ernst, pers. obs.). The courtship sequence described

above is in general agreement with that observed by Ernst (1974b), except that he observed the male bite the female's hindquarters prior to the claw vibration phase.

Graptemys p. kohnii usually lays its eggs in June (Carr, 1952; Dundee and Rossman, 1989). The nesting season of a community of three species of *Graptemys*, including *G. p. pseudogeographica*, in Wisconsin lasts from mid-May to late July, with the first clutch of the season laid from mid-May to mid-June (Vogt, 1980). Nests are excavated between 0545 and 2030, but most clutches are deposited from 0630 to 1000. Nesting occurs throughout the day on overcast days, but is interrupted by rain. Cloacal temperatures of nesting females range from 24.6 to 28.2°C at air temperatures ranging from 21.1 to 32.0°C.

Large numbers of females gather within 3–15 m of nesting beaches waiting for environmental cues to emerge and nest, and they may wander 5–150 m on the beach before digging a nest. Nests may be located in open sand areas or in areas dominated by low shrubs. Most are dug adjacent to clumps of *Carex* or other herbaceous plants, and none are located in dense vegetation (Vogt and Bull, 1984). The flask-shaped nest cavity is dug with the hind limbs and is 10–16 cm deep. The neck of the hole broadens at 4–8 cm beneath the surface. Several "test holes" may be excavated, but a body pit is not constructed as in some other turtle species.

The female extends her head and bobs it vertically as each egg is dropped. Eggs are positioned and packed into the cavity with the hind feet. After oviposition is complete the female fills the nest and packs it down by alternately raising her hind limbs 5 cm above ground and slapping the surface. Females also void bladder water on the nest. The return trip to the water often follows the same track on which the turtle emerged. Some females repeatedly use the same beach to nest (Vogt and Bull, 1982b).

Two and possibly three clutches are laid per year. Clutch size ranges from 8–22 eggs (mean, 14.1) in *G. p. pseudogeographica* to 2–8 eggs in *G. p. kohnii*, with larger females laying larger clutches (Vogt, 1980; Dundee and Rossman, 1989). Eggs in clutches laid by *G. p. pseudogeographica* examined by Vogt (1980) had the following ranges of mean dimensions: length, 32.3–37.4 mm; width, 17.9–24.7 mm; weight, 5.89–11.16 g. The elliptical eggs of *G. p. kohnii* are 35–41.0 mm long and 20.7–26.2 mm wide (Dundee and Rossman, 1989).

In Wisconsin, nests experience daily temperature fluctuations of 2.2–12.2°C. Eggs incubated in the laboratory develop droplets of liquid on the shell within one or two days before hatching, and expand in width and decrease in length as hatching approaches. Hatching begins with one or two longitudinal slits in the shell 5–20 mm long that are presumably cut with the caruncle (egg tooth). The slits increase in size until the hatchling's head is forced through. Hatchlings may pull themselves out of the egg and bury in the incubation medium, but some may remain in the eggshell for three to six days. The egg tooth is lost within three weeks of hatching. The incubation period in nature lasts from 60 to 82 days (Ewert, 1979a; Vogt, 1980). Hatchlings usually remain in the nest until the yolk sac is completely absorbed, but they rarely, if ever, overwinter in the nest (Vogt, 1980). Emergence from the nest may occur at any time of day.

Ewert (1979a) noted that the laboratory incubation period of Minnesota *G. pseudogeographica* was 89.3 days at 22–25°C, 81 days at 25–25.5°C, and 52.1 days at 29.5–30°C. Hatching success was approximately 95% in 285 nests observed over a six-year period in Wisconsin (Vogt, 1980).

Three eggs dissected from a Louisiana female on 13 June hatched 76 days later on 28 August (Dundee and Rossman, 1989). Ewert (1985) reported that during development blood islands associated with embryonic stage 5 are present in *G. p. kohnii* after three or four days incubation at 25°C and two or three days at 30°C; similarly, vitelline circulation (stage 8+), eye pigmentation (stage 12), and body pigmentation (stage 20) are first seen during incubation at 25°C at 6–7 days, 13–15 days, and 35–37 days, respectively, but when incubated at 30°C these stages are attained in 4–5, 8–9, and 23–25 days, respectively. Pipping of the eggshell occurs in 75–79 days at 25°C incubation, and at 51–56 days at 30°C.

Hatchlings are nearly round, and those of each subspecies are patterned like the adults. The carapacial keel is well developed on the first three vertebrals, and the posterior rim of the carapace is even more serrate than that of the adult. The carapace of *G. p. pseudogeographica* is bright olive with yellow markings, that of *G. p. kohnii* is grayer. The plastron patterns of both subspecies are darker than in adults. Hatchling *G. p. pseudogeographica* have carapaces 25.0–33.0 mm long and 26.6–33.7 mm wide; the plastron is 23.8–31.6 mm long (Vogt, 1980). They weigh 1.8–6.6 g (Vogt, 1980), or about 68.5% of freshly laid egg weight (Ewert, 1979a). Hatchling *G. p. kohnii* are 33.8–37.0 mm in carapace length, and weigh 6–9 g.

Incubation temperature influences hatchling head pattern and the frequency of scute anomalies. Five percent of hatchlings incubated at 25°C develop scute anomalies, but 29% of hatchlings incubated at 35°C have them. Ewert (1979a) observed that eggs of *Graptemys* collected along the Mississippi River at Winona, Minnesota, produced some hatchlings with *G. p. kohnii* head patterns and some with patterns typical of *G. p. pseudogeographica*. At incubation temperatures of 25°C, most hatchlings had head patterns like *G. p. kohnii*, but at 30°C the *kohnii* pattern was rare. Vogt (1980) also observed significant differences in the pattern of head blotches of hatchlings from the same clutch incubated at different temperatures.

The sex of *G. pseudogeographica* is determined by incubation temperature (Bull, 1985; Bull and Vogt, 1979; Bull et al., 1982b; Ewert and Nelson, 1991; Vogt, 1980; Vogt and Bull, 1982b, 1984; Janzen and Paukstis, 1991). Eggs incubated at 25°C or lower produce a preponderance of males, but eggs incubated at 30°C or higher produce mostly females. Laboratory-determined threshold temperature (that temperature producing an equal number of males and females) was lower in Tennessee turtles than in Wisconsin turtles in some situations. Nests that produced mostly females were located in open, sandy areas with low, scattered vegetative cover, but those that produced mostly males were associated with denser cover. Nest temperatures were several degrees cooler in shaded areas than in open areas. Because of variation in the availability of these two general habitat types, different beaches often had different hatchling sex ratios (Vogt and Bull, 1982b, 1984).

Incubation periods for *G. p. pseudogeographica* and *G. ouachitensis* nests in Wisconsin ranged from 52 to 73 days (median, 56) for nests producing 100% females and 58 to 85 days (median, 71) for those producing only males. Higher incubation temperatures occur early in the season, so most hatchlings emerging early in the season are females; males are produced late in the season. Thirty percent of the nests observed produced intermediate sex ratios (Vogt and Bull, 1982b).

GROWTH AND LONGEVITY: Growth rates of captive hatchlings were studied by Vogt (1980). Both sexes increase in weight and shell proportions at about the same rate for the first three years. Male growth slows at three to four years of age (at about the onset of sexual maturity), but females continue to grow. During the first three years, male and female carapace growth averages 0.50 mm/month and 0.43 mm/month, respectively. From ages five to six, males and females grow at monthly rates of 0.56

Juvenile *Graptemys pseudogeographica kohnii*

Plastron of juvenile *Graptemys pseudogeographica kohnii*

mm and 1.6 mm, respectively. Females increase in weight about 96 g during their fifth year of growth. Growth rings seem reliable indicators of age in males and females younger than 6 and 12 years, respectively. Recapture of free-living mature females after one to five years revealed increases in carapace length of about 1.0 mm/yr.

Snider and Bowler (1992) reported that a "subspecies" of the false map turtle lived for over 32 years in captivity, but it is not clear if this record applies to *G. pseudogeographica* or to *G. ouachitensis*. A male *G. p. kohnii,* wild caught as a juvenile, lived for 35 years,

five months at the Columbus Zoo (Snider and Bowler, 1992).

FOOD HABITS: *Graptemys p. pseudogeographica* is a generalist omnivore that in the northern part of the range overlaps both *G. geographica* and *G. ouachitensis* in prey types and feeding habitats, but in some more southern areas, where the other two species are absent, *G. p. pseudogeographica* is a mollusk specialist, possibly because of lack of competition (Vogt, 1981b). Females collected in Wisconsin by Vogt (1980) during June, July, and August contained the following percentages (by volume) of prey items: mollusks, 19%; plant material including *Vallisneria, Potamogeton,* and *Lemna,* 42.4%; and insects, including caddisfly cases, mayfly larvae, and damselfly larvae, 21.9%. Males eat the same insects as females, as well as beetles, flies, and other insect larvae, mollusks, fish carrion, and trace amounts of vegetation (Vogt, 1980, 1981b).

Feeding begins in Wisconsin in late May and continues until mid-September (Vogt, 1980). Neustophagic-like surface feeding is sometimes used, but not as often as a search and grab mode (Vogt, 1981b; Ernst, pers. obs.).

Graptemys p. kohnii is also considered omnivorous, and though this may be true of juveniles and males, adult females are probably more molluscivorous. Prey reported for this subspecies includes aquatic plants (*Cabomba, Ceratophyllum, Potamogeton, Lemna*), muscadine grapes (*Vitis*), bivalves (*Carunculina, Corbicula, Lampsilis, Obovaria, Quadrula, Sphaerium*), snails (*Campeloma*), crayfish, dragonfly and damselfly nymphs, and a skink (*Eumeces*) (Carr, 1952; Ernst and Barbour, 1972; Shively and Vidrine, 1984; Johnson, 1987).

Captives of both subspecies readily consume fish, snails, clams, earthworms, crickets, and romaine lettuce (Ernst, pers. obs.).

PREDATORS AND DEFENSE: Maggots of the fly *Metoposarcophaga importans* devoured 36% of the hatchlings found in 23 Wisconsin clutches. The maggots entered the yolk scar of the hatchling once the turtle egg was pipped (Vogt, 1981c). Nests and eggs are also destroyed by red foxes (*Vulpes fulva*), raccoons (*Procyon lotor*), and river otters (*Lutra canadensis*). Over 90% of nests can be destroyed by predators within the first 24 hours after laying. Emerging hatchlings are subject to predation by gulls (*Larus delawarensis*), red-winged blackbirds (*Agelaius phoeniceus*), grackles, crows (*Corvus brachyrhynchos*), and, possibly, great blue herons (*Ardea herodias*) (Vogt, 1980). Bass, catfish, and pike are potential fish predators of hatchlings once they reach the water. At Reelfoot Lake, Tennessee, rice rats (*Oryzomys palustris*) prey on young turtles (Goodpaster and Hoffmeister, 1952). Humans cause mortality of adults through drowning in gill nets, shooting, and setlines for fish (Vogt, 1981a).

Graptemys pseudogeographica is very timid and quickly flees when approached. It rarely attempts to bite when handled, but may void bladder water.

POPULATIONS: Eighty-two percent of the female *G. p. pseudogeographica* captured by Vogt (1980) in Wisconsin were between 21 and 25 cm, and 79% weighed from 1,100 to 1,800 g. The adult males were more uniform in size and weight than females.

Timken (1968) collected 180 *G. p. pseudogeographica* in the Missouri River, of which 144 were females, for a male:female sex ratio of 0.25:1. The female sample included 36 mature and 108 immature turtles. All of the males were sexually mature. Vogt (1980) also reported highly female-biased sex ratios. During a 10-week period he collected 299 females and 27 males in fyke nets, for a male:female ratio of 0.09:1. Other subsamples of his data resulted in estimates of sex ratios of 0.16 and 0.48 males per female.

Vogt (1980) acknowledged that the sex ratios he observed were somewhat biased by concentrating collecting efforts near nesting beaches and other areas frequented by females. It is tempting to speculate that biased sex ratios are partially attributed to the effects of temperature-dependent sex determination. The microhabitat of the nest largely determines the hatchling sex ratio of *G. p. pseudogeographica* (Vogt and Bull, 1982b, 1984). The influence of sampling bias and alternative explanations of biased sex ratios need to be carefully considered in any analysis (Gibbons, 1990; Lovich and Gibbons, 1990).

Graptemys p. kohnii is common in the Ouachita and Sabine rivers of Louisiana (Chaney and Smith, 1950), and at Reelfoot Lake, Tennessee (Ernst and Barbour, pers. obs.). Tinkle (1958a) found it and *Pseudemys concinna* to be the dominant species in the Tensas River. This turtle is declining in Missouri, possibly as a result of several factors including water pollution, river channelization, reduction of suitable nesting sites, siltation, and unlawful shooting (Johnson, 1987). In the past the pet trade also adversely affected some Mississippi map turtle populations.

REMARKS: Vogt (1993) reviewed the systematics of the false map turtle complex, and Carr (1949) and Dundee (1974) commented on the differences between *G. pseudogeographica* and *G. kohnii*. Bour and Dubois (1983b) examined the type specimens of *Emys pseudogeographica* Gray, 1831 and *E. lesueuri* Gray, 1831, and determined that the latter is a junior synonym of the former.

Commercial fishermen told Anderson (1965) that this species was abundant 25 or more years earlier in the Missouri and Mississippi rivers, but had become uncommon. They attributed the decline to stream pollution and asserted that an increasing discharge of pollutants in recent years had virtually eradicated turtles for many miles below Kansas City and St. Louis.

Graptemys ouachitensis Cagle, 1953a
Ouachita map turtle
PLATE 49

RECOGNITION: *Graptemys ouachitensis* is a medium-sized to large (male carapace length to 14 cm, female, to 24 cm) map turtle with a distinct median keel bearing conspicuous low spines and serrated posterior marginals. The oval carapace is olive to brown, and each pleural scute has yellow vermiculations and dark blotches. The upper and lower surfaces of the marginals have a yellow ocellus at each seam, and the bridge is patterned with dark bars. The cream to olive-yellow plastron has a pattern of dark, seam-following lines in adults; the plastron pattern is more extensive in juveniles, but fades with age. The head is narrow to moderately broad with a nonprotruding snout and no medial notch or hook on the upper jaw. Skin color is olive to brown or black with many narrow yellow stripes on the legs, tail, chin, and neck. The postorbital mark may be extensive, and it varies in shape from square to rectangular or elongate to oval, and commonly consists of a downward extension of a neck stripe behind the orbit; one to nine neck stripes reach the orbit. Two large, light spots may occur on each side of the face, one just under the eye and another on the lower jaw, and light transverse bars are present under the chin.

Adult males have long, thick tails, with the vent posterior to the carapacial rim, and elongated foreclaws (especially the third). Sexually mature females are, on average, more than twice the size of mature males (Gibbons and Lovich, 1990).

KARYOTYPE: Diploid chromosomes total 50: 26 macrochromosomes with 48 arms, and 24 microchromosomes with 24 arms (McKown, 1972; Killebrew, 1977a).

FOSSIL RECORD: No fossil specimens have been found.

DISTRIBUTION: *Graptemys ouachitensis* ranges from Texas and Louisiana north and eastward to eastern Kansas, eastern Iowa, Minnesota, Wisconsin, Illinois, Indiana, Kentucky, Tennessee, and northern Alabama. Disjunct populations also exist in Mitchell and Pawnee counties, Kansas, more than 200 km west of the main range (Taggart, 1992; Joseph T. Collins, pers. comm.), and in south-central Ohio.

GEOGRAPHIC VARIATION: The two subspecies of *Graptemys ouachitensis* were first considered subspecies of *G. pseudogeographica* (Cagle, 1953a), but Vogt (1980, 1993) demonstrated that the northern subspecies *G. o. ouachitensis* was taxonomically distinct from sympatric *G. pseudogeographica*. *Graptemys o. ouachitensis* Cagle, 1953a ranges from the Ouachita River system of northern Louisiana west to Oklahoma and northward to Kansas, Iowa, Minnesota, Wisconsin, Illinois, Indiana, and Ohio. It has an extensive square to rectangular postorbital mark, one to three neck stripes touching the orbit, and two large, light spots on each side of the face, one just under the eye and another on the lower jaw. *Graptemys o. sabinensis* Cagle, 1953a, the Sabine map turtle, is restricted to the Sabine River system of Texas and Louisiana. It has an elongate or oval postorbital mark, five to nine neck stripes reach the orbit, and the two light spots on each side of the face are reduced in size.

CONFUSING SPECIES: *Graptemys pseudogeographica kohnii* has a curved bar behind the eye that prevents neck stripes from contacting the orbit, a white iris, and broad-headed females. *Graptemys p. pseudogeographica* has a small, but variable, postorbital mark consisting of a narrow downward extension of a neck stripe behind the orbit, and four to seven neck stripes commonly touching the orbit. *Grapemys versa*

Female *Graptemys ouachitensis ouachitensis*

Male *Graptemys ouachitensis ouachitensis*

has a low keel and commonly a light J-shaped postorbital mark extending backward from the eye. *Graptemys geographica* has a low, relatively spineless vertebral keel, the postorbital mark reduced to a spot, and a relatively broad head.

HABITAT: The Ouachita map turtle is primarily a riverine turtle, inhabiting areas with swift currents and submerged vegetation (Vogt, 1980; Black et al.,

1987; Harvey, 1992), but it also lives in impoundments, lakes, oxbows, and river-bottom swamps. Sand and silt bottoms are preferred over those of gravel, stone, or mud (Ewert, 1979b).

Environmental factors limiting the upstream distribution of *G. o. sabinensis* in Louisiana were examined by Shively and Jackson (1985). The most important proximate determinants of its density were the amount of algal growth on logs and basking site area,

Plastron of *Graptemys*
ouachitensis ouachitensis

Distribution of *Graptemys ouachitensis*

Male *Graptemys ouachitensis sabinensis*

Plastron of *Graptemys ouachitensis sabinensis*

but stream width was the ultimate determinate restricting the upstream limit of distribution.

BEHAVIOR: The behavior of this species is similar to that of *Graptemys pseudogeographica* and the reader is referred to that account for more details. However, several important differences between the two species are worth noting. In Wisconsin, where the two species are sympatric, male *G. ouachitensis*

remain in river channels during the summer but *G. pseudogeographica* moves into quiet backwaters to forage. Female *G. ouachitensis* move to patches of vegetation adjacent to sloughs or river channels after laying their second clutch (Vogt, 1980).

Like *G. pseudogeographica*, the Ouachita map turtle spends most of the day basking during the active season, and may pile up several deep on a log. The cloacal temperatures of seven basking turtles were taken by Vogt (1980) just after they submerged when the air temperature was 21.5°C and the water temperature 22.5°C. Cloacal temperatures of the six females ranged from 23.8 to 27°C (mean 25.8) but that of the male was the same as the water. Basking males were observed to gape more often than females (see Lovich, 1990). Hutchison et al. (1966) reported that the mean critical thermal maximum was 41.0°C (40.4–42.0), and that the loss of the righting response occurred at mean 38.9°C (38.5–39.4).

The feeding symbiosis between Ouachita map turtles and common grackles (*Quiscalus quiscula*) is discussed in the account of *G. pseudogeographica*.

REPRODUCTION: The reproductive cycle of the Ouachita map turtle in Wisconsin is similar to that of *Graptemys pseudogeographica* and is discussed in that account. Males mature in their second or third year. In Louisiana, male *G. o. sabinensis* mature at sizes larger than about 6 cm in plastron length (Cagle, 1953a), but males in Oklahoma mature at a plastron length of about 7 cm (Webb, 1961).

Webb (1961) collected sexually mature females in Oklahoma in early June that had swollen, convoluted oviducts 7–10 mm wide, corpora lutea or atretic follicles less than 4 mm in diameter, and follicles between 3 and 5 mm in diameter. Those collected in June and July had follicles ranging from 9.5 to 23.3 mm, corpora lutea ranging from 4 to 9 mm, and some had oviducal eggs. He concluded that Oklahoma females mature at about 15–16 cm in plastron length in their sixth or seventh year.

Mating in Wisconsin probably takes place in April, October, and November (Vogt, 1980). Courtship behavior is similar to that of *G. pseudogeographica* (see that account), with some noteworthy exceptions. In both species, males vibrate (titillate) their foreclaws against the ocular region of the female during courtship. The mean number of contacts per vibration bout in *G. ouachitensis* is 5.2, or about half the number made by *G. pseudogeographica*. Also, male Ouachita map turtles may or may not bob their heads up and down during courtship as do male false map turtles (Ernst, pers. obs.).

Courtship behavior between a captive male *G. ouachitensis* and a female *G. geographica* was described by Jenkins (1979). The male positioned himself about 3–5 cm in front of the female and began bobbing his head vertically. He then touched his nose to hers. After three or four seconds of nose contact, the male moved back, stopped bobbing, and began to vibrate his foreclaws against the female's orbits. Between vibration episodes he bit her on the neck, forelimbs,

and tail. The female remained passive throughout most of his overtures. When she attempted to move away, the male repeatedly bit her until she emerged from the water and he returned to the bottom of the tank. Copulation is described in the account on *G. pseudogeographica*.

The nesting season of a Wisconsin community of three species of *Graptemys*, including *G. ouachitensis*, lasts from mid-May to late July (Vogt, 1980). The first clutch of the season is laid from mid-May to mid-June. Nests are constructed between 0545 and 2030, but most are dug between 0630 and 1000. Nesting occurs throughout the day on overcast days, but is interrupted by rain. Cloacal temperatures of nesting females range from 24.6 to 28.2°C at air temperatures ranging from 21.1 to 32.0°C. Details of nesting behavior and ecology are summarized in the account on *G. pseudogeographica*.

Two, and possibly three, clutches are laid per year in Oklahoma and Wisconsin (Webb, 1961; Vogt, 1980). Mean clutch size ranges from 6 to 15 for various size classes of females, with an overall mean of about 10.5 eggs per clutch, or an annual reproductive potential of about 21 eggs, assuming that females produce two clutches per year (Vogt, 1980). Webb (1961) also calculated an annual reproductive potential of 21 eggs with an annual realized potential of 19.5 eggs for Oklahoma females, but assumed that females deposit three clutches per year. Clutch size increases with increasing female body size. Egg dimensions are: length, 30.2–40.3 mm; width, 18.7–23.8 mm; weight, 9.2–10.8 g (Webb, 1961; Vogt, 1980; Dundee and Rossman, 1989). Mean clutch weight for females in various size classes ranges from 74 to 153 g (Vogt, 1980). Dry weight of nonlipid components of the egg ranges from 1.36 to 2.54 g (mean 1.94), and lipid weight and percent are 0.45–0.83 g (mean 0.62) and 15.97–34.00% (mean 24.36), respectively (Congdon et al., 1983c).

Nest temperatures, incubation periods, and the influence of incubation temperature on hatchling head pattern and frequency of scute anomalies are discussed in the account on *G. pseudogeographica*. Hatching is described there as well.

Hatchlings rarely, if ever, overwinter in the nest. They are nearly round, with a well-developed keel on the first three vertebrals and a very serrate posterior carapacial rim. The carapace is olive to brown, and the plastron has an extensive dark figure. The carapace is 27.1–35.0 mm long, 26.5–34.0 wide, and 7.7–8.4 mm deep; the plastron is 22.2–34.0 mm long, and hatchlings weigh 1.5–6.2 g (Cagle, 1953a; Webb, 1961; Vogt, 1980).

As in *G. pseudogeographica,* the sex of Ouachita map turtles is determined by incubation temperature (see references and discussion in the account of *G. pseudogeographica* and Bull and Vogt, 1981; Vogt and Bull, 1982; Bull et al., 1990), although a heritable component has been demonstrated (Bull et al., 1982a). Eggs incubated at 28°C produce 100% males, whereas eggs incubated at 30°C produce almost no males (Bull et al., 1982b; Ewert and Nelson, 1991). The sensitive period for sex determination extends throughout most of the middle third of development. Sex is more readily influenced by 25°C than by 31°C, which implies that maleness can be determined earlier in development than can femaleness (Bull and Vogt, 1981). Bull et al. (1990) incubated eggs at a male-producing temperature of 26°C for 31 days and then switched them to female-producing temperatures of either 31°C or 32.5°C. Sex ratio was significantly more male-biased in the 26 to 31°C shift than in the 26 to 32.5°C shift. The results imply that 32.5°C has greater female potency than lower temperatures.

GROWTH AND LONGEVITY: Webb (1961) estimated size at various ages of Oklahoma *G. ouachitensis* using scute proportions. At the end of their first year six free-living males were 4.8–5.3 cm in plastron length and had increased 1.6–2.6 cm, and 17 females were 3.6–6.0 cm and had increased 0.7–3.5 cm. At the end of the second year two males were 6.3–7.3 cm and had increased 1.1–2.4 cm, and eight females were 6.0–8.1 cm and had grown 1.4–2.6 cm. One female in her third year was 9.5 cm. and had grown 2.3 cm. A subadult female studied by Cagle (1953a) was 1.72 cm in plastron length at hatching, 3.63 cm at the end of the first season of growth, 5.13 cm at the end of the second, 5.96 cm at the end of the third, and 7.45 cm at the end of the fifth year.

Moll (1976a) compared the growth rates of two populations of Ouachita map turtles. One population was in an organic, mud-bottomed lake where juveniles were primarily carnivorous. The other was in a section of the Mississippi River with an inorganic sand bottom where juveniles were primarily herbivorous. Juvenile growth was much more rapid in the lake population, but adults grew very slowly, regardless of diet or habitat. Growth slows as sexual maturity is reached.

Growth rates of captive hatchling *G. pseudogeographica* and *G. ouachitensis* in Wisconsin were studied by Vogt (1980) and are summarized in the account on *G. pseudogeographica.*

Snyder and Bowler (1992) reported that Ouachita map turtles have lived for more than eight years in captivity, and Ernst has kept *G. o. ouachitensis* of both sexes alive in his laboratory for more than 10 years.

FOOD HABITS: The relatively narrow crushing surfaces of its jaws probably restrict *Graptemys ouachitensis* from feeding predominantly on mollusks, and so it is basically omnivorous. In Wisconsin, females feed on the surface as well as below it. They graze opportunistically on surface vegetation and insects (Vogt, 1981a). Females collected in Wisconsin during June, July, and August contained the following percentages of food items, by volume: mollusks, 2.8%; plant material including *Vallisneria, Potamogeton,* and *Lemna,* 31.5%; and insects including caddisfly cases, mayfly larvae, and damselfly larvae, 51%. Males eat the same insects as females, as well as beetles, flies, and other insect larvae, mollusks, fish carrion, and trace amounts of vegetation. Feeding begins in late May and continues until mid-September (Vogt, 1980).

In Louisiana, Sabine map turtles have been observed clinging to submerged logs and grazing on the attached filamentous green algae, or eating aquatic insects on the surface of the logs (Shively, 1982; Shively and Jackson, 1985). The males were insectivorous, actively selecting caddisfly larvae (*Hydropsyche*), as do the juveniles, but the juveniles are more omnivorous (Shively, 1982). Prey included algae, bryophytes, trichopterans (Hydropsychidae larvae), beetles (Elmidae adults and larvae), dipterans (Simuliidae, Chironomidae, Tipulidae), megalopterans, dragonflies, mayflies, and small clams (*Corbicula*). Adult females ate mostly algae. Other prey consumed in other parts of the range include leaves, seeds, and fruits of various plants (*Chelone glabra,* wetland grasses, various dicots, *Ulmus americana*), bryozoans, snails, crayfish, spiders, ants and other hymenopterans, dead fish, and fledgling birds (carrion?). Male captives we have kept have readily eaten both fish and romaine lettuce, but our captive females have only taken fish. Terrestrial vegetation is eaten during high-water periods when it is more readily available. Males and juveniles are more carnivorous than are mature females (Webb, 1961; Moll, 1976b).

Resource partitioning in a community of three sympatric *Graptemys* (*ouachitensis, geographica,* and *pseudogeographica*) in the Mississippi River was examined by Vogt (1981b). *G. ouachitensis* was an omnivore, specializing in surface feeding, whereas *G. geographica* was primarily a mollusk feeder, and *G. pseudogeographica* was a general omnivore.

PREDATORS AND DEFENSE: Maggots of the fly *Metoposarcophaga importans* may devour developing embryos in Wisconsin (Vogt, 1981c). Other predators, causes of mortality, and defensive behavior are reviewed in the account of *G. pseudogeographica*.

POPULATIONS: *Graptemys ouachitensis* made up 66% of a sample of three sympatric species of the genus in Wisconsin (Vogt, 1981b). Densities of 2.1–6.7 turtles per 1,000 m² were reported in a Louisiana River (Shively and Jackson, 1985). Of the females captured by Vogt (1980), 85% had carapace lengths between 19 and 23 cm and weights between 800 and 1,400 g. Most of the specimens collected by Webb (1961) were immature owing to the wary nature of large adult females.

Chaney and Smith (1950) collected 175 *G. o. ouachitensis* and *G. pseudogeographica kohnii* from the Ouachita River near Harrisonburg, Louisiana, and 325 *G. o. sabinensis* and *G. p. kohnii* from the Sabine River near Negreet, Louisiana. Webb (1961) reported that Ouachita map turtles made up 15% of the 156 turtles he trapped in Lake Texoma, Oklahoma. These numbers show how abundant these turtles have been at certain localities.

Female-biased sex ratios were reported by Vogt (1980) and Shively and Jackson (1985). Also, of 26 hatchlings sexed by Webb (1961), 19 were females, a 3:1 sex ratio at hatching. Biased sex ratios may be due either to the effects of temperature-dependent sex determination or to sampling bias.

REMARKS: So little is known of the ecology and behavior of this often common species in the southern part of its range that an extensive study of its life history is needed.

Graptemys versa Stejneger, 1925
Texas map turtle
PLATE 50

RECOGNITION: *Graptemys versa* is a small, narrow-headed map turtle with an olive carapace (to 21.4 cm) patterned with yellow reticulations on each scute, a vertebral keel of commonly dark-tipped low knobs having yellow areas anterior to each, and a strongly serrate posterior rim. The carapacial scutes are distinctly convex. All marginals are patterned dorsally with reticulating yellow lines and ventrally with fine dark lines surrounding irregular yellow blotches. The bridge is patterned with fine, dark longitudinal bars; the hingeless plastron is yellow and has a pattern of dark lines along the seams. The skin is olive, with many dark lines surrounding yellowish areas. The orange or yellow postorbital stripes (one on each side) are horizontal or J-shaped and extend backward at their lower (outer) edge; these stripes may be interrupted. Fine yellow stripes extend up the neck from the tympanum to the orbit, and the chin may have a pattern of orange or yellow blotches with dark borders.

Adult males are 6.5–11.2 cm in carapace length, adult females, 9–21.4 cm. Males have long, thick tails, with the vent posterior to the carapacial rim.

KARYOTYPE: The karyotype is composed of 50 chromosomes: 11 pairs of metacentric or submetacentric and 2 pairs of acrocentric macrochromosomes, and 12 pairs of microchromosomes (McKown, 1972).

FOSSIL RECORD: Unknown.

DISTRIBUTION: This turtle is primarily restricted to the Edwards Plateau of central Texas, where it occurs in the Colorado River drainage (Dixon, 1987).

GEOGRAPHIC VARIATION: No subspecies are recognized.

CONFUSING SPECIES: *Trachemys scripta elegans* lacks a vertebral keel and has black plastral smudges. *Pseudemys texana* also lacks a vertebral keel and has broad stripes, spots, or vertical bars on the head. *Graptemys pseudogeographica kohnii* has a crescent-shaped postorbital mark that prevents any neck stripes from reaching the eye. *Graptemys ouachitensis* and *G. p. pseudogeographica* are larger and lack the horizontal or J-shaped postorbital mark. *Graptemys caglei* has a cream-colored transverse bar across the lower jaw.

REMARKS: Little has been reported on the life history of *G. versa*. The record length female had an enlarged head (width, 40 mm), possibly an adaptation to a molluscivorous diet as it passed snail shells in its feces (Kizirian et al., 1990). Captives will eat fresh and canned fish, chicken, beef, hamburger, dog food, insects, and occasionally lettuce.

A captive male kept by Ernst was observed on several occasions to bob its head at a rate of approximately five bobs per second toward a male *G. barbouri* kept in the same tank (Ernst and Barbour, 1972). This behavior is part of the courtship pattern.

Graptemys versa is apparently most closely related to *G. ouachitensis* and *G. pseudogeographica*, with which it was formerly considered conspecific. The relationship of *G. versa* to *G. caglei* and other species of *Graptemys* is discussed in the account of *G. caglei*. Additional information on this species is found in Vogt (1981d).

410

Male *Graptemys versa*

Female *Graptemys versa*

Plastron of *Graptemys versa*

Head pattern of *Graptemys versa*

Distribution of *Graptemys versa*

Graptemys oculifera (Baur, 1890)
Ringed map turtle
PLATE 51

RECOGNITION: *Graptemys oculifera* is a small, narrow-headed map turtle with laterally compressed, black, spinelike vertebral projections and a serrated posterior carapacial margin. Vertebral projections are more pronounced in adult males and juveniles. The carapace (to 21.6 cm) is dark olive-green; each pleural has a broad yellow or orange ocellus, and each marginal is marked with a wide yellow bar or semicircle. The hingeless plastron is yellow or orange, with an olive-brown pattern extending along the seams; this pattern fades with age. The skin is black with yellow stripes, and the ventral surface of the neck bears three wide longitudinal stripes. The variable postorbital marks (one on each side) are ovoid, rectangular, or rounded and usually not connected with the narrow dorsal longitudinal stripe. Two broad yellow stripes enter the orbit. The intraorbital stripe is wide and equal to or greater than the width of the broadest neck stripes. The lower jaw is marked with longitudinal yellow stripes as wide as the black interspaces.

Adult males have long, thick tails, with the anal opening posterior to the carapace rim and closer to the tail tip. Males also have elongated foreclaws. Adult females are 10–22 cm in carapace length, adult males, 6.5–11.0 cm.

KARYOTYPE: The diploid chromosome number is 50: 26 macrochromosomes and 24 microchromosomes (Killebrew, 1977a).

FOSSIL RECORD: No fossils have been found.

DISTRIBUTION: *Graptemys oculifera* is restricted to the Pearl River and its major tributaries in Mississippi and Louisiana, but is not found in the tidally influenced lowermost section of the West Pearl River (McCoy and Vogt, 1988).

GEOGRAPHIC VARIATION: No subspecies are recognized.

CONFUSING SPECIES: *Graptemys flavimaculata* has olive-green skin, a light cream-colored plastron, the postorbital mark connected to the longitudinal dorsal neckstripe, and a large yellow blotch on each pleural. *Graptemys nigrinoda* has broad, rounded, knoblike projections on the vertebrals, postorbital marks connected dorsally to form a Y-shaped mark, and four yellow neckstripes entering the orbit. Other features that separate *G. oculifera*, *G. flavimaculata*, and *G. nigrinoda* are summarized by Cagle (1954a). *Graptemys pulchra*, *G. ernsti*, and *G. gibbonsi* have a wider head and a longitudinal light bar on the chin. *Graptemys pulchra* has narrow yellow markings on each marginal.

HABITAT: *Graptemys oculifera* prefers wide rivers with strong currents, adjacent white sand beaches, and an abundance of basking sites in the form of brush, logs, and debris.

BEHAVIOR: Almost nothing has been published regarding the life history of *Graptemys oculifera*.

It spends much of the day basking, and is wary and difficult to approach at such times. Basking sites are shared with *G. gibbonsi*, *G. pseudogeographica kohnii*, *Trachemys scripta*, *Pseudemys concinna*, *P. floridana*, *Sternotherus carinatus*, *Trionyx muticus*, and *T. spiniferus*. At night it rests on branches and snags just beneath the water.

Hatchlings display negative reactions to bright sunlight. Those placed on the sand within 0.6 m of water turn and move to the nearest shade. Tests suggest that the dark shadows formed by forest background might affect orientation, but that there is a possible negative reaction to dark objects at night. Light reflected from the water is not considered to be

Male *Graptemys oculifera;*
note elongated foreclaws

Plastron of *Graptemys
oculifera*

an important factor in orientation. Hatchlings leave the nest within three hours after sunset, the only time in their lives when they are known to be nocturnally active (Anderson, 1958).

REPRODUCTION: Males become sexually mature at about 65 mm in plastron length. A male of this size collected by Cagle (1953a) had motile sperm in its testes, but the foreclaws and preanal area were not conspicuously elongated. It was apparently in its

first season of maturity but fifth season of growth. Kofron (1991) reported that male maturity was attained in the fourth or fifth year at plastron lengths of 60–70 mm; one male he examined was mature by its third year. Immature males he examined had combined testes lengths of 10.5–29.6 mm, and showed testicular linear growth without recrudescence. Testes attained maximum size in August and September. Combined testes lengths varied seasonally as follows: April to July—10.2–16.0 mm, August—

Head pattern of *Graptemys oculifera*

Distribution of *Graptemys oculifera*

16.0–27.0 mm, and September—24.3–29.6 mm; spermatogenesis apparently occured in August and September.

The smallest mature female collected by Cagle (1953a) had a 12.8-cm plastron. This female, captured on 4 June, had three eggs in the left oviduct and none in the right. Two of the oviducal eggs measured 40.3 by 20.6 mm and 40.0 by 21.0 mm. The ovaries contained four follicles, which were 16, 16, 21, and 23 mm in diameter. When found, this turtle was depositing her first clutch of the season, and she probably would have deposited a second clutch of four eggs. Another female collected in April had four follicles, 7–15 mm in diameter, in each ovary. The two largest immature females examined by Kofron (1991) were 93 and 99 mm (both were of unknown age); adult females ranged from 12.7 to 18.9 cm. From this data, Kofron concluded that females mature at seven or eight years at plastron lengths greater than 10 cm, but Jones (1991) estimated that females mature at an age of about 11 years.

Immature females only have follicles less than 1.0 mm in diameter; follicle classes observed by Kofron are as follows: class I—0.1–4.0 mm, class II—4.1–8.0 mm, class III—8.1–16.0 mm, and class IV—16.1–24.0 mm. Class III and IV follicles have yellow yolk, and the latter are ready for ovulation.

No description of courtship and mating behavior is available, but a copulation was observed near midday on 27 April by Jones (1991).

The eggs are deposited on sandbars in early June. Cagle (1953a) described an incomplete nest as a hole 30 mm in diameter and 30 mm deep leading to a cavity 90 mm in depth; the temperature was 28.8°C in the nest and 29.2°C at the surface. Jones (1991) found nests 7.0–17.4 m from the edge of the water, and 0.06–3.5 m from the nearest vegetation.

Eggs are about 39 × 24 mm (Jones, 1991). Under artificial conditions they hatch in an average of 62.8 days when incubated between 29.5 and 30°C. Several days before pipping the eggshell, sharp-tipped features of the embryo, such as claws and shell margins, are coated with gelatinlike sheaths.

Hatchlings have plastron lengths of about 33 mm (Jones, 1991), and average 9.5 g or approximately 80.1% of freshly laid egg weight (Ewert, 1979a).

GROWTH AND LONGEVITY: Hatchlings were estimated to be 22.3–32.7 mm in plastron length by Cagle (1953a), but no individuals under 31 mm were found in the series of museum specimens examined by Kofron (1991).

Juveniles are 35.7–53.7 mm long in the early part of their first growing season and 39–58 mm long in their second growing season. Kofron (1991) estimated that growth of immature *Graptemys oculifera* of both sexes averaged about 8.4 mm/yr. Juvenile females may grow more rapidly than juvenile males: a 68-mm female was in the second growing season and one 71.2 mm long was in its fifth growing season (Cagle, 1953a). However, Kofron pointed out that Cagle's conclusion was based on assigning an incorrect age to one Tulane University specimen.

Jones (1991) estimated growth rates using adjusted scute annuli measurements that tended to underestimate growth when compared to individuals of known age. His results suggest that males and females grow at the same rate during the first year, but that females grow faster than males afterward. Growth in both sexes slows as maturity is reached (Cagle, 1953a).

A captive female *G. oculifera* lived 12 years, eight months, and 11 days (Snider and Bowler, 1992).

FOOD HABITS: The stomach contents of six juveniles, three mature males, and one large female examined by Cagle (1953a) contained only fragments of insects. He observed two feeding on material growing on the undersurface of a log projecting from the water. Dundee and Rossman (1989) reported that stomach contents included aquatic beetles and their larvae, mayflies and mayfly nymphs, damselflies, dragonfly nymphs, chironomid fly larvae, homopterans, snails, small quantities of algae, and small nematodes, but thought that the nematodes were probably parasites.

The stomachs of 29 *Graptemys oculifera* examined by Kofron (1991) contained 1,078 items in the following frequencies: adult and larval caddisflies were 27% of the prey items with 79% frequency of occurrence; dipteran flies and mayflies, 35% and 23% of the prey items and 14% and 10% frequency of occurrence, respectively; and beetles and plant material, 6% of the prey items each and 45% and 28% frequency of occurrence, respectively. Most plant material consisted of flowers of the Asteraceae and seeds that were the same size and color of a frequently eaten beetle species. Dragonfly larvae and earthworms were found in small numbers, and 66% of the stomachs examined contained small pieces of wood, which probably was ingested incidentally while feeding on materials attached to submerged logs. No observable differences were detected between the stomach contents of adults and subadults.

PREDATORS AND DEFENSE: Eggs and juveniles are undoubtedly preyed upon by a wide variety of animals. Humans are responsible for some forms of adult mutilation and mortality, especially in areas with high boat traffic (Jones, 1991), and fisherman often kill them when they become hooked on their lines.

The ringed map turtle's best defense is to flee when disturbed. If held, a few will bite or expel bladder water, but most retire into their shells.

POPULATIONS: The density and population structure of *Graptemys oculifera* were assessed by Jones (1991) at various locations along the Pearl River. The maximum estimated densities of *G. oculifera* with secondary sexual characters were 341–848 turtles/km of river, depending on the method of calculation. Sex ratios in three of five samples, which included some juveniles with secondary sexual characters, were significantly male biased. Females predominated in samples taken early in the year; males were captured more often in late summer and fall.

Another sample of 51 *G. oculifera* included six mature males, three mature females, and 42 juveniles, 35 of which were hatchlings with seven in their second year of growth (Cagle, 1953a). Kofron (1991) reported 93 males, 40 females, and 30 sex undetermined *G. oculifera* in a sample of museum specimens. McCoy and Vogt (1980b) observed female-biased sex ratios ranging from 0.36 to 0.48 male per female, but their numbers may be biased in favor of females because they used some nets that possibly allowed small males to escape. Chaney and Smith (1950) collected as many as 34 *G. oculifera* and *G. gibbonsi* in a single night near Angie, Louisiana.

REMARKS: Little was known of this species from its original description in 1890 until Cagle's work (1953a), owing partly to errors in locality data such as Mandeville, Louisiana, and Pensacola, Florida. Although *Graptemys oculifera* has recently been reported from the Tangipahoa River (Dundee and Rossman, 1989), available evidence suggests that this species is restricted to the Pearl River. The taxonomic status of the "narrow-headed" group of *Graptemys* has been controversial and reviews are given by Killebrew (1979) and Bertl and Killebrew (1983). *Graptemys oculifera* seems to be most closely related to *G. flavimaculata*.

Along with *G. flavimaculata* and *G. nigrinoda*, *G. oculifera* forms the sawback group of map turtles, in which the spines or knobs of the vertebral keel are prominent.

Graptemys oculifera was classified as a Federally Threatened species in December 1986. Reasons for the decline of this turtle include habitat modification and water-quality degradation (McCoy and Vogt, 1980b; Stewart, 1988). The literature for this species is reviewed by McCoy and Vogt (1988).

Graptemys flavimaculata Cagle, 1954a
Yellow-blotched map turtle
PLATE 52

RECOGNITION: *Graptemys flavimaculata* is a small, narrow-headed turtle with laterally compressed, black, spinelike vertebral projections and a serrated posterior carapacial margin. The carapace (to 18.0 cm) is olive to brown; each pleural has a broad ring or yellow blotch covering most of its surface, and each marginal has a wide yellow bar or semicircle. The hingeless plastron is cream colored, with a black pattern extending along the seams which fades with age. The skin is olive with yellow stripes. About 19 longitudinal yellow stripes adorn the neck; those on the ventral surface are twice as wide as the stripes of the dorsal surface. The postorbital mark commonly is rectangular, and it joins a longitudinal dorsal neck stripe that is at least twice as wide as the next widest neck stripe. Two to four neck stripes reach the orbit. The interorbital stripe is narrower than the neck stripes. The lower jaw is marked with longitudinal yellow stripes, which are wider than the olive-green interstices; thus the yellow is predominant.

Adult males have long, thick tails, with the anal opening posterior to the carapacial rim; they also have elongated foreclaws. Adult females have broader heads and are larger than males. Adult females are 14.9–18.0 cm in carapace length, adult males, 6.7–11.0 cm.

KARYOTYPE: The diploid chromosome number is 50: 26 macrochromosomes and 24 microchromosomes (Killebrew, 1977a).

FOSSIL RECORD: None

DISTRIBUTION: *Graptemys flavimaculata* is restricted to the Pascagoula River and its major tributaries in Mississippi, to within 25 km of the mouth of the Pascagoula River (Cliburn, 1971; McCoy and Vogt, 1980a; U.S. Fish and Wildlife Service, 1992).

GEOGRAPHIC VARIATION: No subspecies are recognized.

CONFUSING SPECIES: *Graptemys oculifera* usually has the postorbital mark separated from the longitudinal dorsal stripes, black skin, a broad yellow or orange circle on each pleural, and a yellow or orange plastron. *Graptemys nigrinoda* has broad, rounded, knoblike vertebral projections, postorbital marks connected dorsally to form a Y-shaped mark, black skin, a narrow yellow or orange semicircle or circle on each pleural, and a yellow plastron. *Graptemys pulchra*, *G. ernsti* and *G. gibbonsi* have wider heads and a longitudinal light bar on the chin; *G. pulchra* also has narrower yellow markings on the marginals.

HABITAT: This species prefers wide rivers with strong currents, sandbars, and nesting beaches, and an abundance of basking sites in the form of snags, brush, and debris.

BEHAVIOR: *Graptemys flavimaculata* spends much of the day basking. Basking may occur at temperatures below 4°C and even during rain showers. It is more likely to bask under cloudy conditions than sympatric *Pseudemys* or *Sternotherus* (McCoy and Vogt, 1980a). This species is an excellent climber and basking sites may be elevated more than 3.7 m above the water line. Aggregations of basking individuals often stack three deep (Floyd, 1973). Like other map turtles it is extremely wary. Little else is known of its nonreproductive behavior.

REPRODUCTION: The reproductive habits of this turtle have not been adequately studied. Cagle (1954a) reported that females were mature at a plastron length of 13.3 cm and males at 6.7 cm.

Male *Graptemys flavimaculata*

Female *Graptemys flavimaculata*

During courtship the male approaches the female with his neck extended. She faces him and extends her neck. He then stretches out his forelimbs and strokes the sides of her head with his claws while she simultaneously attempts to stroke him (Wahlquist, 1970). The behavior is similar to that of *Chrysemys picta*.

Courtship between a male *G. pseudogeographica* and a 13-cm female *G. flavimaculata* is described in the account of the former species.

Cagle (1955) observed a captive hatchling *G. flavimaculata* of unknown sex exhibiting courtshiplike behavior to a larger juvenile female on three occasions. The behavior was not prolonged and consistent as in mature males.

GROWTH AND LONGEVITY: Males may reach sexual maturity in their second year. Cagle (1954a) reported that three males in their third and fourth years were 7.5–8.0 cm long. Growth rings of females become obscured prior to reaching maturity and females larger than 14 cm normally have no measurable growth rings. Nothing has been published on the longevity of this species.

FOOD HABITS: According to the late Fred Cagle's field notes this species feeds predominantly on insects, including caddisfly and chironomid larvae. In contrast, Floyd (1973) reported that fragments of mollusks were abundant in the fecal masses of recently captured *G. flavimaculata*. Perhaps there is a sexual

Plastron of *Graptemys flavimaculata*

Distribution of *Graptemys flavimaculata*

difference in food preferences, as occurs in some other map turtles.

PREDATORS AND DEFENSE: A juvenile alligator mapping turtle, *Macroclemys temminckii,* in Ernst's laboratory consumed two adult male *G. flavimaculata.* Nothing has been published on predation in the wild, but surely raccoons (*Procyon lotor*) destroy many nests.

Adult females will bite when handled, but adult males and juveniles usually withdraw into the shell and remain calm.

POPULATIONS: According to Cagle (1954a), *G. flavimaculata* is the dominant turtle species in the Pascagoula and Chickasawhay river system. He speculated that although the Pascagoula River basin was badly polluted by sewage, waste from wood pulp, and chemical industries, these factors had little effect on *Graptemys* populations. In 1986 Lovich visited the Leaf River in Perry County, Mississippi, and found *G. flavimaculata* and *G. gibbonsi* to be common upstream from a pulp processing plant, but absent below the point of discharge for an undetermined distance. The highly tannic effluent may have been detrimental to the insect and mollusk populations upon which these map turtles feed.

Floyd (1973) reported that more than 400 basking individuals (mostly males) could be sighted on a clear summer day along the lower Pascagoula River. McCoy and Vogt (1980a) reported sex ratios ranging from 0.5 to 0.7 male per female, but their numbers may be biased in favor of females, as they used some nets that possibly allowed small males to escape. Population densities seem to have declined in recent years (U.S. Fish and Wildlife Service, 1992).

Hundreds of these turtles are killed each year during target practice by so-called "sportsmen" (McCoy and Vogt, 1980a). *Graptemys flavimaculata* is listed as threatened by the U.S. Fish and Wildlife Service and endangered by the State of Mississippi.

REMARKS: The yellow-blotched map turtle has the most restricted range of any sawback species, making it very susceptible to habitat degradation, particularly from pollution.

Relationships within the "narrow-headed" group of *Graptemys* based on osteological characters were studied by Killebrew (1976, 1977c, 1979) and Bertl and Killebrew (1983). This species seems to be most closely related to *G. oculifera.*

McCoy and Vogt (1987) summarized the literature on *G. flavimaculata.*

Graptemys nigrinoda Cagle, 1954a
Black-knobbed map turtle

PLATE 53 ·

RECOGNITION: This small, narrow-headed turtle has broad, rounded, black, knoblike vertebral projections and a strongly serrated posterior carapacial rim. Its carapace (to 22.1 cm) is dark olive; each pleural and marginal has a narrow yellow or orange, semicircular or circular mark. The hingeless yellow plastron is commonly tinted with red and has a black, branching pattern. The skin is black, with yellow stripes on the head, neck, limbs, and tail. The postorbital mark is a vertical crescent connecting dorsally with that of the opposite side to form a Y-shaped mark. Commonly two to four neck stripes enter the orbit, and the interorbital stripe is narrower than the neck stripes. The lower jaw has longitudinal yellow stripes as wide as the black interstices.

Adult males have elongated foreclaws and long thick tails, with the anal opening posterior to the carapacial rim. Adult females are 10–22.1 cm in carapace length, adult males, 7.5–12.2.

KARYOTYPE: The diploid chromosome number is 50: 26 macrochromosomes and 24 microchromosomes (Killebrew, 1977a).

FOSSIL RECORD: Unknown.

DISTRIBUTION: The black-knobbed map turtle occurs below the fall line in the Alabama, Tombigbee, Black Warrior, Coosa, Tallapoosa, and Cahaba rivers of Alabama and Mississippi (Shoop, 1967; Cliburn, 1971; Tinkle, 1959a).

GEOGRAPHIC VARIATION: Two subspecies are recognized. *Graptemys nigrinoda nigrinoda* Cagle, 1954a, the black-knobbed map turtle, is restricted to the upper parts of the Tombigbee and Alabama river systems of Alabama and Mississippi. It has a poorly developed plastral figure, which never occupies more than 30% of the plastron. The postocular mark is, typically, crescentic and strongly recurved. The light lines that reach the eye are seldom interrupted. The soft parts are predominantly yellow. *Graptemys n. delticola* Folkerts and Mount, 1969, the delta map turtle, inhabits the interconnecting streams and lakes in the delta of the Mobile Bay drainage, in Baldwin and Mobile counties, Alabama. It differs from the nominate race in having a plastral figure that occupies more than 60% of the plastron. The postocular mark is neither crescentic nor strongly recurved laterally. In many *G. n. delticola* the light lines that reach the eye are interrupted. The soft parts are predominantly black. The validity of *G. n. delticola* was contested by Freeman (1970) and defended by Folkerts and Mount (1970).

CONFUSING SPECIES: *Graptemys oculifera* commonly has the postorbital mark separate from the broad longitudinal dorsal stripe; the carapace rim only slightly serrated; and laterally compressed, spinelike vertebral projections. *Graptemys flavimaculata* has olive skin; the carapace rim slightly serrated; laterally compressed, spinelike vertebral projections; a large yellow blotch on each pleural; and a cream-colored plastron. *Graptemys pulchra* has a large head and a longitudinal light bar on the chin, and *G. ernsti* and *G. gibbonsi* have a large head, a longitudinal light bar on the chin, and relatively wide yellow markings on the marginals.

HABITAT: Sand- and clay-bottomed streams with moderate currents and abundant basking sites of brush, logs, and debris are the favorite habitats. At such sites, *Graptemys nigrinoda* is found in deeper waters than either *G. oculifera* or *G. flavimaculata*.

BEHAVIOR: Basking behavior is well developed in *Graptemys nigrinoda*. Basking may occur during any month of the year, but this species is not

Distribution of *Graptemys nigrinoda*

Plastron of *Graptemys nigrinoda nigrinoda*

active at water temperatures under 10°C (Waters, 1974). Very little basking occurs when light intensity is less than 5,000 footcandles. Under laboratory conditions basking individuals may attain cloacal temperatures as high as 39°C without showing signs of apparent discomfort. Cloacal temperatures of basking turtles are 2–14°C higher than water tempera-

tures with a mean difference of 7.6°C, and 1–5°C higher than air temperatures with a mean difference of 3.5°C (Waters, 1974). Optimum basking conditions occur at water temperatures higher than 15°C, at air temperatures higher than 20°C, light intensities greater than 8,000 footcandles, during periods of time with little or no rainfall, and when favorable

Plastron of *Graptemys nigrinoda delticola*

conditions are preceded by several days unfavorable conditions (Waters, 1974).

Individual turtles have basking-site fidelity, returning to the same site day after day. This species prefers to bask on stationary logs or tangles of logs separated from the shoreline by an area of open water. During periods of high water when preferred basking sites are submerged, it will bask on the river bank. Juveniles bask on branches near shore that are 15–60 mm in diameter, but adults, in particular, prefer basking sites surrounded by open water. Adult males and subadult females bask on branches 50–125 mm in diameter, while mature females select branches 70–200 mm in diameter. Substantial algal growths occur only on adult males (40%), which suggests that females bask for longer periods of time (Waters, 1974).

Waters (1974) has seen as many as four other turtle species basking on the same log with *G. nigrinoda,* but aggressive interactions have not been observed within or between species under these circumstances.

Graptemys nigrinoda spends the night sleeping on brush piles and logs. It seldom leaves the water except to bask or lay eggs.

REPRODUCTION: Much of what we know of reproductive biology of the black-knobbed map turtle comes from the research of Lahanas (1982) on the subspecies *Graptemys nigrinoda delticola.* All of the information reported in this section, unless cited otherwise, is from his work, conducted on the Tensaw River (Gravine Island) in southern Alabama.

The smallest sexually mature male, as evidenced by the presence of sperm in the epididymides, was 71.3 mm in plastron length and five years old. Lahanas did not histologically examine males smaller than this, but noted that secondary sexual characteristics were present by the end of the third growth season at a mean plastron length of 73 mm. Cagle (1954a) reported that males are sexually mature at 68 mm in plastron length in their third season of growth. The smallest females with enlarged follicles were 16.7–17.7 cm in plastron length. Absence of discernable growth annuli on the shells of these females suggests that they were at least nine years old. A female with a plastron length of 13.5 cm collected in the Tombigbee River of Mississippi contained enlarged ova 3–4 mm in diameter (Shoop, 1967).

The sexual cycle of males is as follows. Seminiferous tubules are regressed from April to June but spermatogonia and Sertoli cells are abundant along the basement membrane, and the epididymides are full of mature sperm. Seminiferous tubules begin to expand in June with the start of spermatogenesis. By August spermatogenesis reaches its peak and spermatogonia, spermatocytes, and spermatids are abundant. Spermiogenesis begins in August and the empty lumina start to fill with mature sperm, the epididymides have no sperm within them and their walls are contracted. Testis size and seminiferous tubule diameter reach a maximum in September when spermiogenesis peaks and mature sperm completely fill the lumina. There is a reduction in numbers of spermatogonia and spermatocytes as spermatogenesis declines to completion in October. Mature sperm are clustered around Sertoli cells at this time and spermatids are still fairly abundant. Other mature sperm are contained in the rapidly expanding epididymides. Spermiation begins, spermiogenesis ends, and seminiferous tubules start to contract by November. At this time, some sperm remain in the testes, but the lumina are empty except for cellular debris. The epididymides are packed with mature sperm and remain filled until the next spring when amounts begin to decline.

In female *G. nigrinoda*, vitellogenesis begins in August or September after final clutch deposition. Lahanas divided ovarian follicles into four size classes as follows: Class I (less than 5 mm in diameter), Class II (5–10 mm), Class III (11–16 mm), and Class IV (>17 mm). Class IV follicles were considered to be preovulatory based on measurements of yolks in shelled oviducal eggs. Class I and II follicles are more abundant from September to October than at any other time. Preovulatory and Class III follicles are absent during these months and ovarian weight is probably minimal. The first clutch complement of follicles is thought to reach size Class III in October and November and finish development in March or April, at least one month prior to the nesting season.

The courtship and mating behaviors of this species under natural conditions have not been described. However, Lahanas (1982) observed what he interpreted as courtship behavior between two yearlings maintained in the laboratory. The individuals swam toward each other, just above the substrate, with necks outstretched. They stopped when their noses were within 1 mm. With shells tilted posteriorly, one turtle began to bob its head vertically at the rate of five or six bobs per second. Three bobbing bouts were observed, each punctuated by a two-second pause. Courtshiplike behavior has been observed in juveniles of other species of *Graptemys* as well (Cagle, 1955; Wahlquist, 1970). The fact that the epididymides of adult male *G. nigrinoda* are filled with sperm in the spring suggests that mating occurs in late spring and early summer. Since spermiation begins in September–November the possibility also exists for fall mating.

The nesting season on Gravine Island begins in late May, peaks from mid-June to mid-July, and ends in early August. The nesting season is approximately 72 days long. Oviposition always takes place after dark with peak nesting activity between 2100 and 2400. Optimal nesting habitat on the island is found on beaches near deep water at locations 2–4 m above the mean water level. Most nests are located within 50 m of the water line in open, sunny areas with widely separated clumps of short grass (*Panicum*). Eighty-three percent of the nests are constructed in fine quartz sand with no organic matter. Lahanas suspected that three or four clutches could be oviposited by a female in a single year based on the presence of several size classes of enlarged follicles. Assuming that three clutches are produced annually, the internesting interval could be as long as 30 days.

The nesting process on Gravine Island begins as females congregate 30–50 m from shore about an hour before dark. Females are very cautious when they emerge and will return to the water at the first sign of danger. Once on land the females wander about apparently looking for a suitable nest site. They pause occasionally and perform a sand-sniffing behavior in which the head is extended downward as if gathering olfactory information. This behavior is accompanied by a test scratch in which sand is excavated with sweeping motions of the front feet to a depth of 1 cm. In addition to these test scratches, 40.6% of the nest crawls observed by Lahanas (1982) were accompanied by a total of 16 test nests. In cases where test nests were observed, 14.3% of the females dug more than one. The distribution of test nests along the nesting crawl was bimodal, with 43.1% placed near the water and 30.1% placed near the actual nest. This behavior suggests that females test the substrate soon after emergence and prior to actual nest construction. Test nest behavior probably provides the female with information regarding the suitability of nesting microhabitat. Environmental conditions at test nests were virtually identical to those at actual nest sites in 87.5% of the observed cases. Obstructions were found in two test nests including one with roots under a river birch and one with large pebbles. Test nests were generally 3–5 cm deep. A few were excavated with the hind limbs, but 81% appeared to have been constructed by pushing sand with the shell or by sweeping motions of the front limbs. Total time spent in prenesting activities (wandering, test scratch, and test nest construction) ranged from a few minutes to an hour or more. Once a suitable nest site is located excavation begins after the female achieves a body posture in which the anterior part of the shell midline is tilted upward 15–30° from horizontal. This posturing is accomplished by utilizing available surface irregularities such as grass clumps, or by "bulldozing" behavior in which the female pushes sand forward with the anterior part of the shell, thus creating a tilted platform. Excavation involves alternate scraping with the hind limbs while pivoting the body from side to side as each limb is inserted into the cavity. The rate of nest construction proceeds at about a scoop every four to six seconds. Excavation time varies from 16 to 34 minutes with an average time of 23 minutes.

Average dimensions of six flask-shaped nests were as follows: total depth, 15.2 cm; depth to cavity, 5.6 cm; cavity diameter, 8.9 cm; and neck diameter, 4.8 cm.

Upon completion of the nest, eggs are released at intervals of one to two minutes. Females nod or draw in their heads and slightly raise their hind legs as each egg is released. After each egg is deposited, a hind limb is inserted into the nest and moved about, to position the egg. The duration of oviposition is related to clutch size but generally lasts 8–10 minutes. After the last egg is laid, the clutch is buried with alternating sweeps of the hind limbs. No nest plug is constructed. When the nest is filled with sand, some females toss additional dry sand over the nest with quick sweeping motions of the forelimbs. This serves effectively to camouflage the nest. Burial time for seven clutches ranged from 15 to 25 minutes with an average of 20 minutes, and total nesting time averaged about an hour. Most females return to the water immediately after completing the nest having spent from one to three hours on the shore.

The clutch size of eight nests ranged from three to seven eggs (mean, 5.5). Lahanas observed no correlation between clutch size and egg size, nor between female body size and clutch size, possibly owing to small sample size. Freshly laid eggs are turgid, elliptical, have a smooth surface, and are translucent pink in color. The flexible shell resumes its original shape after being indented slightly. Egg length and width of 42 eggs averaged 37.03 and 23.78 mm, respectively. A sample of six eggs weighed between 13.95 and 16.55 g (mean, 15.38). Eggs enlarge and become turgid after a few weeks of incubation. A clutch of six eggs deposited on 5 August and removed from the nest on 27 September had increased 5.5% and 11.47% in length and width, respectively.

The ability of eggs to tolerate water loss was tested by Lahanas. Six eggs were placed in a one-gallon plastic container with moist sand. The container was then placed under the shade of a tree; the only moisture the eggs received came from occasional precipitation. The sand became completely dry between precipitation events. The eggs were uncovered 72 days later for examination. The lower portion of each egg had collapsed creating a concave fold. The eggs had an average water loss of 45.9% of their original weight. Fertile eggs contained embryos that appeared normal but were only 50% developed in spite of the fact that the elapsed time period was 10 days longer than the average incubation period. Nine clutches incubated under both natural and artificial conditions hatched after 60–68 days with an average incubation period of 62.9 days. The average incubation temperature of most natural nests during August was 30°C (Lahanas, 1982).

Observations of hatching were recorded under artificial conditions. Several days prior to pipping, the lower, formerly translucent part of the eggshell becomes opaque and dry. Three to four days prior to hatching small droplets of liquid form on the outer surface of the eggshell. Lahanas (1982) suggested that these droplets represented extra-embryonic fluid escaping through pores in the eggshell. Hatchlings pip the shell with their caruncle producing a small (2–3 mm), jagged, longitudinal tear in the eggshell. Within hours the opening is widened by movements of the head and forelimbs. Hatchlings remain within the nest for 8–13 days (mean, 10) until the yolk sac is absorbed.

Hatching dates on Gravine Island (as predicted from emergence dates) range from 17 August to 7 October. Overwintering in the nest was not observed. There is considerable hatching asynchrony within a given clutch. Eggs in the same nest may range from unpipped to those in which the eggshell is open and the hatchling yolk sac is completely absorbed. Nest emergence may extend over two or three days in a given clutch. Under artificial conditions, most hatchlings that were buried in sand emerged about one hour after dark.

Hatchling *G. n. delticola* are slightly wider than long. Average shell measurements for 21 hatchlings that still had yolk sacs were: carapace length, 36.5 mm; carapace width, 36.7 mm; and plastron length, 32.8 mm. The serrated carapacial margins of hatchlings are more pronounced than those of adults. The vertebral spines are somewhat compressed laterally and touch at their bases, forming a prominent and conspicuous keel. The relative length of vertebral spines in hatchlings (11.7% of carapace length) is more than twice the value of adult males and more than four times that of adult females. The yolk sacs of 25 hatchlings measured less than one hour after hatching measured from 15 to 21 mm in diameter with an average of 17 mm. Umbilical scars measured approximately 3 mm in length following absorption of the yolk sac. Hatchlings retain the caruncle from a few days to two months after hatching under artificial conditions. Hatchlings are colored and patterned much like adults.

Lahanas (1982) concluded that hatchling orientation patterns from natural nests were random. Of ten

Juvenile *Graptemys nigrinoda delticola*

nests located on level ground with a total of 25 hatchlings, four went north toward the nearest water, six traveled east, eight traveled west, and seven traveled south away from the water. Similar results were observed when hatchlings were tested in orientation arenas. However, when hatchlings were tested in arenas located on sloped surfaces there was a strong tendency to move uphill or downhill.

GROWTH AND LONGEVITY: In the delta region of the Alabama River, *Graptemys nigrinoda* has a growing season of 170–180 days (Lahanas, 1982). Ten individuals showed an average seasonal growth increase of 38.9% by May. Growth increases about 15% per month until September, by which time turtles have accumulated about 95% of their yearly growth.

Females grow significantly faster than males. Estimated average plastron length and yearly growth increases for males examined by Lahanas (1982) were as follows at the end of the indicated age: one year, 50.98 mm, 16.3%; two years, 66.01 mm, 15.03%; three years, 73.36 mm, 7.35%; four years, 81.00 mm, 7.64%; and five years, 84.08 mm, 3.08%. Estimated values for females were: one year, 57.51 mm, 25.32%; two years, 77.30 mm, 19.79%; three years, 101.49 mm, 24.19%; four years, 116.30 mm, 14.81%; five years, 130.49 mm, 14.19%; six years, 141.32 mm, 10.83%; seven years, 158.49 mm, 17.17%; eight years, 165.17 mm, 6.68%; and nine years, 178.50 mm, 13.33%.

A wild-caught male survived 12 years, eight months, and 11 days in captivity (Snider and Bowler,

1992), and Ernst has kept a male collected as a hatchling for more than 13 years.

FOOD HABITS: Wild *Graptemys nigrinoda* have been observed eating beetles and dragonflies that had fallen into the water (Wahlquist, 1970). This feeding behavior was corroborated by Mount (1975) who reported that insects were the only identifiable component in the feces of freshly caught Alabama turtles.

The most detailed study of food habits is that of Lahanas (1982), who reported that *G. nigrinoda* grazes primarily on sessile organisms such as bryozoans, sponges, and freshwater algae. The percent volume of various food types dissected from the gastrointestinal tracts of 15 males were as follows: animal matter, 58.3% including 36.5% sponges (*Corvospongilla, Trochospongilla*), 11.7% bryozoans (*Plumatella*), and 9.6% mollusks (*Modiolus*); plant matter, 40.4% including 11.6% *Cladophora*, 9.2% *Ulothrix*, and 19.6% *Spirogyra*. Values obtained from 17 females were: animal matter, 69.2% including 23.7% *Plumatella*, 27.6% sponges, and 17.9% mollusks; plant material, 28.1% including 17.3% *Spirogyra* and 7.8% *Cladophora*. The percent frequency of occurrence of food items from the same males was as follows: plants—*Cladophora* 13.3%, *Ulothrix* 13.3%, and *Spirogyra* 20.0%; animals—*Corvospongilla/Trochospongilla* 46.7%, *Plumatella* 20.0%, *Modiolus* 20.0%, blue crab (*Callinectes*) 6.6%, barnacles (*Balanus*) 26.7%, and insects 6.7%. Values for females were: plants—*Cladophora* 23.5%, *Ulothrix* 5.9%, *Spirogyra* 17.6%; animals—*Corvo-*

spongilla/Trochospongilla 35.3%, *Plumatella* 29.4%, *Modiolus* 23.5%, *Callinectes* 5.9%, *Balanus* 58.8%, and insects 5.8%.

Although the sexes eat slightly different proportions of the same major food items, Lahanas concluded that the diets were essentially the same owing to high overlap. A clear relationship was observed between the size of the turtle and the size of mollusks consumed with larger turtles eating larger mollusks.

According to the late Fred Cagle's field notes, *G. nigrinoda* eats insects including mayflies, damselflies, midges, dragonflies, beetles (adults and larvae), chironomids, clams, spiders, insect eggs, and small fish. Lahanas reported that captives fed on raw and cooked beef, pork, chicken, dead fish, insects, and occasionally the plant *Elodea*. Captive males in Ernst's laboratory readily eat fish, shrimp, romaine lettuce, and commercial trout chow.

PREDATORS AND DEFENSE: Eighty-two percent of all *Graptemys nigrinoda* nests discovered on Gravine Island by Lahanas (1982) were destroyed by fish crows (*Corvus ossifragus*). Most nests were destroyed within 5–10 minutes, by flocks of 5–10 birds, between 0500 and 0600, and within 12 hours of oviposition. Most eggs are carried away to perches for consumption. Several adult male *G. nigrinoda* collected by Lahanas (1982) had shell injuries that could have been inflicted by alligators.

The human, however, is undoubtedly the greatest enemy of this turtle. Lahanas (1982) reported that delta residents used to collect and eat large numbers of turtle eggs on Gravine Island, and a market existed for adult turtles in the region as late as the early 1980s. Recreational use of the delta also takes its toll on the turtle population. Adults are drowned in gill nets, nests are destroyed by picnickers and explorers, and two *G. nigrinoda* were discovered by Lahanas with their carapaces cracked open by the propellers of outboard motors.

Graptemys nigrinoda relies primarily on its wariness and strong swimming ability to avoid predators. When confronted it will withdraw into its shell, and does not readily bite.

POPULATIONS: Tinkle (1959a) noted that *Graptemys nigrinoda* constituted 66% of the turtles collected in the Tombigbee River and 30% of the turtles collected in the Alabama River during a four-year period. Relative abundance of this species in yearly samples from the Tombigbee River were as follows: 1953, 71%; 1954, 70%; 1955, 61%; and 1956, 69%. *Graptemys nigrinoda* has declined in Mississippi and is now listed as endangered by that state.

Additional information on the population structure of *G. nigrinoda* was provided by Lahanas (1982). Of 186 turtles captured in the vicinity of Gravine Island during 13 months, 77 (41.4%) were *G. nigrinoda*, 56 (30.1%), *Pseudemys alabamensis*, 46 (24.7%), *Pseudemys concinna*, and 7 (3.8%), *Trachemys scripta*. Of the *G. nigrinoda* collected, 31 (40.2%) were adult males (carapace length >83 mm), 29 (37.7%) were adult females (carapace length >183 mm), and 17 (22.1%) were juvenile females.

The almost even sex ratio reported from this data may be a result of sampling error (Lovich and Gibbons, 1990). Lahanas (1982) used turtle nets with 76-mm nylon mesh that only caught animals larger than 80 mm. Thus, adult males smaller than 80 mm were likely to be underrepresented in the sample. Most male *G. nigrinoda* captured by Lahanas were between 106 and 110 mm and most adult females were between 201 and 210 mm.

REMARKS: Skeletal features of *Graptemys nigrinoda* and *G. flavimaculata* were compared by Killebrew (1979). The prefrontal process of the frontal bone and the rostral projection of the basisphenoid are both wider in *flavimaculata*. The relatively flattened carapace of adult *nigrinoda* is highest through the spines of the second and third vertebral scutes. In contrast, the steeply sloped carapace of adult *flavimaculata* is highest through the spine of the second vertebral scute. Spines are high and laterally compressed in *flavimaculata* and low, broad, and knoblike in *nigrinoda*. Killebrew concluded that these and other character differences not only served effectively to separate these two species, but also reinforced the notion of separating the genus *Graptemys* into "narrow-headed" and "broad-headed" species groups (see Dobie, 1981).

Further information on *G. nigrinoda* is summarized in Lahanas (1986).

Malaclemys terrapin (Schoepff, 1793)
Diamondback terrapin
PLATE 54

RECOGNITION: *Malaclemys terrapin* is a small to medium-sized turtle of estuaries and salt marshes characterized by concentric markings and grooves on the vertebral and pleural scutes and, typically, light-colored skin with dark flecks, spots, and other markings. Its carapace (to 23.8 cm) is oblong; its posterior marginals may be curled slightly upward and slightly serrated. The vertebral keel may be low and inconspicuous or knobby and prominent. The carapace is gray, light brown, or black with the grooves often ringed concentrically with darker pigment. The undersides of the marginals and bridge may be marked with dark patterns. The hingeless plastron is yellow to green or black, and may be marked with dark figures and blotches. The skin varies from light gray to black and is marked with dark specks, blotches, or stripes. The head is relatively small in males and large in females. The eyes are black. The jaws are light colored and a dark mustachelike marking may be present on the upper jaw. Females have broad crushing plates on the jaws. The feet are strongly webbed and the hind feet are large.

Adult males are significantly smaller than females in carapace length; males range from 10 to 14 cm, females, 15 to 23 cm. Females also have wider heads, deeper shells, and shorter tails than males.

KARYOTYPE: Diploid chromosomes total 50 (Stock, 1972; Sachsse, 1984): 20 metacentric or submetacentric, 10 subtelocentric, and 20 acrocentric or telocentric. Collectively the diploid complement has 80 arms (Stock, 1972). McKown (1972) noted a similar diploid chromosome number with 26 macrochromosomes and 24 microchromosomes, but recorded only 72 arms (48 macro and 24 micro).

FOSSIL RECORD: Pleistocene (Rancholabrean) fossils are known from Edisto Beach, Colleton County, South Carolina (Dobie and Jackson, 1979).

DISTRIBUTION: The diamondback terrapin lives along the Atlantic and Gulf coasts from Cape Cod to Texas, including the Florida Keys. Records for Mexico have been unsubstantiated (Smith and Smith, 1979). This species was released into San Francisco Bay in May 1943, but did not become established (Taft, 1944; Hildebrand and Prytherch, 1947).

GEOGRAPHIC VARIATION: Seven subspecies have been formally described. *Malaclemys terrapin terrapin* (Schoepff, 1793), the northern diamondback terrapin, ranges along the Atlantic Coast from Cape Cod to Cape Hatteras. Its median keel does not have knobs and the sides of the carapace diverge posteriorly. Carapace color varies from black to light brown with distinct concentric rings, and the plastron is orangish to greenish gray. *Malaclemys t. centrata* (Latreille, in Sonnini and Latreille, 1802), the Carolina diamondback terrapin, ranges from Cape Hatteras to northern Florida. Its median keel does not have knobs, the sides of the carapace are parallel, and the posterior marginals are curled upward. *Malaclemys t. tequesta* (Schwartz, 1955), the Florida east coast diamondback terrapin, occurs along the Atlantic coast of Florida. Its medial keel has posterior-facing knobs. The carapace is dark or tan with no pattern of concentric light circles, but the centers of the large carapace scutes may be lighter than surrounding areas. *Malaclemys t. rhizophorarum* (Fowler, 1906), the mangrove diamondback terrapin, is restricted to the Florida Keys. Its medial keel has bulbous knobs, and its shell is strongly oblong. The carapacial scutes are brown or black without light centers, and the plastral scute seams are outlined with black pigmentation. The neck and forelimbs are commonly uniform gray, the gray hind limbs may be striated with black. *Malaclemys t. macrospilota* (Hay, 1904), the ornate diamondback terrapin, ranges from Florida Bay to the panhandle of Florida. Its median keel has terminal

Male *Malaclemys terrapin terrapin*

Plastron of *Malaclemys terrapin terrapin*

knobs, which may be bulbous, and the carapacial scutes have orange or yellow centers. *Malaclemys t. pileata* (Wied-Neuwied, 1865), the Mississippi diamondback terrapin, ranges from the Florida Panhandle to western Louisiana. Its medial keel has terminal tuberculate knobs. The scutes of the oval carapace lack light centers. The dorsal surfaces of the head, neck, and limbs are dark brown or black, and the upturned edges of the marginals are orange or yellow. Its plastron is yellow and often dusky. *Malaclemys t. littoralis* (Hay, 1904), the Texas diamondback terra-

pin, ranges from western Louisiana to western Texas. Its deep carapace has terminal knobs on the medial keel, and scutes without light centers. The plastron is pale or white. The dorsal surface of the head is whitish, and the neck and legs are greenish gray with heavy black spotting.

In general, geographic variation is poorly defined and may be clinal. Analysis has shown that mitochondrial DNA genotypic diversity and divergence levels are exceptionally low among putative subspecies. One restriction site polymorphism was geographically

Malaclemys terrapin often has a handsome "mustache"

Distribution of *Malaclemys terrapin*

Male *Malaclemys terrapin*
centrata

Male *Malaclemys terrapin*
tequesta

informative and clearly distinguished populations on either side of Cape Canaveral, Florida. This break is congruent with the geographic distribution of populations with and without knobby medial keels (Lamb and Avise, 1992).

CONFUSING SPECIES: Few turtles are found in association with the diamondback terrapin. *Trachemys scripta* and the species of *Pseudemys* have prominent yellow stripes on the head and neck,

Chelydra serpentina and *Macroclemys temminckii* have long saw-toothed tails and reduced, cross-shaped plastra, mud turtles (*Kinosternon*) have hinged plastra, and the various sea turtles have paddle-shaped front flippers.

HABITAT: The diamondback terrapin is a resident of coastal salt marshes, estuaries, and tidal creeks. Juveniles seem to spend the first years of their life under mats of tidal wrack and flotsam (Pitler, 1985).

Female *Malaclemys terrapin rhizophorarum*

Female *Malaclemys terrapin macrospilota*

BEHAVIOR: The annual activity cycle of diamondback terrapins varies because of the extensive
latitudinal distribution of the species. In South
Carolina the active season extends from March to
November. *Malaclemys* is diurnal, except when nesting, spending the day feeding in the marsh and
basking on the banks of tidal creeks. It apparently
spends the night buried in the mud as efforts to seine
them from creeks at night are unsuccessful.

In the northern part of the range along the Atlantic
Coast terrapins enter hibernation from November
through December and emerge between April and
May. Captive juveniles reportedly become dormant at
5–7°C (Dimond, 1987). Yearicks et al. (1981) found
terrapins hibernating individually or in small groups
resting on the bottom under water, buried in the mud
atop creek banks near the high tide line, and beneath
undercut banks. Juveniles were never found in these
sites. Although southern terrapins may emerge from
hibernation on warm days, northern terrapins remain
dormant throughout the winter. Yearicks and his
coauthors concluded that mortality was low among
hibernating terrapins because most of those collected
during hibernation were alive. A juvenile terrapin was
found hibernating in moist sand on 7 November in
Virginia (Lawler and Musick, 1972). Its hibernacu-

Male *Malaclemys terrapin pileata*

lum was approximately 8 m from the high-tide line at a depth of about 0.3 m. Weekly examination revealed vertical and horizontal movements of 2–8 cm. Emergence apparently took place on the night of 23 April.

Living in a euryhaline environment of 11.3–31.8 parts per thousand salinity (Dunson, 1970) has presented *Malaclemys* with a variety of osmotic challenges. It meets these with several behavioral, physiological, and anatomical adaptations, and, as these are critical to its ecology, they are presented in detail below.

Malaclemys terrapin is apparently capable of discriminating among different salinities. When salt-loaded it avoids drinking when salinities range from 27.2 to 34.0%, drinks small amounts when salinities range from 13.6 to 20.0%, and drinks large amounts when they range from 0 to 10.2%. Total body weight decreases significantly if it is exposed to 100% seawater. Fasting individuals lose weight at 0.32% per day in seawater, versus a loss of only 0.21% per day in fresh water (Robinson and Dunson, 1976). Most sodium uptake from seawater is orally at a low rate (Robinson and Dunson, 1976). After exposure to seawater (34%) for seven days terrapins are capable of rehydrating in less than 15 minutes if given access to fresh water. Under experimental conditions, simulated rainfall causes terrapins to swim to the surface or emerge from the water and drink from films of fresh water as thin as 1.6 mm. When simulated rainfall is heavy they stretch their necks upward with mouth open to catch water, and will also drink water collected on the marginal scutes, limbs, or limb sockets of themselves or other terrapins (Davenport and Macedo, 1990).

Osmoregulation in hibernating terrapins was examined by Gilles-Baillien (1973a) with captive animals maintained in seawater and fresh water. Blood osmotic pressures were lowest in both groups during July. Prior to entering hibernation in September osmotic pressure increased in the freshwater group, and then declined progressively during hibernation. Pressure increased in the seawater group from September through hibernation, peaking in mid-April at the end of hibernation. Pressure decreased in May following regular feeding. Similar seasonal patterns were observed in the urea concentrations of both groups. Ionic concentrations (sodium, chloride, potassium) were high from May to September, decreased progressively during hibernation, and then increased dramatically prior to arousal from hibernation. Salt gain at the end of hibernation is probably linked to passive entry of seawater into the terrapin. *Malaclemys* kept in seawater had greater body weights at arousal than they did three months later: a difference due to osmotic factors as they were not fed during hibernation. In contrast, those kept in fresh water maintained almost equal weights during the same period. Terrapins have higher potassium concentrations during the active season than during hibernation (Gilles-Baillien, 1973b).

Osmotic balance of terrapins exposed to sea or fresh water is regulated by blood and intracellular fluids, but osmotic regulation of various tissue types varies (Gilles-Baillien, 1973c). Muscle responds to higher blood osmotic pressure with increased concentrations in ammonia, taurine, urea, and, to a lesser extent, all amino acids except aspartate. The bladder mucosa of individuals kept in seawater also contains high concentrations of these same compounds. Urea is largely responsible for the higher osmotic pressure. The mucosa of the colon shows increases in total amino-acid content, sodium, chloride, and urea. In the jejunum mucosa concentrations of amino acids, urea, and potassium are much higher in terrapins exposed to seawater.

The blood of terrapins transferred from fresh water to 50% seawater shows a rapid increase in osmotic pressure, due mainly to greater sodium and chloride concentrations, within three days. Blood osmotic pressure continues to rise, but at a slower rate, until it stabilizes at 25 days (Cowan, 1981a). Blood of turtles living in seawater compared to that of those in 50% seawater shows higher osmotic pressure due solely to a higher urea concentration, not sodium and chloride. The urine of *Malaclemys* living in water with salinities greater than 50% is generally isosmotic to the blood, but that of freshwater terrapins is usually hyposmotic. The bladder plays an important role in reducing water loss in seawater terrapins, but is not implicated in salt balance. Bladder urine contains low amounts of sodium, but significant chloride (Cowan, 1981a). Urea concentration in the urine is always higher than in the serum, suggesting that the high urea concentration in the blood of terrapins kept in seawater is due to concentration in the bladder (Gilles-Baillien, 1970).

Malaclemys terrapin kept in seawater always has higher hematocrit values and red cell counts at any time of the year than if kept in fresh water, but seasonal variations in the hematological data differ according to whether the turtle is in seawater or in fresh water. The red blood cell inorganic ion content is rather similar for *Malaclemys* in both conditions of salinity, and it changes in the same manner during the year. During the summer, sodium content is much lower, the potassium content has a tendency to be higher, and the chloride content tends to be lower. However, just before spring arousal a special phenomenon takes place in terrapins kept in seawater that is not experienced by those in fresh water. Both the hematocrit and the red blood cell count are greatly augmented, and the volume of the red blood cell is greatly increased together with its sodium and chloride content (Gilles-Baillien, 1973d). Some blood parameters may also vary slightly geographically; Dorfman (1979) compares *Malaclemys* collected in New Jersey with others obtained in Virginia.

Terrapins have orbital glands that were long thought to function as extrarenal salt glands. The ultrastructure of the Harderian gland is similar to that of other emydid turtles, and its primary role is secretion of organic compounds, with no role related to environmental salinity. However, the ultrastructure of the lachrymal gland is unlike any other emydid and strongly suggests a role in active transport and osmoregulation (Cowan, 1969, 1971). Lachrymal gland weight does not increase in seawater-acclimated *Malaclemys* in terms of absolute weight, but does show a small but significant increase in terms of relative weight (Cowan, 1974). The terrapin is able to ion regulate when acclimated to fresh water, 55% seawater, or 100% seawater, but when in 100% seawater it does not volume regulate successfully (Cowan, 1981b). Orbital gland secretions are very low in individuals from all three salinities without a salt load. After salt loading, turtles from all three salinities produce an orbital gland secretion with a sodium concentration greater than seawater. The concentration of ions and kinetics of the response are similar in all three salinities, and orbital gland secretion returns to control preload levels well before an introduced salt load is excreted. There is no correlation between the sodium concentration in the orbital secretion or the rate of sodium excretion and the level of potassium ion stimulated activity in the lachrymal gland (Cowan, 1981b).

Malaclemys acclimated to seawater show a 2.4-fold increase in the sodium concentration of orbital fluid, compared to a 1.4-fold increase in two species of saltwater crocodiles (*Crocodylus acutus, C. porosus*). Maximum rates of salt gland secretion range from 16.8 to 26.6 μmol Na/100 g hr in terrapins acclimated to seawater to 1 μmol/100 g hr in those acclimated to fresh water (Dunson, 1970).

Despite the above results, research by Cowan (1990) casts some doubt on the efficiency of the lachrymal gland as an osmoregulatory organ. Although the gland is capable of secreting tears with sodium chloride concentrations exceeding 500 mM, the absolute amount of sodium chloride secreted and the generation of "free water" is relatively low. In addition, the lachrymal gland responds to irritating fumes unrelated to osmotic or ionic regulation. The contents of tears resulting from ionic and nonionic stimuli are similar, supporting the contention that the gland is not dedicated to salt excretion. The gland is adapted to carry out its role with minimal water loss as expected for a euryhaline animal.

Hatchling *M. terrapin* have a body water content of 77.0% in comparison to the 64.5% of adults, and a slightly higher body dry mass sodium concentration (Dunson, 1985). However, wet mass sodium concentration is only 71% that of adults. When feeding begins, body wet mass sodium concentration soon rises to adult levels. Further increases occur in salinities up to 50% seawater, but an inverse relation between juvenile body size and water efflux occurs when they are kept in 100% seawater. This difference seems to be one cause of the lesser tolerance of juveniles to saline water. In contrast, sodium influx in hatchlings is only slightly elevated. The rate of sodium efflux in fed juveniles is directly correlated with feeding rate, but the main source of sodium uptake at higher salinities seems to be incidental swallowing of water during feeding, not the salt content of the food itself (Dunson, 1985).

Little is known regarding the movements of diamondback terrapins. Hurd et al. (1979) reported that a tag from a marked female was found 8 km from the original point of capture. In the salt marshes around Kiawah Island, South Carolina, *M. t. centrata* show remarkable site fidelity from year to year. Individuals were often recaptured within several meters of the original point of capture in as many as three consecutive years, including periods before and after hurricanes and major tropical storms. Movements of 100–200 m were observed in only six terrapins despite a sample size of 414 marked turtles and 588 total captures (Lovich and Gibbons, 1990). Unpublished observations by Lovich, Gibbons, and other associates at the Savannah River Ecology Laboratory show that rates of movement by terrapins in a South Carolina salt marsh range from 3.9 m/min against the tide to 6.2 m/min with the tide. A small sample of terrapins was observed to move an average distance of 276 m in five hours.

REPRODUCTION: The size and age of sexual maturity varies somewhat geographically (Seigel, 1984). Males mature at about 9 cm before the end of their third year (Cagle, 1952a; Seigel, 1984; Lovich and Gibbons, 1990). Females mature after the sixth year at about 13.2–17.6 cm (Cagle, 1952a; Montevecchi and Burger, 1975; Lovich and Gibbons, 1990). Maturity may come at smaller sizes under conditions of accelerated growth in captivity, as females as small as 12 cm have oviposited (Hildebrand, 1932). Of 11 juvenile females collected by Cagle (1952a) the smallest had oocytes 3 mm in diameter and shrunken oviducts, and the largest had enlarged oviducts and oocytes 7 mm in diameter. Egg-laying females in New Jersey range from 13.2 to 18.4 cm in plastron length (Montevecchi and Burger, 1975).

In Brevard County, Florida, courtship and mating take place in March and April in small canals and ditches surrounding lagoons. Terrapins form large breeding aggregations of as many as 75–250 individuals in a 200-m^2 area. Mating occurs from 1040 to 1610 at water temperatures ranging from 24.8 to 27.0°C and air temperatures ranging from 22.8 to 27.0°C. Courtship begins with the female floating on the surface. The male approaches from the rear, nuzzles or nudges her cloacal region with his snout, and mounts and copulates if the female remains motionless. Females that swim away may be actively pursued for long distances by their suitors. The actual mating process is of short duration with the approach phase lasting 30–60 seconds and copulation lasting only one or two minutes (Seigel, 1980b). Captive male *M. t. centrata* sometimes bob their head rapidly in front of the female prior to copulation (Seigel, 1980b), and some captive males have been observed to stroke females with their foreclaws much as occurs in the *Chrysemys, Pseudemys, Trachemys* complex (Sachsse, 1984).

The nesting season extends from April through July, depending on location. Burger (1977) recorded nesting in New Jersey from 9 June to 23 July, and Lazell and Auger (1981) observed nesting in Massachusetts from 10 June to 20 July. Farther south the nesting season begins earlier. Seigel (1980c) found gravid females in Florida from 28 April to 1 July, and Lovich has observed nesting in South Carolina as early as April, and captive South Carolina females have laid eggs as late as August. In Louisiana egg laying may still occur as late as September (Burns and Williams, 1972). Female *M. terrapin* apparently have the ability to store sperm as some isolated from males after mating have laid fertile eggs four years later (Hildebrand, 1929); however, a marked decrease in fertility occurs after the second year.

Nesting takes place during the day, usually near high tide, but turtles do not nest during heavy or prolonged rains (Burger and Montevecchi, 1975). In Florida the nests are dug from 1040 to 1610 at air temperatures of 28–36°C (mean 31). Female *M. t. tequesta* observed by Seigel (1980c) nested only on dike roads in spite of the availability of nearby sand dunes and spoil piles.

Females are wary when moving overland in search of a nest site and during nest excavation. Those that have laid fewer than three eggs will abandon the nest if disturbed; in contrast, females that have already laid four or more eggs tend to complete the nesting process before leaving (Burger, 1977). Females continue to lay eggs, even when disturbed, after 30% of their clutch is laid. Females disturbed by potential predators move to another location and continue to lay eggs after digging a new nest.

When females are searching for a suitable nest site they occasionally touch their snouts to the sand (Lazell and Auger, 1981). Nest excavation begins with the female digging an area about 105 mm wide, 175 mm long and 50 mm deep with alternating strokes of her front feet. The female then walks forward until her hind legs are over the hole and continues to dig, the webbing of the hind feet acting as a shovel. After oviposition is completed, the female packs sand over the eggs (Montevecchi and Burger, 1975). As many as ten sites may be tested until the final nest is constructed, and test sites may be from 10 mm to several meters apart. The number of rejected sites increases after rain when sand is wet. In New Jersey, females may dig up 2% of the previous clutches laid by other females (Burger, 1977). A complete description of the nest-digging sequence is provided by Burger (1977) and the reader is referred to that reference for details.

Nest site location relative to random points was studied by Burger and Montevecchi (1975) in New Jersey. Nest sites are generally located in vegetated dunes facing away from the sea. Most nests were in relatively flat locations with a mean slope of 7.2°. The distance of beach grass (*Ammophila breviligulata*) to random points and terrapin nests was not significantly different (beach grass was the closest plant species to nests 80% of the time). Nests were usually less than 20 cm from the closest vegetation (mean 1.2 cm). Although random points were often farther away from nests, the difference was not statistically significant. Available vegetative cover ranged from 0 to 100%. Nests were located in areas of less than 20% cover (mean 8.2%), and the cover selected was significantly different from those at random points. Similar nest site selection occurs in South Carolina. The general sites selected for nesting are located in areas above high tide with minimum erosion (Burger, 1977).

Nests are flask shaped and wider than deep. Dimensions (cm) in New Jersey are as follows: depth, 10.80–20.30 (mean 14.98); depth to top egg, 5.08–14.61 (mean 10.65); egg compartment depth, 2.21–8.89 (mean 4.67); and egg compartment width, 4.45–10.15 (mean 7.29) (Montevecchi and Burger, 1975). No relationships were detected between nest dimensions and the plastron length of females.

Clutch size ranges from 4 to 18 with females in the southern part of the range producing fewer but larger eggs than females in the north (Seigel, 1980c). Montevecchi and Burger (1975) reported a mean clutch size of 9.7 eggs in New Jersey, and Seigel (1980c) reported a mean clutch size of 6.7 in Florida.

Larger females lay larger clutches of greater total weight, but no relationship has been detected between body size and individual egg dimensions or weight (Montevecchi and Burger, 1975; Seigel, 1980c). Captives have produced up to five clutches a year (Hildebrand and Hatsel, 1926); in Massachusetts, wild females tend to lay two clutches per year (Lazell, 1979).

Terrapin eggs are pinkish white, dimpled, and leathery. The dimples disappear during the early stages of development. Each egg is symmetrical with the poles being blunter than the curvature of a true ellipsoid. Abnormally small or yolkless eggs are not known in terrapins (Montevecchi and Burger, 1975); within a clutch there is a high positive correlation between mean egg lengths and widths. Clutch size is highly correlated with clutch weight, but shows no relationship with any measure of egg size. Variability in mean egg length and width is much greater between clutches than within them (Montevecchi and Burger, 1975). Egg dimensions vary geographically within the following ranges: length 2.6–4.20 cm; width 1.59–2.70 cm; weight 5.0–13.2 g (Seigel, 1980c; Lovich, pers. obs.). Egg length, width, and breadth decrease as the nesting season advances, a trend not related to changes in female size, clutch size, or clutch weight (Montevecchi and Burger, 1975).

Eggs contain an average of 68.9% water and 8.2% lipid. Lipid dry weight accounts for 26.4% of the total dry weight. Average energy content of eggs is approximately 2.14 kcal/g wet weight and 6.88 kcal/g dry weight. Lighter eggs contain proportionally less water than heavier eggs, but egg weight has little effect on the proportion of lipid dry weight in the egg (Ricklefs and Burger, 1977).

Incubation time is a function of temperature. In New Jersey, eggs in natural nests develop in 61–104 days and hatching occurs from 20 August to 12 October (Burger, 1977). Nests on south-facing slopes hatch in an average of 71 days, whereas nests on north-facing slopes require an average incubation period of 79 days (Burger, 1976b). Incubation period is shorter for nests laid earlier in the season. Clutches deposited in June have a mean incubation period of 74.5 days, but those deposited in July require an average incubation period of 86 days. Nest depth influences not only the timing of hatching, but also the viability of clutches. In shallow nests the top eggs may not hatch, but in deep nests the bottom eggs may not hatch (Burger, 1976a). Hatching occurs over one to four days (mean 2) in an individual nest with the top eggs always hatching first (Burger, 1976a,b).

Hatching time is negatively correlated with egg

length, egg width, and hatchling size (Burger, 1976a,b, 1977): larger eggs and larger hatchlings have shorter incubation times. Seigel (1980c) reported that terrapin eggs from Florida incubated at 20–34°C hatched in 60–73 days (mean 65.6). Dimond (1987) reported that eggs incubated at 24.5–26.0°C hatched in 82 days and eggs incubated at 28.5–29.5°C hatched in 54 days. Clutches incubated outdoors by Cunningham (1939) at normal incubation temperatures hatched in 61–68 days, eggs incubated indoors at relatively high constant temperatures (35–40°C) failed to produce offspring, 24 eggs incubated indoors at a constant medium-high temperature of 30°C produced 23 hatchlings in 61–68 days, and eggs incubated indoors at fluctuating room temperatures (18–33°C) hatched in 61–68 days. Hatchlings in some areas may overwinter in the nest (Gibbons and Nelson, 1978; Lazell and Auger, 1981).

Burger (1976b) studied temperature relationships in terrapin nests in New Jersey. Daily variation in sand temperatures 5 cm from the nest range from 2 to 12°C with a low at 0600 and a high at 1500. Surface sand temperatures at the nest vary from 0 to 30°C during a daily cycle (the mean low and high during a 10-week period ranged from 19 to 24°C and 23 to 31°C, respectively). Short variations in surface temperature caused by rain, cloud cover, and fog do not normally cause changes in the daily temperature pattern of nests. The mean daily temperatures for nests on north-facing and south-facing slopes are 20.9°C and 21.8°C, respectively (nest temperatures averaged 0.9°C lower per day during a 70-day period on north-facing slopes than on south-facing slopes). Development stops completely when the incubation temperature drops to approximately 13°C, but eggs in natural nests may develop despite temperatures climbing to 46°C for short periods (Cunningham, 1939).

Nests produce metabolic heat. The mean difference between temperatures in the nest and temperatures 5 cm from the nest (at similar depths) averaged between 2 and 7°C/day. Differences cannot be detected in empty nests or fresh nests. As noted above, the viability of eggs and incubation time are associated with nest depth. Shallow nests exposed to high temperatures do not develop properly and deep nests may experience low temperature stress or oxygen and moisture deficits. Estimated fertility rates range from 89 to 92% in New Jersey (Burger, 1977).

In Massachusetts the eggs begin hatching in September, and nests continue to release hatchlings through the autumn, with a few baby turtles overwintering in the nest cavity (Lazell, 1979). In midwinter those remaining in the nests are torpid, poised beneath a crust of surface ice; they are well within the frost zone, but they do not freeze and emerge the next spring. The mechanism by which they withstand such low temperatures is unknown.

Malaclemys terrapin has temperature-dependent sex determination. Sachsse (1984) reported that eggs incubated at 25–29°C had a hatchling success rate of 50% with a sex ratio of 52 males and 2 females, but he did not report the sex ratio of hatchlings that did not live, which suggests that differential mortality is responsible for the sex ratio observed (Lovich and Gibbons, 1990). However, the pattern of low incubation temperatures producing a predominance of males is typical for an emydid turtle. Ewert and Nelson (1991) indicated that terrapin eggs incubated at 24°C produce all males while eggs incubated at 30°C hatch out females.

Hatchling terrapins have a carapace length ranging from 2.5 to 3.4 cm and weigh between 5 and 10.8 g (Reid, 1955; Burger, 1977; Seigel, 1980c). Hatchlings emerge from the nest 0–11 days after hatching, and most leave the nest between 1200 and 1700. Hatchlings emerging on relatively flat areas devoid of vegetation for two meters show no orientation preference in the first meter. In contrast, most hatchlings that emerge from nests on slopes walk downslope. This behavior is consistent under controlled experimental conditions regardless of the compass direction faced by hatchlings. On slopes greater than 10° hatchling trails do not radiate more than 30°. On slopes less than 10° the trails radiate more than 75° from the nest. Hatchlings move to the closest vegetation upon emergence and continue to move to other clumps of vegetation, even if the vegetation is uphill from the turtle. The righting response of overturned hatchlings becomes more developed as they approach emergence (Burger, 1976a). Hatchlings show an avoidance of open water and a propensity to move toward vegetation and burrow into tidal wrack at the high-tide line (Lovich et al., 1991b, South Carolina; Ernst, pers. obs., New Jersey).

The commercial importance of terrapins around the turn of the 20th century led the United States Bureau of Fisheries, Department of Commerce, to experiment with captive propagation for many years. Details on breeding and rearing terrapins under artificial conditions are summarized by Coker (1906, 1920), Barney (1922), Hildebrand and Hatsel (1926), and Hildebrand (1929, 1932, 1933).

GROWTH AND LONGEVITY: Growth of *Malaclemys t. tequesta* in Florida was calculated by

Hatchling *Malaclemys terrapin terrapin*

Seigel (1984) using the relationship between plastron length and the length of various growth annuli. Both sexes grow at about the same rate during the first two years after hatching. Growth is most rapid at plastron lengths of between 3.0 and 3.9 cm. Male growth slows as sexual maturity is reached at about three years of age, but female growth continues at a relatively rapid rate until attainment of sexual maturity and an age of at least four years. Growth slows to less than 5% per year in mature turtles.

Malaclemys shows considerable variation in growth rates and timing of maturity within and among populations (Seigel, 1984; Lovich and Gibbons, 1990). Growth rates of Florida *M. t. tequesta* are faster than those of terrapins in Louisiana (Cagle, 1952a), which are somewhat faster than growth rates of captives in North Carolina (Hildebrand, 1932). Growth rates are probably affected by differences in the length of activity and growing seasons, not by initial hatchling size. Growth rates of hatchlings incubated at high temperatures are faster, before and after winter dormancy, than those of hatchlings incubated at lower temperatures (Dimond, 1987).

Until juvenile *Malaclemys* reach about 50 g they cannot grow in salinities above 67% seawater (Dunson, 1985). However, salinities near the nests are above this level. Very small terrapins reared in 100% seawater and offered one drink of fresh water every two weeks can achieve limited growth. In 25% seawater at 28°C, growth of hatchlings is stimulated in comparison with those in fresh water or 50%

seawater. Hatchlings grown in 0.25 Molal glycerol solutions, osmotically similar to 25% seawater, have the same growth rates as small turtles kept in fresh water (Dunson, 1985).

Information on the growth rates of captive terrapins is summarized in Coker (1906), Barney (1922), Hildebrand (1929, 1932), and Allen and Littleford (1955).

Malaclemys terrapin has lived in captivity for more than 14 years (Snider and Bowler, 1992); but Hildebrand (1932) estimated they may live longer than 40 years, and the life span of Florida *M. t. tequesta* was estimated to be 20 years by Seigel (1984).

FOOD HABITS: Diamondback terrapins, especially females, are well adapted for eating hard-shelled prey including salt marsh periwinkles and other gastropods (*Littorina irrorata, Melampus*), crabs (*Uca, Callinectes, Gelasimus, Sesarma*) and small bivalves including blue mussels (*Mytilus edulis*) (Coker, 1906; Allen and Littleford, 1955; Cagle, 1952a; Carr, 1952; Hurd et al., 1979). Other prey items include carrion, fish (*Menidia menidia*), marine annelids (*Nereis*), and plant material (Coker, 1906; Cochran, 1978; Middaugh, 1981; Bishop, 1983). Allen and Littleford (1955) conducted prey choice experiments with captive juveniles, which preferred shellfish and snails over beef, liver, salmon, and tuna. Newly hatched young were less discriminating, but after three weeks began to refuse certain food items.

Unpublished data by Lovich, Gibbons, and other associates at the Savannah River Ecology Laboratory demonstrate the importance of *Littorina* in the diet of free-living South Carolina terrapins. More than 60 terrapins were captured and held in individual containers until they defecated. The number of *Littorina* eaten was measured as the number of opercula excreted and the size of each snail eaten was estimated from the length of each operculum. The usual number of *Littorina* passed through the digestive tract of each turtle was 16, but some *Malaclemys* passed as many as 90. Males eat *Littorina* ranging in shell length from 2 to 15 mm and females eat *Littorina* ranging from 4 to 21 mm. In feeding trials, however, captive terrapins selected *Uca* over *Littorina* when given a choice.

PREDATORS AND DEFENSE: Burger (1977) reported that up to 73% of eggs and 71% of nests detected in single year were destroyed by predators, and Iverson (1991a) estimated the annual survivorship of eggs and hatchlings in this population to be only 23%. Of the turtles that hatched during a two-year study, 22% were killed by predators. Nests located in areas of sparse vegetation, as well as those nests within a meter of other nests, were preyed upon more frequently than were those without such characteristics. The mean clutch size of nests that were destroyed did not differ significantly from that of nests that were not preyed upon.

Terrapin nests and hatchlings are preyed upon by a wide variety of predators including the ghost crab (*Ocypode quadrata*) (Arndt, 1991), crows (*Corvus*), shrikes (*Lanius*), gulls (*Larus*), hogs (*Sus*), rats (*Rattus*), muskrats (*Ondatra*), foxes (*Vulpes*), raccoons (*Procyon;* Seigel, 1980a), skunks (*Mephitis*), and mink (*Mustela*) (Ernst and Barbour, 1972; Burger, 1977). During Burger's (1977) study predators destroyed the following percentages of nests: red fox (*Vulpes vulpes*) 34%, raccoon (*Procyon lotor*) 48%, laughing gulls (*Larus atricilla*) 8%, crows (*Corvus brachyrhynchos*) 6%, and others 4%. Foxes and raccoons are nocturnal predators. Foxes leave partially opened shells near the nest, but eat every egg or turtle present. Raccoons usually eat the entire egg and may leave some eggs or hatchlings uneaten. Eggs left behind by raccoons were usually eaten by gulls in the morning.

Crows and gulls preyed on eggs during the day and were most effective during the laying period. Both species fly over the dunes or perch on nearby poles to watch for females laying eggs. The number of gulls flying over the dunes was directly related to the number of turtles observed digging. Gulls would land near laying females, eat two or three eggs, and fly away with one in its beak. Terrapins usually continued to lay while the gulls were eating. Once the nest was covered gull predation stopped, but crows dug up the eggs with their bills.

Most predation occurs during the laying and hatching periods. Nests constructed in June have a lower rate of predation (58%) than nests constructed in July (80%). During the 4–10-day emergence period, 45% of nests with hatchlings are preyed upon. Nest survival over time was generally linear (Burger, 1977).

Terrapin eggs are also destroyed by the invasion of beachgrass (*Ammophila breviligulata*) roots. Five of 20 terrapin nests examined by Lazell and Auger (1981), 50% of those located in vegetation, were infiltrated by rootlets of beachgrass. In several cases the rootlets entered the bottom center egg of a nest (these eggs appeared to be infertile) and actually caused it to burst. Two nests which overwintered but failed to hatch were completely surrounded by rootlets. Stegmann et al. (1988) documented nutrient uptake from diamondback terrapin eggs by beachgrass. Eggs were collected from the field within 48 hours of laying and injected with radioactive markers of selenium, cesium, manganese, and iron. All isotopes were found in the roots and shoots of beachgrass more than 30 cm from terrapin eggs within 45 days. Beachgrass absorbs important nutrients from terrapin eggs as an adaptation to living in the mineral-deficient soils of barrier dunes.

Nesting females are attacked by raccoons. Seigel (1980a) found 24 freshly killed terrapins (86% adult females) along a 0.5-km dike in Florida during two nesting seasons. In one case a raccoon was observed to kill an adult female and remove the terrapin's internal organs through an opening where the hind limb had been severed. Terrapins are also used as a food source by nesting bald eagles (*Haliaeetus leucocephalus*) (Clark, 1982). Lovich and Gibbons (1990) observed that 12% of females and 8% of males in their South Carolina study population were missing limbs, probably as a result of encounters with unknown predators.

Malaclemys is occasionally fouled by barnacles, including *Balanus eburneus*, *Chelonibia manati*, and *C. testudinaria* (Ross and Jackson, 1972; Jackson et al., 1973; Seigel, 1983). In Florida up to 76% of a terrapin sample may be infested. Barnacles are more likely to be found on the carapace than on the plastron. Males are just as likely as females to be infested. Barnacles may interfere with nesting and mating activities, and in some cases may cause death. The common oyster (*Crassostrea virginica*) and the slipper shell snail (*Crepidula plana*) also occasionally attach to the shell of *Malaclemys* (Jackson and Ross, 1971b; Ross and Jackson, 1972).

Humans are the main enemy of adult diamondback terrapins. *Malaclemys* was considered to be a gourmet food in the late 19th and early 20th century and was exploited until its numbers fell to levels that would not support commercial harvest. An excellent history of this exploitation is given by Carr (1952). A more recent human source of terrapin mortality occurs in crab pots. Bishop (1983) observed that at least 10% of terrapins captured incidentally in South Carolina crab pots drowned, and Ernst has seen as many as 10 drowned *Malaclemys* in a trap in the Chesapeake Bay. Adult males drown more often than adult females because the design of crab pots restricts entry by large females, and, perhaps, males are more prone to prey upon crabs. The most sinister threat facing *Malaclemys,* however, is coastal development and pollution which destroy its feeding grounds, kill off its shellfish prey, and make nesting beaches unsuitable.

If *Malaclemys* can escape when disturbed, it will do so, but if captured it may bite or void its bladder contents. Large females can produce a painful bite with their strong jaws.

POPULATIONS: The flesh of the diamondback terrapin makes excellent soup stock, which almost brought about extirpation of many populations near coastal metropolitan areas during the 1920s. As the turtle was exploited for the soup trade, its numbers became so decimated and the price of its flesh became so high that it became unprofitable to commercially harvest it. Since then most populations south of New York have recovered and now support large numbers of individuals.

Previously reported adult sex ratios range from male biased to female biased (see review in Lovich and Gibbons, 1990). Earlier reports of female-biased hatchling sex ratios (Hildebrand, 1929, 1932; Hildebrand and Hatsel, 1926) were undoubtedly due to the artificial conditions under which terrapins were cultivated in the past. Lovich and Gibbons (1990) reported a strongly male-biased adult sex ratio in South Carolina *M. t. centrata* in spite of the fact that the probability of recapturing individuals of either sex was the same. The observed difference was not attributable to sampling bias, seasonal effects, environmental sex determination, differential mortality, or differential immigration or emigration. After reviewing data from their study and previously published studies Lovich and Gibbons concluded that a male-biased sex ratio is expected in terrapin populations owing to the differential age of maturity in males and females. Males mature earlier than females, so adult males are expected to outnumber adult females, assuming that other factors are minimized and that the population experiences regular recruitment.

Seigel (1984) reported that 31% of the *M. t. tequesta* in a sample from the Banana River of Florida were over 17 cm in plastron length (this would include only females) compared to 3% in the nearby Indian River sample. During two years of sampling, the most frequent carapace length of males in a Delaware salt marsh was 11 cm but females usually had a carapace between 10 and 11 cm long (Hurd et al., 1979).

Population density for Delaware *M. t. terrapin* was estimated to be approximately 1.8 individuals per linear meter of tidal creek (Hurd et al., 1979). Density and biomass at two Florida study sites ranged from 53 to 72 terrapins/ha, and 355 to 390 kg/ha, respectively (Seigel, 1984).

Virtually nothing is known about diamondback terrapins from the time they leave the nest until attainment of sexual maturity. Research emphasis should be focused on these "lost years."

REMARKS: Additional literature on terrapins is summarized by Ernst and Bury (1982) and Palmer and Cordes (1988). Relationships between *Malaclemys* and *Graptemys* are discussed by Wood (1977) and Dobie (1981).

Testudinidae
Tortoises

This family consists of 12 genera and about 50 living species of tortoises (Ernst and Barbour, 1989) which live in the Americas, Europe, Africa, and Asia and on certain oceanic islands. The giant tortoises of the *Geochelone elephantopus* complex of the Galapagos Islands and *G. gigantea* of the Seychelles are the largest living land turtles. Three species of gopher tortoises (genus *Gopherus*) are found in the United States, and another lives in northern Mexico.

Tortoises are medium-sized to large, strictly terrestrial turtles with columnar, elephantine hind limbs. The forelimbs are covered anteriorly with thick, hard scales. The feet are short and broad, with heavy-clawed, webless toes having no more than two bones in any digit. The high-arched carapace is firmly sutured to the bridge; the plastron is well developed and contains an entoplastron. The nuchal bone lacks lateral costiform processes, and there are 11 peripherals. Two biconvex cervical vertebrae are present, and the dorsal rib-heads are often vestigial. The temporal region of the skull is widely emarginated posteriorly; the frontal bones enter the orbit. The quadrate bone always encloses the stapes. The maxilla rarely touches the quadratojugal, and its crushing surface is ridged. The premaxilla also bears a medial ridge. Complex mental glands are present under the chin, and rostral pores on the internarial region may act as mechanoreceptors.

The four living species of North American gopher tortoises are closely related to the extinct genus *Stylemys* (Eocene–Miocene of North America) and show many adaptations for burrowing. Forelimbs are flattened for digging with two to four subradial carpals and five claws; hind limbs are club shaped. No toe webbing is present, and the tail lacks a large terminal scale.

On the basis of differences in carpus structure as well as a number of other anatomical features, two species-groups of *Gopherus* may be recognized (Auffenberg, 1966a, 1976): a *polyphemus*-group, comprising *G. polyphemus* and the Mexican *G. flavomarginatus,* and an *agassizii*-group, comprising *G. agassizii* and *G. berlandieri*. Further evidence of the close relationship of *G. agassizii* and *G. berlandieri* was presented by Woodbury (1952), who described hybrids produced by a mating in captivity of these two species. In *G. flavomarginatus* and *G. polyphemus,* the sacculus contains a large otolithic structure and the inner ear chambers are hypertrophied, but in *G. agassizii* and *G. berlandieri,* the sacculus contains only a small otolithic mass and the inner ear chambers are only slightly inflated. In *flavomarginatus* and *polyphemus,* the cervical vertebrae are short and stout with enlarged, closely joined pre- and postzygapophyses, and a specialized, interlocking joint links the eighth cervical and the first dorsal vertebra. In *agassizii* and *berlandieri,* these vertebrae are not appreciably shortened, their pre- and postzygapophyses not enlarged, and the eighth cervical vertebra does not form a specialized, interlocking joint with the first dorsal vertebra (Bramble, 1982). The first dorsal vertebra is also attached to a distinct, bony strut on the nuchal bone in *flavomarginatus* and *polyphemus,* but not in *agassizii* and *berlandieri.* Instead, there are a small zygapophysis and a neural arch sutured to the first neural (Bramble, 1982). Mental glands are better developed in *agassizii* and *berlandieri* than in *polyphemus* or *flavomarginatus* (Winokur and Legler, 1975). Other characters differentiating the two groups are listed in Auffenberg (1976).

Germano (1993) examined the morphometric differences among the four living species of *Gopherus* and found that carapace length differs significantly among species. After adjusting for size differences, carapace shape is more similar between the largest species, G. *flavomarginatus,* and the smallest species, G. *berlandieri,* than between the two intermediate-sized tortoises, G. *agassizii* and G. *polyphemus.* The results of his morphological data analyses are not congruent with previous studies of morphological variation (Winokur and Legler, 1975; Auffenberg, 1976; Bramble, 1982) and genetic variation (Lamb et al., 1989), nor are they correlated with environmental data.

A controversy has arisen as to what is the proper generic name of the North American gopher tortoises. Bramble (1982) assigned the two species from the western United States, *agassizii* and *berlandieri,* to his newly created genus, *Scaptochelys,* while retaining the species *polyphemus* and *flavomarginatus* in the genus *Gopherus.* In 1984, Bour and Dubois proved that the name *Scaptochelys* is a junior subjective synonym of *Xerobates* Agassiz, 1857, and thus not available. They proposed *Xerobates* as the valid name for the genus, and a number of researchers have followed this designation. Anatomical studies by Crumly (1984), however, have shown that these four tortoise species have a unique suite of characters unknown in most other turtles: a medium premaxillary ridge, shared with the extinct *Stylemys;* prefrontal pits; class I type mental glands (Winokur and Legler, 1975); and absence of dorsal crests on the postzygapophyses of the sixth to eighth cervical vertebrae (dorsal crests are almost absent in the African pancake tortoise, *Malacochersus*). Because of this, Crumly recommended that all living gopher tortoises be retained in the genus *Gopherus.* We follow his recommendation.

Gopherus agassizii (Cooper, 1863)
Desert tortoise
PLATE 55

RECOGNITION: The desert tortoise is a large terrestrial turtle of the southwestern United States that has large, elephantine hind feet, shovellike forefeet, and a gular projection on the plastron. The rough, ridged, but keelless carapace (to 37 cm) is oblong and is highest behind the middle; the rear rim is serrated, and the marginals above the hind limbs are flared. The carapacial scutes are black to tan, and many have brownish or orange centers, particularly in younger individuals. The bridge is well developed and has a single axillary scute. The plastron is large and hingeless; its elongated gular scutes project anteriorly and may bend upward. The plastral scutes are black to tan; some may have yellowish centers. Skin of the limbs is brown and that of the limb sockets and neck yellowish; the head commonly is tan but may be reddish. The head is somewhat rounded, and the crushing ridges of the upper jaws form less than a 65° angle with each other. Well-developed mental glands are present beneath the chin, and two to five rostral pores lie on the internarial region (Winokur and Legler, 1974, 1975). The iris usually is greenish yellow. Forefeet and hind feet are about the same size; the distance from the base of the first claw to the base of the fourth on the forefoot approximately equals the same measurement on the hind foot. The toes are not webbed, and a single, large femoral spur is present.

Males are larger than females and have longer, thicker tails, longer gular projections, concave plastra, and more massive claws. Male mental glands are larger and more complex than those of females, and possibly their secretions are important in sex recognition (Winokur and Legler, 1975).

KARYOTYPE: Diploid chromosomes number 52 (26 macrochromosomes and 26 microchromosomes): 20 metacentric and submetacentric, 10 subtelocentric, and 22 acrocentric and telocentric (Stock, 1972; Dowler and Bickham, 1982).

FOSSIL RECORD: Pleistocene (Rancholabrean) fossils of Gopherus agassizii have been found in Arizona, California, New Mexico, and Nevada (see Brattstrom, 1961; Van Devender et al., 1976; Van Devender and Moodie, 1977; and Van Devender and Mead, 1978, for more details). Remains of the desert tortoise have also been found at archeological sites in Arizona, southern California, and southern Nevada; apparently some Indian tribes used it for food and medicine, and in various rituals and ceremonies (Schneider and Everson, 1989).

DISTRIBUTION: The main range of Gopherus agassizii extends from southern Nevada and extreme southwestern Utah, southward through southeastern California, southwestern Arizona, and western Sonora (including Tiburón Island in the Gulf of California) to northwestern Sinaloa (Hulse and Middendorf, 1979; Patterson, 1982). Ottley and Velázques Solis (1989) reported it from Baja California.

GEOGRAPHIC VARIATION: No subspecies have been designated; however, populations vary in allozymes, plasma protein markers, and mitochondrial DNA (Rainboth et al., 1989; Lamb et al., 1989; Glenn et al., 1990). Allozyme variation, as quantified by genetic distance measures, is not significant between desert tortoises from the western Mojave Desert (Kramer Hills) and those from the eastern Mojave (Chemehuevi Valley), California (Rainboth et al., 1989). However, other statistical analyses of these same populations indicate significant allozyme variation. Lamb et al. (1989) identified five different mitochondrial DNA clones. The first major assemblage consists of three closely related clones (a1–a3) confined to and fixed in populations north and west of the Colorado River. The most common genotype, a1, is found throughout the Colorado and Mojave deserts in California and extends into southern

445

Gopherus agassizii

Plastron of *Gopherus agassizii*

Nevada along the Piute Valley. Clones a2 and a3 are restricted to tortoises living in the northeastern Mojave Desert and are geographically coincident with the northern distributional limits of the species. A second major assemblage, clone a4, occurs from west-central and southern Arizona to central Sonora. Tortoises from southern Sonora have genotype a5, the third major assemblage. A plasma protein marker resembling albumin was found to be polymorphic for electromorphs in northern Mojave Desert populations but Sonoran desert populations to the south were monomorphic (Glenn et al., 1990). These results support those previously reported by Lamb et al. (1989) which show divergence between desert tortoise populations on either side of the Colorado River.

A tortoise from Baja California has been described recently as a new taxon, *Xerobates lepidocephalus* (Ottley and Velázques Solis, 1989), but Crumly and Grismer (in press) have shown the adult female holotype is a *Gopherus agassizii*.

The general concordance between molecular-based

Forelegs of all *Gopherus* are broad and flattened as in this *Gopherus agassizii;* note also gular extension of plastron beneath chin

studies and traditional morphometric analysis (Weinstein and Berry, 1987) suggests that the desert tortoise comprises more than one taxonomic unit.

CONFUSING SPECIES: North of Mexico, only the terrestrial *Terrapene ornata* and aquatic *Kinosternon sonoriense* and *K. flavescens* could be confused with young desert tortoises; each of these has a hinged plastron and lacks a gular projection.

HABITAT: The desert tortoise inhabits desert alluvial fans, washes, canyon bottoms, and rocky hillsides in drylands having sandy or gravelly soil; it reaches an altitude of at least 1,070 m. The particular habitat types utilized vary geographically, gradually changing to rocky slopes in the eastern part of the range (Schamberger and Turner, 1986; Barrett, 1990). Creosote bush, cheese bush, black bush, salt bush, hop sage, paloverde, ironwood, smoke tree, grasses, and cacti are often present in the habitat. The spatial distribution of desert tortoises in relation to plant communities is not random (Baxter, 1988). High-diversity plant ecotones and communities, and possibly soil characteristics, are important features in determining tortoise densities (Wilson and Stager, 1992). Although *Terrapene ornata luteola* occurs with *Gopherus agassizii* at some Arizona localities, no other

Distribution of *Gopherus agassizii*

North American turtle shares the more severe microhabitats occupied by this species.

BEHAVIOR: *Gopherus agassizii* has a relatively long annual period of activity, usually emerging from hibernation in February to late April, and retiring for the winter in late September to November. Of course, this cycle depends on both the latitude and altitude of the population, as well as precipitation patterns. Most surface activity occurs from late April through June, July, and, at some localities, from late August through September. In Mexico, the period of greatest surface activity seems to occur in late summer and early fall (Osorio and Bury, 1982). In the warm season the daily activity of *G. agassizii* is governed largely by temperature, although it becomes active during most diurnal rainstorms. It forages for a short period after sunrise and again in the late afternoon. Between active periods the tortoise rests in its burrow. This pattern is followed over most of the range, but in California Luckenbach (1982) found the period of activity varied according to the season. During early spring (March–April), tortoises usually emerge from their burrows in late morning. Once emerged and warmed, tortoises may be found on the surface throughout the remaining daylight hours, foraging or engaging in courtship. During summer, activity bouts become bimodal because daytime heat causes a cessation of above-ground activities from about 1000 to 1900. This pattern grades into a unimodal late morning to sunset pattern again in the fall (September–November). The desert tortoise is diurnal except, perhaps, during rare rainstorms that may trigger nocturnal emergence (Luckenbach, 1982).

Some desert tortoises first become active at air temperatures as low as 15°C; activity gradually increases with rising temperature, until at about 26.7–29.4°C all are active (Woodbury and Hardy, 1948). McGinnis and Voigt (1971) reported that deep core body temperatures may be up to 10°C cooler than the temperature of the shell surface, and thought the carapace scutes act as a buffer against solar radiation. Brattstrom (1965) and McGinnis and Voigt (1971) found that the temperatures of active *G. agassizii* were 15.0–38.3°C, and that the critical thermal maximum was 39.5°C. On the other hand, Hutchison et al. (1966) found that a *G. agassizii* lost its righting ability at 39.0°C and that the critical thermal maximum was 43.1°C. The latter figure seems more reasonable. Berry and Turner (1984) observed that tortoises less than 60 mm in carapace length were active at significantly lower air temperatures than were larger individuals. An individual kept on its back in direct sunlight will die in a short time, but tortoises can right themselves by using their head, neck, and forelimbs.

Voigt (1975) measured heating and cooling rates of desert tortoises. Heating rates in the field were as much as 10 times faster than cooling rates, and heart rates during heating were significantly faster than during cooling at any particular body temperatures. Difference in the rates of heating and cooling presumably allows maintenance of suitable body temperatures for digestive and reproductive activities for a period after the tortoise has retreated into its burrow. Measurements of oxygen consumption (VO_2) were taken over a temperature range of 8–42°C by Naegle and Bradley (1975). The Q_{10} for VO_2 at 10–20°C, 20–30°C, and 30–40°C were 3.2, 2.3, and 1.8, respectively, and tortoises less than 500 g had significantly higher VO_2 rates than those heavier than 500 g.

Besides overheating, the other major environmental problems of *G. agassizii* are water retention and salt balance. Desert tortoises lose water by evaporation and urination. Some water is always lost by evaporation from the lungs; however, the skin permits the passage of less water than that of turtles in damper climates (Schmidt-Nielsen and Bentley, 1966). Dantzler and Schmidt-Nielsen (1966) showed that the urinary bladder of the desert tortoise is more permeable to water than that of freshwater turtles and that the tortoise excretes nitrogenous wastes in the semisolid form of urates. When water is available it excretes liquid urine, but it is able to go for months without discharging water from the bladder.

July thunderstorms in Nevada trigger emergence from estivation, and the tortoises drink much rainwater, void concentrated urine, accumulate dilute urine, restore normal plasma osmotic concentration, resume feeding on the still-dry grasses and forbs, and accumulate surplus energy (Nagy and Medica, 1986). However, body weight declines during this period owing to negative water balance, and osmotic concentration in bladder urine increases. More rain in September relieves osmotic stress as again tortoises drink, urinate, and store dilute urine. Energy balance remains strongly positive until the *Gopherus* begin feeding on succulent new sprouts of annual plants germinated in late September, and the tortoises return to a springlike physiological condition in mid-November when hibernation begins. Tortoises apparently relinquish maintenance of internal homeostasis on a daily basis during most of the year, while tolerating large imbalances in their water, salt, and energy budgets (Nagy and Medica, 1986). This ability lets them exploit resources that are only periodically available, while balancing water and salt budgets on an annual basis and showing an energy profit.

The desert tortoise occupies a rather small home range wherein water may not be available (Woodbury and Hardy, 1948; Auffenberg, 1969). In the driest parts of its range the desert tortoise has opportunities for drinking only after rains, which are infrequent. When water is available the tortoise will drink (Nagy and Medica, 1977, 1986; Medica et al., 1980; Nagy, 1988). Desert tortoises occasionally construct small catchment basins during showers and thunderstorms that are capable of holding water for up to six hours (Medica et al., 1980). Miller (1932) reported that individuals increased their weights as much as 43% and Medica et al. (1980), as much as 9.2% by drinking. However, the basic water supply of a desert tortoise must come from food: the plants eaten are not entirely dry, and additional water is produced metabolically from them. Tortoises accumulate fat for hibernation, and this is also a source of metabolic water. Nagy and Medica (1977; 1986) reported tortoises gained weight during the spring while eating 3–4% of their body mass in succulent annual plants each day, but by summer, water intake rates dropped from about 25 to 5 ml/day, and metabolic rates also declined. During most of the summer, water turnover rates are very low, 0.36 ml/100 g/day, and only slightly greater than rates of water metabolic production, 0.31 ml/day (Minnich, 1976, 1977).

The desert tortoise enters hibernation in October or November. In southwestern Utah, desert tortoises congregate in large communal dens during the winter (Woodbury and Hardy, 1948). These were dug as deep as 10 m into gravel banks, and some had multiple openings. As many as 23 tortoises were found in one burrow, and some returned to the same burrow annually. Auffenberg (1969) reported that in Pima County, Arizona, individuals often returned year after year to particular hibernacula. These winter burrows were always located well above the floor of arroyos and usually were enlarged ground-squirrel burrows. The typical burrow extended just far enough so that the rear portion of the tortoise's shell was even with the arroyo wall. This depth apparently was sufficient to shelter the tortoise from the cold night winds but allowed the exposure of a part of the shell to the rays of the afternoon sun: the burrows were always located in a south-facing slope, and four or five tortoises sometimes occupied adjacent burrows. Nichols (1953) saw several captives combine their efforts to dig a communal hibernaculum. Nichols (1957) reported that several young captive tortoises hatched in California did not hibernate during their first winter, but all hibernated the second winter.

Gopherus agassizii spends most of its life underground. It constructs a burrow which provides a special microhabitat: the humidity is higher and the temperature is lower and more constant in the burrow than outside it. By retreating into the burrow the tortoise relieves the problems of evaporative water loss and high body temperature. In extremely hot weather the tortoise may stay in its burrow all day. On the other hand, they are especially active during rains when the cooler temperature and higher humidity make conditions outside the burrow more tolerable. In the wild, this turtle seldom basks except on cool days, but captives in more temperate climates often spend considerable time lying in the sun.

The tortoise digs by scraping alternately with the forelimbs; when the hole becomes deep enough the turtle turns around and pushes the dirt out with the sides of its shell. The burrows are dug in dry, gravelly or sandy soil and are often located under a bush in an arroyo bank or at the base of a cliff. In cross-section they are somewhat semicircular; may be straight, curved, or forked; and many have enlarged chambers. Although sometimes just long enough to admit the tortoise, they are rarely up to 10 m in length (Woodbury and Hardy, 1948).

Several types of burrows are constructed for different reasons, and the type and depth of burrows may be related to soil type and to winter and summer temperature extremes (Berry, 1978). Burge (1978) found four types of cover sites in southern Nevada: den, burrow, pallet, and nonburrow. The average density of cover sites used repeatedly (pallets or burrows) was 3.5/ha. Of 783 burrows and pallets, 665 (85%) were in soil with varying amounts of gravel, 564 (72%) were located under shrubs, and 203 (26%) were dug into banks or beds of dry washes. Individual tortoises used 12–25 cover sites per year, and most were repeatedly used.

Dens are horizontal tunnels dug in banks of washes, usually for distances of 2–4.5 m but occasionally for 6–10 m. Summer burrows are scattered over the flats and benches and are dug downward at angles of about 20–40° for a distance of 1.8–2.4 m. Pallets are only about 25 cm to 1.5 m deep. In Sonora, Mexico, Auffenberg (1969) found that the summer retreat was most commonly a shallow hollow dug into the base of an arroyo wall; several tortoises may use the same shelter during a single season. In Utah, woodrats (*Neotoma*) and western rattlesnakes (*Crotalus viridis*) may share the winter burrows with desert tortoises (Woodbury and Hardy, 1948).

Gopherus agassizii is a surprisingly good climber and often digs its winter den at the top of a steep bank. Woodbury and Hardy (1948) reported that to enter one such den a tortoise had to climb 15.5 m at an angle of about 45°, ascend a vertical gravel ledge 30 cm high, at its lowest point, and then climb an additional 1.2 m at an angle of about 40°. At another den the tortoise had to climb 40 cm; the first 20 cm led to a narrow ledge, just wide enough to accommodate the hind feet. Above this a vertical 25 cm led to a 5-cm slope, which in turn led to the entrance to the den. A captive female kept by Ernst spent much time attempting to climb walls and pieces of furniture. On several occasions she climbed vertically 15–20 cm up a living room sofa. In accomplishing this she reached up with her forefeet, hooked them under the sofa cushions, and then did a pull-up, raising her hind limbs clear of the floor.

Once in their burrows, desert tortoises resist almost all attempts to remove them. They brace their forefeet against the walls or else firmly plant them on the floor of the burrow, lean forward, and raise their backs against the roof. This is quite effective, and they are difficult to extract. A captive female that shared the house with Ernst often successfully used these tactics to resist removal from beneath furniture.

Gopherus agassizi is a slow and deliberate animal. Woodbury and Hardy (1948) measured rates of travel as being 219–483 m/hr. At this speed it would take 3.3–7.3 hours to travel 1.6 km (1 mile). The velocity in centimeters/second ranged from 7.6 at 25.8°C to 13.5 at 33.0°C.

Utah desert tortoises perform yearly migrations between the winter hibernacula and the summer feeding grounds, where their home ranges usually cover 4.0–40.5 ha and overlap the ranges of other desert tortoises. There is no evidence that they defend territories in Utah (Woodbury and Hardy, 1948). In California, home ranges seem more variable in size. Marlow (in Luckenbach, 1982) reported 10–14-ha home ranges, and Vaughan (1983) noted mean home range areas of 7.0 ha (1.7–34.0) for females and 5.5 ha (0.4–9.5) for males. Berry (1986a) observed that California desert tortoises know the locations of burrows, mates, water sources, and mineral licks within their home ranges, which are 1–268 ha in size. Despite the home range areas reported by Vaughan (1983), males usually occupy larger ranges than females. Hatchlings and juveniles have restricted home ranges usually associated with no more than two burrows.

In Arizona, Barrett (1990) recorded average home ranges of 19 ha (3–53) for 14 tortoises and found no sexual differences nor any correlation with carapace length. Tortoises used an average of eight burrows each and repeatedly used old burrows. Larger burrows were occupied in the summer; winters were spent in steeper rocky slopes.

Desert tortoises may occasionally move outside of their home ranges. Berry (1986a) reported such movements of 1.4–7.3 km in 16 days to five years. During movements, steep dropoffs are avoided (Patterson, 1971c).

Gopherus agassizii has rather unusual social relationships. When two tortoises meet, each nods its head rapidly, and sometimes they touch noses before they pass. When two males meet, a fight is likely to ensue. After the preliminary nodding they separate a little distance, then, with heads pulled partway into their shells, rush toward one another. They meet head-on, and the gular projections are butted violently together. Fights usually do no damage, but one of the tortoises may be turned over; the vanquished struggles for some time, with one foreleg vibrating vigorously in the air and the other pawing for a foothold on the ground, before he rights himself. If he cannot, the tortoise may die of exposure to the sun.

Campbell and Evans (1967) found that the desert tortoise makes two types of sounds: a short grunt and a drawn-out moan. The fundamental frequency varies by at least an octave—from 0.5 kc to 1.0 kc—and in most cases the signal contains two or three harmonics. These sounds are not involved in courtship or in combat, and their biologic significance is not known.

Other vocalizations by desert tortoises may elicit behavior from other individuals (Patterson, 1976). Hisses emitted by startled tortoises or males engaged in aggressive interactions may produce listening or flight behavior. Long calls, if emitted by subordinate males during combat, may bring on feeding or flight responses in dominant males. Pops and poinks may also cause flight, and, in a few cases, may cause dominant male assistance for overturned subordinate males.

Nichols (1957) reported that after one of her adults drank water it occasionally urinated in its house. Until the house had been thoroughly hosed and aired, other tortoises—one male especially—would not sleep inside unless forced to do so. Patterson (1971b) observed that *G. agassizii* avoided sleeping areas contaminated with fecal matter from other desert tortoises and urine from male *G. berlandieri*. A captive adult female *G. agassizii* kept by Ernst, when first introduced to an adult male *G. polyphemus* of about the same size, rammed him several times, causing him to withdraw into his shell. She then walked away and never again showed such aggressiveness toward him during the several years they were kept together; indeed, they often were in each other's company, especially at night. When a small male *G. berlandieri* was introduced to the female she circled and sniffed him for about a minute and then ignored him.

Relocated tortoises may disrupt the social structure of resident populations by displacing those with established home ranges or they may be driven out by resident tortoises (Berry, 1986a).

REPRODUCTION: Woodbury and Hardy (1948) estimated that sexual maturity in Utah is reached in 15–20 years, when females are 230–265 mm in carapace length and males are 250–316, but in California, Berry (1978) estimated females first reproduced at 215–220 mm in carapace length at ages of 15–20 years, and Turner et al. (1986) reported that females in the Mojave Desert reproduce at 189 mm, indicating they probably mature between 180 and 190 mm. A shorter annual growing season in Utah may account for this difference. Miller (1955) reported that male secondary sexual characteristics begin to appear at 16 years, are definite at 17 years, and are complete at 20 years. A female 165 mm in carapace length (10–11 years old) stimulated courting activity in a large male. Tortoises kept in captivity on an enriched diet and active all year grow faster and may reach mature size in much less time; 12–13 years (Stewart, in Berry, 1978), but possibly as short as four years (D. C. Jackson et al., 1976, 1978).

Neither the male nor the female sexual cycles have been described. The ovarian follicle walls are separated into two components, an outer layer and an inner layer; the inner layer responds to gonadotropin stimulation by producing progesterone (Crews and Licht, 1975).

Courtship and mating begin shortly after spring emergence (possibly as early as 25 March; Medica et al., 1982) and continue through the summer and into the fall as late as October (Tomko, 1972; Luckenbach, 1982). Observations by Weaver (1970) and Black (1976) indicated that courtship begins with the male approaching the female. If she remains motionless, or bobs her head at the male, he may touch parts of her shell and head, perhaps to verify her sex through olfactory cues. The male may also bob his head at this stage. However, if the female crawls away, the male will trail her with low-intensity head bobs and his neck not fully extended. Intensity increases as the female speeds up her walking, and the male now stretches his neck to the fullest. When she is caught he continues high-intensity head bobbing while circling her (usually in a counterclockwise direction). She usually tries to move on or circles him. Once she stops, the male reduces the frequency of head bobbing and starts to bite her on the nose, forelegs, and shell. She usually pulls in at this stage, and may continue to circle to avoid the male. The male rams her with the gular projection, and the female finally ceases to move. Whereupon, the male attempts to mount her from the rear, assuming a nearly erect position with his forelimbs resting on her carapace. He then performs vertical pumping movements, accompanied by puffing and grunting noises.

Most reports of vocalizing during breeding activities suggest that the sounds are a by-product of the copulatory effort; nothing indicates that they serve as an auditory signal (Weaver, 1970).

Oviducts of female *Gopherus agassizii* contain tubules capable of supporting viable sperm for some time, so possibly sperm from one mating may be used to fertilized several clutches of eggs (Gist and Jones, 1989).

Nichols (1953) reported that each spring a captive male chose a mate for the season—usually a different female from that of the previous year. Nichols (1957) reported a female initiating courtship. Several of the complete courtships observed by Black (1976) took over 80 minutes.

The nesting season extends from mid-May through July. Early morning and late afternoon seem to be the favorite nesting times. Females have been known to lay eggs as late as September and October and to nest two or three times in one season (Luckenbach, 1982). The eggs normally are deposited in cavities dug in sandy or friable soil but are also laid in the mouths of burrows or are deposited singly at random. Hampton (1981) found most nests in the Fremont Valley, Kern County, California, were located at the entrance of a large burrow; 12 of 15 were located in the shade of a creosote bush, while only 3 were in the open.

In the days just prior to nesting the female often becomes extremely restless and spends considerable time scratching the soil with her forefeet. She may refuse to eat during this period. After oviposition, females spend less time above ground than do males (Luckenbach, 1982). Males remain above ground longer than females and apparently continue sexual activity throughout the summer. Of 124 tortoises examined in the field in August 1973 by Luckenbach (1982), 80% were adult males.

The nest cavity is usually dug by the hind feet, but the area may first be cleared and the initial scraping done by the forefeet (Luckenbach, 1982). The hind feet are used to dig the nest, to arrange the eggs in the nest, and to scratch and drag soil back into the cavity after the eggs are laid. The female may urinate into the nest cavity before filling it or on it after filling it. The urine may soften the soil for digging, repulse egg predators, camouflage the nest cavity and compact the soil over the finished nest to make nest excavation by predators difficult (Patterson, 1971a). Excavation of the nest may take one to several hours, and oviposition 15–30 minutes.

The nest is funnel shaped; that is, wider at the entrance than in the egg chamber. The depth is 8–25 cm. Nichols (1953) gave the measurements of a typical nest as approximately 15 cm deep, 23 cm in diameter at the top and 18 cm across at the bottom. Nests of captives listed in Hampton (1981) varied from 10 to 20 cm in diameter and 10 to 25 cm in depth.

Clutches consist of 2–15 eggs; about 5–6 is the usual number. Clutch size is directly correlated to the carapace length of the female, and one to three clutches may be laid each year. The eggs vary from elliptical to nearly spherical in shape; four elliptical ones were 41.6–48.7 mm in length, 36.7–39.6 mm in maximum transverse diameter, and 34.9–38.2 mm in minimum transverse diameter (Miller, 1932). Fresh eggs weigh 33–34 g and are moist, translucent, and extremely hard, with a coarse, rough texture and without gloss, chalky layer, or pigment. The translucence, which permits observation of a small gas bubble within the egg, disappears upon drying. The gas bubble remains for several months without change in volume, an indication that the shell is moisture-proof.

Marlow and Tollestrup (1982) observed female desert tortoises consuming the soil of a lime layer on an exposed site. The calcium content of this soil was significantly higher than that of adjacent areas, and all geophagous episodes involved reproductively mature females during the nesting season, a period when the females probably had their greatest calcium need for the shelling of eggs and embryo shell and skeletal development. Also, Berry (1978) reported that it is possible that females do not lay eggs in years when forage production is low.

Mean clutch frequencies per year determined by X-rays taken by Turner et al. (1986) were 1.57–1.89 clutches for 1983–1985. The tortoises typically laid one or two clutches during May and June, but one female did not oviposit in 1984 and single tortoises laid three clutches in 1983 and 1985. If females laid two clutches, the second was faintly visible in X-rays within 9–10 days after the first was laid. Eggs were laid about 22 days after first visible in X-rays. Usually it was the larger females that laid multiple clutches.

Clutch sizes were positively correlated with female body size, but when this effect was removed, clutch size did not differ between years, the first and second clutches laid in a season did not differ in size, females laying only one clutch laid larger clutches than females laying more than one clutch per season, and variation in clutch sizes of different individuals was greater than comparable variation within the same tortoises. Mean clutch frequencies were positively correlated with winter rainfall, but summer rains also apparently contributed to reproductive energetics of the females. Adult females had two periods of distinct weight (mass) loss in 1980 (15–28 May, 12–25 June) which were interpreted as evidence of egg laying by Turner et al. (1984).

Hatching occurs from mid-August to October, with peak emergence in September and early October. Natural incubation periods usually last 90–120 days, but artificially incubated eggs have hatched in 82–92 days. In captivity, a hatching rate of 89% is considered high, the normal rate being about 60% (Luckenbach, 1982). Turner et al. (1986) reported that only 26 (46%) of 57 eggs moved to predator-proof nests in May and June hatched by the end of October; however, none of the 17 apparently viable eggs left in the protected nests until 3 May hatched. Grant (1936b) reported a case of an egg overwintering and hatching the following spring.

Hatchlings are nearly as wide as long and are 36–48 in carapace length, 35–43 mm in carapace width, and 20–24 mm in depth. The carapace varies from dull yellow to brownish, with darker brown areas on each of the scutes. It is pliable, and has wrinkles on the sides and a deep crease across the plastron that allowed curling of the fetus in the egg. In the center of the plastron is a yolk sac about one-third the size of the young turtle; the sac greatly impedes its movements. This is rapidly resorbed over a two-day period, leaving only a soft umbilical scar by the third day; it remains visible for several weeks and does not completely heal for several months. The caruncle disappears gradually. The cervical and the twelfth marginals are incomplete at hatching and are deeply notched and bluntly serrate on the rim. Color and shape of the hatchling are such as to render it practically invisible among stones and dry grasses.

Spotila and Standora (1986) suggested that sex determination may be temperature dependent, as in the European tortoise *Testudo graeca,* with a threshold temperature of 30–31°C.

GROWTH AND LONGEVITY: In nature, the annual feeding period may last only 6–12 weeks

Juvenile *Gopherus agassizii*

Plastron of juvenile *Gopherus agassizii*

in good forage years, which occur on an average of once every five years (Luckenbach, 1982). Lean years may delay growth and maturation, as both are apparently enhanced with greater food availability and quality in captivity (D. C. Jackson et al., 1976, 1978). The juvenile shell remains soft for 5–10 years. There are many reports on the growth rates of captive *Gopherus agassizii* (Miller, 1932, 1955; Patterson and Brattstrom, 1972; D. C. Jackson et al., 1976, 1978; Patterson, 1977, 1978), but relatively few on natural growth rates.

Bogert (1937) reported that a wild female grew 22 mm in 680 days and a smaller female grew 70 mm in 818 days. Woodbury and Hardy (1948) found that many young *G. agassizii* grew to a carapace length of about 100 mm in five years. The most rapid growth recorded by them was a tortoise that grew from 206 to 302 mm in a little more than 52 months. Growth is more rapid up to a carapace length of about 150 mm and then slows in larger tortoises.

Natural growth and age-size relationships in desert tortoises from Nevada were studied by Medica et al. (1975) and Turner et al. (1987). Growth was affected by variations in rainfall, which controlled the growth of food plants. The average annual growth between 1963 and 1973 was about 9 mm (1.8–12.3), and growth generally occurred between April and June. None of the animals measured during this period was mature, and they had original plastron lengths of 47–74 mm. By 1985, all of the tortoises were at least 20 years old. Growth of males and females over this period did not differ significantly. Tortoises reached plastron lengths of 100 mm in 6–7 years, 130 mm in 10–11 years, 150 mm in 13–14 years, and were more than 200 mm at estimated ages of 24 years. Scute annuli produced during the first 20–25 years of growth can be used to age desert tortoises, but annuli counts on most individuals are one or two rings less than actual age (Germano, 1988). Germano (1992) found that the growth rate of desert tortoises varied between populations, with the greatest rates of growth (0–25 years) in tortoises from the western Mojave and Sinaloan deserts, and the slowest rate of growth in those from the eastern Mojave and Sonoran deserts. At age one tortoises from the western Mojave and Sinaloan deserts have average carapace lengths of 51 mm and 59 mm, respectively, while those from the eastern Mojave and Sonoran deserts are only 46 mm and 49 mm, respectively. At age 10, tortoises from the eastern Mojave and Sonoran populations have only grown to an average of 122 mm and 125 mm, being surpassed by the western Mojave and Sinaloan tortoises that have grown to 140 mm and 139 mm, respectively. By age 20, *G. agassizii* from the eastern Mojave average 207 mm in carapace length and those from the Sonoran population, 211 mm; desert tortoises from the western Mojave Desert are 239 mm long, and those from the Sinaloan population have grown to 211 mm.

Many wild adult *G. agassizii* are between 20 and 30 years of age, but, based on minimum estimates of longevity, few live 50 years. Approximately 29% of the desert tortoises from the Sonoran population, 11% of those from the eastern Mojave, and approximately 5% of the tortoises from the western Mojave Desert live past 25 years (Germano, 1992). The greatest estimate of longevity for any wild tortoise is 48–53 years for one from the eastern Mojave Desert. The oldest individual from the western Mojave Desert is estimated to be 32 years old, and the oldest from the Sonoran population is estimated to be 35 years old (Germano, 1992). However, some captives have been very long-lived. Nichols (1953, 1957) reported that a male *G. agassizii* captured in 1929, when four or five years old, was still alive when 32 or 33 years old, and Patterson and Brattstrom (1972) also reported individuals older than 30 years. Snider and

Bowler (1992) reported that one lived 55 years, one month, and 30 days in captivity. Jennings (1981) reported a male potentially 67–72 years old, and Glenn (1983) noted a female that may have been 80+ years, and possibly a centenarian, when she died.

FOOD HABITS: *Gopherus agassizii* is mostly herbivorous, subsisting on various grasses, cacti, and the blossoms of desert Compositae. Lists of plants eaten by wild desert tortoises are presented in Burge and Bradley (1976), Hansen et al. (1976), and Luckenbach (1982). The most important foods seem to be desert annuals, plants that often have a life span of less than 30 days and are generally available only from April to June. Both flowers and vegetative parts are eaten, but, when available, flowers are preferred (Luckenbach, 1982; Ernst, pers. obs.), and peak tortoise activity corresponds to the period of spring blooming. Since food quality decreases dramatically after June, tortoises must eat enough to carry them through summer estivation and winter hibernation, and females must accumulate extra energy reserves for egg yolking. Grasses and other desert scrub plants have been thought to be mostly secondary foods used only to support limited summer activity, but they may be more important, especially as a factor in the annual energy budget (H. Avery, pers. comm.). Cacti (*Opuntia*) may become important secondary foods and water sources in dry years (Turner et al., 1984).

In northern Arizona and southern Utah, Hansen et al. (1976) found that three grasses (*Aristida, Tridens,* and *Bromus*) amounted to 61% of the diet. They also found sand, bird feathers, mammal hairs, snake and lizard skins, and arthropod parts in fecal scats. Desert tortoises from southern Nevada fed on desert mallow (*Sphaeralcea*) and plaintain (*Plantago*) 61% of the time.

The serrated jaws of *G. agassizii* are well adapted to the shredding of vegetation. Tortoises may wander from plant to plant while foraging if these are far apart, but if a cluster of food plants is available they will remain at one spot until satiated. After feeding, tortoises usually seek shelter.

Like other vertebrate herbivores, *G. agassizii* is incapable of producing the enzymes necessary to digest cellulose. These enzymes are produced by microorganisms in its gut that are first obtained as a juvenile by eating the feces of adults.

Captives eat radishes, dandelions, watermelon, cantaloupe, romaine lettuce, tomatoes, apples, strawberries, shaved carrots, spinach, beans, peas and other legumes, bananas, figs, peaches, clover, grasses, grapes, and bird eggshells. Nichols (1953) reported that captives will consume the eggs of their own species.

Little food is available during the period of late summer hatching, and hatchlings spend little time on the surface (Luckenbach, 1982). They dig their own small burrows, or use an existing larger burrow. Dormancy follows shortly, probably before hatchlings have eaten or taken in water. Luckenbach's (1982) observations of captive hatchlings suggest that they ignore food between the time of emergence from the nest and the beginning of winter dormancy.

PREDATORS AND DEFENSE: Coyotes (*Canis latrans*), bobcats (*Lynx rufus*), ravens (*Corvus corax*), golden eagles (*Aquila chrysaetos*), and Gila monsters (*Heloderma suspectum*) are known predators of either eggs, juveniles or adults (Hensley, 1950; Barrow, 1979; Luckenbach, 1982; Barrett and Humphrey, 1986), and ring-tailed cats (*Bassariscus*), badgers (*Taxidea*), skunks (*Mephitis, Spilogale*), kit foxes (*Vulpes*), domestic dogs (*Canis familiaris*), large hawks (*Buteo*), owls (*Athene*), roadrunners (*Geococcyx*), bullsnakes (*Pituophis*), and coachwhip snakes (*Masticophis*) are suspected predators (Ernst and Barbour, 1972; Luckenbach, 1982; H. Avery, pers. comm.).

The presence of a high density of local ravens (*Corvus corax*) has a detrimental affect on populations of *Gopherus agassizii* through predation on young tortoises (Boarman, 1993). Ravens have become subsidized native predators in the Mojave Desert, taking advantage of food and water provided by increased human development and activity. Food from landfills and trash containers, and water from irrigation, swimming pools, sewage lagoons, and other sources appear to have allowed raven populations to increase 1,528% in the Mojave Desert between 1968 and 1988 (estimate based on U.S. Fish and Wildlife Service breeding bird surveys).

Ravens prey primarily on tortoises less than 11.0 cm in carapace length, pecking through soft parts of the shell and feeding on the viscera, or pulling the head and limbs from the body. Large numbers of tortoise shells have been found under raven perches and nests, and preliminary analysis has shown a decrease in the number of small tortoises in populations associated with the presence of many ravens.

Humans sometimes eat desert tortoises, run over them on the highways or with off-road vehicles, or shoot them (Bury and Marlow, 1973; Luckenbach, 1982; Berry, 1986b). This wanton destruction must cease if the desert tortoise is to survive.

When molested, *G. agassizii* retreats into its shell, protecting its head with its forelimbs. It may tilt its shell so that its dorsum is facing a would-be attacker. The desert tortoise seldom bites, but may release bladder water on a handler. The urine may be distasteful to a potential predator; Patterson (1971a) reported it puckered the mouth of a kit fox. If near a burrow the tortoise will quickly retreat underground if disturbed.

Barrett and Humphrey (1986) observed two agonistic interactions between adult female desert tortoises and Gila monsters that appeared to be digging for eggs at the entrance of tortoise dens. The females rushed, rammed, nipped at, and finally drove away the lizards. These behaviors may have been cases of nest defense against egg predators.

Hatchlings differ radically from adults in their disposition; they are very pugnacious—advancing, hissing, and biting when touched; adults are quite docile (Grant, 1936b; Booth, 1958) .

POPULATIONS: Woodbury and Hardy (1948) found approximately 300 *Gopherus agassizii* in about 486 hectares in Utah (0.62/ha; biomass, 2.05 kg/ha; Iverson, 1982a). Of the 281 tortoises they studied, 101 were males, 151 were females, 10 were of indeterminate sex but were thought to be equally divided between males and females, and the sex of the remainder was unrecorded. They estimated that young tortoises made up less than 5% of the population and that the average annual mortality was 1–5%.

More recent studies of 27 desert tortoise populations in southern California have yielded density estimates. Berry (1986a) reported that eight had estimated densities of eight or fewer tortoises/km², six had 8–39/km², and 13 sites supported 42–184 tortoises/km². Most sites had about equal numbers of nonadults (less than 208 mm in carapace length) and adults (208 mm or longer). Only samples from four of 18 populations analyzed suggested sex ratios differing significantly from equality. California populations studied by Barrow (1979) had densities of 0.29–0.31 tortoises per hectare (biomasses, 0.59–0.64 kg/ha; Iverson, 1982a). Other density estimates reported for southern California populations were given in Bickett (1980), Schneider (1980), Luckenbach (1982), and Berry et al. (1983).

Population estimates can vary depending on what method is used. Schneider (1980) calculated the density of a California population using three capture/recapture methods. The Lincoln Index gave density estimates of 80–124 tortoises/km², the Schnabel Method, 75–93/km², and the Stratified Lincoln Index estimates, as high as 174 tortoises/km².

Four populations (two from southern California,

and one each from Nevada and Utah) had similar values for size or age classes: 42–58% adults, 14–17% subadults, 18–33% juveniles, 5–10% very small tortoises, and only 1–2% hatchlings (Berry, 1976).

The annual adult mortality rate is probably about 5% (Luckenbach, 1982), but during very extended dry periods may rise to over 18% (Turner et al., 1984). Survivorship of adults is about 88% per year (Turner et al., 1984). An apparent high rate of mortality at the Piute Valley in southern Nevada between 1979 and 1983 significantly decreased the mean carapace length and average age of the tortoise population by 1983, but not its density (Germano and Joyner, 1988). By 1987, average size and age of the population had increased and the density remained stable. Annual mortality rate for hatchlings to 14-year-old juveniles was 14.5% between 1979 and 1983, while those of 15–25-year-old tortoises and adults older than 25 years were 24.7% and 19.5%, respectively. From 1983 to 1987 the annual mortality rates for the three groups were 6.1%, 9.3%, and 10.3%, respectively. During both periods the lower juvenile mortality rate insured repopulation.

Another important protected population of *G. agassizii* at the Desert Tortoise Natural Area, Kern County, California, has declined since the 1970s, from 149 tortoises\km^2 to 75 tortoises\km^2 in 1989 (Berry, 1991). Some of this mortality was due to Upper Respiratory Tract Disease and raven predation on juveniles.

REMARKS: The range of the desert tortoise has been severely restricted, and today the species is listed as threatened under the Endangered Species Act in all states in which it occurs except Arizona. Mojave Desert populations north and west of the Colorado River were listed by the U.S. Fish and Wildlife Service as threatened in April 1990.

Large areas of desert tortoise habitat in the Mojave Desert have been negatively affected by urbanization, off-road vehicle use, overgrazing of domestic livestock, agriculture, construction of roads and utility corridors, and military training activities. Secondary contributions to degradation include the proliferation of exotic plant species and a higher frequency of human-caused fire. Effects of these impacts include alteration or destruction of macro- and micro-vegetation elements, establishment of disclimax plant communities, destruction of soil stabilizers, soil compaction, erosion, and pollution (Lovich, 1993).

Off-road vehicle (ORV) use is one of the most widespread and destructive human activities to desert habitat (Webb and Wilshire, 1983), and tortoise populations have declined significantly in some areas of ORV use (Luckenbach, 1982). Vehicle use may contribute to declines of tortoise populations directly by crushing individuals (above or below ground), or by collapsing burrows. Vehicle activity may also destroy vegetation used by tortoises for food or cover, making habitat unsuitable for sustaining their populations.

Livestock may compete for food plants with desert tortoises, and livestock grazing possibly reduces tortoise populations (Berry, 1978; Coombs, 1979). Certain key tortoise food plants may constitute over 40% of the cattle diet, and, as cattle are larger and more mobile than tortoises, these plants may be severely depleted with heavy grazing. However, Bostick (1990) argued (based largely on circumstantial evidence and speculation) that the highest tortoise densities historically occurred at a time when livestock overgrazing was at its peak level, and that the fewer the cattle on a range, the smaller the population of resident tortoises present.

Disease has contributed to declines of some desert tortoise populations. Wild and captive desert tortoises are afflicted with Upper Respiratory Tract Disease (URTD) in many areas within the geographic range. Jacobson et al. (1991) isolated a species of *Mycoplasma*, a small bacterium lacking a cell wall, as a potential pathogen causing URTD. Introductions of infected captive tortoises into the desert may have caused the spread of this potentially lethal disease in wild tortoise populations.

Tortoise relocations may or may not be successful (Berry, 1986a). Wild populations contain dominance hierarchies, and to become established in areas where wild tortoises exist, released *G. agassizii* must displace residents, thus disrupting the local social structure. Failing in this, a newly released tortoise may be driven out by local residents. Relocated tortoises may settle at release sites, travel in straight lines (Type II navigation), or disperse for distances over 6 km; therefore, areas to be restocked should be at least 14 km in diameter (Berry, 1986a).

The four species of *Gopherus* contain an os transiliens, a small sesamoid bone in the central raphe of the external adductor muscle, found in no other Recent tortoises (Patterson, 1973a; Bramble, 1974a), that seems to be an adaption for feeding on coarse xerophytic vegetation.

For further information and lists of references on *G. agassizii*, see Douglas (1975, 1977a), Auffenberg and Franz (1978b), the *Proceedings of the Desert Tortoise Council,* and the proceedings of a workshop on the management of the desert tortoise in California published in 1986 in the journal *Herpetologica* (42:56–138).

Gopherus berlandieri (Agassiz, 1857)
Texas tortoise
PLATE 56

RECOGNITION: The Texas tortoise is a small to medium-sized terrestrial turtle having elephantine hind feet, shovellike forefeet, and a gular projection on the plastron. Its short, oblong, keelless carapace (to 22.8 cm) has the highest point posterior to the middle and drops off sharply to a serrated rear rim. It has a somewhat rough, ridged appearance, caused by the commonly well-marked growth rings. The carapace is brown, and the scutes may have yellow centers in young individuals. The marginals above the hind limbs are flared. The bridge is well developed and commonly has two axillary scutes. The hingeless, yellowish plastron is large, and the gular scutes are elongated and project anteriorly, and may bend upward. Limbs, neck, and head are yellowish to brown. The head is wedge shaped, and the snout is somewhat pointed. The angle between the upper crushing ridges is commonly more than 65° but less than 70°. Well-developed mental glands are present beneath the rami of the lower jaw, and two to four rostral pores lie on the internarial region (Winokur and Legler, 1974, 1975). The iris often is greenish yellow. The forefeet are large and shovellike and have thick, blunt claws; the hind feet are large and flat. The distance from the base of the first claw to the base of the fourth claw on the forefoot approximately equals the same measurement on the hindfoot. The toes are not webbed.

Males have slightly longer and narrower carapaces than females, a longer and more deeply forked gular projection, a concave plastron, a longer tail, and larger, more complex mental glands.

KARYOTYPE: As in *Gopherus agassizii* (see for details).

FOSSIL RECORD: No fossil remains have been assigned to this species; however, the Pleistocene fossil species *Gopherus hexagonata*, which seems closer

to *G. polyphemus,* has been found in southeastern Texas (Auffenberg and Franz, 1978c). Its relationship to *G. berlandieri* needs further study.

DISTRIBUTION: *Gopherus berlandieri* occurs from Texas south of Del Rio and San Antonio through eastern Coahuila, Nuevo León, and Tamaulipas to northeastern San Luis Potosí, Mexico.

GEOGRAPHIC VARIATION: No subspecies have been described, but populations differ in carapace length (Rose and Judd, 1982).

CONFUSING SPECIES: Within the Texas tortoise's range, *Terrapene ornata* is the only other turtle that habitually lives on land; it has a hinged plastron and lacks a gular projection.

HABITAT: *Gopherus berlandieri* is found in habitats ranging from near-desert in Mexico to scrub forests in humid and subtropical parts of southern Texas. Sandy, well-drained soils are preferred, and open scrub woods seem to be particularly favored. In southern Texas the tortoise occurs from sea level to 100 or 200 m, but in Tamaulipas it ranges to 884 m.

Unlike the other two *Gopherus* in the United States, *G. berlandieri* usually does not dig an extensive burrow. Instead, it uses its gular projection, forelimbs, and the lateral edges of the shell to push away the surface debris and soil to create a resting place, to which it often returns. This so-called pallet normally is located under a bush or the edge of a clump of cactus and is simply a ramp sloping just steeply enough to accommodate the anterior edge of the shell below the surface. Usually several separate pallets occur within a tortoise's home range. Continued use of a pallet, together with the clearing away of accumulated soil and debris, tends to deepen it; the deepest found by Auffenberg and Weaver (1969) was 10 cm at its

Gopherus berlandieri

Plastron of *Gopherus berlandieri*

anterior end and 33 cm long. Use of pallets is seasonal. Pallets in thick brush near Brownsville, Texas, are used throughout the year, but in summer proportionately more tortoises are found in pallets in such places. In winter a greater proportion of tortoises occupy pallets in open brush or in grassland.

Texas tortoises sometimes live in empty mammal burrows of suitable size, and occasionally will excavate burrows as much as 1.2 m long and 30 cm deep. Where digging is difficult *G. berlandieri* excavates

barely enough to hide itself or else takes shelter beneath rocks, stumps, or debris.

Auffenberg and Weaver (1969) thought that the factors governing the kind and use of shelters by all three species of *Gopherus* were the extent of seasonal surface-temperature extremes and the composition of the substrate.

BEHAVIOR: Weather permitting, *Gopherus berlandieri* may be active in all months, although less so

Distribution of *Gopherus berlandieri*

during the hottest and coldest months. However, Rose and Judd (1975) found none above ground near Port Isabel, Texas, from December to February, even on days with suitable air temperatures, so some populations may hibernate. Possibly some fats are put on for energy and insolation, but the amount is relatively low; Rose (1980) reported that the total lipid index of *G. berlandieri* is only 0.04. Carr (1952) reported that in Tamaulipas in December, Texas tortoises go into a state of semihibernation during periods of chilly weather. Because the soils there are too heavy for effective burrowing, they passively await warmer temperatures, often with no more than half the shell under cover.

The two principle daily activity periods are in the morning and the afternoon. At the Laguna Atascosa National Wildlife Refuge, tortoises are active in April and early May from 0900 to 1959, with the primary peak in midmorning (Bury and Smith, 1986). From 0900 to 0959, tortoises become active, peak activity is from 1000 to 1059, and then activity declines for the next two hours. Few are active from 1300 to 1700. Finally, a secondary peak of activity takes place from 1700 to 1959. Auffenberg and Weaver (1969) reported that the greatest activity in April is at midday, but as the season progresses, two periods become better defined. By July most tortoises are active in the late afternoon (1500 to 1600), but by November, midday movements again become more common at the expense of the morning and late afternoon excursions. There are no apparent differences in the activity period with respect to size or sex. In May, Texas tortoises are active from 0930 to 1830 with peaks from 1030 to 1230 and 1530 to 1730; fewer tortoises are active during the morning than in the afternoon (Rose and Judd, 1975). The two activity periods are related to avoidance of high midday temperatures, particularly increases in substrate temperature (Rose and Judd, 1975; Bury and Smith, 1986).

Some estivation may occur in the summer. Voigt and Johnson (1976) noted curtailed activity during the hottest days at Laguna Atascosa. Tortoises retreated into the shade of dense grass clumps or under clumps of *Opuntia* cacti. Estivating tortoises maintained lower average body temperatures than active individuals. Fasting during estivation results in metabolic changes. After 80 days of fasting, liver glucose and glycogen drop to 33% and 5% of the active feeding values (Horne and Findeisen, 1977). As carbohydrate reserves are depleted, ureogenesis increases, as shown by a rise in blood urea (56 to 363 mg/100 ml) and urine (229 to 600 mg/100 ml), but changes in uric acid are insignificant.

Before emerging, *G. berlandieri* spends a prolonged "warm-up" period inside its pallet (Voigt and Johnson, 1976). It does not emerge until body temperature rises higher than 28°C. The Texas tortoises do not bask long; in its natural habitat, prolonged exposure to the direct rays of the sun is fatal. Grant (1960a) reported that a healthy male exposed to direct sunlight died in 20 minutes while several others, kept in the shade at 39.4°C, were not affected. Hutchison et al. (1966) reported that four tortoises lost righting response at mean 40.4°C (39.8–40.7) and that the mean critical thermal maximum was 42.85°C (42.5–43.2). Two active *G. berlandieri* had mean body temperatures of 32.2 and 33.1°C (Voigt and Johnson, 1976). Active tortoises monitored by Judd and Rose (1977) had temperatures of 24.1–39°C, but 91% of these fell between 30 and 35°C. There is a significant positive correlation between air temperature and body temperature of active tortoises and between substrate temperature and body temperature of inactive individuals. Mean body temperature of *G. berlandieri* active in spring (31.1°C) was significantly lower than that of individuals active during the summer (33.1°C). In the laboratory, heat stress began at 37.5°C, but the critical thermal maximum was near 43.7°C. Nine hibernating tortoises found in winter by Judd and Rose (1977) had a mean body temperature of 9.9°C (6.5–18.5).

Gopherus berlandieri heats significantly faster than it cools (Voigt and Johnson, 1977). Withdrawal of the head greatly affects the head-body temperature relationship. When the head is exposed it heats and cools faster than the body; when withdrawn, slower. When tucked under the shell, the head gains additional insulation. Head temperature probably plays a major role in the determination of daily activity.

In semiarid country *G. berlandieri* may not have access to free water for long periods. Like other species of *Gopherus* it has adapted to this lack by reabsorbing water through the bladder and excreting nitrogenous wastes as semisolids. Baze and Horne (1970) found that in freshly collected *G. berlandieri*, ammonia is most concentrated in the blood and uric acid is highest in the urine (the liver mitochondria of *G. berlandieri* contain several enzymes which are used to detoxify ammonia; Campbell et al., 1985). The rise in osmotic concentration associated with high levels of urea in dehydrated *Gopherus* may be important in reducing evaporative water loss during hibernation or other times of stress; this is especially critical to tortoises living in arid or semiarid habitats. The integument of *Gopherus* is relatively impermeable by comparison with that of other turtles; this, too, is important in water conservation. In many localities the most important, and sometimes the only, water available to *G. berlandieri* is that which it extracts metabolically from its food.

Olson (1976, 1987, 1989) studied body water loss in *G. berlandieri* during summer activity (without the benefit of cover), and winter dormancy (at 5–10°C and 20–25°C, without burrowing). During the summer, water (weight) loss in g/24 hours was 0.78% for a 120-g individual and 0.03% for a 2.15-kg tortoise; water (weight) loss was generally inversely related to body weight. Percentages of water (weight) loss for 24 hours for winter dormant tortoises kept at 20–25°C ranged from 0.014% to 0.13%, and for those kept at 5–10°C, 0.003 to 0.06%.

Auffenberg and Weaver (1969) found that the cumulative average yearly movement for males more than 150 mm in length was 98.6 m for one year, 153 m for two years, and 130 m for three years. Males under 150 mm had average movements of 30 m, 149.1 m, and 178 m for one, two, and three years, respectively. The cumulative average for females over 150 mm in length was 94.1 m for one year, 92.4 m for two years, and 164.1 m for three years; those under 150 mm had movements of 93.7 m, 162 m, and 302 m for the same time periods. The average maximum distance traveled per day was 20.6 m (5.2–52.5). The tracks made by four *G. berlandieri* in a single day across wind-blown silt measured 46 m, 161 m, 142 m, and 480 m. The mean distance of daily movement for three years was 267 m. Daily movements indicated that the tortoises, although nomadic, maintained restricted home ranges for short periods of time.

Gopherus berlandieri occupies a defined home range (Judd and Rose, 1983; Rose and Judd, 1975). Mean distances moved between captures reported by Judd and Rose (1983) and Rose and Judd (1975) were 56.7 m for males, 42 m for females, and 41.3 m for juveniles; mean home ranges were 2.38 ha for males and 1.4 ha for females. After five years of study, the estimation of home range area had changed little; males, 2.57 ha, females, 1.42 ha (Judd and Rose, 1983). The close association between *G. berlandieri* and *Opuntia* cacti may limit the home range needed to fulfill dietary demands.

Hamilton (1944) reported an apparent migration of *G. berlandieri* just after the cessation of torrential rains near Corpus Christi Lake, Texas. Sixteen solitary tortoises were counted on a road in about 4.8 km, and at least as many more were observed beside the road. Most were headed generally east, away from the lake, but the directions varied from NNE to SSE. They were moving as individuals, not as any sort of group.

Grant (1936b) also reported a migration of these tortoises in southern Texas but did not give details.

In a test of homing ability, Auffenberg and Weaver (1969) released *G. berlandieri* at various distances from the pallets in which they found them and traced their movements for 36 hours. One individual removed 77.6 m to the east returned to its pallet and another removed 42.5 m to the east was 20.7 m from its pallet at the end of the test. The distance and direction removed and final distance from the pallet of three other tortoises were: 31 m S, 31.0 m; 49.6 m WSW, 27.9 m; and 100.1 m SSE, 37.2 m. Of 11 tortoises released on flats at distances of 49.6 to 108.5 m from their homes on bushy lomas (broad-topped hills) only four returned.

Visual or olfactory cues are probably used in homing (Auffenberg and Weaver, 1969). That local features may aid the turtle in remaining on the home range is suggested by the movements of the tortoises released on the featureless flats: they showed no consistent ability to reach the loma from release points 50 and 125 m distant from its edge. Tortoises apparently avoid wandering onto the flats; there is no evidence that tortoises regularly cross them from one loma to another, or that they even make short forays onto the flats from a home loma.

As in other terrestrial tortoises, *G. berlandieri* responds to a steep bank by avoidance of the deep drop. The perception of depth when used in conjunction with forelimb tactile sensing may be related to avoidance of falling (Patterson, 1971c).

Males often engage in combat before the breeding season, but the frequency of fighting declines sharply before the breeding season ends. Weaver (1970) saw combat between captive males (in an outdoor pen in Gainesville, Florida) as early as 12 March and in the field as late as July. In confrontations where neither male is subordinate, both engage in ramming and biting, and each attempts to overturn the other with his gular projections. Dominance is apparently established when one overturns the other or when one flees the combat ground after a ramming and pushing contest. Evidence of the combat often remains on the ground in the form of a circle within which the soil has been tamped down by the feet and plastra of the combatants. At the end of combat the victorious male holds his head higher than that of the defeated male. If combat ends with one tortoise fleeing, the loser retreats with his head extended directly forward and the winner pursues with his head inclined upward about 30°.

When only one of the two males is aggressive, the combat takes a different form. The aggressive tortoise rams and bites the other on the front feet, head, and shell in a series of movements similar to those of courtship. The unaggressive male tries to avoid him by pivoting about. The aggression ends when the shy male escapes to a pallet or withdraws his head and limbs and remains still (Weaver, 1970).

Male combat bouts have also been observed in the wild (Rose and Judd, 1982). Of 32 encounters, 24 involved only one aggressive individual. One of these lasted 38 minutes, with the aggressive smaller male repeatedly attempting to mount the other.

The function of these bouts is unknown, as the advantage gained is not clear. At times males may walk closely by other males with no notice. Other meetings immediately spur combat, and the vanquished of one bout may be the aggressive victor in a later encounter.

REPRODUCTION: Auffenberg and Weaver (1969) found that secondary sex characters are clearly evident only in individuals larger than 105 mm in carapace length, but Judd and Rose (1989) reported secondary sexual characters were not evident in tortoises less than 125 mm long.

Sexual maturity is apparently attained at a carapace length of 125 mm or more when three to five years of age. Females 145–150 mm examined by Rose and Judd (1982) were immature but those 155–165 mm long contained shelled eggs.

Chromatographic analyses of chin-gland secretions of adult male *Gopherus berlandieri* by Rose (1970) revealed the presence of nine fatty acids, and behavioral analyses he conducted indicate that these served as an olfactory cue during courtship or combat.

The mating season in Texas lasts from June to September. Weaver (1970), who studied reproductive activities in the wild and in captivity, divided the precopulatory behavior into four stages. Stage one is a relatively passive phase during which the female shows little active response to the male's presence but modulates his behavior (in later stages her behavior is modulated by the male's). Courtship behavior begins with the male trailing a female. Initially he walks 1–3 m behind her, stops whenever she stops, and often bobs his head in her direction. During the early part of the trailing stage the male usually walks with his neck only partly extended. During this initial stage of courtship the female's behavioral role is largely one of indifference and she does not bob her head at any time. She normally grazes and noses at various items on the ground, displaying the same movements and activity as lone, unattended females. Occasionally she makes one or more stops in the shade, during which the male seems to lose interest and may even graze. When she resumes walking the male continues his trailing. These shade stops may be temperature-regulating behavior. Late in the trailing stage, which may last from a few minutes to nearly an hour, the male shortens the distance between himself and the female. When he is about a meter directly behind her he increases the frequency and vigor of head bobbing and when not bobbing holds his head parallel to the ground in a high, arched position, his neck inclined between 25° and 35°. At this point the female increases her walking speed, and ceases all grazing. This shift in the female's behavior marks the end of the first stage.

The second stage of courtship is more intense than the first and begins when the male tries to overtake the female and confront her face to face. On overtaking the female he stops her by biting her head, front feet, and the top front edge of her carapace, and ramming her forcibly with his massive, elongate gular projection. She at first avoids him by turning away from him so that both tortoises move in a circular path of constantly diminishing diameter. As the male increases the intensity of his biting and ramming, the female finally withdraws her head and front legs but continues to pivot her anterior end away from his by driving with her rear feet. With his increased biting tempo, the male's head bobbing stops or loses any recognizable pattern, and he increasingly confines his biting to the female's cervical and anterior marginal scutes. His bites now become quite forceful; he often grasps the female's shell in his mouth and alternately pushes and pulls her. She soon withdraws her head and front feet, leaving her rear feet extended so she is in an incline with the rear of her shell raised. She no longer pivots, and the male attempts to mount her. The stimulus for mounting seems to be the female's inclined position. Observations Walter Auffenberg made near Laredo, Texas, suggest that the female selects the place where this second stage and the subsequent stages occur, usually one relatively free of underbrush.

In the third stage, the male may try to mount from any place on the female's shell. If the initial attempts occur at other than the rear of the female's shell, he works his way posteriorly with his front feet on the dorsal surface of her carapace and his rear feet on the ground.

Coitus occurs in the fourth stage. None of the unions observed by Weaver (1970) lasted 10 minutes and all were terminated when the female walked out from under the male. Housholder (1950) reported that a female *G. berlandieri* (which he thought was a female *G. agassizii*) everted part of her cloaca, apparently to facilitate intromission by the male. This occurs in female *G. polyphemus,* but Weaver did not witness it in courtships by *G. berlandieri*. Each thrust by the male during copulation pushes the female forward. To compensate for her change of position the male performs a series of hopping steps with his rear feet. Occasionally his rear legs become tangled in grass, which impedes his hop-stepping and interrupts copulation. Thus the female's selection of a relatively clear area helps ensure successful coition.

The oviducts of *G. berlandieri* contain tubules capable of storing sperm (Gist and Jones, 1989), so possibly sperm from one mating may be used to fertilize several later clutches.

The length of the nesting season has not been determined. Most observed nestings have been in June or July, but Rose and Judd (1982) found a fresh nest on 29 April and Judd and McQueen (1980) discovered an egg that had been laid on the ground on 4 August. Auffenberg and Weaver (1969) found small holes that appeared to be trial nest sites in late April and in August. They also found shelled eggs in a female accidentally killed in November, and freshly caught females sacrificed in the laboratory contained shelled eggs as late as 16 September and ovarian eggs larger than 10 mm in diameter as late as November. Shelled eggs have been found in the oviducts as early as April and eggs 10 mm or larger as early as March. Ovarian eggs were present in sacrificed females in March and April and again in September, October, and November. Two mature females sacrificed in June and July had no ovarian eggs. These data, which are supported by field observations, suggest two periods of egg laying in Texas: one in late June and July, the other in late August and September. However, a more recent study of female reproduction by Judd and Rose (1989) has showed that egg production begins in April and ends in July, but eggs were found on the ground under prickly pear on 10 and 31 July. About a third of the females radiographed 20–30 April had eggs, and about half had eggs in May and June. No evidence was found that females produced more than one clutch each season. Females apparently retained shelled eggs for up to 39 days, and portioned the ovipositing of their single clutch in time and space. Approximately 33% of the females did not produce a clutch each year.

Soil texture, soil moisture, and orientation with respect to the sun influence the choice of nest site (Auffenberg and Weaver, 1969). Field data permit some generalizations as to nest sites. The nest normally is dug in soil relatively free of vegetation, usually under or near the drip zone of bushes, but no correlation is evident between the chosen site and the shade pattern of the bushes, even though Vermersch (1992) reported nests are usually dug beneath the cover of an overhanging bush. A positive correlation does exist between density of nest sites and density of tortoises. Females use no special nesting grounds. Nests are usually found in small clusters, and there is considerable distance between clusters regardless of tortoise density. Nests are often found near, and even in, the same spot under a particular bush in successive years.

Auffenberg and Weaver (1969) observed the nesting of a captive. At 0745 she scraped the bare floor of the pallet occupied the previous night, using her gular projection as a scoop. Starting at the pallet's shallow end, she pushed a small amount of dirt before her to the deep end. At that end of the pallet, and with her plastron still in contact with the ground, she twisted her shell from side to side so as to shift the loose dirt laterally. She then used her front feet alternately to push the dirt either outside the pallet or onto her carapace. She then backed up to her original starting position, at the shallow end of the pallet, and repeated the sequence. In 30 minutes she deepened the pallet's far end about 12.5 mm, then turned in the pallet to face in the opposite direction, and, with the rear portion of her shell in the deep end, started to dig the nest hole with her hind limbs. Alternately, she placed each hind leg medially under the plastron; as she drew the leg back to its normal position the outer edge of the plantar surface picked up a small amount of dirt and deposited it forward and to the side. After repeating the scraping movement two to four times she shifted the rear of her shell in the direction of the leg last used, thus bringing the opposite leg over the nest. By 0900 she was removing less dirt with each stroke: the hole was now so deep that she had to draw each foot vertically to the surface, which meant that she could bring up less soil; furthermore, the soil became increasingly hard with depth. The hardness she partly overcame by urinating into the cavity. Bladder release seemed correlated with digging activity, for she dug more rapidly immediately after urinating, and at the increased tempo she removed considerably more earth (since the soil was moistened, it stuck better to the edge of her foot). As the soil again became dry the digging tempo decreased.

The nest is somewhat flask shaped, the opening not as wide as the chamber below. Auffenberg and Weaver (1969) gave the measurements of two nests: greatest depth 64 mm and 50 mm; greatest width 64 mm and 70 mm; and diameter of the opening 38 mm and 44 mm, respectively. Vermersch (1992) reported that the egg chamber was usually about 60 mm deep, and Sabath (1960) reported a nest 44 mm in diameter and 76 mm deep.

The number of eggs per clutch usually ranges from one to three. Of 60 nests examined by Auffenberg and Weaver (1969), 38 contained one egg each, 19 contained two eggs each, and three had three eggs each. Judd and Rose (1989) found that clutch size varied from one to five eggs, but averaged about 2.65 eggs per clutch; previously, however, they had reported finding females with as many as seven large ovarian eggs with 21.0–30.5-mm diameters (Rose and Judd, 1982).

Grant (1960a) reported that a captive female laid three eggs in a nest on 8 June and deposited single eggs on the surface on 19 June and on 9 and 13 July. Auffenberg and Weaver (1969) thought that under normal conditions this female probably would have made at least two nests. Judd and Rose (1989) reported that the typical nest could only accommodate two eggs.

The elongate, white, hardened eggs have granular surfaces and are 40.0–53.7 mm in length, and 29.0–34.1 mm in width. The average width/length ratio of nine eggs measured by Auffenberg and Weaver (1969) was 0.71 (0.61–0.80) to one, and the same ratio of six eggs measured by Grant (1960a) was 0.73 (0.66–0.82) to one.

The eggs of *G. berlandieri* must be flexible to be laid (Grant, 1960a; Paxson, 1962). Measurements of eggs and of the maximum space between the posterior carapacial and plastral rims shows that a firm (hardened) egg could not possibly be expelled from the body. The pelvic girdle opening is enlarged (45 × 39 mm) to allow passage of the eggs (Long and Rose, 1989). The xiphiplastra are not sutured to the hypoplastra (except in extreme lateral aspect), and the xiphiplastral-hypoplastral connections serve as hinges to lower the xiphiplastra during oviposition, while the posterior carapace is forced upward, allowing more freedom for egg passage (Rose and Judd, 1991).

Thirteen eggs artificially incubated by Judd and McQueen (1980) hatched in 88–118 days (mean 105 days); hatching success was 60.6%, and the young emerged from 27 August to 5 November.

Hatchlings are nearly round, about 40–50 mm in both length and width, and weigh 20–22 g. The umbilical scar disappears at about 50 mm. Pigmented areas of the hatchling shell are brown, unpigmented areas are creamy white. The unpigmented areas are restricted to the posterior edge of the anterior marginals, to the free edges of the lateral and posterior marginals, and to the center of each pleural and vertebral scute. On the plastron, pigment is restricted to the seam areas except on the femoral scutes, where pigment covers all but the free lateral edges. The head has a yellowish stripe extending from below the anterior corner of the eye to the angle of the jaw. The tympanic region is unpigmented. There is a faint, yellowish patch and a small unpigmented spot around the egg tooth and both nostrils. The throat and chin are creamy white, with a dark spot at the mandibular symphysis. The horny mandibles are dark; the remainder of the head is brown. Scales at the base of the forefeet and the hind feet are black, and the dark scales on the hind feet continue around the side of the heel and up the leg for a short distance; the remainder of the hind leg is creamy white except for yellowish thigh scales. The dorsal tail surface is grayish. The outer brachial scales are black, those of the middle anterior portion of the forelimb have light yellowish centers, and those of the inner edge are creamy white. The scales of the posterior brachial surface are dark dorsally and lighter below, the sharp differentiation occurring just above the elbow. The gular scute is greatly projected. Laminal spurs and marginal denticulations are absent (Auffenberg and Weaver, 1969).

Hybridization between *G. berlandieri* and *G. agassizii* has occurred in captivity (Mertens, 1956).

GROWTH AND LONGEVITY: Auffenberg and Weaver (1969) found that at one year of age *Gopherus berlandieri* is 70–81 mm in length; the mean increase in length during the first year is 50.3%. When three to five years old they are 105–128 mm in length, and they are about 130 mm long in their sixth year. After the sixth year the growth rate slows markedly and remains more or less constant, at approximately 5%/yr. The maximum number of major growth rings counted by Auffenberg and Weaver in any individual was 18 (at 201 mm), but the number could not be counted accurately in most tortoises that were more than 180 mm long. The average absolute growth of males was 7.9 mm per year and 12.5 mm for two years, of females 11.1 mm per year and 18.9 mm for two years; this suggests that females grow faster than males.

Hatchlings studied by Judd and McQueen (1980) grew until about the first of November, after which growth ceased during the winter. Growth resumed in March and continued through the summer. The most rapid increases were in weight followed by carapace length, plastron length, carapace width, and shell height, respectively. Olson (1976) reported the following estimated ages for weight ranges in *G. berlandieri*:

200 g, six years; 500 g, nine years; 860 g, 10 years; and 875 g, 11 years.

Adults of both sexes have lived for 52 years in captivity (Judd and McQueen, 1982).

FOOD HABITS: Wild Texas tortoises seem to prefer the stems, fruits, and flowers of *Opuntia* cacti (Rose and Judd, 1982); grasses, violets, asters, and other plants also are eaten. When a tortoise eats stems, leaves, or fruits, the item is rarely eaten at one time, and older parts are often too tough to be consumed in large quantities. Water content of cacti stems ranges from 90.8–92.2% in old plants to 93.7–94.9% in younger plants; the water content of *Opuntia* fruits is about 84.5% (Rose and Judd, 1982). The pH of *Opuntia* stems is low (3.5–4.8), and it is not known how the tortoise metabolizes the organic acids. Baze and Horne (1970) have found very high ammonia levels in *Gopherus berlandieri*, and it may be the excess acids in its diet that cause the release of ammonia.

In addition to plant remains, a crayfish claw, landsnail shells, and a few fragments of beetles have been recovered from feces. Auffenberg and Weaver (1969) observed individuals feeding on the feces of other tortoises and of rabbits, and they also saw them biting the bleached bones of cows and rabbits, and Mares (1971) saw them feeding on the plant remains embedded in peccary feces. Captives eat romaine lettuce, tomatoes, shaved carrots, grass, clover, apples, and bananas; some captives occasionally eat raw meat.

Several studies (Grant 1960a; Auffenberg, 1969; Auffenberg and Weaver, 1969) have shown that Texas tortoises prefer red and green foods over blue. They prefer green in spring and shift to red in August and September. This matches natural color changes, as the red fruits of *Opuntia* mature at that time.

PREDATORS AND DEFENSE: Skunks (*Mephitis, Spilogale*), raccoons (*Procyon*), and possibly the woodrat (*Neotoma micropus*) prey on the eggs of the Texas tortoise. The young are eaten by almost any predator that encounters them: foxes (*Urocyon, Vulpes*), coyotes (*Canis*), skunks (*Mephitis, Spilogale*), bobcats (*Lynx*), raccoons (*Procyon*), and various snakes. Coyotes and bobcats may prey on adults, but predation pressure on adults is surely low. Tortoises are sometimes parasitized by flesh flies which may seriously weaken them (Neck, 1977).

Collection for the pet trade has removed adults from some populations, thus reducing the available gene pool, but *Gopherus berlandieri* is now protected by strict Texas laws. Unfortunately many are still crushed by automobiles, and a few uninformed ranchers kill them because of a mistaken belief that they eat quail eggs.

When disturbed *G. berlandieri* pulls its head and limbs under its shell, protecting its head with its forelimbs. If tapped on one side of the body, the tortoise will tilt that side of the shell downward while elevating the opposite side with its legs. If handled, some wild individuals may void their bladders, but this happens only rarely.

POPULATIONS: Auffenberg and Weaver (1969) reported the following parameters for three populations in southeast Texas: Loma Tio Alejos, 27.7% adult males, 57.6% adult females, and 14.7% subadults; Port Isabel Loma, 46.6% adult males and 53.4% adult females; and Mesa del Gavilon, 20% adult males, 40% adult females and 40% subadults. On Loma Tio Alejos the minimum overall density was 1/430 m², but densities in the major plant associations differed widely, as follows: in brush, 1/82 m², in the *Baccharis* zone, 1/300 m², in grass and cactus, 1/1,231 m², and in the clay zone, 1/1,575 m². In the open, drier brush of Falcon Dam State Park, Starr County, Texas, the density was about 1/42,000 m². Iverson (1982a) estimated the biomass of a typical population to be 54.5 kg/ha.

At Cameron County, Texas, Judd and Rose (1983) estimated the population size for *Gopherus berlandieri* to be approximately 71–72 animals per 3.3 ha, or a density of 15–16/ha. A total of 102 tortoises were marked (43 males, 30 females, 26 juveniles, and 3 unsexed adults). The male to female ratio of 1.4:1 was not significantly different from equality. Juveniles composed 9–27% of the population over the five-year study.

Bury and Smith (1986) located 107 (106 adults) tortoises on about 3 ha of dirt roads and adjacent areas at the Laguna Atascos National Wildlife Refuge in extreme southwestern Texas. The overall sex ratio was 1.72:1 (67 males: 39 females).

Gopherus berlandieri has been given legal protection by the state of Texas.

REMARKS: Although most human activities are harmful to *Gopherus berlandieri,* Auffenberg and Weaver (1969) have pointed out that several human activities, notably managed grazing, favor them. The most dramatic and long-range effects can be seen where brush control is practiced. This practice initially kills many tortoises but in the long run increases grass production; under current practices, the scattered brush cover the tortoises need reappears very quickly. If the area is grazed by cattle, it is maintained in a dynamic equilibrium in which tortoises can maintain their minimum densities over long periods of time. Slight overgrazing under these conditions encourages the growth of prickly pear (*Opuntia*), one of the staple foods of *G. berlandieri* when grasses become dry in the summer.

Auffenberg and Franz (1978c) have compiled the latest literature summary on this species.

Gopherus polyphemus (Daudin, 1802)
Gopher tortoise
PLATE 57

RECOGNITION: This large terrestrial turtle of the southeastern United States has elephantine hind feet, shovellike forefeet, and a gular projection on the plastron. The keelless, oblong carapace (to 38.1 cm) is widest in front of the bridge and commonly highest in the sacral region; in a few individuals the carapace is somewhat constricted behind the bridge. It drops off abruptly to the rear, and the posterior marginals are only slightly serrated. The growth rings (annuli) are usually well marked in juveniles and young adults, and give the dark-brown to grayish-black carapace a somewhat rough, ridged appearance, but most older adults have smooth carapaces. Juvenile scutes often have light centers. The bridge is well developed and commonly has a single axillary scute. The gular scutes of the large, hingeless, yellowish plastron are elongated, project anteriorly, and may curve upward. Skin of the head and limbs is grayish black, that of the limb sockets yellowish. The head is large and rounded, with an angle between the upper crushing ridges of 73° or more. Well-developed mental glands lie beneath the chin, and four to six rostral pores lie on the internarial region (Winokur and Legler, 1974, 1975). The iris is dark brown. The hind feet are relatively small; the distance from the base of the first claw to the base of the third claw on the forefoot approximately equals the distance from the base of the first claw to the base of the fourth claw on the hind foot. The toes are not webbed.

Males have more concave plastra and larger mental glands under the chin than females. McRae et al. (1981a) found that the shell dimensions and anal notch were significantly larger in adult females than in adult males, but the degree of plastral concavity width between the posterior points of the anal scutes, thickness of the anal scutes, and length of the gular projections were significantly greater in males. These dimorphic characters are best observed in older individuals.

KARYOTYPE: The diploid chromosome number is 52 (26 macrochromosomes, 26 microchromosomes): 20 metacentric and submetacentric, 10 subtelocentric, and 22 acrocentric and telocentric chromosomes (Stock, 1972; Dowler and Bickham, 1982). Little karyotypical variation occurs within the genus *Gopherus* (Dowler and Bickham, 1982).

FOSSIL RECORD: Many Pleistocene fossils of *Gopherus polyphemus* are known: Irvingtonian of Florida, Rancholabrean of Florida and South Carolina (Auffenberg and Franz, 1978d; Holman, 1978); fossil remains of *Gopherus* from Pleistocene deposits in Kansas and Texas may also represent this species (Auffenberg, 1974; Auffenberg and Franz, 1978d).

DISTRIBUTION: *Gopherus polyphemus* ranges from extreme southern South Carolina south through peninsular Florida and west through southern Georgia, Florida, southern Alabama and Mississippi to extreme southeastern Louisiana.

GEOGRAPHIC VARIATION: No subspecies are recognized, but individuals from the western end of the range seem lighter in color, and they seem to have slightly differently shaped heads and carapaces than those from Florida (Ernst, pers. obs.). This needs verification.

CONFUSING SPECIES: This species can be separated from all the other turtles within its range by its elongate gular projection, small elephantine hind limbs, shovellike forelimbs, and lack of a plastral hinge.

HABITAT: The gopher tortoise usually lives on well-drained, deep, sandy soils in contiguous areas situated in pine-oak, beach scrub, oak hammocks or pine flatwoods. Adequate herbaceous foods and

An old Florida *Gopherus polyphemus*

Plastron of *Gopherus polyphemus*

sunny nesting sites must be present. Tortoise densities and movements are both directly related to herbaceous biomass, and densities are highest in fire-adapted plant associations (sand pine–scrub oak and longleaf pine–oak) (Auffenberg and Franz, 1982; Diemer, 1986).

Burrowing, mound-building, and grazing by gopher tortoises may significantly alter the habitat. In oak-pine sandhill woodlands in Florida, Kaczor and Hartnett (1990) found that these activities promoted an environmental heterogeneity that benefited tortoises. Tortoise mounds were characterized by lower concentrations of soil nutrients and organic matter, higher light intensities, and greater daily temperature fluctuations than adjacent undisturbed areas. Temperatures during prescribed spring fires were significantly lower on mounds and near burrow openings than in heavily vegetated areas. Microsuccession of plant species was increased in tortoise-cleared areas, resulting in greater plant diversity at the mounds. Old

Distribution of *Gopherus polyphemus*

mounds had the highest species richness. Tortoise disturbance increased the frequency of recruitment by seed relative to vegetative reproduction in the forb *Pityopsis graminifolia,* a common food plant.

BEHAVIOR: In Florida the gopher tortoise is essentially active all year: it remains in the burrow during cold spells but emerges on warm days. The peak activity period occurs from May to August (Douglass and Layne, 1978). Farther north it may become briefly torpid during severe winter weather.

The daily activity cycle in Florida is unimodal (Douglass and Layne, 1978), with tortoises often active during the warmest hours of the day. From about 1000 to 1400 they wander about, browsing as they go; other times usually are spent in the burrow. On cool days they bask at the entrance before starting on their journeys, but warm rain does not seem to upset the daily routine. Males seem more active both annually and during the day (Douglass and Layne, 1978). Fluctuations of light and temperature entrain their internal clock, which under constant light and temperature (26°C) shows a mean period length of 22:33·4 hours (Gourley, 1972).

A survey of aboveground activities of *G. polyphemus* in Putnam County, Florida, showed it basks 76.4% of the time, walks 16.5%, feeds 4.1%, nests 1%, and mates 1% (L. L. Smith, 1992).

Gopherus polyphemus characteristically basks with its head in an elevated position, in marked contrast to *G. berlandieri* and *G. agassizii.* Often it extends its forefeet to the sides and its hind feet to the rear.

It can withstand high body temperatures. Bogert and Cowles (1947) found 34–35°C to be normal for active individuals, and Douglass and Layne (1978) reported the average body temperature of active turtles is 34.7°C. Hutchison et al. (1966) recorded a critical thermal maximum of 43.9°C—the highest they found in any turtle. When heat stressed, wild tortoises breathe more rapidly, froth at the mouth, and seek shade; they may heat at a rate of 0.12°C/min at 30°C (Spray and May, 1972). Once in the shade, *G. polyphemus* cools rather fast (0.17°C/minute; Spray and May, 1972). A *G. polyphemus* kept in a desiccation chamber at 38°C and 37% humidity lost moisture at a mean rate of 0.42% of the initial weight per hour for more than 79 hours (Bogert and Cowles, 1947). A total loss of 30.4% of the original weight (43% water loss) was recorded; the tortoise died. Of all the species of *Gopherus, G. polyphemus* desiccates most rapidly in captivity if deprived of a burrow (Auffenberg and Weaver, 1969). Cutaneous and respiratory water loss by *G. polyphemus* is two or three times greater than that of *G. agassizii* (Ross, 1977). The average water intake for *G. polyphemus* per day is 3.1±0.13 ml (100 g), while the average water loss is 3.0±0.13 ml (100 g)

An Alabama *Gopherus polyphemus*

A Florida *Gopherus polyphemus*

(Minnich and Ziegler, 1977). This may explain why this species is so consistently associated with burrows over most of its range; the only place where they do not dig extensive burrows is both warm and moist.

The gopher tortoise will drink when water is available. Often it drinks rain water that has collected at the entrance to its burrow (Ashton and Ashton, 1991). The tortoise positions itself so that the entrance of the burrow is blocked with its head at the corner where the wall and floor of the burrow meet. The foreleg facing the entrance is extended forward and into the soil at the entrance, thus stopping any surface flow of water into the burrow. The head is forced into the soil to nearly eye level before the tortoise begins to drink.

Like other members of the genus, *G. polyphemus* is a burrower; however, its forelimbs and feet are more specialized for digging and more closely resemble those of the Mexican *G. flavomarginatus* than those of its two U.S. congeners. In *G. agassizii* and *G. berlandieri* the wrist is movable to a limited degree, but in *G. polyphemus* and *G. flavomarginatus* it is kept virtually immovable by strong, sheetlike ligaments that bind the bones into a relatively solid unit (Auffenberg, 1966a). Thus the forelimbs of the gopher tortoise are notably effective soil-moving devices—a pair of built-in shovels.

Gopherus polyphemus is capable of digging a long burrow, and usually excavates several during its life. Gopher tortoises also use the abandoned burrows of other tortoises (Diemer, 1992b), and it is not known if they continuously use a burrow throughout their lives. The burrow is dug in sandy soil, which may be moist and cohesive at depths of less than 30 cm. The deepest part of the burrow may be enlarged into a chamber, particularly at the periphery of the range where the soil subzone is clay. Both forelimbs are not used simultaneously during digging; the tortoise pivots from one side to the other as it alternates the power stroke from foreleg to foreleg (Wilson et al., 1991). Within the burrow the temperature and humidity remain relatively constant throughout the year; that is, the burrow is a microhabitat in which the gopher tortoise is relatively unaffected by climatic changes on the surface.

The burrows usually are straight and unbranched, but sometimes curve around obstructions. Hansen (1963) recorded the dimensions of 13 burrows as follows: length, 2.7–6.1 m; depth, 1.4–2.8 m; angle of decline, 17–39°; entrance width, 18.5–31.8 cm; entrance depth, 6.4–16.5 cm; width at 60 cm, 13.4–22.9 cm; and depth at 60 cm, 6.4–14 cm. He also reported one burrow 14.5 m long. In 54 burrows the height/width ratio of the burrow entrance was 0.51 to 1, and at 60 cm down it became 0.54 to 1. Burrow widths are positively correlated to the carapace length of the resident tortoise (Martin and Layne, 1987; Wilson et al., 1991).

An enlarged chamber is usually present at the end of the burrow; there the tortoise sleeps and can turn around. The tortoise often defecates in its burrow, and fecal matter frequently accumulates in this terminal chamber. Brode (1959) saw gopher tortoises in late summer backing out of their burrows, dragging and scraping dung and trash and depositing it several feet beyond the entrance.

The number of burrows used in northern Florida increases in April, peaks in July, and remains high through October (Diemer, 1992b). Burrow surveys also indicate a continous cycle of burrow creation and abandonment.

Ultsch and Anderson (1986, 1988) measured the concentrations of O_2 and CO_2 along the lengths and at the ends of occupied gopher tortoise burrows. Hypoxia and hypercarbia occur at all times of the year, but are most pronounced in burrows dug in clay soils. Breathing conditions are worst during the summer, but probably represent no significant problems to tortoises living in sandy areas ($O_2 = 20.1\%$; $CO_2 = 0.78\%$). Burrows in clay soils have moderate hypoxia (average O_2 18.2%, but as low as 12%) and have CO_2 concentrations high enough (to 6.8%) to cause the tortoise some stress. The additional CO_2 in the burrows comes from three sources: tortoise metabolism, commensal metabolism (particularly on decomposing feces), and the surrounding soil. Burrows dug in clay soils through which the gas cannot easily diffuse average only 3.2 m in length, as compared to an average length of 4.1 m in sandy, more porous soils through which gases can more easily escape. The normal critical oxygen tension of 10–11 mm Hg is not affected by CO_2 concentrations as high as 6% (Ultsch and Anderson, 1988). In moderate hypoxia (15% O_2), hypercarbia elicits an increase in the rate of O_2 uptake of 72% after 0.75 hours. After 12–18 hours of hypercarbia this rate still remains elevated by 22%. The tortoise hyperventilates continuously, with CO_2 loading occurring in 8–10 hours.

While the tortoises are overwintering, water may accumulate in their burrows (Means, 1982; Breininger et al., 1991). Means (1982) found water lying in burrows for periods of up to 48 consecutive days. The tortoises were either totally or partially submerged most of the time during these wet periods, indicating a preference for immersion even when water levels were low in the burrows. Immersion may have some thermoregulatory advantages, and it certainly retards body moisture loss while the tortoises are fasting. However, should the soil become softened enough to cause the tunnel to collapse, it could force the tortoise to dig itself out (Burke, 1989a).

Many animals find the burrow of a gopher tortoise a suitable permanent home or a temporary shelter. Among the vertebrates living in the burrows are opossums (*Didelphis*), mice and rats (*Neotoma, Podomys, Peromyscus, Sigmodon*), cottontails (*Sylvilagus*), weasels (*Mustela*), skunks (*Mephitis, Spilogale*), river otters (*Lutra*), red foxes (*Vulpes*), coyotes (*Canis*), burrowing owls (*Speotyto*), quail (*Colinus*), snakes (*Agkistrodon, Cemophora, Coluber, Crotalus, Drymarchon, Elaphe, Heterodon, Masticophis, Micrurus, Pituophis, Sistrurus, Thamnophis*), amphisbaenians (*Rhineura*), lizards (*Anolis, Cnemidophorus, Eumeces, Ophisaurus, Sceloporus, Scincella*), and frogs, toads, and treefrogs (*Acris, Bufo, Eleutherodactylus, Gastrophryne, Rana, Scaphiopus*) (Carr, 1952; Brode, 1959; Lawler, 1977; Franz, 1986a; Frank and Lips, 1989; Jackson and Milstrey, 1989; Jones and Franz, 1990; Lips, 1991; Toland, 1991; Witz et al., 1991; Ernst, pers. obs.) Many arthropods are also commensals or obligates in these burrows: Young and Goff (1939) listed 32 species and Lago (1991) 38 species of spiders, ticks, and insects, and new species of insect inhabitants are still being described (Davis and Milstrey, 1988).

Young *G. polyphemus* also construct small burrows, but some bury themselves in sandy soil or push under vegetable debris (Douglass, 1978). Adults may use a minimum of three burrows during the activity season; McRae et al. (1981b) reported that females use an average of four burrows and males seven in southwestern Georgia.

L. L. Smith (1992) estimated that in the center of a sandhill habitat in Putnam County, Florida, there were only 2.4 burrows/ha, and that the tortoises that used them had a mean carapace length of 209 mm. At the periphery of the sandhill, burrow density increased to 10.6/ha and the tortoises averaged 218 in carapace length. At an oldfield site in the same county, burrow density was 6/ha at the center (mean tortoise carapace length, 248 mm), and 7.6/ha at the perimeter (mean tortoise carapace length 239 mm).

The gopher tortoise has a well-defined home range. As a tortoise becomes older and larger it increases the size of its home range, which for some old individuals may be extensive. At the Ordway Reserve, Putnam County, Florida, adult females have home ranges of 0.002–1.435 ha (L. L. Smith, 1992). The largest recorded home range is 3.14 ha for a 20.3-cm Florida tortoise (Gourley, 1969). Several alternate burrows may be made within the home range, and well-marked pathways often connect them. Burrows seldom are located more than 50 m from places where the tortoise grazes, and well-defined trails usually connect the burrows with feeding areas. Breininger et al. (1991) reported that less than 20% of the active and inactive burrows in an area are occupied during an activity season, but this seems the exception rather than the rule (see Diemer, 1992b). Burke (1989a) reported a movement of 1.1 km by a displaced 25.7-cm male.

In southwestern Georgia, the movement patterns and home ranges of gopher tortoises vary seasonally and are largely determined by social interactions (McRae et al., 1981b). Adults are reproductively active in early spring. During the spring and summer, males move more often than females. Male move-

ments and burrow preferences are mostly determined by reproductive and dominance behaviors. Males occupy home ranges of 0.6–1.44 ha, females have home ranges of 0.04–0.14 ha, but home range area probably depends on the habitat. By late summer, Georgia tortoises begin to move toward adjacent fall-winter home ranges on more mesic soils, possibly because of better food supplies in such areas (McRae et al., 1981b). Georgia adults use at least three burrows during the annual activity period, and do not share burrows overnight. Juveniles typically move only short distances and use only one or two burrows, but do not leave the breeding areas until subadults.

In northern Florida, the home range of *G. polyphemus* is smaller (Diemer, 1992a). The mean home range of six radio-bearing adult males was 0.88 ha, and that of five adult females, 0.31 ha, four subadults, 0.05 ha, and seven juveniles, 0.01 ha. The combined home range of adults averaged 0.52 ha. Juveniles moved from 3 to 99 m between recaptures, subadults, 6–744 m, adult females, 0–186 m, and adult males, 3–474 m. The movement of 744 m was accomplished by a two-year-old tortoise in approximately four days. Juveniles used an average of 2.6 (1–4) different burrows from 1985 to 1987, and an average of 2.1 (1–4) known burrows during the annual activity season from April to December. Similarly, subadults used 4.5 (1–8) and 2.9 (1–6), adult females, 3.0 (2–4) and 2.7 (2–3), and adult males, 7.7 (5–10) and 5.5 (4–7) burrows over the same two periods. Diemer (1992a) observed co-occupancy of a single burrow by one or more adult males and an adult female at least 14 times from mid-May to mid-November. Co-occupancy of one burrow by two adult males or by two immature tortoises was also observed several times. Diemer also noted burrow defense on several occasions, during which the defending tortoise turned sideways in the burrow to block others from entering.

Layne (in Goin and Goin, 1962) trapped a gopher tortoise in its burrow and released it at 1020 in a fire lane about 140 m from the mouth of the burrow. A few minutes later it had moved to within 45 m of the burrow. It progressed at a steady pace, pausing momentarily now and then to nip at some vegetation. When near the burrow site the tortoise turned and headed directly for the burrow, which was about 18 m from the fire lane and screened by brush; it arrived back at the burrow at 1032. Layne then took the tortoise about 180 m west of the burrow into thick brush and released it at about 1040. He then removed the trap from the burrow entrance, smoothed the soil, and departed. At 1430 he discovered tracks leading into the burrow, presumably those of the tortoise handled in the morning.

Some form of orientation is used by *G. polyphemus* to return to a particular burrow. Gibbons and Smith (1968) recorded the compass bearings of tortoises crossing roads in Florida. Each of the tortoises was then put into a closed cardboard box, taken 1.6 km farther down the road, released in the middle of the road, and pointed in a randomly chosen direction. The sun was visible at the time of release in all instances. Most captures and releases were made between 0900 and 1100 and between 0400 and 1800. Of 18 released, nine went in the direction of their original movement, six moved in the opposite direction, and three at right angles to the original direction. Gibbons and Smith thought the simplest explanation was that the tortoises were using the sun to find a particular compass direction.

Gourley (1974) conducted orientation tests on *G. polyphemus* in an open field and in an arena. In the field, 56.6% of individuals showed statistically significant direction preferences. The chosen direction had no relation to the homeward direction and were widely divergent for tortoises from the same population. In the arena, 51.4% showed significant direction preferences. A comparison of the preferred directions in the field and the arena indicated that landmarks may have had a disruptive effect on orientation. Gourley also subjected the tortoises to an advanced phase shift of six hours. This resulted in a change in the expected (counterclockwise) direction, and the mean shift was not significantly different from the expected shift of 90°. These data indicate that the gopher tortoise is probably capable of sun compass orientation.

Gopherus polyphemus has an aversion to dropoffs: at heights of about 30 cm the tortoise hesitates at the edge, whereas at 182 cm the edge is avoided (Yerkes, 1904); Patterson (1971c) also found hesitation and avoidance of deep dropoffs by gopher tortoises. Visual depth perception and forelimb tactile sensing help in avoiding falls.

The gopher tortoise will swim of its own accord in both fresh and brackish water. Brode (1959) observed one at the Gulf Coast Research Laboratory in Mississippi swim the boat slip—a dredged channel about 18 m wide—in order to get to a woodlot. It was a slow swimmer and maintained a fairly regular course. Ernst has also seen them swim across narrow canals and shallow streams.

Carr (1952) observed fights between male and female *G. polyphemus.* Weaver (1970) saw ramming between a captive male and female, but it was not clear whether this was courtship or combat. He also saw one moderate-sized, malformed male *G. polyphemus* repeatedly ram a subadult *Geochelone elephantopus* and an adult *Geochelone pardalis,* each of which was at least 9 kg heavier than its assailant. Ernst had a 19.7-cm male who, when introduced to a 35.6-cm male, first sniffed and bobbed its head and then repeatedly rammed the larger male and drove it into a shelter.

Weaver (1970) studied combat in *G. polyphemus* by watching confrontations between captive males. When a newcomer was introduced, males either remained still, immediately proceeded toward the intruder, or (in a few cases) retreated into a corner. When approaching an intruder, a highly motivated tortoise walked rapidly with his neck fully extended; under normal circumstances the pace was slower and the neck was only partly extended. When the tortoises were about 76 cm apart, head bobbing began. The fact that the bobbing head was always pointed in the direction of another tortoise suggests that a visual cue is involved, but a highly motivated tortoise would walk toward another tortoise in the absence of reciprocal bobbing or locomotion. At contact the vertical bobs of both males became more lateral and finally lost any recognizable pattern. Each sniffed the head and feet of the other. The vertical bobs associated with sniffing movements often were interrupted by a lateral wiping motion across the surface of one of its forelegs. After one or two minutes of mutual sniffing, one of the tortoises became more active than the other, and they clearly demonstrated dominance relationships by their postures. The dominant tortoise supported its weight on all four of its extended legs. He sometimes walked around the submissive one, stopping often to smell his rear legs. The dominant male sometimes rammed the subordinate male, hooked its gular extension under the other tortoise, jerked upward, and overturned it (see Hailman et al., 1991). The submissive tortoise held his head low, with his neck only partly extended. If the dominant tortoise continued to investigate, the submissive one positioned himself at an angle of approximately 45° to the dominant one and maneuvered to keep one side or the other presented to the front of the dominant individual. He did this with his hind legs by pivoting on the anterior portion of the plastron, keeping the front legs withdrawn. After one or two minutes of this behavior, the dominant individual turned away, apparently having lost interest in the other tortoise (but while passing in front of the submissive male, he might kick sand into his face; Hailman et al., 1991).

Perhaps in meetings between two males, or a male

and a female *G. polyphemus* in the nonbreeding season, noncombative recognition of dominance results in the subordinate tortoise leaving the dominant individual's presence. Weaver's (1970) experiments demonstrate that a resident *G. polyphemus* does not necessarily dominate when an intruder is introduced into its home pen; instead, certain individuals tended markedly to be dominant both in their own pen and in those of others.

REPRODUCTION: Sexual maturity in female gopher tortoises is reached in 10–21 years at carapace lengths of 220–265 mm. In Florida, Iverson (1980a) found the smallest mature females with either oviducal eggs or corpora lutea to be 10–15 years old and 229–244 mm, Diemer (1986) found a mature female with a 232-mm carapace (14–15 years), and L. L. Smith (1992) reported that some females less than 225 mm were mature. Landers et al. (1980) reported that females from southwestern Georgia mature at 250–265 mm in carapace length at 19–21 years. Sexual development of tortoises living in the sand ridges of southwestern Georgia was delayed about seven years.

A period of ovarian regression during the summer follows nesting (Iverson, 1980a). However, vitellogenesis resumes by September. Follicles then continue to enlarge until ovulation in April or May, although yolking is somewhat retarded overwinter. In Florida, oviducal eggs may be found as early as 26 April (Iverson, 1980a), and all females have probably ovulated by the end of May. Nonovulated follicles are 10–20 mm in diameter in June, but only 10 mm in July or August. Corpora lutea are barely identifiable by August or September.

Palmer and Guillette (1988, 1990) studied the histology and functional morphology of the female gopher tortoise's reproductive tract. The oviduct is composed of five morphologically distinct regions: infundibulum, uterine tube, isthmus, uterus, and vagina. The epithelium consists of ciliated cells and microvillous secretory cells throughout the oviduct, whereas bleb secretory cells are unique to the infundibulum. The epithelium and endometrial glands of the uterine tube histologically resemble those of the avian magnum which produce egg albumen and may be functionally homologous. The isthmus is a short, nonglandular region of the oviduct and seems to contribute little to either albumen or eggshell formation.

The uterus retains the eggs until oviposition and may form both the fibrous and calcareous eggshell. The endometrial glands are histologically similar to the endometrial glands of the isthmus of birds, which are known to secrete the fibers of the eggshell. Epithelial cells of these glands enlarge during vitellogenesis but shrink during the gravid period, as do oviductal epithelial cells (Palmer and Guillette, 1990). Oviductal hypertrophy during vitellogenesis coincides with elevated plasma estradiol, whereas during the gravid period plasma progesterone levels peak (Taylor, 1982a). The ratio of secretory to ciliated epithelial cells in the oviduct increases during the cycle. The uterine epithelium may supply additional water to the egg albumen as well as transport calcium ions for eggshell formation. The vagina is extremely muscular and serves as a sphincter to retain the eggs until oviposition.

Sperm are found within the oviductal lumen and endometrial glands from the posterior tube to the anterior uterus throughout the reproductive cycle (Palmer and Guillette, 1988, 1990; Gist and Jones, 1989). This indicates sperm storage within the female tract, although the viability and reproductive significance of these sperm are unknown.

In Georgia, males mature in 16–18 years at carapace lengths of 230–240 mm (Landers et al., 1980).

Courtship occurs principally in the spring, but has also been observed in the fall (Landers et al., 1980; Diemer, 1992a; C. K. Dodd, Jr., pers. comm.); two or three males may simultaneously pursue a single female (Diemer, 1992a). Courtship apparently consists of several basic sequential activities. The first of these Auffenberg (1966b) termed the "male orientation circle": the male walks in a circle and periodically stops and bobs his head, perhaps to attract the attention of a sexually responsive female. When a female approaches he bobs his head violently, then bites her on the forelegs, head, anterior edge of the carapace, and particularly the gular projection (this may be the method of sex identification; females do not bite one another or males). The female then backs in a semicircle, stops, and stretches her hind legs. Later she pivots 180°, so that the posterior part of her shell is nearest the male's head, possibly a form of presentation. The attempts to mount, usually unsuccessful, are followed by more biting, which in turn may be followed by a successful mounting and coition. When mounted, the male's head and neck are extended and his mouth usually open. The male may stroke or tap lightly on the female's carapace with his foreclaws.

Landers et al. (1980) and C. K. Dodd, Jr. (pers. comm.) observed several cases in Georgia and Florida, respectively, in which the burrows of known females seemed to be the object of male courtship activity. The females did not emerge, but could be seen in the burrow opening, so probably the male was interested in the female. In three of the Georgia episodes (July and August) females turned sideways in the burrow entrance and remained there during 1–3.5 hours of courtship by the males. Apparently the females were receptive only in the spring, but males were sexually active to some extent from spring to fall.

Auffenberg (1969) found that in some instances, just before the male's behavior changed from head bobbing to biting, the female rubbed the side of her face and chin across her outstretched front legs. Adults of all four species of *Gopherus* have a pair of glands on the chin; although they are small most of the year, these glands usually become swollen in the breeding season. Both sexes have an enlarged scale, more prominent than the rest, on each front leg near the elbow. Scent possibly is transferred by the female from her chin to her front legs by means of this scale. Her chin rubbing seems to be a response to the male's head bobbing, and Auffenberg speculated that this action causes the male to change his behavior from bobbing to biting. His bobbing may provide the female with more than just a visual cue: he has glands beneath the lower jawbone, and the bobbing may also serve to spread a scent signal to the female. Landers et al. (1980) noted that these glands are quite active (enlarged and contained copious fluid) during spring and summer. Those of adult females are active during spring and regress after mid-June.

Eggs may be deposited from late April to mid-July, but most nesting occurs from mid-May to mid-June. Over 70% of the known or estimated nestings in Georgia occur from the last week of May through the second week of June (Landers et al., 1980). Some nests are located at a considerable distance from the burrow, but most in Georgia are dug in the burrow entrances. Landers et al. (1980) reported that at their study site in Georgia 85% of the nests are within 15–80 cm of the burrow entrance. The soil above the eggs is usually exposed to the full rays of the sun.

In Florida less than 2% of the clutches are deposited in the burrow apron; instead most nests are dug some distance from the burrow (L. L. Smith, 1992). Perhaps those studied in Georgia by Landers et al. (1980) are a specialized case caused by altered habitat.

Perhaps the best description of the nesting process has been given by Kenefick (1954). On 27 June, at 1050, a captive female started digging a nest (she had been found mating on 23 April). She first swung her body in a circle while scraping a shallow, bowl-shaped depression with her front feet; it was about 76 cm in diameter. Then, using her hind feet only, she dug a cylindrical cavity, slightly flared at the bottom, about 150 cm in diameter and 150 cm deep—apparently as far as she could reach. At 1100, while straddling the cavity with her rear feet, she laid her first egg. This action was accompanied by long sighs as the neck was moved in and out of the shell. As each egg was laid in the cavity it was pushed to the front by a hind foot. The last of seven eggs was laid at 1130. After this she scraped dirt from the sides of the hole with her hind feet, lightly covering the eggs, and then used her front feet to complete the covering—in all, a 20-minute undertaking. After the nest was filled she walked back and forth over it, brushing it lightly with her foreclaws. The entire procedure, from first digging to final brushing took one hour.

Nesting in Georgia takes place only on warm, sunny days and apparently is not contingent on a preceding rainfall (Landers et al., 1980). Nests there are flask shaped and the eggs are usually 15–25 cm below the soil surface. Eggs in small clutches are in one layer, but larger clutches are commonly in two layers. The eggs are only rarely touched, as some soil usually falls into the cavity as each egg is laid.

A clutch may contain 1–25 eggs; however, mean clutch size varies by population: South Carolina, 3.9 (Wright, 1982); northern Florida, Georgia, and Mississippi, 5–7 (Brode, 1959; Iverson, 1980a; Landers et al., 1980; L. L. Smith, 1992); and southern Florida, 8.9 (Burke, 1987). A clutch from central Florida may contain as many as 25 eggs (L. Macdonald, in L. L. Smith, 1992). Clutch size is directly correlated to female carapace length (Landers et al., 1980; L. L. Smith, 1992). Only one clutch is laid per year. The white, brittle eggs commonly are almost spherical. The diameter is 37.9–53.2 mm, with the larger diameter commonly about 42–43 mm and the smaller about 41 mm; often there is less than 1 mm difference between the greatest and least diameters of individual eggs. Eleven eggs weighed by Arata (1958) were approximately 33.5–47.0 g. Egg size is not significantly correlated with clutch size (Iverson, 1980a). Thirty-seven eggs from Florida *G. polyphemus* contained 33.6% lipid and 62.3% insoluble protein; whole eggs contained 346.7 kJ of energy, egg contents contained 246.4 kJ (Linley, 1987). Eggs are composed of approximately 65% water (Congdon and Gibbons, 1985).

Brode (1959) studied 40 nests in Mississippi and found that most of the eggs in each hatched, but that only about half the young dug their way out. He attributed this mortality to the fact that the overburden was hard packed, and this may be particularly true

Hatching *Gopherus polyphemus*

in Louisiana and Mississippi because of the soils there. Landers et al. (1980) reported that 86% of the eggs hatch in Georgia, and Arata (1958) noted a 92% hatch rate in Florida.

Hatching and emergence occur from August to October. In Florida, incubation in the field probably requires 80–90 days (Iverson, 1980a), in Georgia, 97–106 days (Landers et al., 1980), and in South Carolina it may take as long as 110 days (Wright, 1982). At hatching, the yolk sac is large, averaging 10 × 10 × 5 mm, but it is completely resorbed within 18–24 hours. The deep transverse flexure across the yellow plastron essentially disappears within three days. The granular carapace is almost round, being only slightly longer than wide. The dorsal scutes have yellow centers; their edges and the marginals range from a deep grayish brown to brown. Two tiny points project from the anterior edge of each gular, a similar one occurs at the tip of each anal scute, and an even more minute one can be found on the lateral rim of each femoral scute. A hard, sharp laminal spur on the posterolateral margin of each humeral scute later disappears (Allen, 1983). Young at hatching are 32.0–51.8 mm in carapace length and weigh 18.2–43.0 g (L. L. Smith, 1992). Length and weight of hatchlings may differ significantly from one year to the next: in 1990, L. L. Smith (1992) recorded an average carapace length of 48.0 mm and an average

weight of 30 g, but in 1991 these measurements were 42.3 mm and 33.3 g, respectively.

All parts of the hatchling, except the liver and reserve yolk, are composed predominantly of insoluble protein (Linley, 1987). Lipid constitutes 76.9% of the liver. Reserve yolk is 38.6% and 49.1% lipid at hatching and on day two after hatching, respectively. Hatchlings contain 209.1 kJ of energy. The percent conversion of energy from egg to hatchling averages 76.2% (66.9–93.6) (Linley, 1987).

Landers et al. (1980) calculated the reproductive capacity for female *G. polyphemus* in Georgia. Assuming that all mature females lay one clutch annually, fecundity of the average female in this population would be 7.0 eggs per year. The annual hatching rate (number of young hatched alive) is only a small percentage of the fecundity, owing primarily to nest depredation. Alford (1980) estimated that mean mortality of *G. polyphemus* in northern Florida is 92.2% between egg laying and one year of age. In Georgia, there was an average of only one successful clutch per 9.5 nests. Thus, the average female would have a successful clutch only once in about 9–10 years. A mean of 1.2 eggs per clutch did not hatch, reducing the average hatch to 5.8 (7.0 eggs per clutch minus 1.2). Therefore, the effective rate of reproduction is (again, assuming annual egg laying) about 5.8 hatchlings per mature female per 10 years.

GROWTH AND LONGEVITY: Gopher tortoises from southwestern Georgia grow at an annual increment of 11–12 mm per year (Landers et al., 1982), but this varies with carapace length. Growth increments are greatest for tortoises with 100–190-mm carapaces (about 4–11 years of age), and gradually decrease thereafter. Body volume increments reached a peak in individuals of 220–230 mm in carapace length. Once maturity is reached, growth slows in both sexes, but females grow at a greater rate and become significantly larger than males. Over 90% of the annual growth is from April to October.

Goin and Goff (1941) recovered 33 of 131 marked Florida individuals. The greatest growth was that of a female, which increased in length from 148 mm to 190 mm between June 1937 and March 1938; during this period her weight increased from 545 g to 800 g. The average gain in length for all 33 tortoises was 10.5 mm for an average period of a little less than a year. The average gain in weight was 137.3 g, the greatest, 535 g. Iverson (1980a) reported the average carapace length for 11 Florida hatchlings about one week old to be 48.2 mm (45.0–50.9). Two hatchlings weighed 30.1 and 35.7 g. Juveniles from Florida collected during their first year measured 49.5–41.9 mm in carapace length in October, 54 mm in late April, and 48.6–54.3 mm in June (Iverson, 1980a).

Many wild tortoises have growth annuli showing them to be over 25 years of age.

FOOD HABITS: *Gopherus polyphemus* is herbivorous, and probably ingests animal foods only accidentally. Digestive tracts of wild individuals examined by Carr (1952) contained large amounts of grass and leaves, with occasional bits of hard fruits, bones, charcoal, and, once, insect chitin. Many herbaceous plants are eaten, but these usually reflect the dominant plants in the habitat, and the tortoises may be selective as to genera. In Florida, Macdonald and Mushinsky (1988) found the following families the most frequent components of the diet: Poaceae (*Aristida*, 98% of scats), Asteraceae (60% of scats), Fabaceae (65% of scats), Pinaceae (*Pinus*, 84% of scats), and Fagaceae (79% of scats). Sixty-eight genera from 26 families were identified in the diet. Other than *Aristida* and *Pinus,* the genera of other common plants eaten were *Quercus, Galactia, Cnidoscolus, Tillandsia, Pityopsis,* and *Richardia.* Some scats also contained insects and charcoal.

In southwestern Georgia, grasses and grasslike plants (Cyperaceae and Asteraceae) are the principal foods throughout the activity season, particularly broad-leaved plants (Poaceae, 90%) (Garner and Landers, 1981). Wiregrass (*Aristida*) is eaten mainly in early spring and late fall. In southern Mississippi, *G. polyphemus* subsists mostly on grasses (Poaceae), particularly broomsedge (*Andropogon*) and panic-grasses (*Panicum*) (Lohoefener and Lohmeier, 1981). Brode (1959) observed them eating mushrooms.

Juveniles feed essentially on the same plants as adults (Douglass, 1978; Garner and Landers, 1981). Douglass (1978) observed two juveniles eating grasses and forbs, and their digestive tracts were filled with vegetation. In Mississippi, a juvenile was seen eating leaves of lupine (Fabaceae, *Lupinus*) and morning glory (Convolvulaceae, *Stylisma*) (Jones, 1992). Garner and Landers (1981) found a small juvenile eating raccoon feces composed chiefly of blackberry seeds and insects, and Anderson and Herrington (1992) saw a small adult consume fox scat.

Auffenberg (1969) thought *G. polyphemus* a possible seed dispersal agent for plants, and Hayes and Le Corff (1989) reported that some seeds from injested tallowwood fruits (*Ximenia*) were capable of germinating after defecation by the tortoise.

Gopher tortoises may consume carrion (Garner and Landers, 1981; Anderson and Herrington, 1992), and sometimes even scavenge: Tobey (1979) found one eating discarded stale biscuits. Captives eat romaine lettuce, shaved carrots, grasses, dandelions, various fruits, canned salmon, hamburger, dog food, hard-boiled eggs and cracked eggshells, but vegetable matter is clearly preferred.

Bjorndal (1987) measured the digestive efficiency of *G. polyphemus* fed leaves of the legume *Aeschynomene americana* (intake was held constant relative to body mass). Mean apparent digestive efficiencies were 68% of organic matter, 61% of energy, 73% of cell walls, and 71% of nitrogen. Mean passage time was 13 days. Most individuals ate in the morning, close to the burrow entrance. Environmental temperatures of 21–25°C are needed to stimulate foraging activity (McRae et al., 1981b).

PREDATORS AND DEFENSE: Auffenberg and Weaver (1969) reported that, in Florida, nests destroyed before hatching usually are lost within the first week. Scents associated with nest building and egg laying probably are more important in leading predators to a nest than is the scent of the eggs themselves. These associated scents probably disappear or become masked after a few days. Landers et al. (1980) observed that of 38 nests monitored by them, only four (11%) survived to hatching. Wright (in Diemer, 1986) reported that

74% of the eggs were destroyed at his South Carolina site during a two-year study; the predation rate on hatchlings was 70% the first year and 41% the second. In Florida 43% of the hatchlings released from protected nests were alive after 280 days, compared to less than 20% at unprotected nests (L. L. Smith, 1992). Alford (1980) estimated that from the time of oviposition through the first year of life, 94% of the young are killed by predators. In contrast, monthly survival rates among radio-tagged Florida juveniles were: October–November, 69%; December–January, 100%; February–March, 89%; April–May, 74%; and June–September, 100% (Wilson, 1991).

The leading predators on eggs and juveniles are raccoons (*Procyon),* gray foxes (*Urocyon*), skunks (*Mephitis*), opossums (*Didelphis*), armadillos (*Dasypus*), snakes (*Crotalus, Drymarchon, Masticophis*), and fire ants (*Conomyrma, Solenopsis*) (Douglass and Winegarner, 1977; Thomas, 1978; Landers et al., 1980; Diemer, 1986; Martin, 1989; L. L. Smith, 1992). Red-tailed hawks (*Buteo*) occasionally take juveniles (Fitzpatrick and Woolfenden, 1978).

Adults have few natural predators, although Causey and Cude (1978) reported that in Alabama feral dog (*Canis familiaris*) packs may excavate the burrows and kill the inhabitants, and some Florida raccoons (*Procyon lotor*) may flip a tortoise on its back and reach up through its cloaca to literally clean it out (this seems to be a learned behavior; Dodd, pers. comm.). Humans are the leading killers of adults: many are crushed on the highways, and they are also slaughtered for food. Many juveniles and adults were captured and sold in the pet trade, where they did poorly and usually died soon after removal from their natural habitat. Rattlesnake hunts in parts of the range may have reduced some populations, because the gases introduced into the burrows to induce the snakes to emerge also kill the tortoises (Speake and Mount, 1973). Many populations are being destroyed by the steady press of housing developments, shopping centers, and agriculture; this is the greatest threat in Florida (Dodd, pers. comm.). Taylor (1982b) has made an extensive study of human predation on *G. polyphemus* in Florida.

When surprised away from its burrow, *G. polyphemus* may retreat into its shell or merely try to walk away. It seldom bites but most often scratches or occasionally voids its bladder water if picked up.

POPULATIONS: As of 1988, some federal lands in Florida still supported large numbers of gopher tortoises: Merritt Island National Wildlife Refuge, 57,990; Ocala National Forest, 39,253; St. Marks National Wildlife Refuge, 3,472; Egmont Key National Wildlife Refuge, 2,128; and Everglades National Park, 1,137 (McCoy and Mushinsky, 1992), but the overall population throughout the range seems to be declining.

Alford (1980) studied the mathematical relationship of the width of 430 gopher tortoise burrows and the carapace lengths of their occupants at 13 colonies in northern Florida. The overall approximate frequency distribution of individuals in carapacial size classes for the 13 colonies (interpreted from a bar graph) was 48–66 mm, 0.8%; 66–84 mm, 4%; 84–102 mm, 5%; 102–120 mm, 5%; 120–138 mm, 5.7%; 138–156 mm, 3.6%; 156–174 mm, 5.7%; 174–192 mm, 7%; 192–210 mm, 14%; 210–228 mm, 14.2%; 228–246 mm, 12%; 246–264 mm, 11.4%; 264–282 mm, 4%; 282–300 mm, 4%; 300–318 mm, 1.4%; 318–336 mm, 2%; and 354–372 mm, 0.4%.

In a more recent study in northern Florida, Diemer (1992b) found juveniles composed 27–28% of the population at one site and 43–47% at another; subadults and adults were 19–22% and 50–54%, respectively, at the first locality and 13–16% and 40–41%, respectively, at the second site.

Auffenberg and Franz (1982) found that of all Florida habitats, tortoise populations were most dense in disturbed types, where the animals formed colonies of up to 57 individuals. Mean densities were 266/ha within colonies and 8/ha overall. McRae et al. (1981b) captured a total of 455 tortoises along a 32-km course of roads in southwestern Georgia between March 1978 and June 1980. The densities of gopher tortoises using different sandhill habitats at two sites in southern Georgia were: slash pine plantation, 10.1 and 9.3/ha; longleaf pine–scrub oak, 3.3 and 15.8/ha (Landers and Speake, 1980). The southernmost colony of gopher tortoises at Cape Sable, Florida, occupies 113 ha of unstable coastal dunes where the tortoise density is approximately 11.3/ha and the total population is more than 1,200 tortoises (Kushlan and Mazzotti, 1984). Individuals there range in carapace length from less than 50 mm to more than 380 mm. Iverson (1982a) estimated the biomass of tortoises at a colony in Florida studied by Auffenberg to be approximately 220 kg/ha.

A correction factor of 0.614 multiplied by the sum of the active and inactive gopher tortoise burrows in a study area has been proposed to estimate the population size (Auffenberg and Franz, 1982; Kushlan and Manzotti, 1984; Burke, 1989b,c), but this factor may be too high. The ratio of captured *G. polyphemus* to active and inactive burrows in Putnam County, Florida, varied among years and study sites, ranging from 0.45 to 0.69, with a mean of 0.54 (Diemer, 1992b). Obviously, no general correction factor can apply to all populations, and, to be meaningful, a separate factor must be generated for each population sampled.

The combined male to female ratio for adult *G. polyphemus* in six groups in southern Georgia was 1.1:1.0, and the combined juvenile to adult ratio was 1.0:3.3 (Landers and Speake, 1980). At three sites in northern Florida the adult male to adult female ratio was 1:2, 1:1.5, and 1:0.9 (Diemer, 1992b). The percentages of adults in these three populations ranged from 40% to 62%.

Survivorship of eggs in the nest is 11–45% (Landers et al., 1980; Marshall, 1987), from egg to one year, 5.8% (Alford, 1980), and from subadult to adult, 89% (Layne, 1989).

REMARKS: The range of *G. polyphemus* has decreased dramatically owing to habitat destruction and fragmentation. Threats to the continued survival of populations include land conversion for urbanization, agriculture, forest management, mining, collection for food, the pet trade, and many other factors (see discussion under Predators and defense, and Dodd, 1986, and Diemer, 1989). Tortoises may also be killed during rattlesnake roundups when snake collectors pour gasoline into tortoise burrows to drive out serpents (Wahlquist, 1991). The gopher tortoise is listed as a federally threatened species in western Alabama, eastern Louisiana, and Mississippi.

Recent relocation experiments of gopher tortoises in southern Mississippi have produced mixed results (Lohoefener and Lohmeier, 1986). Only 2 of 19 individuals became established when released in areas where there were feral tortoises, but four of five individuals became established if placed in a started burrow and penned in an area with feral tortoises. Three groups of three tortoises each and one of two placed in started burrows and pens in an area with feral tortoises had a 73% (eight individuals) success rate. The best results (100% establishment) occurred when groups with three and two tortoises were placed in started burrows and pens in areas with no other tortoises.

In contrast, Burke (1989b) concluded that a relocation experiment in Florida was "fairly successful." Two years after the release of 85 tortoises, 35 reproductively active transplants remained at the new site. Dodd and Seigel (1991) emphasized that there was a 50–60% desertion rate in Burke's relocation experiment, which was based on only two years of observation. In an extensive review of the literature, Dodd and Seigel concluded that the success rate of relocation, repatriation, and translocations of reptiles and amphibians was low. Additional information on gopher tortoise relocation is summarized in Diemer et al. (1989).

Gopher tortoises are surprisingly strong for their size, although it is debatable whether one can easily carry a full-grown man on its back as reported by Knight (in Carr, 1952). A large male kept at home by Ernst often moved the furniture around.

Auffenberg (1969) found that in at least one locality on the west coast of Florida some tortoises do not dig burrows, but do construct feeding trailways characteristic of the species. However, they live on land that is close to sea level which has soil only a few centimeters thick over limestone bedrock. Ground conditions make burrowing impossible, and suitable temperature and humidity the year around permit tortoises to survive there without burrows.

More information on the life history and conservation of *Gopherus polyphemus* can be found in Cox et al. (1987) and various issues of the *Proceedings of the Gopher Tortoise Council*. Additional references are listed in Auffenberg and Franz (1978d).

Glossary of scientific names

Derivations of the names are those given by the original author of the taxon or are based on Jaeger (1944), Brown (1956), or the accounts in the Catalog of American Amphibians and Reptiles. The phonetic spellings represent a consensus of a poll of herpetologists and classicists from various parts of the country. Primary (′) and secondary (″) stress marks follow the stressed syllable. Otherwise, phonetic notation generally follows Webster III and includes the following sounds: \a\ as in cap, rarity; \ā\ as in rate; \ä\ as in calm, box; \au̇\ as in plow; \e\ as in get, ferry; \ē\ as in me; \i\ as in big; \ī\ as in bite; \ō\ as in hope; \ȯ\ as in saw, cork, fall; \ȯi\ as in boy, coin; \u̇\ as in pull, book; \ü\ as in rule, too; \ŋ\ as in sing; and the schwa \ə\, which sounds like the a in alone, the e in system, the i in easily, the o in gallop, and the u in circus, hurt. The reader is reminded of E. B. White's advice: If you don't know how to pronounce a word, say it loud.

agassizii (ag′-ə-sē-ī), (ag-ə-sē′-zē-ī), (ag-ə-zē′-zē-ī): named for Jean Louis R. Agassiz

alabamensis (al″-ə-bam-en′-səs): from Alabama

arizonense (ar″-ə-zō-nen′-sē): from Arizona

asper (as′-pər): L., rough, referring to the carapacial surface

barbouri (bar′-bər-ī): named for Thomas Barbour

bauri (bau̇r′-ī): named for Georg H. C. L. Baur

baurii (bau̇r′-ī), (bau̇r′-ē-ī): named for Georg H. C. L. Baur

bellii (bel′-ī), (bel′-ē-ī): named for Thomas Bell

berlandieri (bər-lan′-dē″-ər-ī), (ber-lan′-dēr″-ē): named for Jean Louis Berlandier

bissa (bis′-ə), (bis′-ä): from *bissa*, the local Abyssinian name for the male of this species at its Red Sea type locality

blandingii (blan′-diŋ-ī), (blan-din′-jē-ī): named for William Blanding

caglei (kā′-gəl-ī): named for Fred R. Cagle

calvatus (cal-vā′-təs): from L. *calvus*, smooth, bald, referring to the carapacial surface

Caretta (kə-ret′-ə): from Fr. *caret*, turtle, tortoise, sea turtle

carinatus (kar-ə-nā′-təs): L., keeled

carolina (kar-ə-lī′-nə), (kar″-ō-lī′-nə): named for the Carolina region

centrata (sen-trä′-tə), (sen-trā′-tə): from L. *centrum*, midpoint of a circle, point, referring to the configuration of growth annuli on each carapacial scute

Chelonia (ki-lō′-nē-ə), (chə-lō′-nē-ə): from Gr. *chelōnē*, a tortoise

Chelydra (chə-lī′-drə), (kə-lī′-drə), (kə-lē′-drə): from Gr. *chelydros*, a water serpent

chrysea (krī′-sē-ə), (kris′-ē-ə): from Gr. *chrysos*, gold, referring to the color of the carapacial rim or plastron

Chrysemys (krī′-sə-mēz), (kris′-ə-mēz), (kri-sem′-ēz): from Gr. *chrysos*, gold, referring to the yellow head and shell markings, and Gr. *emys*, tortoise

Clemmys (klem′-ēz): from Gr. *klemmys*, tortoise

concinna (kän″-sin′-ə), (kən-sī′-nə): L., neat, skillfully joined, probably referring to the relatively smooth shell

coriacea (kȯr″-ē-ā′-sē-ə), (kȯr-ə-sē′-ə), (kȯr-ē-ä′-sē-ə): leathery, from L. *corium*, leather, referring to its skin

Deirochelys (dīr-ə-kē′-lēz), (dī″-rō-kē′-lēz): possibly from Gr. *deiras*, hill, hump, referring to the domed carapace of the female, or from Gr. *deire*, neck, "apparently in allusion to the extremely long neck" (Zug and Schwartz, 1971), and Gr. *chelys*, a tortoise

delticola (del-tik′-ə-lə): delta-inhabiting, from *delta* and L. *colo*, to inhabit

depressus (də-pres′-əs), (dē″-pres′-əs): L., pressed down, flattened

Dermochelys (dər-mō-kē′-lēz), (dər-mō-kē′-ləs), (dər-məkel'-ēs): from Gr. *derma*, skin, leather, and Gr. *chelys*, a tortoise

dorsalis (dòr-sal'-əs), (dòr-sā'-ləs): from L. *dorsum*, the back, referring to the conspicuous middorsal stripe

elegans (el'-ə-gänz), (el'-ə-ganz): L., choice, elegant

emoryi (em'-ər-ē-ī''), (em'-rē-ī'): named for William H. Emory

Emydoidea (em''-ə-dòi'-dē-ə), (em''-ē-dòi'-dē-ə): resembling the genus *Emys*

Eretmochelys (ə-ret''-mō-kē'-lēz), (ə-ret'' mō-kel'-ēz): from Gr. *eretmon*, an oar, and Gr. *chelys*, a tortoise, referring to its oarlike forelimbs

ernsti (ərnst'-ī): named for Carl H. Ernst

ferox (fer'-äks), (fir'-äks'), (fēr'-äks): L., fierce, wild, bold

flavescens (flə-ves'-enz), (flav'-ə-senz): yellowish, from L. *flavus*, yellow

flavimaculata (fla''-vē-mak''-yü-lä'-tə), (fla''-vi-mak''-yə-lä'-tə): yellow-spotted, from L. *flavus*, yellow, and L. *macula*, spot

floridana (flor-ə-dā'-nə), (flor-i-dan'-ə): named for Florida

gaigeae (gā'-jē), (gā'-jē-ē): named for Helen T. Gaige

geographica (jē''-ō-graf'-ə-kə), (jē''-ō-graf'-i-cä): named for its carapacial pattern resembling contour lines on a map

gibbonsi (gib'-əns-ī): named for J. Whitfield Gibbons

gigas (gī'-gəs), (jī'-gas): Gr., giant

Gopherus (gō-fer'-əs), (gō'-fər-əs): named after the gopher, for its burrowing habit

gorzugi (gòr-zùg'-ī): named for George R. Zug

Graptemys (grap-tem'-ēz), (grap'-tə-mēz): from Gr. *graptos*, inscribed, and Gr. *emys*, tortoise, probably referring to its carapacial pattern

guadalupensis (gwäd'-ə-lü-pen'-səs): from the Guadalupe (river in Texas)

guttata (gü-tä'-tə), (gə-tät'-ə): L., spotted

hartwegi (härt'-weg-ī), (härt'-wig-ī), (härt'-veg-ī): named for Norman E. Hartweg

hieroglyphica (hī-rō-glif'-i-kə), (hī''-ə-rō-glif'-ə-kə): named for its carapacial pattern resembling hieroglyphics

hippocrepis (hip''-ō-krē'-pəs), (hip-ō-krep'-əs): horseshoe, from Gr. *hippos*, horse, and Gr. *krēpis*, shoe, apparently referring to the head stripe pattern

hirtipes (her'-tə-pēz), (hər-tē'-pēz): rough-footed, from L. *hirtus*, rough, and L. *pes*, foot, referring to the rough scales on the feet

imbricata (im''-bri-kā'-tə), (im'-brə-kä'-tä): L., covered with tiles, referring to the overlapping scutes

insculpta (in-skəlp'-tə), (in-skülp'-tä): L., engraved, referring to its sculptured carapace

kempii (kemp'-ī), (kemp'-ē-ī): named for Richard M. Kemp

Kinosternon (kī''-nō-stər'-nän), (kē''-nō-stərn'-ən): from Gr. *kineō*, to move, and Gr. *sternon*, breast, referring to the plastral hinges

kohnii (kōn'-ī), (kōn'-ē-ī'): named for Gustave Kohn

Lepidochelys (lep''-ə-dō-kē'-lēz), (lep''-ə-dō-kel'-ēz): scaly turtle, from Gr. *lepis*, *lepidos*, scale, and Gr. *chelys*, a tortoise

littoralis (lit''-ə-ral'- s), (lit''-ō-rā'-ləs): from L. *litoralis*, of the seashore

longifemorale (loŋ''-gi-fem''-ər-äl'-ē) (loŋ''-gi-fem''-ō-rā'-lē) (loŋ-ji-fem''-ər-al'-ē): named for its long femoral scute

luteola (lü''-tē-ō'-lə): L., yellowish

Macroclemys (mak''-rō-klem'-ēz): from Gr. *makros*, long, large, and Gr. *klemmys*, tortoise

macrospilota (mak''-rō-spi-lō'-tə): from Gr. *makros*, long, large, and Gr. *spilōtos*, spotted, referring to the large yellow spot on each carapacial scute

major (mā'-jər): L., larger, referring to its size

Malaclemys (mal''-ə-klem'-ēz): from Gr. *malakos*, soft, apparently referring to their soft-bodied molluscan prey, and Gr. *klemmys*, tortoise

marginata (mär''-ji-nā'-tə), (mär''-ji-nä'-tə): from L. *marge*, *marginis*, edge, border, probably referring to the pattern on the marginal scutes

marmorata (mär''-mə-rā'-tə), (mär''-mə-rä'-tə): L., marbled, referring to its carapacial pattern

metteri (met'-ər-ī): named for Dean E. Metter

miaria (mē-ar'-ē-ə), (mī''-ar'-e-ə), (mir'-ē-ə): from Gr. *miaros*, stained with blood, referring to the dark plastral pattern

minor (mī'-nər): L., smaller, referring to its size

mobilensis (mō''-bēl''-en'-səs), (mō''-bəl-en'-səs): from Mobile (Mobile Bay, Alabama)

muhlenbergii (myü''-lən-bərg'-ē-ī), (myü''-lən-bərg''-ī), (myü''-lən-bər'-jē-ī): named for G. H. E. Mühlenberg

murrayi (mər'-ē-ī): named for Leo T. Murray

muticus (myü''-tə-kəs), (myü'-ti-kəs): L., curtailed, cut off, referring to the absence of tubercles on the anterior edge of the carapace (Webb, 1973b)

mydas (mī'-dəs), (mī'-das): from Gr. *mydos*, wetness, referring to its aquatic habitat

nelsoni (nel'-sən-ī): named for George Nelson

nigrinoda (nī''-grə-nō'-də), (ni-grē-nō'-dä), (ni-gri-nō'-dä): black-knobbed, from L. *niger*, black, and L. *nodus*, knot

oculifera (äk''-yü-li'-fər-ə), (ō''-kə-lif'-ər-ə): from L. *oculus*, eye, and L. *fero*, to bear, referring to the ocelli on the carapace

odoratus (ōd''-ə-rā'-təs), (ōd''-ə-rä'-təs): L., sweet-smelling, fragrant, a whimsical reference to malodorous musk glands

olivacea (äl''-ə-vā'-sē-ə): olive-colored, from L. *oliva*, an olive *ornata* (òr-nä′-tə), (òr-nā′-tə): L., decorated, ornate

osceola (äs″-ē-ō′-lə): named for Osceola (Florida)

ouachitensis (wäch″-ə-tò-en′-səs), (wäsh″-i-ten′-səs): from Ouachita (river in Louisiana)

pallida (*Clemmys*) (pal′-ə-də): L., pale, referring to the color of the throat and neck

pallidus (*Trionyx*) (pal′-ə-dəs): L., pale, referring to the overall color

peltifer (pel′-tə-fər), (pel-ti′-fər): from L. *pelta,* small shield, and L. *fero,* to bear, referring to the shape of its small, slender bridge scutes

peninsularis (pə-nin″-sə-lar′-əs), (pə-nin″-sü-lar′-is), (pə-nin″-syü-lar′-əs): named for its restriction to peninsular Florida

picta (pik′-tə), (pik′-tä): L., painted, referring to the carapacial pattern

pileata (pī″-lē-ä′-tə), (pil″-ē-ä′-tə): L., capped, covered with a cap, referring to the dark dorsal surface of the head

polyphemus (päl″-ē-fē′-məs): probably named after Polyphemus, the cave-dwelling giant in the *Odyssey,* for its burrowing habit and its great strength

Pseudemys (süd′-ə-mēz), (sü-dem′-ēz): a genus that resembles but is not *Emys*

pseudogeographica (sü″-dō-je″-ō-graf′-ə-kə): a species that resembles but is not *geographica*

pulchra (pul′-krə), (pul′-krä): L., beautiful

reticularia (rə-tik″-yü-lar′-ē-ə), (rə-tik″-yü-lär′-ē-ə): L., netted, referring to the reticulate carapacial pattern

rhizophorarum (rī″-zō-fə-rär′-əm), (rī″-zō-fòr-ar′-əm): named after the mangrove genus *Rhizophora,* for the type locality

rubriventris (rü″-brə-ven′-trəs), (rüb″-ri-ven′-tris): red-bellied, from L. *ruber,* red, and L. *venter, ventris,* the belly

sabinensis (sə-bēn″-en′-səs), (sā″-bi-nen′-səs): from the Sabine (river in Louisiana)

schlegelii (shlā′-gəl-ī), (shlā′-gəl-ē-ī): named for Hermann Schlegel

scripta (skrip′-tə), (skrip′-tä): L., written, referring to markings on the carapace

serpentina (sər″-pən-tē′-nə), (sər″-pən-tī′-nə): L., snake-like, referring to the long neck

sinensis (si-nen′-səs), (sī″-nen′-səs): from China

sonoriense (sə-nòr″-ē-en′-sē), (sə-nòr″-ə-en′-sē): from Sonora (Mexico)

spiniferus (spə-nif″-ə-rəs), (spī″-nif′-ə-rəs), (spī″-nif″-ə-rəs): L., bearing spines, referring to the rough carapacial surface

steindachneri (stīn″-däk′-nər-ī), (stīn″-dac′-nər-ī′), (shtīn″-däk′-nər-ī): named for Franz Steindachner

Sternotherus (stər″-nō-ther′-əs), (stər-nä′-thər-əs): from Gr. *sternon,* breast, chest, and Gr. *thairos,* hinge

subrubrum (səb-rü′-brəm): from L. *sub-,* prefix meaning under, below, somewhat, and L. *rubrum,* red: not very red, probably referring to the mottling on the hatchling plastron

suwanniensis (sə-wän″-ē-en′-səs), (sü-wan″-ē-en′-sis), from Suwannee (river in Florida)

temminckii (tə-mink′-ē-ī), (tem′-ink-ī′): named for Coenraad J. Temminck

tequesta (tə-kwes′-tə): named for the Tequesta Indians of eastern Florida

Terrapene (ter″-ə-pē′-nē): from the Algonquin name for turtle

terrapin (ter′-ə-pən), (ter′-ə-pin): see *Terrapene*

texana (teks-ā′-nə), (teks-an′-ə): named for Texas

Trachemys (trā″-kem′-ēz), (trāk′-ə-mēz), (trä-kem′-ēz): from Gr. *trachys,* rough, referring to the rough carapacial surface, and Gr. *emys,* tortoise

Trionyx (trī-ō′-niks), (trī-ä′-niks), (trē″-ō′-niks): three-clawed, from Gr. *tris,* thrice, and Gr. *onyx,* claw

triunguis (trī-ən′-gwis), (trī-ən′-gü-is): three-clawed, from L. *tri,* three, and L. *unguis,* claw

troostii (trüst′-ē-ī), (trüst′-ī′), (trōst′-ē-ī): named for Gerard Troost

versa (vər′-sə): from L. *versus,* changed, probably referring to the head pattern differing from that of *Graptemys pseudogeographica* (Vogt, 1981d)

Bibliography

We have attempted to include all papers on the ecology, behavior, and systematics of North American turtles published between 1 January 1970 and 1 October 1992, but have also included material from papers that our colleagues or we have "in press." Only the more pertinent papers on biochemistry, physiology, and morphology have been included, and then only if they are related to the above fields of study. Some important papers published before 1970 are listed, but the reader is referred to Carr (1952) and Ernst and Barbour (1972) for other pre-1970 papers.

Those who are seriously interested in turtle research should regularly consult the following journals: *Copeia*, published by the American Society of Ichthyologists and Herpetologists, *Herpetologica*, published by the Herpetologists' League, and the *Journal of Herpetology*, published by the Society for the Study of Amphibians and Reptiles. Furthermore, anyone with a serious and lasting interest in turtles should join one or more of these societies.

The turtle hobbyist may want to consult one of the local or state amateur herpetological societies, or the California or New York Turtle and Tortoise societies. These groups are dedicated to the conservation of turtles throughout the world and to the proper care of captives. Their newsletters contain much useful information of a general nature on the biology and care of turtles.

Abel, B. 1992. Snapping turtle attacks on trumpeter swan cygnets in Wisconsin. Passenger Pigeon 54:209–213.

Ackerman, R. A. 1977. The respiratory gas exchange of sea turtle nests (*Chelonia, Caretta*). Resp. Physiol. 31:19–38.

———. 1980. Physiological and ecological aspects of gas exchange by sea turtle eggs. Amer. Zool. 20:575–583.

———. 1981a. Oxygen consumption by sea turtle (*Chelonia, Caretta*) eggs during development. Physiol. Zool. 54:316–324.

———. 1981b. Growth and gas exchange of embryonic sea turtles (*Chelonia, Caretta*). Copeia 1981:757–765.

Ackerman, R. A., and F. N. White. 1979. Cyclic carbon dioxide exchange in the turtle *Pseudemys scripta*. Physiol. Zool. 52:378–389.

Ackerman, R. A., R. C. Seagrove, R. Dmi'el, and A. Ar.

1985. Water and heat exchange between parchment-shelled reptile eggs and their surroundings. Copeia 1985:703–711.

Ackman, R. G., and R. D. Burgher. 1965. Cod liver oil fatty acids as secondary reference standards in the GLC of polyunsaturated fatty acids of animal origin: Analysis of a dermal oil of the Atlantic leatherback turtle. J. Amer. Oil Chem. Soc. 42:38–42.

Ackman, R. G., S. N. Hooper, and W. Frair. 1971. Comparison of the fatty acid compositions of depot fats from fresh-water and marine turtles. Comp. Biochem. Physiol. 40B:931–944.

Ackman, R. G., S. N. Hooper, and J. C. Sipos. 1972. Distribution of trans-6-hexadecenoic and other fatty acids in tissues and organs of the Atlantic leatherback turtle, *Dermochelys coriacea coriacea* L. Int. J. Biochem. 3:171–179.

Acuña-Mesén, R. A. 1984. La ultraestructura superficial de la cascara del huevo de la tortuga marina

Lepidochelys olivacea Eschscholtz. Brenesia 22:299–308.

———. 1988. Influencia del cautiverio, peso y tamaño en la migración de los neonatos de *Lepidochelys olivacea* Eschscholtz (Testudines: Chelonidae). Rev. Biol. Trop. 36:97–106.

———. 1989a. Anatomia microscopica de la cascara del huevo de la tortuga carey *Eretmochelys imbricata* (Linnaeus, 1766). Brenesia 31:33–41.

———. 1989b. Ultraestructura de la cáscara del huevo de la tortuga *Pseudemys scripta* (Testudines: Emydidae). Rev. Biol. Trop. 37:193–200.

———. 1990. Ultraestructura de la piel de los neonatos de *Lepidochelys olivacea* (Testudines: Cheloniidae). Rev. Biol. Trop. 38:55–62.

Acuña-Mesén, R. A., and P. E. Hanson. 1990. Phorid fly larvae as predators of turtle eggs. Herpetol. Rev. 21:13–14.

Adams, N. A., D. L. Claussen, and J. Skillings. 1989. Effects of temperature on voluntary locomotion of the eastern box turtle, *Terrapene carolina carolina*. Copeia 1989:905–915.

Adams, S. R., and M. C. deCarvalho, Jr. 1984. Rates of heat exchange in the ornate box turtle, *Terrapene ornata*. Comp. Biochem Physiol. 79A:359–361.

Adler, K. K. 1960. Notes on lateral expansion of the periphery in juveniles of *Sternothaerus odoratus*. Copeia 1960:156.

———. 1961. Egg-laying in the spotted turtle, *Clemmys guttata* (Schneider). Ohio J. Sci. 61:180–182.

———. 1968. Turtles from archeological sites in the Great Lakes region. Michigan Archaeol. 14:147–163.

———. 1970. The influence of prehistoric man on the distribution of the box turtle. Ann. Carnegie Mus. Natur. Hist. 41:263–280.

Agassiz, L. 1857. Contributions to the natural history of the United States of America, vol. 1, 2. Little, Brown and Co., Boston. 452 pp.

Aitken, R. N. C., and S. E. Solomon. 1976. Observations on the ultrastructure of the oviduct of the Costa Rican green turtle (*Chelonia mydas* L.). J. Exp. Mar. Biol. Ecol. 21:75–90.

Alderton, D. 1988. Turtles & tortoises of the world. Facts on File Publications, New York. 191 pp.

Alexander, M. M. 1943. Food habits of the snapping turtle in Connecticut. J. Wildl. Mgt. 7:278–282.

Alford, R. A. 1980. Population structure of *Gopherus polyphemus* in northern Florida. J. Herpetol. 14:177–182.

Allard, H. A. 1935. The natural history of the box turtle. Science Monthly 41:325–338.

———. 1939. Mating of the box turtle ending in death to the male. Copeia 1939:109.

———. 1948. The eastern box-turtle and its behavior. J. Tennessee Acad. Sci. 23:307–321.

Alleman, A. R., E. R. Jacobson, and R. E. Raskin. Morphologic and cytochemical characteristics of blood cells from the desert tortoise (*Gopherus agassizii*). Amer. J. Vet. Res. 53:1645–1651.

Allen, E. R. 1938. Notes on the feeding and egg-laying habits of the *Pseudemys*. Proc. Florida Acad. Sci. 3:105–108.

———. 1950. Sounds produced by Suwannee terrapin. Copeia 1950:62.

———. 1982. *Trionyx ferox* (Florida softshell). Size. Herpetol. Rev. 13:49.

Allen, E. R., and W. T. Neill. 1950. The alligator snapping turtle *Macrochelys temminckii* in Florida. Spec. Publ. Ross Allen's Reptile Inst. (4):1–15.

Allen, J. F., and R. A. Littleford. 1955. Observations on the feeding habits and growth of immature diamondback terrapins. Herpetologica 11:77–80.

Allen, W. B., Jr. 1983. Observations on the laminal spurs of *Gopherus polyphemus*. Herpetol. Rev. 14: 37–38.

Allgower, K. 1980. Effect of the scarab beetle *Trox suberosus* on the hatching success of the East Pacific green turtle *Chelonia mydas agassizii* in the Galapagos Islands. Ann. Rept. Charles Darwin Res. Stn. 1979 (1980):150–152.

Alsop, F. J., III, and G. O. Wallace. 1978. Eastern box turtle (*Terrapene carolina*) feeding on TV tower-killed birds. J. Tennessee Acad. Sci. 53:134.

Altland, P. D. 1951. Observations on the structure of the reproductive organs of the box turtle. J. Morphol. 89:599–621.

Alvarado D., J., and A. Figueroa L. 1991. Comportamiento reproductivo de la tortuga negra *Chelonia agassizi*. Ciencia y Desarrollo 17:43–49.

Alvarez S., T. 1975. Restos óseos animales de las Cuevas del Texcal y Tepeyolo, Puebla, México. Apuntes Arqueológia, México 12:1–55.

———. 1976. Restos óseos de las excavaciones de Tlatilco, Edo. de México. Restos óseos rescatados del Cenote Sagrado de Chichén Itzá, Yucatán. Apuntes Arqueológia, México 15:1–39.

Anderson, J. D., and V. Curcione. 1973. A basic bibliography of the bog turtle (*Clemmys muhlenbergi*). HERP, Bull. New York Herpetol. Soc. 10(1&2):33–36.

Anderson, O. F., and R. E. Herrington. 1992. *Gopherus polyphemus* (gopher tortoise). Diet. Herpetol. Rev. 23:59.

Anderson, P. K. 1958. The photic responses and water-approach behavior of hatchling turtles. Copeia 1958:211–215.

———. 1965. The reptiles of Missouri. Univ. Missouri Press, Columbia. 330 pp.

Andre, J. B., and L. West. 1981. Nesting management of the Atlantic loggerhead, *Caretta caretta caretta* (Linnaeus) (Testudines: Cheloniidae) on Cape Island, South Carolina in 1979. Brimleyana (6):73–82.

Anon. 1990. Navigational secrets identified. Marine Turtle Newsl. (51):4–5.

———. 1991. Kemp's ridley nests in Texas. Marine Turtle Newsl. (55):23.

———. 1992a. First leatherback nest reported in Florida park. Marine Turtle Newsl. (59):21.

———. 1992b. First Kemp's ridley nesting in South Carolina. Marine Turtle Newsl. (59):23.

Anton, T. G. 1987. Notes on winter activity in a red-eared slider, *Trachemys scripta elegans*. Bull. Chicago Herpetol. Soc. 22:131.

———. 1990. Predation on the house sparrow, *Passer domesticus*, by the Gulf Coast box turtle, *Terrapene carolina major*, under seminatural conditions. Bull. Chicago Herpetol. Soc. 25:143–144.

Applegate, R. D. 1974. Some notes on the nest of the midland painted turtle (*Chrysemys picta marginata* Agassiz). Bull. Chicago Herpetol. Soc. 9:42.

Arata, A. A. 1958. Notes on the eggs and young of *Gopherus polyphemus* (Daudin). Quart. J. Florida Acad. Sci. 21:274–280.

Arndt, R. G. 1972. Additional records of *Clemmys muhlenbergi* in Delaware, with notes on reproduction. Bull. Maryland Herpetol. Soc. 8:1–5.

———. 1975a. Meet our turtles. Delaware Conserv. 19(1):11–14.

———. 1975b. The occurrence of barnacles and algae on the red-bellied turtle, *Chrysemys r. rubriventris* (Le Conte). J. Herpetol. 9:357–359.

———. 1977. Notes on the natural history of the bog turtle, *Clemmys muhlenbergi* (Schoepff), in Delaware. Chesapeake Science 18:67–76.

———. 1978. The bog turtle . . . an endangered species? Delaware Conserv. 22(2):18–21, 25.

———. 1986. Notes on the bog turtle, *Clemmys muhlenbergi*, in Warren County, New Jersey. Bull. Maryland Herpetol. Soc. 22:56–61.

———. 1991. Predation on hatchling diamondback terrapin, *Malaclemys terrapin* (Schoepff), by the ghost crab, *Ocypode quadrata* (Fabricius). Florida Scientist 54:215–217.

Arndt, R. G., and W. A. Potter. 1973. A population of the map turtle, *Graptemys geographica*, in the Delaware River, Pennsylvania. J. Herpetol. 7:375–377.

Ashley, L. M. 1962. Laboratory anatomy of the turtle. Wm. C. Brown Co. Publ., Dubuque, Iowa. 48 pp.

Ashton, R. E., Jr., and K. J. Ashton. 1991. *Gopherus polyphemus* (gopher tortoise). Drinking behavior. Herpetol. Rev. 22:55–56.

Ashton, R. E., Jr., and P. S. Ashton. 1985. Handbook of the reptiles and amphibians of Florida. Part 2. Lizards, turtles and crocodilians. Windward Publ., Inc., Miami, Florida. 191 pp.

Auffenberg, W. 1957. The status of the turtle *Macroclemys floridana* Hay. Herpetologica 13:123–126.

———. 1958. Fossil turtles of the genus *Terrapene* in Florida. Bull. Florida St. Mus. Biol. Sci. 3:53–92.

———. 1963. Fossil testudinine turtles of Florida genera *Geochelone* and *Floridemys*. Bull. Florida St. Mus. Biol. Sci. 7:53–97.

———. 1964. A redefinition of the fossil tortoise genus *Stylemys* Leidy. J. Paleontol. 38:316–324.

———. 1966a. The carpus of land tortoises (Testudininae). Bull. Florida St. Mus. Biol. Sci. 10:159–192.

———. 1966b. On the courtship of *Gopherus polyphemus*. Herpetologica 22:113–117.

———. 1969. Tortoise behavior and survival. Rand McNally and Co., Chicago. 38 pp.

———. 1974. Checklist of fossil land tortoises (Testudinidae). Bull. Florida St. Mus. Biol. Sci. 18:121–251.

———. 1976. The genus *Gopherus* (Testudinidae): Pt. I. Osteology and relationships of extant species. Bull. Florida St. Mus. Biol. Sci. 20:47–110.

Auffenberg, W., and R. Franz. 1978a. *Gopherus*. Catalog. Amer. Amphib. Rept. 211:1–2.

———. 1978b. *Gopherus agassizii*. Catalog. Amer. Amphib. Rept. 212:1–2.

———. 1978c. *Gopherus berlandieri*. Catalog. Amer. Amphib. Rept. 213:1–2.

———. 1978d. *Gopherus polyphemus*. Catalog. Amer. Amphib. Rept. 215:1–2.

———. 1982. The status and distribution of the gopher tortoise (*Gopherus polyphemus*). *In* Bury, R. B., ed. North American tortoises: Conservation and ecology, 95–126. U.S. Fish Wildl. Serv. Wildl. Res. Rept. (12).

Auffenberg, W., and W. G. Weaver, Jr. 1969. *Gopherus berlandieri* in southeastern Texas. Bull. Florida St. Mus. Biol. Sci. 13:141–203.

Auger, P. J., and P. Giovannone. 1979. On the fringe of existence: Diamondback terrapins at Sandy Neck. The Cape Naturalist 8:44–58.

Auth, D. L. 1975. Behavioral ecology of basking in the yellow-bellied turtle, *Chrysemys scripta scripta* (Schoepff). Bull. Florida St. Mus. Biol. Sci. 20:1–45.

Avery, H. A., J. R. Spotila, J. D. Congdon, R. U. Fischer, Jr., E. A. Standora, and S. B. Avery. 1993. Roles of diet protein and temperature in the growth and nutritional energetics of juvenile slider turtles, *Trachemys scripta*. Physiol. Zool. 66:902–925.

Avise, J. C., B. W. Bowen, T. Lamb, A. B. Meylan, and E. Bermingham. 1992. Mitochondrial DNA evolution at a turtle's pace: Evidence for low genetic variability and reduced microevolutionary rate in the Testudines. Mol. Biol. Evol. 9:457–473.

Awbrey, F. T., S. Leatherwood, E. D. Mitchell, and W. Rogers. 1984. Nesting green sea turtles (*Chelonia mydas*) on Isla Clarion, Islas Revillagigedos, Mexico. Bull. Southern California Acad. Sci. 83:69–75.

Axtel, R. W. 1959. Amphibians and reptiles of the Black Gap Wildlife Management Area, Brewster County, Texas. Southwest. Natur. 4:88–109.

Babcock, H. L. 1919. The turtles of New England. Mem. Boston Soc. Natur. Hist. 8:323–431.

———. 1937. A new subspecies of the red-bellied terrapin *Pseudemys rubriventris* (Le Conte). Occ. Pap. Boston Soc. Natur. Hist. 8:293–294.

———. 1939. Growth of an individual box turtle. Copeia 1939:175.

Bachère, E. 1981. Le caryotype de la Tortue verte, *Chelonia mydas* L. dans l'Océan Indien (Canal du Mozambique). C. R. Acad. Sci., Paris, ser. 3, 292:1129–1131.

Bacon, P. R. 1970. Studies on the leatherback turtle, *Dermochelys coriacea* (L.), in Trinidad, West Indies. Biol. Conserv. 2:213–217.

———. 1973. The orientation circle in the beach ascent crawl of the leatherback turtle, *Dermochelys coriacea*, in Trinidad. Herpetologica 29:343–348.

Baird, S. F., and C. Girard. 1852. Descriptions of new species of reptiles collected by the U.S. Exploring Expedition under the command of Capt. Charles Wilkes, U.S.N. Proc. Acad. Natur. Sci. Philadelphia 6:174–177.

Baird, T. and. S. E. Soloman. 1979. Calcite and aragonite in the egg shell of *Chelonia mydas* L. J. Exp. Mar. Biol. Ecol. 36:295–303.

Baker, R. E., and J. C. Gillingham. 1983. An analysis of courtship behavior in Blanding's turtle, *Emydoidea blandingi.* Herpetologica 39:166–173.

Balazs, G. H. 1973. Status of marine turtles in the Hawaiian Islands. 'Elepaio (J. Hawaii Audubon Soc.) 33:127–132.

———. 1976. Green turtle migrations in the Hawaiian Archipelago. Biol. Conserv. 9:125–140.

———. 1979a. Hawaiian green turtle (*Chelonia mydas*) and monk seals (*Monachus schauinslandi*) basking [photo]. Herpetol. Rev. 10:123.

———. 1979b. Loggerhead turtle recovered from a tiger shark at Kure Atoll. 'Elepaio (J. Hawaii Audubon Soc.) 39:145–147.

———. 1980. Synopsis of biological data on the green turtle in the Hawaiian Islands. NOAA-TM-NMFS-SWFC-7. 141 pp.

———. 1982a. Growth rates of immature green turtles in the Hawaiian Archipelago. *In* Bjorndal, K. A., ed. Biology and conservation of sea turtles, 117–125. Smithsonian Institution Press, Washington, D.C.

———. 1982b. Status of sea turtles in the Central Pacific Ocean. *In* Bjorndal, K. A., ed. Biology and conservation of sea turtles, 243–252. Smithsonian Institution Press, Washington, D.C.

———. 1982c. Driftnets catch leatherback turtles. Oryx 16:428–430.

———. 1984. Researcher seeks information on hawksbill poisoning. Marine Turtle Newsl. (28):3.

———. 1985. Impact of ocean debris on marine turtles: Entanglement and ingestion. *In* Shomura, R. S., and H. O. Yoshida, eds. Proceedings of the workshop on the fate and impact of marine debris, 387–429. NOAA-TM-NMFS-SWFC-54.

———. 1986. Ontogenetic changes in the plastron pigmentation of hatchling Hawaiian green turtles. J. Herpetol. 20:280–282.

Balazs, G. H., and E. Ross. 1974a. Observations on the basking habit in the captive juvenile Pacific green turtle. Copeia 1974:542–544.

———. 1974b. Observations on the preemergence behavior of the green turtle. Copeia 1974:986–988.

Balazs, G. H., R. G. Forsyth, and A. K. H. Kam. 1987. Preliminary assessment of habitat utilization by Hawaiian green turtles in their resident foraging pastures. NOAA-TM-NMFS-SWFC-71. 107 pp.

Balcombe, J. P., and L.E. Licht. 1987. Some aspects of the ecology of the midland painted turtle, *Chrysemys picta marginata,* in Wye Marsh, Ontario. Can. Field-Natur. 101:98–100.

Baldwin, J., and E. Gyuris. 1983. Loggerhead turtle lactate dehydrogenases. How general is the apparent adaptation to prolonged anaerobiosis displayed by the lacate dehydrogenase isoenzymes from turtles of the genus *Pseudemys*? Comp. Biochem. Physiol. 76B:191–195.

Bancroft, G. T., J. S. Godley, D. T. Gross, N. N. Rojas, D. A. Sutphen, and R. W. McDiarmid. 1983. Large-scale operations management test of use of the white amur for control of problem aquatic plants. The herpetofauna of Lake Conway: Species accounts. Misc. Pap. A-83–5. Army Engineer Waterways Exp. Stat., Vicksburg, Mississippi. 354 pp.

Bane, G. 1992. First report of a loggerhead sea turtle from Alaska. Marine Turtle Newsl. (58):1–2.

Banicki, L. H. 1981. New records of the spotted turtle, *Clemmys guttata* in northern Florida. Florida Scientist 44:253–254.

Bannikov, A. G., I. S. Darevskii, and A. K. Rustamov. 1971. Zemnovodnyi i Presmykayshchie. USSR Isdatel'sto Mysl. Moscow. 304 pp.

Barbour, R. W. 1950. The reptiles of Big Black Mountain, Harlan County, Kentucky. Copeia 1950:100–107.

———. 1971. Amphibians & reptiles of Kentucky. University of Kentucky Press, Lexington. 334 pp.

Barnes, S. B., J. H. Black, and J. Pigg. 1986. New distributional records of the genus Sternotherus in Oklahoma. Bull. Chicago Herpetol. Soc. 21:98–99.

Barney, R. L. 1922. Further notes on the natural history and artificial propagation of the diamond-back terrapin. Bull. Bur. Fish. 38:91–111.

Barone, M. C., and F. A. Jacques. 1975. The effects of induced cold torpor and time of year on blood coagulation in Pseudemys scripta elegans and Chrysemys picta belli. Comp. Biochem. Physiol. 50A:717–721.

Barrett, S. L. 1990. Home range and habitat of the desert tortoise (Xerobates agassizi) in the Picacho Mountains of Arizona. Herpetologica 46:202–206.

Barrett, S. L., and J.A. Humphrey. 1986. Agonistic interactions between Gopherus agassizii (Testudinidae) and Heloderma suspectum (Helodermatidae). Southwest. Natur. 31:261–263.

Barrow, J. 1979. Aspects of ecology of the desert tortoise, Gopherus agassizi, in Joshua Tree National Monument, Pinto Basin, Riverside County, California. Proc. Symp. Desert Tortoise Council 1979:105–131.

Barten, S. L. 1980. The consumption of turtle eggs by a western hognose snake, Heterodon nasicus: a field observation. Bull. Chicago Herpetol. Soc. 15:97–98.

Bartley, J. A. 1971. A histological and hormonal analysis of physiological and morphological chromatophore responses in the soft-shelled turtle Trionyx sp. J. Zool. (London) 163:125–144.

Barton, A. J., and J. W. Price, Sr. 1955. Our knowledge of the bogturtle, Clemmys muhlenbergii, surveyed and augmented. Copeia 1955:159–165.

Barzilay, S. 1980. Aggressive behavior in the wood turtle, Clemmys insculpta. J. Herpetol. 14:89–91.

Baur, G. 1889. The relationship of the genus Deirochelys. Amer. Natur. 23:1099–1100.

———. 1890. Two new species of tortoises from the South. Science 16:262–263.

———. 1893a. Notes on the classification and taxonomy of the Testudinata. Proc. Amer. Phil. Soc. 31:210–225.

———. 1893b. Two new species of North American Testudinata. Amer. Natur. 27:675–677.

Baxter, G. T., and M. D. Stone. 1980. Amphibians and reptiles of Wyoming. Wyoming Game Fish Dept. Bull. (16):1–137.

Baxter, R. J. 1988. Spatial distribution of desert tortoises (Gopherus agassizii) at Twentynine Palms, California: Implications for relocations. In Szaro, R. C., K. E. Severson, and D. R. Patton, eds. Management of amphibians, reptiles, and small mammals in North America, 180–189. USDA Tech. Serv. Gen. Tech. Rept. Rm-166.

Bayless, L. E. 1972. A new turtle record, Chrysemys floridana, for West Virginia. J. Herpetol. 6:39–41.

———. 1975. Population parameters for Chrysemys picta in a New York pond. Amer. Midl. Natur. 93:168–176.

Baze, W. B., and F. R. Horne. 1970. Ureogenesis in chelonia. Comp. Biochem. Physiol. 34:91–100.

Bearse, L. 1985. Loggerheads mate off Cape Hatteras. Marine Turtle Newsl. (34):8.

Becak W., M. L. Becak, H.R.S. Nazareth, and S. Ohno. 1964. Close karyological kinship between the reptilian suborder Serpentes and the class Aves. Chromosoma 15:606–617.

Becker, H. 1992. Beobachtungen bei der Haltung und Nachzucht von Sternotherus carinatus (Gray, 1856). Salamandra 28:9–13.

Behler, J. L., and F. W. King. 1979. The Audubon Society field guide to North American reptiles and amphibians. Alfred A. Knopf, New York. 743 pp.

Behrend, D. F., and R. W. Sage, Jr. 1974. Unusual feeding behavior by black bears. J. Wildl. Mgt. 38:570.

Beissinger, S. R. 1990. Alternative foods of a diet specialist, the snail kite. Auk 107:327–333.

Belkin, D. A. 1964. Variations in heart rate during voluntary diving in the turtle, Pseudemys concinna. Copeia 1964:321–330.

———. 1968a. Anaerobic brain function: Effects of stagnant and anoxic anoxia on persistence of breathing in reptiles. Science 162:1017–1018.

———. 1968b. Aquatic respiration and underwater survival of two freshwater turtle species. Resp. Physiol. 4:1–14.

Belkin, D. A., and C. Gans. 1968. An unusual chelonian feeding niche. Ecology 49:768–769.

Belmore, B. 1972. Firewell spotted turtles. Int. Turtle and Tortoise Soc. J. 6(4):26–27.

———. 1973. Clemmys guttata–notes on reproduction. HERP, Bull. New York Herpetol. Soc. 10(1&2):37–38.

———. 1980. The basic ecology of the spotted turtle Clemmys guttata (Schneider) in Massachusetts. J. Northern Ohio Assoc. Herpetol. 6:5–13.

Bels, V., and R. LiBois. 1983. Etude comparée des parades sexuelles de quelques espèces de cheloniens: Pelomedusa subrufa subrufa (Lacépède), Sternotherus *minor* (Agassiz) et *Kinixys belliana nogueyi* (Bell). Cahiers Ethol. Appl. 3:39–58.

Beltz, R. E. 1954a. Miscellaneous observations on captive Testudininae. Herpetologica 10:45–47.

———. 1954b. Notes on the winter behavior of captive non-indigenous chelonia in southern California. Herpetologica 10:124.

Bennett, D. H. 1972. Notes on the terrestrial wintering of mud turtles (*Kinosternon subrubrum*). Herpetologica 28:245–247.

Bennett, D. H., J. W. Gibbons, and J. C. Franson. 1970. Terrestrial activity in aquatic turtles. Ecology 51:738–740.

Bennett, J. A., and H. Kleerekoper. 1978. A preliminary investigation of the effects of chemical stimulation on the locomotor behavior of hatchling green turtles (*Chelonia mydas*). *In* Henderson, G. E., ed. 1978. Proceedings of the Florida and Interregional Conference on sea turtles, 3–7. Florida Marine Res. Publ. 33.

Bennett, J. M., L. E. Taplin, and G. C. Grigg. 1986. Sea water drinking as a homeostatic response to dehydration in hatchling loggerhead turtles *Caretta caretta*. Comp. Biochem. Physiol. 83A:507–513.

Bentley, P. J., W. L. Bretz, and K. Schmidt-Nielsen. 1967. Osmoregulation in the diamondback terrapin, *Malaclemys terrapin centrata*. J. Exp. Biol. 46:161–167.

Bentley, P. J., and K. Schmidt-Nielsen. 1970. Comparison of the water exchange in two aquatic turtles, *Trionyx spinifer* and *Pseudemys scripta*. Comp. Biochem. Physiol. 32:363–365.

Berkson, H. 1966. Physiological adjustments to prolonged diving in the Pacific green turtle (*Chelonia mydas agassizii*). Comp. Biochem. Physiol. 18:101–119.

———. 1967. Physiological adjustments to deep diving in the Pacific green turtle (*Chelonia mydas agassizii*). Comp. Biochem. Physiol. 21:507–524.

Berry, J. F. 1975. The population effects of ecological sympatry on musk turtles in northern Florida. Copeia 1975:692–701.

Berry, J. F., and C. M. Berry. 1983. A re-analysis of geographic variation and systematics in the yellow mud turtle, *Kinosternon flavescens* (Agassiz). Ann. Carnegie Mus. Natur. Hist. 53:185–206.

Berry, J. F., and C. S. Gidden. 1974. The spotted turtle in Florida and southern Georgia. Florida Scientist 36:198–200.

Berry, J. F., and R. Shine. 1980. Sexual size dimorphism and sexual selection in turtles (Order Testudines). Oecologia (Berlin). 44:185–191.

Berry, K. H. 1976. A comparison of size classes and sex ratios in four populations of the desert tortoise. Proc. Symp. Desert Tortoise Council 1976:38–50.

———. 1978. Livestock grazing and the desert tortoise. Trans. 43rd N.A. Wildl. Natur. Res. Conf.:505–519.

———. 1986a. Desert tortoise (*Gopherus agassizii*) relocation: Implications of social behavior and movements. Herpetologica 42:113–125.

———. 1986b. Incidence of gunshot deaths in desert tortoise populations in California. Wildl. Soc. Bull. 14:127–132.

———. 1991. The status of the desert tortoise in 1990: Current population issues in California. *In* Beaman, K. R., F. Caporaso, S. McKeown, and M. D. Graff, eds. Proceedings of the First International Symposium on Turtles and Tortoises: Conservation and Captive Husbandry, 80–82. Chapman Univ., Orange, California.

Berry, K. H., and F. B. Turner. 1984. Notes on the behavior and habitat preferences of juvenile desert tortoises (*Gopherus agassizii*) in California. Proc. Symp. Desert Tortoise Council 1984:111–130.

Berry, K. H., A. P. Woodman, L. L. Nicholson, and B. L. Burge. 1983. The distribution and abundance of the desert tortoise (*Gopherus agassizii*) on the Chocolate Mountains Aerial Gunnery Range. Proc. Symp. Desert Tortoise Council 1983:47–65.

Bertl, J., and F. C. Killebrew. 1983. An osteological comparison of *Graptemys caglei* Haynes and McKown and *Graptemys versa* Stejneger (Testudines: Emydidae). Herpetologica 39:375–382.

Bethea, N. J. 1972. Effects of temperature on heart rate and rates of cooling and warming in *Terrapene ornata*. Comp. Biochem. Physiol. 41A:301–305.

Bhunya, S. P., and P. Mohanty-Hejmadi. 1986. Somatic chromosome study of a sea turtle, *Lepidochelys olivacea* (Chelonia, Reptilia). Chromosome Inform. Serv. (40):12–14.

Bickett, J. E. 1980. A baseline study of the desert tortoise, *Gopherus agassizi*, at the Interpretive Center Site, Desert Tortoise Natural Area. Proc. Symp. Desert Tortoise Council 1980:174–176.

Bickham, J. W. 1975. A cytosystematic study of turtles in the genera *Clemmys, Mauremys* and *Sacalia*. Herpetologica 31:198–204.

———. 1976. A meiotic analysis of four species of turtles. Genetica 46:193–198.

———. 1979. Karyotypes of sea turtles and the karyological relationships of the Cheloniidae. Amer. Zool. 19:983.

———. 1981. Two-hundred million year old chromosomes: Deceleration of the rate of karyotypic evolution in turtles. Science 212:1291–1293.

Bickham, J. W., and R. W. Baker. 1976. Chromosome

homology and evolution of emydid turtles. Chromosoma 54:201–219.

Bickham, J. W., and J. L. Carr. 1983. Taxonomy and phylogeny of the higher categories of cryptodiran turtles based on a cladistic analysis of chromosomal data. Copeia 1983:918–932.

Bickham, J. W., K. A. Bjorndal, M. W. Haiduk, and W. E. Rainey. 1980. The karyotype and chromosomal banding patterns of the green turtle (*Chelonia mydas*). Copeia 1980:540–543.

Bickham, J. W., J. J. Bull, and J. M. Legler. 1983. Karyotypes and evolutionary relationships of trionychid turtles. Cytologia 48:177–183.

Bickham, J. W., B. G. Hanks, M. J. Smolen, T. Lamb, and J. W. Gibbons. 1988. Flow cytometric analysis of the effects of low-level radiation exposure on natural populations of slider turtles (*Pseudemys scripta*). Arch. Environ. Contam. Toxicol. 17:837–841.

Bickham, J. W., M. D. Springer, and B. J. Galloway. 1984. Distributional survey of the yellow mud turtle (*Kinosternon flavescens*) in Iowa, Illinois, and Missouri: A proposed endangered species. Southwest. Natur. 29:123–132.

Bider, J. R., and W. Hoek. 1971. An efficient and apparently unbiased sampling technique for population studies of painted turtles. Herpetologica 27:481;b2484.

Birchard, G. F., M. J. Packard, and G. C. Packard. 1990. Effect of temperature and hydric conditions on blood pH in embryonic snapping turtles (*Chelydra serpentina*). Can. J. Zool. 68:190–193.

Birkenmeier, E. 1971. Juvenile leathery turtles *Dermochelys coriacea* (Linnaeus), in captivity. Brunei Mus. J. 2:160–172.

Birse, R. F., and J. Davenport. 1987. A study of gut function in young loggerhead sea turtles, *Caretta caretta* L. at various temperatures. Herpetol. J. 1:170–175.

Bishop, C. A., R. J. Brooks, J. H. Carey, P. Ng, R.J Norstrom, and D. R. S. Lean. 1991. The case for a cause-effect linkage between environmental contamination and development in eggs of the common snapping turtle (*Chelydra s. serpentina*) from Ontario, Canada. J. Toxicol. Environ. Health. 33:521–547.

Bishop, J. M. 1983. Incidental capture of diamondback terrapin by crab pots. Estuaries 6:426–430.

Bishop, S. C., and W. J. Schoonmacher. 1921. Turtle hunting in midwinter. Copeia 96:37–38.

Bishop, S. C., and F. J. W. Schmidt. 1931. The painted turtles of the genus *Chrysemys*. Zool. Ser. Field Mus. Natur. Hist. (293)18:123–139.

Bissett, D. 1968. Box turtle nesting. Int. Turtle and Tort. Soc. J. 2(6):12–16, 36.

Bjorndal, K. A. 1979a. Cellulose digestion and volatile fatty acid production in the green turtle, *Chelonia mydas*. Comp. Biochem. Physiol. 63A:127–133.

———. 1979b. Urine concentrations of ammonia, urea and uric acid in the green turtle, *Chelonia mydas*. Comp. Biochem. Physiol. 63A:509–510.

———. 1980a. Nutrition and grazing behavior of the green turtle *Chelonia mydas*. Marine Biol. 56:147–154.

———. 1980b. Demography of the breeding population of the green turtle, *Chelonia mydas*, at Tortuguero, Costa Rica. Copeia 1980:525–530.

———, ed. 1982a. Biology and conservation of sea turtles. Smithsonian Institution Press, Washington, D.C. 583 pp.

———. 1982b. The consequences of herbivory for the life history pattern of the Caribbean green turtle, *Chelonia mydas*. *In* Bjorndal, K. A., ed. Biology and conservation of sea turtles, 111–116. Smithsonian Institution Press, Washington, D.C.

———. 1985. Nutritional ecology of sea turtles. Copeia 1985:736–751.

———. 1986. Effect of solitary vs. group feeding on intake in *Pseudemys nelsoni*. Copeia 1986:234–235.

———. 1987. Digestive efficiency in a temperate herbivorous reptile, *Gopherus polyphemus*. Copeia 1987:714–720.

———. 1990. Digestibility of the sponge *Chondrilla nucula* in the green turtle, *Chelonia mydas*. Bull. Marine Sci. 47:567–570.

———. 1991. Diet mixing: Nonadditive interactions of diet items in an omnivorous freshwater turtle. Ecology 72:1234–1241.

Bjorndal, K. A., and A. B. Bolten. 1988a. Growth rates of juvenile loggerheads, *Caretta caretta*, in the southern Bahamas. J. Herpetol. 22:480–482.

———. 1988b. Growth rates of immature green turtles, *Chelonia mydas*, on feeding grounds in the southern Bahamas. Copeia 1988:555–564.

———. 1989. Comparisons of straight-line and over-the-curve measurements for growth rates of green turtles, *Chelonia mydas*. Bull. Marine Sci. 45:189–192.

———. 1990. Digestive processing in a herbivorous freshwater turtle: Consequences of small-intestine fermentation. Physiol. Zool. 63:1232–1247.

———. 1992a. Spatial distribution of green turtle (*Chelonia mydas*) nests at Tortuguero, Costa Rica. Copeia 1992:45–53.

———. 1992b. Body size and digestive efficiency in a herbivorous freshwater turtle: Advantages of small bite size. Physiol. Zool. 65:1028–1039.

Bjorndal, K. A., and A. Carr. 1989. Variation in clutch

size and egg size in the green turtle nesting population at Tortuguero, Costa Rica. Herpetologica
45:181–189.

Bjorndal, K. A., A. Carr, A. B. Meylan, and J. A.
Mortimer. 1985. Reproductive biology of the
hawksbill *Eretmochelys imbricata* at Tortuguero, Costa
Rica, with notes on the ecology of the species in the
Caribbean. Biol. Conserv. 34:353–368.

Bjorndal, K. A., A. B. Meylan, and B. J. Turner. 1983.
Sea turtles nesting at Melbourne Beach, Florida, I.
Size, growth and reproductive biology. Biol. Conserv.
26:65–77.

Bjorndal, K. A., H. Suganuma, and A. B. Bolten. 1991.
Digestive fermentation in green turtles, *Chelonia
mydas,* feeding on algae. Bull. Marine Sci. 48:166–
171.

Black, J. H. 1970. Turtles of Montana. Montana Wildl.
November 1970:26–32.

———. 1976. Observations on courtship behavior of the
desert tortoise. Great Basin Natur. 36:467–470.

———. 1987. Do ornate box turtles prey on birds? Bull.
Maryland Herpetol. Soc. 23:130–132.

Black, J. H., J. Pigg, and R. L. Lardie. 1987. Distribution records of *Graptemys* in Oklahoma. Bull. Maryland Herpetol. Soc. 23:65–68.

Blair, W. F. 1976. Some aspects of the biology of the
ornate box turtle, *Terrapene ornata*. Southwest. Natur.
21:89–103.

Blake, S. F. 1922. Sexual differences in coloration in the
spotted turtle, *Clemmys guttata*. Proc. U.S. Natl.
Mus. 59:463–469.

Bleakney, J. S. 1958a. The significance of turtle bones
from archaeological sites in southern Ontario and
Quebec. Can. Field-Natur. 72:1–5.

———. 1958b. Postglacial dispersal of the turtle
Chrysemys picta. Herpetologica 14:101–104.

———. 1963. Notes on the distribution and life histories
of turtles in Nova Scotia. Can. Field-Natur. 77:67–
76.

———. 1965. Reports of marine turtles from New
England and eastern Canada. Can. Field-Natur.
79:120–128.

Bloomer, T. J. 1977. *Clemmys muhlenbergi* and friends:
Herptiles that share the bog turtle's habitat. J.
Northern Ohio Assoc. Herpetol. 3:30–34.

———. 1978. Hibernacula congregating in the *Clemmys*
genus. J. Northern Ohio Assoc. Herpetol. 4:37–42.

Bloomer, T. J., and D. M. Bloomer. 1973. New Jersey's
bog turtle: Destined to extinction? HERP, Bull. New
York Herpetol. Soc. 9(3&4):8–12.

Boarman, W. I. 1993. When a native predator becomes a
pest: A case study. *In* Majumdar, S. K., E. W. Miller,
D. E. Miller, J. R. Pratt, R. F. Schmalz, and E. K.

Brown, eds. Conservation and resource management,
186–201. Pennsylvania Academy of Science.

Bocourt, F. 1868. Description de quelques chéloniens
nouveaux appartenant à la faune Mexicaine. Ann. Sci.
Nat. Zool. Paris, ser. 5, 10:121–122.

Bogert, C. M. 1937. Note on the growth rate of the desert
tortoise, *Gopherus agassizi*. Copeia 1937:191–192.

Bogert, C. M., and R. B. Cowles. 1947. Results of the
Archbold Expeditions. No. 58. Moisture loss in
relation to habitat selection in some Floridian reptiles.
Amer. Mus. Novitates (1358):1–34.

Boice, R. 1970. Competitive feeding behaviors in captive
Terrapene c. carolina. Anim. Behav. 18:703–710.

Bolten, A. B., H. R. Martins, M. L. Natali, J. C. Thome,
and M. A. Marcovaldi. 1990. Loggerhead released in
Brazil recaptured in Azores. Marine Turtle Newsl.
(48):24–25.

Bolten, A. B., J. C. Santana, and K. A. Bjorndal. 1992.
Transatlantic crossing by a loggerhead turtle. Marine
Turtle Newsl. (59):7–8.

Bonhomme, F., S. Salvidio, A. LeBeau, and G. Pasteur.
1987. Comparaison génétique des tortues vertes
(*Chelonia mydas*) des Oceans Alantique, Indien et
Pacifique: une illustration apparente de la théorie
mullerienne classique de la structure génétique des
populations? Genetica 74:89–94.

Booth, J. 1975. Boobies ride on backs of turtles. Sea
Swallow 25:51.

Booth, J., and J. A. Peters. 1972. Behavioural studies on
the green turtle (*Chelonia mydas*) in the sea. Anim.
Behav. 20:808–812.

Booth, K. 1958. Development of eggs and young of
desert tortoise. Herpetologica 13:261–263.

———. 1980. Forty years with tortoises. Quadco Print
Co., Orland, California. 110 pp.

Booth, K., and Buskirk. 1988. Three generations of
captive-hatched desert tortoises, *Xerobates agassizii*.
Herpetol. Rev. 19:55–56.

Bostick, V. 1990. The desert tortoise in relation to cattle
grazing. Rangelands 12:149–151.

Boulenger, G. A. 1889. Catalogue of the chelonians,
rhynchocephalians, and crocodiles in the British
Museum (Natural History). Taylor and Francis,
London. 311 pp.

Boulon, R., Jr., K. Eckert and S. Eckert. 1988.
Dermochelys coriacea (leatherback sea turtle). Migration. Herpetol. Rev. 19:88.

Boulon, R. H., Jr., and N. B. Frazer. 1990. Growth of
wild juvenile Caribbean green turtles, *Chelonia mydas*.
J. Herpetol. 24:441–445.

Boundy, J. 1991. A possible native population of the
painted turtle, *Chrysemys picta,* in Arizona. Bull.
Chicago Herpetol. Soc. 26:33.

Bour, R. 1987. Type-specimen of the alligator snapper, *Macroclemys temminckii* (Harlan, 1835). J. Herpetol. 21:340–343.

Bour, R., and A. Dubois. 1983a. Nomenclatural availability of *Testudo coriacea* Vandelli, 1761: A case against a rigid application of the Rules to old, well-known zoological works. J. Herpetol. 17:356–361.

———. 1983b. Statut nomenclatural et specimens-types d'*Emys pseudogeographica* Gray, 1831 et d'*Emys lesueuri* Gray, 1831 (Reptilia, Chelonii, Emydidae). Bull. Mens. Soc. Linn. Lyon 52:42–46.

———. 1984. *Xerobates* Agassiz, 1857, synonyme plus ancien de *Scaptochelys* Bramble, 1982 (Reptilia, Chelonii, Testudinidae). Bull. Mens. Soc. Linn. Lyon 53:30–32.

Bourne, A. R., and P. Licht. 1985. Steroid biosynthesis in turtle testes. Comp. Biochem. Physiol. 81B:793–796.

Bouskila, A. 1986. On the danger of spreading the red eared terrapin, *Chrysemys scripta*, in natural habitats in Israel. Hardun 3:63.

Bowen, B. W. 1988. Population structure of the green sea turtle, *Chelonia mydas*. Progr. Abstr. Comb. Herpetol. Meet., Ann Arbor, Michigan, 1988:66.

Bowen, B. W., A. B. Meylan, and J. C. Avise. 1989. An odyssey of the green sea turtle: Ascension Island revisited. Proc. Natl. Acad. Sci. 86:573–576.

———. 1991. Evolutionary distinctiveness of the endangered Kemp's ridley sea turtle. Nature 352:709–711.

Bowen, B. W., A. B. Meylan, J. P. Ross, C. J. Limpus, G. H. Balazs, and J. C. Avise. 1992. Global population structure and natural history of the green turtle (*Chelonia mydas*) in terms of matriarchal phylogeny. Evolution 46:865–881.

Bowler, J. K. 1977. Longevity of reptiles and amphibians in North American collections as of 1 November 1975. Soc. Stud. Amphib. Rept. Misc. Publ., Herpetol. Circ. (6):1–32.

Boyer, D. R. 1965. Ecology of the basking habit in turtles. Ecology 46:99–118.

Bramble, D. M. 1973. Media dependent feeding in turtles. Amer. Zool. 13:1342.

———. 1974a. Occurrence and significance of the os transiliens in gopher tortoises. Copeia 1974:102–109.

———. 1974b. Emydid shell kinesis: Biomechanics and evolution. Copeia 1974:707–727.

———. 1982. *Scaptochelys:* generic revision and evolution of gopher tortoises. Copeia 1982:852–867.

Bramble, D. M., J. H. Hutchison, and J. M. Legler. 1984. Kinosternid shell kinesis: Structure, function and evolution. Copeia 1984:456–475.

Branch, B. 1988. Bill Branch's field guide to the snakes and other reptiles of southern Africa. Struik Publ., Cape Town. 328 pp.

Brandner, R. L. 1983. A sea turtle nesting at Island Beach State Park, Ocean County, New Jersey. Herpetol. Rev. 14:110.

Brattstrom, B. H. 1953. The amphibians and reptiles from Rancho La Brea. Trans. San Diego Soc. Natur. Hist. 11:365–392.

———. 1955. Small herpetofauna from the Pleistocene of Carpinteria, California. Copeia 1955:138–139.

———. 1961. Some new fossil tortoises from western North America with remarks on the zoogeography and paleoecology of tortoises. J. Paleontol. 35:543–560.

———. 1965. Body temperatures of reptiles. Amer. Midl. Natur. 73:376–422.

———. 1988. Habitat destruction in California with special reference to *Clemmys marmorata:* A perspective. *In* DeLisle, H. F., P. R. Brown, B. Kaufman, and B. M. McGurty, eds. Proceedings of the Conference on California Herpetology, 13–24. Southwest. Herpetol. Soc., Van Nuys, California.

Brattstrom, B. H., and D. F. Messer. 1988. Current status of the southwestern pond turtle, *Clemmys marmorata pallida*, in southern California. Final Report. California Dept. Fish and Game Contract C-2044, 62 pp.

Brattstrom, B. H., and A. Sturn. 1959. A new species of fossil turtle from the Pliocene of Oregon, with notes on other fossil *Clemmys* from western North America. Bull. Southern California Acad. Sci. 58:65–71.

Braun, J., and G. R. Brooks, Jr. 1987. Box turtles (*Terrapene carolina*) as potential agents for seed dispersal. Amer. Midl. Natur. 117:312–318.

Brecke, B., and J. J. Moriarty. 1989. *Emydoidea blandingi* (Blanding's turtle). Longevity. Herpetol. Rev. 20:53.

Breckenridge, W. J. 1944. Reptiles and amphibians of Minnesota. Univ. Minnesota Press, Minneapolis. 202 pp.

———. 1955. Observations on the life history of the soft-shelled turtle *Trionyx ferox,* with especial reference to growth. Copeia 1955:5–9.

———. 1960. A spiny soft-shelled turtle nest study. Herpetologica 16:284–285.

Breininger, D. R., P. A. Schmalzer, and C. R. Hinkle. 1991. Estimating occupancy of gopher tortoise (*Gopherus polyphemus*) burrows in coastal scrub and slash pine flatwoods. J. Herpetol. 25:317–321.

Breitenbach, G. L., J. D. Congdon and R. C. van Loben Sels. 1984. Winter temperatures of *Chrysemys picta* nests in Michigan: Effects on hatchling survival. Herpetologica 40:76–81.

Brenner, F. J. 1970. The influence of light and temperature on fat utilization in female *Clemmys insculpta*. Ohio J. Sci. 70:233–237.

Brewer, K., and F. C. Killebrew. 1986. The annual testicular cycle of *Pseudemys scripta elegans* (Emydidae) in the Texas panhandle. Southwest. Natur. 31:299–305.

Brewster, C. M. 1985. Wood turtle, *Clemmys insculpta*, research in northern Wisconsin. Bull. Chicago Herpetol. Soc. 20:13–20.

Brewster, K. N. 1982. *Emydoidea blandingi* (Blanding's turtle). Reproduction. Herpetol. Rev. 13:48.

Brewster, K. N., and C. M. Brewster. 1986. *Clemmys insculpta* (wood turtle). Ectoparasitism. Herpetol. Rev. 17:48.

———. 1988. Notes on aggression and courtship in the wood turtle, *Clemmys insculpta*. Bull. Chicago Herpetol. Soc. 23:144.

———. 1991. Movement and microhabitat use by juvenile wood turtles introduced into a riparian habitat. J. Herpetol. 25:379–382.

Brimley, C. S. 1942–1943. Reptiles and amphibians of North Carolina. The turtles, tortoises or terrapins. Carolina Tips 5:22–23; 6:2–3, 6–7, 10–11, 14–15, 18–19.

Brisbin, I. L., Jr. 1972. Seasonal variations in the live weights and major body components of captive box turtles. Herpetologica 28:70–75.

Brisbin, I. L., Jr., M. C. Newman, S. G. McDowell, and E. L. Peters. 1990. Prediction of contaminant accumulation by free-living organisms: Applications of a sigmoidal model. Env. Toxicol. Chem. 9:141–149.

Brock, V. E. 1947. The establishment of *Trionyx sinensis* in Hawaii. Copeia 1947:142.

Brode, W. E. 1958. Prehensility of the tails of two turtles (family Chelydridae). Copeia 1958:48.

———. 1959. Notes on behavior of *Gopherus polyphemus*. Herpetologica 15:101–102.

Brongersma, L. D. 1972. European Atlantic turtles. Zool. Verh. Rijksmus. Natuur. Hist. Leiden 121:1–318.

Brooke, M. de L., and M. C. Garnett. 1983. Survival and reproductive performance of hawksbill turtles *Eretmochelys imbricata* L. on Cousin Island, Seychelles. Biol. Conserv. 25:161–170.

Brooks, R. J., M. L. Bobyn, D. A. Galbraith, J. A. Layfield, and E. G. Nancekivell. 1991. Maternal and environmental influences on growth and survival of embryonic and hatchling snapping turtles (*Chelydra serpentina*). Can. J. Zool. 69:2667–2676.

Brooks, R. J., G. P. Brown, and D. A. Galbraith. 1991. Effects of a sudden increase in natural mortality of adults on a population of the common snapping turtle (*Chelydra serpentina*). Can. J. Zool. 69:1314–1320.

Brooks, R. J., D. A. Galbraith, and J. A. Layfield. 1990. Occurrence of *Placobdella parasitica* (Hirudinea) on snapping turtles, *Chelydra serpentina*, in southeastern Ontario. J. Parasitol. 76:190–195.

Brooks, R. J., D. A. Galbraith, E. G. Nancekivell, and C. A. Bishop. 1988. Developing management guidelines for snapping turtles. *In* Szaro, R. C., K. E. Severson, and D. R. Patton, eds. Management of amphibians, reptiles, and small mammals in North America, 174–179. USDA Tech. Serv. Gen. Tech. Rept. Rm-166.

Brooks, R. J., C. M. Shilton, G. P. Brown, and N. W. S. Quinn. 1992. Body size, age distribution, and reproduction in a northern population of wood turtles *Clemmys insculpta*. Can. J. Zool. 70:462–469.

Brooks, W. B., and W. D. Webster. 1988. How tides affect loggerhead emergence activities on Bald Head Island, North Carolina. *In* Schroeder, B. A., ed. Proceedings of the Eighth Annual Workshop on Sea Turtle Conservation and Biology, 3–5. NOAA-TM-NMFS-SEFC-214.

Brown, B. C., and J. Haver. 1952. An unusually large congregation of turtles. Herpetologica 8:2.

Brown, E. E. 1992. Notes on amphibians and reptiles of the western piedmont of North Carolina. J. Elisha Mitchell. Sci. Soc. 108:38–54.

Brown, G. P., and R. J. Brooks. 1991. Thermal and behavioral responses to feeding in free-ranging turtles, *Chelydra serpentina*. J. Herpetol. 25:273–278.

Brown, G. P., R. J. Brooks, and J. A. Layfield. 1990. Radiotelemetry of body temperatures of free-ranging snapping turtles (*Chelydra serpentina*) during summer. Can. J. Zool. 68:1659–1663.

Brown, L. E., and D. Moll. 1979. The status of the nearly extinct Illinois mud turtle with recommendations for its conservation. Milwaukee Publ. Mus. Spec. Publ. Biol. Geol. (3):1–49.

Brown, P. S., R. Giuliano, and G. Hough. 1974. Pituitary regulation of appetite and growth in the turtles *Pseudomys* [sic] *scripta elegans* and *Chelydra serpentina*. J. Exp. Zool. 187:205–216.

Brown, R. A., G. C. McN. Harvey, and L. A. Wilkins. 1982. Growth of Jamaican hawksbill turtles (*Eretmochelys imbricata*) reared in captivity. British J. Herpetol. 6:233–236.

Brown, R. W. 1956. Composition of scientific words. Smithsonian Institution Press, Washington. 882 pp.

Brumwell, M. J. 1940. Notes on the courtship of the turtle, *Terrapene ornata*. Trans. Kansas Acad. Sci. 43:391–392.

Brunton, D. F. 1981. Additional records of stinkpot turtle in the Ottawa District. Trail & Landscape 15:140–142.

Bryan, A. M., W. B. Stone, and P. G. Olafsson. 1987.

Disposition of toxic PCB congenors in snapping turtle eggs: Expressed as toxic equivalents of TCDD. Bull. Environ. Contam. Toxicol. 39:791–796.

Budhabhatti, J., and E. O. Moll. 1990. *Chelydra serpentina* (common snapping turtle). Feeding behavior. Herpetol. Rev. 21:19.

Buhlmann, K. A., and J. C. Mitchell. 1989. *Clemmys insculpta* (wood turtle). USA: Virginia. Herpetol. Rev. 20:76.

Buhlmann, K. A., and M. R. Vaughan. 1985. *Pseudemys concinna* (river cooter). USA: West Virginia. Herpetol. Rev. 16:84–85.

———. 1991. Ecology of the turtle *Pseudemys concinna* in the New River, West Virginia. J. Herpetol. 25:72–78.

Bull, J. J. 1980. Sex determination in reptiles. Quart. Rev. Biol. 55:3–21.

———. 1985. Sex ratio and nest temperature in turtles: Comparing field and laboratory data. Ecology 66:1115–1122.

Bull, J. J., J. M. Legler, and R. C. Vogt. 1985. Non-temperature dependent sex determination in two suborders of turtles. Copeia 1985:784–786.

Bull, J. J., and R. C. Vogt. 1979. Temperature-dependent sex determination in turtles. Science 206:1186–1188.

———. 1981. Temperature-sensitive periods of sex determination in emydid turtles. J. Exp. Zool. 218:435–440.

Bull, J. J., R. C. Vogt, and M. G. Bulmer. 1982a. Heritability of sex ratio in turtles with environmental sex determination. Evolution 36:333–341.

Bull, J. J., R. C. Vogt, and C. J. McCoy. 1982b. Sex determining temperatures in turtles: A geographic comparison. Evolution 36:326–332.

Bull, J. J., T. Wibbels, and D. Crews. 1990. Sex-determining potencies vary among female incubation temperatures in a turtle. J. Exp. Zool. 256:339–341.

Bullen, R. P. 1949. Excavations in northeastern Massachusetts. Pap. Robert S. Peabody Found. Archaeol. 1(3):129–132.

Bundy, R. E. 1951. New locality records of reptiles in New Mexico. Copeia 1951:314.

Burge, B. L. 1978. Physical characteristics and patterns of utilization of cover sites used by *Gopherus agassizi* in southern Nevada. Proc. Symp. Desert Tortoise Council 1978:80–111.

Burge, B. L., and W. G. Bradley. 1976. Population density, structure and feeding habits of the desert tortoise, *Gopherus agassizi*, in a low desert study area in southern Nevada. Proc. Symp. Desert Tortoise Council 1976:51–76.

Burger, J. 1976a. Behavior of hatchling diamondback terrapins (*Malaclemys terrapin*) in the field. Copeia 1976:742–748.

———. 1976b. Temperature relationships in nests of the northern diamondback terrapin, *Malaclemys terrapin terrapin*. Herpetologica 32:412–418.

———. 1977. Determinants of hatching success in diamondback terrapin, *Malaclemys terrapin*. Amer. Midl. Natur. 97:444–464.

Burger, J., and W. A. Montevecchi. 1975. Nest site selection in the terrapin *Malaclemys terrapin*. Copeia 1975:113–119.

Burger, J. W. 1937. Experimental sexual photoperiodicity in the male turtle, *Pseudemys elegans* (Wied). Amer. Natur. 71:481–487.

Burger, W. L. 1952. A neglected subspecies of the turtle *Pseudemys scripta*. J. Tennessee Acad. Sci. 27:75–79.

Burghardt, G. M., and E. H. Hess. 1966. Food imprinting in the snapping turtle, *Chelydra serpentina*. Science 151:108–109.

Burke, A. C. 1991. The development and evolution of the turtle body plan: Inferring intrinsic aspects of the evolutionary process from experimental embryology. Amer. Zool. 31:616–627.

Burke, R. L. 1987. An experimental relocation and reintroduction of a gopher tortoise population. Master's thesis, University of Florida, Gainesville.

———. 1989a. *Gopherus polyphemus* (gopher tortoise). Mortality. Herpetol. Rev. 20:54.

———. 1989b. Florida gopher tortoise relocation: Overview and case study. Biol. Conserv. 48:295–309.

———. 1989c. Burrow-to-tortoise conversion factors: Comparison of three gopher tortoise survey techniques. Herpetol. Rev. 20:92–94.

Burke, V. J., E. A. Standora, and S. J. Morreale. 1991. Factors affecting strandings of cold-stunned juvenile Kemp's ridley and loggerhead sea turtles in Long Island, New York. Copeia 1991:1136–1138.

Burkholder, P. R., L. M. Burkholder, and J. A. Rivero. 1959. Some chemical constituents of turtle grass, *Thalassia testudinum*. Bull. Torrey Bot. Club 86:88–93.

Burne, B. A. 1905. Notes on the muscular and visceral anatomy of the leathery turtle (*Dermochelys coriacea*). Proc. Zool. Soc. London 1905:291–324.

Burns, T. A., and K. L. Williams. 1972. Notes on the reproductive habits of *Malaclemys terrapin pileata*. J. Herpetol. 6:237–238.

Bury, R. B. 1963. Occurrence of *Clemmys m. marmorata* in north coastal California. Herpetologica 18:283.

———. 1970. *Clemmys marmorata*. Catalog. Amer. Amphib. Rept. 100:1–3.

———. 1972. Habits and home range of the Pacific pond turtle, *Clemmys marmorata,* in a stream community. Ph.D. dissertation, University of California, Berkeley. 219 pp.

———. 1979a. Population ecology of freshwater turtles. *In* Harless, M., and H. Morlock, eds. Turtles: Perspectives and research, 571–602. John Wiley & Sons, New York.

———. 1979b. Review of the ecology and conservation of the bog turtle, *Clemmys muhlenbergii.* U.S. Fish Wildl. Serv. Spec. Sci. Rept. Wildl. (219):1–9.

———. 1982. North American tortoises: Conservation and ecology. U.S. Fish Wildl. Serv. Wildl. Res. Rept. 12. 126 pp.

———. 1986. Feeding ecology of the turtle, *Clemmys marmorata.* J. Herpetol. 20:515–521.

———. 1989. Turtle of the month–*Clemmys marmorata*–a true western turtle (Pacific pond). Tortuga Gazette 25(2):3–4.

Bury, R. B., and C. H. Ernst. 1977. *Clemmys.* Catalog. Amer. Amphib. Rept. 203:1–2.

Bury, R. B., and R. W. Marlow. 1973. The desert tortoise–will it survive? Natl. Parks Conserv. Mag. 47(6):9–12.

Bury, R. B., and E. L. Smith. 1986. Aspects of the ecology and management of the tortoise *Gopherus berlandieri* at Laguna Atascosa, Texas. Southwest. Natur. 31:387–394.

Bury, R. B., and J. H. Wolfheim. 1973. Aggression in free-living pond turtles (*Clemmys marmorata*). Bioscience 23:659–662.

Bury, R. B., J. H. Wolfheim, and R. A. Luckenbach. 1979. Agonistic behaviour in free-living painted turtles (*Chrysemys picta belli*). Biol. Behav. 4:227–239.

Bush, F. M. 1959. Foods of some Kentucky herptiles. Herpetologica 15:73–77.

Buskirk, J. R. 1991. An overview of the western pond turtle, *Clemmys marmorata. In* Beaman, K. R., F. Caporaso, S. McKeown, and M. D. Graff, eds. Proceedings of the First International Symposium on Turtles and Tortoises: Conservation and Captive Husbandry, 16–23. Chapman Univ., Orange, California.

Bustard, H. R. 1967. Mechanism of nocturnal emergence from the nest in green turtle hatchlings. Nature 214:317.

———. 1970. The adaptive significance of coloration in hatchling green sea turtles. Herpetologica 26:224–227.

———. 1971. Temperature and water tolerance of incubating sea turtle eggs. British J. Herpetol. 4:196–198.

———. 1973. Sea turtles: Their natural history and conservation. Taplinger Publ. Co., Inc., New York. 220 pp.

Bustard, H. R., P. Greenham, and C. Limpus. 1975. Nesting behavior of loggerhead and flatback turtles in Queensland, Australia. Proc. Kon. Nederl. Akad. Wetensch., ser. C, 78:111–122.

Bustard, H. R., and C. Limpus. 1970. First international recapture of an Australian tagged loggerhead turtle. Herpetologica 26:358–359.

———. 1971. Loggerhead turtle movements. British J. Herpetol. 4:228–230.

Bustard, H. R., K. Simkiss, N. K. Jenkins, and J. H. Taylor. 1969. Some analyses of artificially incubated eggs and hatchlings of green and loggerhead sea turtles. J. Zool. (London) 158:311–315.

Bustard, H. R., and K. P. Tognetti. 1969. Green sea turtles: A discrete simulation of density-dependent population regulation. Science 163:939–941.

Butler, B. O. 1992. Bay State Blanding's turtles. Massachusetts Wildlife 42(3):17–25.

Buxton, C. D., and W. R. Branch. 1983. Octopus predation on the hawksbill turtle, *Eretmochelys imbricata* (Cryptodira: Cheloniidae). J. Herpetol. Assoc. Africa (29):15–17.

Cagle, F. R. 1937. Egg laying habits of the slider turtle (*Pseudemys troostii*), the painted turtle (*Chrysemys picta*), and the musk turtle (*Sternotherus odoratus*). J. Tennessee Acad. Sci. 12:87–95.

———. 1942. Turtle populations in southern Illinois. Copeia 1942:155–162.

———. 1944a. Activity and winter changes of hatchling *Pseudemys.* Copeia 1944:105–109.

———. 1944b. Home range, homing behavior and migration in turtles. Misc. Publ. Mus. Zool. Univ. Michigan (61):1–34.

———. 1944c. Sexual maturity in the female of the turtle *Pseudemys scripta elegans.* Copeia 1944:149–152.

———. 1946. Growth of the slider turtle, *Pseudemys scripta elegans.* Amer. Midl. Natur. 36:685–729.

———. 1948a. Sexual maturity in the male turtle, *Pseudemys scripta troostii.* Copeia 1948:108–111.

———. 1948b. The growth of turtles in Lake Glendale, Illinois. Copeia 1948:197–203.

———. 1949. Notes on the raccoon, *Procyon lotor megalodous* Lowery. J. Mammal. 30:45–47.

———. 1950. The life history of the slider turtle, *Pseudemys scripta troostii* (Holbrook). Ecol. Monogr. 20:31–54.

———. 1952a. A Louisiana terrapin population (*Malaclemys*). Copeia 1952:74–76.

———. 1952b. The status of the turtles *Graptemys pulchra* Baur and *Graptemys barbouri* Carr and Marchand, with notes on their natural history. Copeia 1952:223–234.

———. 1953a. The status of the turtle *Graptemys oculifera* (Baur). Zoologica (New York) 38:137–144.

———. 1953b. Two new subspecies of *Graptemys pseudogeographica*. Occ. Pap. Mus. Zool. Univ. Michigan (546).1–17.

———. 1954a. Two new species of the genus *Graptemys*. Tulane Stud. Zool. 1:167–186.

———. 1954b. Observations on the life cycles of painted turtles (genus *Chrysemys*). Amer. Midl. Natur. 52:225–235.

———. 1955. Courtship behavior in juvenile turtles. Copeia 1955:307.

Cagle, F. R., and A. H. Chaney. 1950. Turtle populations in Louisiana. Amer. Midl. Natur. 43:383–388.

Cagle, F. R., and J. Tihen. 1948. Retention of eggs by the turtle *Deirochelys reticularia*. Copeia 1948:66.

Cahn, A. R. 1937. The turtles of Illinois. Illinois Biol. Monogr. (35):1–218.

Caillouet, C. W., Jr., M. J. Duronslet, A. M. Landry, Jr., D. B. Revera, D. J. Shaver, K. M. Stanley, R. W. Heinly, and E. K. Stabenau. 1991. Sea turtle strandings and shrimp fishing effort in the northwestern Gulf of Mexico, 1986–1989. U.S. Fish Wildl. Serv. Fish. Bull. 89:712–718.

Calliouet, C. W., Jr., and A. M. Landry, Jr., eds. Proceedings of the First International Symposium on Kemp's Ridley Sea Turtle Biology, Conservation and Management. Texas A & M Univ. Sea Grant College Progr. Spec. Publ.-89 (105). 260 pp.

Caillouet, C. W., Jr., D. B. Koi, C. T. Fontaine, T. D. Williams, W. J. Browning, and R. M. Harris. 1986. Growth and survival of Kemp's ridley sea turtle, *Lepidochelys kempi*, in captivity. NOAA-TM-NMFS-SEFC-186. 34 pp.

Caldwell, D. K. 1958. On the status of the Atlantic leatherback turtle, *Dermochelys coriacea coriacea*, as a visitant to Florida nesting beaches, with natural history notes. Quart. J. Florida Acad. Sci. 21:285–291.

———. 1959. The loggerhead turtles of Cape Romain, South Carolina. Bull. Florida St. Mus. Biol. Sci. 4:319–348.

———. 1962a. Comments on the nesting behavior of Atlantic loggerhead sea turtles, based primarily on tagging returns. Quart. J. Florida Acad. Sci. 25:287–302.

———. 1962b. Growth measurements of young captive Atlantic sea turtles in temperate waters. Los Angeles Co. Mus. Cont. Sci. 50:1–8.

———. 1962c. Sea turtles in Baja Californian waters (with special reference to those of the Gulf of California), and the description of a new subspecies of north-eastern Pacific green turtle. Los Angeles Co. Mus. Cont. Sci. (61):1–31.

———. 1962d. Carapace length-body weight relationship and size and sex ratio of the northeastern Pacific green turtle, *Chelonia mydas carrinegra*. Los Angeles Co. Mus. Cont. Sci. (62):1–10.

———. 1963. Second record of the loggerhead sea turtle, *Caretta caretta gigas,* from the Gulf of California. Copeia 1963:568–569.

———. 1969. Baby loggerhead turtles associated with sargassum weed. Quart. J. Florida Acad. Sci. (1968)31:271–272.

Caldwell, D. K., A. Carr, and T. R. Hellier, Jr. 1955a. A nest of the Atlantic leatherback turtle, *Dermochelys coriacea coriacea* (Linnaeus), on the Atlantic Coast of Florida, with a summary of American nesting records. Quart. J. Florida Acad. Sci. 18:279–284.

———. 1955b. Natural history notes on the Atlantic loggerhead turtle, *Caretta caretta caretta*. Quart. J. Florida Acad. Sci. 18:292–302.

Caldwell, D. K., A. F. Carr, and L. H. Ogren. 1959. Nesting and migration of the Atlantic loggerhead turtle. Bull. Florida St. Mus. Biol. Sci. 4:295–308.

Caldwell, D. K., and W. F. Rathjen. 1969. Unrecorded West Indian nesting sites for the leatherback and hawksbill sea turtles, *Dermochelys coriacea* and *Eretmochelys i. imbricata*. Copeia 1969:622–623.

Caldwell, J. P., and J. T. Collins. 1981. Turtles in Kansas. AMS Publ., Lawrence, Kansas. 67 pp.

Callard, I. P., G. V. Callard, V. Lance, and S. Eccles. 1976. Seasonal changes in testicular structure and function and the effects of gonadotropins in the freshwater turtle, *Chrysemys picta*. Gen. Comp. Endocrinol. 30:347–356.

Callard, I. P., and M. Hirsch. 1976. The influence of oestradiol-17 β and progesterone on the contractility of the oviduct of the turtle, *Chrysemys picta, in vitro*. J. Endocrinol. 68:147–152.

Callard, I. P., V. Lance, A. R. Salanick, and D. Barad. 1978. The annual ovarian cycle of *Chrysemys picta*: correlated changes in plasma steroids and parameters of vitellogenesis. Gen. Comp. Endocrinol. 35:245–257.

Camp, C. D. 1986. *Sternotherus minor* (loggerhead musk turtle). Size. Herpetol. Rev. 17:89,91.

Campbell, H. W. 1974. Turtles at the brink: Our endangered species. Bull. Maryland Herpetol. Soc. 10:1–7.

Campbell, H. W., and W. E. Evans. 1967. Sound production in two species of tortoises. Herpetologica 23:204–209.

Campbell, J. W., D. D. Smith, Jr., and J. E. Vorhaben. 1985. Avian and mammalian mitochondrial ammonia–detoxifying systems in tortoise liver. Science 228:349–351.

Cantor, T. 1842. General features of Chusan, with remarks on the flora and fauna of that island. Ann. Mag. Natur. Hist. (London) 11:481–493.

Carpenter, C. C. 1956. Carapace pits in the three-toed box turtle, *Terrapene carolina triunguis* (Chelonia-Emydidae). Southwest. Natur. 1:83–86.

———. 1957. Hibernation, hibernacula and associated behavior of the three-toed box turtle (*Terrapene carolina triunguis*). Copeia 1957:278–282.

———. 1981. *Trionyx spiniferus* (spiny softshell turtle). Morphology. Herpetol. Rev. 12:82.

Carpenter, C. C., and G. W. Ferguson. 1977. Variation and evolution of stereotyped behavior in reptiles. *In* Gans, C., and D. W. Tinkle, eds. Biology of the Reptilia, vol. 7, 335–554. Academic Press, London.

Carr, A. F., Jr. 1937. A new turtle from Florida, with notes on *Pseudemys floridana mobiliensis* (Holbrook). Occ. Pap. Mus. Zool. Univ. Michigan (348):1–7.

———. 1938a. A new subspecies of *Pseudemys floridana,* with notes on the *floridana* complex. Copeia 1938:107–109.

———. 1938b. *Pseudemys nelsoni,* a new turtle from Florida. Occ. Pap. Boston Soc. Natur. Hist. 8:305–310.

———. 1940. A contribution to the herpetology of Florida. Univ. Florida Biol. Sci. Ser. 3:1–118.

———. 1949. The identity of *Malacoclemmys kohnii* Baur. Herpetologica 5:9–10.

———. 1952. Handbook of turtles. The turtles of the United States, Canada, and Baja California. Comstock Publ. Assoc., Cornell University Press, Ithaca, New York. 542 pp.

———. 1954. The zoogeography and migrations of sea turtles. Yrbk. Amer. Philos. Soc. 1954:138–140.

———. 1957. Notes on the zoogeography of the Atlantic sea turtles of the genus *Lepidochelys.* Rev. Biol. Trop. 5:45–61.

———. 1967a. So excellant a fishe. A natural history of sea turtles. Natural History Press, Garden City, New York. 248 pp.

———. 1967b. Adaptive aspects of the scheduled travel of *Chelonia. In* Storm, R. M., ed. Animal orientation and navigation, 35–55. Oregon State University Press, Corvallis.

———. 1967c. The Windward road: Adventures of a naturalist on remote Caribbean shores. Alfred A. Knopf, New York. 258 pp.

———. 1975. The Ascension Island green turtle colony. Copeia 1975:547–555.

———. 1980. Some problems of sea turtle ecology. Amer. Zool. 20:489–498.

———. 1982. Notes on the behavioral ecology of sea turtles. *In* Bjorndal, K. A., ed. Biology and conservation of sea turtles, 19–26. Smithsonian Institution Press, Washington, D.C.

———. 1987. New perspectives on the pelagic stage of sea turtle development. Conserv. Biol. 1:103–121.

Carr, A. F., and D. K. Caldwell. 1956. The ecology and migrations of sea turtles, 1. Results of field work in Florida, 1955. Amer. Mus. Novitates (1793):1–23.

———. 1958. The problem of the Atlantic ridley turtle. Rev. Biol. Trop. 6:245–262.

Carr, A. F., and M. H. Carr. 1970. Modulated reproductive periodicity in *Chelonia.* Ecology 51:335–337.

———. 1972. Site fixity in the Caribbean green turtle. Ecology 53:425–429.

Carr, A. F., M. H. Carr, and A. B. Meylan. 1978. The ecology and migrations of sea turtles, 7. The West Caribbean green turtle colony. Bull. Amer. Mus. Natur. Hist. 162:1–46.

Carr, A. F., and P. J. Coleman. 1974. Seafloor spreading theory and the odyssey of the green turtle. Nature 249:128–130.

Carr, A. F., and J. W. Crenshaw, Jr. 1957. A taxonomic reappraisal of the turtle *Pseudemys alabamensis* Baur. Bull. Florida St. Mus. Biol. Sci. 2:25–42.

Carr, A. F., and L. Giovannoli. 1957. The ecology and migrations of sea turtles, 2. Results of field work in Costa Rica, 1955. Amer. Mus. Novitates (1835):1–32.

Carr, A. F., and C. J. Goin. 1955. Guide to the reptiles, amphibians and freshwater fishes of Florida. University of Florida Press, Gainesville. 341 pp.

Carr, A. F., and H. Hirth. 1961. Social facilitation in green turtle siblings. Anim. Behav. 9:68–70.

———. 1962. The ecology and migrations of sea turtles, 5. Comparative features of isolated green turtle colonies. Amer. Mus. Novitates (2091):1–42.

Carr, A. F., H. Hirth, and L. Ogren. 1966. The ecology and migrations of sea turtles, 6. The hawksbill turtle in the Caribbean Sea. Amer. Mus. Novitates (2248):1–29.

Carr, A. F., and L. T. Marchand. 1942. A new turtle from the Chipola River, Florida. Proc. New England Zool. Club 20:95–100.

Carr, A. F., and A. B. Meylan. 1980a. Evidence of passive migrations of green turtle hatchlings in *Sargassum.* Copeia 1980:366–368.

———. 1980b. Extinction or rescue for the hawksbill? Oryx 15:449–450.

———. 1984. *Dermochelys coriacea* (leatherback sea turtle). Migration. Herpetol. Rev. 15:113.

Carr, A., A. Meylan, J. Mortimer, K. Bjorndal, and T. Carr. 1982. Surveys of sea turtle populations and habitats in the western Atlantic. NOAA-TM-NMFS-SEFC-91. 82 pp.

Carr, A. F., and L. Ogren. 1959. The ecology and migrations of sea turtles, 3. *Dermochelys* in Costa Rica. Amer. Mus. Novitates (1958):1–29.

———. 1960. The ecology and migrations of sea turtles, 4. The green turtle in Caribbean Sea. Bull. Amer. Mus. Natur. Hist. 121:1–48.

Carr, A. F., L. Ogren, and C. McVea. 1981. Apparent hibernation by the Atlantic loggerhead turtle *Caretta caretta* off Cape Canaveral, Florida. Biol. Conserv. 19:7–14.

Carr, A. F., P. Ross, and S. Carr. 1974. Internesting behavior of the green turtle, *Chelonia mydas*, at a mid-ocean island breeding ground. Copeia 1974:703–706.

Carr, A. F., and S. Stancyk. 1975. Observations on the ecology and survival outlook of the hawksbill turtle. Biol. Conserv. 8:161–172.

Carr, J. L., and T. W. Houseal. 1981. Post-hibernation behavior in *Terrapene carolina triunguis* (Emydidae). Southwest. Natur. 26:199–200.

Carr, T., and N. Carr. 1986. *Dermochelys coriacea* (leatherback sea turtle). Copulation. Herpetol. Rev. 17:24–25.

Carroll, D. M. 1991. The year of the turtle: A natural history. Camden House Publ., Inc., Charlotte, Vermont. 172 pp.

Carroll, R. L. 1969. Origin of reptiles. *In* Gans, C., A. d'A. Bellairs, and T. S. Parsons, eds. Biology of the Reptilia, vol. 1, Morphology A, 1–44. Academic Press, London.

Carroll, T. E., and D. H. Ehrenfeld. 1978. Intermediate-range homing in the wood turtle, *Clemmys insculpta*. Copeia 1978:117–126.

Casas-Andreu, G. 1971. National and regional reports: Mexico. IUCN Publ. (n.s.), Suppl. Pap. 31:41–46.

———. 1978. Análisis de la anidación de las tortugas marinas del género *Lepidochelys* en México. An Centro Cienc. Mar. Limnol. Univ. Nac. Autón. México. 5:141–158.

Causey, M. K., and C. A. Cude. 1978. Feral dog predation of the gopher tortoise, *Gopherus polyphemus* (Reptilia, Testudines, Testudinidae) in southeast Alabama. Herpetol. Rev. 9:94–95.

Chabot, J., and D. St-Hilaire. 1991. Première mention de la Tortue musquée, *Sternotherus odoratus,* au Québec. Can. Field-Natur. 105:411–412.

Chace, F. E. 1951. The oceanic crabs of the genera *Planes* and *Pachygrapsus*. Proc. U.S. Natl. Mus. 101:65–103.

Chan, E.-H. 1988. A note on the feeding of leatherback (*Dermochelys coriacea*) hatchlings. Pertanika 11:147–149.

———. 1989. White spot development, incubation and hatchling success of leatherback turtle (*Dermochelys coriacea*) eggs from Rantau Abang, Malaysia. Copeia 1989:42–47.

Chan, E.-H., H. U. Salleh, and H. C. Liew. 1985. Effects of handling on hatchability of eggs of the leatherback turtle, *Dermochelys coriacea* (L.). Pertanika 8:265–271.

Chaney, A., and C. L. Smith. 1950. Methods for collecting mapturtles. Copeia 1950:323–324.

Chase, J. D., K. R. Dixon, J. E. Gates, D. Jacobs, and G. J. Taylor. 1989. Habitat characteristics, population size, and home range of the bog turtle, *Clemmys muhlenbergii*, in Maryland. J. Herpetol. 23:356–362.

Chávez, H. 1966. Propositos y finalidades. Bol. Progr. Nac. Marc. Tortugas Mar., Mexico 1(1):1–16.

———. 1967. Nota preliminar sobre la recaptura de ejemplares marcados de tortuga lora, *Lepidochelys olivacea kempii*. Bol. Prog. Nac. Marc. Tortugas Mar., Mexico 1(6):1–5.

———. 1969. Tagging and recapture of the lora turtle (*Lepidochelys kempi*). Int. Turtle and Tortoise Soc. J. 3(4):14–19, 32–36.

Chávez, H., M. Contreras G., and T. P. E. Hernandez D. 1968a. On the coast of Tamaulipas. Part 1. Int. Turtle and Tortoise Soc. J. 2(4):20–29, 37.

———. 1968b. On the coast of Tamaulipas, Part 2. Int. Turtle and Tortoise Soc. J. 2(5):16–19, 27–34.

Chávez, H., and R. Kaufmann. 1974. Información sobre la tortuga marina *Lepidochelys kempi* (Garman), con referencia a un ejemplar marcado en Mexico y observado en Columbia. Bull. Marine Sci. 24:372–377.

Cherepanov, G. O. 1989. New morphogenetic data on the turtle shell: Discusion [*sic*] on the origin of the horny and bony parts. Studia Palaeocheloniologica 3(1):9–24.

Chippindale, P. 1989. Courtship and nesting records for spotted turtles, *Clemmys guttata,* in the Mer Bleue Bog, southeastern Ontario. Can. Field-Natur. 103:289–291.

Choo, B. L., and L. M. Chou. 1987. Effect of temperature on the incubation period and hatchability of *Trionyx sinensis* Weigmann eggs. J. Herpetol. 21:230–232.

———. 1992. Does incubation temperature influence the sex of embryos in *Trionyx sinensis*? J. Herpetol. 26:341–342.

Chou, L. M., and P. Venugopal. 1982. Effect of light intensity on the early growth of *Pseudemys scripta elegans*. J. Singapore Natl. Acad. Sci. 9:1–3.

Christens, E. 1990. Nest emergence lag in loggerhead sea turtles. J. Herpetol. 24:400–402.

Christens, E., and J. R. Bider. 1986. Reproductive ecology of the painted turtle (*Chrysemys picta marginata*) in southwestern Quebec. Can. J. Zool. 64:914–920.

———. 1987. Nesting activity and hatching success of the painted turtle (*Chrysemys picta marginata*) in southwestern Quebec. Herpetologica 43:55–65.

Christiansen, J. L., and R. M. Bailey. 1988. The lizards and turtles of Iowa. Iowa Dept. Natur. Res., Nongame Tech. Ser. (3):1–19.

Christiansen, J. L., and J. W. Bickham. 1989. Possible historic effects of pond drying and winter kill on the behavior of *Kinosternon flavescens* and *Chrysemys picta*. J. Herpetol. 23:91–94.

Christiansen, J. L., and R. R. Burken. 1979. Growth and maturity of the snapping turtle (*Chelydra serpentina*) in Iowa. Herpetologica 35:261–266.

Christiansen, J. L., J. A. Cooper, and J. W. Bickham. 1984. Reproduction of *Kinosternon flavescens* (Kinosternidae) in Iowa. Southwest. Natur. 29:349–351.

Christiansen, J. L., J. A. Cooper, J. W. Bickham, B. J. Gallaway, and M. A. Springer. 1985. Aspects of the natural history of the yellow mud turtle *Kinosternon flavescens* (Kinosternidae) in Iowa: A proposed endangered species. Southwest. Natur. 30:413–425.

Christiansen, J. L., and A. E. Dunham. 1972. Reproduction of the yellow mud turtle (*Kinosternon flavescens flavescens*) in New Mexico. Herpetologica 28:130–137.

Christiansen, J. L., and B. J. Gallaway. 1984. Raccoon removal, nesting success, and hatchling emergence in Iowa turtles with special reference to *Kinosternon flavescens* (Kinosternidae). Southwest. Natur. 29:343–348.

Christiansen, J. L., B. J. Gallaway, and J. W. Bickham. 1990. Population estimates and geographic distribution of the yellow mud turtle (*Kinosternon flavscens*) in Iowa. J. Iowa Acad. Sci. 97:105–108.

Christiansen, J. L., and E. O. Moll. 1973. Latitudinal reproductive variation within a single subspecies of painted turtle, *Chrysemys picta bellii*. Herpetologica 29:152–163.

Christy, E. J., J. O. Farlow, J. E. Bourque, and J. W. Gibbons. 1974. Enhanced growth and increased body size of turtles living in thermal and post-thermal aquatic systems. *In* Gibbons, J. W., and R. R. Sharitz, eds. Thermal Ecology, 277–284. Atomic Energy Commission Symp. Ser. (CONF-730505). National Technical Information Service, Springfield, VA.

Chu, B. 1989. The technology of using ground heat for soft-shelled turtle overwintering culture. *In* Wang, W.-H., ed. Proceedings of the International Symposium of Agricultural Engineering (89–ISAE), vol. II, 993–994. Beijing, China.

Churcher, C. S., J. J. Pilny, and A. V. Morgan. 1990. Late Pleistocene vertebrate, plant and insect remains from the Innerkip site, southwestern Ontario. Geogr. Phys. Quat. 44:299–308.

Churchill, T. A., and K. B. Storey. 1991. Metabolic responses to freezing by organs of hatchling painted turtles *Chrysemys picta marginata* and *C. p. bellii*. Can. J. Zool. 69:2978–2984.

———. 1992. Responses to freezing exposure of hatchling turtles *Trachemys scripta elegans:* factors influencing the development of freeze tolerance in reptiles. J. Exp. Biol. 167:221–233.

Cink, C. L. 1991. Snake predation on nesting eastern phoebes followed by turtle predation on snake. Kansas Ornithol. Soc. Bull. 42:29.

Clark, D. B., and J. W. Gibbons. 1969. Dietary shift in the turtle *Pseudemys scripta* (Schoepff) from youth to maturity. Copeia 1969:704–706.

Clark, D. R., Jr., and A. J. Krynitsky. 1980. Organochlorine residues in eggs of loggerhead and green sea turtles nesting at Merritt Island, Florida–July and August 1976. Pesticides Monit. J. 14:7–10.

———. 1985. DDE residues and artificial incubation of loggerhead sea turtle eggs. Bull. Environ. Contam. Toxicol. 34:121–125.

Clark, H. W., and J. B. Southall. 1920. Fresh water turtles: A source of meat supply. U.S. Bull. Fish. Doc. 889:3–20.

Clark, P. J., M. A. Ewert, and C. E. Nelson. 1986. Physiological aspects of temperature dependent sex. Proc. Indiana Acad. Sci. 95:519.

Clark, W. S. 1982. Turtles as a food source of nesting bald eagles in the Chesapeake Bay Region. J. Field Ornithol. 53:49–51.

Clarke, R. F. 1981. A record of the alligator snapping turtle, *Macroclemys temmincki* (Testudines: Chelydridae), in Kansas. Trans. Kansas Acad. Sci. 84:59–60.

Claussen, D. L., M. P. Daniel, S. Jiang, and N. A. Adams. 1991. Hibernation in the eastern box turtle, *Terrapene c. carolina*. J. Herpetol. 25:334–341.

Cliburn, J. W. 1971. The ranges of four species of *Graptemys* in Mississippi. J. Mississippi Acad. Sci. 16:16–19.

Cliffton, K., D. O. Cornejo, and R. S. Felger. 1982. Sea turtles of the Pacific Coast of Mexico. *In* Bjorndal, K. A., ed. Biology and conservation of sea turtles, 199–209. Smithsonian Institution Press, Washington, D.C.

Cloudsley-Thompson, J. L. 1982. Rhythmic activity in young red-eared terrapins (*Pseudemys scripta elegans*). British J. Herpetol. 6:188–194.

Cochran, D. M., and C. J. Goin. 1970. The new field book of reptiles and amphibians. G. P. Putnam's Sons, New York. 359 pp.

Cochran, J. D. 1978. A note on the behavior of the diamondback terrapin, *Malaclemys t. terrapin* (Schoepff) in Maryland. Bull. Maryland Herpetol. Soc. 14:100.

Cochran, P. A. 1987. *Graptemys geographica* (map turtle). Adult mortality. Herpetol. Rev. 18:37.

Cochran, P. A., and R. M. Korb. 1987. Recent sightings of the Blanding's turtle, *Emydoidea blandingii*, a threatened species, in Wisconsin. Bull. Chicago Herpetol. Soc. 22:145–147.

Cochran, P. A., and D. R. McConville. 1983. Feeding by *Trionyx spiniferus* in backwaters of the upper Mississippi River. J. Herpetol. 17:82–86.

Coker, R. E. 1906. The natural history and cultivation of the diamond-back terrapin with notes on other forms of turtles. North Carolina Geol. Surv. Bull. 14:1–69.

———. 1920. The diamond-back terrapin: Past, present and future. Science Monthly 11:171–186.

Collard, S. B. 1990. Guest editorial: Speculation on the distribution of oceanic-stage sea turtles, with emphasis on Kemp's ridley in the Gulf of Mexico. Marine Turtle Newsl. (48):6–8.

Collard, S. B., and T. J. Hansknecht. 1990. *Caretta caretta* (loggerhead sea turtle). Habitat. Herpetol. Rev. 21:60.

Collard, S. B., and L. H. Ogren. 1990. Dispersal scenarios for pelagic post-hatchling sea turtles. Bull. Marine Sci. 47:233–243.

Collazo, J. A., R. Boulon, Jr., and T. L. Tallevast. 1992. Abundance and growth patterns of *Chelonia mydas* in Culebra, Puerto Rico. J. Herpetol. 26:293–300.

Collins, D. E. 1990. Western New York bog turtles: Relicts of ephemeral islands or simply elusive? *In* Mitchell, R. S., C. J. Sheviak, and D. J. Leopold, eds. Ecosystem management: Rare species and significant habitats, 151–153. Bulletin No. 471, New York State Museum, Proc. 15th Annual Natural Areas Conference.

Collins, J. T. 1990. Standard common names and current scientific names for North American amphibians and reptiles, 3d ed. Soc. Stud. Amphib. Rept. Herpetol. Circ. (19):1–41.

———. 1991. Viewpoint: A new taxonomic arrangement for some North American amphibians and reptiles. Herpetol. Rev. 22:42–43.

———. 1992. New records of amphibians and reptiles in Kansas for 1991. Kansas Herpetol. Soc. Newsl. 87:12–17.

Combs, S. A. 1971. Nest building and egg laying of the wood turtle. HERP, Bull. New York Herpetol. Soc. 7(3&4):28–29.

Conant, R. 1951a. The reptiles of Ohio. Univ. Notre Dame Press, Notre Dame, Indiana. 284 pp.

———. 1951b. The red-bellied terrapin, *Pseudemys rubriventris* (Le Conte), in Pennsylvania. Ann. Carnegie Mus. Natur. Hist. 32:281–290.

Conant, R., and R. M. Bailey. 1936. Some herpetological records from Monmouth and Ocean counties, New Jersey. Occ. Pap. Mus. Zool. Univ. Michigan (328):1–10.

Conant, R., and J. F. Berry. 1978. Turtles of the family Kinosternidae in the southwestern United States and adjacent Mexico: Identification and distribution. Amer. Mus. Novitates (2642):1–18.

Conant, R., and J. T. Collins. 1991. A field guide to reptiles and amphibians: Eastern and central North America. Houghton Mifflin Co., Boston. 450 pp.

Conant, R., and C. J. Goin. 1948. A new subspecies of soft-shelled turtle from the central United States, with comments on the application of the name *Amyda*. Occ. Pap. Mus. Zool. Univ. Michigan 510:1–19.

Conant, R., and R. G. Hudson. 1949. Longevity records for reptiles and amphibians in the Philadelphia Zoological Garden. Herpetologica 5:1–8.

Conceição, M. B., J. A. Levy, L. F. Marins, and M. A. Maracovaldi. 1990. Electrophoretic characterization of a hybrid between *Eretmochelys imbricata* and *Caretta caretta* (Cheloniidae). Comp. Biochem. Physiol. 97B:275–278.

Congdon, J. D. 1989. Proximate and evolutionary constraints on energy relations of reptiles. Physiol. Zool. 62:356–373.

Congdon, J. D., G. L. Breitenbach, R. C. van Loben Sels, and D. W. Tinkle. 1987. Reproduction and nesting ecology of snapping turtles (*Chelydra serpentina*) in southeastern Michigan. Herpetologica 43:39–54.

Congdon, J. D., A. E. Dunham, and D. W. Tinkle. 1982. Energy budgets and life histories of reptiles. *In* Gans, C., ed. Biology of the Reptilia, vol. 13, Physiology D, 233–271. Academic Press, New York.

Congdon, J. D., and R. E. Gatten, Jr. 1989. Movements and energetics of nesting *Chrysemys picta*. Herpetologica 45:94–100.

Congdon, J. D., R. E. Gatten, Jr., and S. J. Morreale. 1989. Overwintering activity of box turtles (*Terrapene carolina*) in South Carolina. J. Herpetol. 23:179–181.

Congdon, J. D., and J. W. Gibbons. 1983. Relationships of reproductive characteristics to body size in *Pseudemys scripta*. Herpetologica 39:147–151.

———. 1985. Egg components and reproductive characteristics of turtles: Relationships to body size. Herpetologica 41:194–205.

———. 1987. Morphological constraint on egg size: A challenge to optimal egg size theory? Proc. Natl. Acad. Sci. 84:4145–4147.

———. 1989. Biomass productivity of turtles in freshwater wetlands: A geographic comparison. *In* Sharitz, R. R., and J. W. Gibbons, eds. Freshwater wetlands and wildlife, 583–592. DOE Symp. Ser. (61).

———. 1990. Turtle eggs: Their ecology and evolution. *In* Gibbons, J. W., ed. Life history and ecology of the slider turtle, 109–123. Smithsonian Institution Press, Washington, D.C.

Congdon, J. D., J. W. Gibbons, and J. L. Greene. 1983. Parental investment in the chicken turtle (*Deirochelys reticularia*). Ecology 64:419–425.

Congdon, J. D., J. L. Greene, and J. W. Gibbons. 1986. Biomass of freshwater turtles: A geographic comparison. Amer. Midl. Natur. 115:165–173.

Congdon, J. D., and D. W. Tinkle. 1982. Reproductive energetics of the painted turtle (*Chrysemys picta*). Herpetologica 38:228–237.

Congdon, J. D., D. W. Tinkle, G. L. Breitenbach, and R. C. van Loben Sels. 1983. Nesting ecology and hatching success in the turtle *Emydoidea blandingi*. Herpetologica 39:417–429.

Congdon, J. D., D. W. Tinkle, and P. C. Rosen. 1983. Egg components and utilization during development in aquatic turtles. Copeia 1983:264–268.

Congdon, J. D., and R. C. van Loben Sels. 1991. Growth and body size in Blanding's turtles (*Emydoidea blandingi*): Relationships to reproduction. Can. J. Zool. 69:239–245.

———. In press. Relationships of reproductive traits and body size with attainment of sexual maturity and age in Blanding's turtles (*Emydoidea blandingi*). J. Evol. Biol.

Congello, K. 1978. Nesting and egg laying behavior in *Terrapene carolina*. Proc. Pennsylvania Acad. Sci. 52:51–56.

Conley, W. J., and B. A. Hoffman. 1987. Nesting activity of sea turtles in Florida, 1979–1985. Florida Scientist 50:201–210.

Cook, F. R. 1984. Introduction to Canadian amphibians and reptiles. Natl. Mus. Canada, Ottawa. 200 pp.

Cook, F. R., J. D. LaFontaine, S. Black, L. Luciuk, and R. V. Lindsay. 1980. Spotted turtles (*Clemmys guttata*) in eastern Ontario and adjacent Quebec. Can. Field-Natur. 94:411–415.

Cook, S., D. Abb, and W. Frair. 1972. A new record size box turtle. Int. Turtle and Tortoise Soc. J. 6(3):9–17.

Coombs, E. M. 1979. Food habitats and livestock competition with the desert tortoise on the Beaver Dam Slope, Utah. Proc. Symp. Desert Tortoise Council 1979:132–147.

Cooper, J. 1977. Vest-pocket turtle. Natur. Hist. 86(4):53–57.

Cooper, J. G. 1863. Description of *Xerobates agassizii*. Proc. California Acad. Sci. 2:118–123.

Corgan, J. X. 1976. Vertebrate fossils of Tennessee. Tennessee Div. Geol. Bull. (77):1–100.

Corliss, L. A., J. I. Richardson, C. Ryder, and R. Bell. 1989. The hawksbills of Jumby Bay, Antigua, West Indies. Proc. Ninth Ann. Workshop Sea Turtle Conserv. Biol. 33–35.

Cornelius, S. E. 1976. Marine turtle nesting activity at Playa Naranjo, Costa Rica. Brenesia 8:1–27.

———. 1982. Status of sea turtles along the Pacific Coast of Middle America. *In* Bjorndal, K. A., ed. Biology and conservation of sea turtles, 211–219. Smithsonian Institution Press, Washington, D.C.

———. 1983. *Lepidochelys olivacea* (Lora, Carpintera, Pacific Ridley Sea Turtle). *In* Janzen, D. H., ed. Costa Rican natural history, 402–405. University of Chicago Press.

Cornelius, S. E., M. Alvarado Ulloa, J. C. Castro, M. Mata del Valle, and D. C. Robinson. 1991. Management of the olive ridley sea turtles (*Lepidochelys olivacea*) nesting at Playas Nancite and Ostional, Costa Rica. *In* Robinson, J. G., and K. H. Redford, eds. Neotropical wildlife use and conservation, 111–135. University of Chicago Press.

Cornelius, S. E., and D. C. Robinson. 1982. Tag recoveries for ridleys nesting in Costa Rica. Marine Turtle Newsl. (21):2–3.

Costanzo, J. P. 1982. Heating and cooling rates of *Terrapene ornata* and *Chrysemys picta* in water. Bios (Madison, New Jersey). 53:159–166.

Costanzo, J. P., and D. L. Claussen. 1990. Natural freeze tolerance in the terrestrial turtle, *Terrapene carolina*. J. Exp. Zool. 254:228–232.

Coulter, M. W. 1957. Predation by snapping turtles upon aquatic birds in Maine marshes. J. Wildl. Mgt. 21:17–21.

———. 1958. Distribution, food, and weight of the snapping turtle in Maine. Maine Field Natur. 14:53–62.

Cowan, F. B. M. 1969. Gross and microscopic anatomy of the orbital glands of *Malaclemys* and other emydine turtles. Can. J. Zool. 47:723–729.

———. 1971. The ultrastructure of the lachrymal "salt" gland and the Harderian gland in the euryhaline *Malaclemys* and some closely related stenohaline emydines. Can. J. Zool. 49:691–697.

———. 1974. Observations on extrarenal excretion by

orbital glands and osmoregulation in *Malaclemys terrapin*. Comp. Biochem. Physiol. 48A:489–500.

———. 1981a. Short term acclimation of *Malaclemys terrapin* to saltwater. Comp. Biochem. Physiol. 68A:55–59.

———. 1981b. Effects of salt loading on salt gland function in the euryhaline turtle, *Malaclemys terrapin*. J. Comp. Physiol. 145:101–108.

———. 1990. Does the lachrymal salt gland of *Malaclemys terrapin* have a significant role in osmoregulation? Can. J. Zool. 68:1520–1524.

Cox, J., D. Inkley, and R. Kautz. 1987. Ecology and habitat protection needs of gopher tortoise (*Gopherus polyphemus*) populations found on lands slated for large-scale development in Florida. Florida Game Fresh Water Fish Comm., Nongame Wildl. Progr. Tech. Rept. 4. Tallahassee, Florida. 75 pp.

Cox, W. A., J. B. Hazelrig, M. E. Turner, R. A. Angus, and K. R. Marion. 1991. A model for growth in the musk turtle, *Sternotherus minor*, in a north Florida spring. Copeia 1991:954–968.

Cox, W. A., and K. R. Marion. 1972. Winter reproduction and multiple clutches in a spring-dwelling population of *Sternotherus minor minor* (Reptilia: Chelonia: Kinosternidae). ASB Bull. 24:45.

———. 1979. Population structure and survivorship in the musk turtle, *Sternotherus minor*, in a north Florida spring (Reptilia: *Chelonia*). ASB Bull. 26:84.

Cox, W. A., M. C. Nowak, and K. R. Marion. 1980. Observations on courtship and mating behavior in the musk turtle, *Sternotherus minor*. J. Herpetol. 14:200–204.

Cox, W. A., S. T. Wyatt, W. E. Wilhelm, and K. R. Marion. 1988. Infection of the turtle, *Sternotherus minor*, by the lung fluke, *Heronimus mollis*: incidence of infection and correlations to host life history and ecology in a Florida spring. J. Herpetol. 22:488–490.

Craig, R. J., M. W. Klemens, and S. S. Craig. 1980. The northeastern range limit of the eastern mud turtle *Kinosternon s. subrubrum* (Lacépède). J. Herpetol. 14:295–297.

Crastz, F. 1982. Embryological stages of the marine turtle *Lepidochelys olivacea* (Eschscholtz). Rev. Biol. Trop. 30:113–120.

Crawford, E. C., Jr., R. N. Gatz, H. Magnussen, S. F. Perry, and J. Piiper. 1976. Lung volumes, pulmonary blood flow and carbon monoxide diffusing capacity of turtles. J. Comp. Physiol. 107:169–178.

Crawford, K. M. 1991a. The effect of temperature and seasonal acclimatization on renal function of painted turtles, *Chrysemys picta*. Comp. Biochem Physiol. 99A:375–380.

———. 1991b. The winter environment of painted turtles: *Chrysemys picta*: temperature, dissolved oxygen, and potential cues for emergence. Can. J. Zool. 69:2493–2498.

Crawford, K. M., J. R. Spotila, and E. A. Standora 1983. Operative environmental temperatures and basking behavior of the turtle *Pseudemys scripta*. Ecology 64:989–999.

Crawshaw, L. I., M. H. Johnston, and D. E. Lemmons. 1980. Acclimation, temperature selection, and heat exchange in the turtle, *Chrysemys scripta*. Amer. J. Physiol. 238:R443–R446.

Crenshaw, J. W. 1965. Serum protein variation in an interspecies hybrid swarm of turtles of the genus *Pseudemys*. Evolution 19:1–15.

Crews, D., J. J. Bull, and T. Wibbels. 1991. Estrogen and sex reversal in turtles: A dose-dependent phenomenon. Gen. Comp. Endocrinol. 81:357–364.

Crews, D., and P. Licht. 1975. Site of progesterone production in the reptilian ovarian follicle. Gen. Comp. Endocrinol. 27:553–556.

Crews, D., T. Wibbels, and W. H. N. Gutzke. 1989. Action of sex steroid hormones on temperature-induced sex determination in the snapping turtle (*Chelydra serpentina*). Gen. Comp. Endocrinol. 76:159–166.

Cribb, R. B. 1972. Observations on the green turtle, Hoskyn Island. Queensland Natur. 20:116–117.

Critchley, K. 1987. Tar covered turtles recovered on Grand Cayman. Marine Turtle Newsl. (40):11–12.

Crouse, D. T. 1984. Incidental capture of sea turtles by commercial fisheries. Abridged from report to the Center for Environmental Education, March 1982. Smithsonian Herpetol. Inform. Serv. (62):1–8.

———. 1989. Guest editorial: "Large juveniles" also crucial to future breeding success of sea turtle populations. Marine Turtle Newsl. (46):4–5.

Crouse, D. T., L. B. Crowder, and H. Caswell. 1987. A stage-based population model for loggerhead sea turtles and implications for conservation. Ecology 68:1412–1423.

Crowell Comuzzie, D. K., and D. W. Owens. 1990. A quantitative analysis of courtship behavior in captive green sea turtles (*Chelonia mydas*). Herpetologica 46:195–202.

Crumly, C. R. 1984. The genus name for North American gopher tortoises. Proc. Symp. Desert Tortoise Council 1984:147–148.

Crumly, C. R., and L. L. Grismer. In press. Validity of the tortoise, *Xerobates lepidocephalus* Ottley and Velázquez, in Baja California. *In* Biology of North American Tortoises. U.S. Fish and Wildlife Service, Fish and Wildlife Research.

Culbertson, G. 1907. Some notes on the habits of the common box turtle (*Cistudo carolina*). Proc. Indiana Acad. Sci. 1907:78–79.

Cunningham, B. 1939. Effect of temperature upon the developmental rate of the embryo of the diamond back terrapin (*Malaclemys centrata* Lat.). Amer. Natur. 73:381–384.

Cyrus, R. V., I. Y. Mahmoud, and J. Klicka. 1978. Fine structure of the corpus luteum of the snapping turtle, *Chelydra serpentina*. Copeia 1978:622–627.

Czarnowsky, R. 1976. A note on the feeding behavior of a *Clemmys insculpta*. Bull. Maryland Herpetol. Soc. 12:103.

Dalrymple, G. H. 1977. Intraspecific variation in the cranial feeding mechanism of turtles of the genus *Trionyx* (Reptilia, Testudines, Trionychidae). J. Herpetol. 11:255–285.

Dalrymple, G. H., J. C. Hampp, and D. J. Wellins. 1985. Male-biased sex ratio in a cold nest of a hawksbill sea turtle (*Eretmochelys imbricata*). J. Herpetol. 19:158–159.

Daniel, R. S., and K. V. Smith. 1947. Migration of newly hatched loggerhead turtles toward the sea. Science 106:398–399.

Danton, C., and R. Prescott. 1988. Kemp's ridley in Cape Cod Bay, Massachusetts–1987 field research. *In* Schroeder, B. A., ed. Proceedings of the Eighth Annual Workshop on Sea Turtle Conservation and Biology, 17–18. NOAA-TM-NMFS-SEFC-214.

Dantzler, W., and W. Holmes. 1974. Water and mineral metabolism in Reptilia. *In* Florkin, M., and B. Scheer, eds. Chemical zoology, vol. 9, Amphibia and Reptilia, 277–336. Academic Press, New York.

Dantzler, W. H., and B. Schmidt-Nielsen. 1966. Excretion in fresh-water turtle (*Pseudemys scripta*) and desert tortoise (*Gopherus agassizii*). Amer. J. Physiol. 210:198–210.

D'Aoust, J.-Y., E. Daley, M. Crozier, and A. M. Sewell. 1990. Pet turtles: A continuing international threat to public health. Amer. J. Epidemiol. 132:233–238.

Daudin, F. M. 1802. Histoire naturelle, générale et particulière, des Reptiles. 2. F. Dufart, Paris. 432 pp.

Davenport, J. 1987. Locomotion in hatchling leatherback turtles *Dermochelys coriacea*. J. Zool. (London) 212:85–101.

———. 1988. Do diving leatherbacks pursue glowing jelly? British Herpetol. Soc. Bull. (24):20–21.

Davenport, J., S. Antipas, and E. Blake. 1989. Observations of gut function in young green turtles *Chelonia mydas* L. Herpetol. J. 1:336–342.

Davenport, J., and G. H. Balazs. 1991. 'Fiery bodies'–are pyrosomas an important component of the diet of

leatherback turtles? British Herpetol. Soc. Bull. (37):33–38.

Davenport, J., and W. Clough. 1985. The use of limbscales or "pseudoclaws" in food handling by young loggerhead turtles. Copeia 1985:786–788.

———. 1986. Swimming and diving in young loggerhead sea turtles (*Caretta caretta* L.). Copeia 1986: 53–57.

Davenport, J., D. L. Holland, and J. East. 1990. Thermal and biochemical characteristics of the lipids of the leatherback turtle *Dermochelys coriacea:* evidence of endothermy. J. Marine Biol. Assoc. United Kingdom 70:33–41.

Davenport, J., G. Ingle, and A. K. Hughes. 1982. Oxygen uptake and heart rate in young green turtles (*Chelonia mydas*). J. Zool. (London) 198:399–412.

Davenport, J., and Macedo E.-A. 1990. Behavioural osmotic control in the euryhaline diamondback terrapin *Malaclemys terrapin:* responses to low salinity and rainfall. J. Zool. (London) 220:487–496.

Davenport, J., S. A. Munks, and P. J. Oxford. 1984. A comparison of the swimming of marine and freshwater turtles. Proc. Royal Soc. London, ser. B, 220:447–475.

Davenport, J., and P. J. Oxford. 1984. Feeding, gut dynamics, digestion and oxygen consumption in hatchling green turtles (*Chelonia mydas* L.). British J. Herpetol. 6:351–358.

Davenport, J., and T. M. Wong. 1986. Observations on the water economy of the estuarine turtles *Batagur baska* (Gray) and *Callagur borneoensis* (Schlegel and Müller). Comp. Biochem. Physiol. 84A:703–707.

David, W. D., Jr. 1975. Notes on the egg laying habits of *Deirochelys reticularia*. Herpetol. Rev. 6:127.

Davidson, J. M., and R. H. Mount. 1972. Geographic variation in the pond slider, *Pseudemys scripta*, in Alabama. ASB Bull. 19:63.

Davis, B. J. 1991. Developmental changes in the blood oxygen transport system of Kemp's ridley sea turtle, *Lepidochelys kempi*. Can. J. Zool. 69:2660–2666.

Davis, D. R., and E. G. Milstrey. 1988. Description and biology of *Acrolophus pholeter* (Lepidoptera: Tineidae), a new moth commensal from gopher tortoise burrows in Florida. Proc. Entomol. Soc. Washington 90:164–178.

Davis, J. D., and C. G. Jackson, Jr. 1970. Copulatory behavior in the red-eared turtle, *Pseudemys scripta elegans* (Wied). Herpetologica 26:238–240.

———. 1973. Notes on the courtship of a captive male *Chrysemys scripta taylori*. Herpetologica 29:62–64.

Davis, R. A. 1977. Greater Cincinnati chelonians. Cincinnati Mus. Natur. Hist. Quart. 14(3):15–19.

Day, J. F., and G. A. Curtis. 1983. Opportunistic blood-feeding on egg laying sea turtles by salt marsh mosquitos (Diptera: Culicidae). Florida Entomol. 66:359–360.

Degenhardt, W. G., and J. L. Christiansen. 1974. Distribution and habitats of turtles in New Mexico. Southwest. Natur. 19:21–46.

Deitz, D. C., and D. R. Jackson. 1979. Use of American alligator nests by nesting turtles. J. Herpetol. 13:510–512.

Delany, M. F., and C. L. Abercrombie. 1986. American alligator food habits in northcentral Florida. J. Wildl. Mgt. 50:348–353.

Delikat, D. S. 1981. Ixtoc 1 oil spill–Atlantic ridley sea turtle survival. Underwater Natur. 13:13–15.

De Lisle, H. F. 1991. Sex determination in reptiles: Genetic vs environmental. J. Sm. Exotic Anim. Med. 1:20–25.

Demas, S., M. Duronslet, S. Wachtel, C. Caillouet, and D. Nakamura. 1990. Sex-specific DNA in reptiles with temperature sex determination. J. Exp. Zool. 253:319–324.

Den Hartog, J. C. 1980. Notes on the food of sea turtles: *Eretmochelys imbricata* (Linnaeus) and *Dermochelys coriacea* (Linnaeus). Netherlands J. Zool. 30:595–610.

Den Hartog, J. C., and M. M. Van Nierop. 1984. A study on the gut contents of six leathery turtles *Dermochelys coriacea* (Linnaeus) (Reptilia: Testudines: Dermochelyidae) from British waters and from the Netherlands. Zool. Verh. Rijksmus. Natuur. Hist. Leiden 209:1–36.

Denver, R. J., and P. Licht. 1988. Thyroid status influences in vitro thyrotropin and growth hormone responses to thyrotropin-releasing hormone by pituitary glands of hatchling slider turtles (*Pseudemys scripta elegans*). J. Exp. Zool. 246:293–304.

———. 1991. Dependence of body growth on thyroid activity in turtles. J. Exp. Zool. 258:48–59.

DePari, J. A., M. H. Linck, and T. E. Graham. 1987. Clutch size of the Blanding's turtle, *Emydoidea blandingi*, in Massachusetts. Can. Field-Natur. 101: 440–442.

Deraniyagala, P. E. P. 1933. The loggerhead turtles (Carettidae) of Ceylon. Ceylon J. Sci. (B) 18:61–72.

———. 1939. The tetrapod reptiles of Ceylon, vol. 1, Testudinates and crocodilians. Dulau and Co., Ltd., London. 412 pp.

DeRosa, C. T., and D. H. Taylor. 1978. Sun-compass orientation in the painted turtle, *Chrysemys picta* (Reptilia, Testudines, Testudinidae). J. Herpetol. 12:25–28.

———. 1980. Homeward orientation mechanisms in three species of turtles (*Trionyx spinifer, Chrysemys

picta,* and *Terrapene carolina*). Behav. Ecol. Sociobiol. 7:15–23.

———. 1982. A comparison of compass orientation mechanisms in three turtles (*Trionyx spinifer, Chrysemys picta,* and *Terrapene carolina*). Copeia 1982:394–399.

de Silva, G. S. 1982. The status of sea turtle populations in East Malaysia and the South China Sea. *In* Bjorndal, K. A., ed. Biology and conservation of sea turtles, 327–337. Smithsonian Institution Press, Washington, D.C.

DeSmet, W. H. O. 1978. The chromosomes of 11 species of Chelonia (Reptilia). Acta Zool. Pathol. Antverp. 70:15–34.

Dial, B. E. 1987. Energetics and performance during nest emergence and the hatchling frenzy in the loggerhead sea turtles (*Caretta caretta*). Herpetologica 43:307–315.

Dickerson, D. D., and D. A. Nelson. 1988. Use of long wavelength lights to prevent disorientation of hatchling sea turtles. *In* Schroeder, B. A., ed. Proceedings of the Eighth Annual Workshop on Sea Turtle Conservation and Biology, 19–21. NOAA-TM-NMFS-SEFC-214.

Diemer, J. E. 1986. The ecology and management of the gopher tortoise in the southeastern United States. Herpetologica 42:125–133.

———. 1989. *Gopherus polyphemus,* gopher tortoise. *In* Swingland, I. R., and M. W. Klemens, eds. The conservation biology of tortoises, 14–16. Occ. Pap. IUCN Species Survival Commission No. 5.

———. 1992a. Home range and movements of the tortoise *Gopherus polyphemus* in northern Florida. J. Herpetol. 26:158–165.

———. 1992b. Demography of the tortoise *Gopherus polyphemus* in northern Florida. J. Herpetol. 26:281–289.

Diemer, J. E., and P. E. Moler. 1982. Gopher tortoise response to site preparation in northern Florida. Proc. Conf. Southeast. Assoc. Fish. Wildl. Agencies 36:634–637.

Diemer, J. E., D. R. Jackson, J. L. Landers, J. N. Layne, and D. A. Wood. 1989. Gopher tortoise relocation symposium proceedings. Florida Game and Fresh Water Fish Commission, Nongame Wildlife Program Technical Report No. 5. Tallahassee, Florida. 109 pp.

Dimond, M. T. 1983. Sex of turtle hatchlings as related to incubation temperature. Proc. 6th Reptile Symp. Captive Prop. Husb. Zool. Conserv. (Thurmont, Maryland, 1982), 88–101.

———. 1985. Some effects of temperature on turtle egg incubation. *In* Suresh, C. G., and C. B. L. Srivastava, eds. Recent advances in developmental biology of animals, 35–39. Indian Soc. Develop. Biol., Poona.

———. 1987. The effects of incubation temperature on hatching time, sex, and growth of hatchlings of the diamondback terrapin, *Malaclemys terrapin* (Schoepff). Pranikee 8:1–5.

Dinkins, A. 1954. A brief observation on male combat in *Clemmys insculpta*. Herpetologica 10:20.

Dix, M. W., and J. I. Richardson. 1972. Reproductive periodicity of the loggerhead sea-turtle, *Caretta caretta* (Reptilia: Chelonia). ASB Bull. 19:65.

Dixon, J. R. 1987. Amphibians and reptiles of Texas with keys, taxonomic synopses, bibliography, and distribution maps. Texas A&M University Press, College Station, Texas. 434 pp.

Dizon, A. E., and G. H. Balazs. 1982. Radiotelemetry of Hawaiian green turtles at their breeding colony. Marine Fish. Rev. 44:13–20.

Dobie, J. L. 1968a. A new turtle species of the genus *Macroclemys* (Chelydridae) from the Florida Pliocene. Tulane Stud. Zool. Bot. 15:59–63.

———. 1968b. Shelled eggs in the urinary bladder of an alligator snapping turtle, *Macroclemys temmincki*. Herpetologica 24:328–330.

———. 1971. Reproduction and growth in the alligator snapping turtle, *Macroclemys temminckii* (Troost). Copeia 1971:645–658.

———. 1972. Correction of distributional records for *Graptemys barbouri* and *Graptemys pulchra*. Herpetol. Rev. 4:23.

———. 1981. The taxonomic relationship between *Malaclemys* Gray, 1844 and *Graptemys* Agassiz, 1857 (Testudines: Emydidae). Tulane Stud. Zool. Bot. 23:85–102.

Dobie, J. L., and F. M. Bagley. 1988. Recovery plan for the Alabama red-bellied turtle (*Pseudemys alabamensis*). U.S. Fish Wildl. Serv. Tech. Rev. Draft, 20 pp.

Dobie, J. L., and D. R. Jackson. 1979. First fossil record for the diamondback terrapin, *Malaclemys terrapin* (Emydidae), and comments on the fossil record of *Chrysemys nelsoni* (Emydidae). Herpetologica 35:139–145.

Dobie, J. L., L. H. Ogren, and J. F. Fitzpatrick, Jr. 1961. Food notes and records of the Atlantic ridley turtle (*Lepidochelys kempi*) from Louisiana. Copeia 1961:109–110.

Dobson, R. B. 1971. A range extension and basking observation of Blanding's turtle in Nova Scotia. Can. Field-Natur. 85:255–256.

Dodd, C. K., Jr. 1981. Nesting of the green turtle, *Chelonia mydas* (L.), in Florida: Historic review and present trends. Brimleyana (7):39–54.

———. 1982. A controversy surrounding an endangered species listing: The case of the Illinois mud turtle. Smithsonian Herpetol. Inform. Serv. (55):1–22.

———. 1983. A review of the status of the Illinois mud turtle *Kinosternon flavescens spooneri* Smith. Biol. Conserv. 27:141–156.

———. 1986. Desert and gopher tortoises: Perspectives on conservation approaches. *In* Jackson, D. R., and R. J. Bryant, eds. The gopher tortoise and its community, 54–72. Proc. 5th Ann. Mtg. Gopher Tortoise Council.

———. 1987. A bibliography of the loggerhead sea turtle *Caretta caretta* (Linnaeus), 1758. U.S. Fish Wildl. Serv. Endang. Spec. Rept. 16. 64 pp.

———. 1988a. Patterns of distribution and seasonal use of the turtle *Sternotherus depressus* by the leech *Placobdella parasitica*. J. Herpetol. 22:74–81.

———. 1988b. Disease and population declines in the flattened musk turtle *Sternotherus depressus*. Amer. Midl. Natur. 119:394–401.

———. 1988c. Synopsis of the biological data on the loggerhead sea turtle *Caretta caretta* (Linnaeus 1758). U.S. Fish Wildl. Serv. Biol. Rept. 88(14). 110 pp.

———. 1989a. Population structure and biomass of *Sternotherus odoratus* (Testudines: Kinosternidae) in a northern Alabama lake. Brimleyana (15):47–56.

———. 1989b. Secondary sex ratio variation among populations of the flattened musk turtle, *Sternotherus depressus*. Copeia 1989:1041–1045.

———. 1990a. Effects of habitat fragmentation on a stream-dwelling species, the flattened musk turtle *Sternotherus depressus*. Biol. Conserv. 54:33–45.

———. 1990b. *Caretta*. Catalog. Amer. Amphib. Rept. 482:1–2.

———. 1990c. *Caretta caretta*. Catalog. Amer. Amphib. Rept. 483:1–7.

Dodd, C. K., Jr., and E. D. Brodie, Jr. 1975. Notes on the defensive behavior of the snapping turtle, *Chelydra serpentina*. Herpetologica 31:286–288.

Dodd, C. K., Jr., K. M. Enge, and J. N. Stuart. 1988. Aspects of the biology of the flattened musk turtle, *Sternotherus depressus*, in northern Alabama. Bull. Florida St. Mus. Biol. Sci. 34:1–64.

Dodd, C. K., Jr., and G. S. Morgan. 1992. Fossil sea turtles from the early Pliocene Bone Valley Formation, central Florida. J. Herpetol. 26:1–8.

Dodd, C. K., Jr., and R. A. Seigel. 1991. Relocation, repatriation, and translocation of amphibians and reptiles: Are they conservation strategies that work? Herpetologica 47:336–350.

Dodge, C. H., M. T. Dimond, and C. C. Wunder. 1978. Effect of temperature on the incubation time of eggs of the eastern box turtle (*Terrapene carolina carolina* Linné). *In* Henderson, G. E., ed. 1978. Proceedings of the Florida and Interregional Conference on sea turtles, 8–11. Florida Marine Res. Publ. 33.

Dodge, C. H., and C. C. Wunder. 1963. Growth of juvenile red-eared turtles as influenced by gravitational field intensity. Nature 197:922–923.

Dolbeer, R. A. 1969. Population density and home range size of the eastern box turtle (*Terrapene c. carolina*) in eastern Tennessee. ASB Bull. 16:49.

———. 1971. Winter behavior of the eastern box turtle, *Terrapene c. carolina* L., in Tennessee. Copeia 1971:758–760.

Donnelly, M. 1991. Japan bans import of hawksbill shell effective December 1992. Marine Turtle Newsl. (54):1–3.

Dorando, S. L. 1979. A method to reduce error in weight estimation of freshwater turtles. Copeia 1979:346.

Dorfman, D. 1979. Some blood characteristics of the diamondback terrapin, *Malaclemys terrapin*. Bull. New Jersey Acad. Sci. 24:38–40.

Doroff, A. M., and L. B. Keith. 1990. Demography and ecology of an ornate box turtle (*Terrapene ornata*) population in south-central Wisconsin. Copeia 1990: 387–399.

Douglass, J. F. 1975. Bibliography of the North American land tortoises (genus *Gopherus*). U.S. Fish Wildl. Serv. Spec. Sci. Rept. Wildl. 190. 60 pp.

———. 1977a. Supplement to the bibliography of the North American land tortoises (Genus *Gopherus*). Smithsonian Herpetol. Inform. Serv. (39):1–18.

———. 1977b. Abnormalities of scutellation in a population of *Gopherus polyphemus* (Reptilia: Testudinidae). Florida Scientist 40:256–258.

———. 1978. Refugia of juvenile gopher tortoises, *Gopherus polyphemus* (Reptilia, Testudines, Testudinidae). J. Herpetol. 12:413–415.

Douglass, J. F., and J. N. Layne. 1978. Activity and thermoregulation of the gopher tortoise (*Gopherus polyphemus*) in southern Florida. Herpetologica 34:359–374.

Douglass, J. F., and C. E. Winegarner. 1977. Predators of egg and young of the gopher tortoise, *Gopherus polyphemus* (Reptilia, Testudines, Testudinidae) in southern Florida. J. Herpetol. 11:236–238.

Dowler, R. C., and J. W. Bickham. 1982. Chromosomal relationships of the tortoises (family Testudinidae). Genetica 58:189–197.

Drennen, D., D. Cooley, and J. E. Devore. 1989. Armadillo predation on loggerhead turtle eggs at two national wildlife refuges in Florida, USA. Marine Turtle Newsl. (45):7–8.

Drummond, H., and E. R. Gordon. 1979. Luring in the neonate alligator snapping turtle (*Macroclemys temminckii*): Description and experimental analysis. Z. Tierpsychol. 50:136–152.

Dubois, W., and I. P. Callard. 1985. Characterization of the testicular binding site for iodinated rat FSH in the turtle, *Chrysemys picta*. Comp. Biochem. Physiol. 82A:891–897.

Dubois, W., J. Pudney, and I. P. Callard. 1988. The annual testicular cycle in the turtle, *Chrysemys picta:* a histochemical and electron microscopic study. Gen. Comp. Endocrinol. 71:191–204.

Duellman, W. E., and A. Schwartz. 1958. Amphibians and reptiles of southern Florida. Bull. Florida St. Mus. Biol. Sci. 3:181–324.

Duever, M. 1972. The striped mud turtle (*Kinosternon bauri* Garman) in South Carolina. Herpetol. Rev. 4:131.

Dundee, H. A. 1974. Evidence for specific status of *Graptemys kohni* and *Graptemys pseudogeographica*. Copeia 1974:540–542.

———. 1989. Higher category name usage for amphibians and reptiles. Syst. Zool. 38:398–406.

Dundee, H. A., and D. A. Rossman. 1989. The amphibians and reptiles of Louisiana. Louisiana State University Press, Baton Rouge. 300 pp.

Dunham, A. E., and J. W. Gibbons. 1990. Growth of the slider turtle. *In* Gibbons, J. W., ed. Life history and ecology of the slider turtle, 135–145. Smithsonian Institution Press, Washington, D.C.

Dunn, E. R. 1917. Reptile and amphibian collections from the North Carolina mountains, with especial reference to salamanders. Bull. Amer. Mus. Natur. Hist. 37:593–634.

Dunson, M. K., and W. A. Dunson. 1975. The relation between plasma Na concentration and salt gland Na-K ATPase content in the diamondback terrapin and the yellow-bellied sea snake. J. Comp. Physiol. 101:89–97.

Dunson, W. A. 1960. Aquatic respiration in *Trionyx spinifer asper*. Herpetologica 16:277–283.

———. 1970. Some aspects of electrolyte and water balance in three estuarine reptiles, the diamondback terrapin, American and "salt water" crocodiles. Comp. Biochem. Physiol. 32:161–174.

———. 1981. Behavioral osmoregulation in the Key mud turtle, *Kinosternon b. baurii*. J. Herpetol. 15:163–173.

———. 1985. Effect of water salinity and food salt content on growth and sodium efflux of hatchling diamondback terrapins (*Malaclemys*). Physiol. Zool. 58:736–747.

———. 1986. Estuarine populations of the snapping turtle (*Chelydra*) as a model for the evolution of marine adaptations in reptiles. Copeia 1986:741–756.

Dunson, W. A., and H. Heatwole. 1986. Effect of

relative shell size in turtles on water and electrolyte composition. Amer. J. Physiol. 250:R1133–R1137.

Dunson, W. A., and M. E. Seidel. 1986. Salinity tolerance of estuarine and insular emydid turtles (*Pseudemys nelsoni* and *Trachemys decussata*). J. Herpetol. 20:237–245.

DuPonte, M. W., R. M. Nakamura, and E. M. L. Chang. 1978. Activation of latent *Salmonella* and *Arizona* organisms by dehydration in red-eared turtles, *Pseudemys scripta elegans*. Amer. J. Vet. Res. 39:529–530.

Durán Nájera, J. J. 1991. Anidación de la tortuga blanca, *Chelonia mydas* (Linnaeus, 1758) (Testudines: Cheloniidae), en Isla Contoy, México. Rev. Biol. Trop. 39:149–152.

Duron-Dufrenne, M. 1978. Contribution a l'étude de la biologie de *Dermochelys coriacea* (Linné) dans les Pertuis Charentais. Ph.D. dissertation, University of Bordeaux, France.

———. 1987. Premier suivi par satellite en Atlantique d'une tortue Luth *Dermochelys coriacea*. C. R. Acad. Sci. Paris, ser. 3, 304:399–402.

Duron-Dufrenne, M., and R. Bour. 1988. Caractères diagnostiques offerts par le crâne des tortues marines. Mésogée 48:29–32.

Dutton, P., D. McDonald, and R. Boulon. 1992. 1991 a 'record year' for leatherback productivity on St. Croix, U.S. Virgin Islands. Marine Turtle Newsl. (57):15–17.

Dutton, P. H., C. P. Whitmore, and N. Mrosovsky. 1985. Masculinisation of leatherback turtle *Dermochelys coriacea* hatchlings from eggs incubated in styrofoam boxes. Biol. Conserv. 31:249–264.

Eckert, K. L. 1987. Environmental unpredictability and leatherback sea turtle (*Dermochelys coriacea*) nest loss. Herpetologica 43:315–323.

Eckert, K. L., and S. A. Eckert. 1988. Pre-reproductive movements of leatherback sea turtles (*Dermochelys coriacea*) nesting in the Caribbean. Copeia 1988:400–406.

———. 1990. Embryo mortality and hatch success in *In situ* and translocated leatherback sea turtle *Dermochelys coriacea* eggs. Biol. Conserv. 53:37–46.

Eckert, K. L., S. A. Eckert, T. W. Adams, and A. D. Tucker. 1989. Inter-nesting migrations by leatherback sea turtles (*Dermochelys coriacea*) in the West Indies. Herpetologica 45:190–194.

Eckert, K. L., and C. Luginbuhl. 1988. Death of a giant. Marine Turtle Newsl. (43):2–3.

Eckert, S. A., K. L. Eckert, P. Ponganis, and G. L. Kooyman. 1989. Diving and foraging behavior of leatherback sea turtles (*Dermochelys coriacea*). Can. J. Zool. 67:2834–2840.

Eckert, S. A., and H. R. Martins. 1989. Transatlantic travel by juvenile loggerhead turtle. Marine Turtle Newsl. (45):15.

Eckert, S. A., D. W. Nellis, K. L. Eckert, and G. L. Kooyman. 1986. Diving patterns of two leatherback sea turtles (*Dermochelys coriacea*) during internesting intervals at Sandy Point, St. Croix, U.S. Virgin Islands. Herpetologica 42:381–388.

Eckler, J. T., A. R. Breisch, and J. L. Behler. 1990. Radio telemetry techniques applied to the bog turtle (*Clemmys muhlenbergii* Schoepff 1801). *In* Mitchell, R. S., C. J. Sheviak, and D. J. Leopold, eds. Ecosystem management: Rare species and significant habitats, 69–70. Bulletin No. 471, New York State Museum, Proc. 15th Annual Natural Areas Conference.

Ecksdine, V. 1985. Meteorological influence on fall basking of the map turtle, *Graptemys geographica,* in a north temperate stream. Bull. Chicago Herpetol. Soc. 20:82–85.

Edgren, R. A. 1942. A nesting rendezvous of the musk turtle. Chicago Natur. 5:63.

———. 1943. *Pseudemys scripta troostii* in Michigan. Copeia 1943:249.

———. 1948. Some additional notes on Michigan *Pseudemys*. Natur. Hist. Misc. (22):1–2.

———. 1960. Ovulation time in the musk turtle, *Sternothaerus odoratus*. Copeia 1960:60–61.

Edgren, R. A., and M. K. Edgren. 1955. Thermoregulation in the musk turtle, *Sternotherus odoratus* Latreille. Herpetologica 11:213–217.

Edwards, S. 1976. Leatherback turtle, *Dermochelys coriacea*. Drum and Croaker 16:25–28.

Eggers, J. M., M. W. Haberland, and J. C. Griffin. 1992. Growth of juvenile loggerhead sea turtles near PSE&G's Salem Generating Station, Delaware Bay, New Jersey. Marine Turtle Newsl. (59):5–7.

Ehrenfeld, D. W. 1968. The role of vision in the sea-finding orientation of the green turtle (*Chelonia mydas*). 2. Orientation mechanisms and range of spectral sensitivity. Anim. Behav. 16:281–287.

Ehrenfeld, D. W., and A. Carr. 1967. The role of vision in the sea-finding orientation of the green turtle (*Chelonia mydas*). Anim. Behav. 15:25–36.

Ehrenfeld, D. W., and A. L. Koch. 1967. Visual accommodation in the green turtle. Science 155:827–828.

Ehrenfeld, J. G., and D. W. Ehrenfeld. 1973. Externally secreting glands of freshwater and sea turtles. Copeia 1973:305–314.

Ehrhardt, N. M., and R. Witham. 1992. Analysis of growth of the green sea turtle (*Chelonia mydas*) in the western central Atlantic. Bull. Marine Sci. 50:275–281.

Ehrhart, L. M. 1980. Marine turtle nesting in north

Brevard County, Florida, in 1979. Florida Scientist 43:27.

———. 1982. A review of sea turtle reproduction. *In* Bjorndal, K. A., ed. Biology and conservation of sea turtles, 29–38. Smithsonian Institution Press, Washington, D.C.

———. 1983. Marine turtles of the Indian River Lagoon system. Florida Scientist 46:337–346.

Ehrhart, L. M., and B. E. Witherington. 1987. Human and natural causes of marine turtle nest and hatchling mortality and their relationship to hatchling production on an important Florida nesting beach. Florida Game Fresh Water Fish Comm., Nongame Wildl. Progr. Tech. Rept. 1. Tallahassee, Florida. 141 pp.

Einem, G. E. 1956. Certain aspects of the natural history of the mudturtle, *Kinosternon bauri*. Copeia 1956:186–188.

Eisenberg, J. F., and J. Frazier. 1983. A leatherback turtle (*Dermochelys coriacea*) feeding in the wild. J. Herpetol. 17:81–82.

Eisner, T., W. E. Conner, K. Hicks, K. R. Dodge, H. I. Rosenberg, T. H. Jones, M. Cohen, and J. Meinwald. 1977. Stink of stinkpot turtle identified: ω-phenylalkanoic acids. Science 196:1347–1349.

Elgar, M. A., and L. J. Heaphy. 1989. Covariation between clutch size, egg weight and egg shape: Comparative evidence for chelonians. J. Zool. (London) 219:137–152.

Elghammer, R. W., and R. E. Johnson. 1976. Heat production by the eastern box turtle (*Terrapene carolina carolina*) as measured by direct calorimetry. Trans. Illinois St. Acad. Sci. 69:200–206.

Elghammer, R. W., R. O. Swan, R. E. Johnson, and D. Murphy. 1979. Physical characteristics of male and female eastern box turtles (*Terrapene carolina carolina*) found in Illinois. Trans. Illinois St. Acad. Sci. 72:1–8.

Emlen, S. T. 1969. Homing ability and orientation in the painted turtle *Chrysemys picta marginata*. Behaviour 33:58–76.

Engbring, J., N. Idechong, C. Cook, G. Wiles, and R. Bauer. 1992. Observations on the defensive and aggressive behavior of the leatherback turtle (*Dermochelys coriacea*) at sea. Herpetol. Rev. 23:70–71.

England, L. 1979. Notes on the distribution of the ornate box turtle (*Terrapene ornata ornata*) in Arkansas. Proc. Arkansas Acad. Sci. 33:75–76.

Ernst, C. H. 1964a. Further suggestions for the care of juvenile aquatic turtles. Philadelphia Herpetol. Soc. Bull. 12:18.

———. 1964b. Social dominance and aggressiveness in a juvenile *Chrysemys picta picta*. Philadelphia Herpetol. Soc. Bull. 12:18–19.

———. 1965. Bait preferences of some freshwater turtles. J. Ohio Herpetol. Soc. 5:53.

———. 1966. Overwintering of hatchling *Chelydra serpentina* in southeastern Pennsylvania. Philadelphia Herpetol Soc. Bull. 14:8–9.

———. 1967a. Intergradation between the painted turtles *Chrysemys picta picta* and *Chrysemys picta dorsalis*. Copeia 1967:131–136.

———. 1967b. Serum protein analysis: A taxonomic tool. Int. Turtle and Tortoise Soc. J. 1(3):34–36.

———. 1967c. A mating aggregation of the turtle *Clemmys guttata*. Copeia 1967:473–474.

———. 1967d. Notes on the herpetofauna of the White Oak Bird Sanctuary. Philadelphia Herpetol. Soc. Bull. 15:32–36.

———. 1968a. Homing ability in the spotted turtle, *Clemmys guttata* (Schneider). Herpetologica 24:77–78.

———. 1968b. Evaporative water-loss relationships of turtles. J. Herpetol. 2:159–161.

———. 1968c. A turtle's territory. Int. Turtle and Tortoise Soc. J. 2(6):9, 34.

———. 1969. Natural history and ecology of the painted turtle, *Chrysemys picta* (Schneider). Ph.D. dissertation, University of Kentucky. 202 pp.

———. 1970a. Home range of the spotted turtle, *Clemmys guttata* (Schneider). Copeia 1970:391–393.

———. 1970b. Reproduction in *Clemmys guttata*. Herpetologica 26:228–232.

———. 1970c. *Chrysemys picta* and its parasites. Int. Turtle and Tortoise Soc. J. 4(3):28–30.

———. 1970d. The status of the painted turtle *Chrysemys picta* in Tennessee and Kentucky. J. Herpetol. 4:39–45.

———. 1970e. Homing ability in the painted turtle, *Chrysemys picta* (Schneider). Herpetologica 26:399–403.

———. 1971a. Seasonal incidence of leech infestation in the painted turtle, *Chrysemys picta*. J. Parasitol. 57:32.

———. 1971b. Sexual cycles and maturity of the turtle *Chrysemys picta*. Biol. Bull. 140:191–200.

———. 1971c. Growth in the painted turtle, *Chrysemys picta* in southeastern Pennsylvania. Herpetologica 27:135–141.

———. 1971d. *Chrysemys picta*. Catalog. Amer. Amphib. Rept. 106:1–4.

———. 1971e. Population dynamics and activity cycles of *Chrysemys picta* in southeastern Pennsylvania. J. Herpetol. 5:151–160.

———. 1971f. Observations of the painted turtle, *Chrysemys picta*. J. Herpetol. 5:216–220.

———. 1971g. Observations on the egg and hatchling of the American turtle, *Chrysemys picta*. British J. Herpetol. 4:224–227.

———. 1972a. *Clemmys guttata.* Catalog. Amer. Amphib. Rept. 124:1–2.

———. 1972b. *Clemmys insculpta.* Catalog. Amer. Amphib. Rept. 125:1–2.

———. 1972c. Temperature-activity relationships in the painted turtle, *Chrysemys picta.* Copeia 1972:217–222.

———. 1973. The distribution of the turtles of Minnesota. J. Herpetol. 7:42–47.

———. 1974a. Effects of Hurricane Agnes on a painted turtle population. J. Herpetol. 8:237–240.

———. 1974b. Observations on the courtship of male *Graptemys pseudogeographica.* J. Herpetol. 8:377–378.

———. 1974c. *Kinosternon baurii.* Catalog. Amer. Amphib. Rept. 161:1–2.

———. 1975. Growth of the spotted turtle, *Clemmys guttata.* J. Herpetol. 9:313–318.

———. 1976. Ecology of the spotted turtle, *Clemmys guttata* (Reptilia, Testudines, Testudinidae), in southeastern Pennsylvania. J. Herpetol. 10:25–33.

———. 1977. Biological notes on the bog turtle, *Clemmys muhlenbergii.* Herpetologica 33:241–246.

———. 1981. Courtship behavior of male *Terrapene carolina major* (Reptilia, Testudines, Emydidae). Herpetol. Rev. 12:7–8.

———. 1982a. Why are tropical emydid turtles black? Biotropica 14:68.

———. 1982b. Environmental temperatures and activities in wild spotted turtles, *Clemmys guttata.* J. Herpetol. 16:112–120.

———. 1983. *Clemmys guttata* (spotted turtle) × *Clemmys muhlenbergii* (bog turtle). Natural hybrid. Herpetol. Rev. 14:75.

———. 1985a. Red-bellied turtle. *In* Genoways, H. H., and F. J. Brenner, eds. Species of special concern in Pennsylvania, 267–270. Carnegie Museum of Natural History Special Publication 11, Pittsburgh, Pennsylvania.

———. 1985b. Bog turtle, *Clemmys muhlenbergii* (Schoepff). *In* Genoways, H. H., and F. J. Brenner, eds. Species of special concern in Pennsylvania, 270–273. Carnegie Museum of Natural History Special Publication 11, Pittsburgh, Pennsylvania.

———. 1985c. Blanding's turtle, *Emydoidea blandingii* (Holbrook). *In* Genoways, H. H., and F. J. Brenner, eds. Species of special concern in Pennsylvania, 293–294. Carnegie Museum of Natural History Special Publication 11, Pittsburgh, Pennsylvania.

———. 1985d. Midland smooth softshell *Trionyx muticus* LeSueur. *In* Genoways, H. H., and F. J. Brenner, eds. Species of special concern in Pennsylvania, 294–295. Carnegie Museum of Natural History Special Publication 11, Pittsburgh, Pennsylvania.

———. 1986a. Environmental temperatures and activities in the wood turtle, *Clemmys insculpta.* J. Herpetol. 20:222–229.

———. 1986b. Ecology of the turtle, *Sternotherus odoratus,* in southeastern Pennsylvania. J. Herpetol. 20:341–352.

———. 1988. *Chrysemys.* Catalog. Amer. Amphib. Rept. 438:1–8.

———. 1990a. *Pseudemys gorzugi.* Catalog. Amer. Amphib. Rept. 461:1–2.

———. 1990b. Systematics, taxonomy, variation, and geographic distribution of the slider turtle. *In* Gibbons, J. W., ed. Life history and ecology of the slider turtle, 57–67. Smithsonian Institution Press, Washington, D.C.

———. 1992a. *Trachemys gaigeae.* Catalog. Amer. Amphib. Rept. 538:1–4.

———. 1992b. Venomous reptiles of North America. Smithsonian Institution Press, Washington, D.C. 236 pp.

Ernst, C. H., and R. W. Barbour. 1972. Turtles of the United States. University of Kentucky Press, Lexington. 347 pp.

———. 1989. Turtles of the World. Smithsonian Institution Press, Washington, D.C. 313 pp.

Ernst, C. H., R. W. Barbour, and J. R. Butler. 1972. Habitat preferences of two Florida turtles, genus *Kinosternon.* Trans. Kentucky Acad. Sci. 33:41–42.

Ernst, C. H., R. W. Barbour, E. M. Ernst, and J. R. Butler. 1973. Growth of the mud turtle, *Kinosternon subrubrum,* in Florida. Herpetologica 29:247–250.

———. 1974a. Subspecific variation and intergradation in Florida *Kinosternon subrubrum.* Herpetologica 30:317–320.

Ernst, C. H., and R. B. Bury. 1977. *Clemmys muhlenbergii.* Catalog. Amer. Amphib. Rept. 204:1–2.

———. 1982. *Malaclemys terrapin.* Catalog. Amer. Amphib. Rept. 299:1–4.

Ernst, C. H., W. A. Cox, and K. R. Marion. 1983. The distribution and status of the flattened musk turtle in the Warrior Basin in Alabama. Contract Report, Alabama Coal Assoc. 136 pp.

———. 1989. The distribution and status of the flattened musk turtle, *Sternotherus depressus* (Testudines: Kinosternidae). Tulane Stud. Zool. Bot. 27:1–20.

Ernst, C. H., and E. M. Ernst. 1969. Turtles of Kentucky. Int. Turtle and Tortoise Soc. J. 3(5):13–15.

———. 1971. The taxonomic status and zoogeography of the painted turtle, *Chrysemys picta,* in Pennsylvania. Herpetologica 27:390–396.

———. 1973. Biology of *Chrysemys picta bellii* in

southwestern Minnesota. J. Minnesota Acad. Sci. 38:77–80.

———. 1979. Synopsis of protozoans parasitic in native turtles of the United States. Bull. Maryland Herpetol. Soc. 15:1–15.

——— 1980. Relationships between North American turtles of the *Chrysemys* complex as indicated by their endoparasitic helminths. Proc. Biol. Soc. Washington 95:339–345.

Ernst, C. H., and J. A. Fowler. 1977. The taxonomic status of the turtle, *Chrysemys picta,* in the northern peninsula of Michigan. Proc. Biol. Soc. Washington 90:685–689.

Ernst, C. H., J. W. Gibbons, and S. S. Novak. 1988a. *Chelydra.* Catalog. Amer. Amphib. Rept. 419:1–4.

Ernst, C. H., and M. J. Gilroy. 1979. Are leatherback turtles, *Dermochelys coriacea,* common along the middle Atlantic coast? Bull. Maryland Herpetol. Soc. 15:16–19.

Ernst, C. H., and H. F. Hamilton. 1969. Color preferences of some North American turtles. J. Herpetol. 3:176–180.

Ernst, C. H., M. F. Hershey, and R. W. Barbour. 1974b. A new coding system for hardshelled turtles. Trans. Kentucky Acad. Sci. 35:27–28.

Ernst, C. H., and B. G. Jett. 1969. An intergrade population of *Pseudemys scripta elegans* × *Pseudemys scripta troosti* in Kentucky. J. Herpetol. 3:103.

Ernst, C. H., and J. F. McBreen. 1991a. *Terrapene.* Catalog. Amer. Amphib. Rept. 511:1–6.

———. 1991b. *Terrapene carolina.* Catalog. Amer. Amphib. Rept. 512:1–13.

———. 1991c. Wood turtle. *Clemmys insculpta* (Le-Conte). *In* Terwilliger, K., ed. Virginia's endangered species, 455–457. McDonald and Woodward Publ. Co., Blacksburg, Virginia.

Ernst, C. H., and B. S. McDonald, Jr. 1989. Preliminary report on enhanced growth and early maturity in a Maryland population of painted turtles, *Chrysemys picta.* Bull. Maryland Herpetol. Soc. 25:135–142.

Ernst, C. H., J. L. Miller, K. R. Marion, and W. A. Cox. 1988b. Comparisons of shell morphology among turtles of the *Kinosternon minor* complex. Amer. Midl. Natur. 120:282–288.

Ernst, C. H., and J. N. Norris. 1978. Observations on the algal genus *Basicladia* and the red-bellied turtle, *Chrysemys rubriventris.* Estuaries 1:54–57.

Ernst, C. H., S. Soenarjo, and H. F. Hamilton. 1970. The retinal histology of the stinkpot, *Sternotherus odoratus.* Herpetologica 26:222–223.

Ernst, C. H., R. T. Zappalorti, and J. E. Lovich. 1989. Overwintering sites and thermal relations of hibernating bog turtles, *Clemmys muhlenbergii.* Copeia 1989:761–764.

Ernst, C. H., and G. R. Zug. In press. Observations on the reproductive biology of the spotted turtle, *Clemmys guttata,* in southeastern Pennsylvania. J. Herpetol.

Ernst, E. M., and C. H. Ernst. 1975. New hosts and localities for turtle helminths. Proc. Helminthological Soc. Washington 42(2):176–178.

———. 1977. Synopsis of helminths endoparasitic in native turtles of the United States. Bull. Maryland Herpetol. Soc. 13:1–75.

Erskine, D. J., and V. H. Hutchison. 1981. Melatonin and behavioral thermoregulation in the turtle, *Terrapene carolina triunguis.* Physiol. Behav. 26:991–994.

Eschscholtz, J. F. 1829. Zoologischer Atlas, enthaltend Abbildungen und Beschreibungen neuer Thierarten, während des Flottcapitains von Kotzebue zweiter Reise um die Welt, auf der Russisch-Kaiserlichen Kriegsschlupp Predpriaetië in den Jahren 1823–1826, part 1, iv + 17 + 15. G. Reimer, Berlin.

Estridge, R. E. 1970. The taxonomic status of *Sternothaerus depressus* (Testudinata, Kinosternidae) with observations on its ecology. Master's thesis, Auburn University, Auburn, Alabama. 49 pp.

Etchberger, C. R. 1988. The reproductive biology of the male loggerhead musk turtle, *Sternotherus minor minor,* from the southern limit of its range in central Florida. Progr. Comb. Meet. Herpetol. League, . . . Soc. Stud. Amphib. Rept., and American Soc. Ichthyol. Herpetol., 90.

Etchberger, C. R., and L. M. Ehrhart. 1987. The reproductive biology of the female loggerhead musk turtle, *Sternotherus minor minor,* from the southern part of its range in central Florida. Herpetologica 43:66–73.

Etchberger, C. R., M. A. Ewert, J. B. Phillips, C. E. Nelson, and H. D. Prange. 1992. Physiological responses to carbon dioxide in embryonic red-eared slider turtles, *Trachemys scripta.* J. Exp. Zool. 264:1–10.

Etchberger, C. R., and J. B. Iverson. 1990. *Pseudemys texana.* Catalog. Amer. Amphib. Rept. 485:1–2.

Etchberger, C. R., J. B. Phillips, M. A. Ewert, C. E. Nelson, and H. D. Prange. 1991. Effects of oxygen concentration and clutch on sex determination and physiology in red-eared slider turtles (*Trachemys scripta*). J. Exp. Zool. 258:394–403.

Etchberger, C. R., and R. H. Stovall. 1990. Seasonal variation in the testicular cycle of the loggerhead musk turtle, *Sternotherus minor minor,* from central Florida. Can. J. Zool. 68:1071–1074.

Evans, L. T. 1952. Endocrine relationships in turtles. III. Some effects of male hormone in turtles. Herpetologica 8:11–14.

———. 1953. The courtship pattern of the box turtle, *Terrapene c. carolina*. Herpetologica 9:189–192.

———. 1961. Aquatic courtship of the wood turtle, *Clemmys insculpta*. Amer. Zool. 1:353.

———. 1967. How are age and size related to mating in the wood turtle, *Clemmys insculpta*? Amer. Zool. 7:799.

———. 1968. The evolution of courtship in the turtle species, *Terrapene carolina*. Amer. Zool. 8:695–696.

Evans, R. H. 1983. Chronic bacterial pneumonia in free-ranging eastern box turtles (*Terrapene carolina carolina*). J. Wildl. Dis. 19:349–352.

Evenden, F. G., Jr. 1948. Distribution of the turtles of western Oregon. Herpetologica 4:201–204.

Evermann, B. W., and H. W. Clark. 1916. The turtles and batrachians of the Lake Maxinkuckee region. Proc. Indiana Acad. Sci. 1916:472–518.

Ewert, M. A. 1976. Nests, nesting and aerial basking of *Macroclemys* under natural conditions, and comparisons with *Chelydra* (Testudines: Chelydridae). Herpetologica 32:150–156.

———. 1979a. The embryo and its egg: Development and natural history. *In* Harless, M., and H. Morlock, eds. Turtles: Perspectives and research, 333–413. John Wiley & Sons, New York.

———. 1979b. *Graptemys pseudogeographica ouachitensis* (Ouachita map turtle). USA: Indiana. Herpetol. Rev. 10:102.

———. 1979c. *Trionyx muticus muticus* (midland smooth softshell). USA: Indiana. Herpetol. Rev. 10:102.

———. 1985. Embryology of turtles. *In* Gans, C., F. Billett, and P. F. A. Maderson, eds. Biology of the Reptilia, vol. 14, Development A, 75–267. John Wiley & Sons, New York.

———. 1991. Cold torpor, diapause, delayed hatching and aestivation in reptiles and birds. *In* Deeming, D. C., and M. W. J. Ferguson, eds. Egg incubation: Its effects on embryonic development in birds and reptiles, 173–191. Cambridge University Press, New York.

Ewert, M. A., and J. M. Legler. 1978. Hormonal induction of oviposition in turtles. Herpetologica 34:314–318.

Ewert, M. A., and C. E. Nelson. 1991. Sex determination in turtles: Diverse patterns and some possible adaptive values. Copeia 1991:50–69.

Ewing, H. E. 1926. The common box-turtle, a natural host for chiggers. Proc. Biol. Soc. Washington 39:19–20.

———. 1933. Reproduction in the eastern box turtle *Terrapene carolina carolina* (Linné). Copeia 1933:95–96.

———. 1943. Continued fertility in female box turtles following mating. Copeia 1943:112–114.

Fahey, K. M. 1980. A taxonomic study of the cooter turtles, *Pseudemys floridana* (LeConte) and *Pseudemys concinna* (LeConte), in the lower Red River, Atchafalaya River, and Mississippi River basins. Tulane Stud. Zool. Bot. 22:49–66.

Farrell, R. F., and T. E. Graham. 1991. Ecological notes on the turtle *Clemmys insculpta* in northwestern New Jersey. J. Herpetol. 25:1–9.

Fay, L. P. 1984. Mid-Wisconsinan and mid-Holocene herpetofaunas of eastern North America: A study in minimal contrast. Spec. Publ. Carnegie Mus. Natur. Hist. 8:14–19.

———. 1988. Late Wisconsinian Appalachian herpetofaunas: Relative stability in the midst of change. Ann. Carnegie Mus. Natur. Hist. 57:189–220.

Feder, M. E. 1983. The relation of air breathing and locomotion to predation on tadpoles, *Rana berlandieri,* by turtles. Physiol. Zool. 56:522–531.

Feder, M. E., S. L. Satel, and A. G. Gibbs. 1982. Resistance of the shell membrane and mineral layer to diffusion of oxygen and water in flexible-shelled eggs of the snapping turtle (*Chelydra serpentina*). Resp. Physiol. 49:279–291.

Federal Register. 1992. Endangered and threatened wildlife and plants; 90-day finding and commencement of status reviews for a petition to list the western pond turtle and California red-legged frog. Federal Register 57(193):45761–45762.

Feehan, T. 1986. Turtle trade controversy reignited. Traffic (USA) 7:4–5.

Fehring, W. K. 1972. Hue discrimination in hatchling loggerhead turtles (*Caretta caretta caretta*). Anim. Behav. 20:632–636.

Feldman, M. 1982. Notes on reproduction in *Clemmys marmorata*. Herpetol. Rev. 13:10–11.

———. 1983. Effects of rotation on the viability of turtle eggs. Herpetol. Rev. 14:76–77.

Felger, R. S., K. Cliffton, and P. J. Regal. 1976. Winter dormancy in sea turtles: Independent discovery and exploitation in the Gulf of California by two local cultures. Science 191:283–285.

Fenchel, T. M. 1980. The protozoan fauna from the gut of the green turtle, *Chelonia mydas* L. with a description of *Balantidium bacteriophorus* sp. nov. Arch. Protistenk 123:22–26.

Fenchel, T. M., C. P. McRoy, J. C. Ogden, P. Parker, and W. E. Rainey. 1979. Symbiotic cellulose degradation in green turtles, *Chelonia mydas* L. Ap. Env. Microbiol. 37:348–350.

Ferguson, D. E. 1962. Fish feeding on imported fire ants. J. Wildl. Mgt. 26:206–207.

Ferguson, D. E. 1963. Notes concerning the effects of heptachlor on certain poikilotherms. Copeia 1963: 441–443.

Fernando, A. B. 1983. Nesting site and hatchlings of the hawksbill turtle along Tirunelveli Coast of Tamil Nadu. Marine Fish. Inform. Serv. 50:33–34.

Feuer, R. C. 1970. Key to the skulls of Recent adult North American and Central American turtles. J. Herpetol. 4:69–75.

———. 1971a. Ecological factors in success and dispersal of the snapping turtle Chelydra serpentina (Linnaeus). Philadelphia Herpetol. Soc. Bull. 19:3–14.

———. 1971b. Intergradation of the snapping turtles Chelydra serpentina serpentina (Linnaeus, 1758) and Chelydra serpentina osceola Stejneger, 1918. Herpetologica 27:379–384.

———. 1979. Basking in snapping turtles. Philadelphia Herpetol. Soc. Bull. 27:9–10.

Fichter, L. S. 1969. Geographical distribution and osteological variation in fossil and Recent specimens of two species of Kinosternon (Testudines). J. Herpetol. 3:113–119.

Figler, R. A., D. S. MacKenzie, D. W. Owens, P. Licht, and M. S. Amoss. 1989. Increased levels of arginine vasotocin and neurophysin during nesting in sea turtles. Gen. Comp. Endocrinol. 73:223–232.

Finneran, L. C. 1948. Reptiles at Branford, Connecticut. Herpetologica 4:123–126.

Fitch, H. S. 1956. Temperature responses in free-living amphibians and reptiles of northeastern Kansas. Univ. Kansas Publ. Mus. Natur. Hist. 8:417–476.

———. 1958. Home ranges, territories, and seasonal movements of vertebrates of the University of Kansas Natural History Reservation. Univ. Kansas Publ. Mus. Natur. Hist. 11:63–326.

———. 1981. Sexual size differences in reptiles. Univ. Kansas Mus. Natur. Hist. Misc. Publ. 70. 72 pp.

———. 1982. Reproductive cycles in tropical reptiles. Occ. Pap. Mus. Natur. Hist. Univ. Kansas (96):1–53.

———. 1985. Variation in clutch and litter size in New World reptiles. Univ. Kansas Mus. Natur. Hist. Misc. Publ. 76. 76 pp.

Fitch, H. S., and M. V. Plummer. 1975. A preliminary ecological study of the soft-shelled turtle Trionyx muticus in the Kansas River. Israel J. Zool. 24:28–42.

Fitzpatrick, J. W., and G. E. Woolfenden. 1978. Red-tailed hawk preys on juvenile gopher tortoise. Florida Field Natur. 6:49.

Flaherty, N., and J. R. Bider. 1984. Physical structures and the social factor as determinants of habitat use by Graptemys geographica in southwestern Quebec. Amer. Midl. Natur. 111:259–266.

Fletemeyer, J. R. 1978. Underwater tracking evidence of neonate loggerhead sea turtles seeking shelter in drifting sargassum. Copeia 1978:148–149.

———. 1990. Kemp's ridley sea turtle nests in Palm Beach. Florida Natur. 63:5.

Flickinger, E. L., and B. M. Mulhern. 1980. Aldrin persists in yellow mud turtle. Herpetol. Rev. 11:29–30.

Flower, S. S. 1925. Contributions to our knowledge of the duration of life in vertebrate animals. III. Reptiles. Proc. Zool. Soc. (London) 95:911–981.

Floyd, P. 1973. Singing River sawbacks. Int. Turtle and Tortoise Soc. J. 7(2):8–10.

Foley, R. E., and J. R. Spotila. 1978. Effect of wind speed, air temperature, body size and vapor density difference on evaporative water loss from the turtle Chrysemys scripta. Copeia 1978:627–634.

Folkerts, G. W. 1967. Notes on a hybrid musk turtle. Copeia 1967:479–480.

———. 1968. Food habits of the striped-necked musk turtle, Sternotherus minor peltifer Smith and Glass. J. Herpetol. 2:171–173.

Folkerts, G. W., and R. H. Mount. 1969. A new subspecies of the turtle Graptemys nigrinoda Cagle. Copeia 1969:677–682.

———. 1970. Reply to H. L. Freeman's (Herpetol. Rev. 2:3) comments on: A new subspecies of the turtle Graptemys nigrinoda Cagle. Herpetol. Rev. 2:3–4.

Fontaine, C. T., K. T. Marvin, T. D. Williams, W. J. Browning, R. M. Harris, K. L. Williams, Iridelicato, G. A. Shattuck, and R. A. Sadler. 1985. The husbandry of hatchling to yearling Kemp's ridley sea turtles (Lepidochelys kempi). NOAA-TM-NMFS-SEFC-158. 34 pp.

Fontaine, C. T., T. D. Williams, and C. Turner. 1988. Hatchling Kemp's ridley strands at Galveston Island, Texas. Marine Turtle Newsl. 43:9.

Forbes, W. C. 1966. A cytological study of the Chelonia. Ph.D. dissertation, University of Connecticut, Storrs. 285 pp.

Forks, T. 1979. Kingsnake "lays turtle eggs." Bull. Chicago Herpetol. Soc. 14:119.

Fowler, H. W. 1906. Some cold blooded vertebrates from the Florida Keys. Proc. Acad. Natur. Sci. Philadelphia 58:77–113.

Fowler, L. E. 1979. Hatchling success and nest predation in the green sea turtle, Chelonia mydas, at Tortuguero, Costa Rica. Ecology 60:946–955.

Frair, W. 1972. Taxonomic relations among chelydrid and kinosternid turtles elucidated by serological tests. Copeia 1972:97–108.

———. 1979. Taxonomic relations among sea turtles elucidated by serological tests. Herpetologica 35:239–244.

———. 1982. Serum electrophoresis and sea turtle classification. Comp. Biochem. Physiol. 72B:1–4.

———. 1983. Serological survey of softshells with other turtles. J. Herpetol. 17:75–79.

Frair, W., R. G. Ackman, and N. Mrosovsky. 1972. Body temperature of *Dermochelys coriacea:* warm turtle from cold water. Science 177:791–793.

Frank, P. A., and K. R. Lips. 1989. Gopher tortoise burrow use by long-tailed weasels and spotted skunks. Florida Field Natur. 17:20–22.

Franz, R. 1986a. *Gopherus polphemus* (gopher tortoise). Burrow commensals. Herpetol. Rev. 17:64.

———. 1986b. *Pseudemys floridana peninsularis* (peninsula cooter). Egg predation. Herpetol. Rev. 17:64–65.

Franz, R., and R. J. Bryant, eds. 1980. The dilemma of the gopher tortoise–is there a solution? Proc. First Ann. Meet. Gopher Tortoise Council. Auburn University, Auburn, Alabama. 80 pp.

Franz, R., C. K. Dodd, Jr., and A. M. Bard. 1992. The non-marine herpetofauna of Egmont Key, Hillsborough County, Florida. Florida Scientist 55:179–183.

Frazer, N. B. 1983a. Survivorship of adult female loggerhead sea turtles, *Caretta caretta,* nesting on Little Cumberland Island, Georgia, USA. Herpetologica 39:436–447.

———. 1983b. Effect of tidal cycles on loggerhead sea turtles (*Caretta caretta*) emerging from the sea. Copeia 1983:516–519.

———. 1984. A model for assessing mean age-specific fecundity in sea turtle populations. Herpetologica 40:281–291.

———. 1986. Survival from egg to adulthood in a declining population of loggerhead turtles, *Caretta caretta.* Herpetologica 42:47–55.

———. 1987. Preliminary estimates of survivorship for wild juvenile loggerhead sea turtles (*Caretta caretta*). J. Herpetol. 21:232–235.

———. 1989. A philosophical approach to population models. *In* Ogren, L., ed. Proceedings of the Second Western Atlantic Turtle Symposium, 198–207. NOAA-TM-NMFS-SEFC-226.

———. 1992. Sea turtle conservation and halfway technology. Conserv. Biol. 6:179–184.

Frazer, N. B., and L. M. Ehrhart. 1983. Relating straight-line to over-the-curve measurements for loggerheads. Marine Turtle Newsl. (24):4–5.

———. 1985. Preliminary growth models for green, *Chelonia mydas,* and loggerhead, *Caretta caretta,* turtles in the wild. Copeia 1985:73–79.

Frazer, N. B., J. W. Gibbons, and J. L. Greene. 1990a. Exploring Faben's growth interval model with data on a long-lived vertebrate, *Trachemys scripta* (Reptilia: Testudinata). Copeia 1990:112–118.

———. 1990b. Life tables of a slider turtle population. *In* Gibbons, J. W., ed. Life history and ecology of the slider turtle, 183–200. Smithsonian Institution Press, Washington, D.C.

———. 1991a. Life history of the common mud turtle *Kinosternon subrubrum* in South Carolina, USA. Ecology 72:2218–2231.

———. 1991b. Growth, survivorship and longevity of painted turtles, *Chrysemys picta* in a southwestern Michigan marsh. Amer. Midl. Natur. 125:245–258.

Frazer, N. B., and J. I. Richardson. 1985a. Seasonal variation in clutch size for loggerhead sea turtles, *Caretta caretta,* nesting on Little Cumberland Island, Georgia, USA. Copeia 1985:1083–1085.

———. 1985b. Annual variation in clutch size and frequency for loggerhead turtles, *Caretta caretta,* nesting at Little Cumberland Island, Georgia, USA. Herpetologica 41:246–251.

———. 1986. The relationship of clutch size and frequency to body size in loggerhead sea turtles, *Caretta caretta.* J. Herpetol. 20:81–84.

Frazer, N. B., and F. J. Schwartz. 1984. Growth curves for captive loggerhead turtles, *Caretta caretta,* in North Carolina, USA. Bull. Marine Sci. 34:485–489.

Frazier, J. G. 1983. Analisis estadistico de la tortuga golfina *Lepidochelys olivacea* (Eschscholtz) de Oaxaca, Mexico. Cienc. Pesq. Inst. Nac. Pesca, Mexico 4:49–75.

Freeman, H. L. 1970. A comment on: A new subspecies of the turtle *Graptemys nigrinoda* Cagle. Herpetol. Rev. 2:3.

French, T. W. 1986. Archaeological evidence of *Emydoidea blandingii* in Maine. Herpetol. Rev. 17:40.

Fretey, J. 1977. Causes de mortalité des tortues luths adultes (*Dermochelys coriacea*) sur le littoral guyanais. Courrier de la Nature 52:1–10.

———. 1978. Accompagnement à terre de tortues luths, *Dermochelys coriacea* (Linné) pardes Rèmoras. Rev. Fr. Aquariol. 2:49–54.

Fretey, J., and R. Bour. 1980. Redécouverte du type de *Dermochelys coriacea* (Vandelli) (Testudinata, Dermochelyidae). Boll. Zool. 47:193–205.

Fretey, J., and J. Lescure. 1981. Prédation des tortues marines par les oiseaux en Guyane française. L'Oiseau 51:139–145.

Frick, J. 1976. Orientation and behaviour of hatchling green turtles (*Chelonia mydas*) in the sea. Anim. Behav. 24:849–857.

Friedman, J. M., S. R. Simon, and T. W. Scott. 1985. Structure and function of sea turtle hemoglobins. Copeia 1985:679–694.

Fritts, T. H. 1981a. Pelagic feeding habits of turtles in the eastern Pacific. Marine Turtle Newsl. (17):4–5.

———. 1981b. Marine turtles of the Galápagos Islands and adjacent areas of the eastern Pacific on the basis of observations made by J. R. Slevin 1905–1906. J. Herpetol. 15:293–301.

———. 1982. Plastic bags in the intestinal tracts of leatherback marine turtles. Herpetol. Rev. 13:72–73.

Fritts, T. H., and W. Hoffman. 1982. Diurnal nesting of marine turtles in southern Brevard County, Florida. J. Herpetol. 16:84–86.

Fritts, T. H., W. Hoffman, and M. A. McGehee. 1983. The distribution and abundance of marine turtles in the Gulf of Mexico and nearby Atlantic waters. J. Herpetol. 17:327–344.

Fritts, T. H., M. L. Stinson, and R. Marquez M. 1982. Status of sea turtle nesting in southern Baja California, Mexico. Bull. Southern California Acad. Sci. 81:51–60.

Fritz, U. 1989. Beitrag zur Kenntnis der Texas-Schmuckschildkröte (Pseudemys texana Baur 1893) (Reptilia: Testudines: Emydidae). Sauria (Berlin-W.) 11:9–14.

———. 1990. Balzverhalten und Systematik in der Subtribus Nectemydina 1. Die Gattung Trachemys, besonders Trachemys scripta callirostris (Gray, 1855). Salamandra 26:221–245.

———. 1991. Balzverhalten und Systematik in der Subtribus Nectemydina 2. Vergleich oberhalb des Artniveaus und Anmerkungen zur Evolution. Salamandra 27:129–142.

Froese, A. D. 1978. Habitat preferences of the common snapping turtle, Chelydra s. serpentina (Reptilia, Testudines, Chelydridae). J. Herpetol. 12:53–58.

Froese, A. D., and G. M. Burghardt. 1974. Food competition in captive juvenile snapping turtles, Chelydra serpentina. Anim. Behav. 22:735–740.

———. 1975. A dense natural population of the common snapping turtle (Chelydra s. serpentina). Herpetologica 31:204–208.

Fucik, E. 1991. On the value of the orbitotemporal region for the reconstruction of reptilian phylogeny: Ontogeny and adult skull analyses of the chelonian skull. Zool. Anz. 227:209–217.

Fukada, H. 1965. Breeding habits of some Japanese reptiles (critical review). Bull. Kyoto Gakugei Univ., ser. B, 27:65–82.

Gad, J. 1989. Drehversuche an Schildkröteneiern im Hinblick auf Schildanomalien, hier bei Sternotherus odoratus (Latreille, 1801). Salamandra. 25:109–111.

Gaffney, E. S. 1972. An illustrated glossary of turtle skull nomenclature. Amer. Mus. Novitates (2486):1–33.

———. 1975a. A phylogeny and classification of the higher categories of turtles. Bull. Amer. Mus. Natur. Hist. 155:387–436.

———. 1975b. Phylogeny of the chelydrid turtles. A study of shared derived characters in the skull. Fieldiana: Geol. 33:157–178.

———. 1979. Comparative cranial morphology of Recent and fossil turtles. Bull. Amer. Mus. Natur. Hist. 164:65–376.

———. 1984. Historical analysis of theories of chelonian relationship. Syst. Zool. 33:282–301.

Gaffney, E. S., and P. A. Meylan. 1988. A phylogeny of turtles. In Benton, M. J., ed. The phylogeny and classification of the tetrapods, vol. 1, Amphibians, reptiles, birds, 157–219. System Assoc. Spec. Vol. 35A, Clarendon Press, Oxford, England.

Gage, S. H., and S. P. Gage. 1886. Aquatic respiration in soft-shelled turtles: A contribution to the physiology of respiration in vertebrates. Amer. Natur. 20:233–236.

Galbraith, D. A., C. A. Bishop, R. J. Brooks, W. L. Simser, and K. P. Lampman. 1988a. Factors affecting the density of common snapping turtles (Chelydra serpentina serpentina). Can. J. Zool. 66:1233–1240.

Galbraith, D. A., and R. J. Brooks. 1987a. Addition of animal growth lines in adult snapping turtles Chelydra serpentina. J. Herpetol. 21:359–363.

———. 1987b. Survivorship of adult females in a northern population of common snapping turtles, Chelydra serpentina. Can J. Zool. 65:1581–1586.

———. 1989. Age estimates for snapping turtles. J. Wildl. Mgt. 53:502–508.

Galbraith, D. A., R. J. Brooks, and M. E. Obbard. 1989. The influence of growth rate on age and body size at maturity in female snapping turtles (Chelydra serpentina). Copeia 1989:896–904.

Galbraith, D. A., M. W. Chandler, and R. J. Brooks. 1987. The fine structure of home ranges of male Chelydra serpentina: are snapping turtles territorial? Can. J. Zool. 65:2623–2629.

Galbraith, D. A., C. J. Graesser, and R. J. Brooks. 1988b. Egg retention by a snapping turtle, Chelydra serpentina, in central Ontario. Can. Field-Natur. 102:734.

Galbreath, E. C. 1948. Pliocene and Pleistocene records of fossil turtles from western Kansas and Oklahoma. Univ. Kansas Publ. Mus. Natur. Hist. 1:281–284.

———. 1961. Two alligator snappers, Macroclemys temmincki, from southern Illinois. Trans. Illinois St. Acad. Sci. 54:134–135.

Gallaway, B. J., J. W. Bickham, and M. D. Springer.

1985. A controversy surrounding an endangered species listing: The case of the Illinois mud turtle. Another perspective. Smithsonian Herpetol. Inform. Serv. (64):1–17.

Gangarosa, E. J. 1985. Boundaries of conscience. J. Amer. Med. Assoc. 254:265–266.

Ganzhorn, D., and P. Licht. 1983. Regulation of seasonal gonadal cycles by temperature in the painted turtle, *Chrysemys picta*. Copeia 1983:347–358.

Garber, S. D. 1989. A comparison of two populations of *Clemmys insculpta*, the North American wood turtle. Plastron Papers 19:32–35.

Garbin, C. P., and J. Rowe. 1992. An initial study of hatchling food preferences and group feeding behaviors of four species of Nebraskan turtles. Bull. Chicago Herpetol. Soc. 27:57–62.

Garman, S. 1880. On certain species of Chelonioidae. Bull. Mus. Comp. Zool. 6:123–126.

———. 1884. The reptiles of Bermuda. U.S. Natl. Mus. Bull. (25):285–303.

———. 1891. On a tortoise found in Florida and Cuba, *Cinosternum baurii*. Bull. Essex Inst. 23:141–144.

Garner, J. A., and J. L. Landers. 1981. Foods and habitat of the gopher tortoise in southwestern Georgia. Proc. Conf. Southeast. Assoc. Fish Wildl. Agencies 35:120–134.

Garnett, S. T., I. R. Price, and F. J. Scott. 1985. The diet of the green turtle, *Chelonia mydas* (L.), in Torres Strait. Australian Wildl. Res. 12:103–112.

Garrett, J. M., and D. G. Barker. 1987. A field guide to reptiles and amphibians of Texas. Texas Monthly Press, Austin. 225 pp.

Garstka, W. R., W. E. Cooper, Jr., K. W. Wasmund, and J. E. Lovich. 1991. Male sex steroids and hormonal control of male courtship behavior in the yellow-bellied slider turtle, *Trachemys scripta*. Comp. Biochem. Physiol. 98A:271–280.

Gatten, R. E., Jr. 1974a. Effects of temperature and activity on aerobic and anaerobic metabolism and heart rate in the turtles *Pseudemys scripta* and *Terrapene ornata*. Comp. Biochem. Physiol. 48A:619–648.

———. 1974b. Percentage contribution of increased heart rate to increased oxygen transport during activity in *Pseudemys scripta, Terrapene ornata* and other reptiles. Comp. Biochem. Physiol. 48A:649–652.

———. 1974c. Effect of nutritional status on the preferred body temperature of the turtles *Pseudemys scripta* and *Terrapene ornata*. Copeia 1974:912–917.

———. 1975. Effects of activity on blood oxygen saturation, lactate, and pH in the turtles *Pseudemys scripta* and *Terrapene ornata*. Physiol. Zool. 48:24–35.

———. 1978. Aerobic metabolism in snapping turtles, *Chelydra serpentina*, after thermal acclimation. Comp. Biochem. Physiol. 61A:325–337.

———. 1980. Aerial and aquatic oxygen uptake by freely-diving snapping turtles (*Chelydra serpentina*). Oecologia (Berlin). 46:266–271.

———. 1981. Anaerobic metabolism in freely diving painted turtles (*Chrysemys picta*). J. Exp. Zool. 216:377–385.

———. 1984. Aerobic and anaerobic metabolism of freely-diving loggerhead musk turtles (*Sternotherus minor*). Herpetologica 40:1–7.

———. 1987. Cardiovascular and other physiological correlates of hibernation in aquatic and terrestrial turtles. Amer. Zool. 27:59–68.

Gatz, R. N., M. L. Glass, and S. C. Wood. 1987. Pulmonary function of the green sea turtle, *Chelonia mydas*. J. Appl. Physiol. 62:459–463.

Gaudette, A. 1983. Turtle sightings in Québec. Bull Canadian Amphib. Rept. Conserv. Soc. 20(5):1–2.

Gazey, W. J., and M. J. Staley. 1986. Population estimation from mark-recapture experiments using sequential Bayes algorithm. Ecology 67:941–951.

Gehlbach, F. 1965. Amphibians and reptiles from the Pliocene and Pleistocene of North America: A chronological summary and selected bibliography. Texas J. Sci. 17:56–70.

George, G. 1991. Status and conservation of *Graptemys barbouri, Graptemys flavimaculata, Graptemys oculifera* and *Graptemys caglei*. *In* Beaman, K. R., F. Caporaso, S. McKeown, and M. D. Graff, eds. Proceedings of the First International Symposium on Turtles and Tortoises: Conservation and Captive Husbandry, 24–30. Chapman Univ., Orange, California.

George, G. A. 1987. The current status of the alligator snapping turtle, *Macroclemys temmincki*, with a review of its natural history. *In* Rosenberg, M., ed. Proceedings 11th International Herpetological Symposium (Chicago, Illinois), 75–81.

Gerholdt, J. E., and B. Oldfield. 1987. *Chelydra serpentina serpentina* (common snapping turtle). Size. Herpetol. Rev. 18:73.

Germano, D. J. 1988. Age and growth histories of desert tortoises using scute annuli. Copeia 1988:914–920.

———. 1992. Longevity and age-size relationships of populations of desert tortoises. Copeia 1992:367–374.

———. 1993. Shell morphology of North American tortoises. Amer. Midl. Natur. 129:319–335.

Germano, D. J., and M. A. Joyner. 1988. Changes in a desert tortoise (*Gopherus agassizii*) population after a period of high mortality. *In* Szaro, R. C., K. E. Severson, and D. R. Patton, eds. Management of amphibians, reptiles, and small mammals in North America, 190–198. USDA Tech. Serv. Gen. Tech. Rept. Rm-166.

Gettinger, R. D., G. L. Paukstis, and W. H. N. Gutzke. 1984. Influence of hydric environment on oxygen consumption by embryonic turtles *Chelydra serpentina* and *Trionyx spiniferus*. Physiol. Zool. 57:468–473.

Gibbons, J. W. 1967a. Variation in growth rates in three populations of the painted turtle *Chrysemys picta*. Herpetologica 23:296–303.

———. 1967b. Possible underwater thermoregulation by turtles. Can. J. Zool. 45:585.

———. 1968a. Carapacial algae in a population of the painted turtle, *Chrysemys picta*. Amer. Midl. Natur. 79:517–519.

———. 1968b. Population structure and survivorship in the painted turtle, *Chrysemys picta*. Copeia 1968:260–268.

———. 1968c. Reproductive potential, activity, and cycles in the painted turtle, *Chrysemys picta*. Ecology 49:399–409.

———. 1968d. Observations on the ecology and population dynamics of the Blanding's turtle, *Emydoidea blandingi*. Can. J. Zool. 46:288–290.

———. 1968e. Growth rates of the common snapping turtle, *Chelydra serpentina*, in a polluted river. Herpetologica 24:266–267.

———. 1969a. Structure and dynamics of the yellow-bellied turtle, *Pseudemys scripta* (Reptilia: Chelonia: Emydidae) in an artificially heated reservoir. ASB Bull. 16:52.

———. 1969b. Ecology and population dynamics of the chicken turtle, *Deirochelys reticularia*. Copeia 1969:669–676.

———. 1970a. Terrestrial activity and the population dynamics of aquatic turtles. Amer. Midl. Natur. 83:404–414.

———. 1970b. Reproductive characteristics of a Florida population of musk turtles (*Sternothaerus odoratus*). Herpetologica 26:268–270.

———. 1970c. Reproductive dynamics of a turtle (*Pseudemys scripta*) population in a reservoir receiving heated effluent from a nuclear reactor. Can. J. Zool. 48:881–885.

———. 1970d. Sex ratios in turtles. Res. Popul. Ecol. 12:252–254.

———. 1982. Reproductive patterns in freshwater turtles. Herpetologica 38:222–227.

———. 1983. Reproductive characteristics and ecology of the mud turtle, *Kinosternon subrubrum*. Herpetologica 39:254–271.

———. 1986. Movement patterns among turtle popula-tions: Applicability to management of the desert tortoise. Herpetologica 42:104–113.

———. 1987. Why do turtles live so long? Bioscience 37:262–269.

———, ed. 1990a. Life history and ecology of the slider turtle. Smithsonian Institution Press, Washington, D.C. 368 pp.

———. 1990b. Sex ratios and their significance among turtle populations. *In* Gibbons, J. W., ed. Life history and ecology of the slider turtle, 171–182. Smithsonian Institution Press, Washington, D.C.

Gibbons, J. W., and J. W. Coker. 1977. Ecological and life history aspects of the cooter, *Chrysemys floridana* (LeConte). Herpetologica 33:29–33.

———. 1978. Herpetofaunal colonization patterns of Atlantic Coast barrier islands. Amer. Midl. Natur. 99:219–233.

Gibbons, J. W., and G. W. Esch. 1970. Some intestinal parasites of the loggerhead musk turtle (*Sternothaerus m. minor*). J. Herpetol. 4:79–80.

Gibbons, J. W., and J. L. Greene. 1978. Selected aspects of the ecology of the chicken turtle, *Deirochelys reticularia* (Latreille) (Reptilia, Testudines, Emydidae). J. Herpetol. 12:237–241.

———. 1979. X-ray photography: A technique to determine reproductive patterns of freshwater turtles. Herpetologica 35:86–89.

———. 1990. Reproduction in the slider and other species of turtles. *In* Gibbons, J. W., ed. Life history and ecology of the slider turtle, 124–134. Smithsonian Institution Press, Washington, D.C.

Gibbons, J. W., J. L. Greene, and J. D. Congdon. 1983. Drought-related responses of aquatic turtle popula-tions. J. Herpetol. 17:242–246.

———. 1990. Temporal and spatial movement patterns of sliders and other turtles. *In* Gibbons, J. W., ed. Life history and ecology of the slider turtle, 201–215. Smithsonian Institution Press, Washington, D.C.

Gibbons, J. W., J. L. Greene, and K. K. Patterson. 1982. Variation in reproductive characteristics of aquatic turtles. Copeia 1982:776–784.

Gibbons, J. W., J. L. Greene, and J. P. Schubauer. 1979a. Variability in clutch size in aquatic chelonians. British J. Herpetol. 6:13–14.

Gibbons, J. W., and J. R. Harrison III. 1981. Reptiles and amphibians of Kiawah and Capers Islands, South Carolina. Brimleyana (5):145–162.

Gibbons, J. W., G. H. Keaton, J. P. Schubauer, J. L. Greene, D. H. Bennett, J. R. McAuliffe, and R. R. Sharitz. 1979b. Unusual population size structure in freshwater turtles on barrier islands. Georgia J. Sci. 37:155–159.

Gibbons, J. W., and J. E. Lovich. 1990. Sexual

dimorphism in turtles with emphasis on the slider turtle (*Trachemys scripta*). Herpetol. Monogr. (4):1–29.

Gibbons, J. W., and D. H. Nelson. 1978. The evolutionary significance of delayed emergence from the nest by hatchling turtles. Evolution 32:297–303.

Gibbons, J. W., S. S. Novak, and C. H. Ernst. 1988. *Chelydra serpentina*. Catalog. Amer. Amphib. Rept. 420:1–4.

Gibbons, J. W., and R. D. Semlitsch. 1981. Terrestrial drift fences with pitfall traps: An effective technique for quantitative sampling of animal populations. Brimleyana (7):1–16.

———. 1982. Survivorship and longevity of a long-lived vertebrate species: How long do turtles live? J. Anim. Ecol. 51:523–527.

———. 1991. Guide to the reptiles and amphibians of the Savannah River Site. University of Georgia Press, Athens. 131 pp.

Gibbons, J. W., R. D. Semlitsch, J. L. Greene, and J. P. Schubauer. 1981. Variation in age and size at maturity of the slider turtle (*Pseudemys scripta*). Amer. Natur. 117:841–845.

Gibbons, J. W., and M. H. Smith. 1968. Evidence of orientation by turtles. Herpetologica 24:331–334.

Gibbons, J. W., and D. W. Tinkle. 1969. Reproductive variation between turtle populations in a single geographic area. Ecology 50:340–341.

Gilbert, C. R., and D. P. Kelso. 1971. Fishes of the Tortuguero area, Caribbean Costa Rica. Bull. Florida St. Mus. Biol. Sci. 16:1–54.

Gilbert, H., and J. Gilbert. 1992. Possible geographic record of the three-toed box turtle, *Terrapene carolina triunguis* (Agassiz), in Illinois. Bull. Chicago Herpetol. Soc. 27:132–133.

Gilhen, J., and B. Grantmyre. 1973. The wood turtle, *Clemmys insculpta* (LeConte): An addition to the herpetofauna of Cape Breton Island, Nova Scotia. Can. Field-Natur. 87:308–310.

Gilles-Baillien, M. 1970. Urea and osmoregulation in the diamondback terrapin *Malaclemys centrata centrata* (Latreille). J. Exp. Biol. 52:691–697.

———. 1973a. Hibernation and osmoregulation in the diamondback terrapin *Malaclemys centrata centrata* (Latreille). J. Exp. Biol. 59:45–51.

———. 1973b. Seasonal changes in inorganic ions in red blood cells of terrestrial and aquatic chelonia. Biochem. Syst. 1:123–125.

———. 1973c. Isosmotic regulation in various tissues of the diamondback terrapin *Malaclemys centrata centrata* (Latreille). J. Exp. Biol. 59:39–43.

———. 1973d. Seasonal variations and osmoregulation in the red blood cells of the diamondback terrapin

Malaclemys centrata centrata (Latreille). Comp. Biochem. Physiol. 46A:505–512.

Gillette, D. D. 1974. A proposed revision of the evolutionary history of *Terrapene carolina triunguis*. Copeia 1974:537–539.

Gilmore, C. W. 1922 [1923]. A new fossil turtle, *Kinosternon arizonense*, from Arizona. Proc. U.S. Natl. Mus. 62(2451):1–8.

———. 1937. A new marine turtle from the Miocene of California. Proc. California Acad. Sci. 23:171–174.

Gist, D. H., R. A. Hess, and R. J. Thurston. 1992. Cytoplasmic droplets of painted turtle spermatozoa. J. Morphol. 214:153–158.

Gist, D. H., and J. M. Jones. 1987. Storage of sperm in the reptilian oviduct. Scanning Microscopy 1:1839–1849.

———. 1989. Sperm storage within the oviduct of turtles. J. Morphol. 199:379–384.

Gist, D. H., J. A. Michaelson, and J. M. Jones. 1990. Autumn mating in the painted turtle, *Chrysemys picta*. Herpetologica 46:331–336.

Glass, B. P., and N. Hartweg. 1951. *Kinosternon murrayi*, a new musk turtle of the *hirtipes* group from Texas. Copeia 1951:50–52.

Glass, M. L., R. G. Boutilier, and N. Heisler. 1985. Effects of body temperature on respiration, blood gases and acid-base status in the turtle *Chrysemys picta bellii*. J. Exp. Biol. 114:37–51.

Glass, M. L., J. W. Hicks, and M. L. Riedesel. 1979. Respiratory responses to long term temperature exposure in the box turtle, *Terrapene ornata*. J. Comp. Physiol. 131:353–359.

Glenn, J. L. 1983. A note on the longevity of a captive desert tortoise (*Gopherus agassizi*). Proc. Symp. Desert Tortoise Council 1983:131–132.

Glenn, J. L., R. C. Straight, and J. W. Sites, Jr. 1990. A plasma protein marker for population genetic studies of the desert tortoise (*Xerobates agassizi*). Great Basin Natur. 50:1–8.

Glidewell, J. R., T. L. Bettinger, and L. C. Fitzpatrick. 1981. Heat exchange in submerged red-eared turtle, *Chrysemys scripta*. Comp. Biochem. Physiol. 70A:141–143.

Glüsing, G. 1973. Zum Mageninhalt zweier Lederschildkröten, *Dermochelys coriacea*. Salamandra 9:77–80.

Godley, B., K. Kirkwood, S. Raffan, and R. Taylor. 1991. Leatherback turtles in Trinidad. Marine Turtle Newsl. (52):16–17.

Goff, C. C., and D. S. Goff. 1932. Egg laying and incubation of *Pseudemys floridana*. Copeia 1932:92–93.

Goff, D. S., and C. C. Goff. 1935. On the incubation of a clutch of eggs of *Amyda ferox* (Schneider). Copeia 1935:156.

Goff, G. P., and J. Lien. 1988. Atlantic leatherback turtles, *Dermochelys coriacea*, in cold water off Newfoundland and Labrador. Can. Field-Natur. 102:1–5.

Goff, G. P., and G. B. Stenson. 1988. Brown adipose tissue in leatherback sea turtles: A thermogenic organ in an endothermic reptile? Copeia 1988:1071–1075.

Goin, C. J., and C. C. Goff. 1941. Notes on the growth rate of the gopher turtle, *Gopherus polyphemus*. Herpetologica 2:66–68.

Goin, C. J., and O. B. Goin. 1962. Introduction to herpetology. W. H. Freeman and Co., San Francisco. 341 pp.

Goin, C. J., O. B. Goin, and G. R. Zug. 1978. Introduction to herpetology, 3d ed. W. H. Freeman and Co., San Francisco. 378 pp.

Goldsmith, W. M. 1945. Notes on the egg laying habits of the soft shell turtles. Proc. Iowa Acad. Sci. (1944) 51:447–449.

Goode, M. 1983. *Trionyx ferox* (Florida softshell). Reproduction. Herpetol. Rev. 14:122.

Goodpaster, W. W., and D. F. Hoffmeister. 1952. Notes on the mammals of western Tennessee. J. Mammal. 33:362–371.

Goodwin, T. M., and W. R. Marion. 1977. Occurrence of Florida red-bellied turtle eggs in north-central Florida alligator nests. Florida Scientist 40:237–238.

Gordon, D. M. 1990. Geographic variation in painted turtles, *Chrysemys picta*, from eastern Ontario and southern Quebec. Can. Field-Natur. 104:347–353.

Gordon, D. M., and R. D. MacCulloch. 1980. An investigation of the ecology of the map turtle, *Graptemys geographica* (LeSueur), in the northern part of its range. Can. J. Zool. 58:2210–2219.

Gorman, G. C. 1973. The chromosomes of the Reptilia, a cytotaxonomic interpretation. *In* Chiarelli, A. B., and E. Capanna, eds. Cytotaxonomy and vertebrate evolution, 349–424. Academic Press, New York.

Gotte, S. W. 1988. Nest site selection in the snapping turtle, mud turtle, and painted turtle. Master's thesis, George Mason University, Fairfax, Virginia.

———. 1992. *Chrysemys picta picta* (eastern painted turtle). Predation. Herpetol. Rev. 23:80.

Gould, E. 1957. Orientation in box turtles, *Terrapene c. Carolina* (Linnaeus). Biol. Bull. 112:336–348.

———. 1959. Studies on the orientation of turtles. Copeia 1959:174–176.

Gourley, E. V. 1969. Orientation of the gopher tortoise, *Gopherus polyphemus* (Daudin). Diss. Abstr. Int. B. 31:446.

———. 1972. Circadian activity rhythm of the gopher tortoise (*Gopherus polyphemus*). Anim. Behav. 20:13–20.

———. 1974. Orientation of the gopher tortoise, *Gopherus polyphemus*. Anim. Behav. 22:158–169.

Gouveia, J. F., and W. D. Webster. 1988. Nest temperature and sex determination in the loggerhead sea turtle. *In* Schroeder, B. A., ed. Proceedings of the Eighth Annual Workshop on Sea Turtle Conservation and Biology, 27–28. NOAA-TM-NMFS-SEFC-214.

Graham, R. W., J. A. Holman, and P. W. Parmalee. 1983. Taphonomy and paleoecology of the Christiansen Bog mastodon bone bed, Hancock County, Indiana. Rept. Invest. Illinois St. Mus. Natur. Hist. 38:1–29.

Graham T. E. 1969. Pursuit of the Plymouth turtle. Int. Turtle and Tortoise Soc. J. 3(1):10–13.

———. 1970. Growth rate of the spotted turtle, *Clemmys guttata*, in southern Rhode Island. J. Herpetol. 4:87–88.

———. 1971. Growth rate of the red-bellied turtle, *Chrysemys rubriventris*, at Plymouth, Massachusetts. Copeia 1971:353–356.

———. 1978. Preliminary notes on locomotor behavior in juvenile snapping turtles, *Chelydra serpentina*, under controlled conditions. Bull. Maryland Herpetol. Soc. 14:266–268.

———. 1979a. Red-bellied blues. Animals (1979):17–21.

———. 1979b. Locomotor activity in the Blanding's turtle, *Emydoidea blandingii* (Reptilia, Testudines, Emydidae): The phasing effect of temperature. J. Herpetol. 13:365–366.

———. 1981a. New approaches to endangered turtle research. Bios 52:121–126.

———. 1981b. Troubled turtles. Massachusetts Wildlife 32(3):18–19.

———. 1982a. Revelations on red-bellies. Sanctuary, May/June, 8, 11.

———. 1982b. The Blanding's turtle in Massachusetts. Sanctuary, May/June, 9, 11.

———. 1984a. *Pseudemys rubriventris* (red-bellied turtle). Predation. Herpetol. Rev. 15:19.

———. 1984b. *Pseudemys rubriventris* (red-bellied turtle). Food. Herpetol. Rev. 15:50–51.

———. 1988. Recovery in red. Preservation of the Plymouth redbelly turtle. South Shore Mag. 1(2):23–26, 45.

———. 1989. Map and softshell turtles from Vermont. Bull. Maryland Herpetol. Soc. 25(2):35–39.

———. 1991a. *Apalone spinifera spinifera* (eastern spiny softshell). Pattern dimorphism. Herpetol. Rev. 22:97.

———. 1991b. *Pseudemys rubriventris*. Catalog. Amer. Amphib. Rept. 510:1–4.

Graham, T. E., and J. M. Dadah-Tosti. 1981. Temperature effects on locomotor patterns in the wood turtle, *Clemmys insculpta*. Bull. Maryland Herpetol. Soc. 17:74–77.

Graham, T. E., and T. S. Doyle. 1973. The Blanding's

turtle *Emydoidea blandingi* Holbrook in Maine. HISS News-J. 1:29.

———. 1977. Growth and population characteristics of Blanding's turtle, *Emydoidea blandingii,* in Massachusetts. Herpetologica 33:410–414.

———. 1979. Dimorphism, courtship, eggs, and hatchlings of the Blanding's turtle, *Emydoidea blandingii* (Reptilia, Testudines, Emydidae) in Massachusetts. J. Herpetol. 13:125–127.

Graham, T. E., and J. E. Forsberg. 1986. Clutch size in some Maine turtles. Bull. Maryland Herpetol. Soc. 22:146–148.

———. 1991. Aquatic oxygen uptake by naturally wintering wood turtles *Clemmys insculpta.* Copeia 1991:836–838.

Graham, T. E., J. E. Forsberg, and J. J. Albright. 1987. Updated distribution of Blanding's turtle, *Emydoidea blandingi* in Maine. Bull. Maryland Herpetol. Soc. 23:119–121.

Graham, T. E., and A. A. Graham. 1991. *Trionyx spiniferus spiniferus* (eastern spiny softshell). Burying behavior. Herpetol. Rev. 22:56–57.

Graham, T. E., and V. H. Hutchison. 1969. Centenarian box turtles. Int. Turtle and Tortoise Soc. J. 3(3):25–29.

———. 1978. Locomotor activity in *Chrysemys picta:* response to asychronous cycles of temperature and photoperiod. Copeia 1978:364–367.

———. 1979a. Turtle diel activity: Response to different regimes of temperature and photoperiod. Comp. Biochem. Physiol. 63A:299–305.

———. 1979b. Effect of temperature and photoperiod acclimatization on thermal preferences of selected freshwater turtles. Copeia 1979:165–169.

Graham, T. E., and R. W. Perkins. 1976. Growth of the common snapping turtle, *Chelydra s. serpentina,* in a polluted marsh. Bull. Maryland Herpetol. Soc. 12:123–125.

Graham, T. E., and P. J. Petokas. 1989. Correcting for magnification when taking measurements directly from radiographs. Herpetol. Rev. 20:46–47.

Grannan, L. T., Jr., and R. Anderson. 1992. *Macroclemys temminckii* (alligator snapping turtle). USA: Indiana. Herpetol. Rev. 23:88.

Grant, C. 1935. Notes on the spotted turtle in northern Indiana. Proc. Indiana Acad. Sci. 44:244–247.

———. 1936a. Herpetological notes from northern Indiana. Proc. Indiana Acad. Sci. 45:323–333.

———. 1936b. The southwestern desert tortoise, *Gopherus agassizii.* Zoologica (New York) 21:225–229.

———. 1960a. Differentiation of the southwestern tortoises (genus *Gopherus*) with notes on their habits. Trans. San Diego Soc. Natur. Hist. 12:441–448.

———. 1960b. *Gopherus.* Herpetologica 16:29–31.

Grassman, A., and D. Owens. 1981. Evidence of olfactory imprinting in loggerhead turtles. Marine Turtle Newsl. (19):7–10.

———. 1987. Chemosensory imprinting in juvenile green sea turtles, *Chelonia mydas.* Anim. Behav. 35:929–931.

———. 1989. A further evaluation of imprinting in Kemp's ridley sea turtle. *In* Calliouet, C. W., Jr., and A. M. Landry, Jr., eds. Proceedings of the First International Symposium on Kemp's Ridley Sea Turtle Biology, Conservation and Management, 90–95. Texas A & M Univ. Sea Grant College Progr. Spec. Publ.-89 (105).

Grassman, M. A., D. W. Owens, J. P. McVey, and R. Márquez M. 1984. Olfactory-based orientation in artificially imprinted sea turtles. Science. 224:83–84.

Gray, J. E. 1831. Synopsis reptilium or short descriptions of the species of reptiles. Part 1. Cataphracta, tortoises, crocodiles, and enaliosaurians. London. 85 pp.

———. 1844. Catalogue of the tortoises, crocodiles, and amphisbaenians in the collection of the British Museum. London. 80 pp.

———. 1855. Catalogue of the shield reptiles in the collection of the British Museum. Part 1. Testudinata (tortoises). Trustees British Museum, London. 79 pp.

———. 1856. On some new species of freshwater tortoises from North America, Ceylon and Australia, in the collection of the British Museum. Proc. Zool. Soc. London. 1855:197–202.

Green, D. 1984. Long-distance movements of Galápagos green turtles. J. Herpetol. 18:121–130.

Green, N. B., and T. K. Pauley. 1987. Amphibians & reptiles in West Virginia. University of Pittsburgh Press, Pittsburgh, Pennsylvania. 241 pp.

Greer, A. E., J. D. Lazell, Jr., and R. M. Wright. 1973. Anatomical evidence for a counter-current heat exchanger in the leatherback turtle (*Dermochelys coriacea*). Nature 244:181.

Griffin, H. C., Jr., and C. H. Ernst. 1974. A xanthic *Chrysemys scripta elegans.* Herpetol. Rev. 5:105.

Grimpe, R. 1987. Maintenance, behavior, and reproduction of the alligator snapping turtle, *Macroclemys temminckii,* at the Tulsa Zoological Park. Bull. Oklahoma Herpetol. Soc. 12:1–6.

Grobman, A. B. 1990. The effect of soil temperatures on emergence from hibernation of *Terrapene carolina* and *T. ornata.* Amer. Midl. Natur. 124:366–371.

Grogan, W. L., Jr., and G. L. Williams. 1973. Notes on hatchling painted turtles, *Chrysemys pp. picta,* from Maryland. Bull. Maryland Herpetol. Soc. 9:108–110.

Groves, J. D. 1983. Taxonomic status and zoogeography of the painted turtle *Chrysemys picta* (Testudines: Emydidae), in Maryland. Amer. Midl. Natur. 109: 274–279.

———. 1985. Eastern mud turtle, *Kinosternon subrubrum subrubrum* (Lacépède). *In* Genoways, H. H., and F. J. Brenner, eds. Species of special concern in Pennsylvania, 265–267. Carnegie Museum of Natural History Special Publication 11, Pittsburgh, Pennsylvania.

Guilday, J. E., H. W. Hamilton, E. Anderson, and P. W. Parmalee. 1978. The Baker Bluff Cave deposit, Tennessee, and the Late Pleistocene faunal gradient. Bull. Carnegie Mus. Natur. Hist. 11:1–67.

Guillette, L. J., Jr., K. A. Bjorndal, A. B. Bolten, T. S. Gross, B. D. Palmer, B. E. Witherington, and J. M. Matter. 1991. Plasma estradiol-17β, progesterone prostaglandin F, and prostaglandin E$_2$ concentrations during natural oviposition in the loggerhead turtle (*Caretta caretta*). Gen. Comp. Endocrinol. 82:121–130.

Gustafson, E. P. 1978. The vertebrate faunas of the Pliocene Ringold Formation, south-central Washington. Bull. Mus. Natur. Hist. Univ. Oregon (23):1–62.

Gutzke, W. H. N., and J. J. Bull. 1986. Steroid hormones reverse sex in turtles. Gen. Comp. Endocrinol. 64:368–372.

Gutzke, W. H. N., and D. B. Chymiy. 1988. Sensitive periods during embryogeny of hormonally induced sex determination in turtles. Gen. Comp. Endocrinol. 71:265–267.

Gutzke, W. H. N., and G. C. Packard. 1985. Hatching success in relation to egg size in painted turtles (*Chrysemys picta*). Can. J. Zool. 63:67–70.

———. 1986. Sensitive periods for the influence of the hydric environment on eggs and hatchlings of painted turtles (*Chrysemys picta*). Physiol. Zool. 59:337–343.

———. 1987. The influence of temperature on eggs and hatchlings of Blanding's turtles, *Emydoidea blandingii*. J. Herpetol. 21:161–163.

Gutzke, W. H. N., G. C. Packard, M. J. Packard, and T. J. Boardman. 1987. Influence of the hydric and thermal environments of eggs and hatchlings of painted turtles (*Chrysemys picta*). Herpetologica 43:393–404.

Gutzke, W. H. N., and G. L. Paukstis. 1984. A low threshold temperature for sexual differentiation in the painted turtle, *Chrysemys picta*. Copeia 1984:546–547.

Haas, A. 1985. Ganzjährige Freilandhaltung der Schnappschildkröte *Chelydra serpentina serpentina* (Linnaeus, 1758) im Süddentschen Raum (Testudines: Chelydridae). Salamandra 21:1–9.

Haiduk, M. W., and J. W. Bickham. 1982. Chromosomal homologies and evolution of testudinoid turtles with emphasis on the systematic placement of *Platysternon*. Copeia 1982:60–66.

Hailman, J. P., and A. M. Elowson. 1992. Ethogram of the nesting female loggerhead (*Caretta caretta*). Herpetologica 48.1–30.

Hailman, J. P., J. N. Layne, and R. Knap. 1991. Notes on aggressive behavior of the gopher tortoise. Herpetol. Rev. 22:87–88.

Halk, J. H. 1986. *Trionyx spiniferus* (spiny softshell turtle). Size. Herpetol. Rev. 17:65.

Hall, K. V. 1988. The relationship between body size and reproductive characteristics in the leatherback sea turtle (*Dermochelys coriacea*). *In* Schroeder, B. A., ed. Proceedings of the Eighth Annual Workshop on Sea Turtle Conservation and Biology, 29–32. NOAA-TM-NMFS-SEFC-214.

Hall, R. J. 1980. Effects of environmental contaminants on reptiles: A review. U.S. Fish. Wildl. Serv. Spec. Sci. Rept. Wildl. (228):1–12.

Hall, R. J., A. A. Belisle, and L. Sileo. 1983. Residues of petroleum hydrocarbons in tissues of sea turtles exposed to the Ixtoc I oil spill. J. Wildl. Dis. 1982–1983:106–109.

Halstead, B. W. 1970. Poisonous and venomous marine animals of the world, vol. 3. Vertebrates [continued]. U.S. Gov't. Print. Off., Washington, D.C. 1006 pp.

Hamilton, R. D. 1944. Notes on mating and migration in Berlandier's turtle. Copeia 1944:62.

Hamilton, W. J., Jr. 1947. Egg laying of *Trionyx ferox*. Copeia 1947:209.

Hammer, D. A. 1969. Parameters of a marsh snapping turtle population, Lacreek Refuge, South Dakota. J. Wildl. Mgt. 33:995–1005.

———. 1971. The durable snapping turtle. Natur. Hist. 80(6):59–65.

Hammond, K. A., J. R. Spotila, and E. A. Standora. 1988. Basking behavior of the turtle *Pseudemys scripta:* Effects of digestive state, acclimation temperature, sex, and season. Physiol. Zool. 61:69–77.

Hampton, A. M. 1981. Field studies of natality in the desert tortoise, *Gopherus agassizi*. Proc. Symp. Desert Tortoise Council 1981:128–138.

Hansen, K. L. 1963. The burrow of the gopher tortoise. Quart. J. Florida Acad. Sci. 26:353–360.

Hansen, R. M., M. K. Johnson, and T. R. Van Devender. 1976. Foods of the desert tortoise, *Gopherus agassizii*, in Arizona and Utah. Herpetologica 32:247–251.

Harding, J. H. 1977. Record egg clutches for *Clemmys insculpta*. Herpetol. Rev. 8:34.

———. 1979. A case of interspecific aggression in captive turtles. HERP, Bull. New York Herpetol. Soc. 14(2):3–6.

———. 1985. *Clemmys insculpta* (wood turtle). Predation-mutilation. Herpetol. Rev. 16:30.

———. 1989. More about Blanding's turtle. Tortuga Gazette 25(2):5.

———. 1990. Blanding's turtle *Emydoidea blandingii*. Tortuga Gazette 26(1):3–4.

———. 1991. A twenty year wood turtle study in Michigan: Implications for conservation. *In* Beaman, K. R., F. Caporaso, S. McKeown, and M. D. Graff, eds. Proceedings of the First International Symposium on Turtles and Tortoises: Conservation and Captive Husbandry, 31–35. Chapman Univ., Orange, California.

Harding, J. H., and T. J. Bloomer. 1979. The wood turtle, *Clemmys insculpta* . . . a natural history. HERP, Bull. New York Herpetol. Soc. 15(1):9–26.

Harding, J. H., and J. A. Holman. 1987. The paleohistory of turtles: A brief review. Bull. Chicago Herpetol. Soc. 22:109–116.

———. 1990. Michigan turtles and lizards. A field guide and pocket reference. Michigan St. Univ. Cooperat. Ext. Serv. 94 pp.

Harlan, R. 1835. Genera of North American Reptilia and a synopsis of the species. Medical and Physical Researches. Lydia R. Bailey, Philadelphia, Pennsylvania. pp 84–160.

Harless, M. 1970. Social behavior in wood turtles. Amer. Zool. 10:289.

Harless, M. D., and C. W. Lambiotte. 1971. Behavior of captive ornate box turtles. J. Biol. Psychol. 13:17–23.

Harless, M. D., and H. Morlock, eds. 1979. Turtles: Perspectives and research. John Wiley & Sons, New York. 695 pp.

Harris, C. G. 1983. A sighting of the western painted turtle from Morgan Creek, Killdeer Badlands, Saskatchewan. Blue Jay 41:145.

Harris, J. L., J. Laerm, and L. J. Vitt. 1982. *Graptemys pulchra* (Alabama map turtle). USA: Georgia. Herpetol. Rev. 13:24.

Harrison, T. 1963. Notes on marine turtles: 13. Growth rate of the hawksbill. Sarawak Mus. J. (n.ser.) 11:302–303.

Harry, J. L., and D. A. Briscoe. 1988. Multiple paternity in the loggerhead turtle (*Caretta caretta*). J. Heredity 79:96–99.

Harry, J. L., and K. L. Williams. 1991. Differential growth of male and female urinogenital systems of *Caretta caretta*, within the sex-determining period. J. Exp. Zool. 258:204–211.

Harry, J. L., K. L. Williams, and D. A. Briscoe. 1990. Sex determination in loggerhead turtles: Differential expression of two hnRNP proteins. Development 109:305–312.

Hart, D. R. 1982. Growth of painted turtles, *Chrysemys picta*, in Manitoba and Louisiana. Can. Field-Natur. 96:127–130.

———. 1983. Dietary and habitat shift with size of red-eared turtles (*Pseudemys scripta*) in a southern Louisiana population. Herpetologica 39:285–290.

Hartman, W. L. 1958. Intergradation between two subspecies of painted turtle, genus *Chrysemys*. Copeia 1958:261–265.

Hartweg, N. 1939. A new American *Pseudemys*. Occ. Pap. Mus. Zool. Univ. Michigan 397:1–4.

Harvey, M. B. 1992. The distribution of *Graptemys pseudogeographica* on the upper Sabine River. Texas J. Sci. 44:257–258.

Hattan, L. R., and D. H. Gist. 1975. Seminal receptacles in the eastern box turtle, *Terrapene carolina*. Copeia 1975:505–510.

Hay, O. P. 1907. Descriptions of seven new species of turtles from the Tertiary of the United States. Bull. Amer. Mus. Natur. Hist. 23:847–863.

———. 1908. The fossil turtles of North America. Carnegie Inst. Washington Publ. 75:1–568.

———. 1911. A fossil specimen of the alligator snapper (*Macrochelys temminckii*) from Texas. Proc. Amer. Philos. Soc. 50:452–455.

———. 1916. Descriptions of some Floridian fossil vertebrates, belonging mostly to the Pleistocene. Florida St. Geol. Surv. 8th Ann. Rept., 39–76.

———. 1917. Vertebrata mostly from stratum no. 3 at Vero, Florida, together with descriptions of new species. Florida St. Geol. Surv. 9th Ann. Rept., 17–82.

———. 1923. The Pleistocene of North America and its vertebrated animals from the states east of the Mississippi River and from the Canadian provinces east of longitude 95°. Carnegie Inst. Washington Publ. 322:1–499.

———. 1924. The Pleistocene of the middle region of North America and its vertebrated animals. Carnegie Inst. Washington Publ. 322A:1–385.

Hay, O. P., and H. J. Cook. 1930. Fossil vertebrates collected near or in association with human artifacts at localities near Colorado, Texas; Frederick, Oklahoma; and Folsom, New Mexico. Proc. Colorado Mus. Natur. Hist. 9:4–40.

Hay, W. P. 1904. A revision of *Malaclemmys*, a genus of turtles. Bull. U.S. Bur. Fish. 24:1–20.

Hayes, F. E. 1987. Intraspecific kleptoparasitism and aggression in young, captive red-eared sliders (*Pseudemys scripta elegans*). Bull. Maryland Herpetol. Soc. 23:109–112.

———. 1989. Defensive stances in turtles. Herpetol. Rev. 20:4–5.

Hayes, M. P., and J. Le Corff. 1989. *Gopherus polyphemus* (gopher tortoise). Food. Herpetol. Rev. 20:55.

Haynes, D. 1976. *Graptemys caglei*. Catalog. Amer. Amphib. Rept. 184:1–2.

Haynes, D., and R. R. McKown. 1974. A new species of map turtle (genus *Graptemys*) from the Guadalupe River system in Texas. Tulane Stud. Zool. Bot. 18:143–152.

Hays, G. C., and J. R. Speakman. 1991. Reproductive investment and optimum clutch size of loggerhead sea turtles (*Caretta caretta*). J. Anim. Ecol. 60:455–462.

Heath, M. E., and S. M. McGinnis. 1980. Body temperature and heat transfer in the green sea turtle, *Chelonia mydas*. Copeia 1980:767–773.

Heidt, G. A., and R. G. Burbidge. 1966. Some aspects of color preference, substrate preference, and learning in hatchling *Chrysemys picta*. Herpetologica 22:288–292.

Henderson, G. E., ed. 1978. Proceedings of the Florida and Interregional Conference on sea turtles, 24–25 July 1976, Jensen Beach, Florida. Florida Marine Res. Publ. 33. 66 pp.

Hendrickson, J. R. 1958. The green sea turtle, *Chelonia mydas* (Linn.) in Malaya and Sarawak. Proc. Zool. Soc. London 130:455–535.

———. 1980. The ecological strategies of sea turtles. Amer. Zool. 20:597–608.

Hendrickson, J. R., and E. Balasingam. 1966. Nesting beach preferences of Malayan sea turtles. Bull Natl. Mus. Singapore (33):69–76.

Hendrickson, J. R., J. R. Wood, and R. S. Young. 1977. Lysine: Histidine ratios in marine turtle shells. Comp. Biochem. Physiol. 57B:285–286.

Hennemann, W. W. III. 1979. The influence of environmental cues and nutritional status on frequency of basking in juvenile Suwannee terrapins (*Chrysemys concinna*). Herpetologica 35:129–131.

Hensley, M. M. 1950. Notes on the natural history of *Heloderma suspectum*. Trans. Kansas Acad. Sci. 53:268–269.

Henwood, T. A. 1987a. Movements and seasonal changes in loggerhead turtle *Caretta caretta* aggregations in the vicinity of Cape Canaveral, Florida (1978–84). Biol. Conserv. 40:191–202.

———. 1987b. Distribution and migrations of immature Kemp's ridley turtles (*Lepidochelys kempi*) and green turtles (*Chelonia mydas*) off Florida, Georgia, and South Carolina. Northeast Gulf Sci. 9:153–160.

Herald, E. S. 1949. Effects of DDT-oil solutions upon amphibians and reptiles. Herpetologica 5:117–120.

Herbert, C. V., and D. C. Jackson. 1985. Temperature effects on the responses to prolonged submergence in the turtle *Chrysemys picta bellii*. I. Blood acid-base and ionic changes during and following anoxic submergence. II. Metabolic rate, blood acid base and ionic changes, and cardiovascular function in aerated and anoxic water. Physiol. Zool. 58:655–681.

Herman, D. W. 1981. Status of the bog turtle in the southern Appalachians. *In* Proceedings of the Nongame/Endangered Wildlife Symposium, 77–80. Technical Bull. WL-5, Georgia Department of Natural Resources, Game and Fish Division.

———. 1983. *Clemmys muhlenbergi* (bog turtle). Reproduction. Herpetol. Rev. 14:122.

———. 1986a. *Clemmys muhlenbergi* (bog turtle). Nest predation. Herpetol. Rev. 17:24.

———. 1986b. *Clemmys muhlenbergi* (bog turtle). Reproduction. Herpetol. Rev. 17:24.

———. 1987. An incident of twinning in the bog turtle, *Clemmys muhlenbergii* Schoepff. Bull. Maryland Herpetol. Soc. 23:122–124.

———. 1990. Tracking the rare bog turtle. Tortuga Gazette. 26(1):8–10.

———. 1991. Captive husbandry of the eastern *Clemmys* group at Zoo Atlanta. *In* Beaman, K. R., F. Caporaso, S. McKeown, and M. D. Graff, eds. Proceedings of the First International Symposium on Turtles and Tortoises: Conservation and Captive Husbandry, 54–62. Chapman Univ., Orange, California.

Herman, D. W., and G. A. George. 1986. Research, husbandry, and propagation of the bog turtle *Clemmys muhlenbergii* (Schoepff) at the Atlanta Zoo. *In* McKeown, S., et al., eds. Proceedings of the 9th International Herpetological Symposium on Captive Propagation and Husbandry, 125–135. University of San Diego.

Herman, D. W., and R. D. Pharr. 1986. *Clemmys muhlenbergi* (bog turtle). Elevation. Herpetol. Rev. 17:24.

Hibbard, C. W. 1963. The presence of *Macroclemys* and *Chelydra* in the Rexroad fauna from the upper Pliocene of Kansas. Copeia 1963:708–709.

Hibbard, C. W., and D. W. Taylor. 1960. Two late Pleistocene faunas from southwestern Kansas. Contrib. Mus. Paleontol. Univ. Michigan (16):1–223.

Higginson, J. 1989. Sea turtles in Guatemala: Threats and conservation efforts. Marine Turtle Newsl. (45):1–5.

Hildebrand, H. H. 1982. A historical review of the status of sea turtle populations in the western Gulf of Mexico. *In* Bjorndal, K. A., ed. Biology and conservation of sea turtles, 447–453. Smithsonian Institution Press, Washington, D.C.

Hildebrand, S. F. 1929. Review of experiments on artificial culture of diamond-back terrapin. Bull. U.S. Bur. Fish. 45:25–70.

———. 1932. Growth of diamond-back terrapins: Size attained, sex ratio and longevity. Zoologica (New York) 9:551–563.

———. 1933. Hybridizing diamond-back terrapins. J. Heredity 24:231–238.

Hildebrand, S. F., and C. Hatsel. 1926. Diamond-back terrapin culture at Beaufort, N.C. U.S. Bur. Fish., Econ. Circ. 60:1–20.

———. 1927. On the growth, care and age of loggerhead turtles in captivity. Proc. Natl. Acad. Sci. 13:374–377.

Hildebrand, S. F., and H. F. Prytherch. 1947. Diamondback terrapin culture. U.S. Fish Wildl. Serv. Leafl. 216:1–5.

Hinton, T. G., and D. E. Scott. 1990. Radioecological techniques for herpetology, with an emphasis on freshwater turtles. In Gibbons, J. W., ed. Life history and ecology of the slider turtle, 267–287. Smithsonian Institution Press, Washington, D.C.

Hinton, T. G., F. W. Whicker, J. E. Pinder III, and S. A. Ibrahim. 1992. Comparative kinetics of ^{47}Ca, ^{85}Sr and ^{226}Ra in the freshwater turtle, Trachemys scripta. J. Environ. Radioactivity 16:25–47.

Hirsch, K. F. 1983. Contemporary and fossil chelonian eggshells. Copeia 1983:382–397.

Hirschfeld, S. E. 1968. Vertebrate fauna of Nichol's Hammock, a natural trap. Quart. J. Florida Acad. Sci. 31:177–189.

Hirth, H. F. 1962. Cloacal temperatures of the green and hawksbill sea turtles. Copeia 1962:647–648.

———. 1971. Synopsis of biological data on the green turtle Chelonia mydas (Linnaeus) 1758. FAO Fish. Synopsis 85.

———. 1978. A model of the evolution of green turtle (Chelonia mydas) remigrations. Herpetologica 34:141–147.

———. 1980a. Some aspects of the nesting behavior and reproductive biology of sea turtles. Amer. Zool. 20:507–523.

———. 1980b. Chelonia. Catalog. Amer. Amphib. Rept. 248:1–2.

———. 1980c. Chelonia mydas. Catalog. Amer. Amphib. Rept. 249:1–4.

———. 1982. Weight and length relationships of some adult marine turtles. Bull. Marine Sci. 32:336–341.

———. 1988. Intrapopulation reproductive traits of green turtles, (Chelonia mydas) at Tortuguero, Costa Rica. Biotropica. 20:322–325.

Hirth, H. F., and A. Carr. 1970. The green turtle in the Gulf of Aden and the Seychelles Islands. Verh. Kon. Nederl. Akad. Wetensch. Nat. 58:1–44.

Hirth, H. F., and L. H. Ogren. 1987. Some aspects of the ecology of the leatherback turtle Dermochelys coriacea at Laguna Jalova, Costa Rica. NOAA Tech. Rept. NMFS 56. 14 pp.

Hirth, H. F., and D. A. Samson. 1987. Nesting behavior of green turtles (Chelonia mydas) at Tortuguero, Costa Rica. Caribbean J. Sci. 23:374–379.

Hirth, H. F., and W. M. Schaffer. 1974. Survival rate of the green turtle, Chelonia mydas, necessary to maintain stable populations. Copeia 1974:544–546.

Ho, S.-M., J. L'Italien, and I. P. Callard. 1980. Studies on reptilian yolk: Chrysemys vitellogenin and phosvitin. Comp. Biochem. Physiol. 65B:139–144.

Ho, S.-M., S. Kleis, R. McPherson, G. J. Heisermann, and I. P. Callard. 1982. Regulation of vitellogenesis in reptiles. Herpetologica 38:40–50.

Hochachka, P. W., T. G. Owen, J. F. Allen, and G. C. Whittow. 1975. Multiple end products of anaerbiosis in diving vertebrates. Comp. Biochem. Physiol. 50B:17–22.

Hodge, R. P. 1979. Dermochelys coriacea schlegeli (Pacific leatherback). USA: Alaska. Herpetol. Rev. 10:102.

———. 1981. Chelonia mydas agassizi (Pacific green turtle). USA: Alaska. Herpetol. Rev. 12:83–84.

———. 1982. Caretta caretta gigas (Pacific loggerhead). USA: Washington. Herpetol. Rev. 13:24.

———. 1992. Caretta caretta (loggerhead). USA: Alaska. Herpetol. Rev. 23:87.

Hoffman, W., and T. H. Fritts. 1982. Sea turtle distribution along the boundary of the Gulf Stream current off eastern Florida. Herpetologica 38:405–409.

Hoggard, W. 1991. First recorded turtle nesting on Mississippi's man-made beach. Marine Turtle Newsl. (52):11–12.

Hohman, J. P., R. D. Ohmart, and J. Schwartzmann. 1980. An annotated bibliography of the desert tortoise (Gopherus agassizi). Desert Tortoise Council Spec. Publ. (1):1–121.

Holbrook, J. E. 1836–1838. North American herpetology; or a description of the reptiles inhabiting the United States. J. Dobson, Philadelphia 1:1–152, 2:1–142, 3:1–122.

Holcomb, C. M., and W. S. Parker. 1979. Mirex residues in eggs and livers of two long-lived reptiles (Chrysemys scripta and Terrapene carolina) in Mississippi, 1970–1977. Bull. Environ. Contam. Toxicol. 23:369–371.

Holland, D. C. 1985. Clemmys marmorata (western pond turtle). Feeding. Herpetol. Rev. 16:112–113.

———. 1988. Clemmys marmorata (western pond turtle). Behavior. Herpetol. Rev. 19:87–88.

Holland, D. L., J. Davenport, and J. East. 1990. The fatty acid composition of the leatherback turtle Dermochelys coriacea and its jellyfish prey. J. Marine Biol. Assoc. United Kingdom 70:761–770.

Holman, J. A. 1959. Amphibians and reptiles from the Pleistocene (Illinoian) of Williston, Florida. Copeia 1959:96–102.

———. 1963. Late Pleistocene amphibians and reptiles of the Clear Creek and Ben Franklin local faunas of Texas. J. Grad. Res. Cent. Southern Methodist Univ. 31:152–167.

———. 1964. Pleistocene amphibians and reptiles of Texas. Herpetologica 20:73–83.

———. 1966. Some Pleistocene turtles from Illinois. Trans. Illinois St. Acad. Sci. 59:214–216.

———. 1967. A Pleistocene herpetofauna from Ladds, Georgia. Bull. Georgia Acad. Sci. 25:154–166.

———. 1969a. Herpetofauna of the Pleistocene Slaton local fauna of Texas. Southwest. Natur. 14:203–212.

———. 1969b. The Pleistocene amphibians and reptiles of Texas. Publ. Mus. Michigan St. Univ., Biol. Ser. 4:161–192.

———. 1972. Herpetofauna of the Kanopolis local fauna (Pleistocene: Yarmouth) of Kansas. Michigan Acad. 5:87–98.

———. 1973. Reptiles of the Egelhoff local fauna (upper Miocene) of Nebraska. Contrib. Mus. Paleontol. Univ. Michigan. 24:125–134.

———. 1975. Herpetofauna of the Wakeeney local fauna (lower Pliocene: Clarendonian) of Trego County, Kansas. Mus. Paleontol. Univ. Michigan Pap. Paleontol. (12):49–66.

———. 1976. The herpetofauna of the lower Valentine formation, north-central Nebraska. Herpetologica 32:262–268.

———. 1977a. Comments on turtles of the genus *Chrysemys* Gray. Herpetologica 33:274–276.

———. 1977b. The Pleistocene (Kansan) herpetofauna of Cumberland Cave, Maryland. Ann. Carnegie Mus. Natur. Hist. 46:157–172.

———. 1978. The late Pleistocene herpetofauna of Devil's Den Sinkhole, Levy County, Florida. Herpetologica 34:228–237.

———. 1981a. A review of North American Pleistocene snakes. Publ. Mus. Michigan St. Univ., Paleontol. Ser. 1:261–306.

———. 1981b. Fossil amphibians and reptiles of Nebraska and Kansas. Natl. Geogr. Soc. Res. Rept. 13:253–262.

———. 1982. New herpetological species and records from the Norden Bridge fauna (Miocene: late Barstovian) of Nebraska. Trans. Nebraska Acad. Sci. 10:31–36.

———. 1984. *Terrapene carolina carolina* (eastern box turtle). Morphology and behavior. Herpetol. Rev. 15:114.

———. 1985a. Herpetofauna of Ladds Quarry. Natl. Geogr. Res. 1:423–436.

———. 1985b. New evidence in the status of Ladds Quarry. Natl. Geogr. Res. 1:569–570.

———. 1986a. Butler Spring herpetofauna of Kansas (Pleistocene: Illinoian) and its climatic significance. J. Herpetol. 20:568–570.

———. 1986b. Turtles from the late Wisconsinan of west-central Ohio. Amer. Midl. Natur. 116:213–214.

———. 1987. Climatic significance of a late Illinoian herpetofauna from southwestern Kansas. Contrib. Mus. Paleontol. Univ. Michigan 27:129–141.

———. 1988. The status of Michigan's Pleistocene herpetofauna. Michigan Acad. 20:125–132.

———. 1990. Vertebrates from the Harper Site and rapid climatic warming in mid-Holocene Michigan. Michigan Acad. 22:205–217.

———. 1991. North American Pleistocene herpetofaunal stability and its impact on the interpretation of modern herpetofaunas: An overview. *In* Purdue, J. R., W. E. Klippel, and B. W. Styles, eds. Beamers, bobwhites, and blue-points: Tributes to the career of Paul W. Parmalee, 227–235. Illinois St. Mus. Sci. Pap. 23.

Holman, J. A., G. Bell, and J. Lamb. 1990. A late Pleistocene herpetofauna from Bell Cave, Alabama. Herpetol. J. 1:521–529.

Holman, J. A., and C. J. Clausen. 1984. Fossil vertebrates associated with paleo-Indian artifact at Little Salt Spring, Florida. J. Vert. Paleontol. 4:146–154.

Holman, J. A., and R. G. Corner. 1985. A Miocene *Terrapene* (Testudines: Emydidae) and other Barstovian turtles from south-central Nebraska. Herpetologica 41:88–93.

Holman, J. A., and F. Grady. 1989. The fossil herpetofauna (Pleistocene: Irvingtonian) of Hamilton Cave, Pendleton County, West Virginia. NSS Bull. 51:34–41.

Holman, J. A., and J. N. McDonald. 1986. A late Quaternary herpetofauna from Saltville, Virginia. Brimleyana (12):85–100.

Holman, J. A., and M. E. Schloeder. 1991. Fossil herpetofauna of the Lisco C Quarries (Pliocene: early Blancan) of Nebraska. Trans. Nebraska Acad. Sci. 18:19–29.

Holman, J. A., and R. M. Sullivan. 1981. A small herpetofauna from the type section of the Valentine Formation (Miocene: Barstovian), Cherry County, Nebraska. J. Paleontol. 55:138–144.

Holman, J. A., and A. J. Winkler. 1987. A mid-Pleistocene (Irvingtonian) herpetofauna from a cave in southcentral Texas. Texas Mem. Mus., Univ. Texas Pearce-Sellards Ser. (44):1–17.

Holub, R. J., and T. J. Bloomer. 1977. The bog turtle,

Clemmys muhlenbergii . . . a natural history. HERP, Bull. New York Herpetol. Soc. 13(2):9–23.

Hooker, D. 1908. Preliminary observations of the behavior of some newly hatched loggerhead turtles (*Thallassochelys caretta*). Carnegie Inst. Washington Yrbk. 6:111–112.

———. 1911. Certain reactions to color in the young loggerhead turtle. Carnegie Inst. Washington Publ. 132:71–76.

Hooper, D. F. 1992. Turtles, snakes and salamanders of east-central Saskatchewan. Blue Jay. 50:72–77.

Hopkins, S. R., and Y. M. Murphy. 1981. Reproductive ecology of *Caretta caretta* in South Carolina. Rept. South Carolina Wildl. Marine Res. Dept. Div. Wildl. Freshwater Fish. 97 pp.

Horne, F., and C. Findeisen. 1977. Aspects of fasting metabolism in the desert tortoise *Gopherus berlandieri*. Comp. Biochem. Physiol. 58(B):21–26.

Horrocks, J. 1989. Leatherback injured off Barbados, West Indies. Marine Turtle Newsl. (46):9–10.

Horrocks, J. A., and N. McA. Scott. 1991. Nest site location and nest success in the hawksbill turtle *Eretmochelys imbricata* in Barbados, West Indies. Marine Ecol. Progr. Ser. 69:1–8.

Hotaling, E. C., D. C. Wilhoft, and S. B. McDowell. 1985. Egg position and weight of hatchling snapping turtles, *Chelydra serpentina*, in natural nests. J. Herpetol. 19:534–536.

Houseal, T. W., J. W. Bickham, and M. D. Springer. 1982. Geographic variation in the yellow mud turtle, *Kinosternon flavescens*. Copeia 1982:567–580.

Houseal, T. W., and J. L. Carr. 1983. Notes on the reproduction of *Kinosternon subrubrum* (Testudines: Kinosternidae) in East Texas. Southwest. Natur. 28:237–239.

Housholder, V. H. 1950. Courtship and coition of the desert tortoise. Herpetologica 6:11.

Hubbs, C. L. 1977. First record of mating of ridley turtles in California, with notes on commensals, characters, and systematics. California Fish and Game 63:262–267.

Hudson, D. M., and P. L. Lutz. 1986. Salt gland function in the leatherback sea turtle, *Dermochelys coriacea*. Copeia 1986:247–249.

Hughes, D. A., and J. D. Richard. 1974. The nesting of the Pacific ridley turtle *Lepidochelys olivacea* on Playa Nancite, Costa Rica. Marine Biol. 24:97–107.

Hughes, G. R. 1974. The sea turtles of south-east Africa. II. The biology of the Tongaland loggerhead turtle *Caretta caretta* L. with comments on the leatherback turtle *Dermochelys coriacea* L., and the green turtle *Chelonia mydas* L. in the study region. Inv. Rept. Oceangr. Res. Inst. Durban 36:1–96.

———. 1978. Diving record for leatherback sea turtle. Lammergeyer 26:64.

———. 1982. Nesting cycles in sea turtles–typical or atypical? *In* Bjorndal, K. A., ed. Biology and conservation of sea turtles, 81–89. Smithsonian Institution Press, Washington, D.C.

Hughes, G. R., A. J. Bass, and M. T. Mentis. 1967. Further studies on marine turtle in Tongaland. I. Lammergeyer 7:1–55.

Hulse, A. C. 1974. Food habits and feeding behavior of *Kinosternon sonoriense* (Chelonia: Kinosternidae). J. Herpetol. 8:195–199.

———. 1976a. Carapacial and plastral flora and fauna of the Sonora mud turtle, *Kinosternon sonoriense* Le Conte (Reptilia, Testudines, Kinosternidae). J. Herpetol. 10:45–48.

———. 1976b. Growth and morphometrics of *Kinosternon sonoriense* (Reptilia, Testudines, Kinosternidae). J. Herpetol. 10:341–348.

———. 1980. Notes on the occurrence of introduced turtles in Arizona. Herpetol. Rev. 11:16–17.

———. 1982. Reproduction and population structure in the turtle, *Kinosternon sonoriense*. Southwest. Natur. 27:447–456.

Hulse, A. C., and G. A. Middendorf. 1979. Notes on the occurrence of *Gopherus agassizi* (Testudinidae) in extreme eastern Arizona. Southwest. Natur. 24:545–546.

Hulse, A. C., and E. J. Routman. 1982. Leech (*Placobdella parasitica*) infestations on the wood turtle, *Clemmys insculpta*. Herpetol. Rev. 13:116–117.

Humphreys, G. B., and F. F. Mallory. 1977. Colour preferences of the pond slider, *Chrysemys scripta elegans* (Schoepff), and the spotted turtle, *Clemmys guttata* (Schneider). Ontario Field Biol. 31:41–44.

Hunt, R. H., and J. J. Ogden. 1991. Selected aspects of the nesting ecology of American alligators in the Okefenokee Swamp. J. Herpetol. 25:448–453.

Hunt, T. J. 1958. The ordinal name for tortoises, terrapins, and turtles. Herpetologica 14:148–150.

Hurd, L. E., G. W. Smedes, and T. A. Dean. 1979. An ecological study of a natural population of diamondback terrapins (*Malaclemys t. terrapin*) in a Delaware salt marsh. Estuaries 2:28–33.

Hutchison, A. M. 1992. A reproducing population of *Trachemys scripta elegans* in southern Pinellas County, Florida. Herpetol. Rev. 23:74–75.

Hutchison, J. H. 1981. *Emydoidea* (Emydidae, Testudines) from the Barstovian (Miocene) of Nebraska. Paleobios (37):1–6.

Hutchison, J. H., and D. M. Bramble. 1981. Homology of the plastral scales of the Kinosternidae and related turtles. Herpetologica 37:73–85.

Hutchison, V. H., and R. J. Kosh. 1965. The effect of photoperiod on the critical thermal maxima of painted turtles (*Chrysemys picta*). Herpetologica 20:233–238.

Hutchison, V. H., A. Vinegar, and R. J. Kosh. 1966. Critical thermal maxima in turtles. Herpetologica 22:32–41.

Hutton, K. E., D. R. Boyer, J. C. Williams, and P. M. Campbell. 1960. Effects of temperature and body size upon heart rate and oxygen consumption in turtles. J. Cell. Comp. Physiol. 55:87–93.

Ingold, D. A., and W. E. Patterson. 1988. Population parameters of red-eared turtles in a Texas farm pond. Bull. Maryland Herpetol. Soc. 24:27–40.

Ingold, D. A., S. E. Willbern, and D. M. Roberts. 1986. A population estimation technique for aquatic turtles. Bull. Maryland Herpetol. Soc. 22:1–5.

International Commission of Zoological Nomenclature. 1982. Opinion 1236 *Trionyx steindachneri* Siebenrock, 1906 (Reptilia, Testudines): conserved. Bull. Zool. Nomencl. 39:258–259.

Ireland, L. C. 1979. Optokinetic behavior of the hatchling green turtle (*Chelonia mydas*) soon after leaving the nest. Herpetologica 35:365–370.

Iverson, J. B. 1975. Notes on Nebraska reptiles. Trans. Kansas Acad. Sci. 78:51–62.

———. 1976. *Kinosternon sonoriense*. Catalog Amer. Amphib. Rept. 176:1–2.

———. 1977a. Reproduction in freshwater and terrestrial turtles of North Florida. Herpetologica 33:205–212.

———. 1977b. *Kinosternon subrubrum*. Catalog Amer. Amphib. Rept. 193:1–4.

———. 1977c. *Sternotherus depressus*. Catalog. Amer. Amphib. Rept. 194:1–2.

———. 1977d. *Sternotherus minor* (Agassiz). Catalog. Amer. Amphib. Rept. 195:1–2.

———. 1977e. Geographic variation in the musk turtle, *Sternotherus minor*. Copeia 1977:502–517.

———. 1977f. Further notes on Nebraska reptiles. Trans. Kansas Acad. Sci. 80:55–59.

———. 1978a. Reproductive cycle of female loggerhead musk turtles (*Sternotherus minor minor*) in Florida. Herpetologica 34:33–39.

———. 1978b. Distributional problems of the genus *Kinosternon* in the American Southwest. Copeia 1978:476–479.

———. 1978c. Variation in striped mud turtles, *Kinosternon baurii* (Reptilia, Testudines, Kinosternidae). J. Herpetol. 12:135–142.

———. 1979a. *Sternotherus carinatus*. Catalog. Amer. Amphib. Rept. 226:1–2.

———. 1979b. On the validity of *Kinosternon arizonense* Gilmore. Copeia 1979:175–177.

———. 1979c. A taxonomic reappraisal of the yellow mud turtle, *Kinosternon flavescens* (Testudines: Kinosternidae). Copeia 1979:212–225.

———. 1979d. Reproduction and growth of the mud turtle, *Kinosternon subrubrum* (Reptilia, Testudines, Kinosternidae), in Arkansas. J. Herpetol. 13:105–111.

———. 1979e. The female reproductive cycle in north Florida *Kinosternon baurii* (Testudines: Kinosternidae). Brimleyana (1):37–46.

———. 1980a. The reproductive biology of *Gopherus polyphemus* (Chelonia: Testudinidae). Amer. Midl. Natur. 103:353–359.

———. 1980b. Biosystematics of the *Kinosternon hirtipes* species group. Paper presented at Carnegie Museum Powdermill Turtle Conference, 19–21 Sept.

———. 1981. Biosystematics of the *Kinosternon hirtipes* species group (Testudines, Kinosternidae). Tulane Stud. Zool. Bot. 23:1–74.

———. 1982a. Biomass in turtle populations: A neglected subject. Oecologia (Berlin). 55:69–76.

———. 1982b. Ontogenetic changes in relative skeletal mass in the painted turtle *Chrysemys picta*. J. Herpetol. 16:412–414.

———. 1984. Proportional skeletal mass in turtles. Florida Scientist 47:1–11.

———. 1985a. *Kinosternon hirtipes*. Catalog Amer. Amphib. Rept. 361:1–4.

———. 1985b. Geographic variation in sexual dimorphism in the mud turtle *Kinosternon hirtipes*. Copeia 1985:388–393.

———. 1985c. Reproduction in the Florida softshell turtle, *Trionyx ferox*. Florida Scientist 48:41–44.

———. 1985d. Checklist of the turtles of the world with English common names. SSAR Herpetol. Circular 14:1–14.

———. 1988a. Distribution and status of Creaser's mud turtle, *Kinosternon creaseri*. Herpetol. J. 1:285–291.

———. 1988b. Neural bone patterns and the phylogeny of the turtles of the subfamily Kinosterninae. Milwaukee Publ. Mus. Contrib. Biol. Geol. (75):1–12.

———. 1988c. Growth in the common map turtle, *Graptemys geographica*. Trans. Kansas Acad. Sci. 91:153–157.

———. 1989. The Arizona mud turtle, *Kinosternon flavescens arizonense* (Kinosternidae), in Arizona and Sonora. Southwest. Natur. 34:356–368.

———. 1990. Nesting and parental care in the mud turtle, *Kinosternon flavescens*. Can. J. Zool. 68:230–233.

———. 1991a. Patterns of survivorship in turtles (order Testudines). Can. J. Zool. 69:385–391.

———. 1991b. Phylogenetic hypotheses for the evolution of modern kinosternine turtles. Herpetol. Monogr. 5:1–27.

———. 1991c. Life history and demography of the yellow mud turtle, *Kinosternon flavescens*. Herpetologica 47: 373–395.

———. 1992a. Species richness maps of the freshwater and terrestrial turtles of the World. Smithsonian Herpetol. Inform. Serv. (88):1–18.

———. 1992b. A revised checklist with distribution maps of the turtles of the World. Privately printed, Richmond, Indiana. 363 pp.

———. 1992c. Correlates of reproductive output in turtles (order Testudines). Herpetol. Monogr. 6:25–42.

Iverson, J. B., E. L. Barthelmess, G. R. Smith, and C. E. DeRivera. 1991. Growth and reproduction in the mud turtle *Kinosternon hirtipes* in Chihuahua, Mexico. J. Herpetol. 25:64–72.

Iverson, J. B., and C. R. Etchberger. 1989. The distribution of the turtles of Florida. Florida Scientist 52:119–144.

Iverson, J. B., and M. A. Ewert. 1991. Physical characteristics of reptilian eggs and a comparison with avian eggs. *In* Deeming, D. C., and M. W. J. Ferguson, eds. Egg incubation: Its effects on embryonic development in birds and reptiles, 87–100. Cambridge University Press, New York.

Iverson, J. B., and T. E. Graham. 1990. Geographic variation in the redbelly turtle, *Pseudemys rubriventris* (Reptilia: Testudines). Ann. Carnegie Mus. Natur. Hist. 59:1–13.

Iverson, J. B., and S. A. Iverson. 1980. A bibliography to the mud and musk turtle family Kinosternidae. Smithsonian Herpetol. Inform. Serv. 48:1–72.

Jackson, C. G., Jr. 1964. The status of *Deirochelys floridana* Hay with comments on the fossil history of the genus. Tulane Stud. Geol. 2:103–106.

———. 1969. Agonistic behavior in *Sternotherus minor minor* Agassiz. Herpetologica 25:53–54.

———. 1970. A biometrical study of growth in *Pseudemys concinna suwanniensis* I. Copeia 1970:528–534.

———. 1974a. An unusual pattern of cervical central articulation in *Deirochelys reticularia*. Copeia 1974: 788.

———. 1974b. The status of *Trachemys jarmani* Hay with clarification of the fossil record of *Deirochelys*. Copeia 1974:536–537.

Jackson, C. G., Jr., and C. E. Cantrell. 1964. Total body water in neonatal Suwannee terrapins, *Pseudemys concinna suwanniensis* Carr. Comp. Biochem. Physiol. 12:527–528.

Jackson, C. G. Jr., and J. D. Davis. 1972a. A quantitative

study of the courtship display of the red-eared turtle, *Chrysemys scripta elegans* (Wied). Herpetologica 28:58–64.

———. 1972b. Courtship display behavior of *Chrysemys concinna suwanniensis*. Copeia 1972:385–387.

Jackson, C. G., Jr., C. M. Holcomb, and M. M. Jackson. 1974. Aortic calcification, serum calcium, magnesium, sodium and cholesterol in *Gopherus polyphemus*. Comp. Biochem. Physiol. 49A:603–605.

———. 1975. Serum levels of urea and inorganic phosphorus in the loggerhead musk turtle, *Sternotherus minor minor*. Comp. Biochem. Physiol. 51A: 963–964.

Jackson, C. G., Jr., and M. M. Jackson. 1968. The egg and hatchling of the Suwannee terrapin. Quart. J. Florida Acad. Sci. 31:199–204.

Jackson, C. G., Jr., M. M. Jackson, and J. D. Davis. 1969. Cutaneous myiasis in the three-toed box turtle, *Terrapene carolina triunguis*. Bull. Wildl. Dis. Assoc. 5:114.

Jackson, C. G., Jr., and J. M. Kaye. 1974a. The occurrence of Blanding's turtle, *Emydoidea blandingii*, in the late Pleistocene of Mississippi (Testudines: Testudinidae). Herpetologica 30:417–419.

———. 1974b. Occurrence of box turtles, *Terrapene* (Testudines: Testudinidae) in the Pleistocene of Mississippi. Herpetologica 30:11–13.

———. 1975. Giant tortoises in the late Pleistocene of Mississippi. Herpetologica 31:421.

Jackson, C. G., Jr., and A. Ross. 1971a. The occurrence of barnacles on the alligator snapping turtle, *Macroclemys temminckii* (Troost). J. Herpetol. 5:188–189.

———. 1971b. Molluscan fouling of the ornate diamondback terrapin, *Malaclemys terrapin macrospilota* Hay. Herpetologica 27:341–344.

———. 1974. Balanomorph barnacles on *Chrysemys alabamensis*. Quart. J. Florida Acad. Sci. (1972) 35:173–176.

———. 1975. Epizoic occurrence of a bryozoan, *Electra crustulenta*, on the turtle *Chrysemys alabamensis*. Trans. Amer. Microsc. Soc. 94:135–136.

Jackson, C. G., Jr., A. Ross, and G. L. Kennedy. 1973. Epifaunal invertebrates of the ornate diamondback terrapin, *Malaclemys terrapin macrospilota*. Amer. Midl. Natur. 89:495–497.

Jackson, C. G., Jr., J. A. Trotter, T. H. Trotter, and M. W. Trotter. 1976. Accelerated growth rate and early maturity in *Gopherus agassizi* (Reptilia: Testudines). Herpetologica 32:139–145.

Jackson, C. G., Jr., and M. W. Trotter. 1980. Extra carapacial bones in the chicken turtle, *Deirochelys reticularia*. Natur. Hist. Misc. (209):1–3.

Jackson, C. G., Jr., T. H. Trotter, J. A. Trotter, and M. W. Trotter. 1978. Further observations of growth and sexual maturity in captive desert tortoises (Reptilia: Testudines). Herpetologica 34:225–227.

Jackson, D. C. 1968. Metabolic depression and oxygen depletion in the diving turtle. J. Appl. Physiol. 24:503–509.

———. 1969. Buoyancy control in the freshwater turtle, *Pseudemys scripta elegans*. Science 166:1649–1651.

———. 1971. The effect of temperature on ventilation in the turtle, *Pseudemys scripta elegans*. Resp. Physiol. 12:131–140.

———. 1973. Ventilatory response to hypoxia in turtles at various temperatures. Resp. Physiol. 18:178–187.

———. 1976. Non-pulmonary CO_2 loss during diving in the turtle, *Pseudemys scripta elegans*. Comp. Biochem. Physiol. 55A:237–241.

———. 1978. Respiratory control and CO_2 conductance: Temperature effects in a turtle and a frog. Resp. Physiol. 33:103–114.

———. 1985. Respiration and respiratory control in the green turtle, *Chelonia mydas*. Copeia 1985:664–671.

Jackson, D. C., J. Allen, and P. K. Strup. 1976. The contribution of non-pulmonary surfaces to CO_2 loss in 6 species of turtles at 20°C. Comp. Biochem Physiol. 55A:243–246.

Jackson, D. C., C. V. Herbert, and G. R. Ultsch. 1984. The comparative physiology of diving in North American freshwater turtles. II. Plasma ion balance during prolonged anoxia. Physiol. Zool. 57:632–640.

Jackson, D. C., and R. D. Kagen. 1976. Effects of temperature transients on gas exchange and acid-base status of turtles. Amer. J. Physiol. 230:1389–1393.

Jackson, D. C., D. R. Kraus, and H. D. Prange. 1979. Ventilatory response to inspired CO_2 in the sea turtle: Effects of body size and temperature. Resp. Physiol. 38:71–81.

Jackson, D. C., S. E. Palmer, and W. L. Meadow. 1974. The effects of temperature and carbon dioxide breathing on ventilation and acid-base status of turtles. Resp. Physiol. 20:131–146.

Jackson, D. C., and K. Schmidt-Nielsen. 1966. Heat production during diving in the freshwater turtle, *Pseudemys scripta*. J. Cell. Physiol. 67:225–231.

Jackson, D. C., and G. R. Ultsch. 1982. Long-term submergence at 3°C of the turtle, *Chrysemys picta bellii*, in normoxic and severely hypoxic water. II. Extracellular ionic responses to extreme lactic acidosis. J. Exp. Biol. 96:29–43.

Jackson, D. R. 1975. A Pleistocene *Graptemys* (Reptilia: Testudines) from the Santa Fe River of Florida. Herpetologica 31:213–219.

———. 1976. The status of the Pliocene turtles *Pseudemys caelata* Hay and *Chrysemys carri* Rose and Weaver. Copeia 1976:655–659.

———. 1978a. *Chrysemys nelsoni*. Catalog. Amer. Amphib. Rept. 210:1–2.

———. 1978b. Evolution and fossil record of the chicken turtle *Deirochelys*, with a re-evaluation of the genus. Tulane Stud. Zool. Bot. 20:35–55.

———. 1985. Florida's "desert" tortoise. Nature Conserv. News. 35(5):24–26.

———. 1987. Preliminary studies of reproduction in the Suwannee cooter, *Pseudemys concinna suwanniensis*. Progr. Jt. Meet. SSAR–Herpetol. League, Vera Cruz, Mexico, 94.

———. 1988a. Reproductive strategies of sympatric freshwater emydid turtles in northern peninsular Florida. Bull. Florida St. Mus. Biol. Sci. 33:113–158.

———. 1988b. A re-examination of fossil turtles of the genus *Trachemys* (Testudines: Emydidae). Herpetologica 44:317–325.

———. 1991a. Multiple clutches and nesting behavior in the Gulf Coast box turtle. Florida Field Natur. 19:14–16.

———. 1991b. *Trionyx ferox* (Florida softshell). Reproduction. Herpetol. Rev. 22:56.

Jackson, D. R., and E. G. Milstrey. 1989. The fauna of gopher tortoise burrows. *In* Diemer, J. E., et al., eds. Proceedings Gopher Tortoise Relocation Symposium, 86–98. Florida Game and Fresh Water Fish Commission, Nongame Wildlife Program Technical Report No. 5. Tallahassee, Florida.

Jackson, J. F. 1990. Evidence for chemosensor-mediated predator avoidance in musk turtles. Copeia 1990 :557–560.

Jacobson, E. R., J. M. Gaskin, M. B. Brown, R. K. Harris, C. H. Gardiner, J. L. LaPointe, H. P. Adams, and C. Reggiardo. 1991. Chronic upper respiratory tract disease of free-ranging desert tortoises (*Xerobates agassizii*). J. Wildl. Dis. 27:296–316.

Jaeger, E. C. 1944. A source-book of biological names and terms. Charles C Thomas, Springfield, Ill.; Baltimore. xxvi + 256 pp.

Janzen, F. J. 1992. Heritable variation for sex ratio under environmental sex determination in the common snapping turtle (*Chelydra serpentina*). Genetics 131:155–161.

Janzen, F. J., and S. O'Steen. 1990. An instance of male combat in the common snapping turtle (*Chelydra serpentina*). Bull. Chicago Herpetol. Soc. 25:11.

Janzen, F. J., G. C. Packard, M. J. Packard, T. J. Boardman, and J. R. zumBrunnen. 1990. Mobilization of lipid and protein by embryonic snapping turtles in wet and dry environments. J. Exp. Zool. 255:155–162.

Janzen, F. J., and G. L. Paukstis. 1991. A preliminary test of the adaptive significance of environmental sex determination in reptiles. Evolution 45:435–440.

Janzen, F. J., G. L. Paukstis, and E. D. Brodie III. 1992. Observations on basking behavior of hatchling turtles in the wild. J. Herpetol. 26:217–219.

Jarling, C., M. Scarperi, and A. Bleichert. 1984. Thermoregulatory behavior of the turtle, *Pseudemys scripta elegans*, in a thermal gradient. Comp. Biochem. Physiol. 77A:675–678.

———. 1989. Circadian rhythm in the temperature preference of the turtle, *Chrysemys* (= *Pseudemys*) *scripta elegans*, in a thermal gradient. J. Therm. Biol. 14:173–178.

Jenkins, J. D. 1979. Notes on the courtship of the map turtle *Graptemys pseudogeographica* (Gray) (Reptilia, Testudines, Emydidae). J. Herpetol. 13:129–131.

Jenkins, J. T., and H. A. Semken. 1972. Faunal analysis of the Lane Enclosure, Allamakee County, Iowa. Proc. Iowa Acad. Sci. 78:76–78.

Jennings, M. R. 1981. *Gopherus agassizi* (desert tortoise). Longevity. Herpetol. Rev. 12:81–82.

Joeckel, R. M. 1988. A new late Miocene herpetofauna from Franklin County, Nebraska. Copeia 1988:787–789.

Johnson, E. W. 1984. A longevity record for the mud turtle (*Kinosternon bauri*). Proc. Staten Island Inst. Arts Sci. 33:47–48.

Johnson, K. A. 1983. The decline of the spotted turtle, *Clemmys guttata*, in northeastern Illinois. Bull. Chicago Herpetol. Soc. 18:37–41.

Johnson, R. M. 1954. The painted turtle, *Chrysemys picta picta*, in eastern Tennessee. Copeia 1954:298–299.

Johnson, T. R. 1987. The amphibians and reptiles of Missouri. Missouri Dept. Conserv., Jefferson City. 369 pp.

Johnson, W. R., Jr. 1952. *Lepidochelys kempii* and *Caretta c. caretta* from a south Florida Indian mound. Herpetologica 8:36.

Jones, C. A. 1992. *Gopherus polyphemus* (gopher tortoise). Herpetol. Rev. 23:59.

Jones, C. A., and R. Franz. 1990. Use of gopher tortoise burrows by Florida mice (*Podomys floridanus*) in Putnam County, Florida. Florida Field Natur. 18:45–51.

Jones, R. L. 1991. Density and population structure of the ringed sawback turtle, *Graptemys oculifera* (Baur). Final Report. Mississippi Dept. Wildl. Fish. Parks, Mus. Natur. Sci., Mus. Tech. Rept. (17):1–55.

Jones, R. L., T. C. Majure, and K. R. Macaro. 1991.

Graptemys kohnii (Mississippi map turtle). Herpetol. Rev. 22:24–25.

Joseph, J. D., R. G. Ackman, and G. T. Seaborn. 1985. Effect of diet on depot fatty acid composition in the green turtle *Chelonia mydas*. Comp. Biochem. Physiol. 80B:15–22.

Judd, F. W., and J. C. McQueen. 1980. Incubation, hatching, and growth of the tortoise, *Gopherus berlandieri*. J. Herpetol. 14:377–380.

———. 1982. Notes on longevity of *Gopherus berlandieri* (Testudinidae). Southwest. Natur. 27:230–232.

Judd, F. W., H. Nieuwendaal, and D. L. Hockaday. 1991. The leatherback turtle, *Dermochelys coriacea*, in southernmost Texas. Texas J. Sci. 43:101–103.

Judd, F. W., and F. L. Rose. 1977. Aspects of the thermal biology of the Texas tortoise, *Gopherus berlandieri* (Reptilia, Testudines, Testudinidae). J. Herpetol. 11:147–153.

———. 1983. Population structure, density and movements of the Texas tortoise *Gopherus berlandieri*. Southwest. Natur. 28:387–398.

———. 1989. Egg production by the Texas tortoise, *Gopherus berlandieri*, in southern Texas. Copeia 1989:588–596.

Judd, W. W. 1976. Records of snakes and turtles in Ontario in the 1960's. Bull. Can. Amphib. Rept. Conserv. Soc. 13(6):1–2.

Kaczor, S. A., and D. C. Hartnett. 1990. Gopher tortoise (*Gopherus polyphemus*) effects on soils and vegetation in a Florida sandhill community. Amer. Midl. Natur. 123:100–111.

Kajihara, T., and I. Uchida. 1974. The ecology and fisheries of the hawksbill turtle, *Eretmochelys imbricata*, in Southeast Asia. Japanese J. Herpetol. 5:48.

Kam, A. K. H. 1984. An unusual example of basking by a green turtle in the northwestern Hawaiian Islands. 'Elepaio (J. Hawaii Audubon Soc.) 45:3–4.

Kamezaki, N. 1983. The possibility of hybridization between the loggerhead turtle, *Caretta caretta*, and the hawksbill turtle, *Eretmochelys imbricata*, in specimens hatched from eggs collected in Chita peninsula. Japanese J. Herpetol. 10:52–53.

———. 1989. Karyotypes of the loggerhead turtle, *Caretta caretta*, from Japan. Zool. Sci. (Japan) 6:421–422.

———. 1990. Karyotype of the hawksbill turtle, *Eretmochelys imbricata*, from Japan, with notes on a method for preparation of chromosomes from liver cells. Japanese J. Herpetol. 13:111–113.

Kanamoto, Z., and C. Teruya. 1978. Biotechniques of growing the turtle *Trionyx sinensis* in the subtropics. Agriculture 26:31–35.

Kangas, D. A. 1986a. Population size and some statistical predictors of abundance of *Kinosternon flavescens* in north Missouri. Trans. Missouri Acad. Sci. 20:98.

———. 1986b. Survivorship and life table calculations for *Kinosternon flavescens*. Trans. Missouri Acad. Sci. 20:99.

Kaplan, H. M., S. S. Glaezenski, and T. Hirano. 1966. Electron microscope study of turtle sperm. Cytologia 31:99–104.

Karl, S. A., B. W. Bowen, and J. C. Avise. 1992. Global population genetic structure and male mediated gene flow in the green turtle (*Chelonia mydas*): RFLP analyses of anonymous nuclear loci. Genetics 131:163–173.

Kauffmann, R. 1975. Observaciones sobre el crecimiento de tortugas marinas en cautividad. Caldasia 11:139–150.

Kaufmann, J. H. 1986. Stomping for earthworms by wood turtles, *Clemmys insculpta:* A newly discovered foraging technique. Copeia 1986:1001–1004.

———. 1989a. The wood turtle stomp. Natur. Hist. 8:8, 10.

———. 1991. *Clemmys insculpta* (wood turtle). Cleaning symbiosis. Herpetol. Rev. 22:98.

———. 1992a. Habitat use by wood turtles in central Pennsylvania. J. Herpetol. 26:315–321.

———. 1992b. The social behavior of wood turtles, *Clemmys insculpta,* in central Pennsylvania. Herpetol. Monogr. 6:1–25.

Kaufmann, J. H., J. H. Harding, and K. N. Brewster. 1989. Worm stomping by wood turtles revisited. Bull. Chicago Herpetol. Soc. 24:125–126.

Keinath, J. A., and J. A. Musick. 1990. *Dermochelys coriacea* (leatherback sea turtle). Migration. Herpetol. Rev. 21:92.

Keinath, J. A., J. A. Musick, and R. A. Byles. 1987. Aspects of the biology of Virginia's sea turtles: 1979–1986. Virginia J. Sci. 38:329–336.

Kelderman, D. 1992. De Muskusschildpadden *Kinosternon carinatum, K. odoratum* en *K. m. minor* in het terrarium. Lacerta 50:98–102.

Kenefick, J. H. 1954. Observations on egg laying of the tortoise *Gopherus polyphemus*. Copeia 1954:228–229.

Kennedy, M. E. 1969. *Salmonella* serotypes isolated from turtle environment. Can. J. Microbiol. 15:130–132.

Kepenis, V., and J. J. McManus. 1974. Bioenergetics of young painted turtles, *Chrysemys picta*. Comp. Biochem. Physiol. 48A:309–317.

Khosatzky, L. I. 1981. Some peculiar features of heat exchange exhibited by the soft-shelled turtle *Trionyx sinensis* (Weigm.). *In* Borkin, L. J., ed. Herpetological investigations in Siberia and the Far East, 113–117. Leningrad.

Kiester, A. R., C. W. Schwartz, and E. R. Schwartz. 1982.

Promotion of gene flow by transient individuals in an otherwise sedentary population of box turtles (*Terrapene carolina triunguis*). Evolution 36:617–619.

Killebrew, F. C. 1975. Mitotic chromosomes of turtles. III. The Kinosternidae. Herpetologica 31:398–403.

———. 1976. An unusual basisphenoid in one specimen of *Graptemys flavimaculata*. Herpetol. Rev. 7:167–168.

———. 1977a. Mitotic chromosomes of turtles. IV. The Emydidae. Texas J. Sci. 29:245–253.

———. 1977b. Mitotic chromosomes of turtles. V. The Chelydridae. Southwest. Natur. 21:547–548.

———. 1977c. An extra costal in one specimen of *Graptemys flavimaculata* Cagle (Testudines, Emydidae). Southwest. Natur. 22:400–401.

———. 1979. Osteological variation between *Graptemys flavimaculata* and *Graptemys nigrinoda* (Testudines: Emydidae). Herpetologica 35:146–153.

Killebrew, F. C., T. L. James, and J. Bertl. 1984. *Graptemys versa* (Texas map turtle). USA: Texas. Herpetol. Rev. 15:77.

Killebrew, F. C., and R. R. McKown. 1978. Mitotic chromosomes of *Gopherus berlandieri* and *Kinixys belliana belliana* (Testudines, Testudinidae). Southwest. Natur. 23:162–164.

Killebrew, F. C., and D. Porter. 1989. *Pseudemys texana* (Texas river cooter). Size maximum. Herpetol. Rev. 20:70.

———. 1990. *Graptemys caglei* (Cagle's map turtle). Size. Herpetol. Rev. 21:92.

King, F. W. 1982. Historical review of the decline of the green turtle and the hawksbill. *In* Bjorndal, K. A., ed. Biology and conservation of sea turtles, 183–188. Smithsonian Institution Press, Washington, D.C.

King, F. W., and J. V. Griffo, Jr. 1958. A box turtle fatality apparently caused by *Sarcophaga cistudinis* larvae. Florida Entomol. 41:44.

Kingsmill, S. F., and N. Mrosovsky. 1982. Sea-finding behaviour of loggerhead hatchlings: The time course of transient circling following unilateral and asynchronous bilateral blindfolding. Brain, Behav. Evol. 20:29–42.

Kinney, J. L., and F. N. White. 1977. Oxidative cost of ventilation in a turtle, *Pseudemys floridana*. Resp. Physiol. 31:327–332.

Kinney, J. L., D. T. Matsuura, and F. N. White. 1977. Cardiorespiratory effects of temperature in the turtle, *Pseudemys floridana*. Resp. Physiol. 31:309–325.

Kirschvink, J. 1980. Magnetic material in turtles: A preliminary report and a request. Marine Turtle Newsl. (15):7–9.

Kiviat, E. 1978a. Bog turtle habitat ecology. Bull. Chicago Herpetol. Soc. 13:29–42.

———. 1978b. Vertebrate use of muskrat lodges and burrows. Estuaries 1:196–200.

———. 1980. A Hudson River tidemarsh snapping turtle population. Trans. Northeast. Sect. Wildl. Soc. 37:158–168.

Kizirian, D. A., W. K. King, and J. R. Dixon. 1990. *Graptemys versa* (Texas map turtle). Size maximum and diet. Herpetol. Rev. 21:60.

Klemens, M. W., and J. L. Warner. 1983. The status of *Clemmys muhlenbergii* (Schoepff) in Connecticut. Herpetol. Rev. 14:124–125.

Klicka, J., and I. Y. Mahmoud. 1973. Conversion of cholesterol to progesterone by turtle corpus luteum. Steroids 21:483–495.

———. 1977. The effects of hormones on the reproductive physiology of the painted turtle, *Chrysemys picta*. Gen. Comp. Endocrinol. 31:407–413.

———. 1978. Effect of mammalian LH on ascorbic acid depletion in turtle corpus luteum (Reptilia, Testudines, Testudinidae). J. Herpetol. 12:43–45.

Klima, E. F., and J. P. McVey. 1982. Headstarting the Kemp's ridley sea turtle, *Lepidochelys kempi*. *In* Bjorndal, K. A., ed. Biology and conservation of sea turtles, 481–487. Smithsonian Institution Press, Washington, D.C.

Klimstra, W. D. 1951. Notes on late summer snapping turtle movements. Herpetologica 7:140.

———. 1959a. Food habits of the cottonmouth in southern Illinois. Natur. Hist. Misc. (168):1–8.

———. 1959b. Foods of the racer, *Coluber constrictor,* in southern Illinois. Copeia 1959:210–214.

Klimstra, W. D., and F. Newsome. 1960. Some observations on the food coactions of the common box turtle, *Terrapene c. carolina*. Ecology 41:639–647.

Knight, J. L., and R. K. Loraine. 1986. Notes on turtle egg predation by *Lampropeltis getulus* (Linnaeus) (Reptilia: Colubridae) on the Savannah River Plant, South Carolina. Brimleyana (12):1–4.

Knight, T. W., J. A. Layfield, and R. J. Brooks. 1990. Nutritional status and mean selected temperature of hatchling snapping turtles (*Chelydra serpentina*): Is there a thermophilic response to feeding? Copeia 1990:1067–1072.

Koch, A. L., A. Carr, and D. W. Ehrenfeld. 1969. The problem of open-sea navigation: The migration of the green turtle to Ascension Island. J. Theoret. Biol. 22:163–179.

Koffler, B. R., R. A. Seigel, and M. T. Mendonça. 1978. The seasonal occurrence of leeches on the wood turtle, *Clemmys insculpta* (Reptilia, Testudines, Emydidae). J. Herpetol. 12:571–572.

Kofron, C. P. 1991. Aspects of ecology of the threatened ringed sawback turtle, *Graptemys oculifera*. Amphibia-Reptilia 12:161–168.

Kofron, C. P., and A. A. Schreiber. 1985. Ecology of two endangered aquatic turtles in Missouri: *Kinosternon flavescens* and *Emydoidea blandingii*. J. Herpetol. 19:27–40.

———. 1987. Observations on aquatic turtles in a northeastern Missouri marsh. Southwest. Natur. 32:517–521.

Kosh, R. J., and V. H. Hutchison. 1968. Daily rhythmicity of temperature tolerance in eastern painted turtles, *Chrysemys picta*. Copeia 1968:244–246.

Kozuch, L. 1989. *Clemmys guttata* (spotted turtle). USA: Louisiana. Herpetol. Rev. 20:76.

Kraemer, J. E., and R. Bell. 1980. Rain-induced mortality of eggs and hatchlings of loggerhead sea turtles (*Caretta caretta*) on the Georgia coast. Herpetologica 36:72–77.

Kraemer, J. E., and S. H. Bennett. 1981. Utilization of posthatching yolk in loggerhead sea turtles, *Caretta caretta*. Copeia 1981:406–411.

Kraemer, J. E., and J. I. Richardson. 1979. Volumetric reduction in nest contents of loggerhead sea turtles (*Caretta caretta*) (Reptilia, Testudines, Cheloniidae) on the Georgia coast. J. Herpetol. 13:255–260.

Kramer, D. C. 1973. Geophagy in *Terrepene* [sic] *ornata ornata* Agassiz. J. Herpetol. 7:138–139.

Kramer, M. 1984. *Pseudemys nelsoni* (Florida red-bellied turtle). Behavior. Herpetol. Rev. 15:113–114.

———. 1986. Field studies on a freshwater Florida turtle, *Pseudemys nelsoni*. *In* Drickamer, L. C., ed. Behavioral ecology and population biology, 29–34. I. E. C. Univ. Paul Sabatier, Toulouse, France.

———. 1987. Why do juvenile turtles (*Pseudemys nelsoni*) exhibit courtship behavior? Progr. Jt. Meet. SSAR–Herpetol. League, Vera Cruz, Mexico, 100.

———. 1989. Individual discrimination in juveniles of two turtles, *Pseudemys nelsoni* and *Pseudemys floridana* (Chelonia, Emydidae). Biol. Behav. 14:148–156.

Kramer, M., and U. Fritz. 1989. Courtship of the turtle, *Pseudemys nelsoni*. J. Herpetol. 23:84–86.

Kraus, D. R., and D. C. Jackson. 1980. Temperature effects on ventilation and acid-base balance of the green turtle. Amer. J. Physiol. 239:R254–R258.

Krefft, G. 1951. *Deirochelys reticularia* (Latreille), eine wenig bekante Schmuckschildkröte der USA. Aquar. u. Terrar. Z. (Stuttgart) 4:157–160.

Kushlan, J. A. 1986. Atlantic loggerhead turtle nesting status in southwest Florida. Herpetol. Rev. 17:51–52.

Kushlan, J. A., and M. S. Kushlan. 1980. Everglades alligator nests: Nesting sites for marsh reptiles. Copeia 1980:930–932.

Kushlan, J. A., and F. J. Mazzotti. 1984. Environmental effects on a coastal population of gopher tortoises. J. Herpetol. 18:231–239.

Lacépède, B. G. E. 1788. Histoire naturelle des quadrupèdes ovipares et des serpens, vol. 1 [Ovipares]. 18 + 651 pp. Paris.

Laemmerzahl, A. F. 1990. Variation in the spotted turtle, *Clemmys guttata*. Master's thesis, George Mason University, Fairfax, Virginia.

Lagler, K. F. 1943. Food habits and economic relations of the turtles of Michigan with special reference to fish management. Amer. Midl. Natur. 29:257–312.

Lagler, K. F., and V. C. Applegate. 1943. Relationship between the length and the weight in the snapping turtle *Chelydra serpentina* Linnaeus. Amer. Natur. 77:476–478.

Lago, P. K. 1991. A survey of the arthropods associated with gopher tortoise burrows in Mississippi. Entomol. Newsl. 102:1–13.

Lagveux, C. L. 1991. Ecomomic analysis of sea turtle eggs in a coastal community on the Pacific Coast of Honduras. *In* Robinson, J. G., and K. H. Redford, eds. Neotropical wildlife use and conservation, 136–144. University of Chicago Press.

Lahanas, P. N. 1982. Aspects of the life history of the southern black-knobbed sawback, *Graptemys nigrinoda delticola* Folkerts and Mount. Master's thesis, Auburn University, Auburn, Alabama. 293 pp.

———. 1986. *Graptemys nigrinoda*. Catalog. Amer. Amphib. Rept. 396:1–2.

Lamb, T. 1983a. On the problematic identification of *Kinosternon* (Testudines: Kinosternidae) in Georgia, with new state localities for *Kinosternon bauri*. Georgia J. Sci. 41:115–120.

———. 1983b. The striped mud turtle (*Kinosternon bauri*) in South Carolina: A confirmation through multivariate character analysis. Herpetologica 39:383–390.

Lamb, T., and J. C. Avise. 1992. Molecular and population genetic aspects of mitochondrial DNA variability in the diamondback terrapin, *Malaclemys terrapin*. J. Heredity. 83:262–269.

Lamb, T., J. C. Avise, and J. W. Gibbons. 1989. Phylogeographic patterns in mitochondrial DNA of the desert tortoise (*Xerobates agassizi*), and evolutionary relationships among the North American gopher tortoises. Evolution 43:76–87.

Lamb, T., J. W. Bickham, J. W. Gibbons, M. J. Smolen, and S. McDowell. 1991. Genetic damage in a population of slider turtles (*Trachemys scripta*) inhabiting a radioactive reservoir. Arch. Environ. Contam. Toxicol. 20:138–142.

Lamb, T., and J. D. Congdon. 1985. Ash content:

Relationships to flexible and rigid eggshell types of turtles. J. Herpetol. 19:527–530.

Lamb, T., and J. Lovich. 1990. Morphometric validation of the striped mud turtle (*Kinosternon baurii*) in the Carolinas and Virginia. Copeia 1990:613–618.

Lambie, I. 1983. Two tagging records from Trinidad. Marine Turtle Newsl. (24):17.

Landers, J. L., J. A. Garner, and W. A. McRae. 1980. Reproduction of gopher tortoises (*Gopherus polyphemus*) in southwestern Georgia. Herpetologica 36:353–361.

Landers, J. L., W. A. McRae, and J. A. Garner. 1982. Growth and maturity of the gopher tortoise in southwestern Georgia. Bull. Florida St. Mus. Biol. Sci. 27:81–110.

Landers, J. L., and D. W. Speake. 1980. Management needs of sandhill reptiles in southern Georgia. Proc. Conf. Southeast. Assoc. Fish Wildl. Agencies 34:515–529.

Landry, A. M., Jr. 1989. Morphometry of captive-reared Kemp's ridley sea turtles. *In* Calliouet, C. W., Jr., and A. M. Landry, Jr., eds. Proceedings of the First International Symposium on Kemp's Ridley Sea Turtle Biology, Conservation and Management, 220–231. Texas A & M Univ. Sea Grant College Progr. Spec. Publ.-89 (105).

Landry, J. L. 1979. A bibliography of the bog turtle, *Clemmys muhlenbergii* (biology, ecology and distribution). Smithsonian Herpetol. Inform. Serv. (44):1–21.

Langille, B. L., and B. Crisp. 1980. Temperature dependence of blood viscosity in frogs and turtles: Effect on heat exchange with environment. Amer. J. Physiol. 239:R248–R253.

Lapennas, G. N., and P. L. Lutz. 1982. Oxygen affinity of sea turtle blood. Resp. Physiol. 48:59–74.

Lardie, G. E., and R. L. Lardie. 1980. Notes on hatching eggs of common snapping turtle after natural underwater deposition. Bull. Oklahoma Herpetol. Soc. 4:71.

Lardie, R. L. 1965. Pugnacious behavior in the softshell *Trionyx spinifer pallidus* and implications of territoriality. Herpetologica 20:281–284.

———. 1973a. Notes on eggs and young of *Trionyx ferox* (Schneider). J. Herpetol. 7:377–378.

———. 1973b. Notes on courtship, eggs, and young of the Florida red-bellied turtle, *Chrysemys nelsoni*. HISS News-J. 1:183–184.

———. 1975a. Courtship and mating behavior in the yellow mud turtle, *Kinosternon flavescens flavescens*. J. Herpetol. 9:223–227.

———. 1975b. Notes on eggs and young of *Clemmys marmorata marmorata* (Baird and Girard). Occ. Pap. Mus. Natur. Hist. Univ. Puget Sound (47):654.

———. 1975c. Observations on reproduction in *Kinosternon*. J. Herpetol. 9:260–264.

———. 1976. Incubation of turtle eggs from a road kill. Bull. Oklahoma Herpetol. Soc. 1:23.

———. 1978. Additional observation on courtship and mating in the plains yellow mud turtle, *Kinosternon flavescens flavescens*. Bull. Oklahoma Herpetol. Soc. 3:70–72.

———. 1979. Eggs and young of the plains yellow mud turtle. Bull. Oklahoma Herpetol. Soc. 4:24–32.

———. 1980. Winter activity of *Chrysemys scripta elegans* (Wied-Neuwied) in north central Texas. Bull. Oklahoma Herpetol. Soc. 4:72–76.

———. 1983a. Aggressive interactions and territoriality in the yellow mud turtle, *Kinosternon flavescens flavescens* (Agassiz). Bull. Oklahoma Herpetol. Soc. 8:68–83.

———. 1983b. Aggressive interactions among melanistic males of the red-eared slider, *Pseudemys scripta elegans* (Wied). Bull. Oklahoma Herpetol. Soc. 8:105–117.

Lauder, G. V., and T. Prendergast. 1992. Kinematics of aquatic prey capture in the snapping turtle *Chelydra serpentina*. J. Exp. Biol. 164:55–78.

Lawler, A. R., and J. A. Musick. 1972. Sand beach hibernation by a northern diamondback terrapin, *Malaclemys terrapin terrapin* (Schoepff). Copeia 1972:389–390.

Lawler, H. E. 1977. The status of *Drymarchon corias couperi* (Holbrook), the eastern indigo snake, in the southeastern United States. Herpetol. Rev. 8:76–79.

Layne, J. N. 1952. Behavior of captive loggerhead turtles, *Caretta c. caretta* (Linnaeus). Copeia 1952:115.

———. 1989. Comparison of survival rates and movements of relocated and resident gopher tortoises in a south central Florida population. *In* Diemer, J. E., et al., eds. Proceedings Gopher Tortoise Relocation Symposium, 73–79. Florida Game and Fresh Water Fish Commission, Nongame Wildlife Program Technical Report No. 5. Tallahassee, Florida.

Lazell, J. D., Jr. 1976. This broken archipelago: Cape Cod and the islands, amphibians and reptiles. Demeter Press, New York. 260 pp.

———. 1979. Diamondback terrapins at Sandy Neck. Aquasphere, J. New England Aquarium 13:28–31.

———. 1980. New England waters: Critical habitat for marine turtles. Copeia 1980:290–295.

Lazell, J. D., Jr., and P. J. Auger. 1981. Predation on diamondback terrapin (*Malaclemys terrapin*) eggs by dunegrass (*Ammophila breviligulata*). Copeia 1981:723–724.

Leary, T. R. 1957. A schooling of leatherback turtles, *Dermochelys coriacea coriacea,* on the Texas coast. Copeia 1957:232.

LeBuff, C. R., Jr. 1974. Unusual nesting relocation in the loggerhead turtle, *Caretta caretta*. Herpetologica 30:29–31.

———. 1990. The loggerhead turtle in the eastern Gulf of Mexico. *Caretta* Research, Inc., Sanibel, Florida. 236 pp.

LeBuff, C. R., Jr., and R. W. Beatty. 1971. Some aspects of nesting of the loggerhead turtle, *Caretta caretta caretta* (Linne), on the Gulf Coast of Florida. Herpetologica 27:153–156.

Le Conte, J. 1830. Description of the species of North American tortoises. Ann. Lyceum Natur. Hist. New York 3:91–131.

———. 1854. Description of four new species of *Kinosternum*. Proc. Acad. Natur. Sci. Philadelphia 7:180–190.

Lee, D. S., R. Franz, and R. A. Sanderson. 1975. A note on the feeding habits of male Barbour's map turtles. Florida Field Natur. 3:45–46.

Lee, D. S., and W. M. Palmer. 1981. Records of leatherback turtles, *Dermochelys coriacea* (Linnaeus), and other marine turtles in North Carolina waters. Brimleyana (5):95–106.

Legere, R. H. 1989. Mid-winter spotted turtle emergence in Maryland. Notes from Northern Ohio Assoc. Herpetol. 16(6):11–14.

Legler, J. M. 1955. Observations on the sexual behavior of captive turtles. Lloydia 18:95–99.

———. 1956. A social relationship between snapping and painted turtles. Trans. Kansas Acad. Sci. 59:461–462.

———. 1958. The Texas slider (*Pseudemys floridana texana*) in New Mexico. Southwest. Natur. 3:230–231.

———. 1960a. Natural history of the ornate box turtle, *Terrapene ornata ornata* Agassiz. Univ. Kansas Publ. Mus. Natur. Hist. 11:527–669.

———. 1960b. Remarks on the natural history of the Big Bend slider, *Pseudemys scripta gaigeae* Hartweg. Herpetologica 16:139–140.

———. 1990. The genus *Pseudemys* in Mesoamerica: Taxonomy, distribution, and origins. *In* Gibbons, J. W., ed. Life history and ecology of the slider turtle, 82–105. Smithsonian Institution Press, Washington, D.C.

Legler, W. K. 1971. Radiotelemetric observations of cardiac rates in the ornate box turtle. Copeia 1971:760–761.

Lehmann, H. 1984. Ein Zwillingsschlupf bei *Sternotherus minor minor* (Agassiz, 1857). Salamandra 20:192–196.

Lemkau, P. J. 1970. Movements of the box turtle, *Terrapene c. carolina* (Linnaeus) in unfamiliar territory. Copeia 1970:781–783.

Lenarz, M. S., N. B. Frazer, M. S. Ralston, and R. B. Mast. 1981. Seven nests recorded for the loggerhead turtle (*Caretta caretta*) in one season. Herpetol. Rev. 12:9.

Lescure, J., J. Rimblot, J. Fretey, S. Renous, and C. Pieau. 1985. Influence de la temperature d'incubation des oeufs sur la sex-ratio des nouveaux-nes de la tortue luth, *Dermochelys coriacea*. Bull. Soc. Zool. Fr. 110:355–359.

Lestrel, P. E., B. G. Sarnat, and E. G. McNabb. 1989. Carapace growth of the turtle *Chrysemys scripta:* a longitudinal study of shape using Fourier analysis. Anat. Anz., Jena 168:135–143.

Le Sueur, C. A. 1817. An account of the American species of tortoise, not noticed in the systems. J. Acad. Natur. Sci. Philadelphia 1:86–88.

———. 1827. Note sur deux espèces de tortues du genre *Trionyx* Gffr. St. H. Mém. Mus. Hist. Nat. Paris 15:257–268.

Leuck, B. E., and C. C. Carpenter. 1981. Shell variation in a population of three-toed box turtles (*Terrapene carolina triunguis*). J. Herpetol. 15:53–58.

Levell, J. P. 1985. Some observations on the mating behavior of *Terrapene carolina triunguis* in captivity. Bull. Chicago Herpetol. Soc. 20:40–41.

Levin, T. 1992. Hulks roaming the seas: Warm-blooded leatherback. Reptile & Amphib. Mag. Nov./Dec., 22–24, 26–27.

Lewis, G. B. 1940. The Cayman Islands and marine turtle. Bull. Inst. Jamaica 2 (appendix):56–65.

Lewis, S. H., C. Ryder, and K. Benirschke. 1992. Omphalopagus twins in *Chelonia mydas*. Herpetol. Rev. 23:69–70.

Licht, P. 1972. Actions of mammalian pituitary gonadotropins (FSH and LH) in reptiles. II. Turtles. Gen. Comp. Endocrinol. 19:282–289.

———. 1980. Evolutionary and functional aspects of pituitary gonadotropins in the green turtle, *Chelonia mydas*. Amer. Zool. 20:565–574.

———. 1982. Endocrine patterns in the reproductive cycle of turtles. Herpetologica 38:51–61.

Licht, P., G. L. Breitenbach, and J. D. Congdon. 1985a. Seasonal cycles in testicular activity, gonadotropin, and thyroxine in the painted turtle, *Chrysemys picta*, under natural conditions. Gen. Comp. Endocrinol. 59:130–139.

Licht, P., P. Khorrami-Yaghoobi, and D. A. Porter. 1985b. Effects of gonadectomy and steroid treatment on plasma gonadotropins and the response of superfused pituitaries to gonadotropin-releasing hormone in the turtle *Sternotherus odoratus*. Gen. Comp. Endocrinol. 60:441–449.

Licht, P., D. W. Owens, K. Cliffton, and C. Peñaflores.

1982. Changes in LH and progesterone associated with the nesting cycle and ovulation in the olive ridley sea turtle, *Lepidochelys olivacea*. Gen. Comp. Endocrinol. 48:247–253.

Licht, P., and H. Papkoff. 1985. Reevaluation of the relative activities of the pituitary glycoprotein hormones (follicle-stimulating hormone, luteinizing hormone, and thyrotrophin) from the green sea turtle, *Chelonia mydas*. Gen. Comp. Endocrinol. 58:443–451.

Licht, P., and D. A. Porter. 1985a. LH secretion in response to gonadotropin releasing hormone (Gm RH) by superfused pituitaries from two species of turtles. Gen. Comp. Endocrinol. 59:442–448.

———. 1985b. *In vivo* and *in vitro* responses to gonadotropin releasing hormone in the turtle, *Chrysemys picta*, in relation to sex and reproductive stage. Gen. Comp. Endocrinol. 60:75–85.

Licht, P., W. Rainey, and K. Cliffton. 1980. Serum gonadotropin and steroids associated with breeding activities in the green sea turtle, *Chelonia mydas* II. Mating and nesting in natural populations. Gen. Comp. Endocrinol. 40:116–122.

Licht, P., J. Wood, D. W. Owens, and F. Wood. 1979. Serum gonodotropins and steroids associated with breeding activities in the green sea turtle *Chelonia mydas* I. Captive animals. Gen. Comp. Endocrinol. 39:274–289.

Licht, P., J. F. Wood, and F. E. Wood. 1985c. Annual and diurnal cycles in plasma testosterone and thyroxine in the male green sea turtle *Chelonia mydas*. Gen. Comp. Endocrinol. 57:335–344.

Limpus, C. J. 1980. Observations on the hawksbill turtle (*Eretmochelys imbricata*) nesting along the Great Barrier Reef. Herpetologica 36:265–271.

———. 1984. A benthic feeding record from netritic waters for the leathery turtle (*Dermochelys coriacea*). Copeia 1984:552–553.

———. 1985. A study of the loggerhead sea turtle, *Caretta caretta*, in eastern Australia. Ph.D. dissertation, University of Queensland, St. Lucia, Australia.

———. 1987. A turtle fossil on Raine Island, Great Barrier Reef. Search 18:254–256.

Limpus, C. J., V. Baker, and J. D. Miller. 1979. Movement induced mortality of loggerhead eggs. Herpetologica 35:335–338.

Limpus, C. J., and N. C. McLachlan. 1979. Observations on the leatherback turtle, *Dermochelys coriacea* (L.), in Australia. Australian Wildl. Res. 6:105–116.

Limpus, C. J., J. D. Miller, and P. Reed. 1982. Intersexuality in a loggerhead sea turtle, *Caretta caretta*. Herpetol. Rev. 13:32–33.

Limpus, C. J., P. C. Reed, and J. D. Miller. 1983. Islands

and turtles: The influence of choice of nesting beach on sex ratio. *In* Baker, J. T., R. M. Carter, P. W. Sammarco, and K. P. Stark, eds. Proceedings Inaugural Great Barrier Reef Conference, August 28–September 2, 1983, 397–402. James Cook University Press, Townsville, Queenland, Australia.

Lin, Z., Z. Wang, and K. Pan. 1988. The karyotypes of *Trionyx steindachneri*. Zool. Res. (China) 9:161–164.

Linck, M. H., J. A. DePari, B. O. Butler, and T. E. Graham. 1989. Nesting behavior of the turtle, *Emydoidea blandingi,* in Massachusetts. J. Herpetol. 23:442–444.

Lindeman, P. V. 1989. *Chrysemys picta belli* (western painted turtle). Egg retention. Herpetol. Rev. 20:69.

———. 1990. Closed and open model estimates of abundance and tests of model assumption for two populations of the turtle, *Chrysemys picta*. J. Herpetol. 24:78–81.

———. 1991. Survivorship of overwintering hatchling painted turtles, *Chrysemys picta,* in northern Idaho. Can. Field-Natur. 105:263–266.

———. 1992. Nest-site fixity among painted turtles (*Chrysemys picta*) in northern Idaho. Northwest. Natur. 73:27–30.

Lindeman, P. V., and F. W. Rabe. 1990. Effect of drought on the western painted turtle, *Chrysemys picta belli,* in a small wetland ecosystem. J. Freshwater Ecol. 5:359–364.

Liner, E. A. 1954. The herpetofauna of Lafayette, Terrebonne, and Vermilion parishes, Louisiana. Proc. Louisiana Acad. Sci. 17:65–85.

Linley, T. A. 1987. Proximate organic composition and energy content of eggs and hatchlings of the gopher tortoise, *Gopherus polyphemus* (Daudin). Master's thesis, University of South Florida, Tampa.

Linnaeus, C. 1758. Systema naturae. 10th ed. Holmiae, Sweden. 1:1–824.

Linnaeus, C. 1766. Systema naturae. 12th ed. Halae Magdeborgicae, Sweden. 1:1–532.

Linsdale, J. M., and J. L. Gressitt. 1937. Soft-shelled turtles in the Colorado River Basin. Copeia 1937: 222–225.

Lips, K. R. 1991. Vertebrates associated with tortoise (*Gopherus polyphemus*) burrows in four habitats in south-central Florida. J. Herpetol. 25:477–481.

Lipske, M. 1979. Trawlers vs. turtles. Defenders 54:380–385.

Little, R. B. 1973. Variation in the plastral scutellation of *Graptemys pulchra* (Reptilia, Chelonia, Emydidae). ASB Bull. 20:65–66.

Litwin, S. C. 1981. *Chelonia mydas mydas* (green turtle). Nesting. Herpetol. Rev. 12:81.

Lockwood, S. F., B. S. Holland, J. W. Bickham, B. G. Hanks, and J. J. Bull. 1991. Intraspecific genome size variation in a turtle (*Trachemys scripta*) exhibiting temperature-dependent sex determination. Can. J. Zool. 69:2306–2310.

Lofts, B., and H. W. Tsui. 1977. Histological and histochemical changes in the gonads and epididymides of the male soft-shelled turtle *Trionyx sinensis*. J. Zool. (London) 181:57–68.

Lohmann, K. J. 1991. Magnetic orientation by hatchling loggerhead sea turtles (*Caretta caretta*). J. Exp. Biol. 155:37–49.

———. 1992. How sea turtles navigate. Sci. Amer. 266(1):82–88.

Lohmann, K. J., M. Salmon, and J. Wyneken. 1990. Functional autonomy of land and sea orientation systems in sea turtle hatchlings. Biol. Bull. 179:214–218.

Lohmeier, L. 1988. Turtle in trouble. Animal Kingdom 91(6):26–33.

Lohoefener, R. R., W. Hoggard, C. L. Roden, K. D. Mullin, and C. M. Rodgers. 1988. Distribution and relative abundance of surfaced sea turtles in the north-central Gulf of Mexico: Spring and fall 1987. *In* Schroeder, B. A., ed. Proceedings of the Eighth Annual Workshop on Sea Turtle Conservation and Biology, 47–50. NOAA-TM-NMFS-SEFC-214.

Lohoefener, R., and L. Lohmeier. 1981. Comparison of gopher tortoise (*Gopherus polyphemus*) habitats in young slash pine and old longleaf pine areas of southern Mississippi. J. Herpetol. 15:239–242.

———. 1986. Experiments with gopher tortoise (*Gopherus polyphemus*) relocation in southern Mississippi. Herpetol. Rev. 17:37, 39–40.

Loncke, D. J., and M. E. Obbard. 1977. Tag success, dimensions, clutch size and nesting site fidelity for the snapping turtle, *Chelydra serpentina* (Reptilia, Testudines, Chelydridae) in Algonquin Park, Ontario, Canada. J. Herpetol. 11:243–244.

Long, D. R. 1984. Inter-specific comparisons of growth relationships in chelonians. British J. Herpetol. 6:405–407.

———. 1985. Lipid utilization during reproduction in female *Kinosternon flavescens*. Herpetologica 41:58–65.

———. 1986a. Clutch formation in the turtle, *Kinosternon flavescens* (Testudines: Kinosternidae). Southwest. Natur. 31:1–8.

———. 1986b. Lipid content and delayed emergence of hatchling yellow mud turtles. Southwest. Natur. 31:244–246.

Long, D. R., and F. L. Rose. 1989. Pelvic girdle size relationships in three turtle species. J. Herpetol. 23:315–318.

Loveridge, A., and E. E. Williams. 1957. Revision of the African tortoises and turtles of the suborder Cryptodira. Bull. Mus. Comp. Zool. Harvard 115:163–557.

Lovich, J. E. 1982. *Terrapene carolina carolina* (eastern box turtle). USA: Pennsylvania. Herpetol. Rev. 13:25.

———. 1985. *Graptemys pulchra*. Catalog. Amer. Amphib. Rept. 360:1–2.

———. 1988a. Geographic variation in the seasonal activity cycle of spotted turtles, *Clemmys guttata*. J. Herpetol. 22:482–485.

———. 1988b. Aggressive basking behavior in eastern painted turtles (*Chrysemys picta picta*). Herpetologica 44:197–202.

———. 1989a. The spotted turtles of Cedar Bog: Historical analysis of a declining population. *In* Glotzhober, R. C., A. Kochman, and W. T. Schultz, eds. Cedar Bog Symposium II, 23–28. Ohio Historical Society, Columbus, Ohio.

———. 1989b. Another exotic turtle record for Hawaii? 'Elepaio (J. Hawaii Audubon Soc.). 49:86–87.

———. 1990a. Spring movement patterns of two radio-tagged male spotted turtles. Brimleyana (16):67–71.

———. 1990b. Gaping behavior in basking eastern painted turtles. J. Pennsylvania Acad. Sci. 64:78–80.

———. 1993. Restoration and revegetation of degraded habitat as a management tool in recovery of the threatened desert tortoise. Contract Report prepared for California Dept. Parks and Recreation, Off-Highway Motor Vehicle Recreation Div. U.S. Dept. Interior, Bureau of Land Management, California Desert District. 228 pp.

Lovich, J. E., and C. H. Ernst. 1989. Variation in the plastral formulae of selected turtles with comments on taxonomic utility. Copeia 1989:304–318.

Lovich, J. E., C. H. Ernst, and J. F. McBreen. 1990a. Growth, maturity, and sexual dimorphism in the wood turtle, *Clemmys insculpta*. Can. J. Zool. 68:672–677.

Lovich, J. E., W. R. Garstka, and W. E. Cooper, Jr. 1990b. Female participation in courtship behavior of the turtle *Trachemys scripta*. J. Herpetol. 24:422–424.

Lovich, J. E., W. R. Garstka, and C. J. McCoy. 1990c. The development and significance of melanism in the slider turtle. *In* Gibbons, J. W., ed. Life history and ecology of the slider turtle, 233–254. Smithsonian Institution Press, Washington, D.C.

Lovich, J. E., and J. W. Gibbons. 1990. Age at maturity influences adult sex ratio in the turtle *Malaclemys terrapin*. Oikos 59:126–134.

———. 1992. A review of techniques for quantifying sexual size dimorphism. Growth, Develop. Aging 56:269–281.

Lovich, J. E., D. W. Herman, and K. M. Fahey. 1992. Seasonal activity and movements of bog turtles (*Clemmys muhlenbergii*) in North Carolina. Copeia 1992:1107–1111.

Lovich, J. E., and T. R. Jaworski. 1988. Annotated checklist of amphibians and reptiles reported from Cedar Bog, Ohio. Ohio J. Sci. 88:139–143.

Lovich, J. E., A. F. Laemmerzahl, C. H. Ernst, and J. F. McBreen. 1991a. Relationships among turtles of the genus *Clemmys* (Reptilia, Testudines, Emydidae) as suggested by plastron scute morphology. Zool. Scripta 20:425–429.

Lovich, J. E., and C. J. McCoy. 1992. Review of the *Graptemys pulchra* group (Reptilia: Testudines: Emydidae), with descriptions of two new species. Ann. Carnegie Mus. Natur. Hist. 61:293–315.

———. In press. *Graptemys pulchra*, Alabama map turtle. *In* Pritchard, P. C. H., and A. Rhodin, eds. Conservation of freshwater turtles. IUCN Species Survival Commission.

Lovich, J. E., A. D. Tucker, D. E. Kling, J. W. Gibbons, and T. D. Zimmerman. 1991b. Behavior of hatchling diamondback terrapins (*Malaclemys terrapin*) released in a South Carolina salt marsh. Herpetol. Rev. 22:81–83.

Lowell, W. R. 1990. Aerobic metabolism and swimming energetics of the painted turtle, *Chrysemys picta*. Exp. Biol. 48:349–355.

Lucey, E. C. 1974. Heart rate and physiological thermoregulation in a basking turtle, *Pseudemys scripta elegans*. Comp. Biochem. Physiol. 48A:471–482.

Lucey, E. C., and E. W. House. 1977. Effect of temperature on the pattern of lung ventilation and on the ventilation-circulation relationship in the turtle, *Pseudemys scripta*. Comp. Biochem. Physiol. 57A: 239–243.

Luckenbach, R. A. 1982. Ecology and management of the desert tortoise (*Gopherus agassizii*) in California. *In* Bury, R. B., ed. North American tortoises: Conservation and ecology, 1–37. U.S. Fish Wildl. Serv. Wildl. Res. Rept. (12).

Lund, F. 1986. Nest production and nesting-site tenacity of the loggerhead turtle, *Caretta caretta*, on Jupiter Island, Florida. Master's thesis, University of Florida, Gainesville. 32 pp.

Lund, P. F. 1985. Hawksbill turtle (*Eretmochelys imbricata*) nesting on the east coast of Florida. J. Herpetol. 19:164–166.

Lutcavage, M. E., P. G. Bushnell, and D. R. Jones. 1990. Oxygen transport in the leatherback sea turtle *Dermochelys coriacea*. Physiol. Zool. 63:1012–1024.

————. 1992. Oxygen stores and aerobic metabolism in the leatherback sea turtle. Can. J. Zool. 70:348–351.

Lutcavage, M., and P. L. Lutz. 1986. Metabolic rate and food energy requirements of the leatherback sea turtle, *Dermochelys coriacea*. Copeia 1986:796–798.

————. 1991. Voluntary diving metabolism and ventilation in the loggerhead sea turtle. J. Exp. Mar. Biol. Ecol. 147:287–296.

Lutcavage, M., P. L. Lutz, and H. Baier. 1987. Gas exchange in the loggerhead sea turtle *Caretta caretta*. J. Exp. Biol. 131:365–372.

————. 1989. Respiratory mechanics of the loggerhead sea turtle, *Caretta caretta*. Resp. Physiol. 76:13–24.

Lutcavage, M., and J. A. Musick. 1985. Aspects of the biology of sea turtles in Virginia. Copeia 1985:449–456.

Lutz, P. L. 1989. Interaction between hypometabolism and acid-base balance. Can. J. Zool. 67:3018–3023.

Lutz, P. L., and T. B. Bentley. 1985. Respiratory physiology of diving in the sea turtle. Copeia 1985:671–679.

Lutz, P. L., A. Bergey, and M. Bergey. 1989. Effects of temperature on gas exchange and acid-base balance in the sea turtle *Caretta caretta* at rest and during routine activity. J. Exp. Biol. 144:155–169.

Lutz, P. L., and A. Dunbar-Cooper. 1987. Variations in the blood chemistry of the loggerhead sea turtle, *Caretta caretta*. Fish. Bull. 85:37–43.

Lutz, P. L., and G. N. Lapennas. 1982. Effects of pH, CO_2 and organic phosphates on oxygen affinity of sea turtle hemoglobins. Resp. Physiol. 48:75–87.

Lutz, P. L., and M. Lutcavage. 1989. The effects of petroleum on sea turtles: Applicability to Kemp's ridley. *In* Calliouet, C. W., Jr., and A. M. Landry, Jr., eds. Proceedings of the First International Symposium on Kemp's Ridley Sea Turtle Biology, Conservation and Management, 52–54. Texas A & M Univ. Sea Grant College Progr. Spec. Publ.-89 (105).

Lyons, D. J. 1972. New animals for Maryland–eastern spiny soft-shelled turtle. Maryland Conserv. 48(4): 22–25.

MacAskie, I. B., and C. R. Forrester. 1962. Pacific leatherback turtles (*Dermochelys*) off the coast of British Columbia. Copeia 1962:646.

MacCulloch, R. D. 1981a. Variation in the shell of *Chrysemys picta belli* from southern Saskatchewan. J. Herpetol. 15:181–185.

————. 1981b. Leech parasitism on the western painted turtle, *Chrysemys picta belli*, in Saskatchewan. J. Parasitol. 67:128–129.

MacCulloch, R. D., and D. M. Secoy. 1983a. Movement in a river population of *Chrysemys picta bellii* in southern Saskatchewan. J. Herpetol. 17:283–285.

————. 1983b. Demography, growth, and food of western painted turtles, *Chrysemys picta bellii* (Gray), from southern Saskatchewan. Can. J. Zool. 61:1499–1509.

MacCulloch, R. D., and W. F. Weller. 1988. Some aspects of reproduction in a Lake Erie population of Blanding's turtle, *Emydoidea blandingii*. Can. J. Zool. 66:2317–2319.

MacDonald, L. A., and H. R. Mushinsky. 1988. Foraging ecology of the gopher tortoise, *Gopherus polyphemus*, in a sandhill habitat. Herpetologica 44:345–353.

Maginniss, L. A., S. S. Tapper, and L. S. Miller. 1983. Effect of chronic cold and submergence on blood oxygen transport in the turtle, *Chrysemys picta*. Resp. Physiol. 53:15–29.

Mahmoud, I. Y. 1967. Courtship behavior and sexual maturity in four species of kinosternid turtles. Copeia 1967:314–319.

————. 1968a. Nesting behavior in the western painted turtle, *Chrysemys picta bellii*. Herpetologica 24:158–162.

————. 1968b. Feeding behavior in kinosternid turtles. Herpetologica 24:300–305.

————. 1969. Comparative ecology of the kinosternid turtles of Oklahoma. Southwest. Natur. 14:31–66.

Mahmoud, I. Y., A. E. Colás, M. J. Woller, and R. V. Cyrus. 1986. Cytoplasmic progesterone receptors in uterine tissue of the snapping turtle (*Chelydra serpentina*). J. Endocrinol. 109:385–392.

Mahmoud, I. Y., and R. V. Cyrus. 1992. The testicular cycle of the common snapping turtle, *Chelydra serpentina*, in Wisconsin. Herpetologica 48:193–201.

Mahmoud, I. Y., R. V. Cyrus, T. M. Bennett, M. J. Woller, and D. M. Montag. 1985. Ultrastructural changes in testes of the snapping turtle, *Chelydra serpentina* in relation to plasma testosterone ;GD^5-3β-hydroxysteroid dehydrogenase, and cholesterol. Gen. Comp. Endocrinol. 57:454–464.

Mahmoud, I. Y., R. V. Cyrus, and D. L. Wright. 1987. The effect of arginine, vasotocin and ovarian steroids on uterine contractility in the snapping turtle, *Chelydra serpentina*. Comp. Biochem. Physiol. 86A:559–564.

Mahmoud, I. Y., G. L. Hess, and J. Klicka. 1973. Normal embryonic stages of the western painted turtle, *Chrysemys picta belli*. J. Morphol. 141:269–280.

Mahmoud, I. Y., and J. Klicka. 1972. Seasonal gonadal changes in kinosternid turtles. J. Herpetol. 6:183–189.

————. 1975. Extra-uterine egg migration in a snapping turtle, *Chelydra serpentina serpentina*. J. Herpetol. 9:242–243.

Mahmoud, I. Y., and N. Lavenda. 1969. Establishment

and eradication of food preferences in red-eared turtles. Copeia 1969:298–300.

Major, P. D. 1975. Density of snapping turtles, *Chelydra serpentina* in western West Virginia. Herpetologica 31:332–335.

Makino, S. 1952. The chromosomes of the sea turtle, *Chelonia japonica,* with evidence of female heterogamety. Ann. Zool. (Japan) 25:250–257.

Makris, V., and A. J. Rotermund, Jr. 1989. High energy organophosphate levels in the myocardia of cold acclimated and cold-hypoxic freshwater turtles, *Chrysemys picta.* Comp. Biochem. Physiol. 92A:259–262.

Manchester, D., Sr. 1982. Redeared sliders in Pennsylvania. Testudo 2(1):27–30.

Manns, B. 1969. Notes on *Clemmys guttata* as a scavenger in a Parksville, Maryland pond. Bull. Maryland Herpetol. Soc. 5:57.

Manton, M., A. Karr, and D. W. Ehrenfeld. 1972a. Chemoreception in the migratory sea turtle, *Chelonia mydas.* Biol. Bull. 143:184–195.

———. 1972b. An operant method for the study of chemoreception in the green turtle, *Chelonia mydas.* Brain, Behav. Evol. 5:188–201.

Manzella, S. A., and C. T. Fontaine. 1988. Loggerhead sea turtle travels from Padre Island, Texas to the mouth of the Adriatic Sea. Marine Turtle Newsl. (42):7.

Manzella, S. A., and J. A. Williams. 1992. The distribution of Kemp's ridley sea turtle (*Lepidochelys kempi*) along the Texas coast: An atlas. NOAA Tech. Rept. NMFS 110. 52 pp.

Manzella, S., J. Williams, B. Schroeder, and W. Teas. 1991. Juvenile head-started Kemp's ridleys found in floating grass mats. Marine Turtle Newsl. (52):5–6.

Marchand, L. J. 1942. A contribution to a knowledge of the natural history of certain freshwater turtles. Master's thesis, University of Florida, Gainesville. 83 pp.

———. 1944. Notes on the courtship of a Florida terrapin. Copeia 1944:191–192.

———. 1945. The individual range of some Florida turtles. Copeia 1945:75–77.

Mares, M. A. 1971. Coprophagy in the Texas tortoise, *Gopherus berlandieri.* Texas J. Sci. 23:300–301.

Marion, K. R. 1986. Alabama map turtle. *In* Mount, R. H., ed. Vertebrate animals of Alabama in need of special attention, 50–52. Auburn University, Auburn, Alabama.

Marion, K. R., W. A. Cox, and C. H. Ernst. 1984. *Sternotherus depressus* (flattened musk turtle). Coloration. Herpetol. Rev. 15:51.

———. 1991. Prey of the flattened musk turtle, *Sternotherus depressus.* J. Herpetol. 25:385–387.

Marlow, R. W., and K. Tollestrup. 1982. Mining and exploration of natural mineral deposits by the desert tortoise, *Gopherus agassizii.* Anim. Behav. 30:475–478.

Márquez M., R. 1972. Resultados preliminares sobre edad y crecimiento de la tortuga lora *Lepidochelys kempi* (Garman). Mem. IV Congr. Nac. Oceanogr. (Mexico), 419–427.

———. 1983. Atlantic ridley project 1983: Preliminary account. Marine Turtle Newsl. (26):3–4.

———. 1990. Sea turtles of the world. An annotated and illustrated catalogue of sea turtle species known to date. FAO Fish Synops. no. 125, vol. 11. 81 pp.

Márquez M., R., and T. Doi. 1973. Ensayo teórico sobre el análisis de la población de tortuga prieta, *Chelonia mydas carrinegra* Caldwell, en aguas del Golfo de California, México. Bull. Tokai Fish. Res. Lab. (73):1–22.

Márquez M., R., C. Peñaflores S., A. Villanueva O., and J. Díaz F. 1982. A model for diagnosis of populations of olive ridleys and green turtles of West Pacific tropical coasts. *In* Bjorndal, K. A., ed. Biology and conservation of sea turtles, 153–158. Smithsonian Institution Press, Washington, D.C.

Márquez M., R., M. Sanchez P., J. Díaz Flores, and I. Arguello. 1989. Kemp's ridley research at Rancho Nuevo, 1987. Marine Turtle Newsl. (44):6–7.

Márquez M., R., M. Sanchez P., J. Díaz F., J. Vasconcelos, I. Flores, I. Arguello, M. A. Carrasco, and A. Villanueva. 1992. Research at Rancho Nuevo, Tamaulipas, Mexico in 1990. Marine Turtle Newsl. (58):15.

Márquez M., R., M. Sanchez P., D. Rios O., J. Díaz F., A. Villanueva O., and I. Arguello. 1987. Rancho Nuevo operation, 1986. Marine Turtle Newsl. (40):12–15.

Márquez M., R., A. Villanueva O., and C. Peñaflores S. 1976. Sinopsis de datos biologicos sobre la tortuga golfina *Lepidochelys olivacea* (Eschscholts, 1892). Inst. Nac. Pesca, Sinopsis 2. 61 pp.

———. 1981. Anidacion de la tortuga laud (*Dermochelys coriacea schlegelii*) en el Pacifico Mexicano. Cienc. Pesq. Inst. Nac. Pesca, Mexico. 1:45–52.

Márquez M., R., A. Villanueva O., and M. Sanchez Perez. 1982. The population of the Kemp's ridley sea turtle in the Gulf of Mexico–*Lepidochelys kempii.* *In* Bjorndal, K. A., ed. Biology and conservation of sea turtles, 159–164. Smithsonian Institution Press, Washington, D.C.

Marshall, A. T., and S. R. Saddlier. 1989. The duct system of the lachrymal salt gland of the green sea turtle, *Chelonia mydas.* Cell. Tissue Res. 257:399–404.

Marshall, J. E. 1987. The effects of nest predation on hatching success in gopher tortoises (*Gopherus polyphemus* Daudin, 1802). Master's thesis, University of South Alabama, Mobile.

Martin, P. L., and J. N. Layne. 1987. Relationship of gopher tortoise body size to burrow size in a southcentral Florida population. Florida Scientist 50:264–267.

Martin, R. P. 1989. Notes on Louisiana gopher tortoise (*Gopherus polyphemus*). Reproduction. Herpetol. Rev. 20:36–37.

Martof, B. S., W. M. Palmer, J. R. Bailey, and J. R. Harrison III. 1980. Amphibians and reptiles of the Carolinas and Virginia. University of North Carolina Press, Chapel Hill. 264 pp.

Mason, E. B. 1977. Serum thyroxine levels in *Chrysemys picta marginata* (Reptilia, Testudines, Testudinidae) exposed to different thermal environments. J. Herpetol. 11:232–234.

Mast, R. B., and J. L. Carr, Jr. 1985. Macrochelid mites in association with Kemp's ridley hatchlings. Marine Turtle Newsl. (33):11–12.

Mather, C. M. 1982. Record of a turtle eaten by a catfish. Bull. Oklahoma Herpetol. Soc. 7:5.

Mathis, A., and F. R. Moore. 1988. Geomagnetism and the homeward orientation of the box turtle, *Terrapene carolina*. Ethology 78:265–274.

McAllister, C. T. 1987. *Phaenicia* (Diptera: Calliphoridae) myiasis in a three-toed turtle, *Terrapene carolina triunguis* (Reptilia: Emydidae), from Arkansas. Texas J. Sci. 39:377–378.

McAllister, C. T., and W. W. Lamar. 1987. *Pseudemys texana* (Texas river cooter). Size maxima. Herpetol. Rev. 18:73.

McAlpine, D. F. 1980. Nesting behaviour of the leatherback turtle (*Dermochelys coriacea*) on the Caribbean coast of Panama. J. New Brunswick Mus. 1980:32–40.

McAlpine, D. F., and G. Godin. 1986. New records of snapping turtles, *Chelydra serpentina,* and painted turtles, *Chrysemys picta,* from New Brunswick. Can. Field-Natur. 100:63–68.

McAuliffe, J. R. 1975. A preliminary report on some aspects of the life history of the western painted turtle (*Chrysemys picta belli*) in Douglas County, Nebraska. Proc. Nebraska Acad. Sci. 85:17–18.

———. 1978. Seasonal migrational movements of a population of the western painted turtle, *Chrysemys picta bellii* (Reptilia, Testudines, Testudinidae). J. Herpetol. 12:143–149.

McCauley, R. H. 1945. The reptiles of Maryland and the District of Columbia. Privately printed, Hagerstown, Maryland. 194 pp.

McCord, R. D., R. E. Strauss, and C. H. Lowe. 1990. Morphometric variation in *Kinosternon* turtles of the western United States and adjacent Mexico. J. Herpetol. 24:297–301.

McCoy, C. J. 1973. *Emydoidea, Emydoidea blandingii.* Catalog. Amer. Amphib. Rept. 136:1–4.

McCoy, C. J., A. V. Bianculli, and R. C. Vogt. 1978. *Sternotherus minor* (Reptilia, Kinosternidae) in the Pascagoula River system, Mississippi. Herpetol. Rev. 9:109.

McCoy, C. J., and J. F. Jacobs. 1991. Phalangeal formulae in the turtle genera *Chrysemys, Pseudemys,* and *Trachemys* (Testudines: Emydidae). J. Herpetol. 25:211–212.

McCoy, C. J., and J. E. Lovich. In press a. *Graptemys ernsti,* Escambia map turtle. *In* Pritchard, P. C. H., and A. Rhodin, eds. Conservation of freshwater turtles. IUCN Species Survival Commission.

———. In press b. *Graptemys gibbonsi,* Pascagoula map turtle. *In* Pritchard, P. C. H., and A. Rhodin, eds. Conservation of freshwater turtles. IUCN Species Survival Commission.

McCoy, C. J., and R. C. Vogt. 1979. Distribution and population status of the Alabama red-bellied turtle, *Pseudemys alabamensis.* Final Report. U.S. Fish and Wildl. Serv. Contract No. 14–16–0004–79–038, 12 pp.

———. 1980a. Distribution and population status of the yellow-blotched sawback *Graptemys flavimaculata* Cagle in Mississippi. Final Report. U.S. Fish and Wildl. Serv. Contract No. 14–16–0004–79–038. 23 pp.

———. 1980b. Distribution and population status of the ringed sawback *Graptemys oculifera* (Baur) in Mississippi and Louisiana. Final Report. U.S. Fish and Wildl. Serv. Contract No. 14–16–0004–79–038. 23 pp.

———. 1985. *Pseudemys alabamensis.* Catalog. Amer. Amphib. Rept. 371:1–2.

———. 1987. *Graptemys flavimaculata.* Catalog. Amer. Amphib. Rept. 403:1–2.

———. 1988. *Graptemys oculifera.* Catalog. Amer. Amphib. Rept. 422:1–2.

———. 1990. *Graptemys geographica.* Catalog. Amer. Amphib. Rept. 484:1–4.

———. 1992. *Graptemys kohnii* in the Pearl River: An alternative explanation. Herpetol. Rev. 23:28.

McCoy, C. J., R. C. Vogt, and E. J. Censky. 1983. Temperature-controlled sex determination in the sea turtle *Lepidochelys olivacea.* J. Herpetol. 17:404–406.

McCoy, E. D., and H. R. Mushinsky. 1992. Studying a species in decline: Changes in populations of the gopher tortoise on federal lands in Florida. Florida Scientist. 55:116–124.

McDiarmid, R. W., ed. 1978. Rare and endangered biota of Florida, vol. 3, Amphibians and reptiles. University of Florida Press, Gainesville. 74 pp.

McDowell, S. B. 1964. Partition of the genus *Clemmys* and related problems in the taxonomy of the aquatic Testudinidae. Proc. Zool. Soc. London. 143:239–279.

McEwan, B. 1982. Bone anomalies in the shell of *Gopherus polyphemus*. Florida Scientist 45:189–195.

McFarlane, R. W. 1963. Disorientation of loggerhead hatchlings by artificial road lighting. Copeia 1963:153.

McGehee, M. A. 1990. Effects of moisture on eggs and hatchlings of loggerhead sea turtles (*Caretta caretta*). Herpetologica 46:251–258.

McGinnis, S. M., and W. G. Voigt. 1971. Thermoregulation in the desert tortoise, *Gopherus agassizii*. Comp. Biochem. Physiol. 40A:119–126.

McKeown, S. 1978. Hawaiian reptiles and amphibians. Oriental Publ. Co., Honolulu. 80 pp.

McKeown, S., and D. C. Holland. 1985. *Clemmys marmorata* (western pond turtle). Size. Herpetol. Rev. 16:59.

McKeown, S., and R. G. Webb. 1982. Softshell turtles in Hawaii. J. Herpetol. 16:107–111.

McKim, J. M., Jr., and K. L. Johnson. 1983. Polychlorinated biphenyls and p,p'-DDE in loggerhead and green postyearling Atlantic sea turtles. Bull. Environ. Contam. Toxicol. 31:53–60.

McKown, R. R. 1972. Phylogenetic relationships within the turtle genera *Graptemys* and *Malaclemys*. Ph.D. dissertation, University of Texas, Austin. 111 pp.

McMurtray, J. D., and J. I. Richardson. 1985. A northern nesting record for the hawksbill turtle. Herpetol. Rev. 16:16–17.

McPherson, R. J., L. R. Boots, R. MacGregor III, and K. R. Marion. 1982. Plasma steroids associated with seasonal reproductive changes in a multiclutched freshwater turtle, *Sternotherus odoratus*. Gen. Comp. Endocrinol. 48:440–451.

McPherson, R. J., and K. R. Marion. 1981a. Seasonal testicular cycle of the stinkpot turtle (*Sternotherus odoratus*) in central Alabama. Herpetologica 37:33–40.

———. 1981b. The reproductive biology of female *Sternotherus odoratus* in an Alabama population. J. Herpetol. 15:389–396.

———. 1982. Seasonal changes in total lipids in the turtle *Sternotherus odoratus*. Comp. Biochem. Physiol. 71A:93–98.

———. 1983. Reproductive variation between two

populations of *Sternotherus odoratus* in the same geographic area. J. Herpetol. 17:181–184.

McRae, W. A., J. L. Landers, and G. D. Cleveland. 1981. Sexual dimorphism in the gopher tortoise (*Gopherus polyphemus*). Herpetologica 37:46–52.

McRae, W. A., J. L. Landers, and J. A. Garner. 1981. Movement patterns and home range of the gopher tortoise. Amer. Midl. Natur. 106:165–179.

McVey, J. P., and T. Wibbels. 1984. The growth and movements of captive-reared Kemp's ridley sea turtles, *Lepidochelys kempi*, following their release in the Gulf of Mexico. NOAA-TM-NMFS-SEFC-145. 25 pp.

Means, D. B. 1982. Responses to winter burrow flooding of the gopher tortoise (*Gopherus polyphemus* Daudin). Herpetologica 38:521–525.

Meany, D. B. 1979. Nesting habits of the Alabama red-bellied turtle, *Pseudemys alabamensis*. J. Alabama Acad. Sci. 50:113.

Medem, F. 1977. Contribución al conocimiento sobre la taxonomía, distribución geográfica y ecología de la tortuga "Bache" (*Chelydra serpentina acutirostris*). Caldasia 12:41–101.

Medica, P. A., R. B. Bury, and R. A. Luckenbach. 1980. Drinking and construction of water catchments of the desert tortoise, *Gopherus agassizii*, in the Mojave Desert. Herpetologica 36:301–304.

Medica, P. A., R. B. Bury, and F. B. Turner. 1975. Growth of the desert tortoise (*Gopherus agassizi*) in Nevada. Copeia 1975:639–643.

Medica, P. A., C. L. Lyons, and F. B. Turner. 1982. A comparison of 1981 populations of desert tortoises (*Gopherus agassizi*) in grazed and ungrazed areas in Ivanpah Valley, California. Proc. Symp. Desert Tortoise Council 1982:99–124.

Medrano, L., M. Dorizzi, F. Rimblot, and C. Pieau. 1987. Karyotype of the sea-turtle *Dermochelys coriacea* (Vandelli, 1761). Amphibia-Reptilia 8:171–178.

Meeks, R. L., and G. R. Ultsch. 1990. Overwintering behavior of snapping turtles. Copeia 1990:880–884.

Mehrtens, J. 1949. Copulation of *Clemmys guttata* and *Pseudemys troostii elegans*. Herpetologica 5:150.

Meissl, H., and M. Ueck. 1980. Extracellular photoreception of the pineal gland of the aquatic turtle *Pseudemys scripta elegans*. J. Comp. Physiol. 140:173–179.

Mendonça, M. T. 1981. Comparative growth rates of wild immature *Chelonia mydas* and *Caretta caretta* in Florida. J. Herpetol. 15:447–451.

———. 1983. Movements and feeding ecology of immature green turtles (*Chelonia mydas*) in a Florida lagoon. Copeia 1983:1013–1023.

———. 1987. Photothermal effects on the ovarian cycle

of the musk turtle, *Sternotherus odoratus*. Herpetologica 43:82–90.

Mendonça, M. T., and L. M. Ehrhart. 1982. Activity, population size and structure of immature *Chelonia mydas* and *Caretta caretta* in Mosquito Lagoon, Florida. Copeia 1982:161–167.

Mendonça, M. T., and P. Licht. 1986. Photothermal effects on the testicular cycle in the musk turtle, *Sternotherus odoratus*. J. Exp. Zool. 239:117–130.

Mendonça, M. T., and P. C. H. Pritchard. 1986. Offshore movements of post-nesting Kemp's ridley sea turtles (*Lepidochelys kempi*). Herpetologica 42:373–381.

Merchant-Larios, H., and I. Villalpando. 1990. Effect of temperature on gonadal sex differentiation in the sea turtle *Lepidochelys olivacea:* An organ culture study. J. Exp. Zool. 254:327–331.

Merchant-Larios, H., I. Villalpando Fierro, and B. Centeno Urruiza. 1989. Gonadal morphogenesis under controlled temperature in the sea turtle *Lepidochelys olivacea*. Herpetol. Monogr. 3:43–61.

Meritt, D. A., Jr. 1980. The wood turtle, *Clemmys insculpta* (LeConte) natural history, behavior and food habits. Bull. Chicago Herpetol. Soc. 15:6–9.

Merkle, D. A. 1975. A taxonomic analysis of the *Clemmys* complex (Reptilia: Testudines) utilizing starch gel electrophoresis. Herpetologica 31:162–166.

Mertens, R. 1956. ber Reptilienbastarde, II. Senck. Biol. 37:383–394.

Mertens, R. 1973. Das Alter bei der Geschlechtsreife der Dosenschildkröte *Terrapene c. carolina*. Salamandra 9:34–35.

Meshaka, W. E., Jr. 1986. *Chelydra serpentina* (snapping turtle). Foraging. Herpetol. Rev. 17:24.

———. 1988. *Pseudemys nelsoni* (Florida red-bellied slider). Mutualism. Herpetol. Rev. 19:88.

Metcalf, A. L., and E. Metcalf. 1978. An experiment with homing in ornate box turtles (*Terrapene ornata ornata* Agassiz). J. Herpetol. 12:411–412.

———. 1985. Longevity in some ornate box turtles (*Terrapene ornata ornata*). J. Herpetol. 19:157–158.

Metcalf, E. L., and A. L. Metcalf. 1970. Observations on ornate box turtles (*Terrapene ornata ornata* Agassiz). Trans. Kansas Acad. Sci. 73:96–117.

———. 1979. Mortality in hibernating ornate box turtles, *Terrapene ornata*. Herpetologica 35:93–96.

Meylan, A. B. 1982a. Behavioral ecology of the West Caribbean green turtle (*Chelonia mydas*) in the internesting habitat. *In* Bjorndal, K. A., ed. Biology and conservation of sea turtles, 67–80. Smithsonian Institution Press, Washington, D.C.

———. 1982b. Sea turtle migration–evidence from tag returns. *In* Bjorndal, K. A., ed. Biology and conserva-

tion of sea turtles, 91–100. Smithsonian Institution Press, Washington, D.C.

———. 1982c. Estimation of population size in sea turtles. *In* Bjorndal, K. A., ed. Biology and conservation of sea turtles, 135–138. Smithsonian Institution Press, Washington, D.C.

———. 1983. Marine turtles of the Leeward Islands, Lesser Antilles. Atoll. Res. Bull. 278:1–39.

———. 1988. Spongivory in hawksbill turtles: A diet of glass. Science. 239:393–395.

———. 1989. Hawksbill turtle (*Eretmochelys imbricata*). Status report of the hawksbill turtle. Proc. 2d West. Atlantic Turt. Symp., 101–115.

Meylan, A. B., K. A. Bjorndal, and B. J. Turner. 1983. Sea turtles nesting at Melbourne Beach, Florida, II. Post-nesting movements of *Caretta caretta*. Biol. Conserv. 26:79–90.

Meylan, A. B., B. W. Bowen, and J. C. Avise. 1990. A genetic test of the natal homing versus social facilitation models for green turtle migration. Science 248:724–727.

Meylan, A., P. Castaneda, C. Coogan, T. Lozon, and J. Fletemeyer. 1990a. *Lepidochelys kempi* (Kemp's ridley sea turtle). Reproduction. Herpetol. Rev. 21:19–20.

———. 1990b. First recorded nesting by Kemp's ridley in Florida, USA. Marine Turtle Newsl. (48):8–9.

Meylan, A., and S. Sadove. 1986. Cold-stunning in Long Island Sound, New York. Marine Turtle Newsl. (37):7–8.

Meylan, P. A. 1984. Evolutionary relationships of Recent trionychid turtles: Evidence from shell morphology. Studia Geologica Salmanticensia spec. vol. 1, 169–188.

———. 1987. The phylogenetic relationships of soft-shelled turtles (family Trionychidae). Bull. Amer. Mus. Natur. Hist. 186:1–101.

Meylan, P. A., C. A. Stevens, M. E. Barnwell, and E. D. Dohm. 1992. Observations on the turtle community of Rainbow Run, Marion Co., Florida. Florida Scientist 55:219–228.

Middaugh, D. P. 1981. Reproductive ecology and spawning periodicity of the Atlantic silverside, *Menidia menidia* (Pisces: Atherinidae). Copeia 1981:766–776.

Miller, J. D. 1985. Embryology of marine turtles. *In* Gans, C., F. Billett, and P. F. A. Maderson, eds. Biology of the Reptilia, vol. 14, Development A, 269–328. John Wiley & Sons, New York.

Miller, K. 1987. Hydric conditions during incubation influence locomotor performance of hatchling snapping turtles. J. Exp. Biol. 127:401–412.

Miller, K., G. F. Birchard, and G. C. Packard. 1989.

Chelydra serpentina (common snapping turtle). Fecundity. Herpetol. Rev. 20:69.

Miller, K., G. F. Birchard, M. J. Packard, and G. C. Packard. 1989. *Trionyx spiniferus* (spiny softshell turtle). Fecundity. Herpetol. Rev. 20:56.

Miller, L. 1932. Notes on the desert tortoise (*Testudo agassizii*). Trans. San Diego Soc. Natur. Hist. 7:187–208.

———. 1955. Further observations on the desert tortoise, *Gopherus agassizi* of California. Copeia 1955:113–118.

Miller, W. E. 1971. Pleistocene vertebrates of the Los Angeles Basin and vicinity (exclusive of Rancho La Brea). Bull. Los Angeles Co. Mus. Natur. Hist. 10:1–24.

Milsom, W. K. 1975. Development of bouyancy control in juvenile Atlantic loggerhead turtles, *Caretta c. caretta*. Copeia 1975:758–762.

Milsom, W. K., and K. Johansen. 1975. The effect of buoyancy induced lung volume changes on respiratory frequency in a chelonian (*Caretta caretta*). J. Comp. Physiol. 98:157–160.

Milsom, W. K., B. L. Langille, and D. R. Jones. Vagal control of pulmonary vascular resistance in the turtle *Chrysemys scripta*. Can. J. Zool. 55:359–367.

Milstead, W. W. 1967. Fossil box turtles (*Terrapene*) from central North America, and box turtles of eastern Mexico. Copeia 1967:168–179.

———. 1969. Studies on the evolution of box turtles (genus *Terrapene*). Bull. Florida St. Mus. Biol. Sci. 14:1–108.

Milstead, W. W., J. S. Mecham, and H. McClintock. 1950. The amphibians and reptiles of the Stockton Plateau in northern Terrell County, Texas. Texas J. Sci. 2:543–562.

Minarik, C. 1985. *Lepidochelys olivacea* (olive ridley sea turtle). Reproduction. Herpetol. Rev. 16:82.

Minckley, W. L. 1966. Coyote predation on aquatic turtles. J. Mammal. 47:137.

Minnich, J. E. 1976. Water procurement and conservation by desert reptiles in their natural environment. Israel J. Med. Sci. 12:740–758.

———. 1977. Adaptive responses in water electrolyte budgets of native and captive desert tortoises, *Gopherus agassizi*, to chronic drought. Proc. Symp. Desert Tortoise Council 1977:102–129.

———. 1979. Comparison of maintenance electrolyte budgets of free-living desert and gopher tortoises (*Gopherus agassizi* and *G. polyphemus*). Proc. Symp. Desert Tortoise Council 979:166–174.

Minnich, J. E., and M. R. Ziegler. 1977. Water turnover of free-living gopher tortoises, *Gopherus polyphemus*, in central Florida. Proc. Symp. Desert Tortoise Council 1977:130–151.

Minton, S. A., Jr. 1972. Amphibians and reptiles of Indiana. Indiana Acad. Sci. Monogr. 3:1–346.

Minx, P. 1992. Variation in the phalangeal formulae in the turtle genus *Terrapene*. J. Herpetol. 26:234–238.

Mitchell, J. C. 1974. Statistics of *Chrysemys rubriventris* hatchlings from Middlesex County, Virginia. Herpetol. Rev. 5:71.

———. 1979. The concept of phenology and its application to the study of amphibians and reptile life histories. Herpetol. Rev. 10:51–54.

———. 1985a. Variation in the male reproductive cycle in a population of painted turtles, *Chrysemys picta*, from Virginia. Herpetologica 41:45–51.

———. 1985b. Variation in the male reproductive cycle in a population of stinkpot turtles, *Sternotherus odoratus*, from Virginia. Copeia 1985:50–56.

———. 1985c. Female reproductive cycle and life history attributes in a Virginia population of painted turtles, *Chrysemys picta*. J. Herpetol. 19:218–226.

———. 1985d. Female reproductive cycle and life history attributes in a Virginia population of stinkpot turtles, *Sternotherus odoratus*. Copeia 1985:941–949.

———. 1988. Population ecology and life histories of the freshwater turtles *Chrysemys picta* and *Sternotherus odoratus* in an urban lake. Herpetol. Monogr. 2:40–61.

———. 1989. An historical review of the Fairfax County, Virginia, bog turtle record. Catesbeiana 9:3–7.

Mitchell, J. C., and K. A. Buhlmann. 1991. Eastern chicken turtle. *Deirochelys reticularia reticularia* (Latreille). *In* Terwilliger, K., ed. Virginia's endangered species, 459–461. McDonald and Woodward Publ. Co., Blacksburg, Virginia.

Mitchell, J. C., K. A. Buhlmann, and C. H. Ernst. 1991. Bog turtle. *Clemmys muhlenbergii*. *In* Terwilliger, K., ed. Virginia's endangered species, 457–459. McDonald and Woodward Publ. Co., Blacksburg, Virginia.

Mitchell, J. C., and C. A. Pague. 1990. Body size, reproductive variation, and growth in the slider turtle at the northeastern edge of its range. *In* Gibbons, J. W., ed. Life history and ecology of the slider turtle, 146–151. Smithsonian Institution Press, Washington, D.C.

———. 1991. Ecology of freshwater turtles in Back Bay, Virginia. *In* Marshall, H. G., and M. D. Norman, eds. Proceedings of the Back Bay Ecological Symposium, 183–187. Old Dominion Univ., Norfolk, Virginia.

Mitsukuri, K. 1905. The cultivation of marine and freshwater animals in Japan. The snapping turtle, or softshelled tortoise, "suppon." Bull. U.S. Bur. Fish. 24:260–266.

Mohanty-Hejmadi, P., M. Behera, and M. T. Dimond. 1985. Temperature dependent sex differentiation in the olive ridley *Lepidochelys olivacea* and its implications for conservation. Proc. Symp. Endang. Mar. Anim. Marine Parks 1:260–263.

Mohanty-Hejmadi, P., and M. T. Dimond. 1986. Temperature dependent sex determination in the olive ridley turtle. *In* Progress in Developmental Biology. Part A, 159–162. Alan R. Liss, Inc.

Moler, P. E., ed. 1992. Rare and endangered biota of Florida. Vol. 3, Amphibians and reptiles. University of Florida Press, Gainesville. 291 pp.

Moll, D. L. 1974. Notes on the behavior of Isle Royale painted turtles (*Chrysemys picta belli*). J. Herpetol. 8:254–255.

———. 1976a. Environmental influence on growth rate in the Ouachita map turtle, *Graptemys pseudogeographica ouachitensis*. Herpetologica 32:439–443.

———. 1976b. A review of supposed insect catching by basking *Graptemys geographica*. Trans. Illinois St. Acad. Sci. 69:302–303.

———. 1976c. Food and feeding strategies of the Ouachita map turtle (*Graptemys pseudogeographica ouachitensis*). Amer. Midl. Natur. 96:478–482.

———. 1979. Subterranean feeding by the Illinois mud turtle, *Kinosternon flavescens spooneri* (Reptilia, Testudines, Kinosternidae). J. Herpetol. 13:371–373.

———. 1985. The marine turtles of Belize. Oryx 19:155–157.

Moll, D. L., and L. E. Brown. 1976. The mud turtle *Kinosternon flavescens spooneri*—nearly extinct in Illinois. Explorer 1(5):6–7.

Moll, D. L., and E. O. Moll. 1990. The slider turtle in the neotropics: Adaptation of a temperate species to a tropical environment. *In* Gibbons, J. W., ed. Life history and ecology of the slider turtle, 152–161. Smithsonian Institution Press, Washington, D.C.

Moll, E. O. 1973. Latitudinal and intersubspecific variation in reproduction of the painted turtle, *Chrysemys picta*. Herpetologica 29:307–318.

Moll, E. O., and J. M. Legler. 1971. The life history of a neotropical slider turtle, *Pseudemys scripta* (Schoepff), in Panama. Bull. Los Angeles Co. Mus. Natur. Hist. (11):1–102.

Moll, E. O., and M. A. Morris. 1991. Status of the river cooter, *Pseudemys concinna,* in Illinois. Trans. Illinois St. Acad. Sci. 84:77–83.

Monagas, W. R., and R. E. Gatten, Jr. 1983. Behavioural fever in the turtles *Terrapene carolina* and *Chrysemys picta*. J. Therm. Biol. 8:285–288.

Montevecchi, W. A., and J. Burger. 1975. Aspects of the reproductive biology of the northern diamondback terrapin *Malaclemys terrapin terrapin*. Amer. Midl. Natur. 94:166–178.

Moodie, K. B., and T. R. Van Devender. 1974. Pleistocene turtles from the Whitlock Oil Well locality, Graham County, Arizona. J. Arizona Acad. Sci. 9 (suppl.):35.

———. 1977. Additional late Pleistocene turtles from Jones Spring, Hickory County, Missouri. Herpetologica 33:87–90.

———. 1978. Fossil box turtles (genus *Terrapene*) from southern Arizona. Herpetologica 34:172–174.

Moore, J. C. 1953. Shrew on box turtle menu. Everglades Natur. Hist. 1:129.

Moorhouse, F. W. 1933. Notes on the green turtle (*Chelonia mydas*). Rept. Great Barrier Reef Comm. 4:1–22.

Mora, J. M., and D. C. Robinson. 1982. Discovery of a blind olive ridley turtle (*Lepidochelys olivacea*) nesting at Playa Ostional, Costa Rica. Rev. Biol. Trop. 30:178–179.

———. 1984. Predation of sea turtle eggs (*Lepidochelys*) by the snake *Loxocemus bicolor* Cope. Rev. Biol. Trop. 32:161–162.

Morgareidge, K. R., and H. T. Hammel. 1975. Evaporative water loss in box turtles: Effects of rostral brainstem and other temperatures. Science 187:366–368.

Morreale, S. J., and J. W. Gibbons. 1986. Habitat suitability index models: Slider turtle. U.S. Fish Wildl. Serv. Biol. Rept. 82(10.125). 14 pp.

Morreale, S. J., J. W. Gibbons, and J. D. Congdon. 1984. Significance of activity and movement in the yellow-bellied turtle (*Pseudemys scripta*). Can. J. Zool. 62:1038–1042.

Morreale, S. J., A. B. Meylan, S. S. Sandove, and E. A. Standora. 1992. Annual occurrence and winter mortality of marine turtles in New York waters. J. Herpetol. 26:301–308.

Morreale, S. J., G. J. Ruiz, S. R. Spotila, and E. A. Standora. 1982. Temperature-dependent sex determination: Current practices threaten conservation of sea turtles. Science 216:1245–1247.

Morris, K. A., G. C. Packard, T. J. Boardman, G. L. Paukstis, and M. J. Packard. 1983. Effect of the hydric environment on growth of embryonic snapping turtles (*Chelydra serpentina*). Herpetologica 39:272–285.

Morris, M. A. 1976. Courtship-like behavior of immature turtles. Herpetol. Rev. 7:110–111.

Morris, M. A., and M. J. Sweet. 1985. Size, age, and growth of an alligator snapping turtle, *Macroclemys temmincki,* from Illinois. Trans. Illinois Acad. Sci. 78:241–245.

Mortimer, J. A. 1981. The feeding ecology of the west

Caribbean green turtle (*Chelonia mydas*) in Nicaragua. Biotropica 13:49–58.

———. 1982. Feeding ecology of sea turtles. *In* Bjorndal, K. A., ed. Biology and conservation of sea turtles, 103–109. Smithsonian Institution Press, Washington, D.C.

———. 1990. The influence of beach sand characteristics on the nesting behavior and clutch survival of green turtles (*Chelonia mydas*). Copeia 1990:802–817.

Mortimer, J. A., and A. Carr. 1984. Reproductive ecology and behavior of the green turtle (*Chelonia mydas*) at Ascension Island. Natl. Geogr. Soc. Res. Rept. 17:257–270.

———. 1987. Reproduction and migrations of the Ascension Island green turtle (*Chelonia mydas*). Copeia 1987:103–113.

Mortimer, J. A., and K. M. Portier. 1989. Reproductive homing and internesting behavior of the green turtle (*Chelonia mydas*) at Ascension Island, South Atlantic Ocean. Copeia 1989:962–977.

Mosimann, J. E., and J. R. Bider. 1960. Variation, sexual dimorphism, and maturity in a Quebec population of the common snapping turtle, *Chelydra serpentina*. Can. J. Zool. 38:19–38.

Motz, V. A., and I. P. Callard. 1991. Seasonal variations in oviductal morphology of the painted turtle, *Chrysemys picta*. J. Morphol. 207:59–71.

Mount, R. H. 1975. The reptiles and amphibians of Alabama. Auburn University Agricultural Experiment Station, Auburn, Alabama. 347 pp.

———. 1981. The status of the flattened musk turtle, *Sternotherus minor depressus* Tinkle and Webb. U.S. Fish Wildl. Serv. Final Report, Contract »14–16–0004–80–096. 118 pp.

Mrosovsky, N. 1968. Nocturnal emergence of hatchling sea turtles: Control by thermal inhibition of activity. Nature 220:1338–1339.

———. 1971. Black vultures attack live turtle hatchlings. Auk 88:672–673.

———. 1972. Spectrographs of the sounds of leatherback turtles. Herpetologica 28:256–258.

———. 1977. Individual differences in the sea-finding mechanism of hatchling leatherback turtles. Brain, Behav. Evol. 14:261–273.

———. 1978. Effects of flashing lights on sea-finding behavior of green turtles. Behav. Biol. 22:85–91.

———. 1980. Thermal biology of sea turtles. Amer. Zool. 20:531–547.

———. 1981. Plastic jellyfish. Marine Turtle Newsl. 17:5–7.

———. 1982. Sex ratio bias in hatchling sea turtles from artificially incubated eggs. Biol. Conserv. 23:309–314.

———. 1983a. Conserving sea turtles. British Herpetological Society, London. 176 pp.

———. 1983b. Ecology and nest-site selection of leatherback turtles *Dermochelys coriacea*. Biol. Conserv. 26:47–56.

———. 1988. Pivotal temperatures for loggerhead turtles (*Caretta caretta*) from northern and southern nesting beaches. Can. J. Zool. 66:661–669.

Mrosovsky, N., A. Bass, L. A. Corliss, J. I. Richardson, and T. H. Richardson. 1992. Pivotal and beach temperatures for hawksbill turtles nesting in Antigua. Can. J. Zool. 70:1920–1925.

Mrosovsky, N., and A. Carr. 1967. Preference for light of short wavelengths in hatchling green sea turtles, *Chelonia mydas*, tested on their natural nesting beaches. Behaviour 28:217–231.

Mrosovsky, N., P. H. Dutton, and C. P. Whitmore. 1984a. Sex ratios of two species of sea turtle nesting in Suriname. Can. J. Zool. 62:2227–2239.

Mrosovsky, N., and W. Frair. 1974. Reply to Neill and Stevens. Science 184:1010.

Mrosovsky, N., A. M. Granda, and T. Hay. 1979. Seaward orientation of hatchling turtles: Turning systems in the optic tectum. Brain, Behav. Evol. 16:203–221.

Mrosovsky, N., S. R. Hopkins-Murphy, and J. I. Richardson. 1984b. Sex ratio of sea turtles: Seasonal changes. Science 225:739–741.

Mrosovsky, N., and S. F. Kingsmill. 1985. How turtles find the sea. Z. Tierpsychol. 67:237–256.

Mrosovsky, N., and P. C. H. Pritchard. 1971. Body temperatures of *Dermochelys coriacea* and other sea turtles. Copeia 1971:624–631.

Mrosovsky, N., and J. Provancha. 1989. Sex ratio of loggerhead sea turtles hatching on a Florida beach. Can. J. Zool. 67:2533–2539.

Mrosovsky, N., and S. J. Shettleworth. 1968. Wavelength preferences and brightness cues in the water finding behaviour of sea turtles. Behaviour 32:211–257.

———. 1974. Further studies of the sea-finding mechanism in green turtle hatchlings. Behaviour 51:195–208.

———. 1975. On the orientation circle of the leatherback turtle, *Dermochelys coriacea*. Anim. Behav. 23:568–591.

Mrosovsky, N., and C. L. Yntema. 1980. Temperature dependence of sexual differentiation in sea turtles: Implications for conservation practices. Biol. Conserv. 18:271–280.

———. 1982. Temperature dependence of sexual differentiation in sea turtles: Implications for conservation practices. *In* Bjorndal, K. A., ed. Biology and conservation of sea turtles, 59–65. Smithsonian Institution Press, Washington, D.C.

Muir, J. H. 1984. Commercial exploitation of *Graptemys* and *Sternotherus* turtles. Bull. Chicago Herpetol. Soc. 19:98–100.

———. 1989. A description of the painted turtles (*Chrysemys picta* ssp.) from Town Creek, Jackson County, Alabama. Bull. Chicago Herpetol. Soc. 24:9–10.

Mull, M. E. 1987. 'I'iwi portrayed on 22-cent postage stamp. 'Elepaio (J. Hawaii Audubon Soc.). 47:102.

Muller, J. F. 1921. Notes on the habits of the soft-shell turtle *Amyda mutica*. Amer. Midl. Natur. 7:180–184.

Murphy, G. G. 1970. Orientation of adult and hatchling red-eared turtles, *Pseudemys scripta elegans*. Diss. Abst. B. 31:4398.

Murphy, J. 1976. The natural history of the box turtle. Bull. Chicago Herpetol. Soc. 11:2–45.

Murphy, J. C., and M. J. Corn. 1977. A turtle vanishes. Natur. Hist. 86(7):8.

Murphy, T. D. 1964. Box turtle, *Terrapene carolina*, in stomach of copperhead, *Agkistrodon contortrix*. Copeia 1964:221.

Murphy, T. M., and S. R. Hopkins-Murphy. 1984. Aerial and ground surveys of marine turtle nesting beaches in the southeast region, U.S.A. Final Report. National Marine Fisheries Service, Southeast Fisheries Center. 73 pp.

Mushinsky, H. R., and D. S. Wilson. 1992. Seasonal occurrence of *Kinosternon baurii* on a sandhill in central Florida. J. Herpetol. 26:207–209.

Musick, J. A. 1979. The marine turtles of Virginia (families Chelonidae and Dermochelyidae) with notes on identification and natural history. Sea Grant Progr., Virginia Inst. Marine Sci., Ed. Ser. (24):1–17.

Musquera, S., J. Massegú, and J. Planas. 1976. Blood proteins in turtles (*Testudo hermanni, Emys orbicularis* and *Caretta caretta*). Comp. Biochem. Physiol. 55A:225–230.

Myers, C. W. 1956. An unusual feeding habit in the box turtle. Herpetologica 12:155.

Naegle, S. R., and W. G. Bradley. 1975. Influence of temperature and body weight on oxygen consumption in the desert tortoise *Gopherus agassizii*. Herpetol. Rev. 6:71.

Nagy, K. A. 1988. Seasonal patterns of water and energy balance in desert vertebrates. J. Arid Environ. 14:201–210.

Nagy, K. A., and P. A. Medica. 1977. Seasonal water and energy relations of free-living desert tortoises in Nevada: A preliminary report. Proc. Symp. Desert Tortoise Council 1977:152–157.

———. 1986. Physiological ecology of desert tortoises in southern Nevada. Herpetologica 42:73–92.

Nakamura, K. 1937. On the chromosomes of some chelonians. (A preliminary note). Japanese J. Genetics 13:240.

National Research Council, USA. 1990. Decline of the sea turtles: Causes and prevention. National Academy Press, Washington, D.C. 259 pp.

Neck, R. W. 1977. Cutaneous myiasis in *Gopherus berlandieri* (Reptilia, Testudines, Testudinidae). J. Herpetol. 11:96–98.

Neill, W. H., and E. D. Stevens. 1974. Thermal inertia versus thermoregulation in "warm" turtles and tunas. Science 184:1008–1010.

Neill, W. T. 1948a. Hibernation of amphibians and reptiles in Richmond County, Georgia. Herpetologica 4:107–114.

———. 1948b. Use of scent glands by prenatal *Sternotherus minor*. Herpetologica 4:148.

———. 1948c. Odor of young box turtles. Copeia 1948:130.

———. 1948d. The musk turtles of Georgia. Herpetologica 4:181–183.

———. 1951a. The taxonomy of North American soft-shelled turtles, genus *Amyda*. Publ. Res. Div. Ross Allen's Reptile Inst. 1:7–24.

———. 1951b. Notes on the role of crawfishes in the ecology of reptiles, amphibians, and fishes. Ecology 32:764–766.

———. 1951c. Notes on the natural history of certain North American snakes. Publ. Res. Div. Ross Allen's Reptile Inst. 1:47–60.

———. 1957. Historical biogeography of present-day Florida. Bull. Florida St. Mus. Biol. Sci. 2:175–220.

———. 1958. The occurrence of amphibians and reptiles in saltwater areas, and a bibliography. Bull. Marine Sci. Gulf Caribbean 8:1–97.

Neill, W. T., and E. R. Allen. 1954. Algae on turtles: Some additional considerations. Ecology 35:581–584.

———. 1957. The laminal spurs of the juvenile gopher tortoise, *Gopherus polyphemus* (Daudin). Copeia 1957:307.

Nellis, D. W., and V. Small. 1983. Mongoose predation on sea turtle eggs and nests. Biotropica 15:159–160.

Nelson, D. A. 1988. Life history and environmental requirements of loggerhead turtles. U.S. Fish Wildl. Serv. Biol. Rept. 88(23):iii–viii + 34.

Nemuras, K. T. 1966. Spotted turtles in Maryland. HERP, Bull. New York Herpetol. Soc. 3(1):6–9.

———. 1967. Notes on the natural history of *Clemmys muhlenbergi*. Bull. Maryland Herpetol. Soc. 3:80–96.

———. 1974a. The bog turtle: Profile of an endangered species. Virginia Wildl. 35(6):7–9.

————. 1974b. The bog turtle. Wildl. North Carolina 38(2):13–15.

————. 1976. Vanishing bog turtle. Defenders 51(1):38–39.

————. 1979. Turtles of a woodland bog. Conservationist (New York) 33(6):7–10.

Nemuras, K. T., and J. A. Weaver. 1974a. The bog turtle: Synonym for extinction? Natl. Parks Conserv. Mag. 48(6):17–20.

————. 1974b. The bog turtle: A little reptile with big problems. Pennsylvania Angler 43(7):15–18.

Netting, M. G. 1932. Blanding's turtle, *Emys blandingii* (Holbrook), in Pennsylvania. Copeia 1932:173–174.

————. 1936. Hibernation and migration of the spotted turtle, *Clemmys guttata* (Schneider). Copeia 1936:112.

Neville, A., W. D. Webster, J. F. Gouveia, E. L. Hendricks, I. Hendricks, G. Marvin, and W. H. Marvin. 1988. The effects of nest temperature on hatchling emergence in the loggerhead sea turtle (*Caretta caretta*). *In* Schroeder, B. A., ed. Proceedings of the Eighth Annual Workshop on Sea Turtle Conservation and Biology, 71–73. NOAA-TM-NMFS-SEFC-214.

Newman, H. H. 1906. The habits of certain tortoises. J. Comp. Neurol. Psychol. 16:126–152.

Newman, V. 1970. Barbour's map turtle. Florida Wildl. July, 4–5.

Nicholls, E. L., T. T. Tokaryx, and L. V. Hills. 1990. Cretaceous marine turtle from the Western Interior Seaway of Canada. Can. J. Earth. Sci. 27:1288–1298.

Nichols, J. T. 1914. Mud turtle attacked by crab. Copeia (12):3.

————. 1939a. Data on size, growth and age in the box turtle, *Terrapene carolina*. Copeia 1939:14–20.

————. 1939b. Range and homing of individual box turtles. Copeia 1939:125–127.

————. 1947. Notes on the mud turtle. Herpetologica 3:147–148.

Nichols, U. G. 1953. Habits of the desert tortoise, *Gopherus agassizii*. Herpetologica 9:65–69.

————. 1957. The desert tortoise in captivity. Herpetologica 13:141–144.

Nichols, V. A., and C. H. Du Toit. 1983. A leatherback returns to Flagler County: A new northern nesting record for the U.S. Atlantic Coast. Herpetol. Rev. 14:107.

Nicholson, F. A., and P. L. Risley. 1942. A study of the urogenital systems of *Emys blandingii*, with observations on the occurrence of Mullerian ducts in males. Proc. Iowa Acad. Sci. 47:343–360.

Nickol, B. B., and C. H. Ernst. 1987. *Neoechinorhynchus lingulatus* sp. n. (Acanthocephala: Neoechinorhynchidae) from *Pseudemys nelsoni* (Reptilia: Emydidae) of Florida. Proc. Helminthol. Soc. Washington 54:146–149.

Nicol, B., and E. Nicol. 1985. The poor man's snakeneck. Newsl. Chicago Herpetol. Soc. December. 2 pp.

Nicol, E. 1989. Twinning in three turtle species. Bull. Chicago Herpetol. Soc. 24:129–130.

Nicol, R. 1970. Striped mud turtle has tiny offspring. Tortuga Gazette 6(2):4–5.

Nicolson, S. W., and P. L. Lutz. 1989. Salt gland function in the green sea turtle *Chelonia mydas*. J. Exp. Biol. 144:171–184.

Nijs, J., and C. Navez. 1990. Delayed fertilization in the striped mud turtle, *Kinosternon baurii*. Bull. Chicago Herpetol. Soc. 25:146.

Nilsson, G. E., P. L. Lutz, and T. L. Jackson. 1991. Neurotransmitters and anoxic survival of the brain: A comparison of anoxia-tolerant and anoxia-intolerant vertebrates. Physiol. Zool. 64:638–652.

Noble, G. A., and E. R. Noble. 1940. A brief anatomy of the turtle. Stanford University Press, California. 45 pp.

Noble, G. K., and A. M. Breslau. 1938. The senses involved in the migration of young fresh-water turtles after hatching. J. Comp. Psychol. 25:175–193.

Norman, M. D. 1989. Preliminary survey of the freshwater turtles of the Blackwater River. Catesbeiana 9:9–14.

Norris, K. S., and R. G. Zweifel. 1950. Observations on the habits of the ornate box turtle, *Terrapene ornata* (Agassiz). Natur. Hist. Misc. (58):1–4.

Nuitja, I. N. S., and I. Uchida. 1983. Studies in the sea turtles–II. The nesting site characteristics of the hawksbill and the green turtle. Treubia 29:63–79.

Nussbaum, R. A., E. D. Brodie, Jr., and R. M. Storm. 1983. Amphibians and reptiles of the Pacific Northwest. University Press of Idaho, Moscow. 332 pp.

Obbard, M. E., and R. J. Brooks. 1979. Factors affecting basking in a northern population of the common snapping turtle, *Chelydra serpentina*. Can. J. Zool. 57:435–440.

————. 1980. Nesting migrations of the snapping turtle (*Chelydra serpentina*). Herpetologica 36:158–162.

————. 1981a. Fate of overwintering clutches of the common snapping turtle (*Chelydra serpentina*) in Algonquin Park, Ontario. Can. Field-Natur. 95:350–352.

————. 1981b. A radio-telemetry and mark-recapture study of activity in the common snapping turtle, *Chelydra serpentina*. Copeia 1981:630–637.

———. 1987. Prediction of the onset of the annual nesting season of the common snapping turtle, *Chelydra serpentina*. Herpetologica 43:324–328.

Obbard, M. E., and N. E. Down. 1984. A recent specimen of the eastern spiny softshell, *Trionyx spiniferus spiniferus,* from Hamilton Harbour, Lake Ontario. Can. Field-Natur. 98:254–255.

Obst, F. J. 1985. Schmuckschildkröten. Die Gattung *Chrysemys*. A. Ziemsen Verlag, Wittenberg Lutherstadt. 127 pp.

———. 1986. Turtles, tortoises and terrapins. St. Martin's Press, New York. 231 pp.

Odum, R. A. 1985. *Pseudemys scripta elegans* (red-eared slider). Deformity. Herpetol. Rev. 16:113.

Ogden, J. C., L. Robinson, K. Whitlock, H. Daganhardt, and R. Cebula. 1983. Diel foraging patterns in juvenile green turtles (*Chelonia mydas* L.) in St. Croix, United States Virgin Islands. J. Exp. Marine Biol. Ecol. 66:199–205.

Ogren, L. H. 1989. Distribution of juvenile and subadult Kemp's ridley turtles: Preliminary results from the 1984–1987 surveys. *In* Calliouet, C. W., Jr., and A. M. Landry, Jr., eds. Proceedings of the First International Symposium on Kemp's Ridley Sea Turtle Biology, Conservation and Management, 116–123. Texas A & M Univ. Sea Grant College Progr. Spec. Publ.-89 (105).

Ogren, L., and C. McVea, Jr. 1982. Apparent hibernation by sea turtles in North American waters. *In* Bjorndal, K. A., ed. Biology and conservation of sea turtles, 127–132. Smithsonian Institution Press, Washington, D.C.

Ogren, L. H., J. W. Watson, Jr., and D. A. Wickham. 1977. Loggerhead sea turtles, *Caretta caretta,* encountering shrimp trawls. Marine Fish. Rev. 39:15–17.

Oguma, K. 1937. Studies on sauropsid chromosomes III. The chromosomes of the soft-shelled turtle, *Amyda japonica* (Temminck & Schleg.), as additional proof of female heterogamety in the Reptilia. Japanese J. Genetics 24:247–264.

O'Hara, J. 1980. Thermal influences on the swimming speed of loggerhead turtle hatchlings. Copeia 1980:773–780.

O'Hara, J., and J. R. Wilcox. 1990. Avoidance responses of loggerhead turtles, *Caretta caretta,* to low frequency sound. Copeia 1990:564–567.

Olafsson, P. G., A. M. Bryan, B. Bush, and W. Stone. 1983. Snapping turtle: A biological screen for PCBs. Chemosphere 12:1525–1532.

Oliver, J. A. 1955. The natural history of North American amphibians and reptiles. D. Van Nostrand Co., Princeton, New Jersey. 359 pp.

Olson, J. M., and K. M. Crawford. 1989. The effect of seasonal acclimatization on the buffering capacity and lactate dehydrogenase activity in tissues of the freshwater turtle *Chrysemys picta marginata*. J. Exp. Biol. 145:471–476.

Olson, R. E. 1976. Weight regimes in the tortoise *Gopherus berlandieri*. Texas J. Sci. 27:321–323.

———. 1987. Evaporative water loss in the tortoise *Gopherus berlandieri* in ambient temperature regimes. Bull. Maryland Herpetol. Soc. 23:93–100.

———. 1989. Notes on evaporative water loss in terrestrial chelonians. Bull. Maryland Herpetol. Soc. 25:49–57.

Ortleb, E. P., and O. J. Sexton. 1964. Orientation of the painted turtle, *Chrysemys picta*. Amer. Midl. Natur. 71:320–334.

Osorio, S. R., and R. B. Bury. 1982. Ecology and status of the desert tortoise (*Gopherus agassizii*) on Tiburón Island, Sonora. *In* Bury, R. B., ed. North American tortoises: Conservation and ecology, 39–49. U.S. Fish Wildl. Serv. Wildl. Res. Rept. (12).

Ottley, J. R., and V. M. Velázques Solis. 1989. An extant, indigenous tortoise population in Baja California Sur, Mexico, with the description of a new species of *Xerobates* (Testudines: Testudinidae). Great Basin Natur. 49:496–502.

Overmann, S. R., and R. Boice. 1970. Social facilitation of feeding in box turtles and American toads. Ecol. Soc. Amer. Bull. 51(4):23.

Owens, D. W. 1980. The comparative reproductive physiology of sea turtles. Amer. Zool. 20:549–563.

Owens, D., D-C. Comuzzie, and M. Grassman. 1985. Chemoreception in the homing and orientation behavior of amphibians and reptiles, with special reference to sea turtles. *In* Duvall, D., D. Müller-Schwarze, and R. M. Silverstein, eds. Chemical signals in vertebrates, vol. 4, Ecology, evolution and comparative biology, 341–355. Plenum Publ. Corp., New York.

Owens, D. W., M. A. Grassman, and J. R. Hendrickson. 1982. The imprinting hypothesis and sea turtle reproduction. Herpetologica 38:124–135.

Owens, D. W., and J. R. Hendrickson. 1978. Endocrine studies and sex ratios of the green sea turtle, *Chelonia mydas. In* Henderson, G. E., ed. 1978. Proceedings of the Florida and Interregional Conference on sea turtles, 12–14. Florida Marine Res. Publ. 33.

Owens, D. W., J. R. Hendrickson, V. Lance, and I. P. Callard. 1978. A technique for determining sex of immature *Chelonia mydas* using radioimmunoassay. Herpetologica 34:270–273.

Owens, D. W., and Y. A. Morris. 1985. The comparative endocrinology of sea turtles. Copeia 1985:723–735.

Packard, G. C., and M. J. Packard. 1983. Patterns of

nitrogen excretion by embryonic softshell turtles (*Trionyx spiniferus*) developing in cleidoic eggs. Science 221:1049–1050.

———. 1984. Coupling of physiology of embryonic turtles to the hydric environment. *In* Seymour, R. S., ed. Respiration and metabolism of embryonic vertebrates, 99–119. Junk Publ., Dordrecht.

———. 1988. The physiological ecology of reptilian eggs and embryos. *In* Gans, C., and R. B. Huey, eds. Biology of the Reptilia, vol. 16, 523–605, Alan R. Liss, New York.

———. 1989. Control of metabolism and growth in embryonic turtles: A test of the urea hypothesis. J. Exp. Biol. 147:203–216.

———. 1990a. Growth of embryonic softshell turtles is unaffected by uremia. Can. J. Zool. 68:841–844.

———. 1990b. Patterns of survival at subzero temperatures by hatchling painted turtles and snapping turtles. J. Exp. Zool. 254:233–236.

Packard, G. C., M. J. Packard, and L. Benigan. 1991. Sexual differentiation, growth, and hatching success by embryonic painted turtles incubated in wet and dry environments at fluctuating temperatures. Herpetologica 47:125–132.

Packard, G. C., M. J. Packard, and G. F. Birchard. 1989. Sexual differentiation and hatching success by painted turtles incubating in different thermal and hydric environments. Herpetologica 45:385–392.

Packard, G. C., M. J. Packard, and T. J. Boardman. 1981. Patterns and possible significance of water exchange by flexible-shelled eggs of painted turtles (*Chrysemys picta*). Physiol. Zool. 54:165–178.

———. 1982. An experimental analysis of the water relations of eggs of Blanding's turtles (*Emydoidea blandingii*). Zool. J. Linnean Soc. 75:23–34.

———. 1984a. Influence of hydration of the environment on the patterns of nitrogen excretion by embryonic snapping turtles (*Chelydra serpentina*). J. Exp. Biol. 108:195–204.

———. 1984b. Effects of the hydric environment on metabolism of embryonic snapping turtles do not result from altered patterns of sexual differentiation. Copeia 1984:547–550.

Packard, G. C., M. J. Packard, T. J. Boardman, and M. D. Ashen. 1981. Possible adaptive value of water exchanges in flexible-shelled eggs of turtles. Science 213:471–473.

Packard, G. C., M. J. Packard, T. J. Boardman, K. A. Morris, and R. D. Shuman. 1983. Influence of water exchanges by flexible-shelled eggs of painted turtles *Chrysemys picta* on metabolism and growth of embryos. Physiol. Zool. 56:217–230.

Packard, G. C., M. J. Packard, and W. H. N. Gutzke.

1985. Influence of hydration of the environment on eggs and embryos of the terrestrial turtle *Terrapene ornata*. Physiol. Zool. 58:564–575.

Packard, G. C., M. J. Packard, K. Miller, and T. J. Boardman. 1987. Influence of moisture, temperature, and substrate on snapping turtle eggs and embryos. Ecology 68:983–993.

Packard, G. C., T. L. Taigen, T. J. Boardman, M. J. Packard, and C. R. Tracy. 1979. Changes in mass of softshell turtle (*Trionyx spiniferus*) eggs incubated on substrates differing in water potential. Herpetologica 35:78–86.

Packard, G. C., T. L. Taigen, M. J. Packard, and T. J. Boardman. 1980. Water relations of pliable-shelled eggs of common snapping turtles (*Chelydra serpentina*). Can. J. Zool. 58:1404–1411.

———. 1981. Changes in mass of eggs of softshell turtles (*Trionyx spiniferus*) incubated under hydric conditions simulating those of natural nests. J. Zool. (London). 193:81–90.

Packard, G. C., T. L. Taigen, M. J. Packard, and R. D. Shuman. 1979. Water-vapor conductance of testudinian and crocodilian eggs (class Reptilia). Resp. Physiol. 38:1–10.

Packard, M. J., K. F. Hirsch, and J. B. Iverson. 1984. Structure of shells from eggs of kinosternid turtles. J. Morphol. 181:9–20.

Packard, M. J., J. B. Iverson, and G. C. Packard. 1984. Morphology of shell formation in eggs of the turtle *Kinosternon flavescens*. J. Morphol. 181:22–28.

Packard, M. J., and G. C. Packard. 1979. Structure of the shell and tertiary membranes of eggs of softshell turtles (*Trionyx spiniferus*). J. Morphol. 159:131–144.

———. 1986. Effect of water balance on growth and calcium mobilization of embryonic painted turtles (*Chrysemys picta*). Physiol. Zool. 59:398–405.

———. 1991. Sources of calcium, magnesium, and phosphorus for embryonic softshell turtles (*Trionyx spiniferus*). J. Exp. Zool. 258:151–157.

Packard, M. J., G. C. Packard, and T. J. Boardman. 1982. Structure of eggshells and water relations of reptilian eggs. Herpetologica 38:136–155.

Paladino, F. V., M. P. O'Connor, and J. R. Spotila. 1990. Metabolism of leatherback turtles, gigantothermy, and thermoregulation of dinosaurs. Nature 344:858–860.

Pallas, D. C. 1960. Observations on a nesting of the wood turtle, *Clemmys insculpta*. Copeia 1960:155–156.

Palmer, B. D., and L. G. Guillette, Jr. 1988. Histology and functional morphology of the female reproductive tract of the tortoise *Gopherus polyphemus*. Amer. J. Anat. 183:200–211.

———. 1990. Morphological changes in the oviductal endometrium during the reproductive cycle of the tortoise, *Gopherus polyphemus*. J. Morphol. 204:323–333.

Palmer, W. M., and C. L. Cordes. 1988. Habitat suitability index models: Diamondback terrapin (nesting)–Atlantic Coast. U.S. Fish Wildl. Serv. Biol. Rept. 82(10.151):1–18.

Pappas, M. J., and B. J. Brecke. 1992. Habitat selection of juvenile Blanding's turtles, *Emydoidea blandingii*. J. Herpetol. 26:233–234.

Parker, G. H. 1922. The crawling of young loggerhead turtles toward the sea. J. Exp. Zool. 6:323–331.

———. 1929. The growth of the loggerhead turtle. Amer. Natur. 63:367–373.

Parker, J. W. 1982. Opportunistic feeding by an ornate box turtle under the nest of a Mississippi kite. Southwest. Natur. 27:365.

Parker, M. V. 1939. The amphibians and reptiles of Reelfoot Lake and vicinity, with a key for the separation of species and subspecies. J. Tennessee Acad. Sci. 14:72–101.

Parker, W. S. 1984. Immigration and dispersal of slider turtles *Pseudemys scripta* in Mississippi farm ponds. Amer. Midl. Natur. 112:280–293.

———. 1990. Colonization of a newly constructed farm pond in Mississippi by slider turtles and comparisons with established populations. *In* Gibbons, J. W., ed. Life history and ecology of the slider turtle, 216–222. Smithsonian Institution Press, Washington, D.C.

Parkes, A. S. 1981. Reproduction in the green sea turtle, *Chelonia mydas*. Symp. Zool. Soc. London (46):253–265.

Parmalee, P. W. 1989. Muskrat predation on softshell turtles. J. Tennessee Acad. Sci. 64:225–227.

Parmalee, P. W., and W. E. Klippel. 1981. Remains of the wood turtle *Clemmys insculpta* (LeConte) from a late Pleistocene deposit in middle Tennessee. Amer. Midl. Natur. 105:413–416.

Parmenter, R. R. 1980. Effects of food availability and water temperature on the feeding ecology of pond sliders (*Chrysemys scripta*). Copeia 1980:503–514.

———. 1981. Digestive turnover rates in freshwater turtles: The influence of temperature and body size. Comp. Biochem. Physiol. 70A:235–238.

Parmenter, R. R., and H. W. Avery. 1990. The feeding ecology of the slider turtle. *In* Gibbons, J. W., ed. Life history and ecology of the slider turtle, 257–266. Smithsonian Institution Press, Washington, D.C.

Parmley, D. 1986. Herpetofauna of the Rancholabrean Schulze Cave local fauna of Texas. J. Herpetol. 20:1–10.

———. 1988. Additional Pleistocene amphibians and reptiles from the Seymour Formation, Texas. J. Herpetol. 22:82–87.

———. 1990. A late Holocene herpetofauna from Montague County, Texas. Texas J. Sci. 42:412–415.

———. 1992. Turtles from the late Hemphillian (latest Miocene) of Knox County, Nebraska. Texas J. Sci. 44:339–348.

Parrish, F. K. 1958. Miscellaneous observations on the behavior of captive sea turtles. Bull. Marine Sci. Gulf Caribbean. 8:348–355.

Parsons, J. J. 1962. The green turtle and man. University of Florida Press, Gainesville. 126 pp.

———. 1972. The hawksbill turtle and the tortoise shell trade. *In* Etude de géographie tropicale offertes à Pierre Gourou, 45–60. Mouton & Co., Paris.

Parsons, T. S. 1968. Variation in the choanal structure of Recent turtles. Can. J. Zool. 46:1235–1263.

Pathak, S., and L. Dey. 1956. The fatty acid composition of Indian turtle fat. Biochem. J. 62:448–451.

Patterson, R. 1971a. The role of urination in egg predator defense in the desert tortoise (*Gopherus agassizi*). Herpetologica 27:197–199.

———. 1971b. Aggregation and dispersal behavior in captive *Gopherus agassizi*. J. Herpetol. 5:214–216.

———. 1971c. Visual cliff perception in tortoises. Herpetologica 27:339–341.

———. 1973a. The os transiliens in four species of tortoises, genus *Gopherus*. Bull. South. California Acad. Sci. 72:51–52.

———. 1973b. Why tortoises float. J. Herpetol. 7:373–375.

———. 1976. Vocalization in the desert tortoise. Proc. Symp. Desert Tortoise Council 1976:77–83.

———. 1977. Growth and shell relationships in the desert tortoise. Proc. Symp. Desert Tortoise Council 1977:158–166.

———. 1978. Shell growth in the desert tortoise and in the box turtles. Proc. Symp. Desert Tortoise Council 1978:60–68.

———. 1982. The distribution of the desert tortoise (*Gopherus agassizii*). *In* Bury, R. B., ed. North American tortoises: Conservation and ecology, 51–55. U.S. Fish Wildl. Serv. Wildl. Res. Rept. (12).

Patterson, R., and B. Brattstrom. 1972. Growth in captive *Gopherus agassizi*. Herpetologica 28:169–171.

Paukstis, G. L., W. H. N. Gutzke, and G. C. Packard. 1984. Effects of substrate water potential and fluctuating temperatures on sex ratios of hatchling painted turtles (*Chrysemys picta*). Can. J. Zool. 62:1491–1494.

Paukstis, G. L., and F. J. Janzen. 1988. An additional specimen of *Terrapene carolina triunguis* (Reptilia:

Testudines) from southern Illinois. Trans. Illinois Acad. Sci. 81:283–286.

———. 1990. Sex determination in reptiles: Summary of effects of constant temperatures of incubation on sex ratios of offspring. Smithsonian Herpetol. Infor. Serv. (83):1–28.

Paukstis, G. L., and R. D. Shuman. 1989. Supercooling and freeze tolerance in hatchling painted turtles (*Chrysemys picta*). Can. J. Zool. 67:1082–1084.

Pavalko, P. 1986. Shell and scute anomalies in some Midwestern turtles. Bull. Chicago Herpetol. Soc. 21:36–38.

Pawley, R. 1987. Measurements of a large alligator snapping turtle, *Macroclemys temmincki,* in the Brookfield Zoo. Bull. Chicago Herpetol. Soc 22:134.

Paxson, D. W. 1962. An observation of eggs in a tortoise shell. Herpetologica (1961) 17:278–279.

Pearse, A. S. 1923. The abundance and migration of turtles. Ecology 4:24–28.

Penn, G. H. 1950. Utilization of crawfishes by cold-blooded vertebrates in the eastern United States. Amer. Midl. Natur. 44:643–658.

Peretti, P. O., and T. Zrout. 1975. Conditioning in the spinal turtle, *Emydoidea blandingi.* J. Biol. Psychol. 17(2):10–16.

Perry, A., G. B. Bauer, and A. E. Dizon. 1986. Magnetoreception and biomineralization of magnetite in amphibians and reptiles. Topics Geobiol. 5:439–453.

Perry, S. F., C. Darian-Smith, J. Alston, C. J. Limpus, and J. E. Maloney. 1989. Histological structure of the lungs of the loggerhead turtle, *Caretta caretta,* before and after hatching. Copeia 1989:1000–1010.

Peters, E. L., and I. L. Brisbin, Jr. 1988. Radiocaesium elimination in the yellow-bellied turtle (*Pseudemys scripta*). J. Appl. Ecol. 25:461–471.

Peters, J. A. 1948. The box turtle as a host for dipterous parasites. Amer. Midl. Natur. 40:472–474.

Peters, K. 1959. A physiological study of the effect of hibernation on the ornate box turtle. Trans. Kansas Acad. Sci. 62:15–20.

Petersen, A. 1984. *Dermochelys coriacea* (order Chelonia) recorded in Iceland. Natturufraedingurinn 53:161–163.

Peterson, C., G. Monahan, and F. Schwartz. 1985. Tagged green turtle returns and nests again in North Carolina. Marine Turtle Newsl. (35):5–6.

Peterson, C. C. 1987. Thermal relations of hibernating painted turtles, *Chrysemys picta.* J. Herpetol. 21:16–20.

Peterson, E. A. 1966. Hearing in the lizard: Some comments on the auditory capacities of a nonmammalian ear. Herpetologica 22:161–171.

Petokas, P. J. 1981a. A. S. Pearse's density estimates for turtles: The correction of a long-standing error. Bull. Maryland Herpetol. Soc. 17:68–70.

———. 1981b. Snapping turtle predation on ring-billed gulls. Bull. Maryland Herpetol. Soc. 17:111–115.

Petokas, P. J., and M. M. Alexander. 1980. The nesting of *Chelydra serpentina* in northern New York. J. Herpetol. 14:239–244.

———. 1981. Occurrence of the Blanding's turtle in northern New York. New York Fish Game J. 28:119–120.

Petranka, J. W., and A. Phillippi. 1978. Observations on the courtship behavior of juvenile *Chrysemys concinna concinna* and *Chrysemys floridana hoyi* (Reptilia, Testudines, Emydidae). J. Herpetol. 12:417–419.

Pewtress R. K. 1990. The stinkpot musk turtle; its natural history and captive maintenance. *In* Coote, J., ed. Proceedings of the 1988 U.K. Herpetological Societies Symposium on Captive Breeding, 73–78. British Herpetol. Soc., London.

Phasuk, B., and S. Rongmuangsart. 1973. Growth studies on the ridley turtle, *Lepidochelys olivacea olivacea* Eschscholtz, in captivity and the effect of food preferences on growth. Phuket Marine Biol. Center. Res. Bull. (1):1–14.

Philibosian, R. 1976. Disorientation of hawksbill turtle hatchlings, *Eretmochelys imbricata,* by stadium lights. Copeia 1976:824.

Philippi, R. A. 1899. Los tortugas chilenas. Anal. Univ. Chile (Santiago). 104:727–736.

Phillips, E. J. 1977. Raising hatchlings of the leatherback turtle, *Dermochelys coriacea.* British J. Herpetol. 5:677–678.

Pilch, J., Jr. 1981. *Chrysemys concinna texana* (Texas river cooter). Morphology. Herpetol. Rev. 12:81.

Pinckney, J. 1990. Correlation analysis of adult female, egg and hatchling sizes in the loggerhead turtle, *Caretta caretta* (L.), nesting at Kiawah Island, South Carolina, USA. Bull. Marine Sci. 47:670–679.

Pitler, R. 1985. *Malaclemys terrapin terrapin* (northern diamondback terrapin). Behavior. Herpetol. Rev. 16:82.

Pitts, N. 1978. Soil maps on trail of bog turtle. Soil Conserv. 42:22–23.

Platt, S. G., and C. G. Brantley. 1991. *Apalone spinifera* (spiny softshell). Behavior. Herpetol. Rev. 22:57.

Platz, C. C. Jr., G. Mengden, H. Quinn, F. Wood, and J. Wood. 1980. Semen collection, evaluation and freezing in the green sea turtle, Galapagos tortoise, and red-eared pond turtle. Ann. Proc. Amer. Assoc. Zoo Vet. 1980:47–54.

Plotkin, P., M. Polak, and D. W. Owens. 1991. Observations on olive ridley sea turtle behavior prior to an arribada at Playa Nancite, Costa Rica. Marine Turtle Newsl. (53):9–10.

Plummer, M. V. 1976. Some aspects of nesting success in the turtle, *Trionyx muticus*. Herpetologica 32:353–359.

———. 1977a. Notes on the courtship and mating behavior of the soft-shell turtle, *Trionyx muticus* (Reptilia, Testudines, Trionychidae). J. Herpetol. 11:90–92.

———. 1977b. Activity, habitat, and population structure in the turtle, *Trionyx muticus*. Copeia 1977:431–440.

———. 1977c. Reproduction and growth in the turtle *Trionyx muticus*. Copeia 1977:440–447.

Plummer, M. V., and D. B. Farrar. 1981. Sexual dietary differences in a population of *Trionyx muticus*. J. Herpetol. 15:175–179.

Plummer, M. V., and H. W. Shirer. 1975. Movement patterns in a river population of the softshell turtle *Trionyx muticus*. Occ. Pap. Mus. Natur. Hist. Univ. Kansas (43):1–26.

Pluto, T. G., and E. D. Bellis. 1986. Habitat utilization by the turtle, *Graptemys geographica*, along a river. J. Herpetol. 20:22–31.

———. 1988. Seasonal and annual movements of riverine map turtles, *Graptemys geographica*. J. Herpetol. 22:152–158.

Pond, C. M., and C. A. Mattacks. 1984. Anatomical organization of adipose tissue in chelonians. British J. Herpetol. 6:402–405.

Pope, C. H. 1935. Natural history of central Asia. Vol. 10. The reptiles of China. American Museum of Natural History, New York. 604 pp.

———. 1939. Turtles of the United States and Canada. Alfred A. Knopf., Inc., New York. 343 pp.

Porter, K. R. 1972. Herpetology. W. B. Saunders Co., Philadelphia. 524 pp.

Posey, M. H. 1979. A study of the homing instinct in *Terrapene c. carolina* in Maryland. Bull. Maryland Herpetol. Soc. 15:139–140.

Pough, F. H., and M. B. Pough. 1968. The systematic status of painted turtles (*Chrysemys*) in the northeastern United States. Copeia 1968:612–618.

Powders, V. N. 1978. Observations of oviposition and natural incubation of eggs of the alligator snapping turtle, *Macroclemys temmincki*, in Georgia. Copeia 1978:154–156.

Powell, C. B. 1967. Female sexual cycles of *Chrysemys picta* and *Clemmys insculpta* in Nova Scotia. Can. Field-Natur. 81:134–140.

Powell, R., N. A. Laposha, D. D. Smith, and J. S. Parmerlee. 1984. New distributional records for some semiaquatic amphibians and reptiles from the Rio Sabinas Basin, Coahuila, Mexico. Herpetol. Rev. 15:78–79.

Powell, R., and S. Phillips. 1984. *Sternotherus odoratus* (stinkpot). Reproduction. Herpetol. Rev. 15:51.

Prange, H. D. 1976. Energetics of swimming of a sea turtle. J. Exp. Biol. 64:1–12.

———. 1985. Renal and extra-renal mechanisms of salt and water regulation of sea turtles: A speculative review. Copeia 1985:771–776.

Prange, H. D., and L. Greenwald. 1980. Effects of dehydration on the urine concentration and salt gland secretion of the green sea turtle. Comp. Biochem. Physiol. 66A:133–136.

Prange, H. D., and D. C. Jackson. 1976. Ventilation, gas exchange and metabolic scaling of a sea turtle. Resp. Physiol. 27:369–377.

Praschag, R. 1983. Zur Fortpflanzungsbiologie von *Kinosternon baurii* (Garman, 1891) mit Bemerkungen über eine abnorme Gelegehäufigkeit und die Embryonalentwiklung (Testudines: Kinosternidae). Salamandra 19:141–150.

Prescher, T. 1972. Chronologically speaking. Int. Turtle and Tortoise Soc. J. 6(5):13–14.

Preston, R. E. 1971. Pleistocene turtles from the Arkalon local fauna of southwestern Kansas. J. Herpetol. 5:208–211.

———. 1979. Late Pleistocene cold-blooded vertebrate faunas from the mid-continental United States. I. Reptilia: Testudines, Crocodilia. Univ. Michigan Mus. Paleontol. Pap. Paleontol. (19):1–53.

Preston, R. E., and C. J. McCoy. 1971. The status of *Emys twentei* Taylor (Reptilia: Testudinidae) based on new fossil records from Kansas and Oklahoma. J. Herpetol. 5:23–30.

Pritchard, P. C. H. 1969. Sea turtles of the Guianas. Bull. Florida St. Mus. Biol. Sci. 13:85–140.

———. 1971. The leatherback or leathery luth, *Dermochelys coriacea*. IUCN Monogr. 1. 39 pp.

———. 1973. International migrations of South American sea turtles (Cheloniidae and Dermochelidae). Anim. Behav. 21:18–27.

———. 1976. Post-nesting movements of marine turtles (Cheloniidae and Dermochelyidae) tagged in the Guianas. Copeia 1976:749–754.

———. 1979. Encyclopedia of turtles. T. F. H. Publications, Inc., Neptune, New Jersey. 895 pp.

———. 1980a. *Dermochelys, D. coriacea*. Catalog Amer. Amphib. Rept. 238:1–4.

———. 1980b. Record size turtles from Florida and South America. Chelonologica 1:113–123.

———. 1982. Nesting of the leatherback turtle, *Dermochelys coriacea* in Pacific Mexico, with a new estimate of the World population status. Copeia 1982:741–747.

———. 1985. Recovery of a tagged leatherback. Marine Turtle Newsl. (32):8.

———. 1988. The loggerhead in Guyana. Marine Turtle Newsl. (43):6–7.

———. 1989. The alligator snapping turtle: Biology and conservation. Milwaukee Public Museum, Milwaukee, Wisconsin. 104 pp.

———. 1990. Kemp's ridleys are rarer than we thought. Marine Turtle Newsl. (49):1–3.

Pritchard, P. C. H., and W. Greenhood. 1968. The sun and the turtle. Int. Turtle and Tortoise Soc. J. 2(1):20–25, 34.

Pritchard, P. C. H., and R. Márquez M. 1973. Kemp's ridley turtle or Atlantic ridley, Lepidochelys kempi. IUCN Monogr. 2. 30 pp.

Pritchard, P. C. H., and P. Trebbau. 1984. The turtles of Venezuela. Soc. Stud. Amphib. Rept. Contrib. Herpetol. (2). 403 pp.

Provancha, J. A., and N. Mrosovsky. 1988. Sex ratio of loggerhead sea turtles hatching on a Florida beach in 1986. In Schroeder, B. A., ed. Proceedings of the Eighth Annual Workshop on Sea Turtle Conservation and Biology, 89–90. NOAA-TM-NMFS-SEFC-214.

Punzo, F. 1974. A qualitative and quantitative study of food items of the yellow mud turtle, Kinosternon flavescens (Agassiz). J. Herpetol. 8:269–271.

———. 1975. Studies on the feeding behavior, diet, nesting habits and temperature relationships of Chelydra serpentina osceola (Chelonia: Chelydridae). J. Herpetol. 9:207–210.

———. 1976. Analysis of the pH and electrolyte components found in the blood plasma of several species of West Texas reptiles. J. Herpetol. 10:49–52.

Quammen, R. 1992. A latest Cretaceous (Maestrictian) lower vertebrate faunule from the Hell Creek Formation of North Dakota. North Dakota Acad. Sci. Proc. 46:41.

Quay, W. B. 1972. Sexual and relative growth differences in brain regions of the turtle Pseudemys scripta (Schoepff). Copeia 1972:541–546.

Quinn, A. J., and J. L. Christiansen. 1972. The relationship between pond bottom type and growth rate of western painted turtles Chrysemys picta belli in Iowa, a preliminary report. Proc. Iowa Acad. Sci. 78:67–69.

Rabalais, S. C., and N. N. Rabalais. 1980. The occurrence of sea turtles on the south Texas coast. Contrib. Marine Sci. 23:123–129.

Radhakrisna, G., C. C. Q. Chin, F. Wold, and P. J. Weldon. 1989. Glycoproteins in Rathke's gland secretions of loggerhead (Caretta caretta) and Kemp's ridley (Lepidochelys kempi) sea turtles. Comp. Biochem. Physiol. 94B:375–378.

Ragotzkie, R. A. 1959. Mortality of loggerhead turtle eggs from excessive rainfall. Ecology 40:303–305.

Rainboth, W. J., D. C. Buth, and F. B. Turner. 1989. Allozyme variation in Mojave populations of the desert tortoise, Gopherus agassizi. Copeia 1989:115–123.

Rainey, D. G. 1953. Death of an ornate box turtle parasitized by dipterous larvae. Herpetologica 9: 109–110.

Rainey, W. E. 1981. Guide to sea turtle visceral anatomy. NOAA-TM-NMFS-SEFC-82. 82 pp.

Raney, E. C., and E. A. Lachner. 1942. Summer food of Chrysemys picta marginata in Chautauqua Lake, New York. Copeia 1942:83–85.

Rathbun, G. B., N. Siepel, and D. Holland. 1992. Nesting behavior and movements of western pond turtles, Clemmys marmorata. Southwest. Natur. 37:319–324.

Ratterman, R. J., and R. A. Ackerman. 1989. The water exchange and hydric microclimate of painted turtle (Chrysemys picta) eggs incubating in field nests. Physiol. Zool. 62:1059–1079.

Raymond, P. W. 1984. Sea turtle hatchling disorientation and artificial beachfront lighting: A review of the problem and potential solutions. Rept. Center Environ. Ed. Sea Turtle Rescue Fund. 72 pp.

Reagan, D. P. 1974. Habitat selection in the three-toed box turtle, Terrapene carolina triunguis. Copeia 1974:512–527.

Ream, C., and R. Ream. 1966. The influence of sampling methods on the estimation of population structure in painted turtles. Amer. Midl. Natur. 75:325–338.

Rebel, T. P., ed. 1974. Sea turtles and the turtle industry of the West Indies, Florida, and the Gulf of Mexico. University of Miami Press, Coral Gables, Florida. 250 pp.

Redfoot, W. E., L. M. Ehrhart, and P. W. Raymond. 1985. A juvenile Atlantic hawksbill turtle, Eretmochelys imbricata, from Brevard County, Florida. Florida Scientist 48:193–196.

Redmond, A. 1979. Observations on the alligator snapping turtle. Bull. Georgia Herpetol. Soc. 5(3–4):5–6.

Reeves, R. R., and S. Leatherwood. 1983. Autumn sightings of marine turtles (Cheloniidae) off south Texas. Southwest Natur. 28:281–288.

Reid, G. K., Jr. 1955. Reproduction and development in the northern diamondback terrapin, Malaclemys terrapin terrapin. Copeia 1955:310–311.

Reid, M., and A. Nichols. 1970. Predation by reptiles on the periodic cicada. Bull. Maryland Herpetol. Soc. 6:57.

Reilly, S. M. 1983. *Sternotherus odoratus* (stinkpot). Algal relationships. Herpetol. Rev. 14:76.

Reisz, R. 1992. The chelonian story. Turtle are the only survivors of an obscure vertebrate lineage. The Sciences, July/August, 37–43.

Renous, S., and V. Bels. 1991. Etude cinématique de la palette natatoire antérieure de la tortue Luth, *Dermochelys coriacea* (Vandelli, 1761), au cours de sa locomotion terrestre. Can. J. Zool. 69:495–503.

Renous, S., F. Rimblot-Baly, J. Fretey, and C. Pieau. 1989. Caractéristiques de développement embryonnaire de la tortue luth, *Dermochelys coriacea* (Vandelli, 1761). Ann. Sci. Natur. Zool. Paris, ser. 13, 10:197–229.

Reynolds, S. L., and M. E. Seidel. 1982. *Sternotherus odoratus*. Catalog. Amer. Amphib. Rept. 287:1–4.

———. 1983. Morphological homogeneity in the turtle *Sternotherus odoratus* (Kinosternidae) throughout its range. J. Herpetol. 17:113–120.

Rhijn, F. A. van. 1979. Optic orientation in hatchlings of the sea turtle, *Chelonia mydas* I. Brightness: Not the only optic cue in sea finding orientation. Marine Behav. Physiol. 6:105–121.

Rhodin, A. G. J. 1985. Comparative chondro-osseous development and growth of marine turtles. Copeia 1985:752–771.

Rhodin, A. G. J., and T. Largy. 1984. Prehistoric occurrence of the redbelly turtle (*Pseudemys rubriventris*) at Concord, Middlesex County, Massachusetts. Herpetol. Rev. 15:107.

Rhodin, A. G. J., J. A. Ogden, and G. J. Conlogue. 1980. Preliminary studies on skeletal morphology of the leatherback turtle. Marine Turtle Newsl. 16:7–9.

———. 1981. Chondro-osseous morphology of *Dermochelys coriacea*, a marine reptile with mammalian skeletal features. Nature 290:244–246.

Rhodin, A. G. J., and R. C. Schoelkopf. 1982. Reproductive data on a female leatherback turtle, *Dermochelys coriacea*, stranded in New Jersey. Copeia 1982:181–183.

Rhodin, A. G. J., and H. M. Smith. 1982. The original authorship and type specimen of *Dermochelys coriacea*. J. Herpetol. 16:316–317.

Richardson, J. I. 1978. Results of a hatchery for incubating loggerhead sea turtle (*Caretta caretta* Linné) eggs on Little Cumberland Island, Georgia. *In* Henderson, G. E., ed. 1978. Proceedings of the Florida and Interregional Conference on sea turtles, 15. Florida Marine Res. Publ. 33.

Richardson, J. I., and P. McGillivary. 1991. Post-hatchling loggerhead turtles eat insects in *Sargassum* community. Marine Turtle Newsl. (55):2–5.

Richardson, J. I., and T. H. Richardson. 1982. An experimental population model for the loggerhead sea turtle (*Caretta caretta*). *In* Bjorndal, K. A., ed. Biology and conservation of sea turtles, 165–176. Smithsonian Institution Press, Washington, D.C.

Richardson, T. H., J. I. Richardson, C. Ruckdeschel and M. W. Dix. 1978. Remigration patterns of loggerhead sea turtles (*Caretta caretta*) nesting on Little Cumberland and Cumberland Islands, Georgia. *In* Henderson, G. E., ed. 1978. Proceedings of the Florida and Interregional Conference on sea turtles, 39–44. Florida Marine Res. Publ. 33.

Richmond, N. D. 1945. Nesting habits of the mud turtle. Copeia 1945:217–219.

———. 1958. The status of the Florida snapping turtle *Chelydra osceola* Stejneger. Copeia 1958:41–43.

———. 1964. Fossil amphibians and reptiles of Frankstown Cave, Pennsylvania. Ann. Carnegie Mus. Natur. Hist. 36:225–228.

Rickard, R. S., R. M. Engeman, G. O. Zerbe, and R. B. Bury. 1989. A nonparametric comparison of mono-molecular growth curves: Application to western painted turtle data. Growth, Develop. Aging 53:47–56.

Ricklefs, R. E., and J. Burger. 1977. Composition of the eggs of the diamondback terrapin. Amer. Midl. Natur. 97:232–235.

Ridgway, S. H., E. G. Wever, J. G. McCormick, J. Palin, and J. H. Anderson. 1969. Hearing in the giant sea turtle *Chelonia mydas*. Proc. Natl. Acad. Sci. 64:884–890.

Riedesel, M. L., J. L. Cloudsley-Thompson, and J. A. Cloudsley-Thompson. 1971. Evaporative thermoregulation in turtles. Physiol. Zool. 44:28–32.

Riemer, D. N. 1981. Multiple nesting by a female box turtle (*Terrapene c. carolina*). Chelonologica 2:53–56.

Rigley, L. 1974. Agonistic behavior of the eastern mud turtle *Kinosternon subrubrum subrubrum*. Bull. Maryland Herpetol. Soc. 10:22–23.

Rimblot, F., J. Fretey, N. Mrosovsky, J. Lescure, and C. Pieau. 1985. Sexual differentiation as a function of the incubation temperature of eggs in the sea-turtle *Dermochelys coriacea* (Vandelli, 1761). Amphibia-Reptilia. 6:83–92.

Rimblot-Baly, F., J. Lescure, J. Fretey, and C. Pieau. 1987. Sensibilité à la température de la différenciation sexuelle chez la Tortue Luth, *Dermochelys coriacea* (Vandelli, 1761); application des données de l'incubation artificielle à l'étude de la sex-ratio dans la nature. Ann. Sci. Natur. Zool. Paris, ser. 13, 8:277–290.

Risher, J. F., and D. L. Claussen. 1987. The effects of cold acclimation on electrocardiogram parameters in five species of turtles. Comp. Biochem Physiol. 87A:73–80.

Risley, P. L. 1930. Anatomical differences in the sexes of the musk turtle, *Sternotherus odoratus* (Latreille). Pap. Michigan Acad. Sci. Arts Lett. 11:445–464.

———. 1933. Observations on the natural history of the common musk turtle, *Sternotherus odoratus* (Latreille). Pap. Michigan Acad. Sci. Arts Lett. 17:685–711.

———. 1934. The activity of the coelomic (germinal) epithelium of the male musk turtle, *Sternotherus odoratus* (Latreille). J. Morphol. 56:59–99.

———. 1937. A preliminary study of sex development in turtle embryos following administration of testosterone. Anat. Rec. 70:103.

———. 1938. Seasonal changes in the testes of the musk turtle *Sternotherus odoratus* L. J. Morphol. 63:301–317.

———. 1941. Some observations on hermaphroditism in turtles. J. Morphol. 68:101–117.

Rivers, J. J. 1889. Description of a new turtle from the Sacramento River, belonging to the family Trionychidae. Proc. California Acad. Sci. ser. 2, 2:233–236.

Robertson, S. L., and E. N. Smith. 1982. Evaporative water loss in the spiny soft-shelled turtle *Trionyx spiniferus*. Physiol. Zool. 55:124–129.

Robinson, C., and J. R. Bider. 1988. Nesting synchrony—a strategy to decrease predation of snapping turtle (*Chelydra serpentina*) nests. J. Herpetol. 22:470–473.

Robinson, G. D., and W. A. Dunson. 1976. Water and sodium balance in the estuarine diamondback terrapin (*Malaclemys*). J. Comp. Physiol. 105:129–152.

Robinson, K. M., and G. C. Murphy. 1978. The reproductive cycle of the eastern spiny softshell turtle (*Trionyx spiniferus spiniferus*). Herpetologica 34:137–140.

Roby, C. Y., and E. C. Loveless. 1977. Range extension of *Trionyx spiniferus emoryi* into Utah (Reptilia). Great Basin Natur. 37:259.

Rodda, G. H., T. H. Fritts, and J. D. Reichel. 1991. The distributional patterns of reptiles and amphibians in the Mariana Islands. Micronesica 24:195–210.

Rogers, K. L. 1976. Herpetofauna of the Beck Ranch local fauna (upper Pliocene: Blancan) of Texas. Publ. Mus. Michigan St. Univ., Paleontol. ser. 1:163–200.

———. 1982. Herpetofaunas of the Courtland Canal and Hall Ash local faunas (Pleistocene: early Kansas) of Jewell Co., Kansas. J. Herpetol. 16:174–177.

Romer, A. S. 1956. Osteology of reptiles. University of Chicago Press, Chicago, Illinois. 772 pp.

Romeyn, T., and G. T. Haneveld. 1956. Turtle meat (*Eretmochelys imbricata*) poisoning in Netherlands New-Guinea. Doc. Med. Geogr. Trop. 8:380–382.

Root, R. W. 1949. Aquatic respiration in the musk turtle. Physiol. Zool. 22:172–178.

Rosato, P., and D. E. Ferguson. 1968. The toxicity of endrin-resistant mosquitofish to eleven species of vertebrates. Bioscience 18:783–784.

Rose, F. L. 1970. Tortoise chin gland fatty acid composition: Behavioral significance. Comp. Biochem. Physiol. 32:577–580.

———. 1980. Turtles in arid and semi-arid regions. Bull. Ecol. Soc. Amer. 61:89.

———. 1986. Carapace regeneration in *Terrapene* (Chelonia: Testudinidae). Southwest. Natur. 31:131–134.

Rose, F. L., and F. W. Judd. 1975. Activity and home range size of the Texas tortoise, *Gopherus berlandieri*, in south Texas. Herpetologica 31:448–456.

———. 1982. The biology and status of Berlandier's tortoise (*Gopherus berlandieri*). *In* Bury, R. B., ed. North American tortoises: Conservation and ecology, 57–70. U.S. Fish Wildl. Serv. Wildl. Res. Rept. (12).

———. 1991. Egg size versus carapace-xiphiplastron aperture size in *Gopherus berlandieri*. J. Herpetol. 25:248–250.

Rose, F. L., M. E. T. Scioli, and M. P. Moulton. 1988. Thermal preferentia of Berlandier's tortoise (*Gopherus berlandieri*) and the ornate box turtle (*Terrapene ornata*). Southwest. Natur. 33:357–361.

Rosen, P. C. 1987. Variation in female reproduction among populations of Sonoran mud turtles (*Kinosternon sonoriense*). Master's thesis, Arizona State University, Tempe.

Rosene, W., Jr., P. Stewart, and V. Adomaitis. 1961. Responses of heptachlor epoxide in wild animals. Proc. Ann. Conf. Southeast. Assoc. Game Fish Comm. 15:107–113.

Ross, A., and C. G. Jackson, Jr. 1972. Barnacle fouling of the ornate diamondback terrapin, *Malaclemys terrapin macrospilota*. Crustaceana 22:203–205.

Ross, D. A. 1987. Blanding's turtle: Not many left in Wisconsin. Wisconsin Natur. Res. 11:8–10.

———. 1988. *Chrysemys picta* (painted turtle). Predation. Herpetol. Rev. 19:85, 87.

Ross, D. A. 1989a. Population ecology of painted and Blanding's turtles (*Chrysemys picta* and *Emydoidea blandingi*) in central Wisconsin. Trans. Wisconsin Acad. Sci. Arts Lett. 77:77–84.

———. 1989b. Amphibians and reptiles in the diets of North American raptors. Wisconsin Endang. Res. Rept. (59):1–33.

Ross, D. A., and R. K. Anderson. 1990. Habitat use, movements, and nesting ecology of *Emydoidea blandingi* in central Wisconsin. J. Herpetol. 24:6–12.

Ross, D. A., K. N. Brewster, R. K. Anderson, N. Ratner, and C. M. Brewster. 1991. Aspects of the ecology of wood turtles, *Clemmys insculpta*, in Wisconsin. Can. Field-Natur. 105:363–367.

Ross, D. A., and J. E. Lovich. 1992. Does the color pattern of two species of turtles imitate duckweed? J. Pennsylvania Acad. Sci. 66:39–42.

Ross, J. P. 1977. Water loss in the turtle *Gopherus polyphemus*. Comp. Biochem. Physiol. 56A:477–480.

———. 1982. Historical decline of loggerhead, ridley, and leatherback sea turtles. *In* Bjorndal, K. A., ed. Biology and conservation of sea turtles, 189–195. Smithsonian Institution Press, Washington, D.C.

———. 1983. The leatherback sea turtle, *Dermochelys coriacea*, nesting in the Dominican Republic. *In* Rhodin, A. G. J., and K. Miyata, eds. Advances in herpetology and evolutionary biology. Essays in honor of Ernest E. Williams, 706–713. Mus. Comp. Zool., Harvard University. Cambridge.

———. 1984. Adult sex ratio in the green sea turtle. Copeia 1984:774–776.

Ross, J. P., S. Beavers, D. Mundell, and M. Airth-Kindree. 1989. The status of Kemp's ridley. Center Marine Conserv. 51 pp.

Rostal, D. C., J. A. Williams, and P. J. Weldon. 1991. Rathke's gland secretion by loggerhead (*Caretta caretta*) and Kemp's ridley (*Lepidochelys kempi*) sea turtles. Copeia 1991:1129–1132.

Roth, J. A., and J. Laerm. 1980. A late Pleistocene vertebrate assemblage from Edisto Island, South Carolina. Brimleyana (3):1–29.

Rowe, J. W. 1992. Observations of body size, growth, and reproduction in Blanding's turtle (*Emydoidea blandingii*) from western Nebraska. Can. J. Zool. 70:1690–1695.

Rowe, J. W., and E. O. Moll. 1991. A radiotelemetric study of activity and movements of the Blanding's turtle (*Emydoidea blandingi*) in northeastern Illinois. J. Herpetol. 25:178–185.

Ruckdeschel, C., L. Ellis, and C. R. Shoop. 1982. *Dermochelys coriacea* (leatherback sea turtle). Nesting. Herpetol. Rev. 13:126.

Ruckdeschel, C., and G. R. Zug. 1982. Mortality of sea turtles *Caretta caretta* in coastal waters of Georgia. Biol. Conserv. 22:5–9.

Rudloe, A., J. Rudloe, and L. Ogren. 1991. Occurrence of immature Kemp's ridley turtles, *Lepidochelys kempi*, in coastal waters of northwest Florida. Northeast Gulf Sci. 12:49–53.

Rudloe, J. 1980. Time of the turtle. Penguin Books Ltd., Harmondsworth, England. 273 pp.

Rudloff, H.-W. 1986. Schlammschildkröten-Terrarientiere der Zukunft. Aquar. Terrar. 33:166–169.

Rüppell, E. 1835. Neue wilbelthiere zu der Fauna von Abyssinian gehörig. III. Amphibien. Frankfurt am. M. 18 pp.

Ryan, J. J. 1981. A record size female and egg clutch for the bog turtle *Clemmys muhlenbergi*. Bull. Maryland Herpetol. Soc. 17:102–106.

Ryan, J. J., B. P.-Y. Lau, and J. A. Hardy. 1986. 2,3,7,8,-tetrachlorodibenzo—P—dioxin and related dioxins and furans in snapping turtle (*Chelydra serpentina*) tissues from the upper St. Lawrence River. Chemosphere 15:537–548.

Sabath, M. 1960. Eggs and young of several Texas reptiles. Herpetologica 16:72.

Sachsse, W. 1974. Zum Fortpflanzungsverhalten von *Clemmys muhlenbergii* bei weitgehender Nachahmung der natürlichen Lebensbedingungen im Terrarium. Salamandra 10:1–14.

———. 1977a. Normale und pathologische Phänomene bei Zuchtversuchen mit Schildkröten, hier anhand von *Kinosternon bauri* (Reptilia, Testudines, Kinosternidae). Salamandra 13:22–35.

———. 1977b. *Sternotherus m. minor,* seine Nachzucht und die damit verbundenen biologischen Beobachtungen (Reptilia: Testudines: Kinosternidae). Salamandra 13:157–165.

———. 1984. Long term studies of the reproduction of *Malaclemys terrapin centrata*. In Bels, M. V. L., and A. P. Van den Sande, eds. Maintenance and reproduction of reptiles in captivity, vol. 1, 297–308. Acta Zoologica et Pathologica Antverpiensia, no. 78.

Saint-Girons, H. 1991. Histologie comparée des fosses nasales de quelques tortues marines (*Dermochelys coriacea* et *Chelonia mydas*) et d'eaux douces (*Emys orbicularis* et *Pseudemys scripta*) (Reptilia, Dermochelyidae, Cheloniidae, Emydidae). Bijd. Dierk., Hague 61:51–61.

Sakamoto, W., Y. Naito, I. Uchida, and K. Kureha. 1990. Circadian rhythm on diving motion of the loggerhead turtle *Caretta caretta* during inter-nesting and its fluctuations induced by the oceanic environmental events. Nippon Suisan Gakkaishi 56:263–272.

Sakamoto, W., I. Uchida, Y. Naito, K. Kureha, M. Tujimura, and K. Sato. 1990. Deep diving behavior of the loggerhead turtle near the frontal zone. Nippon Suisan Gakkaishi 56:1435–1443.

Salmon, M., and K. J. Lohmann. 1989. Orientation cues used by hatchling loggerhead sea turtles (*Caretta caretta* L.) during their offshore migration. Ethology 83:215–228.

Salmon, M., and J. Wyneken. 1987. Orientation and swimming behavior of hatchling loggerhead turtles *Caretta caretta* L. during their offshore migration. J. Exp. Marine Biol. Ecol. 109:137–153.

———. 1990. Do swimming loggerhead sea turtles

(*Caretta caretta* L.) use light cues for offshore orientation? Marine Behav. Physiol. 17:233–246.

Salmon, M., J. Wyneken, E. Fritz, and M. Lucas. 1992. Seafinding by hatchling sea turtles: Role of brightness, silhouette and beach slope as orientation cues. Behaviour 122:56–77.

Sanderson, R. A. 1974. Sexual dimorphism in the Barbour's map turtle, *Malaclemys barbouri* (Carr and Marchand). Master's thesis, University of South Florida, Tampa. 94 pp.

Sanderson, R. A., and J. E. Lovich. 1988. *Graptemys barbouri*. Catalog. Amer. Amphib. Rept. 421:1–2.

Santhuff, S. D., and L. A. Wilson. 1990. *Graptemys pulchra* (Alabama map turtle). USA: Georgia. Herpetol. Rev. 21:39.

Sapsford, C. W. 1978. Anatomical evidence for intracardiac blood shunting in marine turtles. Zool. Africana 13:57–62.

Sapsford, C. W., and G. R. Hughes. 1978. Body temperature of loggerhead sea turtle *Caretta caretta* and the leatherback sea turtle *Dermochelys coriacea* during nesting. Zool. Africana 13:63–69.

Sapsford, C. W., and M. Van Der Riet. 1979. Uptake of solar radiation by the sea turtle, *Caretta caretta,* during voluntary surface basking. Comp. Biochem. Physiol. 63A:471–474.

Sarnat, B. G., E. McNabb, and M. Glass. 1981. Growth of the turtle *Chrysemys scripta* under constant controlled laboratory conditions. Anat. Rec. 199:433–439.

Scarpulla, E. J. 1991. First records for the leatherback turtle (*Dermochelys coriacea*) along Maryland's Atlantic Coast. Maryland Natur. 33:59–60.

Schamberger, M. L., and F. B. Turner. 1986. The application of habitat modeling to the desert tortoise (*Gopherus agassizii*). Herpetologica 42:134–138.

Schilb, T. P. 1978. Bicarbonate ion transport: A mechanism for the acidification of urine in the turtle. Science 200:208–209.

Schipperijn, A. J. M. 1987. Een ongewilde kruising tussen de modderschildpadden *Kinosternon subrubrum* en *K. flavescens.* Lacerta 45:62–67.

Schmidt, J. 1916. Marking experiments with turtles in the Danish West Indies. Med. Kom. Havundersøgel. Sci. Fisk. 5:1–26.

Schmidt-Nielsen, K., and P. J. Bentley. 1966. Desert tortoise *Gopherus agassizii:* cutaneous water loss. Science 154:911.

Schmidt-Nielsen, K., and R. Fange. 1958. Salt glands in marine reptiles. Nature 182:783–785.

Schneider, J. G. 1783. Allgemeine Naturgeschichte der Schildkröten, nebst einem System. Verseichnisse der einzeinen Arten, Leipzig. 364 pp.

———. 1792. Beschreibung und Abbildung einer neun Art von Wasserschildkröte. Schr. Ges. Naturf. Fruende Berlin 10:259–283

Schneider, J. S., and G. D. Everson. 1989. The desert tortoise (*Xerobates agassizii*) in the prehistory of the southwestern Great Basin and adjacent areas. J. California Great Basin Anthropol. 11:175–202.

Schneider, P. B. 1980. A comparison of three methods of population analysis of the desert tortoise, *Gopherus agassizi.* Proc. Symp. Desert Tortoise Council 1980: 156–162.

Schoepff, J. D. 1792–1801. Historia Testudinum iconibus illustrata. Palm, Erlangae. 136 pp. [Latin version of Naturgeschichte der Schildkröten mit Abbildungen erlautert. Palm, Erlangen. 160 pp. 1792:1–32; 1793:33–88; 1795:89–136; 1801: 137–160.].

Schroeder, B. A., ed. 1988. Proceedings of the Eighth Annual Workshop on Sea Turtle Conservation and Biology. NOAA-TM-NMFS-SEFC-214.

Schubauer, J. P., J. W. Gibbons, and J. R. Spotila. 1990. Home range and movement patterns of slider turtles inhabiting Par Pond. *In* Gibbons, J. W., ed. Life history and ecology of the slider turtle, 223–232. Smithsonian Institution Press, Washington, D.C.

Schubauer, J. P., and R. R. Parmenter. 1981. Winter feeding by aquatic turtles in a southeastern reservoir. J. Herpetol. 15:444–447.

Schueler, F. W. 1983. Reticulate melanism in Canadian western painted turtles. Blue Jay 41:83–91.

Schuett, G. W., and R. E. Gatten, Jr. 1980. Thermal preference in snapping turtles (*Chelydra serpentina*). Copeia 1980:149–152.

Schultz, G. E. 1965. Pleistocene vertebrates from the Butler Spring local fauna, Meade County, Kansas. Pap. Michigan Acad. Sci. Arts. Lett. 50:235–265.

Schulz, J. P. 1972. Nesting beaches of sea turtles in west French Guiana. Proc. Kon. Nederl. Akad. Wetensch., ser. C, 74:398–404.

———. 1975. Sea turtles nesting in Surinam. Zool. Verh. Rijksmus. Natuur. Hist. Leiden (143):1–144.

———. 1982. Status of sea turtle populations nesting in Surinam with notes on sea turtles nesting in Guyana and French Guiana. *In* Bjorndal, K. A., ed. Biology and conservation of sea turtles, 435–437. Smithsonian Institution Press, Washington, D.C.

Schumacher, G.-H. 1972. Die Kopf- und Halsregion der Lederschildkröte *Dermochelys coriacea* (Linneaus, 1766). Abh. Akad Wiss. D.D.R. (2):1–60.

Schwartz, A. 1955. The diamondback terrapins (*Malaclemys terrapin*) of peninsular Florida. Proc. Biol. Soc. Washington. 68:157–164.

———. 1956a. Geographic variation in the chicken

turtle *Deirochelys reticularia* Latreille. Fieldiana: Zool. 34:461–503.

———. 1956b. The relationships and nomenclature of the soft-shelled turtles (genus *Trionyx*) of the southeastern United States. Charleston Mus. Leafl. 26:1–21.

Schwartz, C. W., and E. R. Schwartz. 1974. The three-toed box turtle in central Missouri: Its population, home range, and movements. Missouri Dept. Conserv. Terr. Ser. (5):1–28.

Schwartz, E. R., and C. W. Schwartz. 1991. A quarter-century study of survivorship in a population of three-toed box turtles in Missouri. Copeia 1991:1120–1123.

Schwartz, E. R., C. W. Schwartz, and A. R. Kiester. 1984. The three-toed box turtle in central Missouri, part II: A nineteen-year study of home range, movements and populations. Missouri Dept. Conserv. Terr. Ser. (12):1–29.

Schwartz, F. J. 1978. Behavioral and tolerance responses to cold water temperatures by three species of sea turtles (Reptilia, Cheloniidae) in North Carolina. *In* Henderson, G. E., ed. 1978. Proceedings of the Florida and Interregional Conference on sea turtles, 16–18. Florida Marine Res. Publ. 33.

———. 1989. Biology and ecology of sea turtles frequenting North Carolina. Natl. Undersea Res. Progr. Res. Rept. 89–2:307–331.

Schwartz, F. J., and N. B. Frazer. 1984. Growth in weight for loggerhead turtles, *Caretta caretta,* reared in captivity for 14 years in North Carolina. ASB Bull. 31:81.

Schwartz, F. J., and C. F. Jensen. 1991. Breathing and swimming activities and behaviors exhibited by two species of captive sea turtles (*Chelonia mydas* and *Caretta caretta*) in North Carolina. J. Elisha Mitchell Sci. Soc. 107:21–33.

Schwartz, F. J., C. Peterson, H. Passingham, J. Fridell, and J. Wooten. 1981. First successful nesting of the green turtle, *Chelonia mydas* in North Carolina and north of Georgia. ASB Bull. 28:96.

Schwartz, S. R. 1968. December emergence of hatchling *Terrapene carolina* in Philadelphia, PA. Philadelphia Herpetol. Soc. Bull. 16:20.

Schwarzkopf, L., and R. J. Brooks. 1985a. Sex determination in northern painted turtles: Effect of incubation at constant and fluctuating temperatures. Can. J. Zool. 63:2543–2547.

———. 1985b. Application of operative environmental temperatures to analysis of basking behavior in *Chrysemys picta.* Herpetologica 41:206–212.

———. 1986. Annual variations in reproductive characteristics of painted turtles (*Chrysemys picta*). Can. J. Zool. 64:1148–1151.

———. 1987. Nest-site selection and offspring sex ratio in painted turtles, *Chrysemys picta.* Copeia 1987:53–61.

Schweigger, A. F. 1812. Monographiae Cheloniorum. Königsberg. Arch. Naturwiss. Math. 1:271–368, 406–458.

———. 1814. Prodromi monographie cheloniorum. Regiomonti. 58 pp.

Scott, D. E., F. W. Whicker, and J. W. Gibbons. 1986. Effect of season on the retention of ^{137}Cs and ^{90}Sr by the yellow-bellied slider turtle (*Pseudemys scripta*). Can. J. Zool. 64:2850–2853.

Scribner, K. T., J. E. Evans, S. J. Morreale, M. H. Smith, and J. W. Gibbons. 1986. Genetic divergence among populations of the yellow-bellied slider turtle (*Pseudemys scripta*) separated by aquatic and terrestrial habitats. Copeia 1986:691–700.

Scribner, K. T., M. H. Smith, and J. W. Gibbons. 1984. Genetic differentiation among local populations of the yellow-bellied slider turtle (*Pseudemys scripta*). Herpetologica 40:382–387.

Seabrook, W. 1989. Feral cats (*Felis catus*) as predators of hatchling green turtles (*Chelonia mydas*). J. Zool. (London) 219:83–88.

Seeliger, L. M. 1945. Variation in the Pacific mud turtle. Copeia 1945:150–159.

Seidel, M. E. 1974. Seasonal fluctuation of plasma protein in the spiny softshell turtle, *Trionyx spiniferus.* Herpetologica 30:283–285.

———. 1975. Osmoregulation in the turtle *Trionyx spiniferus* from brackish and freshwater. Copeia 1975:124–128.

———. 1977. Respiratory metabolism of temperate and tropical American turtles (genus *Chrysemys*). Comp. Biochem. Physiol. 57A:297–298.

———. 1978a. Terrestrial dormancy in the turtle *Kinosternon flavescens:* Respiratory metabolism and dehydration. Comp. Biochem. Physiol. 61A:1–4.

———. 1978b. *Kinosternon flavescens.* Catalog Amer. Amphib. Rept. 216:1–4.

———. 1980. Interspecific comparisons of blood protein and urea concentrations in musk turtles (*Sternotherus*), with notes on fasting in *Sternotherus odoratus.* J. Herpetol. 14:167–170.

———. 1981. A taxonomic analysis of pseudemyd turtles (Testudines: Emydidae) from the New River, and phenetic relationships in the subgenus *Pseudemys.* Brimleyana (6):25–44.

Seidel, M. E., and M. D. Adkins. 1989. Variation in turtle myoglobins (subfamily Emydinae: Testudines) examined by isoelectric focusing. Comp. Biochem. Physiol. 94B:569–573.

Seidel, M. E., and N. B. Green. 1982. On the

occurrence of cooter turtles (subgenus *Pseudemys*) in the upper Ohio River Valley. Herpetol. Rev. 13:132–134.

Seidel, M. E., J. B. Iverson, and M. D. Adkins. 1986. Biochemical comparisons and phylogenetic relationships in the family Kinosternidae (Testudines). Copeia 1986:285–294.

Seidel, M. E., and D. R. Jackson. 1990. Evolution and fossil relationships of slider turtles. *In* Gibbons, J. W., ed. Life history and ecology of the slider turtle, 68–73. Smithsonian Institution Press, Washington, D.C.

Seidel, M. E., and R. V. Lucchino. 1981. Allozymic and morphological variation among the musk turtles *Sternotherus carinatus, S. depressus,* and *S. minor* (Kinosternidae). Copeia 1981:119–128.

Seidel, M. E., and W. M. Palmer. 1991. Morphological variation in turtles of the genus *Pseudemys* (Testudines: Emydidae) from central Atlantic drainages. Brimleyana (17):105–135.

Seidel, M. E., and S. L. Reynolds. 1980. Aspects of evaporative water loss in the mud turtles *Kinosternon hirtipes* and *Kinosternon flavescens*. Comp. Biochem. Physiol. 67A:593–598.

Seidel, M. E., S. L. Reynolds, and R. V. Lucchino. 1981. Phylogenetic relationships among musk turtles (genus *Sternotherus*) and genic variation in *Sternotherus odoratus*. Herpetologica 37:161–165.

Seidel, M. E., and H. M. Smith. 1986. *Chrysemys, Pseudemys, Trachemys* (Testudines: Emydidae): Did Agassiz have it right? Herpetologica 42:242–248.

Seigel, R. A. 1978. Simultaneous mortality in the diamondback terrapin. HERP, Bull. New York Herpetol. Soc. 14(1):31–32.

———. 1980a. Predation by raccoons on diamondback terrapins, *Malaclemys terrapin tequesta*. J. Herpetol. 14:87–89.

———. 1980b. Courtship and mating behavior of the diamondback terrapin *Malaclemys terrapin tequesta*. J. Herpetol. 14:420–421.

———. 1980c. Nesting habits of diamondback terrapins (*Malaclemys terrapin*) on the Atlantic Coast of Florida. Trans. Kansas Acad. Sci. 83:239–246.

———. 1983. Occurrence and effects of barnacle infestations on diamondback terrapins (*Malaclemys terrapin*). Amer. Midl. Natur. 109:34–39.

———. 1984. Parameters of two populations of diamondback terrapins (*Malaclemys terrapin*) on the Atlantic Coast of Florida. *In* Seigel, R. A., L. E. Hunt, J. L. Knight, L. Malaret, and N. L. Zuschlag, eds. Vertebrate ecology and systematics: A tribute to Henry S. Fitch, 77–87. Univ. Kansas Mus. Natur. Hist. Spec. Publ. 10.

Semlitsch, R. D., and J. W. Gibbons. 1989. Lack of largemouth bass predation on hatchling turtles (*Trachemys scripta*). Copeia 1989:1030–1031.

Semple, R. E., D. Sigsworth, and J. D. Stitt. 1969. Composition and volume of fluids in winter and summer of turtles native to Ontario, Canada. J. Physiol. 204:39P-40P.

Sever, D. M. 1984. Comments on the occurrence of Blanding's turtle, *Emydoidea blandingi*, in LaPorte and Saint Joseph counties, Indiana. Proc. Indiana Acad. Sci. 93:460–461.

Sexton, O. J. 1959a. Spatial and temporal movements of a population of the painted turtle, *Chrysemys picta marginata* (Agassiz). Ecol. Monogr. 29:113–140.

———. 1959b. A method of estimating the age of painted turtles for use in demographic studies. Ecology 40:716–718.

———. 1965. The annual cycle of growth and shedding in the midland painted turtle, *Chrysemys picta marginata*. Copeia 1965:314–318.

Seyle, W. 1987. Transient reproductive failure in *Caretta*. Marine Turtle Newsl. (40):9–10.

Shaffer, L. L. 1991. Pennsylvania amphibians & reptiles. Pennsylvania Fish. Comm., Harrisburg. 161 pp.

Shah, R. V. 1963. The neck musculature of a cryptodire (*Deirochelys*) and a pleurodire (*Chelodina*) compared. Bull. Mus. Comp. Zool. 129:343–368.

Shalet, L. C. 1977. Social hierarchy in eastern box turtles. Philadelphia Herpetol. Soc. Bull. 25:9–13.

Shane, S. M., R. Gilbert, and K. S. Harrington. 1990 *Salmonella* colonizaton in commercial pet turtles (*Pseudemys scripta elegans*). Epidemiol. Infect. 105:307–316.

Shaver, D. J. 1989. *Chelonia mydas* (green turtle). USA: Texas. Herpetol. Rev. 20:14.

———. 1990. Hypothermic stunning of sea turtles in Texas. Marine Turtle Newsl. (48):25–27.

———. 1991. Feeding ecology of wild and head-started Kemp's ridley sea turtle of south Texas waters. J. Herpetol. 25:327–334.

———. 1992. *Lepidochelys kempii* (Kemp's ridley sea turtle). Reproduction. Herpetol. Rev. 23:59.

Shaver, D. J., and A. Amos. 1988. Sea turtle nesting on Texas beaches in 1987. Marine Turtle Newsl. (42):7–8.

Shaver, D. J., D. W. Owens, A. H. Chaney, C. W. Caillouet, Jr., P. Burchfield, and R. Márquez M. 1988. Styrofoam box and beach temperatures in relation to and sex ratios of Kemp's ridley sea turtle. *In* Schroeder, B. A., ed. Proceedings of the Eighth Annual Workshop on Sea Turtle Conservation and Biology, 103–108. NOAA-TM-NMFS-SEFC-214.

Shealy, R. M. 1976. The natural history of the Alabama

map turtle, *Graptemys pulchra* Baur, in Alabama. Bull. Florida St. Mus. Biol. Sci. 21:47–111.

Sheeky, E. A. 1982. Green turtles basking on Tern Island, French Frigate Shoals. 'Elepaio (J. Hawaii Audubon Soc.). 43:45–47.

Shipman, P., D. Edds, and D. Blex. 1991. Report on the recapture of an alligator snapping turtle (*Macroclemys temminckii*) in Kansas. Kansas Herpetol. Soc. Newsl. 85:8–9.

Shively, S. H. 1982. Factors limiting the upstream distribution of the Sabine map turtle. Master's thesis, University of Southwestern Louisiana, Lafayette.

Shively, S. H., and J. F. Jackson. 1985. Factors limiting the upstream distribution of the Sabine map turtle. Amer. Midl. Natur. 114:292–303.

Shively, S. H., and M. F. Vidrine. 1984. Freshwater mollusks in the alimentary tract of a Mississippi map turtle. Proc. Louisiana Acad. Sci. 47:27–29.

Shoop, C. R. 1967. *Graptemys nigrinoda* in Mississippi. Herpetologica 23:56.

———. 1980. Innuit turtle song: Leatherback turtles near Baffin Island? Marine Turtle Newsl. (15):5–6.

Shoop, C. R., and R. D. Kenney. 1992. Seasonal distributions and abundances of loggerhead and leatherback sea turtles in waters of the northeastern United States. Herpetol. Monogr. 6:43–67.

Shoop, C. R., and C. Ruckdeschel. 1982. Increasing turtle strandings in the southeast United States: A complicating factor. Biol. Conserv. 23:213–215.

———. 1986. New herpetological records for Cumberland Island, Georgia. Herpetol. Rev. 17:51.

———. 1989. Long-distance movement of a juvenile loggerhead sea turtle. Marine Turtle Newsl. (47):15.

Siebenrock, K. F. 1906a. Zur Kenntnis der Schildkrötenfauna der Insel Hainan. Zool. Anz. 30:578–586.

———. 1906b. Eine neue *Cinosternum*-Art aus Florida. Zool. Anz. 30:727–728.

Siebold, P. F., von. 1835. Fauna Japonica, sive descriptio animalium, quae in intinereper Japonium . . . Reptilia elaborantilous C. J. Temminck et H. Schlegel. I. Chelonii. Lugduni Batavorum, 144 pp.

Sievert, L. M., G. A. Sievert, and P. V. Cupp, Jr. 1988. Metabolic rate of feeding and fasting juvenile midland painted turtles, *Chrysemys picta marginata*. Comp. Biochem. Physiol. 90A:157–159.

Silva-Batiz, F., E. Godinez-Dominguez, and J. E. Michel-Morfin. 1992. Rearing and release of yearling olive ridley turtles. Marine Turtle Newsl. (59):8–10.

Simkiss, K. 1962. The sources of calcium for the ossification of the embryos of the giant leathery turtle. Comp. Biochem. Physiol. 7:71–79.

Simon, L. M., and E. D. Robin. 1970. Changes in heart and skeletal muscle cytochrome oxidase activity during anaerobiosis in the freshwater turtle *Pseudemys scripta elegans*. Comp. Biochem. Physiol. 37:437–443.

Simon, M. H. 1975. The green sea turtle (*Chelonia mydas*); collection, incubation and hatching of eggs from natural rookeries. J. Zool. (London) 176:39–48.

Simon, M. H., G. F. Ulrich, and A. S. Parkes. 1975. The green turtle (*Chelonia mydas*): Mating, nesting and hatching on a farm. J. Zool. (London) 177:411–423.

Sites, J. W., Jr., J. W. Bickham, M. W. Haiduk, and J. B. Iverson. 1979. Banded karyotypes of six taxa of kinosternid turtles. Copeia 1979:692–698.

Skorepa, A. C. 1966. The deliberate consumption of stones by the ornate box turtle, *Terrapene o. ornata* Agassiz. J. Ohio Herpetol. Soc. 5:108.

Skorepa, A. C., and J. E. Ozment. 1968. Habitat, habits, and variation of *Kinosternon subrubrum* in southern Illinois. Trans. Illinois St. Acad. Sci. 61:247–251.

Slater, J. R. 1962. Variations and new range of *Clemmys marmorata marmorata*. Occ. Pap. Mus. Natur. Hist. Univ. Puget Sound. 20:204–205.

Slaughter, B. H., W. W. Crook, R. K. Harris, D. C. Allen, and M. Seifert. 1962. The Hill-Shuler local faunas of the upper Trinity River, Dallas and Denton counties, Texas. Univ. Texas Bur. Econ. Geol. Rept. Invest. (48):1–75.

Sloan, K. N., and D. Taylor. 1987. Habitats and movements of adult alligator snapping turtles in northeast Louisiana. Proc. Ann. Conf. Southeast. Assoc. Fish Wildl. Agencies 41:343–348.

Small, P., and T. Ragan. 1991. *Caretta caretta* (loggerhead). Predation. Herpetol. Rev. 22:97.

Small, V. 1982. Sea turtle nesting at Virgin Islands National Park and Buck Island Reef National Monument, 1980 and 1981. Natl. Park Serv. Research/ Resources Manag. Resp. Ser. 61:1–54.

Smith, E. N., and M. C. deCarvalho, Jr. 1985. Heart rate response to threat and diving in the ornate box turtle, *Terrepene* [*sic*] *ornata*. Physiol. Zool. 58:236–241.

Smith, E. N., N. C. Long, and J. Wood. 1986. Thermoregulation and evaporative water loss of green sea turtles, *Chelonia mydas*. J. Herpetol. 20:325–332.

Smith, E. N., S. L. Robertson, and S. R. Adams. 1981. Thermoregulation of the spiny soft-shelled turtle *Trionyx spinifer*. Physiol. Zool. 54:74–80.

Smith, G. W. 1992. Hawksbill turtle nesting at Manatee Bar, Belize, 1991. Marine Turtle Newsl. (57):1–5.

Smith, H[obart]. M. 1958. Total regeneration of the carapace in a box turtle. Turtox News 36:234–235.

———. 1961. Function of the choanal rakers of the green sea turtle. Herpetologica 17:214.

Smith, H. M., and E. D. Brodie, Jr. 1982. A guide to field identification. Reptiles of North America. Golden Press, New York. 240 pp.

Smith, H. M., and B. P. Glass. 1947. A new musk turtle from southeastern United States. J. Washington Acad. Sci. 37:22–24.

Smith, H. M., D. C. Kritsky, and R. L. Holland. 1969. Reticulate melanism in the painted turtle. J. Herpetol. 3:173–176.

Smith, H. M., and L. W. Ramsey. 1952. A new turtle from Texas. Wasmann J. Biol. 10:45–54.

Smith, H. M., and O. Sanders. 1952. Distributional data on Texan amphibians and reptiles. Texas J. Sci. 4:204–219.

Smith, H. M., and R. B. Smith. 1979 [1980]. Synopsis of the herpetofauna of Mexico, vol. 6, Guide to Mexican turtles. Bibliographic addendum III. John Johnson, North Bennington, Vermont. 1044 pp.

———. 1980. *Sternotherus* Gray, 1825, correct spelling; and *Pelusios* Wagler, 1830, proposed conservation (Reptilia, Testudines). Z.N. (S.) 2278. Bull. Zool. Nomencl. 37:124–128.

Smith, H[ugh]. M. 1904. Notes on the breeding of the yellow-bellied terrapin. Smithsonian Misc. Coll. 45:252–253.

Smith, L. L. 1992. Nesting ecology, female home range and activity patterns, and hatchling survivorship in the gopher tortoise (*Gopherus polyphemus*). Master's thesis, University of Florida, Gainesville. 106 pp.

Smith, M. H., and K. T. Scribner. 1990. Population genetics of the slider turtle. *In* Gibbons, J. W., ed. Life history and ecology of the slider turtle, 74–81. Smithsonian Institution Press, Washington, D.C.

Smith, M. H., H. O. Hillestad, M. N. Manlove, D. O. Straney, and J. M. Dean. 1977. Management implications of genetic variability in loggerhead and green sea turtles. XIIIth Congr. Game Biol., 302–312.

Smith, P. W. 1951. A new frog and a new turtle from the western Illinois sand prairies. Bull. Chicago Acad. Sci. 9:189–199.

———. 1961. The amphibians and reptiles of Illinois. Illinois Natur. Hist. Surv. Bull. (28):1–298.

Smith, S. A., and W. J. Houck. 1984. Three species of sea turtles collected from northern California. California Fish and Game 70:60–62.

Smith, S. H. 1988. Cleaning of the hawksbill turtle (*Eretmochelys imbricata*) by adult French angelfish (*Pomecanthus paru*). Herpetol. Rev. 19:55.

Smith, W. G. 1968. A neonate Atlantic loggerhead turtle, *Caretta caretta caretta*, captured at sea. Copeia 1968:880–881.

Snell, H. L., and T. H. Fritts. 1983. The significance of diurnal terrestrial emergence of green turtles (*Chelonia mydas*) in the Galapagos Archipelago. Biotropica 15:285–291.

Snider, A. T., and J. K. Bowler. 1992. Longevity of reptiles and amphibians in North American collections, second edition. Soc. Stud. Amphib. Rept. Herpetol. Circ. (21):1–40.

Snow, J. E. 1980. Second clutch laying by painted turtles. Copeia 1980:534–536.

———. 1982. Predation on painted turtle nests: Nest survival as a function of nest age. Can. J. Zool. 60:3290–3292.

Snyder, L. L. 1921. Some observations on Blanding's turtle. Can. Field-Natur. 35:17–18.

Solomon, S. E., and T. Baird. 1976. Studies on the egg shell (oviducal and oviposited) of *Chelonia mydas*. J. Exp. Marine Biol. Ecol. 22:145–160.

———. 1977. Studies on the soft shell membranes of the egg shell of *Chelonia mydas* L. J. Exp. Marine Biol. Ecol. 27:83–92.

———. 1979. Aspects of the biology of *Chelonia mydas* L. Oceangr. Marine Biol. Ann. Rev. 17:347–361.

———. 1980. The effect of fungal penetration on the egg-shell of the green turtle. Electr. Micros. 2:434–435.

Solomon, S. E., J. R. Hendrickson, and L. P. Hendrickson. 1986. The structure of the carapace and plastron of juvenile turtles, *Chelonia mydas* (the green turtle) and *Caretta caretta* (the loggerhead). J. Anat. 145:123–131.

Solomon, S. E., and M. Purton. 1984. The respiratory epithelium of the lung in the green turtle (*Chelonia mydas* L.). J. Anat. 139:353–370.

Solomon, S. E., and J. Reid. 1983. The effect of the mammillary layer on eggshell formation in reptiles. Anim. Tech. 34:1–10.

Solomon, S. E., and R. Tippett. 1987. The intra-clutch localisation of fungal hyphae in the eggshells of the leatherback turtle (*Dermochelys coriacea*). Anim. Tech. 38:73–79.

Solomon, S. E., and J. M. Watt. 1985. The structure of the eggshell of the leatherback turtle (*Dermochelys coriacea*). Anim. Tech. 36:19–27.

Sonnini de Manoncourt, C. S., and P. A. Latreille. 1802. Histoire naturelle des reptiles avec figures dessinées d'apres nature. I. Deterville, Paris. 280 pp.

Speake, D. W., and R. H. Mount. 1973. Some possible ecological effects of "Rattlesnake Roundups" in the southeastern coastal plain. Proc. Ann. Conf. Southeast. Assoc. Game Fish Comm. 27:267–277.

Spindel, E. L., J. L. Dobie, and D. F. Buxton. 1987. Functional mechanisms and histologic composition of the lingual appendage in the alligator snapping turtle, *Macroclemys temmincki* (Troost) (Testudines: Chelydridae). J. Morphol. 194:287–301.

Spotila, J. R., R. E. Foley, J. P. Schubauer, R. D. Semlitsch, K. M. Crawford, E. A. Standora, and J. W. Gibbons. 1984. Opportunistic behavioral thermoregulation of turtles, *Pseudemys scripta,* in response to microclimatology of a nuclear reactor cooling reservoir. Herpetologica 40:299–308.

Spotila, J. R., R. E. Foley, and E. A. Standora. 1990. Thermoregulation and climate space of the slider turtle. *In* Gibbons, J. W., ed. Life history and ecology of the slider turtle, 288–298. Smithsonian Institution Press, Washington, D.C.

Spotila, J. R., and E. A. Standora. 1985. Environmental constraints on the thermal energetics of sea turtles. Copeia 1985:694–702.

———. 1986. Sex determination in the desert tortoise: A conservative management strategy is needed. Herpetologica 42:67–72.

Spotila, J. R., E. A. Standora, D. P. Easton, and P. S. Rutledge. 1989. Bioenergetics, behavior, and resource partitioning in stressed habitats: Biophysical and molecular approaches. Physiol. Zool. 62:253–285.

Spotila, J. R., E. A. Standora, S. J. Morreale, and G. J. Ruiz. 1987. Temperature dependent sex determination in the green turtle (*Chelonia mydas*): Effects on the sex ratio on a natural nesting beach. Herpetologica 43:74–81.

Sprando, R. L., and L. D. Russell. 1988. Spermiogenesis in the red-ear turtle (*Pseudemys scripta*) and the domestic fowl (*Gallus domesticus*): A study of cytoplasmic events including cell volume changes and cytoplasmic elimination. J. Morphol. 198:95–118.

Spray, D. C. 1972. Weight shifts in the intact turtle during heating and cooling. Comp. Biochem. Physiol. 43A:491–494.

Spray, D. C., and M. L. May. 1972. Heating and cooling rates in four species of turtles. Comp. Biochem. Physiol. 41A:507–522.

St. Clair, R. C., and P. T. Gregory. 1990. Factors affecting the northern range limit of painted turtles (*Chrysemys picta*): Winter acidosis or freezing? Copeia 1990:1083–1089.

Stamper, D. L., R. J. Denver, and P. Licht. 1990. Effects of thyroidal status on metabolism and growth of juvenile turtles, *Pseudemys scripta elegans.* Comp. Biochem. Physiol. 96A:67–73.

Stancyk, S. E. 1982. Non-human predators of sea turtles and their control. *In* Bjorndal, K., ed. Biology and conservation of sea turtles, 139–152. Smithsonian Institution Press, Washington, D.C.

Stancyk, S. E., and J. P. Ross. 1978. An analysis of sand from green turtle nesting beaches on Ascension Island. Copeia 1978:93–99.

Stancyk, S. E., O. R. Tabert, and J. M. Dean. 1980. Nesting activity of the loggerhead turtle *Caretta caretta* in South Carolina, II. Protection of nests from raccoon predation by transplantation. Biol. Conserv. 18:289–298.

Standora, E. A., S. J. Morreale, R. Estes, R. Thompson, and M. Hilburger. 1989. Growth rates of juvenile Kemp's ridleys and their movement in New York waters. *In* Eckert, S. A., K. L. Eckert, and T. A. Richardson, eds. Proceedings of the Ninth Annual Workshop on Sea Turtle Conservation and Biology, 175–177. NOAA-TM-NMFS-SEFC-232.

Standora, E. A., and J. R. Spotila. 1985. Temperature dependent sex determination in sea turtles. Copeia 1985:711–722.

Standora, E. A., J. R. Spotila, and R. E. Foley. 1982. Regional endothermy in the sea turtle, *Chelonia mydas.* J. Therm. Biol. 7:159–165.

Standora, E. A., J. R. Spotila, J. A. Keinath, and C. R. Shoop. 1984. Body temperatures, diving cycles, and movement of a subadult leatherback turtle, *Dermochelys coriacea.* Herpetologica 40:169–176.

Stearns, S. C., and R. E. Crandall. 1984. Plasticity for age and size at sexual maturity: A life-history response to unavoidable stress. *In* Potts, G. W., and R. J. Wooton, eds. Fish reproduction: Strategies and tactics, 13–33. Academic Press, London.

Stebbins, R. C. 1954. Amphibians and reptiles of western North America. McGraw Hill Book Co., Inc. New York. 537 pp.

———. 1985. A field guide to western reptiles and amphibians, 2d ed. Houghton Mifflin Co., Boston. 336 pp.

Steele, C. W., M. A. Grassman, D. W. Owens, and J. H. Matis. 1989. Application of decision theory in understanding food choice behavior of hatchling loggerhead sea turtles and chemosensory imprinting in juvenile loggerhead sea turtles. Experientia 45:202–205.

Stegmann, E. W., R. B. Primack, and G. S. Ellmore. 1988. Absorption of nutrient exudates from terrapin eggs by roots of *Ammophila breviligulata* (Gramineae). Can. J. Bot. 66:714–718.

Stein, R. J., W. K. Eames, and D. C. Parris. 1977. Recent occurrences of beached dead leatherback turtles (*Dermochelys coriacea coriacea*) along the New Jersey coast. Sci. Notes New Jersey St. Mus. 15:1–6.

———. 1980. *Chrysemys scripta elegans* (red-eared slider). USA: New Jersey. Herpetol. Rev. 11:115.

Stejneger, L. 1918. Description of a new snapping turtle and a new lizard from Florida. Proc. Biol. Soc. Washington. 31:89–92.

———. 1925. New species and subspecies of American turtles. J. Washington Acad. Sci. 15:462–463.

——. 1944. Notes on the American soft-shell turtles with special reference to *Amyda agassizii*. Bull. Mus. Comp. Zool. Harvard. 94:1–75.

Stewart, J. H. 1988. A recovery plan for the ringed sawback turtle *Graptemys oculifera*. U.S. Fish Wildl. Serv., Southeast Region. 28 pp.

Stickel, L. F. 1950. Populations and home range relationships of the box turtle, *Terrapene c. carolina* (Linnaeus). Ecol. Monogr. 20:351–378.

——. 1951. Wood mouse and box turtle populations in an area treated annually with DDT for five years. J. Wildl. Mgt. 15:161–164.

——. 1978. Changes in a box turtle population during three decades. Copeia 1978:221–225.

——. 1989. Home range behavior among box turtles (*Terrapene c. carolina*) of a bottomland forest in Maryland. J. Herpetol. 23:40–44.

Stickel, L. F., and C. M. Bunck. 1989. Growth and morphometrics of the box turtle, *Terrapene c. carolina*. J. Herpetol. 23:216–223.

Stickney, R. R., D. B. White, and D. Perlmutter. 1973. Growth of green and loggerhead sea turtles in Georgia on natural and artificial diets. Bull. Georgia Acad. Sci. 31:37–44.

Stinson, M. L. 1984. Biology of sea turtles in San Diego Bay, California, and in the northeastern Pacific Ocean. Master's thesis, San Diego State University, San Diego, California.

Stitt, J. T., and R. E. Semple. 1971. Sites of plasma sequestration induced by body cooling in turtles. Amer. J. Physiol. 221:1189–1191.

Stitt, J. T., R. E. Semple, and D. W. Sigsworth. 1971. Plasma sequestration produced by acute changes in body temperature in turtles. Amer. J. Physiol. 221:1185–1188.

Stock, A. D. 1972. Karyological relationships in turtles (Reptilia: Chelonia). Can. J. Genet. Cytol. 14:859–868.

Stockard, M. E., and R. E. Gatten, Jr. 1983. Activity metabolism of painted turtles (*Chrysemys picta*). Copeia 1983:214–221.

Stone, P. A., J. L. Dobie, and R. P. Henry. 1992a. Cutaneous surface area and bimodal respiration in soft-shelled (*Trionyx spiniferus*), stinkpot (*Sternotherus odoratus*), and mud turtles (*Kinosternon subrubrum*). Physiol. Zool. 65:311–330.

——. 1992b. The effect of aquatic O_2 levels on diving and ventilatory behavior in soft-shelled (*Trionyx spiniferus*), stinkpot (*Sternotherus odoratus*), and mud turtles (*Kinosternon subrubrum*). Physiol. Zool. 65:331–345.

Stone, W. B., E. Kiviat, and S. A. Butkas. 1980. Toxicants in snapping turtles. New York Fish Game J. 27:39–50.

Stoneburner, D. L. 1980. Body depth: An indicator of morphological variation among nesting groups of adult loggerhead sea turtles (*Caretta caretta*). J. Herpetol. 14:205–206.

——. 1982. Satellite telemetry of loggerhead sea turtle movement in the Georgia Bight. Copeia 1982:400–408.

Stoneburner, D. L., and L. M. Ehrhart. 1981. Observations on *Caretta c. caretta*: A record internesting migration in the Atlantic. Herpetol. Rev. 12:66.

Stoneburner, D. L., D. Gilmore, J. Hinesley, D. Gross, D. Hall, and J. I. Richardson. 1979. Observations on *Chelonia mydas mydas*: A northerly extension of known nesting range. Herpetol. Rev. 10:103–104.

Stoneburner, D. L., M. N. Nicora, and E. R. Blood. 1980. Heavy metals in loggerhead sea turtle eggs (*Caretta caretta*): Evidence to support the hypothesis that demes exist in the western Atlantic population. J. Herpetol. 14:171–175.

Stoneburner, D. L., and J. I. Richardson. 1981. Observations on the role of temperature in loggerhead nest site selection. Copeia 1981:238–241.

Storer, T. I. 1930. Notes on the range and life history of the Pacific fresh-water turtle, *Clemmys marmorata*. Univ. California Publ. Zool. 32:429–441.

Storey, K. B., J. M. Storey, S. P. J. Brooks, T. A. Churchill, and R. J. Brooks. 1988. Hatchling turtles survive freezing during winter hibernation. Proc. Natl. Acad. Sci. 85:8350–8354.

Strang, C. A. 1983. Spatial and temporal activity patterns in two terrestrial turtles. J. Herpetol. 17:43–47.

Strass, P. K., K. J. Miles, B. S. McDonald, Jr., and I. L. Brisbin, Jr. 1982. An assessment of factors associated with the daytime use of resting forms by eastern box turtles (*Terrapene carolina carolina*). J. Herpetol. 16:320–322.

Strecker, J. K. 1926. Chapters from the life histories of Texas reptiles and amphibians. Contrib. Baylor Univ. Mus. 8:1–12.

——. 1927. Observations on the food habits of Texas amphibians and reptiles. Copeia (162):6–9.

Stuart, J. N., and C. S. Clark. 1990. *Apalone spinifera emoryi* (Texas spiny softshell). Defensive behavior. Herpetol. Rev. 21:91–92.

Stuart, M. 1974. Reptile breeding data at Louisiana Purchase Gardens and Zoo. Amer. Assoc. Zool. Parks Aquar. Reg. Conf. Proc., 275–276.

Stuart, M. D., and G. C. Miller. 1987. The eastern box turtle, *Terrapene c. carolina* (Testudines: Emydidae), in North Carolina. Brimleyana (13):123–131.

Sturbaum, B. A. 1981. Responses of the three-toed box turtle, *Terrapene carolina triunguis*, to heat stress. Comp. Biochem. Physiol. 70A:199–204.

———. 1982. Temperature regulation in turtles. Comp. Biochem. Physiol. 72A:615–620.

Sturbaum, B. A., and J. L. Bergman. 1981. Changes in selected blood components of the three-toed box turtle, *Terrapene carolina triunguis,* during heat stress. Comp. Biochem. Physiol. 70A:599–602.

Sturbaum, B. A., and M. L. Riedesel. 1974. Temperature regulation responses of ornate box turtles, *Terrapene ornata,* to heat. Comp. Biochem. Physiol. 48A:527–538.

———. 1977. Dissipation of stored body heat by the ornate box turtle, *Terrapene ornata.* Comp. Biochem. Physiol. 58A:93–97.

Surface, H. A. 1908. First report on the economic features of the turtles of Pennsylvania. Zool. Bull. Div. Zool. Pennsylvania Dept. Agric. 6:105–196.

Suwelo, I. S. 1971. Sea turtles in Indonesia. IUCN Publ. (n.s.), Suppl. Pap. 31:85–89.

Suyama, M., T. Hirano, K. Sato and H. Fukada. 1979. Nitrogenous constituents of meat extract of freshwater softshell turtle. Bull. Japanese Soc. Sci. Fish. 45:595–599.

Swan, R. O., and R. E. Johnson. 1977. Heat production by box turtles. Trans. Illinois St. Acad. Sci. 70:239.

Swanson, P. L. 1952. The reptiles of Venango County, Pennsylvania. Amer. Midl. Natur. 47:161–182.

Swingland, I. R., and M. W. Klemens, eds. 1989. The conservation biology of tortoises. Occ. Pap. IUCN Species Survival Comm. (5):1–202.

Tachibana, K. 1979. On the Miocene turtle from Arikawa in the Goto Islands, Nagasaki Prefecture. Ann. Pap. Fac. Educ. Univ. Iwate 39:77–84.

Taft, A. C. 1944. Diamond-back terrapin introduced into California. California Fish and Game 30:101–102.

Taggart, T. W. 1992. *Graptemys pseudogeographica* (false map turtle). USA: Kansas. Herpetol. Rev. 23:88.

Talbert, O. R., Jr., S. E. Stancyk, J. M. Dean, and J. M. Will. 1980. Nesting activity of the loggerhead turtle (*Caretta caretta*) in South Carolina I: A rookery in transition. Copeia 1980:709–718.

Taubes, G. 1992a. A dubious battle to save the Kemp's ridley sea turtle. Science 256:614–616.

———. 1992b. Response to Wibbles. Science 257:466–467.

Tauxe, R. V., J. G. Rigau-Perez, J. G. Wells, and P. A. Blake. 1985. Turtle-associated salmonellosis in Puerto Rico. J. Amer. Med. Assoc. 254:237–239.

Taylor, E. H. 1933. Observations on the courtship of turtles. Univ. Kansas Sci. Bull. 21:269–271.

———. 1935. Arkansas amphibians and reptiles in the Kansas University Museum. Univ. Kansas Sci. Bull. 22:207–218.

———. 1943. An extinct turtle of the genus *Emys* from the Pleistocene of Kansas. Univ. Kansas Sci. Bull. 29:249–254.

Taylor, G. M., and E. Nol. 1989. Movements and hibernation sites of overwintering painted turtles in southern Ontario. Can. J. Zool. 67:1877–1881.

Taylor, R. W., Jr. 1982. Seasonal aspects of the reproductive biology of the gopher tortoise, *Gopherus polyphemus.* Ph.D. dissertation, University of Florida, Gainesville.

———. 1982. Human predation on the gopher tortoise (*Gopherus polyphemus*) in north-central Florida. Bull. Florida St. Mus. Biol. Sci. 28:79–102.

Taylor, R. W., Jr., and E. R. Jacobson. 1982. Hematology and serum chemistry of the gopher tortoise, *Gopherus polyphemus.* Comp. Biochem. Physiol. 72A:425–428.

Taylor, W. E. 1895. The box turtles of North America. Proc. U.S. Natl. Mus. 17:573–588.

Teller, S., and D. Bardak. 1975. New records of late Pleistocene vertebrates from the southern end of Lake Michigan. Amer. Midl. Natur. 94:179–189.

Temple, S. A. 1987. Predation on turtle nests increases near ecological edges. Copeia 1987:250–252.

Tenney, S. M., D. Bartlett, Jr., J. P. Farber, and J. E. Remmers. 1974. Mechanics of the respiratory cycle in the green turtle (*Chelonia mydas*). Resp. Physiol. 22:361–368.

Thayer, G. W., K. A. Bjorndal, J. C. Ogden, S. L. Williams, and J. C. Zieman. 1984. Role of larger herbivores in seagrass communities. Estuaries 7:351–376.

Thayer, G. W., D. W. Engel, and K. A. Bjorndal. 1982. Evidence for short-circuiting of the detritus cycle of seagrass beds by the green turtle, *Chelonia mydas* L. J. Exp. Marine Biol. Ecol. 62:173–183.

Thieme, V. 1979. Erfahrungen mit Weichschildkröten 12. Erste Nachzucht der chinesischen Weichschildkrote *Trionyx sinensis.* Aquar. Terrar. 26:26–29.

Thomas, E. S., and M. B. Trautman. 1937. Segregated hibernaculum of *Sternotherus odoratus* (Latreille). Copeia 1937:231.

Thomas, K., and R. Mount. 1973. The annual cycle of reproduction of the turtle, *Pseudemys floridana floridana* (Testudinata, Testudinidae) with observations on its ecology. ASB Bull. 20:87.

Thomas, M. 1978. Gopher tortoise. Florida Natur. 51(3):2–4.

Thomasson, J. R. 1980. Ornate box turtle, *Terrapene ornata* (Testudinae), feeding on pincushion cactus, *Coryphantha vivipara* (Cactaceae). Southwest. Natur. 25:438.

Thompson, N. B. 1989. The status of the loggerhead,

Caretta caretta; Kemp's ridley, *Lepidochelys kempi;* and green *Chelonia mydas,* sea turtles in US Waters. Marine Fish Rev. 50:16–23.

Thompson, S. W. 1982. Turtles of South Dakota. South Dakota Conserv. Digest 49(3):12–15.

Thornhill, G. M. 1982. Comparative reproduction of the turtle, *Chrysemys scripta elegans,* in heated and natural lakes. J. Herpetol. 16:347–353.

Threlfall, W. 1978. First record of the Atlantic leatherback turtle (*Dermochelys coriacea*) from Labrador. Can. Field-Natur. 92:287.

Thunberg, C. P. 1785–1788. [No title]. Museum naturalium Academiae Upsaliensis . . . . Kongliga Svenska Vetenskapsakademien, Stockholm. Handliger 8.

Timken, R. L. 1968. *Graptemys pseudogeographica* in the upper Missouri River of the northcentral United States. J. Herpetol. 1:76–82.

Timko, R. E., and A. L. Kolz. 1982. Satellite sea turtle tracking. Marine Fish Rev. 44:19–24.

Tinkle, D. W. 1958a. The systematics and ecology of the *Sternothaerus carinatus* complex (Testudinata, Chelydridae). Tulane Stud. Zool. 6:3–56.

———. 1958b. Experiments with censusing of southern turtle populations. Herpetologica 14:172–175.

———. 1959a. The relation of the fall line to the distribution and abundance of turtles. Copeia 1959:167–170.

———. 1959b. Observations of reptiles and amphibians in a Louisiana swamp. Amer. Midl. Natur. 62:189–205.

———. 1959c. Additional remarks on extra-uterine migration of ova in turtles. Herpetologica 15:161–162.

———. 1961. Geographic variation in reproduction size, sex ratio and maturity of *Sternothaerus odoratus* (Testudinata: Chelydridae). Ecology 42:68–76.

———. 1962. Variation in shell morphology of North American turtles. I. The carapacial seam arrangements. Tulane Stud. Zool. 9:331–349.

Tinkle, D. W., J. D. Congdon, and P. C. Rosen. 1981. Nesting frequency and success: Implications for the demography of painted turtles. Ecology 62:1426–1432.

Tinkle, D. W., and R. G. Webb. 1955. A new species of *Sternothaerus* with a discussion of the *Sternotherus carinatus* complex (Chelonia, Kinosternidae). Tulane Stud. Zool. 3:52–67.

Tinklepaugh, O. L. 1932. Maze learning of a turtle. J. Comp. Psych. 13:201–206.

Tobey, F. J., Jr. 1979. Observations on *Gopherus polyphemus* in west-central Georgia. Bull. Maryland Herpetol. Soc. 15:27–28.

———, ed. 1985. Virginia's amphibians and reptiles: A distributional survey. Virginia Herpetol. Soc., Purcellville. 714 pp.

Toland, B. 1991. Spotted skunk use of a gopher tortoise burrow for breeding. Florida Scientist 54:10–12.

Tomko, D. S. 1972. Autumn breeding of the desert tortoise. Copeia 1972:895.

Trobec, T. N., and J. G. Stanley. 1971. Uptake of ions and water by the painted turtle, *Chrysemys picta.* Copeia 1971:537–542.

Tryon, B. W. 1988. The rare little bog turtle of East Tennessee. Tennessee Wildl. 11(4):6–9.

———. 1990. Bog turtles (*Clemmys muhlenbergii*) in the South: A question of survival. Bull. Chicago Herpetol. Soc. 25:57–66.

Tryon, B. W., and D. W. Herman. 1991. Status, conservation, and management of the bog turtle, *Clemmys muhlenbergii,* in the southeastern United States. *In* Beaman, K. R., F. Caporaso, S. McKeown, and M. D. Graff, eds. Proceedings of the First International Symposium on Turtles and Tortoises: Conservation and Captive Husbandry, 36–53. Chapman Univ., Orange, California.

Tryon, B. W., and T. G. Hulsey. 1977. Breeding and rearing the bog turtle *Clemmys muhlenbergii* at the Fort Worth Zoo. Int. Zoo Yrbk. 17:125–130.

Tucker, A. D. 1989. Revised estimate of annual reproductive capacity for leatherback sea turtles (*Dermochelys coriacea*) based on intraseasonal clutch frequency. *In* Ogren, L., ed. Proceedings of the Second Western Atlantic Turtle Symposium, 345–346. NOAA-TM-NMFS-SEFC-226.

Tucker, A. D., and N. B. Frazer. 1991. Reproductive variation in leatherback turtles, *Dermochelys coriacea,* at Culebra National Wildlife Refuge, Puerto Rico. Herpetologica 47:115–124.

Tucker, J. K. 1978. Variation in reproductive potential and growth in *Chrysemys picta* within a single body of water. Bull. Maryland Herpetol. Soc. 14:223–232.

Tucker, J. K., R. S. Funk, and G. L. Paukstis. 1978. The adaptive significance of egg morphology in two turtles (*Chrysemys picta* and *Terrapene carolina*). Bull. Maryland Herpetol. Soc. 14:10–22.

Turkowski, F. J. 1972. Grass sprout grows through embryo of yellow-bellied turtle (*Chrysemys scripta*). Herpetol. Rev. 4:165.

Turner, F. B., P. Hayden, B. L. Burge, and J. B. Roberson. 1986. Egg production by the desert tortoise (*Gopherus agassizii*) in California. Herpetologica 42:93–104.

Turner, F. B., P. A. Medica, and R. B. Bury. 1987. Age-size relationships of desert tortoises (*Gopherus agassizi*) in southern Nevada. Copeia 1987:974–979.

Turner, F. B., P. A. Medica, and C. L. Lyons. 1984.

Reproduction and survival of the desert tortoise (*Scaptochelys agassizii*) in Ivanpah Valley, California. Copeia 1984:811–820.

Tyler, J. D. 1979. A case of swimming in *Terrapene carolina* (Testudines: Emydidae). Southwest. Natur. 24:189–190.

———. 1991. Vertebrate prey of the loggerhead shrike in Oklahoma. Proc. Oklahoma Acad. Sci. 71:17–20.

Tyning, T. F. 1990. A guide to amphibians and reptiles. Little, Brown and Co., Boston. 400 pp.

Uchida, I. 1967. On the growth of the loggerhead turtle, *Caretta caretta*, under rearing conditions. Bull. Japanese Soc. Sci. Fish. 33:497–507.

———. 1979. Brief report on the hawksbill turtle (*Eretmochelys imbricata*) in the waters adjacent to Indonesia and Malaysia. Japanese Tort. Shell Assoc. 47 pp.

Ulrich, G. F., and A. S. Parkes. 1978. The green sea turtle (*Chelonia mydas*): Further observations on breeding in captivity. J. Zool. (London) 185:237–251.

Ultsch, G. R. 1985. The viability of Nearctic freshwater turtles submerged in anoxia and normoxia at 3 and 10°C. Comp. Biochem. Physiol. 81A:607–611.

———. 1988. Blood gases, hematocrit, plasma ion concentrations, and acid-base status of musk turtles (*Sternotherus odoratus*) during simulated hibernation. Physiol. Zool. 61:78–94.

———. 1989. Ecology and physiology of hibernation and overwintering among freshwater fishes, turtles, and snakes. Biol. Rev. 64:435–516.

Ultsch, G. R., and J. F. Anderson. 1986. The respiratory microenvironment within the burrows of gopher tortoises (*Gopherus polyphemus*). Copeia 1986:787–795.

———. 1988. Gas exchange during hypoxia and hypercarbia of terrestrial turtles: A comparison of a fossorial species (*Gopherus polyphemus*) with a sympatric nonfossorial species (*Terrapene carolina*). Physiol. Zool. 61:142–152.

Ultsch, G. R., R. W. Hanley, and T. R. Bauman. 1985. Responses to anoxia during simulated hibernation in northern and southern painted turtles. Ecology 66:388–395.

Ultsch, G. R., C. V. Herbert, and D. C. Jackson. 1984. The comparative physiology of diving in North American freshwater turtles. I. Submergence tolerance, gas exchange, and acid-base balance. Physiol. Zool. 57:620–631.

Ultsch, G. R., and D. C. Jackson. 1982a. Long-term submergence at 3°C of the turtle, *Chrysemys picta bellii*, in normoxic and severely hypoxic water. I. Survival, gas exchange and acid-base status. J. Exp. Biol. 96:11–28.

———. 1982b. Long-term submergence at 3°C of the turtle *Chrysemys picta bellii* in normoxic and severely hypoxic water. III. Effects of changes in ambient P_{O2} and subsequent air breathing. J. Exp. Biol. 97:87–99.

Ultsch, G. R., and D. Lee. 1983. Radiotelemetric observations of wintering snapping turtles (*Chelydra serpentina*) in Rhode Island. J. Alabama Acad. Sci. 54:200–206.

Ultsch, G. R., and J. S. Wasser. 1990. Plasma ion balance of North American freshwater turtles during prolonged submergence in normoxic water. Comp. Biochem. Physiol. 97A:505–512.

United States Fish and Wildlife Service. 1992. Agency draft yellow-blotched map turtle (*Graptemys flavimaculata*) recovery plan. U.S. Fish and Wildlife Service. Jackson, Mississippi. 30 pp.

Van Devender, T. R., and J. E. King. 1975. Fossil Blanding's turtles, *Emydoidea blandingi* (Holbrook), and the late Pleistocene vegetation of western Missouri. Herpetologica 31:208–212.

Van Devender, T. R., and C. H. Lowe, Jr. 1977. Amphibians and reptiles of Yepómera, Chihuahua, Mexico. J. Herpetol. 11:41–50.

Van Devender, T. R., and J. I. Mead. 1978. Early Holocene and late Pleistocene amphibians and reptiles in Sonoran Desert packrat middens. Copeia 1978:464–475.

Van Devender, T. R., and K. B. Moodie. 1977. The desert tortoise in the late Pleistocene with comments about its earlier history. Proc. Symp. Desert Tortoise Council 1977:41–45.

Van Devender, T. R., K. B. Moodie, and A. H. Harris. 1976. The desert tortoise (*Gopherus agassizi*) in the Pleistocene of the northern Chihuahuan desert. Herpetologica 32:298–304.

Van Devender, T. R., A. M. Rea, and M. L. Smith. 1985. The Sangamon interglacial vertebrate fauna from Rancho la Brisca, Sonora, Mexico. Trans. San Diego Soc. Natur. Hist. 21:23–55.

Van Devender, T. R., and N. T. Tessman. 1975. Late Pleistocene snapping turtles (*Chelydra serpentina*) from southern Nevada. Copeia 1975:249–253.

Van Meter, V. B. 1983. Florida's sea turtles. Florida Power & Light Co. Miami. 46 pp.

Van Nierop, M. M., and J. C. Den Hartog. 1984. A study on the gut contents of five juvenile loggerhead turtles, *Caretta caretta* (Linnaeus) (Reptilia, Cheloniidae), from the south-eastern part of the North Atlantic Ocean, with emphasis on coelenterate identification. Zool. Med. (Leiden) 59:35–54.

Vargas Molinar, T. P. E. 1973. Resultados preliminares del marcado de Tortugas Marinas en aguas Mexicanas

(1966–1970). Inst. Nac. Pesca, Mexico, ser. inf. INP/ SI no. 112. 27 pp.

Vaughan, P., and S. Spring. 1980. Long distance hawksbill recovery. Marine Turtle Newsl. (16):6–7.

Vaughan, S. L. 1983. Update of the home range and habitat use study of the desert tortoise, *Gopherus agassizii,* in the Pichaco Mountains, Arizona. Proc. Symp. Desert Tortoise Council 1983:115–116.

Verheijen, F. J., and J. T. Wildschut. 1973. The photic orientation of hatchling sea turtles during water finding behaviour. Netherlands J. Sea Res. 7:53–67.

Vermersch, T. G. 1992. Lizards and turtles of south-central Texas. Eakin Press, Austin, Texas. 170 pp.

Vesely, D. L., D. A. Baeyens, C. J. Winters, R. Elder, and G. Wewers. 1991. Diving increases the N-terminus of the atrial natriuretic factor prohormone in fresh water diving turtles. Comp. Biochem. Physiol. 98A:67–70.

Vitt, L. J., and A. E. Dunham. 1980. *Chrysemys nelsoni* (Florida redbelly turtle). USA: Georgia. Herpetol. Rev. 11:80.

Vogt, R. C. 1979a. Spring aggregating behavior of painted turtles, *Chrysemys picta* (Reptilia, Testudines, Testudinidae). J. Herpetol. 13:363–365.

———. 1979b. Cleaning/feeding symbiosis between grackles (*Quiscalus:* Icteridae) and map turtles (*Graptemys:* Emydidae). Auk 96:609.

———. 1980. Natural history of the map turtles *Graptemys pseudogeographica* and *G. ouachitensis* in Wisconsin. Tulane Stud. Zool. Bot. 22:17–48.

———. 1981a. Natural history of amphibians and reptiles of Wisconsin. Milwaukee Public Museum, Milwaukee, Wisconsin. 205 pp.

———. 1981b. Food partitioning in three sympatric species of map turtle, genus *Graptemys* (Testudinata, Emydidae). Amer. Midl. Natur. 105:102–111.

———. 1981c. Turtle egg (*Graptemys:* Emydidae) infestation by fly larvae. Copeia 1981:457–459.

———. 1981d. *Graptemys versa.* Catalog. Amer. Amphib. Rept. 280:1–2.

———. 1993. Systematics of the false map turtles (*Graptemys pseudogeographica* complex: Reptilia, Testudines, Emydidae). Ann. Carnegie Mus. Natur. Hist. 62:1–46.

Vogt, R. C., and J. J. Bull. 1982a. Genetic sex determination in the spiny softshell *Trionyx spiniferus* (Testudines: Trionychidae) (?). Copeia 1982:699–700.

———. 1982b. Temperature controlled sex-determination in turtles: Ecological and behavioral aspects. Herpetologica 38:156–164.

———. 1984. Ecology of hatchling sex ratio in map turtles. Ecology 65:582–587.

Vogt, R. C., J. J. Bull, C. J. McCoy, and T. W. Houseal.

1982. Incubation temperature influences sex determination in kinosternid turtles. Copeia 1982:480–482.

Vogt, R. C., and C. J. McCoy. 1980. Status of the emydine turtle genera *Chrysemys* and *Pseudemys.* Ann. Carnegie Mus. Natur. Hist. 49:93–102.

Voigt, W. G. 1975. Heating and cooling rates and their effects upon heart rate and subcutaneous temperatures in the desert tortoise, *Gopherus agassizii.* Comp. Biochem Physiol. 52A:527–531.

Voigt, W. G., and C. R. Johnson. 1976. Aestivation and thermoregulation in the Texas tortoise, *Gopherus berlandieri.* Comp. Biochem. Physiol. 53A:41–44.

———. 1977. Physiological control of heat exchange rates in the Texas tortoise, *Gopherus berlandieri.* Comp. Biochem. Physiol. 56A:495–498.

Voorhies, M. R., J. A. Holman, and X. Xiang-Xu. 1987. The Hottell Ranch rhino quarries (basal Ogallala: medial Barstovian), Banner County, Nebraska. Part I: Geologic setting, faunal lists, lower vertebrates. Contrib. Geol. Univ. Wyoming 25:55–69.

Vosjoli, P. de. 1991. The general care and maintenance of box turtles. Advanced Vivarium Systems, Lakeside, California. 36 pp.

———. 1992. The general care and maintenance of red-eared sliders. Advanced Vivarium Systems, Lakeside, California. 47 pp.

Wagler, J. 1830. Natürlisches System der Amphibien, mit Vorangehander Classification der Säugthiere und Vögel. J. G. Cotta'schen Buchhandlung, München. 354 pp.

Wahlquist, H. 1970. Sawbacks of the Gulf Coast. Int. Turtle and Tortoise Soc. J. 4(4):10–13, 28.

———. 1991. Gopher tortoise conservation. *In* Beaman, K. R., F. Caporaso, S. McKeown, and M. D. Graff, eds. Proceedings of the First International Symposium on Turtles and Tortoises: Conservation and Captive Husbandry, 77–79. Chapman Univ., Orange, California.

Wahlquist, H., and G. W. Folkerts. 1973. Eggs and hatchlings of Barbour's map turtle, *Graptemys barbouri* Carr and Marchand. Herpetologica 29:236–237.

Walker, W. F., Jr. 1959. Closure of the nostrils in the Atlantic loggerhead and other sea turtles. Copeia 1959:257–259.

Wallin, L. 1985. A survey of Linnaeus's material of *Chelone mydas, Caretta caretta* and *Eretmochelys imbricata.* (Reptilia, Cheloniidae). Zool. J. Linn. Soc. 85:121–130.

Wang, Z.-X., and N.-S. Liu. 1986. Studies on diving bradycardia of *Trionyx sinensis.* Acta Herpetol. Sinica 5:17–23.

Wang, Z.-X., N.-Z. Sun, and W.-F. Sheng. 1989. Aquatic

respiration in soft-shelled turtles, *Trionyx sinensis*. Comp. Biochem. Physiol. 92A:593–598.

Ward, F. P., C. J. Hohmann, J. F. Ulrich, and S. E. Hill. 1976. Seasonal microhabitat selections of spotted turtles (*Clemmys guttata*) in Maryland elucidated by radioisotope tracking. Herpetologica 32:60–64.

Ward, J. P. 1968. Presumed hybridization of two species of box turtles. Copeia 1968:874–875.

———. 1978. *Terrapene ornata*. Catalog Amer. Amphib. Rept. 217:1–4.

———. 1984. Relationships of chrysemyd turtles of North America (Testudines: Emydidae). Spec. Publ. Mus. Texas Tech. Univ. (21):1–50.

Warner, J. L. 1982. *Terrapene c. carolina* (eastern box turtle). Reproduction. Herpetol. Rev. 13:48–49.

Warwick, C. 1986. Red-eared terrapin farms and conservation. Oryx 20:237–240.

Warwick, C., C. Steedman, and T. Holford. 1990. Ecological implications of the red-eared turtle trade. Texas J. Sci. 42:419–422.

Waters, J. C. 1974. The biological significance of the basking habit in the black-knobbed sawback, *Graptemys nigrinoda* Cagle. Master's thesis, Auburn University, Auburn, Alabama.

Waters, J. H. 1962. Former distribution of the red-bellied turtle in the Northeast. Copeia 1962:649–651.

———. 1964. Subspecific intergradation in the Nantucket Island, Massachusetts, population of the turtle *Chrysemys picta*. Copeia 1964:550–553.

———. 1966. Second find of red-bellied turtle on Martha's Vineyard Island, Massachusetts. Copeia 1966:592.

———. 1969. Additional observations of southeastern Massachusetts insular and mainland populations of painted turtles, *Chrysemys picta*. Copeia 1969:179–182.

Watts, M. R., and J. L. Christiansen. 1989. Turtle use and succession in a pool created in the bottom of a dry lake. J. Iowa Acad. Sci. 96(1, suppl.): A37.

Weaver, W. G., Jr. 1970. Courtship and combat behavior in *Gopherus berlandieri*. Bull. Florida St. Mus. Biol. Sci. 15:1–43.

Weaver, W. G., Jr., and J. S. Robertson. 1967. A re-evaluation of fossil turtles of the *Chrysemys scripta* group. Tulane Stud. Geol. 5:53–66.

Weaver, W. G., Jr., and F. L. Rose. 1967. Systematics, fossil history, and evolution of the genus *Chrysemys*. Tulane Stud. Zool. 14:63–73.

Webb, R. G. 1956. Size at sexual maturity in the male softshell turtle, *Trionyx ferox emoryi*. Copeia 1956:121–122.

———. 1959. Description of a new softshell turtle from the southeastern United States. Univ. Kansas Publ. Mus. Natur. Hist. 11:517–525.

———. 1961. Observations on the life histories of turtles (genus *Pseudemys* and *Graptemys*) in Lake Texoma, Oklahoma. Amer. Midl. Natur. 65:193–214.

———. 1962. North American Recent soft-shelled turtles (Family Trionychidae). Univ. Kansas Publ. Mus. Natur. Hist. 13:429–611.

———. 1973a. *Trionyx ferox*. Catalog. Amer. Amphib. Rept. 138:1–3.

———. 1973b. *Trionyx muticus*. Catalog. Amer. Amphib. Rept. 139:1–2.

———. 1973c. *Trionyx spiniferus*. Catalog. Amer. Amphib. Rept. 140:1–4.

———. 1975. Taxonomic status of *Aspidonectes californiana* Rivers, 1889 (Testudines, Trionychidae). Copeia 1975:771–773.

———. 1978. *Steindachneri* (*Trionyx*) Siebenrock, 1906: Proposed validation under the plenary powers (Reptilia, Testudines). Z.N. (S.) 2162. Bull. Zool. Nomencl. 35:47–48.

———. 1980. The trionychid turtle *Trionyx steindachneri* introduced in Hawaii? J. Herpetol. 14:206–207.

———. 1990. *Trionyx*. Catalog. Amer. Amphib. Rept. 487:1–7.

Webb, R. G., and J. M. Legler. 1960. A new softshell turtle (genus *Trionyx*) from Coahuila, Mexico. Univ. Kansas Sci. Bull. 40:21–30.

Webb, R. H., and H. G. Wilshire. 1983. Environmental effects of off-road vehicles: Impacts and management in arid regions. Springer-Verlag, New York. 534 pp.

Webb, W. J., and E. D. Cashatt. 1985. *Chrysemys picta marginata* (midland painted turtle). Size. Herpetol. Rev. 16:59.

Webster, C. 1986. Substrate preference and activity in the turtle, *Kinosternon flavescens flavescens*. J. Herpetol. 20:477–482.

Weedy, J. B. 1981. Kemp's ridley; preliminary 1981 nesting information. Marine Turtle Newsl. (19):13.

Weigel, R. D. 1962. Fossil vertebrates of Vero, Florida. Florida Geol. Surv. Spec. Publ. (10):1–59.

Weinstein, M. N., and K. H. Berry. 1987. Morphometric analysis of desert tortoise populations. Bur. Land Mgmt. Rept. CA950–CT7–003. 39 pp.

Weldon, P. J., and M. S. Cannon. In press. Histology and histochemistry of Rathke's glands of juvenile Kemp's ridley sea turtle (*Lepidochelys kempi*). Zool. Jb. Anat. 122.

Weldon, P. J., R. T. Mason, M. J. Tanner, and T. Eisner. 1990. Lipids in the Rathke's gland secretions of hatchling Kemp's ridley sea turtles (*Lepidochelys kempi*). Comp. Biochem. Physiol. 96B:705–708.

Weldon, P. J., and M. J. Tanner. 1990. Lipids in the

Rathke's gland secretions of hatchling loggerhead sea turtles (*Caretta caretta*). Copeia 1990:575–578.

Wellins, D. J. 1987. Use of H-Y antigen assay for sex determination in sea turtles. Copeia 1987:46–52.

Wemple, P. 1971. The eastern spiny soft-shelled turtle *Trionyx spinifer spinifer* Le Sueur in Maryland. Bull. Maryland Herpetol. Soc. 7:35–37.

Werler, J. E. 1951. Miscellaneous notes on the eggs and young of Texan and Mexican reptiles. Zoologica (New York) 36:37–48.

Wermuth, H., and R. Mertens. 1961. Schildkröten, Krokodile, Brükenechsen. G. Fisher, Jena. 422 pp.

———. 1977. Liste der rezenten Amphibien und Reptilien. Testudines, Crocodylia, Rhynchocephalia. Das Tierreich 1(27):1–174.

West, N. H., P. J. Butler, and R. M. Bevan. 1992. Pulmonary blood flow at rest and during swimming in the green turtle, *Chelonia mydas*. Physiol. Zool. 65:287–310.

West, N. H., A. W. Smits, and W. W. Burggren. 1989. Factors terminating nonventilatory periods in the turtle *Chelydra serpentina*. Resp. Physiol. 77:337–350.

Wever, E. G., and J. A. Vernon. 1956a. The sensitivity of the turtle's ear as shown by its electrical potentials. Proc. Natl. Acad. Sci. 42:213–220.

———. 1956b. Sound transmission in the turtle's ear. Proc. Natl. Acad. Sci. 42:292–299.

———. 1956c. Auditory responses in the common box turtle. Proc. Natl. Acad. Sci. 42:962–965.

Whetstone, K. N. 1978. Additional record of the fossil snapping turtle *Macroclemys schmidti* from the Marsland Formation (Miocene) of Nebraska with notes on interspecific skull variation within the genus *Macroclemys*. Copeia 1978:159–162.

Whillans, T. H., and E. J. Crossman. 1977. Morphological parameters and spring activities in a central Ontario population of midland painted turtle, *Chrysemys picta marginata* (Agassiz). Can. Field-Natur. 91:47–57.

White, C. P., and W. R. Curtsinger. 1986. Freshwater turtles: Designed for survival. Natl. Geogr. 169:40–59.

White, D., Jr., and D. Moll. 1991. Clutch size and annual reproductive potential of the turtle *Graptemys geographica* in a Missouri stream. J. Herpetol. 25:493–494.

———. 1992. Restricted diet of the common map turtle *Graptemys geographica* in a Missouri stream. Southwest. Natur. 37:317–318.

White, D. S. 1989. Defense mechanisms in riffle beetles (Coleoptera: Dryopoidea). Ann. Entomol. Soc. Amer. 82:237–241.

White, J. B., and G. G. Murphy. 1973. The reproductive cycle and sexual dimorphism of the common snapping turtle, *Chelydra serpentina serpentina*. Herpetologica 29:240–246.

Whitmore, C. P., and P. H. Dutton. 1985. Infertility, embryonic mortality and nest-site selection in leatherback and green sea turtles in Suriname. Biol. Conserv. 34:251–272.

Whittow, G. C., and G. H. Balazs. 1982. Basking behavior of the Hawaiian green turtle (*Chelonia mydas*). Pacific Sci. 36:129–139.

Wibbels, T. 1983. A transatlantic movement of a headstarted Kemp's ridley. Marine Turtle Newsl. (24):15–16.

———. 1984. Orientation characteristics of immature Kemp's ridley sea turtles, *Lepidochelys kempi*. NOAA-TM-NMFS-SEFC-131. 67 pp.

———. 1992. Kemp's ridley sea turtles. Science 257:465.

Wibbels, T., J. J. Bull, and D. Crews. 1991. Chronology and morphology of temperature-dependent sex determination. J. Exp. Zool. 260:371–381.

Wibbels, T., and D. Crews. 1992. Specificity of steroid hormone-induced sex determination in a turtle. J. Endocrinol. 133:121–129.

Wibbels, T., F. C. Killebrew, and D. Crews. 1991. Sex determination in Cagle's map turtle: Implications for evolution, development, and conservation. Can. J. Zool. 69:2693–2696.

Wibbels, T. A., Y. A. Morris, D. W. Owens, G. A. Dienberg, J. Noell, J. K. Leong, R. E. King, and R. Márquez Millan. 1989. Predicted sex ratios from the International Kemp's Ridley Sea Turtle Head Start Research Project. *In* Calliouet, C. W., Jr., and A. M. Landry, Jr., eds. Proceedings of the First International Symposium on Kemp's Ridley Sea Turtle Biology, Conservation and Management, 77–81. Texas A & M Univ. Sea Grant College Progr. Spec. Publ.-89 (105).

Wibbels, T., D. W. Owens, and M. S. Amoss. 1987. Seasonal changes in the serum testosterone titers of loggerhead sea turtles captured along the Atlantic Coast of the United States.

In Witzell, W. N., ed. Ecology of east Florida sea turtles, 59–64. NOAA Tech. Rept. NMFS 53.

Wibbels, T., D. W. Owens, P. Licht, C. Limpus, P. C. Reed, and M. S. Amoss, Jr. 1992. Serum gonadotropins and gonadal steroids associated with ovulation and egg production in sea turtles. Gen. Comp. Endocrinol. 87:71–78.

Wibbels, T., D. W. Owens, C. J. Limpus, P. C. Reed, and M. S. Amoss, Jr. 1990. Seasonal changes in serum gonadal steroids associated with migration, mating, and nesting in the loggerhead sea turtle (*Caretta caretta*). Gen. Comp. Endocrinol. 79:154–164.

Wibbels, T., D. W. Owens, Y. A. Morris, and M. S. Amoss. 1987. Sexing techniques and sex ratios for immature loggerhead sea turtles captured along the Atlantic Coast of the United States. *In* Witzell, W. N., ed. Ecology of east Florida sea turtles, 65–74. NOAA Tech. Rept. NMFS 53.

Wibbels, T., D. W. Owens, and D. Rostal. 1991. Soft plastra of adult male sea turtles: An apparent secondary sexual characteristics. Herpetol. Rev. 22:47–49.

Wickham, M. M. 1922. Notes on the migration of *Macrochelys lacertina*. Proc. Oklahoma Acad. Sci. 2:20–22.

Wied-Neuwied, M. A. P. 1839. Reise in das innere Nörd-America in den Jahren 1832 bis 1834. J. Hoelscher, Coblenz. 653 pp.

———. 1865. Verzeichniss der Reptilien, welche auf einer Reise im nördlichen America beobachtet wurden. Nova Acta Acad. Leopold.-Carol. 32(1):viii + 146 pp.

Wiegmann, A. F. A. 1835. Beiträge zur Zoologie, gesammelt auf einer Reise um die Erde, von Dr. F. J. F. Meyen. Amphibien. Nova Acta Acad. Leopold.-Carol. 17:185–268.

Wiewandt, T. A., C. H. Lowe, and M. W. Larson. 1972. Occurrence of *Hypopachus variolosus* (Cope) in the short-tree Forest of southern Sonora, Mexico. Herpetologica 28:162–164.

Wilbern, S. E. 1982. Climbing ability of box turtles. Bull. Maryland Herpetol. Soc. 18:170–171.

Wilbern, S. E., and D. A. Ingold. 1983. Sexual dimorphism in *Terrapene* shells. Bull. Chicago Herpetol. Soc. 18:34–36.

Wilbur, H. M. 1975a. The evolutionary and mathematical demography of the turtle *Chrysemys picta*. Ecology 56:64–77.

———. 1975b. A growth model for the turtle *Chrysemys picta*. Copeia 1975:337–343.

Wilbur, H. M., and P. J. Morin. 1988. Life history evolution in turtles. *In* Gans, C., and R. B. Huey, eds. Biology of the Reptilia, vol. 16, 387–439. Alan R. Liss, New York.

Wiley, J. W., and F. E. Lohrer. 1973. Additional records of non-fish prey taken by osprey. Wilson Bull. 85:468–470.

Wilhoft, D. C. 1986. Eggs and hatchling components of the snapping turtle (*Chelydra serpentina*). Comp. Biochem. Physiol. 84A:483–486.

Wilhoft, D. C., M. G. del Baglivo, and M. D. del Baglivo. 1979. Observations on mammalian predation of snapping turtle nests (Reptilia, Testudines, Chelydridae). J. Herpetol. 13:435–438.

Wilhoft, D. C., E. Hotaling, and P. Franks. 1983. Effects of temperature on sex determination in embryos of the snapping turtle, *Chelydra serpentina*. J. Herpetol. 17:38–42.

Williams, E. C., Jr. 1961. A study of the box turtle, *Terrapene carolina carolina* (L.), population in Allee Memorial Woods. Proc. Indiana Acad. Sci. 71:399–406.

Williams, E. C., Jr., and W. S. Parker. 1987. A long-term study of a box turtle (*Terrapene carolina*) population at Allee Memorial Woods, Indiana, with emphasis on survivorship. Herpetologica 43:328–335.

Williams, E. E. 1950. Variation and selection of the cervical central articulations of living turtles. Bull. Amer. Mus. Natur. Hist. 94:505–562.

Williams, J. D., Jr., and W. D. Brown. 1976. Characterization of myoglobins from Atlantic and Pacific green sea turtles. Comp. Biochem. Physiol. 54B:253–259.

Williams, J. E. 1952. Homing behavior of the painted turtle and muskturtle in a lake. Copeia 1952:76–82.

Williams, K. L., H. M. Smith, and P. S. Chrapliwy. 1960. Turtles and lizards from northern Mexico. Trans. Illinois St. Acad. Sci. 53:36–45.

Williams, S. L. 1988. *Thalassia testudinum* productivity and grazing by green turtles in a highly disturbed seagrass bed. Marine Biol. 98:447–455.

Williams, T. A., and J. L. Christiansen. 1981. The niches of two sympatric softshell turtles, *Trionyx muticus* and *Trionyx spiniferus*, in Iowa. J. Herpetol. 15:303–308.

Williamson, L. U., J. R. Spotila, and E. A. Standora. 1989. Growth, selected temperature and CTM of young snapping turtles, *Chelydra serpentina*. J. Therm. Biol. 14:33–39.

Wilson, D. S. 1991. Estimates of survival for juvenile gopher tortoises, *Gopherus polyphemus*. J. Herpetol. 25:376–379.

Wilson, D. S., H. R. Mushinsky, and E. D. McCoy. 1991. Relationship between gopher tortoise body size and burrow width. Herpetol. Rev. 22:122–124.

Wilson, P. R. 1989. *Clemmys guttata* (spotted turtle). Reproduction. Herpetol. Rev. 20:69–70.

Wilson, R. L. 1967. The Pleistocene vertebrates of Michigan. Pap. Michigan Acad. Sci. Arts. Letts. 52:197–234.

———. 1968. Systematic and faunal analysis of a lower Pliocene vertebrate assemblage from Trego County, Kansas. Contrib. Mus. Paleontol. Univ. Michigan 22:75–126.

Wilson, R. L., and G. R. Zug. 1966. A fossil map turtle (*Graptemys pseudogeographica*) from central Michigan. Copeia 1966:368–369.

Wilson, R. V., and G. R. Zug. 1991. *Lepidochelys kempii*. Catalog. Amer. Amphib. Rept. 509:1–8.

Wilson, R. W., and R. D. Stager. 1992. Desert tortoise population densities and distribution, Piute Valley, Nevada. Rangelands 14:239–242.

Winegarner, M. S. 1985. Bobcat family utilizes tortoise burrow. Florida Field Natur. 13:32–33.

Winokur, R. M. 1982. Integumentary appendages of chelonians. J. Morphol. 172:59–74.

Winokur, R. M., and J. M. Legler. 1974. Rostral pores in turtles. J. Morphol. 143:107–120.

———. 1975. Chelonian mental glands. J. Morphol. 147:275–292.

Witham, R. 1974. Neonate sea turtles from the stomach of a pelagic fish. Copeia 1974:548.

———. 1980. The "lost year" question in young sea turtles. Amer. Zool. 20:525–530.

———. 1991. On the ecology of young sea turtles. Florida Scientist 54:179–190.

Witham, R., and C. R. Futch. 1977. Early growth and oceanic survival of pen-reared sea turtles. Herpetologica 33:404–409.

Witherington, B. E. 1991. Orientation of hatchling loggerhead turtles at sea off artificially lighted and dark beaches. J. Exp. Marine Biol. Ecol. 149:1–11.

———. 1992. Behavioral responses of nesting sea turtles to artificial lighting. Herpetologica 48:31–39.

Witherington, B. E., and K. A. Bjorndal. 1991a. Influences of artificial lighting on the seaward orientation of hatchling loggerhead turtles Caretta caretta. Biol. Conserv. 55:139–149.

———. 1991b. Influences of wavelength and intensity on hatchling sea turtle phototaxis: Implications for sea-finding behavior. Copeia 1991:1060–1069.

Witherington, B. E., and L. M. Ehrhart. 1989. Hypothermic stunning and mortality of marine turtles in the Indian River Lagoon system, Florida. Copeia 1989:696–703.

Witherington, B. E., and M. Salmon. 1992. Predation on loggerhead turtle hatchlings after entering the sea. J. Herpetol. 26:226–228.

Witkowski, S. A., and J. G. Frazier. 1982. Heavy metals in sea turtles. Marine Pollution Bull. 13:254–255.

Witz, B. W., D. S. Wilson, and M. D. Palmer. 1991. Distribution of Gopherus polyphemus and its vertebrate symbionts in three burrow categories. Amer. Midl. Natur. 126:152–158.

Witzell, W. N. 1980. Growth of captive hawksbill turtles, Eretmochelys imbricata, in western Samoa. Bull. Marine Sci. 30:909–912.

———. 1981. Predation on juvenile green sea turtles, Chelonia mydas by a grouper, Promicrops lanceolatus (Pisces; Serranidae) in the Kingdom of Tonga, South Pacific. Bull. Marine Sci. 31:935–936.

———. 1983. Synopsis of biological data on the hawksbill turtle, Eretmochelys imbricata (Linnaeus, 1766). FAO Fish. Synopsis 137. 78 pp.

———. 1985. Variation of size at maturity of female hawksbill turtles (Eretmochelys imbricata), with speculation on life-history tactics relative to proper stock management. Japanese J. Herpetol. 11:46–51.

———, ed. 1987. Ecology of east Florida sea turtles. Proceedings of the Cape Canaveral, Florida Sea Turtle Workshop, Miami, Florida, February 26–27, 1985. NOAA Tech. Rept. NMFS 53. 80 pp.

Witzell, W. N., and A. C. Banner. 1980. The hawksbill turtle (Eretmochelys imbricata) in western Samoa. Bull. Marine Sci. 30:571–579.

Wolke, R. E., and A. George. 1981. Sea turtle necropsy manual. NOAA-TM-NMFS-SEFC-24. 20 pp.

Wood, F. E., and J. R. Wood. 1982. Sex ratios in captive-reared green turtles, Chelonia mydas. Copeia 1982:482–485.

———. 1990. Successful production of captive F2 generation of the green sea turtle. Marine Turtle Newsl. (50):3–4.

Wood, F. G. 1953. Mating behavior of captive loggerhead turtles, Caretta caretta caretta. Copeia 1953:184–186.

Wood, J. R. 1982. Captive rearing of Atlantic ridleys at Cayman Turtle Farm Ltd. Marine Turtle Newsl. (20):7–9.

Wood, J. R., and F. E. Wood. 1977. Quantitative requirements of the hatchling green sea turtle for lysine, tryptophan, and methionine. J. Nutrition 107:171–175.

———. 1980. Reproductive biology of captive green sea turtles Chelonia mydas. Amer. Zool. 20:499–505.

———. 1984. Captive breeding of the Kemp's ridley. Marine Turtle Newsl. (29):12.

———. 1988. Captive reproduction of Kemp's ridley Lepidochelys kempi. Herpetol. J. 1:247–249.

Wood, J. R., F. E. Wood, and K. Critchley. 1983. Hybridization of Chelonia mydas and Eretmochelys imbricata. Copeia 1983:839–842.

Wood, R. C. 1976. $25.00 per egg! New Jersey Outdoors 3(3):14–15, 26.

———. 1977. Evolution of the emydine turtles Graptemys and Malaclemys (Reptilia, Testudines, Emydidae). J. Herpetol. 11:415–421.

Wood, S. C., R. N. Gatz, and M. L. Glass. 1984. Oxygen transport in the green sea turtle. J. Comp. Physiol. 154B:275–280.

Woodbury, A. M. 1952. Hybrids of Gopherus berlandieri and G. agassizii. Herpetologica 8:33–36.

Woodbury, A. M., and R. Hardy. 1948. Studies of the desert tortoise, Gopherus agassizii. Ecol. Monogr. 18:145–200.

Woodin, M. C., and C. D. Woodin. 1981. Everglades

kite predation on a soft-shelled turtle. Florida Field Natur. 9:64.

Woods, G. T. 1945. Rate of travel of the wood turtle. Copeia 1945:49.

Woody, J. B. 1990. Guest editorial: Is "headstarting" a reasonable conservation measure? "On the surface, yes; in reality, no." Marine Turtle Newsl. (50):8–11.

———. 1991. Guest editorial: It's time to stop headstarting Kemp's ridley. Marine Turtle Newsl. (55):7–8.

Worth, D. F., and J. B. Smith. 1976. Marine turtle nesting on Hutchinson Island, Florida, in 1973. Florida Marine Res. Publ. 18. 17 pp.

Wright, A. H. 1918. Notes on *Clemmys*. Proc. Biol. Soc. Washington. 31:51–57.

Wright, A. H., and S. C. Bishop. 1915. A biological reconnaissance of the Okefinokee Swamp in Georgia: The reptiles. II. Snakes. Proc. Acad. Natur. Sci. Philadelphia 1915:107–192.

Wright, S. 1982. The distribution and population biology of the gopher tortoise (*Gopherus polyphemus*) in South Carolina. Master's thesis, Clemson University, Clemson, South Carolina.

Wygoda, M. L. 1979. Terrestrial activity of striped mud turtles, *Kinosternon baurii* (Reptilia, Testudines, Kinosternidae) in west-central Florida. J. Herpetol. 13:469–480.

Wygoda, M. L., and C. M. Chmura. 1990. Effects of shell closure on water loss in the Sonoran mud turtle, *Kinosternon sonoriense*. Southwest. Natur. 35:228–229.

Wyneken, J., T. J. Burke, M. Salmon, and D. K. Pedersen. 1988. Egg failure in natural and relocated sea turtle nests. J. Herpetol. 22:88–96.

Wyneken, J., and J. Hicklin. 1988. A confirmed hawksbill, *Eretmochelys imbricata* nesting in Broward County Florida. Marine Turtle Newsl. (42):6.

Wyneken, J., and M. Salmon. 1992. Frenzy and postfrenzy swimming activity in loggerhead, green, and leatherback hatchling sea turtles. Copeia 1992:478–484.

Wyneken, J., M. Salmon, and K. J. Lohmann. 1990. Orientation by hatchling loggerhead sea turtles *Caretta caretta* L. in a wave tank. J. Exp. Marine Biol. Ecol. 139:43–50.

Yahner, R. H. 1974. Weight change, survival rate and home range change in the box turtle, *Terrapene carolina*. Copeia 1974:546–548.

Yearicks, E. F., R. C. Wood, and W. S. Johnson. 1981. Hibernation of the northern diamondback terrapin, *Malaclemys terrapin terrapin*. Estuaries 4:78–80.

Yeh, H. K. 1963. Fossil turtles of China. Paleontol. Sinica, n. ser. C, 18:1–111.

Yerkes, R. M. 1904. Space perception of tortoises. J. Comp. Neurol. 2:15–26.

———. 1905. The color-pattern of *Nanemys guttata* Schneider (a preliminary report). Science 21:386.

Yntema, C. L. 1968. A series of stages in the embryonic development of *Chelydra serpentina*. J. Morphol. 125:219–252.

———. 1971. Incidence and survival of twin embryos of the common snapping turtle, *Chelydra serpentina*. Copeia 1971:755–758.

———. 1976. Effects of incubation temperatures on sex differentiation in the turtle, *Chelydra serpentina*. J. Morphol. 150:453–462.

———. 1978. Incubation times for eggs of the turtle *Chelydra serpentina* (Testudines: Chelydridae) at various temperatures. Herpetologica 34:274–277.

———. 1979. Temperature levels and periods of sex determination during incubation of eggs of *Chelydra serpentina*. J. Morphol. 159:17–28.

———. 1981. Characteristics of gonads and oviducts in hatchlings and young of *Chelydra serpentina* resulting from three incubation temperatures. J. Morphol. 167:297–304.

Yntema, C. L., and N. Mrosovsky. 1979. Incubation temperature and sex ratio in hatchling loggerhead turtles: A preliminary report. Marine Turtle Newsl. (11):9–10.

———. 1980. Sexual differentiation in hatchling loggerheads (*Caretta caretta*) incubated at different controlled temperatures. Herpetologica 36:33–36.

———. 1982. Critical periods and pivotal temperatures for sexual differentiation in loggerhead sea turtles. Can. J. Zool. 60:1012–1016.

Young, F. N., and C. C. Goff. 1939. An annotated list of the arthropods found in the burrows of the Florida gopher tortoise, *Gopherus polyphemus* (Daudin). Florida Entomol. 12:53–62.

Young, R. 1992. Tiger shark consumes young sea turtle. Marine Turtle Newsl. (59):14.

Yun, L., L. Chuwu, C. Shuqun, Y. Hongtao, and F. Zhigang. 1984. Studies on the gonadal development of a chinese turtle (*Trionyx sinensis*). Acta Hydrobiol. Sinica 8:145–156.

Zangerl, R. 1945. Fossil specimens of *Macrochelys* from the Tertiary of the plains. Fieldiana: Geol. 10:5–12.

———. 1958. Die oligocänen Meerschildkröten von Glarus. Schweiz. Palaeontol. Abh. 73:5–55.

———. 1969. The turtle shell. *In* Gans, C., A. d'A. Bellairs, and T. S. Parsons, eds. Biology of the Reptilia, vol. 1, Morphology A, 311–339. Academic Press, London.

———. 1980. Patterns of phylogenetic differentiation in

the toxochelyid and cheloniid sea turtles. Amer. Zool. 20:585–596.

Zappalorti, R. T. 1976. The amateur zoologist's guide to turtles and crocodilians. Stackpole Books, Harrisburg, Pennsylvania. 208 pp.

———. 1978. The bog turtle, smallest of North American turtles. Bull. Chicago Herpetol. Soc. 13:75–81.

Zieman, J. C., R. L. Iverson, and J. C. Ogden. 1984. Herbivory effects on *Thalassia testudinum* leaf growth and nitrogen content. Marine Ecol. Progr. Ser. 15:151–158.

Zipko, S. J. 1982. Basking behavior of painted turtles. Amer. Biol. Teach. 44:406–412.

Zovickian, W. H. 1971a. Observations on the nesting of *Clemmys muhlenbergi* in a simulated environment. Bull. Maryland Herpetol. Soc. 7:43–44.

———. 1971b. Humidity as a growth factor in hatchlings of *Clemmys muhlenbergi*. Bull. Maryland Herpetol. Soc. 7:93–95.

Zug, G. R. 1966. The penial morphology and the relationships of cryptodiran turtles. Occ. Pap. Mus. Zool. Univ. Michigan 647:1–24.

———. 1971. American musk turtles, *Sternothaerus* or *Sternotherus?* Herpetologica 27:446–449.

———. 1986. *Sternotherus*. Catalog. American Amphib. Rept. 397:1–3.

———. 1990. Age determination of long-lived reptiles: Some techniques for seaturtles. Ann. Sci. Natur. Zool. Paris, ser. 13, 11:219–222.

———. 1991a. Estimates of age and growth in *Lepidochelys kempii* from skeletochronological data. *In* Tenth Annual Workshop on Sea Turtle Biology and Conservation, 285–286. NOAA-TM-NMFS-SEFC-278.

———. 1991b. Age determination in turtles. Soc. Stud. Amphib. Rept. Herpetol. Circ. (20):1–28.

———. 1993. Herpetology. An introductory biology of the amphibians and reptiles. Academic Press, New York. 507 pp.

———. In press. Turtles of Lee Creek Mine (Pliocene: North Carolina). Smithsonian Contrib. Paleobiol.

Zug, G. R., and G. H. Balazs. 1985. Skeletochronological age estimates for Hawaiian green turtles. Marine Turtle Newsl. (33):9–10.

Zug, G. R., and C. H. Ernst. In press. *Lepidochelys*. Catalog. Amer. Amphib. Rept.

Zug, G. R., and H. J. Kalb. 1989. Skeletochronological age estimates for juvenile *Lepidochelys kempii* from Atlantic Coast of North America. *In* Eckert, S. A., K. L. Eckert, and T. A. Richardson, eds. Proceedings of the Ninth Annual Workshop on Sea Turtle Conservation and Biology, 271–273. NOAA-TM-NMFS-SEFC-232.

Zug, G. R., and A. Schwartz. 1971. *Deirochelys, D. reticularia*. Catalog. Amer. Amphib. Rept. 107:1–3.

Zug, G. R., A. H. Wynn, and C. Ruckdeschel. 1983. Age estimates of Cumberland Island loggerhead sea turtles. Marine Turtle Newsl. (25):9–11.

———. 1986. Age determination of loggerhead sea turtles, *Caretta caretta*, by incremental growth marks in the skeleton. Smithsonian Contrib. Zool. 427. 34 pp.

Zweifel, R. G. 1989. Long-term ecological studies on a population of painted turtles *Chrysemys picta*, on Long Island, New York. Amer. Mus. Novitates (2952):1–55.

Zwinenberg, A. J. 1974. The leatherback (*Dermochelys coriacea*), one of the largest living reptiles. Bull. Maryland Herpetol. Soc. 10:42–49.

———. 1976. The olive ridley *Lepidochelys olivacea* (Eschscholtz, 1829): Probably the most numerous marine turtle today. Bull. Maryland Herpetol. Soc. 12:75–95.

———. 1977. Kemp's ridley, *Lepidochelys kempii* (Garman, 1880), undoubtedly the most endangered marine turtle today (with notes on the current status of *Lepidochelys olivacea*). Bull. Maryland Herpetol. Soc. 13:170–192.

Index

DATE DUE

MAY 1 2001	AUG 2 5 2008
MAY 0 6	JUL 2 1 2008
	NOV 1 3 2012
MAR 2 2 2003	
MAR 2 0 2003	
MAY 0 6 2003	
APR 2 9 2003	
MAY 1 6 2008	
MAY 1 9 2005	
3 2005	
MAY 1 2 2006	
AUG 1 4 2007	
AUG 2 0 2007	
AUG 2 7 2007	
MAY 1 2 2008	

GAYLORD

PRINTED IN U.S.A.